Life-Span Development

NINTH EDITION

 Higher Education

Boston   Burr Ridge, IL   Dubuque, IA   Madison, WI   New York   San Francisco   St. Louis
Bangkok   Bogotá   Caracas   Kuala Lumpur   Lisbon   London   Madrid   Mexico City
Milan   Montreal   New Delhi   Santiago   Seoul   Singapore   Sydney   Taipei   Toronto

The McGraw·Hill Companies

Higher Education

LIFE-SPAN DEVELOPMENT, NINTH EDITION

Published by McGraw-Hill, a business unit of The McGraw-Hill Companies, Inc., 1221 Avenue of the Americas, New York, NY 10020. Copyright © 2004, 2002, 1999, 1997 by The McGraw-Hill Companies, Inc. All rights reserved. No part of this publication may be reproduced or distributed in any form or by any means, or stored in a database or retrieval system, without the prior written consent of The McGraw-Hill Companies, Inc., including, but not limited to, in any network or other electronic storage or transmission, or broadcast for distance learning.

Some ancillaries, including electronic and print components, may not be available to customers outside the United States.

 This book is printed on recycled, acid-free paper containing 10% postconsumer waste.

International   1 2 3 4 5 6 7 8 9 0 QPD/QPD 0 9 8 7 6 5 4 3
Domestic   1 2 3 4 5 6 7 8 9 0 QPD/QPD 0 9 8 7 6 5 4 3

ISBN 0-07-282049-7
ISBN 0-07-121393-7 (ISE)

Vice president and editor-in-chief: *Thalia Dorwick*
Publisher: *Stephen D. Rutter*
Senior sponsoring editor: *Rebecca H. Hope*
Senior developmental editor: *Judith Kromm*
Marketing manager: *Melissa Caughlin*
Senior project manager: *Marilyn Rothenberger*
Manager, New book production: *Sandra Hahn*
Media technology producer: *Ginger Bunn*
Design coordinator: *Gino Cieslik*
Interior designer: *Ellen Pettengell*
Art editor: *Robin Mouat*
Illustrators: *John and Judy Waller*
Photo research coordinator: *Alexandra Ambrose*
Photo researcher: *LouAnn Wilson*
Senior supplement producer: *David A. Welsh*
Compositor: *GAC—Indianapolis*
Typeface: *9.5/12 Meridian*
Printer: *Quebecor World Dubuque, IA*

The credits section for this book begins on page C-1 and is considered an extension of the copyright page.

Library of Congress Cataloging-in-Publication Data

Santrock, John W.
   Life-span development / John W. Santrock.— 9th ed.
      p. cm.
   Includes bibliographical references and indexes.
      ISBN 0-07-282049-7 (alk. paper) — ISBN 0-07-121393-7 (ISE : alk. paper)
      1. Developmental psychology. I. Title.

BF713 .S26 2004
155—dc21

                                                                                2003514125

INTERNATIONAL EDITION ISBN 0-07-121393-7
Copyright © 2004. Exclusive rights by The McGraw-Hill Companies, Inc., for manufacture and export. This book cannot be re-exported from the country to which it is sold by McGraw-Hill. The International Edition is not available in North America.

www.mhhe.com

With special appreciation to my parents,
Ruth and John Santrock

About the Author

John W. Santrock

John Santrock received his Ph.D. from the University of Minnesota in 1973. He taught at the University of Charleston and the University of Georgia before joining the Program in Psychology and Human Development at the University of Texas at Dallas, where he currently teaches a number of undergraduate courses. In 1982, John created the life-span development course at UT–Dallas and has taught it every year since then.

John has been a member of the editorial boards of Child Development and Developmental Psychology. His research on father custody is widely cited and used in expert witness testimony to promote flexibility and alternative considerations in custody disputes. John also has authored these exceptional McGraw-Hill texts: Psychology (7th edition), Child Development (9th edition), Children (7th edition), Adolescence (9th edition), and Educational Psychology (2nd edition).

For many years, John was involved in tennis as a player, teaching professional, and coach of professional tennis players. He has been married for more than 35 years to his wife, Mary Jo, who is a realtor. He has two daughters—Tracy, who is a technology specialist at Nortel in Raleigh, North Carolina, and Jennifer, who is a medical sales specialist at Medtronic. He has one granddaughter, Jordan, age 9. Tracy recently completed the New York Marathon, and Jennifer was in the top 100 ranked players on the Women's Professional Tennis Tour. In the last decade, John also has spent time painting expressionist art.

John Santrock, teaching in his undergraduate course in life-span development.

Brief Contents

Contents

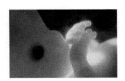

SECTION 2
Beginnings 77

SECTION 3
Infancy 145

S E C T I O N   4
Early Childhood 231

SECTION 5
Middle and Late Childhood 299

SECTION 6
Adolescence 367

SECTION 7
Early Adulthood 437

SECTION 8
Middle Adulthood 511

SECTION 9
Late Adulthood 565

SECTION 10
Endings 651

Preface

Preparing a new edition of *Life-Span Development* is both a joy and a challenge. I enjoy revising this text because the feedback from instructors and students on each edition has been consistently enthusiastic. The challenge of revising a successful text is always to continue meeting readers' needs and expectations, while keeping the material fresh and up to date. For the ninth edition of *Life-Span Development*, I have emphasized three kinds of revisions to meet this challenge. I have expanded coverage in key areas, incorporated the latest research and applications, and honed the elements of the book that make learning easier and more engaging. Here I describe the thrust of these changes in general terms. A list of chapter-by-chapter changes subsequently provides more detail.

CHANGES IN THE NINTH EDITION

> "I am a huge fan of John Santrock's style and textbooks. I thought the 8th edition was very good. The 9th edition promises to be even better."
>
> —JAMES REID, *Washington University in St. Louis*

Expanded Coverage of Adult Development, Aging, and Diversity

Instructors have said repeatedly that most life-span texts don't give enough attention to adult development and aging. In the ninth edition, I have significantly modified, expanded, and updated the content on adult development and aging, continuing a process I began some time ago. Examples of added coverage are new sections on stress in early adulthood (chapter 14), work in midlife (chapter 16), and self-esteem in late adulthood (chapter 20).

> "I continue to believe that this book remains the most comprehensive life-span text suitable for undergraduates now available. The major efforts made in the 8th edition to give greater coverage and depth to the 75 percent of the life span spent in adulthood and old age have been continued in this edition. Most other life-span texts still think of development as practically ending by adolescence or early adulthood and treat the remainder of the life course as an appendix "also to be mentioned." John Santrock makes the conscious effort to understand the early parts of life as prologue for the much longer period of adulthood. Thus, he conveys to the reader early-on that we must understand the beginnings of human development in order to understand what happens later."
>
> —K. WARNER SCHAIE, *Pennsylvania State University*

Diversity is another very important aspect of life-span development, one that has come under increasing scrutiny from researchers in recent years. Every effort was made to explore diversity issues in a sensitive manner in every chapter of this edition. In addition to weaving diversity into discussions of life-span topics, I've included a Sociocultural Worlds of Development box in each chapter to highlight a diversity topic related to the chapter's content. New coverage of diversity includes discussions of early childhood education in Japan (chapter 8), attitudes toward corporal punishment in different cultures (chapter 9), the relationship of gender and ethnicity to obesity (chapter 14), and why people live longer in Okinawa (chapter 18).

> "John Santrock seems to have a special manner about issues of culture and diversity. I have many different cultures represented in my classes and I have never had one express any difficulties with the manner in which these issues are discussed."
>
> —BARBA PATTON, *University of Houston–Victoria*

> "I find this text to be the most comprehensive and culturally inclusive text. The coverage of cultural issues allows me, without apology, to include lectures in my course covering cultural issues and human development."
>
> —YVETTE HARRIS, *Miami University*

Research and Applications

Above all, a text on life-span development must include a solid research foundation. This edition of *Life-Span Development* presents the latest, most contemporary research on each period of the human life span and includes more than 800 citations from the past three years. For example, in chapter 5, I discuss new research on the stressful aspects of co-sleeping (Hunsley & Thoman, 2002); chapter 11 presents recent studies on gender differences in brain structure and function in middle childhood (Frederikse & others, 2000; Halpern, 2001; Swaab & others, 2001); and chapter 16 covers new research on hormonal changes in middle-aged men and women (Sommer, 2001), as well as on hormone replacement therapy for menopausal women (Hlatky & others, 2002).

This edition also includes many more graphs and tables of research data, so that students can see how data from research studies can be visually presented. There are more than 60 new figures and tables of data in *Life-Span Development*, ninth edition. Special care was taken to make sure that these illustrations are designed clearly so that students can interpret and understand them.

It is important not only to present the scientific foundations of life-span development to students, but also to demonstrate that research has real-world applications, to include many applied examples of concepts, and to give students a sense that the field of life-span development has personal meaning for them. For example, a new addition to chapter 10 focuses on recommendations for helping children cope effectively with terrorist attacks.

In addition to giving special attention throughout the text to health, parenting, and educational applications, the ninth edition emphasizes careers. Every chapter has one or more Careers in Life-Span Development inserts that profile an individual whose career relates to the chapter's content. Most of these inserts include a photograph of the person at work. In addition, a new Careers in Life-Span appendix that follows chapter 1 describes a number of careers in the education/research, clinical/counseling, medical/nursing/ physical, and families/relationship categories. Numerous Web links provide students with opportunities to read about these careers in greater depth.

> *"Careers in Life-Span Development is an excellent and exciting addition to the text. A presentation of career vignettes throughout the text will help spark career interest as well as create an atmosphere of the 'applicability' of the material they are learning."*
> —CHRISTINE KERRES MALECKI, *Northern Illinois University*

Improved Accessibility and Interest

I strongly believe that students not only should be challenged to study hard and think more deeply and productively about life-span development, but also should be provided with an effective learning system. Instructors and students alike have commented on many occasions about how student-friendly this text is. However, I strive to keep making the learning system better, and I am truly excited about the improvements for this edition.

Now more than ever, students struggle to find the main ideas in their courses, especially in courses like life-span development, which includes so much material. The new learning headings and learning system center on learning goals that, together with the main text headings, keep the key ideas in front of the reader from the beginning to the end of a chapter. Each chapter has no more than six main headings and corresponding learning goals, which are presented side by side on the chapter-opening spread. At the end of each main section of a chapter, the learning goal is repeated in a new feature called Review and Reflect, which prompts students to review the key topics in the section and poses a question to encourage them to think critically about what they have read. At the end of the chapter, under the heading Reach Your Learning Goals, the learning goals guide students through the bulleted chapter review.

In addition to the verbal tools just described, maps that link up with the learning goals are presented at the beginning of each major section in the chapter. At the end of each chapter, the section maps are assembled into a complete map of the chapter that provides a visual review guide. The complete learning system, including many additional features not mentioned here, is presented later in the Preface in a section titled To the Student.

> *"The learning goals were very informative. They provide direction for the readers. The concept maps are very useful."*
> —TORO SATO, *Shippensburg University*

As important as it is to provide students with an effective learning system, it is imperative to present theories and research at a level that students can understand them and are motivated to learn about them. In each edition of the book, I have carefully rewritten much of the material to make sure it is at a level that challenges students but is also clearly written so they can understand it. I also continually seek better examples of concepts and material that will interest students.

> *"The prose is clear, direct, compelling, and authoritative."*
> —MARIAN UNDERWOOD, *University of Texas at Dallas*

CHAPTER-BY-CHAPTER CHANGES

A number of changes were made in all 21 chapters of *Life-Span Development,* ninth edition. The highlights of these changes include:

CHAPTER 1
Introduction

- Deletion of section on Careers in Life-Span Development from chapter 1 and creation of a careers appendix that now follows chapter 1. The appendix provides considerably expanded coverage of life-span careers and is accompanied by a self-assessment on careers on the book's website. A large number of connections to websites on life-span careers have been added.
- Addition of research descriptions to each section of contemporary concerns: health and well-being, parenting, education, and sociocultural contexts. Each of the research studies described is from the twenty-first century.
- New figure 1.4, illustrating that the main differences in the home environments of children from different ethnic groups are due to poverty rather than ethnicity (Bradley & others, 2001).
- New figure 1.7, showing no differences in happiness across age groups.

> *"I like the reorganization of the chapter. It should make teaching easier."*
> —K. WARNER SCHAIE, *Pennsylvania State University*

"I like the new 'research' sections that highlight the recent research being conducted on that specific topic."

—DEBBIE TINDELL, *Wilkes University*

CHAPTER 2
The Science of Life-Span Development

- Extensive reworking of section on research methods
- Reorganization of types of research; new headings are Descriptive Research, Correlational Research, and Experimental Research
- New discussion of naturalistic observation research (Crowley & others, 2001) and new figure 2.8, illustrating the results of this research
- Expanded and updated coverage of ethics
- Extensively revised discussion of Vygotsky's theory for better student understanding
- Two new photographs to illustrate how research might produce different results depending on how homogeneous or diverse the sample is

"The strengths of this chapter are the depths and clarity of explanations of theories."

—MYRA MARCUS, *Florida Gulf Coast University*

CHAPTER 3
Biological Beginnings

- Important new section, The Collaborative Gene, that discusses why DNA does not determine heredity in a completely independent manner (Gottlieb, 2002)
- Clear, improved discussion of mitosis and meiosis
- New section on genetic imprinting
- Expanded, updated coverage of sex-linked genes
- Updated description of test-tube babies with new recent research studies (Golombok, MacCallum, & Goodman, 2001; Hahn & DiPietro, 2001) and new figure 3.10 on research data
- Expanded, contemporary discussion of the Human Genome Project, including the finding that humans only have about 30,000 to 35,000 genes
- New high-interest figure 3.6: Exploring Your Genetic Future

"The chapter is really rather remarkable in the sheer amount of new and older useful and relevant information that it covers. . . . The chapter for the 9th edition is much improved . . . the breadth of coverage is really admirable and the examples are well chosen."

—GILBERT GOTTLIEB, *University of North Carolina*

CHAPTER 4
Prenatal Development and Birth

- Expanded coverage of teratogens in terms of dose, time of exposure, and genetic susceptibility
- Updated research on cocaine babies
- New teratology section on incompatibility of blood types
- New discussion of cultural variations in childbirth
- New coverage of small for date infants and their comparison to preterm infants
- New discussion of low-birthweight infant rates around the world and very up-to-date information about this topic, including new figure 4.7 (UNICEF, 2001).

"This is a strong chapter."

—LESLEE POLLINA, *Southeast Missouri State University*

CHAPTER 5
Physical Development in Infancy

- Considerable expansion of material on the development of the brain, including new figure 5.4 on synaptic pruning
- Extensive research updating of breast-feeding
- New figure 5.8 on plasticity in the human brain; also new, the fascinating story of Michael Rehbein's loss of his left hemisphere and how his right hemisphere started taking over the functions of speech
- New research on the stressful aspects of co-sleeping (Hunsley & Thoman, 2002)
- Expanded discussion of cultural variations in infants' motor skills

"This is an outstanding chapter. The strengths are the comprehensive coverage of milestones of motor development, excellent figures, and attention to issues of cultural diversity."

—MARIAN S. HARRIS, *University of Illinois, Chicago*

CHAPTER 6
Cognitive Development in Infancy

- New section on infants' understanding of physical reality, including new figure 6.3 on infants' knowledge of cause-and-effect
- New figure 6.5, illustrating the concepts of habituation and dishabituation with seven-hour-old infants
- Expanded, updated coverage of infant memory that focuses on Patricia Bower's recent research
- New section on language production and language comprehension

- New section on language sounds, including Patricia Kuhl's research; also new figure 6.7 on Kuhl's research showing EEG recording of a baby in her research on the transition from a universal to a specialized linguist
- New figure 6.9, summarizing language milestones in infancy
- New discussion of link between level of maternal language and vocabulary growth in infants, including new figure 6.10

"This chapter is a very good one; excellent."

—JULIA RUX, *Georgia Perimeter College*

CHAPTER 7
Socioemotional Development in Infancy

- New section on social referencing
- New section on self-regulation of emotion and coping in infancy
- New discussion of separation protest, including new figure 7.1, showing how separation protest peaks between 13 and 15 months of age in four different cultures
- Discussion of contextual influences on self-regulation of emotion in infancy
- Expanded coverage of the contemporary view of temperament in terms of positive affect and approach, negative affectivity, and effortful control (self-regulation)
- New section on gender, culture, and temperament including recent theory and research (Putnam, Sanson, & Rothbart, 2002)
- Expanded discussion of culture and attachment, including new figure 7.5 on infant attachment in the United States, Germany, and Japan

"The sections on temperament and attachment are very good. In general, this chapter is very strong."

—ALAN FOGEL, *University of Utah*

CHAPTER 8
Physical and Cognitive Development in Early Childhood

- Expansion of discussion on changes in the brain in early childhood, including recent research on neural circuits (Krimel & Golman-Rakic, 2001), and new figure 8.2 on the prefrontal cortex's role in attention and memory
- Expanded coverage of handedness, including new material on the origin and development of handedness, the brain and language, and links of handedness to other abilities
- Addition of recent research on the effects of environmental tobacco smoke on children's respiratory problems and levels of vitamin C (Maninno & others, 2001; Strauss, 2001)

- New figure 8.5, showing the main causes of death in young children in the United States (National Vital Statistics Reports, 2001)
- New discussion of recent study comparing children from a traditional school and children from a Vygotsky-based collaborative school (Matusov, Bell, & Rogoff, 2001)
- New study showing a link between speed of processing information and children's math and reading achievement (Hitch, Towse, & Hutton, 2001)
- Clearer presentation of theory of mind and new figure 8.15 on developmental changes in false belief (Wellman, Cross, & Watson, 2001)
- Expanded coverage of language development in young children

"This is a textbook that I have used for a number of years, and I continue to use it because it is written in an approachable way and its heart is in the right place."

—JEAN BERKO GLEASON, *Boston University*

CHAPTER 9
Socioemotional Development in Early Childhood

- New section on the development of self-conscious emotions, such as pride, shame, and guilt
- New section on co-parenting
- New section on punishment and discipline in discussion of parenting, including cross-cultural comparisons of punishment, and new figure 9.5 on recent cross-cultural research
- New figure 9.7 on Hetherington and Kelly's (2002) research on the effects of divorce on children's adjustment
- Extensive revision and updating of culture, ethnicity, and families, including recent research (Coll & Pachter, 2002; McAdoo, 2002)
- New Sociocultural Worlds of Development box, Acculturation and Ethnic Minority Parenting, based on Cynthia Garcia Coll and Lee Patcher's ideas
- New discussion of recent longitudinal study on the effects of watching educational TV programs on children's achievement and aggression (Anderson & others, 2001).

"The coverage in this chapter is excellent and the new work on punishment and TV are welcome updates."

—ROSS PARKE, *University of California–Riverside*

CHAPTER 10
Physical and Cognitive Development in Middle and Late Childhood

- Recent data on the percentage increase of U.S. children who are overweight (NHANES, 2001)

- New figure 10.1, showing the dramatic decrease in the percentage of children taking daily P.E. classes in the U.S. from 1969 to 1999 (Health Management Resources, 2001)
- New research on Ritalin, behavior management, and ADHD (Swanson & others, 2001)
- Updated, expanded discussion of whether there is evidence for general intelligence (Brody, 2001)
- Updated coverage of language development
- Substantial update of reading issues, including new figure 10.10 on the link between daily reading time and reading achievement
- Expanded coverage of bilingual education, including Kenji Hakuta's (2000) research on how long it takes for language minority students to learn to read and speak English
- New figure 10.11, showing the relation of age of arrival in the United States with grammar proficiency

"Overall, I think this is an excellent chapter. . . . All of the important topics in this area are covered and the topics are well-balanced."
—TORU SATO, *Shippensburg University*

CHAPTER 11
Socioemotional Development in Middle and Late Childhood

- New section on coping with stress, including recommendations on how to help children cope effectively with terrorist attacks, such as 9/11/01 (Gurwitch & others, 2001; La Greca & others, 2002)
- New material on gender differences in brain structure and function (Frederikse & others, 2001; Halpern, 2001; Swaab & others, 2001)
- New data presented from the National Assessment of Educational Progress (2001) on gender and science and gender and reading scores, including new figure 11.3 on reading
- Updated coverage of stepfamilies, including Hetherington's most recent findings (Hetherington & Kelly, 2002)
- New graph (figure 11.5) of bullying behaviors in the United States (Nansel & others, 2001)
- New graph of data (figure 11.6) of Stevenson's research on Asian and U.S. children's math achievement

"Very well done with extremely current reference material."
—MYRA MARCUS, *Florida Gulf Coast University*

CHAPTER 12
Physical and Cognitive Development in Adolescence

- Added recent cross-cultural data on the age of initiation of intercourse (Singh & others, 2000)

- New research on pathways to adversity in early childbearers (Jaffe, 2002)
- Revised and updated coverage of adolescent drug use (Johnston, O'Malley, & Bachman, 2001)
- New figure 12.7, Ecstasy and the adolescent's brain, including two brain scans, one of a normal adolescent brain, the other of an adolescent brain under the influence of Ecstasy
- New studies on links between parents, peers, and drug use in adolescence (National Center on Addiction and Substance Abuse, 2001; Simons-Morton & others, 2001). Also new longitudinal study focused on early childhood predictors of early onset of substance abuse in 10- to 12-year-olds (Kaplow & others, 2002)
- New overview of research on eating disorders in adolescents with descriptions of a number of recent studies (Dowda & others, 2001; Field & others, 2001; Graber & Brooks-Gunn, 2001), including new figure 12.8 on the dramatic increase in obesity in adolescence in the last 40 years
- New study on factors involved in binge eating in adolescent girls (Stice, Presnell, & Spangler, 2002)
- New graph (figure 12.9) on U.S. high school dropouts from different ethnic groups
- New section on how to improve U.S. high schools (Dornbusch & Kaufman, 2001; National Commission on the High School Senior Year, 2001)

"This chapter is so well written and the illustrations are so effective that I cannot add any suggestions to make it stronger."
—BARBA PATTON, *University of Houston–Victoria*

CHAPTER 13
Socioemotional Development in Adolescence

- New section on self-esteem, highlighting the decline in self-esteem during adolescence, especially for girls, including new figure 13.1 (Robins & others, in press)
- New discussion of gender differences in autonomy granting by parents based on recent research (Bumpus, Crouter, & McHale, 2001)
- Recent research comparing parent-adolescent conflict, autonomy, and peer orientation in Japanese and U.S. youth
- New research showing the link between active parental monitoring and guidance and more positive adolescent peer relations and lower drug use (Mounts, 2002)
- New figure 13.5 on developmental changes in the age of onset of romantic activity (Buhrmester, 2001)
- New coverage of research on dating and romantic involvement of Latinas (Raffaelli & Ontai, in press)
- New research on Fast Track, a intervention designed to prevent adolescent problems (The Conduct Problems Prevention Research Group, 2002)
- New research by Richard Savin-Williams (2001) showing that earlier statements about estimates of suicide by gay youth were exaggerated

- New research showing links between degree of acculturation and adolescent problems (Gonzales & others, in press; Roosa & others, 2002)

"The new additions to this chapter are excellent."

—ROSS PARKE, *University of California–Riverside*

CHAPTER 14
Physical and Cognitive Development in Early Adulthood

- Expanded discussion of emerging adulthood, including cross-cultural comparisons, and new figure 14.1 on self-perceptions of adult status
- Extensive new research on adapting to college, including stress in college, what makes college students very happy, the role of ethnicity and gender in health, and the roles of optimism and family factors in adapting to college (Brisette, Scheier, & Carver, 2002; Courtenay, McCreary, & Merighi, 2002; Diener & Seligman, 2002; Sax & others, 2001)
- Recent research on alcohol use during college and new coverage of cultural variations in alcohol use (Wechsler & others, 2002) and new figure 14.7 on the decline in substance use after college (Bachman & others, 2002)
- New figure 14.4 on the role of leptin in obesity
- New section on gender, ethnicity, and obesity
- Completely updated discussion of dual-career couples, including recent data on the increased time spent by men in family tasks; new figure 14.14 (Hyde & Barnett, 2001)

"This chapter rates an 'A.' The text covers the material very well. . . . The topics are most interesting and insightful. . . . The clarity is just what you would expect from John Santrock. . . . I have reviewed almost every other text available for this course and have not found one that I think would be comparable to John Santrock's text."

—BARBA PATTON, *University of Houston–Victoria*

CHAPTER 15
Socioemotional Development in Early Adulthood

- New figure 15.2 on the effects that mere exposure to someone has on the extent to which the person is liked
- New study on women's and men's views of love (Fehr & Broughton, 2001)
- Completely revamped discussion of loneliness, including new section on loneliness and technology
- New national survey on young adults' perceptions of marriage (Whitehead & Popenoe, 2001)
- New discussion of the anxiety that many childless, highly successful women have (Hewlett, 2002)

- New coverage of Hetherington's recent research on the six pathways that divorced adults follow (Hetherington & Kelly, 2002) and new discussion of recommended strategies for divorced adults

"This chapter covers a wider range of topics than some other texts and I consider that a strength."

—CYNTHIA REED, *Tarrant County College*

CHAPTER 16
Physical and Cognitive Development in Middle Adulthood

- New coverage of recent research suggesting that many people in their sixties and even seventies say that they are in middle age (Lachman, Maier, & Budner, 2000; National Council on Aging, 2000)
- New discussion of George Vaillant's recent presentation of new data from his longitudinal study of aging and new figure 16.1 based on this study that focuses on the link between characteristics in middle age and successful aging at 75 to 80 years of age
- New figure 16.2 on the relation of age and gender to cardiovascular disease and new section on lungs, including figure 16.3 on the relation of lung capacity to age and cigarette smoking
- New figure 16.4 on self-rated health at different points in adulthood (National Center for Health Statistics, 1999)
- New research on links between personality factors and health in a large longitudinal study (Aldwin & others, 2001)
- Updated, revised discussion of menopause and hormone replacement therapy
- New discussion of researcher Denise Park's (2001) view on why working memory declines in middle age
- New section on work in midlife

"I was very impressed with the quality of this chapter. . . . It is well conceived, well-written, and attractive."

—JAMES BIRREN, *University of California, Los Angeles*

CHAPTER 17
Socioemotional Development in Middle Adulthood

- New discussion of Vaillant's (2002) longitudinal study showing a link between generativity in middle age and marital quality at 75 to 80 years of age
- Discussion of recent longitudinal study of generativity and identity certainty from the thirties through the fifties (Stewart, Ostrove, & Helson, 2001), including two new figures, figure 17.1 and figure 17.2

- Updated information about the women in the Mills College study conducted by Ravenna Helson, who most recently were assessed in their fifties
- New research on link between earlier support by parents and later support of aging parents by adult children (Silverstein & others, 2002)
- New description of six characteristics in midlife, including purpose in life, autonomy, and environmental mastery, based on Ryff and Keyes' (1998) research, including new figure 17.5
- New discussion of recent study on gender differences in personality traits in 26 countries (Costa, Terracciano, & McCrae, 2001)
- Updated and expanded conclusions about stability and change in personality development in middle adulthood, including the view of Caspi and Roberts (2001) that stability increases in the fifties and sixties

"Both chapters 16 and 17 are great. . . . The coverage is very good."
—JAMES REID, *Washington University*

CHAPTER 18
Physical Development in Late Adulthood

- New Sociocultural Worlds of Development box on living longer in Okinawa, including new figure 18.2 (Willcox, Willcox, & Suzuki, 2002)
- New figure 18.4 on the decrease in brain lateralization in older adults based on recent research (Cabeza, 2002)
- New research from the McArthur Studies of Successful Aging on factors linked with improved physical functioning in older adults (Seeman & Chen, 2002)
- New discussion of ethnicity and U.S. death rates (Centers for Disease Control and Prevention, 2002)
- Recent data on the percentage of men from 65 to 80 and over 80 who have erection difficulties (Butler & Lewis, 2002)
- Expanded, updated discussion of calorie restriction and longevity (Goto & others, 2002; Johannes, 2002)
- Extensive updating of research on exercise and aging (Singh, 2002)
- New discussion of general slowdown in central nervous system functioning
- New dramatic figure 18.5 showing new brain cells generated in an adult male as a consequence of exercise and an enriched environment
- New research on the link between B vitamins and cognitive performance in older adults (Calvaresi & Bryan, 2001)

"In many ways, John Santrock has successfully translated the data on aging into terms that will be understandable to the undergraduate and has done an excellent job of presenting material that focuses on positive images of aging."
—SUSAN WHITBOURNE, *University of Massachusetts, Amherst*

CHAPTER 19
Cognitive Development in Late Adulthood

- New section on aging and attention that focuses on selective attention, divided attention, and sustained attention
- New section on prospective memory and the complexity of age changes involved
- New figure 19.2 on the relation of age to speed of processing as measured by reaction time and new research on the role of exercise in preventing cognitive decline in older adults (Yaffe & others, 2001)
- New discussion of longitudinal study on engaging in stimulating cognitive activities and its link to a lower incidence of Alzheimer's disease (Wilson & others, 2002)
- New research on the link between chronic mild depression in older adults and reduced immune system functioning (McGuire, Kiecolt-Glaser, & Glaser, 2002)
- New research on the link between gender, depression, and aging from 50 to 80, including new figure 19.5 (Barefoot & others, 2001)
- Discussion of new research on religiosity and church attendance in the last year of life (Idler, Stanislav, & Hays, 2001)

"This chapter provides a good overview of major issues and findings."
—JOANN MONTEPARE, *Emerson College*

CHAPTER 20
Socioemotional Development in Late Adulthood

- New figure 20.3 based on national study of changes in positive and negative emotions in older and younger adults
- New section on self-esteem, including discussion of recent large-scale study of developmental changes in self-esteem and new figure 20.5 (Robins & others, 2002)
- New section on changes in self-acceptance across the adult years, including new figure 20.6
- New section on personal control, highlighting Heckhausen's theory and research on primary and secondary control strategies and new figure 20.7 to illustrate developmental changes in these processes across the life span
- New material on links of depression and lower life satisfaction to not having a close friend as an older adult (Antonucci, Lansford, & Akiyama, 2001)

"This chapter has good coverage of major issues."
—JOANN MONTEPARE, *Emerson College*

CHAPTER 21
Death and Grieving

- New research on the economic consequences of widowhood in the U.S. and Germany (Hungerford, 2001)
- New research on the role of psychological and religious factors in the well-being of older adults after the death of a spouse (Fry, 2001)
- New discussion of palliative care (Chochinov, 2002)
- Update on Oregon's active euthanasia through 2001
- Increased coverage of end-of-death issues (Wilson & Truman, 2002)

"This chapter is another 'A.' It is very insightful about the last stanza of human life."

—BARBA PATTON, *University of Houston–Victoria*

ACKNOWLEDGMENTS

I very much appreciate the support and guidance provided to me by many people at McGraw-Hill. Steve Debow, President, and Thalia Dorwick, Editor-in-Chief, have been truly outstanding in their administration of the social sciences area of McGraw-Hill Higher Education. Steve Rutter, Publisher, has brought a wealth of publishing knowledge and vision to bear on improving this book. This is the second edition of *Life-Span Development* that Rebecca Hope has been the editor. She is a wonderful editor who has made very competent decisions and provided valuable advice about many aspects of the ninth edition. Judith Kromm, Senior Developmental Editor, orchestrated important changes in the manuscript. The new edition has considerably benefited also from the energy, organization, and wisdom of Kate Russillo, Editorial Assistant. Melissa Caughlin, Marketing Manager, has contributed in numerous creative ways to this book, as did Chris Hall, the former Marketing Manager. Marilyn Rothenberger was a superb project manager and Bea Sussman did a stellar job in copyediting the book.

EXPERT CONSULTANTS

Life-span development has become an enormous, complex field and no single author can possibly be an expert in all areas of the field. To solve this problem, beginning with the sixth edition, I have sought the input of leading experts in many different areas of life-span development. This tradition continues in the ninth edition. The experts have provided me with detailed recommendations on new research to include for every period of the life span.

The panel of experts who contributed to the ninth edition literally is a who's who register for the field of life-span development. Their photographs and biographies appear on pages xxvii through xxix. Here are the names and areas of expertise of those individuals, whose invaluable feedback and evaluations I gratefully acknowledge:

K. Warner Schaie, *Pennsylvania State University* One of the architects of the field of adulthood and aging

James Birren, *University of California, Los Angeles* A major contributor to the field of aging

Yvette R. Harris, *Miami University (Ohio)* An expert on the effects of ethnicity on cognitive, intellectual, academic, and occupational development

Ross Parke, *University of California at Riverside* One of the world's leading authorities on family processes and children's socioemotional development

Jean Berko Gleason, *Boston University* One of the world's leading experts on children's language development

Scott Miller, *University of Florida* An authority on children's cognitive development

Carolyn Saarni, *Sonoma State University* An expert on children's emotional development

Alan Fogel, *University of Utah* A leading figure in the study of infant development

Susan Whitbourne, *University of Massachusetts, Amherst* An expert on adult development and aging

James Reid, *Washington University* An expert on middle adulthood and aging

Marian Underwood, *University of Texas at Dallas* An expert on peer relations and socioemotional development

Gilbert Gottlieb, *University of North Carolina* A leading figure in biological foundations of development

Barba Patton, *University of Houston–Victoria* An expert on education

Bert Hayslip, *University of North Texas* An expert on the topics of death and grieving

GENERAL TEXT REVIEWERS

I also owe special gratitude to the instructors teaching the life-span course who have provided detailed feedback about the book. Many of the changes in *Life-Span Development,* ninth edition, are based on their feedback. In this regard, I thank these individuals:

Pre-Revision Reviewers

Leslie Ault, *Hostos Community College–CUNY*
Dana Davidson, *University of Hawaii at Manoa*
Marian S. Harris, *University of Illinois at Chicago*
Donna Henderson, *Wake Forest University*
Donna Horbury, *Appalachian State University*
Steven J. Kohn, *Nazareth College*
Christine Malecki, *Northern Illinois University*
Robert McLaren, *California State University at Fullerton*
Leslee Pollina, *Southeast Missouri State University*

Cynthia Reed, *Tarrant County College–Northeast Campus*
Edythe Schwartz, *California State University at Sacramento*

Ninth Edition Reviewers

John Biondo, *Community College of Allegheny County*
Michelle Boyer-Pennington, *Middle Tennessee State University*
Andrea Clements, *East Tennessee State University*
Caroline Gould, *Eastern Michigan University*
Tom Gray, *Laredo Community College*
Michele Gregoire, *University of Florida–Gainesville*
Gary Gute, *University of Northern Iowa*
Derek Isaacowitz, *Brandeis University*
Christina Jose-Kampfner, *Eastern Michigan University*
Amanda Kowal, *University of Missouri*
Myra Marcus, *Florida Gulf Coast University*
Joann Montepare, *Emerson College*
Kimberley Howe Norris, *Cape Fear Community College*
Laura Overstreet, *Tarrant County College–Northeast*
Julia Rux, *Georgia Perimeter College*
Gayla Sanders, *Community College of Baltimore County–Essex*
Toru Sato, *Shippensburg University*
Lisa Scott, *University of Minnesota*
Collier Summers, *Florida Community College*
Debbie Tindell, *Wilkes University*

EXPERT CONSULTANTS FOR PREVIOUS EDITIONS

Beginning with the sixth edition, expert consultants have provided extremely valuable feedback to me. These leading figures in the field of life-span development served as expert consultants on editions 6 through 8: **Toni C. Antonucci**, *University of Michigan, Ann Arbor;* **Paul Baltes**, *Max Planck Institute for Human development;* **Diana Baumrind**, *University of California, Berkeley;* **Carol Beal**, *University of Massachusetts at Amherst;* **Marc H. Bornstein**, *National Institute of Child Health & Development;* **Sue Bredekamp**, *National Association for the Education of Young Children;* **Urie Bronfenbrenner**, *Cornell University;* **Rosalind Charlesworth**, *Weber State University;* **Florence Denmark**, *Pace University;* **Joseph Durlack**, *Loyola University;* **Glen Elder**, *University of North Carolina, Chapel Hill;* **Tiffany Field**, *University of Miami;* **Julia Graber**, *Columbia University;* **Sandra Graham**, *University of California, Los Angeles;* **Jane Halonen**, *Alverno College;* **Algea O. Harrison-Hale**, *Oakland University;* **Craig Hart**, *Brigham Young University;* **Ravenna Helson**, *University of California, Berkeley;* **Cigdem Kagitcibasi**, *Koc University (Turkey);* **Robert Kastenbaum**, *Arizona State University;* **Gisela Labouvie-Vief**, *Wayne State University;* **Barry M. Lester**, *Women and Infant's Hospital;* **Jean M. Mandler**, *University of California—San Diego;* **James Marcia**, *Simon Fraser University;* **Phyllis Moen**, *Cornell University;* **K. Warner Schaie**, *Pennsylvania State University;* **Jan Sinnott**, *Towson State University;* **Margaret Beale Spencer**, *University of Pennsylvania;* **Ross A. Thompson**, *University of Nebraska—Lincoln.*

REVIEWERS OF PREVIOUS EDITIONS

I also remain indebted to the following individuals who reviewed previous editions and whose suggestions have been carried forward into the current edition: **Patrick K. Ackles,** *Michigan State University;* **Berkeley Adams,** *Jamestown Community College;* **Joanne M. Alegre,** *Yavapai College;* **Gary L. Allen,** *University of South Carolina;* **Lilia Allen,** *Charles County Community College:* **Susan E. Allen,** *Baylor University;* **Doreen Arcus,** *University of Massachusetts, Lowell;* **Frank R. Ashbury,** *Valdosta State College;* **Renee L. Babcock,** *Central Michigan University;* **Daniel R. Bellack,** *Trident Technical College;* **Helen E. Benedict,** *Baylor University;* **Alice D. Beyrent,** *Hesser College;* **James A. Blackburn,** *University of Wisconsin, Madison;* **Stephanie Blecharczyk,** *Keene State College;* **Belinda Blevin-Knabe,** *University of Arkansas, Little Rock;* **Karyn Mitchell Boutin,** *Massasoit Community College;* **Donald Bowers,** *Community College of Philadelphia;* **Saundra Y. Boyd,** *Houston Community College;* **Michelle Boyer-Pennington,** *Middle Tennessee State University;* **Ann Brandt-Williams,** *Glendale Community College;* **Jack Busky,** *Harrisburg Area Community College;* **Joan B. Cannon,** *University of Lowell;* **Jeri Carter,** *Glendale Community College;* **Vincent Castranovo,** *Community College of Philadelphia;* **Ginny Chappeleau,** *Muskingum Area Technical College;* **M. A. Christenberry,** *Augusta College;* **Meredith Cohen,** *University of Pittsburg;* **Diane Cook,** *Gainesville College;* **Ava Craig,** *Sacramento City College;* **Kathleen Crowley-Long,** *College of Saint Rose;* **Cynthia Crown,** *Xavier University;* **Diane Davis,** *Bowie State University;* **Tom L. Day,** *Weber State University;* **Doreen DeSantio,** *West Chester University;* **Jill De Villiers,** *Smith College;* **Darryl M. Dietrich,** *College of St. Scholastica;* **Mary B. Eberly,** *Oakland University;* **Margaret Sutton Edmonds,** *University of Massachusetts, Boston;* **Martha M. Ellis,** *Collin County Community College;* **Richard Ewy,** *Penn State University;* **Dan Fawaz,** *Georgia Perimeter College;* **Shirley Feldman,** *Stanford University;* **Roberta Ferra,** *University of Kentucky;* **Linda E. Flickinger,** *St. Claire Community College;* **Lynne Andreozzi Fontaine,** *Community College of Rhode Island;* **Tom Frangicetto,** *Northhampton Community College;* **Kathleen Corrigan Fuhs,** *J. Sargeant Reynolds Community College;* **J. Steven Fulks,** *Utah State University;* **Cathy Furlong,** *Tulsa Junior College;* **Duwayne Furman,** *Western Illinois University;* **John Gat,** *Humboldt State University;* **Marvin Gelman,** *Montgomery County College;* **Rebecca J. Glare,** *Weber State College;* **Jean Berko Gleason,** *Boston University;* **David Goldstein,** *Temple University;* **Judy Goodell,** *National University;* **Mary Ann Goodwyn,** *Northeast Louisiana University;* **Peter C. Gram,** *Pensacola Junior College;* **Dan Grangaard,** *Austin Community College;* **Michael Green,** *University of North Carolina;* **Rea Gubler,** *Southern Utah University;* **Laura Hanish,** *Arizona State University;* **Ester Hanson,** *Prince George's Community College;* **Amanda W. Harrist,** *Oklahoma State University;* **Robert Heavilin,** *Greater Hartford Community College;* **Debra Hollister,** *Valencia Community College;* **Heather Holmes-Lonergan,** *Metropolitan State College of Denver;* **Ramona O. Hopkins,** *Brigham Young University;* **Susan Horton,** *Mesa Community College;* **Sharon C. Hott,** *Allegany College of Maryland;* **Stephen Hoyer,** *Pittsburgh State University;*

Kathleen Day Hulbert, *University of Massachusetss, Lowell;* Kathryn French Iroz, *Utah Valley State College;* Erwin Janek, *Henderson State University;* James Jasper-Jacobsen, *Indiana University—Purdue;* Ursula Joyce, *St. Thomas Aquinas College;* Seth Kalichman, *Loyola University;* Barbara Kane, *Indiana State University;* Kevin Keating, *Broward Community College;* James L. Keeney, *Middle Georgia College;* Elinor Kinarthy, *Rio Hondo College;* Karen Kirkendall, *Sangamon State University;* A. Klingner, *Northwest Community College;* Jane Krump, *North Dakota State College of Science;* Joseph C. LaVoie, *University of Nebraska at Omaha;* Jean Hill Macht, *Montgomery County Community College;* Salvador Macias, *University of South Carolina— Sumter;* Karen Macrae, *University of South Carolina;* Kathy Manuel, *Bossier Parish Community College;* Allan Mayotte, *Riverland Community College;* Susan McClure, *Westmoreland Community College;* Dorothy H. McDonald, *Sandhills Community College;* Robert C. McGinnis, *Ancilla College;* Clara McKinney, *Barstow College;* Sharon McNeeley, *Northeastern Illinois University;* Heather E. Metcalfe, *University of Windsor;* Karla Miley, *Black Hawk College;* Jessica Miller, *Mesa State College;* Teri M. Miller-Schwartz, *Milwaukee Area Technical College;* David B. Mitchell, *Loyola University;* Martin D. Murphy, *University of Akron;* Malinda Muzi, *Community College of Philadelphia;* Gordon K. Nelson, *Pennsylvania State University;* Michael Newton, *Sam Houston State University;* Beatrice Norrie, *Mount Royal College;* Jean O'Neil, *Boston College;* Pete Peterson, *Johnson County Community College;* Richard Pierce, *Pennsylvania State University—Altoona;* David Pipes, *Caldwell Community College;* Robert Poresky, *Kansas State University;* Christopher Quarto, *Middle Tennessee State University;* Bob Rainey, *Florida Community College;* Nancy Rankin, *University of New England;* H. Ratner, *Wayne State University;* Russell Riley, *Lord Fairfax Community College;* Mark P. Rittman, *Cuyahogo Community College;* Clarence Romeno, *Riverside Community College;* Paul Roodin, *SUNY— Oswego;* Ron Russac, *University of North Florida;* Nancy Sauerman, *Kirkwood Community College;* Cynthia Scheibe, *Ithica College;* Robert Schell, *SUNY—Oswego;* Owen Sharkey, *University of Prince Edward Island;* Elisabeth Shaw, *Texarkana College;* Susan Nakayama Siaw, *California State Polytechnical University;* Vicki Simmons, *Univeristy of Victoria;* Gregory Smith, *University of Maryland;* Jon Snodgrass, *California State University—LA;* Donald Stanley, *North Dallas Community College;* Jean A. Steitz, *The University of Memphis;* Barbara Thomas, *National University;* Stacy D. Thompson, *Oklahoma State University;* Stephen Truhon, *Winston-Salem State University;* James Turcott, *Kalamazoo Valley Community College;* Gaby Vandergiessen, *Fairmount State College;* Stephen Werba, *The Community College of Baltimore County—Catonsville;* B. D. Whetstone, *Birmingham Southern College;* Nancy C. White, *Reynolds Community College;* Lyn W. Wickelgren, *Metropolitan State College;* Ann M. Williams, *Luzerne County Community College;* Myron D. Williams, *Great Lakes Bible College;* Linda B. Wilson, *Quincy College.*

SUPPLEMENTS

The ninth edition of *Life-Span Development* is accompanied by a comprehensive and fully integrated array of supplemental materials, both print and electronic, written specifically for instructors and students of life-span development. In addition, a variety of generic supplements are available to further aid in the teaching and learning of life-span development.

For the Instructor

Once again, based on comprehensive and extensive feedback from instructors, we spent considerable time and effort in expanding and improving the ancillary materials.

Instructor's Manual *Christine Malecki* This comprehensive manual provides a variety of useful tools for both seasoned instructors and those new to the life-span development course. The instructor's manual provides these tools, all of which are tied to the text's Learning Goals as appropriate:

- A focused introductory section on teaching life-span development. This section covers helpful material for new instructors, including course-planning ideas, teaching tips, and teaching resources.
- A Total Teaching Package Outline begins each chapter. It features a fully integrated outline to help instructors better use the many resources for the course. Most of the supplementary materials offered in conjunction with *Life-Span Development*, ninth edition, are represented in this outline and have been correlated to the main concepts in each chapter.
- Lecture suggestions, classroom activities, out-of-class activities, research projects, and critical thinking multiple-choice and essay exercises, all of which provide answers where appropriate.
- Classroom activities now provide logistics for required materials, such as accompanying handouts, varying group sizes, and time needed for completion.
- Greatly expanded chapter outlines and personal application projects where students can apply development topics to their own lives.
- Comprehensive transparency, film, and video resources, updated URLs for useful Internet sites, and chapter maps derived from the textbook that can be used for lecture aids.

Printed Test Bank *Angela Sadowski* This comprehensive Test Bank has once again been extensively revised to include over 2,400 multiple-choice and short-answer/brief essay questions for the text's 21 chapters. Each multiple-choice item is classified as factual, conceptual, or applied, as defined by Benjamin Bloom's taxonomy of educational objectives. New to this edition, each test question is now keyed to a chapter learning goal, and the test bank notes which learning goal each item addresses. In response to customer feedback, this Test Bank also provides page references that indicate where in the text the answer to each item can be found.

PowerPoint Slide Presentations The chapter-by-chapter PowerPoint lectures for this edition integrate the text's learning goals, and provide key text material and illustrations, as well as additional illustrations and images not found in the textbook. These presentations are designed to be useful in both small- and large-lecture settings, and are easily tailored to suit an individual instructor's lectures.

Computerized Test Bank on CD-ROM The computerized test bank contains all of the questions in the printed test bank and can be used in both Windows and Macintosh platforms. This CD-ROM provides a fully functioning editing feature that enables instructors to integrate their own questions, scramble items, and modify questions.

The McGraw-Hill Developmental Psychology Image Bank This set of 200 full-color images was developed using the best selection of our human development art and tables and is available online for both instructors and students on the text's Online Learning Center.

Online Learning Center The extensive website designed specifically to accompany Santrock, *Life-Span Development*, ninth edition, offers an array of resources for both instructor and student. For instructors, the website includes a full set of PowerPoint Presentations, hotlinks for the text's topical web links that appear in margins and for the Taking It to the Net exercises that appear at the end of each chapter. These resources and more can be found by logging on to the website at http://www.mhhe.com/santrockld9.

Annual Editions—Developmental Psychology Published by Dushkin/McGraw-Hill, this is a collection of articles on topics related to the latest research and thinking in human development. These editions are updated annually and contain helpful features including a topic guide, an annotated table of contents, unit overviews, and a topical index. An Instructor's Guide containing testing materials is also available.

Sources: Notable Selections in Human Development This volume presents a collection of more than 40 articles, book excerpts, and research studies that have shaped the study of human development and our contemporary understanding of it. The selections are organized topically around major areas of study within human development. Each selection is preceded by a headnote that establishes the relevance of the article or study and provides biographical information about the author.

Taking Sides This debate-style reader is designed to introduce students to controversial viewpoints on the field's most crucial issues. Each issue is carefully framed for the student, and the pro and con essays represent the arguments of leading scholars and commentators in their fields. An Instructor's Guide containing testing material is available.

For the Student

Student Study Guide *Barba Patton* The revised Study Guide provides a complete introduction for students on how best to use each of the various study aids plus invaluable strategies on setting goals, benefiting from class, reading for learning, taking tests, and memory techniques in the section "Being an Excellent Student." Each Study Guide chapter begins with an outline of the chapter that also directs students to additional resources available for the study of specific topics or concepts. Resources referenced include the text's Online Learning Center and Student CD-ROM. The Study Guide also now thoroughly integrates the learning goals provided in each text chapter. The self-test sections contain multiple-choice questions and comprehensive essays with suggested answers, all of which are keyed to the learning goals. Self-tests also include matching sets on key people found in the text and word scramblers on key terms found in the text. Finally, the Study Guide also includes out-of-class projects such as personal application projects and Internet exercises that complement the revised student research projects and allow for more effective student learning.

Interactive CD-ROM for Students This user-friendly CD-ROM gives students an opportunity to test their comprehension of the course material. Prepared specifically to accompany Santrock, *Life-Span Development*, ninth edition, this CD-ROM provides 25 multiple-choice questions for each chapter to help students further test their understanding of key concepts. Feedback is provided for each question's answer. In addition, the CD-ROM provides a Learning Assessment questionnaire to help students discover which type of learner they are, of the three types covered in the program.

Online Learning Center The extensive website designed specifically to accompany Santrock, *Life-Span Development*, ninth edition, offers an array of resources for instructors and students. For students, the website includes interactive quizzing and exercises as well as hotlinks for the text's topical web links that appear in the margins and for the *Taking It to the Net* exercises that appear at the end of each chapter. An important new feature in this edition is the inclusion of many self-assessments related to chapter topics. These resources and more can be found by logging on to the website at http://www.mhhe.com/santrockld9.

Guide to Life-Span Development for Future Educators and ***Guide to Life-Span Development for Future Nurses*** These new course supplements help students apply the concepts of human development to education. They contain information, exercises, and sample tests designed to help students prepare for certification and understand human development from a professional perspective.

Resources for Improving Human Development This informative booklet provides descriptions and contact information for organizations and agencies that can provide helpful information, advice, and support related to particular problems or issues in life-span development. Recommended books and journals are also described and included. The booklet is organized by chronological order of the periods of the life span.

Expert Consultants

K. Warner Schaie

K. Warner Schaie was one of the pioneers who created and shaped the field of life-span development. He continues to be one of the world's leading experts on adult development and aging. Schaie is currently the Evan Pugh Professor of Human Development and Psychology and Director of the Gerontology Center at the Pennsylvania State University. He also holds an appointment as Affiliate Professor of Psychiatry and Behavioral Science at the University of Washington. Schaie received his Ph.D. in psychology from the University of Washington and an honorary doctorate from the Friedrich-Schiller-University of Jena, Germany. He was honored with the Kleemeier Award for Distinguished Research Contributions from the Gerontological Society of America and the Distinguished Scientific Contributions award from the American Psychological Association. He is author or editor of 32 books including the textbook *Adult Development and Aging* (with S. L. Willis) and the *Handbook of the Psychology of Aging* (with J. E. Birren), both of which are now in their fifth edition. He has directed the Seattle Longitudinal Study of cognitive aging since 1956 and is the author of more than 250 journal articles and chapters on the psychology of aging. His current research interest focuses on the life course of adult intelligence, its antecedents and modifiability, as well as methodological issues in the developmental sciences.

James E. Birren

James E. Birren is a pioneering figure in the field of life-span development and continues to be one of the world's leading experts on adult development and aging. He currently is Associate Director of the UCLA Center on Aging and is also Professor Emeritus of Gerontology and Psychology at the University of Southern California. Birren received his M.A. and Ph.D. from Northwestern University, and has been a Visiting Scientist at the University of Cambridge, England, and a Fellow at the Center for Advanced Study in the Behavioral Sciences at Stanford University. Birren's career includes serving as founding Executive Director and Dean of the Gerontology Center at the University of Southern California, as well as Past President of the Gerontological Society of America, the Western Gerontological Society, and the Division on Adult Development and Aging of the American Psychological Association. In addition, he has served as Chief of the Section on Aging of the National Institutes of Mental Health. His awards include the Brookdale Foundation Award for Gerontological Research; honorary doctorates from the University of Gothenberg, Sweden, Northwestern University, and St. Thomas University, Canada; the Gerontological Society Award for Meritorious Research; the Sandoz Prize for Gerontological Research; and the Canadian Association of Gerontology Award for Outstanding Contribution to Gerontology. Birren is Series Editor of the internationally recognized *Handbooks on Aging* and has published more than 250 academic journal articles and books.

Yvette R. Harris

Yvette R. Harris is a leading expert on diversity. She received her Ph.D. from the University of Florida and is currently a faculty member in the Department of Psychology at Miami University in Oxford, Ohio. Harris, a cognitive-developmental psychologist, has authored and co-authored articles on African-American children and academic achievement, and maternal-child learning interaction in African-American families. She has been the recipient of awards from the National Science Foundation and the Murray Research Center to support her research on maternal-child interaction.

Ross Parke

Ross Parke is one of the world's leading experts on socioemotional development. He currently is Distinguished Professor of Psychology and Director of the Center for Family Studies at the University of California, Riverside. Parke obtained his Ph.D. from the University of Waterloo, Ontario, Canada. He is a Past President of Division 7 (Developmental Psychology) of the American Psychological Association and has received the G. Stanley Hall Award from this APA division. He is a Fellow of the American Association for the Advancement of Science. Parke currently is editor of the *Journal of Family Psychology,* having previously served as editor of *Developmental Psychology* and as associate editor of *Child Development*. He is the author of *Fatherhood* and co-author of two books: *Throwaway Dads* and *Child Psychology,* fifth edition, revised. Park is also the co-editor of these books: *Family-Peer Relationships; Children in Time and Place;* and *Exploring Family Relationships with Other Social Contexts.* Parke is well known for his pioneering research on punishment, aggression, child abuse, and the father's role. His current work focuses on the links between family and peer social systems and on the impact of economic stress on families of diverse ethnic backgrounds.

Jean Berko Gleason

Jean Berko Gleason is one of the world's leading experts on child language. She is a Professor in the Department of Psychology at Boston University and also a faculty member and former director of Boston University's Graduate Program in Applied Linguistics. Berko Gleason has been a Visiting Scholar at Stanford University, Harvard, and the Linguistics Institute of the Hungarian Academy of Sciences in Budapest. She received her undergraduate and graduate degrees from Harvard/Radcliffe and has been President of the International Association for the Study of Child Language. Berko Gleason is the author and editor of leading textbooks on language development and psycholinguistics. Since writing her doctoral dissertation on how children learn to make plurals and past tenses in English, she has published over one hundred articles on aphasia, language attrition, language development in children, gender differences in parents' speech, and cross-cultural differences. Her work is frequently cited in the professional literature, and has been featured in the popular press and on television.

Carolyn Saarni

Carolyn Saarni is one of the world's leading experts on children's emotional development. She received her Ph.D. from the University of California at Berkeley and her first academic appointment was at New York University. Since 1980 Saarni has been a Professor and subsequently Chair of the Graduate Department of Counseling at Sonoma State University in California where she trains prospective marriage, family, child counselors and school counselors. Her research has focused on how children learn that they can adopt an *emotional front*—that is, what they express emotionally does not need to match what they really feel. She has also investigated how children use this knowledge strategically in their interpersonal relations with others as well as when coping with aversive feelings. Her research has been funded by the National Science Foundation and the Spencer Foundation, among others. Saarni has co-edited several books on children's emotional development and most recently published *The Development of Emotional Competence.* The thesis of this book is that the skills of emotional competence are contextualized by culture, including moral values and beliefs about "how emotion works." She has also authored numerous chapters and articles on children's emotional development and is regularly consulted by the popular media on topics concerning emotional development in children and youth.

Alan Fogel

Alan Fogel is one of the world's leading experts on infant development. He is currently a Professor of Psychology at the University of Utah in Salt Lake City and previously held a faculty position at Purdue University. Fogel obtained his undergraduate degree at the University of Miami (Florida), his masters degree at Columbia University, and his Ph.D. at the University of Chicago. He is a Fellow of the American Psychological Association and has been an active contributor to research on infant socioemotional development. He especially is known for his application of dynamic systems theory to the study of developmental change. Fogel's theoretical perspective is best summarized in two books he has authored: *Developing through Relationships* and *Infancy: Infant, Family, and Society,* fourth edition. Further information about Alan Fogel's perspective and research can be found at **http://www.psych.utah.edu/alan_fogels_infant_lab/**.

Susan Krauss Whitbourne

Susan Krauss Whitbourne is a leading expert on adult development and aging. She is currently a Professor of Psychology at the University of Massachusetts at Amherst. Whitbourne obtained her Ph.D. in developmental psychology from Columbia University and completed postdoctoral training in clinical psychology at University of Massachusetts. Prior to joining the University of Massachusetts faculty, she was a faculty member at the University of Rochester and SUNY College at Geneseo. Her teaching has been recognized with the College Outstanding Teacher Award and the University Distinguished Teaching Award. Over the past 25 years, Whitbourne has held a variety of elected and appointed positions in Division 20 (Adult Development and Aging) of the American Psychological Association (APA), including President. Whitbourne is also a Fellow of the Gerontological Society of America. Her publications include 14 published books and 2 in preparation, as well as nearly 100 articles and chapters in leading research journals and books. She has been a consulting editor for *Psychology and Aging,* and serves on the editorial board of the *Journal of Gerontology.* Whitbourne has made more than 175 presentations, including a number of invited addresses, at professional conferences.

Marion K. Underwood

Marion K. Underwood is a leading researcher in children's socioemotional development. She obtained her undergraduate degree from Wellesley College and her doctoral degree in clinical psychology from Duke University. Underwood began her faculty career at Reed College in Portland, Oregon, and is currently a Professor at the University of Texas at Dallas. Her research examines anger, aggression, and gender, with special attention to the development of social aggression among girls. Underwood's research has been published in numerous scientific journals and her research program has been supported by the National Institutes of Mental Heath. She authored the forthcoming book, *Ice and Fire: Social Aggression in Girls.* Underwood also received the 2001 University of Texas Chancellor's Council Outstanding Teacher of the Year Award.

Gilbert Gottlieb

Gilbert Gottlieb is one of the world's leading experts on early development. He currently is Research Professor of Psychology in the Center for Developmental Science at the University of North Carolina at Chapel Hill. He held positions at the University of North Carolina at Greensboro and Dorothea Dix Hospital in Raleigh, after receiving his Ph.D. from Duke University, where he was the first graduate from the joint Psychology-Zoology Graduate Training Program in Animal Behavior. Gottlieb helped to revive interest in the field of behavioral embryology by editing a volume by that name. His interest in the developmental basis of evolution resulted in the book, *Individual Development and Evolution.* Gottlieb summarized his career-long research and theoretical efforts in *Synthesizing Nature–Nurture* (1997), which won the 1998 Eleanor Maccoby Award of the Developmental Psychology Division of the American Psychological Association. In 1999 Clark University Press published his monograph, *Probabilistic Epigenesis and Evolution,* which is based upon the Heinz Werner Lectures he gave there. Gottlieb has been a recipient of research grants from the National Institutes of Mental Health and from Child Health and Human Development, as well as from the National Science Foundation. He is Past President of the International Society for Developmental Psychobiology, and he is a recipient of the Distinguished Scientific Contributions to Child Development Award from the Society for Research in Child Development.

Barba Patton

Barba Patton is a leading expert on education. She received her Ed.D. from the University of Houston and is currently a faculty member at the University of Houston-Victoria, where she is Director of the Center for Excellence. Patton presents her views on education each year at national, regional, and local conferences on child development, mathematics, and learning. She has extensively reviewed articles for journals and manuscripts for books. Patton enjoys teaching and the interaction it involves with students. She actively assists teachers in classrooms with students who have learning problems, especially in the area of mathematics and science. She is currently conducting research on dyscalculia.

Bert Hayslip, Jr.

Bert Hayslip, Jr. is a leading expert on death and grieving. He obtained his doctorate in experimental developmental psychology from the University of Akron. He was a faculty member at Hood College and currently is Regents Professor of Psychology at the University of North Texas. Hayslip is a Fellow of the American Psychological Association, the Gerontological Society of America, and the Association for Gerontology in Higher Education. He has held research grants from the National Institute of Aging and other agencies. Hayslip is currently editor of *The International Journal of Aging and Human Development* and associate editor of *Experimental Aging Research.* His research focuses on cognitive processes in aging, interventions to enhance cognitive functioning in later life, personality-ability linkages in older adults, grandparents who raise their grandchildren, grief and bereavement, hospice care, death anxiety, and mental health and aging. He is the co-author of *Hospice Care; Psychology and Aging: An Annotated Bibliography; Grandparents Raising Grandchildren; Adult Development and Aging,* third edition; *Working with Custodial Grandparents;* and *Historical Shifts in Attitudes Toward Death, Dying, and Bereavement.*

TO THE STUDENT

This book provides you with important study tools to help you more effectively learn about life-span development. Especially important is the learning goals system that is integrated throughout each chapter. In the visual walk-through of features, pay special attention to how the learning goals system works.

The Learning Goals System

Using the learning goals system will help you to learn more material more easily. Key aspects of the learning goals system are the learning goals, chapter maps, Review and Reflect, and Reach Your Learning Goals sections, which are all linked together.

At the beginning of each chapter, you will see a page that includes both a chapter outline and three to six learning goals that preview the chapter's main themes and underscore the most important ideas in the chapter. Then, at the beginning of

each major section of a chapter, you will see a mini–chapter map that provides you with a visual organization of the key topics you are about to read in the section. At the end of each section is Review and Reflect, in which the learning goal for the section is restated, a series of review questions related to the mini–chapter map are asked, and a question that encourages you to think critically about a topic related to the section appears. At the end of the chapter, you will come to a section titled Reach Your Learning Goals. This includes an overall chapter map that visually organizes all of the main headings, a restatement of the chapter's learning goals, and a summary of the chapter's content that is directly linked to the chapter outline at the beginning of the chapter and the questions asked in the Review part of Review and Reflect within the chapter. The summary essentially answers the questions asked in the within-chapter Review sections.

A visual presentation of the learning goals system is provided on this and the following pages.

Chapter Opening Outline and Learning Goals

The outline shows the organization of topics by headings. Primary topic headings are printed in blue capital letters. The Learning Goals highlight the main ideas in the chapter by section.

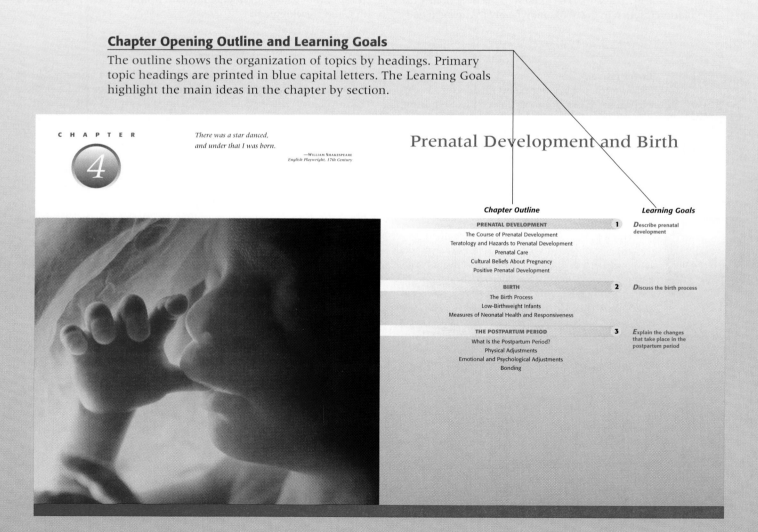

CHAPTER

4

There was a star danced, and under that I was born.

—WILLIAM SHAKESPEARE
English Playwright, 17th Century

Prenatal Development and Birth

Chapter Outline

PRENATAL DEVELOPMENT
The Course of Prenatal Development
Teratology and Hazards to Prenatal Development
Prenatal Care
Cultural Beliefs About Pregnancy
Positive Prenatal Development

BIRTH
The Birth Process
Low-Birthweight Infants
Measures of Neonatal Health and Responsiveness

THE POSTPARTUM PERIOD
What Is the Postpartum Period?
Physical Adjustments
Emotional and Psychological Adjustments
Bonding

Learning Goals

1 *Describe prenatal development*

2 *Discuss the birth process*

3 *Explain the changes that take place in the postpartum period*

1 PRENATAL DEVELOPMENT

- The Course of Prenatal Development
- Teratology and Hazards to Prenatal Development
- Prenatal Care
- Cultural Beliefs About Pregnancy
- Positive Prenatal Development

Mini–Chapter Map

This visual preview displays the main headings and subheadings for each section of the chapter.

Imagine how Tanner Roberts came to be. Out of thousands of eggs and millions of sperm, one egg and one sperm united to produce him. Had the union of sperm and egg come a day or even an hour earlier or later, he might have been very different—maybe even of the opposite sex. Conception occurs when a single sperm cell from the male unites with an ovum (egg) in the female's fallopian tube in a process called fertilization. Remember from chapter 3 that the fertilized egg is called a zygote.

The Course of Prenatal Development

The course of prenatal development lasts approximately 266 days, beginning with fertilization and ending with birth. Prenatal development is divided into three periods: germinal, embryonic, and fetal.

The Germinal Period The **germinal period** is the period of prenatal development that takes place in the first two weeks after conception. It includes the creation of the zygote, continued cell division, and the attachment of the zygote to the uterine wall. By approximately one week after conception, the differentiation of cells has already commenced, as inner and outer layers of the organism are formed. The **blastocyst** is the inner layer of cells that develops during the germinal period. These cells later develop into the embryo. The **trophoblast** is the outer layer of cells that develops during the germinal period. It later provides nutrition and support for the embryo. *Implantation*, the attachment of the zygote to the uterine wall, takes place about 10 to 14 days after conception. Figure 4.1 on page 114 illustrates some of the most significant de

The En ment t riod, t organs change

> **germinal period** The period of prenatal development that takes place in the first two weeks after conception. It includes the creation of the zygote, continued cell division,

Reach Your Learning Goals

This section includes a complete chapter map and a summary restating the Learning Goals and answering the bulleted review questions from the chapter. Use it as a guide to help you organize your study of the chapter, *not* as a substitute for reading and studying the chapter.

Reach Your Learning Goals

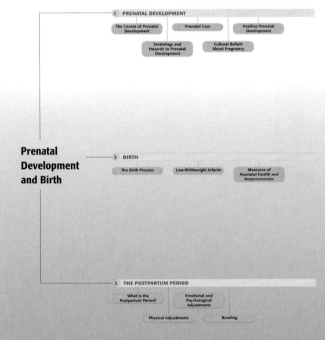

Prenatal Development and Birth

1 PRENATAL DEVELOPMENT

- The Course of Prenatal Development
- Teratology and Hazards to Prenatal Development
- Prenatal Care
- Cultural Beliefs About Pregnancy
- Positive Prenatal Development

2 BIRTH

- The Birth Process
- Low-Birthweight Infants
- Measures of Neonatal Health and Responsiveness

3 THE POSTPARTUM PERIOD

- What Is the Postpartum Period?
- Emotional and Psychological Adjustments
- Physical Adjustments
- Bonding

140

Summary

1 Describe prenatal development

- Prenatal development is divided into three periods: germinal (conception until 10 to 14 days later), which ends when the zygote (a fertilized egg) attaches to the uterine wall; embryonic (two to eight weeks after conception), during which the embryo differentiates into three layers, life-support systems develop, and organ systems form (organogenesis); and fetal (two months after conception until about nine months, or when the infant is born), a time when organ systems have matured to the point at which life can be sustained outside of the womb.
- Teratology is the field that investigates the causes of congenital (birth) defects. Any agent that causes birth defects is called a teratogen. The dose, time of exposure, and genetic susceptibility influence the severity of the damage to an unborn child and the type of defect that occurs. Prescription drugs that can be harmful include antibiotics, some depressants, and certain hormones. Nonprescription drugs that can be harmful include diet pills, aspirin, and coffee. Fetal alcohol syndrome (FAS) is a cluster of abnormalities that appear in offspring of mothers who drink heavily during pregnancy. When pregnant women drink moderately (one to two drinks a day), negative effects on their offspring have been found. Cigarette smoking by pregnant women has serious adverse effects on prenatal and child development (such as low birthweight). Illegal drugs that are potentially harmful to offspring include marijuana, cocaine, and heroin. Incompatibility of the mother's and the father's blood types can also be harmful to the fetus. Potential environmental hazards include radiation, environmental pollutants, toxic wastes, and prolonged exposure to heat in saunas and hot tubs. Rubella (German measles) can be harmful. Syphilis, genital herpes, and AIDS are other teratogens. A developing fetus depends entirely on its mother for nutrition. One nutrient that is especially important early in development is folic acid. High anxiety and stress in the mother are linked with less than optimal prenatal and birth outcomes. Maternal age can negatively affect the offspring's development if the mother is an adolescent or over 30. Paternal factors that can adversely affect prenatal development include exposure to lead, radiation, certain pesticides, and petrochemicals.
- Prenatal care varies extensively but usually involves medical care services with a defined schedule of visits.
- Specific actions in pregnancy are often determined by cultural beliefs. Certain behaviors are expected if a culture views pregnancy as a medical condition or a natural occurrence. For example, prenatal care may not be a priority for expectant mothers who view pregnancy as a natural occurrence.
- It is important to remember that, although things can and do go wrong during pregnancy, most of the time pregnancy and prenatal development go well. Avoiding teratogens helps ensure a positive outcome.

2 Discuss the birth process

- Childbirth occurs in three stages. The first stage, which lasts about 12 to 24 hours for a woman having her first child, is the longest stage. The cervix dilates to about 4 inches at the end of the first stage. The second stage begins when the baby's head moves through the cervix and ends with the baby's complete emergence. The third stage is afterbirth. Being born involves considerable stress for the baby, but the baby is well prepared and adapted to handle the stress. Anoxia—insufficient oxygen supply to the fetus/newborn—is a potential hazard. Childbirth strategies involve the childbirth setting and attendants. In many countries, a doula attends a childbearing woman. Methods of delivery include medicated, natural and prepared, and cesarean.
- Low-birthweight infants weigh less than 5½ pounds and they may be preterm (born three weeks or more before the pregnancy has reached full term) or small for date (also called small for gestational age, which refers to infants whose birthweight is below norm when the length of pregnancy is considered). Small for date infants may be preterm or full term. Although most low-birthweight infants are normal and healthy, as a group they have more health and developmental problems than normal-birthweight infants.
- For many years, the Apgar Scale has been used to assess the newborn's health. The Brazelton Neonatal Behavioral Assessment Scale examines the newborn's neurological development, reflexes, and reactions to people.

3 Explain the changes that take place in the postpartum period

- The postpartum period is the name given to the period after childbirth or delivery. In this period, the woman's body adjusts physically and psychologically to the process of childbearing. The period lasts for about six weeks or until the body has completed its adjustment.
- Physical adjustments in the postpartum period include fatigue, involution (the process by which the uterus returns to its prepregnant size five or six weeks after birth), hormonal changes, when to resume sexual intercourse, and exercises to recover body contour and strength.
- Emotional fluctuations on the part of the mother are common in this period, and they can vary a great deal from one mother to the next. The father also goes through a postpartum adjustment.
- Bonding is the formation of a close connection, especially a physical bond between parents and the newborn shortly after birth. Early bonding has not been found to be critical in the development of a competent infant.

141

Summary

Mexican American culture, the indigenous healer is called a *curandero*. In some Native American tribes, the medicine woman or man fulfills the healing role. Herbalists are often found in Asian cultures, and faith healers, root doctors, and spiritualists are sometimes found in African American culture. When health-care providers come into contact with expectant mothers, they need to assess whether such cultural practices pose a threat to the expectant mother and the fetus. If they pose no threat, there is no reason to try to change them. On the other hand, if certain cultural practices do pose a threat to the health of the expectant mother or the fetus, the health-care provider should consider a culturally sensitive way to handle the problem. For example, some Filipinos will not take any medication during pregnancy.

Positive Prenatal Development

Much of our discussion so far in this chapter has focused on what can go wrong with prenatal development. It is important to keep in mind that most of the time, prenatal development does not go awry and development occurs along the positive path that we described at the beginning of the chapter (Lester, 2000). That said, it is still important for prospective mothers and those who are pregnant to avoid the vulnerabilities to fetal development that we have described.

Review and Reflect

1 Describe prenatal development

REVIEW

- What is the course of prenatal development?
- What are some of the main hazards to prenatal development?
- What are some good prenatal care strategies?
- What are some cultural beliefs about pregnancy?
- Why is it important to take a positive approach to prenatal development?

REFLECT

- What can be done to convince women who are pregnant not to smoke or drink? Consider the role of health-care providers, the role of insurance companies, and specific programs targeted at women who are pregnant.

Review and Reflect

Review questions enable you to quiz yourself on the key ideas and find out whether you've met the learning goals for one section of a chapter before continuing to the next main topic. The question for reflection helps you to think about what you've just read and apply it. Answering these questions will help you to remember key points and concepts.

OTHER LEARNING SYSTEM FEATURES

Ted Kaczynski, the convicted Unabomber, traced his difficulties to growing up as a genius in a kid's body and not fitting in when he was a child.

Alice Walker won the Pulitzer Prize for her book *The Color Purple*. Like the characters in her book, Walker overcame pain and anger to triumph and celebrate the human spirit.

1 THE LIFE-SPAN PERSPECTIVE

Images of Life-Span Development
How Did Ted Kaczynski Become Ted Kaczynski and Alice Walker Become Alice Walker?

The intellectual Ted Kaczynski sprinted through high school, not bothering with his junior year and making only passing efforts at social contact. Off to Harvard at age 16, Kaczynski was a loner during his college years. One of his roommates at Harvard said that he had a special way of avoiding people by quickly shuffling by them and slamming the door behind him. After obtaining his Ph.D. in mathematics at the University of Michigan, Kaczynski became a professor at the University of California at Berkeley. His colleagues there remember him as hiding from social circumstances—no friends, no allies, no networking. After several years at Berkeley, Kaczynski resigned and moved to a rural area of Montana where he lived as a hermit in a crude shack for 25 years. Town residents described him as a bearded eccentric. Kaczynski traced his own difficulties to growing up as a genius in a kid's body and sticking out like a sore thumb in his surroundings as a child. In 1996, he was arrested and charged with being the notorious Unabomber, America's most wanted killer who sent sixteen mail bombs in 17 years that left 23 people wounded and maimed, and 3 people dead. In 1998, he pleaded guilty to the offenses and was sentenced to life in prison.

A decade before Kaczynski allegedly mailed his first bomb, Alice Walker, who would later win a Pulitzer Prize for her book *The Color Purple*, spent her days battling racism in Mississippi. She had recently won her first writing fellowship, but rather than use the money to follow her dream of moving to Senegal, Africa, she put herself

Images of Life-Span Development

Each chapter opens with a high-interest story that is linked to the chapter's content.

 Sociocultural Worlds of Development

Women's Struggle for Equality: An International Journey

There are serious concerns about the educational and psychological conditions of women around the world (Maracek & others, 2003; United Nations, 2001). The countries with the fewest women being educated are in Africa, where in some areas women are receiving no education at all. Canada, the United States, and Russia have the highest percentages of educated women. In developing countries, 67 percent of women and 50 percent of men over the age of 25 have never been to school. At the beginning of the twenty-first century, 80 million more boys than girls were in primary and secondary educational settings around the world (United Nations, 2002).

Women in every country experience violence, often from someone close to them. Partner abuse occurs in one of every six households in the United States, with the vast majority of the abuse being directed at women by men (Walker, 2001). In a survey, "The New Woman Ethics Report," wife abuse was listed as number one among fifteen of the most pressing concerns facing society today (Johnson, 1990). Although most countries around the world now have battered women's shelters, beating women continues to be accepted and expected behavior in some countries.

In a study of depression in high-income countries, women were twice as likely as men to be diagnosed as depressed (Nolen-Hoeksema, 1990). In the United States, from adolescence through adulthood, females are more likely than males to be depressed (Davison & Neale, 2001; Hammen, 2003). Many sociocultural

inequities and experiences have contributed to the greater incidence of depression in females than males (Whiffen, 2001). Also, possibly more women are diagnosed with depression than actually have depression (Nolen-Hoeksema, 2001).

Around the world women too often are treated as burdens rather than assets in the political process. *What can be done to strengthen women's roles in the political process?*

Sociocultural Worlds of Development

Life-Span Development gives special attention to culture, ethnicity, and gender. Most chapters have a box that highlights the sociocultural dimensions of life-span development.

We will discuss sociocultural contexts in each chapter. In addition, a Sociocultural Worlds of Development box appears in most chapters. Look at the one above for a discussion of women's international struggle for equality.

Research on Children's Ethnicity, Poverty, and Type of Home Environment One study recently examined the home environments of three ethnic groups: European American, African American, and Latino (Bradley & others, 2001). The home environments were assessed (by a combination of observations and maternal interviews) at five points in children's lives from infancy through early adolescence. There were some ethnic differences, but the most consistent result involved poverty, which was a much more powerful indicator of the type of home environment children experienced than ethnicity was (see figure 1.4 on page 16).

Social Policy Social policy is a national government's course of action designed to promote the welfare of its citizens. The shape and scope of social policy is strongly tied to the political system. Our country's policy agenda and the welfare of the nation's citizens are influenced by the values held by individual lawmakers, by the nation's economic strengths and weaknesses, and by partisan politics.

Out of concern that policy makers are doing too little to protect the well-being of children and older adults, life-span researchers increasingly are undertaking studies that they hope will lead to effective social policy (Bogenschneider, 2002; Bornstein & Bradley, 2003; Maccoby, 2001; Zigler & Hall, 2000). When more than 15 percent of all children and almost half of all ethnic minority children are being raised in poverty, when 40 to 50 percent of all children can expect to spend at least 5 years in a single-parent home, when children and young adolescents are giving birth, when the use and

social poli of action de citizens.

Careers in Life-Span Development

Every chapter has one or more Careers in Life-Span Development inserts, which feature a person working in a life-span field related to the chapter's content.

A Careers in Life-Span Development Appendix that describes a number of careers appears between Chapter 1 and Chapter 2.

Careers in Life-Span Development

Pam Reid, Educational and Developmental Psychologist

As a child, Pam Reid played with chemistry sets, and at the university she was majoring in chemistry, planning to become a medical doctor. Because some of her friends signed up for a psychology course as an elective, she decided to join them. She was so intrigued by learning more about how people think, behave, and develop that she changed her major to psychology. She says, "I fell in love with psychology." Dr. Reid went on to obtain her Ph.D. in educational psychology ◆(p. 3).

Today, Pamela Trotman Reid is a professor of education and psychology at the University of Michigan. She is also a research scientist for the UM Institute for Research on Women and Gender. Her main interest is how children and adolescents develop social skills, and especially how gender, socioeconomic status, and ethnicity are involved in development (Reid & Zalk, 2001). Because many psychological findings have been based on research with middle-socioeconomic-status non-Latino White populations, She believes it is important to study people from different ethnic groups. She stresses that by understanding the expectations, attitudes, and behavior of diverse groups, we enrich the theory and practice of psychology. Currently Dr. Reid is working with her graduate students on a project

involving middle school girls. She is interested in why girls, more often than boys, stop taking classes in mathematics.

Pam Reid (back row, center) with graduate students she is mentoring at the University of Michigan.

• How might research on topics of primary interest to females, such as relationships, feelings, and empathy, challenge existing theory? For example, in the study of moral development, the highest level has often been portrayed as based on a principle of "justice for the individual" (Kohlberg, 1976). However, more recent theorizing notes individuality and autonomy tend to be male concerns,

Theories are part of the science of life-span development. Some individuals have difficulty thinking of life-span development as a science like physics, chemistry, and biology. Can a discipline that studies how parents nurture children, whether watching TV long hours is linked with being overweight, and the factors involved in life satisfaction among older adults be equated with disciplines that study the molecular structure of a compound and how gravity works? The answer is yes. Science is defined not by *what* it investigates, but by *how* it investigates. Whether you're studying photosynthesis, butterflies, Saturn's moons, or human development, it is the way you study that makes the approach scientific or not.

This chapter introduces the theories and methods that are the foundation of the science of life-span development. At the end of the chapter we will explore some of the ethical challenges and biases that researchers must guard against to protect the integrity of their results and respect the rights of the participants in their studies.

1 THEORIES OF DEVELOPMENT

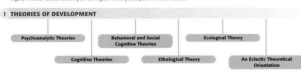

All scientific knowledge stems from a rigorous, systematic method of investigation (Pittenger, 2003; Salkind, 2003). The *scientific method* is essentially a four-step process:

1. Conceptualize a process or problem to be studied.
2. Collect research information (data).
3. Analyze data.
4. Draw conclusions.

In step 1, when researchers are formulating a problem to study, they often draw on *theories* and develop *hypotheses* (Miller, 2001). A **theory** is an interrelated, coherent set of ideas that helps to explain and make predictions. **Hypotheses** are specific assumptions and predictions that can be tested to determine their accuracy. For example, a theory on mentoring might attempt to explain and predict why sustained support, guidance, and concrete experience make a difference in the lives of children from impoverished backgrounds. The theory might focus on children's opportunities to model the behavior and strategies of mentors, or it might focus on the effects of individual attention, which might be missing in the children's lives.

The diversity of theories makes understanding life-span development a challenging undertaking. Just when you think one theory has the correct explanation of life-span development, another theory crops up and makes you rethink your earlier conclusion. To keep from getting frustrated, remember that life-span development is a complex, multifaceted topic. No single theory has been able to account for all aspects of it. Each theory contributes an important piece to the life-span development puzzle. Although the theories sometimes disagree about certain aspects of life-span development, much of their information is complementary rather than contradictory. Together they let us see the total landscape of life-span development in all its richness.

We will briefly explore five major theoretical perspectives on development: psychoanalytic, cognitive, behavioral and social cognitive, ethological, and ecological. In chapter 1, we described the three major processes involved in development: biological, cognitive, and socioemotional. The theoretical approaches that we will describe reflect these processes. Biological processes are very important in Freud's psychoanalytic and

theory An interrelated, coherent set of ideas that helps to explain and make predictions.

hypotheses Specific assumptions and predictions that can be tested to determine their accuracy.

Key Terms and Glossary

Key terms appear in boldface. Their definitions appear in the margin near where they are introduced.

Key terms also are listed and page-referenced at the end of each chapter.

Key terms are alphabetically listed, defined, and page-referenced in a Glossary at the end of the book.

---

opportunities for exercise, the infants often attain motor milestones earlier than infants whose caregivers have not provided these physical activities. For example, Jamaican mothers expect their infants to sit and walk alone two to three months earlier than English mothers do (Hopkins & Westra, 1990). Also, Jamaican mothers regularly massage their infants and stretch their arms and legs, and this is linked with advanced motor development (Hopkins, 1991). In the Gusii culture of Kenya, mothers encourage vigorous movement in their babies (Hopkins & Westra, 1988).

In developing countries, mothers often attempt to stimulate their infants' motor skills more than mothers in more advanced cultures (Hopkins, 1991). This stimulation of infants' motor skills in developing countries may be necessary to improve the infants' chances of survival. In some cases, the emphasis on early stimulation may occur because the caregivers recognize that motor skills are required for important jobs in the culture. Others factors such as climate and spiritual beliefs also may influence the way that caregivers guide their infants' motor development.

Although infants in some cultures, such as Jamaica, reach motor milestones earlier than infants in many cultures, nonetheless, regardless of how much practice takes place, infants around the world reach these motor milestones within the same age range. For example, Algonquin infants in Quebec, Canada, spend much of their first year strapped to a cradle board. Despite such inactivity, these infants still sit up, crawl, and walk within an age range similar to infants in other cultures who have much greater opportunity for activity. In sum, there are slight variations in the age at which infants reach motor milestones depending on their activity opportunities in different cultures, but the variations are not substantial and they are within normal ranges.

Fine Motor Skills Infants have hardly any control over fine motor skills at birth, although they have many components of what later become finely coordinated arm, hand, and finger movements (Rosenblith, 1992). The onset of reaching and grasping marks a significant achievement in infants' functional interactions with their surroundings (McCarty & Ashmead, 1999).

For many years it was believed that reaching for an object is visually guided—that is, the infant must continuously have sight of the hand and the target (White, Castle, & Held, 1964). However, in one study, Rachel Clifton and her colleagues (1993) demonstrated that infants do not have to see their own hands when reaching for an object. They concluded that, because the infants could not see their hand or arm in the dark in the experiment, proprioceptive muscle, tendon, joint sense) cues, not sight of limb, guided the early reaching of the 4-month-old infants.

The development of reaching and grasping becomes more refined during the first two years of life. Initially, infants show only crude shoulder and elbow movements, but later they show wrist movements, hand rotation, and coordination of the thumb and forefinger. The maturation of hand-eye coordination over the first two years of life is reflected in the improvement of fine motor skills. Figure 5.12 on page 166 provides an overview of the development of fine motor skills in the first two years of life.

The infant's grasping system is very flexible and the environment plays a stronger role in grasping than previously thought. One way to show that the environment influences grasping is to vary the motor task and examine if this influences the infant's responses. This can be done by changing the size and shape of the objects for the infant to grasp. Indeed, infants vary their grip on

A baby is an angel whose wings decrease as his legs increase.
—FRENCH PROVERB

(Top) In the Algonquin culture in Quebec, Canada, babies are strapped to a cradle board for much of their infancy. *(Bottom)* In Jamaica, mothers massage and stretch their infants' arms and legs. *To what extent do cultural variations in infants activities influence the time at which they reach motor milestones?*

Quotations

These appear at the beginning of the chapter and occasionally in the margins to stimulate further thought about a topic.

Critical Thinking and Content Questions in Photograph Captions

Most photographs have a caption that ends with a critical thinking or knowledge question in italics to stimulate further thought about a topic.

Web Links

Web icons appear a number of times in each chapter. They signal you to go to the book's website where you will find connecting links that provide additional information on the topic discussed in the text. The labels under the Web icon appear as Web links at the Santrock *Life-Span Development*, ninth edition, website, under that chapter for easy access.

FIGURE 2.5 Bronfenbrenner's Ecological Theory of Development
Bronfenbrenner's ecological theory consists of five environmental systems: microsystem, mesosystem, exosystem, macrosystem, and chronosystem.

Ecological Theory

While ethological theory stresses biological factors, ecological theory emphasizes environmental factors. One ecological theory that has important implications for understanding life-span development was created by Urie Bronfenbrenner (1917–   ). **Ecological theory** is Bronfenbrenner's (1986, 2000; Bronfenbrenner & Morris, 1998) environmental system of development. It consists of five environmental systems ranging from the fine-grained inputs of direct interactions with people to the broad-based inputs of culture (see figure 2.5).

- *Microsystem:* The setting in which the individual lives. These contexts include the person's family, peers, school, and neighborhood ◀▬ p. 13. It is in the microsystem that the most direct interactions with social agents take place—with parents, peers, and teachers, for example. The individual is viewed not as a passive recipient of experiences in these settings, but as someone who helps to construct the settings.
- *Mesosystem:* Involves relations between microsystems or connections between contexts. Examples are the relation of family experiences to school experiences, school experiences to church experiences, and family experiences to peer experiences. For example, children whose parents have rejected them may have difficulty developing positive relations with teachers.
- *Exosystem:* Is involved when experiences in another social setting—in which the individual does not have an active role—influence what the individual experiences in an immediate context. For example, work experiences can affect a

mhhe.com/
santrockld9

Bronfenbrenner's Theory
Bronfenbrenner and a
Multicultural Framework

ecological theory Bronfenbrenner's environmental systems theory that focuses on five environmental systems: microsystem, mesosystem, exosystem, macrosystem, and chronosystem.

Cross-Linkage

A specific page reference appears in the text with a backward-pointing arrow each time a key concept occurs in a chapter subsequent to its initial coverage. When you see the cross-linkage, go back to the page listed to obtain a foundation for the concept.

Online Learning Center

This directs you to the Online Learning Center for this book, where you will find many learning activities to improve your knowledge and understanding of the chapter. A new feature in this edition is the inclusion of a number of self-assessments.

Key People

The most important theorists and researchers in the chapter are listed and page-referenced at the end of each chapter.

Key Terms

theory 43	information-processing	laboratory 59	longitudinal approach 64
hypotheses 43	theory 50	naturalistic observation 59	sequential approach 64
psychoanalytic theory 44	social cognitive theory 52	standardized test 60	cohort effects 65
Erikson's theory 46	ethology 53	case study 61	ethnic gloss 71
Piaget's theory 47	ecological theory 55	life-history records 61	
assimilation 48	eclectic theoretical	correlational research 61	
accommodation 48	orientation 56	experiment 62	
Vygotsky's theory 50	descriptive research 59	cross-sectional approach 63	

Key People

Sigmund Freud 44	Karen Horney 48	Ivan Pavlov 51	Walter Mischel 52
Erik Erikson 45	Lev Vygotsky 50	B. F. Skinner 52	Konrad Lorenz 53
Jean Piaget 47	Robert Siegler 50	Albert Bandura 52	Urie Bronfenbrenner 54

mhhe.com/
santrockld9 **Taking It to the Net**

1. Like many students of life-span psychology, Ymelda has a hard time with Freud's theory, insisting that it is "all about sex." Is that the extent of Freud's theoretical perspective?
2. Juan's life-span psychology teacher asked the class to read about Albert Bandura's famous "Bobo" doll experiment and determine if there were any gender differences in the responses of boys and girls who (a) saw aggressive behavior rewarded and (b) who saw aggressive behavior punished. What should Juan's conclusions be?
3. A requirement for Wanda's methods course is to design and

carry out an original research project. Among the many decisions she must make is what type of data she will collect. She decides to research adapting to college life. Her instructor asks if she will use an interview or a survey. What are the distinctions between surveys and interviews, and what are the benefits and difficulties of each?

Connect to www.mhhe.com/santrockld9 to research the answers and complete these exercises.

mhhe.com/
santrockld9 **E-Learning Tools**

To help you master the material in this chapter, you'll find a number of valuable study tools on the Student CD-ROM that accompanies this book. In addition, visit the Online Learning Center for *Life-Span Development*, ninth edition, where you'll find these valuable resources for chapter 2, "The Science of Life-Span Development."

- Complete the self-assessment, *Models and Mentors in My Life*, to help you evaluate the role models and mentors who have

played an important part in your life and think about the type of role model you want to be.
- View video clips of key developmental psychology experts discussing their views on research methods, developmental theories, and ethics in research.
- Build your decision-making skills by trying your hand at the parenting and education "Scenarios."

Life-Span Development

The Life-Span Developmental Perspective

All the world's a stage. And all the men and women merely players. They have their exits and their entrances. And one man in his time plays many parts. . .

—WILLIAM SHAKESPEARE
English Playwright, 17th Century

This book is about human development—its universal features, its individual variations, its nature. Every life is distinct, a new biography in the world. Examining the shape of human development allows us to understand it better. *Life-Span Development* is about the rhythm and meaning of people's lives, about turning mystery into understanding, and about weaving a portrait of who each of us was, is, and will be. In Section 1, you will read two chapters: "Introduction" (chapter 1) and "The Science of Life-Span Development" (chapter 2).

We reach backward to our parents and forward to our children, and through their children to a future we will never see, but about which we need to care.

—CARL JUNG
*Swiss Psychiatrist,
20th Century*

Introduction

Learning Goals

1 Discuss the life-span perspective of development

2 Identify the most important developmental processes and periods

3 Describe three key developmental issues

Images of Life-Span Development
How Did Ted Kaczynski Become Ted Kaczynski and Alice Walker Become Alice Walker?

Ted Kaczynski, the convicted Unabomber, traced his difficulties to growing up as a genius in a kid's body and not fitting in when he was a child.

Alice Walker won the Pulitzer Prize for her book *The Color Purple*. Like the characters in her book, Walker overcame pain and anger to triumph and celebrate the human spirit.

The intellectual Ted Kaczynski sprinted through high school, not bothering with his junior year and making only passing efforts at social contact. Off to Harvard at age 16, Kaczynski was a loner during his college years. One of his roommates at Harvard said that he had a special way of avoiding people by quickly shuffling by them and slamming the door behind him. After obtaining his Ph.D. in mathematics at the University of Michigan, Kaczynski became a professor at the University of California at Berkeley. His colleagues there remember him as hiding from social circumstances—no friends, no allies, no networking. After several years at Berkeley, Kaczynski resigned and moved to a rural area of Montana where he lived as a hermit in a crude shack for 25 years. Town residents described him as a bearded eccentric. Kaczynski traced his own difficulties to growing up as a genius in a kid's body and sticking out like a sore thumb in his surroundings as a child. In 1996, he was arrested and charged with being the notorious Unabomber, America's most wanted killer who sent sixteen mail bombs in 17 years that left 23 people wounded and maimed, and 3 people dead. In 1998, he pleaded guilty to the offenses and was sentenced to life in prison.

A decade before Kaczynski allegedly mailed his first bomb, Alice Walker, who would later win a Pulitzer Prize for her book *The Color Purple*, spent her days battling racism in Mississippi. She had recently won her first writing fellowship, but rather than use the money to follow her dream of moving to Senegal, Africa, she put herself into the heart and heat of the civil rights movement. Walker grew up knowing the brutal effects of poverty and racism. Born in 1944, she was the eighth child of Georgia sharecroppers who earned $300 a year. When Walker was 8, her brother accidentally shot her in the left eye with a BB gun. By the time her parents got her to the hospital a week later (they had no car), she was blind in that eye and it had developed a disfiguring layer of scar tissue. Despite the counts against her, Walker went on to become an essayist, a poet, an award-winning novelist, a short-story writer, and a social activist who, like her characters (especially the women), has overcome pain and anger.

What leads one individual, so full of promise, to commit brutal acts of violence and another to turn poverty and trauma into a rich literary harvest? If you have ever wondered why people turn out the way they do, you have asked yourself the central question we will explore in this book.

1 THE LIFE-SPAN PERSPECTIVE

What Is Life-Span Development?

Characteristics of the Life-Span Perspective

The Historical Perspective

Some Contemporary Concerns

Why study life-span development? Perhaps you are or will be a parent or teacher, and responsibility for children is or will be a part of your everyday life. The more you learn about children, the better you can guide them. Perhaps you hope to gain an understanding of your own history—as an infant, a child, an adolescent, or a young adult.

Perhaps you want to know what your life will be like as you grow into middle age or old age. Or perhaps you accidentally came across the course description and found it intriguing. Whatever your reasons, you will discover that the study of life-span development is provocative, intriguing, and informative. The life-span perspective offers insights into who we are, how we came to be this way, and where our future will take us.

This chapter previews the themes and issues that we will consider throughout our study of life-span development. First, we will familiarize ourselves with the life-span perspective, then we will explore the processes and periods that characterize human development. Finally, we will examine the primary issues that developmentalists debate, issues that will come up repeatedly in this text.

What Is Life-Span Development?

Development is the pattern of movement or change that begins at conception and continues throughout the human life span. Most development involves growth, although it also includes decline brought on by aging and dying. Thus, we will explore development from the point in time when life begins until the time when it ends. You will see yourself as an infant, as a child, and as an adolescent, and be stimulated to think about how those years influenced the kind of individual you are today. And you will see yourself as a young adult, as a middle-aged adult, and as an adult in old age, and be stimulated to think about how your experiences today will influence your development through the remainder of your adult years.

Life-span development is linked with many different areas of psychology. Neuroscience/biological psychology, cognitive psychology, abnormal psychology, social psychology, and virtually all other areas of psychology explore how people develop in these areas. For example, how memory works is a key aspect of cognitive psychology. In this book you will read about how memory develops from infancy through old age.

The Historical Perspective

Interest in the development of children has a long and rich history, but interest in adults began to develop seriously only in the latter half of the twentieth century. Prior to that time, the number of people living into their sixties and seventies in the United States was small compared with the rest of the population, and development was considered to be something that happened only during childhood. Although development in childhood is very important, a complete view of development now requires that we also consider developmental changes in the adult years. In this section, we will look briefly at how the prevailing view of children and adults has changed.

Child Development Throughout history, philosophers have speculated about the nature of children and how they should be reared. Three influential philosophical views are based on the ideas of original sin, tabula rasa, and innate goodness:

- In the **original sin view,** especially advocated during the Middle Ages, children were perceived as being basically bad, born into the world as evil beings. The goal of child rearing was salvation, which was believed to remove sin from the child's life.
- Toward the end of the seventeenth century, the **tabula rasa view** was proposed by English philosopher John Locke. He argued that children are not innately bad. Instead they are like a "blank tablet," a "tabula rasa" as he called it. They acquire their characteristics through experience. Locke believed that childhood experiences are important in determining adult characteristics. He advised parents to spend time with their children and help them become contributing members of society.
- In the eighteenth century, the **innate goodness view** was presented by Swiss-born French philosopher Jean-Jacques Rousseau. He stressed that children are inherently good. Rousseau said that because children are basically good,

development The pattern of change that begins at conception and continues through the life cycle.

original sin view Advocated during the Middle Ages, the belief that children were born into the world as evil beings and were basically bad.

tabula rasa view The idea, proposed by John Locke, that children are like a "blank tablet."

innate goodness view The idea, presented by Swiss-born philosopher Jean-Jacques Rousseau, that children are inherently good.

they should be permitted to grow naturally with little parental monitoring or constraint.

During the past century and a half, interest in the nature of children and ways to improve their well-being have continued to be important concerns of our society (Booth & Crouter, 2000; Graham, 2001; Wertlieb, 2003). We now conceive of childhood as a highly eventful and unique period of life that lays an important foundation for the adult years and is highly differentiated from them. In most approaches to childhood, distinct periods are identified in which special skills are mastered and new life tasks are confronted. Childhood is no longer seen as an inconvenient "waiting" period during which adults must suffer the incompetencies of the young. We now value childhood as a special time of growth and change, and we invest great resources in caring for and educating our children. We protect them from the stresses and responsibilities of adult work through strict child labor laws. We treat their crimes against society under a special system of juvenile justice. We also have government provisions for helping them when ordinary family support systems fail or when families seriously interfere with the child's well-being.

As we see next, although development in childhood is important, a complete view of development requires that we also consider developmental changes in the adult years.

Life-Span Development The *traditional approach* to the study of development emphasizes extensive change from birth to adolescence, little or no change in adulthood, and decline in old age. Infancy is especially thought to be a time of considerable change. In contrast, the *life-span approach* emphasizes developmental change throughout adulthood as well as childhood (Birren & Schaie, 2001; Overton, 2003; Salthouse, 2000).

In 1900, human life expectancy in the United States was 47 years. It took 5,000 years to extend human life expectancy from 18 to 41 years of age (see figure 1.1). Then, in the twentieth century alone, life expectancy increased by 30 years. Improvements in sanitation, nutrition, and medical knowledge led to this amazing increase in life expectancy. Today, for most individuals, childhood and adolescence represent only about one-fourth of the life span (Schaie, 2000; Schaie & Willis, 2001).

How much has the older adult population grown in the United States? Figure 1.2 reveals a dramatic increase in the over-65 age group since 1900 and projects continued increases through 2040. A significant increase also will occur in the number of individuals in the 85-and-over and in the 100-and-over age categories. Currently, fewer than 50,000 Americans are 100 years of age or older; in 2050, the projected number is more than 800,000. A baby girl born today has a 1-in-3 chance of living to be 100 years of age!

Although we are living longer, on the average, than we did in the past, the maximum life span of humans has not changed since the beginning of recorded history. The upper boundary of the life span is approximately 120 years, and, as indicated in figure 1.3, our only competition from other species for the maximum recorded life span is the Galápagos turtle.

For too long we believed that development was something that happened only to children. To be sure, growth and development are dramatic in the first two decades of life, but a great deal of change goes on in the next five or six decades of life, too. Consider these descriptions of adult development:

The next five or six decades are every bit as important, not only to those adults who are passing through them but to their children, who must live with and understand parents and grandparents. The changes in body, personality, and abilities through these later decades is great. Developmental tasks are imposed by marriage and parenthood, by the

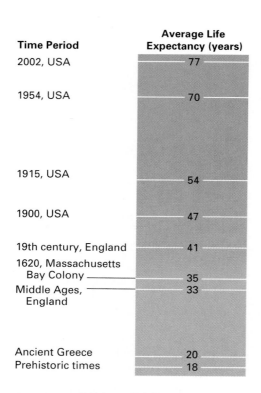

mhhe●com/ santrockld9
History of Childhood
Children's Issues
Children's Rights
UNICEF

FIGURE 1.1 Human Life Expectancy at Birth from Prehistoric to Contemporary Times

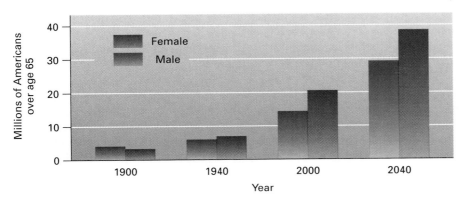

FIGURE 1.2 The Aging of America
Millions of Americans over age 65 from 1900 to the present and projected to the year 2040.

waxing and waning of physical prowess and of some intellectual capacities, by the children's flight from the nest, by the achievement of an occupational plateau, and by retirement and the prospect of final extinction. Parents have always been fascinated by their children's development, but it is high time adults began to look objectively at themselves, to examine the systematic changes in their own physical, mental, and emotional qualities, as they pass through the life span, and to get acquainted with the limitations and assets they share with so many others of their age.
(Sears & Feldman, 1973, pp. v–vi)

As the older population continues to increase in the twenty-first century, there is concern about the increasing number of older adults who will be without either a spouse or children (traditionally the main sources of support for older adults). In recent decades, American adults were less likely to be married, more likely to be childless, and more likely to be living alone than earlier in the twentieth century. As these individuals become older, their need for social relationships, networks, and supports is increasing at the same time as the supply is dwindling.

Characteristics of the Life-Span Perspective

The belief that development is lifelong is central to the life-span perspective, but according to life-span development expert Paul Baltes (1987, 2000), the **life-span perspective** includes several additional characteristics. Baltes describes the life-span perspective as lifelong, multidimensional, multidirectional, plastic, multidisciplinary, and contextual, and involves growth, maintenance, and regulation. Let's look at each of these concepts.

Development Is Lifelong   In the life-span perspective, early adulthood is not the endpoint of development; rather, no age period dominates development. Researchers increasingly study the experiences and psychological orientations of adults at different points in their development. Later in this chapter we will describe the age periods of development and their characteristics.

Development Is Multidimensional   Development consists of biological, cognitive, and socioemotional dimensions. Even within a dimension, such as intelligence, there

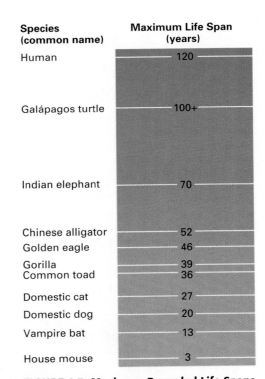

FIGURE 1.3 Maximum Recorded Life Spans for Different Species

life-span perspective The view that development is lifelong, multidimensional, multidirectional, plastic, multidisciplinary, involves growth, maintenance, and regulation, and is contextual.

are many components, such as abstract intelligence, nonverbal intelligence, and social intelligence. K. Warner Schaie is one of the leading theorists and researchers who has studied intellectual development in the adulthood years. You can read further about him in the Careers in Life-Span Development insert.

Development Is Multidirectional   Some dimensions or components of a dimension expand and others shrink. In language development, when one language (such as English) is acquired early in development, the capacity for acquiring second and third languages (such as French and Spanish) decreases later in development, especially after early childhood (Levelt, 1989). In socioemotional development, heterosexual individuals begin to have more relationships with opposite-sex peers during adolescence. As they establish intimate relationships with opposite-sex peers their relationships with same-sex peers might decrease. In cognitive development, older adults might become wiser by being able to call on experience to guide their intellectual decision making (Baltes, 2000). However, they perform more poorly on tasks that require speed in processing information (Madden, 2001; Salthouse, 2000).

Development Is Plastic   A key developmental research agenda is the search for plasticity and its constraints (Maurer, 2001). *Plasticity* means the degree to which characteristics change or remain stable. For example, can intellectual skills still be improved through education for individuals in their seventies or eighties? Or might these intellectual skills be fixed by the time people are in their thirties so that further improvement is impossible? In one research study, the reasoning abilities of older adults were improved through retraining (Willis & Schaie, 1994). However, developmentalists debate how much plasticity people have at different points in their development; possibly we possess less capacity for change when we become old (Baltes, 2000). Later in the chapter we will discuss the issue of stability and change in development, which has close ties with the concept of plasticity.

Development Is Multidisciplinary   Psychologists, sociologists, anthropologists, neuroscientists, and medical researchers all study human development and share an interest in unlocking the mysteries of development through the life span. Research questions that cut across disciplines include:

- What constraints on intelligence are set by the individual's heredity and health status?
- How universal are cognitive and socioemotional changes?
- How do environmental contexts influence intellectual development?

Development Is Contextual   The individual continually responds to and acts on contexts, which includes a person's biological makeup, physical environment, cognitive processes, historical contexts, social contexts, and cultural contexts. In the contextual view, individuals are thought of as changing beings in a changing world.

Baltes and other life-span developmentalists (Baltes, 2000; Baltes, Reese, & Lipsitt, 1980; Schaie, 1996, 2000) believe that three important sources of contextual influences

mhhe ● com/
santrockld9

Exploring Aging Issues
National Aging Information Center
Global Resources on Aging

Careers in Life-Span Development

K. Warner Schaie, Professor of Human Development

K. Warner Schaie is a professor of human development and psychology at Pennsylvania State University, where he teaches and conducts research on adult development and aging. He also directs the Gerontology Center there. He is one of the pioneering psychologists who helped to create the life-span perspective. He is the author or editor of more than 25 books and more than 250 journal articles and book chapters on adult development and aging. Dr. Schaie conducted the Seattle Longitudinal Study of intellectual development, a major research investigation which revealed that many intellectual skills are maintained or even increase in middle age. *To what extent do you think that your intelligence will change during the remainder of your adult years?*

Life-span developmentalist K. Warner Schaie *(right)* with two older adults who are actively using their cognitive skills.

are (1) normative age-graded influences, (2) normative history-graded influences, and (3) nonnormative life events.

Normative age-graded influences are biological and environmental influences that are similar for individuals in a particular age group. These influences include biological processes such as puberty and menopause. They also include sociocultural, environmental processes such as entry into formal education (usually at about age 6 in most cultures) and retirement (which takes place in the fifties and sixties in most cultures).

Normative history-graded influences are common to people of a particular generation because of the historical circumstances they experience. Examples include economic changes (such as the Great Depression in the 1930s), war (such as World War II in the 1940s), the changing role of women, the technology revolution we currently are experiencing, and political upheaval and change (such as the decrease in hard-line communism in the 1990s and into the twenty-first century) (Modell & Elder, 2002).

Nonnormative life events are unusual occurrences that have a major impact on the individual's life and usually are not applicable to many people. These events might include the death of a parent when a child is young, pregnancy in early adolescence, a disaster (such as a fire that destroys a home), or an accident. Nonnormative life events also can include positive events (such as winning the lottery or getting an unexpected career opportunity with special privileges). An important aspect of understanding the role of nonnormative life events is to focus on how people adapt to them.

Development Involves Growth, Maintenance, and Regulation   Baltes and his colleagues (Baltes, 2000; Baltes, Staudinger, & Lindenberger, 1999) believe that the mastery of life often involves conflicts and competition among three goals of human development: growth, maintenance, and regulation. As individuals age into middle and late adulthood, the maintenance and regulation of their capacities takes center stage away from growth. Thus, for many individuals, the goal is not to seek growth in intellectual capacities (such as memory) or physical capacities (such as physical strength), but to maintain those skills or minimize their deterioration. In Section 9, "Late Adulthood," we will discuss these ideas about maintenance and regulation in greater depth.

Earlier in the chapter, we examined life-span development from a historical perspective. As you will see next, the life-span perspective also addresses a number of contemporary concerns from infancy through old age.

Some Contemporary Concerns

Consider some of the topics you read about every day in newspapers and magazines: genetic research, child abuse, mental retardation, parenting, intelligence, career changes, divorce, addiction and recovery, the increasing ethnic minority population, gender issues, homosexuality, midlife crises, stress and health, retirement, and aging. What life-span experts are discovering in each of these areas has direct and significant consequences for understanding children and adults and our decisions as a society about how they should be treated.

Of particular interest in this textbook are the roles that health and well-being, parenting, education, and sociocultural contexts play in life-span development, and their importance in social policy. Here we will preview these themes and highlight a research study pertaining to each one.

Health and Well-Being   Health and well-being have been important goals for just about everyone for most of human history. Asian physicians in 2600 B.C. and Greek physicians in 500 B.C. recognized that good habits are essential for good health. They did not blame the gods for illness or think that magic would cure it—they realized that people have some control over their health and well-being. A physician's role became that of a guide, assisting patients to restore a natural physical and emotional balance.

Adult Development and Aging
The Gerontological Society of America
Geropsychology Resources

In the twenty-first century, we once again recognize the power of lifestyles and psychological states in health and well-being (Baum, Revenson, & Singer, 2001; Brown, Steele, & Walsh-Childers, 2002; Hahn & Payne, 2003; Siegler, Bosworth, & Poon, 2003). In every chapter of this book, issues of health and well-being are integrated into our discussion of life-span development. They also are highlighted in the Internet connections that appear with World Wide Web icons throughout the book.

The topics on health and well-being we will discuss include:

- Drug and alcohol use during pregnancy
- Genetic counseling
- Breast- versus bottle-feeding
- Early intervention
- School health programs
- At-risk adolescents
- Women's health issues
- Exercise
- Addiction and recovery
- Loneliness
- Adaptive physical skills in aging adults
- Coping with death

Clinical psychologists are among the health professionals who help people improve their well-being. Luis Vargas is a child clinical psychologist who has a deep concern about helping adolescents who have become juvenile delinquents and/or substance abusers get their lives on track. You can read further about Luis Vargas and his work in the Careers in Life-Span Development insert.

Research on Premature Infants Tiffany Field's (2001) research focuses on how massage therapy can facilitate weight gain in premature infants. In their original research, Field and her colleagues (1986) found that massage therapy conducted three times per day for 15 minutes with preterm infants led to 47 percent greater weight gain than standard medical treatment. The massaged infants also showed improved social and motor skills. The same positive results for massage therapy has been found in the Philippines and Israel (Goldstein-Ferber, 1997; Jinon, 1996). We will further discuss Field's massage therapy research in chapter 4, "Prenatal Development and Birth."

Parenting We hear a lot about pressures on the contemporary family (Borwkowsi, Ramey, & Bristol-Power, 2002; Cowen & Cowen, 2002; Fitzgerald & others, 2003; Maccoby, 2002; Pruett & Jackson, 2001). In later chapters, we will evaluate issues related to family functioning and parenting. Some of the topics we will consider are:

- Day care
- Working parents and latchkey children
- Effects of divorce on children
- The best way to parent
- Child maltreatment
- Support systems for families

Careers in Life-Span Development

Luis Vargas, Child Clinical Psychologist

Luis Vargas is Director of the Clinical Child Psychology Internship Program and a professor in the Department of Psychiatry at the University of New Mexico Health Sciences Center. He also is Director of Psychology at the University of New Mexico Children's Psychiatric Hospital.

Dr. Vargas obtained an undergraduate degree in psychology from St. Edwards University in Texas, a master's degree in psychology from Trinity University in Texas, and a Ph.D. in clinical psychology from the University of Nebraska–Lincoln.

His main interests are cultural issues and the assessment and treatment of children, adolescents, and families. He is motivated to find better ways to provide culturally responsive mental health services. One of his special interests is the treatment of Latino youth for delinquency and substance abuse. He recently coauthored (with Joan Koss-Chioino) *Working with Latino Youth* (Koss-Chioino & Vargas, 1999), which spells out effective strategies for improving the lives of at-risk Latino youth. *Do you have an interest in helping children and adolescents cope more effectively with problems in their lives? If so, how do you think you could accomplish this goal?*

Luis Vargas (*left*) conducting a child therapy session.

- Marital relationships
- Intergenerational relations
- Aging parents

Research on Family and Peer Relations   One issue that interests researchers who study families and parents focuses on links between family and peer functioning. In one recent study of maltreated children (children who have been abused) and nonmaltreated children, the maltreated children were more likely to be repeatedly rejected across the childhood and adolescent years (Bolger & Patterson, 2001). The main reason for the rejection was the high rate of aggressive behavior shown by the children who had been abused by their parents. Why do you think the abuse by parents resulted in more aggression toward their peers by the children? We will have more to say about maltreated children in chapter 9, "Socioemotional Development in Early Childhood."

Education   In the past decade the American educational system has come under attack (Johnson & others, 2002; McCombs, 2003; Rogoff, Turkanis, & Bartlett, 2001; Sadker & Sadker, 2003). A national committee appointed by the Office of Education concluded that children are being poorly prepared for the increasingly complex future they will face. The educational topics we will explore include these:

- Variations in early childhood education
- Ethnicity, poverty, and schools
- Programs to improve children's critical thinking
- School and family coordination
- Cooperative learning
- How to avoid stifling children's creativity
- Bilingual education
- The best schools for adolescents

Children learn to love when they are loved

Research on Mentoring   Mentoring programs are increasingly being advocated as a strategy for improving the achievement of children and adolescents who are at risk for academic failure. One study focused on 959 adolescents who had applied to the Big Brothers/Big Sisters program (Rhodes, Grossman, & Resch, 2000). Half of the adolescents were mentored through extensive discussions about school, careers, and life, as well as participation in leisure activities with other adolescents. The other half were not mentored. Mentoring led to reduced unexcused absences from school, improvements in classroom performance, and better relationships with parents.

Sociocultural Contexts   The tapestry of American culture has changed dramatically in recent years. Nowhere is the change more dramatic than in the increasing ethnic diversity of America's citizens. This changing demographic tapestry promises not only the richness that diversity produces, but also difficult challenges in extending the American dream to all individuals (Fuligni & Yoshikawa, 2003).

Sociocultural contexts include four important concepts: context, culture, ethnicity, and gender. A **context** is the setting in which development occurs. This setting is influenced by historical, economic, social, and cultural factors. Contexts include homes, schools, peer groups, churches, cities, neighborhoods, university laboratories, countries, and many others. Each of these settings has meaningful historical, economic, social, and cultural legacies (Matsumoto, 2001; Triandis, 2001).

Culture encompasses the behavior patterns, beliefs, and all other products of a particular group of people that are passed on from generation to generation. Culture results from the interaction of people over many years. A cultural group can be as large as the United States or as small as an African hunter-gatherer group. Whatever

mhhe●com/
santrockld9

Health Links
Prevention Programs
AskERIC
Diversity
Social Policy
**Trends in the Well-Being of
Children and Youth**

context The settings, influenced by historical, economic, social, and cultural factors, in which development occurs.

culture The behavior patterns, beliefs, and all other products of a group that are passed on from generation to generation.

Two Korean-born children on the day they became United States citizens. Asian American and Latino children are the fastest-growing immigrant groups in the United States. *How diverse are the students in this class on life-span development that you now are taking? How are their experiences in growing up likely similar to or different than yours?*

its size, the group's culture influences the behavior of its members (Saraswathi & Mistry, 2003; Shiraev & Levy, 2001; Valsiner, 2000). **Cross-cultural studies** involve a comparison of a culture with one or more other cultures. The comparison provides information about the degree to which development is similar, or universal, across cultures, or is instead culture-specific. For example, the United States is an achievement-oriented culture with a strong work ethic. However, recent cross-cultural studies of American and Japanese children showed that Japanese children are better at math, spend more time working on math at school, and do more math homework than American children (Stevenson, 1995, 2000). The topics on culture that we will discuss include:

- Child-care policy around the world
- Vygotsky's sociocultural cognitive theory
- Gender roles in Egypt and China
- Cross-cultural comparisons of secondary schools
- Marriage around the world
- Death and dying in different cultures

Race and ethnicity are sometimes misrepresented. *Race* is a controversial classification of people according to real or imagined biological characteristics such as skin color and blood group membership (Corsini, 1999). An individual's ethnicity can include his or her race but also many other characteristics. Thus, an individual might be White (a racial category) and a fifth-generation Texan who is a Catholic and speaks English and Spanish fluently.

Ethnicity (the word *ethnic* comes from the Greek word for "nation") is rooted in cultural heritage, nationality characteristics, race, religion, and language. Not only is there diversity within a culture such as found in the United States, there also is diversity within each ethnic group. These groups include African Americans, Latinos, Asian Americans, Native Americans, Polish Americans, Italian Americans, and so on. Not all African Americans live in low-income circumstances. Not all Latinos are Catholics. Not all Native Americans are high school dropouts. It is easy to fall into the trap of stereotyping an ethnic group by thinking that all of its members are alike. A more accurate ethnic group portrayal is diversity (Cushner, 2003; Eccles, 2001; Jenkins & others, 2003; McLoyd, 2000).

Among the ethnicity topics we will examine in later chapters are:

- Similarities, differences, and diversity
- Immigration
- Support systems for ethnic minority individuals
- Ethnicity and schooling
- Value conflicts
- Being old, female, and ethnic

Gender involves the psychological and sociocultural dimensions of being female or male. *Sex* refers to the biological dimension of being female or male. Few aspects of our development are more central to our identity and social relationships than gender (Eagly, 2001; Maracek & others, 2003; Worell, 2001). Our society's attitudes about gender are changing. But how much? The gender-related topics we will discuss include these:

- The mother's role and the father's role
- Parental and peer roles in gender development
- Gender similarities and differences
- Femininity, masculinity, and androgyny
- Carol Gilligan's care perspective
- Gender communication patterns
- Family work
- Gender and aging

cross-cultural studies Comparisons of one culture with one or more other cultures. These provide information about the degree to which development is similar, or universal, across cultures, and to the degree to which it is culture-specific.

ethnicity A characteristic based on cultural heritage, nationality characteristics, race, religion, and language.

gender The social dimension of being male or female.

Women's Struggle for Equality: An International Journey

There are serious concerns about the educational and psychological conditions of women around the world (Maracek & others, 2003; United Nations, 2001). The countries with the fewest women being educated are in Africa, where in some areas women are receiving no education at all. Canada, the United States, and Russia have the highest percentages of educated women. In developing countries, 67 percent of women and 50 percent of men over the age of 25 have never been to school. At the beginning of the twenty-first century, 80 million more boys than girls were in primary and secondary educational settings around the world (United Nations, 2002).

Women in every country experience violence, often from someone close to them. Partner abuse occurs in one of every six households in the United States, with the vast majority of the abuse being directed at women by men (Walker, 2001). In a survey, "The New Woman Ethics Report," wife abuse was listed as number one among fifteen of the most pressing concerns facing society today (Johnson, 1990). Although most countries around the world now have battered women's shelters, beating women continues to be accepted and expected behavior in some countries.

In a study of depression in high-income countries, women were twice as likely as men to be diagnosed as depressed (Nolen-Hoeksema, 1990). In the United States, from adolescence through adulthood, females are more likely than males to be depressed (Davison & Neale, 2001; Hammen, 2003). Many sociocultural inequities and experiences have contributed to the greater incidence of depression in females than males (Whiffen, 2001). Also, possibly more women are diagnosed with depression than actually have depression (Nolen-Hoeksema, 2001).

Around the world women too often are treated as burdens rather than assets in the political process. *What can be done to strengthen women's roles in the political process?*

We will discuss sociocultural contexts in each chapter. In addition, a Sociocultural Worlds of Development box appears in most chapters. Look at the one above for a discussion of women's international struggle for equality.

Research on Children's Ethnicity, Poverty, and Type of Home Environment One study recently examined the home environments of three ethnic groups: European American, African American, and Latino (Bradley & others, 2001). The home environments were assessed (by a combination of observations and maternal interviews) at five points in children's lives from infancy through early adolescence. There were some ethnic differences, but the most consistent result involved poverty, which was a much more powerful indicator of the type of home environment children experienced than ethnicity was (see figure 1.4 on page 16).

Social Policy **Social policy** is a national government's course of action designed to promote the welfare of its citizens. The shape and scope of social policy is strongly tied to the political system. Our country's policy agenda and the welfare of the nation's citizens are influenced by the values held by individual lawmakers, by the nation's economic strengths and weaknesses, and by partisan politics.

Out of concern that policy makers are doing too little to protect the well-being of children and older adults, life-span researchers increasingly are undertaking studies that they hope will lead to effective social policy (Bogenschneider, 2002; Bornstein & Bradley, 2003; Maccoby, 2001; Zigler & Hall, 2000). When more than 15 percent of all children and almost half of all ethnic minority children are being raised in poverty, when 40 to 50 percent of all children can expect to spend at least 5 years in a single-parent home, when children and young adolescents are giving birth, when the use and

social policy A national government's course of action designed to promote the welfare of its citizens.

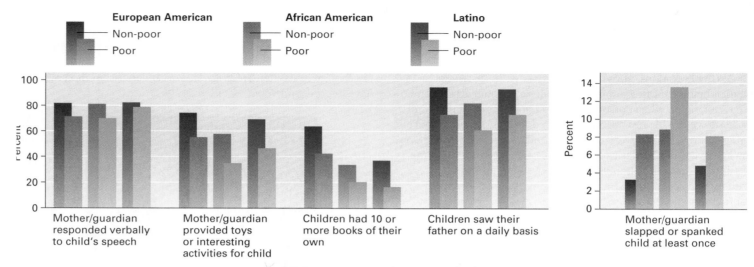

FIGURE 1.4 Home Environments of Infants by Ethnicity and Poverty Status

These data are based on home observations and maternal interviews obtained in the first three years of children's lives. Although there are some differences across ethnic groups, the most consistent differences were found between families classified as poor and non-poor. For example, regardless of their ethnic group, children growing up in non-poor home environments were more likely to have their speech responded to, be provided with toys or interesting activities, have ten or more books of their own, see their father on a daily basis, and be less likely to be slapped or spanked. Similar findings occurred when children were older.

abuse of drugs is widespread, when the specter of AIDS is present, and when the provision of health care for older adults is inadequate, our nation needs revised social policy.

Marian Wright Edelman, president of the Children's Defense Fund, has been a tireless advocate of children's rights (Children's Defense Fund, 2002). Especially troublesome to Edelman (1997) are the indicators of social neglect that place the United States at or near the lowest rank for industrialized nations in the treatment of children. Edelman says that parenting and nurturing the next generation of children is our society's most important function and that we need to take it more seriously than we have in the past. She points out that we hear a lot from politicians these days about "family values," but that when we examine our nation's policies for families, they don't reflect the politicians' words.

Marian Wright Edelman, president of the Children's Defense Fund (shown here interacting with young children), has been a tireless advocate of children's rights and has been instrumental in calling attention to the needs of children. *What are some of these needs?*

At the other end of the life span, our aging society and older persons' status in this society raise policy issues about the well-being of older adults. Special concerns are escalating health-care costs and the access of older adults to adequate health care (Hill & others, 2002).

The need for social welfare resources is far greater than policy makers have seen fit to provide. Then who should get the bulk of government dollars for improved well-being? Children? Their parents? Older adults? **Generational inequity,** a social policy concern, is the condition in which an aging society is being unfair to its younger members. It occurs because older adults pile up advantages by receiving disproportionately large allocations of resources, such as Social Security and Medicare. Generational inequity raises questions about whether the young should have to pay to care for the old and whether an "advantaged" older population is using up resources that should go to disadvantaged children. The argument is that older adults are advantaged because they have publicly financed pensions, health care, food stamps, housing subsidies, tax breaks, and other benefits that younger groups do not have. While the trend of greater services for the elderly has been occurring, the percentage of children in poverty has been rising.

Bernice Neugarten (1988) says the problem should be viewed not as one of generational inequity, but rather as a major shortcoming of our broader economic and social policies. She believes we need to develop a spirit of support for improving the range of options for all people in our society. Also, it is important to keep in mind that children will one day become older adults and will in turn be supported by the efforts of their children (Williams & Nussbaum, 2001). If there were no Social Security system, many adult children would have to bear the burden of supporting their aging parents and spend less of their resources on educating their children (Schaie, 2000).

Research on How Children Acquire Democratic Values   If a democracy like the United States is to remain secure and stable, each new generation of citizens must believe in the system and believe it works for people like them. Research by Constance Flanagan and her colleagues (Flanagan & Faison, 2001; Flanagan, Gill, & Galley, 1998) with different ethnic groups of American youth points to the pivotal role of teaching in this regard (Flanagan, Gill, & Galley, 1998). They have found that the extent to which teachers ensure that all students are treated equally and listen to and respect each other is related to the students' endorsement of democracy.

Maggie Kuhn, founder of the Gray Panthers, an international advocacy group that began in 1970 with five older women committed to improving the social conditions of older adults.

Review and Reflect

1 Discuss the life-span perspective of development

REVIEW

- What is meant by the term *life-span development*?
- What is the historical background of life-span development?
- What are seven main characteristics of the life-span perspective?
- What are some contemporary concerns in life-span development?

REFLECT

- Imagine what your development would have been like in a culture that offered fewer or distinctly different choices than your own. How might your development have been different if your family had been significantly richer or poorer than it was?

Earlier in the chapter we described Paul Baltes' view of the life-span perspective's characteristics. Next, we will further explore the nature of development, examining in greater detail some of the concepts Baltes presented along with other ways of thinking about development.

generational inequity An aging society's being unfair to its younger members because older adults pile up advantages by receiving inequitably large allocations of resources.

2 DEVELOPMENTAL PROCESSES AND PERIODS

Biological, Cognitive, and Socioemotional Processes

Age and Happiness

Periods of Development

Conceptions of Age

Each of us develops partly like all other individuals, partly like some other individuals, and partly like no other individuals. Most of the time, our attention is directed to an individual's uniqueness. But psychologists who study life-span development are drawn to our shared characteristics as well as what makes us unique. As humans, we all have traveled some common paths. Each of us—Leonardo da Vinci, Joan of Arc, George Washington, Martin Luther King, Jr., you—walked at about 1 year, engaged in fantasy play as a young child, and became more independent as a youth. Each of us, if we live long enough, will experience hearing problems and the deaths of family members and friends.

At the beginning of the chapter, we defined *development* as the pattern of movement or change that begins at conception and continues through the life span. The pattern of movement is complex because it is the product of biological, cognitive, and socioemotional processes.

Biological, Cognitive, and Socioemotional Processes

Biological processes produce changes in an individual's physical nature. Genes inherited from parents, the development of the brain, height and weight gains, changes in motor skills, the hormonal changes of puberty, and cardiovascular decline all reflect the role of biological processes in development.

One area of biological research that has immense importance for development seeks to extend the human life span. Although researchers have not yet succeeded, they are making significant strides in understanding the cellular processes that might enable people to live longer (Aisner, Wright, & Shay, 2001; Shay & Wright, 2000). We will have more to say about the biological processes involved in aging in chapter 18, "Physical Development in Late Adulthood."

Cognitive processes refer to changes in the individual's thought, intelligence, and language. Watching a colorful mobile swinging above the crib, putting together a two-word sentence, memorizing a poem, imagining what it would be like to be a movie star, and solving a crossword puzzle all involve cognitive processes.

Researchers have found that the responsiveness of caregivers provides important support for children's advances in cognitive development. In one recent study, the mother's responsiveness was linked with a number of language milestones in children's development (Tamis-LeMonda, Bornstein, & Baumwell, 2001). Children with responsive mothers (such as mothers who respond to a child's bids for attention and to a child's play) spoke their first words earlier and combined parts of speech earlier than children whose mothers responded to them infrequently. We will have much more to say about language development, including how to talk with babies and toddlers, in chapter 6, "Cognitive Development in Infancy."

Socioemotional processes involve changes in the individual's relationships with other people, changes in emotions, and changes in personality. An infant's smile in response to her mother's touch, a young boy's aggressive attack on a playmate, a girl's development of assertiveness, an adolescent's joy at the senior prom, and the affection of an elderly couple all reflect the role of the socioemotional processes in development.

biological processes Changes in an individual's physical nature.

cognitive processes Changes in an individual's thought, intelligence, and language.

socioemotional processes Changes in an individual's relationships with other people, emotions, and personality.

One socioemotional process that interests researchers is marital relations. In a number of research studies, John Gottman and his colleagues (Gottman, 1994; Gottman & others, 2002) found that an important factor in whether wives or husbands felt satisfied with the sex, romance, and passion in their marriage was the quality of the couple's friendship. We will have more to say about marital relations and Gottman's research in chapter 15, "Socioemotional Development in Early Adulthood."

Biological, cognitive, and socioemotional processes are inextricably intertwined. For example, consider a baby smiling in response to its mother's touch. This response depends on biological processes (the physical nature of touch and responsiveness to it), cognitive processes (the ability to understand intentional acts), and socioemotional processes (the act of smiling often reflects a positive emotional feeling and smiling helps to connect us in positive ways with other human beings).

Also, in many instances biological, cognitive, and socioemotional processes are bidirectional. For example, biological processes can influence cognitive processes and vice versa. In Section 9, "Late Adulthood," you will read about how poor health (a biological process) is linked to lower intellectual functioning (a cognitive process). You also will read about how positive thinking about the ability to control one's environment (a cognitive process) can have a powerful effect on an individual's health (a biological process).

Thus, although usually we will study the different processes (biological, cognitive, and socioemotional) in separate locations, keep in mind that we are talking about the development of an integrated individual with a mind and body that are interdependent (see figure 1.5).

Periods of Development

The concept of *developmental period* refers to a time frame in a person's life that is characterized by certain features. For the purposes of organization and understanding, we commonly describe development in terms of these periods. The most widely used classification of developmental periods involves this sequence: prenatal period, infancy, early childhood, middle and late childhood, adolescence, early adulthood, middle adulthood, and late adulthood. Approximate age ranges are listed here for the periods to provide a general idea of when a period begins and ends.

The *prenatal period* is the time from conception to birth. It involves tremendous growth—from a single cell to an organism complete with brain and behavioral capabilities, produced in approximately a nine-month period.

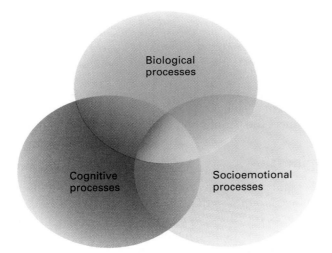

FIGURE 1.5 Developmental Changes Are the Result of Biological, Cognitive, and Socioemotional Processes

These processes interact as individuals develop.

> *One's children's children's children. Look back to us as we look to you; we are related by our imaginations. If we are able to touch, it is because we have imagined each other's existence, our dreams running back and forth along a cable from age to age.*
>
> —ROGER ROSENBLATT
> *American Writer, 20th Century*

Infancy is the developmental period from birth to 18 or 24 months. Infancy is a time of extreme dependence upon adults. Many psychological activities are just beginning—language, symbolic thought, sensorimotor coordination, and social learning, for example.

Early childhood is the developmental period from the end of infancy to about 5 or 6 years. This period is sometimes called the "preschool years." During this time, young children learn to become more self-sufficient and to care for themselves, develop school readiness skills (following instructions, identifying letters), and spend many hours in play with peers. First grade typically marks the end of early childhood.

Middle and late childhood is the developmental period from about 6 to 11 years of age, approximately corresponding to the elementary school years. This period is sometimes called the "elementary school years." The fundamental skills of reading, writing, and arithmetic are mastered. The child is formally exposed to the larger world and its culture. Achievement becomes a more central theme of the child's world, and self-control increases.

Adolescence is the developmental period of transition from childhood to early adulthood, entered at approximately 10 to 12 years of age and ending at 18 to 22 years of age. Adolescence begins with rapid physical changes—dramatic gains in height and weight, changes in body contour, and the development of sexual characteristics such as enlargement of the breasts, development of pubic and facial hair, and deepening of the voice. At this point in development, the pursuit of independence and an identity are prominent. Thought is more logical, abstract, and idealistic. More time is spent outside the family.

Early adulthood is the developmental period that begins in the late teens or early twenties and lasts through the thirties. It is a time of establishing personal and economic independence, career development, and, for many, selecting a mate, learning to live with someone in an intimate way, starting a family, and rearing children.

Middle adulthood is the developmental period from approximately 40 years of age to about 60. It is a time of expanding personal and social involvement and responsibility; of assisting the next generation in becoming competent, mature individuals; and of reaching and maintaining satisfaction in a career.

Late adulthood is the developmental period that begins in the sixties or seventies and lasts until death. It is a time of adjustment to decreasing strength and health, life review, retirement, and adjustment to new social roles.

Life-span developmentalists increasingly distinguish between two age groups in late adulthood: the *young old,* or *old age* (65 to 74 years of age), and the *old old,* or *late old age* (75 years and older). Still others distinguish the *oldest old* (85 years and older) from younger older adults (Pearlin, 1994). Beginning in the sixties and extending to more than 100 years of age, late adulthood has the longest span of any period of development. Combining this lengthy span with the dramatic increase in the number of adults living to older ages, we will see increased attention given to differentiating the late adulthood period.

The periods of the human life span are shown in figure 1.6, along with the processes of development—biological, cognitive, and socioemotional. The interplay of these processes produces the periods of the human life span.

Age and Happiness

When individuals report how happy they are and how satisfied they are with their lives, no particular age group says they are happier or more satisfied than any other age group (Diener, Lucas, & Oishi, 2002). When nearly 170,000 people in 16 countries were surveyed, no differences in their happiness from adolescence into the late adulthood years were found (Inglehart, 1990) (see figure 1.7). About the same percentage of people in each age group—slightly less than 20 percent—reported that they were "very happy."

Periods of Development

| Prenatal period (conception to birth) | Infancy (Birth to 18–24 months) | Early childhood (2–5 years) | Middle and late childhood (6–11 years) | Adolescence (10–12 to 18–21 years) | Early adulthood (20s to 30s) | Middle adulthood (35–45 to 60s) | Late adulthood (60s–70s to death) |

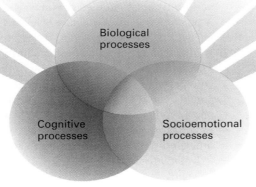

Processes of Development

FIGURE 1.6 Processes and Periods of Development

The unfolding of life's periods of development is influenced by the interaction of biological, cognitive, and socioemotional processes.

Why might older people report just as much happiness and life satisfaction as younger people? Every period of the life span has its stresses, pluses and minuses, hills and valleys. Although adolescents must cope with developing an identity, feelings of insecurity, mood swings, and peer pressure, the majority of adolescents develop positive perceptions of themselves, feelings of competence about their skills, positive relationships with friends and family, and an optimistic view of their future. And while older adults face a life of reduced income, less energy, decreasing physical skills, and concerns about death, they are also less pressured to achieve and succeed, have more time for leisurely pursuits, and have accumulated many years of experience that help them adapt to their lives with a wisdom they may not have had in their younger years. Because growing older is a certain outcome of living, we can derive considerable pleasure from knowing that we are likely to be just as happy as older adults as when we were younger.

Conceptions of Age

In our description of the periods of the life span, we associated approximate age ranges with the periods. However, life-span expert Bernice Neugarten (1988) believes we are rapidly becoming an age-irrelevant society. She says we are already familiar with the 28-year-old mayor, the 35-year-old grandmother, the 65-year-old father of a preschooler, the 55-year-old widow who starts a business, and the 70-year-old student. Neugarten stresses that choices and dilemmas do not spring forth at

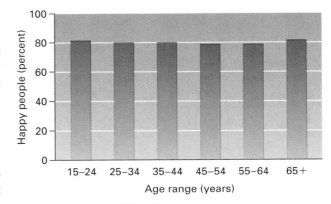

FIGURE 1.7 Age and Happiness

Analysis of surveys of nearly 170,000 people in 16 countries found no age differences in happiness from adolescence into the late adulthood years.

How old would you be if you didn't know how old you were?

—SATCHEL PAIGE
American Baseball Pitcher, 20th Century

Chronological age
Number of years since birth

Biological age
Age in terms of physical health

Psychological age
Adaptive capacity compared to others of the same chronological age

Social age
Social roles and expectations relative to chronological age

FIGURE 1.8 Conceptions of Age

10-year intervals. Decisions are not made and then left behind as if they were merely beads on a chain. Neugarten argues that most adulthood themes appear and reappear throughout the human life span. The issues of intimacy and freedom can haunt couples throughout their relationship. Feeling the pressure of time, reformulating goals, and coping with success and failure are not the exclusive property of adults of a particular age.

Neugarten's ideas raise questions about how age should be conceptualized. Some of the ways in which age has been conceptualized are as chronological age, biological age, psychological age, and social age (Hoyer, Rybash, & Roodin, 1999):

- **Chronological age** is the number of years that have elapsed since birth. Many people consider chronological age to be synonymous with the concept of age. However, some developmentalists argue that chronological age is not very relevant to understanding a person's psychological development (Botwinick, 1978). A person's age does not cause development. Time is a crude index of many events and experiences, and it does not cause anything.
- **Biological age** is a person's age in terms of biological health. Determining biological age involves knowing the functional capacities of a person's vital organs. One person's vital capacities may be better or worse than those of others of comparable age. The younger the person's biological age, the longer the person is expected to live, regardless of chronological age.
- **Psychological age** is an individual's adaptive capacities compared with those of other individuals of the same chronological age. Thus, older adults who continue to learn, are flexible, are motivated, control their emotions, and think clearly are engaging in more adaptive behaviors than their chronological agemates who do not continue to learn, are rigid, are unmotivated, do not control their emotions, and do not think clearly.
- **Social age** refers to social roles and expectations related to a person's age. Consider the role of "mother" and the behaviors that accompany the role (Huyck & Hoyer, 1982). In predicting an adult woman's behavior, it may be more important to know that she is the mother of a 3-year-old child than to know whether she is 20 or 30 years old. We still have some expectations for when certain life events—such as getting married, having children, becoming a grandparent, and retiring—should occur. However, as Neugarten concluded, chronological age has become a less accurate predictor of these life events in our society.

From a life-span perspective, an overall age profile of an individual involves more than just chronological age. It also consists of biological age, psychological age, and social age (see figure 1.8). For example, a 70-year-old man (chronological age) might be in good physical health (biological age), be experiencing memory problems and not be coping well with the demands placed on him by his wife's recent hospitalization (psychological age), and have a number of friends with whom he regularly golfs (social age).

chronological age The number of years that have elapsed since a person's birth; what is usually meant by "age."

biological age A person's age in terms of biological health.

psychological age An individual's adaptive capacities compared to those of other individuals of the same chronological age.

social age Social roles and expectations related to a person's age.

Review and Reflect

2 Identify the most important developmental processes and periods

REVIEW

- What are three key developmental processes?
- What are eight main developmental periods?
- How is age related to happiness?
- What are four ways age can be conceptualized?

REFLECT

- Do you think there is a best age to be? If so, what is it? Why?

3 DEVELOPMENTAL ISSUES

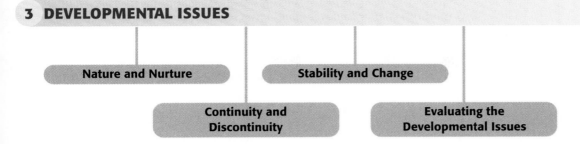

The most important issues in the study of development include nature and nurture, continuity and discontinuity, and stability and change.

Nature and Nurture

The **nature-nurture issue** involves the debate about whether development is primarily influenced by nature or by nurture. *Nature* refers to an organism's biological inheritance, *nurture* to its environmental experiences. "Nature" proponents claim that the most important influence on development is biological inheritance. "Nurture" proponents claim that environmental experiences are the most important influence.

According to the nature advocates, just as a sunflower grows in an orderly way—unless defeated by an unfriendly environment—so does the human grow in an orderly way. The range of environments can be vast, but the nature approach argues that a genetic blueprint produces commonalities in growth and development. We walk before we talk, speak one word before two words, grow rapidly in infancy and less so in early childhood, experience a rush of sexual hormones in puberty, reach the peak of our physical strength in late adolescence and early adulthood, and then physically decline. The nature proponents acknowledge that extreme environments—those that are psychologically barren or hostile—can depress development. However, they believe that basic growth tendencies are genetically wired into humans.

By contrast, other psychologists emphasize the importance of nurture, or environmental experiences, in development. Experiences run the gamut from the individual's biological environment (nutrition, medical care, drugs, and physical accidents) to the social environment (family, peers, schools, community, media, and culture).

Continuity and Discontinuity

Think about your own development for a moment. Did you become the person you are gradually, like the seedling that slowly, cumulatively grows into a giant oak? Or did you experience sudden, distinct changes in your growth, like the caterpillar that changes into a butterfly (see figure 1.9 on page 24)? For the most part, developmentalists who emphasize nurture usually describe development as a gradual, continuous process. Those who emphasize nature often describe development as a series of distinct stages.

The **continuity-discontinuity issue** focuses on the extent to which development involves gradual, cumulative change (continuity) or distinct stages (discontinuity). In terms of continuity, as the oak grows from seedling to giant oak, it becomes *more* oak—its development is continuous. Similarly, a child's first word, though seemingly an abrupt, discontinuous event, is actually the result of weeks and months of growth and practice. Puberty, another seemingly abrupt, discontinuous occurrence, is actually a gradual process occurring over several years.

In terms of discontinuity, each person is described as passing through a sequence of stages in which change is qualitatively rather than quantitatively different. As the caterpillar changes to a butterfly, it is not just more caterpillar, it is a *different kind* of organism—its development is discontinuous. Similarly, at some point a child moves

nature-nurture issue *Nature* refers to an organism's biological inheritance, *nurture* to environmental influences. The "nature" proponents claim biological inheritance is the most important influence on development; the "nurture" proponents claim that environmental experiences are the most important.

continuity-discontinuity issue The issue regarding whether development involves gradual, cumulative change (continuity) or distinct stages (discontinuity).

FIGURE 1.9 Continuity and Discontinuity in Development

Is our development like that of a seedling gradually growing into a giant oak? Or is it more like that of a caterpillar suddenly becoming a butterfly?

stability-change issue The issue of whether development is best described as involving stability or as involving change. This issue involves the degree to which we become older renditions of our early experience or instead develop into someone different from who we were at an earlier point in development.

from not being able to think abstractly about the world to being able to. This is a qualitative, discontinuous change in development, not a quantitative, continuous change.

Stability and Change

Another important developmental topic is the **stability-change issue,** which addresses whether development is best described by stability or change. The stability-change issue involves the degree to which we become older renditions of our early experience or whether we develop into someone different from who were at an earlier point in development. Will the shy child who hides behind the sofa when visitors arrive be a wallflower at college dances, or will the child become a sociable, talkative individual? Will the fun-loving, carefree adolescent have difficulty holding down a 9-to-5 job as an adult or become a straitlaced, serious conformist?

The stability-change issue is linked with Paul Baltes' (1987, 2000) belief, which we discussed earlier, that plasticity or change is an important life-span issue. Recall that in the life-span perspective, plasticity or change is possible throughout the life span, although experts such as Baltes argue that older adults often show less capacity for change than younger adults.

One of the reasons why adult development was ignored by researchers until fairly recently was the predominant belief for many years that nothing much changes in adulthood. The major changes were believed to take place in childhood, especially during the first 5 years of life. Today, most developmentalists believe that some change is possible throughout the human life span, although they disagree, sometimes vehemently, about just how much change can take place, and how much stability there is.

An important dimension of the stability-change issue is the extent to which early experiences (especially in infancy) or later experiences determine a person's development. That is, if infants experience negative, stressful circumstances in their lives, can the effects of those experiences be counteracted by later, more positive experiences? Or are the early experiences so critical, possibly because they are the infant's first, prototypical experiences, that they cannot be overridden by an enriched environment later in development?

The early-later experience issue has a long history and continues to be hotly debated among developmentalists (Gottlieb, 2002). Some believe that unless infants experience warm, nurturant caregiving in the first year or so of life, their development will not likely be optimal (Waters & others, 2000). Plato was sure that infants who were rocked frequently became better athletes. Nineteenth-century New England ministers told parents in Sunday sermons that the way they handled their infants would determine their children's future character. The emphasis on the importance of early experience rests on the belief that each life is an unbroken trail on which a psychological quality can be traced back to its origin (Kagan, 1992, 1998, 2000).

The early-experience doctrine contrasts with the later-experience view that development, like a river, ebbs and flows continuously. The later-experience advocates argue that children are malleable throughout development and that later sensitive caregiving is just as important as earlier sensitive caregiving. A number of life-span developmentalists stress that too little attention has been given to later experiences in development (Baltes, 2000; Birren & Schaie, 2001). They argue that early experiences are important contributors to development, but no more important than later experiences. Jerome Kagan (2000) points out that even children who show the qualities of an inhibited temperament, which is linked to heredity, have the capacity to change their behavior. In his research, almost one-third of a group of children who had an inhibited temperament at 2 years of age were not unusually shy or fearful when they were 4 years of age.

People in Western cultures, especially those steeped in the Freudian belief that the key experiences in development are children's relationships with their parents in the first 5 years of life, have tended to support the idea that early experiences are more important than later experiences. But the majority of people in the world do not share this belief. For example, people in many Asian countries believe that experiences oc-curring after about 6 to 7 years of age are more important to development than earlier experiences. This stance stems from the long-standing belief in Eastern cultures that children's reasoning skills begin to develop in important ways in the middle childhood years.

One recent book—*The Myth of the First Three Years*—supports the later experience argument (Bruer, 1999). The argument is made, based on the available research evi-dence, that learning and cognitive development do not occur only in the first 3 years of life but rather are lifelong. The author concludes that too many parents act as though a switch goes off when a child turns 3, after which further learning either does not take place or is greatly diminished. That is not to say experiences in the first 3 years are unimportant, but rather that later experiences are too. This book has been highly controversial, with early-experience advocates being especially critical of it (Bornstein, 2000).

Evaluating the Developmental Issues

It is important to keep in mind that most life-span developmentalists do not take extreme positions on the three developmental issues. They acknowledge that develop-ment is not all nature or all nurture, not all continuity or all discontinuity, and not all stability or all change (Lerner, 2002). Nature and nurture, continuity and discontinuity, and stability and change characterize development throughout the human life span. With respect to the nature-nurture issue, then, the key to development is the *interaction* of nature and nurture rather than either factor alone (Rutter, 2002). For instance, an in-dividual's cognitive development is the result of heredity-environment interaction, not heredity or environment alone. (Much more about heredity-environment interaction appears in chapter 3.)

Although most developmentalists do not take extreme positions on these three important issues, there is spirited debate regarding how strongly development is in-fluenced by each of these factors (Waters, 2001). Are girls less likely to do well in math because of their "feminine" nature, or because of society's masculine bias? How ex-tensively can the elderly be trained to reason more effectively? How much, if at all, does our memory decline in old age? Can techniques be used to prevent or reduce the decline? Can enriched experiences in adolescence remove "deficits" resulting from childhood experiences of poverty, neglect by parents, and poor schooling? The an-swers given by developmentalists to such questions depend on their stances regarding the issues of nature and nurture, continuity and discontinuity, and stability and change. The answers to these questions also have a bearing on public policy decisions about children, adolescents, and adults, and consequently, on each of our lives.

What is the nature of the early- and later-experience issue in development?

Review and Reflect

3 Describe three key developmental issues

REVIEW

- What is the nature and nurture issue?
- What is the continuity and discontinuity issue?
- What is the stability and change issue?
- What is a good strategy for evaluating the developmental issues?

REFLECT

- Can you identify an early experience that you believe contributed in important ways to your development? Can you identify a recent or current (later) experi-ence that you think had (is having) a strong influence on your development?

Reach Your Learning Goals

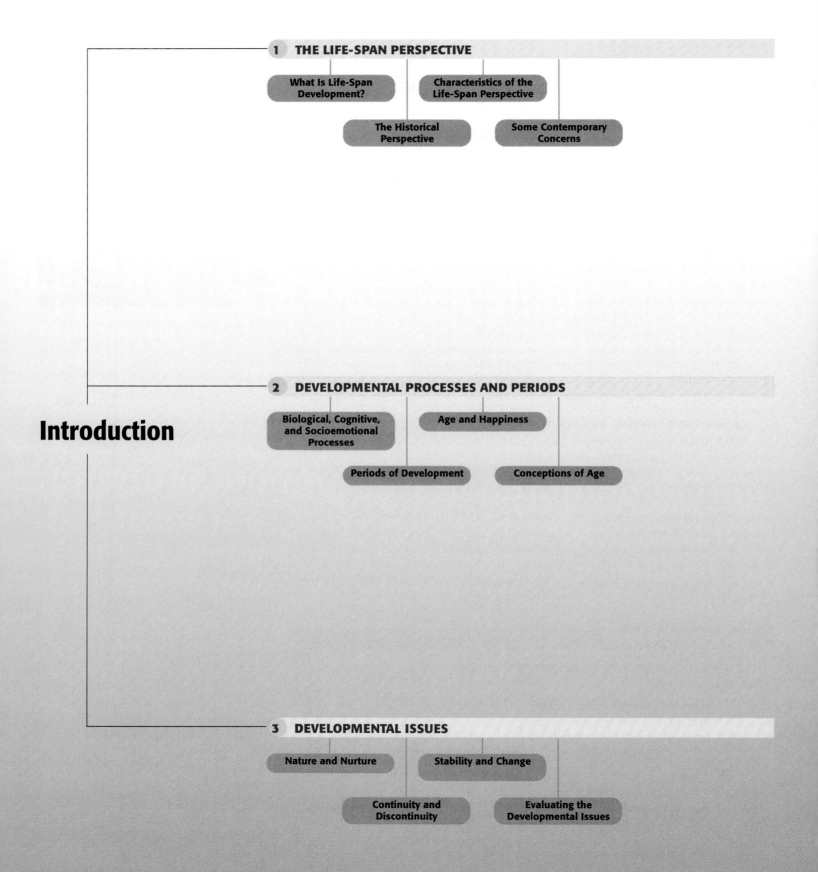

Introduction

1 THE LIFE-SPAN PERSPECTIVE

- What Is Life-Span Development?
- Characteristics of the Life-Span Perspective
- The Historical Perspective
- Some Contemporary Concerns

2 DEVELOPMENTAL PROCESSES AND PERIODS

- Biological, Cognitive, and Socioemotional Processes
- Age and Happiness
- Periods of Development
- Conceptions of Age

3 DEVELOPMENTAL ISSUES

- Nature and Nurture
- Stability and Change
- Continuity and Discontinuity
- Evaluating the Developmental Issues

Summary

1 Discuss the life-span perspective of development

- Development is the pattern of movement or change that begins at conception and continues through the human life span. Development includes growth and decline.
- Interest in children has a long and rich history. Prior to the mid-nineteenth century, philosophical views of childhood were prominent, including the notions of original sin, tabula rasa, and innate goodness. The traditional approach to the study of development emphasizes extensive change in childhood but stability in adulthood; the life-span perspective emphasizes that change is possible throughout the life span. In the twentieth century alone, life expectancy increased by 30 years.
- The life-span perspective includes these basic conceptions: Development is lifelong, multidimensional, multidirectional, plastic, multidisciplinary, and contextual, and involves growth, maintenance, and regulation. Three important sources of contextual influences are (1) normative age-graded influences, (2) normative history-graded influences, and (3) nonnormative life events.
- Today, the development and well-being of children and adults capture the interest of the public, scientists, and policy makers. Among the important contemporary concerns are parenting, education, sociocultural contexts, and social policy. Three important sociocultural contexts are culture, ethnicity, and gender.

2 Identify the most important developmental processes and periods

- Development is influenced by an interplay of biological, cognitive, and socioemotional processes.
- The life-span is commonly divided into these periods of development: prenatal, infancy, early childhood, middle and late childhood, adolescence, early adulthood, middle adulthood, and late adulthood.
- In studies covering adolescence through old age, people report that they are not happier at one point in development than at others.
- Some experts on life-span development believe too much emphasis is placed on chronological age. Neugarten believes we are moving toward a society in which age is a weaker predictor of development in adulthood. However, we often think of age only in terms of chronological age. Nonetheless, a full evaluation of age requires consideration of four dimensions of age: chronological, biological, psychological, and social.

3 Describe three key developmental issues

- The nature-nurture issue focuses on the extent to which development is mainly influenced by nature (biological inheritance) or nurture (experience).
- Developmentalists describe development as continuous (gradual, a cumulative change) or as discontinuous (abrupt, a sequence of stages).
- The stability-change issue focuses on the degree to which we become older renditions of our early experience or develop into someone different from who we were earlier in development. A special aspect of the stability-change issue is the extent to which development is determined by early versus later experiences.
- Most developmentalists recognize that extreme positions on the nature-nurture, continuity-discontinuity, and stability-change issues are unwise. Despite this consensus, there is still spirited debate on these issues.

Key Terms

development 7
original sin view 7
tabula rasa view 7
innate goodness view 8
life-span perspective 9
context 13

culture 13
cross-cultural studies 14
ethnicity 14
gender 14
social policy 15
generational inequity 17

biological processes 18
cognitive processes 18
socioemotional processes 18
chronological age 22
biological age 22
psychological age 22

social age 22
nature-nurture issue 23
continuity-discontinuity issue 23
stability-change issue 24

Key People

John Locke 7
Jean-Jacques Rousseau 8
Paul Baltes 9

Marian Wright Edelman 16
Bernice Neugarten 17, 21
Jerome Kagan 24

mhhe.com/santrockld9 Taking It to the Net

1. Janice plans to join a small family-practice group upon completion of her medical school pediatrics residency. Why should Janice, as a pediatrician, be involved in detecting and helping to prevent violence in the lives of her young patients?
2. Derrick has heard about a recent book that has stirred up a lot of controversy about the role of parents and peers in development. What is the book, what is its premise, and why has it generated so many strong feelings?

3. Carmen is completing her Ph.D. in clinical psychology. She is interested in geropsychology. What are some of the areas in which geropsychologists might conduct research and practice?

Connect to www.mhhe.com/santrockld9 to research the answers and complete these exercises.

mhhe.com/santrockld9 E-Learning Tools

To help you master the material in this chapter, you'll find a number of valuable study tools on the Student CD-ROM that accompanies this book. In addition, visit the Online Learning Center for *Life-Span Development,* ninth edition, where you'll find these valuable resources for chapter 1, "Introduction."

- Learn more about your career options by completing the self-assessment, *Evaluating My Interest in a Career in Life-Span Development.*

- View video clips of key developmental psychology experts discussing their views on the nature-nurture controversy and the concept of understanding contexts of development.
- Build your decision-making skills by trying your hand at the parenting and education "Scenarios."

Appendix *Careers in Life-Span Development*

Some of you may be quite sure about what you plan to make your life's work. Others of you might not have decided on a major yet and might be uncertain about which career path you want to follow. Each of us wants to find a rewarding career and enjoy the work we do. The field of life-span development offers an amazing breadth of career options that can provide extremely satisfying work.

If you decide to pursue a career in life-span development, what career options are available to you? Many. College and university professors teach courses in many different areas of life-span development, education, family development, nursing, and medicine. Teachers impart knowledge, understanding, and skills to children and adolescents. Counselors, clinical psychologists, nurses, and physicians help people of different ages to cope more effectively with their lives and improve their well-being. Various professionals work with families to improve the quality of family functioning.

Although an advanced degree is not absolutely necessary in some areas of life-span development, you usually can considerably expand your opportunities (and income) by obtaining a graduate degree. Many careers in life-span development pay reasonably well. For example, psychologists earn well above the median salary in the United States. Also, by working in the field of life-span development, you can guide people in improving their lives, understand yourself and others better, possibly advance the state of knowledge in the field, and have an enjoyable time while you are doing these things.

If you are considering a career in life-span development, would you prefer to work with infants? children? adolescents? older adults? As you go through this term, try to spend some time with people of different ages. Observe their behavior. Talk with them about their lives. Think about whether you would like to work with people of this age in your life's work.

Another important aspect of exploring careers is to talk with people who work in various jobs. For example, if you have some interest in becoming a school counselor, call a school, ask to speak with a counselor, and set up an appointment to discuss the counselor's career and work. If you have an interest in becoming a nurse, think about whether you would rather work with babies, children, adolescents, or older adults. Call the nursing department at a hospital and set up an appointment to speak with the nursing coordinator about a nursing career.

Something else that should benefit you is to work in one or more jobs related to your career interests while you are in college. Many colleges and universities have internships or work experiences for students who major in such fields as life-span development. Some of these opportunities are for course credit or pay; others are strictly on a volunteer basis. Take advantage of these opportunities. They can provide you with valuable experiences to help you decide if this is the right career area for you, and they can help you get into graduate school, if you decide you want to go.

In the upcoming sections, we will profile a number of careers in four areas: education/research; clinical/counseling; medical/nursing/physical; and families/relationships. These are not the only career options in life-span development, but they should provide you with an idea of the range of opportunities available and information about some of the main career avenues you might pursue. In profiling these careers, we will address the amount of education required, the nature of the training, and a description of the work.

By going to the website for this book, you can obtain more detailed career information about the various careers in life-span development described in this appendix.

EDUCATION/RESEARCH

There are numerous career opportunities in life-span development that involve education and/or research. These range from being a college professor to day-care director to school psychologist.

College/University Professor

Courses in life-span development are taught in many different programs and schools in colleges and universities, including psychology, education, nursing, child and family studies, social work, and medicine. A Ph.D. or master's degree almost always is required to teach in some area of life-span development in a college or university. Obtaining a doctoral degree usually takes 4 to 6 years of graduate work. A master's degree requires approximately 2 years of graduate work. The professional job might be at a research university with one or more master's or Ph.D. programs in life-span development, at a 4-year college with no graduate programs, or at a community college.

The training involves taking graduate courses, learning to conduct research, and attending and presenting papers at professional meetings. Many graduate students work as teaching or research assistants for professors in an apprenticeship relationship that helps them to become competent teachers and researchers. The work that college professors do includes teaching courses either at the undergraduate or graduate level (or both), conducting research in a specific area, advising students and/or directing their research, and serving on college or university committees. Some college instructors do not conduct research as part of their job but instead focus mainly on teaching. However, research is part of the job description at most universities with master's and Ph.D. programs.

If you are interested in becoming a college or university professor, you might want to make an appointment with your instructor in this class on life-span development to learn more about their profession and what their work is like.

Researcher

Some individuals in the field of life-span development work in research positions. Most have either a master's or a Ph.D. in some area of life-span development. They might work at a university, in some cases in a university professor's research program, in government at such agencies as the National Institute of Mental Health, or in private industry. Individuals who have full-time research positions in life-span development generate innovative research ideas, plan studies, and carry out the research by collecting data, analyzing the data, and then interpreting it. Then, they will usually attempt to publish the research in a scientific journal. A researcher often works in a collaborative manner with other researchers on a project and may present the research at scientific meetings, where she or he also learns about other research. One researcher might spend much of his or her time in a laboratory; another researcher might work out in the field, such as in schools, hospitals, and so on.

Elementary or Secondary School Teacher

Becoming an elementary or secondary school teacher requires a minimum of an undergraduate degree. The training involves taking a wide range of courses with a major or concentration in education as well as completing a supervised practice teaching internship. The work of an elementary or secondary school teacher involves teaching in one or more subject areas, preparing the curriculum, giving tests, assigning grades, monitoring students' progress, conducting parent-teacher conferences, and attending in-service workshops.

Exceptional Children (Special Education) Teacher

Becoming a teacher of exceptional children requires a minimum of an undergraduate degree. The training consists of taking a wide range of courses in education and a concentration of courses in educating children with disabilities or children who are gifted. The work of a teacher of exceptional children involves spending concentrated time with individual children who have a disability or are gifted. Among the children a teacher of exceptional children might work with include children with learning disabilities, ADHD, mental retardation, or a physical disability such as cerebral palsy. Some of this work will usually be done outside of the student's regular classroom; some of it will be carried out when the student is in the regular classroom. The exceptional children teacher works closely with the student's regular classroom teacher and parents to create the best educational program for the student. Teachers of exceptional children often continue their education after obtaining their undergraduate degree and attain a master's degree.

Early Childhood Educator

Early childhood educators work on college faculties and have a minimum of a master's degree in their field. In graduate school, they take courses in early childhood education and receive supervisory training in day care or early childhood programs. Early childhood educators usually teach in community colleges that award an associate degree in early childhood education.

Preschool/Kindergarten Teacher

Preschool teachers teach mainly 4-year-old children, and kindergarten teachers primarily teach 5-year-old children. They usually have an undergraduate degree in education, specializing in early childhood education. State certification to become a preschool or kindergarten teacher usually is required. These teachers direct the educational activities of young children.

Family and Consumer Science Educator

Family and consumer science educators may specialize in early childhood education or instruct middle and high school students about such matters as nutrition, interpersonal relationships, human sexuality, parenting, and human development. Hundreds of colleges and universities throughout the United States offer 2- and 4-year degree programs in family and consumer science. These programs usually include an internship requirement. Additional education courses may be needed to obtain a teaching certificate. Some family and consumer educators go on to graduate school for further training, which provides a background for possible jobs in college teaching or research.

Educational Psychologist

An educational psychologist most often teaches in a college or university and conducts research in such areas of educational psychology as learning, motivation, classroom management, and assessment. Most educational psychologists have a doctorate in education, which takes 4 to 6 years of graduate work. They help train students who will take various positions in education, including educational psychology, school psychology, and teaching.

School Psychologist

School psychologists focus on improving the psychological and intellectual well-being of elementary, middle/junior, and high school students. They usually have a master's or doctoral degree in school psychology. In graduate school, they take courses in counseling, assessment, learning, and other areas of education and psychology. School psychologists may work in a centralized office in a school district or in one or more schools. They give psychological tests, interview students and their parents, consult with teachers, and may provide counseling to students and their families.

Gerontologist

Gerontologists usually work in research in some branch of the federal or state government. They specialize in the study of aging with a particular focus on government programs for older adults, social policy, and delivery of services to older adults. In their research, gerontologists define problems to be studied, collect data, interpret the results, and make recommendations for social policy. Most gerontologists have a master's or doctoral degree and have taken a concentration of course work in adult development and aging.

CLINICAL/COUNSELING

There are a wide variety of clinical and counseling jobs that are linked with life-span development. These range from child clinical psychologist to adolescent drug counselor to geriatric psychiatrist.

Clinical Psychologist

Clinical psychologists seek to help people with psychological problems. They work in a variety of settings, including colleges and universities, clinics, medical schools, and private practice. Clinical psychologists have either a Ph.D. (which involves clinical and research training) or a Psy.D. degree (which only involves clinical training). This graduate training usually takes 5 to 7 years and includes courses in clinical psychology and a 1-year supervised internship in an accredited setting toward the end of the training. In most cases, they must pass a test to become licensed in a state and to call themselves a clinical psychologist. Some clinical psychologists only conduct psychotherapy, others do psychological assessment and psychotherapy, and some also do research.

In regard to life-span development, clinical psychologists might specialize in a particular age group, such as children (child clinical psychologist) or older adults (often referred to a geropsychologist). Many geropsychologists pursue a year or two of postdoctoral training.

Psychiatrist

Psychiatrists obtain a medical degree and then do a residency in psychiatry. Medical school takes approximately 4 years, and the psychiatry residency another 3 to 4 years. Unlike psychologists (who do not go to medical school), psychiatrists can administer drugs to clients.

Like clinical psychologists, psychiatrists might specialize in working with children (child psychiatry) or with older adults (geriatric psychiatry). Psychiatrists might work in medical schools in teaching and research roles, in a medical clinic, or in private practice. In addition to administering drugs to help improve the lives of people with psychological problems, psychiatrists also may conduct psychotherapy.

Counseling Psychologist

Counseling psychologists go through much of the same training as clinical psychologists, although in a graduate program in counseling rather than clinical psychology. Counseling psychologists have either a master's degree or a doctoral degree. They also must go through a licensing procedure. One type of master's degree in counseling leads to the designation of licensed professional counselor. They work in the same settings as clinical psychologists, and may do psychotherapy, teach, or conduct research. Many counseling psychologists do not do therapy with individuals who have more severe mental disorders, such as schizophrenia.

School Counselor

School counselors help identify students' abilities and interests, guide students in developing academic plans, and explore career options with students. They may help students cope with adjustment problems. They may work with students individually, in small groups, or even in a classroom. They often consult with parents, teachers, and school administrators when trying to help students with their problems. School counselors usually have a master's degree in counseling.

High school counselors advise students on choosing a major, admissions requirements for college, taking entrance exams, applying for financial aid, and on appropriate vocational and technical training. Elementary school counselors are mainly involved in counseling students about social and personal problems. They may observe children in the classroom and at play as part of their work.

Career Counselor

Career counselors help individuals to identify what the best career options are for them and guide them in applying for jobs. They may work in private industry or at a college or university. They usually interview individuals and give them vocational and/or psychological tests to help provide students with information about appropriate careers that fit their interests and abilities. Sometimes they help individuals to create professional resumes or conduct mock interviews to help them feel comfortable in a job interview. They might create and promote job fairs or other recruiting events to help individuals obtain jobs.

Social Worker

Many social workers are involved in helping people with social or economic problems. They may investigate, evaluate, and attempt to rectify reported cases of abuse, neglect, endangerment, or domestic disputes. They can intervene in families if necessary and provide counseling and referral services to individuals and families. They have a minimum of an undergraduate degree from a school of social work that includes course work in various areas of sociology and psychology. Some social workers also have a master's or doctoral degree. They often work for publicly funded agencies at the city, state, or national level, although increasingly they work in the private sector in areas such as drug rehabilitation and family counseling.

In some cases, social workers specialize in a certain area, as is true of a medical social worker, who has a master's degree in social work (M.S.W.). This involves graduate coursework and supervised clinical experiences in medical settings. A medical social worker might coordinate a variety of support services to people with a severe or long-term disability. Family-care social workers often work with families with children or an older adult who needs support services.

Drug Counselor

Drug counselors provide counseling to individuals with drug-abuse problems. They may work on an individual basis with a substance abuser or conduct group therapy sessions. At a minimum, drug counselors go through an associate's or certificate program. Many have an undergraduate degree in substance-abuse counseling, and some have master's and doctoral degrees. They may work in private practice, with a state or federal government agency, with a company, or in a hospital setting. Some drug counselors specialize in working with adolescents or older adults. Most states provide a certification procedure for obtaining a license to practice drug counseling.

MEDICAL/NURSING/PHYSICAL

This third main area of careers in life-span development includes a wide range of careers in the medical and nursing areas, as well as jobs pertaining to improving some aspect of the person's physical development.

Obstetrician/Gynecologist

An obstetrician/gynecologist prescribes prenatal and postnatal care and performs deliveries in maternity cases. The individual also treats diseases and injuries of the female reproductive system. Becoming an obstetrician/gynecologist requires a medical degree plus 3 to 5 years of residency in obstetrics/gynecology. Obstetricians may work in private practice, in a medical clinic, a hospital, or in a medical school.

Pediatrician

A pediatrician monitors infants' and children's health, works to prevent disease or injury, helps children attain optimal health, and treats children with health problems. Pediatricians have attained a medical degree and then do a 3- to 5-year residency in pediatrics.

Pediatricians may work in private practice, in a medical clinic, in a hospital, or in a medical school. As a medical doctor, they can administer drugs to children and may counsel parents and children on ways to improve the children's health. Many pediatricians on the faculty of medical schools also teach and conduct research on children's health and diseases.

Geriatric Physician

A geriatric physician has a medical degree and has specialized in geriatric medicine by doing a 3- to 5-year residency. Geriatric physicians diagnose medical problems of older adults, evaluate treatment options, and make recommendations for nursing care or other arrangements. As with other doctors, they may work in private practice, in a medical clinic, in a hospital, or in a medical school. They also may primarily treat the diseases and health problems of older adults, but geriatric physicians in medical school settings also may teach future physicians and conduct research.

Neonatal Nurse

A neonatal nurse is involved in the delivery of care to the newborn infant. The neonatal nurse may work to improve the health and well-being of infants born under normal circumstances or be involved in the delivery of care to premature and critically ill neonates. A minimum of an undergraduate degree in nursing with a specialization in the newborn is required. This training involves coursework in nursing and the biological sciences, as well as supervisory clinical experiences.

Nurse-Midwife

A nurse-midwife formulates and provides comprehensive care to selected maternity patients, cares for the expectant mother as she prepares to give birth and guides her through the birth process, and cares for the postpartum patient. The nurse-midwife also may provide care to the newborn, counsel parents on the infant's development and parenting, and provide guidance about health practices. Becoming a nurse-midwife generally requires an undergraduate degree from a school of nursing. A nurse-midwife most often works in a hospital setting.

Pediatric Nurse

Pediatric nurses have a degree in nursing that takes 2 to 5 years to complete. Some also may go on to obtain a master's or doctoral degree in pediatric nursing. Pediatric nurses take courses in biological sciences, nursing care, and pediatrics, usually in a school of nursing. They also undergo supervised clinical experiences in medical settings. They monitor infants' and children's health, work to prevent disease or injury, and help children attain optimal health. They may work in hospitals, schools of nursing, or with pediatricians in private practice or at a medical clinic.

Geriatric Nurse

Geriatric nurses seek to prevent or intervene in the chronic or acute health problems of older adults. They take courses in a school of nursing and obtain a degree in nursing. This takes anywhere from 2 to 5 years. As in the case of a pediatric nurse, a geriatric nurse also may obtain a master's or doctoral degree in his or her specialty. Geriatric nurses take courses in biological sciences, nursing care, and mental health. They also experience supervised clinical training in geriatric settings. They may work in hospitals, nursing homes, schools of nursing, or with geriatric medical specialists or psychiatrists in a medical clinic or in private practice.

Physical Therapist

Physical therapists usually have an undergraduate degree in physical therapy and are licensed by a state. They take courses and experience supervised training in physical therapy. Many physical therapists work with people of all ages, although some specialize in working with a specific age group, such as children or older adults. They work directly with these individuals who have a physical problem either due to disease or injury to help them function as competently as possible. They may consult with other professionals and coordinate services for the individual.

Rehabilitation Counselor

Rehabilitation counselors work directly with individuals who have a physical disability that may have developed because of a disease or an injury. They try to help them function as competently as possible. In their efforts, they consult with other professionals and coordinate services.

Becoming a rehabilitation counselor requires a master's or Ph.D. degree in rehabilitation counseling. This includes graduate coursework, clinical training, training in physical therapy, and possibly research training.

Occupational Therapist

Occupational therapists may have an associate, bachelor's, master's, and/or doctoral degree with education ranging from two to six years. Training includes occupational therapy courses in a specialized program. National certification is required and licensing/registration is required in some states. Occupational Therapy is a health and rehabilitation profession that helps people regain, develop, and build skills that are important for independent functioning, health, well-being, security and happiness. The Occupational Therapist (OTR) initiates the evaluation of clients and manages the treatment process for clients with various impairments.

Therapeutic/Recreation Therapist

Therapeutic/recreation therapists maintain or improve the quality of life for people with special needs through intervention, leisure education, and recreation participation. They work in hospitals, rehabilitation centers, local government agencies, at-risk youth programs, as well as other settings. Becoming a therapeutic/recreation therapist requires an undergraduate degree with coursework in leisure studies and a concentration in therapeutic recreation. National certification is usually required. Coursework in anatomy, special education, and psychology are beneficial.

Audiologist

An audiologist has a minimum of an undergraduate degree in hearing science. This includes courses and supervisory training. Audiologists assess and identify the presence and severity of hearing loss, as well as problems in balance. Some audiologists also go on to obtain a master's or doctoral degree. They may work in a medical clinic, with a physician in private practice, in a hospital, or in a medical school.

Speech Therapist

Speech therapists are health-care professionals who are trained to identify, assess, and treat speech and language problems. They may work with physicians, psychologists, social workers, and other health-care professionals in a team approach to helping individuals with physical or psychological problems in which speech and language are involved in the problem. Speech pathologists have a minimum of an undergraduate degree in speech and hearing science or communications disorders area. They may work in private practice, in hospitals and medical schools, and in government agencies with individuals of any age. Some may specialize in working with children, others with the elderly, or in a particular type of speech disorder.

Genetic Counselor

Genetic counselors are health professionals with specialized graduate degrees and experience in the areas of medical genetics and counseling. Most enter the field after majoring in undergraduate school in such disciplines as biology, genetics, psychology, nursing, public health, and social work.

Genetic counselors work as members of a health-care team, providing information and support to families who have members with birth defects or genetic disorders and to families who may be at risk for a variety of inherited conditions. They identify families at risk and provide supportive counseling. They serve as educators and resource people for other health-care professionals and the public. Almost one-half work in university medical centers, and another one-fourth work in private hospital settings.

FAMILIES/RELATIONSHIPS

A number of careers and jobs are available for working with families and relationship problems across the life span. These range from being a home health aide to working as a marriage and family therapist.

Home Health Aide

No education is required for this position. There is brief training by an agency. A home health aide provides direct services to older adults in the older adults' homes, providing assistance in basic self-care tasks.

Child Welfare Worker

A child welfare worker is employed by the Child Protective Services unit of each state. The child welfare worker protects the child's rights, evaluates any maltreatment of the child, and may have the child removed from the home if necessary. A child social worker has a minimum of an undergraduate degree in social work.

Child Life Specialist

Child life specialists work with children and their families when the child needs to be hospitalized. They monitor the child's activities, seek to reduce the child's stress, help the child cope effectively, and assist the child in enjoying the hospital experience as much as possible. Child life specialists may provide parent education and develop individualized treatment plans based on an assessment of the child's development, temperament, medical plan, and available social supports. Child life specialists have an undergraduate degree, and they take courses in child development and education, as well as usually taking additional courses in a child life program.

Marriage and Family Therapist

Marriage and family therapists work on the principle that many individuals who have psychological problems benefit when psychotherapy is provided in the context of a marital or family relationship. Marriage and family therapists may provide marital therapy, couple therapy to individuals in a relationship who are not married, and family therapy to two or more members of a family.

Marriage and family therapists have a master's or doctoral degree. They go through a training program in graduate school similar to a clinical psychologist but with the focus on marital and family relationships. In most states, it is necessary to go through a licensing procedure to practice marital and family therapy.

WEBSITE CONNECTIONS FOR CAREERS IN LIFE-SPAN DEVELOPMENT

By going to the website for this book, you can obtain more detailed career information about the various careers in life-span development described in this Appendix. Go to the Web connections in the Career Appendix section, where you will read about a description of the websites. Then click on the title and you will be able to go directly to the website described. Here are the website connections:

Education/Research

Careers in Psychology
Elementary and Secondary School Teaching
Exceptional Children Teachers
Early Childhood Education
Family and Consumer Science Education
Educational Psychology
School Psychology

Clinical Counseling

Clinical Psychology
Psychiatry
Counseling Psychology
School Counseling
Social Work
Drug Counseling
Gerontology

Medical/Nursing/Physical Development

Obstetrics and Gynecology
Pediatrics
Nurse-Midwife
Neonatal Nursing
Pediatric Nursing
Gerontological Nursing
Physical Therapy
Occupational Therapy
Therapeutic/Recreation Therapy
Audiology and Speech Pathology
Genetic Counseling

Families/Relationships

Child Welfare Worker
Child Life Specialist
Marriage and Family Therapist

CHAPTER 2

There is nothing quite so practical as a good theory.

—KURT LEWIN
American Social Psychologist, 20th Century

The Science of Life-Span Development

Learning Goals

1 *D*escribe theories of life-span development

2 *E*xplain how research on life-span development is conducted

3 *D*iscuss research challenges in life-span development

Images of Life-Span Development
The Childhoods of Erikson and Piaget

Imagine that you have developed a major theory of development. What would influence you to construct this theory? A person interested in developing such a theory usually goes through a long university training program that culminates in a doctoral degree. As part of the training, the future theorist is exposed to many ideas about a particular area of life-span development, such as biological, cognitive, or socioemotional development. Another factor that could explain why someone develops a particular theory is that person's life experiences. Two important developmental theorists, whose views will be described later in the chapter, are Erik Erikson and Jean Piaget. Let's examine a portion of their lives as they were growing up to discover how their experiences might have contributed to the theories they developed.

Erik Homberger Erikson (1902–1994) was born near Frankfurt, Germany, to Danish parents. Before Erik was born, his parents separated, and his mother left Denmark to live in Germany. At age 3, Erik became ill, and his mother took him to see a pediatrician named Homberger. Young Erik's mother fell in love with the pediatrician, married him, and named Erik after his new stepfather.

Erik attended primary school from the ages of 6 to 10 and then the gymnasium (high school) from 11 to 18. He studied art and a number of languages. Erik did not like the atmosphere of formal schooling, and this attitude was reflected in his grades. Rather than going to college at age 18, the adolescent Erikson wandered around Europe, keeping a diary about his experiences. After a year of travel through Europe, he returned to Germany and enrolled in art school, became dissatisfied, and enrolled in another. Later he traveled to Florence, Italy. Psychiatrist Robert Coles described Erikson at this time:

> To the Italians he was the young, tall, thin Nordic expatriate with long, blond hair. He wore a corduroy suit and was seen by his family and friends as not odd or "sick" but as a wandering artist who was trying to come to grips with himself, a not unnatural or unusual struggle. (Coles, 1970, p. 15)

Contrast Erikson's experiences with those of Jean Piaget. Piaget (1896–1980) was born in Neuchâtel, Switzerland. Jean's father was an intellectual who taught young Jean to think systematically. Jean's mother was also very bright. His father had an air of detachment from his mother, whom Piaget described as prone to frequent outbursts of neurotic behavior.

In his autobiography, Piaget detailed why he chose to study cognitive development rather than social or abnormal development:

> I started to forego playing for serious work very early. Indeed, I have always detested any departure from reality, an attitude which I relate to . . . my mother's poor health. It was this disturbing factor which at the beginning of my studies in psychology made me keenly interested in psychoanalytic and pathological psychology. Though this interest helped me to achieve independence and widen my cultural background, I have never since felt any desire to involve myself deeper in that particular direction, always much preferring the study of normalcy and of the workings of the intellect to that of the tricks of the unconscious. (Piaget, 1952a, p. 238)

These snapshots of Erikson and Piaget illustrate how personal experiences might influence the direction in which a particular theorist goes. Erikson's wanderings and search for self contributed to his theory of identity development, and Piaget's intellectual experiences with his parents and schooling contributed to his emphasis on cognitive development.

Theories are part of the science of life-span development. Some individuals have difficulty thinking of life-span development as a science like physics, chemistry, and biology. Can a discipline that studies how parents nurture children, whether watching TV long hours is linked with being overweight, and the factors involved in life satisfaction among older adults be equated with disciplines that study the molecular structure of a compound and how gravity works? The answer is yes. Science is defined not by *what* it investigates, but by *how* it investigates. Whether you're studying photosynthesis, butterflies, Saturn's moons, or human development, it is the way you study that makes the approach scientific or not.

This chapter introduces the theories and methods that are the foundation of the science of life-span development. At the end of the chapter we will explore some of the ethical challenges and biases that researchers must guard against to protect the integrity of their results and respect the rights of the participants in their studies.

1 THEORIES OF DEVELOPMENT

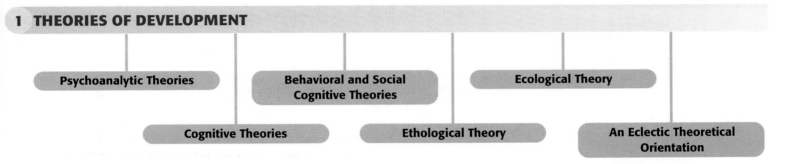

All scientific knowledge stems from a rigorous, systematic method of investigation (Pittenger, 2003; Salkind, 2003). The *scientific method* is essentially a four-step process:

1. Conceptualize a process or problem to be studied.
2. Collect research information (data).
3. Analyze data.
4. Draw conclusions.

In step 1, when researchers are formulating a problem to study, they often draw on *theories* and develop *hypotheses* (Miller, 2001). A **theory** is an interrelated, coherent set of ideas that helps to explain and make predictions. **Hypotheses** are specific assumptions and predictions that can be tested to determine their accuracy. For example, a theory on mentoring might attempt to explain and predict why sustained support, guidance, and concrete experience make a difference in the lives of children from impoverished backgrounds. The theory might focus on children's opportunities to model the behavior and strategies of mentors, or it might focus on the effects of individual attention, which might be missing in the children's lives.

The diversity of theories makes understanding life-span development a challenging undertaking. Just when you think one theory has the correct explanation of life-span development, another theory crops up and makes you rethink your earlier conclusion. To keep from getting frustrated, remember that life-span development is a complex, multifaceted topic. No single theory has been able to account for all aspects of it. Each theory contributes an important piece to the life-span development puzzle. Although the theories sometimes disagree about certain aspects of life-span development, much of their information is complementary rather than contradictory. Together they let us see the total landscape of life-span development in all its richness.

We will briefly explore five major theoretical perspectives on development: psychoanalytic, cognitive, behavioral and social cognitive, ethological, and ecological. In chapter 1, we described the three major processes involved in development: biological, cognitive, and socioemotional. The theoretical approaches that we will describe reflect these processes. Biological processes are very important in Freud's psychoanalytic and

theory An interrelated, coherent set of ideas that helps to explain and make predictions.

hypotheses Specific assumptions and predictions that can be tested to determine their accuracy.

Sigmund Freud, the pioneering architect of psychoanalytic theory. *How did Freud believe each individual's personality is organized?*

mhhe ●com/
santrockld9

Freud's Theory

psychoanalytic theory Describes development as primarily unconscious and heavily colored by emotion. Behavior is merely a surface characteristic and the symbolic workings of the mind have to be analyzed to understand behavior. Early experiences with parents are emphasized.

ethological theory, cognitive processes in Piaget's, Vygotsky's, information-processing, and social cognitive theories. Socioemotional processes are important in Freud's and Erikson's psychoanalytic theories, Vygotsky's sociocultural cognitive theory, behavioral and social cognitive theories, and ecological theory. You will read more about these theories and processes at different points in later chapters in the book.

Psychoanalytic Theories

Psychoanalytic theory describes development as primarily unconscious (beyond awareness) and colored by emotion. Psychoanalytic theorists believe that behavior is merely a surface characteristic and that a true understanding of development requires analyzing the symbolic meanings of behavior and the deep inner workings of the mind. Psychoanalytic theorists also stress that early experiences with parents extensively shape development. These characteristics are highlighted in the main psychoanalytic theory, that of Sigmund Freud.

Freud's Psychosexual Theory   Freud (1856–1939) developed his ideas about psychoanalytic theory while working with mental patients. He was a medical doctor who specialized in neurology. He spent most of his years in Vienna, though he moved to London near the end of his career because of Nazi anti-Semitism.

Freud (1917) believed that personality has three structures: the id, the ego, and the superego. The *id*, he said, consists of instincts, which are an individual's reservoir of psychic energy. In Freud's view, the id is totally unconscious; it has no contact with reality. As children experience the demands and constraints of reality, a new part of personality emerges—the *ego*, the Freudian personality structure that deals with the demands of reality. The ego is called the executive branch of personality because it uses reasoning to make decisions. The id and the ego have no morality. They do not take into account whether something is right or wrong. The *superego* is the Freudian structure of personality that is the moral branch of personality. The superego decides whether something is right or wrong. Think of the superego as what we often refer to as our "conscience." You probably are beginning to sense that both the id and the superego make life rough for the ego. Your ego might say, "I will have sex only occasionally and be sure to take the proper precautions because I don't want the intrusion of a child in the development of my career." However, your id is saying, "I want to be satisfied; sex is pleasurable." Your superego is at work, too: "I feel guilty about having sex."

As Freud listened to, probed, and analyzed his patients, he became convinced that their problems were the result of experiences early in life. Freud believed that we go through five stages of psychosexual development, and that at each stage of development we experience pleasure in one part of the body more than in others.

Freud thought that our adult personality is determined by the way we resolve conflicts between these early sources of pleasure—the mouth, the anus, and then the genitals—and the demands of reality. When these conflicts are not resolved, the individual may become fixated at a particular stage of development. Fixation occurs when the individual remains locked in an earlier developmental stage because needs are under- or overgratified. For example, a parent might wean a child too early, be too strict in toilet training the child, punish the child for masturbation, or "smother" the child with too much attention. Figure 2.1 illustrates the five Freudian stages.

The *oral stage* is the first Freudian stage of development, occurring during the first 18 months of life, in which the infant's pleasure centers around the mouth. Chewing, sucking, and biting are the chief sources of pleasure. These actions reduce tension in the infant.

The *anal stage* is the second Freudian stage of development, occurring between $1\frac{1}{2}$ and 3 years of age, in which the child's greatest pleasure involves the anus or the eliminative functions associated with it. In Freud's view, the exercise of anal muscles reduces tension.

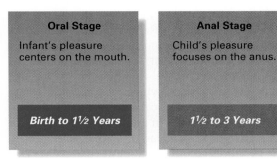

Oral Stage	Anal Stage	Phallic Stage	Latency Stage	Genital Stage
Infant's pleasure centers on the mouth.	Child's pleasure focuses on the anus.	Child's pleasure focuses on the genitals.	Child represses sexual interest and develops social and intellectual skills.	A time of sexual reawakening; source of sexual pleasure becomes someone outside the family.
Birth to 1½ Years	*1½ to 3 Years*	*3 to 6 Years*	*6 Years to Puberty*	*Puberty Onward*

FIGURE 2.1 Freudian Stages

The *phallic stage* is the third Freudian stage of development. The phallic stage occurs between the ages of 3 and 6; its name comes from the Latin word *phallus,* which means "penis." During the phallic stage, pleasure focuses on the genitals as both boys and girls discover that self-manipulation is enjoyable.

In Freud's view, the phallic stage has a special importance in personality development because it is during this period that the Oedipus complex, appears. This name comes from Greek mythology, in which Oedipus, the son of the King of Thebes, unwittingly kills his father and marries his mother. The *Oedipus complex* according to Freudian theory, is the young child's development of an intense desire to replace the same-sex parent and enjoy the affections of the opposite-sex parent.

How is the Oedipus complex resolved? At about 5 to 6 years of age, children recognize that their same-sex parent might punish them for their incestuous wishes. To reduce this conflict, the child identifies with the same-sex parent, striving to be like him or her. If the conflict is not resolved, though, the individual may become fixated at the phallic stage.

The *latency stage* is the fourth Freudian stage of development, which occurs between approximately 6 years of age and puberty. During this period, the child represses all interest in sexuality and develops social and intellectual skills. This activity channels much of the child's energy into emotionally safe areas and helps the child forget the highly stressful conflicts of the phallic stage.

The *genital stage* is the fifth and final Freudian stage of development, occurring from puberty onward. The genital stage is a time of sexual reawakening; the source of sexual pleasure now becomes someone outside of the family. Freud believed that unresolved conflicts with parents reemerge during adolescence. When these conflicts have been resolved, the individual is capable of developing a mature love relationship and functioning independently as an adult.

Freud's theory has undergone significant revisions by a number of psychoanalytic theorists (Eagle, 2000). Many contemporary psychoanalytic theorists place less emphasis on sexual instincts and more emphasis on cultural experiences as determinants of an individual's development. Unconscious thought remains a central theme, but most contemporary psychoanalysts believe that conscious thought makes up more of the mind than Freud envisioned. Next, we will explore the ideas of an important revisionist of Freud's ideas—Erik Erikson.

Erikson's Psychosocial Theory   Erik Erikson recognized Freud's contributions but believed that Freud misjudged some important dimensions of human development. For one thing, Erikson (1950, 1968) said we develop in *psychosocial* stages, rather than in *psychosexual* stages, as Freud maintained. For Freud, the primary motivation for human behavior was sexual in nature, for Erikson it was social and reflected a desire to affiliate with other people. Erikson emphasized developmental change throughout the human life span, whereas Freud argued that our basic personality is shaped in the first five years of life. In **Erikson's theory,** eight stages of development unfold as we go

Erikson's Theory

Erikson's theory Includes eight stages of human development. Each stage consists of a unique developmental task that confronts individuals with a crisis that must be faced.

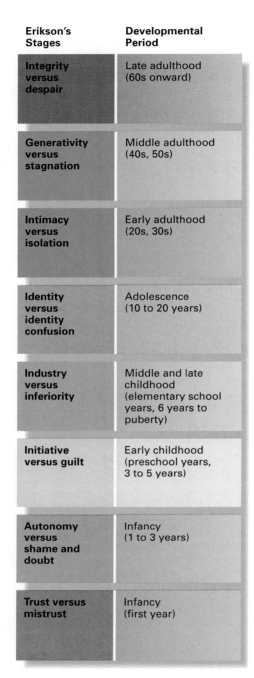

Erikson's Stages	Developmental Period
Integrity versus despair	Late adulthood (60s onward)
Generativity versus stagnation	Middle adulthood (40s, 50s)
Intimacy versus isolation	Early adulthood (20s, 30s)
Identity versus identity confusion	Adolescence (10 to 20 years)
Industry versus inferiority	Middle and late childhood (elementary school years, 6 years to puberty)
Initiative versus guilt	Early childhood (preschool years, 3 to 5 years)
Autonomy versus shame and doubt	Infancy (1 to 3 years)
Trust versus mistrust	Infancy (first year)

FIGURE 2.2 Erickson's Eight Life-Span Stages

through the life span (see figure 2.2). Each stage consists of a unique developmental task that confronts individuals with a crisis that must be resolved. According to Erikson, this crisis is not a catastrophe but a turning point of increased vulnerability and enhanced potential. The more successfully an individual resolves the crises, the healthier development will be (Hopkins, 2000).

Trust versus mistrust is Erikson's first psychosocial stage, which is experienced in the first year of life. A sense of trust requires a feeling of physical comfort and a minimal amount of fear and apprehension about the future. Trust in infancy sets the stage for a lifelong expectation that the world will be a good and pleasant place to live.

Autonomy versus shame and doubt is Erikson's second stage of development. This stage occurs in late infancy and toddlerhood (1 to 3 years). After gaining trust in their caregivers, infants begin to discover that their behavior is their own. They start to assert their sense of independence, or autonomy. They realize their *will*. If infants are restrained too much or punished too harshly, they are likely to develop a sense of shame and doubt.

Initiative versus guilt, Erikson's third stage of development, occurs during the preschool years. As preschool children encounter a widening social world, they are challenged more than when they were infants. Active, purposeful behavior is needed to cope with these challenges. Children are asked to assume responsibility for their bodies, their behavior, their toys, and their pets. Developing a sense of responsibility increases initiative. Uncomfortable guilt feelings may arise, though, if the child is irresponsible and is made to feel too anxious. Erikson has a positive outlook on this stage. He believes that most guilt is quickly compensated for by a sense of accomplishment.

Industry versus inferiority is Erikson's fourth developmental stage, occurring approximately in the elementary school years. Children's initiative brings them in contact with a wealth of new experiences. As they move into middle and late childhood, they direct their energy toward mastering knowledge and intellectual skills. At no other time is the child more enthusiastic about learning than at the end of early childhood's period of expansive imagination. The danger in the elementary school years is that the child can develop a sense of inferiority—feeling incompetent and unproductive. Erikson believed that teachers have a special responsibility for children's development of industry. Teachers should "mildly but firmly coerce children into the adventure of finding out that one can learn to accomplish things which one would never have thought of by oneself" (Erikson, 1968, p. 127).

Identity versus identity confusion is Erikson's fifth developmental stage, which individuals experience during the adolescent years. At this time, individuals are faced with finding out who they are, what they are all about, and where they are going in life. Adolescents are confronted with many new roles and adult statuses—vocational and romantic, for example. Parents need to allow adolescents to explore many different roles and different paths within a particular role. If the adolescent explores such roles in a healthy manner and arrives at a positive path to follow in life, then a positive identity will be achieved. If an identity is pushed on the adolescent by parents, if the adolescent does not adequately explore many roles, and if a positive future path is not defined, then identity confusion reigns.

Intimacy versus isolation is Erikson's sixth developmental stage, which individuals experience during the early adulthood years. At this time, individuals face the developmental task of forming intimate relationships with others. Erikson describes intimacy as finding oneself yet losing oneself in another. If the young adult forms healthy friendships and an intimate relationship with another individual, intimacy will be achieved; if not, isolation will result.

Generativity versus stagnation is Erikson's seventh developmental stage, which individuals experience during middle adulthood. A chief concern is to assist the younger generation in developing and leading useful lives—this is what Erikson means by generativity. The feeling of having done nothing to help the next generation is stagnation.

Integrity versus despair is Erikson's eighth and final stage of development, which individuals experience in late adulthood. During this stage, a person reflects on the past and either pieces together a positive review or concludes that life has not been spent well. Through many different routes, the older person may have developed a positive outlook in most or all of the previous stages of development. If so, the retrospective glances will reveal a picture of a life well spent, and the person will feel a sense of satisfaction—integrity will be achieved. If the older adult resolved many of the earlier stages negatively, the retrospective glances likely will yield doubt or gloom—the despair Erikson talks about.

Erikson did not believe that the proper solution to a stage crisis is always completely positive. Some exposure or commitment to the negative side of the person's conflict is sometimes inevitable—you cannot trust all people under all circumstances and survive, for example. Nonetheless, in the healthy solution to a stage crisis, the positive resolution dominates. We will discuss Erikson's theory again on a number of occasions in the chapters on socioemotional development in this book.

Evaluating the Psychoanalytic Theories   The contributions of psychoanalytic theories include these factors:

- Early experiences play an important part in development.
- Family relationships are a central aspect of development.
- Personality can be better understood if it is examined developmentally.
- The mind is not all conscious; unconscious aspects of the mind need to be considered.
- Changes take place in adulthood as well as the childhood (Erikson).

These are some criticisms of psychoanalytic theories:

- The main concepts of psychoanalytic theories have been difficult to test scientifically.
- Much of the data used to support psychoanalytic theories come from individuals' reconstruction of the past, often the distant past, and are of unknown accuracy.
- The sexual underpinnings of development are given too much importance (especially in Freud's theory).
- The unconscious mind is given too much credit for influencing development.
- Psychoanalytic theories present an image of humans that is too negative (especially Freud).
- Psychoanalytic theories are culture- and gender-biased. To read about culture and gender bias, see the Sociocultural Worlds of Development box on page 48.

Cognitive Theories

Whereas psychoanalytic theories stress the importance of unconscious thoughts, cognitive theories emphasize conscious thoughts. Three important cognitive theories are Piaget's cognitive developmental theory, Vygotsky's sociocultural cognitive theory, and the information-processing theory.

Piaget's theory will be covered in detail later in this book, when we discuss cognitive development in infancy, early childhood, middle and late childhood, and adolescence. Here we briefly present the main ideas of his theory.

Piaget's Cognitive Developmental Theory   **Piaget's theory** states that children actively construct their understanding of the world and go through four stages of cognitive development. Two processes underlie this cognitive construction of the world: organization and adaptation. To make sense of our world, we organize our experiences. For example, we separate important ideas from less important ideas. We connect one idea to another. In addition to organizing our observations and

Erik Erikson with his wife, Joan, an artist. Erikson generated one of the most important developmental theories of the twentieth century. *Which stage of Erikson's theory are you in? Does Erikson's description of this stage characterize you?*

Piaget's theory States that children actively construct their understanding of the world and go through four stages of cognitive development.

Cultural and Gender Bias in Freud's Theory

The Oedipus conflict was one of Freud's most influential concepts. Freud's view that the young child desires to replace the same-sex parent and gain the affections of the opposite-sex parent was developed during the Victorian era of the late nineteenth century when the male was dominant and the female was passive, and when sexual interests were repressed.

Many psychologists believe Freud overemphasized behavior's biological determinants and did not give adequate attention to sociocultural influences. In particular his view on the differences between males and females has a strong biological flavor and focuses on anatomical differences. That is, Freud argued that because they have a penis, boys develop a dominant, powerful personality, and that girls, because they do not have a penis, develop a submissive, weak personality. In basing his view of male/female differences in personality development on anatomical differences, Freud ignored the enormous impact of culture and experience in determining the personalities of the male and the female (Nolen-Hoeksema, 2001).

Three-quarters of a century age, English anthropologist Bronislaw Malinowski (1927) observed the behavior of the Trobriand Islanders of the Western Pacific. He found that the Oedipus complex, is not universal but depends on culture. The family pattern of the Trobriand Islanders is different than in many cultures. In the Trobriand Islands, the biological father is not the head of the household. This role is reserved for the mother's brother, who acts as a disciplinarian. Thus, the Trobriand Islanders tease apart the roles played by the same person in Freud's Vienna and in many other cultures. In Freud's view, this different family constellation should make no difference. The Oedipus complex should still emerge, in which the father is the young boy's hated rival for the mother's love. However, Malinowski found no indication of conflict between fathers and sons in the Trobriand

Islanders. Instead, he observed some negative feelings directed by the boy toward the maternal uncle.

The first feminist-based criticism of Freud's theory was proposed by psychoanalytic theorist Karen Horney (1987). She developed a model of women with positive feminine qualities and self-evaluation. Her critique of Freud's theory included reference to a male-dominant society and culture efforts to eliminate the male bias in psychoanalytic theory continues today.

Karen Horney developed the first feminist-based criticism of Freud's theory. Horney's view emphasizes women's positive qualities and self-evaluation. *Where did Horney think Freud was off base?*

---

mhhe●com/
santrockld9

Horney's Theory
Piaget's Theory

assimilation Occurs when individuals incorporate new information into their existing knowledge.

accommodation Occurs when individuals adjust to new information.

experiences, we *adapt* our thinking to include new ideas because additional information furthers understanding.

Piaget (1954) believed that we adapt in two ways: assimilation and accommodation. **Assimilation** occurs when individuals incorporate new information into their existing knowledge. **Accommodation** occurs when individuals adjust to new information. Consider a circumstance in which a 9-year-old girl is given a hammer and nails to hang a picture on the wall. She has never used a hammer, but from observation and vicarious experience she realizes that a hammer is an object to be held, that it is swung by the handle to hit the nail, and that it is usually swung a number of times. Recognizing each of these things, she fits her behavior into the information she already has (assimilation). However, the hammer is heavy, so she holds it near the top. She swings too hard and the nail bends, so she adjusts the pressure of her strikes. These adjustments reveal her ability to alter slightly her conception of the world (accommodation).

Piaget thought that assimilation and accommodation operate even in the very young infant's life. Newborns reflexively suck everything that touches their lips (assimilation), but, after several months of experience, they construct their understanding of the world differently. Some objects, such as fingers and the mother's breast, can be sucked, but others, such as fuzzy blankets, should not be sucked (accommodation).

Piaget also believed that we go through four stages in understanding the world (see figure 2.3). Each of the stages is age-related and consists of distinct ways of thinking. Remember, it is the *different* way of understanding the world that makes one stage more advanced than another; knowing *more* information does not make the child's thinking more advanced, in the Piagetian view. This is what Piaget meant when he said the child's cognition is *qualitatively* different in one stage compared to another (Vidal, 2000). What are Piaget's four stages of cognitive development like?

The *sensorimotor stage,* which lasts from birth to about 2 years of age, is the first Piagetian stage. In this stage, infants construct an understanding of the world by coordinating sensory experiences (such as seeing and hearing) with physical, motoric actions—hence the term *sensorimotor.* At the beginning of this stage, newborns have little more than reflexive patterns with which to work. At the end of the stage, 2-year-olds have complex sensorimotor patterns and are beginning to operate with primitive symbols.

The *preoperational stage,* which lasts from approximately 2 to 7 years of age, is the second Piagetian stage. In this stage, children begin to represent the world with words, images, and drawings. Symbolic thought goes beyond simple connections of sensory information and physical action. However, although preschool children can symbolically represent the world, according to Piaget, they still lack the ability to perform *operations,* the Piagetian term for internalized mental actions that allow children to do mentally what they previously did physically.

The *concrete operational stage,* which lasts from approximately 7 to 11 years of age, is the third Piagetian stage. In this stage, children can perform operations, and logical reasoning replaces intuitive thought as long as reasoning can be applied to specific or concrete examples. For instance, concrete operational thinkers cannot imagine the steps necessary to complete an algebraic equation, which is too abstract for thinking at this stage of development.

The *formal operational stage,* which appears between the ages of 11 and 15 and continues through adulthood, is the fourth and final Piagetian stage. In this stage, individuals move beyond concrete experiences and think in abstract and more logical terms. As part of thinking more abstractly, adolescents develop images of ideal circumstances. They might think about what an ideal parent is like and compare their parents to this ideal standard. They begin to entertain possibilities for the future and are fascinated with what they can be. In solving problems, formal operational thinkers

Jean Piaget, the famous Swiss developmental psychologist, changed the way we think about the development of children's minds. *What are some key ideas in Piaget's theory?*

Sensorimotor Stage	Preoperational Stage	Concrete Operational Stage	Formal Operational Stage
The infant constructs an understanding of the world by coordinating sensory experiences with physical actions. An infant progresses from reflexive, instinctual action at birth to the beginning of symbolic thought toward the end of the stage.	The child begins to represent the world with words and images. These words and images reflect increased symbolic thinking and go beyond the connection of sensory information and physical action.	The child can now reason logically about concrete events and classify objects into different sets.	The adolescent reasons in more abstract, idealistic, and logical ways.
Birth to 2 Years of Age	*2 to 7 Years of Age*	*7 to 11 Years of Age*	*11 Years of Age through Adulthood*

FIGURE 2.3 Piaget's Four Stages of Cognitive Development

There is considerable interest today in Lev Vygotsky's sociocultural cognitive theory of child development. *What were Vygotsky's three basic claims about children's development?*

mhhe●com/
santrockld9

Vygotsky's Theory

Vygotsky's theory A sociocultural cognitive theory that emphasizes how culture and social interaction guide cognitive development.

information-processing theory Emphasizes that individuals manipulate information, monitor it, and strategize about it. Central to this theory are the processes of memory and thinking.

are more systematic, developing hypotheses about why something is happening the way it is, then testing these hypotheses in a deductive manner. We will examine Piaget's cognitive developmental theory further in chapters 6, 8, 10, 12, and 14.

Vygotsky's Sociocultural Cognitive Theory Like Piaget, the Russian developmentalist Lev Vygotsky (1896–1934) also believed that children actively construct their knowledge. However, Vygotsky gave social interaction and culture far more important roles in cognitive development than Piaget did. **Vygotsky's theory** is a sociocultural cognitive theory that emphasizes how culture and social interaction guide cognitive development. Vygotsky was born the same year as Piaget, but he died much earlier, at the age of 37. Both Piaget's and Vygotsky's ideas remained virtually unknown to American scholars until the 1960s. In the past several decades, American psychologists and educators have shown increased interest in Vygotsky's (1962) views.

Vygotsky portrayed the child's development as inseparable from social and cultural activities. He believed that the development of memory, attention, and reasoning involves learning to use the inventions of society, such as language, mathematical systems, and memory strategies. In one culture, this might consist of learning to count with the help of a computer. In another, it might consist of counting on one's fingers or using beads.

Vygotsky's theory has stimulated considerable interest in the view that knowledge is *situated* and *collaborative* (Greeno, Collins, & Resnick, 1996; John-Steiner & Mahn, 2003; Kozulin, 2000; Rogoff, Turkanis, & Bartlett, 2001). In this view, knowledge is not generated from within the individual but rather is constructed through interaction with other people and objects in the culture, such as books. This suggests that knowing can best be advanced through interaction with others in cooperative activities.

Vygotsky believed that children's social interaction with more-skilled adults and peers is indispensable in advancing cognitive development. It is through this interaction that less-skilled members of the culture learn to use the tools that will help them adapt and be successful in the culture. For example, when a skilled reader regularly helps a child learn how to read, this not only advances a child's reading skills but also communicates to the child that reading is an important activity in the culture.

Vygotsky articulated unique and influential ideas about cognitive development. In chapter 8, "Physical and Cognitive Development in Early Childhood," we will further explore Vygotsky's contributions to our understanding of children's development.

The Information-Processing Theory **Information-processing theory** emphasizes that individuals manipulate information, monitor it, and strategize about it. Central to this theory are the processes of memory and thinking. According to the information-processing theory, individuals develop a gradually increasing capacity for processing information, which allows them to acquire increasingly complex knowledge and skills (Bjorklund & Rosenbaum, 2000; Chen & Siegler, 2000; Siegler, 2001). Unlike Piaget's cognitive developmental theory, the information-processing theory does not describe development as stagelike.

Although a number of factors stimulated the growth of the information-processing theory, none was more important than the computer, which demonstrated that a machine could perform logical operations. Psychologists began to wonder if the logical operations carried out by computers might tell us something about how the human mind works. They drew analogies to computers to explain the relation between cognition or thinking and the brain. The physical brain is said to be analogous to the computer's hardware, cognition is said to be analogous to its software. Although computers and software are not perfect analogies for brains and cognitive activities, the comparison contributed to our thinking about the mind as an active information-processing system.

Robert Siegler (1998), a leading expert on children's information processing, believes that thinking is information processing. He says that when individuals perceive, encode, represent, store, and retrieve information, they are thinking. Siegler especially thinks that an important aspect of development is to learn good strategies for processing information. For example, becoming a better reader might involve learning to monitor the key themes of the material being read.

Evaluating the Cognitive Theories These are some contributions of cognitive theories:

- The cognitive theories present a positive view of development, emphasizing conscious thinking.
- The cognitive theories (especially Piaget's and Vygotsky's) emphasize the individual's active construction of understanding.
- Piaget's and Vygotsky's theories underscore the importance of examining developmental changes in children's thinking.
- The information-processing theory offers detailed descriptions of cognitive processes.

These are some criticisms of cognitive theories:

- There is skepticism about the pureness of Piaget's stages.
- The cognitive theories do not give adequate attention to individual variations in cognitive development.
- The information-processing theory does not provide an adequate description of developmental changes in cognition.
- Psychoanalytic theorists argue that the cognitive theories do not give enough credit to unconscious thought.

mhhe●com/
santrockld9

**Behavioral and
Social Cognitive Theories**

Behavioral and Social Cognitive Theories

Behaviorists essentially believe that scientifically we can study only what can be directly observed and measured. At about the same time as Freud was interpreting patients' unconscious minds through their early childhood experiences, Ivan Pavlov and John B. Watson were conducting detailed observations of behavior in controlled laboratory settings. Out of the behavioral tradition grew the belief that development is observable behavior that can be learned through experience with the environment. The three versions of the behavioral approach that we will explore are Pavlov's classical conditioning, Skinner's operant conditioning, and social cognitive theory.

Pavlov's Classical Conditioning In the early 1900s, the Russian physiologist Ivan Pavlov (1927) knew that dogs innately salivate when they taste food. He became curious when he observed that dogs salivate to various sights and sounds before eating their food. For example, when an individual paired the ringing of a bell with the food, the bell ringing subsequently elicited the salivation response from the dogs when it was presented by itself. With this experiment, Pavlov discovered the principle of *classical conditioning,* in which a neutral stimulus (in our example, ringing a bell) acquires the ability to produce a response originally produced by another stimulus (in our example, food).

In the early twentieth century, John Watson wanted to show that Pavlov's concept of classical conditioning could be applied to human beings. He showed an infant named Albert a white rat to see if he was afraid of it. He was not. As Albert played with the rat, a loud noise was sounded behind his head. As you might imagine, the noise caused little Albert to cry. After several pairings of the loud noise and the white rat, Albert began to fear the rat even when the noise was not sounded (Watson & Rayner, 1920).

B. F. Skinner was a tinkerer who liked to make new gadgets. The younger of his two daughters, Deborah, was raised in Skinner's enclosed Air-Crib, which he invented because he wanted to control her environment completely. The Air-Crib was sound-proofed and temperature controlled. Debbie, shown here as a child with her parents, is currently a successful artist, is married, and lives in London. *What do you think about Skinner's Air-Crib?*

Albert Bandura has been one of the leading architects of social cognitive theory. *What is the nature of his theory?*

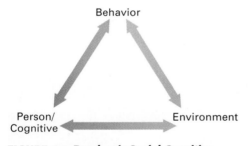

FIGURE 2.4 Bandura's Social Cognitive Model

The arrows illustrate how relations between behavior, person (cognitive), and environment are reciprocal rather than unidirectional.

Albert Bandura

social cognitive theory The view of psychologists who emphasize behavior, environment, and cognition as the key factors in development.

Today, we could not ethically conduct such an experiment, for reasons that we will discuss later in the chapter.

Many of our fears—fear of the dentist from a painful experience, fear of driving from being in an automobile incident, fear of heights from falling off a high chair when we were infants, and fear of dogs from being bitten—can be learned through classical conditioning.

Skinner's Operant Conditioning   In B. F. Skinner's (1938) *operant conditioning*, the consequences of a behavior produce changes in the probability of the behavior's occurrence. If a behavior is followed by a rewarding stimulus it is more likely to recur, but if a behavior is followed by a punishing stimulus it is less likely to recur. For example, when a person smiles at a child after the child has done something, the child is more likely to engage in the activity than if the person gives the child a nasty look.

For Skinner, such rewards and punishments shape individuals' development. For example, Skinner's approach argues that shy people learned to be shy as a result of experiences they had while growing up. It follows that modifications in an environment can help a shy person become more socially oriented.

Social Cognitive Theory   Some psychologists believe that the behaviorists basically are right when they say development is learned and is influenced strongly by environmental interactions. However, they believe that Skinner went too far in declaring that cognition is unimportant in understanding development. **Social cognitive theory** is the view of psychologists who emphasize behavior, environment, and cognition as the key factors in development.

American psychologists Albert Bandura (1986, 2000, 2001) and Walter Mischel (1973, 1995) are the main architects of social cognitive theory's contemporary version, which Mischel (1973) initially labeled *cognitive* social learning theory. Both Bandura and Mischel believe that cognitive processes are important mediators of environment-behavior connections. Bandura's early research program focused heavily on observational learning, learning that occurs through observing what others do. Observational learning is also referred to as imitation or modeling. What is *cognitive* about observational learning in Bandura's view? Bandura (1925–   ) believes that people cognitively represent the behavior of others and then sometimes adopt this behavior themselves. For example, a young boy might observe his father's aggressive outbursts and hostile interchanges with people; when observed with his peers, the young boy's style of interaction is highly aggressive, showing the same characteristics as his father's behavior. A girl might adopt the dominant and sarcastic style of her teacher. When observed interacting with her younger brother, she says, "You are so slow. How can you do this work so slowly?" Social cognitive theorists believe that people acquire a wide range of such behaviors, thoughts, and feelings through observing others' behavior and that these observations form an important part of life-span development.

Bandura's (1986, 1998, 2001) most recent model of learning and development involves behavior, the person/cognition, and the environment. An individual's confidence that he or she can control his or her success is an example of a person factor, and thinking is an example of a cognitive factor. As shown in figure 2.4, behavior, person/cognitive, and environmental factors operate interactively. Behavior can influence person factors and vice versa. The person's cognitive activities can influence the environment, the environment can change the person's cognition, and so on.

Let's consider how Bandura's model might work in the case of a college student's achievement behavior. As the student diligently studies and gets good grades, her behavior produces positive thoughts about her abilities. As part of her effort to make good grades, she plans and develops a number of strategies to make her studying more efficient. In these ways, her behavior has influenced her thought and her thought has influenced her behavior. At the beginning of the term, her college made a special effort to involve students in a study skills program. She decided to join. Her success, along with that of other students who attended the program, has led the college to expand the program next semester. In these ways, environment influenced behavior, and behavior changed the environment. And the college administrators' expectations that the study skills program would work made it possible in the first place. The program's success has spurred expectations that this type of program could work in other colleges. In these ways, cognition changed the environment, and the environment changed cognition.

Evaluating the Behavioral and Social Cognitive Theories   Contributions of the behavioral and social cognitive theories include:

- The importance of scientific research
- The environmental determinants of behavior
- The importance of observational learning (Bandura)
- Person and cognitive factors (social cognitive theory)

Criticisms of the behavioral and social cognitive theories include:

- Too little emphasis on cognition (Pavlov, Skinner)
- Too much emphasis on environmental determinants
- Inadequate attention to developmental changes
- Too mechanical and inadequate consideration of the spontaneity and creativity of humans

Behavioral and social cognitive theories emphasize the importance of environmental experiences in human development. Next we turn our attention to a theory that underscores the importance of biological foundations of development—ethological theory.

mhhe●com/
santrockld9

Exploring Ethology

Ethological Theory

Ethology stresses that behavior is strongly influenced by biology, is tied to evolution, and is characterized by critical or sensitive periods. Ethologists believe that the presence or absence of certain experiences at particular times in the life span influences individuals well beyond the time they first occur and that most psychologists underestimate the importance of these special time frames in early development. Ethologists also stress the powerful roles that evolution and biological foundations play in development (Rosenzweig, 2000).

ethology Stresses that behavior is strongly influenced by biology, is tied to evolution, and is characterized by critical or sensitive periods.

Konrad Lorenz, a pioneering student of animal behavior, is followed through the water by three imprinted greylag geese. Describe Lorenz's experiment with the geese. *Do you think his experiment would have the same results with human babies? Explain.*

Ethology emerged as an important view because of the work of European zoologists, especially Konrad Lorenz (1903–1989). Working mostly with greylag geese, Lorenz (1965) studied a behavior pattern that was considered to be programmed within the birds' genes. A newly hatched gosling seemed to be born with the instinct to follow its mother. Observations showed that the gosling was capable of such behavior as soon as it hatched. Lorenz proved that it was incorrect to assume that such behavior was programmed in the animal. In a remarkable set of experiments, Lorenz separated the eggs laid by one goose into two groups. One group he returned to the goose to be hatched by her. The other group was hatched in an incubator. The goslings in the first group performed as predicted. They followed their mother as soon as they hatched. However, those in the second group, which saw Lorenz when they first hatched, followed him everywhere, as though he were their mother. Lorenz marked the goslings and then placed both groups under a box. Mother goose and "mother" Lorenz stood aside as the box lifted. Each group of goslings went directly to its "mother." Lorenz called this process *imprinting,* the rapid, innate learning within a limited critical period of time that involves attachment to the first moving object seen.

The ethological view of Lorenz and the European zoologists forced American developmental psychologists to recognize the importance of the biological basis of behavior. However, ethological research and theory lacked some ingredients that would elevate it to the ranks of the other theories discussed so far in this chapter. In particular, there was little or nothing in the classical ethological view about the nature of social relationships across the human life span, something that any major theory of development must explain. Also, its concept of *critical period,* a fixed time period very early in development during which certain behaviors optimally emerge, seemed to be overdrawn. Classical ethological theory was weak in stimulating studies with humans. Recent expansion of the ethological view has improved its status as a viable developmental perspective.

One of the most important applications of ethological theory to human development involves John Bowlby's (1969, 1989) theory of attachment. Bowlby argued that attachment to a caregiver over the first year of life has important consequences throughout the life span. In his view, if this attachment is positive and secure, the individual will likely develop more positively in childhood and adulthood. If the attachment is negative and insecure, life-span development will likely not be optimal. In chapter 7, "Socioemotional Development in Infancy," we will explore the concept of infant attachment in much greater detail.

Contributions of ethological theory include:

- Increased focus on the biological and evolutionary basis of development
- Use of careful observations in naturalistic settings
- Emphasis on sensitive periods of development

These are some criticisms of ethological theory:

- The concepts of critical and sensitive periods might be too rigid
- Too strong an emphasis on biological foundations
- Inadequate attention to cognition
- The theory has been better at generating research with animals than with humans

Another theory that emphasizes the biological aspects of human development—evolutionary psychology—will be presented in chapter 3, "Biological Beginnings," along with views on the role of heredity in development. Also, we will examine a number of biological theories of aging in chapter 18, "Physical Development in Late Adulthood."

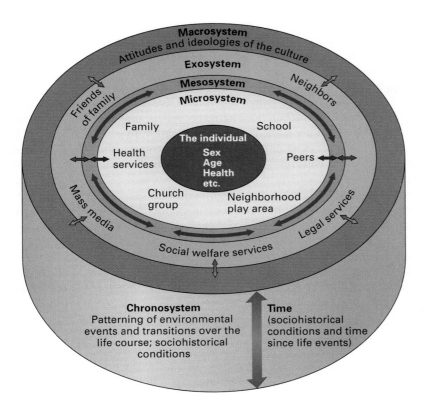

FIGURE 2.5 Bronfenbrenner's Ecological Theory of Development
Bronfenbrenner's ecological theory consists of five environmental systems: microsystem, mesosystem, exosystem, macrosystem, and chronosystem.

Ecological Theory

While ethological theory stresses biological factors, ecological theory emphasizes environmental factors. One ecological theory that has important implications for understanding life-span development was created by Urie Bronfenbrenner (1917–   ).

Ecological theory is Bronfenbrenner's (1986, 2000; Bronfenbrenner & Morris, 1998) environmental system of development. It consists of five environmental systems ranging from the fine-grained inputs of direct interactions with people to the broad-based inputs of culture (see figure 2.5).

- *Microsystem:* The setting in which the individual lives. These contexts include the person's family, peers, school, and neighborhood ◀▥ p. 13. It is in the microsystem that the most direct interactions with social agents take place—with parents, peers, and teachers, for example. The individual is viewed not as a passive recipient of experiences in these settings, but as someone who helps to construct the settings.
- *Mesosystem:* Involves relations between microsystems or connections between contexts. Examples are the relation of family experiences to school experiences, school experiences to church experiences, and family experiences to peer experiences. For example, children whose parents have rejected them may have difficulty developing positive relations with teachers.
- *Exosystem:* Is involved when experiences in another social setting—in which the individual does not have an active role—influence what the individual experiences in an immediate context. For example, work experiences can affect a

Bronfenbrenner's Theory

Bronfenbrenner and a Multicultural Framework

ecological theory Bronfenbrenner's environmental systems theory that focuses on five environmental systems: microsystem, mesosystem, exosystem, macrosystem, and chronosystem.

Urie Bronfenbrenner developed ecological theory, a perspective that is receiving increased attention. His theory emphasizes the importance of both micro and macro dimensions of the environment in which the child lives.

woman's relationship with her husband and their child. The mother might receive a promotion that requires more travel, which might increase marital conflict and change patterns of parent-child interaction. Another example is the federal government through its role in the quality of medical care and support systems for older adults.

- *Macrosystem:* The culture in which individuals live. Remember from chapter 1 that culture refers to the behavior patterns, beliefs, and all other products of a group of people that are passed on from generation to generation ◀ᴵᴵᴵᴵ p. 13. Remember also that cross-cultural studies—the comparison of one culture with one or more other cultures—provide information about the generality of development.
- *Chronosystem:* The patterning of environmental events and transitions over the life course, as well as sociohistorical circumstances. For example, in studying the effects of divorce on children, researchers have found that the negative effects often peak in the first year after the divorce. The effects also are more negative for sons than for daughters (Hetherington, 1993). By two years after the divorce, family interaction is less chaotic and more stable. With regard to sociocultural circumstances, women today are much more likely to be encouraged to pursue a career than they were 20 or 30 years ago.

Bronfenbrenner (2000; Bronfenbrenner & Morris, 1998) has added biological influences to his theory and now describes it as a bioecological theory. Nonetheless, ecological, environmental contexts still predominate in Bronfenbrenner's theory (Ceci, 2000).

The contributions of ecological theory include:

- A systematic examination of macro and micro dimensions of environmental systems
- Attention to connections between environmental settings (mesosystem)
- Consideration of sociohistorical influences on development (chronosystem)

These are some criticisms of ecological theory:

- Even with the added discussion of biological influences in recent years, there is still too little attention to biological foundations of development
- Inadequate attention to cognitive processes

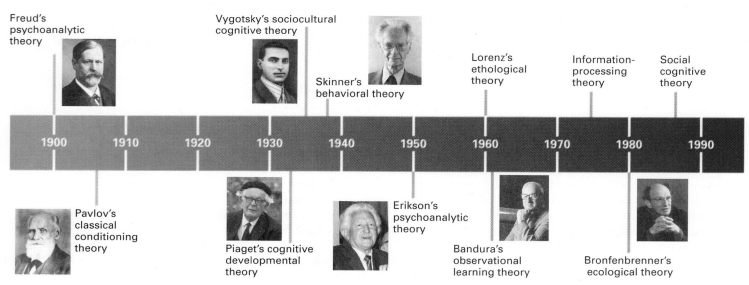

FIGURE 2.6 Time Line for Major Developmental Theories

An Eclectic Theoretical Orientation

An **eclectic theoretical orientation** does not follow any one theoretical approach, but rather selects from each theory whatever is considered its best features. No single theory described in this chapter can explain entirely the rich complexity of life-span development. Each of the theories has made important contributions to our understanding of development, but none provides a complete description and explanation. Psychoanalytic theory best explains the unconscious mind. Erikson's theory best describes the changes that occur in adult development. Piaget's, Vygotsky's, and the information-processing views provide the most complete description of cognitive development. The behavioral and social cognitive and ecological theories have been the most adept at examining the environmental determinants of development. The ethological theories have made us aware of biology's role and the importance of sensitive periods in development. It is important to recognize that, although theories are helpful guides, relying on a single theory to explain development is probably a mistake.

An attempt was made in this chapter to present five theoretical perspectives objectively. The same eclectic orientation will be maintained throughout the book. In this way, you can view the study of development as it actually exists—with different theorists making different assumptions, stressing different empirical problems, and using different strategies to discover information.

The theories that we have discussed were conceived at different points in the twentieth century. For a chronology of when these theories were proposed, see figure 2.6 on page 56. Figure 2.7 compares the main theoretical perspectives in terms of how they view important developmental issues in life-span development.

eclectic theoretical orientation An orientation that does not follow any one theoretical approach, but rather selects from each theory whatever is considered the best in it.

Theory	Issues		
	Continuity/discontinuity, early versus later experiences	**Biological and environmental factors**	**Importance of cognition**
Psychoanalytic	Discontinuity between stages—continuity between early experiences and later development; early experiences very important; later changes in development emphasized in Erikson's theory	Freud's biological determination interacting with early family experiences; Erikson's more balanced biological-cultural interaction perspective	Emphasized, but in the form of unconscious thought
Cognitive	Discontinuity between stages in Piaget's theory; continuity between early experiences and later development in Piaget's and Vygotsky's theory; no stages in Vygotsky's theory or information-processing theory	Piaget's emphasis on interaction and adaptation; environment provides the setting for cognitive structures to develop; information-processing view has not addressed this issue extensively but mainly emphasizes biological-environmental interaction	The primary determinant of behavior
Behavioral and social cognitive	Continuity (no stages); experience at all points of development important	Environment viewed as the cause of behavior in both views	Strongly deemphasized in the behavioral approach but an important mediator in social cognitive theory
Ethological	Discontinuity but no stages; critical or sensitive periods emphasized; early experiences very important	Strong biological view	Not emphasized
Ecological	Little attention to continuity/discontinuity; change emphasized more than stability	Strong environmental view	Not emphasized

FIGURE 2.7 A Comparison of Theories and Issues in Life-Span Development

Review and Reflect

1 Describe theories of life-span development

REVIEW

- What is the relationship between a theory and hypotheses? What are two main psychoanalytic theories? What are some strengths and weaknesses of the psychoanalytic theories?
- What are three main cognitive theories? What are some strengths and weaknesses of the cognitive theories?
- What are three main behavioral and social cognitive theories? What are some strengths and weaknesses of the behavioral and social cognitive theories?
- What is the nature of ethological theory? What are some strengths and weaknesses of the theory?
- What is an eclectic theoretical orientation?

REFLECT

- Which of the life-span theories do you think best explains your own development? Why?

2 RESEARCH IN LIFE-SPAN DEVELOPMENT

Types of Research   **Time Span of Research**

Generally, research in life-span development is designed to test hypotheses, which in some cases, are derived from the theories just described. Through research, theories are modified to reflect new data and occasionally new theories arise. What types of research are conducted in life-span development? If researchers want to study people of different ages, what research designs can they use? These are the questions that we will examine next.

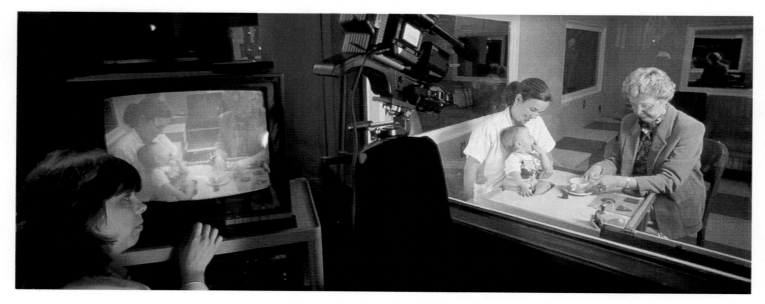

In this research study, mother-child interaction is being videotaped. Later, researchers will code the interaction using precise categories.

Types of Research

This section describes the major methods used to gather data about life-span development. For this purpose, there are three basic types of research: descriptive, correlational, and experimental. Each has strengths and weaknesses.

Descriptive Research   Some important theories have grown out of **descriptive research,** which has the purpose of observing and recording behavior. For example, a psychologist might observe the extent to which people are altruistic or aggressive toward each other. By itself, descriptive research cannot prove what causes some phenomenon, but it can reveal important information about people's behavior and attitudes. Descriptive research methods include observation, surveys and interviews, standardized tests, case studies, and life-history records.

Observation   Scientific observation requires an important set of skills (McMillan & Wergin, 2002). Unless we are trained observers and practice our skills regularly, we might not know what to look for, we might not remember what we saw, we might not realize that what we are looking for is changing from one moment to the next, and we might not communicate our observations effectively.

For observations to be effective, they have to be systematic (Elmes, Kantowitz, & Roedinger, 2003). We have to have some idea of what we are looking for. We have to know whom we are observing, when and where we will observe, and how the observations will be made. In what form they will be recorded: In writing? Tape recording? Video?

Where should we make our observations? We have two choices: the laboratory and the everyday world.

When we observe scientifically, we often need to control certain factors that determine behavior but are not the focus of our inquiry (Hoyle & Judd, 2002). For this reason, some research in life-span development is conducted in a **laboratory,** a controlled setting with many of the complex factors of the "real world" removed.

An experiment conducted by Albert Bandura (1965) found that children behaved more aggressively after observing a model being rewarded for aggression. Bandura conducted this study in a laboratory with adults the child did not know. Thus, he controlled when the child witnessed aggression, how much aggression the child saw, and what form the aggression took. Bandura would not have had as much control over the experiment, or as much confidence in the results, if the study had been conducted in the children's homes and if familiar people had been present, such as the child's parents, siblings, or friends.

Laboratory research does have some drawbacks. First, it is almost impossible to conduct research without the participants' knowing they are being studied. Second, the laboratory setting is unnatural and therefore can cause the participants to behave unnaturally.

Another drawback of laboratory research is that people who are willing to come to a university laboratory may not fairly represent groups from diverse cultural backgrounds. Those who are unfamiliar with university settings, and with the idea of "helping science," may be intimidated by the setting.

Still another problem is that some aspects of life-span development are difficult if not impossible to examine in the laboratory. Laboratory studies of certain types of stress may even be unethical.

Naturalistic observation provides insights that we sometimes cannot achieve in the laboratory (Billman, 2003; Langston, 2002). **Naturalistic observation** means observing behavior in real-world settings, making no effort to manipulate or control the situation. Life-span researchers conduct naturalistic observations at sporting events, day-care centers, work settings, malls, and other places people live in and frequent. Suppose that you wanted to study the level of civility on your campus. Most likely, you would want to include some naturalistic observation of how people treat one another in places like the cafeteria or the library reading room.

*S*cience refines everyday thinking.

—Albert Einstein
German-born American Physicist, 20th Century

descriptive research Has the purpose of observing and recording behavior.

laboratory A controlled setting in which many of the complex factors of the "real world" are removed.

naturalistic observation Observing behavior in real-world settings.

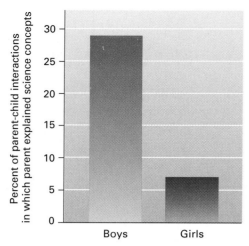

FIGURE 2.8 Parents' Explanations of Science to Sons and Daughters at a Science Museum

In a naturalistic observation study at a children's science museum, parents were three times more likely to explain science to boys than to girls (Crowley & others, 2001). The gender difference occurred regardless of whether the father, the mother, or both parents were with the child, although the gender difference was greatest for fathers' science explanations to sons and daughters.

"Would you say Attila is doing an excellent job, a good job, a fair job, or a poor job?"

standardized test A test with uniform procedures for administration and scoring. Many standardized tests allow a person's performance to be compared with the performance of other individuals.

Naturalistic observation was used in one study that focused on conversations in a children's science museum (Crowley & others, 2001). Parents were three times as likely to engage boys than girls in explanatory talk while visiting different exhibits at the science museum, suggesting a gender bias that encourages boys more than girls in science (see figure 2.8). In another study, Mexican American parents who had completed high school used more explanations with their children when visiting a science museum than Mexican American parents who had not completed high school (Tenenbaum & others, 2002).

Surveys and Interviews   Sometimes the best and quickest way to get information about people is to ask them for it. One technique is to *interview* them directly. A related method that is especially useful when information from many people is needed is the *survey,* sometimes referred to as a questionnaire. A standard set of questions is used to obtain peoples' self-reported attitudes or beliefs about a particular topic. In a good survey, the questions are clear and unbiased, allowing respondents to answer unambiguously.

Surveys and interviews can be used to study a wide range of topics from religious beliefs to sexual habits to attitudes about gun control to beliefs about how to improve schools. Surveys and interviews can be conducted in person or over the telephone. In addition, some surveys are now being conducted over the Internet.

Some survey and interview questions are unstructured and open-ended, such as "Could you elaborate on your optimistic tendencies?" or "How fulfilling would you say your marriage is?" They allow for unique responses from each person surveyed. Other survey and interview questions are more structured and ask about more specific things. For example, one national poll on beliefs about what needs to be done to improve U.S. schools asked: "Of the following four possibilities, which one do you think offers the most promise for improving public schools in the community: a qualified, competent teacher in every classroom; free choice for parents among a number of private, church-related, and public schools; rigorous academic standards; the elimination of social promotion; or don't know? (Rose & Gallup, 2000). More than half of the respondents said that the most important way to improve schools is to have a qualified, competent teacher in every classroom.

One problem with surveys and interviews is the tendency of participants to answer questions in a way that they think is socially acceptable or desirable rather than telling what they truly think or feel (Best & Kahn, 2003). For example, on a survey or in an interview some individuals might say that they do not take drugs even though they do.

Standardized Tests   A **standardized test** has uniform procedures for administration and scoring. Many standardized tests allow a person's performance to be compared with the performance of other individuals (Aiken, 2003). One widely used standardized test in psychology is the Stanford-Binet intelligence test, which is described in chapter 10, "Physical and Cognitive Development in Middle and Late Childhood."

Scores on standardized tests are often stated in percentiles. Suppose you scored in the 92nd percentile on the SAT. This score would mean that 92 percent of a large group of individuals who previously took the test received scores lower than yours.

The main advantage of standardized tests is that they provide information about individual differences among people. One problem with standardized tests is that they do not always predict behavior in non-test situations. Another problem is that standardized tests are based on the belief that a person's behavior is consistent and stable, yet personality and intelligence—two primary targets of standardized testing—can vary with the situation. For example, a person may perform poorly on a standardized intelligence test in an office setting but score much higher at home, where he or she is less anxious.

This criticism is especially relevant for members of minority groups, some of whom have been inaccurately classified as mentally retarded on the basis of their scores on intelligence tests (Valencia & Suzuki, 2001). In addition, cross-cultural psychologists caution that many psychological tests developed in Western cultures might not be appropriate in other cultures (Cushner & Brislin, 1995). People in other cultures may have had experiences that cause them to interpret and respond to questions much differently from the people for whom the test was standardized.

Case Studies   A **case study** is an in-depth look at a single individual. Case studies are performed mainly by mental health professionals when, for either practical or ethical reasons, the unique aspects of an individual's life cannot be duplicated and tested in other individuals (Dattilio, 2001). A case study provides information about one person's fears, hopes, fantasies, traumatic experiences, upbringing, family relationships, health, or anything that helps the psychologist understand the person's mind and behavior.

An example of a case study is Erik Erikson's (1969) analysis of India's spiritual leader Mahatma Gandhi. Erikson studied Gandhi's life in great depth to gain insights into how his positive spiritual identity developed, especially during his youth. In putting the pieces of Ghandi's identity development together, Erikson described the contributions of culture, history, family, and various other factors that might affect the way other people develop an identity.

Other vivid case studies appear in later chapters. One involves Michael Rehbein, who had much of the entire left side of his brain removed at 7 years of age to end severe epileptic seizures. Another concerns a modern-day wild child named Genie, who lived in near isolation during her childhood.

Case histories provide dramatic, in-depth portrayals of people's lives, but remember that we must be cautious when generalizing from this information. The subject of a case study is unique, with a genetic makeup and personal history that no one else shares. In addition, case studies involve judgments of unknown reliability. Psychologists who conduct case studies rarely check to see if other psychologists agree with their observations.

Life-History Records   **Life-history records** are records of information about a lifetime chronology of events and activities. They often involve a combination of data records on education, work, family, and residence. These records may be generated with information from archival materials (public records or historical documents) or interviews, which might include obtaining a life calendar from the respondent. Life calendars record the age (year and month) at which transitions occur in a variety of activity domains and life events, thus portraying an unfolding life course. In compiling life-history records, researchers increasingly use a wide array of materials, including written and oral reports from the subject, vital records, observation, and public documents (Clausen, 1993). One of the advantages of the multiple-materials approach is that information from varied sources can be compared and discrepancies sometimes can be resolved, resulting in a more accurate life-history record.

Correlational Research   In **correlational research,** the goal is to describe the strength of the relationship between two or more events or characteristics. The more strongly the two events are correlated (or related or associated), the more effectively we can predict one event from the other (Whitley, 2002). For example, if researchers find that low-involved, permissive parenting is correlated with a child's lack of self-control, it suggests that low-involved, permissive parenting might be one source of the lack of self-control. This form of research is a key method of data analysis, which you may recall, is the third step in the scientific method.

Mahatma Gandhi was the spiritual leader of India in the middle of the twentieth century. Erik Erikson conducted an extensive case study of his life to determine what contributed to his identity development. *What are some limitations of the case study approach?*

Correlational Research

Experimental Research

case study   An in-depth look at a single individual.

life-history records   Records of information about a lifetime chronology of events and activities that often involve a combination of data records on education, work, family, and residence.

correlational research   The goal is to describe the strength of the relationship between two or more events or characteristics.

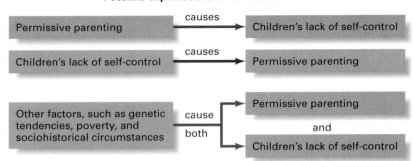

FIGURE 2.9 Possible Explanations for Correlational Data

An observed correlation between two events cannot be used to conclude that one event caused the other. Some possibilities are that the second event caused the first event or that a third, unknown event caused the correlation between the first two events.

A caution is in order, however. *Correlation does not equal causation.* The correlational finding just mentioned does not mean that permissive parenting necessarily causes low self-control in children. It could mean that, but it also could mean that a child's lack of self-control caused the parents to simply throw up their arms in despair and give up trying to control the child. It also could mean that other factors, such as heredity or poverty, caused the correlation between permissive parenting and low self-control in children. Figure 2.9 illustrates these possible interpretations of correlational data.

Throughout this book you will read about numerous correlational research studies. Keep in mind how easy it is to assume causality when two events or characteristics merely are correlated.

Experimental Research   An **experiment** is a carefully regulated procedure in which one or more factors believed to influence the behavior being studied are manipulated while all other factors are held constant. If the behavior under study changes when a factor is manipulated, we say that the manipulated factor has caused the behavior to change (Kirk, 2003). In other words, the experiment has demonstrated cause and effect. The cause is the factor that was manipulated. The effect is the behavior that changed because of the manipulation. Nonexperimental research methods (descriptive and correlational research) cannot establish cause and effect because they do not involve manipulating factors in a controlled way.

Independent and Dependent Variables   Experiments include two types of changeable factors, or variables: independent and dependent. An *independent variable* is a manipulated, influential, experimental factor. It is a potential cause. The label "independent" is used because this variable can be manipulated independently of other factors to determine its effect. Researchers have a vast array of options open to them in selecting independent variables, and one experiment may include several independent variables.

A *dependent variable* is a factor that can change in an experiment, in response to changes in the independent variable. As researchers manipulate the independent variable, they measure the dependent variable for any resulting effect.

Experimental and Control Groups   Experiments can involve one or more experimental groups and one or more control groups.

An *experimental group* is a group whose experience is manipulated. A *control group* is a comparison group that is as much like the experimental group as possible and that is treated in every way like the experimental group except for the manipulated factor (independent variable). The control group serves as a baseline against which the effects of the manipulated condition can be compared.

experiment A carefully regulated procedure in which one or more of the factors believed to influence the behavior being studied are manipulated while all other factors are held constant.

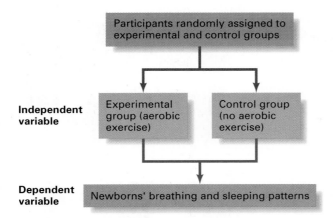

FIGURE 2.10 Principles of Experimental Research
Imagine that you decide to conduct an experimental study of the effects of aerobic exercise by pregnant women on their newborns' breathing and sleeping patterns. You would randomly assign pregnant women to experimental and control groups. The experimental group women would engage in
aerobic exercise over a specified number of sessions and weeks. The control group would not. Then,
when the infants are born, you would assess their breathing and sleeping patterns. If the breathing
and sleeping patterns of newborns whose mothers were in the experimental group are more positive
than those of the control group, you would conclude that aerobic exercise caused the positive effects.

Random assignment is an important principle for deciding whether each participant will be placed in the experimental group or in the control group (Shaughnessy,
Zechmeister, & Zechmeister, 2003). *Random assignment* means that researchers assign
participants to experimental and control groups by chance. It reduces the likelihood
that the experiment's results will be due to any preexisting differences between
groups. Figure 2.10 illustrates the nature of experimental research.

Time Span of Research

A special concern of developmentalists is the time span of a research investigation.
Studies that focus on the relation of age to some other variable are common in life-
span development. We have several options: Researchers can study different individuals of different ages and compare them; they can study the same individuals as they
age over time; or they can use some combination of these two approaches.

Cross-Sectional Approach   The **cross-sectional approach** is a research strategy
in which individuals of different ages are compared at one time. A typical cross-
sectional study might include a group of 5-year-olds, 8-year-olds, and 11-year-olds.
Another might include a group of 15-year-olds, 25-year-olds, and 45-year-olds. The
different groups can be compared with respect to a variety of dependent variables: IQ,
memory, peer relations, attachment to parents, hormonal changes, and so on. All of
this can be accomplished in a short time. In some studies data are collected in a single
day. Even in large-scale cross-sectional studies with hundreds of subjects, data collection does not usually take longer than several months to complete.

The main advantage of the cross-sectional study is that the researcher does not
have to wait for the individuals to grow up or become older. Despite its time efficiency,
the cross-sectional approach has its drawbacks. It gives no information about how individuals change or about the stability of their characteristics. The increases and decreases of development—the hills and valleys of growth and development—can
become obscured in the cross-sectional approach. For example, in a cross-sectional approach to perceptions of life satisfaction, average increases and decreases might be revealed. But the study would not show how the life satisfaction of individual adults

cross-sectional approach A research strategy in which individuals of different ages are
compared at one time.

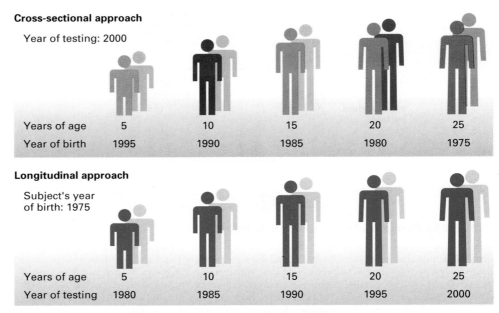

FIGURE 2.11 A Comparison of Cross-Sectional and Longitudinal Approaches

waxed and waned over the years. It also would not tell us whether adults who had positive or negative perceptions of life satisfaction as young adults maintained their relative degree of life satisfaction as middle-aged or older adults.

Longitudinal Approach The **longitudinal approach** is a research strategy in which the same individuals are studied over a period of time, usually several years or more. For example, if a study of life satisfaction were conducted longitudinally, the same adults might be assessed periodically over a 70-year time span—at the ages of 20, 35, 45, 65, and 90, for example. Figure 2.11 compares the cross-sectional and longitudinal approaches.

Although longitudinal studies provide a wealth of information about such important issues as stability and change in development and the importance of early experience for later development, they are not without their problems (Raudenbush, 2001). They are expensive and time-consuming. The longer the study lasts, the more participants drop out—they move, get sick, lose interest, and so forth. Participants can bias the outcome of a study, because those who remain may be dissimilar to those who drop out. Those individuals who remain in a longitudinal study over a number of years may be more compulsive and conformity-oriented, for example, or they might have more stable lives.

Sequential Approach Sometimes developmentalists also combine the cross-sectional and longitudinal approaches to learn about life-span development (Schaie, 1993). The **sequential approach** is the combined cross-sectional, longitudinal design. In most instances, this approach starts with a cross-sectional study that includes individuals of different ages. A number of months after the initial assessment, the same individuals are tested again—this is the longitudinal aspect of the design. At this later time, a new group of participants is assessed at each age level. The new groups at each level are added at the later time to control for changes that might have taken place in the original group—some might have dropped out of the study, or retesting might have improved their performance, for example. The sequential approach is complex, expensive, and time-consuming, but it does provide information that is impossible to obtain from cross-sectional or longitudinal approaches alone. The

longitudinal approach A research strategy in which the same individuals are studied over a period of time, usually several years or more.

sequential approach A combined cross-sectional, longitudinal design.

FIGURE 2.12 Cohort Effects

Cohort effects are due to a person's time of birth or generation but not actually to age. Think for a moment about growing up in (a) the Roaring Twenties, (b) the Great Depression, (c) the 1940s and World War II, (d) the 1950s, (e) the late 1960s, and (f) today. *How might your development be different depending on which of these time frames has dominated your life? your parents' lives? your grandparents' lives?*

sequential approach has been especially helpful in examining cohort effects in life-span development, which we will discuss next.

Cohort Effects   A *cohort* is a group of people who are born at a similar point in history and share similar experiences as a result, such as living through the Great Depression of the 1930s or growing up in the same city around the same time. For example, cohorts can differ in years of education, child-rearing practices, health, attitudes toward sex, religious values, and economic status (see figure 2.12). In life-span development research, **cohort effects** are due to a person's time of birth or

cohort effects Effects due to a person's time of birth or generation but not to actual age.

Research Method	Theory
Observation	• All theories emphasize some form of observation. • Behavioral and social cognitive theories place the strongest emphasis on laboratory observation. • Ethological theory places the strongest emphasis on naturalistic observation.
Survey/interview	• Psychoanalytic and cognitive studies (Piaget, Vygotsky) often use interviews. • Behavioral, social cognitive, and ethological theories are the least likely to use surveys or interviews.
Standardized test	• None of the theories discussed emphasize the use of this method.
Case study	• Psychoanalytic theories (Freud, Erikson) are the most likely to use this method.
Life-history record	• This method is most likely to be advocated by ecological theory and psychoanalytic theories.
Correlational research	• All of the theories use this research method, although psychoanalytic theories are the least likely to use it.
Experimental research	• The behavioral and social cognitive theories and the information-processing theories are the most likely to use the experimental method. • Psychoanalytic theories are the least likely to use it.
Cross-sectional/longitudinal/sequential methods	• No theory described uses these methods more than any other. • The sequential method is the least likely to be used by any theory.

FIGURE 2.13 Connections of Research Methods to Theories

generation but not to actual age. Cohort effects are important because they can powerfully affect the dependent measures in a study ostensibly concerned with age. Researchers have shown it is especially important to be aware of cohort effects in the assessment of adult intelligence (Schaie, 1996). Individuals born at different points in time—such as 1920, 1940, and 1960—have had varying opportunities for education, while individuals born in earlier years had less access ◀️ p. 11.

Cross-sectional studies can show how different cohorts respond but they can confuse age changes and cohort effects. Longitudinal studies are effective in studying age changes but only within one cohort. With sequential studies, both age changes in one cohort can be examined and compared with age changes in another cohort.

A point that is important to make is that theories often are linked with a particular research method or methods. Thus, method(s) researchers use are associated with their particular theoretical approach. Figure 2.13 illustrates the connections between research methods and theories.

Review and Reflect

2 **Explain how research on life-span development is conducted**

REVIEW

- How is research on life-span development conducted?
- What are some ways that researchers study the time span of people's lives?

REFLECT

- You have learned that correlation does not equal causation. Develop an example of two variables (two sets of observations) that are correlated but that you believe almost certainly have no causal relationship.

3 FACING UP TO RESEARCH CHALLENGES

Conducting Ethical Research   **Minimizing Bias**

The scientific foundation of research in life-span development helps to minimize the effect of individual researcher's biases and to maximize the objectivity of the results. Still, some subtle challenges remain to be fully resolved. One is to ensure that research is conducted in an ethical way; another is to recognize, and try to overcome, researchers' deeply buried personal biases.

Conducting Ethical Research

Ethics is an important part of your understanding of the science of life-span development. Even if you have no formal exposure to life-span development beyond this course, you will find that scientific research in this field and related disciplines affects our everyday life. For one thing, decision makers in business, government, schools, and many other institutions use the results of research in life-span development to help people lead happier, healthier, more productive lives.

The explosion in technology has forced society to grapple with looming ethics questions that were unimaginable only a few decades ago. The same line of research that enables previously sterile couples to have children might also let prospective parents "call up and order" the characteristics they prefer in their children and someday tip the balance of males and females in the world. Should embryos left over from procedures for increasing fertility be saved or discarded? The line of research that enables previously sterile couples to have children has also led to the spectacle of frozen embryos being passed about in the courts as a part of divorce settlements.

Ethics in research may affect you more personally if you serve at some point, as is quite likely, as a participant in a study. In that event, you need to know about your rights as a participant and about the responsibilities researchers have in assuring that these rights are safeguarded. The failure to consider participants' well-being can have life-altering consequences for them. For example, one investigation of young dating couples asked them to complete a questionnaire that coincidentally stimulated some of the participants to think about potentially troublesome issues (Rubin & Mitchell, 1976). One year later, when the researchers followed up with the original sample, 9 of 10 participants said they had discussed their answers with their dating partner. In most instances, the discussions helped to strengthen the relationships. In some cases, though, the participants used the questionnaire as a springboard to discuss previously

mhhe●com/
santrockld9

Psychologists' Ethical Principles

hidden problems or concerns. One participant said, "The study definitely played a role in ending my relationship with Larry." In this case, the couple had different views about how long they expected to be together. She was thinking of a short-term dating relationship only, while he was thinking in terms of a lifetime. Their answers to the questions brought the disparity in their views to the surface and led to the end of their relationship. Researchers have a responsibility to anticipate the personal problems their study might cause and to at least inform the participants of the possible fallout.

If you ever become a researcher in life-span development yourself, you will need an even deeper understanding of ethics. You may never become a researcher in the field of psychology, but you may carry out one or more experimental projects in psychology courses. Even smart, conscientious students frequently do not consider the rights of the participants who serve in their experiments. A student might think, "I volunteer in a home for the mentally retarded several hours per week. I can use the residents of the home in my study to see if a particular treatment helps improve their memory for everyday tasks." But without proper permissions the most well-meaning, kind, and considerate studies still violate the rights of the participants.

Ethics Guidelines   Safeguarding the rights of research participants is a challenge because the potential harm is not always obvious (Gall, Borg, & Gall, 2003). At first glance, you might not imagine that a questionnaire on dating relationships among college students would have any substantial impact or that an experiment involving treatment of memory loss in older adults would be anything but beneficial. But researchers increasingly recognize that lasting harm might come to the participants in a study of life-span development.

Today colleges and universities have review boards that evaluate the ethical nature of research conducted at their institutions. Proposed research plans must pass the scrutiny of a research ethics committee before the research can be initiated.

In addition, the American Psychological Association (APA) has developed ethics guidelines for its members. The code of ethics instructs psychologists to protect their participants from mental and physical harm. The participants' best interests need to be kept foremost in the researcher's mind (Rosnow, 1995). APA's guidelines address four important issues:

- *Informed Consent* All participants must know what their participation will involve and what risks might develop. For example, participants in a study on dating should be told beforehand that a questionnaire might stimulate thoughts about issues in their relationship that they have not considered. Participants also should be informed that in some instances a discussion of the issues might improve their relationship, but in others might worsen the relationship and even end it. Even after informed consent is given, participants must retain the right to withdraw from the study at any time and for any reason.
- *Confidentiality* Researchers are responsible for keeping all of the data they gather on individuals completely confidential and when possible, completely anonymous.
- *Debriefing* After the study has been completed, participants should be informed of its purpose and the methods that were used. In most cases, the experimenter also can inform participants in a general manner beforehand about the purpose of the research without leading participants to behave in a way they think that the experimenter is expecting. When preliminary information about the study is likely to affect the results, participants can at least be debriefed after the study has been completed.
- *Deception* This is an ethical issue that researchers debate extensively (Hoyle & Judd, 2002). In some circumstances, telling the participant beforehand what the research study is about substantially alters the participant's behavior and invalidates the researcher's data. In all cases of deception, however, the psychologist must ensure that the deception will not harm the participant and that the partic-

Look at these two photographs, one of all White males, the other of a diverse group of females and males from different ethnic groups, including some White individuals. Consider a topic in psychology, such as parenting, love, or cultural values. *If you were conducting research on this topic, might the results of the study be different depending on whether the participants in your study were the individuals in the photograph on the left or those on the right?*

ipant will be told the complete nature of the study (debriefed) as soon as possible after the study is completed.

Minimizing Bias

Studies of life-span development are most useful when they are conducted without bias or prejudice toward any particular group of people. Of special concern is bias based on gender and bias based on culture or ethnicity ◀ⅢⅢ p. 14.

Gender Bias   For decades, society has had a strong gender bias, a preconceived notion about the abilities of women and men that prevented individuals from pursuing their own interests and achieving their potential. Gender bias also has had a less obvious effect within the field of life-span development (Etaugh & Bridges, 2001; Palvdi, 2002; Shields & Eyssell, 2001). For example, it is not unusual for conclusions to be drawn about females' attitudes and behaviors from research conducted with males as the only participants (Maracek & others, 2003).

Florence Denmark and her colleagues (1988) argue as well that when gender differences are found, they sometimes are unduly magnified. For example, a researcher might report in a study that 74 percent of the men had high achievement expectations versus only 67 percent of the women and go on to talk about the differences in some detail. In reality, this might be a rather small difference. It also might disappear if the study were repeated or the study might have methodological problems that don't allow such strong interpretations.

Researchers giving females equal rights in research have raised some new questions (Tetreault, 1997):

• How might gender bias influence the choice of hypotheses, participants, and research design? For example, the most widely known theory of moral development was proposed by a male (Lawrence Kohlberg) in a male-dominant society (the United States), and males were the main participants in research used to support the theory for many years.

Careers in Life-Span Development

Pam Reid, Educational and Developmental Psychologist

As a child, Pam Reid played with chemistry sets, and at the university she was majoring in chemistry, planning to become a medical doctor. Because some of her friends signed up for a psychology course as an elective, she decided to join them. She was so intrigued by learning more about how people think, behave, and develop that she changed her major to psychology. She says, "I fell in love with psychology." Reid went on to obtain her Ph.D. in educational psychology ◀▥ p. 31.

Today, Pamela Trotman Reid is a professor of education and psychology at the University of Michigan. She is also a research scientist for the UM Institute for Research on Women and Gender. Her main interest is how children and adolescents develop social skills, and especially how gender, socioeconomic status, and ethnicity are involved in development (Reid & Zalk, 2001). Because many psychological findings have been based on research with middle-socioeconomic-status non-Latino White populations, She believes it is important to study people from different ethnic groups. She stresses that by understanding the expectations, attitudes, and behavior of diverse groups, we enrich the theory and practice of psychology. Currently Dr. Reid is working with her graduate students on a project involving middle school girls. She is interested in why girls, more often than boys, stop taking classes in mathematics.

Pam Reid (*back row, center*) with graduate students she is mentoring at the University of Michigan.

- How might research on topics of primary interest to females, such as relationships, feelings, and empathy, challenge existing theory? For example, in the study of moral development, the highest level has often been portrayed as based on a principle of "justice for the individual" (Kohlberg, 1976). However, more recent theorizing notes individuality and autonomy tend to be male concerns, and suggest that a principle based on relationships and connections with others be added to our thinking about high-level moral development (Gilligan, 1982, 1998).
- How has research that has exaggerated gender differences between females and males influenced the way the people think about females? For example, some researchers believe that gender differences in mathematics have often been exaggerated and have been fueled by societal bias (Hyde & Mezulis, 2001; Hyde & Plant, 1995). Such exaggeration of differences can lead to negative expectations for females' math performance.

Cultural and Ethnic Bias The realization that research on life-span development needs to include more people from diverse ethnic groups has also been building (Graham, 1992). Historically, people from ethnic minority groups (African American, Latino, Asian American, and Native American) have been discounted from most research in the United States and simply thought of as variations from the norm or average. Because their scores don't always fit the norm, minority individuals have been viewed as confounds or "noise" in data. Consequently, researchers have deliberately excluded them from the samples they have selected. Given the fact that individuals from diverse ethnic groups were excluded from research on life-span development for so long, we might reasonably conclude that people's real lives are perhaps more varied than research data have indicated in the past (Ponterotto & others, 2001; Stevenson, 1995).

Researchers also have tended to overgeneralize about ethnic groups (Jenkins & others, 2003; Trimble, 1989). **Ethnic gloss** is using an ethnic label such as African American or Latino in a superficial way that portrays an ethnic group as being more homogeneous than it really is. For example, a researcher might describe a research sample like this: "The participants were 20 Latinos and 20 Anglo-Americans." A more complete description of the Latino group might be something like this: "The 20 Latino participants were Mexican Americans from low-income neighborhoods in the southwestern area of Los Angeles. Twelve were from homes in which Spanish is the dominant language spoken, 8 from homes in which English is the main language spoken. Ten were born in the United States, 10 in Mexico. Ten described themselves as Mexican American, 5 as Mexican, 3 as American, 2 as Chicano, and 1 as Latino." Ethnic gloss can cause researchers to obtain samples of ethnic groups that are not representative of the group's diversity, which can lead to overgeneralization and stereotyping.

Pam Reid is a leading researcher who studies gender and ethnic bias in development. To read about Pam's interests, see the Careers in Life-Span Development insert on page 70.

Review and Reflect

3 **Discuss research challenges in life-span development**

REVIEW

- What are researchers' ethical responsibilities to the people they study?
- How can gender, cultural, and ethnic bias affect the outcome of a research study?

REFLECT

- Imagine that you are conducting a research study on the sexual attitudes and behaviors of adolescents? What ethical safeguards should you use in conducting the study?

ethnic gloss Using an ethnic label such as African American or Latino in a superficial way that portrays an ethnic group as being more homogeneous than it really is.

Reach Your Learning Goals

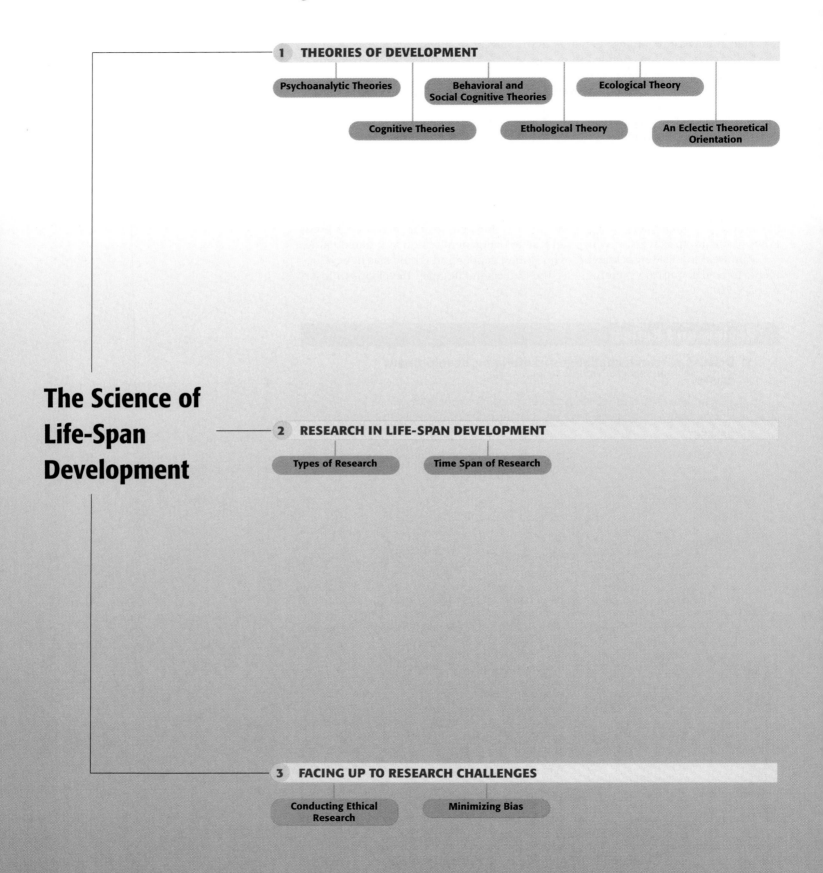

The Science of Life-Span Development

1 THEORIES OF DEVELOPMENT

- Psychoanalytic Theories
- Behavioral and Social Cognitive Theories
- Cognitive Theories
- Ethological Theory
- Ecological Theory
- An Eclectic Theoretical Orientation

2 RESEARCH IN LIFE-SPAN DEVELOPMENT

- Types of Research
- Time Span of Research

3 FACING UP TO RESEARCH CHALLENGES

- Conducting Ethical Research
- Minimizing Bias

Summary

1 Describe theories of life-span development

- The scientific method involves four main steps: (1) conceptualize a problem, (2) collect data, (3) analyze data, and (4) draw conclusions. Theory is often involved in conceptualizing a problem. A theory is an interrelated, coherent set of ideas that helps to explain and to make predictions. Hypotheses are specific assumptions and predictions, often derived from theory, that can be tested to determine their accuracy.
- Psychoanalytic theory describes development as primarily unconscious and as heavily colored by emotion. Psychoanalytic theorists believe that behavior is merely a surface characteristic and that early experiences with parents shape development. Freud said that personality is made up of three structures—id, ego, and superego. The conflicting demands of these structures produce anxiety. Freud also believed that individuals go through five psychosexual stages—oral, anal, phallic, latency, and genital. Erikson's theory emphasizes these eight psychosocial stages of development: trust vs. mistrust, autonomy vs. shame and doubt, initiative vs. guilt, industry vs. inferiority, identity vs. identity confusion, intimacy vs. isolation, generativity vs. stagnation, and integrity vs. despair. Contributions of psychoanaytic theories include an emphasis on a developmental framework. One criticism is that they often lack scientific support.
- Cognitive theories emphasize conscious thoughts. Piaget proposed a cognitive developmental theory in which children use the processes of organization and adaptation (assimilation and accommodation) to understand their world. In Piaget's theory, children go through four cognitive stages: sensorimotor, preoperational, concrete operational, and formal operational. Vygotsky's sociocultural cognitive theory emphasizes how culture and social interaction guide cognitive development. The information-processing theory emphasizes that individuals manipulate information, monitor it, and strategize about it. Contributions of cognitive theories include an emphasis on the active construction of understanding. One criticism is that they give too little attention to individual variations.
- Three versions of the behavioral approach are Pavlov's classical conditioning, Skinner's operant conditioning, and Bandura's social cognitive theory. In Pavlov's classical conditioning, a neutral stimulus acquires the ability to produce a response originally produced by another stimulus. In Skinner's operant conditioning, the consequences of a behavior produce changes in the probability of the behavior's occurrence. In Bandura's social cognitive theory, observational learning is a key aspect of life-span development. Bandura emphasizes reciprocal interactions among the person (cognition), behavior, and environment. Contributions of the behavioral and social cognitive theories include an emphasis on scientific research. One criticism is that they give inadequate attention to developmental changes.
- Ethology stresses that behavior is strongly influenced by biology, is tied to evolution, and is characterized by critical or sensitive periods. Contributions of ethological theory include a focus on the biological and evolutionary basis of development. Criticisms include a belief that the critical and sensitive period concepts might be too rigid.
- Ecological theory is Bronfenbrenner's environmental systems view of development. It consists of five environmental systems: microsystem, mesosystem, exosystem, macrosystem, and chronosystem. Contributions of the theory include a systematic examination of macro and micro dimensions of environmental systems. One criticism is that it gives inadequate attention to biological and cognitive factors.
- An eclectic theoretical orientation does not follow any one theoretical approach, but rather selects from each theory whatever is considered the best in it.

2 Explain how research on life-span development is conducted

- Three main types of research are (1) descriptive, (2) correlational, and (3) experimental. Five types of descriptive research are observation (in a laboratory or a naturalistic setting), survey (questionnaire) or interview, standardized test, case study, and life-history record. In correlational research, the goal is to describe the strength of the relationship between two or more events or characteristics. Experimental research involves conducting an experiment, which can determine cause and effect. An independent variable is the manipulated, influential, experimental factor. A dependent variable is a factor that can change in an experiment, in response to changes in the independent variable. Experiments can involve one or more experimental groups and control groups. In random assignment, researchers assign participants to experimental and control groups by chance.
- When researchers decide about the time span of their research, they can conduct cross-sectional, longitudinal, or sequential studies. Life-span researchers are especially concerned about cohort effects.

3 Discuss research challenges in life-span development

- Researchers' ethical responsibilities include seeking participants' informed consent, ensuring their confidentiality, debriefing them about the purpose and potential personal consequences of participating, and avoiding unnecessary deception of participants.
- Researchers need to guard against gender, cultural, and ethnic bias in research. Every effort should be made to make research equitable for both females and males. More individuals from ethnic minority backgrounds need to be included as participants in life-span research. A special concern is ethnic gloss.

Key Terms

Key People

Taking It to the Net

1. Like many students of life-span psychology, Ymelda has a hard time with Freud's theory, insisting that it is "all about sex." Is that the extent of Freud's theoretical perspective?

2. Juan's life-span psychology teacher asked the class to read about Albert Bandura's famous "Bobo" doll experiment and determine if there were any gender differences in the responses of boys and girls who (a) saw aggressive behavior rewarded and (b) who saw aggressive behavior punished. What should Juan's conclusions be?

3. A requirement for Wanda's methods course is to design and carry out an original research project. Among the many decisions she must make is what type of data she will collect. She decides to research adapting to college life. Her instructor asks if she will use an interview or a survey. What are the distinctions between surveys and interviews, and what are the benefits and difficulties of each?

Connect to www.mhhe.com/santrockld9 to research the answers and complete these exercises.

E-Learning Tools

To help you master the material in this chapter, you'll find a number of valuable study tools on the Student CD-ROM that accompanies this book. In addition, visit the Online Learning Center for *Life-Span Development,* ninth edition, where you'll find these valuable resources for chapter 2, "The Science of Life-Span Development."

- Complete the self-assessment, *Models and Mentors in My Life,* to help you evaluate the role models and mentors who have played an important part in your life and think about the type of role model you want to be.

- View video clips of key developmental psychology experts discussing their views on research methods, developmental theories, and ethics in research.

- Build your decision-making skills by trying your hand at the parenting and education "Scenarios."

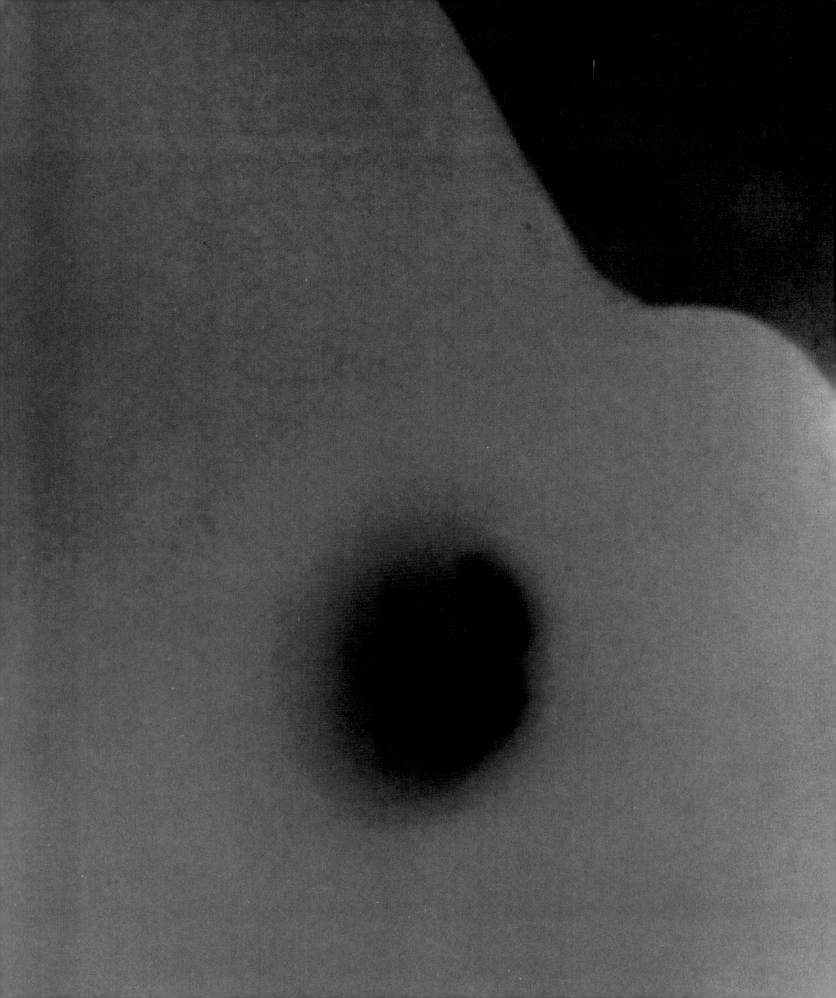

Beginnings

2

What endless questions vex the thought, of whence and whither, when and how.
—SIR RICHARD BURTON
English Explorer, 19th Century

The rhythm and meaning of life involve beginnings. Questions are raised about how, from so simple a beginning, endless forms develop and grow and mature. What was this organism, what will this organism be? Section 2 contains two chapters: "Biological Beginnings" (chapter 3) and "Prenatal Development and Birth" (chapter 4). In these chapters we address questions about our beginnings.

There are one hundred and ninety-three living species of monkeys and apes. One hundred and ninety-two of them are covered with hair. The exception is the naked ape, self-named Homo sapiens.

—DESMOND MORRIS
British Zoologist, 20th Century

Biological Beginnings

Learning Goals

1 Discuss the evolutionary perspective

2 Describe the genetic foundations of development

3 Identify important reproduction challenges and choices

4 Explain heredity-environment interaction

Images of Life-Span Development
The Jim and Jim Twins

Jim Springer and Jim Lewis are identical twins. They were separated at 4 weeks of age and did not see each other again until they were 39 years old. Both worked as part-time deputy sheriffs, vacationed in Florida, drove Chevrolets, had dogs named Toy, and married and divorced women named Betty. One twin named his son James Allan, and the other named his son James Alan. Both liked math but not spelling, enjoyed carpentry and mechanical drawing, chewed their fingernails down to the nubs, had almost identical drinking and smoking habits, had hemorrhoids, put on 10 pounds at about the same point in development, first suffered headaches at the age of 18, and had similar sleep patterns.

But Jim and Jim have some differences. One wears his hair over his forehead, the other slicks it back and has sideburns. One expresses himself best orally; the other is more proficient in writing. But, for the most part, their profiles are remarkably similar.

Jim Lewis (*left*) and Jim Springer (*right*).

Another pair, Daphne and Barbara, are called the "giggle sisters" because, after being reunited, they were always making each other laugh. A thorough search of their adoptive families' histories revealed no gigglers. And the identical sisters handled stress by ignoring it, avoided conflict and controversy whenever possible, and showed no interest in politics.

Two other identical twin sisters were separated at 6 weeks and reunited in their fifties. Both had nightmares, which they describe in hauntingly similar ways: both dreamed of doorknobs and fishhooks in their mouths as they smothered to death! The nightmares began during early adolescence and stopped within the past 10 to 12 years. Both women were bed wetters until about 12 or 13 years of age, and their educational and marital histories are remarkably similar.

These sets of twins are part of the Minnesota Study of Twins Reared Apart, directed by Thomas Bouchard and his colleagues. The study brings identical twins (identical genetically because they come from the same fertilized egg) and fraternal twins (dissimilar genetically because they come from different fertilized eggs) from all over the world to Minneapolis to investigate their lives. There the twins complete a number of personality tests and provide detailed medical histories, including information about diet and smoking, exercise habits, chest X-rays, heart stress tests, and EEGs (brain-wave tests). The twins are interviewed and asked more than 15,000 questions about their family and childhood environment, personal interests, vocational orientation, values, and aesthetic judgments. They also are given ability and intelligence tests (Bouchard & others, 1990).

Critics of the Minnesota identical twins study point out that some of the separated twins were together for several months prior to their adoption, that some of the twins had been reunited prior to their testing (in some cases, a number of years earlier), that adoption agencies often place twins in similar homes, and that even strangers who spend several hours together and start comparing their lives are likely to come up with some coincidental similarities (Adler, 1991). Still, the Minnesota study of identical twins indicates the increased interest scientists have recently shown in the genetic basis of human development and points to the need for further research on genetic and environmental factors (Bouchard, 1995).

The examples of Jim and Jim, the giggle sisters, and the identical twins who had the same nightmares stimulate us to think about our genetic heritage and the biological foundations of our existence. Organisms are not like billiard balls, moved by simple, external forces to predictable positions on life's pool table. Environmental experiences and biological foundations work together to make us who we are. Our coverage of life's biological beginnings in this chapter focuses on evolution, genetic foundations, reproduction challenges and choices, and the interaction of heredity and environment.

1 THE EVOLUTIONARY PERSPECTIVE

Natural Selection and Adaptive Behavior

Evolutionary Psychology

In evolutionary time, humans are relative newcomers to Earth, yet we have established ourselves as the most successful and dominant species. If we consider evolutionary time as a calendar year, humans arrived here in the last moments of December (Sagan, 1977). As our earliest ancestors left the forest to feed on the savannahs, and finally to form hunting societies on the open plains, their minds and behaviors changed. How did this evolution come about?

Natural Selection and Adaptive Behavior

Natural selection is the evolutionary process that favors individuals of a species that are best adapted to survive and reproduce. To understand natural selection, let's return to the middle of the nineteenth century, when the British naturalist Charles Darwin was traveling around the world, observing many different species of animals in their natural surroundings. Darwin, who published his observations and thoughts in *On the Origin of Species* (1859), noted that most organisms reproduce at rates that would cause enormous increases in the population of most species and yet populations remain nearly constant. He reasoned that an intense, constant struggle for food, water, and resources must occur among the many young born each generation, because many of the young do not survive. Those that do survive pass on their genes to the next generation. Darwin believed that those who do survive to reproduce are probably superior in a number of ways to those who do not. In other words, the survivors are better adapted to their world than are the nonsurvivors (Raven & others, 2002). Over the course of many generations, organisms with the characteristics needed for survival would comprise a larger percentage of the population. Over many, many generations, this could produce a gradual modification of the whole population. If environmental conditions change, however, other characteristics might become favored by natural selection, moving the process in a different direction.

To understand the role of evolution in behavior, we need to understand the concept of adaptive behavior. In evolutionary conceptions of psychology, *adaptive behavior* is behavior that promotes an organism's survival in the natural habitat. Adaptive behavior involves the organism's modification of its behavior to include its likelihood of survival (Cosmides & others, 2003). All organisms must adapt to particular places, climates, food sources, and ways of life. Natural selection designs an adaptation to perform a certain function. An example of adaptation is an eagle's claws, designed by natural selection to facilitate predation. In the human realm, attachment is a system designed by natural selection to ensure an infant's closeness to the caregiver for feeding and protection from danger.

Evolutionary Psychology

Although Darwin introduced the theory of evolution by natural selection in 1859, his ideas about evolution only recently have emerged as a popular framework for explaining behavior. Psychology's newest approach, **evolutionary psychology,**

mhhe.com/ santrockld9

Evolution
Evolution and Behavior
Evolutionary Psychology
Handbook of Evolutionary Psychology
Evolutionary Psychology Resources

evolutionary psychology A contemporary approach that emphasizes the importance of adaptation, reproduction, and "survival of the fittest" in explaining behavior.

emphasizes the importance of adaptation, reproduction, and "survival of the fittest" in explaining behavior. Evolution favors organisms that are best adapted to survive and reproduce in a particular environment. The evolutionary psychology approach focuses on conditions that allow individuals to survive or to fail. In this view, the evolutionary process of natural selection favors behaviors that increase organisms' reproductive success and their ability to pass their genes to the next generation (Bjorklund & Bering, 2001; Caporael, 2001; Cosmides & others, 2003; Durrant & Ellis, 2003).

David Buss' (1995, 1999, 2000; Larsen & Buss, 2002) ideas on evolutionary psychology have ushered in a whole new wave of interest in how evolution can explain human behavior. He believes that just as evolution shapes our physical features, such as body shape and height, it also pervasively influences how we make decisions, how aggressive we are, our fears, and our mating patterns.

Evolution and Life-Span Development

According to life-span developmentalist Paul Baltes (1996; Baltes, Staudinger, & Lindenberger, 1999), the benefits of evolutionary selection decrease with age. Why do the later years of life benefit less from the optimizing power of evolutionary selection pressure than the younger years? The main reason is reproductive fitness, which primarily extends from conception through the earlier part of adulthood. As a consequence, says Baltes, selection operates mainly during the first half of life. Also, given the much shorter life span in early human evolution, selection pressure could not function as often in the later years of life. Most individuals died before possible negative genetic attributes were activated or their negative consequences appeared.

A concrete example of a decrease in the benefits of evolutionary selection in older adults involves Alzheimer's disease, a progressive, irreversible brain disorder characterized by gradual deterioration. This disease typically does not appear until age 70 or older. Possibly diseases like Alzheimer's emerge in later life because evolutionary pressures based on reproductive fitness were not able to select against it.

While Baltes believes that the benefits of evolutionary selection decrease following the decline in reproductive capacity, he argues that the need for culture increases (see figure 3.1). Some of the cultural factors needed by older adults are cognitive skills, motivation, socialization, literacy, and medical technology. In other words, as older adults weaken biologically, they need culture-based resources (material, social, economic, psychological). For example, for cognitive skills to continue into old age at levels of performance comparable to those experienced earlier in adulthood, cognitive support and training are needed (Hoyer, Rybash, & Roodin, 2003). And as we indicated in chapter 1, Baltes also stresses that there is a life-span shift in the allocation of resources away from growth and toward maintenance and the regulation of loss.

Evaluating Evolutionary Psychology

Albert Bandura (1998), whose social cognitive theory was described in chapter 2, addressed the "biologizing" of psychology and evolution's role in social cognitive theory ◀|||| p. 52. Bandura acknowledges the important influence of evolution on human adaptation and change. However, he rejects what he calls "one-sided evolutionism," which sees social behavior as the product of evolved biology, in favor of a bidirectional view. According to this view, evolutionary pressures created changes in biological structures for the use of tools, which enabled organisms to manipulate, alter, and construct new environmental conditions. Environmental innovations of increasing complexity produced, in turn, new selection pressures for the evolution of specialized biological systems for consciousness, thought, and language.

Human evolution gave us bodily structures and biological potentialities—in other words, not behavioral dictates. Having evolved, advanced biological capacities can be used to produce diverse cultures: aggressive, pacific, egalitarian, or autocratic. As American scientist

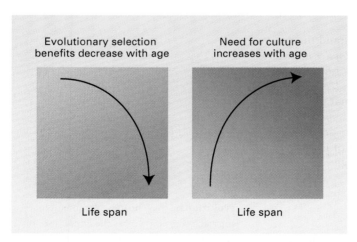

FIGURE 3.1 Baltes' View of Evolution and Culture Across the Life Span

Steven Jay Gould (1981) concluded, in most domains of human functioning, biology allows a broad range of cultural possibilities. The Russian American Theodore Dobzhansky (1977) also reminds us that the human species has been selected for the ability to learn and for plasticity—for the capacity to adapt to diverse contexts, not for biologically fixed behavior. Bandura (1998) points out that the pace of social change shows that biology does permit a range of possibilities.

Review and Reflect

1 Discuss the evolutionary perspective

REVIEW

- How can natural selection and the concept of adaptive behavior be defined?
- What is evolutionary psychology and how has it been criticized?

REFLECT

- Are you more inclined to support the views of evolutionary psychologists or their critics? Why?

2 GENETIC FOUNDATIONS

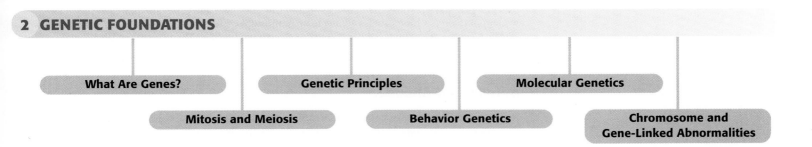

Every species must have a mechanism for transmitting characteristics from one generation to the next. This mechanism is explained by the principles of genetics (Cummings, 2003; Livesley, Jang, & Vernon, 2003). Each of us carries a genetic code that we inherited from our parents. This code is located within every cell in our bodies. Our genetic codes are alike in one important way—they all contain the human genetic code. Because of the human genetic code, a fertilized human egg cannot grow into an egret, eagle, or elephant.

What Are Genes?

Each of us began life as a single cell weighing about one twenty-millionth of an ounce! This tiny piece of matter housed our entire genetic code—information about who we would become. These instructions orchestrated growth from that single cell to a person made of trillions of cells, each containing a perfect replica of the original genetic code (Wilson, 2003).

The nucleus of each human cell contains 46 **chromosomes,** which are threadlike structures that come in 23 pairs, one member of each pair coming from each parent. Chromosomes are made up of deoxyribonucleic acid, or **DNA,** a complex molecule that contains genetic information. DNA's "double helix" shape looks like a spiral staircase. **Genes,** the units of hereditary information, are short segments of DNA. Genes carry information that enables cells to reproduce and manufacture the proteins needed to sustain life. Chromosomes, DNA, and genes can be mysterious. To gain a better understanding of this mystery, see figure 3.2 on page 84.

chromosomes Threadlike structures that come in 23 pairs, one member of each pair coming from each parent. Chromosomes are made up of the genetic substance DNA.

DNA A complex molecule that contains genetic information.

genes Units of hereditary information composed of DNA. Genes carry information that enables cells to reproduce themselves and manufacture the proteins that maintain life.

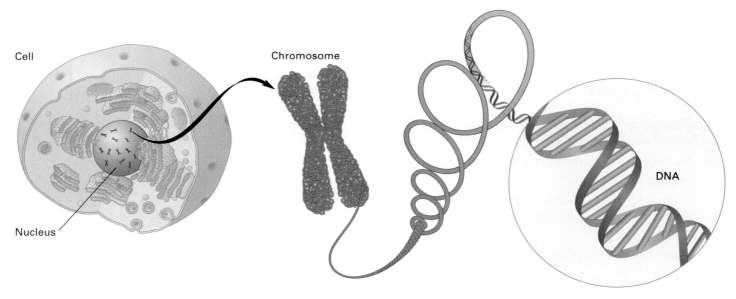

Cell

Nucleus

Chromosome

DNA

FIGURE 3.2 Cells, Chromosomes, Genes, and DNA

(*Left*) The body contains trillions of cells, which are the basic structural units of life. Each cell contains a central structure, the nucleus. (*Middle*) Chromosomes and genes are located in the nucleus of the cell. Chromosomes are made up of threadlike structures composed of DNA molecules. (*Right*) A gene, a segment of DNA that contains the hereditary code. The structure of DNA is a spiraled double chain.

Mitosis and Meiosis

Mitosis and meiosis are processes of cellular reproduction by which DNA is distributed to new cells. **Mitosis** is the process of cell division by which each chromosome in the cell's nucleus duplicates itself. The resulting 46 chromosomes move to the opposite sides of the cell, then the cell separates, and two new cells are formed with each now containing 46 chromosomes. Thus the process of mitosis allows DNA to duplicate itself.

A specialized division of chromosomes occurs during the formation of reproductive cells. **Meiosis** is the process by which cells in the reproductive organs divide into gametes (sperm in males, eggs in females), which have half the genetic material of the parent cell. Mitosis and meiosis differ in these ways:

- In mitosis, the focus is on cell growth and repair, whereas meiosis involves sexual reproduction.
- In mitosis, the number of chromosomes present in the new cells remains the same as in the original cell (the chromosomes copy themselves), whereas in meiosis, the number of chromosomes is cut in half.
- In mitosis, two daughter cells are formed from the dividing cell; in meiosis four daughter cells are produced as a result of two meiotic divisions.

Each human gamete has 23 unpaired chromosomes. The process of human **reproduction** begins when a female gamete, or ovum (egg), is fertilized by a male gamete, or sperm (see figure 3.3). A **zygote** is the single cell formed through fertilization. In the zygote, two sets of unpaired chromosomes combine to form one set of paired chromosomes—one member of each pair from the mother and the other member from the father. In this manner, each parent contributes 50 percent of the offspring's genes.

Genetic Principles

Genetic determination is a complex affair, and much is still unknown about the way genes work (Lewis, 2003). The known genetic principles include dominant-recessive

mitosis The process of cell division by which each chromosome in a cell's nucleus duplicates itself.

meiosis The process by which cells in the reproductive organs divide into gametes (sperm in males, eggs in females), which have half of the genetic material of the parent cell.

reproduction The process that, in humans, begins when a female gamete (ovum) is fertilized by a male gamete (sperm).

zygote A single cell formed through fertilization.

genes, sex-linked genes, genetic imprinting, polygenic inheritance, reaction range, and canalization.

Dominant-Recessive Genes Principle   According to the *dominant-recessive genes principle,* some genes are dominant and will always override so-called recessive genes. In other words, if one gene of a pair is dominant and one is recessive, the dominant gene will be expressed in the characteristic it governs. A recessive gene exerts its influence only if the two genes of a pair are both recessive. If you inherit a recessive gene for a trait from each of your parents, you will show the trait. If you inherit a recessive gene from only one parent, you may never know you carry the gene.

Brown hair and dimples rule over blond hair and freckles in the world of dominant-recessive genes. Can two brown-haired parents have a blond-haired child? Yes, they can. Suppose that in each parent the gene pair that governs hair color includes a dominant gene for brown hair and a recessive gene for blond hair. Since dominant genes override recessive genes, the parents have brown hair, but both are carriers of blondness and can pass on their recessive genes for blond hair. With no dominant gene to override them, if a child receives a gene for blond hair from each parent, the pair of recessive genes will make the child's hair blond. Figure 3.4 illustrates the dominant-recessive genes principle.

Sex-Linked Genes   For thousands of years, people wondered what determined whether we become male or female. Aristotle believed that the father's arousal during intercourse determines the offspring's sex. The more excited the father was, the more likely it would be a son, he reasoned. Of course, he was wrong, but it was not until the 1920s that researchers confirmed the existence of human sex chromosomes, 2 of the 46 chromosomes human beings normally carry. Ordinarily females have two X chromosomes, so-named for their shape, and males have one X and a smaller Y chromosome. Figure 3.5 on page 86, shows the chromosome makeup of a male and a female.

A number of disorders have been traced to the sex chromosomes. *X-linked inheritance* is the term used to describe the inheritance of a defective or mutated gene that is carried on the X chromosome (Trappe & others, 2001). Because males have only one X chromosome, when there is a mutant gene on the X chromosome, males have no "backup" copy and therefore may carry an X-linked disease. Females will be less likely to have an X-linked problem because their second X chromosome is not likely to carry

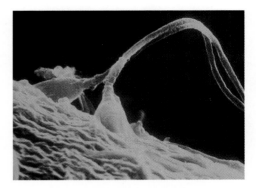

FIGURE 3.3 Union of Sperm and Egg

Landmarks in the History of Genetics

Heredity Resources

Genetics Journals and News

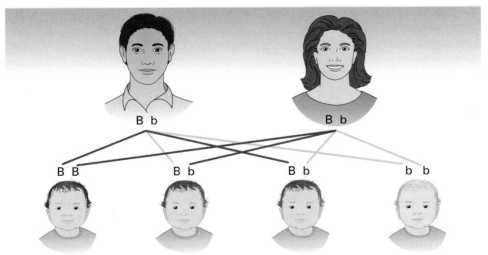

B = Gene for brown hair   b = Gene for blond hair

FIGURE 3.4 How Brown-Haired Parents Can Have a Blond-Haired Child

Although both parents have brown hair, each parent can have a recessive gene for blond hair. In this example, both parents have brown hair, but each parent carries the recessive gene for blond hair. Therefore, the odds of their child having blond hair are one in four—the probability the child will receive a recessive gene (*b*) from each parent.

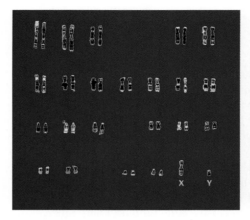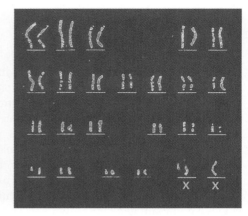

a.   b.

FIGURE 3.5 The Genetic Difference Between Males and Females

Set (*a*) shows the chromosome structure of a male, and set (*b*) shows the chromosome structure of a female. The last pair of 23 pairs of chromosomes is in the bottom right box of each set. Notice that the Y chromosome of the male is smaller than the X chromosome of the female. To obtain this kind of chromosomal picture, a cell is removed from a person's body, usually from the inside of the mouth. The chromosomes are stained by chemical treatment, magnified, and then photographed.

the altered gene. Thus, most individuals who have X-linked diseases are males. Females who have one changed copy of the X gene are known as "carriers," and they usually do not show any signs of the X-linked disease. Hemophilia and fragile X syndrome, which we will discuss later in the chapter, are examples of X-linked inheritance (Gonzales-del Angel & others, 2000).

Genetic Imprinting *Genetic imprinting* is a mechanism in which genes have been modified in one of the parents and have differing effects depending on whether they are transmitted to the offspring through the egg or sperm (Jirtle, Sander, & Barret, 2000). An imprinted gene dominates one that has not been imprinted. Genetic imprinting may explain why individuals who inherit Huntington disease from their father show symptoms of the disease at an earlier age than when they inherit from their mother (Navarrette, Martinez, & Salamanca, 1994). Also, when individuals inherit Turner syndrome (which is characterized by underdeveloped sex organs) from their father, they tend to show better cognitive and social skills than when they inherit the disorder from their mother (Martinez-Pasarell & others, 1999). We will discuss Huntington disease and Turner syndrome later in the chapter.

Polygenic Inheritance Genetic transmission is usually more complex than the simple examples we have examined thus far (Lewis, 2003). *Polygenic inheritance* is the genetic principle by which many genes can interact to produce a particular characteristic. Few psychological characteristics are associated with single pairs of genes. Most are related to the interaction of many different genes. There are about 30,000 to 35,000 genes in the human genome, so you can imagine that possible combinations of these are staggering in number. Traits affected by this mixing of genes are said to be polygenically determined.

No one possesses all the characteristics that our genetic structure makes possible. A **genotype** is the person's genetic heritage, the actual genetic material. However, not all of this genetic material is apparent in our observed and measurable characteristics. A **phenotype** is the way an individual's genotype is expressed in observable and measurable characteristics. Phenotypes include physical traits (such as height, weight, eye color, and skin pigmentation) and psychological characteristics (such as intelligence, creativity, personality, and social tendencies).

genotype A person's genetic heritage; the actual genetic material.

phenotype The way an individual's genotype is expressed in observed and measurable characteristics.

Calvin and Hobbes

by Bill Watterson

For each genotype, a range of phenotypes can be expressed. Imagine that we could identify all of the genes that would make a person introverted or extraverted. Would measured introversion-extraversion be predictable from knowledge of the specific genes? The answer is no, because, even if our genetic model were adequate, introversion-extraversion is a characteristic shaped by experience throughout life. For example, parents may push an introverted child into social situations and encourage the child to become more gregarious.

To understand how introverted a child is, think about a series of genetic codes that predispose the child to develop in a particular way, and imagine environments that are responsive or unresponsive to this development. For instance, the genotype of some persons may predispose them to be introverted in an environment that promotes a turning inward of personality, yet, in an environment that encourages social interaction and outgoingness, these individuals may become more extraverted. However, it would be unlikely for the individual with this introverted genotype to become a strong extravert.

Reaction Range The **reaction range** is the range of possible phenotypes for each genotype. The actual phenotype depends on an environment's restrictiveness or richness. Sandra Scarr (1984) explains reaction range this way: Each of us has a range of potential. For example, an individual with "medium-tall" genes for height who grows up in a poor environment may be shorter than average; however, in an excellent nutritional environment, the individual may grow up to be taller than average. No matter how well fed a person is, though, someone with "short" genes will never be taller than average. Scarr believes that characteristics such as intelligence and introversion work the same way. That is, there is a range within which the environment can modify intelligence, but intelligence is not completely malleable. Reaction range gives us an estimate of how modifiable intelligence is.

Canalization Although some traits have a wide reaction range, others are somewhat immune to extensive changes in the environment. These characteristics seem to stay on a particular developmental course, regardless of the environmental assaults on them (Waddington, 1957). **Canalization** is the term used to describe the narrow path, or developmental course, that certain characteristics take. Apparently, preservative forces help to protect, or buffer, a person from environmental extremes. For example, research by Jerome Kagan (1984) indicates that Guatemalan infants who had experienced extreme malnutrition as infants showed normal social and cognitive development later in childhood.

Although the genetic influence of canalization keeps organisms on a particular developmental path, genes alone do not directly determine human behavior. Developmentalist Gilbert Gottlieb (2000, 2002) points out that genes are an integral part of the organism but that their activity (genetic expression) can be affected by the organism's environment. For example, hormones that circulate in the blood make their way into

reaction range The range of possible phenotypes for each genotype, suggesting the importance of an environment's restrictiveness or richness.

canalization The process by which characteristics take a narrow path, or developmental course. Apparently, preservative forces help to protect a person from environmental extremes.

the cell, where they influence the cell's activity by turning genes "on" and "off." The flow of hormones themselves can be affected by environmental events, such as light, day length, nutrition, and behavior.

Behavior Genetics

Behavior genetics is the study of the degree and nature of behavior's hereditary basis. Behavior geneticists assume that behaviors are jointly determined by the interaction of heredity and environment (Maxson, 2003; Rowe, 2001; Wahlsten, 2000).

At the beginning of the chapter, we described the Minnesota Study of Twins Reared Apart. In their research on the link between heredity and behavior, behavior geneticists often conduct either twin studies or adoption studies. In the most common type of **twin study,** the behavioral similarity of identical twins is compared with the behavioral similarity of fraternal twins. *Identical twins* (called monozygotic twins) develop from a single fertilized egg that splits into two genetically identical replicas, each of which becomes a person. *Fraternal twins* (called dizygotic twins) develop from separate eggs and separate sperm, making them genetically no more similar than ordinary siblings. Although fraternal twins share the same womb, they are no more alike genetically than are non-twin brothers and sisters, and they may be of different sexes. By comparing groups of identical and fraternal twins, behavior geneticists capitalize on the basic knowledge that identical twins are more similar genetically than are fraternal twins (Jacob & others, 2001). In one twin study, 7,000 pairs of Finnish identical and fraternal twins were compared on the personality traits of extraversion and neuroticism (psychological instability) (Rose & others, 1998). On both of these personality traits, the identical twins were much more similar than the fraternal twins were, suggesting that heredity plays a role in both traits. However, several issues crop up as a result of twin studies. Adults might stress the similarities of identical twins more than those of fraternal twins, and identical twins might perceive themselves as a "set" and play together more than fraternal twins do. If so, observed similarities in identical twins could be environmentally influenced.

In an **adoption study,** investigators seek to discover whether, in behavior and psychological characteristics, adopted children are more like their adoptive parents, who have provided a home environment, or more like their biological parents, who have contributed their heredity. Another type of adoption study compares adoptive and biological siblings. In one investigation, the educational levels attained by the biological parents were better predictors of the adopted children's IQ scores than were the IQs of the children's adoptive parents (Scarr & Weinberg, 1983). Because of the genetic relation between the adopted children and their biological parents, the implication is that heredity influences children's IQ scores. However, keep in mind that adoption studies are correlational, so we cannot conclude that heredity alone causes variations in the behavior of adopted and biological children.

Molecular Genetics

In contrast to behavior geneticists who study the effects of heredity on behavior at a global level, molecular genetics is studied at microscopic level (Klug & Cummings, 2003). Today, there is a great deal of enthusiasm about the use of molecular genetics to discover the specific locations on genes that are linked to an individual's susceptibility to many diseases and other aspects of health and well-being (Lewis, 2003).

The Human Genome Project   The Human Genome Project, begun in the 1970s, has made stunning progress in mapping all of the estimated 30,000 to 35,000 genes in the human genome (U.S. Department of Energy, 2001). The Human Genome Project has already linked specific DNA mutations with the increased risk of a number of

mhhe ●com/
santrockld9

Behavior Genetics

Twin Research

Human Genome Project

behavior genetics The study of the degree and nature of behavior's basis in heredity.

twin study A study in which the behavioral similarity of identical twins is compared with the behavioral similarity of fraternal twins.

adoption study A study in which investigators seek to discover whether, in behavior and psychological characteristics, adopted children are more like their adoptive parents, who provided a home environment, or more like their biological parents, who contributed their heredity. Another form of the adoption study is to compare adoptive and biological siblings.

diseases and conditions, including Huntington disease (in which the central nervous system deteriorates), some forms of cancer, asthma, diabetes, hypertension, and Alzheimer's disease (Davies, 2001; Goodstadt & Ponting, 2001).

Every individual carries a number of DNA mutations that might lead to serious physical disease or mental disorder. Identifying the mutations could enable doctors to predict an individual's disease risks, recommend healthy lifestyle regimens, and prescribe the safest and most effective drugs. A decade or two from now, parents of a newborn baby may be able to leave the hospital with a full genomic analysis that would tell them which diseases the infant is at risk for.

However, mining DNA mutations to discover health risks might increasingly threaten an individual's ability to land and hold jobs, obtain insurance, and keep their genetic profile private. For example, should an airline pilot or neurosurgeon who one day will develop a hereditary disorder that makes their hands shake be required to leave that job early? To think further about such issues, see figure 3.6.

The Collaborative Gene   The hope of many biologists was that the Human Genome Project would demonstrate virtually a one-to-one connection between genes and behavior. I remember a conversation I had in the late 1990s with a biologist who had mapped the identity of several genes as part of the Human Genome Project. He strongly believed that the behavior of his two adolescents was solely due to the genes they inherited and was completely unrelated to the myriad of experiences they had while they were growing up.

One of the big surprises in the Human Genome Project was the recent finding that humans have only about 30,000 to 35,000 genes (U.S. Department of Energy, 2001). Previously, biologists were sure that humans had 50,000 to 100,000 or more genes. They also believed that there was a one-to-one correspondence between the number of genes and the number of proteins produced in the human body; that is, each gene was responsible for the synthesis of only one protein. However, it is now accepted that humans have far more proteins (300,000 to 500,000) than they have genes and, thus, there cannot be a one-to-one correspondence between them (Commoner, 2002; Moore, 2001).

	Yes	No	Undecided
1. Would you want you or your loved one to be tested for a gene that increases your risk for a disease, but does not determine whether you will actually develop the disease?	☐	☐	☐
2. Would you want you and your mate to be tested before having offspring to determine your risk for having a child who is likely to contract various diseases?	☐	☐	☐
3. Should testing of unborn children be restricted to traits that are commonly considered to have negative outcomes, such as disease?	☐	☐	☐
4. Should altering a newly conceived person's genes to improve qualities such as intelligence, appearance, and strength be allowed?	☐	☐	☐
5. Should employers be permitted access to your genetic information?	☐	☐	☐
6. Should life insurance companies have access to your genetic information?	☐	☐	☐

FIGURE 3.6 Exploring Your Genetic Future

These athletes, many of whom have Down syndrome, are participating in a Special Olympics competition. Notice the distinctive facial features of the individuals with Down syndrome, such as a round face and a flattened skull. *What causes Down syndrome?*

Developmental psychologist David Moore (2001) titled his recent book *The Dependent Gene* to underscore the concept that DNA does not determine traits in an independent manner. Rather, genes and the environment together influence our characteristics. DNA contains the genetic instructions needed for growth and development. However, DNA information can be modified within the cell as small pieces of DNA are mixed, matched, and linked with RNA (ribonucleic acid) in a process called *RNA editing*. RNA transmits the information for further processing in protein synthesis.

DNA clearly exerts an important influence on inheritance, but it acts only in collaboration with many protein-based processes that prevent and repair incorrect sequences, transform proteins into an active form, and provide genetic information beyond that originating in the gene itself (Commoner, 2002; Gottlieb, 1998). Numerous studies have shown that external sensory and internal neural events can excite or inhibit gene expression (Gottlieb, Wahlsten, & Lickliter, 1998; Mauro & others, 1994; Rusak & others, 1990). In sum, according to an increasing number of developmental psychologists who study molecular genetics, no single gene is solely responsible for a given protein and therefore for the inherited trait (Gottlieb, 2001; Moore, 2001). Rather than being an independent gene, DNA is a collaborative gene.

Most molecular biologists operate under the assumption that DNA is the secret of life. However, environmental scientist Barry Commoner (2002) argues that DNA likely did not create life but instead life created DNA. He concluded that when life was first formed on Earth, proteins must have appeared before DNA because, unlike DNA, proteins have the ability to generate the chemical energy necessary to assemble small molecules into larger ones like DNA. According to Commoner, DNA is a mechanism created by the cell to store information produced in the cell. Once produced by the primitive cell, DNA could become a stable place to store information about the cell's chemistry. Thus, in Commoner's view, the fundamental unit of life is not DNA but rather the cell of which DNA is a component.

Chromosome and Gene-Linked Abnormalities

Earlier in this chapter, we saw that abnormal genes are linked with a number of disorders. Here we will examine some of the abnormalities that can occur in chromosomes and genes.

Chromosome Abnormalities   When gametes are formed, the 46 chromosomes do not always divide evenly. In this case, the resulting sperm or ovum does not have the normal 23 chromosomes. The most notable outcomes of this error are Down syndrome and abnormalities of the sex chromosomes (see figure 3.7).

Down Syndrome   **Down syndrome** is a chromosomally transmitted form of mental retardation that is caused by the presence of an extra (47th) chromosome. An individual with Down syndrome has a round face, a flattened skull, an extra fold of skin over the eyelids, a protruding tongue, short limbs, and retardation of motor and mental abilities. It is not known why the extra chromosome is present, but the health of the male sperm or female ovum may be involved (Davison, Gardiner, & Costa, 2001; MacLean, 2000). Women between the ages of 18 and 38 are less likely to give birth to a child with Down syndrome than are younger or older women. Down syndrome appears approximately once in every 700 live births but rarely in African American children.

mhhe ● com/
santrockld9

Genetic Disorders
Prenatal Testing and Down Syndrome

Down syndrome A form of mental retardation, caused by the presence of an extra (47th) chromosome.

Name	Description	Treatment	Incidence
Down syndrome	An extra chromosome causes mild to severe retardation and physical abnormalities.	Surgery, early intervention, infant stimulation, and special learning programs	1 in 1,900 births at age 20 1 in 300 births at age 35 1 in 30 births at age 45
Klinefelter syndrome	An extra X chromosome causes physical abnormalities.	Hormone therapy can be effective	1 in 800 males
Fragile X syndrome	An abnormality in the X chromosome can cause mental retardation, learning disabilities, or short attention span.	Special education, speech and language therapy	More common in males than in females
Turner syndrome	A missing X chromosome in females can cause mental retardation and sexual underdevelopment.	Hormone therapy in childhood and puberty	1 in 2,500 female births
XYY syndrome	An extra Y chromosome can cause above-average height.	No special treatment required	1 in 1,000 male births

FIGURE 3.7 Some Chromosome Abnormalities

Note: Treatment does not necessarily erase the problem but may improve the individual's adaptive behavior and quality of life.

Some individuals have developed special programs to help children with Down syndrome. One such program was developed by Janet Marchese, an adoptive mother of a Down syndrome baby. She began putting the parents of children with Down syndrome together with couples who wanted to adopt the children. Her adoption network has placed more than 1,500 Down syndrome children and has a waiting list of couples who want to adopt.

Abnormalities of the Sex Chromosomes   Each newborn has at least one X chromosome. However, approximately 1 in every 500 infants either is missing a second X chromosome, or has an X chromosome that is combined with two more sex chromosomes. Four such sex-linked chromosomal disorders are Klinefelter syndrome, fragile X syndrome, Turner syndrome, and XYY syndrome (Baum, 2000).

Klinefelter syndrome is a disorder in which males have an extra X chromosome, making them XXY instead of XY (Lowe & others, 2001). Males with this disorder have undeveloped testes, and they usually have enlarged breasts and become tall. Klinefelter syndrome occurs approximately once in every 800 live male births.

Fragile X syndrome is a disorder that results from an abnormality in the X chromosome, which becomes constricted and tends to break. Mental deficiency often accompanies fragile X syndrome, but its form varies considerably (mental retardation, learning disability, short attention span) (Lewis, 2003). This disorder occurs more frequently in males than in females, possibly because the second X chromosome in females overrides the disorder's negative effects.

Turner syndrome is a disorder in females in which either an X chromosome is missing, making the person XO instead of XX, or the second X chromosome is partially deleted (Bramswig, 2001). These females are short in stature and have a webbed neck. They might be infertile and have difficulty in mathematics, but their verbal ability is often facilitated. Turner syndrome occurs in approximately 1 of every 2,500 live female births.

The **XYY syndrome** is a disorder in which the male has an extra Y chromosome. Early interest in this syndrome focused on the belief that the extra Y chromosome found in some males contributed to their aggression and violence. It was then reasoned that if a male had an extra Y chromosome he would likely be extremely aggressive and possibly develop a violent personality. However, researchers

Klinefelter syndrome A disorder in which males have an extra X chromosome, making them XXY instead of XY.

fragile X syndrome A disorder involving an abnormality in the X chromosome, which becomes constricted and, often, breaks.

Turner syndrome A disorder in females in which either an X chromosome is missing, making the person XO instead of XX, or the second X chromosome is partially deleted.

XYY syndrome A disorder in which males have an extra Y chromosome.

Careers in Life-Span Development

Holly Ishmael, Genetic Counselor

Holly Ishmael is a genetic counselor at Children's Mercy Hospital in Kansas City. She obtained an undergraduate degree in psychology from Sarah Lawrence College and then a master's degree in genetic counseling from the same college. She uses many of the principles discussed in this chapter in her genetic counseling work.

Genetic counselors have specialized graduate degrees in the areas of medical genetics and counseling ◀‖‖‖ p. 36. They enter graduate school in these areas with undergraduate backgrounds from a variety of disciplines, including biology, genetics, psychology, public health, and social work. Genetic counselors, like Ishmael, work as members of a health-care team, providing information and support to families with birth defects or genetic disorders. They identify families at risk by analyzing inheritance patterns and explore options with the family. Genetic counselors may serve as educators and resource people for other health-care professionals and the public. Some genetic counselors also work in administrative positions or conduct research. Some genetic counselors, like Ishmael, become specialists in prenatal and pediatric genetics; others might specialize in cancer genetics or psychiatric genetic disorders.

Holly says, "Genetic counseling is a perfect combination for people who want to do something science-oriented, but

need human contact and don't want to spend all of their time in a lab or have their nose in a book."

There are approximately thirty graduate genetic counseling programs in the United States. If you are interested in this profession, you can obtain further information from the National Society of Genetic Counselors at this website: http://www.nsgc.org.

Holly Ishmael (*left*) in a genetic counseling session.

---

subsequently found that XYY males are no more likely to commit crimes than are XY males (Witkin & others, 1976).

Gene-Linked Abnormalities   Not only can abnormalities be produced by an uneven number of chromosomes, but they also can result from harmful genes (Croyle, 2000). More than 7,000 such genetic disorders have been identified, although most of them are rare.

Phenylketonuria (PKU) is a genetic disorder in which the individual cannot properly metabolize a substance needed for production of proteins in the body. Phenylketonuria is now easily detected, but, if it is left untreated, mental retardation and hyperactivity result. The disorder is treated by diet to prevent an excess accumulation of the substance, phenylalanine. Phenylketonuria involves a recessive gene and occurs about once in every 10,000 to 20,000 live births. Phenylketonuria accounts for about 1 percent of institutionalized mentally retarded individuals, and it occurs primarily in Whites.

The story of phenylketonuria has important implications for the nature-nurture issue. Although phenylketonuria is a genetic disorder (nature), how or whether a gene's influence in phenylketonuria is played out can depend on environmental influences since the disorder can be treated (nurture). That is, restricting the individual's diet (environment) prevents mental retardation. Thus, phenylketonuria is an excellent example of the interaction of heredity and environment (Luciana, Sullivan, & Nelson, 2001; Merrick, Aspler, & Schwartz, 2001).

Sickle-cell anemia, which occurs most often in African Americans, is a genetic disorder that deforms the body's red blood cells. A red blood cell is usually shaped like

phenylketonuria (PKU) A genetic disorder in which an individual cannot properly metabolize a substance needed for production of proteins in the body. PKU is now easily detected but, if left untreated, results in mental retardation and hyperactivity.

sickle-cell anemia A genetic disorder that affects the red blood cells and occurs most often in people of African descent.

a disk, but in sickle-cell anemia, a change in a recessive gene modifies its shape to a hook-shaped "sickle." These cells die quickly, causing anemia, crippling pain in bones and joints, and early death of the individual because they cannot carry oxygen to other cells in the body. About 1 in 400 African American babies is born with sickle-cell anemia. One in 10 African Americans is a carrier, as is 1 in 20 Latin Americans. Treatment of individuals with sickle-cell anemia starts with early diagnosis, preferably in the newborn period and includes penicillin. Treatment of complications often includes antibiotics, pain management, and blood transfusions.

Other genetic abnormalities include cystic fibrosis, diabetes, hemophilia, spina bifida, and Tay-Sachs disease. Figure 3.8 provides information about these conditions.

Some genetic disorders, such as Huntington disease and Tay-Sachs disease, are hereditary. Others, such as spina bifida, can be diagnosed before birth. Genetic counselors, usually physicians or biologists who are well-versed in the field of medical genetics, are familiar with the kinds of problems just described, the odds of encountering them, and helpful strategies for offsetting some of their effects. To read about the career and work of a genetic counselor, see the Careers in Life-Span Development insert on page 92.

During a physical examination for a college football tryout, Jerry Hubbard, 32, learned that he carried the gene for sickle-cell anemia. Daughter Sara is healthy but daughter Avery (in the flowered dress) has sickle-cell anemia. *If you were a genetic counselor, would you recommend that this family have more children? Explain.*

Name	Description	Treatment	Incidence
Cystic fibrosis	Glandular dysfunction that interferes with mucus production; breathing and digestion are hampered, resulting in a shortened life span.	Physical and oxygen therapy, synthetic enzymes, and antibiotics; most individuals live to middle age.	1 in 2,000 births
Diabetes	Body does not produce enough insulin, which causes abnormal metabolism of sugar.	Early onset can be fatal unless treated with insulin.	1 in 2,500 births
Hemophilia	Delayed blood clotting causes internal and external bleeding.	Blood transfusions/injections can reduce or prevent damage due to internal bleeding.	1 in 10,000 males
Huntington disease	Central nervous system deteriorates, producing problems in muscle coordination and mental deterioration.	Doesn't usually appear until age 35 or older; death likely 10 to 20 years after symptoms appear.	1 in 20,000 births
Phenylketonuria (PKU)	Metabolic disorder that, left untreated, causes mental retardation.	Special diet can result in average intelligence and normal life span.	1 in 14,000 births
Sickle-cell anemia	Blood disorder that limits the body's oxygen supply; it can cause joint swelling, as well as heart and kidney failure.	Penicillin, medication for pain, antibiotics, and blood transfusions groups.	1 in 400 African American children (lower among other
Spina bifida	Neural tube disorder that causes brain and spine abnormalities.	Corrective surgery at birth, orthopedic devices, and physical/medical therapy.	2 in 1,000 births
Tay-Sachs disease	Deceleration of mental and physical development caused by an accumulation of lipids in the nervous system.	Medication and special diet are used, but death is likely by 5 years of age.	One in 30 American Jews is a carrier.

FIGURE 3.8 Some Gene-Linked Abnormalities

Review and Reflect

2 **Describe the genetic foundations of development**

REVIEW

- What are genes?
- What are mitosis and meiosis?
- What are some important genetic principles?
- What is behavior genetics?
- What is molecular genetics? What is the nature of the collaborative gene?
- What are some key chromosome- and gene-linked abnormalities?

REFLECT

- What are some possible ethical issues regarding genetics and development that might arise in the future?

3 REPRODUCTION CHALLENGES AND CHOICES

Prenatal Diagnostic Tests   **Infertility**   **Adoption**

mhhe ● com/
santrockld9

Amniocentesis
Obstetric Ultrasound
Chorionic Villi Sampling
Genetic Counseling

Earlier in this chapter we discussed several principles of genetics, including the role of meiosis in reproduction. Having also examined a number of genetic abnormalities that can occur, we now have some background to consider some of the challenges and choices facing prospective parents.

Prenatal Diagnostic Tests

Scientists have developed a number of tests to determine whether a fetus is developing normally, among them amniocentesis, ultrasound sonography, chorionic villi sampling, and the maternal blood test.

Amniocentesis is a prenatal medical procedure in which a sample of amniotic fluid is withdrawn by syringe and tested for any chromosome or metabolic disorders (Tercyak & others, 2001). The amnionic fluid is in the amnion, a thin, membraneous sac in which the embryo is suspended. Amniocentesis is performed between the 12th and 16th weeks of pregnancy. The later amniocentesis is performed, the better its diagnostic potential. The earlier it is performed, the more useful it is in deciding whether to terminate a pregnancy. There is a small risk of miscarriage when amniocentesis is performed; about 1 woman in every 200 to 300 miscarries after amniocentesis.

Ultrasound sonography is a prenatal medical procedure in which high-frequency sound waves are directed into the pregnant woman's abdomen. The echo from the sounds is transformed into a visual representation of the fetus' inner structures. This technique can detect such disorders as microencephaly, a form of mental retardation involving an abnormally small brain. Ultrasound sonography is often used in conjunction with amniocentesis to determine the precise location of the fetus in the

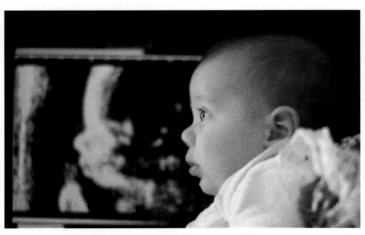

A 6-month-old infant poses with the ultrasound sonography record taken four months into the baby's prenatal development. *What is ultrasound sonography?*

mother's abdomen. When ultrasound sonography is used five or more times, the risk of low birth weight may be increased.

As scientists have searched for more accurate, safer assessments of high-risk prenatal conditions, they have developed a new test. *Chorionic villi sampling* is a prenatal medical procedure in which a small sample of the placenta (the vascular organ that links the fetus to the mother's uterus) is removed at some point between the 8th and 11th weeks of pregnancy (Zoppi & others, 2001). Diagnosis takes approximately 10 days. Chorionic villi sampling allows a decision about abortion to be made near the end of the first 12 weeks of pregnancy, a point when abortion is safer and less traumatic than after amniocentesis. Chorionic villi sampling has a slightly higher risk of miscarriage than amniocentesis and is linked with a slight risk of limb deformities. Both techniques provide valuable information about the presence of birth defects, but they also raise issues pertaining to whether an abortion should be obtained if birth defects are present.

The *maternal blood test (alpha-fetoprotein—AFP)* is a prenatal diagnostic technique that is used to assess blood alphaprotein level, which is associated with neural-tube defects. This test is administered to women 14 to 20 weeks into pregnancy only when they are at risk for bearing a child with defects in the formation of the brain and spinal cord.

Infertility

Approximately 10 to 15 percent of couples in the United States experience *infertility,* which is defined as the inability to conceive a child after 12 months of regular intercourse without contraception. The cause of infertility can rest with the woman or the man (Paseh, 2001). The woman may not be ovulating (releasing eggs to be fertilized), she may be producing abnormal ova, her fallopian tubes by which ova normally reach the womb may be blocked, or she may have a disease that prevents implantation of the ova. The man may produce too few sperm, the sperm may lack motility (the ability to move adequately), or he may have a blocked passageway (Oehnigner, 2001). In one study, long-term use of cocaine by men was related to low sperm count, low motility, and a higher number of abnormally formed sperm (Bracken & others, 1990). Cocaine-related infertility appears to be reversible if users stop taking the drug for at least one year.

In some cases, surgery may correct the cause of infertility. In others, hormone-based drugs may improve the probability of having a child. However, in some instances, fertility drugs have caused superovulation, producing three or more babies at a time. A summary of some of infertility's possible causes and solutions is presented in figure 3.9 on page 96.

In the United States, more than 2 million couples seek help for infertility every year. Of those, about 40,000 try high-tech assisted reproduction. The five most common techniques are these:

- *In vitro fertilization (IVF).* An egg and a sperm are combined in a laboratory dish. If the egg is fertilized, the resulting embryo is transferred into the woman's uterus or womb. The success rate is just under 20 percent.
- *Gamete intrafallopian transfer (GIFT).* A doctor inserts eggs and sperm directly into a woman's fallopian tube. The success rate is almost 30 percent.
- *Intrauterine insemination (IUI).* Frozen sperm—that of the husband or an unknown donor—is placed directly into the uterus. The success rate is 10 percent.

The McCaughey septuplets, born in 1997. *Why has there been such a dramatic increase in multiple births?*

Men

Problem	Possible causes	Treatment
Low sperm count	Hormone imbalance, varicose vein in scrotum, possibly environmental pollutants Drugs (cocaine, marijuana, lead, arsenic, some steroids and antibiotics) Y chromosome gene deletions	Hormone therapy, surgery, avoiding excessive heat
Immobile sperm	Abnormal sperm shape Infection Malfunctioning prostate	None Antibiotics Hormones
Antibodies against sperm	Problem in immune system	Drugs

Women

Problem	Possible causes	Treatment
Ovulation problems	Pituitary or ovarian tumor Underactive thyroid	Surgery Drugs
Antisperm secretions	Unknown	Acid or alkaline douche, estrogen therapy
Blocked fallopian tubes	Infection caused by IUD or abortion or by sexually transmitted disease	Eggs surgically removed from ovary and placed in uterus
Endometriosis (tissue buildup in uterus)	Delayed parenthood until the thirties	Hormones, surgical removal of uterine tissue buildup

FIGURE 3.9 Fertility Problems, Possible Causes, and Treatments

- *Zygote intrafallopian transfer (ZIFT)*. This is a two-step procedure. First, eggs are fertilized in the laboratory. Then, any resulting zygotes are transferred to a fallopian tube. The success rate is approximately 25 percent.
- *Intracytoplasmic sperm injection (ICSI)*. A doctor uses a microscopic pipette to inject a single sperm from a man's ejaculate into an egg in a laboratory dish. The zygote is returned to the uterus. The success rate is approximately 25 percent.

The creation of families by means of the new reproductive technologies raises important questions about the psychological consequences for children. Studies support the idea that "test-tube" babies function well and typically do not differ from naturally conceived children in various behaviors and psychological characteristics (Golombok, MacCallum, & Goodman, 2001; Hahan & Dipietro, 2001) (see figure 3.10).

One consequence of fertility treatments is an increase in multiple births. Twenty-five to 30 percent of pregnancies achieved by fertility treatments—including in vitro fertilization—now result in multiple births. Though parents may be thrilled at the prospect of having children, they also face serious risks. Any multiple birth increases the likelihood that the babies will have life-threatening and costly problems, such as extremely low birthweight.

Adoption

Although surgery and fertility drugs can sometimes solve an infertility problem, another choice is to adopt a child (Moody, 2001). Adoption is the social and legal process by which a parent-child relationship is established between persons unrelated at birth. Researchers have found that adopted children and adolescents often show more psychological and school-related problems than nonadopted children (Brodzinsky & others, 1984; Brodzinsky, Lang, & Smith, 1995). Adopted adolescents are referred to psychological treatment two to five times as often as their nonadopted peers (Grotevant & McRoy, 1990).

In one study of 4,682 adopted adolescents and the same number of nonadopted adolescents, adoptees showed lower levels of adjustment (Sharma, McGue, & Benson, 1996). In another study, adopted adolescents had more school adjustment problems, were more likely to use illicit drugs, and were more likely to engage in delinquent behavior (Sharma, McGue, & Benson, 1998). However, adopted siblings were less withdrawn and engaged in more prosocial behavior (such as being altruistic, caring, and supportive of others) than nonadopted siblings. In one study of 1,587 adopted and 87,165 nonadopted adolescents, the adopted adolescents were at higher risk for all of the domains sampled, including school achievement and problems, substance abuse, psychological well-being, and physical health (Miller & others, 2000). In this study, the effects of adoption were more negative when the adopted parents had low levels of education. Also, in this study, when a subsample consisting of the most negative problem profiles was examined, the differences between adopted and nonadopted even widened with the adopted adolescents far more likely to have the most problems.

In one of these studies, the later adoption occurred, the more problems the adoptees had. Infant adoptees had the fewest adjustment difficulties; those adopted after they were 10 years of age had the most problems (Sharma, McGue, & Benson, 1996). Other research has documented that early adoption often has better outcomes for the child than later adoption. At age 6, children adopted from an orphanage in the first 6 months of their lives showed no lasting negative effects of their early experience. However, children from the orphanage who were adopted after they were 6 months of age had abnormally high levels of cortisol, a stress-regulating hormone, indicating that their stress regulation had not developed adequately (Chisholm, 1998).

These results have policy implications, especially for the thousands of children who are relegated to the foster care system after infancy. Most often, older children are put up for adoption due to parental abuse or neglect. The process of terminating the birth parents' parental rights can be lengthy. In the absence of other relatives, children are turned over to the foster care system, where they must wait for months or even years to be adopted.

A question that virtually every adoptive parent wants answered is, "Should I tell my adopted child that he or she is adopted? If so, when?" Most psychologists believe that adopted children should be told that they are adopted, because they will eventually find out anyway. Many children begin to ask where they came from when they are approximately 4 to 6 years of age. This is a natural time to begin to respond in simple ways to children about their adopted status. Clinical psychologists report that one problem that sometimes surfaces is the desire of adoptive parents to make life too perfect for the adoptive child and to present a perfect image of themselves to the child. The result too often is that adopted children feel that they cannot release any angry feelings and openly discuss problems (Warshak, 2001).

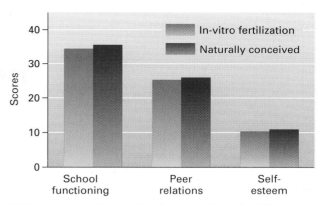

FIGURE 3.10 Socioemotional Functioning of Children Conceived Through In-Vitro Fertilization or Naturally Conceived

In one study, comparisons of the socioemotional functioning of young adolescents who had either been conceived through in-vitro fertilization (IVF) or naturally conceived revealed no differences between the two groups (Golombok & others, 2001). Although the means for the naturally conceived group were slightly higher, this is likely due to chance. The mean scores shown for the different measures are in the normal range of functioning.

Review and Reflect

3 Identify important reproduction challenges and choices

REVIEW

- What are some common prenatal diagnostic tests?
- What are some causes of infertility?
- How does adoption affect children's development?

REFLECT

- We discussed a number of studies indicating that adoption is linked with negative outcomes for children. Does that mean that all adopted children have more negative outcomes than all nonadopted children? Explain.

4 HEREDITY-ENVIRONMENT INTERACTION

```
                    Intelligence              Shared and Nonshared
                                             Environmental Experiences

              Heredity-Environment                 Conclusions About
                  Correlations                     Heredity-Environment
                                                       Interaction
```

In our discussion of adoption, we indicated that children who are adopted later in their development often have more problems than those who are adopted very early in their lives. This finding suggests that the environment plays an important role in children's development. Indeed, heredity and environment interact to produce development (McGuire, 2001). To explore this interaction, we will focus on one important area of development—intelligence—and then explore other aspects of heredity-environment interaction.

Intelligence

One of the hottest areas in the study of intelligence centers on the extent to which intelligence is influenced by genetics and the extent to which it is influenced by environment. Although it is difficult to tease apart these influences, that has not kept psychologists from trying to unravel them.

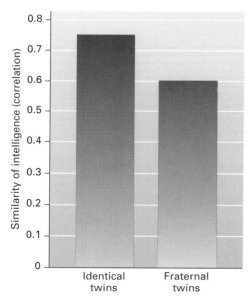

FIGURE 3.11 Correlation Between Intelligence Test Scores and Twin Status

The graph represents a summary of research findings that have compared the intelligence test scores of identical and fraternal twins. An approximate .15 difference has been found with a higher correlation for identical twins (.75) and a lower correlation for fraternal twins (.60).

Heredity   Arthur Jensen (1969) sparked a lively, and at times, hostile debate when he presented his thesis that intelligence is primarily inherited. Jensen believes that environment and culture play only a minimal role in intelligence. Jensen reviewed the research on intelligence, much of which involved comparisons of identical and fraternal twins. Identical twins have exactly the same genetic makeup. If intelligence is genetically determined, Jensen reasoned, identical twins' IQs should be similar. Fraternal twins and ordinary siblings are less similar genetically, so their IQs should be less similar.

The studies on intelligence in identical twins that Jensen reviewed had an average correlation of .82, a very high positive association. Investigations of fraternal twins, however, produced an average correlation of .50, a moderately high positive correlation. A difference of .32 is substantial.

Many scholars have criticized Jensen's work. One criticism concerns his definition of intelligence itself. Jensen believes that IQ as measured by standardized intelligence tests is a good indicator of intelligence. Critics argue that IQ tests tap only a narrow range of intelligence. Everyday problem solving, work, and social adaptability, say the critics, are important aspects of intelligence not measured in the traditional IQ tests used in Jensen's review of studies. A second criticism is that most investigations of heredity and environment do not include environments that differ radically. Thus, it is not surprising that many heredity studies show environment to be a fairly weak influence on intelligence. Further, in a much more recent review than Jensen's, the difference in intelligence between identical and fraternal twins was only .15, substantially less than what Jensen found (Grigorenko, 2000) (See figure 3.11).

The controversy about heredity and intelligence was fueled by the publication of *The Bell Curve: Intelligence and Class Structure in American Life* (1994) by Richard Herrnstein and Charles Murray. They argued that America is rapidly evolving a huge

THE WIZARD OF ID

Reprinted by permission of Johnny Hart and Creators Syndicate, Inc.

underclass of intellectually deprived individuals whose cognitive abilities will never match the future needs of most employers. The authors believe that members of this underclass, a large percentage of whom are African American, might be doomed by their shortcomings to welfare dependency, poverty, crime, and lives devoid of hope of ever reaching the American dream.

Herrnstein and Murray believe that IQ can be quantitatively measured and that IQ test scores vary across ethnic groups. They point out that, in the United States, Asian Americans score several points higher than Whites, while African Americans score about 15 points lower than Whites. They also argue that these IQ differences are at least partly due to heredity and that government money spent on education programs such as Project Head Start is wasted, helping only the government's bloated bureaucracy.

Why do Herrnstein and Murray call their book *The Bell Curve*? A bell curve is a normal distribution graph, which has the shape of a bell—bulging in the middle and thinning out at the edges (see figure 3.12). Normal distribution graphs are used to represent large numbers of people, who are sorted according to a shared characteristic, such as weight, exposure to asbestos, taste in clothing, or IQ.

Herrnstein and Murray often refer to bell curves to make a point: that predictions about any individual based exclusively on the person's IQ are useless. Weak correlations between intelligence and job success have predictive value only when they are applied to large groups of people. Within such large groups, say Herrnstein and Murray, the pervasive influence of IQ on human society becomes apparent.

Significant criticisms have been leveled at *The Bell Curve* (Block, 2002; Moore, 2001). Experts on intelligence generally agree that African Americans score lower than Whites on IQ tests. However, many of these experts raise serious questions about

mhhe ○ com/
santrockld9

Two Views of *The Bell Curve*
Sternberg's Critique of *The Bell Curve*

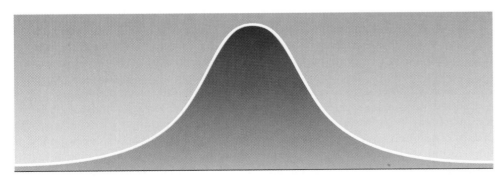

FIGURE 3.12 The Bell Curve
The term *bell curve* is used to describe a normal distribution graph, a symmetrical shape that looks like a bell—bulging in the middle and thinning out at the edges.

the accuracy of IQ tests as a measure of a person's intelligence. Critics contend that IQ tests are culturally biased against African Americans and Latinos (Ogbu, 2002). In 1971, the U.S. Supreme Court endorsed such criticisms and ruled that tests of general intelligence, in contrast to tests that solely measure fitness for a particular job, are discriminatory and cannot be administered as a condition of employment.

How strong is the correlation between parental IQ and children's IQ? The concept of heritability seeks to separate the effects of heredity and environment in a population. **Heritability** refers to the fraction of the variance in IQ in a population that is attributed to genetics. The heritability index is computed using correlational statistical techniques. Thus, the highest degree of heritabilty is 1.00 and correlations of .70 and above suggest a strong genetic influence. A committee of respected researchers convened by the American Psychological Association concluded that by late adolescence, the heritability of intelligence is about .75, which reflects a strong genetic influence (Neisser & others, 1996).

Interestingly, researchers have found that the heritability of intelligence increases from childhood to adulthood (from as low as 35 percent in childhood to as high as 75 percent in adulthood) (McGue & others, 1993). Why might hereditary influences on intelligence increase with age? Possibly as we grow older, our interactions with the environment are shaped less by the influence of others and the environment on us and more by our ability to choose our environments to allow the expression of genetic tendencies we have inherited (Neisser & others, 1996). For example, sometimes parents push children into environments that are not compatible with their genetic inheritance (wanting to be a doctor or an engineer, for example), but as adults these individuals may make their own choices about career and intellectual interests.

It is important to keep in mind that heritability refers to groups (populations), not to individuals (Okagaki, 2000). Researchers rely on the concept of heritability to describe why people differ, not to explain the effects of heredity on a single individual's intelligence.

Environment   Today, most researchers agree that heredity does not determine intelligence to the extent Jensen and Hernnstein and Murray claimed (Moore, 2001; Sternberg & Grigorenko, 2001). For most people, this means modifications in environment can change their IQ scores considerably. It also means that programs designed to enrich a person's environment can have a considerable impact, improving school achievement and fostering the acquisition of skills needed for employment. While genetic endowment may always influence a person's intellectual ability, the environmental influences and opportunities we provide children and adults do make a difference.

Researchers increasingly are interested in manipulating the early environment of children who are at risk for impoverished intelligence (Ramey, Ramey, & Lanzi, 2001). Their emphasis is on prevention rather than remediation. Many low-income parents have difficulty providing an intellectually stimulating environment for their children. Programs that educate parents to be more sensitive caregivers and train them to be better teachers, as well as support services, such as high quality child-care programs, can make a difference in a child's intellectual development. To read about one such early intervention program, see the Sociocultural Worlds of Development box.

Studies of schooling also reveal effects on intelligence (Ceci & Gilstrap, 2000; Christian, Bachnan, & Morrison, 2001). The biggest effects have been found when large groups of children have been deprived of formal education for an extended period of time, resulting in lower intelligence. In one study, the intellectual functioning of Indian children in South Africa whose schooling was delayed for four years because of the unavailability of teachers was investigated (Ramphal, 1962). Compared with children in nearby villages who had teachers, the Indian children whose entry into school was delayed by four years experienced a decrement of 5 IQ points for every year of delay.

heritability A concept that refers to the fraction of variance in IQ in a population that is attributed to genetics.

The Abecedarian Intervention Program

Each morning a young mother waited with her child for the bus that would take the child to school. The unusual part of this is that the child was only 2 months old and "school" was an experimental program at the University of North Carolina at Chapel Hill. There the child experienced a number of interventions designed to improve her intellectual development—everything from bright objects dangled in front of her eyes while she was a baby to language instruction and counting activities when she was a toddler (Wickelgren, 1999).

This child was part of the Abecedarian Intervention Program conducted by Craig Ramey and his associates (Ramey & Campbell, 1984; Ramey & Ramey, 1998; Ramey, Ramey, & Lanzi, 2001). They randomly assigned 111 young children from low-income, poorly educated families either to an intervention group, which experienced full-time, year-round day care along with medical and social work services, or to a control group, which got medical and social benefits but no day care. The day-care program included gamelike learning activities aimed at improving language, motor, social, and cognitive skills. The success of the program in improving IQ was evident by the time the children were 3 years old, at which time the children in the experimental group showed normal IQs averaging 101, a 17-point advantage over the control group. Recent follow-up results suggest that the effects are long-lasting. More than a decade later, at age 15, children from the intervention group still maintained an IQ advantage of 5 points over the control group children (97.7 to 92.6) (Ramey, Campbell, & Blair, 2001; Ramey & others, 2000). They also did better on standardized tests of reading and math, and they were less likely to be held back a year in school (see figure 3.13). The greatest IQ gains were in the children whose mothers had especially low IQs—below 70. At age 15, these children showed a 10-point IQ advantage over a group of children whose mothers had IQs below 70 but did not experience the day-care intervention.

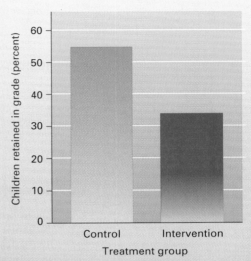

FIGURE 3.13 Early Intervention and Retention in School

When the children in the Abecedarian program were 15 years of age, those who experienced the preschool intervention were less likely to have been retained in a grade than the children in the control group.

Another possible effect of education on intelligence can be seen in rapidly rising IQ test scores around the world (Flynn, 1999). Scores on these tests have been rising so fast that a high percentage of people regarded as having average intelligence in the early 1900s would be considered below average in intelligence today (Howard, 2001) (see figure 3.14 on page 102). If a representative sample of people today took an intelligence test in 1932, about one-fourth would be defined as having very superior intelligence, a label usually accorded to fewer than 3 percent of the population. Because the change has taken place in a relatively short period of time, it can't be due to heredity, but rather may be due to increasing levels of education attained by a much greater percentage of the world's population or to other environmental factors, such as the explosion of information to which people are exposed. The worldwide increase in intelligence test scores that has occurred over a short time frame has been called the *Flynn effect,* after the researcher who discovered it—James Flynn.

Keep in mind that environmental influences are complex. Growing up with all the "advantages," for example, does not necessarily guarantee success. Children from wealthy families may have easy access to excellent schools, books, travel, and tutoring, but they may take such opportunities for granted and fail to develop the motivation to learn and to achieve. By the same token, "poor" or "disadvantaged" does not automatically equal "doomed." Many impoverished children and youth make the best of the opportunities available to them and learn to seek out advantages that can help them improve their lives.

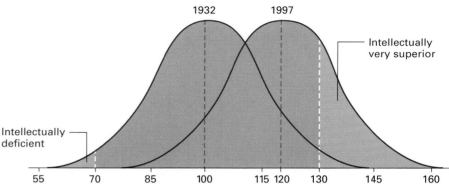

FIGURE 3.14 The Increase in IQ Scores from 1932 to 1997

As measured by the Stanford-Binet intelligence test, American children seem to be getting smarter. Scores of a group tested in 1932 fell along a bell-shaped curve with half below 100 and half above. Studies show that if children took that same test today, half would score above 120 on the 1932 scale. Very few of them would score in the "intellectually deficient" end, on the left side, and about one-fourth would rank in the "very superior" range.

Heredity-Environment Correlations

The notion of heredity-environment correlations involves the concept that individuals' genes influence the types of environments to which they are exposed. That is, individuals inherit environments that are related or linked to their genetic propensities (Plomin & others, 2001). Behavior geneticist Sandra Scarr (1993) described three ways that heredity and environment are correlated: passively, evocatively, and actively (see figure 3.15).

- **Passive genotype-environment correlations** occur because biological parents provide an environment that matches their own genetic tendencies and their children inherit genetic tendencies from their parents. For example, the parents might have a genetic predisposition to be intelligent and read skillfully. Because they read well and enjoy reading, they provide their children with books to read. The likely outcome is that their children, given their own inherited predispositions from their parents, will become skilled readers.
- **Evocative genotype-environment correlations** occur because a child's genotype elicits certain types of physical and social environments. For example, active, smiling children receive more social stimulation than passive, quiet children do. Cooperative, attentive adolescents evoke more pleasant and instructional responses from the adults around them than uncooperative, distractible adolescents do. Athletically inclined youth tend to elicit encouragement to engage in school sports. As a consequence, these adolescents tend to be the ones who try out for sport teams and go on to participate in athletically oriented environments.
- **Active (niche-picking) genotype-environment correlations** occur when children seek out environments that they find compatible and stimulating. Niche-picking refers to finding a niche or setting that is suited to one's abilities. Adolescents select from their surrounding environment some aspect that they respond to, learn about, or ignore. Their active selections of environments are related to their particular genotype. For example, attractive adolescents tend to seek out attractive peers. Adolescents who are musically inclined are likely to select musical environments in which they can successfully perform their skills.

passive genotype-environment correlations Correlations that occur because biological parents provide an environment that matches their own genetic tendencies and their children inherit genetic tendencies from their parents.

evocative genotype-environment correlations Correlations that exist when the child's genotype elicits certain types of physical and social environments.

active (niche-picking) genotype-environment correlations Correlations that exist when children seek out environments they find compatible and stimulating.

Heredity-Environment Correlation	Description	Examples
Passive	Children inherit genetic tendencies from their parents and parents also provide an environment that matches their own genetic tendencies.	Musically inclined parents usually have musically inclined children and they are likely to provide an environment rich in music for their children.
Evocative	The child's genetic tendencies elicit stimulation from the environment that supports a particular trait. Thus genes evoke environmental support.	A happy, outgoing child elicits smiles and friendly responses from others.
Active (niche-picking)	Children actively seek out "niches" in their environment that reflect their own interests and talents and are thus in accord with their genotype.	Libraries, sports fields, and a store with musical instruments are examples of environmental niches children might seek out if they have intellectual interests in books, talent in sports, or musical talents, respectively.

FIGURE 3.15 Exploring Heredity-Environment Correlations

Scarr believes that the relative importance of the three genotype-environment correlations changes as children develop from infancy through adolescence. In infancy, much of the environment that children experience is provided by adults. Thus, passive genotype-environment correlations are more common in the lives of infants and young children than they are for older children and adolescents who can extend their experiences beyond the family's influence and create their environments to a greater degree.

Shared and Nonshared Environmental Experiences

Behavior geneticists also believe that another way the environment's role in heredity-environment interaction is to consider the experiences that children have common with other children living in the same home, as well as experiences that are not shared (Feinberg & Hetherington, 2001; Plomin, Ashbury, & Dunn, 2001). **Shared environmental experiences** are children's common experiences, such as their parents' personalities or intellectual orientation, the family's socioeconomic status, and the neighborhood in which they live. Behavior geneticist Robert Plomin (1993) has found that common rearing, or shared environment, accounts for little of the variation in children's personality or interests. In other words, even though two children live under the same roof with the same parents, their personalities are often very different.

Nonshared environmental experiences are a child's unique experiences, both within the family and outside the family, that are not shared with another sibling. Thus, experiences occurring within the family can be part of the "nonshared environment." Parents often interact differently with each sibling, and siblings interact differently with parents (Hetherington, Reiss, & Plomin, 1994; Reiss & others, 2000). Siblings often have different peer groups, different friends, and different teachers at school.

Conclusions About Heredity-Environment Interaction

Both genes and environment are necessary for a person to even exist. Without genes, there is no person; without environment, there is no person (Scarr & Weinberg, 1980). Heredity and environment operate together—or cooperate—to produce a person's intelligence, temperament, height, weight, ability to pitch a baseball, ability to read, and so on (Gottlieb, 2001, 2002; Gottlieb, Wahlsten, & Lickliter, 1998) ◀ p. 23. If an attractive, popular, intelligent girl is elected president of her senior class in high

shared environmental experiences Children's common environmental experiences that are shared with their siblings, such as their parents' personalities and intellectual orientation, the family's social class, and the neighborhood in which they live.

nonshared environmental experiences The child's own unique experiences, both within the family and outside the family, that are not shared by another sibling. Thus, experiences occurring within the family can be part of the "nonshared environment."

*T*he interaction of heredity and environment is so extensive that to ask which is more important, nature or nurture, is like asking which is more important to a rectangle, height or width.

—WILLIAM GREENOUGH
Contemporary Developmental Psychologist,
University of Illinois at Urbana

mhhe ●com/
santrockld9

Genes and Parenting

What is the theme of Judith Harris' controversial book, The Nurture Assumption? *What is the nature of the controversy?*

school, is her success due to heredity or to environment? Of course, the answer is both. Because the environment's influence depends on genetically endowed characteristics, we say the two factors *interact* (Mader, 2002).

The relative contributions of heredity and environment are not additive. That is, we can't say that such-and-such a percentage of nature and such-and-such a percentage of experience make us who we are. That's the old view. Nor is it accurate to say that full genetic expression happens once, around conception or birth, after which we carry our genetic legacy into the world to see how far it takes us. Genes produce proteins throughout the life span, in many different environments. Or they don't produce these proteins, depending on how harsh or nourishing those environments are.

The emerging view is that many complex behaviors likely have some genetic loading that gives people a propensity for a particular developmental trajectory (Plomin & others, 2001). However, the actual development requires more: an environment. And that environment is complex, just like the mixture of genes we inherit (Sternberg & Grigorenko, 2001). Environmental influences range from the things we lump together under "nurture" (such as parenting, family dynamics, schooling, and neighborhood quality) to biological encounters (such as viruses, birth complications, and even biological events in cells) (Greenough, 1997, 1999; Greenough & others, 2001).

Imagine for a moment that there is a cluster of genes somehow associated with youth violence. (This example is hypothetical because we don't know of any such combination.) The adolescent who carries this genetic mixture might experience a world of loving parents, regular nutritious meals, lots of books, and a series of masterful teachers. Or the adolescent's world might include parental neglect, a neighborhood where gunshots and crime are everyday occurrences, and inadequate schooling. In which of these environments are the adolescent's genes likely to manufacture the biological underpinnings of criminality?

The most recent nature-nurture controversy erupted when Judith Harris (1998) published *The Nurture Assumption.* In this provocative book, she argued that what parents do does not make a difference in their children's and adolescents' behavior. Yell at them. Hug them. Read to them. Ignore them. Harris says it won't influence how they turn out. She argues that genes and peers are far more important than parents in children's and adolescents' development.

Harris is right that genes matter and she is right that peers matter, although her descriptions of peer influences do not take into account the complexity of peer contexts and developmental trajectories (Hartup, 1999). In addition to not adequately considering peer complexities, Harris is wrong that parents don't matter. For example, in the early child years parents play an important role in selecting children's peers and indirectly influencing children's development (Baumrind, 1999).

Child development expert T. Berry Brazelton (1998) commented, *"The Nurture Assumption* is so disturbing it devalues what parents are trying to do. . . . Parents might say, 'If I don't matter, why should I bother?' That's terrifying and it's coming when children and youth need a stronger home base." Even Jerome Kagan (1998), a champion of the view that biology strongly influences development, when commenting about Harris' book, concluded that whether children are cooperative or competitive, achievement-oriented or not, they are strongly influenced by their parents for better or for worse.

There is a huge parenting literature with many research studies documenting the importance of parents in children's development (Collins & others, 2000, 2001; Maccoby, 2002). We will discuss parents' important roles throughout this book.

Review and Reflect

4 Explain heredity-environment interaction

REVIEW

- How is intelligence influenced by heredity and how is it influenced by environment?
- What are three types of heredity-environment correlations? Give your own example of each.
- What are shared and nonshared experiences?
- What conclusions can be reached about heredity-environment interaction?

REFLECT

- Someone tells you that they have analyzed their genetic background and environmental experiences and reached the conclusion that environment definitely has had little influence on their intelligence. What would you say to this person about their ability to make this self-diagnosis?

Reach Your Learning Goals

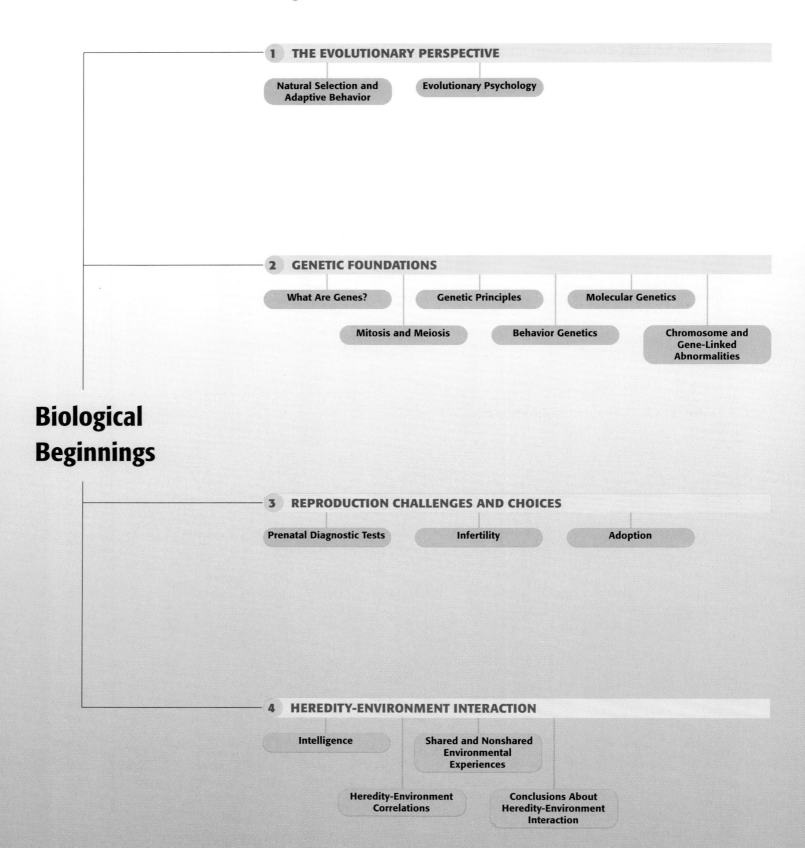

Biological Beginnings

1 THE EVOLUTIONARY PERSPECTIVE

- Natural Selection and Adaptive Behavior
- Evolutionary Psychology

2 GENETIC FOUNDATIONS

- What Are Genes?
- Genetic Principles
- Molecular Genetics
- Mitosis and Meiosis
- Behavior Genetics
- Chromosome and Gene-Linked Abnormalities

3 REPRODUCTION CHALLENGES AND CHOICES

- Prenatal Diagnostic Tests
- Infertility
- Adoption

4 HEREDITY-ENVIRONMENT INTERACTION

- Intelligence
- Shared and Nonshared Environmental Experiences
- Heredity-Environment Correlations
- Conclusions About Heredity-Environment Interaction

Summary

1 Discuss the evolutionary perspective

- Natural selection is the process that favors the individuals of a species that are best adapted to survive and reproduce. The process of natural selection was originally described by Charles Darwin. In evolutionary theory, adaptive behavior is behavior that promotes the organism's survival in a natural habitat. Biological evolution shaped human beings into a culture-making species.
- Evolutionary psychology is the view that adaptation, reproduction, and "survival of the fittest" are important in explaining behavior. According to Baltes, the benefits of evolutionary selection decrease with age mainly because of a decline in reproductive fitness. While evolutionary selection benefits decrease with age, cultural needs increase. Social cognitive theorist Albert Bandura acknowledges evolution's important role in human adaptation and change but argues for a bidirectional view that enables organisms to alter and construct new environmental conditions. Biology allows for a broad range of cultural possibilities.

2 Describe the genetic foundations of development

- The nucleus of each human cell contains 46 chromosomes, which are composed of DNA. Genes are short segments of DNA that provide information to help cells to reproduce and manufacture proteins that sustain life.
- Mitosis is the process of cell division in which each chromosome duplicates itself so that the two daughter cells each have 46 identical chromosomes. Genes are transmitted from parents to offspring by gametes, or sex cells, which contain only half the full complement of chromosomes (23). Gametes are formed by meiosis, a process by which one parent cell splits into four daughter cells. Reproduction takes place when a female gamete (ovum) is fertilized by male gamete (sperm) to create a single-celled zygote.
- Genetic principles include those involving dominant-recessive genes, sex-linked genes, genetic imprinting, polygenic inheritance, genotype-phenotype influences, reaction range, and canalization.
- Behavior genetics is the field concerned with the degree and nature of behavior's hereditary basis. Methods used by behavior geneticists include twin studies and adoption studies.
- The field of molecular genetics seeks to discover the precise locations of genes that determine an individual's susceptibility to various diseases and other aspects of health and well-being. The Human Genome Project has made stunning progress in mapping the human genome. It is important to recognize that there is not a one-to-one correspondence between a gene, a protein, and a human trait or behavior. A gene does not act independently to produce a trait or behavior. Rather, it acts collaboratively.
- Chromosome abnormalities occur when chromosomes do not divide evenly. Down syndrome is the result of a chromosomal abnormality caused by the presence of a 47th chromosome. Abnormalities of the sex chromosomes can result in disorders such as Klinefelter syndrome, fragile X syndrome, Turner syndrome, and XYY syndrome. Gene-linked disorders caused by harmful genes include phenylketonuria (PKU) and sickle-cell anemia.

3 Identify important reproduction challenges and choices

- Amniocentesis, ultrasound sonography, chorionic villi sampling, and the maternal blood test are used to determine the presence of defects once pregnancy has begun.
- Approximately 10 to 15 percent of U.S. couples have infertility problems, some of which can be corrected through surgery or fertility drugs. Additional options include in-vitro fertilization and other more recently developed techniques.
- Adopted children and adolescents have more problems than their nonadopted counterparts. When adoption occurs very early in development, the outcomes for the child are improved.

4 Explain heredity-environment interaction

- The extent to which intelligence is due to heredity or to environment has been the subject of controversy. Jensen's and Herrnstein and Murray's views that intelligence is strongly determined by heredity have prompted critics to attempt to dismantle their arguments. Genetic similarity might explain why identical twins show stronger correlations on intelligence tests than fraternal twins do. Many studies show that intelligence has a reasonably strong heritability component, although the heritabilty concept has been criticized. Environmental influences on intelligence have been demonstrated in studies of intervention programs for children at risk for having low IQs, research on schooling, and in investigations of sociohistorical changes. Intelligence test scores have risen considerably around the world in recent decades. This so-called the Flynn effect supports the idea that environment plays an important role in intelligence.
- Scarr argues that the environments parents select for their children depend on the parents' genotypes. Passive genotype-environment, evocative genotype-environment, and active (niche-picking) genotype-environment are three correlations. Scarr believes the relative importance of these three genotype-environment correlations changes as children develop.
- Behavior geneticists study shared and nonshared environmental experiences to help determine how heredity and environment contribute to development. Shared environmental experiences refer to siblings' common experiences. Nonshared environmental influences refer to the child's unique experiences.
- Many complex behaviors have some genetic loading that gives people a propensity for a particular developmental trajectory. Actual development also requires an environment and that environment is complex. The interaction of heredity and environment is extensive.

Key Terms

Key People

Taking It to the Net

1. Ahmahl, a biochemistry major, is writing a psychology paper on the potential dilemmas that society and scientists may face as a result of the decoding of the human genome. What are some of the main issues or concerns that Ahmahl should address in his class paper?

2. Brandon and Katie are thrilled to learn that they are expecting their first child. They are curious about the genetic make-up of their unborn child and want to know (a) what disorders might be identified through prenatal genetic testing, and

(b) which tests, if any, Katie should undergo to help determine this information?

3. Greg and Courtney have three boys. They would love to have a girl. Courtney read that there is a clinic in Virginia where you can pick the sex of your child. How successful are such efforts? Would you want to have this choice available to you?

Connect to www.mhhe.com/santrockld9 to research the answers and complete these exercises.

E-Learning Tools

To help you master the material in this chapter, you'll find a number of valuable study tools on the Student CD-ROM that accompanies this book. In addition, visit the Online Learning Center for *Life-Span Development,* ninth edition, where you'll find these valuable resources for chapter 3, "Biological Beginnings."

• Learn more about how genetic screening is done by reviewing the sample assessment, Prenatal Genetic Screening

Questionnaire. Then try your hand at developing a family health tree by completing the self-assessment, *My Family Health Tree.*

• View video clips of key researchers, including David Buss as he discusses the importance of evolutionary psychology.

• Build your decision-making skills by trying your hand at the parenting and education "Scenarios."

There was a star danced,
and under that I was born.

—WILLIAM SHAKESPEARE
English Playwright, 17th Century

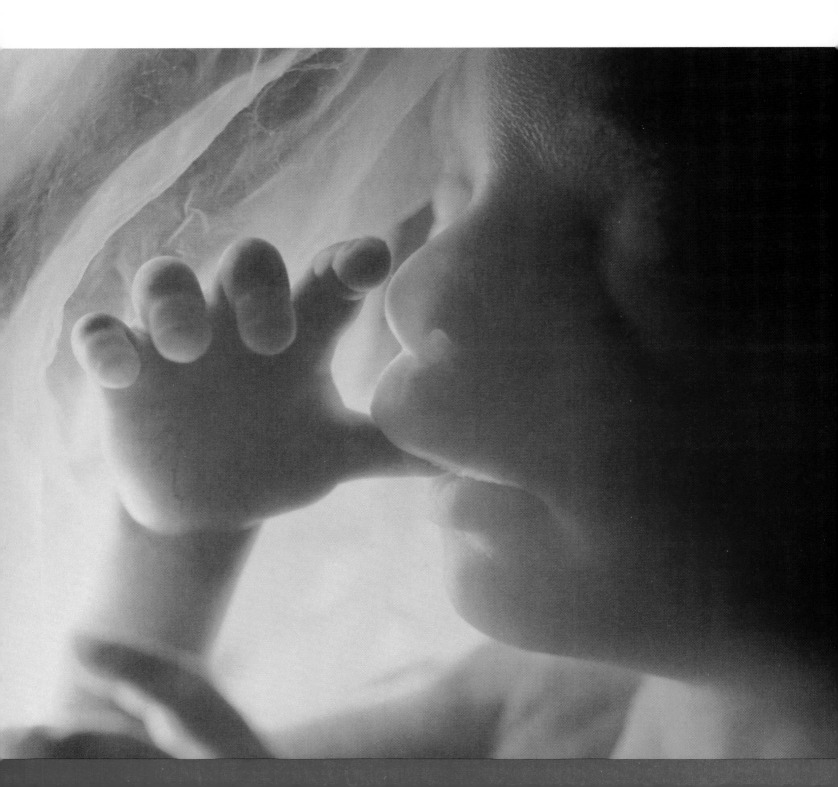

Prenatal Development and Birth

Images of Life-Span Development
Tanner Roberts' Birth: A Fantastic Voyage

Tanner Roberts was born in a suite at St. Joseph's Medical Center in Burbank, California (Warrick, 1992). Let's examine what took place in the hours leading up to his birth. It is day 266 of his mother Cindy's pregnancy. She is in the frozen-food aisle of a convenience store and feels a sharp pain, starting in the small of her back and reaching around her middle, which causes her to gasp. For weeks, painless Braxton Hicks spasms (named for the gynecologist who discovered them) have been flexing her uterine muscles. But these practice contractions were not nearly as intense and painful as the one she just experienced. After six hours of irregular spasms, her uterus settles into a more predictable rhythm.

At 3 A.M., Cindy and her husband, Tom, are wide awake. They time Cindy's contractions with a stopwatch. The contractions are now only six minutes apart. It's time to call the hospital. At the hospital, Cindy goes to a labor-delivery suite. The nurse puts a webbed belt and fetal monitor around Cindy's middle to measure the labor. The monitor picks up the fetal heart rate. With each contraction of the uterine wall, Tanner's heartbeat jumps from its resting state of about 140 beats to 160 to 170 beats per minute. When the cervix is dilated to more than 4 centimeters, or almost half open, Cindy is given her first medication. As Demerol begins to drip in her veins, she becomes more relaxed. Tanner's heart rate dips to 130 and then 120.

Contractions are now coming every three to four minutes, each one lasting about 25 seconds. The Demerol does not completely obliterate Cindy's pain. She hugs her husband as the nurse urges her to "relax those muscles. Breathe deep. Relax. You are almost done."

Each contraction briefly cuts off Tanner's source of oxygen. However, the minutes of rest between each contraction resupply the oxygen and Cindy's deep breathing helps rush fresh blood to the fetal heart and brain.

At 8 A.M., Cindy's obstetrician arrives and determines that her cervix is almost completely dilated. Using a tool made for the purpose, he reaches into the birth canal and tears the membranes of the amnio sac, and about half a liter of clear fluid flows out. Contractions are now coming every two minutes, and each one is lasting a full minute.

By 9 A.M., the labor suite has been transformed into a delivery room. Tanner's body is compressed by his mother's contractions and pushes. As he nears his entrance into the world, the compressions help press the fluid from his lungs in preparation for his first breath.

Squeezed tightly in the birth canal, the top of Tanner's head emerges. His face is puffy and scrunched. Although fiercely squinting because of the sudden light, Tanner's eyes are open. Tiny bubbles of clear mucus are on his lips. Before any more of his body emerges, the obstetrician cradles Tanner's head and suctions his nose and mouth. Tanner takes his first breath, a large gasp followed by whimpering, and then a loud cry. Tanner's body is wet but only slightly bloody as the doctor lifts him onto his mother's abdomen. The umbilical cord, still connecting Tanner with his mother, slows and stops pulsating. The obstetrician cuts it, severing Tanner's connection to his mother's womb. Now Tanner's blood flows not to his mother's blood for nourishment, but to his own lungs, intestines, and other organs. This chapter chronicles the truly remarkable developments from conception through birth. Imagine . . . at one time you were an organism floating in a sea of fluid in your mother's womb. Let's now explore what your development was like from the time you were conceived through the time you were born.

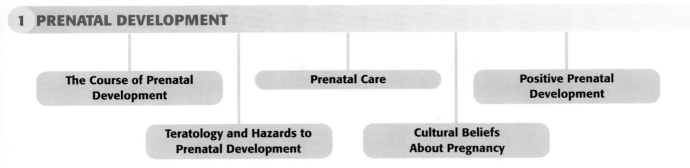

1 PRENATAL DEVELOPMENT

- The Course of Prenatal Development
- Teratology and Hazards to Prenatal Development
- Prenatal Care
- Cultural Beliefs About Pregnancy
- Positive Prenatal Development

Imagine how Tanner Roberts came to be. Out of thousands of eggs and millions of sperm, one egg and one sperm united to produce him. Had the union of sperm and egg come a day or even an hour earlier or later, he might have been very different—maybe even of the opposite sex. Conception occurs when a single sperm cell from the male unites with an ovum (egg) in the female's fallopian tube in a process called fertilization. Remember from chapter 3 that the fertilized egg is called a zygote.

The Course of Prenatal Development

The course of prenatal development lasts approximately 266 days, beginning with fertilization and ending with birth. Prenatal development is divided into three periods: germinal, embryonic, and fetal.

The Germinal Period   The **germinal period** is the period of prenatal development that takes place in the first two weeks after conception. It includes the creation of the zygote, continued cell division, and the attachment of the zygote to the uterine wall. By approximately one week after conception, the differentiation of cells has already commenced, as inner and outer layers of the organism are formed. The **blastocyst** is the inner layer of cells that develops during the germinal period. These cells later develop into the embryo. The **trophoblast** is the outer layer of cells that develops during the germinal period. It later provides nutrition and support for the embryo. *Implantation*, the attachment of the zygote to the uterine wall, takes place about 10 to 14 days after conception. Figure 4.1 on page 114 illustrates some of the most significant developments during the germinal period.

The Embryonic Period   The **embryonic period** is the period of prenatal development that occurs from two to eight weeks after conception. During the embryonic period, the rate of cell differentiation intensifies, support systems for cells form, and organs appear. As the zygote attaches to the uterine wall, the name of the mass of cells changes from *zygote* to *embryo* and three layers of cells are formed. The embryo's *endoderm* is the inner layer of cells, which will develop into the digestive and respiratory systems. The outer layer of cells is divided into two parts. The *ectoderm* is the outermost layer, which will become the nervous system, sensory receptors (ears, nose, and eyes, for example), and skin parts (hair and nails, for example). The *mesoderm* is the middle layer, which will become the circulatory system, bones, muscles, excretory system, and reproductive system. Every body part eventually develops from these three layers. The endoderm primarily produces internal body parts, the mesoderm primarily produces parts that surround the internal areas, and the ectoderm primarily produces surface parts.

As the embryo's three layers form, life-support systems for the embryo mature and develop rapidly. These life-support systems include the placenta, the umbilical cord, and the amnion. The **placenta** is a life-support system that consists of a disk-shaped group of tissues in which small blood vessels from the mother and the

germinal period The period of prenatal development that takes place in the first two weeks after conception. It includes the creation of the zygote, continued cell division, and the attachment of the zygote to the uterine wall.

blastocyst The inner layer of cells that develops during the germinal period. These cells later develop into the embryo.

trophoblast The outer layer of cells that develops in the germinal period. These cells provide nutrition and support for the embryo.

embryonic period The period of prenatal development that occurs two to eight weeks after conception. During the embryonic period, the rate of cell differentiation intensifies, support systems for the cells form, and organs appear.

placenta A life-support system that consists of a disk-shaped group of tissues in which small blood vessels from the mother and offspring intertwine.

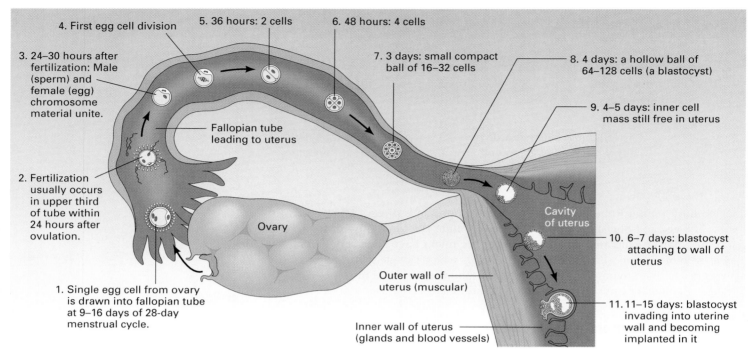

FIGURE 4.1 Significant Developments in the Germinal Period

mhhe●com/
santrockld9

The Visible Embryo
The Trimesters

umbilical cord A life-support system containing two arteries and one vein that connects the baby to the placenta.

amnion The life-support system that is a bag or envelope that contains a clear fluid in which the developing embryo floats.

organogenesis Organ formation that takes place during the first two months of prenatal development.

offspring intertwine but do not join. The **umbilical cord** is a life-support system, containing two arteries and one vein, that connects the baby to the placenta. Very small molecules—oxygen, water, salt, food from the mother's blood, as well as carbon dioxide and digestive wastes from the embryo's blood—pass back and forth between the mother and infant. Large molecules cannot pass through the placental wall; these include red blood cells and harmful substances, such as most bacteria, maternal wastes, and hormones. The mechanisms that govern the transfer of substances across the placental barrier are complex and are still not entirely understood (Gielchinsky & others, 2002; Weeks & Mirembe, 2002). Figure 4.2 provides an illustration of the placenta, the umbilical cord, and the nature of blood flow in the expectant mother and developing child in the uterus. The **amnion,** a bag or an envelope that contains a clear fluid in which the developing embryo floats, is another important life-support system. Like the placenta and umbilical cord, the amnion develops from the fertilized egg, not from the mother's own body. At approximately 16 weeks, the kidneys of the fetus begin to produce urine. This fetal urine remains the main source of the amniotic fluid until the third trimester, when some of the fluid is excreted from the lungs of the growing fetus. Although the amniotic fluid increases in volume tenfold from the 12th to the 40th week of pregnancy, it is also removed in various ways. Some is swallowed by the fetus, and some is absorbed through the umbilical cord and the membranes covering the placenta. The amniotic fluid provides an environment that is temperature and humidity controlled, as well as shockproof.

Before most women even know they are pregnant, some important embryonic developments take place. In the third week, the neural tube that eventually becomes the spinal cord forms. At about 21 days, eyes begin to appear, and at 24 days the cells for the heart begin to differentiate. During the fourth week, the urogenital system becomes apparent, and arm and leg buds emerge. Four chambers of the heart take shape, and blood vessels appear. From the fifth to the eighth week, arms and legs differentiate further; at this time, the face starts to form but still is not very recognizable. The intestinal tract develops and the facial structures fuse. At eight weeks, the developing organism weighs about 1/30 ounce and is just over 1 inch long. **Organogenesis** is the process of

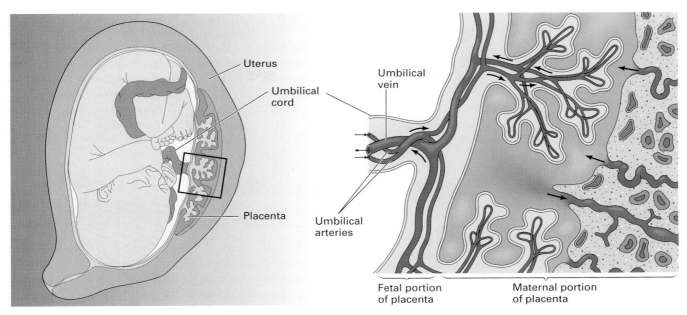

FIGURE 4.2 The Placenta and the Umbilical Cord

Maternal blood flows through the uterine arteries to the spaces housing the placenta, and it returns through the uterine veins to the maternal circulation. Fetal blood flows through the umbilical arteries into the capillaries of the placenta and returns through the umbilical veins to the fetal circulation. The exchange of materials takes place across the layer separating the maternal and fetal blood supplies, so the bloods never come into contact. *Note:* The area bound by the square is enlarged in the right half of the illustration. Arrows indicate the direction of blood flow.

organ formation that takes place during the first two months of prenatal development. When organs are being formed, they are especially vulnerable to environmental changes. Later in the chapter, we will describe the environmental hazards that can adversely affect organogenesis.

The Fetal Period The **fetal period** is the prenatal period of development that begins two months after conception and lasts for seven months, on the average. Growth and development continue their dramatic course during this time. Three months after conception, the fetus is about 3 inches long and weighs about 1 ounce. It has become active, moving its arms and legs, opening and closing its mouth, and moving its head. The face, forehead, eyelids, nose, and chin are distinguishable, as are the upper arms, lower arms, hands, and lower limbs. The genitals can be identified as male or female. By the end of the fourth month, the fetus has grown to 6 inches in length and weighs 4 to 7 ounces. At this time, a growth spurt occurs in the body's lower parts. Prenatal reflexes are stronger; arm and leg movements can be felt for the first time by the mother.

By the end of the fifth month, the fetus is about 12 inches long and weighs close to a pound. Structures of the skin have formed—toenails and fingernails, for example. The fetus is more active, showing a preference for a particular position in the womb. By the end of the sixth month, the fetus is about 14 inches long and has gained another half pound to a pound. The eyes and eyelids are completely formed, and a fine layer of hair covers the head. A grasping reflex is present and irregular breathing movements occur. By the end of the seventh month, the fetus is about 16 inches long, and having gained another pound, now weighs about 3 pounds. During the eighth and ninth months, the fetus grows longer and gains substantial weight—about another 4 pounds. At birth, the average American baby weighs 7½ pounds and is about 20 inches long. In these last two months, fatty tissues develop, and the functioning of various organ systems—heart and kidneys, for example—steps up.

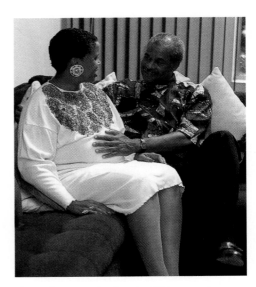

Lines of communication should be open between the expectant mother and her partner during pregnancy. *What are some examples of good partner communication during pregnancy?*

fetal period The prenatal period of development that begins two months after conception and lasts for seven months, on the average.

We have described a number of changes in prenatal development in terms of germinal, embryonic, and fetal periods. Another way to divide prenatal development is in terms of equal periods of three months, called trimesters. An overview of some of the main changes in prenatal development in the three trimesters is presented in figure 4.3. Remember that the three trimesters are not the same as the three prenatal periods we have discussed—germinal, embryonic, and fetal. The germinal and embryonic periods occur in the first trimester. The fetal period begins toward the end of the first trimester and continues through the second and third trimesters. An important point that needs to be made is that the first time a fetus has a chance of surviving

First trimester (first 3 months)

Prenatal growth	Conception to 4 weeks	8 weeks	12 weeks	
	• Is less than ¹⁄₁₀ inch long	• Is less than 1 inch long	• Is about 3 inches long and weighs about 1 ounce	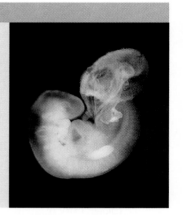
	• Beginning development of spinal cord, nervous system, gastro-intestinal system, heart, and lungs	• Face is forming with rudimentary eyes, ears, mouth, and tooth buds	• Can move arms, legs, fingers, and toes	
	• Amniotic sac envelopes the preliminary tissues of entire body	• Arms and legs are moving	• Fingerprints are present	
		• Brain is forming	• Can smile, frown, suck, and swallow	
	• Is called a "zygote"	• Fetal heartbeat is detectable with ultrasound	• Sex is distinguishable	
		• Is called an "embryo"	• Can urinate	
			• Is called a "fetus"	

Second trimester (middle 3 months)

Prenatal growth	16 weeks	20 weeks	24 weeks	
	• Is about 5¹⁄₂ inches long and weighs about 4 ounces	• Is 10 to 12 inches long and weighs ¹⁄₂ to 1 pound	• Is 11 to 14 inches long and weighs 1 to 1¹⁄₂ pounds	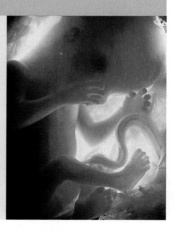
	• Heartbeat is strong	• Heartbeat is audible with ordinary stethoscope	• Skin is wrinkled and covered with protective coating (vernix caseosa)	
	• Skin is thin, transparent	• Sucks thumb	• Eyes are open	
	• Downy hair (lanugo) covers body	• Hiccups	• Waste matter is collected in bowel	
	• Fingernails and toenails are forming	• Hair, eyelashes, eyebrows are present	• Has strong grip	
	• Has coordinated movements; is able to roll over in amniotic fluid			

Third trimester (last 3 months)

Prenatal growth	28 weeks	32 weeks	36 to 38 weeks	
	• Is 14 to 17 inches long and weighs 2¹⁄₂ to 3 pounds	• Is 16¹⁄₂ to 18 inches long and weighs 4 to 5 pounds	• Is 19 inches long and weighs 6 pounds	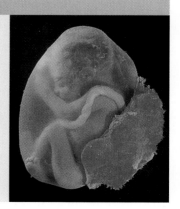
	• Is adding body fat	• Has periods of sleep and wakefulness	• Skin is less wrinkled	
	• Is very active	• Responds to sounds	• Vernix caseosa is thick	
	• Rudimentary breathing movements are present	• May assume the birth position	• Lanugo is mostly gone	
		• Bones of head are soft and flexible	• Is less active	
		• Iron is being stored in liver	• Is gaining immunities from mother	

FIGURE 4.3 The Three Trimesters of Prenatal Development

outside of the womb is the beginning of the third trimester (at about seven months). Even when infants are born in the seventh month, they usually need assistance in breathing.

Teratology and Hazards to Prenatal Development

Some expectant mothers carefully tiptoe about in the belief that everything they do and feel has a direct effect on their unborn child. Others behave casually, assuming that their experiences will have little effect. The truth lies somewhere between these two extremes. Although living in a protected, comfortable environment, the fetus is not totally immune to the larger world surrounding the mother. The environment can affect the child in many well-documented ways. Thousands of babies born deformed or mentally retarded every year are the result of events that occurred in the mother's life, as early as one or two months before conception (Bailey, Forget, & Koren, 2002).

A **teratogen** (the word comes from the Greek word *tera* meaning "monster") is any agent that causes a birth defect. The field of study that investigates the causes of birth defects is called *teratology*. Teratogens include drugs, incompatible blood types, environmental pollutants, infectious diseases, nutritional deficiencies, maternal stress, and advanced maternal and paternal age. So many teratogens exist that practically every fetus is exposed to at least some teratogens. For this reason, it is difficult to determine which teratogen causes which birth defect. In addition, it may take a long time for the effects of a teratogen to show up. Only about half of all potential effects appear at birth.

The dose, the time of exposure to a particular agent, and genetic susceptibility influence the severity of the damage to an unborn child and the type of defect that occurs:

- *Dose* The dose effect is rather obvious—the greater the dose of an agent, such as a drug, the greater the effect.
- *Time of Exposure* Teratogens do more damage when they occur at some points in development rather than at others (Brent & Fawcett, 2000). In general, the embryonic period is a more vulnerable time than the fetal period. As figure 4.4 on page 118 shows, sensitivity to teratogens begins about three weeks after conception. The probability of a structural defect is greatest early in the embryonic period, when organs are being formed. After organogenesis is complete, teratogens are less likely to cause anatomical defects. Exposure later, during the fetal period, is more likely to stunt growth or to create problems in the way organs function. The precision of organogenesis is evident; teratologists point out that the vulnerability of the eyes is greatest at 24 to 40 days, the heart at 20 to 40 days, and the legs at 24 to 36 days.

  In chapter 2, we introduced the concept of *critical period* in our discussion of Lorenz' ethological theory. Recall that a critical period is a fixed time period very early in development during which certain experiences or events can have a long-lasting effect on development. As shown in figure 4.4, each body structure has its own critical period of formation. Thus, the critical period for the central nervous system (week 3) is earlier than for arms and legs (weeks 4 and 5).
- *Genetic Susceptibility* The type or severity of abnormalities caused by a teratogen is linked to the genotype of the pregnant woman and the genotype of the fetus. For example, variation in maternal metabolism of a particular drug can influence the degree to which the drug effects are transmitted to the fetus. Differences in placental membranes and placental transport also affect fetal exposure. The genetic susceptibility of the fetus to a particular teratogen can also affect the extent to which the fetus is vulnerable.

Prescription and Nonprescription Drugs Some pregnant women take prescription and nonprescription drugs without thinking about the possible effects on the fetus (Addis, Magrini & Mastroiacovo, 2001). Occasionally, a rash of deformed babies

*T*he history of man for nine months preceding his birth would, probably, be far more interesting, and contain events of greater moment than all three score and ten years that follow it.

—SAMUEL TAYLOR COLERIDGE
English Poet, Essayist, 19th Century

mhhe com/
santrockld9

Health and Prenatal Development
Exploring Teratology
High-Risk Situations

teratogen From the Greek word *tera,* meaning "monster." Any agent that causes a birth defect. The field of study that investigates the causes of birth defects is called teratology.

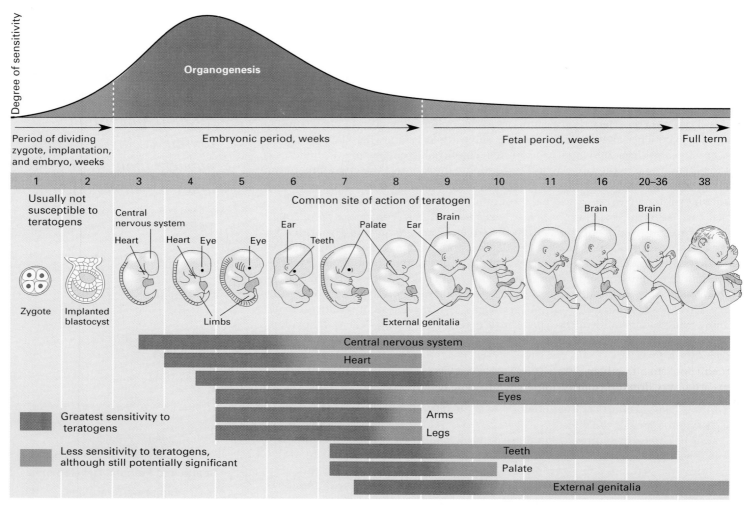

FIGURE 4.4 Teratogens and the Timing of Their Effects on Prenatal Development
The danger of structural defects caused by teratogens is greatest early in embryonic development. The period of organogenesis (red color) lasts for about six weeks. Later assaults by teratogens (blue-green color) mainly occur in the fetal period and instead of causing structural damage are more likely to stunt growth or cause problems of organ function.

is born, bringing to light the damage drugs can have on a developing fetus. This happened in 1961, when many pregnant women took a popular tranquilizer, thalidomide, to alleviate their morning sickness. In adults, the effects of thalidomide are mild; in embryos, however, they are devastating. Not all infants were affected in the same way. If the mother took thalidomide on day 26 (probably before she knew she was pregnant), an arm might not grow. If she took the drug two days later, the arm might not grow past the elbow. The thalidomide tragedy shocked the medical community and parents into the stark realization that the mother does not have to be a chronic drug user for the fetus to be harmed. Taking the wrong drug at the wrong time is enough to physically handicap the offspring for life (Sorokin, 2002).

Prescription drugs that can function as teratogens include antibiotics, such as streptomycin and tetracycline; some depressants; certain hormones, such as progestin and synthetic estrogen; and Accutane (which often is prescribed for acne) (Committee on Drugs, 2000).

Nonprescription drugs that can be harmful include diet pills, aspirin, and caffeine (Cnattingius & others, 2000). Let's explore the research on caffeine. A review of studies on caffeine consumption during pregnancy concluded that a small increase in the risks for spontaneous abortion and low birthweight occurs for pregnant women consuming more than 150 milligrams of caffeine (approximately two cups of brewed coffee or two to three 12-ounce cans of cola) per day (Fernandez & others, 1998). In one study, pregnant women who drank caffeinated coffee were more likely have preterm deliveries and newborns with a lower birthweight than their counterparts who did not drink caffeinated coffee (Eskenazi & others, 1999). In this study, no effects were found for pregnant women who drank decaffeinated coffee. Taking into account such results, the Food and Drug Administration recommends that pregnant women either not consume caffeine or consume it only sparingly.

Psychoactive Drugs   *Psychoactive drugs* are drugs that act on the nervous system to alter states of consciousness, modify perceptions, and change moods. A number of psychoactive drugs, including alcohol and nicotine, as well as illegal drugs such as cocaine, marijuana, and heroin have been studied to determine their links to prenatal and child development (Caulfield, 2001; Fogel, 2001).

Alcohol   Heavy drinking by pregnant women can be devastating to offspring (Barr & Streissguth, 2001; Enoch & Goldman, 2002; Committee on Substance Abuse, 2000). **Fetal alcohol syndrome (FAS)** is a cluster of abnormalities that appears in the offspring of mothers who drink alcohol heavily during pregnancy (Archibald & others, 2001). The abnormalities include facial deformities and defective limbs, face, and heart. Most of these children are below average in intelligence, and some are mentally retarded (Bookstein & others, 2002; Olson, 2000). Although many mothers of FAS infants are heavy drinkers, many mothers who are heavy drinkers do not have children with FAS or have one child with FAS and other children who do not have it. Figure 4.5 shows a child with fetal alcohol syndrome. Although no serious malformations such as those produced by FAS are found in infants born to mothers who are moderate drinkers, in one study, children whose mothers drank moderately (one to two drinks a day) during pregnancy were less attentive and alert, even at 4 years of age (Streissguth & others, 1984). In one study, prenatal alcohol exposure was a better predictor of adolescent alcohol use and its negative consequences than was family history of alcohol problems (Baer & others, 1998). And in another study, adults with fetal alcohol syndrome had a high incidence of mental disorders, such as depression or anxiety (Famy, Streissguth, & Unis, 1998).

Nicotine   Cigarette smoking by pregnant women can also adversely influence prenatal development, birth, and postnatal development. Fetal and neonatal deaths are higher among smoking mothers. There also are higher incidences of preterm births and lower birthweights (Bush & others, 2001; Wang & others, 2000).

In one study, urine samples from 22 of 31 newborns of smoking mothers contained substantial amounts of one of the strongest carcinogens (NNK) in tobacco smoke; the urine samples of the newborns whose mothers did not smoke were free of the carcinogen (Lackmann & others, 1999). In another study, prenatal exposure to cigarette smoking was related to poorer language and cognitive skills at 4 years of age (Fried & Watkinson, 1990). Respiratory problems and sudden infant death syndrome (also known as crib death) are more common among the offspring of mothers who smoked during pregnancy (Schoendorf & Kiely, 1992). Intervention programs designed to help pregnant women stop smoking can reduce some of smoking's negative behaviors, especially by raising birthweights (Klesges & others, 2001; Lightwood, Phibbs, & Glantz, 1999).

Illegal Drugs   Among the illegal drugs that have been studied to determine their effects on prenatal and child development are cocaine, marijuana, and heroin (Fifer & Grose-Fifer, 2001).

FIGURE 4.5 Fetal Alcohol Syndrome
Notice the wide-set eyes, flat bones, and thin upper lip.

mhhe com/
santrockld9

Fetal Alcohol Syndrome
Smoking and Pregnancy

fetal alcohol syndrome (FAS) A cluster of abnormalities that appears in the offspring of mothers who drink alcohol heavily during pregnancy.

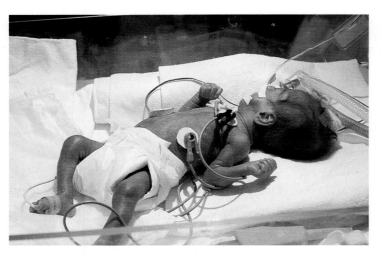

What do we know about the effects of cocaine on children's development?

Cocaine With the increased use of cocaine in the United States, there is concern about its effects on the embryos, fetuses, and infants of pregnant cocaine users (Hand & others, 2001). Cocaine use during pregnancy has recently attracted considerable attention because of possible harm to the developing embryo and fetus (Butz & others, 2001; Smith & others, 2001; Zeskind & others, 1999). The most consistent finding is that cocaine exposure during prenatal development is associated with reduced birthweight, length, and head circumference. Also, in one study, prenatal cocaine exposure was associated with impaired motor development at 2 years of age (Arendt & others, 1999).

Researchers increasingly are finding that fetal cocaine exposure is linked with impaired information processing (Singer, & others, 1999). In one study, prenatal cocaine exposure was moderately related to poor attentional skills through 5 years of age (Bandstra & others, 2000). In another study, prenatal cocaine exposure was related to impaired processing of auditory information after birth (Potter & others, 2000).

Although researchers are finding such deficits in children who are prenatally exposed to cocaine, a cautious interpretation of these findings is in order (Chavkin, 2001; Frank & others, 2001; Potter & others, 2000). Why? Because other factors (such as poverty, malnutrition, and other substance abuse) in the lives of pregnant women who use cocaine often cannot be ruled out as possible contributors to the negative effects on children (Kaugers & others, 2000). For example, cocaine users are more likely than nonusers to smoke cigarettes, use marijuana, drink alcohol, and take amphetamines. Teasing apart these potential influences from the effects of cocaine itself has not yet been adequately accomplished. Obtaining valid information about the frequency and type of drug use by mothers is complicated because many mothers fear prosecution and loss of child custody because of their drug use.

Indeed, there is still controversy about the effects on the offspring of cocaine use by women during pregnancy. One recent review concluded that prenatal exposure to cocaine by itself has not been demonstrated to have negative effects on the offspring (Frank & others, 2001).

Marijuana Marijuana use by pregnant women has detrimental effects on a developing fetus (Fried & Smith, 2001). Marijuana use by pregnant women is associated with increased tremors and startles among newborns and poorer verbal and memory development at 4 years of age (Fried & Watkinson, 1990).

Heroin It is well documented that infants whose mothers are addicted to heroin show several behavioral difficulties (Hulse & others, 2001). The young infants of these mothers are addicted and show withdrawal symptoms characteristic of opiate abstinence, such as tremors, irritability, abnormal crying, disturbed sleep, and impaired motor control. Behavioral problems are still often present at the first birthday, and attention deficits may appear later in the child's development. The most common treatment for heroin addiction, methadone, is associated with very severe withdrawal symptoms in newborns.

Incompatible Blood Types The incompatibility of the mother's and father's blood types is another risk to prenatal development. Variations in the surface structure of red blood cells distinguish different blood types. One type of surface marker borne by red blood cells identifies a person's blood group as A, B, O, or AB. The second type, called the *Rh factor,* is said to be positive if the Rh marker is present or negative if the individual's red blood cells do not carry this marker. If a pregnant woman is Rh negative and her partner is Rh positive, the fetus may be Rh positive (Weiss, 2001). When the fetus' blood is Rh positive and the mother's is Rh negative, the mother's immune system may produce antibodies that will attack the fetus. This can result in any number of problems, including miscarriage or stillbirth, anemia, jaundice, heart defects, brain damage, or death soon after birth (Narang & Jain, 2001).

Generally, the first Rh-positive baby of an Rh-negative mother is not at risk, but with each subsequent pregnancy the risk becomes greater. A vaccine (RhoGAM) may be given to the mother within three days of the child's birth to prevent her body from making antibodies that will attack future Rh-positive fetuses. Also, babies affected by Rh incompatibility can be given blood transfusions before or right after birth (Mannessier & others, 2000).

Environmental Hazards   Radiation, chemicals, and other hazards in our modern industrial world can endanger the fetus (Grigorenko, 2001; Ostrea, Whitehall, & Laken, 2000; Timins, 2001). For instance, radiation can cause a gene mutation (an abrupt, permanent change in genetic material). Chromosomal abnormalities are higher among the offspring of fathers exposed to high levels of radiation in their occupations (Schrag & Dixon, 1985). Radiation from X-rays also can affect the developing embryo and fetus, especially in the first several weeks after conception, when women do not yet know they are pregnant (Barnett & Maulik, 2001). It is important for women and their physicians to weigh the risk of an X-ray when an actual or potential pregnancy is involved (Shaw, 2001).

Environmental pollutants and toxic wastes are also sources of danger to unborn children. Researchers have found that various hazardous wastes and pesticides cause defects in animals exposed to high doses. Among the dangerous pollutants and wastes are carbon monoxide, mercury, and lead. Some children are exposed to lead because they live in houses in which lead-based paint flakes off the walls or near busy highways, where there are heavy automobile emissions from leaded gasoline. Researchers believe that early exposure to lead affects children's mental development (Markowitz, 2000). For example, in one study, 2-year-olds who prenatally had high levels of lead in their umbilical-cord blood performed poorly on a test of mental development (Bellinger & others, 1987).

Researchers also have found that manufacturing chemicals known as PCBs are harmful to prenatal development. In one study, the extent to which pregnant women ate PCB-polluted fish from Lake Michigan was examined, and subsequently their newborns were observed (Jacobson & others, 1984). The women who had eaten more PCB-polluted fish were more likely to have smaller, preterm infants who were more likely to react slowly to stimuli. And, in another study, prenatal exposure to PCBs was associated with problems in visual discrimination and short-term memory in 4-year-old children (Jacobson & others, 1992).

A current environmental concern is the low-level electromagnetic radiation emitted by computer monitors. The fear is that women who spend long hours in front of the monitors might risk adverse effects to their offspring, should they become pregnant. Researchers have not found exposure to computer monitors to be related to miscarriage (Schnorr & others, 1991).

Yet another recent environmental concern for expectant mothers is prolonged exposure to heat produced by saunas or hot tubs. By raising the mother's body temperature, a sauna or a hot tub can cause a fever that endangers the fetus. The high temperature of a fever may interfere with cell division and may cause birth defects or even fetal death if the fever occurs repeatedly for prolonged periods of time. If the expectant mother wants to take a sauna or bathe in a hot tub, prenatal experts recommend that she take her oral temperature while she is exposed to the heat. When the expectant mother's body temperature rises a degree or more, she should get out and cool down. Ten minutes is a reasonable length of time for expectant mothers to spend in a sauna or hot tub, since the body temperature does not usually rise in this length of time. If the expectant mother feels uncomfortably hot in a sauna or hot tub, she should get out, even if she has been there only for a short time.

An explosion at the Chernobyl nuclear power plant in the Ukraine produced radioactive contamination that spread to surrounding areas. Thousands of infants were born with health problems and deformities as a result of the nuclear contamination, including this boy whose arm did not form. *Other than radioactive contamination, what are some other types of environmental hazards to prenatal development?*

Other Maternal Factors   So far we have discussed a number of drugs and environmental hazards that have harmful effects on prenatal and child development. Here we will explore these other potentially harmful maternal factors: infectious diseases, nutrition, emotional states and stress, and age.

Infectious Diseases   Maternal diseases and infections can produce defects in offspring by crossing the placental barrier, or they can cause damage during the birth process itself (Iannucci, 2000). Rubella (German measles) is one disease that can cause prenatal defects. The greatest damage occurs if a mother contracts rubella in the third or fourth week of pregnancy, although infection during the second month is also damaging. A rubella outbreak in 1964–1965 resulted in 30,000 prenatal and neonatal (newborn) deaths, and more than 20,000 affected infants were born with malformations, including mental retardation, blindness, deafness, and heart problems. Elaborate preventive efforts ensure that rubella will never again have such disastrous effects. A vaccine that prevents German measles is now routinely administered to children, and women who plan to have children should have a blood test before they become pregnant to determine if they are immune to the disease (Signore, 2001; Ward, Lambert, & Lester, 2001).

Syphilis (a sexually transmitted disease) is more damaging later in prenatal development—four months or more after conception. Rather than affecting organogenesis, as rubella does, syphilis damages organs after they have formed. Damage includes eye lesions, which can cause blindness, and skin lesions. When syphilis is present at birth, problems can develop in the central nervous system and gastrointestinal tract (Hollier & others, 2001). Most states require that pregnant women be given a blood test to detect the presence of syphilis.

Another infection that has received widespread attention recently is genital herpes. Newborns contract this virus when they are delivered through the birth canal of a mother with genital herpes (Qutub & others, 2001). About one-third of babies delivered through an infected birth canal die; another one-fourth become brain damaged. If an active case of genital herpes is detected in a pregnant woman close to her delivery date, a cesarean section can be performed (in which the infant is delivered through an incision in the mother's abdomen) to keep the virus from infecting the newborn.

AIDS is a sexually transmitted disease that is caused by the human immunodeficiency virus (HIV), which destroys the body's immune system. In the early 1990s, before preventive treatments were available, 1,000 to 2,000 infants were born with HIV infection each year in the United States. Since then, dramatic reductions in the transmission of AIDS from mothers to the fetus/newborn have occurred. Only about one-third as many cases of newborns with AIDS appear today as in the early 1990s. This decline is due to the increase in counseling and voluntary testing of pregnant women for HIV and to the use of zidovudine (AZT) by infected women during pregnancy, and for the infant after birth (Bulterys, 2001; Centers for Disease Control and Prevention, 2000; Committee on Pediatric AIDS, 2000; Rovira & others, 2001).

A mother can infect her offspring with AIDS in three ways: (1) during gestation across the placenta, (2) during delivery through contact with maternal blood or fluids, and (3) postpartum (after birth) through breast-feeding. The transmission of AIDS through breast-feeding is especially a problem in many developing countries (Semba & Neville, 1999).

Babies born to HIV-infected mothers can be (1) infected and symptomatic (show AIDS symptoms), (2) infected but asymptomatic (not show AIDS symptoms), or (3) not infected at all. An infant who is infected and asymptomatic may still develop HIV symptoms up until 15 months of age.

Nutrition   A developing fetus depends completely on its mother for nutrition, which comes from the mother's blood. The nutritional status of the fetus is determined by the mother's total caloric intake, and also by appropriate levels of proteins, vitamins, and minerals. The mother's nutrition even influences her ability to reproduce. In extreme instances of malnutrition, women stop menstruating, thus precluding conception. Children born to malnourished mothers are more likely to be malformed.

Researchers have also found that being overweight before and during pregnancy can be risk factors for the fetus and the child. In two recent studies, obese women had a significant risk of late fetal death, although the risk of preterm delivery was reduced in these women (Cnattingius & others, 1998; Kumari, 2001).

One aspect of maternal nutrition that is important for normal prenatal development is folic acid, a B-complex vitamin (Callender, Rickard, & Rinsky-Eng, 2001). A lack of folic acid is linked with neural tube defects in offspring, such as spina bifida (Honein & others, 2001). The U.S. Public Health Service now recommends that pregnant women consume a minimum of 400 micrograms of folic acid per day (that is about twice the amount the average woman gets in one day). Orange juice and spinach are examples of foods rich in folic acid.

Because the fetus depends entirely on its mother for nutrition, it is important for the pregnant woman to have good nutritional habits. In Kenya, this government clinic provides pregnant women with information about how their diet can influence the health of their fetus and offspring. *What might the information about diet be like?*

Emotional States and Stress   Tales abound about how a pregnant woman's emotional state affects the fetus. For centuries it was thought that frightening experiences—such as a severe thunderstorm or a family member's death—leave birthmarks on the child or affect the child in more serious ways. Today we believe that the mother's stress can be transmitted to the fetus, but we have a better grasp of how this takes place (Monk & others, 2000; Relier, 2001). We now know that when a pregnant woman experiences intense fears, anxieties, and other emotions, physiological changes occur—among them, changes in respiration and glandular secretions. For example, producing adrenaline in response to fear restricts blood flow to the uterine area and can deprive the fetus of adequate oxygen.

The mother's emotional state during pregnancy can influence the birth process too. An emotionally distraught mother might have irregular contractions and a more difficult labor, which can cause irregularities in the baby's oxygen supply or can produce irregularities after birth. Babies born after extended labor also may adjust more slowly to their world and be more irritable.

Maternal anxiety during pregnancy is related to less than optimal outcomes (Brouwers, van Baar, & Pop, 2001). Circumstances that are linked with maternal anxiety during pregnancy include marital discord, death of a husband, and unwanted pregnancy (Field, 1990).

In studies on stress, prenatal development, and birth, Christine Dunkel-Schetter and her colleagues (1998; Dunkel-Schetter & others, 2001) have found that women under stress are about four times as likely to deliver their babies prematurely as are their low-stress counterparts. In another study, maternal stress increased the level of corticotrophin-releasing hormone (CRH) early in pregnancy (Hobel & others, 1999). CRH has been linked with premature delivery. There also is a connection between stress and unhealthy behaviors, such as smoking, drug use, and poor prenatal care (Dunkel-Schetter, 1999). Also, in one recent study, maternal depression was linked with increased fetal activity, possibly as a result of elevated stress hormones in the mother (Dieter & others, 2001). Further, researchers have found that pregnant women who are optimistic thinkers have less-adverse birth outcomes than pregnant women who are pessimistic thinkers (Loebel & Yali, 1999). Optimists believe that they have more control over the outcome of their pregnancy.

Maternal Age   Consideration of possible harmful effects of the mother's age on the fetus and infant focuses on adolescence and the thirties and beyond (Abel, Kruger, &

What are some of the risks for infants born to adolescent mothers?

Burd, 2002). Approximately one of every five births is to an adolescent; in some urban areas, the figure reaches as high as one in every two births. Infants born to adolescents are often premature (Ekwo & Moawad, 2000). In one recent study, low-birthweight delivery increased 11 percent and preterm delivery increased 14 percent for women 35 years and older (Tough & others, 2002). The mortality rate of infants born to adolescent mothers is double that of infants born to mothers in their twenties. Although such figures probably reflect the mothers' immature reproductive system, they also may involve poor nutrition, lack of prenatal care, and low socioeconomic status (Lenders, McElrath, & Scholl, 2000). Prenatal care decreases the probability that a child born to an adolescent girl will have physical problems. However, adolescents are the least likely of women in all age groups to obtain prenatal assistance from clinics, pediatricians, and health services.

Increasingly, women seek to establish their careers before beginning a family, delaying childbearing until their thirties. Down syndrome, a form of mental retardation, is related to the mother's age (Holding, 2002). A baby with Down syndrome rarely is born to a mother under the age of 30, but the risk increases after the mother reaches 30. By age 40, the probability is slightly over 1 in 100, and by age 50 it is almost 1 in 10. The risk also is higher before age 18.

Women also have more difficulty becoming pregnant after the age of 30. One study in a French fertility clinic focused on women whose husbands were sterile (Schwartz & Mayaux, 1982). To make it possible for the women to have a child, women were artificially inseminated once a month for one year. Each woman had 12 chances to become pregnant. Seventy-five percent of the women in their twenties became pregnant, 62 percent of the women 31 to 35 years old became pregnant, and only 54 percent of the women over 35 years old became pregnant.

We still have much to learn about the role of the mother's age in pregnancy and childbirth. As women remain active, exercise regularly, and are careful about their nutrition, their reproductive systems may remain healthier longer than was thought possible in the past.

Paternal Factors So far, we have been considering maternal factors during pregnancy that can influence prenatal development and the development of the child. Might there also be some paternal risk factors? Indeed, there are several. Men's exposure to lead, radiation, certain pesticides, and petrochemicals may cause abnormalities in sperm that lead to miscarriage or diseases, such as childhood cancer (Lindbohm, 1991; Trasler, 2000; Trasler & Doerkson, 2000). When fathers have a diet low in vitamin C, their offspring have a higher risk of birth defects and cancer (Fraga & others, 1991). Also, it has been speculated that, when fathers take cocaine, it may attach itself to sperm and cause birth defects, but the evidence for this is not yet strongly established. In some studies, chronic marijuana use has been shown to reduce testosterone levels and sperm counts, although the results have been inconsistent (Fields, 1998; Nahas, 1984).

The father's smoking during the mother's pregnancy also can cause problems for the offspring. In one investigation, the newborns of fathers who smoked during their wives' pregnancy were 4 ounces lighter at birth for each pack of cigarettes smoked per day than were the newborns whose fathers did not smoke during their wives' pregnancy (Rubin & others, 1986). In another study, in China, the longer the fathers smoked, the stronger the risk was for their children to develop cancer (Ji & others, 1997). In such studies, it is very difficult to tease apart prenatal and postnatal effects.

As is the case with older mothers, older fathers also may place their offspring at risk for certain birth defects. These include Down syndrome (about 5 percent of these children have older fathers), dwarfism, and Marfan syndrome, which involves head and limb deformities.

Early prenatal education classes focus on such topics as changes in the development of the fetus. Later classes focus on preparation for the birth and care of the newborn. *To what extent should fathers, as well as mothers, participate in these classes?*

Prenatal Care

Prenatal care varies enormously, but usually involves a package of medical care services in a defined schedule of visits (McCormick, 2001). In addition to medical care, prenatal care programs often include comprehensive educational, social, and nutritional services (Nichols & Humenick, 2000; Shiono & Behrman, 1995). Women who are pregnant can benefit from the information and advice they receive from health-care personnel, such as Rachel Thompson, an obstetrician/gynecologist whose work is described in the Careers in Life-Span Development insert.

Prenatal care usually includes screening for manageable conditions and/or treatable diseases that can affect the baby or the mother. The education an expectant woman receives about pregnancy, labor and delivery, and caring for the newborn can be extremely valuable, especially for first-time mothers (Cosey & Bechtel, 2001). Prenatal care is also very important for women in poverty because it links them with other social services. The legacy of prenatal care continues after birth, because women who receive this type of care are more likely to seek preventive care for their infants (Bates & others, 1994).

Inadequate prenatal care can occur for a variety of reasons, including the health-care system, provider practices, and individual and social characteristics (Howell, 2001). In one national study, 71 percent of low-income women experienced problems obtaining prenatal care (U.S. General Accounting Office, 1987). Lack of transportation and child care, as well as financial difficulties, were commonly cited as barriers to getting prenatal care. Motivating positive attitudes toward pregnancy is also important. Women who have unplanned or unwanted pregnancies, or who have negative attitudes about being pregnant, are more likely to delay prenatal care or to miss appointments (Joseph, 1989).

Despite the advances made in prenatal care and technology in the United States, the availability of high-quality medical and educational services still needs much improvement. Some countries, especially in Scandinavia and Western Europe, provide more consistent, higher-quality prenatal care than the United States does.

Cultural Beliefs About Pregnancy

A woman's behavior during pregnancy is often determined by cultural beliefs. Certain behaviors are expected if a culture views pregnancy as a medical condition, whereas other behaviors are expected if pregnancy is viewed as a natural occurrence. For example, prenatal care may not be a priority for expectant mothers who view pregnancy as a natural occurrence. Thus, health-care providers need to become aware of the health practices of various cultural groups, including health beliefs about pregnancy and prenatal development. Cultural assessment is an important dimension of providing adequate health care for expectant mothers from various cultural groups. Cultural assessment includes identifying the main beliefs, values, and behaviors related to pregnancy and childbearing. In particular, ethnic background, degree of affiliation with the ethnic group, patterns of decision making, religious preference, language, communication style, and common etiquette practices can significantly affect women's attitudes about the type of medical care needed during pregnancy.

Health-care practices during pregnancy are influenced by numerous factors, including the prevalence of traditional home care remedies and folk beliefs, the importance of indigenous healers, and the influence of professional health-care workers. Many Mexican American mothers are strongly influenced by their mothers and older

Careers in Life-Span Development

Rachel Thompson, Obstetrician/Gynecologist

Rachel Thompson is the senior member of Houston Women's Care Associates, which specializes in health care for women. She has one of Houston's most popular obstetrics/gynecology (OB/GYN) practices ◀‖‖ p. 34. Dr. Thompson's medical degree is from Baylor College of Medicine, where she also completed her internship and residency. Her work focuses on many of the topics we discuss in this chapter on prenatal development, birth, and the postpartum period.

In addition to her clinical practice, Dr. Thompson also is a clinical instructor in the Department of Obstetrics and Gynecology at Baylor College of Medicine. Rachel says that one of the unique features of their health-care group is that the staff is comprised only of women who are full-time practitioners.

Rachel Thompson (*right*), talking with one of her patients at Houston Women's Care Associates.

mhhe ○com/ santrockld9

Reproductive Health Links

Exploring Pregnancy

Childbirth Classes

Prenatal Care

Health-Care Providers

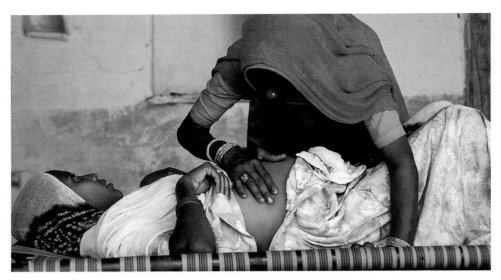

In India, a midwife checks on the size, position, and heartbeat of a fetus. Midwives deliver babies in many cultures around the world. *What are some cultural variations in prenatal care?*

women in their culture, often seeking and following their advice during pregnancy. In Mexican American culture, the indigenous healer is called a *curandero.* In some Native American tribes, the medicine woman or man fulfills the healing role. Herbalists are often found in Asian cultures, and faith healers, root doctors, and spiritualists are sometimes found in African American culture. When health-care providers come into contact with expectant mothers, they need to assess whether such cultural practices pose a threat to the expectant mother and the fetus. If they pose no threat, there is no reason to try to change them. On the other hand, if certain cultural practices do pose a threat to the health of the expectant mother or the fetus, the health-care provider should consider a culturally sensitive way to handle the problem. For example, some Filipinos will not take any medication during pregnancy.

Positive Prenatal Development

Much of our discussion so far in this chapter has focused on what can go wrong with prenatal development. It is important to keep in mind that most of the time, prenatal development does not go awry and development occurs along the positive path that we described at the beginning of the chapter (Lester, 2000). That said, it is still important for prospective mothers and those who are pregnant to avoid the vulnerabilities to fetal development that we have described.

Review and Reflect

1 Describe prenatal development

REVIEW

- What is the course of prenatal development?
- What are some of the main hazards to prenatal development?
- What are some good prenatal care strategies?
- What are some cultural beliefs about pregnancy?
- Why is it important to take a positive approach to prenatal development?

REFLECT

- What can be done to convince women who are pregnant not to smoke or drink? Consider the role of health-care providers, the role of insurance companies, and specific programs targeted at women who are pregnant.

2 BIRTH

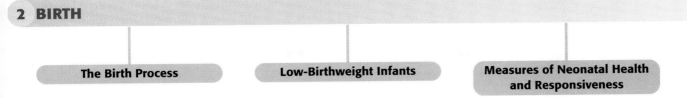

The Birth Process   Low-Birthweight Infants   Measures of Neonatal Health
                                                               and Responsiveness

As we saw in the opening story about Tanner Roberts, many changes take place during the birth of a baby (Verklan, 2002). Let's further explore the birth process.

The Birth Process

Here we will examine the stages of birth, the transition from fetus to newborn, childbirth strategies, low-birthweight infants, and measures of neonatal (newborn) health and responsiveness.

Stages of Birth   Childbirth—or labor—occurs in three stages (see figure 4.6). For a woman having her first child, the first stage lasts an average of 12 to 24 hours; it is the longest of the three stages. In the first stage, uterine contractions are 15 to 20 minutes apart at the beginning and last up to a minute. These contractions cause the woman's cervix, the opening into the birth canal, to stretch and open. As the first stage progresses, the contractions come closer together, appearing every two to five minutes.

mhhe ●com/
santrockld9

Preparing for Birth

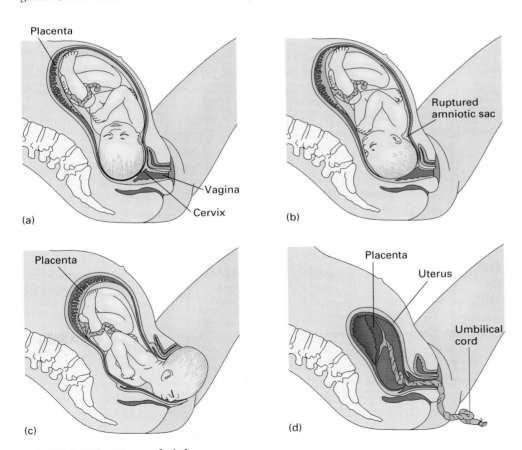

FIGURE 4.6 The Stages of Birth

(*a*) First stage: cervix is dilating; (*b*) late first stage (transition stage): cervix is fully dilated, and the amniotic sac has ruptured, releasing amniotic fluid; (*c*) second stage: birth of the infant; (*d*) third stage: delivery of the placenta (afterbirth).

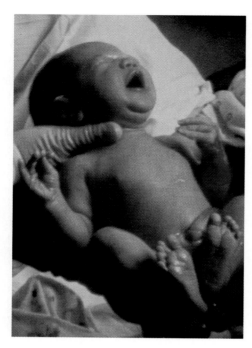

After the long journey of prenatal development, birth takes place. During birth the baby is on a threshold between two worlds. *What is the fetus/newborn transition like?*

W e must respect this instant of birth, this fragile moment. The baby is between two worlds, on a threshold, hesitating...

—FREDERICK LEBOYER
French Obstetrician, 20th Century

Their intensity increases too. By the end of the first birth stage, contractions dilate the cervix to an opening of about 4 inches, so that the baby can move from the uterus to the birth canal.

The second birth stage begins when the baby's head starts to move through the cervix and the birth canal. It terminates when the baby completely emerges from the mother's body. For a first birth, this stage lasts approximately 1½ hours. With each contraction, the mother bears down hard to push the baby out of her body. By the time the baby's head is out of the mother's body, the contractions come almost every minute and last for about a minute.

Afterbirth is the third stage, at which time the placenta, umbilical cord, and other membranes are detached and expelled. This final stage is the shortest of the three birth stages, lasting only minutes.

The Transition from Fetus to Newborn   Being born involves considerable stress for the baby. During each contraction, when the placenta and umbilical cord are compressed as the uterine muscles draw together, the supply of oxygen to the fetus is decreased. If the delivery takes too long, anoxia can develop (Mohan, Golding, & Paterson, 2001). *Anoxia* is the condition in which the fetus/newborn has an insufficient supply of oxygen. Anoxia can cause brain damage.

The baby has considerable capacity to withstand the stress of birth. Large quantities of adrenaline and noradrenalin, hormones that protect the fetus in the event of oxygen deficiency, are secreted in stressful circumstances. These hormones increase the heart's pumping activity, speed up heart rate, channel blood flow to the brain, and raise the blood-sugar level. Never again in life will such large amounts of these hormones be secreted. This circumstance underscores how stressful it is to be born and also how well prepared and adapted the fetus is for birth (Committee on Fetus and Newborn, 2000; Mishell, 2000; Van Beveren, 2002).

As we saw in the case of Tanner Roberts at the beginning of the chapter, the umbilical cord is cut immediately after birth, and the baby is on its own. Now 25 million little air sacs in the lungs must be filled with air. Until now, these air sacs have held fluid, but this fluid is rapidly expelled in blood. The first breaths may be the hardest ones an individual takes. Before birth, oxygen came from the mother via the umbilical cord, but now the baby has to be self-sufficient and breathe on its own.

At the time of birth, the baby is covered with what is called *vernix caseosa,* a protective skin grease. This vernix consists of fatty secretions and dead cells, thought to function in protecting the baby's skin against heat loss before and during birth. After the baby and mother have met and become acquainted with each other, the baby is taken to be cleaned, examined, weighed, and evaluated. Later in the chapter, we will discuss several measures that are used to examine the newborn's health and responsiveness.

Childbirth Strategies   Among the childbirth decisions that need to be made are what the setting will be, who the attendants will be, and which childbirth technique will be used. Here we will discuss the options available to expectant parents.

Childbirth Setting and Attendants   In the United States, 99 percent of births take place in hospitals, and more than 90 percent are attended by physicians (Ventura & others, 1997). Many hospitals now have birthing centers, where fathers or birth coaches may be with the mother during labor and delivery. Some people believe this so-called alternative birthing center offers a good compromise between a technological, depersonalized hospital birth (which cannot offer the emotional experience of a home birth) and a birth at home (which cannot offer the medical backup of a hospital). A birthing room approximates a home setting as much as possible and allows for a full range of birth experiences, from a totally unmedicated, natural birth to the most complex, intensive medical care. Some women with good medical histories and low risk for problem delivery choose a home delivery or a delivery in a freestanding birthing center, which is usually staffed by nurse-midwives (Wong, Perry, & Hockenberry, 2001).

Approximately 6 percent of women who deliver a baby in the United States are attended by a midwife (Ventura & others, 1997). Most midwives are nurses who have been specially trained in delivering babies (Oshio, Johnson, & Fullerton, 2002) p. 35. One study found that the risk of neonatal mortality (an infant death occurring in the first 28 days of life) was 33 percent lower and the risk of a low-birthweight baby was 31 percent lower for births attended by a certified nurse-midwife than for births attended by physicians (MacDorman & Singh, 1998). Compared to physicians, certified nurse-midwives generally spend more time with patients during prenatal visits, place more emphasis on patient counseling and education, provide more emotional support, and are more likely to be with the patient one-on-one during the entire labor and delivery process, which may explain the more positive outcomes for babies delivered by certified nurse-midwives.

In many countries around the world, babies are more likely to be delivered at home than they are in the United States. For example, in Holland, 35 percent of the babies are born at home, and more than 40 percent are delivered by midwives rather than doctors (Treffers & others, 1990).

In many countries, a doula attends a childbearing woman. *Doula* is a Greek word that means "a woman who helps." A **doula** is a caregiver who provides continuous physical, emotional, and educational support for the mother before, during, and after childbirth. Doulas remain with the mother throughout labor, assessing and responding to her needs. In one study, the mothers who received doula support reported less labor pain than the mothers who did not receive doula support (Klaus, Kennell, & Klaus, 1993). Doulas typically function as part of a "birthing team," serving as an adjunct to the midwife or the hospital obstetric staff (McGrath & others, 1999; Pascali-Bonaro, 2002).

In the United States, most doulas work as independent providers hired by the expectant woman. Managed care organizations are increasingly offering doula support as a part of regular obstetric care. In many cultures, the practice of a knowledgeable woman helping a mother in labor is not officially labeled "doula" support but is simply an ingrained, centuries-old custom.

In many cultures, several people attend the mother during labor and delivery. Which persons attend the mother may vary across cultures. In the East African Nigoni culture, men are completely excluded from the childbirth process. In this culture, women even conceal their pregnancy from their husband as long as possible. In the Nigoni culture, when a woman is ready to give birth, female relatives move into the woman's hut and the husband leaves, taking his belongings (clothes, tools, weapons, and so on) with him. He is not permitted to return until after the baby is born.

In some cultures, childbirth is a more open, community affair than in the United States. For example, in the Pukapukan culture in the Pacific Islands, women give birth in a shelter that is open for villagers to observe.

Methods of Delivery   Among the methods of delivery are medicated, natural and prepared, and cesarean. The American Academy of Pediatrics recommends the least possible medication during delivery, although it is up to the mother or attending medical personnel to decide whether drugs are needed (Hotchner, 1997).

There are three basic kinds of drugs that are used for labor: analgesia, anesthesia, and oxytocics. *Analgesia* is used to relieve pain. Analgesics include tranquilizers, barbiturates, and narcotics (such as Demerol). *Anesthesia* is used in late first-stage labor and during expulsion of the baby to block sensation in an area of the body or to block consciousness. There is a trend toward not using general anesthesia, which blocks consciousness, in normal births because it can be transmitted through the placenta to the fetus. However, an epidural anesthesia does not cross the placenta. An *epidural block* is regional anesthesia that numbs the woman's body from the waist down. Even this drug, thought to be relatively safe, has come under recent criticism because it is

A woman in the African !Kung culture giving birth in a sitting position. Notice the help and support being given by another woman. *What are some cultural variations in childbirth?*

mhhe com/ santrockld9

Childbirth Strategies
Childbirth Setting and Attendants
Midwifery
Doula
Fathers and Childbirth
Siblings and Childbirth

doula A caregiver who provides continuous physical, emotional, and educational support for the mother before, during, and after childbirth.

Careers in Life-Span Development

Linda Pugh, Perinatal Nurse

Perinatal nurses work with childbearing women to support health and growth during the childbearing experience ◀▥ p. 35. Linda Pugh, Ph.D., R.N.C., is a perinatal nurse on the faculty at The Johns Hopkins University School of Nursing. She is certified as an inpatient obstetric nurse and specializes in the care of women during labor and delivery. She teaches undergraduate and graduate students, educates professional nurses, and conducts research. In addition, she consults with hospitals and organizations about women's health issues and topics we discuss in this chapter.

Her research interests include nursing interventions with low-income breast-feeding women, discovering ways to prevent and ameliorate fatigue during childbearing, and using breathing exercises during labor.

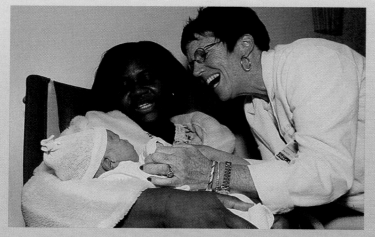

Linda Pugh (*right*), a perinatal nurse, with a mother and her newborn.

natural childbirth Developed in 1914 by Dick-Read, this method attempts to reduce the mother's pain by decreasing her fear through education about childbirth and relaxation techniques during delivery.

prepared childbirth Developed by French obstetrician Ferdinand Lamaze, this childbirth strategy is similar to natural childbirth but includes a special breathing technique to control pushing in the final stages of labor and a more detailed anatomy and physiology course.

associated with fever, extended labor, and increased risk for cesarean delivery (Ransjo-Arvidson & others, 2001). *Oxytocics* are synthetic hormones that are used to stimulate contractions. Pitocin is the most commonly used oxytocic (Carbonne, Tsatsarius, & Goffinet, 2001; Gard & others, 2002).

Predicting how a particular drug will affect an individual pregnant woman and the fetus is difficult. Though we have many commonalities as human beings, we also vary a great deal. Thus, a particular drug might have only a minimal effect on one fetus yet have a much stronger effect on another fetus. The drug's dosage also is a factor. Stronger doses of tranquilizers and narcotics given to decrease the mother's pain have a potentially more negative effect on the fetus than mild doses. It is important for the mother to assess her level of pain and have a voice in the decision of whether she should receive medication or not (Young, 2001).

Though the trend at one time was toward a natural childbirth without any medication, today the emphasis is on using some medication but keeping it to a minimum when possible. The emphasis today also is on broadly educating the pregnant woman so that she can be reassured and confident. The emphasis on education is reflected in the techniques of natural childbirth and prepared childbirth.

Natural childbirth was developed in 1914 by an English obstetrician, Grantley Dick-Read. Its purpose is to reduce the mother's pain by decreasing her fear through education about childbirth and by teaching her to use breathing methods and relaxation techniques during delivery. Dick-Read believed that the doctor's relationship with the mother is an important dimension of reducing her perception of pain. He said the doctor should be present during her active labor prior to delivery and should provide reassurance.

Prepared childbirth was developed by French obstetrician Ferdinand Lamaze. This childbirth strategy is similar to natural childbirth but includes a special breathing technique to control pushing in the final stages of labor, as well as a more detailed anatomy and physiology course. The Lamaze method has become very popular in the United States. The pregnant woman's husband or a friend usually serves as a coach, who attends childbirth classes with her and helps her with her breathing and relaxation during delivery.

Many other prepared childbirth techniques also have been developed (Samuels & Samuels, 1996). They usually include elements of Dick-Read's natural childbirth or Lamaze's method, plus one or more other components. For instance, the Bradley method places special emphasis on the father's role as a labor coach. Virtually all of the prepared childbirth methods emphasize some degree of education, relaxation and breathing exercises, and support. In recent years, new ways of teaching relaxation have been offered, including guided mental imagery, massage, and meditation. In sum, the current belief in prepared childbirth is that, when information and support are provided, women *know* how to give birth. To read about one nurse whose research focuses on discovering ways to prevent and reduce fatigue during childbearing and the use of breathing exercises during labor, see the Careers in Life-Span Development insert.

In a *cesarean delivery,* the baby is removed from the mother's uterus through an incision made in her abdomen. This method also is sometimes known as a cesarean section. A cesarean section is usually performed if the baby is in a **breech position,** which causes the baby's buttocks to be the first part to emerge from the vagina. Normally, the crown of the baby's head comes through the vagina first, but in 1 of every 25 deliveries, the baby's head is still in the uterus when the rest of the body is out. Breech births can cause respiratory problems.

Cesarean deliveries also are performed if the baby is lying crosswise in the uterus, if the baby's head is too large to pass through the mother's pelvis, if the baby develops complications, or if the mother is bleeding vaginally.

The benefits and risks of cesarean sections continue to be debated (Alexander, McIntire, & Leveno, 2001; Green & others, 2001; Peskin & Reine, 2002). Cesarean deliveries are safer than breech deliveries, but they involve a higher infection rate, longer hospital stay, and greater expense and stress that accompany any surgery.

Some critics believe that too many babies are delivered by cesarean section in the United States. More cesarean sections are performed in the United States than in any other country in the world. In the 1980s, births by cesarean section increased almost 50 percent in the United States, with almost one-fourth of babies delivered in this way. In the early 1990s, cesarean births decreased but recently have increased once again (National Center for Health Statistics, 2002).

Low-Birthweight Infants

A **low-birthweight infant** weighs less than 5½ pounds at birth. Two subgroups are those that are very low birthweight (under 3 pounds) and extremely low birthweight (under 2 pounds).

Another way of classifying low-birthweight babies involves whether they are preterm or small for date. **Preterm infants** are those born three weeks or more before the pregnancy has reached its full term. This means that the term "preterm" is given to an infant who is born 35 or less weeks after conception. Most preterm babies are also low-birthweight babies.

A short gestation period does not necessarily harm an infant. It is distinguished from retarded prenatal growth, in which the fetus has been damaged (Kopp, 1992). The neurological development of the preterm baby continues after birth on approximately the same timetable as if the infant were still in the womb. For example, consider a preterm baby born 30 weeks after conception. At 38 weeks, approximately two months after birth, this infant shows the same level of brain development as a 38-week fetus who is yet to be born.

Small for date infants (also called *small for gestational age infants*) are those whose birthweight is below normal when the length of the pregnancy is considered. Small for date infants may be preterm or full term. They weigh less than 90 percent of all babies of the same gestational age. Inadequate nutrition and smoking by pregnant women are among the main factors in producing small for date infants (Chan, Keane, & Robinson, 2001; England & others, 2001).

There has been an increase in low-birthweight infants in the United States in the last two decades (Hall, 2000). The increase is thought to be due to the increasing number of adolescents having babies, drug abuse, and poor nutrition. The incidence of low birthweight varies considerably from country to country (see figure 4.7 on page 132). As shown in figure 4.7, the U.S. low-birthweight rate of 7.6 percent is considerably higher than for many other developed countries (UNICEF, 2001). In the developing world, low birthweight stems mainly from the mother's poor health and nutrition. Diseases such as diarrhea and malaria, which are common in developing countries, can impair fetal growth if the mother becomes infected while she is pregnant. In developed countries, cigarette smoking during pregnancy is the leading cause of low birthweight (UNICEF, 2001). In both developed and developing countries, adolescents who give birth when their bodies have yet to fully mature are at risk for having low-birthweight babies.

Although most low-birthweight infants are normal and healthy, as a group they have more health and developmental problems than normal-birthweight infants

A "kilogram kid," weighing less than 2.3 pounds at birth. *What are some long-term outcomes for weighing so little at birth?*

breech position The baby's position in the uterus that causes the buttocks to be the first part to emerge from the vagina.

low-birthweight infant An infant that weighs less than 5½ pounds at birth.

preterm infants Those born three weeks or more before the pregnancy has reached its full term.

small for date infants Also called small for gestational age infants, these infants' birthweights are below normal when the length of pregnancy is considered. Small for date infants may be preterm or full term.

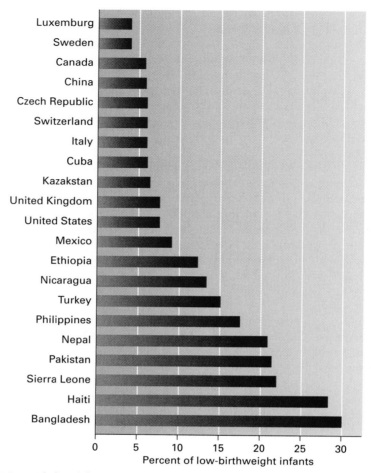

FIGURE 4.7 Low-Birthweight Rates by Country

The graph shows the percentage of children born with low birthweight in a wide range of countries around the world (UNICEF, 2001).

(Hack & others, 2002; Rickards & others, 2001). The number and severity of these problems increase as birthweight decreases (Kilbride, Thorstad, & Daily, 2000). With the improved survival rates for infants who are born very early and very small have come increases in severe brain damage (Yu, 2000). Cerebral palsy and other forms of brain injury are highly correlated with brain weight—the lower the brain weight, the greater the likelihood of brain injury (Watemberg & others, 2002). Approximately 7 percent of moderately low birthweight infants (3 pounds 5 ounces to 5 pounds 8 ounces) have brain injuries. This figure increases to 20 percent for the smallest newborns (1 pound 2 ounces to 3 pounds 5 ounces). Low-birthweight infants are also more likely than normal-birthweight infants to have lung or liver diseases.

At school age, children who were born low-birthweight infants are more likely than their normal-birthweight counterparts to have a learning disability, attention deficit disorder, or breathing problems such as asthma (Taylor, Klein, & Hack, 1994). Very low birthweight children have more learning problems and lower levels of achievement in reading and math than moderately low birthweight children. These problems are reflected in much higher percentages of low-birthweight children being enrolled in special education programs. Approximately 50 percent of all low-birthweight children are enrolled in special education programs.

Not all of these adverse consequences can be attributed solely to low birthweight. Some of the less severe but more common developmental and physical delays occur because many low-birthweight children come from disadvantaged environments (Fang, Madhaven, & Alderman, 1999).

Some of the devastating effects of low birthweight can be reversed (Blair & Ramey, 1996; Shino & Behrman, 1995). Intensive enrichment programs that provide medical and educational services for both the parents and the child have been shown to improve short-term developmental outcomes for low-birthweight children. Federal laws mandate that services for school-age children with a disability (which include medical, educational, psychological, occupational, and physical care) be expanded to include family-based care for infants. At present, these services are aimed at children born with severe congenital disabilities. The availability of services for moderately low birthweight children who do not have severe physical problems varies from state to state, but generally these services are not available.

Tiffany Field's (1998, 2001) research has led to a surge of interest in the role that massage might play in improving the developmental outcomes of low-birthweight infants. In her first study in this area, massage therapy conducted three times per day for 15-minute periods led to 47 percent greater weight gain than standard medical treatment (Field & others, 1986) (see figure 4.8). The massaged infants also were more active and alert, and they performed better on developmental tests. Field and her colleagues have also demonstrated the benefits of massage therapy with women in reducing their labor pain (Field & others, 1997), with cocaine babies (Scafidi & Field, 1996), and with the infants of depressed adolescent mothers (Field & others, 1996)

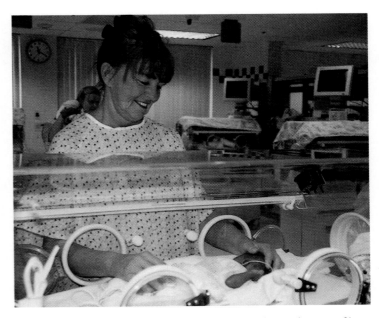

Shown here is Tiffany Field massaging a newborn infant. *What types of infants has massage therapy been shown to help?*

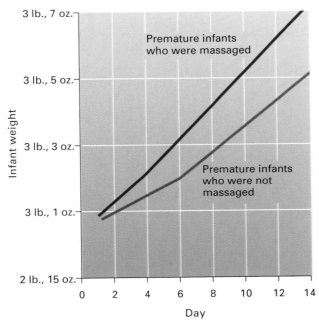

FIGURE 4.8 Weight Gain Comparison of Premature Infants Who Were Massaged or Not Massaged

The graph shows that the mean daily weight gain of premature infants who were massaged was greater than for premature infants who were not massaged.

Score	0	1	2
Heart rate	Absent	Slow—less than 100 beats per minute	Fast—100–140 beats per minute
Respiratory effort	No breathing for more than one minute	Irregular and slow	Good breathing with normal crying
Muscle tone	Limp and flaccid	Weak, inactive, but some flexion of extremities	Strong, active motion
Body color	Blue and pale	Body pink, but extremities blue	Entire body pink
Reflex irritability	No response	Grimace	Coughing, sneezing and crying

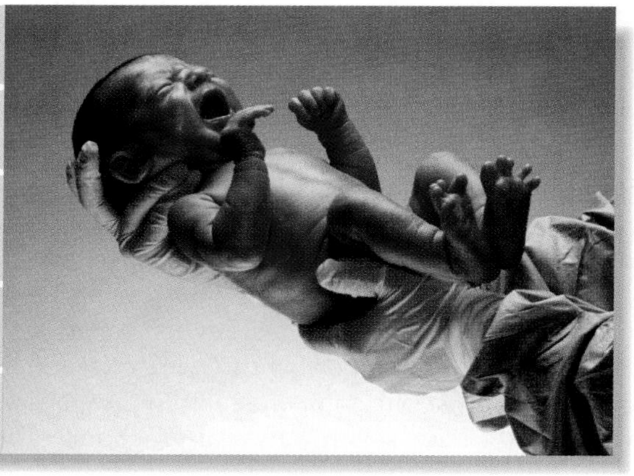

FIGURE 4.9 The Apgar Scale

Measures of Neonatal Health and Responsiveness

Almost immediately after birth, a newborn is weighed, cleaned up, and tested for signs of developmental problems that might require urgent attention. The **Apgar Scale** is widely used to assess the health of newborns at one and five minutes after birth. The Apgar Scale evaluates infants' heart rate, respiratory effort, muscle tone, body color, and reflex irritability. An obstetrician or a nurse does the evaluation and gives the newborn a score, or reading, of 0, 1, or 2 on each of these five health signs (see figure 4.9). A total score of 7 to 10 indicates that the newborn's condition is good. A score of 5 indicates there may be developmental difficulties. A score of 3 or below signals an emergency and indicates that the baby might not survive. The Apgar Scale is especially good at assessing the newborn's ability to respond to the stress of delivery, labor, and the new environment (Casey, McIntire, & Leveno, 2001). The Apgar Scale also identifies high-risk infants who need resuscitation.

To evaluate the newborn more thoroughly, the **Brazelton Neonatal Behavioral Assessment Scale** is performed within 24 to 36 hours after birth. This scale measures the newborn's neurological development, reflexes, and reactions to people. When the Brazelton is given, the newborn is treated as an active participant, and the score attained is based on the newborn's best performance. Sixteen reflexes, such as sneezing, blinking, and rooting, are assessed, along with reactions to circumstances, such as the infant's reaction to a rattle. (We will have more to say about reflexes in the next chapter, when we discuss physical development in infancy.) The examiner rates the newborn on each of 27 categories. As an indication of how detailed the ratings are, consider item 15: "cuddliness." Nine categories are involved in assessing this item, and scoring is done on a continuum that ranges from the infant's being very resistant to being held to the infant's being extremely cuddly and clinging. The Brazelton scale is used not only as a sensitive index of neurological competence in the week after birth, but also as a measure in many research studies on infant development. In scoring the Brazelton scale, T. Berry Brazelton and his colleagues (Brazelton, Nugent, & Lester, 1987) categorize the 27 items into four categories—physiological, motoric, state, and interaction. They also classify the baby in global terms, such as "worrisome," "normal," or "superior," based on these categories (Nugent & Brazelton, 2000).

A very low Brazelton score can indicate brain damage, or it can reflect stress to the brain that may heal in time. However, if an infant merely seems sluggish in responding to social circumstances, parents are encouraged to give the infant attention and become more sensitive to the infant's needs. Parents are shown how the newborn can respond to people and how to stimulate such responses. Researchers have found that the social interaction skills of both high-risk infants and healthy, responsive infants can be improved through such communication with parents (Worobey & Belsky, 1982).

Apgar Scale A widely used method to assess the health of newborns at one and five minutes after birth. The Apgar Scale evaluates infants' heart rate, respiratory effort, muscle tone, body color, and reflex irritability.

Brazelton Neonatal Behavioral Assessment Scale A test given several days after birth to assess newborns' neurological development, reflexes, and reactions to people.

Review and Reflect

2 Discuss the birth process

REVIEW

- What are the three main stages of birth? What is the transition from fetus to newborn like for the infant? What are some different birth strategies?
- What are the outcomes for children if they are born preterm or with a low birthweight?
- What are two measures of neonatal health and responsiveness?

REFLECT

- If you are a female, which birth strategy do you prefer? Why? If you are a male, how involved would you want to be in helping your partner through pregnancy and the birth of your baby?

3 THE POSTPARTUM PERIOD

What Is the Postpartum Period?   **Emotional and Psychological Adjustments**

Physical Adjustments   **Bonding**

The weeks immediately following childbirth present a number of challenges for new parents and their offspring. Many health professionals believe that the best way to meet these challenges is with a family-centered approach that uses the family's resources to support an early and smooth adjustment to the newborn by all family members.

What Is the Postpartum Period?

The **postpartum period** is the period after childbirth or delivery. It is a time when the woman adjusts, both physically and psychologically, to the process of childbearing. It lasts for about six weeks or until the body has completed its adjustment and has returned to a nearly prepregnant state. Some health professionals refer to the postpartum period as the "fourth trimester." Though the time span of the postpartum period does not necessarily cover three months, the term of "fourth trimester" suggests continuity and the importance of the first several months after birth for the mother.

The postpartum period is influenced by what preceded it. During pregnancy, the woman's body gradually adjusted to physical changes, but now it is forced to respond quickly. The method of delivery and circumstances surrounding the delivery affect the speed with which the woman's body readjusts during the postpartum period.

The postpartum period involves a great deal of adjustment and adaptation (Plackslin, 2000). The baby has to be cared for; the mother has to recover from childbirth; the mother has to learn how to take care of the baby; the mother needs to learn to feel good about herself as a mother; the father needs to learn how to take care of his recovering wife; the father needs to learn how to take care of the baby; and the father needs to learn how to feel good about himself as a father.

postpartum period The period after childbirth when the mother adjusts, both physically and psychologically, to the process of childbirth. This period lasts for about six weeks or until her body has completed its adjustment and returned to a near prepregnant state.

Physical Adjustments

A woman's body makes numerous physical adjustments in the first days and weeks after childbirth. She may have a great deal of energy or feel exhausted and let down. Most new mothers feel tired and need rest. Though these changes are normal, the fatigue can undermine the new mother's sense of well-being and confidence in her ability to cope with a new baby and a new family life.

Involution is the process by which the uterus returns to its prepregnant size five or six weeks after birth. Immediately following birth, the uterus weighs 2 to 3 pounds. By the end of five or six weeks, the uterus weighs 2 to $3\frac{1}{2}$ ounces. Nursing the baby helps contract the uterus at a rapid rate.

After delivery, a woman's body undergoes sudden and dramatic changes in hormone production. When the placenta is delivered, estrogen and progesterone levels drop steeply and remain low until the ovaries start producing hormones again. The woman will probably begin menstruating again in four to eight weeks if she is not breast-feeding. If she is breast-feeding, she might not menstruate for several months to a year or more, though ovulation can occur during this time. The first several menstrual periods following delivery might be heavier than usual, but periods soon return to normal.

Some women and men want to resume sexual intercourse as soon as possible after the birth. Others feel constrained or afraid. A sore perineum (the area between

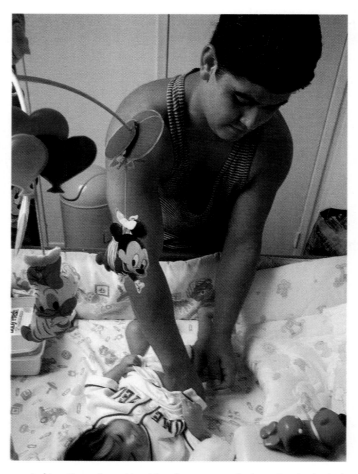

The postpartum period is a time of considerable adjustment and adaptation for both the mother and the father. Fathers can provide an important support system for mothers, especially in helping mothers care for young infants. *As part of supporting the mother, what kinds of tasks might the father of a newborn do?*

the anus and vagina in the female), a demanding baby, lack of help, and extreme fatigue affect a woman's ability to relax and to enjoy making love. Physicians often recommend that women refrain from having sexual intercourse for approximately six weeks following the birth of the baby.

If the woman regularly engaged in conditioning exercises during pregnancy, exercise will help her recover her former body contour and strength during the postpartum period. With a caregiver's approval, the new mother can begin some exercises as soon as one hour after delivery. In addition to recommending exercise in the postpartum period for women, health professionals also increasingly recommend that women practice the relaxation techniques they used during pregnancy and childbirth. Five minutes of slow breathing on a stressful day in the postpartum period can relax and refresh the new mother, as well as the new baby.

Emotional and Psychological Adjustments

Emotional fluctuations are common for mothers in the postpartum period. These emotional fluctuations may be due to any of a number of factors: hormonal changes, fatigue, inexperience or lack of confidence with newborn babies, or the extensive time and demands involved in caring for a newborn. For some women, the emotional fluctuations decrease within several weeks after the delivery and are a minor aspect of their motherhood. For others, they are more long-lasting and can produce feelings of anxiety, depression, and difficulty in coping with stress (Barnes, 2002; Troisi & others, 2002). Mothers who have such feelings, even when they are getting adequate rest, may benefit from professional help in dealing with their problems (Strass, 2002). Here are some of the signs that can indicate a need for professional counseling about postpartum adaptation:

- Excessive worrying
- Depression
- Extreme changes in appetite
- Crying spells
- Inability to sleep

The father also undergoes considerable adjustment in the postpartum period, although in many cases he will be away at work all day, whereas the mother will be at home, at least in the first few weeks. One of the most common reactions of the husband is the feeling that the baby comes first and gets all of the attention. In some marriages, the man may have had that relationship with his wife and now feels that he has been replaced by the baby.

One strategy to help the man's postpartum reaction is for the parents to set aside some special time to be together with each other. The father's postpartum reaction also likely will be improved if he has taken childbirth classes with his wife and is an active participant in caring for the baby.

Important factors for both the mother and the father are the time and thought that go into being a competent parent of a young infant (Cowan & Cowan, 2000; McVeigh, Baafi, & Williamson, 2002). It is important for both the mother and the father to become aware of the young infant's developmental needs—physical, psychological, and emotional. Both the mother and the father need to develop a sensitive, comfortable relationship with the baby.

Some health-care professionals specialize in the postpartum period. To read about the work and career of postpartum specialist Diane Sanford, see the Careers in Life-Span Development insert on page 138.

Bonding

A special component of the parent-infant relationship is **bonding,** the formation of a connection, especially a physical bond between parents and the newborn in the period

bonding The formation of a close connection, especially a physical bond between parents and their newborn in the period shortly after birth.

Careers in Life-Span Development

Diane Sanford, Clinical Psychologist and Postpartum Expert

The information you have read about postpartum adjustment is the focus of Diane Sanford's work. Sanford has a doctorate in clinical psychology and never set out to become a specialist in women's health ◀▥ p. 32. For many years she had a private practice in clinical psychology with a focus on marital and family issues. Then she began collaborating with a psychiatrist whose clients included women with postpartum depression.

For the last 14 years, she has specialized in postpartum problems and other related aspects of female development, including infertility, pregnancy loss, and menopause. Sanford provides clients with practical advice that she believes helps women effectively cope with their problems. She begins by guiding them to think about concrete steps they can take to ease their emotional turmoil during this important postpartum transition. For example, new mothers may need help in figuring out ways to get partners and others to help with their infants. Or they may just need to be reassured that they can handle the responsibilities they face as parents.

After years of practicing on her own, Sanford and a women's health nurse formed Women's Healthcare Partnership five years ago. In addition to the two partners, the staff now includes a full-time counselor in marriage and family relationships, and a social worker. Nurse educators, a dietician, and a fitness expert work on a consulting basis. Dr. Sanford has also co-authored *Postpartum Survival Guide* (Dunnewold & Sanford, 1994), which reflects her strategies for helping women cope with postpartum issues.

Diane Sanford holding an infant of one of the mothers who comes to her for help in coping with postpartum issues.

shortly after birth. Some physicians believe that the period shortly after birth is critical in development. During this time, the parents and child need to form an important emotional attachment that provides a foundation for optimal development in years to come (Kennell & McGrath, 1999). Special interest in bonding stems from concern by pediatricians that the circumstances surrounding delivery often separate mothers and their infants, preventing or making difficult the development of a bond. The pediatricians argued that giving the mother drugs to make her delivery less painful can contribute to the lack of bonding. The drugs can make the mother drowsy, thus interfering with her ability to respond to and stimulate the newborn. Advocates of bonding also assert that preterm infants are isolated from their mothers to an even greater degree than are full-term infants, thereby increasing their difficulty in bonding.

Is there evidence that such close contact between mothers and newborns is critical for optimal development later in life? Although some research supports the bonding hypothesis (Klaus & Kennell, 1976), a body of research challenges the significance of the first few days of life as a critical period (Bakeman & Brown, 1980; Rode & others, 1981). Indeed, the extreme form of the bonding hypothesis—that the newborn must have close contact with the mother in the first few days of life to develop optimally—simply is not true.

Nonetheless, the weakness of the maternal-infant bonding research should not be used as an excuse to keep motivated mothers from interacting with their infants in the postpartum period. Such contact brings pleasure to many mothers. In some mother-infant pairs—including preterm infants, adolescent mothers, or mothers from disadvantaged circumstances—the practice of bonding may set in motion a climate for improved interaction after the mother and infant leave the hospital.

In recognition of the belief that bonding may have a positive effect on getting the parental-infant relationship off to a good start, many hospitals now offer a *rooming-in* arrangement, in which the baby remains in the mother's room most of the time during its hospital stay. However, if parents choose not to use this rooming-in arrangement, the weight of the research evidence suggests that it will not harm the infant emotionally (Lamb, 1994).

Review and Reflect

3 Explain the changes that take place in the postpartum period

REVIEW

- What does the postpartum period involve?
- What physical adjustments does the woman's body make in this period?
- What emotional and psychological adjustments characterize the postpartum period?
- Is bonding critical for optimal development?

REFLECT

- If you are a female, what can you do to adjust effectively in the postpartum period? If you are a male, what can you do to help in the postpartum period?

Reach Your Learning Goals

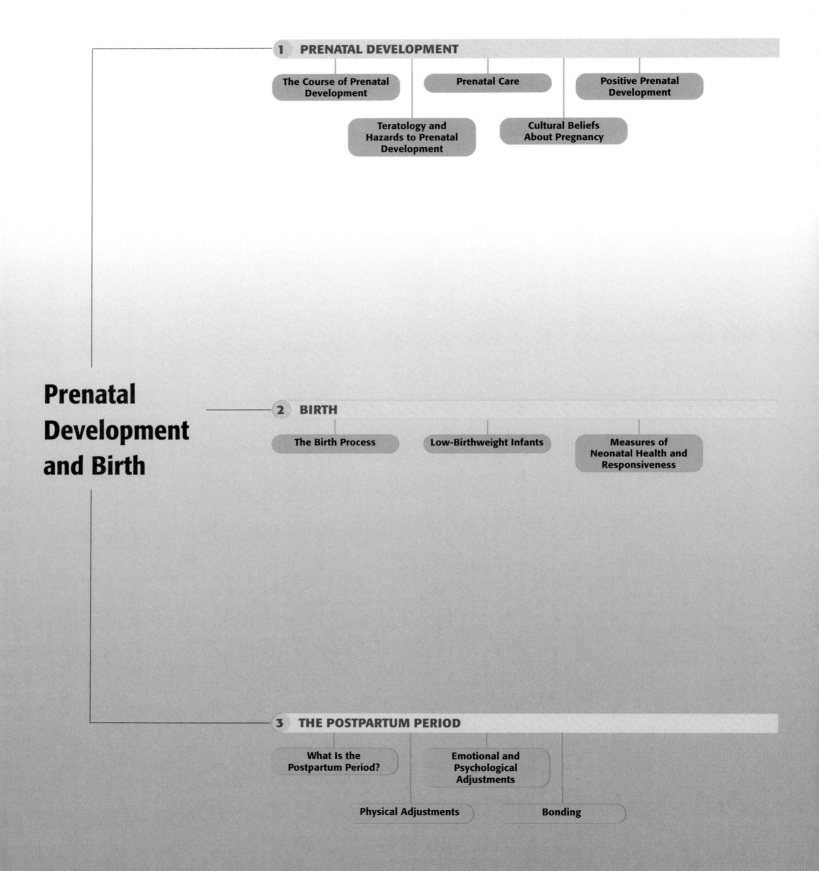

Prenatal Development and Birth

1 PRENATAL DEVELOPMENT

- The Course of Prenatal Development
- Teratology and Hazards to Prenatal Development
- Prenatal Care
- Cultural Beliefs About Pregnancy
- Positive Prenatal Development

2 BIRTH

- The Birth Process
- Low-Birthweight Infants
- Measures of Neonatal Health and Responsiveness

3 THE POSTPARTUM PERIOD

- What Is the Postpartum Period?
- Physical Adjustments
- Emotional and Psychological Adjustments
- Bonding

Summary

1 Describe prenatal development

- Prenatal development is divided into three periods: germinal (conception until 10 to 14 days later), which ends when the zygote (a fertilized egg) attaches to the uterine wall; embryonic (two to eight weeks after conception), during which the embryo differentiates into three layers, life-support systems develop, and organ systems form (organogenesis); and fetal (two months after conception until about nine months, or when the infant is born), a time when organ systems have matured to the point at which life can be sustained outside of the womb.
- Teratology is the field that investigates the causes of congenital (birth) defects. Any agent that causes birth defects is called a teratogen. The dose, time of exposure, and genetic susceptibility influence the severity of the damage to an unborn child and the type of defect that occurs. Prescription drugs that can be harmful include antibiotics, some depressants, and certain hormones. Nonprescription drugs that can be harmful include diet pills, aspirin, and coffee. Fetal alcohol syndrome (FAS) is a cluster of abnormalities that appear in offspring of mothers who drink heavily during pregnancy. When pregnant women drink moderately (one to two drinks a day), negative effects on their offspring have been found. Cigarette smoking by pregnant women has serious adverse effects on prenatal and child development (such as low birthweight). Illegal drugs that are potentially harmful to offspring include marijuana, cocaine, and heroin. Incompatibility of the mother's and the father's blood types can also be harmful to the fetus. Potential environmental hazards include radiation, environmental pollutants, toxic wastes, and prolonged exposure to heat in saunas and hot tubs. Rubella (German measles) can be harmful. Syphilis, genital herpes, and AIDS are other teratogens. A developing fetus depends entirely on its mother for nutrition. One nutrient that is especially important early in development is folic acid. High anxiety and stress in the mother are linked with less than optimal prenatal and birth outcomes. Maternal age can negatively affect the offspring's development if the mother is an adolescent or over 30. Paternal factors that can adversely affect prenatal development include exposure to lead, radiation, certain pesticides, and petrochemicals.
- Prenatal care varies extensively but usually involves medical care services with a defined schedule of visits.
- Specific actions in pregnancy are often determined by cultural beliefs. Certain behaviors are expected if a culture views pregnancy as a medical condition or a natural occurrence. For example, prenatal care may not be a priority for expectant mothers who view pregnancy as a natural occurrence.
- It is important to remember that, although things can and do go wrong during pregnancy, most of the time pregnancy and prenatal development go well. Avoiding teratogens helps ensure a positive outcome.

2 Discuss the birth process

- Childbirth occurs in three stages. The first stage, which lasts about 12 to 24 hours for a woman having her first child, is the longest stage. The cervix dilates to about 4 inches at the end of the first stage. The second stage begins when the baby's head moves through the cervix and ends with the baby's complete emergence. The third stage is afterbirth. Being born involves considerable stress for the baby, but the baby is well prepared and adapted to handle the stress. Anoxia—insufficient oxygen supply to the fetus/newborn—is a potential hazard. Childbirth strategies involve the childbirth setting and attendants. In many countries, a doula attends a childbearing woman. Methods of delivery include medicated, natural and prepared, and cesarean.
- Low-birthweight infants weigh less than 5½ pounds and they may be preterm (born three weeks or more before the pregnancy has reached full term) or small for date (also called small for gestational age, which refers to infants whose birthweight is below norm when the length of pregnancy is considered). Small for date infants may be preterm or full term. Although most low-birthweight infants are normal and healthy, as a group they have more health and developmental problems than normal-birthweight infants.
- For many years, the Apgar Scale has been used to assess the newborn's health. The Brazelton Neonatal Behavioral Assessment Scale examines the newborn's neurological development, reflexes, and reactions to people.

3 Explain the changes that take place in the postpartum period

- The postpartum period is the name given to the period after childbirth or delivery. In this period, the woman's body adjusts physically and psychologically to the process of childbearing. The period lasts for about six weeks or until the body has completed its adjustment.
- Physical adjustments in the postpartum period include fatigue, involution (the process by which the uterus returns to its prepregnant size five or six weeks after birth), hormonal changes, when to resume sexual intercourse, and exercises to recover body contour and strength.
- Emotional fluctuations on the part of the mother are common in this period, and they can vary a great deal from one mother to the next. The father also goes through a postpartum adjustment.
- Bonding is the formation of a close connection, especially a physical bond between parents and the newborn shortly after birth. Early bonding has not been found to be critical in the development of a competent infant.

Key Terms

Key People

1. Denise's sister, Doreen, is pregnant for the first time. Doreen is not particularly known for her healthy lifestyle. What particular things can Denise encourage Doreen to do in order to give birth to a healthy baby?

2. Sienne told her fiancé, Jackson, that he had better stop smoking before they begin trying to conceive a child. Why is Sienne concerned about Jackson's smoking and its effect on their children before they have even started planning their family?

3. Hannah, who gave birth to a healthy baby boy—her first child—two weeks ago, appears to her husband Sean to be sad, lethargic, and is having trouble sleeping. How can Sean determine if Hannah is just going through a natural period of post-baby "blues" or if she might be suffering from postpartum depression?

Connect to www.mhhe.com/santrockld9 to research the answers and complete these exercises.

mhhe ● com/ santrockld9 **E-Learning Tools**

To help you master the material in this chapter, you'll find a number of valuable study tools on the Student CD-ROM that accompanies this book. In addition, visit the Online Learning Center for *Life-Span Development*, ninth edition, where you'll find these valuable resources for chapter 4, "Prenatal Development and Birth."

- Learn how alcohol consumption might affect a pregnancy by completing the self-assessment, *Pregnancy Screening for Alcohol Use*.
- Build your decision-making skills by trying your hand at the parenting and education "Scenarios."

Infancy

Babies are such a nice way to start people.
—DON HEROLD
American Writer, 20th Century

As newborns, we were not empty-headed organisms. We had some basic reflexes, among them crying, kicking, and coughing. We slept a lot, and occasionally we smiled, although the meaning of our first smiles was not entirely clear. We ate and we grew. We crawled and then we walked, a journey of a thousand miles beginning with a single step. Sometimes we conformed, sometimes others conformed to us. Our development was a continuous creation of more complex forms. Our helpless kind demanded the meeting eyes of love. We juggled the necessity of curbing our will with becoming what we could will freely. Section 3 contains three chapters: "Physical Development in Infancy" (chapter 5), "Cognitive Development in Infancy" (chapter 6), and "Socioemotional Development in Infancy" (chapter 7).

Physical Development in Infancy

Learning Goals

1 *D*iscuss physical growth and development in infancy

2 *D*escribe infants' motor development

3 *E*xplain sensory and perceptual development in infancy

Images of Life-Span Development
Bottle- and Breast-Feeding in Africa

Latonya is a newborn baby in the African country of Ghana. The culture of the area in which she was born discourages breast-feeding. She has been kept apart from her mother and bottle-fed in her first days of infancy. Manufacturers of infant formula provide the hospital where she was born with free or subsidized milk powder. Her mother has been persuaded to bottle-feed rather than breast-feed her. When her mother bottle-feeds Latonya, she overdilutes the milk formula with unclean water. Latonya's feeding bottles also have not been sterilized. Latonya becomes very sick. She dies before her first birthday.

By contrast, Ramona lives in the African country of Nigeria. Her mother is breast-feeding her. Ramona was born at a Nigerian hospital where a "baby-friendly" program had been initiated. In this program, babies are not separated from their mothers when they are born, and the mothers are encouraged to breast-feed them. The mothers are told of the perils that bottle-feeding can bring because of unsafe water and unsterilized bottles. They also are informed about the advantages of breast milk, which include its nutritious and hygienic qualities, its ability to immunize babies against common illnesses, and its role in reducing the mother's risk of breast and ovarian cancer. At 1 year of age, Ramona is very healthy.

For the past 10 to 15 years, the World Health Organization and UNICEF have been trying to reverse the trend toward bottle-feeding of infants, which emerged in many impoverished countries. They have instituted the "baby-friendly" program in many countries. They also have persuaded the International Association of Infant Formula Manufacturers to stop marketing their baby formulas to hospitals in countries where the governments support the baby-friendly initiatives. For the hospitals themselves, costs actually will be reduced as infant formula, feeding bottles, and separate nurseries become unnecessary. For example, baby-friendly Jose Fabella Memorial Hospital in the Philippines already has reported saving 8 percent of its annual budget.

Hospitals play a vital role in getting mothers to breast-feed their babies. For many years, maternity units favored bottle-feeding and did not give mothers adequate information about the benefits of breast-feeding. With the initiatives of the World Health Organization and UNICEF, things are changing, but there still are many places in the world where the baby-friendly initiatives have not been implemented (Grant, 1993).

It is very important for infants to get a healthy start. In this chapter we will explore these aspects of the infant's development: physical growth, motor development, and sensory and perceptual development.

1 PHYSICAL GROWTH AND DEVELOPMENT IN INFANCY

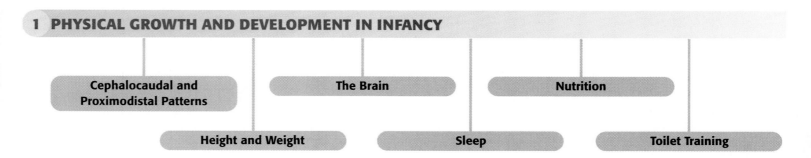

Infants' physical development in the first two years of life is extensive. At birth, neonates have a gigantic head (relative to the rest of the body), which flops around uncontrollably. They also possess reflexes that are dominated by evolutionary movements. In the span of 12 months, infants become capable of sitting anywhere, standing, stooping, climbing, and usually walking. During the second year, growth decelerates, but rapid increases in such activities as running and climbing take place. Let's now examine in greater detail the sequence of physical development in infancy.

Cephalocaudal and Proximodistal Patterns

The **cephalocaudal pattern** is the sequence in which the greatest growth always occurs at the top—the head—with physical growth in size, weight, and feature differentiation gradually working its way down from top to bottom (for example, shoulders, middle trunk, and so on). This same pattern occurs in the head area, because the top parts of the head—the eyes and brain—grow faster than the lower parts, such as the jaw. An extraordinary proportion of the total body is occupied by the head during prenatal development and early infancy (see figure 5.1). Later in the chapter you will see that sensory and motor development proceed according to the cephalocaudal principle. For example, infants see objects before they can control their trunk and they can use their hands long before they can crawl or walk.

The **proximodistal pattern** is the sequence in which growth starts at the center of the body and moves toward the extremities. An example of this is the early maturation of muscular control of the trunk and arms, as compared with that of the hands and fingers. Further, infants use their whole hand as a unit before they can control several fingers.

Height and Weight

The average North American newborn is 20 inches long and weighs 7½ pounds. Ninety-five percent of full-term newborns are 18 to 22 inches long and weigh between 5½ and 10 pounds.

In the first several days of life, most newborns lose 5 to 7 percent of their body weight before they learn to adjust to neonatal feeding. Once infants adjust to sucking, swallowing, and digesting, they grow rapidly, gaining an average of 5 to 6 ounces per week during the first month. They have doubled their birthweight by the age of 4

> **cephalocaudal pattern** The sequence in which the greatest growth occurs at the top—the head—with physical growth in size, weight, and feature differentiation gradually working from top to bottom.
>
> **proximodistal pattern** The sequence in which growth starts at the center of the body and moves toward the extremities.

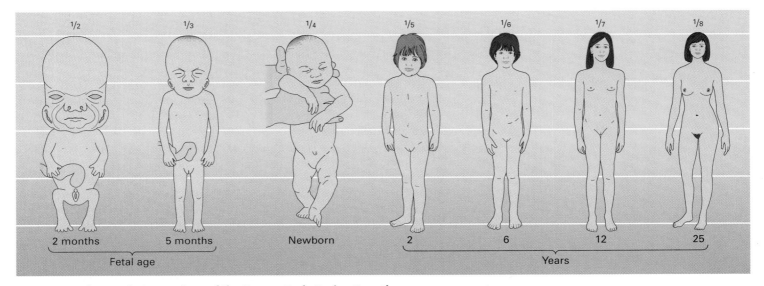

| 1/2 | 1/3 | 1/4 | 1/5 | 1/6 | 1/7 | 1/8 |

| 2 months | 5 months | Newborn | 2 | 6 | 12 | 25 |

Fetal age · Years

FIGURE 5.1 Changes in Proportions of the Human Body During Growth

As individuals develop from infancy through adulthood, one of the most noticeable physical changes is that the head becomes smaller in relation to the rest of the body. The fractions listed refer to head size as a proportion of total body length at different ages.

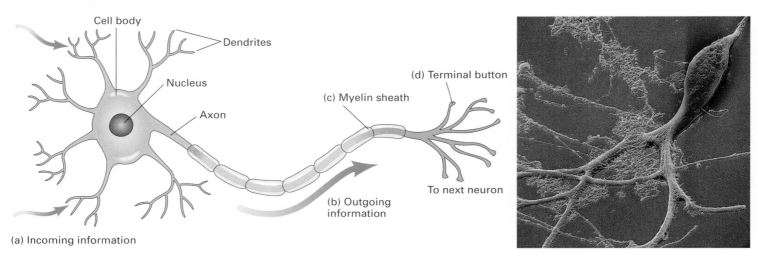

FIGURE 5.2 The Neuron

(*a*) The dendrites of the cell body receive information from other neurons, muscles, or glands through the axon. (*b*) Axons transmit information away from the cell body. (*c*) A myelin sheath covers most axons and speeds information transmission. (*d*) As the axon ends, it branches out into terminal buttons. At the right is an actual photograph of a neuron.

months and have nearly tripled it by their first birthday. Infants grow about 1 inch per month during the first year, reaching approximately 1½ times their birth length by their first birthday.

Infants' rate of growth is considerably slower in the second year of life. By 2 years of age, infants weigh approximately 26 to 32 pounds, having gained a quarter to half a pound per month during the second year; now they have reached about one-fifth of their adult weight. At 2 years of age, the average infant is 32 to 35 inches in height, which is nearly one-half of their adult height.

The Brain

As an infant walks, talks, runs, shakes a rattle, smiles, and frowns, changes are occurring in its brain. Consider that the infant began life as a single cell and nine months later was born with a brain and nervous system that contained approximately 100 billion nerve cells, or neurons. A **neuron** is a nerve cell that handles information processing at the cellular level (see figure 5.2). Indeed, at birth the infant probably has almost all of the neurons it will ever have.

The Brain's Development   Among the most dramatic changes in the brain in the first two years of life are the spreading connections of dendrites to each other. Figure 5.3 illustrates these changes.

A *myelin sheath,* which is a layer of fat cells, encases most axons (see figure 5.2). Not only does the myelin sheath insulate nerve cells, but it also helps nerve impulses travel faster. *Myelination,* the process of encasing axons with fat cells, begins prenatally and continues after birth. Myelination for visual pathways occurs rapidly after birth, being completed in the first six months. Auditory myelination is not completed until 4 or 5 years of age. Some aspects of myelination continue even into adolescence.

In addition to dendritic spreading and the encasement of axons through myelination, another important aspect of the brain's development at the cellular level is the dramatic increase in connections between neurons (Ramey & Ramey, 2000). *Synapses* are tiny gaps between neurons where connections between axons and dendrites take place. As the infant develops, synaptic connections between axons and dendrites proliferate (Baudry, 2003).

neuron Nerve cell that handles information processing at the cellular level.

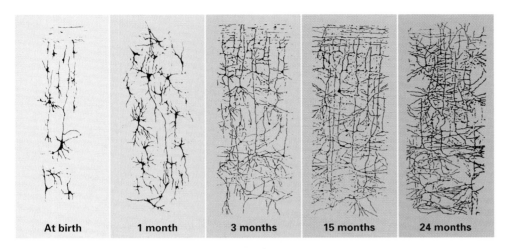

| At birth | 1 month | 3 months | 15 months | 24 months |

FIGURE 5.3 The Development of Dendritic Spreading

Note the increase in connectedness between neurons over the course of the first 2 years of life.

mhhe●com/
santrockld9

Neural Processes

Researchers have discovered an intriguing aspect of synaptic connections. Nearly twice as many of these connections are made as will ever be used (Huttenlocher & others, 1991; Huttenlocher & Dabholkar, 1997). The connections that are used become strengthened and survive while the unused ones are replaced by other pathways or disappear (Casey, Durston, & Fossella, 2001; Varoqueaux, 2003). That is, these connections will be "pruned," in the language of neuroscience. Figure 5.4 on page 152 vividly illustrates the dramatic growth and later pruning of synapses in the visual, auditory, and prefrontal cortex areas of the brain (Huttenlocher & Dabholkar, 1997). These areas are critical for higher-level cognitive functioning in areas like learning, memory, and reasoning.

As shown in figure 5.4, "blooming and pruning" vary considerably by brain region in humans (Thompson & Nelson, 2001). For example, the peak of synaptic overproduction in the visual cortex occurs at about the fourth postnatal month, followed by a gradual retraction until the middle to end of the preschool years (Huttenlocher & Dabholkar, 1997). In areas of the brain involved in hearing and language, a similar, though somewhat later, course is detected. However, in the prefrontal cortex (the area of the brain where higher-level thinking and self-regulation occur), the peak of overproduction takes place at about 1 year of age and it is not until middle to late adolescence that the adult density of synapses is achieved. Both heredity and environment are thought to influence the timing and course of synaptic overproduction and subsequent retraction.

Using the electroencephalogram (EEG), which measures the brain's electrical activity, researchers have found that a spurt in EEG activity occurs from about 1½ to 2 years of age (Fischer & Bidell, 1998; Fischer & Rose, 1995). Other spurts seem to take place at about 9, 12, 15, and 18 to 20 years of age. Researchers believe that these spurts of brain activity may coincide with important changes in cognitive development. For example, the increase in EEG brain activity at 1½ to 2 years of age is likely associated with an increase in conceptual and language growth.

At birth, the newborn's brain is about 25 percent of its adult weight. By the second birthday, the brain is about 75 percent of its adult weight. However, the brain's areas do not mature uniformly. Some areas, such as the primary motor areas, develop earlier than others, such as the primary sensory areas.

Studying the brain's development in infancy is not as easy as it might seem, because even the latest brain-imaging technologies can't make out fine details and they can't be used on the babies. Positron-emission tomography (PET) scans pose a

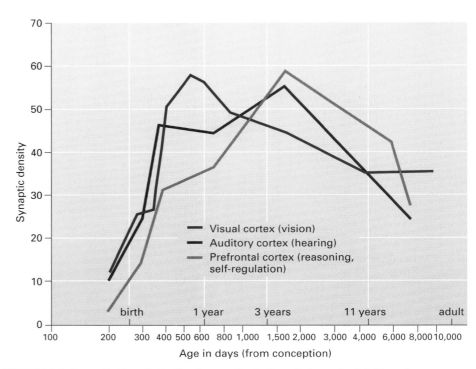

FIGURE 5.4 Synaptic Density in the Human Brain from Infancy to Adulthood

The graph shows the dramatic increase and then pruning in synaptic density for three regions of the brain: visual cortex, auditory cortex, and prefrontal cortex. Synaptic density is believed to be an important indication of the extent of connectivity between neurons.

radiation risk, and infants wriggle too much for magnetic resonance imaging, or an MRI (Marcus, Mulrine, & Wong, 1999). However, one researcher who is making strides in finding out more about the brain's development in infancy is Charles Nelson (1999; deHaan & Nelson, 1999), some of whose research involves attaching up to 128 electrodes to a baby's scalp (see figure 5.5). He has found that even newborns produce distinctive brain waves that reveal they can distinguish their mother's voices from another woman's, even while they are asleep. In other research, Nelson has found that by 8 months of age babies can distinguish the picture of a wooden toy they were allowed to feel, but not see, from pictures of other toys. This achievement coincides with the development of neurons in the brain's hippocampus (an important structure in memory), allowing the infant to remember specific items and events.

The Brain's Lobes and Hemispheres   The highest level of the brain is the forebrain. It consists of a number of structures, including the *cerebral cortex*, which makes up about 80 percent of the brain's volume and covers the lower portions of the brain like a cap. The cerebral cortex plays a critical role in many important human functions, such as perception, language, and thinking.

The cerebral cortex is divided into four main areas called lobes:

- the *frontal lobe* is involved in voluntary movement and thinking.
- the *occipital lobe* is involved in vision.
- the *temporal lobe* is involved in hearing.
- the *parietal lobe* is involved in processing information about body sensations.

The frontal lobe is immature in the newborn. However, as neurons in the frontal lobes become myelinated and interconnected during the first year of life, infants develop an ability to regulate their physiological states (such as sleep) and gain more control over their reflexes. Cognitive skills that require deliberate thinking don't

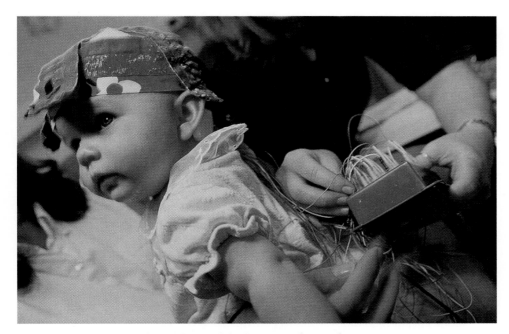

FIGURE 5.5 Measuring the Brain's Activity in Research on Infant Memory

In Charles Nelson's research, electrodes are attached to a baby's scalp to measure the brain's activity to determine its role in the development of an infant's memory. *Why is it so difficult to measure infants' brain activity?*

emerge until later (Bell & Fox, 1992). Indeed, as we saw earlier, the prefrontal region of the frontal lobe has the most prolonged development of any brain region with changes detectable at least into the adolescent years (Johnson, 2001).

The cerebral cortex is divided into two halves, or hemispheres (see figure 5.6). **Lateralization** is the specialization of function in one hemisphere of the cerebral cortex or the other. There continues to be considerable interest in the degree to which each is involved in various aspects of thinking, feeling, and behavior (Hellige, 2003).

The most extensive research on the brain's hemispheres has focused on language. At birth, the hemispheres already have started to specialize: Newborns show greater electrical brain activity in the left hemisphere than the right hemisphere when they are listening to speech sounds (Hahn, 1987). A common misconception is that virtually all language processing is carried out in the left hemisphere. Speech and grammar are localized to the left hemisphere in most people; however, some aspects of language such as appropriate language use in different contexts and the use of metaphor and humor involves the right hemisphere. Thus, language does not occur exclusively in the brain's left hemisphere (Johnson, 2000, 2001).

It is a popular myth that the left hemisphere is the exclusive location of logical thinking and the right hemisphere the exclusive location of creative thinking. However, most neuroscientists agree that complex functions, such as reading, performing music, and creating art, involve both hemispheres. They believe that labeling people as "left-brained" because they are logical thinkers and "right-brained" because they are creative thinkers does not correspond to the way the brain's hemispheres actually work. Such complex thinking in normal people is the outcome of communication between both sides of the brain.

Early Experience and the Brain   Until the middle of the twentieth century, scientists believed that the brain's development was determined almost exclusively by genetic factors. Researcher Mark Rosenzweig (1969) was curious about whether early experiences change the brain's development. He conducted a number of experiments with rats and other animals to investigate this possibility. Animals were randomly

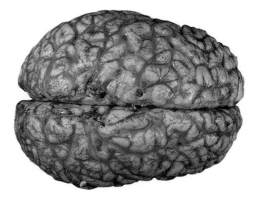

FIGURE 5.6 The Human Brain's Hemispheres

The two halves (hemispheres) of the human brain are clearly seen in this photograph.

lateralization Specialization of function in one hemisphere of the cerebral cortex or the other.

assigned to grow up in different environments. Animals in an enriched early environment lived in cages with stimulating features, such as wheels to rotate, steps to climb, levers to press, and toys to manipulate. In contrast, other animals had the early experience of growing up in standard cages or in barren, isolated conditions.

The results were stunning. The brains of the animals growing up in the enriched environment developed better than the brains of the animals reared in standard or isolated conditions. The brains of the "enriched" animals weighed more, had thicker layers, had more neuronal connections, and had higher levels of neurochemical activity.

Similar findings occurred when older animals were reared in vastly different environments, although the results were not as strong as for the younger animals. Such results give hope that enriching the lives of infants and young children who live in impoverished environments can produce positive changes in their development.

Depressed brain activity has recently been found in children who grow up in a deprived environment (Cicchetti, 2001). As shown in figure 5.7, a child who grew up in the unresponsive and unstimulating environment of a Romanian orphanage showed considerably depressed brain activity compared to a normal child (Begley, 1997).

Scientists also now know that, starting shortly after birth, a baby's brain produces trillions more connections between neurons than it can possibly use. The brain eliminates connections that are seldom or never used. This pruning of brain connections continues at least until about 10 years of age.

The profusion of connections provides the growing brain with flexibility and resilience. Consider 16-year-old Michael Rehbein. At age 4½, he began to experience uncontrollable seizures—as many as 400 a day. Doctors said the only solution was to remove the left hemisphere of his brain where the seizures were occurring. The first major surgery was at age 7 and another at age 10. Recovery was slow but his right hemisphere began to reorganize and take over functions that normally occur in the brain's left hemisphere. One of these functions was speech (see figure 5.8).

Neuroscientists believe that what wires the brain—or rewires it, in the case of Michael Rehbein—is repeated experience (Nash, 1997). Each time a baby tries to

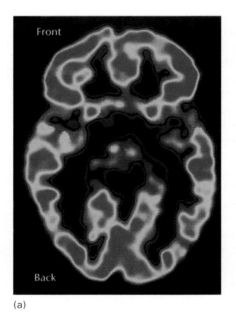
(a)

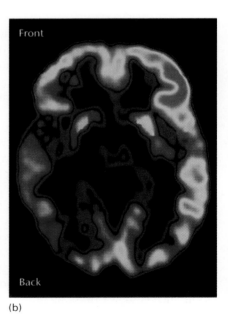
(b)

FIGURE 5.7 Early Deprivation and Brain Activity

These two photographs are PET (positron-emission tomography) scans (which use radioactive tracers to image and analyze blood flow and metabolic activity in the body's organs) of the brains of (a) a normal child and (b) an institutionalized Romanian orphan who experienced substantial deprivation since birth. In PET scans, the highest to lowest brain activity is reflected in the colors of red, yellow, green, blue, and black, respectively. As can be seen, red and yellow show up to a much greater degree in the PET scan of the normal child than the deprived Romanian orphan.

touch an attractive object or gazes intently at a face, tiny bursts of electricity shoot through the brain, knitting together neurons into circuits. The results are some of the behavioral milestones we discuss in this and other chapters. For example, at about 2 months of age, the motor-control centers of the brain develop to the point at which infants can suddenly reach out and grab a nearby object. At about 4 months, the neural connections necessary for depth perception begin to form. And at about 12 months the brain's speech centers are poised to produce one of infancy's magical moments: when the infant utters its first word.

In sum, neural connections are formed early in life. The infant's brain literally is waiting for experiences to determine how connections are made (Greenough, 2001; Johnson, 2000, 2001). Before birth, it appears that genes mainly direct how the brain establishes basic wiring patterns. Neurons grow and travel to distant places awaiting further instructions. After birth, environmental experiences are important in the brain's development. The inflowing stream of sights, sounds, smells, touches, language, and eye contact help shape the brain's neural connections (Black, 2001).

Sleep

When we were infants, sleep consumed more of our time than it does now. Newborns sleep 16 to 17 hours a day, although some sleep more and others less. The range is from a low of about 10 hours to a high of about 21 hours, although the longest period of sleep is not always between 11 P.M. and 7 A.M. Although total sleep remains somewhat consistent for young infants, their sleep during the day does not always follow a rhythmic pattern. An infant might change from sleeping several long bouts of 7 or 8 hours to three or four shorter sessions only a few hours in duration. By about 1 month of age, many American infants have begun to sleep longer at night, and by about 4 months of age, they usually have moved closer to adultlike sleep patterns, spending the most time sleeping at night and the most time awake during the day (Daws, 2000).

There are cultural variations in infant sleeping patterns. For example, in the Kipsigis culture in the African country of Kenya, infants sleep with their mothers at night and are permitted to nurse on demand (Super & Harkness, 1997). During the day they are strapped to their mother's backs, accompanying them on their daily rounds of chores and social activities. As a result, the Kipsigis infants do not sleep through the night until much later than American infants do. During the first eight months of postnatal life, Kipsigis infants rarely sleep longer than three hours at a stretch, even at night. This contrasts with American infants, many of whom begin to sleep up to eight hours a night by 8 months of age.

REM Sleep   Researchers are intrigued by the various forms of infant sleep. They are especially interested in *REM (rapid eye movement) sleep*. Most adults spend about one-fifth of their night in REM sleep, and REM sleep usually appears about 1 hour after non-REM sleep. However, about one-half of an infant's sleep is REM sleep, and infants often begin their sleep cycle with REM sleep rather than non-REM sleep. By the time infants reach 3 months of age, the percentage of time they spend in REM sleep falls to about 40 percent, and REM sleep no longer begins their sleep cycle. The large amount of REM sleep may provide infants with added self-stimulation, since they spend less time awake than do older children (Zuk & Zuk, 2002). REM sleep also might promote the brain's development in infancy (McNamara, Lijowska, & Thach, 2002). Figure 5.9 on page 156 illustrates the average number of total hours spent in sleep and the amount of time spent in REM sleep, across the human life span. As can be seen, infants sleep far more than children and adults, and a much greater amount of time is taken up by REM sleep in infancy than at any other point in the life span.

Shared Sleeping   There is considerable variation across cultures in newborns' sleeping arrangements. Sharing a bed with a mother is a common practice in many

(a)

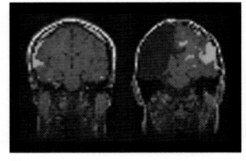

(b)

FIGURE 5.8 Plasticity in the Brain's Hemispheres

(*a*) Michael Rehbein at 14 years of age. (*b*)Michael's right hemisphere (*right*) has reorganized to take over the language functions normally carried out by corresponding areas in the left hemisphere of an intact brain (*left*). However, the right hemisphere is not as efficient as the left, and more areas of the brain are recruited to process speech.

Development of the Brain

Early Development of the Brain

Early Experience and the Brain

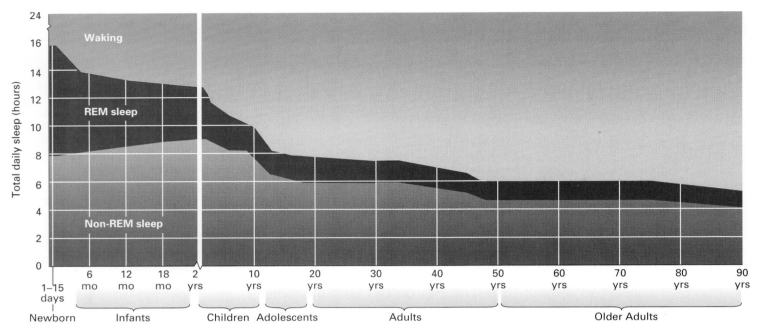

FIGURE 5.9 Sleep Across the Human Life Span

> *S leep that knits up the ravelled sleave of care... Balm of hurt minds, nature's second course. Chief nourisher in life's feast.*
>
> —WILLIAM SHAKESPEARE
> *English Playwright, 17th Century*

sudden infant death syndrome (SIDS) A condition that occurs when an infant stops breathing, usually during the night, and suddenly dies without an apparent cause.

cultures, whereas in others newborns sleep in a crib, either in the same room as the parents or in a separate room. In the United States, sleeping in a crib in a separate room is the most frequent sleeping arrangement for an infant. In one cross-cultural study, American mothers said they have their infants sleep in a separate room to promote the infants' self-reliance and independence (Morelli & others, 1992). By contrast, Mayan mothers in rural Guatemala had infants sleep in their bed until the birth of a new sibling, at which time the infant would sleep with another family member or in a separate bed in the mother's room. The Mayan mothers believed that the cosleeping arrangement with their infants enhanced the closeness of their relationship with the infants and were shocked when told that American mothers have their baby sleep alone.

Some child experts believe there are benefits to shared sleeping, such as promoting breast-feeding, responding more quickly to the baby's cries, and detecting potentially dangerous breathing pauses in the baby (McKenna, Mosko, & Richard, 1997). However, the American Academy of Pediatrics Task Force on Infant Positioning and SIDS (2000; Cohen, 2000) discourages shared sleeping. The Task Force concluded that in some instances bed sharing might lead to sudden infant death syndrome (SIDS), as could be the case if a sleeping mother rolls over on her baby. One recent study found physiological responses indicative of greater stress in co-sleeping infants than non-co-sleeping infants (Hunsley & Thoman, 2002). Thus, shared sleeping remains a controversial issue, with some experts recommending it, others arguing against it.

SIDS **Sudden infant death syndrome (SIDS)** is a condition that occurs when infants stop breathing, usually during the night, and suddenly die without an apparent cause. Since 1992, The American Academy of Pediatrics has recommended that infants be placed to sleep on their backs to reduce the risk of SIDS. Since that time, the frequency of prone sleeping has decreased from 70 percent to 20 percent of U.S. infants (American Academy of Pediatrics Task Force in Infant Positioning and SIDS, 2000). Some researchers now believe that an inability to swallow effectively in the prone (face down) sleeping position is an important reason SIDS occurs (Jeffery & others, 2000). Researchers have found that SIDS decreases when infants sleep on their backs rather than on their stomachs or sides (Smith & Hattersley, 2000). However,

SIDS still remains the highest cause of infant death in the United States with nearly 3,000 infant deaths due to SIDS. Risk of SIDS is highest at 4 to 6 weeks of age.

Unfortunately, at this time there is no definitive way to predict which infants will become the victims of SIDS. However, researchers have found that these are risk factors for SIDS (American Academy of Pediatrics Task Force in Infant Positioning and SIDS, 2000; Goldwater, 2001; Kahn & others, 2002; Maas, 1998):

SIDS

- Low-birthweight infants are 5 to 10 times more likely to die of SIDS than are their normal-weight counterparts (Sowter & others, 1999).
- Infants whose siblings have died of SIDS are two to four times as likely to die of it (Lenoir, Mallet, & Calenda, 2000).
- Six percent of infants with sleep apnea, a temporary cessation of breathing in which the airway is completely blocked, usually 10 seconds or longer, die of SIDS (McNamara & Sullivan, 2000).
- African American and Eskimo infants are four to six times as likely as all others to die of SIDS (Pollock & Frohna, 2001).
- SIDS is more common in lower socioeconomic groups (Mitchell & others, 2000).
- SIDS is more common in infants who are passively exposed to cigarette smoke (Pollack, 2001).
- Soft bedding is not recommended (Flick & others, 2001).

Nutrition

Our coverage of infant nutrition begins with information about nutritional needs and eating behavior, then turns to the issue of breast- versus bottle-feeding, and concludes with an overview of malnutrition.

Nutritional Needs and Eating Behavior   The importance of adequate energy and nutrient intake consumed in a loving and supportive environment during the infant years cannot be overstated (Samour, Helm, & Lang, 2000). From birth to 1 year of age, human infants nearly triple their weight and increase their length by 50 percent. Individual differences among infants in terms of their nutrient reserves, body composition, growth rates, and activity patterns make defining actual nutrient needs difficult. However, because parents need guidelines, nutritionists recommend that infants consume approximately 50 calories per day for each pound they weigh—more than twice an adult's requirement per pound.

Some years ago, controversy surrounded the issue of whether a baby should be fed on demand or on a regular schedule. Behaviorist John Watson (1928) argued that scheduled feeding is superior because it increases the child's orderliness. An example of a recommended schedule for newborns was 4 ounces of formula every six hours. In recent years, demand feeding—in which the timing and amount of feeding are determined by the infant—has become more popular.

Today, Americans are extremely nutrition-conscious. Does the same type of nutrition that makes us healthy adults also make young infants healthy? Some affluent, well-educated parents almost starve their babies by feeding them the low-fat, low-calorie diet they eat themselves. Diets designed for adult weight loss and prevention of heart disease may actually retard growth and development in babies. Fat is very important for babies. Nature's food—breast milk—is not low in fat or calories. No child under the age of 2 should be consuming skim milk.

In one investigation, seven babies 7 to 22 months of age were found to be undernourished by their unwitting health-conscious parents (Lifshitz & others, 1987). In some instances, the parents had been fat themselves and were determined that their child was not going to be. The well-meaning parents substituted vegetables, skim milk, and other low-fat foods for what they called junk food. However, for growing infants, high-calorie, high-energy foods are part of a balanced diet.

Human milk, or an alternative formula, is a baby's source of nutrients for the first 4 to 6 months. The growing consensus is that breast-feeding is better for the baby's health, although controversy still swirls about the issue of breast- versus bottle-feeding. *Why is breast-feeding strongly recommended by pediatricians?*

Breast- Versus Bottle-Feeding Human milk or an alternative formula is the baby's source of nutrients and energy for the first 4 to 6 months of life. For years, debate has focused on whether breast-feeding is better for the infant than bottle-feeding. The growing consensus is that breast-feeding is better for the baby's health (Blum, 2000).

What are some of the benefits of breast-feeding? They include these benefits during the first 2 years of life and later (AAP Work Group on Breastfeeding, 1997; Eiger & Olds, 1999; London & others, 2000):

- Appropriate weight gain
- Fewer allergies (Arshad, 2001; Hoppu & others, 2001)
- Prevention or reduction of diarrhea, respiratory infections (such as pneumonia and bronchitis), bacterial and urinary tract infections, and otitis media (a middle ear infection) (AAP Work Group on Breastfeeding, 1997; Kramer & others, 2001; Silfverdal & others, 2002)
- Denser bones in childhood and adulthood (Gibson & others, 2000; Jones, Riley, & Dwyer, 2000)
- Reduced childhood cancer and reduced incidence of breast cancer in mothers and their female offspring (Bernier & others, 2000)
- Lower incidence of SIDS—in one study, for every month of exclusive breast-feeding, the rate of SIDS was cut in half (Fredrickson, 1993)
- Neurological and cognitive development (Brody, 1994)
- Visual acuity (Makrides & others, 1995)

Which women are least likely to breast-feed? They include mothers who work full-time outside of the home, mothers under age 25, mothers without a high school education, African American mothers, and mothers in low-income circumstances (Ryan, 1997). In one study of low-income mothers in Georgia, interventions (such as counseling focused on the benefits of breast-feeding and the free loan of a breast pump) increased the incidence of breast-feeding (Ahluwalia & others, 2000). Increasingly, mothers who return to work in the infant's first year of life use a breast pump to extract breast milk that can be stored for later feeding of the infant when the mother is not present.

The American Pediatric Association strongly endorses breast-feeding throughout the first year of life (AAP Work Group on Breastfeeding, 1997). Are there circumstances when mothers should not breast-feed? Yes, they are (1) when the mother is infected with AIDS, which can be transmitted through her milk, or has another infectious disease; (2) if she has active tuberculosis; or (3) she is taking any drug that might not be safe for the infant (AAP Committee on Drugs, 1994; AAP Work Group on Breastfeeding, 1997).

This Honduran child has kwashiorkor. Notice the tell-tale sign of kwashiorkor—a greatly expanded abdomen. *What are some other characteristics of kwashiorkor?*

Some women cannot breast-feed their infants because of physical difficulties; others feel guilty if they terminate breast-feeding early (Mozingo & others, 2000). They might worry that they are depriving their infants of important emotional and psychological benefits. Some researchers have found that there are no psychological differences between breast-fed and bottle-fed infants (Ferguson, Harwood, & Shannon, 1987; Young, 1990). To read about a program that gives infants a healthy start in life, see the Sociocultural Worlds of Development box.

Malnutrition in Infancy Early weaning from breast milk to inadequate nutrients, such as unsuitable and unsanitary cow's milk formula, can cause protein deficiency and malnutrition.

A Healthy Start

The Hawaii Family Support/Healthy Start Program began in 1985 (Allen, Brown, & Finlay, 1992). It was designed by the Hawaii Family Stress Center in Honolulu, which had been making home visits to improve family functioning and reduce child abuse for more than a decade. Participation is voluntary. Families of newborns are screened for family risk factors, including unstable housing, histories of substance abuse, depression, parents' abuse as children, late or no prenatal care, fewer than 12 years of schooling, poverty, and unemployment. Early identification workers screen and interview new mothers in the hospital. They also screen families referred by physicians, nurses, and others. Because the demand for services outstrips available resources, only families with a substantial number of risk factors can participate.

Each new participating family receives a weekly visit from a family support worker. Each of the program's eight home visitors works with approximately 25 families at a time. The worker helps the family cope with any immediate crisis, such as unemployment or substance abuse. The family also is linked directly with a pediatrician to ensure that the children receive regular health care. Infants are screened for developmental delays and are immunized on schedule. Pediatricians have been educated about the program. They are notified when a child is enrolled in Healthy Start and when a family at risk stops participating.

The Family Support/Healthy Start Program recently hired a child development specialist to work with families of children with special needs. And in some instances, the program's male family support worker visits a father to talk specifically about his role in the family. The support workers encourage parents to participate in group activities held each week at the program center located in a neighborhood shopping center.

Over time, parents are encouraged to assume more responsibility for their family's health and well-being. Families can participate in Healthy Start until the child is 5 and enters public school.

The Hawaii Family Support/Healthy Start Program provides many home-visitor services for overburdened families of newborns and young children. This program has been very successful in reducing abuse and neglect in families. *What are some examples of the home-visitor services in this program?*

Something that looks like milk but is not, usually a form of tapioca or rice, also might be used. In many of the world's developing countries, mothers used to breast-feed their infants for at least two years. To become more modern, they stopped breast-feeding much earlier and replaced it with bottle-feeding. Comparisons of breast-fed and bottle-fed infants in such countries as Afghanistan, Haiti, Ghana, and Chile document that the death rate of bottle-fed infants is as much as five times that of breast-fed infants (Grant, 1997).

Two life-threatening conditions that can result from malnutrition are marasmus and kwashiorkor. **Marasmus** is a wasting away of body tissues in the infant's first year, caused by severe protein-calorie deficiency. The infant becomes grossly underweight, and its muscles atrophy. **Kwashiorkor** is a condition caused by a deficiency in protein in which the child's abdomen and feet swell with water. This disease usually appears between 1 to 3 years of age. Kwashiorkor makes children sometimes appear to be well-fed even though they are not. Kwashiorkor causes a child's vital organs to collect the nutrients that are present and deprive other parts of the body of them. The child's hair also becomes thin, brittle, and colorless. And the child's behavior often becomes listless.

Even if not fatal, severe and lengthy malnutrition is detrimental to physical, cognitive, and social development (Grantham-McGregor, Ani & Fernald, 2001). In some cases, even moderate malnutrition can produce subtle difficulties in development. In one investigation, two groups of extremely malnourished 1-year-old South African infants were studied (Bayley, 1970). The children in one group were given adequate nourishment during the next six years; no intervention took place in the lives of the

marasmus A wasting away of body tissues in the infant's first year, caused by severe protein-calorie deficiency.

kwashiorkor A condition caused by a deficiency in protein in which the child's abdomen and feet become swollen with water.

Careers in Life-Span Development

T. Berry Brazelton, Pediatrician

T. Berry Brazelton is America's best-known pediatrician as a result of his numerous books, television appearances, and newspaper and magazine articles about parenting and children's health ◀▥ p. 34. He takes a family-centered approach to child development issues and communicates with parents in easy-to-understand ways.

Dr. Brazelton founded the Child Development Unit at Boston Children's Hospital and created the Brazelton Neonatal Behavioral Assessment Scale, a widely used measure of the newborn's health and well-being (which you read about in chapter 4). He also has conducted a number of research studies on infants and children and has been president of the Society for Research in Child Development, a leading research organization.

T. Berry Brazelton, pediatrician, with a young child.

other group. After the seventh year, the poorly nourished group of children performed much worse on tests of intelligence than did the adequately nourished group. Another study linked the diets of rural Guatemalan infants with their social development at the time they entered elementary school (Barrett, Radke-Yarrow, & Klein, 1982). Children whose mothers had been given nutritious supplements during pregnancy and who themselves had been given more nutritious, high-calorie foods in their first two years of life were more active, more involved, more helpful with their peers, less anxious, and happier than their counterparts who had not been given nutritional supplements. The results suggest how important it is for parents to be attentive to the nutritional needs of their infants.

In further research on early supplementary feeding and children's cognitive development, Ernesto Pollitt and his colleagues (1993) conducted a longitudinal investigation over two decades in rural Guatemala. They found that early nutritional supplements in the form of protein and increased calories can have positive long-term effects on cognitive development. The researchers also found that the relation of nutrition to cognitive performance is moderated both by the time period during which the supplement is given and by the sociodemographic context. For example, the children in the lowest socioeconomic groups benefited more than did the children in higher socioeconomic groups. Although there still was a positive nutritional influence when supplementation began after 2 years of age, the effect on cognitive development was less powerful.

To adequately develop physically, as well as cognitively and socioemotionally, children need a nurturant, supportive environment. One individual who has stood out as an advocate of caring for children is T. Berry Brazelton, who is featured in the Careers in Life-Span Development insert.

Toilet Training

The ability to control elimination depends on both muscular maturation and motivation (Schum & others, 2002). Children must be able to control their muscles to eliminate at the appropriate time, and they must want to eliminate in the toilet or potty, rather than in their pants. Many toddlers are physically able to do this by the time they are about 2 years of age (Bakker & others, 2002; Maizels, Rosenbaum, & Keating, 1999). When toilet training is initiated, it should be accomplished in a warm, relaxed, supportive manner (Michel, 2000).

Many parents today are being encouraged to use a "readiness" approach to toilet training—that is, wait until children show signs that they are ready for toilet training. Pediatricians note that toilet training is being delayed until an older age today more than in earlier generations (American Academy of Pediatrics, 2001). One recent study of almost 500 U.S. children found that 50 percent of the girls were toilet trained by 35 months and 50 percent of the boys by 39 months (Schum & others, 2001).

Some developmentalists argue that delaying toilet training until the twos and threes can make it a battleground because many children at these ages are pushing so strongly for autonomy. Another argument is that late toilet training can be difficult for children who go to day care, because older children in diapers or training pants can be stigmatized by peers.

mhhe●com/
santrockld9

Malnutrition in Infancy
Toilet Training

Review and Reflect

1 **Discuss physical growth and development in infancy**

REVIEW

- What are cephalocaudal and proximodistal patterns?
- What changes in height and weight take place in infancy?
- What are some key features of the brain and its development in infancy?
- What changes occur in sleep during infancy?
- What are infants' nutritional needs?
- When should toilet training be instituted?

REFLECT

- What three pieces of advice about the infant's physical development would you want to give a friend who has just had a baby? Why those three?

2 MOTOR DEVELOPMENT

Reflexes   **Gross and Fine Motor Skills**   **Dynamic Systems Theory**

The study of motor development has seen a renaissance in the past decade. New insights are being made into the ways in which infants acquire motor skills. We will begin our exploration of motor development by examining reflexes, then turn our attention to gross and fine motor skills. To conclude, we will cover dynamic systems theory, which is responsible for the awakened interest in the ways in which infants acquire motor skills.

Reflexes

The newborn is not a passive, unresponsive organism. Among other things, it has some basic reflexes, which are genetically endowed survival mechanisms. For example, the newborn has no fear of water, naturally holding its breath and contracting its throat to keep water out if it is submerged in water. Reflexes can serve as important building blocks for subsequent purposeful motor activity.

Reflexes govern the newborn's movements, which are automatic and beyond the newborn's control. They are built-in reactions to stimuli. Reflexes provide infants adaptive responses to the environment before infants have had the opportunity to learn. Let's look at several of these reflexes:

- The **sucking reflex** occurs when newborns automatically suck an object placed in their mouth. The sucking reflex enables newborns to get nourishment before they have associated a nipple with food. The sucking reflex is an example of a reflex that is present at birth but later disappears.
- The **rooting reflex** occurs when the infant's cheek is stroked or the side of the mouth is touched. In response, the infant turns its head toward the side that was touched in an apparent effort to find something to suck. The sucking and rooting reflexes disappear when the infant is 3 to 4 months old. They are replaced by the infant's voluntary eating. The sucking and rooting reflexes have survival value for newborn mammals, who must find the mother's breast to obtain nourishment.

*T*he experiences of the first three years of life are almost entirely lost to us, and when we attempt to enter into a small child's world, we come as foreigners who have forgotten the landscape and no longer speak the native tongue.

—SELMA FRAIBERG
Developmentalist and Child Advocate, 20th Century

sucking reflex A newborn's built-in reaction of automatically sucking an object placed in its mouth. The sucking reflex enables the infant to get nourishment before it has associated a nipple with food.

rooting reflex A newborn's built-in reaction that occurs when the infant's cheek is stroked or the side of the mouth is touched. In response, the infant turns its head toward the side that was touched, in an apparent effort to find something to suck.

- The **Moro reflex** is a neonatal startle response that occurs in response to a sudden, intense noise or movement. When startled, the newborn arches its back, throws back its head, and flings out its arms and legs. Then the newborn rapidly closes its arms and legs to the center of its body. The Moro reflex is a vestige from our primate ancestry, and it also has survival value—it leads the newborn to grab for support while falling. This reflex, which is normal in all newborns, also tends to disappear at 3 to 4 months of age. Steady pressure on any part of the infant's body calms the infant after it has been startled. Holding the infant's arm flexed at the shoulder will quiet the infant.
- The **grasping reflex** occurs in the first three months of life when something touches the infant's palms. The infant responds by grasping tightly.

Some reflexes present in the newborn—coughing, blinking, and yawning, for example—persist throughout life. They are as important for the adult as they are for the infant. Other reflexes, though, disappear several months following birth, as the infant's brain functions mature, and voluntary control over many behaviors develops. The movements of some reflexes eventually become incorporated into more complex, voluntary actions. One example is the grasping reflex. By the end of the third month, the grasping reflex diminishes, and the infant displays a more voluntary grasp, which is often produced by visual stimuli. For example, when an infant sees a mobile whirling above its crib, it may reach out and try to grasp it. As its motor development becomes smoother, the infant will grasp objects, carefully manipulate them, and explore their qualities.

An overview of the main reflexes we have discussed, along with others, is given in figure 5.10.

Sucking is an especially important reflex: It is the infant's route to nourishment. The sucking capabilities of newborns vary considerably. Some newborns are efficient at forceful sucking and obtaining milk; others are not as adept and get tired before they are full. Most newborns take several weeks to establish a sucking style that is coordinated with the way the mother is holding the infant, the way milk is coming out of the bottle or breast, and the infant's sucking speed and temperament.

Moro reflex A neonatal startle response that occurs in reaction to a sudden, intense noise or movement. When startled, the newborn arches its back, throws its head back, and flings out its arms and legs. Then the newborn rapidly closes its arms and legs to the center of the body.

grasping reflex A neonatal reflex that occurs when something touches the infant's palms. The infant responds by grasping tightly.

Reflex	Stimulation	Infant's Response	Developmental Pattern
Blinking	Flash of light, puff of air	Closes both eyes	Permanent
Babinski	Sole of foot stroked	Fans out toes, twists foot in	Disappears after 9 months to 1 year
Grasping	Palms touched	Grasps tightly	Weakens after 3 months, disappears after 1 year
Moro (startle)	Sudden stimulation, such as hearing loud noise or being dropped	Startles, arches back, throws head back, flings out arms and legs and then rapidly closes them to center of body	Disappears after 3 to 4 months
Rooting	Cheek stroked or side of mouth touched	Turns head, opens mouth, begins sucking	Disappears after 3 to 4 months
Stepping	Infant held above surface and feet lowered to touch surface	Moves feet as if to walk	Disappears after 3 to 4 months
Sucking	Object touching mouth	Sucks automatically	Disappears after 3 to 4 months
Swimming	Infant put face down in water	Makes coordinated swimming movements	Disappears after 6 to 7 months
Tonic neck	Infant placed on back	Forms fists with both hands and usually turns head to the right (sometimes called the "fencer's pose" because the infant looks like it is assuming a fencer's position)	Disappears after 2 months

FIGURE 5.10 Infant Reflexes

A study by pediatrician T. Berry Brazelton (1956) involved observations of infants for more than a year to determine the incidence of their sucking when they were nursing and how their sucking changed as they grew older. Over 85 percent of the infants engaged in considerable sucking behavior unrelated to feeding. They sucked their fingers, their fists, and pacifiers. By the age of 1 year, most had stopped the sucking behavior.

Parents should not worry when infants suck their thumb, their fist, or even a pacifier. Many parents, though, do begin to worry when thumb sucking persists into the preschool and elementary school years. As much as 40 percent of children continue to suck their thumbs after they have started school (Kessen, Haith, & Salapatek, 1970). Most developmentalists do not attach a great deal of significance to this behavior and are not aware of parenting strategies that might contribute to it. Individual differences in children's biological makeup may be involved to some degree in the continuation of sucking behavior.

Gross and Fine Motor Skills

Gross motor skills involve large muscle activities, such as moving one's arms and walking. **Fine motor skills** involve more finely tuned movements, such as finger dexterity. Let's examine the changes in gross and fine motor skills in the first two years of life.

Gross Motor Skills   Ask any parents about their baby, and sooner or later you are likely to hear about one or more motor milestones, such as "Cassandra just learned to crawl," "Jesse is finally sitting alone," or "Shauna took her first step last week." It is no wonder that parents proudly announce such milestones. New motor skills are the most dramatic and observable changes in the infant's first year of life. These motor progressions transform babies from being unable to even lift their heads to being able to grab things off the grocery store shelf, to chase the cat, and to participate actively in the family's social life (Thelen, 1995).

At birth, infants have no appreciable coordination of the chest or arms, but in the first month they can lift their head from a prone position. At about 3 months, infants can hold their chest up and use their arms for support after being in a prone position. At 3 to 4 months, infants can roll over, and at 4 to 5 months they can support some weight with their legs. At about 6 months, infants can sit without support, and by 7 to 8 months they can crawl and stand without support. At approximately 8 months, infants can pull themselves up to a standing position, at 10 to 11 months they can walk using furniture for support (this is called cruising), and at 12 to 13 months they can walk without assistance. A summary of the developmental accomplishments in gross motor skills during the first year is shown in figure 5.11 on page 164. The actual month at which the milestones occur varies by as much as 2 to 4 months, especially among older infants. What remains fairly uniform, however, is the sequence of accomplishments. An important implication of these infant motor accomplishments is the increasing degree of independence they bring. Older infants can explore the environment more extensively and initiate social interaction with caregivers and peers more readily than when they were younger.

Although infants usually learn to walk about their first birthday, the neural pathways that control the leg alternation component of walking are thought to be in place from a very early age, possibly even at birth or before (Thelen, 2000). Infants engage in frequent alternating kicking movements throughout the first six months of life when they are lying on their backs. Also, when 1- to 2-month-olds are given support with their feet in contact with a motorized treadmill, they show well-coordinated, alternating steps.

If infants can produce forward stepping movements so early in their first year of life, why does it take them so long to learn to walk? The key skills in learning to walk appear to be stabilizing balance on one leg long enough to swing the other forward

gross motor skills Motor skills that involve large muscle activities, such as walking.

fine motor skills Motor skills that involve more finely tuned movements, such as finger dexterity.

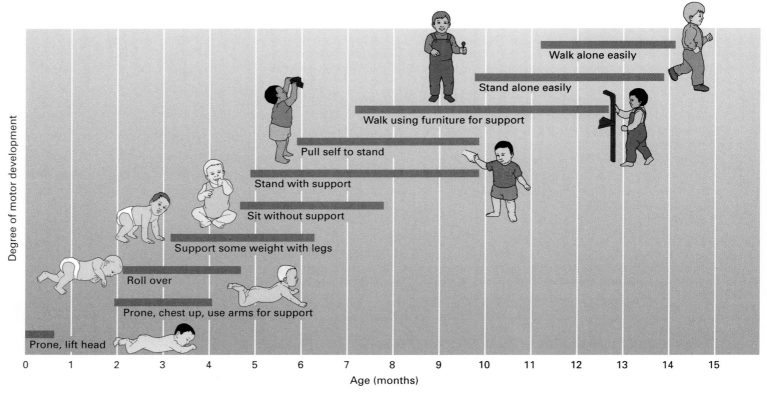

FIGURE 5.11 Milestones in Gross Motor Development

and shifting the weight without falling. This is a difficult biomechanical problem to solve, and it takes infants about a year to do it.

In the second year of life, toddlers become more motorically skilled and mobile. They are no longer content with being in a playpen and want to move all over the place. Child development experts believe that motor activity during the second year is vital to the child's competent development and that few restrictions, except for safety purposes, should be placed on their motoric adventures (Fraiberg, 1959).

By 13 to 18 months, toddlers can pull a toy attached to a string and use their hands and legs to climb up a number of steps. By 18 to 24 months, toddlers can walk quickly or run stiffly for a short distance, balance on their feet in a squat position while playing with objects on the floor, walk backward without losing their balance, stand and kick a ball without falling, stand and throw a ball, and jump in place.

With the increased interest of today's adults in aerobic exercise and fitness, some parents have tried to give their infants a head start on becoming physically fit and physically talented. However, most pediatricians recommend against structured exercise classes for babies. They are seeing more bone fractures and dislocations and more muscle strains in babies now than in the past. They point out that, when an adult is stretching and moving an infant's limbs, it is easy to go beyond the infant's physical limits without knowing it.

Physical fitness classes for infants range from passive fare—with adults putting infants through the paces—to programs called "aerobic" because they demand crawling, tumbling, and ball skills. However, exercise for infants cannot be aerobic, because infants cannot exercise with enough intensity to achieve aerobic benefits.

In most cultures, infants are not exposed to structured physical fitness classes like the ones that are showing up in the United States. However, when parents or other caregivers provide babies with physical guidance by physically handling them in special ways (such as stroking, massaging, or stretching) or providing them with

mhhe●com/
santrockld9

Developmental Milestones
Physical Development in Infancy

opportunities for exercise, the infants often attain motor milestones earlier than infants whose caregivers have not provided these physical activities. For example, Jamaican mothers expect their infants to sit and walk alone two to three months earlier than English mothers do (Hopkins & Westra, 1990). Also, Jamaican mothers regularly massage their infants and stretch their arms and legs, and this is linked with advanced motor development (Hopkins, 1991). In the Gusii culture of Kenya, mothers encourage vigorous movement in their babies (Hopkins & Westra, 1988).

In developing countries, mothers often attempt to stimulate their infants' motor skills more than mothers in more advanced cultures (Hopkins, 1991). This stimulation of infants' motor skills in developing countries may be necessary to improve the infants' chances of survival. In some cases, the emphasis on early stimulation may occur because the caregivers recognize that motor skills are required for important jobs in the culture. Others factors such as climate and spiritual beliefs also may influence the way that caregivers guide their infants' motor development.

Although infants in some cultures, such as Jamaica, reach motor milestones earlier than infants in many cultures, nonetheless, regardless of how much practice takes place, infants around the world reach these motor milestones within the same age range. For example, Algonquin infants in Quebec, Canada, spend much of their first year strapped to a cradle board. Despite such inactivity, these infants still sit up, crawl, and walk within an age range similar to infants in other cultures who have much greater opportunity for activity. In sum, there are slight variations in the age at which infants reach motor milestones depending on their activity opportunities in different cultures, but the variations are not substantial and they are within normal ranges.

Fine Motor Skills Infants have hardly any control over fine motor skills at birth, although they have many components of what later become finely coordinated arm, hand, and finger movements (Rosenblith, 1992). The onset of reaching and grasping marks a significant achievement in infants' functional interactions with their surroundings (McCarty & Ashmead, 1999).

For many years it was believed that reaching for an object is visually guided—that is, the infant must continuously have sight of the hand and the target (White, Castle, & Held, 1964). However, in one study, Rachel Clifton and her colleagues (1993) demonstrated that infants do not have to see their own hands when reaching for an object. They concluded that, because the infants could not see their hand or arm in the dark in the experiment, proprioceptive (muscle, tendon, joint sense) cues, not sight of limb, guided the early reaching of the 4-month-old infants.

The development of reaching and grasping becomes more refined during the first two years of life. Initially, infants show only crude shoulder and elbow movements, but later they show wrist movements, hand rotation, and coordination of the thumb and forefinger. The maturation of hand-eye coordination over the first two years of life is reflected in the improvement of fine motor skills. Figure 5.12 on page 166 provides an overview of the development of fine motor skills in the first two years of life.

The infant's grasping system is very flexible and the environment plays a stronger role in grasping than previously thought. One way to show that the environment influences grasping is to vary the motor task and examine if this influences the infant's responses. This can be done by changing the size and shape of the objects for the infant to grasp. Indeed, infants vary their grip on

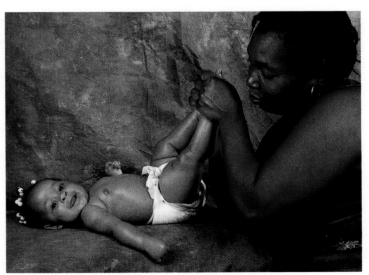

(*Top*) In the Algonquin culture in Quebec, Canada, babies are strapped to a cradle board for much of their infancy. (*Bottom*) In Jamaica, mothers massage and stretch their infants' arms and legs. *To what extent do cultural variations infants activities influence the time at which they reach motor milestones?*

Birth to 6 months

2 months	Holds rattle briefly
2½ months	Glances from one object to another
3 to 4 months	Plays in simple way with rattle; inspects fingers; reaches for dangling ring; visually follows ball across table
4 months	Carries object to mouth
4 to 5 months	Recovers rattle from chest; holds two objects
5 months	Transfers object from hand to hand
5 to 6 months	Bangs in play; looks for object while sitting

6 to 12 months

6 months	Secures cube on sight; follows adult's movements across room; immediately fixates on small objects and stretches out to grasp them; retains rattle
6½ months	Manipulates and examines an object; reaches for, grabs, and retains rattle
7 months	Pulls string to obtain an object
7½ to 8½ months	Grasps with thumb and finger
8 to 9 months	Persists in reaching for toy out of reach on table; shows hand preference, bangs spoon; searches in correct place for toys dropped within reach of hands; may find toy hidden under cup
10 months	Hits cup with spoon; crude release of object
10½ to 11 months	Picks up raisin with thumb and forefinger; pincer grasp; pushes car along
11 to 12 months	Puts three or more objects in a container

12 to 18 months

Places one 2-inch block on top of another 2-inch block (in imitation)

Scribbles with a large crayon on large piece of paper

Turns two to three pages in a large book with cardboard pages while sitting in an adult's lap

Places three 1-inch cube blocks in a 6-inch diameter cup (in imitation)

Holds a pencil and makes a mark on a sheet of paper

Builds a four-block tower with 2-inch cube blocks (in imitation)

18 to 24 months

Draws an arc on a piece of unlined paper with a pencil after being shown how

Turns a doorknob that is within reach, using both hands

Unscrews a lid put loosely on a small jar after being shown how

Places large pegs in a pegboard

Connects and takes apart a pop bead string of five beads

Zips and unzips a large zipper after being shown how

FIGURE 5.12 The Development of Fine Motor Skills in Infancy

an object depending on its size and shape, as well as the size of their own hands relative to the object's size. Infants grip small objects with their thumb and forefinger (and sometimes their middle finger too) while they grip large objects with all of the fingers of one hand or both hands.

In studies of grasping, age differences occur in regard to which perceptual system is most likely to be used in coordinating grasping. Four-month-olds rely more on touch to determine how they will grip an object; eight-month-olds are more likely to use vision as a guide (Newell & others, 1989). This developmental change is efficient because vision lets infants preshape their hands as they reach for an object. As we see next, such perceptual-motor coupling is an important aspect of dynamic systems theory.

Dynamic Systems Theory

The study of motor development has seen a renaissance in the last decade. Historically, researcher Arnold Gesell (1934), as well as others, gave rich descriptions of motor milestones, but they assumed that they were unfolding as a consequence of a genetic plan. In recent years, it has become recognized that motor development is not the result of nature alone or nurture alone. And there has been a shift to focus on *how* motor skills develop.

Esther Thelen (1995, 2000, 2001) has presented a new theory that reflects the new perspective in motor development. **Dynamic systems theory** seeks to explain how motor behaviors are assembled for perceiving and acting. In this theory, "assembly" means the coordination or convergence of a number of factors, such as the development of the nervous system, the body's physical properties and movement possibilities, the goal the infant is motivated to reach, and the environmental support for the skill. This theory also emphasizes that perception and action work together in the infant's mastery of a skill.

The dynamic systems view contrasts with the traditional maturational view by proposing that even the universal milestones, such as crawling, reaching, and walking are learned through a process of adaptation (Goldfield & Wolff, 2002). It emphasizes exploration and selection in finding solutions to new task demands. In other words, infants modify their movement patterns to fit a new task by exploring and selecting various configurations. The assumption is that the infant is motivated by the new challenge—a desire to get a new toy in one's mouth or to cross the room to join other family members. It is the new task, the challenge of the context, not a genetic program that represents the driving force for change.

Let's look at two babies—Gabriel and Hannah—to see how dynamic systems theory describes and explains their behavior and development (Bower, 1999). Each child improvises ways to reach out with one of their arms from a sitting position and wrap their fingers around a new toy. Gabriel and Hannah make all sorts of split-second adjustments to keep each reaching motion on course. Their rapid arm extension requires holding their bodies steady so that their arm and upper torso don't plow into the toy. Muscles in their arm and shoulder contract and stretch in a host of combinations and

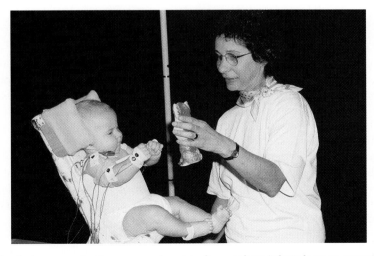

Esther Thelen is shown conducting an experiment to discover how infants learn to control their arms to reach and grasp for objects. A computer device is used to monitor the infant's arm movements and to track muscle patterns. Thelen's research is conducted from a dynamic systems perspective. *What is the nature of this perspective?*

dynamic systems theory The new perspective on motor development in infancy that seeks to explain how motor behaviors are assembled for perceiving and acting.

exert a variety of forces. Their arm movements are not exact, machinelike motions that can be precisely planned out in advance but rather adapt to the goal and context at hand—how to pick up the new toy.

Review and Reflect

2 Describe infants' motor development

REVIEW

- What are some reflexes that infants have?
- How do gross and fine motor skills develop in infancy?
- What is dynamic systems theory?

REFLECT

- Which view of infant motor development do you prefer—the traditional maturational view or the dynamic systems view? Why?

3 SENSORY AND PERCEPTUAL DEVELOPMENT

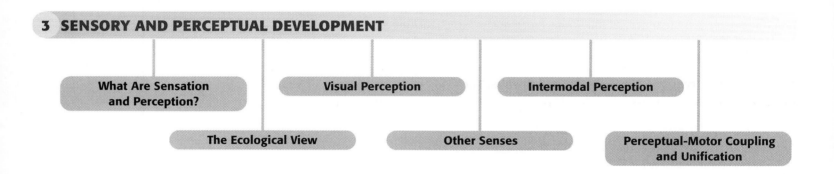

What Are Sensation and Perception?

The Ecological View

Visual Perception

Other Senses

Intermodal Perception

Perceptual-Motor Coupling and Unification

A key theme in the dynamic systems view that we just discussed is that perception and action are coupled when new skills are learned. Keep this idea in mind as you read about sensory and perceptual development (Slater, 2001).

What Are Sensation and Perception?

How does a newborn know that her mother's skin is soft rather than rough? How does a 5-year-old know what color his hair is? How does an 8-year-old know that summer is warmer than winter? How does a 10-year-old know that a firecracker is louder than a cat's meow? Infants and children "know" these things because of their senses. All information comes to the infant through the senses. Without vision, hearing, touch, taste, smell, and other senses, the infant's brain would be isolated from the world; the infant would live in dark silence, a tasteless, colorless, feelingless void.

Sensation occurs when information interacts with sensory receptors—the eyes, ears, tongue, nose, and skin. The sensation of hearing occurs when waves of pulsating air are collected by the outer ear and transmitted through the bones of the inner ear to the auditory nerve. The sensation of vision occurs as rays of light contact the eyes and become focused on the retina.

Perception is the interpretation of what is sensed. The information about physical events that contacts the ears may be interpreted as musical sounds, for example. The physical energy transmitted to the retinas may be interpreted as a particular color, pattern, or shape.

sensation The product of the interaction between information and the sensory receptors—the eyes, ears, tongue, nostrils, and skin.

perception The interpretation of what is sensed.

The Ecological View

In the past several decades, much of the research on perceptual development in infancy has been guided by the ecological view of Eleanor and James J. Gibson (E. J. Gibson, 1969, 1989, 2001; J. J. Gibson, 1966, 1979). They believe that we can directly perceive information that exists in the world around us: We do not have to build up representations of the world in our mind; information about the world is available in the environment. Thus, the **ecological view** states that perception functions to bring organisms in contact with the environment and increase adaptation. In ecological theory, perception is for action. Perception gives people such information as when to duck, when to turn their body through a narrow passageway, and when to put a hand up to catch something.

The Gibsons believe that if complex things can be perceived directly, perhaps they can be perceived even by young infants. Thus, the ecological view has inspired investigators to search for the competencies that young infants possess. Of course, ecological theorists do not deny that perception develops as infants and children develop. In fact, the ecological theorists stress that, as perceptual processes mature, the child becomes more efficient at discovering the properties of objects available to the senses.

For the Gibsons, all objects have **affordances,** which are opportunities for interaction offered by objects that are necessary to perform functional activities. For example, adults immediately know when a chair is appropriate for sitting, a surface is for walking, or an object is within reach. We directly and accurately perceive these affordances by sensing information from the environment—such as the light or sound reflected by the surfaces of the world—and from our own bodies through muscle receptors, joint receptors, skin receptors, and the like. The developmental question, though, is how these affordances are acquired. In one study, infants who were crawlers or walkers recognized the action-specific properties of surfaces (Gibson & others, 1987). When faced with a rigid plywood surface or a squishy waterbed, crawlers crossed both without hesitating. The toddlers, however, stopped and explored the waterbed, then chose to crawl rather than walk across it. Note the coupling of perception and action to adapt to a particular task demand in the world.

In another study, infants who were learning to walk were more cautious about descending a steep slope than younger infants were (Adolph, 1997). The older infants perceived that a slope *affords* the possibility not only for faster locomotion but also for falling.

Visual Perception

Can newborns see? How does visual perception develop in infancy?

Visual Acuity and Color   Psychologist William James (1890/1950) called the newborn's perceptual world a "blooming, buzzing confusion." Was James right? A century later, we can safely say that he was wrong. The infant's perception of visual information is far more advanced than was once thought (Slater, 2001).

Just how well can infants see? The newborn's vision is estimated to be 20/400 to 20/800 on the well-known Snellen chart, with which you are tested when you have your eyes examined (Haith, 1991). This is about 10 to 30 times lower than normal adult vision (20/20). By 6 months of age, though, vision is 20/100 or better, and, by about the first birthday, the infant's vision approximates that of an adult (Banks & Salapatek, 1983). Figure 5.13 on page 170 shows a computer estimation of what a picture of a face looks like to an infant at different points in development from a distance of about 6 inches.

Can newborns see color? At birth, babies can distinguish between green and red (Adams, 1989). Adultlike functioning in all three types (red, blue, green) of color-sensitive receptors is present by 2 months of age.

Perceptual Development

Newborns' Senses

Richard Aslin's Research

International Society on Infant Studies

The infant is by no means as helpless as it looks and is quite capable of some very complex and important actions.

—**HERB PICK**
Contemporary Developmental Psychologist, University of Minnesota

ecological view The view that perception functions to bring organisms in contact with the environment and to increase adaptation.

affordances Opportunities for interaction offered by objects that are necessary to perform functional activities.

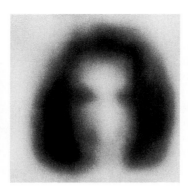

FIGURE 5.13 Visual Acuity During the First Months of Life

The four photographs represent a computer estimation of what a picture of a face looks like to a 1-month-old, 2-month-old, 3-month-old, and 1-year-old (which approximates that of an adult).

Visual Preferences   Robert Fantz (1963) is a pioneer in the study of visual perception in infants. Fantz made an important discovery that advanced the ability of researchers to investigate infants' visual perception: Infants look at different things for different lengths of time. Fantz placed infants in a "looking chamber," which had two visual displays on the ceiling above the infant's head. An experimenter viewed the infant's eyes by looking through a peephole. If the infant was fixating on one of the displays, the experimenter could see the display's reflection in the infant's eyes. This allowed the experimenter to determine how long the infant looked at each display. In figure 5.14, you can see Fantz's looking chamber and the results of his experiment. The infants preferred to look at patterns rather than at color or brightness. For example, they preferred to look at a face, a piece of printed matter, or a bull's-eye longer than at red, yellow, or white discs. In another experiment, Fantz found that younger infants—only 2 days old—look longer at patterned stimuli, such as faces and concentric circles, than at red, white, or yellow discs. Based on these results, it is likely that

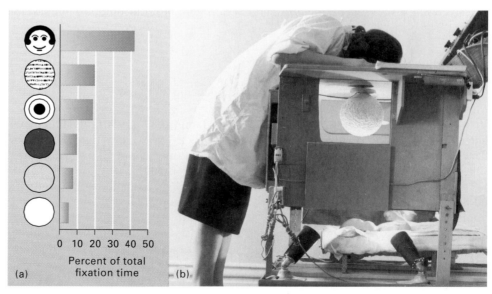

FIGURE 5.14 Fantz's Experiment on Infants' Visual Perception

(*a*) Infants 2 to 3 months old preferred to look at some stimuli more than others. In Fantz's experiment, infants preferred to look at patterns rather than at color or brightness. For example, they looked longer at a face, a piece of printed matter, or a bull's-eye than at red, yellow, or white discs. (*b*) Fantz used a "looking chamber" to study infants' perception of stimuli.

pattern perception has an innate basis, or at least is acquired after only minimal environmental experience. The newborn's visual world is not the blooming, buzzing confusion William James imagined.

Perception of Faces   The human face is perhaps the most important visual pattern for the newborn to perceive. The infant progresses through a sequence of steps to full perceptual appreciation of the face (Gibson, 1969). At about 3½ weeks the infant is fascinated with the eyes, perhaps because the infant notices simple perceptual features such as dots, angles, and circles. At 2 months of age and older, the infant begins to notice the mouth and pay attention to its movements. By 5 months of age the infant has detected other features of the face, such as its three-dimensional surface and the oval shape of the head. Beyond 6 months of age, the infant distinguishes familiar faces from unfamiliar faces—mother from stranger and masks from real faces, for example.

How do young infants scan the human face? In one study, researchers showed human faces to 1- and 2-month-old infants (Maurer & Salapatek, 1976). By use of a special mirror arrangement, the faces were projected as images in front of the infant's eyes so that the infant's eye movements could be photographed. Figure 5.15 shows the plotting of eye fixations of a 1-month-old and a 2-month-old infant. Notice that the 1-month-old scanned only a few portions of the entire face—a narrow segment of the chin and two spots on the head. The 2-month-old scanned a much wider area of the face—the mouth, the eyes, and a large portion of the head. The older infant also spent more time examining the internal details of the face, while the younger infant concentrated more on the outer contour of the face.

Depth Perception   How early can infants perceive depth? To investigate this question, infant perception researchers Eleanor Gibson and Richard Walk (1960) conducted a classic experiment. They constructed a miniature cliff with a drop-off covered by glass. The motivation for this experiment arose when Gibson was eating a picnic lunch on the edge of the Grand Canyon. She wondered whether an infant looking over the canyon's rim would perceive the dangerous drop-off and back up. In their laboratory, Gibson and Walk placed infants on the edge of a visual cliff and had their mothers coax them to crawl onto the glass (see figure 5.16). Most infants would not crawl out on the glass, choosing instead to remain on the shallow side, indicating that they could perceive depth. However, because the 6- to 14-month-old infants had extensive visual experience, this research did not answer the question of whether depth perception is innate.

Exactly how early in life does depth perception develop? Since younger infants do not crawl, this question is difficult to answer. Research with 2- to 4-month-old infants shows differences in heart rate when they are placed directly on the deep side of the visual cliff instead of on the shallow side (Campos, Langer, & Krowitz, 1970). However, an alternative interpretation is that young infants respond to differences in some visual characteristics of the deep and shallow cliffs, with no actual knowledge of depth.

Visual Expectations   Infants not only see forms and figures at an early age but also develop expectations about future events in their world by the time they are 3 months of age. Marshall Haith and his colleagues (Canfield & Haith, 1991; Haith, Hazen, & Goodman, 1988) studied whether babies would form expectations about where an interesting picture would appear. The pictures were presented to the infants in either a regularly

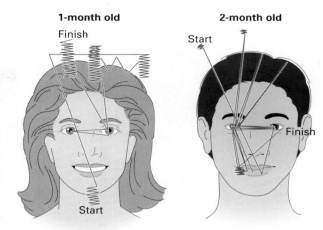

FIGURE 5.15 How 1- and 2-Month-Old Infants Scan the Human Face

FIGURE 5.16 Examining Infants' Depth Perception on the Visual Cliff

Eleanor Gibson and Richard Walk (1960) found that most infants would not crawl out on the glass, which indicated that they had depth perception.

FIGURE 5.17 The Young Infant's Knowledge of the Perceptual World

A 4-month-old in Elizabeth Spelke's infant perception laboratory is tested to determine if it knows that an object in motion will not stop in midair.

mhhe com/
santrockld9

Elizabeth Spelke's Research

alternating sequence—such as left, right, left, right—or an unpredictable sequence—such as right, right, left, right. When the sequence was predictable, the 3-month-old infants began to anticipate the location of the picture, looking at the side on which it was expected to appear. The young infants formed this visual expectation in less than one minute. However, younger infants did not develop expectations about where a picture would be presented.

Elizabeth Spelke (1988, 1991) also has demonstrated that young infants form visual expectations. She placed babies before a puppet stage and showed them a series of unexpected actions—for example, a ball seemed to roll through a solid barrier, another seemed to leap between two platforms, and a third appeared to hang in midair (Spelke, 1979) (see figure 5.17). Spelke measured the babies' looking times and recorded longer intervals for unexpected than expected actions. She concluded that, by 4 months of age, even though infants do not yet have the ability to talk about objects, move around objects, manipulate objects, or even see objects with high resolution, they can recognize where a moving object is when it has left their visual field and can infer where it should be when it comes into their sight again.

Other Senses

Considerable development also takes place in other sensory systems during infancy. We will explore development in hearing, touch and pain, smell, and taste.

Hearing Can the fetus hear? What is the newborn's hearing like? What types of auditory stimulation should be used with infants at different points in the first year?

In the last few months of pregnancy, the fetus can hear sounds: the mother's voice, music, and so on (Kisilevsky, 1995). Given that the fetus can hear sounds, two psychologists wanted to find out if listening to Dr. Seuss' classic story *The Cat in the Hat*, while still in the mother's womb, would produce a preference for hearing the story after birth (DeCasper & Spence, 1986). Sixteen pregnant women read *The Cat in the Hat* to their fetuses twice a day over the last six weeks of their pregnancies. When the babies were born, their mothers read *The Cat in the Hat* or a story with a different rhyme and pace, *The King, the Mice and the Cheese* (which was not read to them during prenatal development). The infants sucked on a nipple in a different way when the mothers read *The Cat in the Hat*, suggesting that the infants recognized its pattern and tone (to which they had been exposed prenatally) (see figure 5.18).

Two important conclusions can be drawn from this investigation. First, it reveals how ingenious scientists have become at assessing the development not only of infants but of fetuses as well, in this case discovering a way to "interview" newborn babies who cannot yet talk. Second, it reveals the remarkable ability of an infant's brain to learn even before birth. However, conclusions from this study should not be overdrawn. It does not suggest that reading to an infant prenatally will produce a child who acquires language and cognitive development more rapidly.

Immediately after birth, infants can hear, although their sensory thresholds are somewhat higher than those of adults (Slater, Field, & Hernandez-Reif, 2002; Trehub & others, 1991). That is, a stimulus must be louder to be heard by a newborn than by an adult. Also, in one study, as infants aged from 8 to 28 weeks, they became more proficient at localizing sounds (Morrongiello, Fenwick, & Chance, 1990).

Babies are born into the world prepared to respond to the sounds of any human language. Even very young infants can discriminate subtle phonetic differences, such as those between the speech sounds of *ba* and *ga*. Young infants also will suck more

FIGURE 5.18 Hearing in the Womb

(*a*) Pregnant mothers read *The Cat in the Hat* to their fetuses during the last few months of pregnancy. (*b*) When they were born, the babies preferred listening to a recording of their mothers reading *The Cat in the Hat*, as evidenced by their sucking on a nipple that produced this recording, rather than another story, *The King, the Mice and the Cheese.*

rapidly on a nipple in order to listen to some sounds rather than others (Flohr & others, 2001; Mehler & others, 1988; Spence & DeCasper, 1987):

- A recording of their mother's voice is preferred to the voice of an unfamiliar woman.
- Their mother's native language is preferred to a foreign language.
- The classical music of Beethoven is preferred to the rock music of Aerosmith.

And an interesting developmental change occurs during the first year of life. Six-month-old infants can discriminate phonetic sound contrasts from languages to which they have never been exposed, but they lose this discriminative ability by their first birthday. This finding demonstrates that experience with a specific language is necessary for retaining this ability (Werker & LaLonde, 1988).

Touch and Pain Do newborns respond to touch? Can newborns feel pain?

Touch Newborns respond to touch. A touch to the cheek produces a turning of the head, whereas a touch to the lips produces sucking movements. An important ability that develops in infancy is to connect information about vision with information about touch. One-year-olds clearly can do this, and it appears that 6-month-olds can, too (Acredolo & Hake, 1982). Whether still younger infants can coordinate vision and touch is yet to be determined.

Pain It once was thought that newborns are indifferent to pain, but we now know that is not true. The main research that has documented newborns' sensitivity to pain involves male infants' stressful reactions to being circumcised (Gunnar, Malone, & Fisch, 1987). For example, newborn males show a higher level of cortisol (a hormonal response to stress) after circumcision than prior to the surgery. As a consequence, anesthesia now is used in some cases of circumcision (Taddio & others, 1997).

For many years, doctors have performed operations on newborns without anesthesia. This medical practice was accepted because of the dangers of anesthesia and the supposition that newborns do not feel pain. Recently, as researchers have convincingly demonstrated that newborns can feel pain, the long-standing practice of operating on newborns without anesthesia is being challenged.

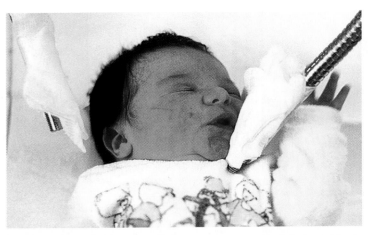

FIGURE 5.19 Newborns' Preference for the Smell of Their Mother's Breast Pad

In the experiment by MacFarlane (1975), 6-day-old infants preferred to smell their mother's breast pad rather than a clean one that had never been used, but 2-day-old infants did not show the preference, indicating that this odor preference requires several days of experience to develop.

Smell   Newborns can differentiate odors. For example, by the expressions on their faces, they seem to indicate that they like the smell of vanilla and strawberry but do not like the smell of rotten eggs and fish (Steiner, 1979). In one investigation, young infants who were breast-fed showed a clear preference for smelling their mother's breast pad when they were 6 days old (MacFarlane, 1975) (see figure 5.19). However, when they were 2 days old, they did not show this preference (compared to a clean breast pad), indicating that they require several days of experience to recognize this odor.

Taste   Sensitivity to taste might be present before birth. When saccharin was added to the amniotic fluid of a near-term fetus, increased swallowing was observed (Windle, 1940). In one study, even at only 2 hours of age, babies made different facial expressions when they tasted sweet, sour, and bitter solutions (Rosenstein & Oster, 1988) (see figure 5.20). At about 4 months of age, infants begin to prefer salty tastes, which as newborns they were averse to (Harris, Thomas, & Booth, 1990).

Intermodal Perception

Imagine yourself playing basketball or tennis. You are experiencing many visual inputs: the ball coming and going, other players moving around, and so on. You are also experiencing many auditory inputs: the sound of the ball bouncing or being hit, the grunts and groans, and so on. There is good correspondence between much of the visual and auditory information: When you see the ball bounce, you hear a bouncing sound; when a player stretches to hit a ball, you hear a groan.

We live in a world of objects and events that can be seen, heard, and felt. When mature observers simultaneously look and listen to an event, they experience a unitary episode. All of this is so commonplace that it scarcely seems worth mentioning, but consider the task of very young infants with little practice at perceiving. Can they put vision and sound together as precisely as adults do?

Intermodal perception is the ability to relate and integrate information about two or more sensory modalities, such as vision and hearing. To test intermodal perception, Elizabeth Spelke (1979) showed 4-month-old infants two films simultaneously. In each film, a puppet jumped up and down, but in one of the films the sound track matched the puppet's dancing movements; in the other film, it did not. By measuring the infants' gaze, Spelke found that the infants looked more at the puppet whose actions were synchronized with the sound track, suggesting that they recognized the visual-sound correspondence. Young infants can also coordinate visual-auditory information involving people (Condry, Smuth, & Spelke, 2001). In one study, infants as young as 3½ months old looked more at their mother when they also heard her voice and longer at their father when they also heard his voice (Spelke & Owsley, 1979).

Might auditory-visual relations be coordinated even in newborns? Newborns do turn their eyes and their head toward the sound of a voice or rattle when the sound is maintained for several seconds (Clifton & others, 1981), but the newborn can localize a sound and look at an object only in a crude way (Bechtold, Bushnell, & Salapatek, 1979). Improved accuracy at auditory-visual coordination likely requires a sharpening through experience with visual and auditory stimuli. Nonetheless, although at a crude level, auditory-visual intermodal perception appears to be present at birth, likely having evolutionary value.

In sum, crude exploratory forms of intermodal perception exist in newborns. These exploratory forms of intermodal perception become sharpened with experience in the first year of life. In the first 6 months, infants have difficulty forming mental representations that connect sensory input from different modes, but in the second half of the first year they show an increased ability to make this connection mentally.

intermodal perception The ability to relate and integrate information about two or more sensory modalities, such as vision and hearing.

Thus, babies come into the world with some innate abilities to perceive relations among sensory modalities, but their intermodal abilities improve considerably through experience. As with all aspects of development, in perceptual development, nature and nurture interact and cooperate.

Perceptual-Motor Coupling and Unification

For the most part our discussion of motor development and sensory/perceptual development have been separated in this chapter. Indeed, the main thrust of research in many studies has been to discover how perception guides action. A less well studied but important issue is how action shapes perception. Motor activities might be crucial because they provide the means for exploring the world and learning about its properties. Only by moving one's eyes, head, hands, and arms and by traversing from one location to another can individuals fully experience their environment and learn to effectively adapt to it.

The distinction between perceiving and doing has been a time-honored tradition in psychology. However, a number of contemporary experts on perceptual and motor development question this distinction (Bornstein & Arterberry, 1999; Lochman, 2000; Pick, 1997; Thelen, 2000, 2001). For example, Esther Thelen (1995) argues that individuals perceive in order to move and move in order to perceive. Thus, there is an increasing belief that perceptual and motor development do not occur in isolation from one another but, rather, are coupled.

Babies are continually coordinating their movements with concurrent perceptual information to learn how to maintain balance, reach for objects in space, and locomote across various surfaces and terrains (Thelen, 2001). To illustrate how infants are motivated to move by what they perceive, consider the sight of an attractive object across the room. In this situation, infants must perceive the current state of their bodies and learn how to use their limbs to get to the goal object. Although their movements at first are awkward and uncoordinated, babies soon learn to select patterns that are appropriate for reaching their goals. Equally important is the other part of the perception-action coupling: action educates perception. For example, watching an object while exploring it manually helps infants to visually discriminate its properties of texture, size, and hardness. Locomoting in the environment teaches babies how objects and people look from different perspectives or whether surfaces will support their weight.

Also think about how often during each day you need to coordinate perceptual input with motor actions to accomplish what you want to do. For example, right now I am looking at my computer screen (perceiving) to make sure the words are appearing accurately as I am typing them (motorically). We develop this ability by physically exploring the world revealed to us by sensation and perception, thus experiencing new sensations and perceptions to be explored.

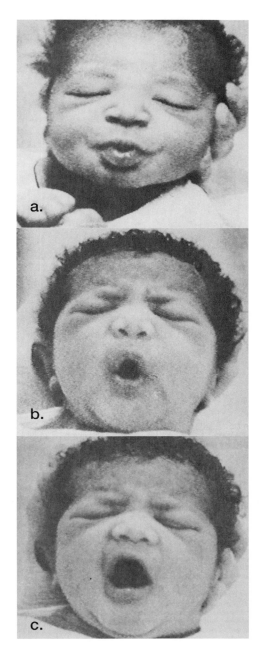

FIGURE 5.20 Newborns' Facial Responses to Basic Tastes

Facial expressions elicited by (*a*) a sweet solution, (*b*) a sour solution, and (*c*) a bitter solution.

Review and Reflect

3 Explain sensory and perceptual development in infancy

REVIEW

- What are sensation and perception?
- What is the ecological view of perception?
- How does visual perception develop in infancy?
- How do hearing, touch and pain, smell, and taste develop in infancy?
- What is intermodal perception?
- How is perceptual-motor development coupled and unified?

REFLECT

- How much sensory stimulation should caregivers provide for infants? A little? A lot? Could an infant be given too much sensory stimulation? Explain.

Reach Your Learning Goals

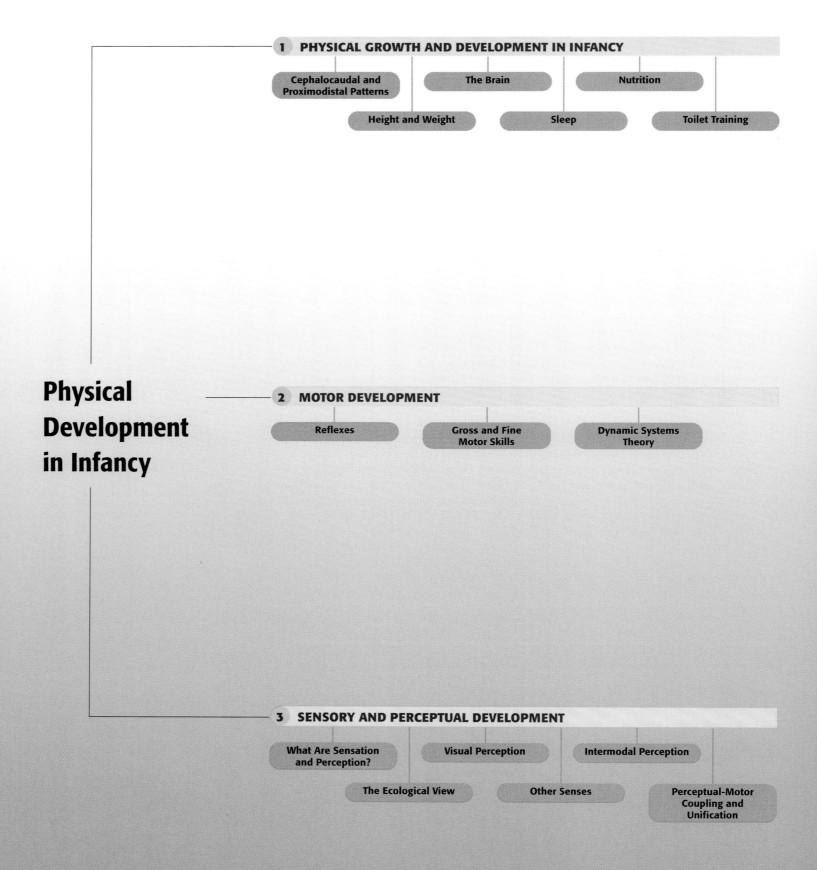

Physical Development in Infancy

1 PHYSICAL GROWTH AND DEVELOPMENT IN INFANCY

- Cephalocaudal and Proximodistal Patterns
- Height and Weight
- The Brain
- Sleep
- Nutrition
- Toilet Training

2 MOTOR DEVELOPMENT

- Reflexes
- Gross and Fine Motor Skills
- Dynamic Systems Theory

3 SENSORY AND PERCEPTUAL DEVELOPMENT

- What Are Sensation and Perception?
- The Ecological View
- Visual Perception
- Other Senses
- Intermodal Perception
- Perceptual-Motor Coupling and Unification

Summary

1   Discuss physical growth and development in infancy

- The cephalocaudal pattern is the sequence in which growth proceeds from top to bottom. The proximodistal pattern is the sequence in which growth starts at the center of the body and moves toward the extremities.
- The average North American newborn is 20 inches long and weighs $7\frac{1}{2}$ pounds. Infants grow about 1 inch per month in the first year and nearly triple their weight by their first birthday. The rate of growth slows in the second year.
- One of the most dramatic changes in the brain in the first two years of life is dendritic spreading. Myelination continues through infancy and even into adolescence. The cerebral cortex has two hemispheres (left and right). Lateralization refers to the specialization of function in one hemisphere or the other. Research with animals suggests that the environment plays a key role in early brain development. Neural connections are formed early in an infant's life. Before birth, genes mainly direct neurons to different locations. After birth, the inflowing stream of sights, sounds, smells, touches, language, and eye contact help shape the brain's neural connections.
- Newborns usually sleep 16 to 17 hours a day. By 4 months of age, many American infants approach adultlike sleeping patterns. REM sleep—during which dreaming occurs—is present more in early infancy than in childhood and adulthood. Sleeping arrangements for infants vary across cultures. In America, infants are more likely to sleep alone than in many other cultures. Some experts believe shared sleeping can lead to sudden infant death syndrome (SIDS), a condition that occurs when a sleeping infant suddenly stops breathing and dies without an apparent cause.
- Infants need to consume about 50 calories per day for each pound they weigh. The growing consensus is that breast-feeding is superior to bottle-feeding. Severe infant malnutrition is still prevalent in many parts of the world. A special concern in impoverished countries is early weaning from breast milk.
- Toilet training is expected to be attained by about 3 years of age in North America. Toilet training should be carried out in a relaxed, supportive manner.

2   Describe infants' motor development

- The newborn is not a passive organism. Reflexes (automatic movements, such as the rooting reflex and the Moro reflex) govern the newborn's behavior. For infants, sucking is an especially important reflex because it provides a means of obtaining nutrition.
- Gross motor skills involve large muscle activities, such as moving one's arms and walking. A number of gross motor milestones occur in infancy although the actual month of these milestones may vary as much as 2 to 4 months, especially in older infants. Although, infants usually learn to walk by their first birthday, the neural pathways that allow walking begin to form earlier. Fine motor skills involve movements that are more finely tuned than gross motor skills. A number of fine motor milestones occur in infancy. The development of reaching and grasping becomes more refined during the first two years of life.
- Dynamic systems theory seeks to explain how motor behaviors are assembled for perceiving and acting. This approach emphasizes the importance of exploration and selection in finding solutions to new task demands. A key theme is that perception and action are coupled when new skills are learned.

3   Explain sensory and perceptual development in infancy

- Sensation occurs when information interacts with the sensory receptors—the eyes, ears, tongue, nose, and skin. Perception is the interpretation of what is sensed.
- In the ecological view, perception functions to bring organisms in contact with the environment and increase adaptation.
- William James was wrong in belief that the newborn's visual world is a "blooming, buzzing confusion." Newborns can see and can distinguish colors, and they prefer to look at patterns rather than at color or brightness. In Fantz's pioneering research, infants only 2 days old looked longer at patterned stimuli, such as faces, than at single-colored discs. The human face is one of the most important visual patterns for infants to perceive and they show developmental changes in how they perceive faces. A classic study by Gibson and Walk demonstrated through the use of the visual cliff that infants as young as 6 months of age have depth perception. Haith has demonstrated that infants develop expectations about future events in their world by the time they are 3 months of age.
- The fetus can hear in the last few months before birth. Immediately after birth, a newborn can hear, and its sensory threshold is higher than that of adults. Newborns respond to touch and can feel pain.
- Intermodal perception is the ability to relate and integrate information about two or more sensory modalities, such as vision and hearing. Spelke's research demonstrated that infants as young as $3\frac{1}{2}$ months of age can link visual and auditory stimuli.
- A time-honored belief in psychology has been that perceptual and motor development are distinct. Increasingly, it is believed that perceptual-motor development is coupled and unified. For example, infants perceive in order to move and move in order to perceive. Babies are continually coordinating their movements with concurrent information to learn how to maintain balance, reach for objects, and locomote.

Key Terms

cephalocaudal pattern 149
proximodistal pattern 149
neuron 150
lateralization 153
sudden infant death syndrome
   (SIDS) 156

marasmus 159
kwashiorkor 159
sucking reflex 161
rooting reflex 161
Moro reflex 162
grasping reflex 162

gross motor skills 163
fine motor skills 163
dynamic systems theory 167
sensation 168
perception 168
ecological view 169

affordances 169
intermodal perception 174

Key People

Charles Nelson 152
Mark Rosenzweig 153
Ernesto Pollitt 159
T. Berry Brazelton 160, 163

Rachel Clifton 165
Esther Thelen 167, 175
Eleanor and James J.
   Gibson 169

William James 169
Robert Fantz 170
Richard Walk 171
Marshall Haith 171

Elizabeth Spelke 172, 174

mhhe com/
santrockld9 **Taking It to the Net**

1. Professor Samuels asked his life-span psychology students to write a one-page report explaining how a child's brain develops during infancy and what role parents play in fostering maximal brain development. What should this report contain that would provide a comprehensive explanation of the research found to date?

2. Huy grew up in a traditional Chinese family, where co-sleeping until adolescence was the norm. He sees no problem with allowing his infant daughter to sleep with him and his wife. His wife, Lori, who was born and raised in the United States, is concerned that allowing her to sleep in their bed places her at risk for SIDS. Is co-sleeping a significant risk factor for SIDS? What else can Huy and Lori do to reduce the risk?

3. Marianne has landed a part-time job as a nanny for Jack, a 2-month-old boy. What can Marianne expect to see in terms of the child's sensory and motor development as she interacts with and observes Jack over the next six months?

Connect to www.mhhe.com/santrockld9 to research the answers and complete these exercises.

mhhe com/
santrockld9 **E-Learning Tools**

To help you master the material in this chapter, you'll find a number of valuable study tools on the Student CD-ROM that accompanies this book. In addition, visit the Online Learning Center for *Life-Span Development,* ninth edition, where you'll find these valuable resources for chapter 5, "Physical Development in Infancy."

- What are your beliefs about an infant's physical development? Use the self-assessment, *My Beliefs About Nurturing a Baby's Physical Development,* to determine what your views are.

- View video clips of key researchers, including Charles Nelson as he discusses his research with infants.
- Build your decision-making skills by trying your hand at the parenting and education "Scenarios."

6

I wish I could travel down by the road that crosses the baby's mind where reason makes kites of her laws and flies them....

—RABINDRANATH TAGORE
*Bengali Poet, Essayist,
20th Century*

Cognitive Development in Infancy

Learning Goals

1 Summarize Piaget's theory of infant development

2 Describe how infants learn and remember

3 Discuss the assessment of intelligence in infancy

4 Explain language development in infancy

Images of Life-Span Development
Laurent, Lucienne, and Jacqueline

The Swiss psychologist Jean Piaget was a meticulous observer of his three children—Laurent, Lucienne, and Jacqueline. His books on cognitive development are filled with his observations. This list provides a glimpse of Piaget's observations of his children's cognitive development in infancy (Piaget, 1952).

- At 21 days of age, Laurent finds his thumb after three attempts; once he finds his thumb, prolonged sucking begins. But, when he is placed on his back, he doesn't know how to coordinate the movement of his arms with that of his mouth; his hands draw back, even when his lips seek them.
- During the third month, thumb sucking becomes less important to Laurent because of new visual and auditory interests. But, when he cries, his thumb goes to the rescue.
- Toward the end of Lucienne's fourth month, while she is lying in her crib, Piaget hangs a doll over her feet. Lucienne thrusts her feet at the doll and makes it move. Afterward, she looks at her motionless foot for a second, then kicks at the doll again. She has no visual control of her foot because her movements are the same whether she only looks at the doll or it is placed over her head. By contrast, she does have tactile control of her foot; when she tries to kick the doll and misses, she slows her foot movements to improve her aim.
- At 11 months, while seated, Jacqueline shakes a little bell. She then pauses abruptly so she can delicately place the bell in front of her right foot; then she kicks the bell hard. Unable to recapture the bell, she grasps a ball and places it in the same location where the bell was. She gives the ball a firm kick.
- At 1 year, 2 months, Jacqueline holds in her hands an object that is new to her: a round, flat box that she turns over and shakes; then she rubs it against her crib. She lets it go and tries to pick it up again. She succeeds only in touching it with her index finger, being unable to fully reach and grasp it. She keeps trying to grasp it and presses to the edge of her crib. She makes the box tilt up, but it nonetheless falls again. Jacqueline shows an interest in this result and studies the fallen box.
- At 1 year, 8 months, Jacqueline arrives at a closed door with a blade of grass in each hand. She stretches her right hand toward the doorknob but detects that she cannot turn it without letting go of the grass, so she puts the grass on the floor, opens the door, picks up the grass again, and then enters. But, when she wants to leave the room, things get complicated. She puts the grass on the floor and grasps the doorknob. Then she perceives that, by pulling the door toward her, she simultaneously chases away the grass that she had placed between the door and the threshold. She then picks up the grass and places it out of the door's range of movement.

For Piaget, these observations reflect important changes in the infant's cognitive development. Later in the chapter, you will learn that Piaget believed that infants go through six substages of development and that the behaviors you have just read about characterize those substages.

The excitement and enthusiasm about infant cognition have been fueled by an interest in what an infant knows at birth and soon after, by continued fascination about innate and learned factors in the infant's cognitive development, and by controversies about whether infants construct their knowledge (as Piaget believed) or whether they know their world more directly. In this chapter we will study Piaget's theory of infant development, learning and remembering, individual differences in intelligence, and language development.

1 PIAGET'S THEORY OF INFANT DEVELOPMENT

The Sensorimotor Stage of Development	Understanding Physical Reality	Evaluating Piaget's Sensorimotor Stage

Poet Noah Perry once asked, "Who knows the thoughts of a child?" Piaget knew as much as anyone. Through careful, inquisitive interviews and observations of his own three children—Laurent, Lucienne, and Jacqueline—Piaget changed the way we think about children's conception of the world. Remember that we studied a general outline of Piaget's cognitive developmental theory in chapter 2 ◀▥ p. 47. You might want to review that discussion now.

Piaget believed that the child passes through a series of stages of thought from infancy to adolescence. Passage through these stages results from biological pressures to *adapt* to the environment (through assimilation and accommodation) and to structure thinking. Recall from chapter 2 that assimilation occurs when individuals incorporate new knowledge into existing knowledge and that accommodation takes place when individuals adjust to new information.

Another important concept in Piaget's theory is **scheme,** a cognitive structure that helps individuals organize and understand their experiences. Schemes change with age. Even newborns have schemes. For instance, they grasp reflexively anything that touches their hand. As children grow older and gain more experience, they gradually shift from using schemes based on physical activities to schemes based on internal mental activities such as strategies and plans. For example, later in infancy an action-based grasping scheme can become part of a plan for obtaining a desirable object.

Piaget's stages are *qualitatively* different from one another. The way children reason at one stage is qualitatively different from the way they reason at another stage. This contrasts with the quantitative assessments of intelligence made through the use of standardized intelligence tests—which focus on what the child knows, or how many questions the child can answer correctly. Remember from chapter 2 that Piaget believed there are four stages of cognitive development: sensorimotor, preoperational, concrete operational, and formal operational. Here our focus is on Piaget's stage of infant cognitive development. In later chapters (8, 10, and 12) we will explore the last three Piagetian stages.

The Sensorimotor Stage of Development

According to Piaget, the sensorimotor stage lasts from birth to about 2 years of age, corresponding to the period of infancy. During this time, mental development is characterized by considerable progression in the infant's ability to organize and coordinate sensations with physical movements and actions—hence the name *sensorimotor* (Piaget, 1952).

At the beginning of the sensorimotor stage, the infant has little more than reflexive patterns with which to work. By the end of the stage, the 2-year-old has complex sensorimotor patterns and is beginning to operate with a primitive system of symbols. Unlike other stages, the sensorimotor stage is subdivided into six substages, each of which involves qualitative changes in sensorimotor organization.

Within a developmental substage, there may be different schemes—sucking, rooting, and blinking in substage 1, for example. In substage 1, the schemes are basically

We are born capable of learning.

—**JEAN-JACQUES ROUSSEAU**
Swiss-Born French Philosopher, 18th Century

mhhe●com/
santrockld9

**Piaget's Stages
Sensorimotor Development**

scheme In Piaget's theory, a cognitive structure that helps individuals organize and understand their experiences.

Simple reflexes

Infants are limited to exercising simple reflexes, such as rooting and sucking.

0 to 1 month of age

First habits and primary circular reactions

Infants' reflexes evolve into adaptive schemes that are more refined and coordinated.

1 to 4 months of age

Secondary circular reactions

Infants become more outwardly oriented, moving beyond self-preoccupation. They discover procedures for producing interesting events.

4 to 8 months of age

Coordination of secondary circular reactions

Infants combine and recombine earlier schemes and engage for the first time in truly intentional behavior. Infants can now separate means and end in trying to reach a goal.

8 to 12 months of age

Tertiary circular reactions, novelty, and curiosity

Infants start to vary schemes to produce new effects.

12 to 18 months of age

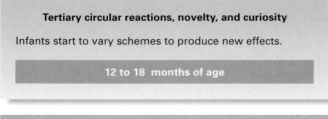
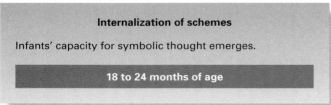

Internalization of schemes

Infants' capacity for symbolic thought emerges.

18 to 24 months of age

FIGURE 6.1 Piaget's Six Substages of Sensorimotor Development

reflexive. From substage to substage, the schemes change in organization. This change is at the heart of Piaget's description of the stages. The six substages of sensorimotor development are (see figure 6.1):

- **Simple reflexes** are the hallmarks of Piaget's first sensorimotor substage, which corresponds to the first month after birth. In this substage, the basic means of coordinating sensation and action is through reflexive behaviors. These include rooting and sucking, which the infant has at birth. In substage 1, the infant exercises these reflexes. More important, the infant develops an ability to produce behaviors that resemble reflexes in the absence of obvious reflexive stimuli. The newborn may suck when a bottle or nipple is only nearby, for example. When the baby was just born, the bottle or nipple would have produced the sucking pattern only when placed directly in its mouth or touched to the lips. Reflexlike actions in the absence of a triggering stimulus are evidence that the infant is initiating action and is actively structuring experiences in the first month of life.

- **First habits and primary circular reactions** characterize Piaget's second sensorimotor stage, which develops between 1 and 4 months of age. In this substage, infants' reflexes have evolved into adaptive schemes that are more refined and coordinated. A *habit* is a scheme based on a simple reflex, such as sucking, that has become completely separated from its eliciting stimulus. For example, an infant in substage 1 might suck when orally stimulated by a bottle or when visually shown the bottle. However, an infant in substage 2 might exercise the sucking scheme even when no bottle is present. A **primary circular reaction** is a scheme based on the infant's attempt to reproduce an interesting or a pleasurable event that initially occurred by chance. In a well-known Piagetian example, a child accidentally sucks his fingers when they are placed near his mouth. Later, he searches for his fingers to suck them again, but the fingers do not cooperate in the search because the infant cannot coordinate visual and manual actions. Habits and circular reactions are stereotyped, in that the infant repeats them the same way each time.

- **Secondary circular reactions** make up Piaget's third sensorimotor stage, which develops between 4 and 8 months of age. In this substage, the infant becomes more object-oriented or focused on the world, moving beyond the preoccupation with the self that characterizes sensorimotor interactions. By chance, the infant might shake a rattle. The infant will repeat this action for the sake of experiencing what it can do in the world. The infant imitates some simple actions of others, such as the baby talk or burbling of adults, and some physical gestures. However, these imitations are limited to actions the infant is already able to produce.

- **Coordination of secondary circular reactions** occurs in Piaget's fourth sensorimotor substage, which develops between 8 and 12 months of age. In this substage, several significant changes take place that involve the coordination of schemes and intentionality. Infants readily combine and recombine previously learned schemes in a *coordinated way*. They might look at an object and grasp it simultaneously, or they might visually inspect a toy, such as a rattle, and finger it simultaneously in obvious tactile exploration. Actions are even more outwardly directed than before. Related to this coordination is the second achievement—the presence of *intentionality,* the separation of means and goals in accomplishing simple feats. For example, infants might manipulate a stick (the means) to bring a desired toy within reach (the goal). They might knock over one block to reach and play with another one.

- **Tertiary circular reactions, novelty, and curiosity** distinguish Piaget's fifth sensorimotor substage, which develops between 12 and 18 months of age. In this substage, infants become intrigued by the variety of properties that objects possess and by the many things they can make happen to objects. A block can be made to fall, spin, hit another object, and slide across the ground. Tertiary circular reactions are schemes in which the infant purposely explores new possibilities with objects, continually changing what is done to them and exploring the results. Piaget says that this stage marks the developmental starting point for human curiosity and interest in novelty. Previously circular reactions were devoted exclusively to reproducing former events, with the exception of imitation of novel acts, which occurs as early as substage 4. The tertiary circular act is the first to be concerned with novelty.

- **Internalization of schemes** occurs in Piaget's sixth and final sensorimotor substage, which develops between 18 and 24 months of age. In this substage, the infant's mental functioning shifts from a purely sensorimotor plane to a symbolic plane, and the infant develops the ability to use primitive symbols. For Piaget, a *symbol* is an internalized sensory image or word that represents an event. Primitive symbols permit the infant to think about concrete events without directly acting them out or perceiving them. Moreover, symbols allow the infant to manipulate and transform the represented events in simple ways. In a favorite Piagetian example, Piaget's young daughter saw a matchbox being opened and closed. Sometime later, she mimicked the event by opening and closing her mouth. This was an obvious expression of her image of the event. In another example, a child opened a door slowly to avoid disturbing a piece of paper lying on the floor on the other side. Clearly, the child had an image of the unseen paper and what would happen to it if the door opened quickly.

Understanding Physical Reality

Piaget thought that children, even infants, are much like little scientists, examining the world to find out how it works. Developmentalists are interested in how infants' knowledge of the physical world develops (Bremner, 2002). Key aspects of infants' understanding of physical reality are object permanence and cause and effect.

Object Permanence **Object permanence** is the Piagetian term for one of an infant's most important accomplishments: understanding that objects and events continue to exist even when they cannot directly be seen, heard, or touched. Imagine what thought would be like if you could not distinguish between yourself and your world. Your thinking would be chaotic, disorganized, and unpredictable. This is what the mental life of a newborn is like, according to Piaget. There is no self-world differentiation and no sense of object permanence. By the end of the sensorimotor period, however, both are present.

The principal way in which object permanence is studied is by watching an infant's reaction when an interesting object or event disappears (see figure 6.2 on page 186). If infants show no reaction, it is assumed they believe the object no longer exists. By contrast, if infants are surprised at the disappearance and search for the object, it is assumed they believe it continues to exist.

In one research study of object permanence, Renée Baillargeon (1986) showed 6- and 8-month-old infants a toy car that moved down an inclined track, disappeared behind a screen, and then reemerged at the other end, still on the track. After this same sequence was repeated several times, the infants then saw something different

simple reflexes Piaget's first sensorimotor substage, which corresponds to the first month after birth. In this substage, the basic means of coordinating sensation and action is through reflexive behaviors, such as rooting and sucking, which the infant has at birth.

first habits and primary circular reactions Piaget's second sensorimotor substage, which develops between 1 and 4 months of age. In this substage, infants' reflexes evolve into adaptive schemes that are more refined and coordinated.

primary circular reaction A scheme based on the infant's attempt to reproduce an interesting or a pleasurable event that initially occurred by chance.

secondary circular reactions Piaget's third sensorimotor substage, which develops between 4 and 8 months of age. In this substage, the infant becomes more object-oriented, or focused on the world, moving beyond preoccupation with the self in sensorimotor interactions.

coordination of secondary circular reactions Piaget's fourth sensorimotor substage, which develops between 8 and 12 months of age. In this substage, several significant changes take place involving the coordination of schemes and intentionality.

tertiary circular reactions, novelty, and curiosity Piaget's fifth sensorimotor substage, which develops between 12 and 18 months of age. In this substage, infants become intrigued by the variety of properties that objects possess and by the multiplicity of things they can make happen to objects.

internalization of schemes Piaget's sixth and final sensorimotor substage, which develops between 18 and 24 months of age. In this substage, the infant's mental functioning shifts from a purely sensorimotor plane to a symbolic plane, and the infant develops the ability to use primitive symbols.

object permanence The Piagetian term for one of an infant's most important accomplishments: understanding that objects and events continue to exist, even when they cannot directly be seen, heard, or touched.

 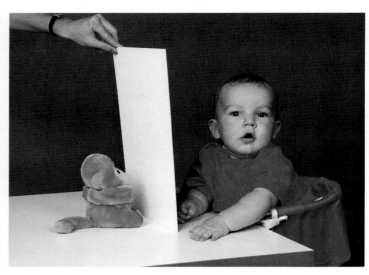

FIGURE 6.2 Object Permanence

Piaget thought that object permanence is one of infancy's landmark cognitive accomplishments. For this 5-month-old boy, "out-of-sight" is literally out of mind. The infant looks at the toy monkey (*left*), but, when his view of the toy is blocked (*right*), he does not search for it. Several months later, he will search for the hidden toy monkey, reflecting the presence of object permanence.

take place. A box was placed behind the screen, in one instance next to the track (a possible event), in another instance directly on the track (an impossible event). Then the infants watched the toy car go from one side of the screen to the other. Infants looked longer at the impossible event than at the possible event. This indicated they remembered not only that the box still existed (object permanence) but its location.

Causality Piaget was very interested in infants' knowledge of cause and effect. His conclusions about infants' understanding of cause and effect were based mainly on his observations of the extent to which infants acted to produce a desired outcome, such as pushing aside an obstacle to reach a goal.

One study on infants' understanding of causality found that even young infants comprehend the size of a moving object determines how far it will move a stationary object if it collides with it (Kotovsky & Baillargeon, 1994 (see figure 6.3). In this research, a cylinder rolls down a ramp and hits a toy bug that is located at the bottom of the ramp. By 5½ to 6½ months of age, infants understand that the bug will roll farther if it is hit by a large cylinder than if it is hit by a small cylinder after they have observed how far it will be pushed by a medium-sized cylinder. Thus, by the middle of the first year of life, these infants understood that the size of the cylinder was a causal factor in determining how far the bug would move when it was hit by the cylinder.

Evaluating Piaget's Sensorimotor Stage

Piaget opened up a whole new way of looking at infants by describing how their main task is to coordinate their sensory impressions with their motor activity. Piaget constructed his view of infancy mainly by observing the development of his own three children. Few laboratory techniques were available at the time. In the past several decades, sophisticated experimental techniques have been devised to study infants, and there have been a large number of research studies on infant development (Cohen & Cashon, 2003). Much of the new research suggests that the infant's cognitive world is not as neatly packaged as Piaget portrayed it (Gounin-Decarie, 1996; Meltzoff & Moore, 1999). The two research areas that have led researchers to a somewhat different understanding of infant development are (1) perceptual development and (2) conceptual development.

Perceptual Development A number of theorists, such as Eleanor Gibson (2001) and Elizabeth Spelke (1991; Spelke & Newport, 1998), believe that infants' perceptual abilities are highly developed very early in development ◀▥ p. 169. For example, Spelke has demonstrated that infants as young as 4 months of age have intermodal perception—the ability to coordinate information from two or more sensory modalities, such as vision and hearing. Other research, by Renée Baillargeon (1995), documents that infants as young as 4 months expect objects to be substantial (in the sense that other objects cannot move through them) and permanent (in the sense that objects continue to exist when they are hidden). In sum, researchers believe that infants see objects as bounded, unitary, solid, and separate from their background, possibly at birth or shortly thereafter, but definitely by 3 to 4 months of age. Young infants still have much to learn about objects, but the world appears both stable and orderly to them and, thus, capable of being conceptualized. Infants are continually trying to structure and make sense of their world (Meltzoff & Gopnik, 1997).

Conceptual Development It is more difficult to study what infants are thinking about than to study what they see. Still, researchers have devised ways to assess whether or not infants are thinking. One strategy is to look for symbolic activity, such as using a gesture to refer to something. Piaget (1952) used this strategy to document infants' motor recognition. For example, he observed his 6-month-old daughter make a gesture when she saw a familiar toy in a new location. She was used to kicking at the toy in her crib. When she saw it across the room, she made a brief kicking motion. However, Piaget did not consider this to be true symbolic activity because it was a motor movement, not a purely mental act. Nonetheless, Piaget suggested that his daughter was referring to, or classifying, the toy through her actions (Mandler, 1998). In a similar way, infants whose parents use sign language have been observed to start using conventional signs at about 6 to 7 months of age (Bonvillian, Orlansky, & Novack, 1983).

In summary, many of today's researchers believe that Piaget wasn't specific enough about how infants learn about their world and that infants are far more competent than Piaget envisioned (Meltzoff, 2000). Recent research on infants' perceptual and conceptual development suggests that infants have more sophisticated perceptual abilities and can begin to think earlier than Piaget envisioned. These researchers believe that infants either are born with or acquire these abilities early in their development (Mandler, 1990, 1998).

Piaget's view is a general, unifying story of how biology and experience sculpt the infant's cognitive development: assimilation and accommodation always take the infant to higher ground through a series of substages. And for Piaget, the motivation for change is general, an internal search for equilibrium. However, like much of the modern world, today the field of infant cognition is very specialized. There are many researchers working on different questions, with no general theory emerging that can connect all of the different findings (Nelson, 1999). Their theories are local theories, focused on specific research questions, rather than grand theories like Piaget's. If there is a unifying theme, it is that investigators in infant development struggle with the big issue of nature and nurture.

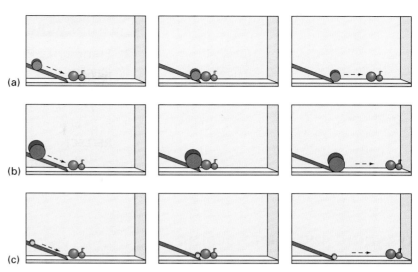

FIGURE 6.3 The Infants' Understanding of Causality

After young infants saw how far the medium-sized cylinder (*a*) pushed a toy bug, they showed more surprise at the event in (*c*) that showed a very small cylinder pushing the toy bug as far as the large cylinder (*b*). Their surprise, indicated by looking at (*c*) longer than (*b*), indicated that they understood the size of a cylinder was a causal factor in determining how far the toy bug would be pushed when it was hit by the cylinder.

mhhe ◯ com/
santrockld9

Cognitive Milestones
Challenges to Piaget

*I*nfants are creating concepts and organizing their world into conceptual domains that will form the backbone of their thought throughout life.

—**JEAN MANDLER**
Contemporary Psychologist,
University of California–San Diego

Review and Reflect

1 **Summarize Piaget's theory of infant development**

REVIEW

- What are some characteristics of Piaget's stage of sensorimotor development?
- What are two key aspects of infants' understanding of physical reality?
- What are some contributions and criticisms of Piaget's sensorimotor stage?

REFLECT

- What are some implications of Piaget's theory of infant development for parenting?

2 LEARNING AND REMEMBERING

- Conditioning
- Habituation and Dishabituation
- Imitation
- Memory

In this section, we will explore these aspects of how infants learn and remember: conditioning; habituation and dishabituation; imitation; and memory. In contrast to Piaget's theory, the approaches we will look at here do not describe infant development in terms of stages.

FIGURE 6.4 The Technique Used in Rovee-Collier's Investigation of Infant Memory

In Rovee-Collier's experiment, operant conditioning was used to demonstrate that infants as young as 2½ months of age can retain information from the experience of being conditioned.

Conditioning

In chapter 2, "The Science of Life-Span Development," we described Pavlov's classical conditioning and Skinner's operant conditioning ◀◼◼◼ p. 51. Both types of conditioning have been demonstrated in infants.

Here we will examine some aspects of operant conditioning (in which the consequences of the behavior produce changes in the probability of the behavior's occurrence) in infants. For example, if an infant's behavior is followed by a rewarding stimulus, the behavior is likely to recur.

Operant conditioning has especially been helpful to researchers in their efforts to determine what infants perceive. For example, infants will suck faster on a nipple when the sucking behavior is followed by a visual display, music, or a human voice (Rovee-Collier, 1987).

Carolyn Rovee-Collier (1987) has also demonstrated how infants can retain information from the experience of being conditioned. In a characteristic experiment, she places a 2½-month-old baby in a crib under an elaborate mobile. She then ties one end of a ribbon to the baby's ankle and the other end to the mobile. Subsequently, she observes that the baby kicks and makes the mobile move. The movement of the mobile is the reinforcing stimulus (which increases the baby's kicking behavior) in this experiment. Weeks later, the baby is returned to the crib, but its foot is not tied to the mobile. The baby kicks, which suggests it has retained the information that if it kicks a leg, the mobile will move (see figure 6.4).

Habituation and Dishabituation

If a stimulus—a sight or sound—is presented to infants several times in a row, they usually pay less attention to it each time. This response suggests they are bored with it. This is the process of **habituation**—repeated presentation of the same stimulus, which causes reduced attention to the stimulus. **Dishabituation** is an increase in responsiveness after a change in stimulation. Among the measures researchers use to study whether habituation is occurring are sucking behavior (sucking behavior stops when the young infant attends to a novel object), heart and respiration rates, and the length of time the infant looks at an object. Newborn infants can habituate to repetitive stimulation in virtually every stimulus modality—vision, hearing, touch, and so on (Rovee-Collier, 1987). Figure 6.5 shows the results of one study of habituation and dishabituation with newborns (Slater, Morison, & Somers, 1988).

Habituation can be used to tell us much about infants' perception, such as the extent to which they can see, hear, smell, taste, and experience touch (Cohen & Cashon, 2003; Slater, 2002). Habituation also can be used to tell whether infants recognize something they have previously experienced.

The extensive assessment of habituation in recent years has resulted in its use as a measure of an infant's maturity and well-being. Infants who have brain damage or have suffered birth traumas, such as insufficient oxygen, do not habituate well and might later have developmental and learning problems.

A knowledge of habituation and dishabituation can benefit parent-infant interaction. Infants respond to changes in stimulation. If stimulation is repeated often, the infant's response will decrease to the point that the infant no longer responds to the parent. In parent-infant interaction, it is important for parents to do novel things and to repeat them often until the infant stops responding. The wise parent senses when the infant shows an interest and that many repetitions of the stimulus may be necessary for the infant to process the information. The parent stops or changes behaviors when the infant redirects her attention (Rosenblith, 1992).

Imitation

Can infants imitate someone else's emotional expressions? If an adult smiles, will the baby follow with a smile? If an adult protrudes her lower lip, wrinkles her forehead, and frowns, will the baby show a sad face? If an adult opens his mouth, widens his eyes, and raises his eyebrows, will the baby follow suit? Can infants only a few days old do these things?

habituation Repeated presentation of the same stimulus, which causes reduced attention to the stimulus.

dishabituation An increase in responsiveness after a change in stimulation.

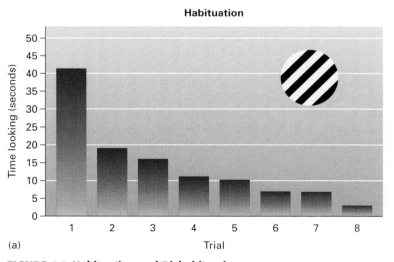

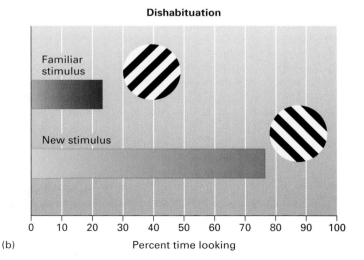

FIGURE 6.5 Habituation and Dishabituation

In the first part of one study, 7-hour-old newborns were shown the stimulus in (*a*). As indicated, the newborns looked at it an average of 41 seconds when it was first presented to them (Slater, Morison, & Somers, 1988). Over seven more presentations of the stimulus, they looked at it less and less. In the second part of study, infants were presented with both the familiar stimulus to which they had just become habituated (*a*) and a new stimulus (shown in *b*, which was rotated 90 degrees). The newborns looked at the new stimulus three times as much as the familiar stimulus.

FIGURE 6.6 Infant Imitation

Infant development researcher Andrew Meltzoff protrudes his tongue in an attempt to get the infant to imitate his behavior.

> *Life is all memory, except for the one present moment that goes by you so quick you hardly catch it going.*
>
> —TENNESSEE WILLIAMS
> *American Playwright, 20th Century*

deferred imitation Imitation that occurs after a time delay of hours or days.

memory A central feature of cognitive development, pertaining to all situations in which an individual retains information over time.

Infant development researcher Andrew Meltzoff (2000; Meltzoff & Moore, 1999) has conducted numerous studies of infants' imitative abilities. He believes infants' imitative abilities are biologically based, because infants can imitate a facial expression within the first few days after birth. This occurs before they have had the opportunity to observe social agents in their environment protruding their tongues and engaging in other behaviors. He also emphasizes that the infant's imitative abilities do not resemble what ethologists conceptualize as a hardwired, reflexive, innate releasing mechanism but, rather, involve flexibility, adaptability, and intermodal perception. In Meltzoff's observations of infants in the first 72 hours of life, the infants gradually displayed a full imitative response of an adult's facial expression, such as protruding the tongue or opening the mouth wide (see figure 6.6).

Not all experts on infant development accept Meltzoff's conclusions that newborns are capable of imitation. Some say that these babies were engaging in little more than automatic responses to a stimulus.

Meltzoff also has studied **deferred imitation,** which occurs after a time delay of hours or days. In one study, Meltzoff (1988) demonstrated that 9-month-old infants could imitate actions that they had seen performed 24 hours earlier. Each action consisted of an unusual gesture—such as pushing a recessed button in a box (which produced a beeping sound). Piaget believed that deferred imitation doesn't occur until about 18 months of age. Meltzoff's research suggested that it occurs much earlier.

Memory

Memory is a central feature of cognitive development that involves the retention of information over time. Sometimes information is retained only for a few seconds, and at other times it is retained for a lifetime.

Can infants remember? Some infant researchers, such as Carolyn Rovee-Collier, argue that infants as young as 2 to 6 months of age can remember some experiences through 1½ to 2 years of age (Rovee-Collier, 2001; Rovee-Collier & Barr, 2002).

However, critics such as Jean Mandler (2000), a leading expert on infant cognition, argue that Rovee-Collier fails to distinguish between retention of a perceptual-motor variety that is involved in conditioning tasks (like that involved in kicking a mobile), often referred to as *implicit memory,* and the ability to consciously recall the past, often referred to as *explicit memory.* When people think about what memory is, they are referring to the latter, which most researchers find does not occur until the second half of the first year (Mandler & McDonough, 1995).

By 9 months of age, infants' explicit memory is readily apparent. For example, in one study, 9-month-old infants long-term recall of a two-step sequence (such as "Make Big Bird turn on the light") occurred (Carver & Bauer, 1999). Five weeks after experiencing such two-step sequences, 45 percent of the infants demonstrated their long-term memory by producing the two actions in the sequence. The other 55 percent did not show evidence of remembering the sequence of actions, reflecting individual differences in infant memory. Also, in a related assessment of these infants, researchers demonstrated changes in the brain activity of the infants as they engaged in recall of the sequences they had experienced five weeks earlier (Carver, Bauer, & Nelson, 2000).

While explicit memory emerges in the second half of the first year of life, the results of other research reveal that it undergoes substantial development and consolidation over the course of the second year of life (Carver & Bower, 2001). In one longitudinal study, infants were assessed several times during the second year of life (Bauer & others, 2000). These older infants showed more accurate memory and required fewer prompts to demonstrate their memory than infants under the age of 1.

Most adults cannot remember anything from the first three years of their life; this is referred to as *infantile amnesia.* When adults seem to be able to recall something from their infancy, it likely is something they have been told about by relatives or something they saw in a photograph or home movie. One explanation of infantile amnesia focuses on the maturation of the brain, especially in the frontal lobes, which occurs after infancy (Boyer & Diamond, 1992).

**mhhe●com/
santrockld9**

**Infant Cognition
Infant Memory Research**

Review and Reflect

2 Describe how infants learn and remember

REVIEW

- How do infants learn through conditioning?
- How does infant learning involve habituation and dishabituation?
- How is imitation involved in infant learning?
- To what extent can infants remember?

REFLECT

- If someone said that they remember being abused by their parents when they were 2 years old, would you believe them? Explain your answer.

3 INDIVIDUAL DIFFERENCES IN INTELLIGENCE

So far, we have discussed how the cognitive development of infants generally progresses. We have emphasized what is typical of the largest number of infants or the average infant, but the results obtained for most infants do not apply to all infants. It is advantageous to know whether an infant is developing at a slow, normal, or advanced pace during the course of infancy. If an infant advances at an especially slow rate, then some form of enrichment may be necessary. If an infant develops at an advanced pace, parents may be advised to provide toys that stimulate cognitive growth in slightly older infants. Individual differences in infant cognitive development have been studied primarily through the use of developmental scales, or infant intelligence tests. For example, the Brazelton Neonatal Behavioral Assessment Scale, which we discussed in chapter 4, is widely used to evaluate newborns ◀▥ p. 134.

The infant testing movement grew out of the tradition of IQ testing of older children. However, the measures for assessing infants are necessarily less verbal than IQ tests that assess the intelligence of older children. The infant developmental scales contain far more perceptual motor items. They also include measures of social interaction.

The most important early contributor to the developmental testing of infants was Arnold Gesell (1934). He developed a measure that was used as a clinical tool to help distinguish potentially normal babies from abnormal ones. This was especially useful to adoption agencies, which had large numbers of babies awaiting placement. Gesell's examination was used widely for many years and is still frequently used by pediatricians to assess infants. The current version of the Gesell test has four categories of behavior: motor, language, adaptive, and personal-social. The **developmental quotient (DQ)** is an overall developmental score that combines subscores in motor, language, adaptive, and personal-social domains in the Gesell assessment of infants.

The **Bayley Scales of Infant Development,** developed by Nancy Bayley, are widely used in the assessment of infant development. The current version has three components: a mental scale, a motor scale, and an infant behavior profile. Unlike Gesell, whose scales were clinically motivated, Bayley (1969) wanted to develop scales that would assess infant behavior and predict later development. The early version of the Bayley scales covered only the first year of development. In the 1950s, the scales

developmental quotient (DQ) An overall developmental score that combines subscores in motor, language, adaptive, and personal-social domains in the Gesell assessment of infants.

Bayley Scales of Infant Development
Scales developed by Nancy Bayley, which are widely used in the assessment of infant development. The current version has three components: a mental scale, a motor scale, and an infant behavior profile.

were extended to assess older infants. In 1993, the Bayley-II was published, with updated norms for diagnostic assessment at a younger age.

Because our discussion in this chapter centers on the infant's cognitive development, our primary interest is in Bayley's mental scale. It includes assessment of:

- Auditory and visual attention to stimuli
- Manipulation, such as combining objects or shaking a rattle
- Examiner interaction, such as babbling and imitation
- Relation with toys, such as banging spoons together
- Memory involved in object permanence, as when the infant finds a hidden toy
- Goal-directed behavior that involves persistence, such as putting pegs in a board
- Ability to follow directions and knowledge of objects' names, such as understanding the concept of "one"

How well should a 6-month-old perform on the Bayley mental scale? The 6-month-old infant should be able to vocalize pleasure and displeasure, persistently search for objects that are just out of immediate reach, and approach a mirror that is placed in front of the infant by the examiner. How well should a 12-month-old perform? By 12 months of age, the infant should be able to inhibit behavior when commanded to do so, imitate words the examiner says (such as *Mama*), and respond to simple requests (such as "Take a drink").

Another assessment tool, the Fagan Test of Infant Intelligence, is increasingly being used (Fagan, 1992). This test focuses on the infant's ability to process information, including encoding the attributes of objects, detecting similarities and differences between objects, forming mental representations, and retrieving these representations. The Fagan test estimates babies' intelligence by comparing the amount of time they look at a new object with the amount of time they spend looking at a familiar object. This test elicits similar performances from infants in different cultures and is correlated with measures of intelligence in older children.

Tests of infant intelligence have been valuable in assessing the effects of malnutrition, drugs, maternal deprivation, and environmental stimulation on the development of infants. However, they do not correlate highly with IQ scores obtained later in childhood. This shortcoming is not surprising because the test items are considerably less verbal than the items on intelligence tests given to older children. Yet specific aspects of infant intelligence are related to specific aspects of childhood intelligence. For example, in one study, infant language abilities assessed by the Bayley test predicted language, reading, and spelling ability at 6 to 8 years of age (Siegel, 1989). Infant perceptual-motor skills predicted visuospatial, arithmetic, and fine motor skills at 6 to 8 years of age. These results indicate that an item analysis of infant scales like Bayley's can provide information about the development of specific intellectual functions.

Toosje Thyssen VanBeveren is an infant assessment specialist who administers tests like the Bayley scales and the Fagan Test of Infant Intelligence. To read about her work with infants, see the Careers in Life-Span Development insert.

The explosion of interest in infant development has produced many new measures, especially using tasks that evaluate the way infants process information. Evidence is accumulating that measures of habituation and dishabituation predict intelligence in childhood (McCall & Carriger, 1993). Less cumulative attention by an infant in the habituation situation and greater amounts of attention in the dishabituation situation reflect more efficient information processing. Both types of attention—decrement and recovery—when measured in the first 6 months of infancy, are related to higher IQ scores on standardized intelligence tests given at various times between infancy and adolescence. In sum, more precise assessments of the infant's cognition with information-processing tasks involving attention have led to the conclusion that continuity between infant and childhood intelligence is greater than was previously believed.

It is important, however, not to go too far and think that the connections between early infant cognitive development and later childhood cognitive development are so

Careers in Life-Span Development

Toosje Thyssen VanBeveren, Infant Assessment Specialist

Toosje Thyssen VanBeveren is a developmental psychologist at the University of Texas Medical Center in Dallas. She has a master's degree in child clinical psychology and a Ph.D. in human development.

Currently, Dr. VanBeveren is involved in a program called New Connections. This 12-week program is a comprehensive intervention for young children (0 to 6 years of age) who were affected by substance abuse prenatally and for their caregivers.

In the New Connections program, VanBeveren conducts assessments of infants' developmental status and progress, identifying delays and deficits. She might refer the infants to a speech, physical, or occupational therapist and monitor the infants' therapeutic services and developmental progress. VanBeveren trains the program staff and encourages them to use the exercises she recommends. She also discusses the child's problems with the primary caregivers, suggests activities they can carry out with their children, and assists them in enrolling their infants in appropriate programs.

During her graduate work at the University of Texas at Dallas, Dr. VanBeveren was author John Santrock's teaching assistant in his undergraduate course on life-span development for four years. As a teaching assistant, she attended classes, graded exams, counseled students, and occasionally gave

lectures. Each semester, VanBeveren returns to give a lecture on prenatal development and infancy in the life-span class. She also teaches part-time in the psychology department at UT-Dallas. She teaches an undergraduate course, "The Child in Society," and a graduate course, "Infant Development."

In Dr. VanBeveren's words, "My days are busy and full. The work is often challenging. There are some disappointments but mostly the work is enormously gratifying."

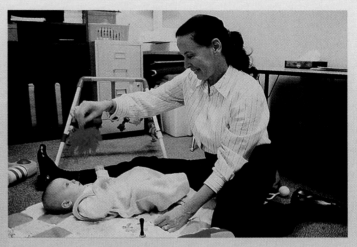

Toosje Thyssen VanBeveren conducting an infant assessment.

strong that no discontinuity takes place. Rather than asking whether cognitive development is continuous *or* discontinuous, perhaps we should be examining the ways cognitive development is both continuous and discontinuous. Some important changes in cognitive development take place after infancy, changes that underscore the discontinuity of cognitive development. We will describe these changes in cognitive development in subsequent chapters, which focus on later periods of development.

Review and Reflect

3 **Discuss the assessment of intelligence in infancy**

REVIEW

- How is infant intelligence measured?

REFLECT

- Parents have their 1-year-old infant assessed with a developmental scale and the infant does very well on it. How confident should they be that the infant is going to be a genius when he or she grows up?

4 LANGUAGE DEVELOPMENT

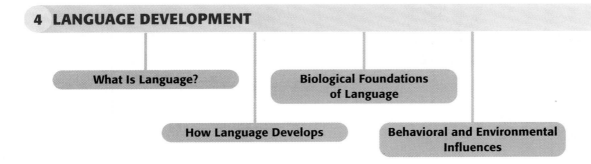

What Is Language?

Biological Foundations of Language

How Language Develops

Behavioral and Environmental Influences

In 1799, a nude boy was observed running through the woods in France. The boy was captured when he was 11 years old. He was called the Wild Boy of Aveyron and was believed to have lived in the woods alone for six years. When found, he made no effort to communicate. Even after a number of years, he never learned to communicate effectively. Sadly, a modern-day wild child named Genie was discovered in Los Angeles in 1970. Despite intensive intervention, Genie never acquired more than a primitive form of language. Both cases—the Wild Boy of Aveyron and Genie—raise questions about the biological and environmental determinants of language, topics that we will examine in greater detail later in this chapter. First, though, we need to define the term *language*.

What Is Language?

Language is a form of communication, whether spoken, written, or signed, that is based on a system of symbols. Think how important language is in our everyday lives. We need language in order to speak with others, listen to others, read, and write. Our language enables us to describe past events in detail and to plan for the future. Language lets us pass down information from one generation to the next and create a rich cultural heritage.

All human languages have some common characteristics. These include infinite generativity and organizational rules. **Infinite generativity** is the ability to produce an endless number of meaningful sentences using a finite set of words and rules. This quality makes language a highly creative enterprise.

How Language Develops

As infants develop, they reach a number of language milestones. At birth they communicate by crying, but by about 2 years of age, most can say approximately 200 words in the language their parents use. How does this remarkable ability develop?

Babbling and Other Vocalizations Babies actively produce sounds from birth onward (Lock, 2002). The purpose of these early communications is to attract attention from caregivers and others in the environment. In the first year, the production of sound goes through this sequence:

- *Crying.* This is present even at birth and can signal distress. However, as you will discover in chapter 7, there are different types of cries that can signal different things.
- *Cooing.* This first occurs at about 1 to 2 months. These are *oo* sounds such as *coo* or *goo* that usually occur during interaction with the caregiver.
- *Babbling.* This first occurs in the middle of the first year and includes strings of consonant-vowel combinations.
- *Gestures.* Infants start using gestures, such as showing and pointing, at about 8 to 12 months of age. Some examples of gestures are waving bye-bye, nodding

language A form of communication based on a system of symbols. In humans language is characterized by infinite generativity and rule systems.

infinite generativity An individual's ability to generate an infinite number of meaningful sentences using a finite set of words and rules, which makes language a highly creative enterprise.

one's head to mean "yes," showing an empty cup to ask for more milk, and pointing to a dog to draw attention to it.

Deaf infants, born to deaf parents who use sign language, babble with their hands and fingers at about the same age as hearing children babble vocally (Bloom, 1998). Such similarities in timing and structure between manual and vocal babbling indicate the presence of a unified language capacity that underlies signed and spoken language (Petitto & Marnetette, 1991).

Recognizing Language Sounds Language is made up of basic sounds or phonemes. **Phonology** is a language's sound system. Phonological rules ensure that certain sound sequences occur (for example, *sp, ba,* or *ar*) and others do not (for example, *zx* or *qp*).

Phonology provides a basis for constructing a large and expandable set of words— all that are or ever will be in that language—out of two or three dozen phonemes. We do not need 500,000 phonemes, only a few dozen.

Patricia Kuhl's (1993, 2000) research reveals that long before they actually learn words, infants can sort through a number of spoken sounds in search of the ones that have meaning. Kuhl argues that from birth up to about 7 months of age, infants are "universal linguists" who are capable of distinguishing each of the 150 sounds that make up human speech. By about 11 months of age, they clearly have started to specialize in the speech sounds of their native language (see figure 6.7).

An important language task for infants is to pick out individual words from the nonstop stream of sound that comprises ordinary speech. To do so, they have to find the boundaries between words, which is very difficult for infants because adults don't pause between words when they speak (Jusczyk, 2002). Still, researchers have found that infants begin to detect word boundaries by 8 months of age. For example, in one study, 8-month-old infants listened at home to recorded stories that contained unusual words, such as *hornbill* and *python* (Jusczyk & Hohne, 1997). Two weeks later, the researchers tested the infants with two lists of words, one made up of words they had already heard in the stories, the other of new, unusual words that did not appear in the stories. The infants listened to the familiar words for a second longer, on average, than to new words.

Language Milestones
The Naming Explosion
Brain and Language Development

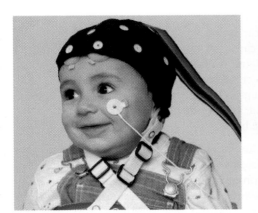 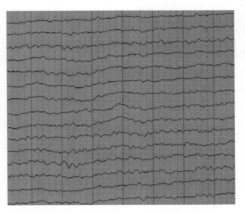

FIGURE 6.7 From Universal to Specialized Linguist
The people of the world speak thousands of languages and babies are born with the ability to learn any of them. In her research, Patricia Kuhl monitors infants' brain waves (an example of a brain wave recording is shown on the right) as they listen to different sounds. She has discovered that up to about the age of 7 months, infants can distinguish between two sounds in a language such as Mandarin Chinese—a subtle difference that English-speaking parents cannot detect. However, by 11 months of age, unused neuronal connections have begun to be pruned away. As infants' brains process a single language over time, they cease to be "universal linguists."

phonology A language's sound system.

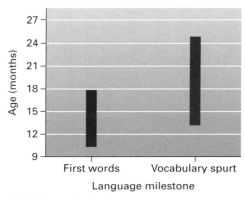

FIGURE 6.8 Variation in Language Milestones

First Words Spoken vocabulary begins when the infant utters its first word, a milestone eagerly anticipated by every parent. This event usually occurs at about 10 to 15 months of age. Many parents view the onset of language development as coincident with this first word. However, as we have seen, some significant language milestones have already occurred, such as cooing and babbling.

The infant's spoken vocabulary rapidly increases once the first word is spoken (Camaioni, 2002). The *vocabulary spurt* is a label that has been given to the rapid increase in an infant's vocabulary that begins to occur at approximately 18 months of age (Bloom, Lifter, & Broughton, 1985). The average 18-month-old can speak about 50 words, but by the age of 2 years can speak about 200 words.

A child's first words include those that name important people (*dada*), familiar animals (*kitty*), vehicles (*car*), toys (*ball*), food (*milk*), body parts (*eye*), clothes (*hat*), household items (*clock*), and greeting terms (*bye*). These were the first words of babies 50 years ago. They are the first words of babies today. At times it is hard to tell what these one-word utterances mean. One possibility is that they stand for an entire sentence in the infant's mind.

There is variation in the timing at which children say their first word and in their vocabulary spurt (Bloom, 1998). Figure 6.8 shows the range for these two language milestones in 14 children. The average ages of these children at the time they reached these milestones were: first word (13 months) and vocabulary spurt (19 months). However, the individual children ranged from 10 to 17 months for their first word and from 13 to 25 months for their vocabulary spurt.

Around the world, young children learn to speak in two-word utterances, in most cases, at about 18 to 24 months of age. *What are some examples of these two-word utterances?*

Two-Word Utterances By the time children are 18 to 24 months of age, they usually utter two-word statements. During this two-word stage, they quickly grasp the importance of expressing concepts and of the role that language plays in communicating with others. To convey meaning with two-word utterances, the child relies heavily on gesture, tone, and context. The wealth of meaning children can communicate with a two-word utterance includes (Slobin, 1972):

- Identification: "See doggie."
- Location: "Book there."
- Repetition: "More milk."
- Nonexistence: "All gone thing."
- Negation: "Not wolf."
- Possession: "My candy."
- Attribution: "Big car."
- Agent-action: "Mama walk."
- Action-direct object: "Hit you."
- Action-indirect object: "Give Papa."
- Action-instrument: "Cut knife."
- Question: "Where ball?"

These examples are from children whose first language is English, German, Russian, Finnish, Turkish, or Samoan. Although these two-word sentences omit many parts of speech, they are remarkably succinct in conveying many messages. In fact, in every language, a child's first combinations of words have this economical quality. **Telegraphic speech** is the use of short and precise words to communicate. When we send a telegram, we try to be short and precise, excluding any unnecessary words. As a result, articles, auxiliary verbs, and other connectives usually are omitted. Young children's two- and three-word utterances are characteristically telegraphic. Of course, telegraphic speech is not limited to two-word phrases. "Mommy give ice cream" and "Mommy give Tommy ice cream" also are examples of telegraphic speech. As children leave the two-word stage, they move rather quickly into three-, four-, and five-word combinations.

telegraphic speech The use of short and precise words to communicate; young children's two- and three-word utterances characteristically are telegraphic.

Language Production and Language Comprehension A distinction is made between language production and language comprehension. *Language production* refers to the words and sentences that children use. *Language comprehension* refers to the language children understand. At about 8 to 12 months, infants often indicate their first word comprehension (Bloom, 1993). But recall that they don't say their first word (language production) until an average of about 13 months. On the average, infants understand about 50 words at about 13 months but can't say this many words until about 18 months (Menyuk, Liebergott, & Schultz, 1995). Thus, in infancy, receptive vocabulary (words the child understands) considerably exceeds spoken vocabulary (words the child uses).

We have discussed a number of language milestones in infancy. Figure 6.9 summarizes the time at which infants typically reach these milestones.

Age	Language Milestones
Birth	Crying
1 to 2 months	Cooing begins
6 months	Babbling begins
8 to 12 months	Use gestures, such as showing and pointing Comprehension of words appears
13 months	First word spoken
18 months	Vocabulary spurt starts
18 to 24 months	Uses two-word utterances Rapid expansion of understanding of words

FIGURE 6.9 Some Language Milestones in Infancy

Biological Foundations of Language

The strongest evidence for the biological basis of language is that children all over the world reach language milestones at about the same time developmentally and in about the same order. This occurs despite the vast variation in the language input they receive. For example, in some cultures, adults never talk to children under 1 year of age, yet these infants still acquire language. Also, there is no other convincing way to explain how *quickly* children learn language than through biological foundations.

With these thoughts in mind, let's now explore these questions about biological influences on language: How strongly is language influenced by biological evolution? Are humans biologically wired to learn language?

Biological Evolution Estimates vary as to how long ago humans acquired language—about 100,000 years ago. In evolutionary time, then, language is a very recent acquisition. A number of experts believe that biological evolution undeniably shaped humans into linguistic creatures (Chomsky, 1957). The brain, nervous system, and vocal apparatus of our predecessors changed over hundreds of thousands of years. Physically equipped to do so, *Homo sapiens* went beyond grunting and shrieking to develop abstract speech. Language clearly gave humans an enormous edge over other animals and increased the chances of survival (Pinker, 1994).

Biological Prewiring Linguist Noam Chomsky (1957) believes humans are biologically prewired to learn language at a certain time and in a certain way. He said that children are born into the world with a **language acquisition device (LAD),** a biological endowment that enables the child to detect certain language categories, such as phonology, syntax, and semantics. The LAD is a theoretical construct that flows from evidence about the biological basis of language.

Is there evidence for the existence of a LAD? Supporters of the LAD concept cite the uniformity of language milestones across languages and cultures, biological substrates for language, and evidence that children create language even in the absence of well-formed input. With regard to the last argument, most deaf children are the offspring of hearing parents. Some of these parents choose not to expose their deaf child to sign language, in order to motivate the child to learn speech while providing the child with a supportive social environment. Susan Goldin-Meadow (1979) has found that these children develop spontaneous gestures that are not based on their parents' gestures.

In the wild, chimps communicate through calls, gestures, and expressions, which evolutionary psychologists believe might be the roots of true language. *How strong is biology's role in language?*

language acquisition device (LAD) A biological endowment, hypothesized by Chomsky, that enables the child to detect certain language categories, such as phonology, syntax, and semantics.

Behavioral and Environmental Influences

Behaviorists view language as just another behavior, such as sitting, walking, and running. They argue that language represents chains of responses (Skinner, 1957) or imitation (Bandura, 1977). But many of the sentences we produce are novel; we have not heard them or spoken them before. For example, a child hears the sentence "The plate fell on the floor" and then says, "My mirror fell on the blanket," after dropping the mirror on the blanket. The behavioral mechanisms of reinforcement and imitation cannot completely explain this.

While spending long hours observing parents and their young children, child language researcher Roger Brown (1973) searched for evidence that parents reinforce their children for speaking in grammatical ways. He found that parents sometimes smile and praise their children for sentences they like. However, they also reinforce sentences that are ungrammatical. Brown concluded that no evidence exists to document that reinforcement is responsible for language's rule systems.

Another criticism of the behavioral view is that it fails to explain the extensive orderliness of language. The behavioral view predicts that vast individual differences should appear in children's speech development because of each child's unique learning history. But, as we have seen, a compelling fact about language is its structure and ever-present rule systems. All infants coo before they babble. All toddlers produce one-word utterances before two-word utterances. All state sentences in the active form before they state them in a passive form.

However, we do not learn language in a social vacuum. Most children are bathed in language from a very early age (Fernald, 2001; Hart & Risley, 1995). We need this early exposure to language to acquire competent language skills. The Wild Boy of Aveyron did not learn to communicate effectively after living in social isolation for years. Genie's language is rudimentary, even after years of extensive training.

Today most language acquisition researchers believe that children from a wide variety of cultural contexts acquire their native language without explicit teaching (Clark, 2000). In some cases, they do so without apparent encouragement. Thus, there appear to be very few aids that are necessary for learning a language. However, the support and involvement of caregivers and teachers greatly facilitate a child's language learning (Berko Gleason, 2000, 2001; Hoff, 2003; Hoff-Ginsberg & Lerner, 1999). Of special concern are children who grow up in impoverished circumstances and are not exposed to guided participation in language. To read about the effects that poverty has on language development, see the Sociocultural Worlds of Development box.

An intriguing aspect of the environment in the young child's acquisition of language is called **infant-directed speech.** This type of speech is often used by parents (in which case it sometimes is called "parentese") and other adults when they talk to babies. It has a higher than normal pitch and involves the use of simple words and sentences.

It is hard to talk this way when not in the presence of a baby, but as soon as you start talking to a baby, you immediately shift into it. Much of this is automatic and something adults often are unaware that they are even doing. Infant-directed speech has the important functions of capturing the infant's attention and maintaining communication. When parents are asked why they use infant-directed speech when talking to their baby, they point out that it is designed to teach their baby to talk. Older child peers and siblings also might use infant-directed speech or "baby talk" when communicating with an infant.

Are there strategies other than infant-directed speech that adults use to enhance the child's acquisition of language? Four candidates are recasting, echoing, expanding, and labeling. *Recasting* is rephrasing something the child has said in a different way, perhaps turning it into a question. For example, if the child says, "The dog was barking," the adult can respond by asking, "When was the dog barking?" The effects of recasting fit with suggestions that "following in order to lead" helps a child learn language. That is, letting a child initially indicate an interest and then proceeding to elaborate that interest—commenting, demonstrating, and explaining—improve

infant-directed speech Speech often used by parents (in which case it sometimes is called "parentese") and other adults when they talk to babies. It has a higher than normal pitch and involves the use of simple words and sentences.

Language Environment, Poverty, and Language Development

In a study conducted by Betty Hart and Todd Risley (1995), the language environments and language development of children from middle-income professional and welfare backgrounds were observed. All of the children developed normally in terms of learning to talk and acquiring all of the forms of English and basic vocabulary. However, there were enormous differences in the sheer amount of language the children were exposed to and the level of the children's language development. For example, in a typical hour, the middle-income professional parents spent almost twice as much time communicating with their children as the welfare parents did. The children from the middle-income professional families heard about 2,100 words an hour, their child counterparts in welfare families only 600 words an hour. The researchers estimated that by 4 years of age, the average welfare family child would have 13 million fewer words of cumulative language experience than the child in the average middle-income professional family. Amazingly, some of the 3-year-old children from middle-income professional families had a recorded vocabulary that exceeded the recorded vocabulary of some of the welfare parents!

In another study, the level of maternal speech to infants was carefully assessed (Huttenlocher & others, 1991). As shown in figure 6.10, mothers who used a higher level of language (more talkative and used far more words) when interacting with their infants had infants with markedly higher vocabularies. By the

second birthday, vocabulary differences were substantial and linked to the level of language input provided by the mother.

In sum, the language environment of children is linked to their vocabulary development. When children grow up in impoverished circumstances, and when their parents do not use a large number of vocabulary words in communicating with them, their vocabulary development suffers.

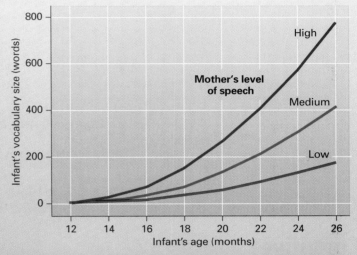

FIGURE 6.10 Level of Maternal Speech and Infant Vocabulary

communication and help language acquisition. In contrast, an overly active, directive approach to communicating with the child may be harmful.

Echoing is repeating what a child says, especially if it is an incomplete phrase or sentence. *Expanding* is restating, in a linguistically sophisticated form, what a child has said. *Labeling* is identifying the names of objects. Young children are forever being asked to identify the names of objects. Roger Brown (1986) identified this as "the great word game" and claimed that much of the early vocabulary acquired by children is motivated by this adult pressure to identify the words associated with objects.

The strategies just described—recasting, echoing, expanding, and labeling—are used naturally and in meaningful conversations. Parents do not (and should not) use any deliberate method to teach their children to talk. Even for children who are slow in learning language, the experts agree that intervention should occur in natural ways, with the goal of being able to convey meaning.

Review and Reflect

4 Explain language development in infancy

REVIEW

- What is language?
- How does language develop in infancy?
- What are some biological foundations of language?
- What are some behavioral and environmental influences on language?

REFLECT

- Would it be a good idea for parents to hold large flash cards of words in front of their infant to help the infant learn language? Why or why not? What do you think Piaget would say about this activity?

Reach Your Learning Goals

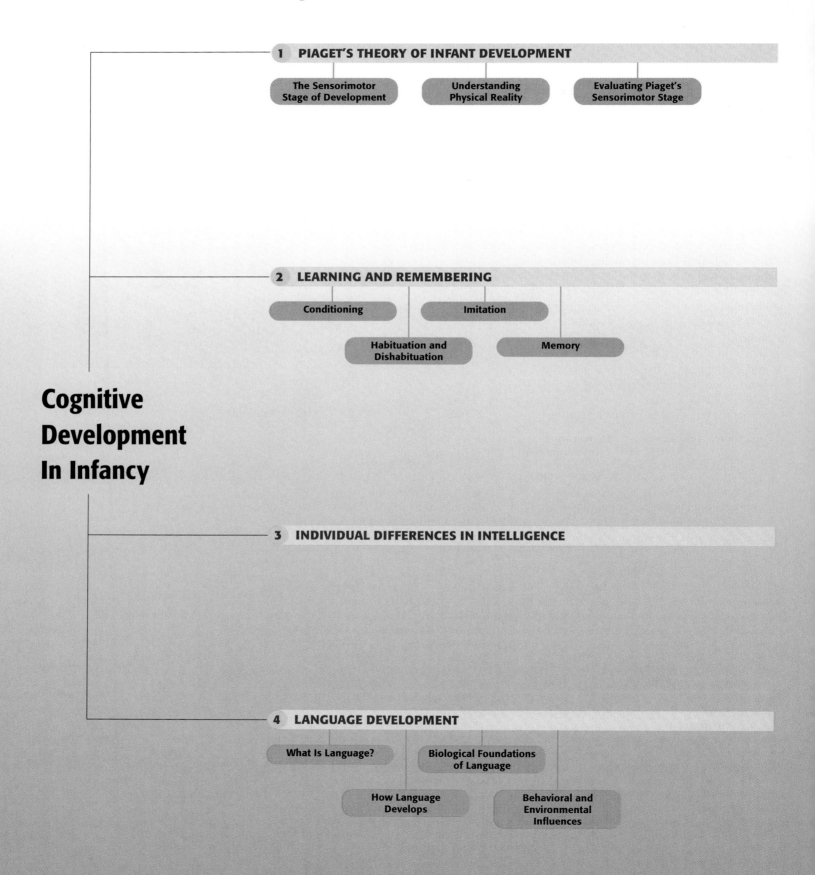

Cognitive Development In Infancy

1 PIAGET'S THEORY OF INFANT DEVELOPMENT

- The Sensorimotor Stage of Development
- Understanding Physical Reality
- Evaluating Piaget's Sensorimotor Stage

2 LEARNING AND REMEMBERING

- Conditioning
- Imitation
- Habituation and Dishabituation
- Memory

3 INDIVIDUAL DIFFERENCES IN INTELLIGENCE

4 LANGUAGE DEVELOPMENT

- What Is Language?
- Biological Foundations of Language
- How Language Develops
- Behavioral and Environmental Influences

Summary

1 Summarize Piaget's theory of infant development

- In Piaget's theory, there are four qualitatively different cognitive stages of development: sensorimotor, preoperational, concrete operational, and formal operational. Assimilation, accommodation, and schemes are important concepts that are involved in the individual's adaptation. In Piaget's first stage—sensorimotor development—the infant is able to organize and coordinate sensations with physical movements. This stage lasts from birth to about 2 years of age and is nonsymbolic throughout, according to Piaget. Sensorimotor development has six substages: simple reflexes; first habits and primary circular reactions; secondary circular reactions; coordination of secondary circular reactions; tertiary circular reactions, novelty, and curiosity; and internalization of schemes.
- Piaget and other developmentalists have been interested in the infant's understanding of physical reality. One aspect of this is reality is object permanence, the ability to understand that objects and events continue to exist even though the infant is no longer observing them. The other aspect involves infant's understanding of cause and effect.
- Piaget opened up a whole new way of looking at infant development in terms of coordinating sensory input with motoric actions. In the last three decades many research studies have suggested that revision of Piaget's view is needed. In perceptual development, researchers have found that a stable and differentiated perceptual world is formed earlier than Piaget envisioned. In conceptual development, researchers have found that memory and other forms of symbolic activity occur at least by the second half of the first year of life, much earlier than Piaget believed.

2 Describe how infants learn and remember

- Both classical and operant conditioning occur in infants. Operant conditioning techniques have especially been useful to researchers in demonstrating infants' perception and retention of information about perceptual-motor actions.
- Habituation is the repeated presentation of the same stimulus, causing reduced attention to the stimulus. If a different stimulus is presented and the infant pays increased attention to it, dishabituation is occurring. Newborn infants can habituate to repetitive stimulation.
- Meltzoff has shown that newborns can match their behaviors (such as protruding their tongue) to a model. His research also shows that deferred imitation occurs as early as 9 months of age.
- Memory is the retention of information over time. Infants as young as 2 months of age can retain information about perceptual-motor actions. However, many experts argue that what we commonly think of as memory (consciously remembering the past) does not occur until the second half of the first year of life.

3 Discuss the assessment of intelligence in infancy

- Developmental scales for infants grew out of the tradition of IQ testing of older children. These scales are less verbal than IQ tests. Gesell was an early developer of an infant test. His scale is still widely used by pediatricians; it provides a developmental quotient (DQ). The Bayley scales are the developmental scales that continue to be widely used today; developed by Nancy Bayley, they consist of a motor scale, a mental scale, and an infant behavior profile. Increasingly used, the Fagan test assesses how effectively the infant processes information. Global infant intelligence measures are not good predictors of childhood intelligence. However, specific aspects of infant intelligence, such as information-processing tasks involving attention, have been better predictors of childhood intelligence, especially in a specific area. There is both continuity and discontinuity between infant cognitive development and cognitive development later in childhood.

4 Explain language development in infancy

- Language is a form of communication, whether spoken, written, or signed, that is based on a system of symbols. Infinite generativity is the ability to produce an endless number of meaningful sentences using a finite set of words and rules.
- Among the milestones in infant language development are crying (birth), cooing (1 to 2 months), babbling (6 months), using gestures (8 to 12 months), comprehension of words (8 to 12 months), first word spoken (13 months), vocabulary spurt (18 months), rapid expansion of understanding words (18 to 24 months), and two-word utterances (18 to 24 months).
- The strongest evidence for a biological foundation for language is that children all over the world reach language milestones at about the same time developmentally despite vast variation in language input. In evolution, language clearly gave humans an enormous edge over other animals and increased their chance of survival. Chomsky proposed the concept of a language acquisition device (LAD) that flows from the evidence about the biological foundations of language.
- The behavioral view—that language reinforcement and imitation are the factors in language acquisition—has not been supported by research. Among the ways that adults teach language to children are infant-directed speech, recasting, echoing, expanding, and labeling. Parents should talk extensively with an infant, especially about what the baby is attending to. Talk primarily should be live talk, not mechanical talk.

Key Terms

Key People

Taking It to the Net

1. Toby must make a 15-minute class presentation on an important theorist who has significantly contributed to our understanding of human development. If Toby were to select Piaget, what types of information (written, spoken, visual) should he include in this presentation to his class?
2. Veronica works in an infant day-care center that serves mothers who are participating in a welfare-to-work program, advising the mothers about nutrition. What do these mothers need to know about the effect of poor nutrition on their child's cognitive development?

3. Taye is worried that his 1-year-old-cousin, Matthew, whom he often baby-sits, is not on track with his language development as compared to his niece, Rita. By this age, what are some of the language-related milestones or tasks that an average child usually has achieved?

Connect to www.mhhe.com/santrockld9 to research the answers and complete these exercises.

E-Learning Tools

To help you master the material in this chapter, you'll find a number of valuable study tools on the Student CD-ROM that accompanies this book. In addition, visit the Online Learning Center for *Life-Span Development*, ninth edition, where you'll find these valuable resources for chapter 6, "Cognitive Development in Infancy."

- What are your beliefs about nurturing an infant's cognitive development? Use the self-assessment, *My Beliefs About Nurturing a Baby's Mind*, to determine what your views are.
- Build your decision-making skills by trying your hand at the parenting and education "Scenarios."

CHAPTER 7

*We never know the love
of our parents until
we have become parents.*

—Henry Ward Beecher
American Writer, 19th Century

Socioemotional Development in Infancy

Learning Goals

1 *D*iscuss emotional and personality development in infancy

2 *D*escribe how attachment develops in infancy

3 *E*xplain how social contexts influence the infant's development

Images of Life-Span Development
The Story of Tom's Fathering

Many fathers are spending more time with their infants.

TOM IS A 1-year-old infant who is being reared by his father during the day. His mother works full-time at her job away from home, and his father is a writer who works at home; they prefer this arrangement over putting Tom in day care. Tom's father is doing a great job of caring for him. Tom's father keeps Tom nearby while he is writing and spends lots of time talking to him and playing with him. From their interactions, it is clear that they genuinely enjoy each other.

Tom's father is a far cry from the emotionally distant, conformist, traditional-gender-role fathers of the 1950s. He looks to the future and imagines the Little League games Tom will play in and the many other activities he can enjoy with Tom. Remembering how little time his own father spent with him, he is dedicated to making sure that Tom has an involved, nurturing experience with his father. Of course, not all fathers in the 1950s behaved like Tom's father and not all fathers today are as emotionally involved with their children as Tom is.

When Tom's mother comes home in the evening, she spends considerable time with him. Tom shows a positive attachment to both his mother and his father. His parents have cooperated and successfully juggled their careers and work schedules to provide 1-year-old Tom with excellent child care.

In chapters 5 and 6, you read about how the infant perceives, learns, and remembers. Infants also are socioemotional beings, capable of displaying emotions and initiating social interaction with people close to them.

1 EMOTIONAL AND PERSONALITY DEVELOPMENT

Emotional Development	Temperament	Personality Development

Anyone who has been around infants for even a brief period of time detects that they are emotional beings. Not only do we notice infants' expressions of emotions, but we sense that they vary in their temperament. Some are shy and others are outgoing. Some are active and others much less so. Let's explore these and other aspects of emotional and personality development in infants.

Emotional Development

Infants can express a number of emotions. We will see what these are and how they develop, but first we need to define *emotion*.

Defining *emotion* is difficult because it is not easy to tell when a child or an adult is in an emotional state. Is a child in an emotional state when her heart beats fast, her palms sweat, and her stomach churns? Or is she in an emotional state when she smiles or grimaces? The body and face play important roles in understanding children's emotion. However, psychologists debate how important each is in determining whether a child is in an emotional state. For our purposes, we will define **emotion** as

emotion Feeling, or affect, that can involve physiological arousal (a fast heartbeat, for example), conscious experience (thinking about being in love with someone, for example), and behavioral expression (a smile or grimace, for example).

feeling, or affect, that can involve physiological arousal (a fast heartbeat, for example), conscious experience (thinking about being in love with someone, for example), and behavioral expression (a smile or grimace, for example). Psychologists debate which of these components is the most important aspect of emotion and how they mix to produce emotional experiences (Izard, 2000; Witherington, Campos, & Hertenstein, 2002).

When we think about children's emotions, a few dramatic feelings, such as rage, fear, and glorious joy, usually spring to mind. However, emotions can be subtle as well—the feeling a mother has when she holds her baby, the mild irritation of boredom, and the uneasiness of being in a new situation.

Affect in Parent-Child Relationships   Emotions are the first language with which parents and infants communicate before the infant acquires speech (Maccoby, 1992). Infants react to their parents' facial expressions and tone of voice. In return, parents "read" what the infant is trying to communicate, responding appropriately when their infants are either distressed or happy. Sensitive, responsive parents help their infants grow emotionally, whether the infants respond in distressed or happy ways (Campos, 2001; Thompson, 1998).

The initial aspects of infant attachment to parents are based on emotion-linked interchanges, as when an infant cries and the caregiver sensitively responds. By the end of the first year, a mother's facial expression—either smiling or fearful—influences whether an infant will explore an unfamiliar environment. And, when children hear their parents quarreling, they often react with distress and inhibit their play (Cummings, 1987). Exceptionally well-functioning families often include humor in their interactions, sometimes making each other laugh and developing light, pleasant mood states to defuse conflicts. And, when a positive mood has been induced in the child, the child is more likely to comply with a parent's directions.

Infant and adult affective communicative capacities make possible coordinated infant-adult interactions (Thompson, 1999). The face-to-face interactions of even 3-month-old infants and adults are bidirectional (mutually regulated). This coordination has led to the characterization of mother-infant interaction as "reciprocal" or "synchronous." These terms attempt to capture the quality of interaction when all is going well.

Crying   Crying is the most important mechanism newborns have for communicating with their world. This statement is true even for the first cry, which tells the mother and doctor the baby's lungs have filled with air. Cries also may tell physicians and researchers something about the central nervous system.

Babies don't have just one type of cry. They have at least three:

- **Basic cry:** a rhythmic pattern that usually consists of a cry, followed by a briefer silence, then a shorter inspiratory whistle that is somewhat higher in pitch than the main cry, then another brief rest before the next cry. Some infancy experts believe that hunger is one of the conditions that incite the basic cry.
- **Anger cry:** a variation of the basic cry in which more excess air is forced through the vocal cords.
- **Pain cry:** stimulated by a high-intensity stimulus, a sudden appearance of a long, initial loud cry followed by breath holding; no preliminary moaning is present.

Most parents, and adults in general, can determine whether an infant's cries signify anger or pain (Zeskind, Klein, & Marshall, 1992). Parents also can distinguish the cries of their own baby better than those of another baby.

To soothe or not to soothe—should a crying baby be given attention and soothed, or does this spoil the infant? Many years ago, the behaviorist John Watson (1928) argued that parents spend too much time responding to infant crying. As a consequence, he said, parents are actually rewarding infant crying and increasing its incidence. More

Blossoms are scattered by the wind
And the wind cares nothing, but
The blossoms of the heart
No wind can touch.

—Youshida Kenko
Buddhist Monk, 14th Century

mhhe com/
santrockld9

Exploring Emotion
International Society for
Research on Emotions

basic cry A rhythmic pattern usually consisting of a cry, a briefer silence, a shorter inspiratory whistle that is higher pitched than the main cry, and then a brief rest before the next cry.

anger cry A cry similar to the basic cry, with more excess air forced through the vocal chords.

pain cry A sudden appearance of loud crying without preliminary moaning and followed by an extended period of breath holding.

*H*e who binds himself
to joy
Does the winged life
destroy;
But he who kisses the joy
as it
Flies lives in eternity's
sun rise.

—**William Blake**
English Poet, 19th Century

What are some developmental changes in emotion during infancy? What are some different types of crying that infants display?

mhhe ○com/
santrockld9

Infant Crying

recently, behaviorist Jacob Gewirtz (1977) found that a caregiver's quick, soothing response to crying increased crying. In contrast, infancy experts Mary Ainsworth (1979) and John Bowlby (1989) stress that you can't respond too much to infant crying in the first year of life. They believe that the caregiver's quick, comforting response to the infant's cries is an important ingredient in the development of a strong bond between the infant and caregiver. In one of Ainsworth's studies, infants whose mothers responded quickly when they cried at 3 months of age cried less later in the first year of life (Bell & Ainsworth, 1972). We will examine Ainsworth's work in more detail later in this chapter.

Controversy, then, still characterizes the issue of whether parents should respond to an infant's cries (Lewis & Ramsay, 1999). However, developmentalists increasingly argue that an infant cannot be spoiled in the first year of life, which suggests that parents should soothe a crying infant rather than be unresponsive; as a result, infants will likely develop a sense of trust and secure attachment to the caregiver in the first year of life.

Smiling   Smiling is another important communicative affective behavior of the infant. Two types of smiling can be distinguished in infants:

- **Reflexive smile:** a smile that does not occur in response to external stimuli and appears during the first month after birth, usually during sleep.
- **Social smile:** a smile that occurs in response to an external stimulus, typically a face in the case of the young infant.

Social smiling does not occur until 2 to 3 months of age (Emde, Gaensbauer, & Harmon, 1976), although some researchers believe that infants grin in response to voices as early as 3 weeks of age (Sroufe & Waters, 1976). The power of the infant's smiles was appropriately captured by British theorist John Bowlby (1969): "Can we doubt that the more and better an infant smiles the better he is loved and cared for? It is fortunate for their survival that babies are so designed by nature that they beguile and enslave mothers."

reflexive smile   A smile that does not occur in response to external stimuli. It happens during the month after birth, usually during irregular patterns of sleep, not when the infant is in an alert state.

social smile   A smile in response to an external stimulus, which, early in development, typically is a face.

Fear   The most frequent expression of an infant's fear involves **stranger anxiety,** in which an infant shows a fear and wariness of strangers. This reaction tends to appear in the second half of the first year of life. There are individual variations in stranger anxiety, and not all infants show distress when they encounter a stranger. Stranger anxiety usually emerges gradually, first appearing at about 6 months of age in the form of wary reactions. By age 9 months, the fear of strangers is often more intense and continues to escalate through the infant's first birthday (Emde, Gaensbauer, & Harmon, 1976).

A number of factors can influence whether an infant shows stranger anxiety, including the social context and the characteristics of the stranger. In terms of the social context, infants show less stranger anxiety when they are in familiar settings. For example, in one study, 10-month-olds showed little stranger anxiety when they met a stranger in their own home but much greater fear when they encountered a stranger in a research laboratory (Sroufe, Waters, & Matas, 1974). Also, infants show less stranger anxiety when they are sitting on their mothers' laps than when placed in an infant seat several feet away from their mothers (Bohlin & Hagekull, 1993). Thus, it appears that, when infants have a sense of security, they are less likely to show stranger anxiety.

Who the stranger is and how the stranger behaves also influence stranger anxiety in infants. Infants are less fearful of child strangers than adult strangers. They also are less fearful of friendly, outgoing, smiling strangers than of passive, unsmiling strangers (Bretherton, Stolberg, & Kreye, 1981).

Another expression of the infant's fear is **separation protest,** the infant's distress over being separated from his or her caregiver. Separation protest tends to peak at about 15 months in U.S. infants. In one study, charted in figure 7.1, separation protest peaked at about 13 to 15 months in four different cultures (Kagan, Kearsley, & Zelazo, 1978). Although the percentage of infants who engaged in separation protest varied across cultures, the infants reached a peak of protest at about the same age—just before the middle of the second year of life.

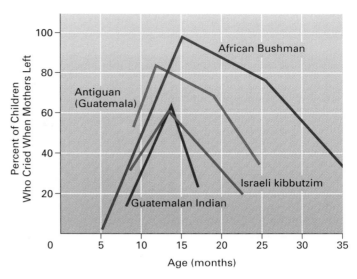

FIGURE 7.1 Separation Protest in Four Cultures

Note that separation protest peaked at about the same time in all four cultures in this study (13 to 15 months of age). However, a higher percentage (100 percent) of infants in an African Bushman culture engaged in separation protest compared to only about 60 percent of infants in Guatemalan Indian and Israeli kibbutzim cultures.

Social Referencing   **Social referencing** involves "reading" emotional cues in others to help determine how to act in a particular situation. The development of social referencing helps infants to interpret ambiguous situations more accurately, as when they encounter a stranger and need to know whether to fear the person (Mumme, Fernald, & Herrera, 1996). Infants become better at social referencing in the second year of life. In their second year, they have a tendency to "check" with their mother before they act. That is, they look at her to see if she is happy, angry, or fearful. In one study, 14- to 22-month-old infants were more likely to look at their mother's face as a source of information about how to act in a situation than were 6- to 9-month-old infants (Walden, 1991).

Emotional Regulation and Coping   **Emotional regulation** consists of effectively managing arousal to adapt and reach a goal (Eisenberg & others, 2002). Arousal involves a state of alertness or activation, which can reach levels that are too high for effective functioning. Crying and anger are two emotions that often require regulation.

During the first year of life, the infant gradually develops an ability to inhibit, or minimize, the intensity and duration of emotional reactions (Eisenberg, 2001). At the same time, infants acquire a greater diversity of emotional responses. Examples of early emotional regulation are infants' soothing themselves by sucking and withdrawing from excessive stimulation. Caregivers play an important role in helping infants learn how to regulate their emotions by attending to their distress and providing them with comfort.

stranger anxiety An infant's fear and wariness of strangers; it tends to appear in the second half of the first year of life.

separation protest An infant's distress over being separated from his or her caregiver.

social referencing "Reading" emotional cues in others to help determine how to act in a particular situation.

emotional regulation Effectively managing arousal to adapt and reach a goal.

"Oh, he's cute, all right, but he's got the temperament of a car alarm."

From early in infancy, babies put their thumbs in their mouths as a self-soothing strategy. In the early part of infancy, infants mainly depend on caregivers to help them sooth their emotions by rocking them to sleep, singing lullabyes to them, gently stroking them, and so on. Many developmentalists believe it is a good strategy for a caregiver to soothe an infant before the infant gets into an intense, agitated, uncontrolled state (Thompson, 1994). Later in infancy, when they become aroused, infants sometimes redirect their attention to something else or distract themselves in order to reduce their arousal (Grolnick, Bridges, & Connell, 1996).

Contexts can influence emotional regulation (Kopp & Neufeld, 2002; Saarni, 1999). Infants are often affected by such factors as fatigue, hunger, time of day, the people around them, and where they are. Infants must learn to increasingly adapt to different contexts that require emotional regulation. Further, new context demands appear as the infant becomes older and parents modify their expectations. For example, a parent may not expect a 1½-year-old to scream loudly in a restaurant but may not have been as bothered by this when the infant was 6 months old.

By 2 years of age, toddlers can use language to define their feeling states and the context that is upsetting them (Kopp & Neufeld, 2002). A toddler might say, "Feel bad. Dog scare." The communication of this type of information about feeling states and context may help caregivers to more effectively assist the child in regulating emotion.

Temperament

Emotional responses to similar situations vary among infants. One infant might be cheerful and happy much of the time; another baby might cry a lot and more often display a negative mood. These behaviors reflect differences in temperament (Halpern & Brand, 1999; Rothbart & Putnam, 2002). Let's explore a definition of temperament, the ways in which it can be classified, and the implications of temperamental variations for parenting.

Defining and Classifying Temperament   **Temperament** is an individual's behavioral style and characteristic way of emotionally responding. A widely debated issue is just what the key dimensions of temperament are. Psychiatrists Alexander Chess and Stella Thomas (Chess & Thomas, 1977; Thomas & Chess, 1991) believe there are three basic types, or clusters, of temperament:

- **Easy child:** This child is generally in a positive mood, quickly establishes regular routines in infancy, and adapts easily to new experiences.
- **Difficult child:** This child reacts negatively and cries frequently, engages in irregular daily routines, and is slow to accept new experiences.
- **Slow-to-warm-up child:** This child has a low activity level, is somewhat negative, and displays a low intensity of mood.

Various dimensions make up these three basic clusters of temperament. In their longitudinal investigation, Chess and Thomas found that 40 percent of the children they studied could be classified as easy, 10 percent as difficult, and 15 percent as slow to warm up (35 percent did not fit any of the three patterns). Researchers have found that these three basic clusters of temperament are moderately stable across the childhood years.

One way of classifying temperament involves comparing a shy, subdued, timid child with a sociable, extraverted, bold child. Jerome Kagan (1997, 2000, 2002; Kagan & Snidman, 1991) regards shyness with strangers, whether peers or adults, as one feature of a broader temperament category called *inhibition to the unfamiliar*. Inhibited

temperament An individual's behavioral style and characteristic way of emotionally responsing.

easy child A child who is generally in a positive mood, who quickly establishes regular routines in infancy, and who adapts easily to new experiences.

difficult child A child who tends to react negatively and cry frequently, who engages in irregular daily routines, and who is slow to accept new experiences.

slow-to-warm-up child A child who has a low activity level, is somewhat negative, shows low adaptability, and displays a low intensity of mood.

children react to many aspects of unfamiliarity with initial avoidance, distress, or subdued affect, especially beginning about 7 to 9 months of age. Kagan has found that inhibition shows considerable stability across the infant and early childhood years.

New classifications of temperament continue to be forged (Bornstein, 2000; Rothbart & Putnam, 2002; Wachs & Bates, 2002; Wachs & Kohnstamm, 2001). In a review of temperament research, Mary Rothbart and John Bates (1998) concluded that the best framework for classifying temperament involves a revision of Chess and Thomas' categories of easy, difficult, and slow to warm up. The general classification of temperament now focuses more on:

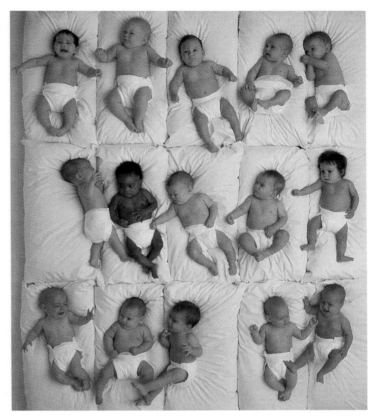

- *Positive affect and approach.* This category is much like the personality trait of extraversion/introversion. This category fits Kagan's concept of uninhibited children.
- *Negative affectivity.* Children whose temperament is characterized by negative affectivity are easily distressed and may fret and cry often. Negative affectivity is closely related to the personality trait of introversion, a tendency toward shyness and inhibition. This category also fits Kagan's concept of inhibition.
- *Effortful control (self-regulation).* This category reflects the child's ability to control his or her emotions and matches the concept of emotional regulation that we discussed earlier in the chapter. Thus, infants who are high on effortful control show an ability to keep their arousal from getting too high and have strategies for soothing themselves. By contrast, children low on effortful control often show an inability to control their arousal and they become easily agitated and intensely emotional.

What are some ways that developmentalists have classified infants' temperaments? Which classification makes the most sense to you, based on your observations of infants?

A number of scholars conceive of temperament as a stable characteristic of newborns, which comes to be shaped and modified by the child's later experiences. This raises the question of heredity's role in temperament (Goldsmith, 1988). Twin and adoption studies have been conducted to answer this question (Plomin & others, 1994). The researchers have found a heritability index in the range of .50 to .60, suggesting a moderate influence of heredity on temperament. However, the strength of the association usually declines as infants become older (Goldsmith & Gottesman, 1981). This finding supports the belief that temperament becomes more malleable with experience. Alternatively, it may be that, as a child becomes older, behavior indicators of temperament are more difficult to spot.

Infant Temperament

Goodness of Fit *Goodness of fit* refers to the match between a child's temperament and the environmental demands the child must cope with (Bates, 2001; Matheny & Phillips, 2001). Goodness of fit can be important to the child's adjustment. For example, consider an active child who is made to sit still for long periods of time or lives in a small apartment. Consider also a slow-to-warm-up child who is abruptly pushed into new situations on a regular basis. A bad fit between the child's temperament and these environmental demands can produce adjustment problems for the child. In our discussion of parenting and the child's temperament, many of the recommendations involve consideration of goodness of fit.

Parenting and the Child's Temperament Many parents don't become believers in temperament's importance until the birth of their second child. They tend to view the first child's behavior as being solely a result of how they socialized the child. However, management strategies that worked with the first child might not be as effective

What are some good strategies for parents to adopt when responding to their infant's temperament?

with the second child. Problems experienced with the first child (such as those involved in feeding, sleeping, and coping with strangers) might not exist with the second child, but new problems might arise. Such experiences strongly suggest that nature as well as nurture influence the child's development, that children differ from each other from very early in life, and that these differences have important implications for parent-child interaction (Kwak & others, 1999).

What are the implications of temperamental variations for parenting? Although answers to this question necessarily are speculative because of the incompleteness of the research literature, these conclusions were reached by temperament expert Mary Rothbart and her colleagues (Putnam, Sanson, & Rothbart, 2002; Sanson & Rothbart, 1995):

- *Attention to and respect for individuality.* An important implication of taking children's individuality seriously is that it becomes difficult to generate prescriptions for "good parenting," other than possibly specifying that parents need to be sensitive and flexible. Parents need to be sensitive to the infant's signals and needs. A goal of parenting might be accomplished in one way with one child and in another way with another child, depending on the child's temperament.

  Some temperament characteristics pose more parenting challenges than others, at least in modern Western societies. Children's proneness to distress, as exhibited by frequent crying and irritability, can contribute to the emergence of avoidant or coercive parental responses. In one research study, though, extra support and training for mothers of distress-prone infants improved the quality of mother-infant interaction (van den Boom, 1989).

- *Structuring the child's environment.* Crowded, noisy environments can pose greater problems for some children (such as a "difficult child") than others (such as an "easygoing" child). We might also expect that a fearful, withdrawing child would benefit from slower entry into new contexts.

- *The "difficult child" and packaged parenting programs.* Some books and programs for parents focus specifically on temperament (Cameron, Hansen, & Rosen, 1989; Turecki & Tonner, 1989). These programs usually focus on children with "difficult" temperaments. Acknowledgment that some children are harder to parent is often helpful, and advice on how to handle particular difficult temperament characteristics can also be useful. However, weighted against these potential advantages are several disadvantages. Whether a particular characteristic is difficult depends on its fit with the environment, whereas the notion of difficult temperament suggests that the problem rests solely with the child. Labeling a child "difficult" risks becoming a self-fulfilling prophecy—that is, if a child is identified as "difficult," the labeling might lead adults to expect the child to behave in this way and contribute to the continuance of the difficult behavior.

A child's temperament needs to be taken into account when considering caregiving behavior (Kochanska, 1999). Research does not yet allow for many highly specific recommendations, but, in general, caregivers should (1) be sensitive to the individual characteristics of the child, (2) be flexible in responding to these characteristics, and (3) avoid negative labeling of the child.

Gender, Culture, and Temperament   Parents might react differently to a child's temperament, depending on whether the child is a girl or a boy (Kerr, 2001). For example, in one study, mothers were more responsive to the crying of irritable girls than to the crying of irritable boys (Crockenberg, 1986).

Children's temperament also can vary across cultures (Putnam, Sanson, & Rothbart, 2002). For example, an active temperament might be valued in some cultures (such as the United States) but not in other cultures (such as China). Indeed, behavioral inhibition is more highly valued in China than in North America and researchers have found that Chinese infants have a more inhibited temperament than Canadian infants (Chen & others, 1998). The cultural differences in temperament were linked to parental attitudes and behaviors. Canadian mothers of inhibited 2-year-olds were less accepting of their infants' inhibited temperament while their Chinese mothers were more accepting.

Personality Development

We have explored some important aspects of emotional development and temperament, which reveal individual variations in infants. Let's now examine the characteristics that often are thought of as central to the infant's personality development: trust and the development of self and independence.

Trust According to Erik Erikson (1968), the first year of life is characterized by the trust-versus-mistrust stage of development ◀▥ p. 46. Following a life of regularity, warmth, and protection in the mother's womb, the infant faces a world that is less secure. Erikson believes that infants learn trust when they are cared for in a consistent, warm manner. If the infant is not well fed and kept warm on a consistent basis, a sense of mistrust is likely to develop.

Trust versus mistrust is not resolved once and for all in the first year of life. It arises again at each successive stage of development, which can have positive or negative outcomes. For example, children who enter school with a sense of mistrust may trust a particular teacher who has taken the time to make herself trustworthy. With this second chance, children overcome their early mistrust. By contrast, children who leave infancy with a sense of trust can still have their sense of mistrust activated at a later stage, perhaps if their parents are separated or divorced under conflicting circumstances.

The Developing Sense of Self and Independence Individuals carry with them a sense of who they are and what makes them different from everyone else. They cling to this identity and begin to feel secure in the knowledge that their identity is becoming more stable. Real or imagined, the sense of self is a strong motivating force in life. When does the individual begin to sense a separate existence from others?

The Self Infants are not "given" a self by their parents or the culture. Rather, they find and construct selves (Rochat, 2002). Studying the self in infancy is difficult mainly because infants are unable to describe with language their experiences of themselves.

To determine whether infants can recognize themselves, psychologists have used mirrors. In the animal kingdom, only the great apes learn to recognize their reflection in the mirror, but human infants accomplish this feat by about 18 months of age. How does the mirror technique work? The mother puts a dot of rouge on her infant's nose. The observer watches to see how often the infant touches its nose. Next, the infant is placed in front of a mirror, and observers detect whether nose touching increases. In two independent investigations in the second half of the second year of life, a majority of infants recognized their own image and coordinated the image they saw with the actions of touching their own body (Amsterdam, 1968; Lewis & Brooks-Gunn, 1979) (see figure 7.2).

Independence Not only does the infant develop a sense of self in the second year of life, but independence also becomes a more central theme in the infant's life. The theories of Margaret Mahler and Erik Erikson have important implications for both self-development and independence. Mahler (1979) believes that the child goes through a separation and then an individuation process. Separation involves the infant's movement away from the mother. Individuation involves the development of self.

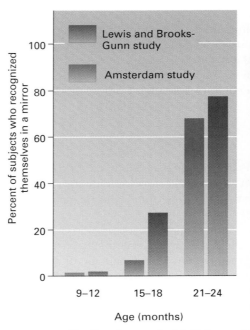

FIGURE 7.2 The Development of Self-Recognition in Infancy
The graph shows the findings of two studies in which infants less than 1 year of age did not recognize themselves in the mirror. A slight increase in the percentage of infant self-recognition occurred around 15 to 18 months of age and then by 2 years of age, a majority of children recognized themselves.

Self-Development in Infancy
Seeking Independence

Erikson (1968), like Mahler, believed that independence is an important issue in the second year of life ◄▥ p. 46. Erikson describes the second stage of development as the stage of autonomy versus shame and doubt. Autonomy builds on the infant's developing mental and motor abilities. At this point in development, not only can infants walk, but they can also climb, open and close, drop, push and pull, and hold and let go. Infants feel pride in these new accomplishments and want to do everything themselves, whether it is flushing a toilet, pulling the wrapping off a package, or deciding what to eat. It is important for parents to recognize the motivation of toddlers to do what they are capable of doing at their own pace. Then they can learn to control their muscles and their impulses themselves. But when caregivers are impatient and do for toddlers what they are capable of doing themselves, shame and doubt develop. Every parent has rushed a child from time to time. It is only when parents consistently overprotect toddlers or criticize accidents (wetting, soiling, spilling, or breaking, for example) that children develop an excessive sense of shame and doubt about their ability to control themselves and their world.

Erikson also believed that the stage of autonomy versus shame and doubt has important implications for the development of independence and identity during adolescence. The development of autonomy during the toddler years gives adolescents the courage to be independent individuals who can choose and guide their own future.

Review and Reflect

1 Discuss emotional and personality development in infancy
REVIEW
- What is the nature of an infant's emotions and how do they change?
- What is temperament and how does it develop in infancy?
- What are some important aspects of personality in infancy and how do they develop?

2 ATTACHMENT

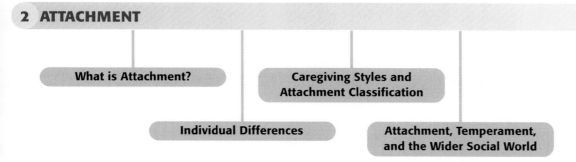

A small curly-haired girl named Danielle, 12 months old, begins to whimper. After a few seconds, she begins to wail. The psychologist observing Danielle is conducting a research study on the nature of attachment between infants and their mothers. Subsequently, Danielle's mother enters the room, and Danielle's crying ceases. Quickly, Danielle crawls over to where her mother is seated and reaches out to be held. This situation is one of the main ways in which psychologists study the nature of attachment during infancy.

What Is Attachment?

In everyday language, attachment is a relationship between two individuals who feel strongly about each other and do a number of things to continue the relationship. Many pairs of people are attached: relatives, lovers, a teacher and student. In the language of developmental psychology, though, attachment is often restricted to a relationship between particular social figures and a particular phenomenon that is thought to reflect unique characteristics of the relationship. In this case, the developmental period is infancy, the social figures are the infant and one or more adult caregivers, and the phenomenon is a bond (Bowlby, 1969, 1989). To summarize, **attachment** is a close emotional bond between an infant and a caregiver.

There is no shortage of theories about infant attachment. Freud believed that infants become attached to the person or object that provides oral satisfaction. For most infants, this is the mother, since she is most likely to feed the infant.

Is feeding as important as Freud thought? A classic study by Harry Harlow (1958) reveals that the answer is no (see figure 7.3). Harlow evaluated whether feeding or contact comfort was more important to infant attachment. Infant monkeys were removed from their mothers at birth and reared for six months by surrogate (substitute) "mothers." One of the mothers was made of wire, the other of cloth. Half of the infant monkeys were fed by the wire mother, half by the cloth mother. Periodically, the amount of time the infant monkeys spent with either the wire or the cloth monkey was computed. Regardless of whether they were fed by the wire or the cloth mother, the infant monkeys spent far more time with the cloth mother. This study clearly demonstrated that feeding is not the crucial element in the attachment process and that contact comfort is important.

Erik Erikson (1968) believed that the first year of life is the key time frame for the development of attachment. Recall his proposal—also discussed in chapter 2—that the

attachment A close emotional bond between an infant and a caregiver.

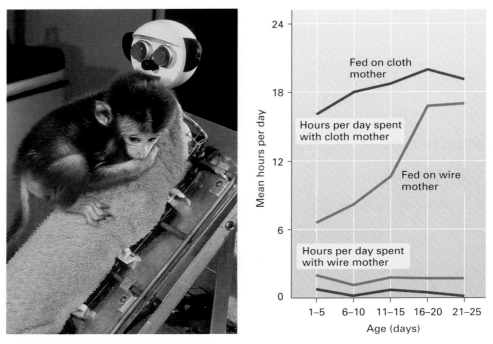

FIGURE 7.3 Contact Time with Wire and Cloth Surrogate Mothers

Regardless of whether the infant monkeys were fed by a wire or a cloth mother, they overwhelmingly preferred to spend contact time with the cloth mother.

first year of life represents the stage of trust versus mistrust ◀‖‖‖ p. 46. A sense of trust requires a feeling of physical comfort and a minimal amount of fear and apprehension about the future. Trust in infancy sets the stage for a lifelong expectation that the world will be a good and pleasant place to be. Erikson also believed that responsive, sensitive parenting contributes to an infant's sense of trust.

The ethological perspective of British psychiatrist John Bowlby (1969, 1989) also stresses the importance of attachment in the first year of life and the responsiveness of the caregiver. Bowlby believes that an infant and his or her primary caregiver form an attachment. He argues that the newborn is biologically equipped to elicit attachment behavior (Weizmann, 2000). The baby cries, clings, coos, and smiles. Later, the infant crawls, walks, and follows the mother. The infant's goal is to keep the primary caregiver nearby.

Attachment does not emerge suddenly but rather develops in a series of phases, moving from a baby's general preference for human beings to a partnership with primary caregivers. Here are four such phases based on Bowlby's conceptualization of attachment (Schaffer, 1996):

Phase 1:   Birth to 2 months   Infants instinctively direct their attachment to human figures. Strangers, siblings, and parents are equally likely to elicit smiling or crying from the infant.

Phase 2:   2 to 7 months   Attachment becomes focused on one figure, usually the primary caregiver, as the baby gradually learns to distinguish familiar from unfamiliar people.

Phase 3:   7 to 24 months   Specific attachments develop. With increased locomotor skills, babies actively seek contact with regular caregivers, such as the mother or father.

Phase 4:   24 months on   A goal-corrected partnership is formed in which children become aware of others' feelings, goals, and plans and begin to take these into account in forming their own actions.

Individual Differences

Although attachment to a caregiver intensifies midway through the first year, isn't it likely that some babies have a more positive attachment experience than others? Mary Ainsworth (1979) thinks so. She says that, in **secure attachment,** infants use the caregiver, usually the mother, as a secure base of attachment from which to explore the environment. Ainsworth believes that secure attachment in the first year of life provides an important foundation for psychological development later in life. The caregiver's sensitivity to the infant's signals increases secure attachment (deWolff & van Ijzendoorn, 1997). The securely attached infant moves freely away from the mother but processes her location through periodic glances. The securely attached infant responds positively to being picked up by others and, when put back down, freely moves away to play. An insecurely attached infant, by contrast, avoids the mother or is ambivalent toward her, fears strangers, and is upset by minor, everyday separations. Ainsworth's concept of secure attachment has much in common with Erikson's ideas about the development of trust.

Ainsworth created the **Strange Situation,** an observational measure of infant attachment that requires the infant to move through a series of introductions, separations, and reunions with the caregiver and an adult stranger in a prescribed order (see figure 7.4). In using the Strange Situation, researchers hope that their observations will provide them with information about the infant's motivation to be near the caregiver and the degree to which the caregiver's presence provides the infant with security and confidence. For example, in the presence of their caregiver, securely attached infants explore the room and examine toys that have been placed in it. When the caregiver departs, securely attached infants might mildly protest, and when the caregiver returns these infants reestablish positive interaction with her, perhaps by smiling or climbing on her lap. Subsequently, the securely attached infant often resumes playing with the toys in the room.

Three types of insecurely attached infants have been described:

- **Insecure avoidant babies** show insecurity by avoiding the mother. In the Strange Situation, these babies engage in little interaction with the caregiver, often display distress by crying when she leaves the room, usually do not reestablish contact with her on her return, and may even turn their back on her at this point. If contact is established, the infant usually leans away or looks away.
- **Insecure resistant babies** often cling to the caregiver and then resist her by fighting against the closeness, perhaps by kicking or pushing away. In the Strange Situation, these babies often cling anxiously to the caregiver and don't explore the playroom. When the caregiver leaves, they often cry loudly and push away if she tries to comfort them on her return.
- **Insecure disorganized babies** show insecurity in being disorganized and disoriented. In the Strange Situation, these babies might appear dazed, confused, and fearful. To be classified as disorganized, strong patterns of avoidance and resistance must be shown or certain select behaviors, such as extreme fearfulness around the caregiver, must be present.

Although the Strange Situation has been used in a large number of studies of infant attachment, some critics believe that the isolated, controlled events of the setting might not necessarily reflect what would happen if infants were observed with their caregiver in a natural environment. The issue of using controlled, laboratory assessments versus naturalistic observations is widely debated in child development circles.

secure attachment The infant uses a caregiver as a secure base from which to explore the environment. Ainsworth believes that secure attachment in the first year of life provides an important foundation for psychological development later in life.

Strange Situation An observational measure of infant attachment that requires the infant to move through a series of introductions, separations, and reunions with the caregiver and an adult stranger in a prescribed order.

insecure avoidant babies Babies that show insecurity by avoiding the caregiver.

insecure resistant babies Babies that often cling to the caregiver, then resist her by fighting against the closeness, perhaps by kicking or pushing away.

insecure disorganized babies Babies that show insecurity by being disorganized and disoriented.

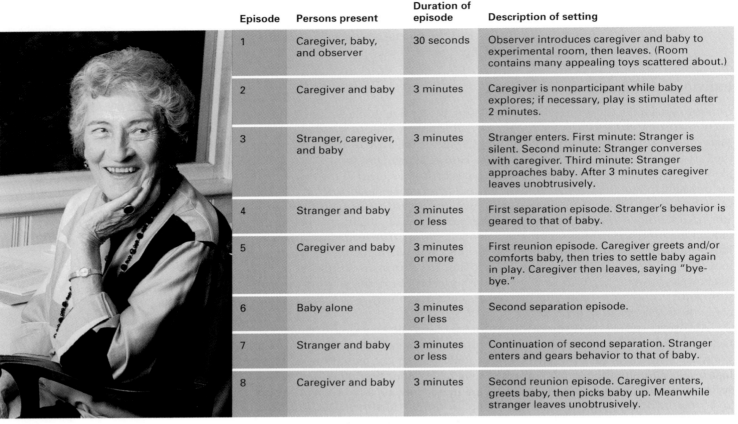

Episode	Persons present	Duration of episode	Description of setting
1	Caregiver, baby, and observer	30 seconds	Observer introduces caregiver and baby to experimental room, then leaves. (Room contains many appealing toys scattered about.)
2	Caregiver and baby	3 minutes	Caregiver is nonparticipant while baby explores; if necessary, play is stimulated after 2 minutes.
3	Stranger, caregiver, and baby	3 minutes	Stranger enters. First minute: Stranger is silent. Second minute: Stranger converses with caregiver. Third minute: Stranger approaches baby. After 3 minutes caregiver leaves unobtrusively.
4	Stranger and baby	3 minutes or less	First separation episode. Stranger's behavior is geared to that of baby.
5	Caregiver and baby	3 minutes or more	First reunion episode. Caregiver greets and/or comforts baby, then tries to settle baby again in play. Caregiver then leaves, saying "bye-bye."
6	Baby alone	3 minutes or less	Second separation episode.
7	Stranger and baby	3 minutes or less	Continuation of second separation. Stranger enters and gears behavior to that of baby.
8	Caregiver and baby	3 minutes	Second reunion episode. Caregiver enters, greets baby, then picks baby up. Meanwhile stranger leaves unobtrusively.

FIGURE 7.4 The Ainsworth Strange Situation

Mary Ainsworth (*left*) developed the Strange Situation to assess whether infants are securely or insecurely attached to their caregiver. The episodes involved in the Ainsworth Strange Situation are described here.

If early attachment to a caregiver is important, it should relate to a child's social behavior later in development. Researchers have found that for some children, early attachments seem to foreshadow later functioning (Schneider, Atkinson, & Tardif, 2001; Sroufe, Egeland, & Carlson, 1999). For other children, there is little continuity (Thompson, 2000). Consistency in caregiving over a number of years is likely an important factor in connecting early attachment and the child's functioning later in development.

Caregiving Styles and Attachment Classification

Attachment is defined as a close emotional bond between the infant and caregiver. Is the parent's caregiving style linked with this close emotional bond called attachment? Securely attached babies have caregivers who are sensitive to their signals and are consistently available to respond to their infants' needs (Gao, Elliot, & Waters, 1999; Main, 2000). These caregivers often let their babies have an active part in determining the onset and pacing of interaction in the first year of life.

How do the caregivers of insecurely attached babies interact with them? Caregivers of insecure avoidant babies tend to be unavailable or rejecting (Berlin & Cassidy, 2000). They often don't respond to their babies' signals and have little physical contact with them. When they do interact with their babies, they may behave in an angry and irritable way toward them. Caregivers of insecure resistant babies tend to be inconsistently available to their babies (Cassidy & Berlin, 1994). That is, sometimes they respond to their babies' needs, and sometimes they don't. In general, they tend not to be very affectionate with their babies and show little synchrony when interacting with them. Caregivers of insecure disorganized babies often neglect or physically abuse their babies (Barnett, Ganiban, & Cicchetti, 1999). In some cases, these caregivers also have depression (Field, 1992; Levy, 1999).

Attachment, Temperament, and the Wider Social World

Not all research reveals the power of infant attachment to predict subsequent development. In one longitudinal study, attachment classification in infancy did not predict attachment classification at 18 years of age (Lewis, 1997). In this study, the best predictor of attachment classification at 18 was the occurrence of parent divorce in intervening years.

Thus, not all developmentalists believe that attachment in infancy is the only path to competence in life. Indeed, some developmentalists believe that too much emphasis is placed on the importance of the attachment bond in infancy. Jerome Kagan (1987, 2000), for example, believes that infants are highly resilient and adaptive; he argues that they are evolutionarily equipped to stay on a positive developmental course, even in the face of wide variations in parenting. Kagan and others stress that genetic and temperament characteristics play a more important role in a child's social competence than the attachment theorists, such as Bowlby, Ainsworth, and Sroufe, are willing to acknowledge (Chaudhuri & Williams, 1999; Young & Shahinfar, 1995). For example, infants may have inherited a low tolerance for stress. This inherited characteristic, rather than an insecure attachment bond, may be responsible for their inability to get along with peers.

Also, researchers have found cultural variations in attachment. German and Japanese babies often show different patterns of attachment than American infants do. As shown in figure 7.5, German infants are more likely to show an avoidant attachment pattern and Japanese infants are less likely to show this pattern than U.S. infants (van Ijzendoorn & Kroonenberg, 1988). The avoidant pattern in German babies likely occurs because their caregivers encourage them to be more independent (Grossmann & others, 1985). Also as shown in figure 7.5, Japanese babies are more likely than American babies to be categorized as resistant. This may have more to do with the Ainsworth Strange Situation as a measure of attachment than with attachment insecurity itself. Japanese mothers rarely let anyone unfamiliar with their babies care for them. Thus, the Ainsworth Strange Situation might create considerably more stress for Japanese infants than for American infants, who are more accustomed to separation from their mothers (Takahashi, 1990). Even though there are cultural variations in attachment classification, the prevailing classification in every culture studied so far is secure attachment (van Ijzendoorn & Kroonenberg, 1988).

Another criticism of attachment theory is that it ignores the diversity of socializing agents and contexts that exists in an infant's world. In some cultures, infants show attachments to many people. Among the Hausa (who live in Nigeria), both grandmothers and siblings provide a significant amount of care for infants (Harkness & Super, 1995). Infants in agricultural societies tend to form attachments to older siblings, who are assigned a major responsibility for younger siblings' care. The attachments formed by infants in group care in Israeli kibbutzim provide another challenge to the singular attachment thesis.

Researchers recognize the importance of competent, nurturant caregivers in an infant's development (Maccoby, 1999; McHale & others, 2001; Parke, 2001). At issue, though, is whether or not secure attachment, especially to a single caregiver, is critical (Thompson, 2000).

What is the nature of secure and insecure attachment?

Forming a Secure Attachment

Attachment Research

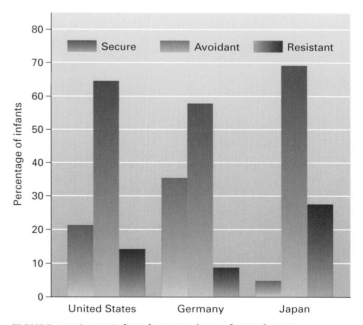

FIGURE 7.5 Cross-Cultural Comparison of Attachment

In one study, infant attachment in three countries—the United States, Germany, and Japan—was measured in the Ainsworth Strange Situation (van Ijzendoorn & Kroonenberg, 1988). The dominant attachment pattern in all three countries was secure attachment. However, German infants were more avoidant and Japanese infants were less avoidant and more resistant than U.S. infants.

Review and Reflect

2 **Describe how attachment develops in infancy**

REVIEW

- What is attachment?
- What are some individual variations in attachment?
- How are caregiving styles related to attachment classifications?
- What are some issues related to attachment?

REFLECT

- How might the infant's temperament be related to the way in which attachment is classified? Look at the temperament categories we described and reflect on how these might be more likely to show up in infants in some attachment categories than others.

3 SOCIAL CONTEXTS

The Family   **Day Care**

Now that we have explored the infant's emotional and personality development and attachment, let's examine the social contexts in which these occur. We will begin by studying a number of aspects of the family and then turn to a social context in which infants increasingly spend time—day care.

The Family

Most of us began our lives in families and spent thousands of hours during our childhood interacting with our parents. Some of you are already parents; others of you may become parents. What is the transition to parenthood like?

The Transition to Parenting

The Transition to Parenthood   When people become parents through pregnancy, adoption, or stepparenting, they face disequilibrium and must adapt (Heincke, 2002; Klitzing, Simoni, & Burgin, 1999). Parents want to develop a strong attachment with their infant, but they still want to maintain strong attachments to their spouse and friends, and possibly continue their careers. Parents ask themselves how this new being will change their lives. A baby places new restrictions on partners; no longer will they be able to rush out to a movie on a moment's notice, and money may not be readily available for vacations and other luxuries. Dual-career parents ask, "Will it harm the baby to place her in day care? Will we be able to find responsible baby-sitters?"

In a longitudinal investigation of couples from late pregnancy until 3½ years after the baby was born, couples enjoyed more positive marital relations before the baby was born than after (Cowan & Cowan, 2000; Cowan & others, 1995). Still, almost one-third showed an increase in marital satisfaction. Some couples said that the baby had both brought them closer together *and* moved them farther apart. They commented that being parents enhanced their sense of themselves and gave them a new, more stable identity as a couple. Babies opened men up to a concern with intimate relationships, and the demands of juggling work and family roles stimulated women to manage family tasks more efficiently and pay attention to their own personal growth.

At some point during the early years of the child's life, parents face the difficult task of juggling their roles as parents and as self-actualizing adults. Until recently in our culture, nurturing our children and having a career were thought to be incompatible. Fortunately, we have come to recognize that the balance between caring and achieving, nurturing and working—although difficult to manage—can be accomplished (Hoffman & Youngblade, 1999).

Reciprocal Socialization   For many years, socialization between parents and children was viewed as a one-way process: Children were considered to be the products of their parents' socialization techniques. Today, however, we view parent-child interaction as reciprocal (Hartup & Laursen, 1999). **Reciprocal socialization** is socialization that is bidirectional. That is, children socialize parents just as parents socialize children. For example, the interaction of mothers and their infants is symbolized as a dance or a dialogue in which successive actions of the partners are closely coordinated. This coordinated dance or dialogue can assume the form of mutual synchrony in which each person's behavior depends on the partner's previous behavior (Feldman, Greenbaum, & Yirmiya, 1999). Or it can be reciprocal in the sense that actions of the partners are matched, as when one partner imitates the other or when there is mutual smiling.

When reciprocal socialization has been studied in infancy, mutual gaze, or eye contact, plays an important role in early social interaction. In one investigation, the mother and infant engaged in a variety of behaviors while they looked at each other. By contrast, when they looked away from each other, the rate of such behaviors dropped considerably (Stern & others, 1977). In sum, the behaviors of mothers and infants involve substantial interconnection, mutual regulation, and synchronization.

An important form of reciprocal socialization is **scaffolding,** in which parents time interactions in such a way that the infant experiences turn-taking with the parents. Scaffolding involves parental behavior that supports children's efforts, allowing them to be more skillful than they would be if they were to rely only on their own abilities. In using scaffolding, caregivers provide a positive, reciprocal framework in which they and their children interact. For example, in the game peek-a-boo, the mother initially covers the baby. Then she removes the cover and registers "surprise" at the infant's reappearance. As infants become more skilled at peek-a-boo, pat-a-cake, and so on, there are other caregiver games that exemplify scaffolding and turn-taking sequences. In one study, infants who had more extensive scaffolding experiences with their parents (especially in the form of turn-taking) were more likely to engage in turn-taking when they interacted with their peers (Vandell & Wilson, 1988). Scaffolding is not confined to parent-infant interaction but can be used by parents to support children's achievement-related efforts in school by adjusting and modifying the amount and type of support that best suits the child's level of development.

The Family as a System   As a social system, the family can be thought of as a constellation of subsystems defined in terms of generation, gender, and role (Kreppner, 2001; Minuchin, 2001). Divisions of labor among family members define particular subunits, and attachments define others. Each family member is a participant in several subsystems. Some are *dyadic* (involving two people), some *polyadic* (involving more than two people). The father and child represent one dyadic subsystem, the mother and father another. The mother-father-child represent one polyadic subsystem, the mother and two siblings another.

Jay Belsky (1981) proposed an organizational scheme that highlights the reciprocal influences of family members and family subsystems (see figure 7.6). Belsky believes that marital relations, parenting, and infant behavior and development can have both direct and indirect effects on each other. An example of a direct effect is the influence of the parents' behavior on the child. An example of an indirect effect is how the relationship between the spouses mediates the way a parent acts toward the child (McHale, Lauretti, & Kuerston-Hogan, 1999). For example, marital conflict might

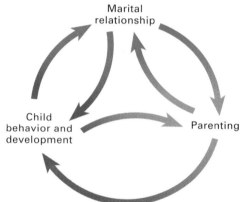

FIGURE 7.6 Interaction Between Children and Their Parents: Direct and Indirect Effects

reciprocal socialization Socialization that is bidirectional; children socialize parents, just as parents socialize children.

scaffolding Parents time interactions so that infants experience turn-taking with the parents.

reduce the efficiency of parenting, in which case marital conflict would indirectly affect the child's behavior.

Maternal and Paternal Infant Caregiving Can fathers take care of infants as competently as mothers can? Observations of fathers and their infants suggest that fathers have the ability to act sensitively and responsively with their infants (Parke, 1995, 2000, 2001, 2002). The strongest evidence of the plasticity of male caregiving abilities is based on male primates, which are notoriously low in their interest in offspring. When forced to live with infants whose female caregivers are absent, the adult male competently rears the infants. Remember, however, that, although fathers can be active, nurturant, involved caregivers with their infants, many do not choose to follow this pattern (Eggebeen & Knoester, 2001; Silverstein, 2001).

Do fathers behave differently toward infants than mothers do? Maternal interactions usually center on child-care activities—feeding, changing diapers, bathing. Paternal interactions are more likely to include play. Fathers engage in more rough-and-tumble play. They bounce infants, throw them up in the air, tickle them, and so on (Lamb, 1986, 2000). Mothers do play with infants, but their play is less physical and arousing than that of fathers.

In stressful circumstances, do infants prefer their mother or father? In one study, 20 12-month-olds were observed interacting with their parents (Lamb, 1977). With both parents present, the infants preferred neither their mother nor their father. The same was true when the infants were alone with the mother or the father. However, the entrance of a stranger, combined with boredom and fatigue, produced a shift in the infants' social behavior toward the mother. In stressful circumstances, then, infants show a stronger attachment to the mother.

In a more recent study, fathers were interviewed about their caregiving responsibilities when their children were 6, 15, 24, and 36 months of age (NICHD Early Child Care Research Network, 2000). A subset was videotaped during father-child play at 6 and 36 months. Caregiving activities (such as bathing, feeding, and dressing the child, and taking the child to day care) and sensitivity during play interactions (such as being responsive to the child's signals and needs, and expressing positive feelings) with their children were predicted by several factors. Fathers were more involved in caregiving when they worked fewer hours and mothers worked more hours, when fathers and mothers were younger, when mothers reported greater marital intimacy, and when the children were boys. Fathers who had less-traditional child-rearing beliefs and reported more marital intimacy were more sensitive during play.

Might the nature of parent-infant interaction be different in families that adopt nontraditional gender roles? This question was investigated by Michael Lamb and his colleagues (1982). They studied Swedish families in which the fathers were the primary caregivers of their firstborn, 8-month-old infants. The mothers were working full-time. In all observations, the mothers were more likely to discipline, hold, soothe, kiss, and talk to the infants than were the fathers. These mothers and fathers dealt with their infants differently, along the lines of American fathers and mothers following traditional gender roles. Having fathers assume the primary caregiving role did not substantially alter the way they interacted with their infants. This may be for biological reasons or because of deeply ingrained socialization patterns in cultures.

Day Care

Many parents worry whether day care will adversely affect their children. They fear that day care will reduce their infants' emotional attachment to them, retard the infants' cognitive development, fail to teach them how to control anger, and allow them to be unduly influenced by their peers. How extensive is day care? Are the worries of these parents justified?

Today far more young children are in day care than at any other time in history; about 2 million children currently receive formal, licensed day care, and more than

mhhe ● com/
santrockld9

Family Resources
Maternal Resources
The Fatherhood Project

We have all the knowledge necessary to provide absolutely first-rate child care in the United States. What is missing is the commitment and the will.

—**Edward Zigler**
Contemporary Developmental Psychologist, Yale University

Child-Care Policy Around the World

Sheila Kammerman (1989, 2000a, b) has conducted extensive examinations of parental leave policies around the world. Parental leaves were first enacted as maternity policies more than a century ago to protect the physical health of working women at the time of childbirth. More recently, child-rearing, parental, and paternity leaves were created in response not only to the needs of working women (and parents), but also because of concern for the child's well being. The European Union (EU) mandated a paid 14-week maternity leave in 1992 and a three-month parental leave in 1998.

Across cultures, policies vary in eligibility criteria, leave duration, benefit level, and the extent to which parents take advantage of these policies. The European policies just mentioned lead the way in creating new standards of parental leave. The United States is alone among advanced industrialized countries in the briefness of parental leave granted and among the few countries with unpaid leave (Australia and New Zealand are the others).

There are five different types of parental leave from employment:

- *Maternity Leave.* In some countries the pre-birth leave is compulsory as is a 6- to 10-week leave following birth.
- *Paternity Leave.* This is usually much briefer than maternity leave. It may be especially important when a second child is born and the first child requires care.
- *Parental Leave.* This is a gender-neutral leave that usually follows a maternity leave and allows either women or men to take advantage of the leave policy and share it or choose which of them will use it.
- *Child-Rearing Leave.* In some countries, this is a supplement to a maternity leave or a variation on a parental leave. A child-rearing leave is usually longer than a maternity leave and is typically paid at a much lower level.
- *Family Leave.* This covers reasons other than the birth of a new baby and can allow time off from employment to care for an ill child or other family members, time to accompany a child to school for the first time, or time to visit a child's school.

Sweden has one of the most extensive leave policies. Paid for by the government at 80 percent of wages, one year of parental leave is allowed (including maternity leave). Maternity leave may begin 60 days prior to expected birth of the baby and ends six weeks after birth. Another six months of parental leave can be used until the child's eighth birthday (Kammerman, 2000a). Virtually all eligible mothers take advantage of the leave policy and approximately 75 percent of eligible fathers take at least some part of the leave they are allowed. In addition, employed grandparents now also have the right to take time off to care for an ill grandchild.

Spain is an example of a relatively poor country that still provides substantial parental leave. Spain allows a 16-week paid maternity leave (paid at 100 percent of wages) at childbirth with up to 6 weeks prior to childbirth allowed. Fathers are permitted two days of leave.

5 million children attend kindergarten. Also, uncounted millions of children are cared for by unlicensed baby-sitters.

In Sweden, mothers or fathers are given paid maternity or paternity leave for up to one year. For this reason, day care for Swedish infants under 1 year of age is usually not a major concern. Sweden and many other European countries have well-developed child care policies. To learn about these policies, see the Sociocultural Worlds of Development box.

Because the United States does not have a policy of paid leave for child care, day care in the United States has become a major national concern. The type of day care that young children receive varies extensively (Burchinal & others, 1996; Scarr, 2000). Many day-care centers house large groups of children and have elaborate facilities. Some are commercial operations; others are nonprofit centers run by churches, civic groups, and employers. Child care is frequently provided in private homes, at times by child care professionals, at others by mothers who want to earn extra money.

A special contemporary interest of researchers is the role of poverty in the quality of day care (Chase-Lansdale, Coley, & Grining, 2001; Huston, McLoyd, & Coll, 1994). In one study, day-care centers that served high-income children delivered better-quality care than did centers that served middle- and low-income children (Phillips & others, 1994). The indices of quality (such as teacher-child ratios) in subsidized centers for the poor were fairly good, but the quality of observed teacher-child interaction was lower than in high-income centers.

What constitutes a high-quality day-care program for infants? The demonstration program developed by Jerome Kagan and his colleagues (Kagan, Kearsley, & Zelazo,

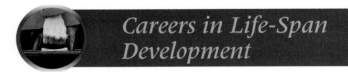

Careers in Life-Span Development

Rashmi Nakhre, Day-Care Director

Rashmi Nakhre has two master's degrees—one in psychology, the other in child development—and is director of the Hattie Daniels Day Care Center in Wilson, North Carolina. At a recent ceremony, "Celebrating a Century of Women," Nakhre received the Distinguished Women of North Carolina Award for 1999–2000.

Nakhre first worked at the day-care center soon after she arrived in the United States 25 years ago. She says that she took the job initially because she needed the money but "ended up falling in love with my job." Nakhre has turned the Wilson, North Carolina, day-care center into a model for other centers. The Center almost closed several years after she began working there because of financial difficulties. Dr. Nakhre played a major role in raising funds not only to keep it open but to improve it. The Center provides quality day care for the children of many Latino migrant workers.

Rashmi Nakhre, day-care director, working with some of the children at her center.

1978) at Harvard University is exemplary. The day-care center included a pediatrician, a nonteaching director, and an infant-teacher ratio of 3 to 1. Teachers' aides assisted at the center. The teachers and aides were trained to smile frequently, to talk with the infants, and to provide them with a safe environment, which included many stimulating toys. No adverse effects of day care were observed in this project. More information about what to look for in a quality day-care center is presented in figure 7.7. Using such criteria, one study discovered that children who entered low-quality child care as infants were least likely to be socially competent in early childhood (less compliant, less self-controlled, less task-oriented, more hostile, and less competent in peer interaction) (Howes, 1988). Unfortunately, children who come from families with few resources (psychological, social, and economic) are more likely to experience poor-quality day care than are children from more-advantaged backgrounds (Lamb, 1994). To read about one individual who provides quality day care to individuals from impoverished backgrounds, see the Careers in Life-Span Development insert.

Aware of the growing use of child care, the National Institute of Child Health and Human Development (NICHD) set out to develop a comprehensive, longitudinal study (a study that follows the same individuals over time, usually several years or more) that focuses on the child-care experiences of children and their development (Burchinal, 2001; Owen, 2001; Peth-Pierce, 1998). The study began in 1991, and data were collected on a diverse sample of almost 1,400 children and their families at 10 locations across the United States over a period of seven years. Researchers used multiple methods (trained observers, interviews, questionnaires, and testing) and measured many facets of children's development, including physical health, cognitive development, and socioemotional development. Here are some of the results of this extensive study to date:

• The infants from low-income families were more likely to receive low-quality child care than were their higher-income counterparts. Quality of care was based on such characteristics as group size, child–adult ratio, physical environment, caregiver characteristics (such as formal education, specialized training, and child-care experience), and caregiver behavior (such as sensitivity to children).

• Child care in and of itself neither adversely affected nor promoted the security of infants' attachments to their mothers. Certain child-care conditions, in combination with certain home environments, did increase the probability that infants would be insecurely attached to their mothers. The infants who received either poor quality of care or more than 10 hours per week of care, or were in more than one setting in the first 15 months of life, were more likely to be insecurely attached, but only if their mothers were less sensitive in responding to them.

• Child-care quality, especially sensitive and responsive attention from caregivers, was linked with fewer child problems. The higher the quality of child care over the first three years of life (more positive language stimulation and interaction between the child and the provider), the greater the child's language and cognitive abilities. No cognitive benefits were found for the children in the exclusive care of their mother.

What constitutes quality child care? These recommendations were made by the National Association for the Education of Young Children (1986). They are based on a consensus arrived at by experts in early childhood education and child development. It is especially important for parents to meet the adults who will care for their child. Caregivers are responsible for every aspect of the program's operation.

1. The adult caregivers

   • The adults should enjoy and understand how infants and young children grow.

   • There should be enough adults to work with a group and to care for the individual needs of children. The recommended ratios of adult caregivers to children of different ages are:

Age of children	Adult to children ratio
0 to 1 Year	1:3
1 to 2 Years	1:5
2 to 3 Years	1:6
3 to 4 Years	1:8
4 to 5 Years	1:10

   • Caregivers should observe and record each child's progress and development.

2. The program activities and equipment

   • The environment should foster the growth and development of young children working and playing together.

   • A good center should provide appropriate and sufficient equipment and play materials and make them readily available.

   • Infants and children should be helped to increase their language skills and to expand their understanding of the world.

3. The relation of staff to families and the community

   • A good program should consider and support the needs of the entire family. Parents should be welcome to observe, discuss policies, make suggestions, and work in the activities of the center.

   • The staff in a good center should be aware of and contribute to community resources. The staff should share information about community recreational and learning opportunities with families.

4. The design of the facility and the program to meet the varied demands of infants and young children, their families, and the staff

   • The health of children, staff, and parents should be protected and promoted. The staff should be alert to the health of each child.

   • The facility should be safe for children and adults.

   • The environment should be spacious enough to accommodate a variety of activities and equipment. More specifically, there should be a minimum of 35 square feet of usable playroom floor space indoors per child and 75 square feet of play space outdoors per child.

FIGURE 7.7 What Is High-Quality Day Care?

**National Child Care
Information Center
NICHD Study of Early Child Care**

Review and Reflect

3 Explain how social contexts influence the infant's development

REVIEW

• What are some important family processes in infant development?

• How does day care influence infant development?

REFLECT

• Imagine that a friend of yours is getting ready to put her baby in day care. What advice would you give to her? Do you think she should stay home with the baby? Why or why not? What type of day care would you recommend?

Reach Your Learning Goals

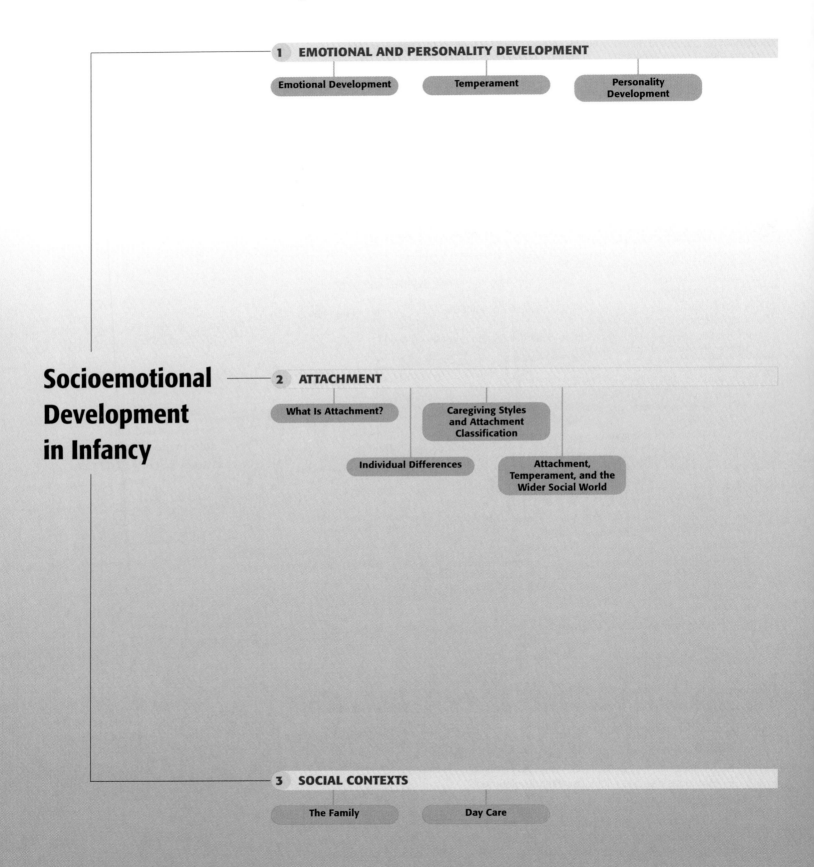

Socioemotional Development in Infancy

1 EMOTIONAL AND PERSONALITY DEVELOPMENT

Emotional Development

Temperament

Personality Development

2 ATTACHMENT

What Is Attachment?

Caregiving Styles and Attachment Classification

Individual Differences

Attachment, Temperament, and the Wider Social World

3 SOCIAL CONTEXTS

The Family

Day Care

Summary

1 Discuss emotional and personality development in infancy

- Emotion is feeling or affect that can involve a mixture of physiological arousal, conscious experience, and overt behavior. Emotions are the way that parents and infants communicate before the infant acquires speech. Expressions of emotion make possible coordinated infant-adult interaction. Babies have at least three types of cries—basic cry, anger cry, and pain cry. Most parents, and adults in general, can tell whether an infant's cry signifies anger or pain. There is controversy about whether babies should be soothed when crying. An increasing number of development researchers support Bowlby and Ainsworth's belief that infant crying should be responded to immediately in the first year of life. Two types of smiles can be distinguished in infants: reflexive and social. Two fears that infants develop are stranger anxiety and separation protest. Social referencing increases in the second year of life. As infants develop it is important for them to engage in emotional regulation.

- Temperament is an individual's behavioral style and characteristic way of emotionally responding. Chess and Thomas classified infants as (1) easy, (2) difficult, or (3) slow to warm up. Kagan believes that inhibition to the unfamiliar is an important temperament category. Recent classifications focus more on (1) positive affect and approach, (2) negative affectivity, and (3) effortful control (self-regulation). Goodness of fit—the match between a child's temperament and the environmental demands the child must cope with—can be an important aspect of a child's adjustment. Although research evidence is sketchy at this point in time, some general recommendations are that caregivers should (1) be sensitive to the individual characteristics of the child, (2) be flexible in responding to these characteristics, and (3) avoid negative labeling of the child. Gender and culture are linked to variations in temperament.

- Erikson argued that an infant's first year is characterized by the stage of trust versus mistrust. At some point in the second half of the second year of life, the infant develops a sense of self. Independence becomes a central theme in the second year of life. Mahler argues that the infant separates herself from her mother and then develops individuation. Erikson stressed that the second year of life is characterized by the stage of autonomy versus shame and doubt.

2 Describe how attachment develops in infancy

- Attachment is a close emotional bond between the infant and caregiver. Feeding is not an important aspect of attachment, although contact comfort and trust are. Bowlby's ethological theory stresses that the caregiver and the infant instinctively form attachment. Attachment develops in four phases, beginning at birth and continuing past 24 months.

- Securely attached babies use the caregiver, usually the mother, as a secure base from which to explore the environment. Three types of insecure attachment are avoidant, resistant, and disorganized. Ainsworth argued that secure attachment in the first year of life is optimal for development. She created the Strange Situation, an observational measure of attachment.

- Caregivers of secure babies are sensitive to the babies' signals and are consistently available to meet their needs. Caregivers of insecure avoidant babies tend to be unavailable or rejecting. Caregivers of insecure resistant babies tend to be inconsistently available to their babies and usually are not very affectionate. Caregivers of insecure disorganized babies often neglect or physically abuse their babies.

- Some critics argue that attachment theorists have not given adequate attention to genetics and temperament. Other critics stress that they have not adequately taken into account the diversity of social agents and contexts. Cultural variations in attachment have been found, but in all cultures studied to date secure attachment is the most common classification.

3 Explain how social contexts influence the infant's development

- The transition to parenthood requires considerable adaptation and adjustment on the part of parents. Children socialize parents just as parents socialize children. Mutual regulation and scaffolding are important aspects of reciprocal socialization. Belsky's model describes direct and indirect effects. The mother's primary role when interacting with the infant is caregiving; the father's is playful interaction.

- Day care has become a basic need of the American family. More children are in day care now than at any earlier point in history. The quality of day care is uneven, and day care remains a controversial topic. Quality day care can be achieved and seems to have few adverse effects on children. In the NICHD child-care study, infants from low-income families were more likely to receive the lowest quality of care. Also, higher quality of child care was linked with fewer child problems.

Key Terms

emotion 206
basic cry 207
anger cry 207
pain cry 207
reflexive smile 208
social smile 208

stranger anxiety 209
separation protest 209
social referencing 209
emotional regulation 209
temperament 210
easy child 210

difficult child 210
slow-to-warm-up child 210
attachment 215
secure attachment 217
Strange Situation 217
insecure avoidant babies 217

insecure resistant babies 217
insecure disorganized
    babies 217
reciprocal socialization 221
scaffolding 221

Key People

John Watson 207
Jacob Gewirtz 208
Mary Ainsworth 208, 217
John Bowlby 208, 216

Alexander Chess and
    Stella Thomas 210
Mary Rothbart and
    John Bates 211

Erik Erikson 213, 215
Margaret Mahler 213
Harry Harlow 215
Jerome Kagan 219, 223

Jay Belsky 221

Taking It to the Net

1. Catherine is conducting a class for new parents at a local clinic. What advice should Catherine give the parents about how parenting practices can affect a child's inborn temperament?
2. Janice is a researcher for a biotech firm. Her husband, Jeff, is a corporate attorney. Both of them have worked hard to establish themselves in their careers, and neither wants to stay home to take care of their 6-month-old daughter, Jessica. Although they are looking into various day-care programs,

both of them are concerned about the potential negative effects. According to the research, does day care have a negative effect on attachment or future development? Does the quality of the program or the amount of time in day care make a difference?

Connect to www.mhhe.com/santrockld9 to research the answers and complete these exercises.

E-learning Tools

To help you master the material in this chapter, you'll find a number of valuable study tools on the Student CD-ROM that accompanies this book. In addition, visit the Online Learning Center for *Life-Span Development*, ninth edition, where you'll find these valuable resources for chapter 7, "Socioemotional Development in Infancy."

- What are your beliefs about nurturing an infant's socioemotional development? Use the self-assessment, *My Beliefs About*

Nurturing a Baby's Socioemotional Development, to determine what your views are.
- View video clips of key researchers, including Alan Sroufe as he discusses his research on attachment.
- Build your decision-making skills by trying your hand at the parenting and education "Scenarios."

Early Childhood

You are troubled at seeing him spend his early years doing nothing. What! Is it nothing to be happy? Is it nothing to skip, to play, to run about all day long? Never in his life will he be so busy as now.

—JEAN-JACQUES ROUSSEAU
Swiss-Born Philosopher, 18th Century

In early childhood, our greatest untold poem was being only 4 years old. We skipped and ran and played all day long, never in our lives so busy, busy being something we had not quite grasped yet. Who knew our thoughts, which we worked up into small mythologies all our own? Our thoughts and images and drawings took wings. The blossoms of our heart, no wind could touch. Our small world widened as we discovered new refuges and new people. When we said "I," we meant something totally unique, not to be confused with any other. Section Four consists of two chapters: "Physical and Cognitive Development in Early Childhood" (chapter 8) and "Socioemotional Development in Early Childhood" (chapter 9).

*The greatest person
ever known
Is one all poets have
outgrown;
The poetry, innate and
untold,
Of being only four
years old.*

—CHRISTOPHER MORLEY
American Novelist, 20th Century

Physical and Cognitive Development in Early Childhood

Images of Life-Span Development
Teresa Amabile and Her Creativity

Teresa Amabile remembers that, when she was in kindergarten, she rushed in every day, excited and enthusiastic about getting to the easel and playing with all those bright colors and big paint brushes. Children also had free access to a clay table with all kinds of art materials on it. Teresa remembers going home every day and telling her mother she wanted to draw, paint, and play with crayons.

Teresa's kindergarten experience, unfortunately, was the high point of her artistic interest. The next year, she entered a traditional elementary school and things began to change. Instead of Teresa's having free access to art materials every day, art became just another subject, something she had for an hour and a half every Friday afternoon.

Week after week, all through elementary school, it was the same art class. According to Teresa, her elementary school art classes were very restricted and demoralizing. She recalls being given small reprints of painting masterpieces, a different one each week. For example, one week in the second grade, children were presented with Leonardo da Vinci's *Adoration of the Magi*. This was meant for art appreciation, but that's not how the teacher used it. Instead, the children were told to take out their art materials and try to copy the masterpiece. For Teresa, and the other children, this was an exercise in frustration. She says that young elementary school children do not have the skill development even to make all those horses and angels fit on the page, let alone make them look like the masterpiece. Teresa easily could tell that she was not doing well at what the teacher asked her to do.

The children were not given any help in developing their skills. Also, the teacher graded the children on the art they produced, adding evaluation pressure to the situation. Teresa was aware at that time that her motivation for doing artwork was being completely destroyed. She no longer wanted to go home and paint at the end of the day.

Teresa Amabile eventually obtained her Ph.D. in psychology and became one of the leading researchers on creativity. Her hope is that more elementary schools will not crush children's enthusiasm for creativity, the way hers did. So many young children, like Teresa, are excited about exploring and creating, but, by the time they reach the third or fourth grade, many don't like school, let alone have any sense of pleasure in their own creativity (Goleman, Kaufman, & Ray, 1993).

Parents and educators who clearly understand how young children develop can play an active role in creating programs that foster their natural interest in learning, rather than stifling it. We will explore different approaches to early childhood education in this chapter, following a discussion of the physical, cognitive, and language changes in young children.

1 PHYSICAL CHANGES

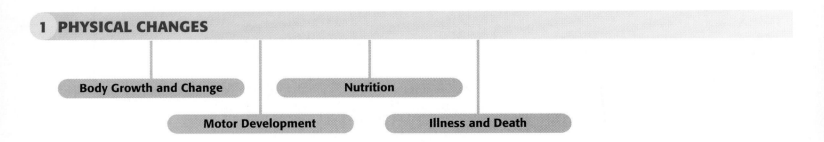

Remember from chapter 5 that an infant's growth in the first year is rapid and follows cephalocaudal and proximodistal patterns ◀▥ p. 149. Around their first birthday, most infants begin to walk. During an infant's second year, the growth rate begins to slow down, but both gross and fine motor skills progress rapidly. The infant develops a sense of mastery through increased proficiency in walking and running. Improvement in fine motor skills—such as being able to turn the pages of a book one at a time—also contributes to the infant's sense of mastery in the second year. The growth rate continues to slow down in early childhood. Otherwise, we would be a species of giants.

Body Growth and Change

Growth in height and weight is the obvious physical change that characterizes early childhood. Unseen changes in the brain and nervous system are no less significant in preparing children for advances in cognition and language.

Height and Weight   The average child grows 2½ inches in height and gains between 5 and 7 pounds a year during early childhood. As the preschool child grows older, the percentage of increase in height and weight decreases with each additional year. Girls are only slightly smaller and lighter than boys during these years, a difference that continues until puberty. During the preschool years, both boys and girls slim down as the trunks of their bodies lengthen. Although their heads are still somewhat large for their bodies, by the end of the preschool years most children have lost their top-heavy look. Body fat also shows a slow, steady decline during the preschool years. The chubby baby often looks much leaner by the end of early childhood. Girls have more fatty tissue than boys; boys have more muscle tissue.

**Preschool Growth
and Development
Development Milestones**

Growth patterns vary individually. Think back to your preschool years. This was probably the first time you noticed that some children were taller than you, some shorter; some were fatter, some thinner; some were stronger, some weaker. Much of the variation is due to heredity, but environmental experiences are involved to some extent. A review of the height and weight of children around the world concluded that the two most important contributors to height differences are ethnic origin and nutrition (Meredith, 1978). The urban, middle-socioeconomic-status, and firstborn children were taller than rural, lower-socioeconomic-status, and later-born children. Children whose mothers smoked during pregnancy were half an inch shorter than the children whose mothers did not smoke during pregnancy. In the United States, African American children are taller than White children.

Why are some children unusually short? The possible culprits are congenital factors (genetic or prenatal problems), physical problems that develop in childhood, or emotional difficulties. An example of a congenital factor is having a mother who smoked regularly during pregnancy. The physical problem of being chronically sick can make a child shorter than age-mates who are rarely sick. Emotional difficulties among children who have been physically abused or neglected might inhibit the secretion of adequate growth hormone, which can restrict physical growth. In many cases, children with growth problems can be treated with hormones. Usually this treatment is directed at the pituitary gland, located at the base of the brain, which secretes growth-related hormones.

The bodies of 5-year-olds and 2-year-olds are different. Notice that the 5-year-old not only is taller and weighs more, but also has a longer trunk and legs than the 2-year-old. *Can you think of some other physical differences between 2- and 5-year-olds?*

The Brain   One of the most important physical developments during early childhood is the continuing development of the brain and nervous system (Byrnes, 2001). The changes that occur during this period enable children to plan their actions, to attend to stimuli more effectively, and to make considerable strides in language development.

Brain Size and Growth   While the brain continues to grow in early childhood, it does not grow as rapidly as in infancy. The

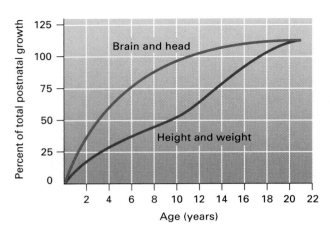

FIGURE 8.1 Growth Curves for the Head and Brain and for Height and Weight

The more rapid growth of the brain and head can easily be seen. Height and weight advance more gradually over the first two decades of life.

brain and the head grow more rapidly than any other part of the body. The top parts of the head, the eyes, and the brain grow faster than the lower portions, such as the jaw. Figure 8.1 reveals how the growth curve for the head and brain advances more rapidly than the growth curve for height and weight.

Changes in Neurons   Communication in the brain is characterized by the transmission of information between neurons, or nerve cells. Some of the brain's increase in size is due to the increase in the number and size of nerve endings within and between areas of the brain. These nerve endings continue to grow at least until adolescence.

Neurons communicate with each other through *neurotransmitters* (chemical substances) that carry information across *synapses* (gaps) between the neurons. The concentration of the neurotransmitter dopamine increases considerably from 3 to 6 years of age (Diamond, 2001). We will discuss the significance of this change shortly.

Some of the brain's increase in size also is due to an increase in **myelination,** the process by which nerve cells are covered and insulated with a layer of fat cells ◀▥ p. 150. This has the effect of increasing the speed of information traveling through the nervous system. Some developmentalists believe myelination is important in the maturation of a number of children's abilities. For example, myelination in the areas of the brain related to hand-eye coordination is not complete until about 4 years of age. Myelination in the areas of the brain related to focusing attention is not complete until the end of the middle or late childhood.

Changes in Brain Structures   Until recently, scientists have not had adequate technology to detect and map sensitive changes in the human brain as it develops. However, the creation of sophisticated brain-scanning techniques has allowed better detection of these changes (Blumenthal & others, 1999; Casey, 2002; Schalagar & others, 2002). Using these techniques, scientists recently have discovered that children's brains undergo dramatic anatomical changes between the ages of 3 and 15 (Thompson & others, 2000). By repeatedly obtaining brain scans of the same children for up to 4 years, they have found that children's brains experience rapid, distinct spurts of growth. The amount of brain material in some areas can nearly double in as little as a year, followed by a drastic loss of tissue as unneeded cells are purged and the brain continues to reorganize itself. The scientists found that the overall size of the brain did not increase dramatically from age 3 to 15. What did dramatically change were local patterns within the brain.

Researchers have found that from 3 to 6 years of age the most rapid growth takes place in the frontal lobe areas involved in planning and organizing new actions, and in maintaining attention to tasks. From age 6 through puberty, the most growth takes place in the temporal and parietal lobes, especially areas that play major roles in language and spatial relations.

The Brain and Cognitive Development   The increasing maturation of the brain, combined with opportunities to experience a widening world, contribute to children's emerging cognitive abilities. Consider a child who is learning to read aloud. Input from the child's eyes is transmitted to the child's brain, then passed through many brain systems, which translate (process) the patterns of black and white into codes for letters, words, and associations. The output occurs in the form of messages to the child's lips and tongue. The child's own gift of speech is possible because brain systems are organized in ways that permit language processing.

The brain is organized in many neural circuits, which consist of neurons with certain functions. One neural circuit has an important function in attention and working memory (a type of memory similar to short-term memory that is like a mental work-

myelination The process in which the nerve cells are covered and insulated with a layer of fat cells, which increases the speed at which information travels through the nervous system.

bench in performing many cognitive tasks) (Krimel & Goldman-Rakic, 2001). This neural circuit involves the *prefrontal cortex* and the neurotransmitter dopamine (Case, Durston, & Fossella, 2001; Diamond, 2001) (see figure 8.2).

In sum, scientists are beginning to chart connections between children's cognitive development (attention and memory, for example), brain structures (prefrontal cortex, for example), and the transmission of information at the level of the neuron (the neurotransmitter dopamine, for example). As advances in technology allow scientists to "look inside" the brain and observe its activity, we will likely understand more precisely how the brain functions in cognitive development.

Motor Development

Running as fast as you can, falling down, getting right back up and running just as fast as you can . . . building towers with blocks . . . scribbling, scribbling, and scribbling some more . . . cutting paper with scissors . . . During your preschool years, you probably developed the ability to perform all of these activities.

Gross Motor Skills   The preschool child no longer has to make an effort simply to stay upright and to move around. As children move their legs with more confidence and carry themselves more purposefully, moving around in the environment becomes more automatic.

At 3 years of age, children enjoy simple movements, such as hopping, jumping, and running back and forth, just for the sheer delight of performing these activities. They take considerable pride in showing how they can run across a room and jump all of 6 inches. The run-and-jump will win no Olympic gold medals, but for the 3-year-old the activity is a source of considerable pride and accomplishment.

At 4 years of age, children are still enjoying the same kind of activities, but they have become more adventurous. They scramble over low jungle gyms as they display their athletic prowess. Although they have been able to climb stairs with one foot on each step for some time, they are just beginning to be able to come down the same way.

At 5 years of age, children are even more adventuresome than when they were 4. It is not unusual for self-assured 5-year-olds to perform hair-raising stunts on practically any climbing object. Five-year-olds run hard and enjoy races with each other and their parents. A summary of development in gross motor skills during early childhood is shown in figure 8.3.

Fine Motor Skills   At 3 years of age, children are still emerging from the infant ability to place and handle things. Although they have had the ability to pick up the tiniest objects between their thumb and forefinger for some time, they are still somewhat

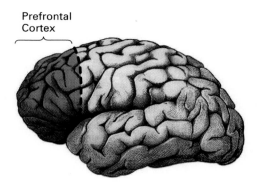

FIGURE 8.2 The Prefrontal Cortex

This evolutionarily advanced portion (shaded in purple) of the brain shows extensive development from 3 to 6 years of age and is believed to play important roles in attention and working memory.

37 to 48 Months	49 to 60 Months	61 to 72 Months
Throws ball underhanded (4 feet)	Bounces and catches ball	Throws ball (44 feet, boys; 25 feet, girls)
Pedals tricycle 10 feet	Runs 10 feet and stops	Carries a 16-pound object
Catches large ball	Pushes/pulls a wagon/doll buggy	Kicks rolling ball
Completes forward somersault (aided)	Kicks 10 inch´ ball toward target	Skips alternating feet
Jumps to floor from 12 inches	Carries 12-pound object	Roller skates
Hops three hops with both feet	Catches ball	Skips rope
Steps on footprint pattern	Bounces ball under control	Rolls ball to hit object
Catches bounced ball	Hops on one foot four hops	Rides bike with training wheels

FIGURE 8.3 The Development of Gross Motor Skills in Early Childhood

The skills are listed in the approximate order of difficulty within each age period.

37 to 48 Months	49 to 60 Months	61 to 72 Months
Approximates a circle in drawing	Strings and laces shoelace	Folds paper into halves and quarters
Cuts paper	Cuts following a line	Traces around hand
Pastes using pointer finger	Strings 10 beads	Draws rectangle, circle, square, and triangle
Builds three-block bridge	Copies figure X	
Builds eight-block tower	Opens and places clothespins (one-handed)	Cuts interior piece from paper
Draws 0 and +		Uses crayons appropriately
Dresses and undresses doll	Builds a five-block bridge	Makes clay object with two small parts
Pours from pitcher without spilling	Pours from various containers	Reproduces letters
	Prints first name	Copies two short words

Note: The skills are listed in the approximate order of difficulty within each age period.

FIGURE 8.4 The Development of Fine Motor Skills in Early Childhood

Handedness

Today, most teachers let children write with the hand they favor. *What are the main reasons children become left- or right-handed?*

clumsy at it. Three-year-olds can build surprisingly high block towers, each block placed with intense concentration but often not in a completely straight line. When 3-year-olds play with a simple jigsaw puzzle, they are rather rough in placing the pieces. Even when they recognize the hole a piece fits into, they are not very precise in positioning the piece. They often try to force the piece in the hole or pat it vigorously.

By 4 years of age, children's fine motor coordination has improved substantially and become much more precise. Sometimes 4-year-old children have trouble building high towers with blocks because, in their desire to place each of the blocks perfectly, they may upset those already stacked. By age 5, children's fine motor coordination has improved further. Hand, arm, and body all move together under better command of the eye. Mere towers no longer interest the 5-year-old, who now wants to build a house or a church, complete with steeple, though adults might still need to be told what each finished project is meant to be. A summary of the development of fine motor skills in early childhood is shown in figure 8.4.

Handedness   For centuries, left-handers have suffered unfair discrimination in a world designed for right-handers. For many years, teachers forced all children to write with their right hand, even if they had a left-hand tendency. Fortunately, today most teachers let children write with the hand they favor.

Origin and Development of Handedness   What is the origin of hand preference? Genetic inheritance seems to be a strong influence. In one study, the handedness of adopted children was not related to the handedness of their adopted parents, but it was related to the handedness of their biological parents (Carter-Saltzman, 1980).

Right-handedness is dominant in all cultures (it appears in a ratio of about 9 right-handers to 1 left-hander) and it appears before the impact of culture. For example, in one study, ultrasound observations of fetal thumb sucking showed that 9 of 10 fetuses were more likely to be sucking their right hand's thumb (Hepper, Shahidullah, & White, 1990). Newborns also show a preference for one side of their body over the other. In one study, 65 percent of the infants turned their head to the right when they were lying on their back in a crib (Michel, 1981). Fifteen percent preferred to face toward the left and the remaining 20 percent showed no preference. These preferences for the right or the left were linked with handedness later in development.

Handedness, the Brain, and Language   Approximately 95 percent of right-handed individuals primarily process speech in the brain's left hemisphere (Springer & Deutsch, 1985). However, left-handed individuals show more variation. More than one-half of left-handers process speech in their left hemisphere, just like right-handers. However, about one-fourth of left-handers process speech equally in both hemispheres (Knecht & others, 2000).

Are there differences in the language development of left- and right-handers? The most consistent finding is that left-handers are more likely to have reading problems (Geschwind & Behan, 1984; Natsopoulos & others, 1998).

Handedness and Other Abilities   Although there is a tendency for left-handers to have more reading problems than right-handers, left-handedness is more common among mathematicians, musicians, architects, and artists (Michelangelo, Leonardo da Vinci, and Picasso were all left-handed) (Schacter & Ransil, 1996). Architects and artists who are left-handed benefit from the tendency of left-handers to have unusually good visual-spatial skills and the ability to imagine spatial layouts (Holtzen, 2000). Also, in one study of more than 100,000 students taking the Scholastic Aptitude Test (SAT), 20 percent of the top-scoring group was left-handed, twice the rate of left-handedness found in the general population (10 percent) (Bower, 1985).

Nutrition

What are a preschool child's energy needs? What is a preschooler's eating behavior like?

Energy Needs   Feeding and eating habits are important aspects of development during early childhood. What children eat affects their skeletal growth, body shape, and susceptibility to disease. Recognizing that nutrition is important for the child's growth and development, the federal government provides money for school lunch programs.

Energy requirements for individual children are determined by the **basal metabolism rate (BMR),** which is the minimum amount of energy a person uses in a resting state. An average preschool child requires 1,700 calories per day, but energy needs of individual children of the same age, sex, and size vary. Although the reasons for these differences are not known, differences in physical activity, basal metabolism, and the efficiency with which children use energy are possible explanations.

Eating Behavior   Caregivers' special concerns involve the appropriate amount of fat in young children's diets (Troiano & Flegal, 1998). While some health-conscious parents may be providing too little fat in their infants' and children's diets, other parents are raising their children on diets in which the percentage of fat is far too high. Our changing lifestyles, in which we often eat on the run and pick up fast-food meals, contribute to the increased fat levels in children's diets. The American Heart Association recommends that the daily limit for calories from fat should be approximately 35 percent, and many fast-food meals have fat content that is too high for good health.

Might being overweight be associated with lower self-esteem, even in young children? In one recent study, the relation of weight status and self-esteem in 5-year-old girls was examined (Davison & Birth, 2001). The girls who were overweight had lower body self-esteem than those who were not overweight.

Being overweight can be a serious problem in early childhood (Behrman, Kliegman, & Jenson, 2000). Except for extreme cases of obesity, overweight preschool children are usually not encouraged to lose a great deal of weight but to slow their rate of weight gain so that they will grow into a more normal weight for their height by thinning out as they grow taller. Prevention of obesity in children includes helping children and parents see food as a way to satisfy hunger and nutritional needs, not as proof of love or as a reward for good behavior (Hill & Trowbridge, 1998). Routine physical activity should be a daily occurrence. The child's life should be centered on activity, not meals (Rothstein, 2001).

Illness and Death

What are the leading causes of death in young children in the United States? What are the greatest health risks for children today? How pervasive is death among young children around the world?

> *This would be a better world for children if parents had to eat the spinach.*
> —GROUCHO MARX
> *American Comedian, 20th Century*

basal metabolism rate (BMR) The minimum amount of energy a person uses in a resting state.

Exploring Childhood Obesity

Helping an Overweight Child

Preschoolers' Health

Harvard Center for Children's Health

Child Health Guide

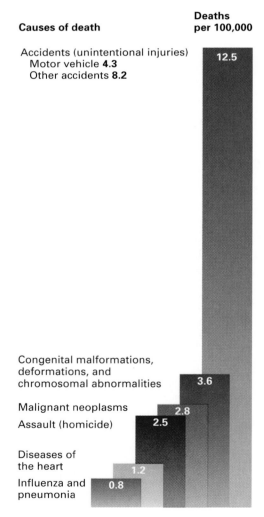

FIGURE 8.5 Main Causes of Death in Children 1 through 4 Years of Age

These figures are based on the number of deaths per 100,000 children 1 through 4 years of age in the United States in 1999 (National Vital Statistics Report, 2001).

The United States If a pediatrician who stopped practicing 50 years ago were to study the illness and health records of young children today, the conclusion might seem to be more like science fiction than medical fact (Elias, 1998). The story of children's health in the past 50 years is a shift toward prevention and out-patient care.

In recent decades, vaccines have nearly eradicated disabling bacterial meningitis and have become available to prevent measles, rubella, mumps, and chicken pox. From 1950 to the present, there has been a dramatic decline in deaths of children under the age of 5 from birth immaturity, birth defects, accidents, cancer, homicide, and heart disease. The disorders most likely to be fatal during early childhood today are birth defects, cancer, and heart disease. Although the dangers of many diseases for children have been greatly diminished, it still is important for parents to keep young children on an immunization schedule to prevent a resurgence of these contagious diseases.

In the United States, accidents are the leading cause of death in young children (National Vital Statistics Reports, 2001) (see figure 8.5). Motor vehicle accidents, drowning, falls, and poisoning are high on the list of causes of death in young children (Brenner & others, 2001).

Today, a special concern about children's illness and health is exposure to parental smoking. An estimated 22 percent of children and adolescents in the United States are exposed to tobacco smoke in the home. An increasing number of studies reach the conclusion that children are at risk for health problems if they live in homes in which a parent smokes (Ehrlich & others, 2001). In one study, if the mother smoked, her children were twice as likely to have respiratory problems as the children of non-smoking mothers (Etzel, 1988). Research studies have found that children exposed to tobacco smoke in the home are more likely to experience wheezing symptoms and asthma than children in nonsmoking homes (Jaakkola, Nafstad, & Magnus, 2001; Mannino & others, 2001). Environmental tobacco smoke also affects the amount of vitamin C, a key nutrient for the immune system, in children and adolescents. In a recent study, when parents smoked at home their 4- to 18-year-old children and adolescents had significantly lower levels of vitamin C in their blood than their counterparts in nonsmoking homes (Strauss, 2001). And the more parents smoked, the less vitamin C the children and adolescents had.

Another contemporary concern in the United States is the poor health status of many young children from low-income families (Karns, 2001). Approximately 11 million preschool children in the United States are malnourished and therefore at risk for health problems. Many have less resistance to diseases, including minor ones, such as colds, and major ones, such as influenza, than other children.

In addition, an estimated 3 million children under 6 years of age are thought to be at risk for lead poisoning (Chisolm, 2001; Geltman, Brown, & Cochran, 2001). Lead can get into children's bloodstreams through food or water that is contaminated by lead, from putting lead-contaminated fingers in their mouths, or from inhaling dust from lead-based paint. The negative effects of high lead levels in children's blood are lower intelligence and achievement, and attention deficit hyperactivity disorder (Soong & others, 1999). Children in poverty are at higher risk for lead poisoning than children living in higher-socioeconomic conditions.

Information about how to avoid environmental smoke, lead contamination, and other hazards to children's health is available from pediatricians and pediatric nurses. To read about the work of one pediatric nurse, Barbara Deloin, see the Careers in Life-Span Development insert.

The State of Illness and Health of the World's Children One of every three deaths in the world is that of a child under 5. Every week more than a quarter of a million children die in developing countries. The most devastating effects occur in countries where poverty rates are high. The poor are the majority in nearly one of every five nations in the world (UNICEF, 2002). They often experience lives of hunger,

Careers in Life-Span Development

Barbara Deloin, Pediatric Nurse

Barbara Deloin is a pediatric nurse in Denver, Colorado. She practices nursing in the Pediatric Oral Feeding Clinic and is involved in research as part of an irritable infant study for the Children's Hospital in Denver. She also is on the faculty of nursing at the Colorado Health Sciences Center. Deloin previously worked in San Diego where she was coordinator of the Child Health Program for the County of San Diego.

Her research interests focus on children with special health-care needs, especially high-risk infants and children and promoting positive parent-child experiences. Deloin was elected president of the National Association of Pediatric Nurse Associates and Practitioners for the 2000–2001 term ◀‖‖ p. 35.

Barbara Deloin, working with a child with special health-care needs.

malnutrition, illness, inadequate access to health care, unsafe water, and inadequate protection from harm.

A leading cause of child death in impoverished countries is diarrhea produced by dehydration. Giving the child a large volume of water and liquids usually prevents dehydration. Measles, tetanus, and whooping cough also still lead to the deaths of many children around the world, although increased immunization programs in the last several decades have led to a decrease in deaths due to these diseases (Foege, 2000).

In the last decade, there has been a dramatic increase in the number of young children who have died because of HIV/AIDS transmitted to them by their parents (UNICEF, 2002). The uneducated are four times more likely to believe there is no way to avoid AIDS and three times more likely to be unaware that the virus can be transmitted from mother to child (UNICEF, 2002).

Review and Reflect

1 Identify physical changes in early childhood

REVIEW

- What is the nature of body growth and change?
- What changes take place in motor development?
- What role does nutrition play in early childhood?
- What are some causes of illness and death among young children in the United States and around the world?

REFLECT

- What were your eating habits as a young child? In what ways are they similar or different to your current eating habits? Were your early eating habits a forerunner of whether or not you have weight problems today?

2 COGNITIVE CHANGES

| Piaget's Preoperational Stage | Vygotksy's Theory | Information Processing |

mhhe●com/
santrockld9

Symbolic Thinking

The cognitive world of the preschool child is creative, free, and fanciful. Preschool children's imaginations work overtime, and their mental grasp of the world improves. Our coverage of cognitive development in early childhood focuses on three theories: Piaget's, Vygotsky's, and information processing.

Piaget's Preoperational Stage

Remember from chapter 6 that, during Piaget's sensorimotor stage of development, the infant progresses in the ability to organize and coordinate sensations and perceptions with physical movements and actions ◀▥ p. 183. What kinds of changes take place in the preoperational stage?

The preoperational stage stretches from approximately 2 to 7 years of age. It is a time when stable concepts are formed, mental reasoning emerges, egocentrism begins strongly and then weakens, and magical beliefs are constructed. The label *preoperational* emphasizes that the child at this stage cannot yet think something through without acting it out.

What are operations? **Operations** are internalized sets of actions that allow children to do mentally what before they did physically. Mentally adding and subtracting numbers are examples of operations.

Thought in the preoperational stage is flawed and not well organized. Preoperational thought is the beginning of the ability to reconstruct at the level of thought what has been established in behavior. Preoperational thought also involves a transition from primitive to more sophisticated use of symbols. Preoperational thought can be divided into two substages: the symbolic function substage and the intuitive thought substage.

Symbolic Function Substage   The **symbolic function substage** is the first substage of preoperational thought, which occurs roughly between 2 and 4 years of age. In this substage, the young child gains the ability to mentally represent an object that is not present. The ability to engage in symbolic thought is called *symbolic function*, and it vastly expands the child's mental world. Young children use scribbled designs to represent people, houses, cars, clouds, and so on. Other examples of symbolism in early childhood are language and the prevalence of pretend play. In sum, the ability to think symbolically and to represent the world mentally predominates in this early substage of preoperational thought (DeLoache, 2001). However, although young children make distinct progress during this substage, their thought still has several important limitations, two of which are egocentrism and animism.

Egocentrism, the inability to distinguish between one's own perspective and someone else's, is an important feature of preoperational thought. This telephone conversation between 4-year-old Mary, who is at home, and her father, who is at work, typifies Mary's egocentric thought:

> **Father:** Mary, is Mommy there?
>
> **Mary:** (Silently nods)
>
> **Father:** Mary, may I speak to Mommy?
>
> **Mary:** (Nods again silently)

operations In Piaget's theory, internalized sets of actions that allow children to do mentally what they formerly did physically.

symbolic function substage Piaget's first substage of preoperational thought, in which the child gains the ability to mentally represent an object that is not present (between 2 and 4 years of age).

egocentrism The inability to distinguish between one's own perspective and someone else's (salient feature of the first substage of preoperational thought).

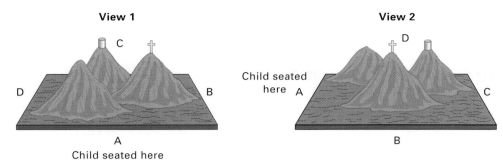

View 1   **View 2**

C   D

D   B   Child seated
here   A   C

A   B

Child seated here

FIGURE 8.6 The Three Mountains Task

View 1 shows the child's perspective from where he or she is sitting. View 2 is an example of the photograph the child would be shown, mixed in with others from different perspectives. To correctly identify this view, the child has to take the perspective of a person sitting at spot (*b*). Invariably, a preschool child who thinks in a preoperational way cannot perform this task. When asked what a view of the mountains looks like from position (*b*), the child selects a photograph taken from location (*a*), the child's view at the time.

Mary's response is egocentric in that she fails to consider her father's perspective before replying. A nonegocentric thinker would have responded verbally.

Piaget and Barbel Inhelder (1969) studied young children's egocentrism by devising the three mountains task (see figure 8.6). The child walks around the model of the mountains and becomes familiar with what the mountains look like from different perspectives. During this walking tour, the child can see that there are different objects on the mountains. The child is then seated on one side of the table on which the mountains are placed. The experimenter moves a doll to different locations around the table, at each location asking the child to select, from a series of photos, the one photo that most accurately reflects the view the doll is seeing. Children in the preoperational stage often pick the view from where they are sitting, rather than the doll's view. Perspective-taking does not develop uniformly in preschool children, who frequently show perspective skills on some tasks but not others.

Animism, another limitation of preoperational thought, is the belief that inanimate objects have "lifelike" qualities and are capable of action. A young child might show animism by saying, "That tree pushed the leaf off, and it fell down," or "The sidewalk made me mad; it made me fall down." A young child who uses animism fails to distinguish the appropriate occasions for using human and nonhuman perspectives (Gelman & Opfer, 2002).

Possibly because young children are not very concerned about reality, their drawings are fanciful and inventive. Suns are blue, skies are yellow, and cars float on clouds in their symbolic, imaginative world. One 3½-year-old looked at a scribble he had just drawn and described it as a pelican kissing a seal (see figure 8.7a). The symbolism is simple but strong, like abstractions found in some modern art. As the famous twentieth-century artist Pablo Picasso commented, "I used to draw like Raphael but it has taken me a lifetime to draw like young children." In the elementary school years, a child's drawings become more realistic, neat, and precise (see figure 8.7b). Suns are yellow, skies are blue, and cars travel on roads (Winner, 1986).

Intuitive Thought Substage   Tommy is 4 years old. Although he is starting to develop his own ideas about the world he lives in, his ideas are still simple, and he is not very good at thinking things out. He has difficulty understanding events he knows are taking place but which he cannot see. His fantasized thoughts bear little resemblance to reality. He cannot yet answer the question "What if . . . ?" in any reliable way. For example, he has only a vague idea of what would happen if a car were to hit him. He also has difficulty negotiating traffic because he cannot do the mental calculations necessary to estimate whether an approaching car will hit him when he crosses the road.

animism The belief that inanimate objects have "lifelike" qualities and are capable of action.

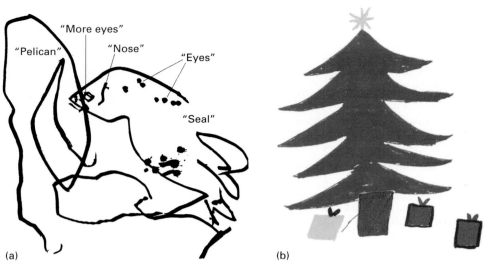

FIGURE 8.7 The Symbolic Drawings of Young Children

(*a*) A 3½-year-old's symbolic drawing. Halfway into this drawing, the 3½-year-old artist said it was "a pelican kissing a seal." (*b*) This 11-year-old's drawing is neater and more realistic but also less inventive.

The **intuitive thought substage** is the second substage of preoperational thought, which occurs between approximately 4 and 7 years of age. In this substage, children begin to use primitive reasoning and want to know the answers to all sorts of questions. Piaget called this time period *intuitive* because, on the one hand, young children seem so sure about their knowledge and understanding, yet they are so unaware of how they know what they know. That is, they say they know something but know it without the use of rational thinking.

An important characteristic of preoperational thought is **centration**—the focusing, or centering, of attention on one characteristic to the exclusion of all others. Centration is most clearly evidenced in young children's lack of **conservation**—awareness that altering an object's or a substance's appearance does not change its quantitative properties. To adults, it is obvious that a certain amount of liquid stays the same, regardless of a container's shape. But this is not at all obvious to young children. Instead, they are struck by the height of the liquid in the container. In the conservation task—Piaget's most famous test—a child is presented with two identical beakers, each filled to the same level with liquid (see figure 8.8). The child is asked if these beakers have the same amount of liquid, and she usually says yes. Then the liquid from one beaker is poured into a third beaker, which is taller and thinner than the first two. The child is then asked if the amount of liquid in the tall, thin beaker is equal to that which remains in one of the original beakers. Children who are less than 7 or 8 years old usually say no and justify their answers in terms of the differing height or width of the beakers. Older children usually answer yes and justify their answers appropriately ("If you poured the milk back, the amount would still be the same").

In Piaget's theory, failing the conservation of liquid task is a sign that children are at the preoperational stage of cognitive development. Passing this test is a sign that they are at the concrete operational stage. In Piaget's view, the preoperational child fails to show conservation not only of liquid but also of number, matter, length, volume, and area (figure 8.9 portrays several of these). Children often vary in their performance on different conservation tasks. Thus, a child might be able to conserve volume but not number.

The child's inability to mentally reverse actions is an important characteristic of preoperational thought. For example, in the conservation of matter shown in figure 8.9, preoperational children say that the longer shape has more clay because they

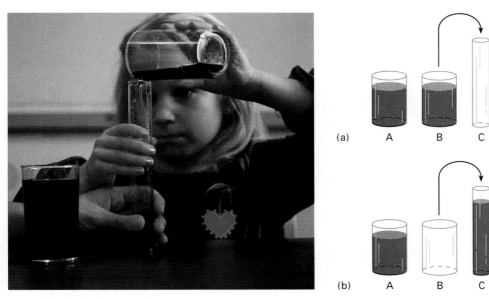

FIGURE 8.8 Piaget's Conservation Task

The beaker test is a well-known Piagetian test to determine whether a child can think operationally—that is, can mentally reverse actions and show conservation of the substance. (*a*) Two identical beakers are presented to the child. Then, the experimenter pours the liquid from B into C, which is taller and thinner than A or B. (*b*) The child is asked if these beakers (A and C) have the same amount of liquid. The preoperational child says "no". When asked to point to the beaker that has more liquid, the preoperational child points to the tall, thin beaker.

assume that "longer is more." Preoperational children cannot mentally reverse the clay-rolling process to see that the amount of clay is the same in both the shorter ball shape and the longer stick shape.

Some developmentalists do not believe Piaget was entirely correct in his estimate of when children's conservation skills emerge. For example, Rochel Gelman (1969) showed that, when the child's attention to relevant aspects of the conservation task is improved, the child is more likely to conserve. Gelman has also demonstrated that attentional training on one dimension, such as number, improves the preschool child's performance on another dimension, such as mass. Thus, Gelman believes that

Type of Conservation	Initial Presentation	Manipulation	Preoperational Child's Answer
Number	Two identical rows of objects are shown to the child, who agrees they have the same number.	One row is lengthened and the child is asked whether one row now has more objects.	Yes, the longer row.
Matter	Two identical balls of clay are shown to the child. The child agrees that they are equal.	The experimenter changes the shape of one of the balls and asks the child whether they still contain equal amounts of clay.	No, the longer one has more.
Length	Two sticks are aligned in front of the child. The child agrees that they are the same length.	The experimenter moves one stick to the right, then asks the child if they are equal in length.	No, the one on the top is longer.

FIGURE 8.9 Some Dimensions of Conservation: Number, Matter, and Length

"I still don't have all the answer, but I'm beginning to ask the right questions."

mhhe●com/ santrockld9

Vygotsky on Language and Thought

Vygotsky: Revolutionary Scientist

---

conservation appears earlier than Piaget thought and that attention is especially important in explaining conservation.

Yet another characteristic of preoperational children is that they ask a barrage of questions. Children's earliest questions appear around the age of 3, and by the age of 5 they have just about exhausted the adults around them with "why" questions. The child's questions yield clues about mental development and reflect intellectual curiosity. These questions signal the emergence of the child's interest in reasoning and figuring out why things are the way they are. Here are some samples of the questions children ask during the questioning period of 4 to 6 years of age (Elkind, 1976):

- "What makes you grow up?"
- "Why does a lady have to be married to have a baby?"
- "Who was the mother when everybody was a baby?"

Vygotsky's Theory

In chapter 2, we described some basic ideas about Vygotsky's theory. Here we expand on Vygotsky's theory of development, beginning with his unique ideas about the zone of proximal development p. 50.

The Zone of Proximal Development   The **zone of proximal development (ZPD)** is Vygotsky's term for the range of tasks that are too difficult for a child to master alone but that can be learned with the guidance and assistance of adults or more-skilled children. Thus, the lower limit of the ZPD is the level of problem solving reached by the child working independently. The upper limit is the level of additional responsibility the child can accept with the assistance of an able instructor (see figure 8.10). Vygotsky's emphasis on the ZPD underscores his belief in the importance of social influences, especially instruction, on children's cognitive development. An example of the ZPD is an adult helping a child put together a jigsaw puzzle.

The ZPD captures the child's cognitive skills that are in the process of maturing and can be mastered only with the assistance of a more-skilled person (Rowe & Wertsch, 2002). Vygotsky (1962) called these the "buds" or "flowers" of development, to distinguish them from the "fruits" of development, tasks that the child already can accomplish independently.

Scaffolding   In chapter 7, we discussed the concept of scaffolding in socioemotional development p. 221. Here we describe its role in cognitive development. Closely linked to the idea of zone of proximal development, **scaffolding** involves changing the level of support. Over the course of a teaching session, a more-skilled person adjusts the amount of guidance to fit the child's current performance level. When the task the student is learning is new, the more-skilled person may use direct instruction. As the student's competence increases, less guidance is given.

Language and Thought   Vygotsky (1962) believed that young children use language not only for social communication but also to plan, guide, and monitor their behavior in a self-regulatory fashion. The use of language for self-regulation is called *inner speech* or *private speech*. For Piaget, private speech is egocentric and immature, but for Vygotsky it is an important tool of thought during the early childhood years.

Vygotsky believed that language and thought initially develop independently of each other and then merge. He said that all mental functions have external, or social, origins. Children must use language to communicate with others before they can focus inward on their own thoughts. Children also must communicate externally and use language for a long period of time before the transition from external to internal speech takes place. This transition period occurs between the ages of 3 and 7 years of age and involves talking to oneself. After a while, the self-talk becomes second nature

---

zone of proximal development (ZPD) Vygotsky's term for tasks too difficult for children to master alone but that can be mastered with assistance.

scaffolding In cognitive development, Vygotsky used this term to describe the changing support over the course of a teaching session, with the more-skilled person adjusting guidance to fit the child's current performance level.

Lee Vygotsky (1896–1934), shown here with his daughter, believed that children's cognitive development is advanced through social interaction with skilled individuals embedded in a sociocultural backdrop. *How is Vygotsky's theory different from Piaget's?*

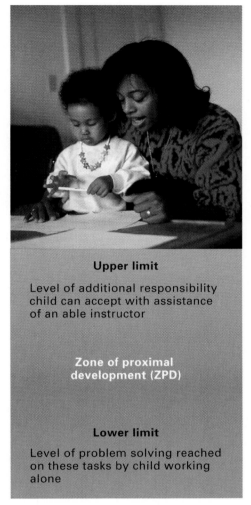

Upper limit

Level of additional responsibility child can accept with assistance of an able instructor

Zone of proximal development (ZPD)

Lower limit

Level of problem solving reached on these tasks by child working alone

FIGURE 8.10 Vygotsky's Zone of Proximal Development

Vygotsky's zone of proximal development has a lower limit and an upper limit. Tasks in the ZPD are too difficult for the child to perform alone. They require assistance from an adult or a skilled child. As children experience the verbal instruction or demonstration, they organize the information in their existing mental structures, so they can eventually perform the skill or task alone.

to children, and they can act without verbalizing. When this occurs, children have internalized their egocentric speech in the form of inner speech, which becomes their thoughts. Vygotsky believed that children who use a lot of private speech are more socially competent than those who don't. He argued that private speech represents an early transition in becoming more socially communicative.

Vygotsky's view challenged Piaget's ideas on language and thought. Vygotsky said that language, even in its earliest forms, is socially based. By contrast, Piaget emphasized young children's egocentric and nonsocial speech. For Vygotsky, when young children talk to themselves, they are using language to govern their behavior and guide themselves. Piaget believed that such self-talk reflects immaturity. However, researchers have found support for Vygotsky's view of the positive role of private speech in children's development (Winsler, Diaz, & Montero, 1997).

Evaluating and Comparing Vygotsky's and Piaget's Theories Although Vygotsky and Piaget were contemporaries, Vygotsky's work was not translated until 1962, long after his death, so it has not yet been evaluated as thoroughly. Vygotsky's theory has been embraced by many teachers and has been successfully applied to education. His view of the importance of sociocultural influences on children's development fits with the current belief that it is important to evaluate the contextual factors in learning (Gojdamaschko, 1999). However, some critics say he overemphasizes the role of language in thinking.

We already have mentioned several comparisons of Vygotsky's and Piaget's theories, such as Vygotsky's emphasis on the role of inner speech in development and Piaget's view that such speech is immature. We also said earlier that both Vygotsky's and Piaget's theories are constructivist, emphasizing that children actively construct knowledge and understanding, rather than being passive receptacles.

Although both theories are constructivist, Vygotsky's is a **social constructivist approach,** which emphasizes the social contexts of learning and the mutual construction of knowledge. Piaget's theory does not have this social emphasis. These analogies reflect the differing degree of social emphasis in the theories. Moving from

social constructivist approach An approach that emphasizes the social contexts of learning and that knowledge is mutually built and constructed. Vygotsky's theory reflects this approach.

Piaget to Vygotsky, the conceptual shift is from the individual to collaboration, social interaction, and sociocultural activity (John-Steiner & Mahn, 2003: Rogoff, 1998). For Piaget, children construct knowledge by transforming, organizing, and reorganizing previous knowledge. For Vygotsky, children construct knowledge through social interaction with others (Hogan & Tudge, 1999). The implication of Piaget's theory for teaching is that children need support to explore their world and discover knowledge. The main implication of Vygotsky's theory for teaching is that students need many opportunities to learn with the teacher and more-skilled peers. In both Piaget's and Vygotsky's theories, teachers serve as facilitators and guides, rather than as directors and molders of learning. Figure 8.11 compares Vygotsky's and Piaget's theories.

Teaching Strategies Based on Vygotsky's Theory Here are some ways that Vygotsky's theory can be incorporated in the classroom:

- *Use the child's zone of proximal development in teaching.* Teaching should begin toward the zone's upper limit, where the child is able to reach the goal only through close collaboration with the instructor. With adequate continuing instruction and practice, the child organizes and masters the behavioral sequences required to perform the target skill. As the instruction continues, the performance transfers from the teacher to the child. The teacher gradually reduces the explanations, hints, and demonstrations until the student is able to perform the skill alone. Once the goal is achieved, it may become the foundation for the development of a new ZPD.
- *Use scaffolding.* Look for opportunities to use scaffolding when children need help with self-initiated learning activities (Elicker, 1996). Also use scaffolding to help children move to a higher level of skill and knowledge. Offer just enough assistance.

	Vygotsky	Piaget
Sociocultural Context	Strong Emphasis	Little Emphasis
Constructivism	Social constructivist	Cognitive constructivist
Stages	No general stages of development proposed	Strong emphasis on stages (sensorimotor, preoperational, concrete operational, and formal operational)
Key Processes	Zone of proximal development, language, dialogue, tools of the culture	Schema, assimilation, accommodation, operations, conservation, classification, hypothetical-deductive reasoning
Role of Language	A major role; language plays a powerful role in shaping thought	Language has a minimal role; cognition primarily directs language
View on Education	Education plays a central role, helping children learn the tools of the culture.	Education merely refines the child's cognitive skills that have already emerged.
Teaching Implications	Teacher is a facilitator and guide, not a director; establish many opportunities for children to learn with the teacher and more skilled peers	Also views teacher as a facilitator and guide, not a director; provide support for children to explore their world and discover knowledge

FIGURE 8.11 Comparison of Vygotsky's and Piaget's Theories

- *Use more-skilled peers as teachers.* Children can benefit from the support and guidance of more-skilled children, as well as from adults.

- *Monitor and encourage children's use of private speech.* Be aware of the developmental change from externally talking to oneself when solving a problem during the preschool years to privately talking to oneself in the early elementary school years. In the elementary school years, encourage children to internalize and self-regulate their talk to themselves.

- *Assess the child's ZPD, not IQ.* Like Piaget, Vygotsky did not believe that formal, standardized tests are the best way to assess children's learning. Rather, Vygotsky argued that assessment should focus on determining the child's zone of proximal development. The skilled helper presents the child with tasks of varying difficulty to determine the best level at which to begin instruction. The ZPD is a measure of learning potential.

- *Transform the classroom with Vygotskian ideas.* What does a Vygotskian classroom look like? In the Kamehameha Elementary Education Program (KEEP), which is based on Vygotsky's theory (Tharp, 1994), the zone of proximal development is the key element of instruction. Children might read a story and then interpret its meaning. Many of the learning activities take place in small groups. All children spend at least 20 minutes each morning in an activity setting called "Center One." In this context, scaffolding is used to improve children's literary skills. The instructor asks questions, responds to students' queries, and builds on the ideas that students generate. Thousands of low-income children have attended KEEP public schools in Hawaii, on an Arizona Navajo Indian reservation, and in Los Angeles. Compared with a control group of non-KEEP children, the KEEP children participate more actively in classroom discussion, are more attentive in class, and have higher reading achievement (Tharp & Gallimore, 1988).

In Vygotsky's theory, an important point is that children need to learn the skills that will help them do well in their culture. Vygotsky believed that this should be accomplished through interaction with more-skilled members of the culture, such as this Mexican-American girl learning to read with the guidance of her mother. *What are some other ways that skilled members of a society can interact with young children?*

In one recent study with a foundation in Vygotsky's theory, pairs of children from two U.S. public schools worked together (Matusov, Bell, & Rogoff, 2001). One member of the pair was always from a school with a traditional format involving only occasional opportunities for children to cooperate in their schoolwork. The other member of the pair was always from a school that emphasizes collaboration throughout the school day. The children with the collaborative school background more often built on each other's ideas in a collaborative way than did the children with the traditional school background. The traditional school children primarily used a "quizzing" form of guidance based on asking known-answer questions and withholding information to test learner's understanding.

Piaget's cognitive development theory and Vygotsky's sociocultural cognitive theory have provided important insights about the way young children think and how this thinking changes developmentally. Next, we will explore a third major view on children's thinking—information processing.

Information Processing

Not only can we study stages of cognitive development, as Piaget did, but we can also study young children's cognitive processes. Two important aspects of preschool children's thinking are attention and memory. What are the limitations and advances in attention and memory during the preschool years?

Attention   In chapter 6, we discussed attention in the context of habituation, which is something like being bored ◀|||| p. 189. In habituation, the infant loses interest in a stimulus and no longer attends to it. Habituation involves a decrement in attention. Dishabituation is the recovery of attention. The importance of these aspects of attention in infancy for the preschool years was underscored by research showing that both decrement and recovery of attention, when measured in the first six months of infancy, were associated with higher intelligence in the preschool years (Bornstein & Sigman, 1986).

The child's ability to pay attention changes significantly during the preschool years in three ways:

- *Control of attention.* Toddlers wander around, shift attention from one activity to another, and seem to spend little time focused on any one object or event. By comparison, the preschool child might be observed watching television for a half hour. In one study, young children's attention to television in the natural setting of the home was videotaped (Anderson & others, 1985). In 99 families comprising 460 individuals who were observed for 4,672 hours, visual attention to television dramatically increased during the preschool years.
- *Salient versus relevant dimensions.* One deficit in attention during the preschool years concerns those dimensions that stand out, or are *salient*, compared with those that are relevant to solving a problem or performing well on a task. For example, a problem might have a flashy, attractive clown that presents the directions for solving a problem. Preschool children are influenced strongly by the features of the task that stand out, such as the flashy, attractive clown. After the age of 6 or 7, children attend more efficiently to the dimensions of the task that are relevant, such as the directions for solving a problem. Developmentalists believe this change reflects a shift to cognitive control of attention, so that children act less impulsively and reflect more.
- *Planfulness.* When experimenters ask children to judge whether two complex pictures are the same, preschool children tend to use a haphazard comparison strategy, not examining all of the details before making a judgment. By comparison, elementary school age children are more likely to systematically compare the details across the pictures, one detail at a time (Vurpillot, 1968) (see figure 8.12).

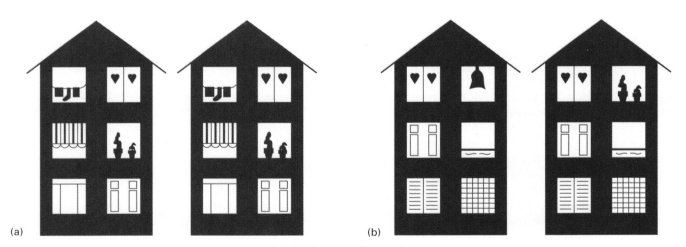

(a)   (b)

FIGURE 8.12 The Planfulness of Attention

In one study, children were given pairs of houses to examine, like the ones shown here (Vurpillot, 1968). For three pairs of houses, what was in the windows was identical (*a*). For the other three pairs, the windows had different items in them (*b*). By filming the reflection in the children's eyes, it could be determined what they were looking at, how long they looked, and the sequence of their eye movements. Children under 6 examined only a fragmentary portion of each display and made their judgments on the basis of insufficient information. By contrast, older children scanned the windows in more detailed ways and were more accurate in their judgments of which windows were identical.

Memory   Memory is a central process in children's cognitive development; it involves the retention of information over time. Conscious memory comes into play as early as 7 months of age, although children and adults have little or no memory of events experienced before the age of 3 ◀||| p. 191. Among the interesting questions about memory in the preschool years are those involving short-term memory.

Short-Term Memory   In **short-term memory,** individuals retain information for up to 30 seconds, assuming there is no rehearsal of the information. Using rehearsal (repeating information after it has been presented), we can keep information in short-term memory for a much longer period. One method of assessing short-term memory is the memory-span task. If you have taken an IQ test, you were probably exposed to one of these tasks. You simply hear a short list of stimuli—usually digits—presented at a rapid pace (one per second, for example). Then you are asked to repeat the digits. Research with the memory-span task suggests that short-term memory increases during early childhood. For example, in one investigation, memory span increased from about 2 digits in 2- to 3-year-old children to about 5 digits in 7-year-old children, yet, between 7 and 13 years of age, memory span increased only by 1½ digits (Dempster, 1981) (see figure 8.13). Keep in mind, though, that memory span varies from one individual to another; it is for this reason that IQ and various aptitude tests were developed.

Why are there differences in memory span because of age? Rehearsal of information is important; older children rehearse the digits more than younger children. Speed and efficiency of processing information are important, too, especially the speed with which memory items can be identified. For example, in one study, children were tested on their speed at repeating words presented orally (Case, Kurland, & Goldberg, 1982). Speed of repetition was a powerful predictor of memory span. Indeed, when the speed of repetition was controlled, the 6-year-olds' memory spans were equal to those of young adults.

The speed-of-processing explanation highlights a key point in the information-processing perspective: The speed with which a child processes information is an important aspect of the child's cognitive abilities (Schneider, 2002). In one recent study, faster processing speed on a memory-span task was linked with higher reading and mathematics achievement (Hitch, Towse, & Hutton, 2001).

How Accurate Are Young Children's Long-Term Memories?   In chapter 6, we saw that most of an infant's memories are fragile and, for the most part, short-lived—except for the memory of perceptual-motor actions, which can be substantial (Mandler, 2000). Does their memory become more accurate when they grow into the early childhood years? Yes, it does. Young children can remember a great deal of information if they are given appropriate cues and prompts.

A current controversy focuses on whether young children should be allowed to testify in court. Increasingly, young children are being allowed to testify, especially if they are the only witnesses to abuse, a crime, and so forth. These conclusions have been reached about children as eyewitnesses (Bruck & Ceci, 1999):

- *Age differences in children's susceptibility to suggestion.* Preschoolers are more suggestible than older children and adults (Koriat, Goldsmith, & Pansky, 2000). Young children can be led, under certain circumstances, to incorporate false suggestions into their accounts of even intimate body touching by adults (Hyman & Loftus, 2001). Despite their greater resistance to suggestibility, there is concern, too, about the effects of suggestive interviews on older children.
- *Individual differences in susceptibility.* Some preschoolers are highly resistant to interviewers' suggestions, while others succumb immediately to the slightest suggestion.

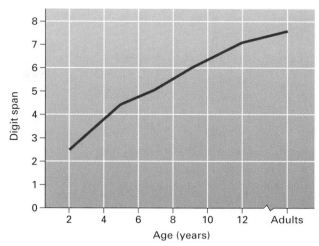

FIGURE 8.13 Developmental Changes in Memory Span

In one study, memory span increased about 3 digits from 2 years of age to 5 digits at 7 years of age (Dempster, 1981). By 12 years of age, memory span had increased on average another 1½ digits to 7 digits.

mhhe.com/santrockld9

Children's Eyewitness Testimony

short-term memory The memory component in which individuals retain information for up to 30 seconds, assuming there is no rehearsal.

Four-year-old Jennifer Royal was the only eyewitness to one of her play-mate's being shot to death. She was allowed to testify in open court and the clarity of her statements helped to convict the gunman. *What are some issues involved in whether young children should be allowed to testify in court?*

- *Young children's accuracy as eyewitnesses.* Despite the evidence that many young children's responses can be influenced by suggestive interviews, they are capable of recalling much that is relevant about an event (Howe, 1997). Children are more likely to accurately recall an event when the interviewer has a neutral tone, does not use misleading questions, and they are not motivated to make a false report (Bruck & Ceci, 1999).

In sum, whether a young child's eyewitness testimony is accurate or not may depend on a number of factors such as the type, number, and intensity of the suggestive techniques the child has experienced. It appears that the reliability of young children's reports have as much to do with the skills and motivation of the interiewer as with any natural limitations on young children's memory.

Strategies   In chapter 2, we mentioned that an especially important aspect of information-processing theory is the use of good strategies ◀▥ p. 50. Strategies consist of deliberate mental activities to improve the processing of information. For example, rehearsing information and organizing it are two typical strategies that older children and adults use to remember more effectively. For the most part, young children do not use rehearsal and organization to remember (Miller & Seier, 1994).

Do young children use any strategies at all? Problem-solving strategies in young children were the focus of research by Zhe Chen and Robert Siegler (2000). They placed young children at a table where an attractive toy was placed too far away for the child to reach it (they were not allowed to crawl on the table). On the table, between the child and the toy, were six potential tools (see figure 8.14). Only one of them was likely to be useful in obtaining the toy. After initially assessing the young children's attempts to obtain the toy on their own, the experimenters either modeled how to obtain the toy (using the appropriate tool) or gave the child a hint (telling the child to use the particular tool). These 2-year-olds learned the strategy and subsequently mapped the strategy onto new problems. Admittedly, this is a rather simple problem-solving strategy—selecting the best tool to use to obtain a desired toy—but it does document that children as young as 2 years of age can learn a strategy.

FIGURE 8.14 The Toy-Retrieval Task in the Study of Young Children's Problem-Solving Strategies

The child needed to choose the target tool (in this illustration, the toy rake) to pull in the toy (in this case, the turtle).

The Young Child's Theory of Mind   **Theory of mind** refers to awareness of one's own mental processes and the mental processes of others. Even young children are curious about the nature of the human mind, and developmentalists have shown a flurry of interest in children's thoughts about what the human mind is like (Flavell, 1999; McCormick, 2003; Wellman, 1997, 2000, 2002).

Children's theory of mind changes as they go through the early childhood years (Flavell, Miller, & Miller, 2002):

theory of mind Refers to the awareness of one's own mental processes and the mental processes of others.

- *2 to 3 years of age.* Children begin to understand three mental states:
  Perceptions. The child realizes that another person sees what is in front of his or her eyes and not necessarily what is in front of the child's eyes.
  Desires. The child understands that if someone wants something, he or she will try to get it. A child might say, "I want my mommy."
  Emotions. The child can distinguish between positive (for example, happy) and negative (sad, for example) emotions. A child might say, "Tommy feels bad."

Careers in Life-Span Development

Helen Schwe, Developmental Psychologist and Toy Designer

Helen Schwe obtained a Ph.D. from Stanford University in developmental psychology. She now spends her days talking with computer engineers and designing "smart" toys for children ◀▐▐▐ p. 30. Smart toys are designed to improve children's problem-solving and symbolic thinking skills.

During graduate school Dr. Schwe worked part-time for Hasbro Toys, testing its children's software on preschoolers. Her first job after graduate school was with Zowie Entertainment, which recently was purchased by LEGO.

While with Zowie and now LEGO, Dr. Schwe helped to design the pirate game called "Redbeard's Pirate Quest" and many other toys for children. She says that even in a toy's most primitive stage of development, you see children creatively responding to challenges and displaying their joy when they solve a problem. Along with conducting experiments and focus groups at different stages of a toy's development, She also helps assess the age-appropriateness of a toy. Most of her current work focuses on 3- to 5-year-old children. (Schlegel, 2000).

Helen Schwe, a developmental psychologist, with some of the toys she designed.

Despite these advances, at 2 to 3 years of age, children have only a minimal understanding of how mental life can be linked to behavior. They think that people are at the mercy of their desires and don't understand how beliefs influence behavior.

- *4 to 5 years of age.* Children come to understand that the mind can represent objects and events accurately or inaccurately. The realization that people can have *false beliefs*—beliefs that are not true—develops in a majority of children by the time they are 5 years old (Wellman, Cross, & Watson, 2001) (see figure 8.15). One study of false beliefs involved showing young children a Band-Aids box and asking them what was inside (Jenkins & Astington, 1996). To the children's surprise, the box actually contained pencils. When asked what a child who had never seen the box would think was inside, 3-year-olds typically responded "pencils." However, the 4- and 5-year-olds, grinning at the anticipation of other children's false beliefs who had not seen what was inside the box, were more likely to say "Band-Aids."

Some developmental psychologists use their training in areas such as cognitive development to pursue careers in applied areas. To read about the work of one individual who followed this path, see the Careers in Life-Span Development insert.

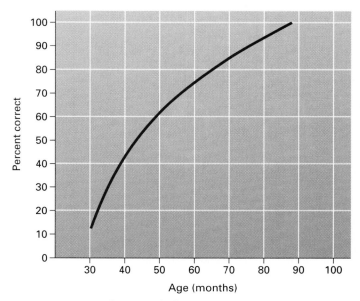

FIGURE 8.15 Developmental Changes in False-Belief Performance

False-belief performance dramatically increases from 2½ years of age through the middle of the elementary school years. In a summary of the results of many studies, 2½-year-olds gave incorrect responses about 80 percent of the time (Wellman, Cross, & Watson, 2001). At 3 years, 8 months, they were correct about 50 percent of the time, and after that, gave increasingly correct responses.

Review and Reflect

2 **Describe three views of the cognitive changes that occur in early childhood**

REVIEW

- What characterizes Piaget's stage of preoperational thought?
- What is Vygotsky's theory of children's cognitive development?
- What are some important ways that young children process information?

REFLECT

- Should children be allowed to develop such concepts as conservation naturally or should the concepts be taught to them? Explain.

3 LANGUAGE DEVELOPMENT

This is a wug.

Now there is another one.
There are two of them.
There are two _____.

FIGURE 8.16 Stimuli in Berko's Study of Young Children's Understanding of Morphological Rules

In Jean Berko's (1958) study, young children were presented cards, such as this one with a "wug" on it. Then the children were asked to supply the missing word; in supplying the missing word, they had to say it correctly too. "Wugs" is the correct response here.

Young children's understanding sometimes gets way ahead of their speech. One 3-year-old, laughing with delight as an abrupt summer breeze stirred his hair and tickled his skin, commented, "I got breezed!" Many of the oddities of young children's language sound like mistakes to adult listeners. However, from the children's point of view, they are not mistakes. They represent the way young children perceive and understand their world at that point in their development.

As children go through the early childhood years, their grasp of the rule systems that govern language increase (Hoff, 2003). These rule systems include phonology (the sound system) morphology (the rules for combining minimal units of meaning), syntax (rules for making sentences), semantics (the meaning system), and pragmatics (the rules for use in social settings).

Children become increasingly capable of producing all the sounds of their language. They can even produce complex consonant clusters.

By the time children move beyond two-word utterances, they demonstrate a knowledge of morphology rules. Children begin using the plural and possessive forms of nouns (such as *dogs* and *dog's*). They put appropriate endings on verbs (such as *-s* when the subject is third-person singular and *-ed* for the past tense. They use prepositions (such as *in* and *on*), articles (such as *a* and *the*), and various forms of the verb *to be* (such as "I *was* going to the store"). Some of the best evidence for changes in children's use of morphological rules occurs in their overgeneralization of the rules. Have you ever heard a preschool child say "foots" instead of "feet," or "goed" instead of "went"? If you do not remember hearing such usage, talk to parents who have young children or to the young children themselves. You will hear some interesting morphological errors.

In a classic experiment that was designed to study children's understanding of morphological rules, Jean Berko (1958) presented preschool children and first-grade children with cards such as the one shown in figure 8.16. Children were asked to look at the card while the experimenter read aloud the words on the card. Then the children were asked to supply the missing word. This might sound easy, but Berko was interested not just in the children's ability to recall the right word but also in their ability to say it "correctly" (with the ending that was dictated by morphological rules). "Wugs" would be the correct response for the card in figure 8.16.

Although the children's answers were not perfect, they were much better than chance. Moreover, the children demonstrated their knowledge of morphological rules,

How do children's language abilities develop during early childhood?

not only with the plural forms of nouns ("There are two wugs") but with possessive forms of nouns and the third-person singular and past-tense forms of verbs. What makes Berko's study impressive is that most of the words were made up for the experiment. Thus, the children could not base their responses on remembering past instances of hearing the words. Instead, they were forced to rely on *rules.*

Young children also learn to manipulate syntax. They can generate questions, passives, clauses, and all the major syntactical structures of their language.

As children move beyond the two-word stage, their knowledge of semantics or meanings also rapidly advances. The speaking vocabulary of a 6-year-old child ranges from 8,000 to 14,000 words. Assuming that word learning began when the child was 12 months old, this translates into a rate of 5 to 8 new word meanings a day between the ages of 1 and 6. After five years of word learning, the 6-year-old child does not slow down. According to some estimates, the average child of this age is moving along at the awe-inspiring rate of 22 words a day! How would you fare if you were given the task of learning 22 new words every day? It is truly miraculous how quickly children learn language.

Although there are many differences between a 2-year-old's language and a 6-year-old's language, the most dramatic differences pertain to pragmatics. A 6-year-old is simply a much better conversationalist than a 2-year-old. What are some of the changes in pragmatics that are made in the preschool years? At about 3 years of age, children improve in their ability to talk about things that are not physically present. That is, they improve their command of the characteristic of language known as "displacement." Children become increasingly removed from the "here and now" and are able to talk about things that are not physically present, as well as things that happened in the past, or may happen in the future. Preschoolers can tell you what they want for lunch tomorrow, something that would not have been possible at the two-word stage in infancy. Preschool children also become increasingly able to talk in different ways to different people.

The advances in language that take place in early childhood lay the foundation for later development in the elementary school years, which we will discuss in chapter 10.

Language Development
Language Growth
Pragmatic Language

4 EARLY CHILDHOOD EDUCATION

- The Child-Centered Kindergarten
- Developmentally Appropriate and Inappropriate Practice in Education
- Education for Children Who Are Disadvantaged
- The Montessori Approach
- Does Preschool Matter?

mhhe●com/
santrockld9

Early Childhood Education
Reggio Emilia
NAEYC
High/Scope: Active Learning

There are many variations in the ways young children are educated. First we will explore the child-centered kindergarten and the Montessori approach, then we will turn our attention to developmentally appropriate and inappropriate practice in education, whether preschool is necessary, and education for children who are disadvantaged.

The Child-Centered Kindergarten

Kindergarten programs vary a great deal (Roopnarine & Johnson, 2000). Some approaches place more emphasis on young children's social development, others on their cognitive development.

In the **child-centered kindergarten,** education involves the whole child and includes concern for the child's physical, cognitive, and socioemotional development. Instruction is organized around the child's needs, interests, and learning styles. The process of learning, rather than what is learned, is emphasized (White & Coleman, 2000). Each child follows a unique developmental pattern, and young children learn best through firsthand experiences with people and materials. Play is extremely important in the child's total development. *Experimenting, exploring, discovering,* and *trying out* are all words that describe excellent kindergarten programs.

The Montessori Approach

Montessori schools are patterned after the educational philosophy of Maria Montessori, an Italian physician-turned-educator, who crafted a revolutionary approach to young children's education at the beginning of the twentieth century (Wentworth, 1999). Although some Montessori schools provide programs for school-age children, most specialize in early childhood education.

In the **Montessori approach,** children are given considerable freedom and spontaneity in choosing activities. They are allowed to move from one activity to another as they desire. The teacher acts as a facilitator rather than a director of learning. The teacher shows the child how to perform intellectual activities, demonstrates interesting ways to explore curriculum materials, and offers help when the child requests it.

child-centered kindergarten Education that involves the whole child by considering both the child's physical, cognitive, and social development and the child's needs, interests, and learning styles.

Montessori approach An educational philosophy in which children are given considerable freedom and spontaneity in choosing activities and are allowed to move from one activity to another as they desire.

Some developmentalists favor the Montessori approach, but others believe that it neglects children's social development. For example, while Montessori fosters independence and the development of cognitive skills, it deemphasizes verbal interaction between the teacher and child and peer interaction. Montessori's critics also argue that it restricts imaginative play.

Developmentally Appropriate and Inappropriate Practice in Education

Developmentally appropriate practice is based on knowledge of the typical development of children within an age span (age-appropriateness) and the uniqueness of the child (individual-appropriateness). Developmentally appropriate practice contrasts with developmentally inappropriate practice, which ignores the concrete, hands-on approach to learning. Direct teaching largely through abstract paper-and-pencil activities presented to large groups of young children is believed to be developmentally inappropriate.

One of the most comprehensive documents addressing the issue of developmentally appropriate practice in early childhood programs is the position statement by the National Association for the Education of Young Children (NAEYC) (Bredekamp, 1987, 1997; National Association for the Education of Young Children, 1986). This document reflects the expertise of many of the foremost experts in the field of early childhood education. In figure 8.17 you can examine some of the NAEYC recommendations for developmentally appropriate practice. In one study, the children who attended developmentally appropriate kindergartens displayed more appropriate classroom behavior and had better conduct records and better work and study habits in the first grade than did the children who attended developmentally inappropriate kindergartens (Hart & others, 1993, 1998).

Does Preschool Matter?

Preschool is rapidly becoming a norm in early childhood education. Twenty-three states already have legislation pending to provide schooling for 4-year-old children, and there are many private preschool programs. The growth in preschool education may benefit many children, but is preschool really a good thing for all children?

According to developmental psychologist David Elkind (1988), parents who are exceptionally competent and dedicated and who have both the time and the energy can provide the basic ingredients of early childhood education in their home. If parents have the competence and resources to provide young children with a variety of learning experiences and exposure to other children and adults (possibly through neighborhood play groups), along with opportunities for extensive play, then home schooling may sufficiently educate young children. However, if parents do not have the commitment, the time, the energy, and the resources to provide young children with an environment that approximates a good early childhood program, then it *does* matter whether a child attends preschool. Thus, the issue is not whether preschool is important but whether home schooling can closely duplicate what a competent preschool program can offer.

There is a concern about preschool and early childhood programs that place too much emphasis on achievement. Researchers have documented that increased academic pressure can be stressful for young children. In one study, Diane Burts and her colleagues (1989) compared the frequencies of stress-related behaviors observed in young children in classrooms with developmentally appropriate instructional practices with those of children in classrooms with developmentally inappropriate instructional practices. They found that the children in the developmentally inappropriate classrooms exhibited more stress-related behaviors than the children in the developmentally appropriate classrooms. In another study, children in a highly academically oriented early childhood education program were compared with children in a low academically

Head Start Resources
Poverty and Learning
Early Childhood Care and Education Around the World

---

developmentally appropriate practice
Education that focuses on the typical developmental patterns of children (age-appropriateness) and the uniqueness of each child (individual-appropriateness).

Component	Appropriate practice	Inappropriate practice
Language development, literacy, and cognitive development	Children are provided many opportunities to see how reading and writing are useful before they are instructed in letter names, sounds, and word identification. Basic skills develop when they are meaningful to children. An abundance of these activities is provided to develop language and literacy: listening to and reading stories and poems; taking field trips; dictating stories; participating in dramatic play; talking informally with other children and adults; and experimenting with writing.	Reading and writing instruction stresses isolated skill development, such as recognizing single letters, reading the alphabet, singing the alphabet song, coloring within predefined lines, and being instructed in correct formation of letters on a printed line.
	Children develop an understanding of concepts about themselves, others, and the world around them through observation, interaction with people and real objects, and the seeking of solutions to concrete problems. Learning about math, science, social studies, health, and other content areas is integrated through meaningful activities.	Instruction stresses isolated skill development through memorization. Children's cognitive development is seen as fragmented in content areas, such as math or science, and times are set aside for each of these.
Physical development	Children have daily opportunities to use large muscles, including running, jumping, and balancing. Outdoor activity is planned daily so children can freely express themselves.	Opportunity for large muscle activity is limited. Outdoor time is limited because it is viewed as interfering with instructional time, rather than as an integral part of the children's learning environment.
	Children have daily opportunities to develop small muscle skills through play activities, such as puzzles, painting, and cutting.	Small motor activity is limited to writing with pencils, coloring predrawn forms, and engaging in similar structured lessons.
Aesthetic development and motivation	Children have daily opportunities for aesthetic expression and appreciation through art and music. A variety of art media are available.	Art and music are given limited attention. Art consists of coloring predrawn forms or following adult-prescribed directions.
	Children's natural curiosity and desire to make sense of their world are used to motivate them to become involved in learning.	Children are required to participate in all activities to obtain the teacher's approval; to obtain extrinsic rewards, such as stickers or privileges; or to avoid punishment.

FIGURE 8.17 NAEYC Recommendations for Developmentally Appropriate and Inappropriate Education

Early Childhood Education in Japan

At a time of low academic achievement by children in the United States, many Americans are turning to Japan, a country of high academic achievement, for possible answers. However, the answers provided by Japanese preschools are not the ones Americans expected to find. In most Japanese preschools, surprisingly little emphasis is put on academic instruction. In one study, 300 Japanese and 210 Americans preschool teachers, child development specialists, and parents were asked about various aspects of early childhood education (Tobin, Wu, & Davidson, 1989). Only 2 percent of the Japanese respondents listed "to give children a good start academically" as one of their top three reasons for a society to have preschools. In contrast, over half the American respondents chose this as one of their top three choices. To prepare children for successful careers in first grade and beyond, Japanese schools do not teach reading, writing, and mathematics but rather skills like persistence, concentration, and the ability to function as a member of a group. The vast majority of young Japanese children are taught to read at home by their parents.

In the comparison of Japanese and American parents, more than 60 percent of the Japanese parents said that the purpose of preschool is to give children experience being a member of the group compared to only 20 percent of the U.S. parents (Tobin, Wu, & Davidson, 1989) (see figure 8.18). Lessons in living and working together grow naturally out of the Japanese culture. In many Japanese kindergartens, children wear the same uniforms, including caps, which are of different colors to indicate the classrooms to which they belong. They have identical sets of equipment, kept in identical drawers and shelves. This is not intended to turn the young children into robots, as some Americans have observed, but to impress on them that other people, just like themselves, have needs and desires that are equally important (Hendry, 1986).

As in America, there is diversity in Japanese early childhood education. Some Japanese kindergartens have specific aims, such as early musical training or the practice of Montessori strategies. In large cities, some kindergartens are attached to universities that have elementary and secondary schools. Some Japanese parents believe that, if their young children attend a university-based program, it will increase the children's chances of eventually being admitted to top-rated schools and universities. Several more progressive programs have introduced free play as an antidote for the heavy intellectual orientation in some Japanese kindergartens.

In Japan, learning how to cooperate and participating in group experiences are viewed as extremely important reasons for early childhood education.

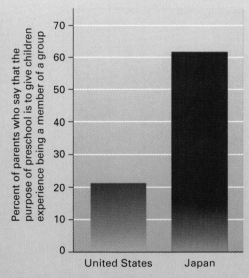

FIGURE 8.18 Comparison of Japanese and U.S. Parents' Views on the Purpose of Preschool

oriented early childhood education program (Hirsch-Pasek & others, 1989). No benefits appeared for children in the highly academically oriented early childhood education program, but some possible harmful effects were noted. Higher test anxiety, less creativity, and a less positive attitude toward school characterized more of the children in the highly academic program than in the low academic program.

In Japan, the goals of early childhood education are quite different from those of American programs. To read about the differences, see the Sociocultural Worlds of Development box.

Careers in Life-Span Development

Yolanda Garcia, Director of Children's Services/Head Start

Yolanda Garcia has worked in the field of early childhood education and family support for three decades. She has been the Director of the Children's Services Department for the Santa Clara, California, County Office of Education since 1980. As director, she is responsible for managing child development programs for 2,500 3- to 5-year-old children in 127 classrooms. Her training includes two master's degrees, one in public policy and child welfare from the University of Chicago and another in educational administration from San Jose State University.

Garcia has served on many national advisory committees that have resulted in improvements in the staffing of Head Start programs. Most notably, she served on the Head Start Quality Committee that recommended the development of Early Head Start and revised performance standards for Head Start programs. Garcia currently is a member of the American Academy of Science Committee on the Integration of Science and Early Childhood Education.

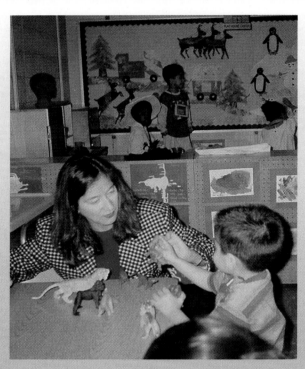

Yolanda Garcia, Director of Children's Services/Head Start, working with some Head Start children in Santa Clara, California.

Education for Children Who Are Disadvantaged

For many years, children from low-income families did not receive any education before they entered the first grade. In the 1960s, an effort was made to try to break the cycle of poverty and poor education for young children in the United States through compensatory education. **Project Head Start** is a government-funded program designed to provide children from low-income families the opportunity to acquire the skills and experiences important for success in school. Project Head Start began in the summer of 1965, funded by the Economic Opportunity Act, and it continues to serve disadvantaged children today.

Evaluations support the positive influence of quality early childhood programs on both the cognitive and social worlds of disadvantaged young children (Goelman & others, 2003; Reynolds, 1999). One high-quality early childhood education program (although not a Head Start program) is the Perry Preschool program in Ypsilanti, Michigan, a 2-year preschool program that includes weekly home visits from program personnel. In an analysis of the long-term effects of the program, young adults who attended the Perry Preschool have higher high school graduation rates, a higher employment rate, less need for welfare, a lower crime rate, and a lower teen pregnancy rate than in a control group from the same background who did not have the enriched early childhood education experience (Weikart, 1993).

Although educational intervention for children who are disadvanted is important, Head Start programs are not all created equal. One estimate is that 40 percent of the

Project Head Start A government-funded program that is designed to provide children from low-income families the opportunity to acquire the skills and experiences important for school success.

1,400 Head Start programs are of questionable quality (Zigler & Styfco, 1994). Developing consistently high-quality Head Start programs should be a national priority.

One individual who is strongly motivated to make Head Start a valuable learning experience for young children from disadvantaged backgrounds is Yolanda Garcia. To read about her work, see the Careers in Life-Span Development insert.

Review and Reflect

4 **Evaluate different approaches to early childhood education**

REVIEW

- What is child-centered kindergarten?
- What is the Montessori approach?
- How is developmentally appropriate practice different from developmentally inappropriate practice?
- Does preschool matter?
- What are the main efforts to educate young children who are disadvantaged?

REFLECT

- Might preschool be more beneficial to children from middle-income than low-income families? Why?

Reach Your Learning Goals

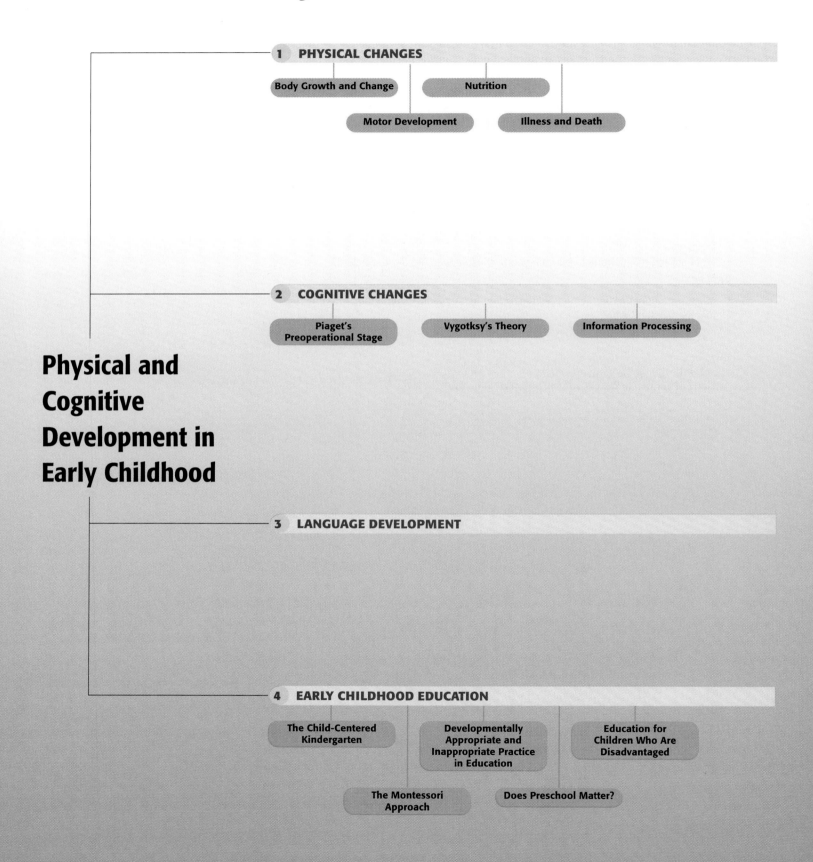

Physical and Cognitive Development in Early Childhood

1 PHYSICAL CHANGES

- Body Growth and Change
- Nutrition
- Motor Development
- Illness and Death

2 COGNITIVE CHANGES

- Piaget's Preoperational Stage
- Vygotksy's Theory
- Information Processing

3 LANGUAGE DEVELOPMENT

4 EARLY CHILDHOOD EDUCATION

- The Child-Centered Kindergarten
- Developmentally Appropriate and Inappropriate Practice in Education
- Education for Children Who Are Disadvantaged
- The Montessori Approach
- Does Preschool Matter?

Summary

1 Identify physical changes in early childhood

- The average child grows 2½ inches in height and gains between 5 and 7 pounds a year during early childhood. Growth patterns vary individually, though. Some children are unusually short because of congenital problems, a physical problem that develops in childhood, or emotional problems. Some of the brain's increase in size in early childhood is due to increases in the number and size of nerve endings, some to myelination. Recently, researchers have found that changes in local patterns in the brain occur between 3 and 15 years of age. These changes often involve spurts of brain activity. From 3 to 6 years of age, the most rapid growth occurs in the frontal lobes; from 6 to puberty, the most substantial changes take place in the temporal and parietal lobes, especially those areas involving language and spatial relations. Increasing brain maturation contributes to improved cognitive abilities.
- Gross motor skills increase dramatically during early childhood. Children become increasingly adventuresome as their gross motor skills improve. Fine motor skills also improve substantially during early childhood. At one point, all children were taught to be right-handed. In today's world, the strategy is to allow children to use the hand they favor. Left-handed children are as competent in motor skills and intellect as right-handed children, although left-handers have more reading problems. Both genetic and environmental explanations of handedness have been given.
- Energy requirements vary according to basal metabolism, rate of growth, and level of activity. A special concern is that too many young children are being raised on diets that are too high in fat. The child's life should be centered on activities, not meals.
- In recent decades, vaccines have virtually eradicated many diseases that once resulted in the deaths of many young children. The disorders still most likely to be fatal for young children are birth defects, cancer, and heart disease, but accidents are the leading cause of death in young children. A special concern is the poor health status of many young children in low-income families. They often have less resistance to disease, including colds and influenza, than do their higher-socioeconomic-status counterparts. One of every three deaths in the world is that of a child under 5. Every week, more than a quarter of a million children die in developing countries. The most common cause of children's death in developing countries is diarrhea. There has been a dramatic increase in HIV/AIDS in young children in developing countries in the last decade.

2 Describe three views of the cognitive changes that occur in early childhood

- Piaget's preoperational stage of thought is the beginning of the ability to reconstruct at the level of thought what has been established in behavior and a transition from primitive to more sophisticated use of symbols. In preoperational thought, the child's thoughts are flawed and not well organized. The symbolic function substage occurs between 2 and 4 years of age and is characterized by symbolic thought, egocentrism, and animism. The intuitive thought substage stretches from 4 to 7 years of age. It is called intuitive because children seem so sure about their knowledge yet are unaware of how they know what they know. The preoperational child lacks conservation and asks a barrage of questions.
- In Vygotsky's theory, the zone of proximal development (ZPD) describes the range of tasks that are too difficult for children to master alone but which can be learned with the guidance and assistance of adults or more-skilled children. Scaffolding involves changing the level of support over the course of a teaching session, with the more-skilled person adjusting guidance to fit the student's current performance level. Vygotsky believed that language plays a key role in guiding cognition. Comparisons of Vygotsky's and Piaget's theories involve constructivism, metaphors for learning, stages, key processes, role of language, views on education, and teaching implications. Vygotsky's theory is social constructivist, Piaget's cognitive constructivist. Applications of Vygotsky's theory in education focus on using the child's zone of proximal development, using scaffolding and more-skilled peers as teachers, monitoring and encouraging children's use of private speech, assessing the child's ZPD rather than IQ, and transforming the classroom with Vygotskian ideas.
- Information-processing theory emphasizes cognitive processes. The child's ability to attend to stimuli dramatically improves during early childhood. One deficit in attention in early childhood is that the child attends to the salient rather than the relevant features of a task. Significant improvement in short-term memory occurs during early childhood. With good prompts, young children's long-term memories can be accurate, although young children can be led into developing false memories. Young children usually don't use strategies to remember, but they can learn rather simple problem-solving strategies. Theory of mind is the awareness of one's own mental processes and the mental processes of others. Children begin to understand mental states involving perceptions, desires, and emotions at 2 to 3 years of age and at 4 to 5 years of age realize that people can have false beliefs.

3 Summarize how language develops in early childhood

- Young children increase their grasp of language's rule systems. These include phonology, morphology, syntax, semantics, and pragmatics. Berko's classic experiment demonstrated that young children understand morphological rules.

4 **Evaluate different approaches to early childhood education**

- The child-centered kindergarten emphasizes the education of the whole child, with particular attention to individual variation, the process of learning, and the importance of play in development.
- The Montessori approach, another well-known strategy for early childhood education, allows children to choose from a range of activities while teachers serve as facilitators.
- Developmentally appropriate practice focuses on the typical patterns of children (age-appropriateness) and the unique-ness of each child (individual-appropriateness). Such prac-tice contrasts with developmentally inappropriate practice, which ignores the concrete, hands-on approach to learning.
- A special concern is the view that education is a race and that an early academic start in preschool will help children win the race. Critics argue that too many preschools are aca-demically oriented and stressful for young children.
- The U.S. government has tried to break the poverty cycle with programs such as Head Start. Model programs have been shown to have positive effects on children from poverty backgrounds.

Key Terms

myelination 236
basal metabolism rate (BMR) 239
operations 242
symbolic function substage 242
egocentrism 242

animism 243
intuitive thought substage 244
centration 244
conservation 244
zone of proximal development (ZPD) 246
scaffolding 246

social constructivist approach 247
short-term memory 251
theory of mind 252
child-centered kindergarten 256
Montessori approach 256

developmentally appropriate practice 258
Project Head Start 260

Key People

Teresa Amabile 234
Jean Piaget 242
Barbel Inhelder 243
Rochel Gelman 245

Lev Vygtosky 246
Zhe Chen and Robert Siegler 252

Jean Berko 254
Maria Montessori 256
David Elkind 258

Taking It to the Net

1. Professor Jackson has asked his students to try and place Piaget's theories in the context of contemporary research. What should students know about how Piaget's theories stack up in relation to recent research findings?

2. Judith and Louis have a 3-year-old son, Mitchell. Many of their friends are enrolling their children in preschool. Judith and Louis do not think they can afford to enroll Mitchell in a preschool program, although both of them think that the benefits of preschool might justify the cost. Are there significant benefits associated with preschool programs? Are there particular types of preschools that seem more beneficial for children?

3. Beyonce, who is working in a prosecutor's office for her senior internship, has been asked to write a memo on the suggestibility of child witnesses and how likely a jury is to believe a child's testimony in court cases. How can she find information for the memo that provides research-based facts as well as guidelines for dealing with child witnesses that will be helpful for the prosecutors?

Connect to www.mhhe.com/santrockld9 to research the answers and complete these exercises.

E-Learning Tools

To help you master the material in this chapter, you'll find a number of valuable study tools on the Student CD-ROM that accompanies this book. In addition, visit the Online Learning Center for *Life-Span Development*, ninth edition, where you'll find these valuable resources for chapter 8, "Physical and Cognitive Development in Early Childhood."

- What do you think are the most important aspects of early childhood education? Use the self-assessment, *What I Think Is Important in Early Childhood Education,* to solidify your opinions on the topic.
- View video clips of key researchers, including Steve Ceci as he discusses his research on child witness testimony.
- Build your decision-making skills by trying your hand at the parenting and education "Scenarios."

*Let us play, for it is
    yet day
And we cannot go to
    sleep;
Besides, in the sky
the little birds fly
And the hills are all
covered with sheep.*

—WILLIAM BLAKE
English Poet, 19th Century

Socioemotional Development in Early Childhood

Chapter Outline

EMOTIONAL AND PERSONALITY DEVELOPMENT

The Self

Emotional Development

Moral Development

Gender

FAMILIES

Parenting

Sibling Relationships and Birth Order

The Changing Family in a Changing Society

PEER RELATIONS, PLAY, AND TELEVISION

Peer Relations

Play

Television

Learning Goals

1 *Discuss emotional and personality development in early childhood*

2 *Explain how families can influence young children's development*

3 *Describe the roles of peers, play, and television in young children's development*

Images of Life-Span Development
Sarah and Her Developing Moral Values

Like many children, Sara Newland loves animals. When she was just 4 years old, she turned that love into social activism. During a trip to the zoo, she learned about the plight of an endangered species and became motivated to help. With her mother's assistance, Sara baked cakes and cookies and sold them on the sidewalk near her apartment building in New York City. She was elated when she raised $35, which she promptly mailed to the World Wildlife Fund. A few weeks later, her smiles turned into tears when the fund wrote Sara asking for more money. Sara was devastated because she thought she had taken care of the animal problem. Her mother told Sara that the endangered species problem and many others are so big that they require continual help from lots of people. That explanation apparently worked because Sara, now 9 years old, helps out at an inner-city child-care center and regularly takes meals to homeless people in her neighborhood (Kantrowitz, 1991). Sara tells her friends not to be scared of homeless people. She says that some people wonder why she gives to them, then says, "If everyone gave food to them, they would all have decent meals."

Sensitive parents can make a difference in encouraging young children's sense of morality and values. Some experts on moral development believe that a capacity for goodness is present from the start, which reflects the "innate goodness" view of the child, which we discussed in chapter 1. But many developmentalists also believe that parents must nurture that goodness, just as they help their children become good readers, musicians, or athletes.

1 EMOTIONAL AND PERSONALITY DEVELOPMENT

The Self

Emotional Development

Moral Development

Gender

In the story that opened the chapter, Sara displayed a positive sense of morality through her motivation to help an endangered species and the homeless. Let's further explore young children's moral development and other aspects of their emotional and personality development, beginning with the self.

The Self

We learned in chapter 7 that toward the end of the second year of life children develop a sense of self ◀▥ p. 213. During early childhood, some important developments in the self take place. Among these developments are facing the issue of initiative versus guilt and enhancing self-understanding.

Initiative Versus Guilt According to Erik Erikson (1968), the psychosocial stage that characterizes early childhood is *initiative versus guilt*. By now, children have become convinced that they are a person of their own; during early childhood, they must discover what kind of person they will become. They intensely identify with their parents, who most of the time appear to them to be powerful and beautiful, although often unreasonable, disagreeable, and sometimes even dangerous. During early childhood, children use their perceptual, motor, cognitive, and language skills to make things happen. They have a surplus of energy that permits them to forget failures quickly and to approach new areas that seem desirable—even if they seem dangerous—with undiminished zest and some increased sense of direction. On their own *initiative*, then, children at this stage exuberantly move out into a wider social world.

The great governor of initiative is *conscience*. Children now not only feel afraid of being found out, but they also begin to hear the inner voice of self-observation, self-guidance, and self-punishment (Bybee, 1999). Their initiative and enthusiasm may bring them not only rewards but also punishments. Widespread disappointment at this stage leads to an unleashing of guilt that lowers the child's self-esteem.

Whether children leave this stage with a sense of initiative that outweighs their sense of guilt depends in large part on how parents respond to their children's self-initiated activities. Children who are given the freedom and opportunity to initiate motor play, such as running, bike riding, sledding, skating, tussling, and wrestling, have their sense of initiative supported. Initiative is also supported when parents answer their children's questions and do not deride or inhibit fantasy or play activity. In contrast, if children are made to feel that their motor activity is bad, that their questions are a nuisance, and that their play is silly and stupid, then they often develop a sense of guilt over self-initiated activities that may persist through life's later stages (Elkind, 1970).

Self-Understanding **Self-understanding** is the child's representation of self, the substance and content of self-conceptions. For example, a 5-year-old girl understands that she is a girl, has blond hair, likes to ride her bicycle, has a friend, and is a swimmer. An 11-year-old boy understands that he is a student, a boy, a football player, a family member, a video-game lover, and a rock music fan. A child's self-understanding is based on the various roles and membership categories that define who children are. Though not the whole of personal identity, self-understanding provides its rational underpinnings (Damon & Hart, 1992).

The rudimentary beginning of self-understanding begins with self-recognition, which takes place by approximately 18 months of age. Since children can verbally communicate their ideas, research on self-understanding in childhood is not limited to visual self-recognition, as it was during infancy. Mainly by interviewing children, researchers have probed children's conceptions of many aspects of self-understanding (Moore & Lemmon, 2001). These include mind and body, self in relation to others, and pride and shame in self. In early childhood, children usually conceive of the self in physical terms. Most young children think the self is part of their body, usually their head. Young children usually confuse self, mind, and body. Because the self is a body part for them, they describe it along many material dimensions, such as size, shape, and color. Young children distinguish themselves from others through many different physical and material attributes. Says 4-year-old Sandra, "I'm different from Jennifer because I have brown hair and she has blond hair." Says 4-year-old Ralph, "I am different from Hank because I am taller, and I am different from my sister because I have a bicycle."

Researchers also believe that the *active dimension* is a central component of the self in early childhood (Keller, Ford, & Meacham, 1978). If we define the category *physical* broadly enough, we can include physical actions as well as body image and material possessions. For example, preschool children often describe themselves in terms of such activities as play. In sum, in early childhood, children frequently think of themselves in terms of a physical self or an active self.

Emotional Development

Children, like adults, experience many emotions during the course of a day. At times, children also try to make sense of other people's emotional reactions and feelings.

Young Children's Emotion Language and Understanding Among the most important changes in emotional development in early childhood are the increased use of emotion language and the understanding of emotion (Kuebli, 1994). Preschoolers

self-understanding The child's cognitive representation of self, the substance and content of the child's self-conceptions.

Approximate Age of Child	Description
2 to 3 years	Increase emotion vocabulary most rapidly
	Correctly label simple emotions in self and others and talk about past, present, and future emotions
	Talk about the causes and consequences of some emotions and identify emotions associated with certain situations
	Use emotion language in pretend play
4 to 5 years	Show increased capacity to reflect verbally on emotions and to consider more complex relations between emotions and situations
	Understand that the same event may call forth different feelings in different people and that feelings sometimes persist long after the events that caused them
	Demonstrate growing awareness about controlling and managing emotions in accord with social standards

FIGURE 9.1 Some Characteristics of Young Children's Emotion Language and Understanding

become more adept at talking about their own and others' emotions. Between 2 and 3 years of age, children continue to increase the number of terms they use to describe emotion (Ridgeway, Waters, & Kuczaj, 1985). However, in the preschool years, children are learning more than just the "vocabulary" of emotion terms, they also are learning about the causes and consequences of feelings (Denham, 1998).

At 4 to 5 years of age, children show an increased ability to reflect on emotions. In this developmental time frame, they also begin to understand that the same event can elicit different feelings in different people. Moreover, they show a growing awareness about controlling and managing emotions to meet social standards (Bruce, Olen, & Jensen, 1999). A summary of the characteristics of young children's emotion language and understanding is shown in figure 9.1.

Self-Conscious Emotions *Self-conscious emotions* require that children be able to refer to themselves and be aware of themselves as distinct from others (Lewis, 1993, 1995, 2002). Pride, shame, embarrassment, and guilt are self-conscious emotions.

Recall from chapter 7, "Socioemotional Development in Infancy," that self-awareness appears in the last half of the second year of life. The self-conscious emotions do not appear to develop, at the very earliest, until this self-awareness is in place. Thus, emotions such as pride and guilt become more common in the early childhood years. They are especially influenced by parents' responses to children's behavior. For example, a young child may experience a twinge of guilt when a parent says, "You should feel bad about biting your sister." Shortly, we will further discuss guilt in the context of moral development.

Moral Development

Moral development involves the development of thoughts, feelings, and behaviors regarding rules and conventions about what people should do in their interactions with other people. Developmentalists study how children think, behave, and feel about such rules and regulations. We will begin our exploration of moral development in children by focusing on a cognitive view of moral development.

Piaget's View of Moral Reasoning Interest in how the child thinks about moral issues was stimulated by Jean Piaget (1932). He extensively observed and interviewed children from the age of 4 to 12. He watched them play marbles, seeking to learn how they used and thought about the game's rules. He also asked children questions about

moral development Development that involves thoughts, feelings, and actions regarding rules and conventions about what people should do in their interactions with other people.

ethical rules—theft, lies, punishment, and justice, for example. Piaget concluded that children think in two distinctly different ways about morality, depending on their developmental maturity:

- **Heteronomous morality** is the first stage of moral development in Piaget's theory, occurring from approximately 4 to 7 years of age. Justice and rules are conceived of as unchangeable properties of the world, removed from the control of people.
- **Autonomous morality** is the second stage of moral development in Piaget's theory, displayed by older children (about 10 years of age and older). The child becomes aware that rules and laws are created by people and that, in judging an action, one should consider the actor's intentions as well as the consequences.

Children 7 to 10 years of age are in a transition between the two stages, showing some features of both.

Let's consider Piaget's two stages of moral development further. The heteronomous thinker judges the rightness or goodness of behavior by considering the consequences of the behavior, not the intentions of the actor. For example, the heteronomous thinker says that breaking 12 cups accidentally is worse than breaking 1 cup intentionally while trying to steal a cookie. For the moral autonomist, the reverse is true. The actor's intentions assume paramount importance. The heteronomous thinker also believes that rules are unchangeable and are handed down by all-powerful authorities. When Piaget suggested that new rules be introduced into the game of marbles, the young children resisted. They insisted that the rules had always been the same and could not be altered. By contrast, older children—who were moral autonomists—accepted change and recognized that rules are merely convenient, socially agreed-upon conventions, subject to change by consensus.

The heteronomous thinker also believes in **imminent justice,** the concept that, if a rule is broken, punishment will immediately be meted out. The young child believes that the violation is connected in some automatic way to the punishment. Thus, young children often look around worriedly after committing a transgression, expecting inevitable punishment. Older children, the moral autonomists, recognize that punishment is socially mediated and occurs only if a relevant person witnesses the wrongdoing and that, even then, punishment is not inevitable.

Piaget argued that, as children develop, they become more sophisticated in thinking about social matters, especially about the possibilities and conditions of cooperation. Piaget believed that this social understanding comes about through the mutual give-and-take of peer relations. In the peer group, where all members have similar power and status, plans are negotiated and coordinated, and disagreements are reasoned about and eventually settled. Parent-child relations, in which parents have the power and the child does not, are less likely to advance moral reasoning, because rules are often handed down in an authoritarian way. Later, in chapter 11, we will discuss another highly influential cognitive view of moral development, that of Lawrence Kohlberg.

Moral Behavior The study of moral behavior is emphasized by behavioral and social cognitive theorists ◀‖‖ p. 51. The processes of reinforcement, punishment, and imitation are used to explain children's moral behavior. When children are rewarded for behavior that is consistent with laws and social conventions, they are likely to repeat that behavior. When models who behave morally are provided, children are likely to adopt their actions. And, when children are punished for immoral behavior, those behaviors are likely to be reduced or eliminated. However, because punishment may have adverse side effects, it needs to be used judiciously and cautiously.

Another important point needs to be made about the social cognitive view of moral development. Moral behavior is influenced extensively by the situation. What children do in one situation is often only weakly related to what they do in other situations. A child might cheat in math class but not in English class; a child might steal

heteronomous morality The first stage of moral development, in Piaget's theory, occurring from approximately 4 to 7 years of age. Justice and rules are conceived of as unchangeable properties of the world, removed from the control of people.

autonomous morality The second stage of moral development, in Piaget's theory, displayed by older children (about 10 years of age and older). The child becomes aware that rules and laws are created by people and that, in judging an action, one should consider the actor's intentions as well as the consequences.

imminent justice The concept that, if a rule is broken, punishment will be meted out immediately.

What is moral is what you feel good after and what is immoral is what you feel bad after.

—ERNEST HEMINGWAY
American Author, 20th Century

a piece of candy when others are not present but not steal it when they are present. More than half a century ago, morality's situational nature was observed in a comprehensive study of thousands of children in many different situations—at home, at school, and at church, for example. The totally honest child was virtually nonexistent; so was the child who cheated in all situations (Hartshorne & May, 1928–1930).

Social cognitive theorists also believe that the ability to resist temptation is closely tied to the development of self-control. Children must overcome their impulses toward something they want that is prohibited. To achieve this self-control, they must learn to be patient and to delay gratification. Social cognitive theorists believe that cognitive factors are important in the child's development of self-control (Bandura, 2002).

Moral Feelings In chapter 2, we discussed Sigmund Freud's psychoanalytic theory ◀◀◀ p. 44. It describes the *superego* as one of the three main structures of personality—the id and ego being the other two. In Freud's classical psychoanalytic theory, the child's superego—the moral branch of personality—develops as the child resolves the Oedipus conflict and identifies with the same-sex parent in the early childhood years. Among the reasons children resolve the Oedipus conflict is the fear of losing their parents' love and of being punished for their unacceptable sexual wishes toward the opposite-sex parent. To reduce anxiety, avoid punishment, and maintain parental affection, children form a superego by identifying with the same-sex parent. Through their identification with the same-sex parent, children internalize the parents' standards of right and wrong that reflect societal prohibitions. And the child turns inward the hostility that was previously aimed externally at the same-sex parent. This inwardly directed hostility is now felt self-punitively as guilt, which is experienced unconsciously (beyond the child's awareness). In the psychoanalytic account of moral development, the self-punitiveness of guilt is responsible for keeping the child from committing transgressions. That is, children conform to societal standards to avoid guilt.

Positive feelings, such as empathy, contribute to the child's moral development. *Empathy* is reacting to another's feelings with an emotional response that is similar to the other's feelings. Although empathy is experienced as an emotional state, it often has a cognitive component. The cognitive component is the ability to discern another's inner psychological states, or what is called "perspective taking." Young infants have the capacity for some purely empathic responses, but for effective moral action children need to learn how to identify a wide range of emotional states in others. They also need to learn to anticipate what kinds of action will improve another person's emotional state.

Gender

While sex refers to the biological dimension of being male or female, **gender** refers to the social and psychological dimensions of being male or female. Two aspects of gender bear special mention:

- **Gender identity** is the sense of being male or female, which most children acquire by the time they are 3 years old.
- **Gender role** is a set of expectations that prescribes how females or males should think, act, and feel.

gender The social and psychological dimension of being male or female.

gender identity The sense of being male or female, which most children acquire by the time they are 3 years old.

gender role A set of expectations that prescribes how females or males should think, act, and feel.

Biological Influences In chapter 3, you learned that humans normally have 46 chromosomes arranged in pairs. The 23rd pair may have two X chromosomes to produce a female, or it may have an X and a Y chromosome to produce a male.

Just as chromosomes are important in understanding biological influences, so are hormones. The two main classes of sex hormones are estrogens and androgens. *Estrogens,* such as estradiol, influence the development of female physical sex characteristics. *Androgens,* such as testosterone, promote the development of male physical sex characteristics. In the first few weeks of gestation, female and male embryos look alike. Male sex organs start to differ from female sex organs when the Y chromosome in the male embryo triggers the secretion of androgens. Low levels of androgens in the female embryo allow the normal development of female sex organs.

In gender development, however, biology is not completely destiny. When gender attitudes and behavior are at issue, children's socialization experiences matter a great deal (Eccles, 2000; Lippa, 2002: Rice, 2002; Travis, 2001).

Social Influences   In the United States, adults discriminate between the sexes shortly after the infant's birth. The "pink and blue" treatment might be applied to boys and girls before they leave the hospital. Soon afterward, differences in hairstyles, clothes, and toys become obvious. Adults and peers reward these differences throughout development. And boys and girls learn gender roles through imitation, or observational learning, by watching what other people say and do. In recent years, the idea that parents are the critical socializing agents in gender-role development has come under fire. Parents are only one of many sources through which the individual learns gender roles (Beal, 1994; Fagot, Rodgers, & Leinbach, 2000). Culture, schools, peers, the media, and other family members are others, yet it is important to guard against swinging too far in this direction because—especially in the early years of development—parents are important influences on gender development.

Psychoanalytic and Social Cognitive Theories   Two prominent theories address the way children acquire masculine and feminine attitudes and behaviors from their parents:

- The **psychoanalytic theory of gender** stems from Freud's view that the preschool child develops a sexual attraction to the opposite-sex parent. At 5 or 6 years of age, the child renounces this attraction because of anxious feelings. Subsequently, the child identifies with the same-sex parent, unconsciously adopting the same-sex parent's characteristics. However, today many child developmentalists do not believe gender development proceeds on the basis of identification, at least not in terms of Freud's emphasis on childhood sexual attraction (Callan, 2001). Children become gender-typed much earlier than 5 or 6 years of age, and they become masculine or feminine even when the same-sex parent is not present in the family.
- The **social cognitive theory of gender** emphasizes that children's gender development occurs through observation and imitation of gender behavior, and through the rewards and punishments children experience for gender-appropriate and -inappropriate behavior. Unlike psychoanalytic theory, social cognitive theory argues that sexual attraction to parents is not involved in gender development. (A comparison of the psychoanalytic and social cognitive views is presented in figure 9.2) Parents often use rewards and punishments to teach their daughters to be feminine ("Karen, you are being a good girl when you play gently with your doll") and their sons to be masculine ("Keith, a boy as big as you is

mhhe ●com/
santrockld9

Gender Resources

Theory	Processes	Outcomes
Freud's psychoanalytic theory	Sexual attraction to opposite-sex parent at 3 to 5 years of age; anxiety about sexual attraction and subsequent identification with same-sex parent at 5 to 6 years of age	Gender behavior similar to that of same-sex parent
Social cognitive theory	Rewards and punishments of gender-appropriate and -inappropriate behavior by adults and peers; observation and initiation of models' masculine and feminine behavior	Gender behavior

FIGURE 9.2 A Comparison of the Psychoanalytic and Social Cognitive Views of Gender Development

Parents influence their children's development by action and example.

psychoanalytic theory of gender A theory deriving from Freud's view that the preschool child develops a sexual attraction to the opposite-sex parent, by approximately 5 or 6 years of age renounces this attraction because of anxious feelings, and subsequently identifies with the same-sex parent, unconsciously adopting the same-sex parent's characteristics.

social cognitive theory of gender A theory that emphasizes that children's gender development occurs through the observation and imitation of gender behavior and through the rewards and punishments children experience for gender-appropriate and -inappropriate behavior.

In childhood, boys and girls tend to gravitate toward others of their own sex. Boys' and girls' groups develop distinct cultures with different agendas.

—ELEANOR MACCOBY

Contemporary Developmental Psychologist, Stanford University

Fathers and Sons

not supposed to cry"). Peers also extensively reward and punish gender behavior (Lott & Maluso, 2001). And, by observing adults and peers at home, at school, in the neighborhood, and on television, children are widely exposed to a myriad of models who display masculine and feminine behavior. Critics of the social cognitive view argue that gender development is not as passively acquired as it indicates. Later, we will discuss the cognitive views of gender development, which stress that children actively construct their gender world.

Parental Influences Parents, by action and by example, influence their children's gender development. Both mothers and fathers are psychologically important in children's gender development. Mothers are more consistently given responsibility for nurturance and physical care. Fathers are more likely to engage in playful interaction and to be given responsibility for ensuring that boys and girls conform to existing cultural norms. And, whether or not they have more influence on them, fathers are more involved in socializing their sons than their daughters. Fathers seem to play an especially important part in gender-role development. They are more likely than mothers to act differently toward sons and daughters. Thus, they contribute more to distinctions between the genders (Huston, 1983).

Many parents encourage boys and girls to engage in different types of play and activities (Fagot, Leinbach, & O'Boyle, 1992). Girls are more likely to be given dolls to play with during childhood. When old enough, they are more likely to be assigned baby-sitting duties. Girls are encouraged to be more nurturant and emotional than boys. Fathers are more likely to engage in aggressive play with their sons than with their daughters.

Peer Influences Parents provide the earliest discrimination of gender roles in development. Before long, though, peers join the societal process of responding to and modeling masculine and feminine behavior (Brannon, 2002). Children who play in sex-appropriate activities tend to be rewarded for doing so by their peers. Those who play in cross-sexed activities tend to be criticized by their peers or left to play alone. Children show a clear preference for being with and liking same-sex peers (Maccoby, 1993, 1998, 2002). This tendency usually becomes stronger during the middle and late childhood years. After extensive observations of elementary school playgrounds, two researchers characterized the play settings as "gender school." They said that boys teach one another the required masculine behavior and enforce it strictly (Luria &

As reflected in this tug-of-war battle between boys and girls, the playground in elementary school is like going to "gender school." Elementary school children show a clear preference for being with and liking same-sex peers. *Think back to when you were in elementary school. How much did you prefer being with peers who were the same sex as you?*

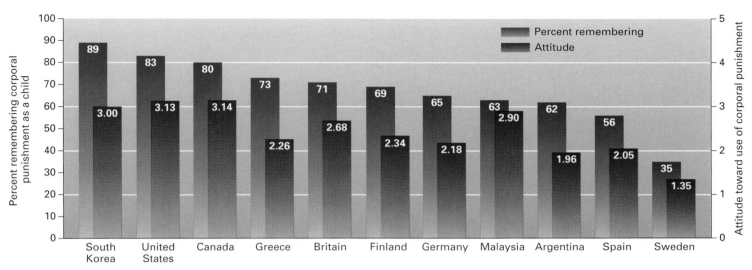

FIGURE 9.5 Corporal Punishment in Different Countries

A 5-point scale was used to assess attitudes toward corporal punishment with scores closer to 1 indicating an attitude against its use and scores closer to 5 suggesting an attitude for its use.

A recent cross-cultural comparison found that individuals in the United States and Canada were among the most favorable toward corporal punishment and remembered it being used by their parents (Curran & others, 2001) (see figure 9.5). People in Sweden especially had an unfavorable attitude toward corporal punishment and were less likely than people in the other countries to remember it being used by their parents.

Most child psychologists recommend reasoning with the child, especially explaining the consequences of the child's actions for others, as the best way to handle children's misbehaviors(Straus, 2003). Time-out, in which the child is removed from a setting where the child experiences positive reinforcement, can also be effective. For example, when the child has misbehaved, a parent might take away TV viewing for a specified period of time.

Child Abuse   Unfortunately, as we just mentioned, punishment sometimes leads to the abuse of infants and children. Child abuse is an increasing problem in the United States. Estimates of its incidence vary, but some authorities say that as many as 500,000 children are physically abused every year. Laws in many states now require doctors and teachers to report suspected cases of child abuse, yet many cases go unreported, especially those of battered infants.

Child abuse is such a disturbing circumstance that many people have difficulty understanding or sympathizing with parents who abuse or neglect their children. Our response is often outrage and anger directed at the parent. This outrage focuses our attention on parents as bad, sick, monstrous, sadistic individuals who cause their children to suffer. Experts on child abuse believe that this view is too simple and deflects attention away from the social context of the abuse and parents' coping skills. It is especially important to recognize that child abuse is a diverse condition, that it is usually mild to moderate in severity, and that it is only partially caused by the individual personality characteristics of parents (Azar, 2002; Field, 2000). The most common kind of abuser is not a raging, uncontrolled physical abuser but an overwhelmed single mother in poverty who neglects the child.

The Multifaceted Nature of Abuse   Whereas the public and many professionals use the term *child abuse* to refer to both abuse and neglect, developmentalists increasingly

Child maltreatment involves grossly inadequate and destructive aspects of parenting.

—DANTE CICCHETTI
*Contemporary Developmental Psychologist,
University of Rochester*

**mhhe ● com/
santrockld9**

Child Abuse Prevention Network

**International Aspects
of Child Abuse**

**National Clearinghouse
on Child Abuse and Neglect**

use the term *child maltreatment* (Cicchetti, 2001). This term does not have quite the emotional impact of the term *abuse* and acknowledges that maltreatment includes several different conditions. Among the different types of maltreatment are physical and sexual abuse; the fostering of delinquency; lack of supervision; medical, educational, and nutritional neglect; and drug or alcohol abuse. In one large survey, approximately 20 percent of the reported cases involved abuse alone, 46 percent neglect alone, 23 percent both abuse and neglect, and 11 percent sexual abuse (American Association for Protecting Children, 1986).

The Cultural Context of Abuse   The extensive violence that takes place in the American culture is reflected in the occurrence of violence in the family (Azar, 2002). A regular diet of violence appears on television screens, and parents often resort to power assertion as a disciplinary technique. In China, where physical punishment is rarely used to discipline children, the incidence of child abuse is reported to be very low. In the United States, many abusing parents report that they do not have sufficient resources or help from others. This may be a realistic evaluation of the situation experienced by many low-income families, who do not have adequate preventive and supportive services.

Family Influences   To understand abuse in the family, the interactions of all family members need to be considered, regardless of who actually performs the violent acts against the child. For example, even though the father may be the one who physically abuses the child, contributions by the mother, the child, and siblings also should be evaluated. Many parents who abuse their children come from families in which physical punishment was used. These parents view physical punishment as a legitimate way of controlling the child's behavior. Physical punishment may be a part of this sanctioning.

Were parents who abuse children abused by their own parents? About one-third of parents who were abused themselves when they were young abuse their own children (Cicchetti & Toth, 1998). Thus, some, but not a majority, of parents are locked into an intergenerational transmission of abuse. Mothers who break out of the intergenerational transmission of abuse often have at least one warm, caring adult in their background, have a close, positive marital relationship, and have received therapy (Egeland, Jacobivitz, & Sroufe, 1988).

Developmental Consequences of Abuse   Among the developmental consequences of child maltreatment are poor emotion regulation, attachment problems, problems in peer relations, difficulty in adapting to school, and other psychological problems (Azar, 2002; Shonk & Cicchetti, 2001). Difficulties in initiating and modulating positive and negative affect have been observed in maltreated infants (Cicchetti, Ganiban, & Barnett, 1991). Maltreated infants also may show excessive negative affect or blunted positive affect (Maughan & Cicchetti, 2002).

Maltreated children appear to be poorly equipped to develop successful peer relations, due to their aggressiveness, avoidance, and aberrant responses to both distress and positive approaches from peers (Bolger & Patterson, 2001; Mueller & Silverman, 1989).

Being physically abused has been linked with children's anxiety, personality problems, depression, conduct disorder, and delinquency (Shonk & Cicchetti, 2001; Toth, Manley, & Cicchetti, 1992). Later, during the adult years, maltreated children show increased violence toward other adults, dating partners, and marital partners, as well as increased substance abuse, anxiety, and depression (Malinosky-Rummell & Hansen, 1993). In sum, maltreated children are at risk for developing a wide range of problems and disorders (Bissada & Briere, 2002).

Coparenting   A dramatic increase in research on coparenting has occurred in the last two decades. The organizing theme of this research is that poor coordination, active undermining and disparagement of the other parent, lack of cooperation and warmth, and disconnection by one parenting partner—either alone or in combination with overinvolvement by the other—are conditions that place children at developmental risk (McHale & others, 2002). By contrast, parental cooperation and warmth show clear ties to children's prosocial behavior and competence in peer relations. For example, in one study, 4-year-old children from families characterized by low levels of mutuality and support in coparenting were more likely than their classmates to show difficulties in social adjustment when observed on the playground (McHale, Johnson, & Sinclair, 1999).

Good Parenting Takes Time and Effort   In today's society, there is an unfortunate theme which suggests that parenting can be done quickly and with little or no inconvenience (Sroufe, 2000). One example of this involves playing Mozart CDs in the hope that they will enrich infants' and young children's brains. Some of these parents might be thinking "I don't have enough time to spend with my children so I'll just play these intellectual CDs and then they won't need me as much." Judith Harris' book *The Nurture Assumption* (which states that heredity and peer relations are the key factors in children's development) fits into this theme that parents don't need to spend much time with their children p. 104. Why did it become so popular? To some degree some people who don't spend much time with their children saw it as supporting their neglect and reducing their guilt.

One-minute bedtime stories also are now being marketed successfully for parents to read to their children (Walsh, 2000). Most of these are brief summaries of longer stories. There are one-minute bedtime bear books, puppy books, and so on. These parents know it is good for them to read with their children, but they don't want to spend a lot of time doing it.

What is wrong with these quick-fix approaches to parenting? Good parenting takes a lot of time and a lot of effort. You can't do it in a minute here and a minute there. You can't do it with CDs.

Parents who do not spend enough time with their children or who have problems in child rearing can benefit from counseling and therapy. To read about the work of marriage and family counselor Darla Botkin, see the Careers in Life-Span Development insert.

Sibling Relationships and Birth Order

What are sibling relationships like? How extensively does birth order influence behavior?

Sibling Relationships   Any of you who have grown up with siblings (brothers or sisters) probably have a rich memory of aggressive, hostile interchanges. But sibling relationships also have many pleasant, caring moments (Zukow-Goldring, 2002). Children's sibling relationships include helping, sharing, teaching, fighting, and playing. Children can act as emotional

Careers in Life-Span Development

Darla Botkin, *Marriage and Family Therapist*

Darla Botkin, a marriage and family therapist who teaches, conducts research, and engages in therapy in the area of marriage and family therapy p. 37. She is on the faculty of the University of Kentucky. Botkin obtained a bachelor's degree in elementary education with a concentration in special education and then went on to receive a master's degree in early childhood education. She spent the next six years working with children and their families in a variety of settings, including day care, elementary school, and Head Start. These experiences led Botkin to recognize the interdependence of the developmental settings that children and their parents experience (such as home, school, and work). She returned to graduate school and obtained a Ph.D. in family studies from the University of Tennessee. She then became a faculty member in the Family Studies program at the University of Kentucky. Completing further coursework and clinical training in marriage and family therapy, she became certified as a marriage and family therapist.

Dr. Botkin's current interests include working with young children in family therapy, gender and ethnic issues in family therapy, and the role of spirituality in family wellness.

Darla Botkin (*left*), conducting a family therapy session.

The one-child family is becoming much more common in China because of the strong motivation to limit the population growth in the People's Republic of China. The policy is still new, and its effects on children have not been fully examined. *In general, what have researchers found the only child to be like?*

Big sisters are the crab grass in the lawn of life.
—CHARLES SCHULZ
American Cartoonist, 20th Century

mhhe com/
santrockld9

Working Parents
Family and the Workplace

supports, rivals, and communication partners. More than 80 percent of American children have one or more siblings. Because there are so many possible sibling combinations, it is difficult to generalize about sibling influences. Among the factors to consider are the number of siblings, the ages of siblings, birth order, age spacing, the sex of siblings, and whether sibling relationships are different from parent-child relationships (Teti, 2001).

Birth Order Birth order is a special interest of sibling researchers. When differences in birth order are found, they usually are explained by variations in interactions with parents and siblings associated with the unique experiences of being in a particular position in the family. This is especially true in the case of the firstborn child (Teti & others, 1993). Parents have higher expectations for firstborn children than for later-born children. They put more pressure on them for achievement and responsibility. They also interfere more with their activities (Rothbart, 1971).

Given the differences in family dynamics involved in birth order, it is not surprising that firstborns and later-borns have different characteristics (Zajonc, 2001). Firstborn children are more adult-oriented, helpful, conforming, anxious, and self-controlled than their siblings. Parents give more attention to firstborns and this is related to firstborns' nurturant behavior (Stanhope & Corter, 1993). Parental demands and high standards established for firstborns result in these children's excelling in academic and professional endeavors. Firstborns are overrepresented in *Who's Who* and Rhodes scholars, for example. However, some of the same pressures placed on firstborns for high achievement may be the reason they also have more guilt, anxiety, and difficulty in coping with stressful situations, as well as higher admission to child guidance clinics.

What is the only child like? The popular conception is that the only child is a "spoiled brat," with such undesirable characteristics as dependency, lack of self-control, and self-centered behavior. But researchers present a more positive portrayal of the only child, who often is achievement-oriented and displays a desirable personality, especially in comparison with later-borns and children from large families (Falbo & Poston, 1993; Jiao, Ji, & Jing, 1996).

Keep in mind, though, that birth order by itself often is not a good predictor of behavior. When factors such as age spacing, sex of the siblings, heredity, temperament, parenting styles, peer influences, school influences, sociocultural factors, and so forth are taken into account, they often are more important in determining a child's behavior than birth order.

The Changing Family in a Changing Society

More children are growing up in diverse family structures than ever before. Many mothers spend the greatest part of their day away from their children, even their infants. More than one of every two mothers with a child under the age of 5 is in the labor force; more than two of every three with a child from 6 to 17 years of age is. And the increasing number of children growing up in single-parent families is staggering. As shown in figure 9.6, the United States has the highest percentage of single-parent families, compared with virtually all other countries.

Working Parents Because household operations have become more efficient and family size has decreased in America, it is not certain that when both parents work outside the home, children receive less attention than children in the past whose mothers were not employed. Outside employment—at least for parents with school-age children—might simply be filling time previously taken up by added household burdens and more children. It also cannot be assumed that, if the mother did not go to

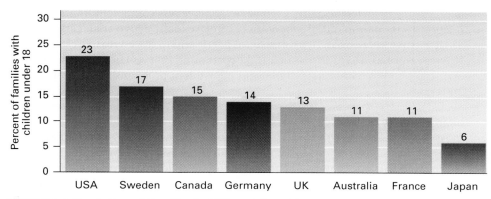

FIGURE 9.6 Single-Parent Families in Different Countries

work, the child would benefit from the time freed up by streamlined household operations and smaller families. Mothering does not always have a positive effect on the child. The educated, nonworking mother may overinvest her energies in her children. This can foster an excess of worry and discourage the child's independence. In such situations, the mother may give more parenting than the child can profitably handle.

As Lois Hoffman (1989) commented, maternal employment is a part of modern life. It is not an aberrant aspect of it but a response to other social changes. The needs of the growing child require the mother to loosen her hold on the child. This task may be easier for the working woman, whose job is an additional source of identity and self-esteem.

A number of researchers have found no detrimental effects of maternal employment on children's development (Gottfried, Gottfried, & Bathurst, 2002; Hoffman & Youngblade, 1999). However, in specific circumstances, work can produce positive or negative effects on parenting. In some families, work-related stress can spill over and harm parenting. In others, a greater sense of overall well-being produced by work can lead to more positive parenting.

Further, researchers are consistently finding when a child's mother works in the first year of life it can have a negative effect on the child's later development (Belsky & Eggebeen, 1991; Hill & others, 2001). For example, a recent major longitudinal study found that the 3-year-old children of mothers who went to work before the children were 9 months old had poorer cognitive outcomes than 3-year-old children who had stayed at home with their mothers in the first nine months of the child's life (Brooks-Gunn, Han, & Waldfogel, 2002). The negative effects of working mothers were less pronounced with the mothers worked less than 30 hours a week, the mothers were more sensitive (responsive and comforting) in their caregiving, and the child care the children received outside the home was higher in quality. Thus, when mothers do go back to work in the infant's first year of life, it clearly is important that they consider how many hours they are going to work, be sensitive in their caregiving, and get the best child care they can afford.

Effects of Divorce on Children   Let's examine some important questions about the effects of divorce on children:

- *Are children better adjusted in intact, never-divorced families than in divorced families?* Most researchers agree that children from divorced families show poorer adjustment than their counterparts in nondivorced families (Amato & Keith, 1991; Hetherington & Kelly, 2002; Hetherington & Stanley-Hagan, 2002) (see figure 9.7). Those that have experienced multiple divorces are at greater risk. Children in divorced families are more likely than children in nondivorced families to have academic problems, to show externalized problems (such as acting out and delinquency) and internalized problems (such as anxiety and

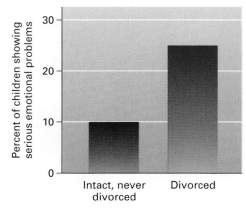

FIGURE 9.7 Divorce and Children's Emotional Problems

In Hetherington's research, 25 percent of children from divorced families showed serious emotional problems compared to only 10 percent of children from intact, never-divorced families. However, keep in mind that a substantial majority (75 percent) of the children from divorced families did not show serious emotional problems.

mhhe●com/
santrockld9

Children and Divorce

Divorce and Family Ties

Divorce Resources

Father Custody

depression), to be less socially responsible, to have less competent intimate relationships, to drop out of school, to become sexually active at an early age, to take drugs, to associate with antisocial peers, and to have low self-esteem (Conger & Chao, 1996). Nonetheless, keep in mind that a majority of children in divorced families do not have significant adjustment problems (Buchanan, 2001).

- *Should parents stay together for the sake of the children?* Whether parents should stay in an unhappy or conflicted marriage for the sake of their children is one of the most commonly asked questions about divorce (Hetherington, 1999, 2000). If the stresses and disruptions in family relationships associated with an unhappy, conflictual marriage that erode the well-being of children are reduced by the move to a divorced, single-parent family, divorce can be advantageous. However, if the diminished resources and increased risks associated with divorce also are accompanied by inept parenting and sustained or increased conflict, not only between the divorced couple but also between the parents, children, and siblings, the best choice for the children would be for an unhappy marriage to be retained (Hetherington & Stanley-Hagan, 2002). These are "ifs," and it is difficult to determine how these will play out when parents either remain together in an acrimonious marriage or become divorced.

- *How much do family processes matter in divorced families?* Family processes matter a lot (Emery & others, 2001; Hetherington & Stanley-Hagan, 2002; Kelly, 2001). When divorced parents' relationship with each other is harmonious and when they use authoritative parenting, the adjustment of children improves (Hetherington, Bridges, & Insabella, 1998). A number of researchers have shown that a disequilibrium, which includes diminished parenting skills, occurs in the year following the divorce but that, by two years after the divorce, restabilization has occurred and parenting skills have improved (Hetherington, 1989).

- *What factors are involved in the child's individual risk and vulnerability in a divorced family?* Among the factors involved in the child's risk and vulnerability are the child's adjustment prior to the divorce, as well as the child's personality and temperament, gender, and custody situation (Hetherington & Stanley-Hagan, 2002). Children whose parents later divorce show poorer adjustment before the breakup (Amato & Booth, 1996).

Personality and temperament also play a role in children's adjustment in divorced families. Children who are socially mature and responsible, who show few behavioral problems, and who have an easy temperament are better able to cope with their parents' divorce. Children with a difficult temperament often have problems in coping with their parents' divorce (Hetherington, 1999).

Earlier studies reported gender differences in response to divorce, with divorce being more negative for girls than boys in mother-custody families. However, more recent studies have shown that gender differences are less pronounced and consistent than was previously believed. Some of the inconsistency may be due to the increase in father custody, joint custody, and increased involvement of noncustodial fathers, especially in their sons' lives. One recent analysis of studies found that children in joint-custody families were better adjusted than children

In Japan, only 6% of children live in single-parent families, compared to 23% in the United States. *What might explain this difference?*

in sole-custody families (Bauserman, 2002). Some studies have shown that boys adjust better in father-custody families, girls in mother-custody families, while other studies have not (Maccoby & Mnookin, 1992; Santrock & Warshak, 1979),

Cultural, Ethnic, and Socioeconomic Variations in Families   Parenting can be influenced by culture, ethnicity, and socioeconomic status. What have cross-cultural studies found about parenting?

Cross-Cultural Studies   Cultures vary on a number of issues involving families, such as what the father's role in the family should be, the extent to which support systems are available to families, and the ways in which children should be disciplined (Harkness & Super, 2002). Although there are cross-cultural variations in parenting (Whiting & Edwards, 1988), in one study of parenting behavior in 186 cultures around the world, the most common pattern was a warm and controlling style, one that was neither permissive nor restrictive (Rohner & Rohner, 1981). The investigators commented that the majority of cultures have discovered, over many centuries, a "truth" that only recently emerged in the Western world—namely, that children's healthy social development is most effectively promoted by love and at least some moderate parental control.

Ethnicity   Families within different ethnic groups in the United States differ in their size, structure, composition, reliance on kinship networks, and levels of income and education (Coll & Pachter, 2002; Parke & Buriel, 1998). Large and extended families are more common among minority groups than among the White majority. For example, 19 percent of Latino families have three or

What are some characteristics of families within different ethnic groups?

more children, compared with 14 percent of African American and 10 percent of White families. African American and Latino children interact more with grandparents, aunts, uncles, cousins, and more-distant relatives than do White children.

Single-parent families are more common among African Americans and Latinos than among White Americans (Weinraub, Houruath, & Gringlas, 2002). In comparison with two-parent households, single parents often have more limited resources of time, money, and energy (Gyamfi, Brooks-Gunn, & Jackson, 2001). Ethnic minority parents also are less educated and more likely to live in low-income circumstances than their White counterparts. Still, many impoverished ethnic minority families manage to find ways to raise competent children (Coll & Pachter, 2002).

Some aspects of home life can help protect ethnic minority children from injustice. The community and the family can filter out destructive racist messages, and parents can present alternative frames of reference to those presented by the majority. The extended family also can serve as an important buffer to stress (McAdoo, 1999, 2002; Wakschlag, Chase-Lansdale, & Brooks-Gunn, 1996). To read further about ethnic minority parenting, see the Sociocultural Worlds of Development box on page 286.

mhhe com/
santrockld9

Family Diversity

Socioeconomic Status   In America and most Western cultures, differences have been found in child rearing among different socioeconomic (SES) groups (Hoff, Laursen, & Tardif, 2002):

- Lower-SES parents (1) are more concerned that their children conform to society's expectations, (2) create a home atmosphere in which it is clear that

Acculturation and Ethnic Minority Parenting

Cynthia Garcia Coll and Lee Pachter (2002) recently described how the cultural context influences ethnic minority parenting. A summary of their views is presented here.

Ethnic minority children and their parents are expected to transcend their own cultural background and incorporate aspects of the dominant culture into their development. Young children's expectations and opportunities for acculturation (the process through which cultural adaptation and change occurs) are mainly influenced by their parents and the extended-family system. The level of family acculturation can affect parenting style by influencing expectations for children's development, parent-child interactions, and the role of the extended family. The appropriateness of caregiving practices may involve conflict or confusion between less acculturated and more acculturated family members. For example, in one study, the level of acculturation and maternal education were the strongest predictors of maternal-infant interaction patterns in Latino families (Perez-Febles, 1992).

In early childhood, the family's level of acculturation continues to influence caregiving practices and important decisions about day care and early childhood education. In day-care centers, school, church, and other community settings, ethnic minority children learn about the dominant culture's values and may be expected to adapt to unfamiliar cultural norms (such as being on the winning team, expressing emotions, and being responsible for one's self). For example, an African American mother might prefer to leave her children with extended-family members while she is at work because historically this has been seen as the best way to cope with an absent mother. However, this well-intentioned, culturally appropriate decision might place the child at an educational and social disadvantage relative to other children of the same age who benefit from preschool experiences that support the transition into the elementary school years.

In middle and late childhood and adolescence, disparity between the acculturation of children, their parents, and the extended family can become magnified. In adolescence, individuals often make decisions about their acculturation status more independently from their family. When immigrant adolescents choose to adopt the values of the dominant U.S. culture (such as unchaperoned dating), they often clash with those of parents and extended-family members who have more traditional values.

It is important to recognize the complexity and individual variation in the acculturative aspects of ethnic minority parenting. This complexity and variation involve the generation of the family members, the recency of their migration, their socioeconomic status, national origin, and many aspects of the social context of the dominant culture in which they now live (such as racial attitudes, quality of schooling, and community support groups).

How is acculturation involved in ethnic minority parenting?

parents have authority over children, (3) use physical punishment more in disciplining their children, and (4) are more directive and less conversational with their children.

- Higher-SES parents (1) are more concerned with developing children's initiative and delay of gratification, (2) create a home atmosphere in which children are more nearly equal participants and in which rules are discussed rather than being laid out in an authoritarian manner, (3) are less likely to use physical punishment, and (4) are less directive and more conversational with their children.

There also are socioeconomic differences in the way that parents think about education (Magnuson & Duncan, 2002; Hoff, Laursen, & Tardiff, 2002). Middle- and upper-income parents more often think of education as something that should be mutually encouraged by parents and teachers. By contrast, low-income parents are more likely to view education as the teacher's job. Thus, increased school-family linkages especially can benefit students from low-income families.

Review and Reflect

2 **Explain how families can influence young children's development**

REVIEW

- What aspects of parenting are linked with young children's development?
- How are sibling relationships and birth order related to young children's development?
- How is children's development affected by having two wage earning parents, having divorced parents, and being part of a particular cultural, ethnic and socioeconomic group?

REFLECT

- Which style or styles of parenting did your mother and father use in rearing you? What effects do you think their parenting styles have on your development?

3 PEER RELATIONS, PLAY, AND TELEVISION

| Peer Relations | Play | Television |

The family is an important social context for children's development. However, children's development also is strongly influenced by what goes on in other social contexts, such as peer relations, play, and television.

Peer Relations

As children grow older, peer relations consume an increasing amount of their time. What is the function of a child's peer group?

Peers are children of about the same age or maturity level. Same-age peer interaction fills a unique role in our culture. Age grading would occur even if schools were not age graded and children were left alone to determine the composition of their own societies. One of the most important functions of the peer group is to provide a source of information and comparison about the world outside the family. Children receive feedback about their abilities from their peer group. Children evaluate what they do in terms of whether it is better than, as good as, or worse than what other children do. It is hard to do this at home because siblings are usually older or younger.

Are peers necessary for development? When peer monkeys who have been reared together are separated, they become depressed and less advanced socially (Suomi, Harlow, & Domek, 1970). The human development literature contains a classic example of the importance of peers in social development. Anna Freud (Freud & Dann, 1951) studied six children from different families who banded together after their parents were killed in World War II. Intensive peer attachment was observed. The children formed a tightly knit group, dependent on one another and aloof with outsiders. Even though deprived of parental care, they neither became delinquent nor developed serious mental disorders.

Thus, good peer relations can be necessary for normal social development. Special concerns focus on children who are withdrawn and aggressive (Coie, 1999; Ladd, 1999). Withdrawn children who are rejected by peers and/or victimized and feeling lonely are at risk for depression. Children who are aggressive with their peers are at

mhhe●com/
santrockld9

Peer Relations

And that park grew up with me; that small world widened as I learned its secrets and boundaries, as I discovered new refuges in its woods and jungles: hidden homes and lairs for the multitudes of imagination, for cowboys and Indians. . . . I used to dawdle on half holidays along the bent and Devon-facing seashore, hoping for gold watches or the skull of a sheep or a message in a bottle to be washed up with the tide.

—DYLAN THOMAS
Welsh Poet , 20th Century

risk for developing a number of problems, including delinquency and dropping out of school. We will have much more to say about peer relations in chapter 11, "Socio-emotional Development in Middle and Late Childhood."

Play

An extensive amount of peer interaction during childhood involves play. Although peer interaction can involve play, social play is but one type of play. *Play* is a pleasurable activity that is engaged in for its own sake. Our coverage of play includes its functions, Parten's classic study of play, and types of play.

Play's Functions   Play is essential to the young child's health. As today's children move into the twenty-first century and continue to experience pressure in their lives, play becomes even more crucial (Van Hoorn & others, 1999). Play increases affiliation with peers, releases tension, advances cognitive development, increases exploration, and provides a safe haven in which to engage in potentially dangerous behavior. Play increases the probability that children will converse and interact with each other. During this interaction, children practice the roles they will assume later in life (Sutton-Smith, 2000).

According to Freud and Erikson, play is an especially useful form of human adjustment, helping the child master anxieties and conflicts. Because tensions are relieved in play, the child can cope with life's problems. Play permits the child to work off excess physical energy and to release pent-up tensions. *Play therapy* allows the child to work off frustrations. Through play therapy, the therapist can analyze the child's conflicts and ways of coping with them. Children may feel less threatened and be more likely to express their true feelings in the context of play.

Piaget (1962) believed that play advances children's cognitive development. At the same time, he said that children's cognitive development *constrains* the way they play. Play permits children to practice their competencies and acquired skills in a relaxed, pleasurable way. Piaget thought that cognitive structures need to be exercised, and play provides the perfect setting for this exercise. For example, children who have just learned to add or multiply begin to play with numbers in different ways as they perfect these operations, laughing as they do so.

Vygotsky (1962), whose developmental theory was discussed in chapter 8, also believed that play is an excellent setting for cognitive development. He was especially interested in the symbolic and make-believe aspects of play, as when a child substitutes a stick for a horse and rides the stick as if it were a horse. For young children, the imaginary situation is real. Parents should encourage such imaginary play, because it advances the child's cognitive development, especially creative thought.

Daniel Berlyne (1960) described play as exciting and pleasurable in itself because it satisfies our exploratory drive. This drive involves curiosity and a desire for information about something new or unusual. Play is a means whereby children can safely explore and seek out new information—something they might not otherwise do. Play encourages this exploratory behavior by offering children the possibilities of novelty, complexity, uncertainty, surprise, and incongruity.

Parten's Classic Study of Play   Many years ago, Mildred Parten (1932) developed an elaborate classification of children's play. Based on observations of children in free play at nursery school, Parten arrived at these play categories:

- **Unoccupied play** is not play as it is commonly understood. The child may stand in one spot or perform random movements that do not seem to have a goal. In most nursery schools, unoccupied play is less frequent than other forms of play.
- **Solitary play** happens when the child plays alone and independently of others. The child seems engrossed in the activity and does not care much about anything else that is happening. Two- and 3-year-olds engage more frequently in solitary play than older preschoolers do.

unoccupied play Play in which the child is not engaging in play as it is commonly understood and might stand in one spot, or perform random movements that do not seem to have a goal.

solitary play Play in which the child plays alone and independently of others.

Mildred Parten classified play into six categories. *Study this photograph. Which of Parten's categories are reflected in the behavior of the children?*

- **Onlooker play** takes place when the child watches other children play. The child may talk with other children and ask questions but does not enter into their play behavior. The child's active interest in other children's play distinguishes onlooker play from unoccupied play.
- **Parallel play** occurs when the child plays separately from others but with toys like those the others are using or in a manner that mimics their play. The older children are, the less frequently they engage in this type of play. However, even older preschool children engage in parallel play quite often.
- **Associative play** involves social interaction with little or no organization. In this type of play, children seem to be more interested in each other than in the tasks they are performing. Borrowing or lending toys and following or leading one another in line are examples of associative play.
- **Cooperative play** consists of social interaction in a group with a sense of group identity and organized activity. Children's formal games, competition aimed at winning, and groups formed by the teacher for doing things together are examples of cooperative play. Cooperative play is the prototype for the games of middle childhood. Little cooperative play is seen in the preschool years.

Types of Play Parten's categories represent one way of thinking about the different types of play. However, today researchers and practitioners who are involved with children's play believe other types of play are important in children's development. Whereas Parten's categories emphasize the role of play in the child's social world, the contemporary perspective on play emphasizes both the cognitive and the social aspects of play. Among the most widely studied types of children's play today are sensorimotor and practice play, pretense/symbolic play, social play, constructive play, and games (Bergin, 1988). We will consider each of these types of play in turn.

Sensorimotor and Practice Play **Sensorimotor play** is behavior that is engaged in by infants to derive pleasure from exercising their existing sensorimotor schemas. The development of sensorimotor play follows Piaget's description of sensorimotor thought, which we discussed in chapter 6. Infants initially engage in exploratory and playful visual and motor transactions in the second quarter of the first year of life. For example, at 9 months of age, infants begin to select novel objects for exploration and play, especially those that are responsive, such as toys that make noise or bounce. At 12 months of age, infants enjoy making things work and exploring cause and effect.

onlooker play Play in which the child watches other children play.

parallel play Play in which the child plays separately from others, but with toys like those the others are using or in a manner that mimics their play.

associative play Play that involves social interaction with little or no organization.

cooperative play Play that involves social interaction in a group with a sense of group identity and organized activity.

sensorimotor play Behavior engaged in by infants to derive pleasure from exercising their existing sensorimotor schemas.

Practice play involves the repetition of behavior when new skills are being learned or when physical or mental mastery and coordination of skills are required for games or sports. Sensorimotor play, which often involves practice play, is primarily confined to infancy, while practice play can be engaged in throughout life. During the preschool years, children often engage in play that involves practicing various skills. While practice play declines in the elementary school years, practice play activities such as running, jumping, sliding, twirling, and throwing balls or other objects are frequently observed on the playgrounds at elementary schools.

Pretense/Symbolic Play Pretense/symbolic play occurs when the child transforms the physical environment into a symbol. Between 9 and 30 months of age, children increase their use of objects in symbolic play. They learn to transform objects—substituting them for other objects and acting toward them as if they were these other objects. For example, a preschool child treats a table as if it were a car and says, "I'm fixing the car," as he grabs a leg of the table.

Many experts on play consider the preschool years the "golden age" of symbolic/pretense play that is dramatic or sociodramatic in nature. This type of make-believe play often appears at about 18 months of age and reaches a peak at 4 to 5 years of age, then gradually declines.

Social Play Social play is play that involves interaction with peers. Parten's categories, described earlier, are oriented toward social play. Social play with peers increases dramatically during the preschool years.

Constructive Play Constructive play combines sensorimotor and practice repetitive activity with symbolic representation of ideas. Constructive play occurs when children engage in self-regulated creation or construction of a product or a problem solution. Constructive play increases in the preschool years as symbolic play increases and sensorimotor play decreases. In the preschool years, some practice play is replaced by constructive play. For example, instead of moving their fingers around and around in finger paint (practice play), children are more likely to draw the outline of a house or a person in the paint (constructive play). Some researchers have found that constructive play is the most common type of play during the preschool years (Rubin, Maioni, & Hornung, 1976). Constructive play is also a frequent form of play in the elementary school years, both in and out of the classroom. Constructive play is one of the few playlike activities allowed in work-centered classrooms. For example, having children create a play about a social studies topic involves constructive play. Whether children consider such activities to be play usually depends on whether they get to choose whether to do it (it is play) or whether the teacher imposes it (it is not play), as well as whether it is enjoyable (it is play(or not)it is not play) (King, 1982).

Constructive play also can be used in the elementary school years to foster academic skill learning, thinking skills, and problem solving. Many educators plan classroom activities that include humor, encourage playing with ideas, and promote creativity (Bergin, 1988). Educators also often support the performance of plays, the writing of imaginative stories, the expression of artistic abilities, and the playful exploration of computers and other technological equipment. However, distinctions between work and play frequently become blurred in the elementary school classroom. Think of constructive play as a midway point between play and work.

Games Activities that are engaged in for pleasure. **Games** include rules and often competition with one or more individuals. Preschool children may begin to participate in social game play that involves simple rules of reciprocity and turn taking. However, games take on a much stronger role in the lives of elementary school children. In one study, the highest incidence of game playing occurred between 10 and 12 years of age (Eiferman, 1971). After age 12, games decline in popularity (Bergin, 1988).

practice play Play that involves repetition of behavior when new skills are being learned or when physical or mental mastery and coordination of skills are required for games or sports.

pretense/symbolic play Play in which the child transforms the physical environment into a symbol.

social play Play that involves social interactions with peers.

constructive play Play that combines sensorimotor/practice repetitive activity with symbolic representation of ideas. Constructive play occurs when children engage in self-regulated creation or construction of a product or a problem solution.

games Activities engaged in for pleasure that include rules and often competition with one or more individuals.

Television

Few developments in society in the second half of the twentieth century had a greater impact on children than television (Bryant & Bryant, 2001; Comstock & Scharrar, 1999; Murray, 2000). Many children spend more time in front of the television set than they do with their parents. Although it is only one of the many forms of mass media that affect children's behavior, television is the most influential. The persuasive capabilities of television are staggering (Kotler, Wright, & Huston, 2001). The 20,000 hours of television watched by the time the average American adolescent graduates from high school are greater than the number of hours spent in the classroom.

Television's Many Roles   Television can have a negative influence by taking children away from homework, making them passive learners, teaching them stereotypes, providing them with violent models of aggression, and presenting them with unrealistic views of the world. However, television can have a positive influence on children's development by presenting motivating educational programs, increasing their information about the world beyond their immediate environment, and providing models of prosocial behavior (Clifford, Gunter, & McAleer, 1995).

Amount of Television Watching by Children   Just how much television do young children watch? They watch a lot. In the 1990s, children watched an average of 26 hours of television each week, which is more than any other activity except sleep (National Center for Children Exposed to Violence, 2001). As shown in figure 9.8, considerably more children in the United States than their counterparts in other developed countries watch television for long periods. For example, seven times as many 9-year-olds in the United States as their counterparts in Switzerland watch television more than 5 hours a day.

Effects of Television on Children's Aggression and Prosocial Behavior   A special concern is the extent to which children are exposed to violence and aggression on television. Up to 80 percent of the prime-time shows include violent acts, including beatings, shootings, and stabbings. The frequency of violence increases on the Saturday morning cartoon shows, which average more than 25 violent acts per hour.

What are the effects of television violence on children's aggression? Does television merely stimulate a child to go out and buy a *Star Wars* ray gun, or can it trigger an attack on a playmate? When children grow up, can television violence increase the likelihood they will violently attack someone?

In one longitudinal study, the amount of violence viewed on television at age 8 was significantly related to the seriousness of criminal acts performed as an adult (Huesmann, 1986). In another study, long-term exposure to television violence was

"Mrs. Horton, could you stop by school today?"
Copyright © Martha F. Campbell.

Children's Television Workshop
Television and Violence
Television and Children

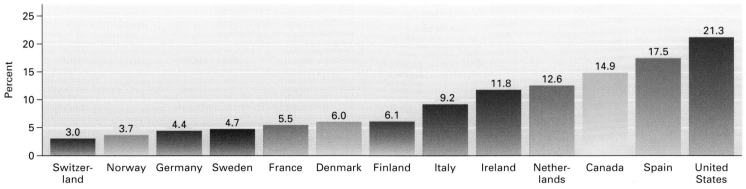

FIGURE 9.8 **Percentage of 9-Year-Old Children Who Report Watching More Than Five Hours of Television per Weekday**

Television is a medium of entertainment which permits millions of people to listen to the same joke at the same time, and yet remain lonesome.

—T. S. ELIOT
*American-Born English Poet,
20th Century*

significantly related to the likelihood of aggression in 1,565 12- to 17-year-old boys (Belson, 1978). Boys who watched the most aggression on television were the most likely to commit a violent crime, swear, be aggressive in sports, threaten violence toward another boy, write slogans on walls, or break windows. These studies are *correlational*, so we cannot conclude from them that television violence *causes* aggressive behavior. In one experiment, children were randomly assigned to one of two groups: One group watched television shows taken directly from violent Saturday morning cartoon offerings on 11 different days; the second group watched television cartoon shows with all of the violence removed (Steur, Applefield, & Smith, 1971). The children were then observed during play at their preschool. The preschool children who saw the TV cartoon shows with violence kicked, choked, and pushed their playmates more than did the preschool children who watched nonviolent TV cartoon shows. Because the children were randomly assigned to the two conditions (TV cartoons with violence versus nonviolent TV cartoons), we can conclude that exposure to TV violence *caused* the increased aggression in the children in this investigation.

Television also can teach children that it is better to behave in positive, prosocial ways than in negative, antisocial ways (Dorr, Rabin, & Irlin, 2002; Wilson, 2001). Aimee Leifer (1973) demonstrated that television is associated with prosocial behavior in young children. She selected a number of episodes from the television show *Sesame Street* that reflected positive social interchanges. She was especially interested in situations that taught children how to use their social skills. For example, in one interchange, two men were fighting over the amount of space available to them. They gradually began to cooperate and to share the space. Children who watched these episodes copied these behaviors, and in later social situations they applied the prosocial lessons they had learned.

Some critics have argued that research results do not warrant the conclusion that TV violence causes aggression (Freedman, 1984). But many experts insist that TV violence can cause aggressive or antisocial behavior in children (Anderson & Bushman, 2002; Bushman & Huesmann, 2001; Perse, 2001). Of course, television violence is not the *only* cause of aggression. There is no *one* cause of any social behavior. Aggression, like all other social behaviors, has multiple determinants (Donnerstein, 2002). The link between TV violence and aggression in children is influenced by children's aggressive tendencies and by their attitudes toward violence and monitoring of children's exposure to it.

Television and Cognitive Development   Children bring various cognitive skills and abilities to their television viewing experience (Rabin & Dorr, 1995). Several important cognitive shifts take place between early childhood and middle and late childhood (Wilson, 2001). Preschool children often focus on the most striking perceptual features of a TV program and are likely to have difficulty in distinguishing reality from fantasy in the portrayals. As children enter elementary school, they are better able to link scenes together and draw causal conclusions from narratives. Judgments of reality also become more accurate in older children.

How does television influence children's creativity and verbal skills? Television is negatively related to children's creativity (Williams, 1986). Also, because television is primarily a visual modality, verbal skills—especially expressive language—are enhanced more by aural or print exposure (Beagles-Roos & Gat, 1983). Educational programming for young children can promote creativity and imagination, possibly because it has a slower pace, and auditory and visual modalities are better coordinated (Anderson & others, 2001). Newer technologies, especially interactive television, hold promise for motivating children to learn and become more exploratory in solving problems (Singer, 1993).

In one recent longitudinal study, viewing educational programs as preschoolers was associated with a host of desirable characteristics in adolescence: getting higher grades, reading more books, placing a higher value on achievement, being more creative, and acting less aggressively (Anderson & others, 2001). These associations were

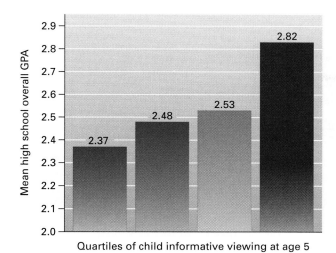

FIGURE 9.9 Educational TV Viewing in educational TV and High School Grade Point Average for Boys

When boys watched more educational television (especially *Sesame Street*) as preschoolers, they had higher grade point averages in high school (Anderson & others, 2001). The graph displays the boys' early TV viewing patterns in quartiles and the means of their grade point averages. The bar on the left is for the lowest 25 percent of boys who viewed educational TV programs, the next bar the next 25 percent, and so on, with the bar on the right for the 25 percent of the boys who watched the most educational TV shows as preschoolers.

more consistent for boys than girls. Figure 9.9 shows the results for boys' high school grade point average. However, girls who were more frequent viewers of violent TV programs in the preschool years had lower grades in adolescence than girls who infrequently watched violent TV programs in the preschool years.

Review and Reflect

3 Describe the roles of peers, play, and television in young children's development

REVIEW

- How do peers affect young children's development?
- What are some theories and types of play?
- How does television influence children's development?

REFLECT

- What guidelines would you recommend to parents that you believe would help them to make television a more positive influence on their children's development? Consider such factors as the child's age, the child's activities other than TV, the parents' patterns of interaction with the children, and types of TV shows.

Reach Your Learning Goals

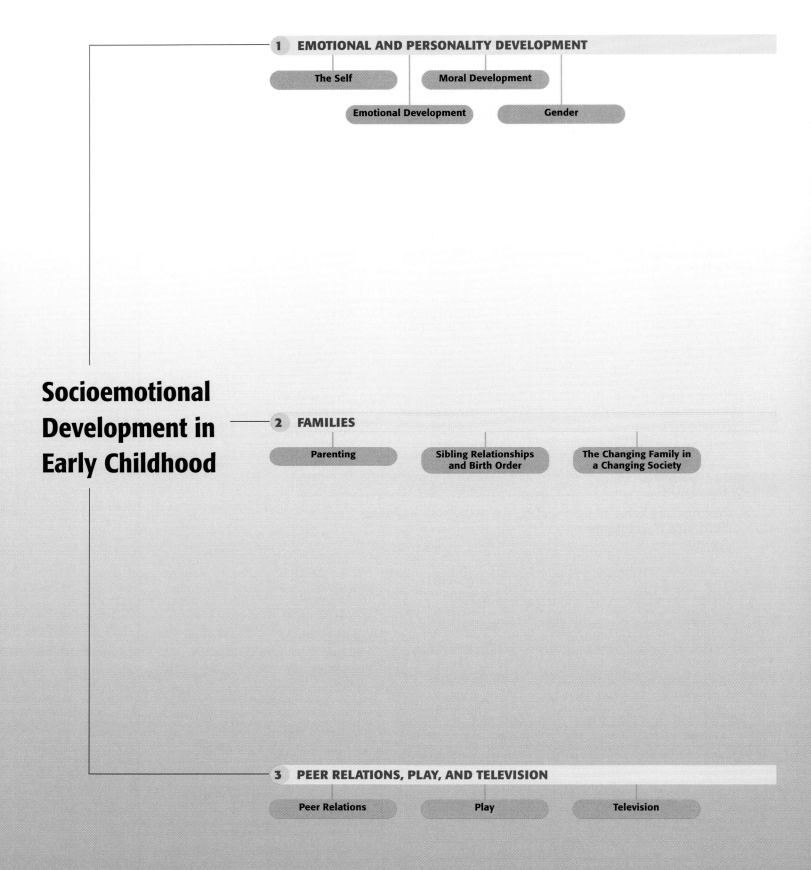

Socioemotional Development in Early Childhood

1 EMOTIONAL AND PERSONALITY DEVELOPMENT

- The Self
- Moral Development
- Emotional Development
- Gender

2 FAMILIES

- Parenting
- Sibling Relationships and Birth Order
- The Changing Family in a Changing Society

3 PEER RELATIONS, PLAY, AND TELEVISION

- Peer Relations
- Play
- Television

Summary

1 **Discuss emotional and personality development in early childhood**

- Erikson believed that early childhood is a period when development involves resolving the conflict of initiative versus guilt. While a rudimentary form of self-understanding occurs at about 18 months in the form of self-recognition, in early childhood the physical self, or active self, emerges.
- Preschoolers become more adept at talking about their own and others' emotions. Two- and 3-year-olds continue to increase the number of terms they use to describe emotion and learn more about the causes and consequences of feelings. At 4 to 5 years of age, children show an increased ability to reflect on emotions and understand that a single event can elicit different emotions in different people. They also show a growing awareness about controlling and managing emotions to meet social standards. Self-conscious emotions, such as pride, shame, and guilt, increase in early childhood.
- Moral development involves thoughts, feelings, and actions regarding rules and regulations about what people should do in their interactions with others. Developmentalists study how children think, behave, and feel about such rules and regulations. Piaget distinguished between the heteronomous morality of younger children and the autonomous morality of older children. Moral behavior is emphasized by behavioral and social cognitive theorists. They believe there is considerable situational variability in moral behavior and that self-control is an important aspect of understanding children's moral behavior. Freud's psychoanalytic theory emphasizes the importance of feelings with regard to the development of the superego, the moral branch of personality, which develops through the Oedipus conflict and identification with the same-sex parent. In Freud's view, children conform to societal standards to avoid guilt. Positive emotions, such as empathy, also are an important aspect of understanding moral feelings. In Damon's view, both positive and negative emotions contribute to children's moral development.
- Gender refers to the social and psychological dimensions of being male or female. Gender identity is acquired by 3 years of age for most children. A gender role is a set of expectations that prescribes how females or males should think, act, and feel. The 23rd pair of chromosomes may have two X chromosomes to produce a female, or one X and one Y chromosome to produce a male. The two main classes of sex hormones are estrogens, which are dominant in females, and androgens, which are dominant in males. Biology is not completely destiny in gender development; children's socialization experiences matter a great deal. Both psychoanalytic theory and social cognitive theory emphasize the adoption of parents' gender characteristics. Peers are especially adept at rewarding gender-appropriate behavior. Both cognitive developmental and gender schema theories emphasize the role of cognition in gender development.

2 **Explain how families can influence young children's development**

- Authoritarian, authoritative, neglectful, and indulgent are four main parenting styles. Authoritative parenting is the style most often associated with children's social competence. Physical punishment is widely used by U.S. parents but there are a number of reasons why it is not a good choice. An understanding of child abuse requires information about cultural and familial influences. Child maltreatment places the child at risk for a number of developmental problems. Coparenting has positive effects on children's development. In today's society, an unfortunate theme is that parenting can be done quickly. However, good parenting takes extensive time and effort.
- Siblings interact with each other in positive and negative ways. Birth order is related in certain ways to child characteristics, but some critics argue that birth order by itself is not a good predictor of behavior.
- Sociocultural and economic factors affect children's development in many ways. In general, having both parents employed full-time outside the home has not been shown to have negative effects on children. However, in specfic circumstances, when a mother works outside the home, such as when the infant is less than 1 year old, negative effects can occur. Divorce can have negative effects on children's adjustment, but so can an acrimonious relationship between parents who stay together for their children's sake. If divorced parents develop a harmonious relationship and practice authoritative parenting, children's adjustment improves. Authoritative parenting is the most widely used style around the world. Cultures vary on a number of issues regarding families. African American and Latino children are more likely than White American children to live in single-parent families and larger families and to have extended family connections. Lower-SES parents create a home atmosphere that involves more authority and physical punishment with children than higher-SES parents. Higher-SES parents are more concerned about developing children's initiative and delay of gratification.

3 **Describe the roles of peers, play, and television in young children's development**

- Peers are powerful socialization agents. Peers are children who are about the same age or maturity level. Peers provide a source of information and comparison about the world outside the family.
- Play's functions include affiliation with peers, tension release, advances in cognitive development, exploration, and provision of a safe haven. Parten developed the categories of unoccupied, solitary, onlooker, parallel, associative, and cooperative play. The contemporary perspective on play emphasizes both the cognitive and the social aspects of play.

Among the most widely studied aspects of children's play today are sensorimotor play, practice play, pretense/symbolic play, social play, constructive play and games.

• Television can have both negative influences (such as turning children into passive learners and presenting them with aggressive models) and positive influences (such as presenting motivating educational programs and providing models of prosocial behavior) on children's development. Children watch huge amounts of television. TV violence is not the only cause of children's aggression, but it can induce aggression. Prosocial behavior on TV is associated with increased positive behavior by children. Children's cognitive skills influence their TV-viewing experiences. Television viewing is negatively related to children's creativity and verbal skills.

Key Terms

Key People

Taking It to the Net

1. Doris and Ken are in the process of getting a divorce. Both of them want full custody of their two children, Kevin, age 10, and Chrissie, age 3. Although the divorce process has been very stressful for both of them, Doris and Ken share concerns about the effects their divorce might have on their children. What immediate effects can they expect, especially given the context of the custody battle? How might Kevin's reactions differ from Chrissie's? What might the long-term effects of the divorce be on their children?

2. Karen's mother is concerned about how to best help her daughter, Teresa, whose husband has abandoned her and their 5-year-old son. What are some of the challenges that Teresa may have to face and how can her mother help her through this difficult time?

3. Jonathan and Diedre want to shield their children from the violence on television, but they are not sure how to go about it—other than by not allowing any television viewing at all. What recommendations does the APA have for parents?

Connect to www.mhhe.com/santrockld9 to research the answers and complete these exercises.

E-Learning Tools

To help you master the material in this chapter, you'll find a number of valuable study tools on the Student CD-ROM that accompanies this book. In addition, visit the Online Learning Center for *Life-Span Development*, ninth edition, where you'll find these valuable resources for chapter 9, "Socioemotional Development in Early Childhood."

- What might your parenting style be, based on what you've read in this chapter? Use the self-assessment, *My Parenting Style*, to get a better idea of what it might be.

- View video clips of key researchers, including Judy Dunn as she discusses her research on sibling relationships.
- Build your decision-making skills by trying your hand at the parenting and education "Scenarios."

Middle and Late Childhood

*Blessed be childhood,
which brings
something of heaven
into the midst of our
rough earthliness.*
—HENRI FREDERIC AMIEL
Swiss Poet, Philosopher, 19th Century

In middle and late childhood, children are on a different plane, belonging to a generation and feeling all their own. It is the wisdom of the human life span that at no time are children more ready to learn than during the period of expansive imagination at the end of early childhood. Children develop a sense of wanting to make things—and not just to make them, but to make them well and even perfectly. Their thirst is to know and to understand. They are remarkable for their intelligence and for their curiosity. Their parents continue to be important influences in their lives, but their growth also is shaped by successive choirs of friends. They don't think much about the future or about the past, but they enjoy the present moment. Section 5 consists of two chapters, "Physical and Cognitive Development in Middle and Late Childhood" (chapter 10) and "Socioemotional Development in Middle and Late Childhood" (chapter 11).

CHAPTER 10

Every forward step we take we leave some phantom of ourselves behind.

—JOHN LANCASTER SPALDING
American Educator, 19th Century

Physical and Cognitive Development in Middle and Late Childhood

Chapter Outline

PHYSICAL CHANGES AND HEALTH

Body Growth and Proportion

Motor Development

Exercise and Sports

Health, Illness, and Disease

CHILDREN WITH DISABILITIES

Who Are Children with Disabilities?

Learning Disabilities

Attention Deficit Hyperactivity Disorder (ADHD)

Educational Issues

COGNITIVE CHANGES

Piaget's Theory

Information Processing

Intelligence

Creativity

LANGUAGE DEVELOPMENT

Vocabulary and Grammar

Reading

Bilingualism

Learning Goals

1 *D*escribe physical changes and health in middle and late childhood

2 *I*dentify children with disabilities and issues in educating them

3 *E*xplain cognitive changes in middle and late childhood

4 *D*iscuss language development in middle and late childhood

Some critics argue that Jessica Dubroff was not allowed to be a child. *Did her parents act irresponsibly?*

Images of Life-Span Development
Jessica Dubroff, Child Pilot

Many parents want their children to be gifted and provide them with many opportunities to achieve this status. Child psychologists believe that some parents go too far and push their children too much, especially when they try to get their children to be a child star in a particular area, like figure skating, tennis, or music. To think further about parents' efforts to get their children to achieve lofty accomplishments, let's examine the tragic story of Jessica Dubroff.

In 1996, Jessica Dubroff took off in cold rain and died when her single-engine Cessna nosedived into a highway. Seven-year-old Jessica was only 4 feet, 2 inches tall and weighed just 55 pounds. What was she doing flying an airplane, especially in quest of being the youngest person ever to fly across the continent?

Jessica's parents seemed determined to give their daughter independence from the beginning. She was delivered in a birthing tub without benefit of a doctor or midwife. Her parents' philosophy was that real life is the best tutor, experience the best preparation for life. As a result, they kept Jessica and her brother (age 9) and sister (age 3) at home without filing a home-schooling plan with local authorities. Jessica had no dolls, only tools. Instead of studying grammar, she did chores and sought what her mother called "mastery." Jessica had few, if any, boundaries. Parenting mainly consisted of cheerleading.

Jessica became interested in flying after her parents gave her an airplane ride for her sixth birthday, only 23 months before her fatal crash. Her father admitted that the cross-country flight was his idea, but claimed that he had presented it to Jessica as a choice. The father became her press agent, courting TV, radio, and newspapers to publicize her flight.

Did Jessica grow up too soon? Did her parents push her too much to achieve in a single activity? Should they instead have encouraged her to have a more well-rounded life and one more typical for her age? Were her parents living vicariously through her?

Later in this chapter, we will explore the real nature of giftedness in children. This chapter is about physical and cognitive development in middle and late childhood. To begin, we will explore some changes in physical development.

1 PHYSICAL CHANGES AND HEALTH

Body Growth and Proportion

Motor Development

Exercise and Sports

Health, Illness, and Disease

Continued change characterizes children's bodies during middle and late childhood and their motor skills improve. It is important for children to engage in regular exercise and avoid illness and disease.

Body Growth and Proportion

The period of middle and late childhood involves slow, consistent growth. This is a period of calm before the rapid growth spurt of adolescence. During the elementary school years, children grow an average of 2 to 3 inches a year until, at the age of 11, the average girl is 4 feet, 10¼ inches tall, and the average boy is 4 feet, 9 inches tall. During the middle and late childhood years, children gain about 5 to 7 pounds a year. The weight increase is due mainly to increases in the size of the skeletal and muscular systems, as well as the size of some body organs. Muscle mass and strength gradually increase as "baby fat" decreases. The loose movements and knock knees of early childhood give way to improved muscle tone. The increase in muscular strength is due to heredity and to exercise. Children also double their strength capabilities during these years. Because of their greater number of muscle cells, boys are usually stronger than girls.

Proportional changes are among the most pronounced physical changes in middle and late childhood. Head circumference, waist circumference, and leg length decrease in relation to body height (Wong & others, 2001). A less noticeable physical change is that bones continue to ossify during middle and late childhood but yield to pressure and pull more than mature bones.

Motor Development

During middle and late childhood, children's motor development becomes much smoother and more coordinated than it was in early childhood. For example, only one child in a thousand can hit a tennis ball over the net at the age of 3, yet by the age of 10 or 11 most children can learn to play the sport. Running, climbing, skipping rope, swimming, bicycle riding, and skating are just a few of the many physical skills elementary school children can master. In gross motor skills involving large activity, boys usually outperform girls.

As children move through the elementary school years, they gain greater control over their bodies and can sit and attend for longer periods of time. However, elementary school children are far from having physical maturity, and they need to be active. Elementary school children become more fatigued by long periods of sitting than by running, jumping, or bicycling. Physical action is essential for these children to refine their developing skills, such as batting a ball, skipping rope, or balancing on a beam. An important principle of practice for elementary school children, therefore, is that they should be engaged in *active*, rather than passive, activities.

Increased myelination of the central nervous system is reflected in the improvement of fine motor skills during middle and late childhood. Children's hands are used more adroitly as tools. Six-year-olds can hammer, paste, tie shoes, and fasten clothes. By 7 years of age, children's hands have become steadier. At this age, children prefer a pencil to a crayon for printing, and reversal of letters is less common. Printing becomes smaller. At 8 to 10 years of age, the hands can be used independently with more ease and precision. Fine motor coordination develops to the point at which children can write rather than print words. Letter size becomes smaller and more even. At 10 to 12 years of age, children begin to show manipulative skills similar to the abilities of adults. The complex, intricate, and rapid movements needed to produce fine-quality crafts or to play a difficult piece on a musical instrument can be mastered. Girls usually outperform boys in fine motor skills.

Exercise and Sports

How much exercise do children get? What are children's sports like?

Exercise Are children getting enough exercise? In a 1997 national poll, only 22 percent of children in grades 4 through 12 were physically active for 30 minutes every day of the week (Harris, 1997). Their parents said their children were too busy watching TV, spending time on the computer, or playing video games to exercise much. Boys were more physically active at all ages than girls. In one historical comparison, the percentage of children involved in daily P.E. programs in schools decreased by 80 percent in 1969 to 20 percent in 1999 (Health Management Resources, 2001) (see figure 10.1).

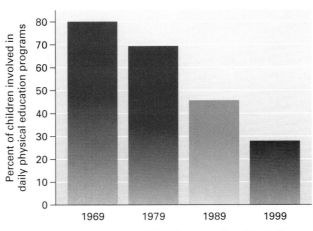

FIGURE 10.1 Percentage of Children Involved in Daily Physical Education Programs in the United States from 1969 to 1999

There has been a dramatic drop in the percentage of children participating in daily physical education programs in the United States from 80 percent in 1969 to only 20 percent in 1999.

mhhe●com/
santrockld9

**Child Health
Child Health Guide**

Here are some ways to get children to exercise more:

- Offer more physical activity programs run by volunteers at school facilities.
- Improve physical fitness activities in schools.
- Have children plan community and school activities that really interest them.
- Encourage families to focus more on physical activity and parents to exercise more (in the national poll more than 50 percent of the parents engaged in no vigorous physical activities on a regular basis).

Sports Sports have become an integral part of American culture. Thus, it is not surprising that more and more children become involved in sports every year. Both in public schools and in community agencies, children's sports programs that involve baseball, soccer, football, basketball, swimming, gymnastics, and other activities have grown to the extent that they have changed the shape of many children's lives.

Participation in sports can have both positive and negative consequences for children. Children's participation in sports can provide exercise, opportunities to learn how to compete, self-esteem, and a setting for developing peer relations and friendships. However, sports also can have negative outcomes for children: the pressure to achieve and win, physical injuries, a distraction from academic work, and unrealistic expectations for success as an athlete (Cheng & others, 2000; Committee on Sports Medicine and Fitness, 2000). Few people challenge the value of sports for children when conducted as part of a school physical education or intramural program. However, some critics question the appropriateness of highly competitive, win-oriented sports teams in schools and communities (Kelm & others, 2001; Washington & others, 2001).

The negative consequences of children's sports was tragically played out when Thomas Junta beat to death another father after their sons' ice hockey game in July 2001. He was sentenced to 6 to 10 years in prison in January 2002.

Six-year-old Zhang Liyin (*third from left*) hopes to someday become an Olympic gymnastics champion. Attending the sports school is considered an outstanding privilege; only 260,000 of China's 200 million children are given this opportunity. *What positive and negative outcomes might children experience from playing sports? Are some sports programs, such as China's sports schools, too intense for children? Should children experience a more balanced life? Is there too much emphasis on sports in the United States?*

Health, Illness, and Disease

For the most part, middle and late childhood is a time of excellent health. Disease and death are less prevalent in this period than in others in childhood and adolescence.

Accidents and Injuries The most common cause of severe injury and death in middle and late childhood is motor vehicle accidents, either as a pedestrian or as a passenger (Wong & others, 2001). The use of safety-belt restraints is important in reducing the severity of motor vehicle injuries (Bolen, Bland, & Sacks, 1999). The school-age child's motivation to ride a bicycle increases the risk of accidents. Other serious injuries involve skateboards, roller skates, and other sports equipment.

Most accidents occur in or near the child's home or school. The most effective prevention strategy is to educate the child about the hazards of risk taking and improper use of equipment. Appropriate safety helmets, protective eye and mouth shields, and protective padding are recommended for children who engage in active sports.

Cancer Cancer is the second leading cause of death (with injuries the leading cause) in children 5 to 14 years of age. Three percent of all children's deaths in this age period are due to cancer. In the 15 to 24 age group, cancer accounts for 13 percent of all deaths. Currently, 1 in every 330 children in the United States develops cancer before the age of 19. Morever, the incidence of cancer in children is increasing (Neglia & others, 2001).

Child cancers have a different profile from adult cancers. Adult cancers attack mainly the lungs, colon, breast, prostate, and pancreas. Child cancers mainly attack the white blood cells (leukemia), brain, bone, lymph system, muscles, kidneys, and nervous system. All are characterized by an uncontrolled proliferation of abnormal cells.

As indicated in figure 10.2, the most common cancer in children is leukemia, a cancer of the tissues that make blood cells. In leukemia, the bone marrow makes an abundance of white blood cells that don't function properly. They invade the marrow and crowd out normal cells, making the child susceptible to bruising and infection. Lymphomas arise in the lymph system. Childhood lymphomas spread to the central nervous system and bone marrow.

Child life specialists are among the health professionals who work to make the lives of children with diseases such as cancer less stressful. To read about the work of child life specialist Sharon McCleod, see the Careers in Life-Span Development insert.

Obesity In one recent analysis, the prevalence of being overweight from 6 to 11 years of age in the United States increased 325 percent from 1974 to 1999 (NHANES, 2001). Girls are more likely than boys to be obese. Obesity at 6 years of age results in approximately a 25 percent probability that the child will be obese as an adult; obesity at age 12 results in approximately a 75 percent chance that the adolescent will be obese as an adult.

Inadequate levels of exercise are linked with being overweight. A child's activity level is influenced by heredity but also by a child's motivation to

Careers in Life-Span Development

Sharon McLeod, Child Life Specialist

Sharon McLeod is a child life specialist who is clinical director of the Child Life and Recreational Therapy Department at the Children's Hospital Medical Center in Cincinnati ◀ p.37.

Under McLeod's direction, the goals of the Child Life Department are to promote children's optimal growth and development, reduce the stress of health-care experiences, and provide support to child patients and their families. These goals are accomplished through therapeutic play and developmentally appropriate activities, educating and psychologically preparing children for medical procedures, and serving as a resource for parents and other professionals regarding children development and health-care issues.

In McLeod's view, "Human growth and development, coping theory, and play provide the foundation for the profession of child life. My most beneficial moments as a student were during my fieldwork and internship when I experienced hands-on theories and concepts learned in courses."

Sharon McLeod, child life specialist, working with a child at Children's Hospital Medical Center in Cincinnati.

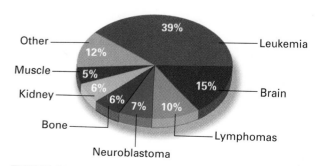

FIGURE 10.2 Types of Cancer in Children

Overweight Children

Heart Smart

Diseases and Illnesses

Medical Links

Cancer in Children

engage in energetic activities and caregivers who model an active lifestyle and provide children with opportunities to be active (French, Story, & Jeffery, 2001; Wardle & others, 2001).

The context in which children eat can influence their eating habits and weight. In one recent study, children who ate with their families were more likely to eat low-fat foods (such as low-fat milk and salad dressing and lean meats), more vegetables, and drank fewer sodas than children who ate alone (Cullen, 2001). In this study, overweight children ate 50 percent of their meals in front of a TV, compared to only 35 percent of normal-weight children.

Obesity is a risk factor for many medical and psychological problems (Kiess & others, 2001; Polivy & Herman, 2002). Obese children can develop pulmonary problems and hip problems. Obese children also are prone to have high blood pressure and elevated blood cholesterol levels. Low self-esteem and depression are common outgrowths of obesity. Furthermore, obese children often are excluded from peer groups. In chapter 14, we will discuss the most effective treatments for obesity, with a special focus on the importance of exercise.

Review and Reflect

1 **Describe physical changes and health in middle and late childhood**

REVIEW

- What are some changes in body growth and proportion in middle and late childhood?
- How do children's motor skills develop in middle and late childhood?
- What roles do exercise and sports play in children's lives?
- What are some characteristics of health, illness, and disease in middle and late childhood?

REFLECT

- Should parents be banned from coaching their children in sports and/or watching their children play in sports? Explain.

2 CHILDREN WITH DISABILITIES

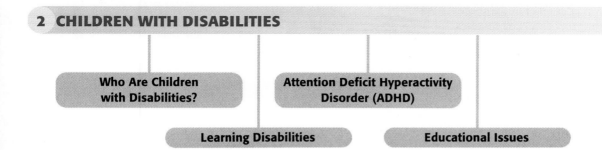

The elementary school years are a time when children with disabilities become more sensitive about their differentness and how it is perceived by others.

Who Are Children with Disabilities?

Approximately 10 percent of all children in the United States receive special education or related services. Figure 10.3 shows the approximate percentages of children with

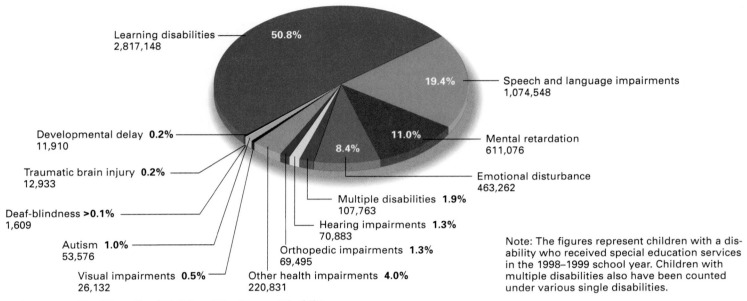

FIGURE 10.3 The Diversity of Children Who Have a Disability

Note: The figures represent children with a disability who received special education services in the 1998–1999 school year. Children with multiple disabilities also have been counted under various single disabilities.

various disabilities who receive special education services (U.S. Department of Education, 2000). Within this group, a little more than half have a learning disability. Substantial percentages of children also have speech or language impairments (19.4 percent of those with disabilities), mental retardation (11 percent), and serious emotional disturbance (8.4 percent).

Educators now prefer to speak of "children with disabilities" rather than "disabled children" to emphasize the person, not the disability. The term *handicapping conditions* is still used to describe impediments to the learning and functioning of individuals with a disability that have been imposed by society (Hallahan & Kaufman, 2003). For example, when children who use a wheelchair do not have adequate access to a bathroom, transportation, and so on, this is referred to as a handicapping condition.

Learning Disabilities

Children with a **learning disability** (1) are of normal intelligence or above, (2) have difficulties in at least one academic area and usually several, and (3) have a difficulty that cannot be attributed to any other diagnosed problem or disorder. The global concept of learning disabilities includes problems in listening, concentrating, speaking, and thinking.

About three times as many boys as girls are classified as having a learning disability (U.S. Department of Education, 1996). Among the explanations for this gender difference are a greater biological vulnerability of boys, as well as referral bias (boys are more likely to be referred by teachers for treatment because of their disruptive, hyperactive behavior).

The most common problem that characterizes children with a learning disability involves reading (Grigorenko, 2001; Siegel, 2003). Such children especially show problems with phonological skills (these involve being able to understand how sounds and letters match up to make words). **Dyslexia** is a severe impairment in the ability to read and spell (Pennington & Lefty, 2001).

Children with a learning disability often have difficulties in handwriting, spelling, or composition. Their writing may be extremely slow, their writing products may be virtually illegible, and they may make numerous spelling errors because of their inability to match up sounds and letters.

Exploring Disabilities

Learning Disabilities

Learning Disabilities Association

learning disability A disability that involves (1) having normal intelligence or above; (2) having difficulties in at least one academic area and usually several; and (3) having no other problem or disorder, such as mental retardation, that can be determined as causing the difficulty.

dyslexia A category of learning disabilities involving a severe impairment in the ability to read and spell.

Many interventions have focused on improving the child's reading ability (Lyon & Moats, 1997; Snowling, 2002). For example, in one study, instruction in phonological awareness at the kindergarten level had positive effects on reading development when the children reached the first grade (Blachman & others, 1994).

Unfortunately, not all children who have a learning disability that involves reading problems have the benefit of appropriate early intervention. Most children whose reading disability is not diagnosed until the third grade or later and who receive standard interventions fail to show noticeable improvement (Lyon, 1996). However, intensive instruction over a period of time by a competent teacher can remediate the deficient reading skills of many children. For example, in one study, 65 severely dyslexic children were given 65 hours of individual instruction in addition to group instruction in phonemic awareness and thinking skills (Alexander & others, 1991). The intensive intervention significantly improved the dyslexic children's reading skills.

ADHD

Attention Deficit Hyperactivity Disorder (ADHD)

Attention deficit hyperactivity disorder (ADHD) is a disbility in which children consistently show one or more of these characteristics over a period of time: (1) inattention, (2) hyperactivity, and (3) impulsivity. Children who are inattentive have difficulty focusing on any one thing and may get bored with a task after only a few minutes. Children who are hyperactive show high levels of physical activity, almost always seeming to be in motion. Children who are impulsive have difficulty curbing their reactions and don't do a good job of thinking before they act. Depending on the characteristics that children with ADHD display, they can be diagnosed as (1) ADHD with predominantly inattention, (2) ADHD with predominantly hyperactivity/impulsivity, or (3) ADHD with both inattention and hyperactivity/impulsivity (Whalen, 2001).

The U.S. Office of Education figures on children with a disability shown in figure 10.3 include children with ADHD in the category of children with specific learning disabilities, an overall category that comprises slightly more than one-half of all children who receive special education services. The number of children diagnosed and treated for ADHD has increased substantially, by some estimates doubling in the 1990s. The disorder occurs as much as four to nine times more in boys than in girls. There is con-

attention deficit hyperactivity disorder (ADHD) A disability in which children consistently show one or more of the following characteristics: (1) inattention, (2) hyperactivity, and (3) impulsivity.

Many children with ADHD show impulsive behavior, such as this child who is jumping out of his seat and throwing a paper airplane at other children. *How would you handle this situation if you were a teacher and this were to happen in your classroom?*

troversy about the increased diagnosis of ADHD (Terman & others, 1996), however. Some experts attribute the increase mainly to heightened awareness of the disorder. Others are concerned that many children are being diagnosed without undergoing extensive professional evaluation based on input from multiple sources.

Definitive causes of ADHD have not been found. For example, scientists have not been able to identify cause-related sites in the brain. However, a number of causes have been proposed, such as low levels of certain neurotransmitters (chemical messengers in the brain), prenatal abnormalities, and postnatal abnormalites (Schweitzer, Cummins, & Kant, 2001). Heredity also may play a role, as 30 to 50 percent of children with ADHD have a sibling or parent who has the disorder (Faraone & Doyle, 2001; Woodrich, 1994).

Students with ADHD have a failure rate in school that is two to three times that of other students. About one-half of students with ADHD have repeated a grade by adolescence and more than one-third eventually drop out of school.

Many experts recommend a combination of academic, behavioral, and medical interventions to help students with ADHD learn and adapt more effectively (Rapport & others, 2001; Whalen, 2001). This intervention requires cooperation and effort on the part of the parents of students with ADHD, school personnel (teachers, administrators, special educators, and school psychologists), and health-care professionals (Whalen, 2001).

It is estimated that about 85 to 90 percent of students with ADHD are taking stimulant medication such as Ritalin to control their behavior (Denney, 2001). Although Ritalin is a stimulant, in many children with ADHD it has the opposite effect, slowing down their nervous system and behavior (Greenhill & others, 2002; Johnson & Leung, 2001). Researchers have found that a combination of medication (such as Ritalin) and behavior management improves the behavior of children with ADHD better than medication alone or behavior management alone (Swanson & others, 2001).

The use of Ritalin and other stimulants to treat ADHD continues to be controversial. Critics argue that physicians are too quick to prescribe Ritalin, especially for mild cases of ADHD, and that long-term studies of the effects of Ritalin on children with ADHD have not been conducted to determine possible negative effects.

Educational Issues

The legal requirement that schools serve all children with a disability is fairly recent. Beginning in the mid 1960s to mid 1970s, legislatures, the federal courts, and the United States Congress laid down special educational rights for children with disabilities. Prior to that time, most children with a disability were either refused enrollment or inadequately served by schools. In 1975, *Public Law 94-142*, the Education for All Handicapped Children Act, required that all students with disabilities be given a free, appropriate public education and be provided the funding to help implement this education.

In 1990, Public Law 94-142 was renamed the *Individuals with Disabilities Education Act (IDEA).* The IDEA spells out broad mandates for services to all children with disabilities. These include evaluation and eligibility determination, appropriate education and the individualized education plan (IEP), and the least restrictive environment (LRE) (Martin, Martin, & Terman, 1996).

The IDEA requires that students with disabilities have an **individualized education plan (IEP),** a written statement that spells out a program that is specifically tailored for the student with a disability. In general, the IEP should be (1) related to the child's learning capacity, (2) specifically constructed to meet the child's individual needs and not merely a copy of what is offered to other children, and (3) designed to provide educational benefits.

Under the IDEA, a child with a disability must be educated in the **least restrictive environment (LRE),** which is a setting that is as similar as possible to the one in which children who do not have a disability are educated. The term **inclusion**

Public Law 94-142 mandates free, appropriate education for all children. *What are the aspects of this education?*

Education of Children Who Are Exceptional

Inclusion

individualized education plan (IEP) A written statement that spells out a program tailored to a child with a disability. The plan should be (1) related to the child's learning capacity, (2) specially constructed to meet the child's individual needs and not merely a copy of what is offered to other children, and (3) designed to provide educational benefits.

least restrictive environment (LRE) The concept that a child with a disability must be educated in a setting that is as similar as possible to the one in which children who do not have a disability are educated.

inclusion Educating a child with special education needs full-time in the regular classroom.

Family-Centered and Culture-Centered Approaches to Working with a Child Who Has a Disability

Best practices in service delivery to children with disabilities are moving toward a family-focused or family-centered approach (Lynch & Hanson, 1993). This approach emphasizes the importance of partnerships between parents and disability professionals and shared decision making in assessment, intervention, and evaluation. It also underscores the belief that services for children must be offered in the context of the entire family and that the entire family system is the partner and the client, not just the child (Lyytinen & others, 1994).

At the same time as services are becoming more family focused, the families served by many intervention programs are becoming increasingly diverse. Many families are characterized by attitudes, beliefs, values, customs, languages, and behaviors that are unfamiliar to interventionists. It is not uncommon for interventionists in some locations to work with families from as many as ten different cultures or more. In a large school district, as many as fifty languages may be spoken.

Who are these interventionists who work with children who have a disability or are at risk for one? They include educators, nurses, speech and language specialists, audiologists, occupational and physical therapists, physicians, social workers, and psychologists. Regardless of the agency, program, service, setting, or professional discipline, having the attitudes and skills that facilitate effective cross-cultural interactions is needed for competent intervention.

Ideally, families in need of services for their children receive assistance from professionals who are knowledgeable and competent in their discipline, who speak the same language as family members, and have the ability to establish rapport and work in partnership with family members to implement interventions for the child and family. However, the current match between many professionals and the families whom they serve is not perfect. This does not mean, though, that families cannot receive high-quality assistance. It simply means that interventionists need to be especially sensitive to the importance of developing cross-cultural competence and learning how to respond in sensitive and appropriate ways.

describes the education of a child with special education needs full-time in the general school program. Not long ago, it was considered appropriate to educate children with disabilities outside the regular classroom. However, today, schools must make every effort to provide inclusion for children with disabilities (Dettmer, Dyck, & Thurston, 2002; Hallahan & Kaufman, 2003). To read further about children with disabilities, see the Sociocultural Worlds of Development box.

Review and Reflect

2 Identify children with disabilities and issues in educating them

REVIEW

- Who are children with disabilities?
- What characterizes children with learning disabilities?
- How would you describe children with attention deficit hyperactivity disorder? What kind of treatment are they typically given?
- What are some issues in educating children with disabilities?

REFLECT

- Think back on your own schooling and how children with learning disabilities or ADHD either were or were not diagnosed. Were you aware of such individuals in your classes? Were they helped by specialists? You may know one or more individuals with a learning disability or ADHD. Ask them about their educational experiences and whether they believe schools could have done a better job of helping them.

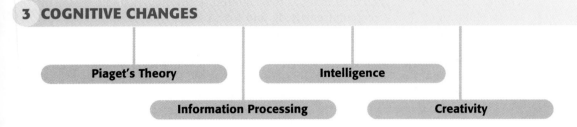

3 COGNITIVE CHANGES

Piaget's Theory

Information Processing

Intelligence

Creativity

Do children enter a new stage of cognitive development in middle and late childhood? How do children process information in this age period? What is the nature of children's intelligence and creativity? Let's explore these questions.

Piaget's Theory

According to Piaget (1952), the preschool child's thought is preoperational ◀▥ p. 242. Preoperational thought involves the formation of stable concepts, the emergence of mental reasoning, the prominence of egocentrism, and the construction of magical belief systems. Thought during the preschool years is still flawed and not well organized. Piaget believed that concrete operational thought does not appear until about the age of 7, but, as we learned in chapter 8, Piaget may have underestimated some of the cognitive skills of preschool children. For example, by carefully and cleverly designing experiments on understanding the concept of number, it was demonstrated that some preschool children show conservation, a concrete operational skill (Gelman, 1969). In chapter 8, we explored concrete operational thought by describing the preschool child's flaws in thinking about such concrete operational skills as conservation; here we will cover the characteristics of concrete operational thought again, this time emphasizing the competencies of elementary school children. Piaget believed that concrete operational thought characterizes children from about 7 to 11 years of age. We will also consider applications of Piaget's ideas to children's education and an evaluation of Piaget's theory.

Remember that, according to Piaget, *concrete operational thought* is made up of operations—mental actions that allow children to do mentally what they had done physically before ◀▥ p. 242. Concrete operations are also mental actions that are reversible. In the well-known test of reversibility of thought involving conservation of matter, the child is presented with two identical balls of clay. The experimenter rolls one ball into a long, thin shape; the other remains in its original ball shape. The child is then asked if there is more clay in the ball or in the long, thin piece of clay. By the time children reach the age of 7 or 8, most answer that the amount of clay is the same. To answer this problem correctly, children have to imagine the clay rolling back into a ball. This type of imagination involves a reversible mental action. Thus, a concrete operation is a reversible mental action on real, concrete objects. Concrete operations allow the child to coordinate several characteristics rather than focus on a single property of an object. In the clay example, the preoperational child is likely to focus on height *or* width. The concrete operational child coordinates information about both dimensions.

Many of the concrete operations Piaget identified focus on the way children reason about the properties of objects. One important skill that characterizes the concrete operational child is the ability to classify or divide things into different sets or subsets and to consider their interrelationships. An example of the concrete operational child's classification skills involves a family tree of four generations (see figure 10.4) (Furth & Wachs, 1975). This family tree suggests that the grandfather (A) has three

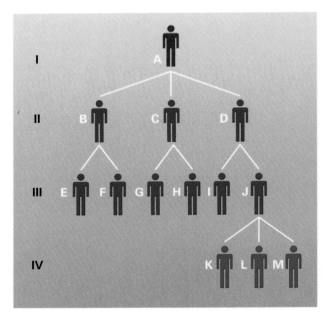

FIGURE 10.4 Classification: An Important Ability in Concrete Operational Thought

A family tree of four generations *(I to IV)*: The preoperational child has trouble classifying the members of the four generations; the concrete operational child can classify the members vertically, horizontally, and obliquely (up and down and across). For example, the concrete operational child understands that a family member can be a son, a brother, and a father, all at the same time.

children (B, C, and D), each of whom has two children (E through J), and that one of these children (J) has three children (K, L, and M). A child who comprehends the classification system can move up and down a level (vertically), across a level (horizontally), and up and down and across (obliquely) within the system. The concrete operational child understands that person J can at the same time be father, brother, and grandson, for example.

Some Piagetian tasks require children to reason about relations between classes. One such task is **seriation,** the concrete operation that involves ordering stimuli along a quantitative dimension (such as length). To see if students can serialize, a teacher might haphazardly place eight sticks of different lengths on a table. The teacher then asks the students to order the sticks by length. Many young children end up with two or three small groups of "big" sticks or "little" sticks, rather than a correct ordering of all eight sticks. Another mistaken strategy they use is to evenly line up the tops of the sticks but ignore the bottoms. The concrete operational thinker simultaneously understands that each stick must be longer than the one that precedes it and shorter than the one that follows it.

Another aspect of reasoning about the relations between classes is **transitivity,** which is the ability to logically combine relations to understand certain conclusions. In this case, consider three sticks (A, B, and C) of differing lengths. A is the longest, B is intermediate in length, and C is the shortest. Does the child understand that, if $A > B$ and $B > C$, then $A > C$? In Piaget's theory, concrete operational thinkers do; preoperational thinkers do not.

mhhe com/
santrockld9

Piaget and Education

Piaget and Education Piaget was not an educator and never pretended to be. However, he provided a sound conceptual framework from which to view learning and education. Here are some more general principles in Piaget's theory that can be applied to teaching (Elkind, 1976; Heuwinkel, 1996):

- *Take a constructivist approach.* In a constructivist vein, Piaget emphasized that children learn best when they are active and seek solutions for themselves. Piaget opposed teaching methods which imply that children are passive receptacles. The educational implication of Piaget's view is that, in all subjects, students learn best by making discoveries, reflecting on them, and discussing them, rather than blindly imitating the teacher or doing things by rote.
- *Facilitate rather than direct learning.* Effective teachers design situations that allow students to learn by doing. These situations promote students' thinking and discovery. Teachers listen, watch, and question students to help them gain better understanding. Don't just examine *what* students think and the product of their learning. Rather, carefully observe them as they find out *how* they think. Ask relevant questions to stimulate their thinking and ask them to explain their answers.
- *Consider the child's knowledge and level of thinking.* Students do not come to class with empty heads. They have many ideas about the physical and natural world. They have concepts of space, time, quantity, and causality. These ideas differ from the ideas of adults. Teachers need to interpret what a student is saying and respond in a mode of discourse that is not too far from the student's level.
- *Promote the student's intellectual health.* When Piaget came to lecture in the United States, he was asked, "What can I do to get my child to a higher cognitive stage sooner?" He was asked this question so often here compared with other countries that he called it the American question. For Piaget, children's learning should occur naturally. Children should not be pushed and pressured into achieving too much too early in their development, before they are maturationally ready. Some parents spend long hours every day holding up large flash cards with words on them to improve their baby's vocabulary. In the Piagetian view, this is not the best way for infants to learn. It places too much emphasis on speeding up intellectual development, involves passive learning, and will not work.

seriation The concrete operation that involves ordering stimuli along a quantitative dimension (such as length).

transitivity The ability to logically combine relations to understand certain conclusions.

- *Turn the classroom into a setting of exploration and discovery.* What do actual class-rooms look like when the teachers adopt Piaget's views? Several first- and second-grade math classrooms provide some good examples (Kamii, 1985, 1989). The teachers emphasize students' own exploration and discovery. The classrooms are less structured than what we think of as a typical classroom. Workbooks and predetermined assignments are not used. Rather, the teachers observe the students' interests and natural participation in activities to deter-mine what the course of learning will be. For example, a math lesson might be constructed around counting the day's lunch money or dividing supplies among students. Teachers encourage peer interaction because students' different view-points can contribute to advances in thinking.

Evaluating Piaget's Theory   What were Piaget's main contributions? Has his the-ory withstood the test of time?

Contributions   Piaget was a giant in the field of developmental psychology, the founder of the present field of children's cognitive development. Psychologists owe him a long list of masterful concepts of enduring power and fascination: assimilation, accommodation, object permanence, egocentrism, conservation, and others. Psychol-ogists also owe him the current vision of children as active, constructive thinkers (Vidal, 2000).

Piaget also was a genius when it came to observing children ◀‖‖ p. 182. His care-ful observations showed us inventive ways to discover how children act on and adapt to their world. Piaget showed us some important things to look for in cognitive devel-opment, such as the shift from preoperational to concrete operational thinking. He also showed us how children need to make their experiences fit their schemas (cogni-tive frameworks) yet simultaneously adapt their schemas to experience. Piaget also re-vealed how cognitive change is likely to occur if the context is structured to allow gradual movement to the next higher level and that a concept does not emerge sud-denly, fully blown but, rather, through a series of partial accomplishments that lead to increasingly comprehensive understanding (Haith & Benson, 1998).

Criticisms   Piaget's theory has not gone unchallenged. Questions are raised about es-timates of children's competence at different developmental levels; stages; the training of children to reason at higher levels; and culture and education.

- *Estimates of children's competence.* Some cognitive abilities emerge earlier than Piaget thought (Meltzoff, 2001; Miller, 2001). For example, as previously noted, some aspects of object permanence emerge earlier than he believed. Even 2-year-olds are nonegocentric in some contexts. Some understanding of the con-servation of number has been demonstrated as early as age 3, although Piaget did not think it emerged until 7. Young children are not as uniformly "pre" this and "pre" that (precausal, preoperational) as Piaget thought. Other cognitive abilities also can emerge later than Piaget thought. Many adolescents still think in concrete operational ways or are just beginning to master formal operations. Even many adults are not formal operational thinkers. In sum, recent theoretical revisions highlight more cognitive competencies of infants and young children and more cognitive shortcomings of adolescents and adults (Flavell, Miller, & Miller, 2002).
- *Stages.* Piaget conceived of stages as unitary structures of thought. Thus, his the-ory assumes developmental synchrony; that is, various aspects of a stage should emerge at the same time. However, some concrete operational concepts do not appear in synchrony. For example, children do not learn to conserve at the same time as they learn to cross-classify. Thus, most contemporary developmentalists agree that children's cognitive development is not as stagelike as Piaget thought.
- *Training children to reason at higher levels.* Some children who are at one cognitive stage (such as preoperational) can be trained to reason at a higher cognitive

Piaget with his wife and three children; he often used his observations of his children to provide examples of his theory.

We owe to Piaget the present field of cognitive development with its image of the developing child, who through its own active and creative commerce with its environment, builds an orderly succession of cognitive structures enroute to intellectual maturity.

—JOHN FLAVELL
Contemporary Developmental Psychologist, Stanford University

An outstanding teacher and education in the logic of science and mathematics are important cultural experiences that promote the development of operational thought. *Might Piaget have underestimated the roles of culture and schooling in children's cognitive development?*

stage (such as concrete operational). This poses a problem for Piaget's theory. He argued that such training is only superficial and ineffective, unless the child is at a maturational transition point between the stages (Gelman & Williams, 1998).

- *Culture and education.* Culture and education exert stronger influences on children's development than Piaget believed (Gelman & Brenneman, 1994). The age at which children acquire conservation skills is related to the extent to which their culture provides relevant practice. An outstanding teacher and education in the logic of math and science can promote concrete and formal operational thought.

Still, some developmental psychologists believe we should not throw out Piaget altogether. These **neo-Piagetians** argue that Piaget got some things right but that his theory needs considerable revision. In their revision of Piaget, more emphasis is given to how children process information through attention, memory, and strategies (Case, 1999). They especially believe that a more accurate vision of children's thinking requires more emphasis on strategies, the speed at which children process information, the particular cognitive task involved, and the division of cognitive problems into smaller, more precise steps (Case & Mueller, 2001; Demetriou, 2001).

Information Processing

Among the changes in information processing during middle and late childhood are those involving memory, critical thinking, and metacognition. Remember also, from chapter 8, that the attention of most children improves dramatically during middle and late childhood and that at this time children attend more to the task-relevant features of a problem than to the salient features ◀‖‖ p. 250.

Memory In chapter 8, we concluded that short-term memory increases considerably during early childhood but after the age of 7 does not show as much increase ◀‖‖ p. 251. Is the same pattern found for **long-term memory,** a relatively permanent and unlimited type of memory? Long-term memory increases with age during middle and late childhood.

neo-Piagetians Developmentalists who have elaborated on Piaget's theory, believing that more emphasis should be given to information processing, strategies, and precise cognitive steps.

long-term memory A relatively permanent type of memory that holds huge amounts of information for a long period of time.

Knowledge and Expertise An especially important influence on memory is the knowledge that individuals have about a particular topic (National Research Council, 1999). The role of knowledge in memory has especially been studied in the context of experts and novices. Experts have acquired extensive knowledge that influences what they notice and how they organize, represent, and interpret information. This in turn, affects their ability to remember, reason and solve problems.

Expertise is a term that is used to describe organized factual knowledge about a particular content area. One child might have a great deal of knowledge about chess while another child is very knowledgeable about sports. When individuals have expertise about a particular subject, their memory also tends to be good regarding material related to the subject.

One study found that 10- and 11-year-olds who were experienced chess players ("experts") were able to remember more information about chess pieces than college students who were not chess players ("novices") (Chi, 1978) (see figure 10.5). In contrast, when the college students were presented with other stimuli, they were able to remember them better than the children were. Thus, the children's expertise in chess gave them superior memories, but only in chess.

There are developmental changes in expertise. Older children usually have more expertise about a subject than younger children do, which can contribute to their better memory for the subject.

Control Processes/Strategies If we know anything at all about long-term memory, it is that long-term memory depends on the learning activities individuals engage in when learning and remembering information (Intons-Peterson, 1996; Mayer, 2003; Pressley, 2000). **Control processes** are cognitive processes that do not occur automatically but require effort and work. They are under the learner's conscious control and can be used to improve memory. They are also appropriately called *strategies*.

One research study found extensive variations in strategy instruction (Moely, Santulli, & Obach, 1995). Some teachers did try to help students with their memory and study strategies, but, overall, strategy instruction was low across a broad range of activities. Strategy instruction was most likely to occur in teaching math and problem solving. In many cases, children develop their own strategies.

Critical Thinking Currently, both psychologists and educators have considerable interest in critical thinking, although it is not an entirely new idea (Santrock & Halonen, 2002). Famous educator John Dewey (1933) proposed a similar idea when he talked about the importance of getting students to think reflectively.

Critical thinking involves thinking reflectively and productively, as well as evaluating the evidence. In this book, the second part of the Review and Reflect sections of each chapter challenge you to think critically about a topic or an issue related to the discussion.

Jacqueline and Martin Brooks (1993, 2001) lament that so few schools really teach students to think critically and develop a deep understanding of concepts. For example, many high school students read *Hamlet* but don't think deeply about it, never transforming their prior notions of power, greed, and relationships. Deep understanding occurs when students are stimulated to rethink their prior ideas.

In Brooks and Brooks' view, schools spend too much time on getting students to give a single correct answer in an imitative way, rather than encouraging them to expand their thinking by coming up with new ideas and rethinking earlier conclusions. They believe that too often teachers ask students to recite, define, describe, state, and list, rather than to analyze, infer, connect, synthesize, criticize, create, evaluate, think, and rethink.

Brooks and Brooks point out that many successful students complete their assignments, do well on tests, and get good grades, yet they don't ever learn to think critically and deeply. They believe our schools turn out students who think too superficially, staying on the surface of problems rather than stretching their minds and becoming deeply engaged in meaningful thinking.

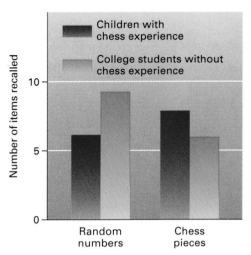

FIGURE 10.5 The Role of Expertise in Memory

Notice that when 10- to 11-year-old children and college students were asked to remember a string of random numbers that had been presented to them, the college students fared better. However, the 10- to 11-year-olds who had experience playing chess ("experts") had better memory for the location of chess pieces on a chess board than college students with no chess experience ("novices") (Chi, 1978).

control processes Cognitive processes that do not occur automatically but require work and effort. These processes are under the learner's conscious control and can be used to improve memory. They are also appropriately called *strategies*.

critical thinking Thinking reflectively and productively, as well as evaluating the evidence.

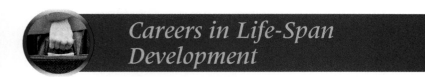

Careers in Life-Span Development

Laura Martin, Science Museum Educator and Research Specialist

After taking a psychology course as an undergraduate, Laura Martin obtained a master's degree from Bank Street College of Education in New York. Martin then worked as a teacher of young children for several years. That experience challenged her to learn more about how children think, so she applied to graduate school in child development and eventually obtained her Ph.D. from the University of California–San Diego. She later returned to Bank Street College and orchestrated projects on technology and learning. Then Martin joined Children's Television Workshop, which produces *Sesame Street*, as research director. Later, she became Vice President for Productions Research at Children's Television Workshop.

Interesting opportunities continued to be presented to her including offers from a software developer, the government, and colleges. She took a job as a science museum education and research specialist at the Arizona Science Center. At the center, Dr. Martin conceptualizes exhibits and researches whether the layout designs are communicating effectively. She organizes programs, classes, and resources. Martin says that as she does these things, her education and training in child development are extremely helpful.

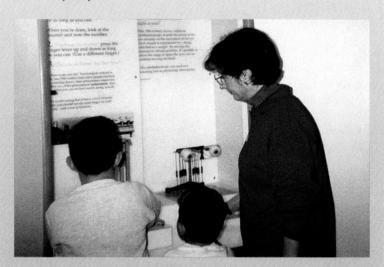

Laura Martin with children at the Arizona Science Center.

Museums are settings that can stimulate children's thinking. To read about the work of Laura Martin, a science museum educator and researcher, see the Careers in Life-Span Development insert ◀▥▥ p. 30.

Metacognition   **Metacognition** is cognition about cognition, or knowing about knowing (Flavell, 1999; Flavell, Miller, & Miller, 2002). One expert on children's thinking, Deanna Kuhn (1999), believes that metacognition should be a stronger focus of efforts to help children become better critical thinkers, especially at the middle school and high school levels. She distinguishes between first-order cognitive skills that enable children to know about the world (these have been the main focus of critical thinking programs) and second-order cognitive skills—*meta-knowing skills*—that entail knowing about one's own (and others') knowing.

The majority of developmental studies classified as "metacognitive" have focused on metamemory, or knowledge about memory (DeMarie, Abshier, & Ferron, 2001). This includes general knowledge about memory, such as knowing that recognition tests are easier than recall tests. It also encompasses knowledge about one's own memory, such as a student's ability to monitor whether she has studied enough for a test that is coming up next week.

By 5 or 6 years of age, children usually know that familiar items are easier to learn than unfamiliar ones, that short lists are easier than long ones, that recognition is easier than recall, and that forgetting is more likely to occur over time (Lyon & Flavell, 1993). However, in other ways young children's metamemory is limited. They don't understand that related items are easier to remember than unrelated ones and that remembering the gist of a story is easier than remembering information verbatim (Kreutzer, Leonard, & Flavell, 1975). By the fifth grade, students understand that gist recall is easier than verbatim recall. Young children also have an inflated opinion of their memory abilities. For example, in one study a majority of young children predicted that they would be able to recall all 10 items on a list of 10 items. When tested for this, none of the young children managed this feat (Flavell, Friedrichs, & Hoyt, 1970). As they move through the elementary school years, children give more realistic evaluations of their memory skills (Schneider & Pressley, 1997).

In the view of Michael Pressley (2000), the key to education is helping students learn a rich repertoire of strategies that result in solutions to problems. Good thinkers routinely use strategies and effective planning to solve problems. Good thinkers also know when and where to use strategies (metacognitive knowledge about strategies). Understanding when and where to use strategies often results from the learner's monitoring of the learning situation (McCormick, 2003).

Summarizing and getting the "gist" of what an author is saying are important strategies for improving one's reading skills. Planning, organizing, rereading, and writing multiple drafts are good strategies for improving writing skills.

metacognition Cognition about cognition, or knowing about knowing.

Intelligence

Just what is meant by the concept of "intelligence"? Some experts describe intelligence as problem-solving skills. Others describe it as the ability to adapt to and learn from life's everyday experiences. Combining these ideas, we can arrive at a definition of **intelligence** as problem-solving skills and the ability to learn from and adapt to life's everyday experiences.

Interest in intelligence has often focused on individual differences and assessment. **Individual differences** are the stable, consistent ways in which people are different from each other. We can talk about individual differences in personality or any other domain, but it is in the domain of intelligence that the most attention has been directed at individual differences. For example, an intelligence test purports to inform us about whether a student can reason better than others who have taken the test. Let's go back in history and see what the first intelligence test was like.

The Binet Tests   In 1904, the French Ministry of Education asked psychologist Alfred Binet to devise a method of identifying children who were unable to learn in school. School officials wanted to reduce crowding by placing students who did not benefit from regular classroom teaching in special schools. Binet and his student Theophile Simon developed an intelligence test to meet this request. The test is called the 1905 Scale. It consisted of 30 questions on topics ranging from the ability to touch one's ear to the ability to draw designs from memory and define abstract concepts.

Binet developed the concept of **mental age (MA),** an individual's level of mental development relative to others. Not much later, in 1912, William Stern created the concept of **intelligence quotient (IQ),** a person's mental age divided by chronological age (CA), multiplied by 100. That is:

$$IQ = \frac{MA}{CA} \times 100$$

If mental age is the same as chronological age, then the person's IQ is 100. If mental age is above chronological age, then IQ is more than 100. If mental age is below chronological age, then IQ is less than 100.

The Binet test has been revised many times to incorporate advances in the understanding of intelligence and intelligence tests. These revisions are called the Stanford-Binet tests (Stanford University is where the revisions have been done). By administering the test to large numbers of people of different ages from different backgrounds, researchers have found that scores on the Stanford-Binet approximate a normal distribution (see figure 10.6 on page 318). A **normal distribution** is symmetrical, with a majority of the scores falling in the middle of the possible range of scores and few scores appearing toward the extremes of the range.

The current Stanford-Binet is administered individually to people from the age of 2 through the adult years. It includes a variety of items, some of which require verbal responses, others nonverbal responses. For example, items that reflect a 6-year-old's performance on the test include the verbal ability to define at least six words, such as *orange* and *envelope,* as well as the nonverbal ability to trace a path through a maze. Items that reflect an average adult's intelligence include defining such words as *disproportionate* and *regard,* explaining a proverb, and comparing idleness and laziness.

The fourth edition of the Stanford-Binet was published in 1985. One important addition to this version was the analysis of the individual's responses in terms of four content areas: verbal reasoning, quantitative reasoning, abstract/visual reasoning, and short-term memory. A general composite score is still obtained to reflect overall intelligence. The Stanford-Binet continues to be one of the most widely used tests to assess a student's intelligence (Naglieri, 2000).

The Wechsler Scales   Another set of widely used tests to assess students' intelligence is called the Wechsler scales, developed by David Wechsler. They include the

intelligence Problem-solving skills and the ability to learn from and adapt to the experiences of everyday life.

individual differences The stable, consistent ways in which people are different from each other.

mental age (MA) Binet's measure of an individual's level of mental development, compared with that of others.

intelligence quotient (IQ) A person's mental age divided by chronological age, multiplied by 100.

normal distribution A symmetrical distribution with most cases falling in the middle of the possible range of scores and a few scores appearing toward the extremes of the range.

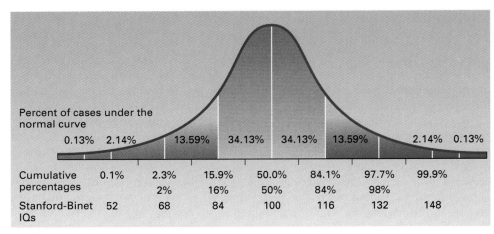

FIGURE 10.6 The Normal Curve and Stanford-Binet IQ Scores

The distribution of IQ scores approximates a normal curve. Most of the population falls in the middle range of scores. Notice that extremely high and extremely low scores are very rare. Slightly more than two-thirds of the scores fall between 84 and 116. Only about 1 in 50 individuals has an IQ of more than 132, and only about 1 in 50 individuals has an IQ of less than 68.

Wechsler Preschool and Primary Scale of Intelligence–Revised (WPPSI-R) to test children 4 to 6½ years of age; the Wechsler Intelligence Scale for Children (WISC-III) for children and adolescents 6 to 16 years of age; and the Wechsler Adult Intelligence Scale (WAIS-III).

Not only do the Wechsler scales provide an overall IQ, but they also yield verbal and performance IQs. Verbal IQ is based on six verbal subscales, performance IQ on five performance subscales. This allows the examiner to quickly see patterns of strengths and weaknesses in different areas of the student's intelligence. Several of the Wechsler subscales are shown in figure 10.7.

Verbal Subscales

Similarities
A child must think logically and abstractly to answer a number of questions about how things might be similar.

Example: "In what way are a lion and a tiger alike?"

Comprehension
This subscale is designed to measure an individual's judgment and common sense.

Example: "What is the advantage of keeping money in a bank?"

Nonverbal Subscales

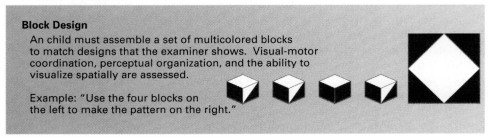

Block Design
An child must assemble a set of multicolored blocks to match designs that the examiner shows. Visual-motor coordination, perceptual organization, and the ability to visualize spatially are assessed.

Example: "Use the four blocks on the left to make the pattern on the right."

The Wechsler includes 11 subscales, 6 verbal and 5 nonverbal.
Three of the subscales are shown here.

FIGURE 10.7 Sample Subscales of the Wechsler Intelligence Scale for Children (WISC-III)

Simulated items similar to those in the *Wechsler Intelligence Scale for Children*, Third Edition. Copyright © 1949, 1955, 1974, 1981, 1991 by The Psychological Corporation, a Harcourt Assessment Company. Reproduced by permission. All rights reserved.

Types of Intelligence   Is it more appropriate to think of a child's intelligence as a general ability or as a number of specific abilities? Binet focused on a child's general intelligence. The IQ concept developed by William Stern was designed to capture this overall intellectual ability. Wechsler believed it was important to describe both a child's general intelligence and specific verbal and performance intelligences. This built on the ideas of Charles Spearman (1927), who said that people have both a general intelligence, which he called *g*, and specific types of intelligence, which he called *s*. As early as the 1930s, L. L. Thurstone (1938) said people have seven of these specific abilities, which he called primary abilities: verbal comprehension, number ability, word fluency, spatial visualization, associative memory, reasoning, and perceptual speed. More recently, the search for specific types of intelligence has heated up.

"You're wise, but you lack tree smarts."
© The New Yorker Collection, 1988, Donald Reilly from cartoonbank.com. All Rights Reserved.

Sternberg's Triarchic Theory   Robert J. Sternberg (1986, 1999, 2002, 2003) developed the **triarchic theory of intelligence,** which states that intelligence comes in three forms:

- *Analytical intelligence.* This refers to the ability to analyze, judge, evaluate, compare, and contrast. Ann has high analytical intelligence. She scores high on traditional intelligence tests, such as the Stanford-Binet, and is a star analytical thinker.
- *Creative intelligence.* This consists of the ability to create, design, invent, originate, and imagine. Todd has high creative intelligence. He does not have the best test scores but has an insightful and creative mind.
- *Practical intelligence.* This involves the ability to use, apply, implement, and put ideas into practice. Art is high on practical intelligence. He is street-smart and has learned to deal in practical ways with his world, although his scores on traditional intelligence tests are average.

Sternberg (1999) says that children with different triarchic patterns "look different" in school. Students with high analytic ability tend to be favored in conventional schooling. They often do well in direct instruction classes, in which the teacher lectures and gives students objective tests. They often are considered to be "smart" students, who get good grades, show up in high-level tracks, do well on traditional tests of intelligence and the SAT, and later get admitted to competitive colleges. Children who are high in creative intelligence are often not in the top rung of their class. Sternberg says that many teachers have expectations about how assignments should be done, and creatively intelligent students may not conform to those expectations. Instead of giving conformist answers, they give unique answers, for which they might get reprimanded or marked down. No teacher wants to discourage creativity, but Sternberg believes that too often a teacher's desire to improve students' knowledge depresses creative thinking.

Like children high in creative intelligence, children who are practically intelligent often do not relate well to the demands of school. However, many of these children do well outside of the classroom's walls. They may have excellent social skills and good common sense. As adults, some become successful managers, entrepreneurs, or politicians, yet they have undistinguished school records.

Gardner's Eight Frames of Mind   Howard Gardner (1983, 1993, 2002) believes there are eight types of intelligence. These are described here, with examples of the types of vocations in which they are reflected as strengths (Campbell, Campbell, & Dickinson, 1999):

- *Verbal skills:* the ability to think in words and to use language to express meaning (authors, journalists, speakers)

mhhe●com/
santrockld9

Sternberg's Theory

triarchic theory of intelligence Sternberg's theory that intelligence consists of analytical intelligence, creative intelligence, and practical intelligence.

Children in the Key School form "pods," in which they pursue activities of special interest to them. Every day, each child can choose from activities that draw on Gardner's eight frames of mind. The school has pods that range from gardening to architecture to gliding to dancing. *What are some of the main ideas of Gardner's theory and its application to education?*

- *Mathematical skills:* the ability to carry out mathematical operations (scientists, engineers, accountants)
- *Spatial skills:* the ability to think three-dimensionally (architects, artists, sailors)
- *Bodily-kinesthetic skills:* the ability to manipulate objects and be physically skilled (surgeons, craftspeople, dancers, athletes)
- *Musical skills:* sensitivity to pitch, melody, rhythm, and tone (composers, musicians, and sensitive listeners)
- *Interpersonal skills:* the ability to understand and effectively interact with others (teachers, mental health professionals)
- *Intrapersonal skills:* the ability to understand oneself and effectively direct one's life (theologians, psychologists)
- *Naturalist skills:* the ability to observe patterns in nature and understand natural and human-made systems (farmers, botanists, ecologists, landscapers)

mhhe ● com/
santrockld9

Multiple Intelligence Links

**Multiple Intelligences
and Education**

The Key School in Indianapolis immerses students in activities that closely resemble Gardner's frames of mind (Goleman, Kaufman, & Ray, 1993). Each day, every student is exposed to materials that are designed to stimulate a range of human abilities, including art, music, computing, language skills, math skills, and physical games. In addition, attention is given to students' understanding of themselves and others.

Evaluating the Multiple-Intelligence Approaches Sternberg's and Gardner's approaches have much to offer. They have stimulated teachers to think more broadly about what makes up children's competencies. And they have motivated educators to develop programs that instruct students in multiple domains. These approaches also have contributed to the interest in assessing intelligence and classroom learning in innovative ways that go beyond conventional standardized and paper-and-pencil memory tasks (Torff, 2000). One way this assessment is carried out is by evaluating students' learning portfolios.

Some critics say that classifying musical skills as a main type of intelligence is off base. They ask whether there are possibly other skill domains that Gardner has left out. For example, there are outstanding chess players, prizefighters, writers, politicians, physicians, lawyers, ministers, and poets, yet we do not refer to chess intelligence, prizefighter intelligence, and so on. Other critics say that the research base to support the three intelligences of Sternberg and the eight intelligences of Gardner as the best ways to categorize intelligence has not yet been developed.

There also are a number of psychologists who support Spearman's concept of *g* (general intelligence) and many of them believe that the multiple-intelligence views have taken the concept of *s* (specific intelligences) too far. For example, one expert on intelligence, Nathan Brody (2000) argues that people who excel at one type of intellectual task are likely to excel in others. Thus, individuals who do well at memorizing lists of digits are also likely to be good at solving verbal problems and spatial layout problems.

Controversies and Issues in Intelligence   The field of intelligence has its controversies. In chapter 3, "Biological Beginnings," we discussed the controversial issue of how extensively intelligence is due to heredity or environment ◀▥ p. 98. We concluded that intelligence is due to an interaction of heredity and environment (Sternberg & Grigorenko, 2001). Here, we will focus on several more issues, involving ethnicity and culture, as well as the use and misuse of intelligence tests.

Ethnicity and Culture   In the United States, children from African American and Latino families score below children from White families on standardized intelligence tests. Most comparisons have focused on African Americans and Whites. On the average, African American schoolchildren score 10 to 15 points lower than do White American schoolchildren (Neisser & others, 1996). Keep in mind that this figure of 10 to 15 points lower represents an average score. Many African American children score higher than many White children. Estimates are that 15 to 25 percent of all African American schoolchildren score higher than half of all White schoolchildren.

Are these differences based on heredity or environment? The consensus is environment (Brooks-Gunn, Klebanov, & Duncan, 1996). For example, in recent decades, as African Americans have experienced improved social, economic, and educational opportunities, the gap between White and African American children on conventional intelligence tests has narrowed (Jones, 1984). Between 1977 and 1996, as African Americans gained more educational opportunities, the gap between their SAT scores and those of their White counterparts shrank 23 percent (College Board, 1996). Also, when children from disadvantaged African American families are adopted by more advantaged middle-SES families, their scores on intelligence tests become closer to the national average for middle-SES children than to the national average for children from low-income families (Scarr & Weinberg, 1983).

Many of the early tests of intelligence were culturally biased, favoring urban children over rural children, children from middle-SES families over children from low-income families, and White children over minority children (Miller-Jones, 1989). The standards for the early tests were almost exclusively based on White middle-SES children. And some of the items were culturally biased. For example, one item on an early test asked what you should do if you find a 3-year-old in the street. The correct answer was "Call the police." However, children from impoverished inner-city families might not choose this answer if they have had bad experiences with the police. Children living in rural areas might not have police nearby. The contemporary versions of intelligence tests attempt to reduce such cultural bias.

Even if the content of test items is appropriate, another problem can characterize intelligence tests. Since many items are verbal, minority groups may encounter problems in understanding the language of the items.

Culture-fair tests are tests of intelligence that are intended to be free of cultural bias. Two types of culture-fair tests have been devised. The first includes items that are familiar to children from all socioeconomic and ethnic backgrounds, or items that at least are familiar to the children taking the test. For example, a child might be asked how a bird and a dog are different, on the assumption that all children have been exposed to birds and dogs. The second type of culture-fair test has no verbal questions. Figure 10.8 on page 322 shows a sample question from the Raven Progressive

culture-fair tests Tests of intelligence that are designed to be free of cultural bias.

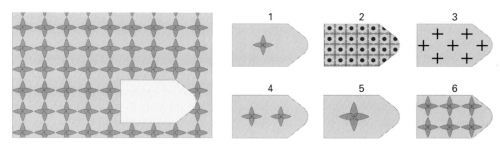

FIGURE 10.8 Sample Item from the Raven Progressive Matrices Test
Individuals are presented with a matrix arrangement of symbols, such as the one at the left of this figure, and must then complete the matrix by selecting the appropriate missing symbol from a group of symbols, such as the ones at the right.

Matrices Test. Even though tests such as the Raven Progressive Matrices are designed to be culture-fair, people with more education still score higher than those with less education do.

These attempts to produce culture-fair tests remind us that conventional intelligence tests probably are culturally biased, yet the effort to create a truly culture-fair test has not yielded a successful alternative. It also is important to consider that what is viewed as intelligent in one culture may not be thought of as intelligent in another (Serpell, 2000). In most Western cultures, children are considered intelligent if they are both smart (have considerable knowledge and can solve verbal problems) and fast (can process information quickly). By contrast, in the Buganda culture in Uganda, children who are wise, slow in thought, and say the socially correct thing are considered intelligent. And, in the widely dispersed Caroline Islands, one of the most important dimensions of intelligence is the ability to navigate by the stars.

The Use and Misuse of Intelligence Tests Psychological tests are tools. Like all tools, their effectiveness depends on the knowledge, skill, and integrity of the user. A hammer can be used to build a beautiful kitchen cabinet, or it can be used as a weapon of assault. Like a hammer, psychological tests can be used for positive purposes, or they can be badly abused. Here are some cautions about IQ that can help you avoid the pitfalls of using information about a child's intelligence in negative ways:

- *Avoid stereotyping and expectations.* A special concern is that the scores on an IQ test easily can lead to stereotypes and expectations about students. Sweeping generalizations are too often made on the basis of an IQ score. An IQ test should always be considered a measure of current performance. It is not a measure of fixed potential. Maturational changes and enriched environmental experiences can advance a student's intelligence.
- *Not a sole indicator of competence.* Another concern about IQ tests occurs when they are used as the main or sole characteristic of competence. A high IQ is not the ultimate human value. As we have seen in this chapter, it is important to consider not only students' intellectual competence in such areas as verbal skills but also their creative and practical skills.
- *Caution in interpreting an overall IQ score.* In evaluating a child's intelligence, it is wiser to think of intelligence as consisting of a number of domains. Keep in mind the different types of intelligence described by Sternberg and Gardner. Remember that, by considering the different domains of intelligence, you can find that every child has at least one or more strengths.

The Extremes of Intelligence Intelligence tests have been used to discover indications of mental retardation or intellectual giftedness, the extremes of intelligence. At times, intelligence tests have been misused for this purpose. Keeping in mind the theme that an intelligence test should not be used as the sole indicator of mental retardation or giftedness, we will explore the nature of these intellectual extremes.

Mental Retardation **Mental retardation** is a condition of limited mental ability in which an individual has a low IQ, usually below 70 on a traditional intelligence test, and has difficulty adapting to everyday life. About 5 million Americans fit this definition of mental retardation.

There are several classifications of mental retardation. About 89 percent of the mentally retarded fall into the mild category, with IQs of 55 to 70. About 6 percent are classified as moderately retarded, with IQs of 40 to 54; these people can attain a second-grade level of skills and may be able to support themselves as adults through some types of labor. About 3.5 percent of the mentally retarded are in the severe category, with IQs of 25 to 39; these individuals learn to talk and engage in very simple tasks but require extensive supervision. Less than 1 percent have IQs below 25; they fall into the profoundly mentally retarded classification and need constant supervision (Drew & Hardman, 2000).

Mental retardation can have an organic cause, or it can be social and cultural in origin:

- **Organic retardation** is mental retardation that is caused by a genetic disorder or by brain damage; the word *organic* refers to the tissues or organs of the body, so there is some physical damage in organic retardation. Down syndrome, one form of mental retardation, occurs when an extra chromosome is present in an individual's genetic makeup (see figure 10.9) ◀▥ p. 90. It is not known why the extra chromosome is present, but it may involve the health or age of the female ovum or male sperm. Most people who suffer from organic retardation have IQs that range between 0 and 50.
- **Cultural-familial retardation** is a mental deficit in which no evidence of organic brain damage can be found; individuals' IQs range from 50 to 70. Psychologists suspect that such mental deficits result from the normal variation that distributes people along the range of intelligence scores above 50, combined with growing up in a below-average intellectual environment.

Giftedness There have always been people whose abilities and accomplishments outshine others'—the whiz kid in class, the star athlete, the natural musician. People who are **gifted** have above-average intelligence (an IQ of 130 or higher) and/or superior talent for something. When it comes to programs for the gifted, most school systems select children who have intellectual superiority and academic aptitude. Children who are talented in the visual and performing arts (arts, drama, dance), athletics, or other special aptitudes tend to be overlooked (Olszewski-Kubilius, 2003).

There has been speculation that giftedness is linked with having a mental disorder. However, no relation between giftedness and mental disorder has been found. Recent studies support the conclusion that gifted people tend to be more mature, have fewer emotional problems than others, and grow up in a positive family climate (Davidson, 2000; Feldman, 2001).

What are the characteristics of children who are gifted? Lewis Terman (1925) conducted an extensive study of 1,500 children whose Stanford-Binet IQs averaged 150. A popular myth is that gifted children are maladjusted, but Terman found in his study that they were not only academically gifted but also socially well adjusted. Many of these gifted children went on to become successful doctors, lawyers, and professors, and scientists.

Ellen Winner (1996) described three criteria that characterize gifted children, whether in art, music, or academic domains:

1. *Precocity.* Gifted children are precocious. They begin to master an area earlier than their peers. Learning in their domain is more effortless for them than for ordinary children. In most instances, these gifted children are precocious because they have an inborn high ability in a particular domain or domains.
2. *Marching to their own drummer.* Gifted children learn in a qualitatively different way than ordinary children. One way that they march to a different drummer is that they need minimal help, or scaffolding, from adults to learn. In many

FIGURE 10.9 A Child with Down Syndrome
What causes a child to develop Down syndrome? In which major classification of mental retardation does the condition fall?

**mhhe●com/
santrockld9**

Mental Retardation

Children Who Are Gifted

Gifted Education

mental retardation A condition of limited mental ability in which an individual has a low IQ, usually below 70 on a traditional test of intelligence, and has difficulty adapting to everyday life.

organic retardation Mental retardation that involves some physical damage and is caused by a genetic disorder or brain damage.

cultural-familial retardation Retardation that is characterized by no evidence of organic brain damage, but the individual's IQ is between 50 and 70.

gifted Having above-average intelligence (an IQ of 130 or higher) and/or superior talent for something.

Careers in Life-Span Development

Sterling Jones, Supervisor of Gifted and Talented Education

Sterling Jones is program supervisor for gifted and talented children in the Detroit Public School System. Jones has been working with children who are gifted for more than three decades. He believes that students' mastery of skills mainly depends on the amount of time devoted to instruction and the length of time allowed for learning. Thus, he believes that many basic strategies for challenging children who are gifted to develop their skills can be applied to a wider range of students than once believed. He has rewritten several pamphlets for use by teachers and parents, including *How to Help Your Child Succeed* and *Gifted and Talented Education for Everyone.*

Jones has undergraduate and graduate degrees from Wayne State University and taught English for a number of years before becoming involved in the program for gifted children. He also has written materials on African Americans,

such as *Voices from the Black Experience,* that are used in the Detroit schools.

Sterling Jones with some of the children in the gifted program in the Detroit Public School System.

---

instances, they resist any kind of explicit instruction. They also often make discoveries on their own and solve problems in unique ways.

3. A *passion to master.* Gifted children are driven to understand the domain in which they have high ability. They display an intense, obsessive interest and an ability to focus. They are not children who need to be pushed by their parents. They motivate themselves, says Winner.

One career opportunity in life-span development involves working with children who are gifted as a teacher or supervisor. To read about the work of a supervisor of gifted and talented education, see the Careers in Life-Span Development insert.

Creativity

creativity The ability to think in novel and unusual ways and to come up with unique solutions to problems.

convergent thinking Thinking that produces one correct answer and is characteristic of the kind of thinking tested by standardized intelligence tests.

divergent thinking Thinking that produces many answers to the same question and is characteristic of creativity.

Creativity is the ability to think in novel and unusual ways and to come up with unique solutions to problems. Thus, intelligence and creativity are not the same thing. This was recognized in Sternberg's account of intelligence earlier in this chapter and by J. P. Guilford (1967). Guilford distinguished between **convergent thinking,** which produces one correct answer and characterizes the kind of thinking that is required on conventional tests of intelligence, and **divergent thinking,** which produces many different answers to the same question and characterizes creativity. For example, a typical item on a conventional intelligence test is "How many quarters will you get in return for 60 dimes?" By contrast, the following question has many possible answers: "What image comes to mind when you hear the phrase 'Sitting alone in a dark room' or 'Can you think of some unique uses for a paper clip?'"

Are intelligence and creativity related? Although most creative children are quite intelligent, the reverse is not necessarily true. Many highly intelligent children (as measured by high scores on conventional intelligence tests) are not very creative. And, if Sternberg were to have his way, creative thinking would become part of a broader definition of intelligence.

An important goal is to help children become more creative. What are the best strategies for accomplishing this goal?

- *Have children engage in brainstorming and come up with as many ideas as possible.* In **brainstorming,** individuals are encouraged to come up with creative ideas in a group, play off each other's ideas, and say whatever comes to mind. The more ideas children produce, the better their chance of creating something unique (Runco, 2000).

- *Provide children with environments that stimulate creativity.* Some settings nourish creativity; others depress it. People who encourage children's creativity often rely on their natural curiosity. They provide exercises and activities that stimulate children to find insightful solutions to problems, rather than asking a lot of questions that require rote answers.

- *Don't overcontrol.* Teresa Amabile (1993) says that telling children exactly how to do things leaves them feeling that any originality is a mistake and any exploration is a waste of time. Letting children select their interests and supporting their inclinations are less likely to destroy their natural curiosity than dictating which activities they should engage in (Csikszentmihalyi, 2000).

- *Encourage internal motivation.* The excessive use of prizes, such as gold stars, money, or toys, can stifle creativity by undermining the intrinsic pleasure children derive from creative activities. Creative children's motivation is the satisfaction generated by the work itself (Amabile & Hennessey, 1992).

- *Foster flexible and playful thinking.* Creative thinkers are flexible and play with problems, which gives rise to a paradox. Although creativity takes effort, the effort goes more smoothly if students take it lightly.

- *Introduce children to creative people.* Teachers can invite these people to their classrooms and ask them to describe what helps them become creative or to demonstrate their creative skills. A writer, poet, musician, scientist, and many others can bring their props and productions to the class, turning it into a theater for stimulating students' creativity.

Review and Reflect

3 Explain cognitive changes in middle and late childhood

REVIEW

- What characterizes Piaget's stage of concrete operational thought? What are some contributions and criticisms of Piaget?
- How do children process information in the middle and late childhood years?
- What is intelligence? What are some different forms of intelligence? What are some issues related to intelligence?
- What is creativity? What are some characteristics of creativity? What are some strategies for helping children to become more creative?

REFLECT

- A CD-ROM, *Children's IQ and Achievement Test,* now lets parents test their child's IQ and how well the child is performing in relation to his or her grade in school. What might be some problems with parents giving their children an IQ test?

brainstorming A technique in which individuals are encouraged to come up with creative ideas in a group, play off each other's ideas, and say practically whatever comes to mind.

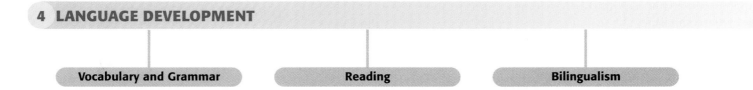

| Vocabulary and Grammar | Reading | Bilingualism |

Children gain new skills as they enter school that make it possible to learn to read and write: these include increasingly using language in a displaced way, learning what a word is, and how to recognize and talk about sounds (Berko Gleason, 2002). They have to learn the alphabetic principle, that the alphabet letters represent sounds of the language. As children develop during middle and late childhood, changes in their vocabulary and grammar also take place (Hoff, 2003).

Vocabulary and Grammar

During middle and late childhood, a change occurs in the way children think about words. They become less tied to the actions and perceptual dimensions associated with words, and they become more analytical in their approach to words.

When asked to say the first word that comes to mind when they hear a word, young children typically provide a word that often follows the word in a sentence. For example, when asked to respond to "dog" the young child may say "barks," or to the word "eat" say "lunch." At about 7 years of age, children begin to respond with a word that is the same part of speech as the stimulus word. For example, a child may now respond to the word "dog" with "cat" or "horse." To "eat," they now might say "drink." This is evidence that children now have begun to categorize their vocabulary by parts of speech (Berko Gleason, 2002).

An important point needs to be made about vocabulary development. Children who begin elementary school with a small vocabulary are at risk when it comes to learning to read (Berko Gleason, 2002).

Children make similar advances in grammar. The elementary school child's improvement in logical reasoning and analytical skills helps in the understanding of such constructions as the appropriate use of comparatives *(shorter, deeper)* and subjectives ("If you were president . . . ").

Reading

What are some approaches to teaching children how to read? Education and language experts continue to debate how children should be taught to read (Combs, 2002). The debate is between those who advocate a basic-skill-and-phonetics approach and those who emphasize a whole-language approach.

- **Basic-skills-and-phonetics approach.** This approach involves teaching both phonemic awareness (breaking apart and manipulating sounds in words) and phonics (learning that sounds are represented by letters of the alphabet which can then be blended together to form words). Early reading materials should involve simple materials (Fox & Hull, 2002). Only after they have learned phonological rules should children be given books and poems.
- **Whole-language approach.** This approach assumes that reading instruction should parallel children's natural language learning. From the outset, reading materials should be whole and meaningful. That is, in early reading instruction, children should be presented with materials in their complete form, such as stories and poems. In this way, say the whole-language advocates, children learn to understand language's communicative function. The whole-language approach implies that all words are essentially "sight" words, which the child recognizes as

mhhe●com/ santrockld9

Reading Research

Reading

Children's Literature

basic-skills-and-phonetics approach The idea that reading instruction should teach both phonemic awareness and phonics.

whole-language approach An approach to reading instruction based on the idea that instruction should parallel children's natural language learning. Reading materials should be whole and meaningful.

a whole without detecting how the individual letters contribute to sounds. In the whole-language approach, reading should be connected with writing and listening skills. Also in this approach, reading is often integrated with other skills such as science and social studies. Most whole-language approaches have students read real-world, relevant materials, such as newspapers and books, and ask them to write about them and discuss them.

Which approach is best? Researchers have found that children can benefit from both approaches. They have found strong evidence that the basic-skills-and-phonetics approach should be used in teaching children to read but that students also benefit from the whole-language approach of being immersed in a natural world of print (Fox & Hull, 2002; Heilman, Blair, & Rupley 2002; Wilson & others, 2001).

These were the conclusions of the National Reading Panel (2000), which conducted the largest, most comprehensive review of research on reading ever conducted. The panel, which included a number of leading experts on reading, found that phonological awareness instruction is especially effective when it is combined with letter training and as part of a total literacy program. The most effective phonological awareness training involve two main skills: blending (listening to a series of separate spoken sounds and blending them, such as /g/ /o/ = go) and segmentation (tapping out/counting out the sounds in a word, such as /g/ /o/ = go, which is two sounds). Researchers also have found that phonological awareness improves when it is integrated with reading and writing, is simple, and is conducted in small groups rather than a whole class (Stahl, 2002). Other conclusions reached by the National Reading Panel (2000) suggest that children's reading benefits from guided oral reading (having them practice what they have learned by reading aloud with guidance and feedback) and applying reading comprehension strategies to guide and improve reading instruction. We will discuss a number of these strategies shortly.

In a recent study, Michael Pressley and his colleagues (2001) examined literacy instruction in five U.S. classrooms. Based on academic and classroom literacy performance of students, the effectiveness of classrooms was analyzed. In the most effective classrooms, teachers exhibited excellent classroom management based on positive reinforcement and cooperation; balanced teaching of skills, literature, and writing; scaffolding and matching task demands to students' skill level; encouragement of student self-regulation; and strong connections across subject areas. In general, the extensive observations did not support any particular reading approach (such as whole-language or basic-skills-and-phonetics approaches); rather, excellent instruction involved multiple, well-integrated components. An important point in this study is that effective reading instruction involves more than a specific reading approach—it also includes effective classroom management, encouragement of self-regulation, and other components (Pressley, 2003).

Reading is like other important skills that children need to develop. It takes time and effort to become a proficient reader. In a recent national assessment, children in the fourth grade had higher scores on a national reading test when they read 11 or more pages daily for school and homework (National Assessment of Educational Progress, 2000) (see figure 10.10). Thus, teachers who required students to read a great deal on a daily basis helped children develop their reading skills.

Bilingualism

As many as 10 million children in the United States come from homes in which English is not the primary language. One major concern regarding such children is to find the best way to help them to succeed in a culture where English is dominant, in school and beyond (Garcia & Willis, 2001; Nieto, 2002).

Bilingual education, which has been the preferred strategy of schools for the last two decades, aims to teach academic subjects to immigrant children in their native languages (most often Spanish), and slowly and simultaneously teach them English

What are the main approaches to teaching children how to read?

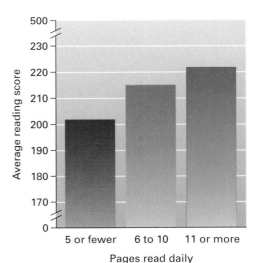

FIGURE 10.10 The Relation of Reading Achievement to Number of Pages Read Daily

In the recent analysis of reading in the fourth grade in the National Assessment of Educational Progress (2000), reading more pages daily in school and as part of homework assignments was related to higher scores on a reading test in which scores ranged from 0 to 500.

Careers in Life-Span Development

Salvador Tamayo, Bilingual Education Teacher

Salvador Tamayo teaches bilingual education in the fifth grade at Turner Elementary School in West Chicago. He recently was given a national educator award by the Milken Family Foundation for his work in bilingual education. Tamayo especially is adept at integrating technology into his bilingual education classes. He and his students have created several award-winning websites about the West Chicago City Museum, the local Latino community, and the history of West Chicago. His students also developed an "I Want to Be an American Citizen" website to assist family and community members in preparing for the U.S. Citizenship Test. Tamayo also teaches a bilingual education class at Wheaton College.

Salvador Tamayo working with students on technology in his bilingual education 5th grade class.

(Garcia & others, 2002). Bilingual education continues to be controversial. To read about the work of one bilingual education teacher, see the Careers in Life-Span Development insert.

Some states have passed laws declaring English to be their official language, eliminating the obligation for schools to teach minority children in languages other than English (Rothstein, 1998). In California, voters repealed bilingual education altogether.

How long does it take language minority students to learn English? Kenji Hakuta and his colleagues (2000) collected data on children in four different school districts to determine how long it takes language minority students to speak and read English effectively. Speaking proficiency took three to five years, while reading proficiency took four to seven years.

A common fear is that early exposure to English will lead to children's loss of their native language. However, researchers have found that bilingualism (the ability to speak two languages) is not detrimental to the child's performance in either language (Hakuta, 2000; Hakuta & Garcia, 1989). In studies of Latino American children, there was no evidence of a loss in Spanish proficiency (productive language, receptive language, and language complexity) for children attending a bilingual preschool (Rodriquez & others, 1995). Children who attended bilingual preschool, compared to those who remained at home, showed significant and parallel gains in both English and Spanish.

Is it better to learn a second language as a child or as an adult? Adults make faster initial progress but their eventual success in the second language is not as great as children's. For example, in one study Chinese and Korean adults who immigrated to the United States at different ages were given a test of grammatical knowledge (Johnson & Newport, 1991). Those who began learning English from 3 to 7 years of age scored as well as native speakers on the test, but those who arrived in the United States (and started learning English) in later childhood or adolescence had lower test scores (see figure 10.11). Children's ability to pronounce a second language with the correct accent also decreases with age, with an especially sharp decline occurring after the age

FIGURE 10.11 Grammar Proficiency and Age at Arrival in the United States

In one study, ten years after arriving in the United States, individuals from China and Korea took a grammar test (Johnson & Newport, 1991). People who arrived before the age of 8 had a better grasp of grammar than those who arrived later.

of about 10 to 12 (Asher & Garcia, 1969). Adolescents and adults can become competent at a second language but this is a more difficult task than learning it as a child.

The United States is one of the few countries in the world in which most students graduate from high school knowing only their own language. For example, in Russia schools have 10 grades, called forms, which roughly correspond to the 12 grades in American schools. Children begin school at age 7 in Russia and begin learning English in the third form. Because of the emphasis on teaching English in Russian schools, most Russian citizens under the age of 40 today are bilingual, able to speak at least some English in addition to their native language.

Review and Reflect

4   Discuss language development in middle and late childhood

REVIEW

- What are some changes in vocabulary and grammar in the middle and late childhood years?
- What controversy characterizes how to teach children to read?
- What is bilingualism? What issues are involved in bilingual education?

REFLECT

- What would be some of the key considerations in a balanced approach to teaching reading?

Reach Your Learning Goals

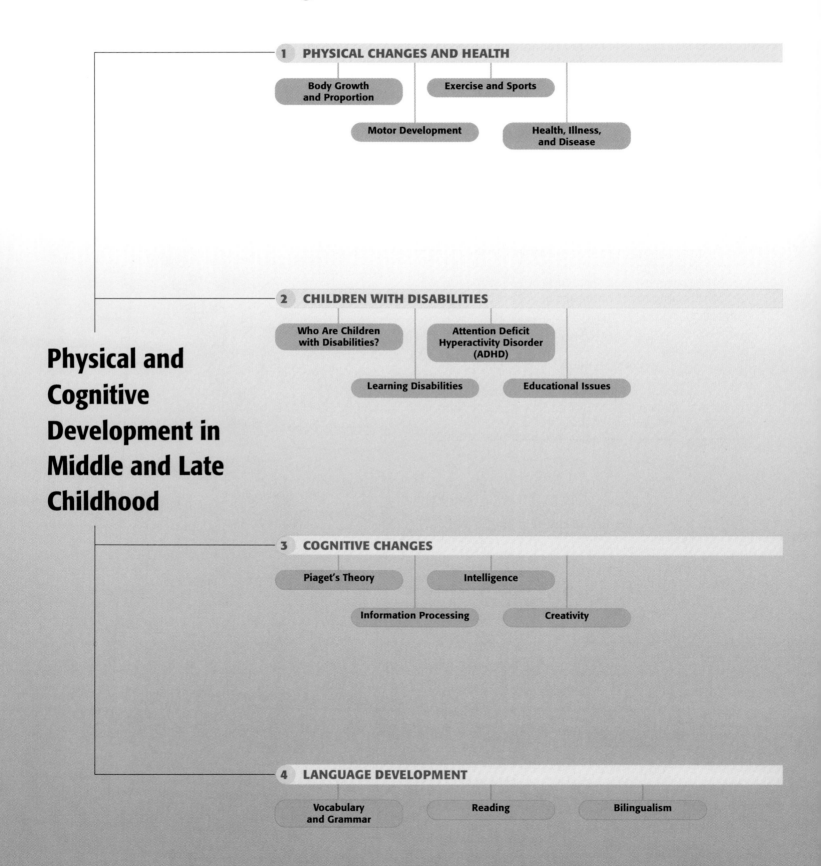

Physical and Cognitive Development in Middle and Late Childhood

1 PHYSICAL CHANGES AND HEALTH

- Body Growth and Proportion
- Exercise and Sports
- Motor Development
- Health, Illness, and Disease

2 CHILDREN WITH DISABILITIES

- Who Are Children with Disabilities?
- Attention Deficit Hyperactivity Disorder (ADHD)
- Learning Disabilities
- Educational Issues

3 COGNITIVE CHANGES

- Piaget's Theory
- Intelligence
- Information Processing
- Creativity

4 LANGUAGE DEVELOPMENT

- Vocabulary and Grammar
- Reading
- Bilingualism

Summary

1 Describe physical changes and health in middle and late childhood

- The period of middle and late childhood involves slow, consistent growth. During this period, children grow an average of 2 to 3 inches a year. Muscle mass and strength gradually increase. Among the most pronounced changes in body growth and proportion are decreases in head circumference, waist circumference, and leg length in relation to body height.

- During the middle and late childhood years, motor development becomes much smoother and more coordinated. Children gain greater control over their bodies and can sit and attend for longer periods of time. However, their lives should be activity-oriented and very active. Increased myelination of the central nervous system is reflected in improved motor skills. Improved fine motor skills appear in the form of handwriting development. Boys are usually better at gross motor skills, girls at fine motor skills.

- Most American children do not get nearly enough exercise. Children's participation in sports can have positive (exercise and self-esteem) or negative (pressure to win and physical injuries) consequences.

- For the most part, middle and late childhood is a time of excellent health. The most common cause of severe injury and death in childhood is motor vehicle accidents, with most occurring at or near the child's home or school. Obesity in children poses serious health risks. Cancer is the second leading cause of death in children (after accidents). Childhood cancers have a different profile from adult cancers—they usually already have spread to other parts of the body and they typically are of a different type. Leukemia is the most common childhood cancer.

2 Identify children with disabilities and issues in educating them

- An estimated 10 percent of U.S. children with a disability receive special education or related services. Slightly more than 50 percent of these students are classified as having a learning disability (in the federal government classification, this includes attention deficit hyperactivity disorder, or ADHD). The term *children with disabilities* is now used instead of the term *disabled children*.

- Children with a learning disability are of normal intelligence or above, have difficulties in at least one academic area and usually several, and have a difficulty that is not attributable to another diagnosed problem or disorder. The most common learning disability in children involves reading. Dyslexia is a severe impairment in the ability to read and spell.

- ADHD is a disability in which children consistently show problems in one or more of these areas: inattention, hyperactivity, and impulsivity. Many experts recommend a combination of academic, behavioral, and medical interventions to help students with ADHD learn and adapt more effectively.

- Beginning in the mid 1960s to mid 1970s, the educational rights for children with disabilities were laid down. In 1975, Public Law 94-142, the Education for All Handicapped Children Act, required that all children be given a free, appropriate public education. In 1990, Public Law 94-142 was renamed the Individuals with Disabilities Education Act (IDEA). An IEP consists of a written plan that spells out a program tailored to a child with a disability. The concept of least restrictive environment, which is contained in the IDEA, states that children with disabilities must be educated in a setting that is as similar as possible to the one in which children without disabilities are educated. The term *inclusion* means educating children with disabilities full-time in the regular classroom.

3 Explain cognitive changes in middle and late childhood

- Piaget said that the stage of concrete operational thought characterizes children from about 7 to 11 years of age. This stage involves operations, conservation, classification, seriation, and transitivity. Thought is not as abstract as later in development. Piaget's ideas have been applied extensively to education. We owe Piaget the field of cognitive development; he was a genius at observing children. However, critics question his estimates of competence at different developmental levels, his stages concept, and other ideas. Neo-Piagetians believe that Piaget got some things right but that his theory needs considerable revision. Neo-Piagetians emphasize how children process information, strategies, speed of information processing, and more precise cognitive steps than Piaget did.

- Long-term memory increases in middle and late childhood. Knowledge and expertise influence memory. Control processes, also called strategies, can be used by children to improve their memory. Critical thinking involves thinking reflectively and productively, as well as evaluating the evidence. A special concern is the lack of emphasis on critical thinking in many schools. Metacognition is cognition about cognition, or knowing about knowing. Most metacognitive studies have focused on metamemory. Pressley believes the key to education is helping students learn a rich repertoire of strategies.

- Intelligence consists of problem-solving skills and the ability to adapt to and learn from life's everyday experiences. Interest in intelligence often focuses on individual differences and assessment. Binet and Simon developed the first intelligence test. Binet developed the concept of mental age and Stern created the concept of IQ as MA/CA X 100. The Stanford-Binet approximates a normal distribution. The Wechsler scales are widely used to assess intelligence and yield an overall IQ, as well as verbal and performance IQs. Spearman proposed that people have a general intelligence (g) and specific types of intelligence (s). Sternberg proposed that intelligence comes in three main forms: analytical, creative, and practical. Gardner believes there are eight types of intelligence: verbal, math, spatial, bodily-kinesthetic, self-insight, insight about others, musical skills, and naturalist skills. The multiple-intelligence approaches have expanded our conception of intelligence, but critics argue that the research base for these approaches is not well established. Issues in intelligence include ethnicity and culture, and the use and misuse of intelligence tests. Mental retardation involves low IQ and problems in adapting to everyday life. One classification of mental retardation consists of organic or cultural-familial. A child who is gifted has above-average intelligence and/or superior talent for something. Terman contributed to our understanding that gifted children are not more maladjusted than nongifted children. Three characteristics of gifted children are precocity, individuality, and a passion to master.

- Creativity is the ability to think in novel and unusual ways and to come up with unique solutions to problems. Guilford distinguished between convergent and divergent thinking. A number of strategies can be used to encourage children's creative thinking, including brainstorming.

4 **Discuss language development in middle and late childhood**

- Children become more analytical and logical in their approach to words and grammar. They become less tied to the actions and perceptual dimensions associated with words, and they become more analytical in their approach to words. In terms of grammar, children now better understand comparatives and subjectives.
- A current debate in reading focuses on the basic-skills-and-phonetics approach versus the whole-language approach. The basic-skills-and-phonetics approach advocates phonetics instruction and giving children simplified materials. The whole-language approach stresses that reading instruction should parallel children's natural language learning and giving children whole-language materials, such as books and poems. The National Reading Panel (2000) concluded that both approaches can benefit children.
- Bilingual education aims to teach academic subjects to immigrant children in their native languages (most often in Spanish) while gradually adding English instruction. Researchers have found that bilingualism does not interfere with performance in either language. Success in learning a second language is greater in childhood than in adolescence.

Key Terms

learning disability 307
dyslexia 307
attention deficit hyperactivity disorder (ADHD) 308
individualized education plan (IEP) 309
least restrictive environment (LRE) 309
inclusion 309
seriation 312

transitivity 312
neo-Piagetians 314
long-term memory 314
control processes 315
critical thinking 315
metacognition 316
intelligence 317
individual differences 317
mental age (MA) 317
intelligence quotient (IQ) 317

normal distribution 317
triarchic theory of intelligence 319
culture-fair tests 321
mental retardation 323
organic retardation 323
cultural-familial retardation 323
gifted 323
creativity 324

convergent thinking 324
divergent thinking 324
brainstorming 325
basic-skills-and-phonetics approach 326
whole-language approach 326

Key People

Jean Piaget 311
John Dewey 315
Jacqueline and Martin Brooks 315
Deanna Kuhn 316

Michael Pressley 316, 327
Alfred Binet 317
Theophile Simon 317
William Stern 317
David Wechsler 317

Charles Spearman 319
L. L. Thurstone 319
Robert J. Sternberg 319
Howard Gardner 319
Nathan Brody 321

Lewis Terman 323
Ellen Winner 323
J. P. Guilford 324
Teresa Amabile 325

Taking It to the Net

1. Clarence wants to teach his fifth-grade students good diet, nutritional, and exercise habits. What lessons can they be taught now that will benefit them later in life?
2. Noah's parents are upset to hear that their fourth-grader may have dyslexia. Noah's father voices to his son's teacher his concern that people will think Noah is stupid. What should Noah's teacher tell these parents about the nature and causes of dyslexia?

3. Carla is the top student in mathematics. Mario displays exceptional talent in art class. Warren is very social and popular with his peers. What do these three students show us about different types of intelligence? How might traditional theories of intelligence miss the unique talents of these students?

Connect to www.mhhe.com/santrockld9 to research the answers and complete these exercises.

E-Learning Tools

To help you master the material in this chapter, you'll find a number of valuable study tools on the Student CD-ROM that accompanies this book. In addition, visit the Online Learning Center for *Life-Span Development,* ninth edition, where you'll find these valuable resources for chapter 10, "Physical and Cognitive Development in Middle and Late Childhood."

- Based on what you've read about Gardner's eight types of intelligence, what areas of intelligence are your strengths? In which are you least proficient? Use the self-assessment, *Evaluating Myself on Gardner's Eight Types of Intelligence,* to find out.
- Build your decision-making skills by trying your hand at the parenting and education "Scenarios."

Children are busy becoming something they have not quite grasped yet, something which keeps changing.

—**ALASTAIR REID**
American Poet,
20th Century

Socioemotional Development in Middle and Late Childhood

Learning Goals

1 *D*iscuss emotional and personality development in middle and late childhood

2 *D*escribe parent-child issues and societal changes in families

3 *I*dentify changes in peer relationships in middle and late childhood

4 *C*haracterize the transition to elementary school and sociocultural aspects of schooling and achievement

Images of Life-Span Development

The Stories of Lafayette and Pharoah: The Tragedy of Poverty and Violence

Alex Kotlowitz (1991) followed the lives of two brothers, 10-year-old Lafayette and 7-year-old Pharoah, for two years. The boys lived in an impoverished housing project in Chicago. Their father had a drug habit and had trouble holding down a job.

Kotlowitz approached their mother, LaJoe, about the possibility of writing a book about Lafayette, Pharoah, and other children in the neighborhood. She liked the idea but hesitated. She then commented, "But you know, there are no children around here. They've seen too much to be children."

Over the two years, Lafayette and Pharoah struggled with school, resisted the lure of gangs, and mourned the deaths of friends. All the time they wondered why they were living in such a violent place and hoped they could get out.

Their older brother, 17-year-old Terrence, was a drug user. Lafayette told one of his friends, "You grow up 'round it. There are a lot of people in the projects who say they're not gonna do drugs, that they're not gonna drop out of school, that they won't be on the streets. But they're doing it now. Never say never. But I say never. My older brother didn't set a good example for me, but I'll set a good example for my younger brother."

A few days later, police arrested Terrence as a robbery suspect. They handcuffed him in the apartment in front of Lafayette and Pharoah. Pharoah told his mother, "I'm just too young to understand how life really is."

Several months later, shooting erupted in the housing complex, and their mother herded Lafayette and Pharoah into the hallway, where they crouched along the walls to avoid stray bullets. Lafayette said to his mother, "If we don't get away, someone's gonna end up dead. I feel it." Shortly thereafter, a 9-year-old friend of the boys was shot in the back of the head as he walked into his building just across the street. The bullet had been meant for someone else.

Poverty, stress, and violence were constants where Lafayette and Pharoah lived. There were so many shootings that many of them didn't even make the newspaper. Both boys wanted to move to a safe, quiet neighborhood, but their mother struggled just to make ends meet in the projects.

How might the stress of poverty and violence affect children's development? How might it affect the parent-child relationship? Although these kinds of circumstances are often harmful to children, might some children be resilient in the face of such stressors and have positive outcomes in life?

Some children triumph over life's adversities (Masten, 1999; Perkins & Borden, 2003). Norman Garmezy (1985, 1993) has studied resilience amid disadvantage for many years. He concluded that three factors help children become resilient to stress and disadvantage: (1) good cognitive skills, especially attention, which helps children focus on tasks, such as schoolwork; (2) a family—even if enveloped in poverty—characterized by warmth, cohesion, and a caring adult, such as a grandparent who takes responsibility in the absence of responsive parents or in the presence of intense marital conflict; and (3) external support, such as a teacher, a neighbor, a mentor, a caring agency, or a church. In one longitudinal study of resilient individuals from birth to 32 years of age in Kauia, these three factors were present in their lives (Werner, 1989). Later in this chapter we will focus on some of the strategies that can be used in schools to help children like Lafayette and Pharoah who live in impoverished conditions.

1 EMOTIONAL AND PERSONALITY DEVELOPMENT

| The Self | | Moral Development |
| Emotional Development | | Gender |

In chapter 9, we discussed the development of the self, emotional development, moral development, and gender in early childhood ◀▥ p. 268. Here, we will focus on these important dimensions of children's development in middle and late childhood.

The Self

What is the nature of the child's self-understanding and self-esteem in the elementary school years?

The Development of Self-Understanding In middle and late childhood, self-understanding increasingly shifts from defining oneself through external characteristics to defining oneself through internal characteristics. Elementary school children are also more likely to define themselves in terms of social characteristics and social comparisons (Harter, 1999). This theme of self-definition will be discussed shortly.

In middle and late childhood, children not only recognize differences between inner and outer states but also are more likely to include subjective inner states in their definition of self. For example, in one study, second-grade children were much more likely than younger children to name psychological characteristics (such as preferences or personality traits) in their self-definition and were less likely to name physical characteristics (such as eye color or possessions) (Aboud & Skerry, 1983). For example, 8-year-old Todd included in his self-description, "I am smart and I am popular." Ten-year-old Tina says about herself, "I am pretty good about not worrying most of the time. I used to lose my temper, but I'm better about that now. I also feel proud when I do well in school."

In addition to the increase of psychological characteristics in self-definition during the elementary school years, the *social aspects* of the self also increase at this point in development. In one investigation, elementary school children often included references to social groups in their self-descriptions (Livesly & Bromley, 1973). For example, some children referred to themselves as Girl Scouts, as Catholics, or as someone who has two close friends.

Children's self-understanding in the elementary school years also includes increasing reference to *social comparison*. At this point in development, children are more likely to distinguish themselves from others in comparative rather than in absolute terms. That is, elementary-school-age children are no longer as likely to think about what they do or do not do but are more likely to think about what they can do *in comparison with others*. This developmental shift provides an increased tendency to establish one's differences from others as an individual.

Self-Esteem and Self-Concept High self-esteem and a positive self-concept are important characteristics of children's well-being (Dusek & McIntyre, 2003; Harter, 1999). **Self-esteem** refers to global evaluations of the self. Self-esteem is also referred to as self-worth or self-image. For example, a child may perceive that she is not merely a person but a *good* person. Of course, not all children have an overall positive image of themselves. **Self-concept** refers to domain-specific evaluations of the self. Children can make self-evaluations in many domains of their lives—academic, athletic,

K̲now yourself.
—SOCRATES
Greek Philosopher, 5th Century B.C.

self-esteem The global evaluative dimension of the self. Self-esteem is also referred to as self-worth or self-image.

self-concept Domain-specific evaluations of the self.

appearance, and so on. In sum, *self-esteem* refers to global self-evaluations, *self-concept* to more domain-specific evaluations.

Investigators have not always made clear distinctions between self-esteem and self-concept, sometimes using the terms interchangeably or not precisely defining them. The distinction between self-esteem as global self-evaluation and self-concept as domain-specific self-evaluation should help you keep the terms straight.

Research on Self-Esteem   One research area explores whether self-esteem fluctuates from day to day or remains stable. Most research studies have found it to be stable at least across a month or so of time (Baumeister, 1993; Tesser, 2000). Self-esteem can change, especially in response to transitions in life. For example, when children go from elementary school to middle school, their self-esteem usually drops (Hawkins & Berndt, 1985).

As children grow through the elementary years, they increasingly engage in social comparison with their peers. This can lower their self-esteem when they evaluate themselves in a less favorable light than their peers (Damon & Hart, 1988; Harter, 1998).

Another research issue involves whether low self-esteem is linked with developmental problems. One area where the research has been consistent is depression—low self-esteem is related to depression (Harter, 1998).

An important point needs to be made about much of the research on self-esteem: It is correlational rather than experimental. Remember from chapter 2, "The Science of Life-Span Development," that correlation does not equal causation. Thus, if a correlational study finds an association between self-esteem and depression, depression might cause low self-esteem or low self-esteem might cause depression.

Increasing Children's Self-Esteem   Four ways children's self-esteem can be improved are listed here (Bednar, Wells, & Peterson, 1995; Harter, 1999):

- *Identify the causes of low self-esteem.* Intervention should target the causes of low-esteem. Children have the highest self-esteem when they perform competently in domains that are important to them. Therefore, children should be encouraged to identify and value areas of competence. These areas might include academic skills, athletic skills, physical attractiveness, and social acceptance.
- *Provide emotional support and social approval.* Some children with low self-esteem come from conflicted families or conditions in which they experienced abuse or neglect—situations in which support was not available. In some cases, alternative sources of support can be implemented either informally through the encouragement of a teacher, a coach, or another significant adult, or more formally, through programs such as Big Brothers and Big Sisters.
- *Help children achieve.* Achievement also can improve children's self-esteem. For example, the straightforward teaching of real skills to children often results in increased achievement and, thus, in enhanced self-esteem. Children develop higher self-esteem because they know the important tasks to achieve goals, and they have experienced performing them or similar behaviors.
- *Help children cope.* Self-esteem is often increased when children face a problem and try to cope with it, rather than avoid it. If coping rather than avoidance prevails, children often face problems realistically, honestly, and nondefensively. This produces favorable self-evaluative thoughts, which lead to the self-generated approval that raises self-esteem.

Industry Versus Inferiority   In chapter 2, we described Erik Erikson's (1968) eight stages of human development ◀▥ p. 46. His fourth stage, industry versus inferiority, appears during middle and late childhood. The term *industry* expresses a dominant theme of this period: Children become interested in how things are made and how they work. It is the Robinson Crusoe age, in that the enthusiasm and minute detail Crusoe uses to describe his activities appeal to the child's budding sense of industry.

When children are encouraged in their efforts to make, build, and work—whether building a model airplane, constructing a tree house, fixing a bicycle, solving an addition problem, or cooking—their sense of industry increases. However, parents who see their children's efforts at making things as "mischief" or "making a mess" encourage children's development of a sense of inferiority.

Children's social worlds beyond their families also contribute to a sense of industry. School becomes especially important in this regard. Consider children who are slightly below average in intelligence. They are too bright to be in special classes but not bright enough to be in gifted classes. They fail frequently in their academic efforts, developing a sense of inferiority. By contrast, consider children whose sense of industry is derogated at home. A series of sensitive and committed teachers may revitalize their sense of industry (Elkind, 1970).

Emotional Development

In chapter 9, we saw that preschoolers become more adept at talking about their own and others' emotions ◀▥ p. 270. They also show a growing awareness about controlling and managing emotions to meet social standards. Further developmental changes characterize emotion in middle and late childhood (Rubin, 2000; Saarni, 1999).

Developmental Changes Here are some important developmental changes in emotions during the elementary school years (Kuebli, 1994; Wintre & Vallance, 1994):

- An increased ability to understand such complex emotions as pride and shame (Kuebli, 1994). These emotions become more internalized and integrated with a sense of personal responsibility.
- Increased understanding that more than one emotion can be experienced in a particular situation
- An increased tendency to take into fuller account the events leading to emotional reactions
- Marked improvements in the ability to suppress or conceal negative emotional reactions
- The use of self-initiated strategies for redirecting feelings ◀▥ p. 319

Emotional Intelligence Both Sternberg's and Gardner's views, which were discussed in chapter 10, include categories of social intelligence. In Sternberg's theory the category is called "practical intelligence" and in Gardner's theory the categories are "insights about self" and "insights about others." However, the greatest interest in recent years in the social aspects of intelligence has focused on the concept of emotional intelligence. The concept of **emotional intelligence** initially was proposed in 1990 as a form of social intelligence that involves the ability to monitor one's own and others' feelings and emotions, to discriminate among them, and to use this information to guide one's thinking and action (Salovy & Mayer, 1990). However, the main interest in emotional intelligence was ushered in with the publication of Daniel Goleman's book *Emotional Intelligence* (1995). Goleman believes that when it comes to predicting an individual's competence, IQ as measured by standardized intelligence tests matters less than emotional intelligence. In Goleman's view, emotional intelligence involves these four main areas:

- *Developing emotional self-awareness* (such as the ability to separate feelings from actions)
- *Managing emotions* (such as being able to control anger)
- *Reading emotions* (such as taking the perspective of others)
- *Handling relationships* (such as the ability to solve relationship problems)

Some schools have begun to develop programs that are designed to help children with their emotional lives. For example, one private school near San Francisco, the

emotional intelligence A form of social intelligence that involves the ability to monitor one's own and others' feelings and emotions, to discriminate among them, and to use this information to guide one's thinking and action.

What are some effective strategies to help children cope with traumatic events, such as the terrorist attacks on the United States on 9/11/2001?

Nueva School, has a class in what is called "self science." The subject in self science is feelings—the child's own and those involved in relationships. Teachers speak to real issues, such as hurt over being left out, envy, and disagreements that could disrupt into a schoolyard battle. The list of the contents for self science matches up with many of Goleman's components of emotional intelligence.

Coping with Stress An important aspect of children's lives is learning how to cope with stress. As children get older, they are able to more accurately appraise a stressful situation and determine how much control they have over it. Older children generate more coping alternatives to stressful conditions and use more cognitive coping strategies (Compas & others, 2001; Saarni, 1999). For example, older children are better at intentionally shifting their thoughts to something that is less stressful than younger children are. Older children are better at reframing (changing one's perception of a stressful situation). For example, younger children may be very disappointed that their teacher did not say hello to them when they arrived at school. Older children may reframe this type of situation and think, "She might have been busy with other things and just forgot to say hello."

By 10 years of age, most children are able to use these cognitive strategies to cope with stress (Saarni, 1999). However, in families that have not been supportive and are characterized by turmoil or trauma, children may be so overwhelmed by stress that they do not use such strategies.

The terrorist attacks on the World Trade Center in New York City and the Pentagon in Washington, D.C., on September 11, 2001, raised special concerns about how to help children cope with such stressful events (La Greca & others, 2002). Children who have a number of coping techniques have the best chance of adapting and functioning competently in the face of such traumatic events. Here are some recommendations for helping children cope with the stress of these types of events (Gurwitch & others, 2001):

- *Reinforce ideas of safety and security.* This may need to be done a number of times.
- *Listen to and tolerate children retelling events.*
- *Encourage children to talk about confusing feelings, worries, daydreams, and disruptions of concentration.* Listen carefully and remind them that these are normal reactions following a scary event.
- *Help children make sense of what happened.* Children may misunderstand what took place. For example, young children may blame themselves. Children may believe things happened that did not happen, believe that terrorists are coming to their home or school, and so on. Gently help children to develop a realistic understanding of the stressful event.
- *Provide reassurance to children so that they will be able to handle stressful feelings over time.*
- *Protect children from reexposure to frightening situations and reminders of the trauma.* This includes limiting conversations about the event in front of children.

Traumatic events may cause individuals to think about the moral aspects of life. Hopelessness and despair may short-circuit moral development when a child is confronted by the violence of war zones and impoverished inner cities (Garbarino & others, 1992; Nadar, 2001). Let's further explore children's moral development.

Moral Development

Remember from chapter 9 our description of Piaget's view of moral development  p. 271. Piaget believed that younger children are characterized by heteronomous morality but that, by 10 years of age, they have moved into a higher stage called "autonomous" morality. According to Piaget, older children consider the intentions of the individual, believe that rules are subject to change, and are aware that punishment does not always follow a wrongdoing.

A second major perspective on moral development was proposed by Lawrence Kohlberg. Kohlberg acknowledged that Piaget's cognitive stages of development (especially preoperational, concrete operational, and formal operational) serve as the underpinnings for his theory. However, Kohlberg believed there was more to moral development than Piaget's stages. Kohlberg especially emphasized the importance of opportunities to take the perspective of others and experiencing conflict between one's current stage of moral thinking and the reasoning of someone at a higher stage.

Kohlberg's Theory of Moral Development   Kohlberg stressed that moral development is based primarily on moral reasoning and unfolds in stages (Kohlberg, 1958, 1976, 1986). Kohlberg arrived at his view after 20 years of using a unique interview with children. In the interview, children are presented with a series of stories in which characters face moral dilemmas. Here is the most well-known Kohlberg dilemma:

> In Europe a woman was near death from a special kind of cancer. There was one drug that the doctors thought might save her. It was a form of radium that a druggist in the same town had recently discovered. The drug was expensive to make, but the druggist was charging ten times what the drug cost him to make. He paid $200 for the radium and charged $2,000 for a small dose of the drug. The sick woman's husband, Heinz, went to everyone he knew to borrow the money, but he could only get together $1,000 which is half of what it cost. He told the druggist that his wife was dying and asked him to sell it cheaper or let him pay later. But the druggist said, "No, I discovered the drug, and I am going to make money from it." So Heinz got desperate and broke into the man's store to steal the drug for his wife. (Kohlberg, 1969, p. 379)

This story is one of eleven that Kohlberg devised to investigate the nature of moral thought. After reading the story, the interviewee answers a series of questions about the moral dilemma. Should Heinz have stolen the drug? Was stealing it right or wrong? Why? Is it a husband's duty to steal the drug for his wife if he can get it no other way? Would a good husband steal? Did the druggist have the right to charge that much when there was no law setting a limit on the price? Why or why not? It is important to note that whether the individual says to steal the drug or not is not important in identifying the person's moral stage. What is important is the individual's moral reasoning behind the decision.

From the answers interviewees gave for this and other moral dilemmas, Kohlberg hypothesized three levels of moral development, each of which is characterized by two stages. A key concept in understanding moral development is **internalization,** the developmental change from behavior that is externally controlled to behavior that is controlled by internal standards and principles. As children and adolescents develop, their moral thoughts become more internalized. Let's look further at Kohlberg's three levels of moral development (see figure 11.1 on page 342).

Kohlberg's Level 1: Preconventional Reasoning   **Preconventional reasoning** is the lowest level in Kohlberg's theory of moral development. At this level, the individual shows no internalization of moral values—moral reasoning is controlled by external rewards and punishments.

- Stage 1. *Heteronomous morality* is the first stage in Kohlberg's theory. At this stage, moral thinking is often tied to punishment. For example, children and adolescents obey adults because adults tell them to obey.
- Stage 2. *Individualism, instrumental purpose, and exchange* is the second Kohlberg stage of moral development. At this stage, individuals pursue their own interests but also let others do the same. Thus, what is right involves an equal exchange. People are nice to others so that they will be nice to them in return.

Kohlberg's Level 2: Conventional Reasoning   **Conventional reasoning** is the second, or intermediate, level in Kohlberg's theory of moral development. At this

Lawrence Kohlberg, the architect of a provocative cognitive developmental theory of moral development. *What is the nature of his theory?*

Kohlberg's Theory

internalization The developmental change from behavior that is externally controlled to behavior that is controlled by internal standards and principles.

preconventional reasoning The lowest level in Kohlberg's theory of moral development. The individual shows no internalization of moral values—moral reasoning is controlled by external rewards and punishment.

conventional reasoning The second, or intermediate, level in Kohlberg's theory of moral development. Internalization is intermediate. Individuals abide by certain standards (internal), but they are the standards of others (external), such as parents or the laws of society.

LEVEL 1 Preconventional Level No Internalization	**LEVEL 2** Conventional Level Intermediate Internalization	**LEVEL 3** Postconventional Level Full Internalization
Stage 1 Heteronomous Morality *Children obey because adults tell them to obey. People base their moral decisions on fear of punishment.*	**Stage 3** Mutual Interpersonal Expectations, Relationships, and Interpersonal Conformity *Individuals value trust, caring, and loyalty to others as a basis for moral judgments.*	**Stage 5** Social Contract or Utility and Individual Rights *Individuals reason that values, rights, and principles undergird or transcend the law.*
Stage 2 Individualism, Purpose, and Exchange *Individuals pursue their own interests but let others do the same. What is right involves equal exchange.*	**Stage 4** Social System Morality *Moral judgments are based on understanding of the social order, law, justice, and duty.*	**Stage 6** Universal Ethical Principles *The person has developed moral judgments that are based on universal human rights. When faced with a dilemma between law and conscience, a personal, individualized conscience is followed.*

FIGURE 11.1 Kohlberg's Three Levels and Six Stages of Moral Development

level, internalization is intermediate. Individuals abide by certain standards (internal), but they are the standards of others (external), such as parents or the laws of society.

- Stage 3. *Mutual interpersonal expectations, relationships, and interpersonal conformity* is Kohlberg's third stage of moral development. At this stage, individuals value trust, caring, and loyalty to others as a basis of moral judgments. Children and adolescents often adopt their parents' moral standards at this stage, seeking to be thought of by their parents as a "good girl" or a "good boy."
- Stage 4. *Social systems morality* is the fourth stage in Kohlberg's theory of moral development. At this stage, moral judgments are based on understanding the social order, law, justice, and duty. For example, adolescents may say that, for a community to work effectively, it needs to be protected by laws that are adhered to by its members.

Kohlberg's Level 3: Postconventional Reasoning **Postconventional reasoning** is the highest level in Kohlberg's theory of moral development. At this level, morality is completely internalized and is not based on others' standards. The individual recognizes alternative moral courses, explores the options, and then decides on a personal moral code.

- Stage 5. *Social contract or utility and individual rights* is the fifth Kohlberg stage. At this stage, individuals reason that values, rights, and principles undergird or transcend the law. A person evaluates the validity of actual laws and social systems can be examined in terms of the degree to which they preserve and protect fundamental human rights and values.
- Stage 6. *Universal ethical principles* is the sixth and highest stage in Kohlberg's theory of moral development. At this stage, the person has developed a moral standard based on universal human rights. When faced with a conflict between law and conscience, the person will follow conscience, even though the decision might involve personal risk.

Kohlberg believed that these levels and stages occur in a sequence and are age related: Before age 9, most children reason about moral dilemmas in a preconventional way; by early adolescence, they reason in more conventional ways. Most adolescents reason at stage 3, with some signs of stages 2 and 4. By early adulthood, a

postconventional reasoning The highest level in Kohlberg's theory of moral development. Morality is completely internalized.

small number of individuals reason in postconventional ways. Figure 11.2 shows the results of a longitudinal investigation of Kohlberg's stages (Colby & others, 1983). A review of data from 45 studies in 27 diverse world cultures provided support for the universality of Kohlberg's first four stages, although there was more cultural diversity at stages 5 and 6 (Snarey, 1987).

Kohlberg's Critics   Kohlberg's provocative theory of moral development has not gone unchallenged (Helwig & Turiel, 2002; Rest, 1999). The criticisms involve the link between moral thought and moral behavior, inadequate consideration of culture's role and the family's role in moral development, and underestimation of the care perspective.

Moral Thought and Moral Behavior   Kohlberg's theory has been criticized for placing too much emphasis on moral thought and not enough emphasis on moral behavior. Moral reasons can sometimes be a shelter for immoral behavior. Bank embezzlers and presidents endorse the loftiest of moral virtues when commenting about moral dilemmas, but their own behavior may be immoral. No one wants a nation of cheaters and thieves who can reason at the postconventional level. The cheaters and thieves may know what is right yet still do what is wrong.

Culture and Moral Development   Yet another criticism of Kohlberg's view is that it is culturally biased (Banks, 1993; Miller, 1995). A review of research on moral development in 27 countries concluded that moral reasoning is more culture-specific than Kohlberg envisioned and that Kohlberg's scoring system does not recognize higher-level moral reasoning in certain cultural groups (Snarey, 1987). Examples of higher-level moral reasoning that would not be scored as such by Kohlberg's system are values related to communal equity and collective happiness in Israel, the unity and sacredness of all life forms in India, and the relation of the individual to the community in New Guinea. These examples of moral reasoning would not be scored at the highest level in Kohlberg's system because they do not emphasize the individual's rights and abstract principles of justice.

Family Processes and Moral Development   Kohlberg believed that family processes are essentially unimportant in children's moral development. He argued that parent-child relationships are usually power-oriented and provide children with little opportunity for mutual give-and-take or perspective taking. Rather, Kohlberg said that such opportunities are more likely to be provided by children's peer relations (Brabeck, 2000).

Kohlberg likely underestimated the contribution of family relationships to moral development. Inductive discipline, which involves the use of reasoning and focuses children's attention on the consequences of their actions for others, positively influences moral development (Hoffman, 1970). Parents' moral values influence children's developing moral thoughts (Gibbs, 1993).

Gender and the Care Perspective   Carol Gilligan (1982, 1992, 1996) believes that Kohlberg's theory of moral development does not adequately reflect relationships and concern for others. The **justice perspective** is a moral perspective that is built on the rights of the individual; individuals stand alone and make moral decisions independently. Kohlberg's theory is a justice perspective. By contrast, the **care perspective** is a moral perspective that views people in terms of their connectedness with others and emphasizes interpersonal communication, relationships with others, and concern for others. Gilligan's theory is a care perspective. According to Gilligan, Kohlberg greatly

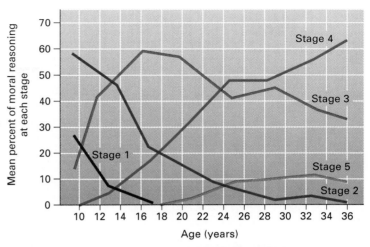

FIGURE 11.2 Age and the Percentage of Individuals at Each Kohlberg Stage

In one longitudinal study of males from 10 to 36 years of age, at age 10 most moral reasoning was at stage 2 (Colby & others, 1983). At 16 to 18 years of age, stage 3 became the most frequent type of moral reasoning, and it was not until the mid-twenties that stage 4 became the most frequent. Stage 5 did not appear until 20 to 22 years of age and it never characterized more than 10 percent of the individuals. In this study, the moral stages appeared somewhat later than Kohlberg envisioned and stage 6 was absent.

justice perspective A moral perspective that focuses on the rights of the individual; individuals independently make moral decisions.

care perspective The moral perspective of Carol Gilligan, that views people in terms of their connectedness with others and emphasizes interpersonal communication, relationships with others, and concern for others.

Carol Gilligan (third from right) is shown with some of the students she has interviewed about the importance of relationships in a female's development. *What is Gilligans's view of moral development?*

mhhe ●com/
santrockld9

Gilligan's Care Perspective

underplayed the care perspective in moral development. She believes that this may have happened because he was a male, because most of his research was with males rather than females, and because he used male responses as a model for his theory.

Gilligan believes that girls reach a critical juncture in their development when they reach adolescence. Usually around 11 to 12 years of age, girls become aware that their intense interest in intimacy is not prized by the male-dominated culture, even though society values women as caring and altruistic. The dilemma is that girls are presented with a choice that makes them look either selfish or selfless. Gilligan believes that, as adolescent girls experience this dilemma, they increasingly silence their "distinctive voice."

Researchers have found support for Gilligan's claim that females' and males' moral reasoning often centers around different concerns and issues (Galotti, Kozberg, & Farmer, 1990). However, one of Gilligan's initial claims—that traditional Kohlbergian measures of moral development are biased against females—has been supported (Walker, 1991).

While females often articulate a stronger care perspective and males a stronger justice perspective, the gender difference is not absolute. For example, in one study, 53 of the 80 females and males showed either a care or a justice perspective, but 27 individuals used both orientations, with neither predominating (Gilligan & Attanucci, 1988).

Prosocial Behavior and Altruism Children's moral behavior can involve negative, antisocial acts—such as lying, cheating, and stealing—or it can involve their *prosocial behavior*—the positive aspects of moral behavior, such as showing empathy to someone or behaving altruistically (Hoffman, 2002). While Kohlberg's and Gilligan's theories have focused primarily on the cognitive, thinking aspects of moral development, the study of prosocial moral behavior has placed more emphasis on its behavioral aspects (Grusec, Davidov, & Lundell, 2002).

Altruism is an unselfish interest in helping someone else. Human acts of altruism are plentiful—the hardworking laborer who places $5 in a Salvation Army kettle; rock concerts to feed the hungry, help farmers, and fund AIDS research; the child who takes in a wounded cat and cares for it, and so on.

William Damon (1988) described a developmental sequence of children's altruism, especially of sharing. Most sharing during the first three years of life is done not for empathy reasons, but for the fun of the social play ritual or out of mere imitation. Then, at about 4 years of age, a combination of empathic awareness and adult encouragement produces a sense of obligation on the part of the child to share with others. This obligation forces the child to share, even though the child may not perceive this as the best way to have fun. Most 4-year-olds are not selfless saints, however. Children believe they have an obligation to share but do not necessarily think they should be as generous to others as they are to themselves.

By the start of the elementary school years, children genuinely begin to express more objective ideas about fairness. It is common to hear 6-year-old children use the word *fair* as synonymous with *equal* or *same*. By the mid to late elementary school years, children also believe that equity means special treatment for those who deserve it.

Missing from the factors that guide children's altruism is one that many adults might expect to be the most influential of all: the motivation to obey adult authority figures. Surprisingly, a number of studies have shown that adult authority has only a small influence on children's sharing (Eisenberg, 1982). Parental advice and prodding certainly foster standards of sharing, but the give-and-take of peer requests and arguments provides the most immediate stimulation of sharing.

Gender

altruism Unselfish interest in helping another person.

In chapter 9, we discussed the biological, cognitive, and social influences on gender development ◀▥ p. 272. Gender is such a pervasive aspect of an individual's identity that we will further consider its role in children's development here. Among the gender-related topics we will examine are gender stereotypes, similarities, and differences; and gender-role classification.

Gender Stereotypes **Gender stereotypes** are broad categories that reflect our general impressions and beliefs about females and males. How widespread is feminine and masculine stereotyping? According to a far-ranging study of college students in 30 countries, stereotyping of females and males is pervasive (Williams & Best, 1982). Males were widely believed to be dominant, independent, aggressive, achievement-oriented, and enduring, while females were widely believed to be nurturant, affiliative, less esteemed, and more helpful in times of distress. Other research continues to find that gender stereotyping is pervasive (Best, 2002; Kite, 2002; Spence & Buckner, 2000).

In a subsequent study, women and men who lived in more highly developed countries perceived themselves as more similar than women and men who lived in less developed countries (Williams & Best, 1989). In the more highly developed countries, the women were more likely to attend college and be gainfully employed. Thus, as sexual equality increases, male and female stereotypes, as well as actual behavioral differences, may diminish. In this study, the women were more likely to perceive similarity between the sexes than the men were (Williams & Best, 1989). And the sexes were perceived more similarly in the Christian than in the Muslim societies.

Gender Similarities and Differences Let's now examine some of the differences between the sexes, keeping in mind that (1) the differences are averages—not all females versus all males; (2) even when differences are reported, there is considerable overlap between the sexes; and (3) the differences may be due primarily to biological factors, sociocultural factors, or both. First, we will examine physical differences, and then we will turn to cognitive and socioemotional differences.

Physical Similarities and Differences From conception on, females have a longer life expectancy than males, and females are less likely than males to develop physical or mental disorders. Estrogen strengthens the immune system, making females more resistant to infection, for example. Female hormones also signal the liver to produce more "good" cholesterol, which makes females' blood vessels more elastic than males'. Testosterone triggers the production of low-density lipoprotein, which clogs blood vessels. Males have twice the risk of coronary disease as females. Higher levels of stress hormones cause faster clotting in males, but also higher blood pressure than in females. Women have about twice the body fat of men, most concentrated around breasts and hips. In males, fat is more likely to go to the abdomen. On the average, males grow to be 10 percent taller than females. Male hormones promote the growth of long bones; female hormones stop such growth at puberty.

Does gender matter when it comes to brain structure and function? Human brains are much alike, whether the brain belongs to a male or a female (Halpern, 2002). However, researchers have found some differences in the brains of males and females (Goldstein & others, 2001; Kimura, 2000) Among the differences that have been discovered are:

- One part of the hypothalamus responsible for sexual behavior is larger in men than in women (Swaab & others, 2001).
- Portions of the corpus callosum—the band of tissues through which the brain's two hemispheres communicate—is larger in females than males (Le Vay, 1994).
- An area of the parietal lobe that functions in visuospatial skills is larger in males than in females (Frederikse & others, 2000).
- The areas of the brain involved in emotional expression show more metabolic activity in females than in males (Gur & others, 1995).

Cognitive Similarities and Differences In a classic review of gender differences, Eleanor Maccoby and Carol Jacklin (1974) concluded that males have better math and

Gender Stereotyping

T here is more difference within the sexes than between them.
—IVY COMPTON-BURNETT
English Novelist, 20th Century

gender stereotypes Broad categories that reflect our impressions and beliefs about females and males.

"So according to the stereotype, you can put two and two together, but I can read the handwriting on the wall."

© 1994 Joel Pett. All Rights Reserved.

visuospatial skills (the kinds of skills an architect needs to design a building's angles and dimensions), while females have better verbal abilities. Subsequently, Maccoby (1987) revised her conclusion about several gender dimensions. She said that the accumulation of research evidence now suggests that verbal differences between females and males have virtually disappeared but that the math and visuospatial differences still exist.

Some experts in gender, such as Janet Shibley Hyde (1993; Hyde & Mezulis, 2002), believe that the cognitive differences between females and males have been exaggerated. For example, Hyde points out that there is considerable overlap in the distributions of female and male scores on math and visuospatial tasks.

In a national study boys did slightly better than girls at math and science (National Assessment of Educational Progress, 2001). Overall, though, girls were far superior students, and they were significantly better than boys in reading (see figure 11.3). In another recent national study, females had better writing skills than males in grades 4, 8, and 12 with the gap widening as students progressed through school (Coley, 2001; National Assessment of Educational Progress, 1998).

Socioemotional Similarities and Differences Two areas of socioemotional development in which gender similarities and differences have been studied extensively are aggression and the self-regulation of emotion.

One of the most consistent gender differences is that boys are more physically aggressive than girls are. The difference occurs in all cultures and appears very early in children's development (White, 2002). The physical aggression difference is especially pronounced when children are provoked. Both biological and environmental factors have been proposed to account for gender differences in aggression. Biological factors include heredity and hormones. Environmental factors include cultural expectations, adult and peer models, and social agents who reward aggression in boys and punish aggression in girls.

Although boys are consistently more physically aggressive than girls, might girls show as much or more verbal aggression, such as yelling, than boys? When verbal aggression is examined, gender differences often disappear or are sometimes even more pronounced in girls (Eagly & Steffen, 1986). Girls are much more likely than boys to engage in what is called *relational aggression*, which involves such behaviors as trying to make others dislike a certain child by spreading malicious rumors about the child or ignoring another child when angry at him or her (Crick, Grotpeter, & Bigbee, 2002; Crick & others, 2001; Underwood, 2002).

An important skill is to be able to regulate and control your emotions and behavior (Eisenberg, 2001). Males usually show less self-regulation than females, and this low self-control can translate into behavioral problems (Eisenberg, Martin, & Fabes, 1996). In one study, children's low self-regulation was linked with greater aggression, the teasing of others, overreaction to frustration, low cooperation, and inability to delay gratification (Block & Block, 1980).

Earlier in the chapter, we discussed Carol Gilligan's belief that many females are more sensitive about relationships and have better relationship skills than males do. In chapter 15, "Socioemotional Development in Early Adulthood," we will further explore this area of gender.

Gender-Role Classification Not very long ago, it was accepted that boys should grow up to be masculine and girls to be feminine, that boys are made of "frogs and snails" and girls are made of "sugar and spice and all that is nice." Let's further explore such gender classifications of boys and girls as "masculine" and "feminine."

In the past, a well-adjusted boy was supposed to be independent, aggressive, and powerful. A well-adjusted girl was supposed to be dependent, nurturant, and unin-

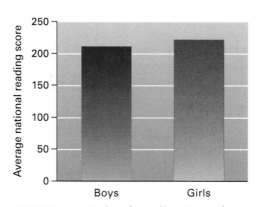

FIGURE 11.3 National Reading Scores for Boys and Girls

In the National Assessment of Educational Progress, data collected in 2000 indicated that girls did better in reading in the fourth grade (National Assessment of Educational Progress, 2001). An earlier study indicated that this gender difference holds for eighth- and twelfth-grade students as well (National Assessment of Educational Progress, 1998). Reading on the national assessment was scored on a scale from 0 to 500.

terested in power. The masculine characteristics were considered to be healthy and good by society; the feminine characteristics were considered undesirable.

In the 1970s, as both females and males became dissatisfied with the burdens imposed by their stereotypic roles, alternatives to femininity and masculinity were proposed. Instead of describing masculinity and femininity as a continuum in which more of one means less of the other, it was proposed that individuals could have both masculine and feminine traits. This thinking led to the development of the concept of **androgyny,** the presence of positive masculine and feminine characteristics in the same person (Bem, 1977; Spence & Helmreich, 1978). The androgynous boy might be assertive (masculine) and nurturant (feminine). The androgynous girl might be powerful (masculine) and sensitive to others' feelings (feminine). In one recent study it was confirmed that societal changes are leading females to be more assertive (Spence & Buckner, 2000).

Measures have been developed to assess androgyny. One of the most widely used measures is the Bem Sex-Role Inventory. To see whether your gender-role classification is masculine, feminine, or androgynous, see figure 11.4.

Gender experts, such as Sandra Bem, argue that androgynous individuals are more flexible, competent, and mentally healthy than their masculine or feminine counterparts. To some degree, though, deciding on which gender-role classification is best depends on the context involved. For example, in close relationships, feminine and androgynous orientations might be more desirable because of the expressive nature of close relationships. However, masculine and androgynous orientations might be more desirable in traditional academic and work settings because of the achievement demands in these contexts.

A special concern involves adolescent boys who adopt a strong masculine role. Researchers have found that high-masculinity adolescent boys often engage in problem behaviors, such as delinquency, drug abuse, and unprotected sexual intercourse (Pleck, 1995). Many of these boys, who present themselves as virile, macho, and aggressive, also do poorly in school. Too many adolescent males base their manhood on the caliber of gun they carry or the number of children they have fathered (Sullivan, 1991).

Gender in Context The concept of gender-role classification involves a personality trait–like categorization of a person. However, it may be helpful to think of personality in terms of person-situation interaction rather than personality traits alone.

Whast are little boys made of? Frogs and snails And puppy-dogs' tails. What are little girls made of? Sugar and spice And all that's nice.
—J.O. HALLIWELL
English Author, 19th Century

mhhe ●com/
santrockld9
Androgyny

The following items are from the Bem Sex-Role Inventory. When taking the BSRI, a person is asked to indicate on a 7-point scale how well each of the 60 characteristics describes herself or himself. The scale ranges from 1 (never or almost never true) to 7 (always or almost always true).

EXAMPLES OF MASCULINE ITEMS	EXAMPLES OF FEMININE ITEMS
Defends open beliefs	Does not use harsh language
Forceful	Affectionate
Willing to take risks	Loves children
Dominant	Understanding
Aggressive	Gentle

Scoring: The items are scored on independent dimensions of masculinity and feminity as well as androgyny and undifferentiate classifications.

FIGURE 11.4 The Bem Sex-Role Inventory: Are You Androgynous?

androgyny The presence of positive masculine and feminine characteristics in the same individual.

In China, females and males are usually socialized to behave, feel, and think differently. The old patriarchal traditions of male supremacy have not been completely uprooted. Chinese women still make considerably less money than Chinese men do, and, in rural China (such as here in the Lixian Village of Sichuan) male supremacy still governs many women's lives.

Thus, in our discussion of gender-role classification, we describe how different gender roles might be more appropriate, depending on the context, or setting, involved.

To see the importance of considering gender in context, let's examine helping behavior and emotion. The stereotype is that females are better than males at helping. But it depends on the situation. Females are more likely than males to volunteer their time to help children with personal problems and to engage in caregiving behavior. However, in situations in which males feel a sense of competence and involve danger, males are more likely than females to help (Eagly & Crowley, 1986). For example, a male is more likely than a female to stop and help a person stranded by the roadside with a flat tire.

"She is emotional; he is not"—that is the master emotional stereotype. However, like differences in helping behavior, emotional differences in males and females depend on the particular emotion involved and the context in which it is displayed (Shields, 1991). Males are more likely to show anger toward strangers, especially male strangers, when they feel they have been challenged. Males also are more likely to turn their anger into aggressive action. Emotional differences between females and males often show up in contexts that highlight social roles and relationships. For example, females are more likely to discuss emotions in terms of relationships, and they are more likely to express fear and sadness.

The importance of considering gender in context is nowhere more apparent than when examining what is culturally prescribed behavior for females and males in different countries around the world (Gibbons, 2000). While there has been greater acceptance of androgyny and similarities in male and female behavior in the United States, in many countries gender roles have remained gender-specific. For example, in many Middle Eastern countries, the division of labor between males and females is dramatic. Males are socialized and schooled to work in the public sphere, females in the private world of home and child rearing. The Islamic religion, which predominates in many Middle Eastern countries, dictates that the man's duty is to provide for his family and the woman's is to care for her family and household. China also has been a male-dominant culture. Although women have made some strides in China, the male role is still dominant. Androgynous behavior and gender equity are not what most males in China want to see happen.

Review and Reflect

1 **Discuss emotional and personality development in middle and late childhood**

REVIEW

- What changes take place in the self in the middle and late childhood years?
- How does emotion change in middle and late childhood?
- What is Kohlberg's theory of moral development and how has it been criticized? How do prosocial behavior and altruism develop in the middle and late childhood years?
- What are some important aspects of gender in middle and late childhood?

REFLECT

- What do you think about the following circumstance? A man who had been sentenced to serve 10 years for selling a small amount of marijuana walked away from a prison camp six months after he was sent there. He is now in his fifties and has been a model citizen. Should he be sent back to prison? Why or why not? At which Kohlberg stage should your response be placed?

2 FAMILIES

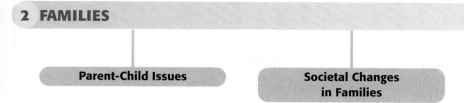

As children move into the middle and late childhood years, parents spend considerably less time with them. In one study, parents spent less than half as much time with their children aged 5 to 12 in caregiving, instruction, reading, talking, and playing as when the children were younger (Hill & Stafford, 1980). This drop in parent-child interaction may be even more extensive in families with little parental education. Although parents spend less time with their children in middle and late childhood than in early childhood, parents continue to be extremely important socializing agents in their children's lives. What are some of the most important parent-child issues in middle and late childhood?

Parent-Child Issues

Parent-child interactions during early childhood focus on such matters as modesty, bedtime regularities, control of temper, fighting with siblings and peers, eating behavior and manners, autonomy in dressing, and attention seeking. While some of these issues—fighting and reaction to discipline, for example—are carried forward into the elementary school years, many new issues have appeared by the age of 7 (Maccoby, 1984). These include whether children should be made to perform chores and, if so, whether they should be paid for them; how to help children learn to entertain themselves, rather than relying on parents for everything; and how to monitor children's lives outside the family in school and peer settings.

School-related matters are especially important for families during middle and late childhood (Collins, Madsen, & Susman-Stillman, 2002). School-related difficulties are the number one reason that children in this age group are referred for clinical help. Children must learn to relate to adults outside the family on a regular basis—adults who interact with the child much differently than parents. During middle and late childhood, interactions with adults outside the family involve more formal control and achievement orientation.

Discipline during middle and late childhood is often easier for parents than it was during early childhood; it may also be easier than during adolescence. In middle and late childhood, children's cognitive development has matured to the point where it is possible for parents to reason with them about resisting deviation and controlling their behavior. By adolescence, children's reasoning has become more sophisticated, and they may be less likely to accept parental discipline. Adolescents also push more strongly for independence, which contributes to parenting difficulties. Parents of elementary school children use less physical discipline than do parents of preschool children. By contrast, parents of elementary school children are more likely to use deprivation of privileges, appeals directed at the child's self-esteem, comments designed to increase the child's sense of guilt, and statements indicating to the child that he or she is responsible for his or her actions.

During middle and late childhood, some control is transferred from parent to child, although the process is gradual and involves *coregulation* rather than control by either the child or the parent alone. The major shift to autonomy does not occur until about the age of 12 or later. During middle and late childhood, parents continue to exercise general supervision and exert control, while children are allowed to engage in

School-Family Linkages

How does living in a stepfamily influence a child's development?

mhhe ● com/
santrockld9

Stepfamilies

Stepfamily Resources

Stepfamily Support

moment-to-moment self-regulation. This coregulation process is a transition period between the strong parental control of early childhood and the increased relinquishment of general supervision of adolescence.

Societal Changes in Families

As we discussed in chapter 9 ◀ p. 282, increasing numbers of children are growing up in divorced and working-mother families. But there are several other major shifts in the composition of family life that especially affect children in middle and late childhood. Parents are divorcing in greater numbers than ever before, but many of them remarry (Dunn & others, 2001). It takes time for parents to marry, have children, get divorced, and then remarry. Consequently, there are far more elementary and secondary school children than infant or preschool children living in stepfamilies.

Stepfamilies   The number of remarriages involving children has grown steadily in recent years. Also, divorces occur at a 10 percent higher rate in remarriages than in first marriages (Cherlin & Furstenberg, 1994). As a result of their parents' successive marital transitions, about half of all children whose parents divorce will have a stepparent within four years of parental separation.

In some cases, the stepfamily may have been preceded by a circumstance in which the spouse died. However, by far the largest number of stepfamilies are preceded by divorce rather than death.

Three common types of stepfamily structure are (1) stepfather, (2) stepmother, and (3) blended or complex. In stepfather families, the mother typically had custody of the children and remarried, introducing a stepfather into her children's lives. In stepmother families, the father usually had custody and remarried, introducing a stepmother into his children's lives. In a blended or complex stepfamily, both parents bring children from previous marriages to live in the newly formed stepfamily.

Researchers have found that children's relationships with custodial parents (mothers in stepfather families, fathers in stepmother families) are often better than with stepparents (Santrock, Sitterle, & Warshak, 1988). Also, children in simple families (stepmother, stepfather) often show better adjustment than their counterparts in complex (blended) families (Anderson & others, 1999; Hetherington & Kelly, 2002).

As in divorced families, children in stepfamilies show more adjustment problems than children in nondivorced families (Hetherington, Bridges, & Isabella, 1998). The adjustment problems are similar to those in divorced children—academic problems and lower self-esteem, for example (Anderson & others, 1999). However, as with divorced children, it is important to recognize that a majority of children in stepfamilies do not have problems. In one recent study, 20 percent of children from stepfamilies showed adjustment problems compared to 10 percent in intact, never-divorced families (Hetherington & Kelly, 2002; Hetherington & Stanley-Hagan, 2002).

In terms of the age of the child, researchers have found that early adolescence is an especially difficult time for the formation of a stepfamily (Anderson & others, 1999). This may occur because the stepfamily circumstances exacerbate normal adolescent concerns about identity, sexuality, and autonomy.

Latchkey Children   We concluded in chapter 9 ◀ p. 282 that when both parents work outside the home it does not necessarily have negative outcomes for their children. However, a certain subset of children from dual-earner families deserves further scrutiny: latchkey children. These children typically do not see their parents from the time they leave for school in the morning until about 6 or 7 P.M. They are called "latchkey" children because they are given the key to their home, take the key to school, and then use it to let themselves into the home while their parents are still at work. Latchkey children are largely unsupervised for two to four hours a day during each school week. During the summer months, they might be unsupervised for entire days, five days a week.

In one study, researchers interviewed more than 1,500 latchkey children (Long & Long, 1983). They concluded that a slight majority of these children had had negative latchkey experiences. Some latchkey children may grow up too fast, hurried by the responsibilities placed on them. How do latchkey children handle the lack of limits and structure during the latchkey hours? Without limits and parental supervision, latchkey children find their way into trouble more easily, possibly stealing, vandalizing, or abusing a sibling. Ninety percent of the juvenile delinquents in Montgomery County, Maryland, are latchkey children. Joan Lipsitz (1983), in testifying before the Select Committee on Children, Youth, and Families, called the lack of adult supervision of children in the after-school hours one of today's major problems. Lipsitz called it the "three-to-six o'clock problem" because it was during this time that the Center for Early Adolescence in North Carolina, when Lipsitz was director, experienced a peak of referrals for clinical help. And, in a 1987 national poll, teachers rated the latchkey children phenomenon the number one reason that children have problems in school (Harris, 1987).

While latchkey children may be vulnerable to problems, the experiences of latchkey children vary enormously, as do the experiences of all children with working parents (Belle, 1999). Parents need to give special attention to the ways in which their latchkey children's lives can be effectively monitored. Variations in latchkey experiences suggest that parental monitoring and authoritative parenting help the child cope more effectively with latchkey experiences, especially in resisting peer pressure (Galambos & Maggs, 1989; Steinberg, 1986). In one study, attending a formal after-school program that included academic, recreational, and remedial activities was associated with better academic achievement and social adjustment, in comparison with other types of after-school care (such as informal adult supervision or self-care) (Posner & Vandell, 1994). Practitioners and policymakers recommend that after-school programs have warm and supportive staff, a flexible and relaxed schedule, multiple activities, and opportunities for positive interactions with staff and peers (Pierce, Hamm, & Vandell, 1997).

Review and Reflect

2 **Describe parent-child issues and societal changes in families**

REVIEW

- What are some important parent-child issues in middle and late childhood?
- What are some societal changes in families that influence children's development?

REFLECT

- What was your relationship with your parents like when you were in elementary school? How do you think it influenced your development?

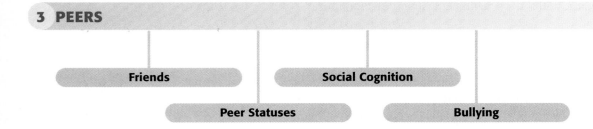

During middle and late childhood, children spend an increasing amount of time with their peers. First, we will explore children's friendships and then turn to other aspects of peer relations.

Friends

"My best friend is nice. She is honest and I can trust her. I can tell her my innermost secrets and know that nobody else will find out about them. I have other friends, but she is my best friend. We consider each other's feelings and don't want to hurt each other. We help each other out when we have problems. We make up funny names for people and laugh ourselves silly. We make lists of which boys we think are the ugliest, which are the biggest jerks, and so on. Some of these things we share with other friends, some we don't." This is a description of a friendship by a 10-year-old girl. It reflects the belief that children are interested in specific peers—not just any peers. They want to share concerns, interests, information, and secrets with them.

Why are children's friendships important? They serve six functions (Gottman & Parker, 1987:

- *Companionship.* Friendship provides children with a familiar partner and playmate, someone who is willing to spend time with them and join in collaborative activities.
- *Stimulation.* Friendship provides children with interesting information, excitement, and amusement.
- *Physical support.* Friendship provides time, resources, and assistance.
- *Ego support.* Friendship provides the expectation of support, encouragement, and feedback, which helps children maintain an impression of themselves as competent, attractive, and worthwhile individuals.
- *Social comparison.* Friendship provides information about where the child stands vis-à-vis others and whether the child is doing okay.
- *Intimacy and affection.* Friendship provides children with a warm, close, trusting relationship with another individual in which self-disclosure takes place.

Willard Hartup (1996, 2000, 2001; Hartup & Abecassis, 2002) has studied peer relations and friendship for more than three decades. He recently concluded that friends can be cognitive and emotional resources from childhood through old age. Friends can foster self-esteem and a sense of well-being. Although having friends can be a developmental advantage, not all friendships are alike. People differ in the company they keep—that is, who their friends are. Developmental advantages occur when children have friends who are socially skilled and supportive. However, it is not developmentally advantageous to have coercive and conflict-ridden friendships (Berndt, 1999).

Two of friendship's most common characteristics are intimacy and similarity. **Intimacy in friendships** is self-disclosure and the sharing of private thoughts. Research reveals that intimate friendships may not appear until early adolescence (Berndt & Perry, 1990). Also, throughout childhood, friends are more similar than dissimilar in terms of age, sex, race, and many other factors. Friends often have similar attitudes toward school, similar educational aspirations, and closely aligned achievement

intimacy in friendships Self-disclosure and the sharing of private thoughts.

orientations. Friends like the same music, the same kind of clothes, and the same kind of leisure activities.

Peer Statuses

Children often think, "What can I do to get all of the kids at school to like me?" or "What's wrong with me? Something must be wrong, or I would be more popular." What makes a child popular with peers? **Popular children** are frequently nominated as a best friend and are rarely disliked by their peers. Researchers have found that popular children give out reinforcements, listen carefully, maintain open lines of communication with peers, are happy, act like themselves, show enthusiasm and concern for others, and are self-confident without being conceited (Hartup, 1983).

Developmentalists have distinguished among three types of children who have a different peer status than popular children (Ladd, 1999; Wentzel & Asher, 1995):

- **Neglected children** are infrequently nominated as a best friend but are not disliked by their peers.
- **Rejected children** are infrequently nominated as someone's best friend and are actively disliked by their peers.
- **Controversial children** are frequently nominated both as someone's best friend and as being disliked.

Rejected children often have more serious adjustment problems later in life than do neglected children (Kupersmidt & Patterson, 1993). For example, in one study, 112 fifth-grade boys were evaluated over a period of seven years until the end of high school (Kupersmidt & Coie, 1990). The key factor in predicting whether rejected children would engage in delinquent behavior or drop out of school later during adolescence was aggression toward peers in elementary school.

Not all rejected children are aggressive (Haselager & others, 2002; Hymel, McDougall, & Renshaw, 2002). Although aggression and its related characteristics of impulsiveness and disruptiveness underlie rejection about half the time, approximately 10 to 20 percent of rejected children are shy.

An important question to ask is how neglected children and rejected children can be trained to interact more effectively with their peers (Ladd, Buhs, & Troop, 2002). The goal of training programs with neglected children is often to help them attract attention from their peers in positive ways and to hold their attention by asking questions, by listening in a warm and friendly way, and by saying things about themselves that relate to the peers' interests. They also are taught to enter groups more effectively.

The goal of training programs with rejected children is often to help them listen to peers and "hear what they say" instead of trying to dominate peer interactions. Rejected children are trained to join peers without trying to change what is taking place in the peer group. Children may need to be motivated to use these strategies by being persuaded that they work effectively and are satisfying. In some programs, children are shown videotapes of appropriate peer interaction; then they are asked to comment on them and to draw lessons from what they have seen. In other training programs, popular children are taught to be more accepting of neglected or rejected peers.

Social Cognition

Social cognitions involve thoughts about social matters (Lewis & Carpendale, 2002). Children's social cognitions about their peers become increasingly important for understanding peer relationships in middle and late childhood. Of special interest are the ways in which children process information about peer relations and their social knowledge (Dodge, 2000).

A boy accidentally trips and knocks a peer's soft drink out of his hand. The peer misinterprets the encounter as hostile, which leads him to retaliate aggressively against the boy. Through repeated encounters of this kind, other peers come to

What are some functions of children's friendships?

popular children Children who are frequently nominated as a best friend and are rarely disliked by their peers.

neglected children Children who are infrequently nominated as a best friend but are not disliked by their peers.

rejected children Children who are infrequently nominated as a best friend and are actively disliked by their peers.

controversial children Children who are frequently nominated both as someone's best friend and as being disliked.

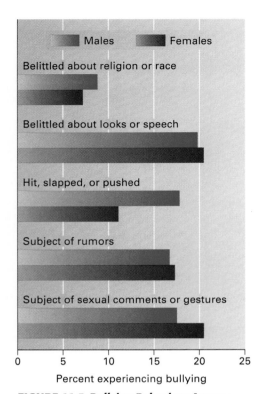

FIGURE 11.5 Bullying Behaviors Among U.S. Youth

This graph shows the type of bullying most often experienced by U.S. youth. The percentages reflect the extent to which bullied students said that they had experienced a particular type of bullying. In terms of gender, note that when they were bullied, boys were more likely to be hit, slapped, or pushed than girls were.

mhhe ●com/
santrockld9

Reducing Bullying

perceive the aggressive boy as habitually acting in inappropriate ways. Kenneth Dodge (1983) argues that children go through five steps in processing information about their social world. They decode social cues, interpret, search for a response, select an optimal response, and enact. Dodge has found that aggressive boys are more likely to perceive another child's actions as hostile when the child's intention is ambiguous. And, when aggressive boys search for cues to determine a peer's intention, they respond more rapidly, less efficiently, and less reflectively than do nonaggressive children. These are among the social cognitive factors believed to be involved in the nature of children's conflicts.

Social knowledge is also involved in children's ability to get along with peers. An important part of children's social life involves knowing what goals to pursue in poorly defined or ambiguous situations. Social relationship goals, such as how to initiate and maintain a social bond, are also important. Children need to know what scripts to follow to get other children to be their friends. For example, as part of the script for getting friends, it helps to know that saying nice things, regardless of what the peer does or says, will make the peer like the child more.

Bullying

Significant numbers of students are victimized by bullies (Pellegrini, 2002; Rigby, 2002; Smith & others, 2002). In one recent national survey of more than 15,000 sixth-through tenth-grade students, nearly one of every three students said that they had experienced occasional or frequent involvement as a victim or perpetrator in bullying (Nansel & others, 2001). In this study, *bullying* was defined as verbal or physical behavior intended to disturb someone less powerful. Boys and younger middle school students were most likely to be affected. As shown in figure 11.5, being belittled about looks or speech was the most frequent type of bullying. Children who said they were bullied reported more loneliness and difficulty in making friends, while those who did the bullying were more likely to have low grades and to smoke and drink alcohol.

In one study, both bullying and victim behavior were linked to parent-child relationships (Olweus, 1980). Bullies' parents were more likely to be rejecting, authoritarian, or permissive about their son's aggression, whereas victims' parents were more likely to be anxious and overprotective.

To reduce bullying, these strategies can be adopted (Limber, 1997):

- Get older peers to serve as monitors for bullying and intervene when they see it taking place.
- Develop schoolwide rules and sanctions against bullying and post them throughout the school.
- Form friendship groups for adolescents who are regularly bullied by peers.
- Incorporate the message of the antibullying program into church, school, and other community activities where adolescents are involved.

Some children who are highly aggressive turn into juvenile delinquents and some become violent youth. We will discuss juvenile delinquency and violent youth in chapter 13, "Socioemotional Development in Adolescence." Next, we will turn our attention to the role of social cognition in peer relations. In part of this discussion, we will explore ideas about reducing the aggression of children in their peer encounters.

Review and Reflect

3 Identify changes in peer relationships in middle and late childhood

REVIEW

- What are children's friendships like?

- How does children's peer status influence their development?
- How is social cognition involved in children's peer relations?
- What is the nature of bullying?

REFLECT

- If you were a school principal, what would you do to reduce bullying in your school?

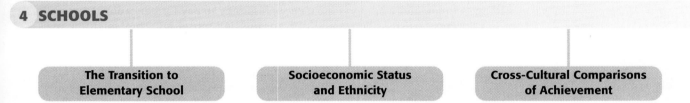

4 SCHOOLS

The Transition to Elementary School	Socioeconomic Status and Ethnicity	Cross-Cultural Comparisons of Achievement

It is justifiable to be concerned about the impact of schools on children: By the time students graduate from high school, they have spent 10,000 hours in the classroom. Children spend many years in schools as members of a small society in which there are tasks to be accomplished, people to be socialized and socialized by, and rules that define and limit behavior, feelings, and attitudes.

The Transition to Elementary School

For most children, entering the first grade signals a change from being a "homechild" to being a "schoolchild"—a situation in which new roles and obligations are experienced. Children take up a new role (being a student), interact and develop relationships with new significant others, adopt new reference groups, and develop new standards by which to judge themselves. School provides children with a rich source of new ideas to shape their sense of self.

A special concern about children's early school experiences is emerging. Evidence is mounting that early schooling proceeds mainly on the basis of negative feedback. For example, children's self-esteem in the latter part of elementary school is lower than it is in the earlier part, and older children rate themselves as less smart, less good, and less hardworking than do younger ones (Blumenfeld & others, 1981).

Children should be given opportunities to actively construct their learning. Let's examine two elementary school classrooms (Katz & Chard, 1989). In one, children spent an entire morning making identical pictures of traffic lights. The teacher made no attempt to get the children to relate the pictures to anything else the class was doing. In the other class, the children were investigating a school bus. They wrote to the district's school superintendent and asked if they could have a bus parked at their school for a few days. They studied the bus, discovered the functions of its parts, and discussed traffic rules. Then, in the classroom, they built their own bus out of cardboard. The children had fun, but they also practiced writing, problem solving, and even some arithmetic. When the class had their parents' night, the teacher was ready with reports on how each child was doing. However, all that the parents wanted to see was the bus because their children had been talking about it at home for weeks. Many contemporary education experts believe that this is the kind of education all children deserve. That is, they believe that children should be active, constructivist learners and taught through concrete, hands-on experience (Bonk & Cunningham, 1999).

ERIC Clearinghouse on Teachers

Elementary Education

Pathways to School Improvement

Socioeconomic Status and Ethnicity

Children from low-income, ethnic minority backgrounds have more difficulties in school than do their middle-socioeconomic status, White counterparts. Why? Critics argue that schools have not done a good job of educating low-income, ethnic minority students to overcome the barriers to their achievement (Scott-Jones, 1995). Let's further explore the roles of socioeconomic status and ethnicity in schools.

The Education of Students from Low-Socioeconomic Backgrounds Many children in poverty face problems at home and at school that present barriers to their learning (Bradley & Corwyn, 2002; Phillips & others, 1999). At home, they might have parents who don't set high educational standards for them, who are incapable of reading to them, and who don't have enough money to pay for educational materials and experiences, such as books and trips to zoos and museums. They might be malnourished and live in areas where crime and violence are a way of life (Ceballo, 1999).

Many of the schools that children from impoverished backgrounds attend have fewer resources than do the schools in higher-income neighborhoods (Bradley & Corwyn, 2002). Schools in low-income areas are more likely to have more students with lower achievement test scores, lower graduation rates, and smaller percentages of students going to college. And they are more likely to have young teachers with less experience than do schools in higher-income neighborhoods. In some instances, though, federal aid has provided a context for improved learning in schools located in low-income areas.

Schools in low-income areas also are more likely to encourage rote learning, while schools in higher-income areas are more likely to work with children to improve their thinking skills (Spring, 1998). Thus far too many schools in low-income neighborhoods provide students with environments that are not conducive to effective learning, and many of the schools' buildings and classrooms are old, crumbling, and poorly maintained.

Jonathan Kozol (1991) vividly described some of the problems that children of poverty face in their neighborhood and at school in *Savage Inequalities*. Here are some of his observations in one inner-city area. East St. Louis, Illinois, which is 98 percent African American, has no obstetric services, no regular trash collection, and few jobs. Nearly one third of the families live on less than $7,500 a year, and 75 percent of its population lives on welfare of some form. Blocks upon blocks of housing consist of dilapidated, skeletal buildings. Residents breathe the chemical pollution of nearby Monsanto Chemical Company. Raw sewage repeatedly backs up into homes. Lead from nearby smelters poisons the soil. Child malnutrition and fear of violence are common. The problems of the streets spill over into the schools, where sewage also backs up from time to time. Classrooms and hallways are old and unattractive, athletic facilities inadequate. Teachers run out of chalk and paper, the science labs are 30 to 50 years out of date, and the school's heating system has never worked correctly. A history teacher has 110 students but only 26 books.

Kozol says that anyone who visits places like East St. Louis, even for a brief time, comes away profoundly shaken. After all, these are innocent children who have done nothing wrong. Kozol's interest was in describing what life is like in the nation's inner-city neighborhoods and schools, which are predominantly African American and Latino. However, as indicated earlier, there are many non-Latino White children who live in poverty, although they often are in suburban or rural areas. Kozol argues that many inner-city schools are still segregated, are grossly underfunded, and do not provide adequate opportunities for children to learn effectively.

One trend in antipoverty programs is to conduct two-generational intervention (Huston, 1999; McLoyd, 1998, 1999, 2000). This involves providing both services for children (such as educational day care or preschool education) and services for parents (such as adult education, literacy training, and job skill training). Recent evaluations of the two-generational programs suggest that they have more positive effects on

mhhe ● com/
santrockld9

**Urban Education and
Children in Poverty**

Interview with Jonathan Kozol

Diversity and Education

In his book *Savage Inequalities,* Jonathan Kozol (*above*) vividly portrayed the problems that children of poverty face in their neighborhood and at school. *What are some of these problems?*

parents than they do on children (St. Pierre, Layzer, & Barnes, 1996). Also discouraging for children is that, when the two-generational programs show benefits, they are more likely to be in the form of health benefits than cognitive gains.

Ethnicity in Schools   School segregation is still a factor in the education of children of color in the United States (Simons, Finlay, & Yang, 1991). Almost one third of all African American and Latino students attend schools in which 90 percent or more of the students are from minority groups.

The school experiences of students from different ethnic groups vary considerably (Nelson-LeGall & Kelly, 2001). African American and Latino students are much less likely than non-Latino White or Asian American students to be enrolled in academic, college preparatory programs and are much more likely to be enrolled in remedial and special education programs. Asian American students are far more likely than other ethnic minority groups to take advanced math and science courses in high school. African American students are twice as likely as Latinos, Native Americans, or Whites to be suspended from school. Ethnic minorities of color constitute the majority in 23 of the 25 largest school districts in the United States, a trend that is increasing (Banks, 1995). However, 90 percent of the teachers in America's schools are non-Latino White, and the percentage of minority teachers is projected to decrease even further in the coming years.

American anthropologist John Ogbu (1989) proposed the view that ethnic minority students are placed in a position of subordination and exploitation in the American educational system. He believes that students of color, especially African Americans and Latinos, have inferior educational opportunities, are exposed to teachers and school administrators who have low academic expectations for them, and encounter negative stereotypes of ethnic minority groups (Ogbu & Stern, 2001). In one study of middle schools in predominantly Latino areas of Miami, Latino and White teachers rated African American students as having more behavioral problems than African American teachers rated the same students as having (Zimmerman & others, 1995).

Like Ogbu, educational psychologist Margaret Beale Spencer (1990) says that a form of institutional racism permeates many American schools. That is, well-meaning teachers, acting out of misguided liberalism, fail to challenge children of color to achieve. Such teachers prematurely accept a low level of performance from these children, substituting warmth and affection for high standards of academic success.

Here are some strategies for improving relationships among ethnically diverse students (Santrock, 2001).

- *Turn the class into a jigsaw classroom.* When Eliot Aronson was a professor at the University of Texas at Austin, the school system contacted him for ideas on how to reduce the increasing racial tension in classrooms. Aronson (1986) developed the concept of "jigsaw classroom," in which students from different cultural backgrounds are placed in a cooperative group in which they have to construct different parts of a project to reach a common goal. Aronson used the term *jigsaw* because he saw the technique as much like a group of students cooperating to put different pieces together to complete a jigsaw puzzle. How might this work? Team sports, drama productions, and music performances are examples of contexts in which students cooperatively participate to reach a common goal.
- *Use technology to foster cooperation with students from around the world.* The Sociocultural Worlds of Development box on page 358 illustrates how to do this.
- *Encourage students to have positive personal contact with diverse other students.* Contact alone does not do the job of improving relationships with diverse others. For example, busing ethnic minority students to predominantly White schools, or vice versa, has not reduced prejudice or improved interethnic relations (Minuchin & Shapiro, 1983). What matters is what happens after children get to school. Especially beneficial in improving interethnic relations is sharing one's worries,

Multicultural Education

The Global Lab

Traditionally, students have learned within the walls of their classroom and interacted with their teacher and other students in the class. With advances in telecommunications, students can learn from and with teachers and students around the world. The teachers and students might be from schools in such diverse locations as Warsaw, Tokyo, Istanbul, and a small village in Israel.

The Global Laboratory Project is one example that has capitalized on advances in telecommunications (Schrum & Berenfeld, 1997). It consists of science investigations that involve environmental monitoring, sharing data via telecommunication hookups, and placing local findings in a global context. In an initial telecommunications meeting, students introduced themselves and described their schools, communities, and study locations. The locations included Moscow, Russia; Warsaw, Poland; Kenosha, Wisconsin; San Antonio, Texas; Pueblo, Colorado; and Aiken, South Carolina. This initial phase was designed to help students develop a sense of community and become familiar with their collaborators from around the world. As their data collection and evaluation evolved, students continued to communicate with their peers worldwide and to learn more not only about science but also about the global community.

Classrooms or schools also can use fax machines to link students from around the country and world (Cushner, McClelland, & Safford, 1996). Fax machines transfer artwork, poetry, essays, and other materials to other students in locations as diverse as Europe, Asia, Africa, and South America. Students also can communicate the same day with pen pals through e-mail, where once it took weeks for a letter to reach someone in a faraway place. An increasing number of schools also use videotelephone technology

in foreign language instruction. Instead of simulating a French café in a typical French language class, American students might talk with French students who have placed a videotelephone in a French café in their country.

Such global technology projects can go a long way toward reducing American students' ethnocentric beliefs. The active building of connections around the world through telecommunications gives students the opportunity to experience others' perspectives, better understand other cultures, and reduce prejudice.

Global technology projects can help students become less ethnocentric. *What is the nature of some of these projects?*

successes, failures, coping strategies, interests, and other personal information with people of other ethnicities. When this happens, people are seen more as individuals than as a heterogeneous cultural group.
- *Encourage students to engage in perspective taking.* Exercises and activities that help students see others' perspectives can improve interethnic relations. This helps students "step into the shoes" of peers who are culturally different and feel what it is like to be treated in fair or unfair ways (Cushner, McClelland, & Safford, 1996).
- *Help students think critically and be emotionally intelligent when cultural issues are involved.* Students who think in narrow ways are prejudiced. Students who learn to think critically and deeply about interethnic relations are likely to decrease their prejudice. Becoming more emotionally intelligent includes understanding the causes of one's feelings, managing anger, listening to what others are saying, and being motivated to share and cooperate.
- *Reduce bias.* Teachers can reduce bias by displaying images of children from diverse ethnic and cultural groups, selecting play materials and classroom activities that encourage cultural understanding, helping students resist stereotyping, and working with parents (Derman-Sparks, 1989).
- *View the school and community as a team to help support teaching efforts.* James Comer (1988; Comer & others, 1996) believes that a community, team approach is the best way to educate children. Three important aspects of the Comer Project for

Careers in Life-Span Development

James Comer, Child Psychiatrist

James Comer grew up in a low-income neighborhood in East Chicago, Indiana, and credits his parents with leaving no doubt about the importance of education. He obtained a BA degree from Indiana University. He went on to obtain a medical degree from Howard University College of Medicine, a Master of Public Health degree from the University of Michigan School of Public Health, and psychiatry training at the Yale University School of Medicine's Child Study Center ◀▥ p. 32. He currently is the Maurice Falk Professor of Child Psychiatry at the Yale University Child Study Center and an associate dean at the Yale University Medical School. During his years at Yale, Comer has concentrated his career on promoting a focus on child development as a way of improving schools. His efforts in support of healthy development of young people are known internationally.

Dr. Comer, perhaps, is best known for the founding of the School Development Program in 1968, which promotes the collaboration of parents, educators, and community to improve social, emotional, and academic outcomes for children. His concept of teamwork is currently improving the educational environment in more than 500 schools throughout America.

James Comer (*left*) is shown with some of the inner-city African American children who attend a school that became a better learning environment because of Comer's intervention.

Change are (1) a governance and management team that develops a comprehensive school plan, assessment strategy, and staff development plan; (2) a mental health or school support team; and (3) a parent's program. Comer believes that the entire school community should have a cooperative rather than an adversarial attitude. The Comer program is currently operating in more than 600 schools in 26 states. To read further about Comer's work and his career, see the Careers in Life-Span Development insert.

- *Be a competent cultural mediator.* Teachers can play a powerful role as a cultural mediator by being sensitive to racist content in materials and classroom interactions, learning more about different ethnic groups, being sensitive to children's ethnic attitudes, viewing students of color positively, and thinking of positive ways to get parents of color more involved as partners with teachers in educating children (Banks, 1997; Cushner, 1999).

Cross-Cultural Comparisons of Achievement

American children are more achievement-oriented than their counterparts in many countries. However, in the past decade, the poor performance of American children in math and science has become well publicized. For example, in one cross-national comparison of the math and science achievement of 9- to 13-year-old students, the United States finished 13th (out of 15) in science and 15th (out of 16) in math

We [the United States] accept performances in students that are nowhere near where they should be.

—**HAROLD STEVENSON**
Contemporary Developmental Psychologist, University of Michigan

Asian grade schools intersperse studying with frequent periods of activities. This approach helps children maintain their attention and likely makes learning more enjoyable. Shown here are Japanese fourth-graders making wearable masks. *What are some differences in the way children in many Asian countries are taught compared to children in the United States?*

achievement (Educational Testing Service, 1992). In this study, Korean and Taiwanese students placed first and second, respectively.

Harold Stevenson's (1995, 2000; Stevenson & Hofer, 1999) research explores reasons for the poor performance of American students. Stevenson and his colleagues have completed five cross-cultural comparisons of students in the United States, China, Taiwan, and Japan. In these studies, Asian students consistently outperform American students. And the longer the students are in school, the wider the gap becomes between Asian and American students—the lowest difference is in the first grade, the highest in the eleventh grade (the highest grade studied).

To learn more about the reasons for these large cross-cultural differences, Stevenson and his colleagues spent thousands of hours observing in classrooms, as well as interviewing and surveying teachers, students, and parents. They found that the Asian teachers spent more of their time teaching math than did the American teachers. For example, more than one fourth of total classroom time in the first grade was spent on math instruction in Japan, compared with only one tenth of the time in the U.S. first-grade classrooms. Also, the Asian students were in school an average of 240 days a year, compared with 178 days in the United States.

In addition to the substantially greater time spent on math instruction in the Asian schools than the American schools, differences were found between the Asian and American parents. The American parents had much lower expectations for their children's education and achievement than did the Asian parents. Also, the American parents were more likely to believe that their children's math achievement was due to innate ability; the Asian parents were more likely to say that their children's math achievement was the consequence of effort and training (Stevenson, Lee, & Stigler, 1986) (see figure 11.6). The Asian students were more likely to do math homework than were the American students, and the Asian parents were far more likely to help their children with their math homework than were the American parents (Chen & Stevenson, 1989).

Critics of the cross-national comparisons argue that, in many comparisons, virtually all U.S. children are being compared with a "select" group of children from other countries, especially in the secondary school comparisons. Therefore, they conclude, it is no wonder that American students don't fare so well. That criticism holds for some international comparisons. However, even when the top 25 percent of students in different countries have been compared, U.S. students move up some, but not a lot (Mullis, 1999).

Review and Reflect

4 **Characterize the transition to elementary school and sociocultural aspects of schooling and achievement**

REVIEW

- What is the transition to elementary school like?
- How do socioeconomic status and ethnicity influence schooling?
- What are some cross-cultural comparisons of achievement?

REFLECT

- Should the United States be worried about the low performance of its students in mathematics and science in comparison to Asian students? Are Americans' expectations for students too low?

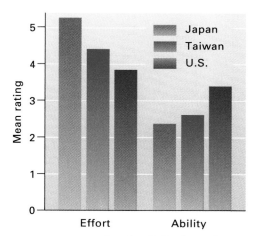

FIGURE 11.6 Mothers' Beliefs About the Factors Responsible for Children's Math Achievement in Three Countries

In one study, mothers in Japan and Taiwan were more likely to believe that their children's math achievement was due to effort rather than innate ability, while U.S. mothers were more likely to believe their children's math achievement was due to innate ability (Stevenson, Lee, & Stigler, 1986). If parents believe that their children's math achievement is due to innate ability and their children are not doing well in math, the implication is that they are less likely to think their children will benefit from putting forth more effort.

Reach Your Learning Goals

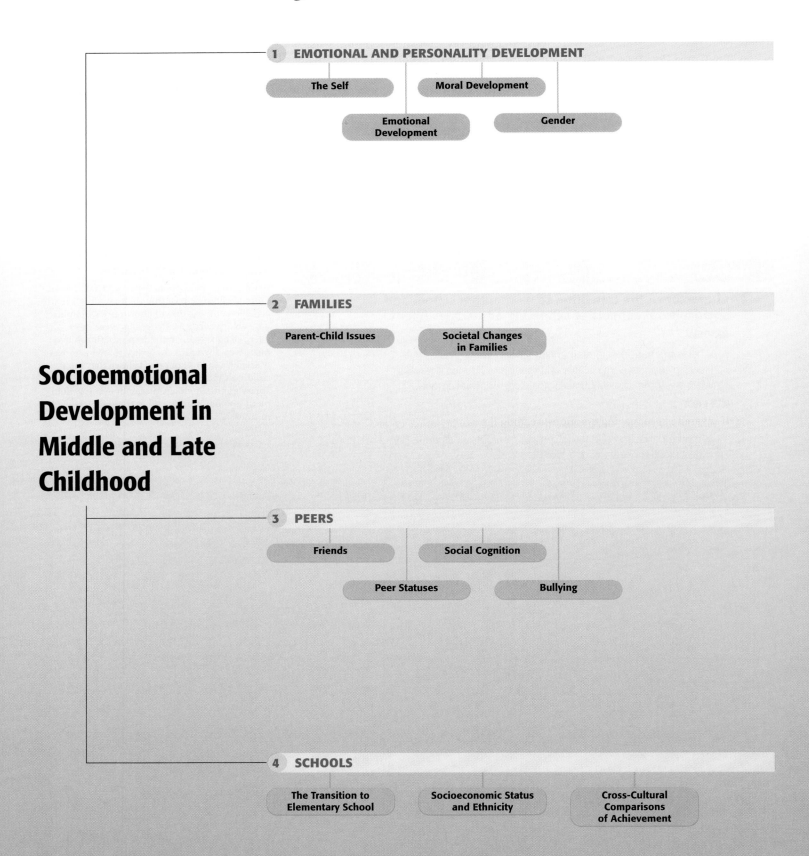

Socioemotional Development in Middle and Late Childhood

1 EMOTIONAL AND PERSONALITY DEVELOPMENT

- The Self
- Moral Development
- Emotional Development
- Gender

2 FAMILIES

- Parent-Child Issues
- Societal Changes in Families

3 PEERS

- Friends
- Social Cognition
- Peer Statuses
- Bullying

4 SCHOOLS

- The Transition to Elementary School
- Socioeconomic Status and Ethnicity
- Cross-Cultural Comparisons of Achievement

Summary

1 Discuss emotional and personality development in middle and late childhood

- The internal self, the social self, and the socially comparative self become more prominent in middle and late childhood. Self-esteem refers to global evaluations of the self and is also referred to as self-worth or self-image. Self-concept refers to domain-specific evaluations of the self. Four ways to increase self-esteem are to (1) identify the causes of low self-esteem, (2) provide emotional support and social approval, (3) help children achieve, and (4) help children cope. Erikson's fourth stage of development, industry versus inferiority, characterizes the middle and late childhood years.

- Developmental changes in emotion include increased understanding of such complex emotions as pride and shame, detecting that more than one emotion can be experienced in a particular situation, taking into account the circumstances that led up to the emotional reaction, improvements in the ability to suppress and conceal emotions, and using self-initiated strategies to redirect emotions. Emotional intelligence is a form of social intelligence that involves the ability to monitor one's own and others' feelings and emotions, to discriminate among them, and to use this information to guide one's own thinking and action. Goleman believes that emotional intelligence involves four main areas: emotional self-awareness, managing emotions, reading emotions, and handling relationships. As children get older, they use a greater variety of coping strategies and more cognitive strategies.

- Kohlberg developed a provocative theory of moral reasoning with three levels—preconventional, conventional, and postconventional—and six stages (two at each level). Increased internalization characterizes movement to levels 2 and 3. Prosocial behavior involves positive moral behaviors. Altruism is an unselfish interest in helping others. Damon described a developmental sequence of altruism.

- Gender stereotypes are widespread around the world. A number of physical differences exist between males and females. Some experts, such as Hyde, argue that cognitive differences between males and females have been exaggerated. In terms of socioemotional differences, males are more physically aggressive than females while females regulate their emotions better. There is controversy about how similar or different males and females are in a number of areas. Gender-role classification focuses on how masculine, feminine, or androgynous individuals are. Androgyny means having both positive feminine and masculine characteristics. It is important to think about gender in terms of context.

2 Describe parent-child issues and societal changes in families

- Parents spend less time with children during middle and late childhood than in early childhood. New parent-child issues emerge and discipline changes. Control is more coregulatory.

- Like in divorced families, children living in stepparent families have more adjustment problems than their counterparts in nondivorced families. However, a majority of children in stepfamilies do not have adjustment problems. Latchkey children may become vulnerable when they are not monitored by adults in the after-school hours.

3 Identify changes in peer relationships in middle and late childhood

- Children's friendships serve six functions: companionship, stimulation, physical support, ego support, social comparison, and intimacy/affection. Intimacy and similarity are two common characteristics of friendship.

- Popular children are frequently nominated as a best friend and rarely disliked by their peers. Neglected children are infrequently nominated as a best friend but are not disliked by their peers. Rejected children are infrequently nominated as a best friend and are actively disliked by their peers. Controversial children are frequently nominated both as a best friend and as being disliked by peers. Rejected children are especially at risk for a number of problems.

- Social information-processing skills and social knowledge are two important dimensions of social cognition in peer relations.

- Significant numbers of children are bullied and this can result in short-term and long-term negative effects for the victim.

4 Characterize the transition to elementary school and sociocultural aspects of schooling and achievement

- Children spend more than 10,000 hours in the classroom as members of a small society in which there are tasks to be accomplished, people to be socialized and socialized by, and rules that define and limit behavior. A special concern is that early schooling too often proceeds on the basis of negative feedback to children.

- Children in poverty face problems at home and at school that present barriers to their learning. It is important that teachers have positive expectations for and challenge children of color to achieve.

- American children are more achievement-oriented than children in many countries, but are less achievement-oriented than many children in Asian countries, such as China, Taiwan, and Japan.

Key Terms

Key People

1. Ling, a third-grade teacher, overheard a talk show discussion on emotional intelligence. She has seen several books on the subject in the local library but was unaware of its impact on learning. What is emotional intelligence and how can Ling and her students' parents facilitate this type of development in children?

2. Frank is researching the latest information on bullying after his younger brother told him of his recent experiences with bullies at his junior high school. What information is available on the prevalence of bullying, the makeup of the children who bully, and why this type of behavior is increasing?

Connect to <u>www.mhhe.com/santrockld9</u> to research the answers and complete these exercises.

To help you master the material in this chapter, you'll find a number of valuable study tools on the Student CD-ROM that accompanies this book. In addition, visit the Online Learning Center for *Life-Span Development,* ninth edition, where you'll find these valuable resources for chapter 11, "Socioemotional Development in Middle and Late Childhood."

- How well do you remember your own socioemotional development? Complete the self-assessment, *My Socioemotional Development as a Child.*

- View video clips of key developmental psychology experts, including Robert Emery discussing his research on children and divorce.
- Build your decision-making skills by trying your hand at the parenting and education "Scenarios."

Adolescence

"Who are you?" asked the caterpillar. Alice replied rather shyly, "I—I hardly know, sir, just at present—at least I know who I was when I got up this morning, but I must have changed several times since then."

—LEWIS CARROLL
English Writer, 19th Century

Adolecents feel like they will live forever. At times, they are sure that they know everything. They clothe themselves with rainbows and go brave as the zodiac, flashing from one end of the world to the other in both mind and body. In many ways, today's adolescents are privileged, wielding unprecedented economic power. At the same time, they move through a seemingly endless preparation for life. They try on one face after another, seeking to find a face of their own. In their most pimply and awkward moments, they become acquainted with sex. They play furiously at "adult games" but are confined to the society of their own peers. They want their parents to understand them. Their generation of young people is the fragile cable by which the best and the worst of their parents' generation is transmitted to the present. In the end, there are only two lasting bequests parents can leave youth, one being roots, the other wings. Section Six contains two chapters: "Physical and Cognitive Development in Adolescence" (chapter 12) and "Socioemotional Development in Adolescence" (chapter 13).

In youth, we clothe ourselves with rainbows, and go brave as the zodiac.

—RALPH WALDO EMERSON
American Poet, 19th Century

Physical and Cognitive Development in Adolescence

Learning Goals

1 *D*iscuss the nature of adolescence

2 *D*escribe pubertal changes and adolescent sexuality

3 *I*dentify adolescent problems in substance use and abuse, eating disorders, and health

4 *E*xplain cognitive changes in adolescence

5 *S*ummarize some key aspects of how schools influence adolescent development

Images of Life-Span Development
The Best of Times and the Worst of Times for Today's Adolescents

It is both the best of times and the worst of times for adolescents. Their world possesses powers and perspectives inconceivable 50 years ago: computers, longer life expectancies, the entire planet accessible through television, satellites, air travel. So much knowledge, though, can be chaotic and dangerous. School curricula have been adapted to teach new topics: AIDS, adolescent suicide, drug and alcohol abuse, incest. The hazards of the adult world—its sometimes fatal temptations—descend upon children and adolescents so early that their ideals may be shattered.

Crack, for example, is far more addictive and deadly than marijuana, the drug of an earlier generation. Strange fragments of violence and sex flash out of the television set and lodge in the minds of youth. The messages are powerful and contradictory. Rock videos suggest orgiastic sex. Public health officials counsel safe sex. Jerry Springer conducts seminars on exotic drugs and serial murders. Television pours a bizarre version of reality into the imaginations of adolescents (Morrow, 1988).

Adolescence is not a time of rebellion, crisis, pathology, and deviance. A far more accurate vision of adolescence is of a time of evaluation, of decision making, of commitment, of carving out a place in the world. Most of the problems of today's youth are not with the youth themselves. What adolescents need is access to a range of legitimate opportunities and to long-term support from adults who care deeply about them (Booth & Crouter, 2001; Larson, Brown, & Mortimer, 2003).

1 THE NATURE OF ADOLESCENCE

As in the development of children, genetic, biological, environmental, and social factors interact in adolescent development. Also, continuity and discontinuity characterize adolescent development. The genes inherited from parents still influence thought and behavior during adolescence, but inheritance now interacts with the social conditions of the adolescent's world—with family, peers, friendships, dating, and school experiences ◀||| p. 103. An adolescent has experienced thousands of hours of interaction with parents, peers, and teachers in the past 10 to 13 years of development. Still new experiences and developmental tasks appear during adolescence. Relationships with parents take a different form, moments with peers become more intimate, and dating occurs for the first time, as do sexual exploration and possibly intercourse. The adolescent's thoughts are more abstract and idealistic. Biological changes trigger a heightened interest in body image. Adolescence, then, has both continuity and discontinuity with childhood.

There is a long history of worrying about how adolescents will turn out. In 1904, G. Stanley Hall proposed the "storm-and-stress" view that adolescence is a turbulent time charged with conflict and mood swings. Today's adolescents face demands and expectations, as well as risks and temptations, that appear to be more numerous and complex than those faced by adolescents only a generation ago. Nonetheless, contrary to the popular stereotype of adolescents as highly stressed and incompetent, the vast majority of adolescents successfully negotiate the path from childhood to adulthood. By some criteria, today's adolescents are doing better than their counterparts from a decade or two earlier. Today, more adolescents complete high school, especially African American adolescents. The majority of adolescents today have positive self-concept and positive relationships with others.

Growing up has never been easy. However, adolescence is not best viewed as a time of rebellion, crisis, pathology, and deviance. A far more accurate vision of adolescence describes it as a time of evaluation, of decision making, of commitment, and of carving out a place in the world. Most of the problems of today's youth are not with the youth themselves. What adolescents need is access to a range of legitimate opportunities and to long-term support from adults who deeply care about them. *What might be some examples of such support and caring?*

Practical Resources and Research
Adolescent Issues
Profile of America's Youth
Trends in the Well-Being
of America's Youth

A cross-cultural study by Daniel Offer and his colleagues (1988) supported the contention that most adolescents have positive images of themselves and contradicted the stereotype that most adolescents have problems or are disturbed in some way. The self-images of adolescents around the world were sampled—in the United States, Australia, Bangladesh, Hungary, Israel, Italy, Japan, Taiwan, Turkey, and West Germany. A healthy self-image characterized at least 73 percent of the adolescents studied. They appeared to be moving toward adulthood with a healthy integration of previous experiences, self-confidence, and optimism about the future. Although there were some differences among the adolescents, they were happy most of the time, they enjoyed life, they perceived themselves as able to exercise self-control, they valued work and school, they expressed confidence about their sexual selves, they expressed positive feelings toward their families, and they felt they had the capability to cope with life's stresses: not exactly a storm-and-stress portrayal of adolescence.

Public attitudes about adolescence emerge from a combination of personal experience and media portrayals, neither of which produce an objective picture of how normal adolescents develop (Feldman & Elliott, 1990). Some of the readiness to assume the worst about adolescents likely involves the short memories of adults. Many adults measure their current perceptions of adolescents by their memories of their own adolescence. Adults may portray today's adolescents as more troubled, less respectful, more self-centered, more assertive, and more adventurous than they were.

However, in matters of taste and manners, the young people of every generation have seemed radical, unnerving, and different from adults—different in how they look, in how they behave, in the music they enjoy, in their hairstyles, and in the clothing they choose. It is an enormous error, though, to confuse adolescents' enthusiasm for trying on new identities and enjoying moderate amounts of outrageous behavior with hostility toward parental and societal standards. Acting out and boundary testing are time-honored ways in which adolescents move toward accepting, rather than rejecting, parental values.

Although the majority of adolescents experience the transition from childhood to adulthood more positively than is portrayed by many adults and the media, too many adolescents today are not provided with adequate opportunities and support to become competent adults (Perkins & Borden, 2003; Pittman & Diversi, 2003). In many ways, today's adolescents are presented with a less stable environment than adolescents of a decade or two ago. High divorce rates, high adolescent pregnancy rates, and increased geographic mobility of families contribute to this lack of stability in adolescents' lives. Today's adolescents are exposed to a complex menu of lifestyle options through the media, and, although the adolescent drug rate is beginning to show signs of decline, the rate of adolescent drug use in the United States is higher than that of any other country in the industrialized Western world. Many of today's adolescents face these temptations, as well as sexual activity, at increasingly young ages.

Our discussion underscores an important point about adolescents: They do not make up a homogeneous group. Most adolescents negotiate the lengthy path to adult maturity successfully, but too large a group does not. Ethnic, cultural, gender, socioeconomic, age, and lifestyle differences influence the actual life trajectory of every adolescent. Different portrayals of adolescence emerge, depending on the particular group of adolescents being described (Call & others, 2003).

Now that we have considered some historical views of adolescents and have evaluated today's adolescents, let's turn our attention to the ways in which adolescents develop physically. We will begin with the dramatic changes of puberty.

Review and Reflect

1 **Discuss the nature of adolescence**

REVIEW

- What characterizes adolescent development?

REFLECT

- How much have adolescents changed or stayed the same over the last 30 to 40 years?

2 PUBERTY AND SEXUALITY

> **Pubertal Changes**

> **Adolescent Sexuality**

One father remarked that the problem with his teenage son was not that he grew, but that he did not know when to stop growing. As we will see, there is considerable variation in the timing of the adolescent growth spurt.

Pubertal Changes

Puberty can be distinguished from adolescence. For most of us, puberty has ended long before adolescence is exited, although puberty is the most important marker of the beginning of adolescence. What is puberty? **Puberty** is a period of rapid physical maturation involving hormonal and bodily changes that occur primarily during early adolescence.

Imagine a toddler displaying all the features of puberty—a 3-year-old girl with fully developed breasts or a boy just slightly older with a deep voice. That is what we would see by the year 2250 if the age at which puberty arrives kept getting younger at

puberty A period of rapid skeletal and sexual maturation that occurs mainly in early adolescence.

From *Penguin Dreams and Stranger Things* by Berkeley Breathed. Copyright © 1985 by The Washington Post Company. By permission of Little, Brown & Company, Inc. Reprinted by permission of International Creative Management. Copyright © 1985 by Berkeley Breathed.

its present pace. In Norway, **menarche**—a girl's first menstruation—occurs at just over 13 years of age, compared to 17 years of age in the 1840s. In the United States—where children mature up to a year earlier than children in European countries—the average age of menarche declined significantly since the mid nineteenth century (see figure 12.1). Fortunately, however, we are unlikely to see pubescent toddlers, since what has happened in the past century is likely the result of a higher level of nutrition and health. The available information suggests that menarche began to occur earlier at about the time of the Industrial Revolution, a period associated with increased standards of living and advances in medical science (Petersen, 1979).

Genetic factors also are involved in puberty. Puberty is not simply an environmental accident. As indicated earlier, while nutrition, health, and other factors affect puberty's timing and variations in its makeup, the basic genetic program is wired into the nature of the species (Plomin, 1993).

Another key factor in puberty's occurrence is body mass. Menarche occurs at a relatively consistent weight in girls. A body weight approximating 106 ± 3 pounds can trigger menarche and the end of the pubertal growth spurt. For menarche to begin and continue, fat must make up 17 percent of the girl's body weight. Both teenage anorexics whose weight drops dramatically and female athletes in certain sports (such as gymnastics) may become amenorrheic (having an absence or suppression of menstrual discharge).

In summary, puberty's determinants include nutrition, health, heredity, and body mass. So far, our discussion of puberty has emphasized its dramatic changes. Keep in mind, though, that puberty is not a single, sudden event (Archibald, Graber, & Brooks-Gunn, 2003). We know when a young boy or girl is going through puberty, but pinpointing its beginning and its end is difficult. Except for menarche, which occurs rather late in puberty, no single marker heralds puberty. For boys, the first whisker or first wet dream is an event that could mark its appearance, but both may go unnoticed.

Hormonal Changes Behind the first whisker in boys and the widening of hips in girls is a flood of **hormones,** powerful chemical substances secreted by the endocrine glands and carried through the body by the bloodstream. The endocrine system's role in puberty involves the interaction of the hypothalamus, the pituitary gland, and the gonads (sex glands). The **hypothalamus** is a structure in the higher portion of the

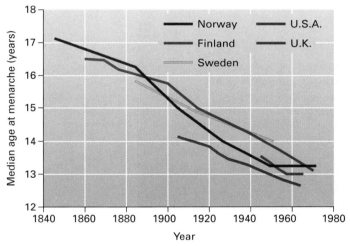

FIGURE 12.1 Median Ages at Menarche in Selected Northern European Countries and the United States from 1845 to 1969

Notice the steep decline in the age at which girls experienced menarche in five different countries. Recently the age at which girls experience menarche has been leveling off.

menarche A girl's first menstruation.

hormones Powerful chemical substances secreted by the endocrine glands and carried through the body by the bloodstream.

hypothalamus A structure in the higher portion of the brain that monitors eating, drinking, and sex.

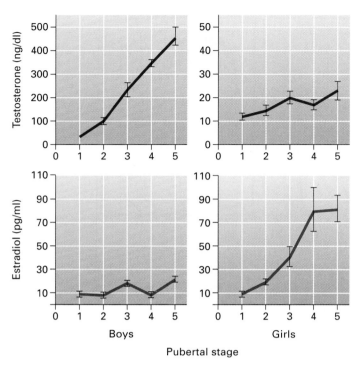

FIGURE 12.2 Hormone Levels by Sex and Pubertal stage for Testosterone and Estradiol

The five stages range from the early beginning of puberty (stage 1) to the most advanced stage of puberty (stage 5). Notice the significant increase in testosterone in boys and the significant increase in estradiol in girls.

brain that monitors eating, drinking, and sex. The **pituitary gland** is an important endocrine gland that controls growth and regulates other glands. The **gonads** are the sex glands—the testes in males, the ovaries in females. How does this hormonal system work? The pituitary sends a signal via gonadotropins (hormones that stimulate the testes or ovaries) to the appropriate gland to manufacture the hormone. Then the pituitary gland, through interaction with the hypothalamus, detects when the optimal level of hormones is reached and responds by maintaining gonadotropin secretion.

The concentrations of certain hormones increase dramatically during adolescence (Dorn & Lucas, 1995; Susman, Dorn, & Schiefelbein, 2003; Susman & others, 1995). *Testosterone* is a hormone associated in boys with the development of genitals, an increase in height, and a change in voice. *Estradiol* is a hormone associated in girls with breast, uterine, and skeletal development. In one study, testosterone levels increased eighteenfold in boys but only twofold in girls during puberty; estradiol increased eightfold in girls but only twofold in boys (Nottelmann & others, 1987) (see figure 12.2).

Note that both testosterone and estradiol are present in the hormonal makeup of both boys and girls but that testosterone dominates in male pubertal development, estradiol in female pubertal development.

The same influx of hormones that puts hair on a male's chest and imparts curvature to a female's breast may contribute to psychological development in adolescence (Dorn & Lucas, 1995). In one study of 108 normal boys and girls ranging in age from 9 to 14, a higher concentration of testosterone was present in boys who rated themselves more socially competent (Nottelmann & others, 1987). In another study of 60 normal boys and girls in the same age range, girls with higher estradiol levels expressed more anger and aggression (Inoff-Germain & others, 1988). However, hormonal effects by themselves do not account for adolescent development (Graber & Brooks-Gunn, 2002). For example, in one study, social factors accounted for two to four times as much variance as did hormonal factors in young adolescent girls' depression and anger (Brooks-Gunn & Warren, 1989). Also, behavior and moods can affect hormones (Paikoff, Buchanan, & Brooks-Gunn, 1991). Stress, eating patterns, exercise, sexual activity, tension, and depression can activate or suppress various aspects of the hormonal system. In sum, the hormone-behavior link is complex.

One additional aspect of the pituitary gland's role in development still needs to be described. Not only does the pituitary gland release gonadotropins that stimulate the testes and ovaries, but through interaction with the hypothalamus the pituitary gland also secretes hormones that either directly lead to growth and skeletal maturation or produce such growth effects through interaction with the thyroid gland, located in the neck region.

Height, Weight, and Sexual Maturation Among the most noticeable physical changes during puberty are increases in height and weight, as well as sexual maturation.

Height and Weight As indicated in figure 12.3, the growth spurt occurs approximately two years earlier for girls than for boys (Abbassi, 1998). The mean beginning of the growth spurt in girls in 9 years of age; for boys, it is 11 years of age. The peak rate of pubertal change occurs at 11.5 years for girls and 13.5 years for boys. During their growth spurt, girls increase in height about 3½ inches per year, boys about 4 inches.

Boys and girls who are shorter or taller than their peers before adolescence are likely to remain so during adolescence. In our society, there is a stigma attached to

pituitary gland An important endocrine gland that controls growth and regulates other glands.

gonads The sex glands—the testes in males and the ovaries in females.

short boys. At the beginning of the adolescent period, girls tend to be as tall as or taller than boys of their age, but by the end of the middle school years most boys have caught up or, in many cases, have even surpassed girls in height. And, even though height in the elementary school years is a good predictor of height later in adolescence, there is still room for the individual's height to change in relation to the height of his or her peers. As much as 30 percent of the height of late adolescence is unexplained by height in the elementary school years.

The rate at which adolescents gain weight follows approximately the same developmental timetable as the rate at which they gain height. Marked weight gains coincide with the onset of puberty. During early adolescence, girls tend to outweigh boys, but, just as with height, by about age 14 boys begin to surpass girls.

Sexual Maturation Think back to the onset of your puberty. Of the striking changes that were taking place in your body, what was the first change that occurred? Researchers have found that male pubertal characteristics develop in this order: increase in penis and testicle size, appearance of straight public hair, minor voice change, first ejaculation (which usually occurs through masturbation or a wet dream), appearance of kinky pubic hair, onset of maximum growth, growth of hair in armpits, more detectable voice changes, and growth of facial hair. Three of the most noticeable areas of sexual maturation in boys are penis elongation, testes development, and growth of facial hair. The normal range and average age of development for these sexual characteristics, along with height spurt, are shown in figure 12.4 on page 376.

What is the order of appearance of physical changes in females? First, either the breasts enlarge or pubic hair appears. Later, hair appears in the armpits. As these changes occur, the female grows in height, and her hips become wider than her shoulders. Her first menstruation comes rather late in the pubertal cycle. Initially, her menstrual cycles may be highly irregular. For the first several years, she might not ovulate every menstrual cycle. Some girls do not become fertile until two years after the period begins. No voice changes comparable to those in pubertal males occur in pubertal females. By the end of puberty, the female's breasts have become more fully rounded. Two of the most noticeable aspects of female pubertal change are pubic hair and breast development. Figure 12.4 shows the normal range and average development of these sexual characteristics and also provides information about menarche and height gain.

Individual Variations in Puberty The pubertal sequence may begin as early as 10 years of age or as late as 13½ for most boys. It may end as early as 13 years or as late as 17 years for most boys. The normal range is wide enough that, given two boys of the same chronological age, one might complete the pubertal sequence before the other one has begun it. For girls, the age range of the first menstrual period is even wider. Menarche is considered within a normal range if it appears between the ages of 9 and 15.

Body Image One psychological aspect of physical change in puberty is certain: Adolescents are preoccupied with their bodies and develop individual images of what their bodies are like. Perhaps you looked in the mirror on a daily and sometimes even hourly basis to see if you could detect anything different about your changing body. Preoccupation with one's body image is strong throughout adolescence, but it is especially acute during puberty, a time when adolescents are more dissatisfied with their bodies than in late adolescence (Wright, 1989).

There are gender differences in adolescents' perceptions of their bodies. In general, girls are less happy with their bodies and have more negative body images, compared with boys, throughout puberty (Brooks-Gunn & Paikoff, 1993). Also, as pubertal change proceeds, girls often become more dissatisfied with their bodies, probably because their body fat increases, while boys become more satisfied as they move through puberty, probably because their muscle mass increases (Gross, 1984).

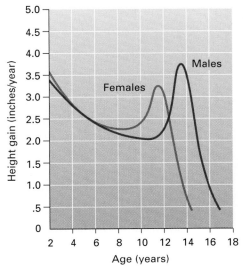

FIGURE 12.3 Pubertal Growth Spurt
On the average, the peak of the growth spurt that characterizes pubertal change occurs 2 years earlier for girls (11½) than for boys (13½).

Biological Changes

Males

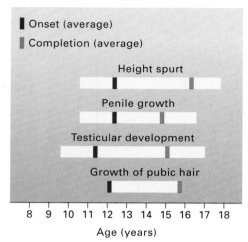

Females

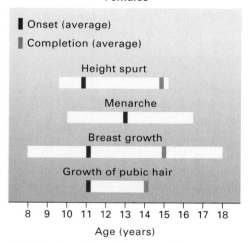

FIGURE 12.4 Normal Range and Average Development of Sexual Characteristics in Males and Females

Early and Late Maturation Some of you entered puberty early, others late, and yet others on time. When adolescents mature earlier or later than their peers, might they perceive themselves differently? In the Berkeley Longitudinal Study some years ago, early-maturing boys perceived themselves more positively and had more successful peer relations than did their late-maturing counterparts (Jones, 1965). The findings for early-maturing girls were similar but not as strong as for boys. When the late-maturing boys were in their thirties, however, they had developed a stronger sense of identity than the early-maturing boys had (Peskin, 1967). Possibly this occurred because the late-maturing boys had more time to explore life's options or because the early-maturing boys continued to focus on their advantageous physical status instead of on career development and achievement.

More recent research confirms, though, that at least during adolescence it is advantageous to be an early-maturing rather than a late-maturing boy (Simmons & Blyth, 1987). The more recent findings for girls suggest that early-maturing girls experience more problems in school but also more independence and popularity with boys. The time that maturation is assessed also is a factor. In the sixth grade, early-maturing girls show greater satisfaction with their figures than do late-maturing girls, but by the tenth grade late-maturing girls are more satisfied (Simmons & Blyth, 1987) (see figure 12.5). The reason for this is that, in late adolescence, early-maturing girls are shorter and stockier, whereas late-maturing girls are taller and thinner. Late-maturing girls in late adolescence have bodies that more closely approximate the current American ideal of feminine beauty—tall and thin.

In the past decade, an increasing number of researchers have found that early maturation increases girls' vulnerability to a number of problems (Brooks-Gunn & Paikoff, 1993). Early-maturing girls are more likely to smoke, drink, be depressed, have an eating disorder, request earlier independence from their parents, and have older friends; and their bodies are likely to elicit responses from males that lead to earlier dating and earlier sexual experiences (Wiesner & Ittel, 2002). In one study, the early-maturing girls had lower educational and occupational attainment in adulthood (Stattin & Magnusson, 1990). Apparently as a result of their social and cognitive immaturity, combined with early physical development, early-maturing girls are easily lured into problem behaviors, not recognizing the possible long-term effects of these on their development (Petersen, 1993; Sarigiani & Petersen, 2000).

Some researchers now question whether the effects of puberty are as strong as once believed (Petersen, 1993). Puberty affects some adolescents more strongly than others and some behaviors more strongly than others. Body image, dating interest, and sexual behavior are affected by pubertal change. The recent questioning of puberty's effects suggests that, in terms of overall development and adjustment in the human life span, pubertal variations (such as early and late maturation) are less dramatic than is commonly thought. In thinking about puberty's effects, keep in mind that an adolescent's world involves cognitive and socioemotional changes, as well as physical changes. As with all periods of development, these processes work in concert to produce who we are in adolescence.

Adolescent Sexuality

Adolescence is a time of sexual exploration and experimentation, of sexual fantasies and realities, of incorporating sexuality into one's identity. Adolescents have an almost insatiable curiosity about sexuality's mysteries. They think about whether they are sexually attractive, how to do sex, and what the future holds for their sexual lives. The majority of adolescents eventually manage to develop a mature sexual identity, but for most there are times of vulnerability and confusion along life's sexual journey.

Adolescence is a bridge between the asexual child and the sexual adult (Feldman, 1999). Every society gives some attention to adolescent sexuality. In some societies, adults clamp down and protect adolescent females from males by chaperoning them. Other societies promote very early marriage. Yet other societies, such as found in the

United States, allow some sexual experimentation, although there is controversy about just how far sexual experimentation should be allowed to go.

An important point to keep in mind as you read about adolescent sexuality is that sexual development and interest are normal aspects of adolescent development and that the majority of adolescents have healthy sexual attitudes and engage in sexual practices that will not compromise their development (Feldman, 1999). In our discussion of adolescent sexuality, we will focus on developing a sexual identity, the progression of adolescent sexual behaviors, risk factors for sexual problems, contraceptive use, sexually transmitted diseases, and adolescent pregnancy. In chapter 14, "Physical and Cognitive Development in Early Adulthood," we will further explore these important aspects of sexuality: heterosexuality and homosexuality, sexually transmitted diseases, and forcible sexual behavior and sexual harassment.

Developing a Sexual Identity Mastering emerging sexual feelings and forming a sense of sexual identity is multifaceted (Brooks-Gunn & Graber, 1999). This lengthy process involves learning to manage sexual feelings (such as sexual arousal and attraction), developing new forms of intimacy, and learning the skills to regulate sexual behavior to avoid undesirable consequences (Crockett, Raffaelli, & Moilanen, 2003). Developing a sexual identity also involves more than just sexual behavior. It includes interfaces with other developing identities. Sexual identities emerge in the context of physical factors, social factors, and cultural factors, with most societies placing constraints on the sexual behavior of adolescents.

An adolescent's sexual identity involves an indication of sexual orientation (homosexual, heterosexual, bisexual), and it also involves activities, interests, and styles of behavior (Buzwell & Rosenthal, 1996). For example, some adolescents have a high anxiety level about sex, others a low level. Some adolescents are strongly aroused sexually, others less so. Some adolescents are very active sexually, others are virgins. Some adolescents are sexually inactive because of a strong religious upbringing, others go to church regularly and it does not inhibit their sexual activity (Thorton & Canburn, 1989).

Although the development of gay or lesbian identity has been widely studied in adults, few researchers have investigated the gay or lesbian identity (often referred to as the coming-out process) in adolescents. In one comprehensive survey of adolescent sexual orientation in almost 35,000 junior and senior high school students in Minnesota, 4.5 percent reported predominantly homosexual attractions (Remafedi & others, 1992). Homosexual identities, attractions, and behaviors increased with age. More than 6 percent of the 18-year-olds said they had predominantly homosexual attractions. How many of these youth later become gay is not known, although it is widely accepted that many adolescents who engage in homosexual behavior in adolescence do not continue the practice into adulthood.

One of the harmful aspects of the stigmatization of homosexuality is the self-devaluation engaged in by gay individuals (Savin-Williams, 2001). The common form of self-devaluation is called *passing,* the process of hiding one's real social identity. Passing strategies include giving out information that hides one's homosexual identity or avoiding one's true sexual identity. Passing behaviors include lying to others and saying, "I'm straight and attracted to opposite-sex individuals." Such defenses against self-recognition are heavily entrenched in our society. Without adequate support, and with fear of stigmatization, many gay and lesbian youth return to the closet and then reemerge at a safer time later, often in college. A special concern is the lack of support gay adolescents receive from parents, teachers, counselors, and peers. We will discuss homosexuality, as well as heterosexuality, in greater depth in chapter 14, "Physical and Cognitive Development in Early Adulthood."

The Progression of Adolescent Sexual Behaviors Adolescents engage in a rather consistent progression of sexual behaviors (DeLamater & MacCorquodale, 1979). Necking usually comes first, followed by petting. Next comes intercourse, or, in

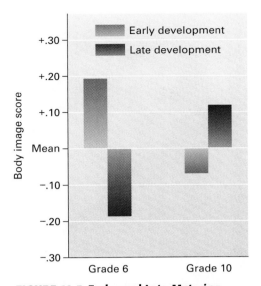

FIGURE 12.5 Early- and Late-Maturing Adolescent Girls' Perceptions of Body Image in Early and Late Adolescence

What is the progression of sexual behaviors in adolescence?

some cases, oral sex, which has increased substantially in adolescence in recent years. In one study, 452 individuals 18 to 25 years of age were asked about their own past sexual experiences (Feldman, Turner, & Araujo, 1999). The following progression of sexual behaviors occurred: kissing preceded petting which preceded sexual intercourse and oral sex (Feldman, Turner, & Araujo, 1999). Male adolescents reported engaging in these sexual behaviors approximately one year earlier than female adolescents.

Here is information from a national survey of adolescents that further reveals the timing of their sexual activities (Alan Guttmacher Institute, 1998):

- Most young adolescents have not had sexual intercourse: 8 in 10 girls and 7 in 10 boys are virgins at age 15.
- The probability that adolescents will have sexual intercourse increases steadily with age, but 1 in 5 individuals have not yet had sexual intercourse by age 19.
- Initial sexual intercourse occurs in the mid- to late-adolescent years for a majority of teenagers, about 8 years before they marry.
- The majority of adolescent females' first voluntary sexual partner are younger, the same age, or no more than 2 years older; 27 percent are 3 to 4 years older; and 12 percent are 5 or more years older.

In some areas of the United States, the percentages of sexually active young adolescents may be even greater. In an inner-city area of Baltimore, 81 percent of the males at age 14 said that they already had engaged in sexual intercourse. Other surveys in inner-city, low-income areas also reveal a high incidence of early sexual intercourse (Clark, Zabin, & Hardy, 1984).

In sum, by the end of adolescence the majority of U.S. adolescents have had sexual intercourse. Male, African American, and inner-city adolescents report being the most sexually active (Feldman, Turner, & Araujo, 1999). Although sexual intercourse can be a meaningful experience for older, mature adolescents, many adolescents are not emotionally prepared to handle sexual experiences, especially in early adolescence. In one study, the earlier boys and girls engaged in sexual intercourse, the more they were likely to show adjustment problems (Bingham & Crockett, 1996).

The timing of teenage sexual initiation varies by country and gender. In one study, among females, the proportion having first intercourse by age 17 ranged from 72 percent in Mali to 47 percent in the United States and 45 percent in Tanzania (Singh & others, 2000). The percentage of males who had their first intercourse by age 17 ranged from 76 percent in Jamaica to 64 percent in the United States and 63 percent in Brazil.

Risk Factors for Sexual Problems   While most adolescents become sexually active at some point during adolescence, some adolescents engage in sex at early ages (before age 16) and experience a number of partners over time. These adolescents are the least effective users of contraception and are at risk for early, unintended pregnancy and for sexually transmitted diseases. Early sexual activity is also linked with other risky behaviors such as excessive drinking, drug use, delinquency, and school-related problems (Dryfoos, 1990). Also, adolescents who live in low-income neighborhoods often are more sexually active and have higher adolescent pregnancy rates than adolescents who live in more affluent circumstances. And as we saw earlier, African American adolescents engage in sexual activities sooner than other ethnic groups, while Asian American adolescents have the most restrictive sexual timetable.

Contraceptive Use   Sexual activity is a normal activity necessary for procreation, but it involves considerable risks if appropriate safeguards are not taken. There are two kinds of risks that youth encounter: unintended/unwanted pregnancy and sexually transmitted diseases. Both of these risks can be reduced significantly by using contraception and barriers (such as condoms). Gay and lesbian youth who do not experiment with heterosexual intercourse are spared the risk of pregnancy, but, like their heterosexual peers, they still face the risk of sexually transmitted diseases.

The good news is that adolescents are increasing their use of contraceptives. Adolescent girls' contraceptive use at first intercourse rose from 48 percent to 65 percent during the 1980s (Forrest & Singh, 1990). By 1995, use at first intercourse reached 78 percent, with two-thirds of that figure involving condom use. A sexually active adolescent who does not use contraception has a 90 percent chance of pregnancy within one year (Alan Guttmacher Institute, 1998). The method adolescent girls use most frequently is the pill (44 percent), followed by the condom (38 percent). About 10 percent use an injectable contraceptive, 4 percent use withdrawal, and 3 percent use an implant (Alan Guttmacher Institute, 1998). Approximately one-third of adolescent girls who rely on condoms also take the pill or practice withdrawal.

Although adolescent contraceptive use is increasing, many sexually active adolescents still do not use contraceptives, or they use them inconsistently (Ford, Sohn, & Lepowski, 2001). Sexually active younger adolescents are less likely than older adolescents to take contraceptive precautions. Younger adolescents are more likely to use a condom or withdrawal, whereas older adolescents are more likely to use the pill or a diaphragm. In one study, adolescent females reported changing their behavior in the direction of safer sex practices more than did adolescent males (Rimberg & Lewis, 1994).

Sexually Transmitted Diseases **Sexually transmitted diseases (STDs)** are contracted primarily through sexual contact, which is not limited to sexual intercourse. Oral-genital and anal-genital contact also can transmit STDs.

Every year more than 3 million American adolescents (about one-fourth of those who are sexually experienced) acquire an STD (Alan Guttmacher Institute, 1999). In a single act of unprotected sex with an infected partner, a teenage girl has a 1 percent risk of getting HIV, a 30 percent risk of acquiring genital herpes, and a 50 percent chance of contracting gonorrhea (Glei, 1999). Chlamydia (which can spread by sexual contact and infects the genitals of both sexes) is more common among adolescents than among young adults. In some areas, as many as 25 percent of sexually active adolescents have contracted chlamydia (Donovan, 1993). In one recent cross-cultural study of sixteen developed countries, the incidence of chlamydia was high among adolescents in all of the countries (Panchaud & others, 2000). Adolescents also have a higher incidence of gonorrhea than young adults.

In chapter 14, we will study sexually transmitted diseases in more depth. Earlier we mentioned that when adolescents are sexually active and do not use contraception, one possible outcome is adolescent pregnancy. Let's further explore the nature of adolescent pregnancy.

FEIFFER®

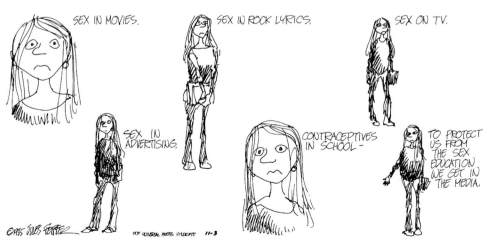

sexually transmitted diseases (STDs) Diseases that are contracted primarily through sexual contact, which is not limited to sexual intercourse. Oral-genital and anal-genital contact also can transmit STDs.

Careers in Life-Span Development

Lynn Blankenship, Family and Consumer Science Educator

Lynn Blankenship is a family and consumer science educator. She has an undergraduate degree in this area from the University of Arizona. She has taught for more than 20 years, the last 14 at Tucson High Magnet School.

Blankenship was awarded the Tucson Federation of Teachers Educator of the Year Award for 1999-2000 and the Arizona Teacher of the Year in 1999.

Blankenship especially enjoys teaching life skills to adolescents. One of her favorite activities is having students care for an automated baby that imitates the needs of real babies. She says that this program has a profound impact on students because the baby must be cared for around the clock for the duration of the assignment. Blankenship also coordinates real-world work experiences and training for students in several child-care facilities in the Tucson area.

Lynn Blankenship, (center) teaching life skills to students.

Adolescent Pregnancy In a recent cross-cultural comparison, the United States continued to have one of the highest adolescent pregnancy and childbearing rates in the industrialized world, despite a considerable decline in the 1990s (Alan Guttmacher Institute, 2000; Centers for Disease Control and Prevention, 2001). U.S. adolescent pregnancy rates are similar to those in Russia and Bulgaria, and at least four times the rates in France, Germany, and Japan. The U.S. adolescent pregnancy rate is eight times as high as in the Netherlands. While U.S. adolescents are no more sexually active than their counterparts in the Netherlands, their adolescent pregnancy is dramatically higher.

There are encouraging trends, though, in U.S. adolescent pregnancy rates. In 2000, births to adolescent girls fell to a record low (Centers for Disease Control and Prevention, 2001). For every 1,000 girls 15 to 19 years of age, there were 49 births—the lowest rate in six decades that the statistic has been kept. The rate of births to adolescent girls has dropped 22 percent since 1991. Reasons for the decline include increased contraceptive use, fear of sexually transmitted diseases such as AIDS, and the economic prosperity of the 1990s, which may have motivated adolescents to delay starting a family so that they could take jobs. The greatest drop in U.S. adolescent pregnancy rates in the 1990s was for 15- to 17-year-old girls. There is a special concern about the continued high rate of adolescent pregnancy in Latinas (Child Trends, 2001).

The consequences of adolescent pregnancy rates are cause for concern (Miller & others, 2003). Adolescent pregnancy creates health risks for both the offspring and the mother. Infants born to adolescent mothers are more likely to have low birthweights—a prominent factor in infant mortality—as well as neurological problems and childhood illness (Dryfoos, 1990). Adolescent mothers often drop out of school. However, often it is not pregnancy alone that leads to negative consequences for an adolescent mother and her offspring (Brooks-Gunn & Paikoff, 1997; Feldman, 1999; Leadbetter & Way, 2001). Adolescent mothers are more likely to come from low-income backgrounds (Hoffman, Foster, & Furstenberg, 1993). Many adolescent mothers also were not good students before they became pregnant. One recent study found that adolescent childbearers were more likely to have a history of conduct problems, less educational attainment, and lower childhood socioeconomic status than later childbearers (Jaffee, 2002). However, in this study, early childbearing exacerbated the difficulties associated with these risks.

Keep in mind that not every adolescent female who bears a child lives a life of poverty and low achievement. Thus, while adolescent pregnancy is a high-risk circumstance and in general adolescents who do not become pregnant fare better than those who don't, some adolescent mothers do well in school and have positive outcomes (Ahn, 1994; Whitman & others, 2001). Serious, extensive efforts are needed to help pregnant adolescents and young mothers enhance their educational and occupational opportunities. Adolescent mothers also need help in obtaining competent day care and in planning for the future.

Family and consumer science educators teach life skills, such as effective decision making, to adolescents. To read about the work of one family and consumer science educator, see the Careers in Life-Span Development insert.

Review and Reflect

2 **Describe pubertal changes and adolescent sexuality**

REVIEW

- What are some key aspects of puberty?
- What are some important aspects of sexuality in adolescence?

REFLECT

- Did you experience puberty on-time or off-time (early or late)? How did this affect your development?

3 ADOLESCENT PROBLEMS AND HEALTH

| Substance Use and Abuse | Eating Problems and Disorders | Adolescent Health |

Problems that can develop in adolescence include substance use and abuse, and eating disorders. We will discuss these problems here, then in chapter 13 explore the adolescent problems of juvenile delinquency, depression, and suicide. Also in this section we will examine adolescent health.

Substance Use and Abuse

The 1960s and 1970s were a time of marked increases in the use of illicit drugs. During the social and political unrest of those years, many youth turned to marijuana, stimulants, and hallucinogens. Increases in alcohol consumption by adolescents also were noted (Robinson & Greene, 1988). More precise data about drug use by adolescents have been collected in recent years. Each year since 1975, Lloyd Johnston, Patrick O'Malley, and Gerald Bachman (2001), working at the Institute of Social Research at the University of Michigan, have carefully monitored drug use by America's high school seniors in a wide range of public and private high schools. From time to time, they also sample the drug use of younger adolescents and adults.

Overall drug use among U.S. secondary school students declined in the 1980s but began to increase in the early 1990s, peaked in the mid-1990s, and has since leveled off (Johnston, O'Malley, & Bachman, 2001). Drugs that reached peak use levels by adolescents in the mid 1990s included inhalants, hallucinogens (such as LSD), marijuana, and amphetamines. Figure 12.6 shows the trends in overall drug use by American high school seniors since 1975.

A special concern in recent years is the increase in the use of "club drugs," so labeled because they are popular at nightclubs and all-night dance parties

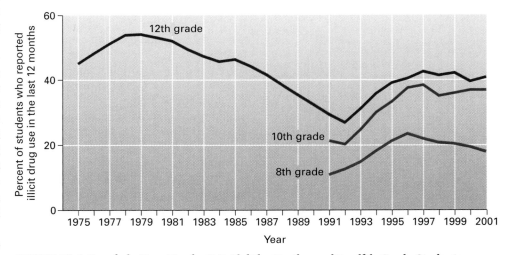

FIGURE 12.6 Trends in Drug Use by U.S. Eighth-, Tenth-, and Twelfth-Grade Students

This graph shows the percentage of U.S. eighth-, tenth-, and twelfth-grade students who reported having taken an illicit drug in the last 12 months, over the period 1975 through 2001.

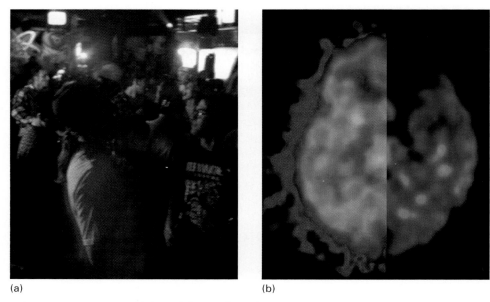

(a)   (b)

FIGURE 12.7 Ecstasy and the Adolescent's Brain

(*a*) In recent years, the use of Ecstasy by adolescents has become increasingly popular at nightclubs and all-night dance parties called "raves." (*b*) Ecstasy stimulates the release of the neurotransmitter serotonin in the brain, producing a euphoric high that lasts for several hours. However, Ecstasy also destroys nerve cells and affects areas of the brain responsible for learning and memory. These images show a brain scan of a normal brain (*left*) and a brain under the influence of Ecstasy (*right*). Notice the dramatic differences in cerebral activity in the two brains as reflected in their different coloring in the brain scans.

called "raves." The main club drug is Ecstasy, a methamphetamine that also has hallucinogenic properties (see figure 12.7). In 2001, Ecstasy use continued to rise among adolescents (Johnston, O'Malley, & Bachman, 2001). Nine percent of the twelfth-graders and six percent of the tenth-graders said they had used Ecstasy in the last year.

Even with the recent leveling off in drug use, the United States still has the highest rate of adolescent drug use of any industrialized nation. Also, the University of Michigan study likely underestimates the percentage of adolescents who take drugs, because it does not include high school dropouts, who have a higher rate of drug use than do students who are still in school.

Alcohol Alcohol is the drug most widely used by adolescents in our society. For them, it has produced many enjoyable moments and many sad ones as well. Alcoholism is the third leading killer in the United States, with more than 13 million people classified as alcoholics, many of whom established their drinking habits during adolescence. Each year, approximately 25,000 people are killed and 1.5 million injured by drunk drivers. In 65 percent of the aggressive male acts against females, the offender is under the influence of alcohol (Goodman & others, 1986). In numerous instances of drunken driving and assaults on females, the offenders are adolescents.

How extensive is alcohol use by adolescents? Alcohol use by high school seniors has gradually declined. Monthly use declined from 72 percent in 1980 to 50 percent in 2001 (Johnston, O'Malley, & Bachman, 2001). The prevalence of drinking five or more drinks in a row in a two-week interval fell from 41 percent in 1980 to 33 percent in 2001. However, data from college students show little drop in alcohol use and an increase in heavy drinking. Heavy drinking at parties among college males is common and is becoming more common (Wechsler & others, 2000).

Cigarette Smoking Smoking begins primarily during childhood and adolescence. One study found that, once young adolescents begin to smoke cigarettes, the addictive properties of nicotine make it extremely difficult for them to stop (Melby & Vargas, 1996).

The good news is that cigarette smoking is decreasing. In the national survey by the Institute of Social Research, the percentage of high school seniors who are current cigarette smokers continued to gradually decline in 2001 (Johnston, O'Malley, & Bachman, 2001). Cigarette smoking peaked in 1997 among high school seniors and since then has been gradually declining. Among high school seniors, a decline from 36.5 percent in 1997 to 29.5 percent in 2000 occurred regarding smoking one or more cigarettes in the past 30 days. Among eighth- and tenth-graders, the decline was even greater. However, despite these recent improvements, about 3 of 10 American youth are active smokers at the end of high school.

The devastating effects of early smoking were brought home in a recent research study that found that smoking in the adolescent years causes permanent genetic changes in the lungs and forever increases the risk of lung cancer, even if the smoker quits (Weincke & others, 1999). Such damage was much less likely among smokers in the study who started in their twenties. One of the remarkable findings in the study was that the early age of onset of smoking was more important in predicting the genetic damage than how much the individuals smoked.

The Roles of Development, Parents, and Peers   Most adolescents become drug users at some point in their development, whether limited to alcohol, caffeine, and cigarettes or extended to marijuana, cocaine, and hard drugs. A special concern involves adolescents using drugs as a way of coping with stress, which can interfere with the development of competent coping skills and responsible decision making. Researchers have found that drug use in childhood or early adolescence has more detrimental long-term effects on the development of responsible, competent behavior than when drug use occurs in late adolescence (Newcomb & Bentler, 1988). When they use drugs to cope with stress, many young adolescents enter adult roles of marriage and work prematurely, without adequate socioemotional growth, and experience greater failure in adult roles.

How early are adolescents beginning drug use? National samples of eighth- and ninth-grade students were included for the first time in 1991 in the Institute for Social Research survey of drug use (Johnston, O'Malley, & Bachman, 1992). Early in the drug use increase in the United States (late 1960s, early 1970s), drug use was much higher among college students than among high school students, who in turn had much higher rates of drug use than middle or junior high school students. However, today the rates for college and high school students are similar, and the rates for young adolescents are not as different from those for older adolescents as might be anticipated.

Parents, peers, and social support play important roles in preventing adolescent drug abuse (Dishion, 2001; Reifman, 2001; Simons-Morton & others, 2001; Windle & Windle, 2003). Positive relationships with parents and others are important in reducing adolescents' drug use (Brody & Ge, 2001). In one recent study, low parental involvement, peer pressure, and associating with problem-behaving friends were linked with higher use of drugs by adolescents (Simons-Morton & others, 2001). Also, in a recent national survey, parents who were more involved in setting limits (such as where adolescents went after school and what they were exposed to on TV and the Internet) were more likely to have adolescents who did not use drugs (National Center on Addiction and Substance Abuse, 2001). Also, one longitudinal study linked the early onset of substance abuse with early childhood predictors (Kaplow & others, 2002). Risk factors at kindergarten for substance use at 10 to 12 years of age included being male, having a parent who abused substances, a low level of verbal reasoning by parents, and low social problem-solving skills.

Substance abuse is a serious problem in adolescence (Jeynes, 2002). As we see next, eating disorders also can become serious problems in adolescence, especially for females.

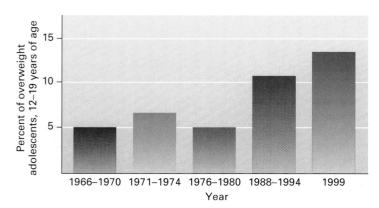

FIGURE 12.8 The Increase in Being Overweight in Adolescence from 1968 to 1999 in the United States

In this study, being overweight was determined by body mass index (BMI), which is computed by a formula that takes into account height and weight (National Center for Health Statistics, 2000). Only adolescents above the 95th percentile in the overweight category were included in the study. There was a substantial increase in the percentage of adolescents who were overweight from 1968 to 1999.

Eating Problems and Disorders

Eating disorders have become increasing problems in adolescence (Garner & Desai, 2001; McVey & others, 2002; Polivy & others, 2003). Here are some research findings involving adolescent eating disorders:

- Girls who felt negatively about their bodies in early adolescence were more likely to develop eating disorders, two years later, than their counterparts who did not feel negatively about their bodies (Attie & Brooks-Gunn, 1989).
- Negative parent-adolescent relationships were linked with increased dieting by girls over a one-year period (Archibald, Graber, & Brooks-Gunn, 1999).
- Girls who were both sexually active with their boyfriends and in pubertal transition were the most likely to be dieting or engaging in disordered eating patterns (Caufmann, 1994).
- Girls who were making a lot of effort to look like same-sex figures in the media were more likely than their peers to become very concerned about their weight (Field & others, 2001).
- Adolescent girls who watched four hours of television or more per day were more likely to be overweight than those who watched less than four hours a day (Dowda & others, 2001).
- A number of studies have revealed that adolescent girls have a strong desire to weigh less (Graber & Brooks-Gunn, 2001).
- Since the 1960s, an increasing percentage of adolescents have become overweight (see figure 12.8).

Let's now examine two eating disorders that may appear in adolescence: anorexia nervosa and bulimia nervosa.

Anorexia Nervosa   **Anorexia nervosa** is an eating disorder that involves the relentless pursuit of thinness through starvation. Anorexia nervosa eventually can lead to death. Three main characteristics of persons with anorexia nervosa are these (Davison & Neale, 2001):

- Weighing less than 85 percent of what is considered normal for their age and height.
- Having an intense fear of gaining weight. The fear does not decrease with weight loss.
- Having a distorted image of their body shape (Smolak & Striegel-Moore, 2002). Even when they are extremely thin, they see themselves as too fat. They never think they are thin enough, especially in the abdomen, buttocks, and thighs. They usually weigh themselves frequently, often take their body measurements, and gaze critically at themselves in mirrors.

Anorexia nervosa typically begins in the early to middle teenage years, often following an episode of dieting and the occurrence of some type of life stress. It is about ten times more likely in females than in males. When anorexia nervosa does occur in males, the symptoms and other characteristics (such as family conflict) are usually similar to those reported by females who have the disorder (Olivardia & others, 1995).

Most anorexics are White adolescent or young adult females from well-educated, middle- and upper-income families that are competitive and high-achieving. They set high standards, become stressed about not being able to reach the standards, and are intensely concerned about how others perceive them (Striegel-Moore, Silberstein, & Rodin, 1993). Unable to meet these high expectations, they turn to something they can control: their weight.

anorexia nervosa An eating disorder that involves the relentless pursuit of thinness through starvation.

The fashion image in the American culture that emphasizes "thin is beautiful" contributes to the incidence of anorexia nervosa. This image is reflected in the saying "You never can be too rich or too thin." The media portrays thin as beautiful in their choice of fashion models, which many adolescent girls want to emulate.

Bulimia Nervosa   Anorexics control their eating by restricting it. Most bulimics cannot. **Bulimia nervosa** is an eating disorder in which the individual consistently follows a binge-and-purge eating pattern. The bulimic goes on an eating binge and then purges by self-inducing vomiting or using a laxative. Most binge-purge eaters are females in their late teens or early twenties. As with anorexics, most bulimics are pre-occupied with food, have a strong fear of becoming overweight, and are depressed or anxious (Davison & Neale, 2000). Unlike anorexia nervosa, the binge-and-purging of bulimia nervosa occurs within a normal weight range, which means that it often is difficult to detect (Mizes & Miller, 2000; Orbanic, 2001).

Although many people binge and purge occasionally and some experiment with it, for a person to be considered to have a serious bulimic disorder, the episodes must occur at least twice a week for 3 months. Many bulimics once were somewhat overweight and began binging and purging during an episode of dieting (Schwitzer & others, 2001). One recent study of adolescent girls found that increased dieting, pressure to be thin, exaggerated importance of appearance, body dissatisfaction, depression symptoms, low self-esteem, and low social support predicted binge eating two years later (Stice, Presnell, & Spangler, 2002).

In chapter 13 we will explore these additional adolescent problems: juvenile delinquency, youth violence, depression, and suicide. Let's now turn our attention to the role of adolescence in the development of health.

Adolescent Health

How important is adolescence in the development of health? What are the leading causes of death in adolescence?

Adolescence: A Critical Juncture in Health   Adolescence is a critical juncture in the adoption of behaviors relevant to health (Maggs, Schulenberg, & Hurrelmann, 1997; Roth & Brooks-Gunn, 2000; Spear & Kolbok, 2001). Many of the factors linked to poor health habits and early death in the adult years begin during adolescence. The early formation of healthy behavioral patterns, such as eating foods low in fat and cholesterol and engaging in regular exercise not only has immediate health benefits but contributes to the delay or prevention of major causes of premature disability and mortality in adulthood—heart disease, stroke, diabetes, and cancer (Jessor, Turbin, & Costa, 1998).

In a recent comparison of adolescent health behavior in 28 countries, U.S. adolescents exercised less and ate more junk food than adolescents in most other countries (World Health Organization, 2000). Just two-thirds of U.S. adolescents exercised at least twice a week, compared to 80 percent or more of adolescents in Ireland, Austria, Germany, and the Slovak Republic. U.S. adolescents were more likely to eat fried food and less likely to eat fruits and vegetables than adolescents in most other countries studied. U.S. adolescents' eating choices were similar to those of adolescents in England. Eleven-year-olds in the United States were as likely as European 11-year-olds to smoke, but by age 15 U.S. adolescents were less likely to smoke.

Many health experts believe that improving adolescent health involves far more than trips to a doctor's office when sick. The health experts increasingly recognize that whether adolescents will develop a health problem or be healthy is primarily based on their behavior. The goals are to (1) reduce adolescents' health-compromising behaviors, such as drug abuse, violence, unprotected sexual intercourse, and dangerous driving; and (2) increase health-enhancing behaviors, such as eating nutritiously, exercising, and wearing seat belts.

Anorexia nervosa has become an increasing problem for adolescent girls and young adult women. *What are some possible causes of anorexia nervosa?*

mhhe ● com/
santrockld9

Adolescent Health

National Longitudinal Study of Adolescent Health

bulimia nervosa An eating disorder in which the individual consistently follows a binge-and-purge pattern.

Leading Causes of Death in Adolescence Medical improvements have increased the life expectancy of today's adolescents compared to their counterparts who lived earlier in the twentieth century. Still, life-threatening factors continue to exist in adolescents' lives.

The three leading causes of death in adolescence are accidents, homicide, and suicide (Gould, 2001). More than half of all deaths in adolescents ages 10 to 19 are due to accidents, and most of those involve motor vehicles, especially for older adolescents. Risky driving habits, such as speeding, tailgating, and driving under the influence of alcohol or other drugs, may be more important causes of these accidents than is lack of driving experience. In about 50 percent of the motor vehicle fatalities involving an adolescent, the driver has a blood alcohol level of 0.10 percent, twice the level needed to be "under the influence" in some states. A high rate of intoxication is also often present in adolescents who die as pedestrians or while using recreational vehicles.

Homicide is the second leading cause of death in adolescence (National Center for Health Statistics, 2001). Homicide is especially high among African American male adolescents, who are three times more likely to be killed by guns than by natural causes (Simons, Finlay, & Yang, 1991).

Suicide accounts for 6 percent of the deaths in the 10-to-14 age group, a rate of 1.3 per 100,000 population. In the 15-to-19 age group, suicide accounts for 12 percent of deaths or 9 per 100,000 population. Since the 1950s, the adolescent suicide rate has tripled. We will discuss suicide further in chapter 13.

Review and Reflect

3 **Identify adolescent problems in substance use and abuse, eating disorders, and health**

REVIEW

- What are some characteristics of adolescence substance use and abuse and eating disorders?
- Why is adolescence a critical juncture in health? What are the leading causes of death in adolescence?

REFLECT

- What do you think should be done to reduce the use of drugs by adolescents?

4 ADOLESCENT COGNITION

Piaget's Theory   **Adolescent Egocentrism**   **Information Processing**

Adolescents' developing power of thought opens up new cognitive and social horizons. Let's examine what their developing power of thought is like, beginning with Piaget's theory (1952).

Piaget's Theory

What are Jean Piaget's ideas about cognitive development in adolescence ◀‖‖ p. 49? To answer this question, we will study Piaget's stage of formal operational thought.

Most significantly, formal operational thought is more abstract than concrete operational thought. Adolescents are no longer limited to actual, concrete experiences as anchors for thought. They can conjure up make-believe situations, events that are purely hypothetical possibilities or strictly abstract propositions, and can try to reason logically about them.

The abstract quality of the adolescent's thought at the formal operational level is evident in the adolescent's verbal problem-solving ability. Whereas the concrete operational thinker needs to see the concrete elements A, B, and C to be able to make the logical inference that, if A = B and B = C, then A = C, the formal operational thinker can solve this problem merely through verbal presentation.

Another indication of the abstract quality of adolescents' thought is their increased tendency to think about thought itself. One adolescent commented, "I began thinking about why I was thinking what I was. Then I began thinking about why I was thinking about what I was thinking about what I was." If this sounds abstract, it is, and it characterizes the adolescent's enhanced focus on thought and its abstract qualities.

Accompanying the abstract nature of formal operational thought in adolescence is thought full of idealism and possibilities. While children frequently think in concrete ways, or in terms of what is real and limited, adolescents begin to engage in extended speculation about ideal characteristics—qualities they desire in themselves and in others. Such thoughts often lead adolescents to compare themselves with others in regard to such ideal standards. And, during adolescence, the thoughts of individuals are often fantasy flights into future possibilities. It is not unusual for the adolescent to become impatient with these newfound ideal standards and to become perplexed over which of many ideal standards to adopt.

At the same time that adolescents think more abstractly and idealistically, they also think more logically. Adolescents begin to think more as a scientist thinks, devising plans to solve problems and systematically testing solutions. This type of problem solving has an imposing name. **Hypothetical-deductive reasoning** is Piaget's formal operational concept that adolescents have the cognitive ability to develop hypotheses, or best guesses, about ways to solve problems, such as an algebraic equation. Then they systematically deduce, or conclude, which is the best path to follow in solving the equation. By contrast, children are more likely to solve problems in a trial-and-error fashion.

One example of hypothetical-deductive reasoning involves a modification of the familiar game Twenty Questions. Individuals are shown a set of 42 color pictures, displayed in a rectangular array (six rows of seven pictures each) and are asked to determine which picture the experimenter has in mind (that is, which is "correct"). The subjects are allowed to ask only questions to which the experimenter can answer yes or no. The object of the game is to select the correct picture by asking as few questions as possible. Adolescents who are deductive hypothesis testers formulate a plan and test a series of hypotheses, which considerably narrows the field of choices. The most effective plan is a "halving" strategy (Q: Is the picture in the right half of the array? A: No. Q: Okay. Is it in the top half? And so on.). A correct halving strategy guarantees the answer in seven questions or less. By contrast, concrete operational thinkers may persist with questions that continue to test some of the same possibilities that previous questions could have eliminated. For example, they may ask whether the correct picture is in row 1 and are told that it is not. Later, they ask whether the picture is X, which is in row 1.

Thus, formal operational thinkers test their hypotheses with judiciously chosen questions and tests. By contrast, concrete operational thinkers often fail to understand the relation between a hypothesis and a well-chosen test of it, stubbornly clinging to ideas that already have been discounted.

Some of Piaget's ideas on formal operational thought are being challenged (Eccles, Wigfield, & Byrnes, 2003; Kuhn, 2000; Overton & Byrnes, 1991). There is much more

hypothetical-deductive reasoning Piaget's formal operational concept that adolescents have the cognitive ability to develop hypotheses, or best guesses, about ways to solve problems, such as an algebraic equation.

Many adolescent girls spend long hours in front of the mirror, depleting cans of hairspray, tubes of lipstick, and jars of cosmetics. *How might this behavior be related to changes in adolescent cognitive and physical development?*

individual variation in formal operational thought than Piaget envisioned. Only about one in three young adolescents is a formal operational thinker. Many American adults never become formal operational thinkers, and neither do many adults in other cultures. Education in the logic of science and mathematics is an important cultural experience that promotes the development of formal operational thinking.

Also, for adolescents who become formal operational thinkers, assimilation (incorporating new information into existing knowledge) dominates the initial development of formal operational thought, and the world is perceived subjectively and idealistically. Later in adolescence, as intellectual balance is restored, these individuals accommodate (adjust to new information) to the cognitive upheaval that has occurred.

In addition to thinking more logically, abstractly, and idealistically, which characterizes Piaget's formal operational thought stage, in what other ways does adolescent cognition change? One important way involves adolescent egocentrism.

Adolescent Egocentrism

"Oh, my gosh! I can't believe it. Help! I can't stand it!" Tracy desperately yells. "What is wrong? What is the matter?" her mother asks. Tracy responds, "Everyone in here is looking at me." The mother queries, "Why?" Tracy says, "Look, this one hair just won't stay in place," as she rushes to the restroom of the restaurant. Five minutes later, she returns to the table in the restaurant after she has depleted an entire can of hairspray.

During a conversation between two 14-year-old girls, the one named Margaret says, "Are you kidding, I won't get pregnant." And, 13-year-old Adam describes himself, "No one understands me, particularly my parents. They have no idea of what I am feeling."

Adolescent egocentrism is the heightened self-consciousness of adolescents. David Elkind (1976) believes that adolescent egocentrism can be dissected into two types of social thinking—imaginary audience and personal fable. The notion of **imaginary audience** involves adolescents' belief that others are as interested in them as they themselves are, as well as attention-getting behavior—attempts to be noticed, visible, and "on stage." Tracy's comments and behavior that we described in the first paragraph of this section reflect the imaginary audience. Another adolescent might think that others are as aware of a small spot on his trousers as he is, possibly knowing that he has masturbated. Another adolescent, an eighth-grade girl, walks into her classroom and thinks that all eyes are riveted on her complexion. Adolescents especially sense that they are "on stage" in early adolescence, believing they are the main actors and all others are the audience.

According to Elkind, the **personal fable** is the part of adolescent egocentrism involving an adolescent's sense of uniqueness and invincibility. The comments of Margaret and Adam, mentioned earlier, reflect the personal fable. Adolescents' sense of personal uniqueness makes them feel that no one can understand how they really feel. For example, an adolescent girl thinks that her mother cannot possibly sense the hurt she feels because her boyfriend has broken up with her. As part of their effort to retain a sense of personal uniqueness, adolescents might craft a story about the self that is filled with fantasy, immersing themselves in a world that is far removed from reality. Personal fables frequently show up in adolescent diaries.

Adolescents also often show a sense of invincibility, believing that they themselves will never suffer the terrible experiences (such as deadly car wrecks) that can happen to other people. This sense of invincibility likely is involved in the reckless

adolescent egocentrism The heightened self-consciousness of adolescents.

imaginary audience Involves adolescents' belief that others are as interested in them as they themselves are; attention-getting behavior motivated by a desire to be noticed, visible, and "on stage."

personal fable The part of adolescent egocentrism that involves an adolescent's sense of uniqueness and invincibility.

behavior of some adolescents, such as drag racing, drug use, suicide, and having sexual intercourse without using contraceptives or barriers against STDs.

Information Processing

Two of the most important aspects of changes in information processing in adolescence involve decision making and critical thinking.

Decision Making   Adolescence is a time of increased decision making—about the future, which friends to choose, whether to go to college, which person to date, whether to have sex, whether to buy a car, and so on (Byrnes, 1997, 2001, 2003; Galotti & Kozberg, 1996; Jacobs & Klaczynski, 2002; Kuhn, 2000). How competent are adolescents at making decisions? In some reviews, older adolescents are described as more competent than younger adolescents, who, in turn, are more competent than children (Keating, 1990). Compared to children, young adolescents are more likely to generate options, to examine a situation from a variety of perspectives, to anticipate the consequences of decisions, and to consider the credibility of sources.

Although driver-training courses can improve adolescents' cognitive and motor skills related to driving, these courses have not been effective in reducing adolescents' high rate of traffic accidents. *Why might this be so?*

The ability to make competent decisions does not guarantee that they will be made in everyday life, where breadth of experience often comes into play (Jacobs & Potenza, 1990; Jacobs & Klaczynski, 2002; Keating, 1990). For example, driver-training courses improve adolescents' cognitive and motor skills to levels equal to, or sometimes superior to, those of adults. However, driver training has not been effective in reducing adolescents' high rate of traffic accidents (Potvin, Champagne, & Laberge-Nadeau, 1988). An important research agenda is to study the ways adolescents make decisions in practical situations.

Another strategy is for parents to involve their adolescents in appropriate decision-making activities. In one study of more than 900 young adolescents and a subsample of their parents, adolescents were more likely to participate in family decision making when they perceived themselves as in control of what happens to them and if they thought that their input would have some bearing on the outcome of the decision-making process (Liprie, 1993).

Critical Thinking   Adolescence is an important transitional period in the development of critical thinking (Keating, 1990). In one study of fifth-, eighth-, and eleventh-graders, critical thinking increased with age but still only occurred in 43 percent of even the eleventh-graders, and many adolescents showed self-serving biases in their reasoning (Klaczynski & Narasimham, 1998).

Among the cognitive changes that allow improved critical thinking in adolescence are:

- Increased speed, automaticity, and capacity of information processing, which free cognitive resources for other purposes
- More breadth of content knowledge in a variety of domains
- Increased ability to construct new combinations of knowledge
- A greater range and more spontaneous use of strategies or procedures for applying or obtaining knowledge, such as planning, considering alternatives, and cognitive monitoring

Although adolescence is an important period in the development of critical-thinking skills, if a solid basis of fundamental skills (such as literacy and math skills) is not developed during childhood, such critical-thinking skills are unlikely to mature in adolescence ◀▥ p. 315. For the subset of adolescents who lack such fundamental skills, potential gains in adolescent thinking are not likely.

Review and Reflect

4 **Explain cognitive changes in adolescence**

REVIEW

- What is Piaget's theory of adolescent cognitive development?
- What is adolescent egocentrism?
- What are some important aspects of decision making and critical thinking in adolescence?

REFLECT

- Using Piaget's theory of cognitive development as a guide, suppose an 8-year-old and a 16-year-old are watching a political convention on television. How might their perceptions of the proceedings differ? What Piagetian concepts would these perceptions reflect?

5 SCHOOLS

```
The Transition to Middle          High School
or Junior High School

        Effective Schools              Service Learning
        for Young Adolescents
```

The impressive changes in adolescents' cognition lead us to examine the nature of schools for adolescents. In chapter 11, we discussed different ideas about the effects of schools on children's development ◀▥ p. 355. Here, we will focus more exclusively on the nature of secondary schools. Questions we will look at include these: What is the transition from elementary to middle or junior high school like? What are effective schools for young adolescents?

mhhe●com/
santrockld9

Schools for Adolescents

National Center for Education Statistics

United States Department of Education

Middle Schools

The Transition to Middle or Junior High School

The emergence of junior high schools in the 1920s and 1930s was justified on the basis of the physical, cognitive, and social changes that characterize early adolescence, as well as the need for more schools for the growing student population. Old high schools became junior high schools, and new regional high schools were built. In most systems, the ninth grade remained a part of the high school in content, although physically separated from it in a 6-3-3 system. Gradually, the ninth grade was restored to the high school, as many school systems developed middle schools that include the seventh and eighth grades, or sixth, seventh, and eighth grades. The creation of middle schools was influenced by the earlier onset of puberty in recent decades.

One worry of educators and psychologists is that junior high and middle schools have simply become watered-down versions of high schools, mimicking their curricular and extracurricular schedules. The critics argue that unique curricular and extracurricular activities reflecting a wide range of individual differences in biological and psychological development in early adolescence should be incorporated into our junior high and middle schools. The critics also stress that many high schools foster passivity rather than autonomy and that schools should create a variety of pathways for students to achieve an identity.

The transition to middle school or junior high school from elementary schools interests developmentalists because, even though it is a normative experience for virtually all children, the transition can be stressful (Eccles, 2000, 2003; Seidman, 2000). Why? The transition takes place at a time when many changes—in the individual, in the family, and in school—are occurring simultaneously. These changes include puberty and related concerns about body image; the emergence of at least some aspects of formal operational thought, including accompanying changes in social cognition; increased responsibility and independence in association with decreased dependency on parents; change from a small, contained classroom structure to a larger, more impersonal school structure; change from one teacher to many teachers and from a small, homogeneous set of peers to a larger, more heterogeneous set of peers; and an increased focus on achievement and performance and their assessment. This list includes a number of negative, stressful features, but there can be positive aspects to the transition. Students are more likely to feel grown up, have more subjects from which to select, have more opportunities to spend time with peers and to locate compatible friends, and enjoy increased independence from direct parental monitoring, and they may be more challenged intellectually by academic work.

When students make the transition from elementary school to middle or junior high school, they experience the **top-dog phenomenon,** the circumstance of moving from the top position (in elementary school, being the oldest, biggest, and most powerful students in the school) to the lowest position (in middle or junior high school, being the youngest, smallest, and least powerful students in the school). Researchers who have charted the transition from elementary to middle or junior high school find that the first year of middle or junior high school can be difficult for many students (Hawkins & Berndt, 1985). For example, in one study of the transition from sixth grade in an elementary school to the seventh grade in a junior high school, adolescents' perceptions of the quality of their school life plunged in the seventh grade (Hirsch & Rapkin, 1987). In the seventh grade, the students were less satisfied with school, were less committed to school, and liked their teachers less. The drop in school satisfaction occurred regardless of how academically successful the students were.

Effective Schools for Young Adolescents

What makes a successful middle school? Joan Lipsitz (1984) and her colleagues searched the nation for the best middle schools. Extensive contacts and observations were made. Based on the recommendations of education experts and observations in schools in different parts of the United States, four middle schools were chosen for their outstanding ability to educate young adolescents. What were these middle schools like? The most striking feature was their willingness and ability to adapt all school practices to their students' individual differences in physical, cognitive, and social development. The schools took seriously the knowledge we have developed about young adolescents. This seriousness was reflected in the decisions about different aspects of school life. For example, one middle school fought to keep its schedule of minicourses on Friday, so that every student could be with friends and pursue personal interests. Two other middle schools expended considerable energy on a complex school organization, so that small groups of students worked with small groups of teachers who could vary the tone and pace of the school day, depending on the students' needs. Another middle school developed an advisory scheme, so that each student had daily contact with an adult who was willing to listen, explain, comfort, and prod the adolescent. Such school policies reflect thoughtfulness and personal concern about individuals who have compelling developmental needs.

Another aspect of the effective middle schools was that early in their existence—the first year in three of the schools and the second year in the fourth school—they emphasized the importance of creating an environment that was positive for adolescents' social and emotional development. This goal was established not only because such environments contribute to academic excellence but also because social and

top-dog phenomenon The circumstance of moving from the top position in elementary school to the lowest position in middle or junior high school.

The transition from elementary to middle or junior high school occurs at the same time as a number of other developmental changes. *What are some of these other developmental changes?*

emotional development were valued as intrinsically important in adolescents' schooling. Recognizing that the vast majority of middle schools do not approach the excellent schools described by Joan Lipsitz (1984), in 1989 the Carnegie Corporation issued an extremely negative evaluation of our nation's middle schools. In the report, "Turning Points: Preparing American Youth for the 21st Century," the conclusion was put forth that most young adolescents attend massive, impersonal schools, learn from seemingly irrelevant curricula, trust few adults in school, and lack access to health care and counseling. The Carnegie Corporation (1989) report includes these recommendations:

- Develop smaller "communities" or "houses" to lessen the impersonal nature of large middle schools.
- Lower student-to-counselor ratios from several-hundred-to-1 to 10-to-1.
- Involve parents and community leaders in schools.
- Develop curricula that produce students who are literate, understand the sciences, and have a sense of health, ethics, and citizenship.
- Have teachers team teach in more flexibly designed curriculum blocks that integrate several disciplines, instead of presenting students with disconnected, rigidly separated 50-minute segments.
- Boost students' health and fitness with more in-school programs and help students who need public health care to get it.

In sum, middle schools throughout the nation need a major redesign if they are to be effective in educating adolescents for becoming competent adults in the twenty-first century.

High School

Just as there are concerns about U.S. middle school education, so are there concerns about U.S. high school education (Dornbusch & Kaufman, 2001; Kaufman, 2001).

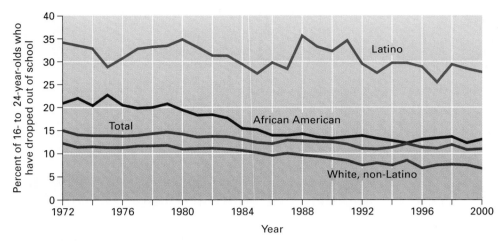

FIGURE 12.9 Trends in High School Dropout Rates

From 1972 through 2000, the school dropout rate for Latinos remained very high (27.8 percent of 16- to 24-year-olds in 2000). The African American dropout rate was still higher (13.1 percent) than the White non-Latino rate (6.9 percent) in 2000. The overall dropout rate declined considerably from the 1940s through the 1960s but has declined only slightly since 1972.

Many students graduate from high school with inadequate reading, writing, and mathematical skills, including many who go on to college and have to enroll in remediation classes there. Other students drop out of high school and do not have skills that will allow them to advance in the work world.

High School Dropouts   In the last half of the twentieth century, high school dropout rates declined overall (National Center for Education Statistics, 2001). For example, in the 1940s, more than half of U.S. 16- to 24-year-olds had dropped out of school but in 2000 this figure had decreased to only 10.9 percent. Figure 12.9 shows the trends in high school dropout rates from 1972 through 2000. Notice that the dropout rate of Latino adolescents remains precariously high (27.8 percent of 16- to 24-year-old Latino adolescents had dropped out of school in 2000). The highest dropout rate in the United States, though, occurs for Native American youth—only about 10 percent finish their high school education.

Students drop out of schools for many reasons. In one study, almost 50 percent of the dropouts cited school-related reasons for leaving school, such as not liking school or being expelled or suspended (Rumberger, 1995). Twenty percent of the dropouts (but 40 percent of the Latino students) cited economic reasons for leaving school. One-third of the female students dropped out for personal reasons, such as pregnancy or marriage.

One of the roles of high school guidance counselors is to work with high-risk students to reduce the likelihood that they will drop out of school, encourage them to go to college, and increase their understanding of careers. To read about the work of one high school guidance counselor, see the Careers in Life-Span Development insert on page 394.

Toward Effective High Schools   Many high school graduates not only are poorly prepared for college, they also are poorly prepared for the demands of the modern, high-performance workplace. In a review of hiring practices at major companies, it was concluded that many companies now have sets of basic skills they want the individuals they hire to have. These include the ability to read at relatively high levels, do at least elementary algebra, use personal computers for straightforward tasks such as word processing, solve semi-structured problems in which hypotheses must be formed

mhhe ○ com/
santrockld9

Reducing the Dropout Rate

High School Education

Careers in Life-Span Development

Armando Ronquillo, High School Counselor/College Advisor

Armando Ronquillo is a high school counselor and college advisor at Pueblo High School, which is in a low-socioeconomic-status area in Tucson, Arizona ◀|||| p. 33. More than 85 percent of the students have a Latino background. Ronquillo was named top high-school counselor in the state of Arizona for the year 2000. He has especially helped to increase the number of Pueblo High School students who go to college.

Ronquillo has an undergraduate degree in elementary and special education, and a master's degree in counseling. He counsels the students on the merits of staying in school and on the lifelong opportunities provided by a college education. Ronquillo guides students in obtaining the academic preparation that will enable them to go to college, including how to apply for financial aid and scholarships. He also works with parents to help them understand that "their child going to college is not only doable but also affordable."

Ronquillo works with students on setting goals and planning. He has students plan for the future in terms of 1-year (short-term), 5-year (mid-range), and 10-plus-year (long-term) time periods. He says he does this "to help students visualize how the educational plans and decisions they make today will affect them in the future." Ronquillo also organizes a number of college campus visitations for students from Pueblo High School each year.

Armando Ronquillo, counseling a Latina high school student about college.

and tested, communicate effectively (orally and in writing), and work effectively in groups with persons of various backgrounds (Murnane & Levy, 1996).

An increasing number of educators believe that the nation's high schools need a new mission for the twenty-first century, which addresses the problems listed here (National Commission on the High School Senior Year, 2001):

1. More support is needed to enable all students to graduate from high school with the knowledge and skills needed to succeed in post–secondary education and careers. Many parents and students, especially those in low-income and minority communties, are unaware of the knowledge and level of skills required to succeed to post–secondary education.
2. High schools need to have higher expectations for student achievement. A special concern is the senior year of high school, which has become too much of a party-time rather than a time to prepare for one of life's most important transition. Some students who have been accepted to college routinely ignore the academic demands of their senior year. Low academic expectations harm students from all backgrounds.
3. U.S. high school students spend too much time working in low-level service jobs. Researchers have found that when tenth graders work more than 14 hours a week their grades drop and when eleventh graders work 20 or more hours a week their grades drop (Greenberger & Steinberg, 1986). At the same time, shorter, higher-quality work experiences, including community service and internships, have been shown to benefit high school students.

Cross-Cultural Comparisons of Secondary Schools

Secondary Schools in different countries share a number of features, but differ on others (Cameron & others, 1983). Let's explore the similarities and differences in secondary schools in six countries: Australia, Brazil, Germany, Japan, Russia, and the United States.

Most countries mandate that children begin school at 6 to 7 years of age and stay in school until they are 14 to 17 years of age. Brazil requires students to go to school only until they are 14 years of age, while Russia mandates that students stay in school until they are 17. Germany, Japan, Australia, and the United States require school attendance until 15 to 16 years of age.

Most secondary schools around the world are divided into two or more levels, such as middle school (or junior high school) and high school. However, Germany's schools are divided according to three educational ability tracks: (1) The main school provides a basic level of education, (2) the middle school gives students a more advanced education, and (3) the academic school prepares students for entrance to a university. German schools, like most European schools, offer a classical education, which includes courses in Latin and Greek.

Japanese secondary schools have an entrance exam, but secondary schools in the other five countries do not. Only Australia and Germany have comprehensive exit exams.

The United States is the only country in the world in which sports are an integral part of the public school system. Only a few private schools in other countries have their own sports teams, sports facilities, and highly organized sports events.

Curriculum is often similar in secondary schools in different countries, although there are some differences in content and philosophy. For example, at least until recently, the secondary schools in Russia have emphasized the preparation of students for work. The "labor education program," which is part of the secondary school curriculum, includes vocational training and on-the-job experience. The idea is to instill in youth a love for manual work and a positive attitude about industrial and work organizations. Russian students who are especially gifted—academically, artistically, or athletically—attend special schools where they are encouraged to develop their talents and are trained to be the very best in their vocation. With the breakup of the Soviet Union, it will be interesting to follow what changes in education take place in Russia.

In Brazil, students are required to take Portuguese (the native language) and four foreign languages (Latin, French, English, and Spanish). Brazil requires these languages because of the country's international character and emphasis on trade and commerce. Seventh-grade students in Australia take courses in sheep husbandry and weaving, two areas of economic and cultural interest in the country. In Japan, students take a number of Western courses in addition to their basic Japanese courses; these courses include Western literature and languages (in addition to Japanese literature and language), Western physical education (in addition to Japanese martial arts classes), and Western sculpture and handicrafts (in addition to Japanese calligraphy). The Japanese school year is also much longer than that of other countries (225 days versus 180 days in the United States, for example).

The juku, or "cramming school," is available to Japanese children and adolescents in the summertime and after school. It provides coaching to help them improve their grades and their entrance exam scores for high schools and universities. The Japanese practice of requiring an entrance exam for high school is a rarity among the nations of the world.

4. There has been too little coordination and communication across the different levels of the K–12, as well as between K–12 schools and institutions of higher education.
5. At the middle and secondary school levels, every student needs strong, positive connections with adults, preferably many of them, as they explore options for school, post–secondary education, and work.

Are American secondary schools different from those in other countries? To explore this question, see Sociocultural Worlds of Development box.

"What are some of the positive effects of service training?"

mhhe●com/
santrockld9

Service Learning

Service Learning

Service learning is a form of education that promotes social responsibility and service to the community. In service learning, students might engage in tutoring, help the elderly, work in a hospital, assist at a day-care center, or clean up a vacant lot to make a play area. An important goal of service learning is for students to become less self-centered and more motivated to help others (Waterman, 1997; Youniss & others, 2003).

Service learning takes education out into the community. One eleventh-grade student worked as a reading tutor for students from low-income homes who had reading skills well below their grade levels. She commented that, until she did the tutoring, she didn't realize how many students had not experienced the same opportunities she had had when she was growing up. An especially rewarding moment was when one young girl told her, "I want to learn to read like you do so I can go to college when I grow up." Thus, service learning can benefit not only the students but also the recipients of their help.

Researchers have found that service learning benefits students in a number of ways:

- Their grades improve, they become more motivated, and they set more goals (Johnson & others, 1998).
- Their self-esteem improves (Hamburg, 1997).
- They become less alienated (Calabrese & Schumer, 1986).
- They increasingly reflect on society's political organization and moral order (Yates, 1995).

Required community service has increased in high schools. In one survey, 15 percent of the nation's largest school districts had such a requirement (National and Community Service Coalition, 1995). Even though required community service has increased in high schools, in another survey of 40,000 adolescents, two thirds said they had never done any volunteer work to help other people (Benson, 1993). The benefits of service learning, for both the volunteer and the recipient, suggest that more adolescents should be required to participate in such programs.

service learning A form of education that promotes social responsibility and service to the community.

Careers in Life-Span Development

Constance Flanagan, Professor of Youth Civic Development

Constance (Connie) Flanagan is a professor of youth civic development in the College of Agricultural Sciences at Pennsylvania State University. Her research focuses on youths' views about justice and the factors in families, schools, and communities that promote civic values, connections, and skills in youth (Flanagan, 2002).

　Dr. Flanagan obtained her undergraduate degree in psychology from Duquesne University, her master's degree in education from the University of Iowa, and her Ph.D. from the University of Michigan. She has a special interest in improving the U.S. social policy for adolescents and serves as co-chair of the Committee on Child Development, Public Policy, and Public Information for the Society for Research in Child Development. In addition to teaching undergraduate and graduate classes, conducting research, and serving on various committees, she also evaluates research for potential publication as a member of the editorial board of *Journal of Adolescent Research* and *Journal of Research on Adolescence.* She also presents her ideas and research at numerous national and international meetings.

Connie Flanagan with adolescents.

　Connie Flanagan conducts research on factors in families, schools, and communities that are related to service learning in adolescents. To read about her work and career, see the Careers in Life-Span Development insert.

Review and Reflect

5　**Summarize some key aspects of how schools influence adolescent development**

REVIEW

- What is the transition to middle or junior high school like?
- What are some characteristics of effective schools for young adolescents?
- What are some important things to know about high school dropouts and improving high schools?
- What is service learning and how does it affect adolescent development?

REFLECT

- What was your middle or junior high school like? How did it measure up to Lipsitz' criteria for effective schools for young adolescents and the Carnegie Foundation's recommendations?

Reach Your Learning Goals

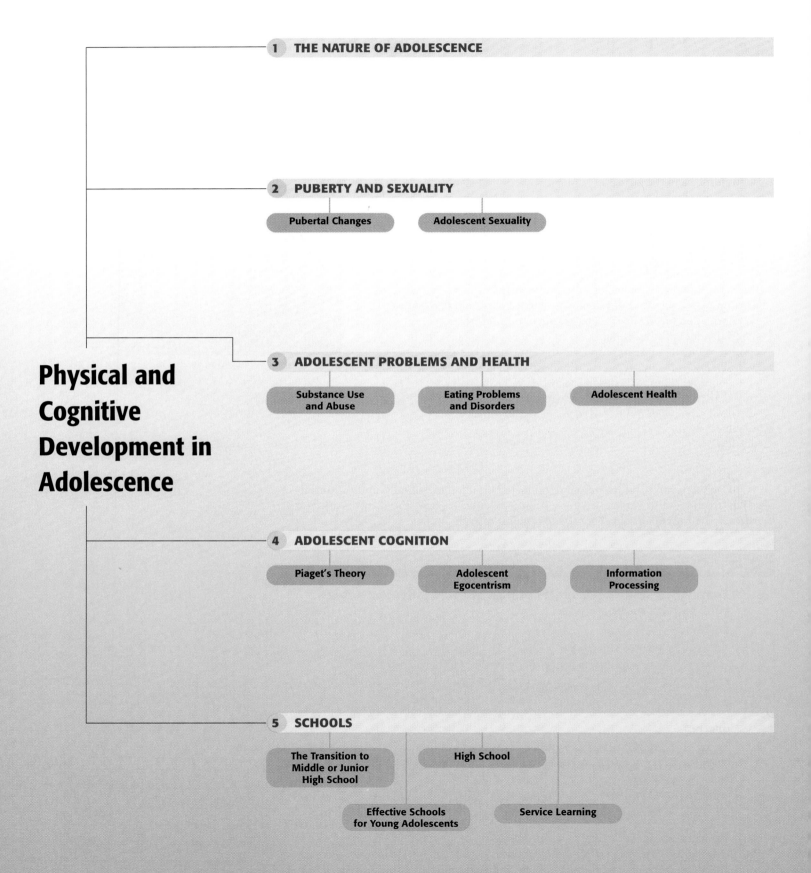

Physical and Cognitive Development in Adolescence

1 THE NATURE OF ADOLESCENCE

2 PUBERTY AND SEXUALITY

- Pubertal Changes
- Adolescent Sexuality

3 ADOLESCENT PROBLEMS AND HEALTH

- Substance Use and Abuse
- Eating Problems and Disorders
- Adolescent Health

4 ADOLESCENT COGNITION

- Piaget's Theory
- Adolescent Egocentrism
- Information Processing

5 SCHOOLS

- The Transition to Middle or Junior High School
- High School
- Effective Schools for Young Adolescents
- Service Learning

Summary

1 Discuss the nature of adolescence

- Many stereotypes of adolescents are too negative. Most adolescents today successfully negotiate the path from childhood to adulthood. However, too many of today's adolescents are not provided with adequate opportunities and support to become competent adults. It is important to view adolescents has a heterogeneous group because different portraits of adolescents emerge depending on the particular set of adolescents being described.

2 Describe pubertal changes and adolescent sexuality

- Puberty is a period of rapid physical maturation involving hormonal and bodily changes that occur primarily during early adolescence. Puberty's determinants include nutrition, health, heredity, and body mass. The endocrine system's influence on puberty involves an interaction of the hypothalamus, the pituitary gland, and the gonads (sex glands). Testosterone plays a key role in the pubertal development of males while estradiol serves this function in females. The initial onset of pubertal growth occurs on the average at 9 years for girls and 11 for boys, reaching a peak change for girls at $11\frac{1}{2}$ and for boys at $13\frac{1}{2}$. Sexual maturation is a predominant feature of pubertal change. Individual variation in pubertal changes is substantial. Adolescents show considerable interest in their body image with girls having more negative body images than boys do. Early maturation favors boys, at least during early adolescence. Early-maturing girls are vulnerable to a number of risks.

- Mastering emerging sexual feelings and forming a sense of sexual identity involve multiple factors. National U.S. data indicate that by age 19, four of five individuals have had sexual intercourse. Risk factors for sexual problems include poverty and early sexual activity. Contraceptive use in adolescence is increasing. More than one in four adolescents has a sexually transmitted disease (STD). America's adolescent pregnancy rate is high but has been decreasing in recent years.

3 Identify adolescent problems in substance use and abuse, eating disorders, and health

- The 1960s and 1970s were times of marked increase in illicit drug use by adolescents. In the 1980s, adolescent drug use declined, but then increased through the mid-1990s, and has leveled off since then. The United States has the highest rate of drug use of any industrialized nation. A special recent concern in the United States is the increased use of Ecstasy by youth. Alcohol abuse is a major adolescent problem, although its rate has been dropping in recent years, as has cigarette smoking. Drug use in childhood or early adolescence has more negative outcomes than drug use that begins in late adolescence. Parents and peers are important in whether adolescents take drugs.

- Eating disorders have increased in adolescence with a substantial increase in the percentage of adolescents who are overweight. Two eating disorders that may emerge in adolescence are anorexia nervosa and bulimia nervosa.

- Adolescence is a critical juncture in health because many of the factors related to poor health habits and early death in the adult years begin during adolescence. The three leading causes of death in adolescence are accidents, homicide, and suicide.

4 Explain cognitive changes in adolescence

- Formal operational thought, Piaget's fourth stage of cognitive development, is more abstract, idealistic, and logical than concrete operational thought. Hypothetical-deductive reasoning is a term used to describe adolescents' more logical reasoning. Formal operational thought occurs in two phases—assimilation (early adolescence) and accommodation (middle years of adolescence). There is individual variation in adolescent cognition and Piaget did not give this adequate attention. Many young adolescents are not formal operational thinkers but rather are consolidating their concrete operational thought.

- Elkind describes the concept of adolescent egocentrism as consisting of two parts: imaginary audience and personal fable.

- Changes in information processing in adolescence include increased decision making and critical thinking. Increased speed of processing, automaticity, and capacity, as well as more breadth of content knowledge and a greater range and spontaneous use of strategies, allow for improved critical thinking in adolescence.

5 Summarize some key aspects of how schools influence adolescent development

- The transition to middle or junior high school coincides with many social, familial, and individual changes in the adolescent's life and this transition is often stressful. The transition involves moving from the top-dog to the lowest position.

- Successful schools for young adolescents take individual differences seriously, show a deep concern for what is known about early adolescence, and emphasize socio-emotional as well as cognitive development. In 1989, the Carnegie Foundation recommended a major redesign of U.S. middle schools.

- The overall high school dropout rate declined considerably in the last half of the twentieth century, but the dropout rates of Latino and Native American youth remain very high. A number of strategies have been proposed for improving U.S. high schools, including better support and higher expectations.

- Service learning involves educational experiences that promote social responsibility and service to the community. Researchers have found that service learning benefits students in a number of ways.

Key Terms

puberty 372
menarche 373
hormones 373
hypothalamus 373
pituitary gland 374

gonads 374
sexually transmitted diseases (STDs) 379
anorexia nervosa 384
bulimia nervosa 385

hypothetical-deductive reasoning 387
adolescent egocentrism 388
imaginary audience 388
personal fable 388

top-dog phenomenon 391
service learning 396

Key People

Lloyd Johnston, Patrick O'Malley, and Gerald Bachman 381

Jean Piaget 386
David Elkind 388
Joan Lipsitz 391

Taking It to the Net

1. Sharon wonders why so much of the talk about adolescent pregnancy focuses on the girl's motivation and behavior. What about the guys, she wonders. What are the risk factors that account for teenage pregnancy?

2. Al is the student member of his high school's substance abuse awareness educational forum. He has been asked to address the incoming freshmen on the latest statistics about teen use of tobacco, marijuana, cocaine, heroin, alcohol, and methamphetamine. What information should his report focus on to best educate the group?

3. Mrs. Karpacz, an elementary school principal, wants to help prepare her fourth-grade students for the transition to middle school. What can parents, teachers, and students do to prepare for a smooth transition and cause the least amount of upheaval for the child?

Connect to www.mhhe.com/santrockld9 to research the answers and complete these exercises.

E-Learning Tools

To help you master the material in this chapter, you'll find a number of valuable study tools on the Student CD-ROM that accompanies this book. In addition, visit the Online Learning Center for *Life-Span Development*, ninth edition, where you'll find these valuable resources for chapter 12, "Physical and Cognitive Development in Adolescence."

- The self-assessment, *My Sexual and Romantic Involvement in Adolescence*, challenges you to explore the romantic and sexual relationships you might have been involved in through high school.

- View video clips of key developmental psychology experts, including Jeanne Brooks-Gunn discussing her research with adolescents.

- Build your decision-making skills by trying your hand at the parenting and education "Scenarios."

In case you're worried about what's going to become of the younger generation, it's going to grow up and start worrying about the younger generation.

—ROGER ALLEN,
Contemporary American Writer

Socioemotional Development in Adolescence

Learning Goals

1 Discuss changes in self-esteem and identity in adolescence

2 Describe the changes that take place in adolescents' relationships with their parents

3 Characterize the changes that occur in peer relations during adolescence

4 Explain how culture influences adolescent development

5 Identify adolescent problems in socioemotional development and strategies for helping adolescents with problems

Images of Life-Span Development
A 15-Year-Old Girl's Self-Description

How do adolescents describe themselves? How would you have described yourself when you were 15 years old? What features would you have emphasized? Here is a self-portrait of one 15-year-old girl:

What am I like as a person? Complicated! I'm sensitive, friendly, outgoing, popular, and tolerant, though I can also be shy, self-conscious, and even obnoxious. Obnoxious! I'd *like* to be friendly and tolerant all of the time. That's the kind of person I *want* to be, and I'm disappointed when I'm not. I'm responsible, even studious now and then, but on the other hand, I'm a goof-off, too, because if you're too studious, you won't be popular. I don't usually do that well at school. I'm a pretty cheerful person, especially with my friends, where I can even get rowdy. At home I'm more likely to be anxious around my parents. They expect me to get all A's. It's not fair! I worry about how I probably *should* get better grades. But I'd be mortified in the eyes of my friends. So I'm usually pretty stressed-out at home, or sarcastic, since my parents are always on my case. But I really don't understand how I can switch so fast. I mean, how can I be cheerful one minute, anxious the next, and then be sarcastic? Which one is the *real* me? Sometimes, I feel phony, especially around boys. Say I think some guy might be interested in asking me out. I try to act different. I'll be flirtatious and fun-loving. And then everybody, I mean *everybody* else is looking at me like they think I'm totally weird. Then I get self-conscious and embarrassed and become radically introverted, and I don't know who I really am! Am I just trying to impress them or what? But I don't really care what they think anyway. I don't *want* to care, that is. I just want to know what my close friends think. I can be my true self with my close friends. I can't be my real self with my parents. They don't understand me. What do *they* know about what it's like to be a teenager? They still treat me like I'm still a kid. At least at school people treat you more like you're an adult. That gets confusing, though. I mean, which am I, a kid or an adult? It's scary, too, because I don't have any idea what I want to be when I grow up. I mean, I have lots of *ideas*. My friend Sheryl and I talk about whether we'll be stewardesses, or teachers, or nurses, veterinarians, maybe mothers, or actresses. But how do you decide all of this? I really don't know. I mean, I think about it a lot, but I can't resolve it. There are days when I wish I could just become immune to myself. (Harter, 1990)

1 SELF-ESTEEM AND IDENTITY

Self-Esteem	Identity

The 15-year-old girl's self-description that you just read reflects the increased interest in self-portrayal and search for an identity in adolescence. Before we explore identity in depth, let's examine how self-esteem changes in adolescence.

Self-Esteem

Controversy characterizes the extent to which self-esteem changes during adolescence and whether there are gender differences in adolescents' self-esteem. In one recent study, both boys and girls had particularly high self-esteem in childhood but their self-esteem dropped considerably during adolescence (Robins & others, 2002). The self-esteem of girls declined more than the self-esteem of boys during adolescence in this study (see Figure 13.1). Another recent study also found that the self-esteem of girls declined during early adolescence, but that the self-esteem of boys increased in early adolescence (Baldwin & Hoffman, 2002). In this study, adolescent self-esteem was related to positive family relationships. Explanations of the decrease in self-esteem for adolescent girls involve the decline in their body image as pubertal change occurs and their interest in social relationships that is not adequately rewarded by society.

Some critics argue that developmental changes and gender differences in self-esteem during adolescents have been exaggerated (Harter, 2002). For example, in one analysis of research studies on self-esteem in adolescence, it was concluded that girls have only slightly more negative self-esteem than boys (Kling & others, 1999).

Identity

By far the most comprehensive and provocative story of identity development has been told by Erik Erikson. As you may remember from chapter 2, identity versus identity confusion is the fifth stage in Erikson's eight stages of the life span, occurring at about the same time as adolescence 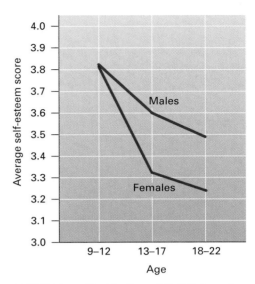 p. 46. It is a time of being interested in finding out who one is, what one is all about, and where one is headed in life.

During adolescence, worldviews become important to the individual, who enters what Erikson (1968) calls a "psychological moratorium," a gap between the security of childhood and the autonomy of adulthood. Adolescents experiment with the numerous roles and identities they draw from the surrounding culture. Youth who successfully cope with these conflicting identities during adolescence emerge with a new sense of self that is both refreshing and acceptable (Bosma & Kunnen, 2001; Moshman, 1999). Adolescents who do not successfully resolve this identity crisis are confused, suffering what Erikson calls "identity confusion." This confusion takes one of two courses: The individuals withdraw, isolating themselves from peers and family, or they lose their identity in the crowd.

Identity is a self-portrait composed of many pieces. These pieces include:

- The career and work path a person wants to follow (vocational/career identity)
- Whether a person is conservative, liberal, or a middle-of-the-roader (political identity)
- A person's spiritual beliefs (religious identity)
- Whether a person is single, married, divorced, and so on (relationship identity)
- The extent to which the person is motivated to achieve and is intellectual (achievement, intellectual identity)
- Whether a person is heterosexual, homosexual, or bisexual (sexual identity)
- Which part of the world or country a person is from and how intensely the person identifies with his or her cultural heritage (cultural/ethnic identity)
- The kind of things a person likes to do, which can include sports, music, hobbies, and so on (interests)
- The individual's personality characteristics (such as being introverted or extraverted, anxious or calm, friendly or hostile, and so on) (personality)
- The individual's body image (physical identity)

Contemporary Views of Identity   Contemporary views of identity development suggest several important considerations. First, identity development is a lengthy process; in many instances, it is a more gradual, less cataclysmic transition than Erikson's term *crisis* implies. Second, identity development is extraordinarily complex.

Identity formation neither begins nor ends with adolescence. It begins with the appearance of attachment, the development of a sense of self, and the emergence of independence in infancy, and it reaches its final phase with a life review and integration in old age. What is important about identity in adolescence, especially late

FIGURE 13.1 The Decline of Self-Esteem in Adolescence

In one study, the self-esteem of both boys and girls declined during adolescence, but declined considerably more for girls than boys (Robins & others, 2002). The self-esteem scores represent the mean self-esteem scores on a 5-point scale with higher scores reflecting higher self-esteem. Note that even though the self-esteem of girls declined in adolescence, their average self-esteem (3.3) was above the neutral point (3.0) on the scale. Thus, even though their self-esteem declined, it cannot be characterized as low.

mhhe●com/
santrockld9

Identity Development

The Society for Research on Identity Development

Identity Development in Literature

As long as one keeps searching, the answers come.

—JOAN BAEZ
American Folk Singer, 20th Century

adolescence, is that for the first time physical development, cognitive development, and social development advance to the point at which the individual can sort through and synthesize childhood identities and identifications to construct a viable pathway toward adult maturity. Resolution of the identity issue at adolescence does not mean that identity will be stable through the remainder of one's life. A person who develops a healthy identity is flexible, adaptive, and open to changes in society, in relationships, and in careers. This openness assures numerous reorganizations of identity features throughout the life of the person who has achieved identity.

Identity formation does not happen neatly, and it usually does not happen cataclysmically. At the bare minimum, it involves commitment to a vocational direction, an ideological stance, and a sexual orientation. Synthesizing the identity components can be a long, drawn-out process, with many negations and affirmations of various roles and faces (Kroger, 2003). Identities are developed in bits and pieces. Decisions are not made once and for all but have to be made again and again. And the decisions may seem trivial at the time: whom to date, whether or not to break up, whether or not to have intercourse, whether or not to take drugs, whether to go to college after high school or get a job, which major to choose, whether to study or whether to play, whether or not to be politically active, and so on. Over the years of adolescence, the decisions begin to form a core of what the individual is all about as a person—what is called "identity."

Identity Statuses and Development Canadian psychologist James Marcia (1980, 1994) analyzed Erikson's theory of identity development and concluded that it is important to distinguish between crisis and commitment in identity development. **Crisis** is a period of identity development during which the adolescent is choosing among meaningful alternatives. Most researchers now use the term *exploration* rather than *crisis*, although, in the spirit of Marcia's original formulation, we will use the term *crisis*. **Commitment** is defined as the part of identity development in which adolescents show a personal investment in what they are going to do.

The extent of an individual's crisis and commitment is used to classify him or her according to one of four identity statuses (see Figure 13.2).

crisis Marcia's term for a period of identity development during which the adolescent is choosing among meaningful alternatives.

commitment Marcia's term for the part of identity development in which adolescents show a personal investment in what they are going to do.

identity diffusion Marcia's term for adolescents who have not yet experienced a crisis (explored meaningful alternatives) or made any commitments.

identity foreclosure Marcia's term for adolescents who have made a commitment but have not experienced a crisis.

identity moratorium Marcia's term for adolescents who are in the midst of a crisis, but their commitments are either absent or vaguely defined.

identity achievement Marcia's term for adolescents who have undergone a crisis and have made a commitment.

- **Identity diffusion** occurs when individuals have not yet experienced a crisis (that is, they have not yet explored meaningful alternatives) or made any commitments. Not only are they undecided about occupational and ideological choices, but they are also likely to show little interest in such matters.
- **Identity foreclosure** occurs when individuals have made a commitment but have not yet experienced a crisis. This occurs most often when parents hand down commitments to their adolescents, more often than not in an authoritarian manner. In these circumstances, adolescents have not had adequate opportunities to explore different approaches, ideologies, and vocations on their own.
- **Identity moratorium** occurs when individuals are in the midst of a crisis but their commitments are either absent or only vaguely defined.
- **Identity achievement** occurs when individuals have undergone a crisis and have made a commitment.

Position on Occupation and Ideology	Identity Status			
	Identity diffusion	Identity foreclosure	Identity moratorium	Identity achievement
Crisis	Absent	Absent	Present	Present
Commitment	Absent	Present	Absent	Present

FIGURE 13.2 Marcia's Four Statuses of Identity

Let's explore some examples of Marcia's identity statuses. A 13-year-old adolescent has neither begun to explore her identity in any meaningful way nor made an identity commitment, so she is *identity diffused*. An 18-year-old boy's parents want him to be a medical doctor so he is planning on majoring in premedicine in college and really has not adequately explored any other options, so he is *identity foreclosed*. Nineteen-year-old Sasha is not quite sure what life paths she wants to follow, but she recently went to the counseling center at her college to find out about different careers, so she is in *identity moratorium* status. Twenty-one-year-old Marcelo extensively explored a number of different career options in college, eventually getting his degree in science education, and is looking forward to his first year of teaching high school students, so he is *identity achieved*. Our examples of identity statuses have focused on the career dimension, but remember that the whole of identity is made up of a number of dimensions.

Young adolescents are primarily in Marcia's identity diffusion, foreclosure, or moratorium status. At least three aspects of the young adolescent's development are important in identity formation: Young adolescents must establish confidence in parental support, develop a sense of industry, and gain a self-reflective perspective on their future. Some researchers believe the most important identity changes take place in the college years, rather than earlier in adolescence. For example, Alan Waterman (1992) has found that, from the years preceding high school through the last few years of college, the number of individuals who are identity achieved increases, along with a decrease in those who are identity diffused. College upperclassmen are more likely than college freshmen or high school students to be identity achieved. Many young adolescents are identity diffused. These developmental changes are especially true in regard to vocational choice. For religious beliefs and political ideology, fewer college students have reached the identity achieved status, with a substantial number characterized by foreclosure and diffusion. Thus, the timing of identity may depend on the particular role involved, and many college students are still wrestling with ideological commitments.

Many identity status researchers believe that a common pattern of individuals who develop positive identities is to follow what are called "MAMA" cycles of *moratorium-achiever-moratorium-achiever*. These cycles may be repeated throughout life. Personal, family, and societal changes are inevitable, and, as they occur, the flexibility and skill required to explore new alternatives and develop new commitments are likely to facilitate an individual's coping skills.

Family Influences on Identity   Parents are important figures in the adolescent's development of identity. In studies that relate identity development to parenting styles, democratic parents, who encourage adolescents to participate in family decision making, foster identity achievement. Autocratic parents, who control the adolescent's behavior without giving the adolescent an opportunity to express opinions, encourage identity foreclosure. Permissive parents, who provide little guidance to adolescents and allow them to make their own decisions, promote identity diffusion (Enright & others, 1980).

In addition to doing studies on parenting styles, researchers have also examined the role of individuality and connectedness in the development of identity. The presence of a family atmosphere that promotes both individuality and connectedness is important in the adolescent's identity development (Cooper & Grotevant, 1989):

- **Individuality** consists of two dimensions: self-assertion, the ability to have and communicate a point of view, and separateness, the use of communication patterns to express how one is different from others.
- **Connectedness** consists of two dimensions: mutuality, sensitivity to, and respect for others' views, and permeability—openness to others' views.

In general, research findings reveal that identity formation is enhanced by family relationships that are both individuated, which encourages adolescents to develop their

Once formed, an identity furnishes individuals with a historical sense of who they have been, a meaningful sense of who they are now, and a sense of who they might become in the future.

—JAMES MARCIA
Contemporary Psychologist,
Simon Fraser University

individuality According to Cooper and her colleagues, individuality consists of two dimensions: self-assertion (the ability to have and communicate a point of view) and separateness (the use of communication patterns to express how one is different from others).

connectedness According to Cooper and her colleagues, connectedness consists of two dimensions: mutuality (sensitivity to and respect for others' views) and permeability (openness to others' views).

*M*any ethnic minority youth must bridge "multiple worlds" in constructing their identities.

—CATHERINE COOPER
Contemporary Psychologist,
University of California at Santa Cruz

mhhe ● com/
santrockld9

Cultural Identity in Canada

Exploring Ethnic Identities

**An Adolescent Talks
About Ethnic Identity**

Ethnic Identity Research

ethnic identity An enduring, basic aspect of the self that includes a sense of membership in an ethnic group and the attitudes and feelings related to that membership.

own point of view, and connected, which provides a secure base from which to explore the widening social worlds of adolescence.

Cultural and Ethnic Aspects of Identity   Erikson was especially sensitive to the role of culture in identity development. He points out that, throughout the world, ethnic minority groups have struggled to maintain their cultural identities while blending into the dominant culture (Erikson, 1968). Erikson said that this struggle for an inclusive identity, or identity within the larger culture, has been the driving force in the founding of churches, empires, and revolutions throughout history.

For ethnic minority individuals, adolescence is often a special juncture in their development (Phinney, 2000, 2003; Spencer & others, 2001). Although children are aware of some ethnic and cultural differences, most ethnic minority individuals consciously confront their ethnicity for the first time in adolescence. In contrast to children, adolescents have the ability to interpret ethnic and cultural information, to reflect on the past, and to speculate about the future.

Jean Phinney (1996) defined **ethnic identity** as an enduring, basic aspect of the self that includes a sense of membership in an ethnic group and the attitudes and feelings related to that membership. Thus, for adolescents from ethnic minority groups, the process of identity formation has an added dimension due to exposure to alternative sources of identification—their own ethnic group and the mainstream or dominant culture. Researchers have found that ethnic identity increases with age and that higher levels of ethnic identity are linked with more positive attitudes not only toward one's own ethnic group but toward members of other ethnic groups as well (Phinney, Ferguson, & Tate, 1997). Many ethnic minority adolescents have bicultural identities—identifying in some ways with their ethnic minority group, in other ways with the majority culture (Comaz-Díaz, 2001; Phinney & Devich-Navarro, 1997).

The ease or difficulty with which ethnic minority adolescents achieve healthy identities depends on a number of factors (Ferrer-Wreder & others, 2002). Many ethnic minority adolescents have to confront issues of prejudice and discrimination, and barriers to the fulfillment of their goals and aspirations (Comaz-Díaz, 2001).

In one investigation, ethnic identity exploration was higher among ethnic minority than among White American college students (Phinney & Alipuria, 1990). In this same investigation, ethnic minority college students who had thought about and resolved issues involving their ethnicity had higher self-esteem than did their ethnic minority counterparts who had not. In another investigation, the ethnic identity development of Asian American, African American, Latino, and White American tenth-grade students in Los Angeles was studied (Phinney, 1989). Adolescents from each of the three ethnic minority groups faced a similar need to deal with their ethnic-group identification in a predominantly White American culture. In some instances, the adolescents from the three ethnic minority groups perceived different issues to be important in their resolution of ethnic identity. For Asian American adolescents, pressures to achieve academically and concerns about quotas that make it difficult to get into good colleges were salient issues. Many African American adolescent females discussed their realization that White American standards of beauty (especially hair and skin color) did not apply to them; African American adolescent males were concerned with possible job discrimination and the need to distinguish themselves from a negative societal image of African American male adolescents. For Latino adolescents, prejudice was a recurrent theme, as was the conflict in values between their Latino cultural heritage and the majority culture.

The contexts in which ethnic minority youth live influence their identity development (Phinney, 2003; Spencer, 1999). Many ethnic minority youth in the United States live in low-income urban settings where support for developing a positive identity is absent. Many of these youth live in pockets of poverty, are exposed to drugs, gangs, and criminal activities, and interact with other youth and adults who have dropped out of school and/or are unemployed. In such settings, effective organizations and programs for youth can make important contributions to developing a positive identity.

One study focused on sixty youth organizations that involved 24,000 adolescents over a period of 5 years (Heath & McLaughlin, 1993). They found that these organizations were especially good at building a sense of ethnic pride in inner-city ethnic youth. Heath and McLaughlin (1993) believe that many inner-city youth have too much time on their hands, too little to do, and too few places to go. Inner-city youth want to participate in organizations that nurture them and respond positively to their needs and interests. Organizations that perceive youth as fearful, vulnerable, and lonely, but also frame them as capable, worthy, and eager to have a healthy and productive life contribute in positive ways to the identity development of ethnic minority youth.

Gender and Identity Development   In Erikson's (1968) classic discussion of identity development, the division of labor between the sexes was reflected in his assertion that males' aspirations were mainly oriented toward career and ideological commitments, while females' were centered around marriage and childbearing. In the 1960s and 1970s, researchers found support for Erikson's assertion about gender differences in identity. For example, vocational concerns were more central to the identity of males, and affiliative concerns were more important in the identity of females. However, in the past two decades, as females have developed stronger vocational interests, sex differences are turning into sex similarities.

Some investigators believe the order of stages proposed by Erikson is different for females and males. One view is that for males identity formation precedes the stage of intimacy, while for females intimacy precedes identity. These ideas are consistent with the belief that relationships and emotional bonds are more important concerns of females, while autonomy and achievement are more important concerns of males (Gilligan, 1990). In one study, the development of a clear sense of self by adolescent girls was related to their concerns about care and response in relationships (Rogers, 1987).

The task of identity exploration may be more complex for females than for males, in that females may try to establish identities in more domains than males. In today's world, the options for females have increased and thus may at times be confusing and conflicting, especially for females who hope to successfully integrate family and career roles (Archer, 1994).

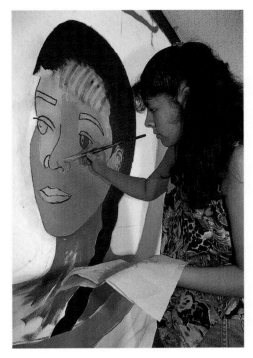

What are some important aspects of ethnic identity in adolescence?

Review and Reflect

1 Discuss changes in self-esteem and identity in adolescence

REVIEW

- What are some changes in self-esteem that take place in adolescence?
- How does identity develop in adolescence?

REFLECT

- Where are you in your identity development? Get out a sheet of paper and list each of the pieces of identity (career/work, political, spiritual, and so on) in a column on the left side of the paper and then write the four identity statuses (diffused, foreclosed, moratorium, and achieved) across the top of the page. Place a check mark in the appropriate space that reflects your identity status for the particular aspect of identity. If you checked diffused or foreclosed for any of the areas, think about what you need to do to move on to a moratorium status in those areas.

2 FAMILIES

Autonomy and Attachment   **Parent-Adolescent Conflict**

In chapter 11, we discussed how, during middle and late childhood, parents spend less time with their children than in early childhood, that discipline involves an increased use of reasoning and deprivation of privileges, and that there is a gradual transfer of control from parents to children but still within the boundary of coregulation ◄|||| p. 349. Among the most important aspects of family relationships in adolescence are those that involve autonomy and attachment, and parent-adolescent conflict.

Autonomy and Attachment

The adolescent's push for autonomy and responsibility puzzles and angers many parents. Parents see their teenager slipping from their grasp. They may have an urge to take stronger control as the adolescent seeks autonomy and responsibility. Heated emotional exchanges may ensue, with either side calling names, making threats, and doing whatever seems necessary to gain control. Parents may seem frustrated because they *expect* their teenager to heed their advice, to want to spend time with the family, and to grow up to do what is right. Most parents anticipate that their teenager will have some difficulty adjusting to the changes that adolescence brings, but few parents can imagine and predict just how strong an adolescent's desires will be to spend time with peers or how much adolescents will want to show that it is they—not their parents—who are responsible for their successes and failures.

The ability to attain autonomy and gain control over one's behavior in adolescence is acquired through appropriate adult reactions to the adolescent's desire for control (Zimmer-Gembeck & Collins, 2003). At the onset of adolescence, the average individual does not have the knowledge to make appropriate or mature decisions in all areas of life. As the adolescent pushes for autonomy, the wise adult relinquishes control in those areas in which the adolescent can make reasonable decisions but continues to guide the adolescent to make reasonable decisions in areas in which the adolescent's knowledge is more limited. Gradually, adolescents acquire the ability to make mature decisions on their own.

Gender differences characterize autonomy-granting in adolescence with boys being given more independence than girls. In one recent study, this was especially true in U.S. families with a traditional gender-role orientation (Bumpus, Crouter, & McHale, 2001).

Cultural differences also characterize adolescent autonomy. In one study, U.S. adolescents sought autonomy earlier than Japanese adolescents (Rothbaum & others, 2000). In the transition to adulthood, Japanese youth are less likely to live outside the home than Americans (Hendry, 1999).

Recall from chapter 7 that one of the most widely discussed aspects of socioemotional development in infancy is secure attachment to caregivers. In the past decade, researchers have explored whether secure attachment also might be an important concept in adolescents' relationships with their parents (Cassidy & Shaver, 1999; Sroufe, 2001). For example, Joseph Allen and his colleagues (Allen & Hauser, 1994; Allen & Kuperminc, 1995; Allen & others, 2002) found that securely attached adolescents were less likely than those who were insecurely attached to engage in problem behaviors, such as juvenile delinquency and drug abuse. In other research, securely attached adolescents had better peer relations than their insecurely attached counterparts (Kobak, 1999; Laible, Carlo, & Raffaeli, 2000).

*W*hen I was a boy of 14, my father was so ignorant I could hardly stand to have the man around. But when I got to be 21, I was astonished at how much he had learnt in 7 years.

—Mark Twain
American Writer and Humorist, 20th Century

Parent-Adolescent Conflict

While attachment to parents remains strong during adolescence, the connectedness is not always smooth. Early adolescence is a time when conflict with parents escalates beyond childhood levels. This increase may be due to a number of factors: the biological changes of puberty, cognitive changes involving increased idealism and logical reasoning, social changes focused on independence and identity, maturational changes in parents, and expectations that are violated by parents and adolescents. The adolescent compares her parents to an ideal standard and then criticizes their flaws. A 13-year-old girl tells her mother, "That is the tackiest-looking dress I have ever seen. Nobody would be caught dead wearing that." The adolescent demands logical explanations for comments and discipline. A 14-year-old boy tells his mother, "What do you mean I have to be home at 10 P.M. because it's the way we do things around here? Why do we do things around here that way? It doesn't make sense to me."

Many parents see their adolescent changing from a compliant child to someone who is noncompliant, oppositional, and resistant to parental standards. When this happens, parents tend to clamp down and put more pressure on the adolescent to conform to parental standards. Parents often expect their adolescents to become mature adults overnight, instead of understanding that the journey takes 10 to 15 years. Parents who recognize that this transition takes time handle their youth more competently and calmly than those who demand immediate conformity to adult standards. The opposite tactic—letting adolescents do as they please without supervision—is also unwise.

In one study, Reed Larson and Marsye Richards (1994) had mothers, fathers, and adolescents carry electronic pagers for a week and report their activities and emotions at random times. The result was a portrait of the hour-by-hour emotional realities lived by families with adolescents. Differences between the fast-paced daily realities lived by each family member created considerable potential for misunderstanding and conflict. Because each family member was often attending to different priorities, needs, and stressors, their realities were often out of sync. Even when they wanted to share leisure activity, their interests were at odds. One father said that his wife liked to shop, his daughter liked to play video games, and he liked to stay home. Although the main theme of this work was the hazards of contemporary life, some of the families with adolescents were buoyant, and their lives were coordinated.

Conflict with parents increases in early adolescence, but it does not reach the tumultuous proportions G. Stanley Hall envisioned at the beginning of the twentieth century (Adams & Laursen, 2001; Holmbeck, 1996; Steinberg & Silk, 2002). Rather, much of the conflict involves the everyday events of family life, such as keeping a bedroom clean, dressing neatly, getting home by a certain time, and not talking forever on the phone. The conflicts rarely involve major dilemmas, such as drugs and delinquency.

It is not unusual to hear parents of young adolescents ask, "Is it ever going to get better?" Things usually do get better as adolescents move from early to late adolescence. Conflict with parents often escalates during early adolescence, remains somewhat stable during the high school years, and then lessens as the adolescent reaches 17 to 20 years of age. Parent-adolescent relationships become more positive if adolescents go away to college than if they stay at home and go to college (Sullivan & Sullivan, 1980).

The everyday conflicts that characterize parent-adolescent relationships may actually serve a positive developmental function. These minor disputes and negotiations facilitate the adolescent's transition from being dependent on parents to becoming an autonomous individual. For example, in one study, adolescents who expressed disagreement with their parents explored identity development more actively than did adolescents who did not express disagreement with their parents (Cooper & others, 1982). As previously mentioned, one way for parents to cope with the adolescent's push for independence and identity is to recognize that adolescence is a 10- to 15-year

Parent-Adolescent Relationships
Parenting Today's Adolescents
Parent-Adolescent Conflict

*I*t is not enough for parents to understand children. They must accord children the privilege of understanding them.

—Milton Sapirstein
American Psychiatrist, 20th Century

transitional period in the journey to adulthood, rather than an overnight accomplishment. Recognizing that conflict and negotiation can serve a positive developmental function can tone down parental hostility too. Understanding parent-adolescent conflict, though, is not simple (Conger & Ge, 1999).

In sum, the old model of parent-adolescent relationships suggested that as adolescents mature they detach themselves from parents and move into a world of autonomy apart from parents. The old model also suggested that parent-adolescent conflict is intense and stressful throughout adolescence. The new model emphasizes that parents serve as important attachment figures and support systems as adolescents explore a wider, more complex social world. The new model also emphasizes that, in most families, parent-adolescent conflict is moderate rather than severe and that the everyday negotiations and minor disputes are normal and can serve the positive developmental function of helping the adolescent make the transition from childhood dependency to adult independence (see figure 13.3).

Still, a high degree of conflict characterizes some parent-adolescent relationships. One estimate of the proportion of parents and adolescents who engage in prolonged, intense, repeated, unhealthy conflict is about one in five families (Montemayor, 1982). While this figure represents a minority of adolescents, it indicates that 4 to 5 million American families encounter serious, highly stressful parent-adolescent conflict. And this prolonged, intense conflict is associated with a number of adolescent problems—movement out of the home, juvenile delinquency, school dropout, pregnancy and early marriage, membership in religious cults, and drug abuse (Brook & others, 1990).

It should be pointed out that in some cultures there is less parent-adolescent conflict than in others. American psychologist Reed Larson (1999) recently spent six months in India studying middle-socioeconomic-status adolescents and their families. He observed that in India there seems to be little parent-adolescent conflict and that many families likely would be described as "authoritarian" in Baumrind's categorization. Larson also observed that in India adolescents do not go through a process of breaking away from their parents and that parents choose their youths' marital partners. Researchers have also found considerably less conflict between parents and adolescents in Japan than in the United States (Rothbaum & others, 2000).

We have seen that parents play very important roles in adolescent development. Although adolescents are moving toward independence, they still need to stay connected with families (Roth & Brooks-Gunn, 2000). In the National Longitudinal Study on Adolescent Health (Council of Economic Advisors, 2000) of more than 12,000 adolescents, those who did not eat dinner with a parent five or more days a week had

Old Model		**New Model**
Autonomy, detachment from parents; parent and peer worlds are isolated		Attachment and autonomy; parents are important support systems and attachment figures; adolescent-parent and adolescent-peer worlds have some important connections
Intense, stressful conflict throughout adolescence; parent-adolescent relationships are filled with storm and stress on virtually a daily basis		Moderate parent-adolescent conflict common and can serve a positive developmental function; conflict greater in early adolescence, especially during the apex of puberty

FIGURE 13.3 Old and New Models of Parent-Adolescent Relationships

dramatically higher rates of smoking, drinking, marijuana use, getting into fights, and initiation of sexual activity. In another recent study, parents who played an active role in monitoring and guiding their adolescents' development were more likely to have adolescents with positive peer relations and lower drug use than parents who had a less active role (Mounts, 2002).

Competent adolescent development is most likely to happen when adolescents have parents who (Small, 1990):

- Show them warmth and mutual respect
- Demonstrate sustained interest in their lives
- Recognize and adapt to their cognitive and socioemotional development
- Communicate expectations for high standards of conduct and achievement
- Display constructive ways of dealing with problems and conflict

These ideas coincide with Diana Baumrind's (1971, 1991) authoritative parenting style, which we discussed in chapter 9, "Socioemotional Development in Early Childhood."

mhhe com/
santrockld9
Reengaging Families with Adolescents
Families as Asset Builders

Review and Reflect

2 **Describe the changes that take place in adolescents' relationships with their parents**

REVIEW

- How do autonomy and attachment develop in adolescence?
- What is the nature of parent-adolescent conflict?

REFLECT

- How much autonomy did your parents give you in adolescence? Too much? Too little? How intense was your conflict with your parents during adolescence? What were the conflicts mainly about? Would you behave differently toward your own adolescents than your parents did with you? If so, how?

3 PEERS

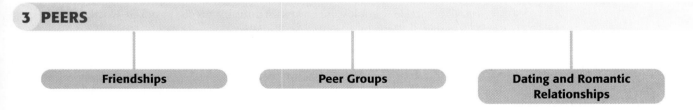

Friendships   Peer Groups   Dating and Romantic Relationships

In chapter 11, we discussed how children spend more time with their peers in middle and late childhood than in early childhood ◀▥ p. 352. We also found that friendships become more important in middle and late childhood and that popularity with peers is a strong motivation for most children. Advances in cognitive development during middle and late childhood also allow children to take the perspective of their peers and friends more readily, and their social knowledge of how to make and keep friends increases.

Imagine you are back in junior or senior high school, especially during one of your good times. Friends, clubs, cliques, dates, and parties probably come to mind. Adolescents spend huge chunks of time with peers, more than in middle and late childhood.

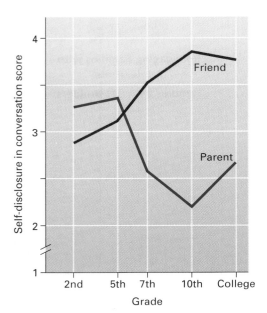

FIGURE 13.4 Developmental Changes in Self-Disclosing Conversations

Self-disclosing conversations with friends increased dramatically in adolescence while declining in an equally dramatic fashion with parents. However, self-disclosing conversations with parents began to pick up somewhat during the college years. The measure of self-disclosure involved a 5-point rating scale completed by the children and youth with a higher score representing greater self-disclosure. The data shown represent the means for each age group.

*E*ach of you, individually, walkest with the tread of a fox, but collectively ye are geese.

—SOLON

Greek Poet, Statesman,
6th Century B.C.

Friendships

Harry Stack Sullivan (1953) was the most influential theorist to discuss the importance of adolescent friendships, and his ideas have withstood the test of time. He argued that there is a dramatic increase in the psychological importance and intimacy of close friends during early adolescence. In contrast to other psychoanalytic theorists' narrow emphasis on the importance of parent-child relationships, Sullivan contended that friends also play important roles in shaping children's and adolescents' well-being and development. In terms of well-being, he argued that all people have a number of basic social needs, including the need for tenderness (secure attachment), playful companionship, social acceptance, intimacy, and sexual relations. Whether or not these needs are fulfilled largely determines our emotional well-being. For example, if the need for playful companionship goes unmet, then we become bored and depressed; if the need for social acceptance is not met, we suffer a lowered sense of self-worth.

Developmentally, friends become increasingly depended on to satisfy these needs during adolescence; thus, the ups-and-downs of experiences with friends increasingly shape adolescents' state of well-being (Berndt, 2002). In particular, Sullivan believed that the need for intimacy intensifies during early adolescence, motivating teenagers to seek out close friends. He felt that, if adolescents fail to forge such close friendships, they experience painful feelings of loneliness, coupled with a reduced sense of self-worth.

Research findings support many of Sullivan's ideas. For example, adolescents report disclosing intimate and personal information to their friends more often than do younger children (Buhrmester, 1998; Buhrmester & Furman, 1987) (see figure 13.4). Adolescents also say they depend more on friends than on parents to satisfy their needs for companionship, reassurance of worth, and intimacy (Furman & Buhrmester, 1992). In one study, daily interviews with 13- to 16-year-old adolescents over a 5-day period were conducted to find out how much time they spent engaged in meaningful interactions with friends and parents (Buhrmester & Carbery, 1992). Adolescents spent an average of 103 minutes per day in meaningful interactions with friends, compared with just 28 minutes per day with parents. In addition, the quality of friendship is more strongly linked to feelings of well-being during adolescence than during childhood. Teenagers with superficial friendships, or no close friendships at all, report feeling lonelier and more depressed, and they have a lower sense of self-esteem than do teenagers with intimate friendships (Yin, Buhrmester, & Hibbard, 1996). In another study, friendship in early adolescence was a significant predictor of self-worth in early adulthood (Bagwell, Newcomb, & Bukowski, 1994).

Although most adolescents develop friendships with individuals who are close to their own age, some adolescents become best friends with younger or older individuals. A common fear, especially among parents, is that adolescents who have older friends will be encouraged to engage in delinquent behavior or early sexual behavior. Researchers have found that adolescents who interact with older youths do engage in these behaviors more frequently, but it is not known whether the older youth guide younger adolescents toward deviant behavior or whether the younger adolescents were already prone to deviant behavior before they developed the friendship with the older youth (Billy, Rodgers, & Udry, 1984).

Peer Groups

How much pressure is there to conform to peers during adolescence? Consider this statement made by an adolescent girl:

Peer pressure is extremely influential in my life. I have never had very many friends, and I spend quite a bit of time alone. The friends I have are older. The closest friend I have had is a lot like me in that we are both sad and depressed a lot. I began to act even more depressed than before when I was with her. I would call her up and try to act even more depressed than I was because that is what I thought she liked. In that relationship, I felt pressure to be like her.

Conformity to peer pressure in adolescence can be positive or negative. Teenagers engage in all sorts of negative conformity behavior—use seedy language, steal, vandalize, and make fun of parents and teachers. However, a great deal of peer conformity is not negative and consists of the desire to be involved in the peer world, such as dressing like friends and wanting to spend large amounts of time with members of a clique. Such circumstances may involve prosocial activities as well, as when clubs raise money for worthy causes.

Young adolescents conform more to peer standards than children do. Investigators have found that, around the eighth and ninth grades, conformity to peers—especially to their antisocial standards—peaks (Leventhal, 1994). At this point, adolescents are most likely to go along with a peer to steal hubcaps off a car, draw graffiti on a wall, or steal cosmetics from a store counter. However, researchers have found that U.S. adolescents are more likely to put pressure on their peers to resist parental influence than Japanese adolescents are (Rothbaum & others, 2000).

Cliques and Crowds Cliques and crowds assume more important roles in the lives of adolescents than children (Brown, 2003). **Cliques** are small groups that range from 2 to about 12 individuals and average about 5 to 6 individuals. The clique members are usually of the same sex and about the same age. Cliques can form because adolescents engage in similar activities, such as being in a club or on a sports team (Ennet & Bauman, 1996). Some cliques also form because of friendship. Several adolescents may form a clique because they have spent time with each other and enjoy each other's company. Not necessarily friends, they often develop a friendship if they stay in the clique. What do adolescents do in cliques? They share ideas, hang out together, and often develop an in-group identity in which they believe that their clique is better than other cliques.

Crowds are a larger group structure than cliques. Adolescents are usually members of a crowd based on reputation and may or may not spend much time together. Crowds are less personal than cliques. Many crowds are defined by the activities adolescents engage in (such as "jocks" who are good at sports or "druggies" who take drugs).

In one study, crowd membership was associated with adolescent self-esteem (Brown & Lohr, 1987). The crowds included jocks (athletically oriented), populars (well-known students who led social activities), normals (middle-of-the-road students who made up the masses), druggies or toughs (known for illicit drug use or other delinquent activities), and nobodies (low in social skills or intellectual abilities). The self-esteem of the jocks and the populars was highest, whereas that of the nobodies was lowest. One group of adolescents not in a crowd had self-esteem equivalent to that of the jocks and the populars; this group was the independents, who indicated that crowd membership was not important to them. Keep in mind that these data are correlational; self-esteem could increase an adolescent's probability of becoming a crowd member, just as crowd membership could increase the adolescent's self-esteem.

Adolescent Groups Versus Children Groups Children groups differ from adolescent groups in several important ways. The members of children groups often are friends or neighborhood acquaintances, and their groups usually are not as formalized as many adolescent groups. During the adolescent years, groups tend to include a broader array of members. In other words, adolescents other than friends or neighborhood acquaintances often are members of adolescent groups. Try to recall the

What changes take place in friendship during the adolescent years?

mhhe●com/
santrockld9

Adolescent Peer Relationships

Peer Pressure

Youth Connections

clique A small group that ranges from 2 to about 12 individuals, averaging about 5 to 6 individuals, and can form because adolescents engage in similar activities.

crowd A larger group structure than a clique, a crowd is usually formed based on reputation and members may or may not spend much time together.

Most adolescents conform to the mainstream standards of their peers. However, the rebellious or anticonformist adolescent reacts counter to the mainstream peer group's expectations, deliberately moving away from the actions or beliefs this group advocates.

student council, honor society, or football team at your junior high school. If you were a member of any of these organizations, you probably remember that they were made up of many people you had not met before and that it was a more heterogeneous group than your childhood peer groups. For example, peer groups in adolescence are more likely to have a mixture of individuals from different ethnic groups than are peer groups in childhood.

Dating and Romantic Relationships

Adolescents spend considerable time either dating or thinking about dating, which has gone far beyond its original courtship function to become a form of recreation, a source of status and achievement, and a setting for learning about close relationships. One function of dating, though, continues to be mate selection.

Types of Dating and Developmental Changes A number of developmental changes characterize dating. In one recent study, announcing that "I like someone" occurred by the sixth grade for 40 percent of the individuals sampled (Buhrmester, 2001) (see figure 13.5). However, it was not until the tenth grade that 50 percent of the adolescents had a sustained romantic relationship that lasted two months or longer. By their senior year, 25 percent still had not engaged in this type of sustained romantic relationship. Also, in this study, girls' early romantic involvement was linked with lower grades, less active participation in class discussion, and school-related problems. A rather large portion of adolescents in dating relationships say that their relationships have persisted 11 months or longer: 20 percent of adolescents 14 or younger, 35 percent of 15- to 16-year-olds, and almost 60 percent of 17- and 18-year-olds (Carver, Joyner, & Udry, in press).

In their early romantic relationships, many adolescents are not motivated to fulfill attachment or even sexual needs. Rather, early romantic relationships serve as a context for adolescents to explore how attractive they are, how they should romantically interact with someone, and how all of this looks to the peer group (Brown,

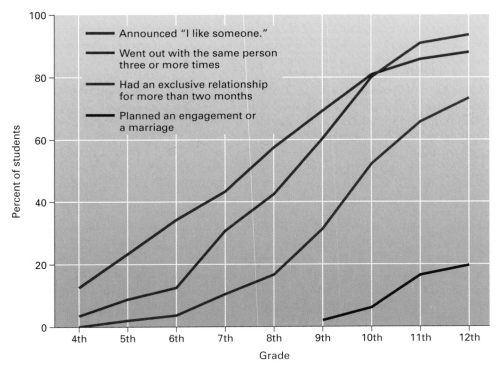

FIGURE 13.5 Age of Onset of Romantic Activity

In this study, announcing that "I like someone" occurred earliest, followed by going out with the same person three or more times, having an exclusive relationship for over two months, and finally planning an engagement or marriage (which characterized only a very small percentage of participants by the twelfth grade) (Buhrmester, 2001).

1999). Only after adolescents acquire some basic competencies in interacting with romantic partners does the fulfillment of attachment and sexual needs become central functions of these relationships (Bouchey & Furman, 2003; Furman & Wehner, 1999).

In their early exploration of romantic relationships, today's adolescents often find comfort in numbers and begin hanging out together in heterosexual groups. Sometimes they just hang out at someone's house or get organized enough to get someone to drive them to a mall or a movie (Peterson, 1997). A special concern is early dating and "going with" someone, which is associated with adolescent pregnancy and problems at home and school (Downey & Bonica, 1997).

Yet another form of dating recently has been added. *Cyberdating* is dating over the Internet (Thomas, 1998). One 10-year-old girl posted this ad on the Net:

> Hi! I'm looking for a Cyber Boyfriend! I'm 10. I have brown hair and brown eyes. I love swimming, playing basketball, and think kittens are adorable!!!

Cyberdating is especially becoming popular among middle school students. By the time they reach high school and are able to drive, dating usually has evolved into a more traditional real-life venture. Adolescents need to be cautioned about the potential hazards of cyberdating and not really knowing who is on the other end of the computer connection.

Dating Scripts **Dating scripts** are the cognitive models that guide individuals' dating interactions. In one study, first dates were highly scripted along gender lines (Rose & Frieze, 1993). The males followed a proactive dating script, the females a reactive one. The male's script involved initiating the date (asking for and planning it), controlling the public domain (driving and opening doors), and initiating sexual interaction (making physical contact, making out, and kissing). The female's script focused on

Dating and Romantic Relationships
Teen Chat

dating scripts The cognitive models that adolescents and adults use to guide and evaluate dating interactions.

the private domain (concern about appearance, enjoying the date), participating in the structure of the date established by the male (being picked up, having doors opened), and responding to his sexual overtures. These gender differences give males more power in the initial stage of a dating relationship.

In another study, male and female adolescents brought different motivations to the dating experience (Feiring, 1996). The 15-year-old girls were more likely to describe romance in terms of interpersonal qualities, the boys in terms of physical attraction. The young adolescents frequently mentioned the affiliative qualities of companionship, intimacy, and support as positive aspects of romantic relationships, but not love and security. Also, the young adolescents described physical attraction more in terms of cute, pretty, or handsome than in sexual terms (such as being a good kisser). Possibly the failure to discuss sexual interests was due to the adolescents' discomfort in talking about such personal feelings with an unfamiliar adult.

Emotion and Romantic Relationships The strong emotions of romantic relationships can thrust adolescents into a world in which things are turned upside down and ordinary reality recedes from view (Larson, Clore, & Wood, 1999). One 14-year-old reports that he is so in love he can't think about anything else. A 15-year-old girl is enraged by the betrayal of her boyfriend. She is obsessed with ways to get back at him. The daily fluctuations in the emotions of romantic relationships can make the world seem almost surreal. Although the strong emotions of romance can have disruptive effects on adolescents, they also provide a source for possible mastery and growth. Learning to manage these strong emotions can give adolescents a sense of competence.

Romantic relationships often are involved in an adolescent's emotional experiences (Collins, 2002). In one study of ninth- to twelfth-graders, girls gave real and fantasized heterosexual relationships as the explanation for more than one-third of their strong emotions and boys gave this reason for 25 percent of their strong emotions (Wilson-Shockley, 1995). Strong emotions were attached far less to school (13%), family (9%), and same-sex peer relations (8%). The majority of the emotions were reported as positive, but a substantial minority (42%), were reported as negative, including feelings of anxiety, anger, jealousy, and depression. The most common trigger of the first episode of major depression in adolescence is a romantic breakup.

What are dating relationships like in adolescence?

Sociocultural Contexts and Dating   The sociocultural context exerts a powerful influence on adolescents' dating patterns. Values and religious beliefs of people in various cultures often dictate the age at which dating begins, how much freedom in dating is allowed, whether dates must be chaperoned by adults or parents, and the roles of males and females in dating. For example, Latino and Asian American cultures have more conservative standards regarding adolescent dating than does the Anglo-American culture. Dating may be a source of cultural conflict for many immigrants and their families who have come from cultures in which dating begins at a late age, little freedom in dating is allowed, dates are chaperoned, and adolescent girl dating is especially restricted. One recent study found that Asian American adolescents were less likely to be involved in a romantic relationship in the past 18 months than African American or Latino adolescents (Carver, Joyner, & Udry, in press).

In one recent study, Latina young adults in the midwestern United States reflected on their experiences in dating during adolescence (Raffaeli & Ontai, in press). They said that their parents placed strict boundaries on their romantic involvement. As a result, the young women said that their adolescent dating experiences were filled with tension and conflict. Over half of the Latinas engaged in "sneak dating" without their parents' knowledge.

Review and Reflect

3 **Characterize the changes that occur in peer relations during adolescence**

REVIEW

- What changes take place in friendship during adolescence?
- What are adolescents' peer groups like?
- What is the nature of adolescent dating and romantic relationships?

REFLECT

- What were your peer relationships like during adolescence? What peer groups were you involved in? How did they influence your development? What were your dating and romantic relationships like in adolescence? If you could change anything about the way you experienced peer relations in adolescence, what would it be?

4 CULTURE AND ADOLESCENT DEVELOPMENT

Cross-Cultural Comparisons   **Ethnicity**

We live in an increasingly diverse world, one in which there is increasing contact between adolescents from different cultures and ethnic groups. In this section, we will explore how adolescents vary cross-culturally, rites of passage, and the nature of ethnic minority adolescents and their development.

Cross-Cultural Comparisons

Ideas about the nature of adolescents and orientation toward adolescents may vary from culture to culture and within the same culture over different time periods

These Congolese Kota boys painted their faces as part of a rite of passage to adulthood. *What rites of passage do American adolescents have?*

(Whiting, 1989). For example, some cultures (such as the Mangaian culture in the South Sea Islands) have more permissive attitudes toward adolescent sexuality than the American culture, and some cultures (the Ines Beag culture off the coast of Ireland, for example) have more conservative attitudes toward adolescent sexuality than the American culture. Over the course of the twentieth century, attitudes toward sexuality—especially for females—have become more permissive in the American culture.

Early in the previous century, overgeneralizations about the universal aspects of adolescents were made based on data and experience in a single culture—the middle-class culture of the United States. For example, it was believed that adolescents everywhere went through a period of "storm and stress," characterized by self-doubt and conflict. However, when Margaret Mead visited the island of Samoa, she found that the adolescents of the Samoan culture were not experiencing much stress.

As we discovered in chapter 1, *cross-cultural studies* involve the comparison of a culture with one or more other cultures, which provides information about the degree to which development is similar, or universal, across cultures, or the degree to which it is culture-specific. The study of adolescence has emerged in the context of Western industrialized society, with the practical needs and social norms of this culture dominating thinking about adolescents. Consequently, the development of adolescents in Western cultures has evolved as the norm for all adolescents of the human species, regardless of economic and cultural circumstances. This narrow viewpoint can produce erroneous conclusions about the nature of adolescents. One variation in the experiences of adolescents in different cultures is whether the adolescents go through a rite of passage.

Some societies have elaborate ceremonies that signal the adolescent's move to maturity and achievement of adult status (Kottak, 2002). A **rite of passage** is a ceremony or ritual that marks an individual's transition from one status to another. Most rites of passage focus on the transition to adult status. In many primitive cultures, rites of passage are the avenue through which adolescents gain access to sacred adult practices, to knowledge, and to sexuality. These rites often involve dramatic practices intended to facilitate the adolescent's separation from the immediate family, especially the mother. The transformation is usually characterized by some form of ritual death and rebirth, or by means of contact with the spiritual world. Bonds are forged between the adolescent and the adult instructors through shared rituals, hazards, and secrets to allow the adolescent to enter the adult world. This kind of ritual provides a forceful and discontinuous entry into the adult world at a time when the adolescent is perceived to be ready for the change.

Africa has been the location of many rites of passage for adolescents, especially sub-Saharan Africa. Under the influence of Western culture, many of the rites are disappearing today, although some vestiges remain. In locations where formal education is not readily available, rites of passage are still prevalent.

Do we have such rites of passage for American adolescents? We certainly do not have universal formal ceremonies that mark the passage from adolescence to adulthood. Certain religious and social groups do have initiation ceremonies that indicate that an advance in maturity has been reached—the Jewish bar mitzvah, the Catholic confirmation, and social debuts, for example. School graduation ceremonies come the closest to being culturewide rites of passage in the United States. The high school graduation ceremony has become nearly universal for middle-class adolescents and increasing numbers of adolescents from low-income backgrounds. Nonetheless, high school graduation does not result in universal changes; many high school graduates continue to live with their parents, continue to be economically dependent on them,

rite of passage A ceremony or ritual that marks an individual's transition from one status to another. Most rites of passage focus on the transition to adult status.

and continue to be undecided about career and lifestyle matters. Another rite of passage for increasing numbers of American adolescents is sexual intercourse (Halonen & Santrock, 1999). By 19 years of age, four out of five American adolescents have had sexual intercourse.

Now that we have discussed the importance of a global perspective in understanding adolescence and the nature of rites of passage, we will turn our attention to the development of ethnic minority adolescents in the United States.

Ethnicity

Earlier in this chapter, we explored the identity development of ethnic minority adolescents. Here we will examine other aspects of ethnicity, beginning with difficulty of separating ethnicity and socioeconomic influences. First, we will examine the nature of ethnicity and socioeconomic status; second, we will examine the nature of differences and diversity; third, we will study the aspects of value conflicts, assimilation, and pluralism.

Ethnicity and Socioeconomic Status   Much of the research on ethnic minority adolescents has failed to tease apart the influences of ethnicity and socioeconomic status. Ethnicity and socioeconomic status can interact in ways that exaggerate the influence of ethnicity because ethnic minority individuals are overrepresented in the lower socioeconomic levels of American society. Consequently, researchers too often have given ethnic explanations of adolescent development that were largely due to socioeconomic status rather than ethnicity. For example, decades of research on group differences in self-esteem failed to consider the socioeconomic status of African American and White children and adolescents. When African American adolescents from low-income backgrounds are compared with White adolescents from middle-income backgrounds, the differences are often large but not informative because of the confounding of ethnicity and socioeconomic status (Scott-Jones, 1995).

Although some ethnic minority youth are from middle-income backgrounds, economic advantage does not entirely enable them to escape their ethnic minority status (Spencer & Dornbusch, 1990). Middle-income ethnic minority youth still encounter much of the prejudice, discrimination, and bias associated with being a member of an ethnic minority group. Often characterized as a "model minority" because of their strong achievement orientation and family cohesiveness, Japanese Americans still experience stress associated with ethnic minority status (Sue, 1990). Even though middle-income ethnic minority adolescents have more resources available to counter the destructive influences of prejudice and discrimination, they still cannot completely avoid the pervasive influence of negative stereotypes about ethnic minority groups.

Not all ethnic minority families are poor. However, poverty contributes to the stressful life experiences of many ethnic minority adolescents. Thus, many ethnic minority adolescents experience a double disadvantage: (1) prejudice, discrimination, and bias because of their ethnic minority status, and (2) the stressful effects of poverty.

Differences and Diversity   There are legitimate differences between various ethnic minority groups, as well as between ethnic minority groups and the majority White group. Recognizing and respecting these differences are important aspects of getting along with others in a multicultural world. Historical, economic, and social experiences produce differences in ethnic groups (Coll, Meyer, & Brillion, 1995). Individuals living in a particular ethnic or cultural group adapt to the values, attitudes, and stresses of that culture. Their behavior, while possibly different from yours, is, nonetheless, often functional for them. It is important for adolescents to take the perspective of individuals from ethnic and cultural groups that are different from theirs and think, "If I were in their shoes, what kind of experiences might I have had?" "How would I feel if I were a member of their ethnic or cultural group?" "How would I think and behave if I had grown up in their world?" Such perspective taking often increases an adolescent's

mhhe com/
santrockld9

Changing Contexts

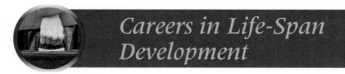

Careers in Life-Span Development

Carola Suarez-Orozco, Lecturer, Researcher, and Co-Director of Immigration Projects

Carola Suarez-Orozco is a researcher and lecturer in the Human Development and Psychology area at Harvard University. She also is co-director of the Harvard Immigration Projects. She obtained her undergraduate degree (development studies) and graduate (clinical psychology) degrees from the University of California at Berkeley ◀▥ p. 32.

Suarez-Orozco has worked both in clinical and public school settings in California and Massachusetts. She currently is co-directing a five-year longitudinal study of immigrant adolescents' (coming from Central America, China, and the Dominican Republic) adaptation to schools and society. One of the courses she teaches at Harvard is on the psychology of immigrant youth. She especially believes that more research needs to be conducted on the intersection of cultural and psychological factors in the adaptation of immigrant and ethnic minority youth.

Carolyn Suarez-Orozco, with her husband Marcelo, who also studies the adaptation of immigrants.

empathy and understanding of individuals from ethnic and cultural groups different from their own.

Another important dimension to continually keep in mind when studying ethnic minority adolescents is their diversity (Burton & Allison, 1995; Cauce & others, 2002; Wilson & Hall, 2000). Ethnic minority groups are not homogeneous; they have different social, historical, and economic backgrounds. For example, Mexican, Cuban, and Puerto Rican immigrants are all Latinos, but they migrated for different reasons, came from varying socioeconomic backgrounds in their native countries, and experience different rates and types of employment in the United States. The federal government now recognizes the existence of 511 different Native American tribes, each having a unique ancestral background with differing values and characteristics. Asian Americans include the Chinese, Japanese, Filipinos, Koreans, and Southeast Asians, each group having a distinct ancestry and language. As an indication of the diversity of Asian Americans, they not only show high educational attainments but also include a high proportion of individuals with no education whatsoever. For example, 90 percent of Korean American males graduate from high school, but only 71 percent of Vietnamese American males do.

Relatively high rates of minority immigration are contributing to the growth in the proportion of ethnic minorities in the U.S. population (McLoyd, 1998, 2000). Because immigrants often experience stressors uncommon to or less prominent among longtime residents (such as language barriers, dislocations and separations from support networks, dual struggle to preserve identity and to acculturate, and changes in SES status), adaptions in intervention programs may be required to achieve optimal cultural sensitivity when working with adolescents and their immigrant families (Chun & Akutsu, 2003).

Although the U.S. immigrant population has been growing, psychologists have been slow to study these families. In one recent study, the cultural values and intergenerational value discrepancies in immigrant (Vietnamese, Armenian, and Mexican) and nonimmigrant families (African American and European American) were studied (Phinney, Ong, & Madden, 2000). Family obligations were endorsed more by parents than adolescents in all groups, and the intergenerational value discrepancy generally increased with time in the United States.

Parents and adolescents may be at different stages of acculturation, which can produce conflict over cultural values (Roosa & others, 2002; Samaniego & Gonzales, 1999; Santisteban & Mitrani, 2003). Research increasingly shows links between acculturation and adolescent problems (Gonzales & others, in press). For example, more-acculturated Latino youths in the United States experience higher rates of conduct problems, substance abuse, and risky sexual behavior than their less-acculturated counterparts (Brook & others, 1998; Epstein, Botvin, & Díaz, 1998).

One individual who is deeply concerned about immigrant youth and conducts research to learn more about ways to help them cope with life in America is Carola Suarez-Orozco. To read about her work, see the Careers in Life-Span Development insert.

El Puente and Quantum

El Puente, which means "the bridge," was opened in New York City in 1983 because of community dissatisfaction with the health, education, and social services youth were receiving (Simons, Finlay, & Yang, 1991). El Puente emphasizes five areas of youth development: health, education, achievement, personal growth, and social growth.

El Puente is located in a former Roman Catholic church on the south side of Williamsburg in Brooklyn, a neighborhood made up primarily of low-income Latino families, many of which are far below the poverty line. Sixty-five percent of the residents receive some form of public assistance. The neighborhood has the highest school dropout rate for Latinos in New York City and the highest felony rate for adolescents in Brooklyn.

When the youth, ages 12 through 21, first enroll in El Puente, they meet with counselors and develop a four-month plan that includes the programs they are interested in joining. At the end of four months, the youth and staff develop a plan for continued participation. Twenty-six bilingual classes are offered in such subjects as the fine arts, theater, photography, and dance. In addition, a medical and fitness center, GED night school, and mental health and social services centers are a part of El Puente.

El Puente is funded through state, city and private organizations and serves about 300 youth. The program has been replicated in Chelsea and Holyoke, Massachusetts, and two other sites in New York are being developed.

The Quantum Opportunities Program, funded by the Ford Foundation, was a four-year, year-around mentoring effort. The students were entering the ninth grade at a high school with high rates of poverty, were minorities, and came from families that received public assistance. Each day for four years, mentors provided sustained support, guidance, and concrete assistance to their students.

The Quantum program required students to participate in (1) academic-related activities outside school hours, including reading, writing, math, science, social studies, peer tutoring, and computer skills training; (2) community service projects, including tutoring elementary school students, cleaning up the neighborhood, and volunteering in hospitals, nursing homes, and libraries; and (3) cultural enrichment and personal development activities, including life skills training and college and job planning. In exchange for their commitment to the program, students were offered financial incentives that encouraged participation, completion, and long-range planning. A stipend of $1.33 was given to students for each hour they participated in these activities. For every 100 hours of education, service, or development activities,

students received a bonus of $100. The average cost per participant was $10,600 for the four years, which is one half the cost of one year in prison.

An evaluation of the Quantum project compared the mentored students with a nonmentored control group. Sixty-three percent of the mentored students graduated from high school, but only 42 percent of the control group did; 42 percent of the mentored students are currently enrolled in college, but only 16 percent of the control group are. Further, the control-group students were twice as likely as the mentored students to receive food stamps or welfare, and they had more arrests. Such programs clearly have the potential to overcome the intergenerational transmission of poverty and its negative outcomes.

These adolescents participate in the programs of El Puente, located in a predominantly low-income Latino neighborhood in Brooklyn, New York. *Which areas of youth development does the El Puente program stress?*

Value Conflicts, Assimilation, and Pluralism   Stanley Sue (1990) believes that value conflicts are often involved when individuals respond to ethnic issues. These value conflicts have been a source of considerable controversy. According to Sue, without properly identifying the assumptions and effects of the conflicting values, it is difficult to resolve ethnic minority issues. Let's examine one of these value conflicts, assimilation versus pluralism, to see how it might influence an individual's response to an ethnic minority issue:

- **Assimilation** is the absorption of ethnic minority groups into the dominant group, which often means the loss of some or virtually all of the behavior and values of the ethnic group. Individuals who adopt an assimilation stance usually advocate that ethnic minority groups become more American.
- **Pluralism** is the coexistence of distinct ethnic and cultural groups in the same society. Individuals who adopt a pluralistic stance usually advocate that cultural differences be maintained and appreciated (Leong, 2000).

assimilation The absorption of ethnic minority groups into the dominant group, which often involves the loss of some or virtually all of the behavior and values of the ethnic minority group.

pluralism The coexistence of distinct ethnic and cultural groups in the same society. Individuals with a pluralistic stance usually advocate that cultural differences be maintained and appreciated.

Sue believes that one way to resolve value conflicts about sociocultural issues is to conceptualize or redefine them in innovative ways. For example, in the assimilation/pluralism conflict, rather than assume that assimilation is necessary for the development of functional skills, one strategy is to focus on the fluctuating criteria defining those skills considered to be functional; another is to consider the possibility that developing functional skills does not prevent the existence of pluralism. For instance, the classroom instructor might use multicultural examples when teaching social studies and still be able to discuss both culturally universal and culturally specific approaches to American and other cultures. To read about two programs that provide support for ethnic minority youth, see the Sociocultural Worlds of Development box on page 423.

Review and Reflect

4 Explain how culture influences adolescent development

REVIEW

- What are some comparisons of adolescents in different cultures? What are rites of passage?
- How does ethnicity influence adolescent development?

REFLECT

- What is your ethnicity? Have you ever been stereotyped because of your ethnicity? How diverse is your ethnicity?

5 ADOLESCENT PROBLEMS

Juvenile Delinquency	Depression and Suicide	The Interrelation of Problems and Successful Prevention/Intervention Programs

In chapter 12, we described these adolescent problems: substance abuse, sexually transmitted diseases, and eating disorders. Here, we will examine the problems of juvenile delinquency, depression, and suicide.

Juvenile Delinquency

juvenile delinquent An adolescent who breaks the law or engages in behavior that is considered illegal.

The label **juvenile delinquent** is applied to an adolescent who breaks the law or engages in behavior that is considered illegal. Like other categories of disorders, juvenile delinquency is a broad concept; legal infractions range from littering to murder. Because the adolescent technically becomes a juvenile delinquent only after being judged guilty of a crime by a court of law, official records do not accurately reflect the number of illegal acts juvenile delinquents commit. Estimates of the number of juvenile delinquents in the United States are sketchy, but FBI statistics indicate that at least 2 percent of all youth are involved in juvenile court cases.

U.S. government statistics reveal that 8 of 10 cases of juvenile delinquency involve males (Snyder & Sickmund, 1999). Although males are still far more likely to engage in juvenile delinquency, in the last two decades there has been a greater increase in female delinquency than male delinquency (Snyder & Sickmund, 1999). For both male and female delinquents, rates for property offenses are higher than for other rates of offenses (such as toward persons, drug offenses, and public order offenses). Arrests of adolescent males for delinquency still are much higher than for adolescent females.

Delinquency rates among African Americans, other minority groups, and lower-socioeconomic-status youth are especially high in proportion to the overall population of these groups. However, such groups have less influence over the judicial decision-making process in the United States and, therefore, may be judged delinquent more readily than their White, middle-socioeconomic-status counterparts.

In the Pittsburgh Youth Study, a longitudinal study focused on more than 1,500 inner-city boys, three developmental pathways to delinquency were (Loeber & Farrington, 2001; Loeber & others, 1998; Stoutheimer-Loeber & others, 2002):

- *Authority conflict.* Youth on this pathway showed stubbornness prior to age 12, then moved on to defiance and avoidance of authority.
- *Covert.* This pathway included minor covert acts, such as lying, followed by property damage and moderately serious delinquency, then serious delinquency.
- *Overt.* This pathway included minor aggression followed by fighting and violence.

One issue in juvenile justice is whether an adolescent who commits a crime should be tried as an adult (Steinberg & Cauffman, 2001). In a recent study, trying adolescent offenders as adults increased rather than reduced their crime rate (Myers, 1999). The study evaluated more than 500 violent youth in Pennsylvania, which has adopted a "get tough" policy. Although these 500 offenders had been given harsher punishment than a comparison group retained in juvenile court, they were more likely to be rearrested—and rearrested more quickly—for new offenses once they were returned to the community. This suggests that the price of short-term public safety attained by prosecuting juveniles as adults might increase the number of criminal offenses over the long run.

Causes of Delinquency What causes delinquency? Many causes have been proposed, including heredity, identity problems, community influences, and family experiences. Erik Erikson (1968), for example, believes that adolescents whose development has restricted them from acceptable social roles or made them feel that they cannot measure up to the demands placed on them may choose a negative identity. Adolescents with a negative identity may find support for their delinquent image among peers, reinforcing the negative identity. For Erikson, delinquency is an attempt to establish an identity, although a negative one.

Although delinquency is less exclusively a phenomenon of lower socioeconomic status (SES) than it was in the past, some characteristics of lower-class culture might promote delinquency. The norms of many lower-SES peer groups and gangs are antisocial, or counterproductive, to the goals and norms of society at large. Getting into and staying out of trouble are prominent features of life for some adolescents in low-income neighborhoods (Flannery & others, 2003). Adolescents from low-income backgrounds may sense that they can gain attention and status by performing antisocial actions. Being "tough" and "masculine" are high-status traits for lower-SES boys, and these traits are often measured by the adolescent's success in performing and getting away with delinquent acts. A community with a high crime rate also lets the adolescent observe many models who engage in criminal activities. These communities

mhhe ●com/
santrockld9

Office of Juvenile Justice and Delinquency Prevention

Justice Information Center

Preventing Crime

Common parenting weaknesses in the families of antisocial boys include a lack of supervision, poor disciplining skills, limited problem-solving abilities, and a tendency to be uncommunicative with sons.

—Gerald Patterson
Contemporary American Psychologist, University of Oregon

may be characterized by poverty, unemployment, and feelings of alienation toward the middle class. Quality schooling, educational funding, and organized neighborhood activities may be lacking in these communities.

Family support systems are also associated with delinquency (Feldman & Weinberger, 1994). Parents of delinquents are less skilled in discouraging antisocial behavior and in encouraging skilled behavior than are parents of nondelinquents. Parental monitoring of adolescents is especially important in determining whether an adolescent becomes a delinquent (Patterson, DeBaryshe, & Ramsey, 1989). Family discord and inconsistent and inappropriate discipline are also associated with delinquency. An increasing number of studies have also found that siblings can have a strong influence on delinquency (Conger & Reuter, 1996). In one recent study, high levels of hostile sibling relationships and older sibling delinquency were linked with younger sibling delinquency in both brother and sister pairs (Slomkowski & others, 2001). Having delinquent peers greatly increases the risk of becoming delinquent (Henry, Tolan, & Gorman-Smith, 2001).

Youth Violence Youth violence is a special concern in the United States today (U.S. Department of Health and Human Services, 2001). In one study, 17 percent of U.S. high school students reported carrying a gun or other weapon the past 30 days (National Center for Health Statistics, 2000). In this same study, a smaller percentage (7 percent) reported bringing a gun or other weapon onto school property. Not all violence-related behaviors involve weapons. In this study, 44 percent of male and 27 percent of female high school students said they had been involved in one or more fights.

In the late 1990s, a series of school shootings gained national attention. In April 1999, two Columbine High School (in Littleton, Colorado) students, Eric Harris (18) and Dylan Klebold (17) shot and killed 12 students and a teacher, wounded 23 others, and then killed themselves. In May 1998, slightly built Kip Kinkel strode into a cafeteria at Thurston High School in Springfield, Oregon, and opened fire on his fellow students, murdering two and injuring many others. Later that day, police went to Kip's home and found his parents lying dead on the floor, also victims of Kip's violence.

In 2001, 15-year-old Charles "Andy" Williams fired shots at Santana High School in Southern California that killed two classmates and injured 13 others. According to students at the school, Andy was a victim of bullying and had joked the previous weekend of his violent plans, but no one took him seriously after he later said he was just kidding.

Is there any way psychologists can predict whether a youth will turn violent? It's a complex task, but researchers have pieced together some clues (Cowley, 1998). Violent youth are overwhelmingly male, and many are driven by feelings of powerlessness. Violence seems to infuse these youth with a sense of power. In one study based on data collected in the National Longitudinal Study of Adolescent Health, secure attachment to parents, living in an intact family, and attending church services with parents were linked with lower incidences of violent behavior in seventh- through twelfth-graders (Franke, 2000).

Small-town shooting sprees attract attention, but youth violence is far greater in poverty-infested areas of inner cities. Urban poverty fosters powerlessness and rage, and many inner-city neighborhoods provide almost daily opportunities to observe violence. Many urban youth who live in poverty also lack adequate parent involvement and supervision (Tolan, 2001).

James Garbarino (1999, 2001) says there is a lot of ignoring that goes on in these kinds of situations. Parents often don't want to acknowledge what might be a very upsetting reality. Harris and Klebold were members of the "Trenchcoat Mafia" clique of Columbine outcasts. The two even had made a video for a school video class the previous fall that depicted them walking down the halls at the school shooting other students. Allegations were made that a year earlier the sheriff's department had been

"Andy" Williams, escorted by police after being arrested for killing two classmates and injuring 13 others at Santana High School. *What factors might contribute to youth murders?*

given information that Harris had bragged openly on the Internet that he and Klebold had built four bombs. Kip Kinkel had an obsession with guns and explosives, a history of abusing animals, and a nasty temper when crossed. When police examined his room, they found two pipe bombs, three larger bombs, and bomb-making recipes Kip had downloaded from the Internet. Clearly, some signs were present in these students' lives to suggest that they had some serious problems, but it is still very difficult to predict whether youth like these will act on their anger and sense of powerlessness to commit murder.

Garbarino (1999, 2001) has interviewed a number of youth killers. He concludes that nobody really knows precisely why a tiny minority of youth kill but that it might be a lack of a spiritual center. In the youth killers he interviewed, Garbarino often found a spiritual or emotional emptiness in which the youth sought meaning in the dark side of life.

Some interventions can reduce or prevent youth violence (Carnegie Council on Adolescent Development, 1995). Efforts at prevention should include developmentally appropriate schools, supportive families, and youth and community organizations. At a more specific level, one promising strategy for preventing youth violence is the teaching of conflict management as part of health education in elementary and middle schools. To build resources for such programs, the Carnegie Foundation is supporting a national network of violence prevention practitioners based at the U.S. Department of Education, linked with a national research center on youth violence at the University of Colorado.

These are some of the Oregon Social Learning Center's recommendations for reducing youth violence (Walker, 1998):

- *Recommit to raising children safely and effectively.* This includes engaging in parenting practices that have been shown to produce healthy, well-adjusted children. Such practices include consistent, fair discipline that is not harsh or severely punitive, careful monitoring and supervision, positive family management techniques, involvement in the child's daily life, daily debriefings about the child's experiences, and teaching problem-solving strategies.
- *Make prevention a reality.* Too often lip service is given to prevention strategies without investing in them at the necessary levels to make them effective.
- *Give more support to schools, which are struggling to educate a population that includes many at-risk children.*
- *Forge effective partnerships among families, schools, social service systems, churches, and other agencies to create the socializing experiences that will provide all youth with the opportunity to develop in positive ways.*

One individual whose goal is to reduce violence in adolescence and help at-risk adolescents cope more effectively with their lives is Rodney Hammond. To read about his work, see the Careers in Life-Span Development insert.

Careers in Life-Span Development

Rodney Hammond, Health Psychologist

When Rodney Hammond went to college at the University of Illinois in Champaign-Urbana, he had not decided on a major. To help finance his education, he took a part-time job in a child development research program sponsored by the psychology department. In this job, he observed inner-city children in contexts designed to improve their learning. He saw firsthand the contributions psychology can make and knew then that he wanted to be a psychologist.

Rodney Hammond went on to obtain a doctorate in school and community psychology with a focus on children's development ◀️ꓲ p. 32. Today, he is Director of Violence Prevention at the National Center for Injury Prevention and Control in Atlanta. Hammond calls himself a "health psychologist," although when he went to graduate school, training for that profession did not exist as it does now. He and his associates teach at-risk youth how to use social skills to manage conflict effectively and to recognize situations that could become violent. They have shown in their research that with this intervention many youth are less likely to become juvenile delinquents. Hammond's message to undergraduates: "If you are interested in people and problem solving, psychology is a great way to combine the two."

Rodney Hammond, counseling an adolescent girl about the risks of adolescence and how to effectively cope with them.

Depression and Suicide

What is the nature of depression in adolescence? What causes an adolescent to commit suicide?

Depression   Depression is more likely to occur in adolescence than in childhood. Also, adolescent girls consistently have higher rates of depression than adolescent boys. (Kaltalia-Heino & others, 2001). Among the reasons for this sex difference are that

- Females tend to ruminate in their depressed mood and amplify it.
- Females' self-images, especially their body images, are more negative than males'.
- Females face more discrimination than males do.
- Puberty occurs earlier for girls than for boys, and as a result girls experience a piling up of changes and life experiences in the middle school years, which can increase depression.

Certain family factors place adolescents at risk for developing depression (Seroczynski, Jacquez, & Cole, 2003). These include having a depressed parent, emotionally unavailable parents, parents who have high marital conflict, and parents with financial problems.

Poor peer relationships also are associated with adolescent depression. Not having a close relationship with a best friend, having less contact with friends, and experiencing peer rejection all increase depressive tendencies in adolescents.

The experience of difficult changes or challenges also is associated with depressive symptoms in adolescence (Compas & Grant, 1993), and parental divorce increases depressive symptoms in adolescents. Also, when adolescents go through puberty at the same time as they move from elementary school to middle or junior high school, they

Depression is more likely to occur in adolescence than in childhood, and female adolescents are more likely than male adolescents to be depressed. *What are some possible reasons adolescents become depressed?*

report being depressed more than do adolescents who go through puberty after the school transition.

Suicide   Suicidal behavior is rare in childhood but escalates in early adolescence. Suicide is the third leading cause of death today among adolescents 13 through 19 years of age in the United States (National Center for Health Statistics, 2000). Although the incidence of suicide in adolescence has increased in recent decades, it still is a relatively rare event. In 1998, 4,135 individuals from 15 through 24 years of age committed suicide in the United States, or about 11 of every 100,000 individuals in this age grouping (National Vital Statistics Reports, 2001).

Far more adolescents contemplate suicide or attempt suicide unsuccessfully (Borowsky, Ireland, & Resnick, 2001). In a national study, one-fifth of U.S. high school students said that they had seriously considered or attempted suicide in the last 12 months (National Center for Health Statistics, 2000). Less than 3 percent reported a suicide attempt that resulted in an injury, poisoning, or drug overdose that had been treated by a doctor. Females were more likely to attempt suicide than males but males were more likely to commit suicide. Males use more lethal means, such as a gun, in their suicide attempts, while adolescent females are more likely to cut their wrists or take an overdose of sleeping pills, which is less likely to result in death.

Homosexual adolescents may be vulnerable to suicide. Early reports suggested that homosexual youth were three to seven times more likely to attempt suicide than heterosexual youth (Ferguson, Horwood, & Beautrais, 1999; Herrill & others, 1999). In one recent study of 12,000 adolescents, approximately 15 percent of gay and lesbian youth said that they had attempted suicide compared to 7 percent of heterosexual youth (Russell & Joyner, 2001). And in another recent study, gay and lesbian adolescents were only slightly more likely than heterosexual adolescents to attempt suicide (Savin-Williams, in press). According to a leading researcher on gay youth, Richard Savin-Williams (2001), the earlier studies likely exaggerated the suicide rates for gay adolescents because they only surveyed the most disturbed youth who were attending support groups or hanging out at shelters for gay youth.

Distal, or earlier, experiences often are involved in suicide attempts as well. The adolescent might have a long-standing history of family instability and unhappiness. Just as a lack of affection and emotional support, high control, and pressure for achievement by parents during childhood are related to adolescent depression, such combinations of family experiences are also likely to show up as distal factors in suicide attempts. The adolescent might also lack supportive friendships.

Just as genetic factors are associated with depression, they are also associated with suicide. The closer a person's genetic relationship to someone who has committed suicide, the more likely that person is to also commit suicide.

What is the psychological profile of the suicidal adolescent? Suicidal adolescents often have depressive symptoms (American Academy of Pediatrics, 2000; Gadpaille, 1996). Although not all depressed adolescents are suicidal, depression is the most frequently cited factor associated with adolescent suicide. A sense of hopelessness, low self-esteem, and high self-blame are also associated with adolescent suicide (Harter & Marold, 1992; Harter & Whitesell, 2001).

The Interrelation of Problems and Successful Prevention/Intervention Programs

We have described some of the major adolescent problems in this chapter and the preceding chapter: substance abuse; juvenile delinquency; school-related problems, such as dropping out of school; adolescent pregnancy and sexually transmitted diseases; depression; and suicide ◀▥ pp. 380, 381.

The most at-risk adolescents have more than one problem. Researchers are increasingly finding that problem behaviors in adolescence are interrelated (Tubman & Windle, 1995). For example, heavy substance abuse is related to early sexual activity,

mhhe●com/
santrockld9

Adolescent Depression
Suicide

lower grades, dropping out of school, and delinquency. Early initiation of sexual activity is associated with the use of cigarettes and alcohol, the use of marijuana and other illicit drugs, lower grades, dropping out of school, and delinquency. Delinquency is related to early sexual activity, early pregnancy, substance abuse, and dropping out of school. As many as 10 percent of all adolescents in the United States have serious multiple-problem behaviors (for example, adolescents who have dropped out of school, are behind in their grade level, are users of heavy drugs, regularly use cigarettes and marijuana, and are sexually active but do not use contraception). Many, but not all, of these very high-risk youth "do it all." Another 15 percent of adolescents participate in many of these behaviors but with slightly lower frequency and less deleterious consequences. These high-risk youth often engage in two- or three-problem behaviors (Dryfoos, 1990).

In addition to understanding that many adolescents engage in multiple-problem behaviors, it also is important to develop programs that reduce adolescent problems. In a review of the programs that have been successful in preventing or reducing adolescent problems, adolescence researcher Joy Dryfoos (1990) described the common components of these successful programs:

1. *Intensive individualized attention.* In successful programs, high-risk children are attached to a responsible adult, who gives the child attention and deals with the child's specific needs. This theme occurs in a number of programs. In a successful substance-abuse program, a student assistance counselor is available full-time for individual counseling and referral for treatment.

2. *Communitywide multiagency collaborative approaches.* The basic philosophy of communitywide programs is that a number of different programs and services have to be in place. In one successful substance-abuse program, a communitywide health promotion campaign has been implemented that uses local media and community education, in concert with a substance-abuse curriculum in the schools.

3. *Early identification and intervention.* Reaching children and their families before children develop problems, or at the beginning of their problems, is a successful strategy. One preschool program serves as an excellent model for the prevention of delinquency, pregnancy, substance abuse, and dropping out of school. Operated by the High Schope Foundation in Ypsilanti, Michigan, the Perry Preschool has had a long-term positive impact on its students. This enrichment program, directed by David Weikart, serves disadvantaged African American children. They attend a high-quality two-year preschool program and receive weekly home visits from program personnel. Based on official police records, by age 19, individuals who had attended the Perry Preschool program were less likely to have been arrested and reported fewer adult offenses than a control group. The Perry Preschool students also were less likely to drop out of school, and teachers rated their social behavior as more competent than that of a control group who had not received the enriched preschool experience.

One current program that seeks to prevent adolescent problems is called Fast Track (Dodge, 2001; The Conduct Problems Prevention Research Group, 2002). High-risk children who show conduct problems at home and at kindergarten were identified. Then, during the elementary school years, the at-risk children and their families are given support and training in parenting, problem-solving and coping skills, peer relations, classroom atmosphere and curriculum, academic achievement, and home-school relations. Ten project interventionists work with the children, their families, and schools to increase the protective factors and decrease the risk factors in these areas. Thus far, results show that the intervention effectively improved parenting practices and children's problem-solving and coping skills, peer relations, reading achievement, and problem behavior at home and school during the elementary school years compared to a control group of high-risk children who did not experience the intervention.

Careers in Life-Span Development

Peter Benson, Director, Search Institute

Peter Benson has been the Director of the Search Institute in Minneapolis since 1985. The Search Institute is an independent, nonprofit organization whose mission is to advance the well-being of adolescents. The Institute conducts applied scientific research, provides information about many aspects of improving adolescents' lives, gives support to communities, and trains people to work with youth.

Peter obtained his undergraduate degree in psychology from Augustana College, master's degree in the psychology of religion from Yale University, and Ph.D. in social psychology from the University of Denver. Peter directs a staff of 80 individuals at the Search Institute, lectures widely about youth, and consults with a number of communities and organizations on adolescent issues.

Under Peter's direction, the Search Institute has determined through research that a number of assets (such as family

support and good schools) serve as a buffer to prevent adolescents from developing problems and increase the likelihood that adolescents will competently make the transition from adolescence to adulthood.

Peter Benson, talking with adolescents.

One individual who has been a leader in improving the well-being of adolescents and seeking to reduce their problems is Peter Benson. To read about his career and work, see the Careers in Life-Span Development insert.

Review and Reflect

5 Identify adolescent problems in socioemotional development and strategies for helping adolescents with problems

REVIEW

- What is juvenile delinquency? What causes it? What is the nature of youth violence?
- What is the nature of depression and suicide in adolescence?
- How are adolescent problems interrelated? What are some components of successful prevention/intervention programs with adolescents?

REFLECT

- Are the consequences of choosing a course of risk-taking in adolescence today more serious than in the past? If so, why?

Reach Your Learning Goals

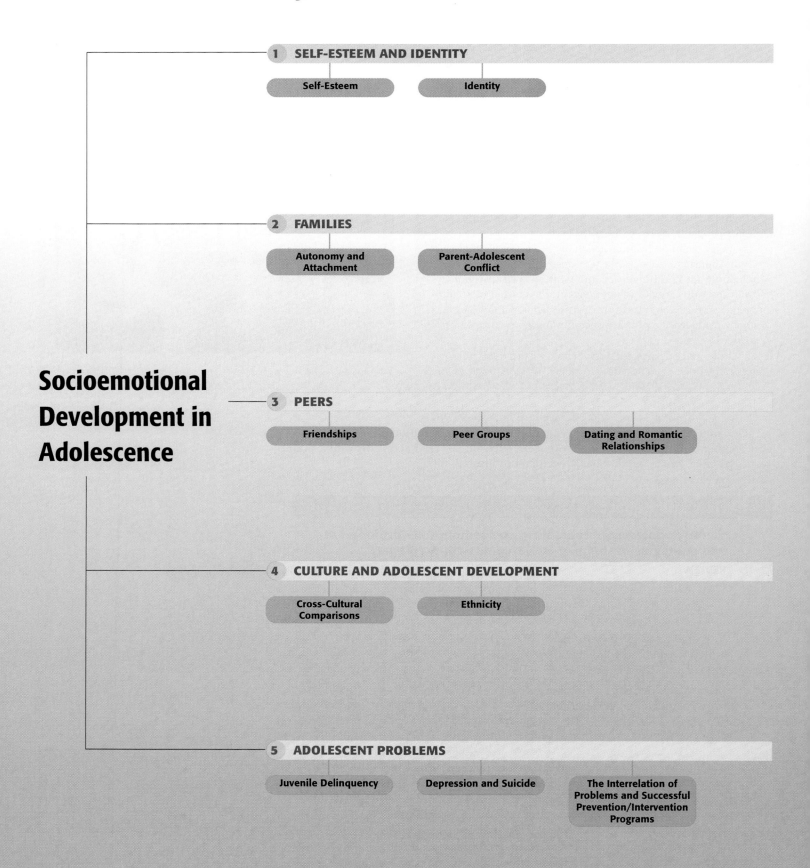

Socioemotional Development in Adolescence

1 SELF-ESTEEM AND IDENTITY

- Self-Esteem
- Identity

2 FAMILIES

- Autonomy and Attachment
- Parent-Adolescent Conflict

3 PEERS

- Friendships
- Peer Groups
- Dating and Romantic Relationships

4 CULTURE AND ADOLESCENT DEVELOPMENT

- Cross-Cultural Comparisons
- Ethnicity

5 ADOLESCENT PROBLEMS

- Juvenile Delinquency
- Depression and Suicide
- The Interrelation of Problems and Successful Prevention/Intervention Programs

Summary

1 Discuss changes in self-esteem and identity in adolescence

- Some researchers have found that self-esteem declines in early adolescence for both boys and girls, but the drop for girls is greater. Other researchers caution that these declines are often exaggerated and actually are small in nature.
- Erikson's theory is the most comprehensive view of identity development. Identity versus identity confusion is the fifth stage in Erikson's theory. Identity is a self-portrait composed of many pieces. Identity development is extraordinarily complex. For the first time in development, during adolescence, individuals are physically, cognitively, and socially mature enough to synthesize their lives and pursue a path toward adult maturity. Marcia proposed that four statuses of identity exist, based on a combination of conflict and commitment: diffusion, foreclosure, moratorium, and achievement. Some experts believe the main identity changes take place in late adolescence or youth. Individuals often follow "moratorium-achievement-moratorium-achievement" cycles. Both individuation and connectedness in parent-adolescent relationships are linked with progress in adolescent identity development. Erikson argued that throughout the world ethnic minority groups have struggled to maintain their cultural identities while blending into the majority culture. Adolescence is often a special juncture in ethnic minority identity development. Erikson's theory argues for gender differences in identity, but some researchers have found gender similarities rather than differences. Others argue that relationships are more central in the identity development of females than of males.

2 Describe the changes that take place in adolescents' relationships with their parents

- Many parents have a difficult time handling the adolescent's push for autonomy, even though the push is one of the hallmarks of adolescence. Adolescents do not simply move into a world isolated from parents; attachment to parents increases the probability that an adolescent will be socially competent.
- Parent-adolescent conflict increases in adolescence. The conflict is usually moderate rather than severe and the increased conflict may serve the positive developmental function of promoting autonomy and identity. A subset of adolescents experiences high parent-adolescent conflict, which is linked with negative outcomes.

3 Characterize the changes that occur in peer relations during adolescence

- Harry Stack Sullivan was the most influential theorist to discuss the importance of adolescent friendships. He argued that there is a dramatic increase in the psychological importance and intimacy of close friends in early adolescence.

- The pressure to conform to peers is strong during adolescence, especially during the eighth and ninth grades. Cliques and crowds assume more importance in the lives of adolescents than in the lives of children. Membership in certain crowds—especially jocks and populars—is associated with increased self-esteem. Independents also show high self-esteem. Children groups are less formal and less heterogeneous than adolescent groups.
- Dating takes on added importance in adolescence, and it can have many functions. Younger adolescents often begin to hang out together in heterosexual groups. A special concern is early dating, which is linked with developmental problems. Male dating scripts are proactive, those of females reactive. Emotions are heavily involved in adolescent dating and romantic relationships. Culture can exert a powerful influence on adolescent dating.

4 Explain how culture influences adolescent development

- As in other periods of development, culture influences adolescents' development. Ceremonies mark an individual's transition from one status to another, especially into adulthood. In primitive cultures, rites of passage are often well defined. In contemporary America, rites of passage to adulthood are ill-defined.
- Much of the research on ethnic minority adolescents has not teased apart the influences of ethnicity and social class. Because of this failure, too often researchers have given ethnic explanations that were largely due to socioeconomic factors. While not all ethnic minority families are poor, poverty contributes to the stress of many ethnic minority adolescents. There are legitimate differences between many ethnic groups, as well as between ethnic groups and the White majority. Recognizing these differences is an important aspect of getting along with others in a diverse, multicultural world. Too often, differences between ethnic groups and the White majority have been interpreted as deficits on the part of the ethnic minority group. Another important dimension of ethnic minority groups is their diversity. Ethnic minority groups are not homogeneous; they have different social, historical, and economic backgrounds. Failure to recognize diversity and individual variations results in the stereotyping of an ethnic minority group. Value conflicts are often involved when individuals respond to ethnic issues. One prominent value conflict involves assimilation versus pluralism.

5 Identify adolescent problems in socioemotional development and strategies for helping adolescents with problems

- A juvenile delinquent is an adolescent who breaks the law or engages in conduct that is considered illegal. Heredity, identity problems, community influences, and family experiences have been proposed as causes of juvenile delinquency. An increasing concern is the high rate of violence among youth.

- Adolescents have a higher rate of depression than children. Female adolescents are more likely to have mood and depressive disorders than male adolescents are. Adolescent suicide is the third leading cause of death in U.S. adolescents. Both proximal and distal factors are likely involved in suicide's causes.

- Researchers are increasingly finding that problem behaviors in adolescence are interrelated. Dryfoos found a number of common components in programs designed to prevent or reduce adolescent problems: They provide individual attention to high-risk adolescents, they develop community-wide intervention, and they include early identification and intervention.

Key Terms

crisis 406
commitment 406
identity diffusion 406
identity foreclosure 406

identity moratorium 406
identity achievement 406
individuality 407
connectedness 407

ethnic identity 408
cliques 415
crowds 415
dating scripts 417

rite of passage 420
assimilation 424
pluralism 424
juvenile delinquent 424

Key People

Erik Erikson 405, 425
James Marcia 406
Alan Waterman 407

Reed Larson and Marsye
   Richards 411
G. Stanley Hall 411

Harry Stack Sullivan 414
Stanley Sue 423
Richard Savin-Williams 429

Joy Dryfoos 430

Taking It to the Net

1. Shelley's mother is Euro-American, and her father is Japanese. Many people who do not know her have a hard time identifying her ethnic background, and she is constantly asked, "What are you?" There are a couple of other students of color at her school, although few of them openly identify as biracial or multiracial. Shelley is now in the process of figuring out who she is. What are some of the challenges biracial or multiracial adolescents face? How might the process of identity development progress?

2. Fourteen-year-old Denise, an only child, and her mother, Doris, always had a great relationship—until recently. Now it seems that they are constantly arguing. Doris is trying to understand what is going on with her daughter. How can she tell if Denise's behavior is normal for a 14-year-old?

3. The local school board wants to try to prevent violent and tragic incidents like those in Littleton, Colorado, and Springfield, Oregon. It has asked its principals and teachers to study an APA publication that identifies warning signs of violence and suggests interventions. What will they learn from it and how can they try and prevent similar situations in their own school district if possible?

Connect to www.mhhe.com/santrockld9 to research the answers and complete these exercises.

E-Learning Tools

To help you master the material in this chapter, you'll find a number of valuable study tools on the Student CD-ROM that accompanies this book. In addition, visit the Online Learning Center for *Life-Span Development*, ninth edition, where you'll find these valuable resources for chapter 13, "Socioemotional Development in Adolescence."

- What do you believe your level of self-esteem to be? Complete the self-assessment, *My Self-Esteem*, to calculated your self-esteem score and learn more about this concept. Then think about how closely your parents were watching you in adolescence by taking the self-assessment, *How Much Did My Parents Monitor My Behavior in Adolescence?* Finally, would you know if you were depressed? The self-assessment, *Am I Depressed?*, will help you better understand some of the signs of depression.

- View video clips of key developmental psychology experts, including Laurence Steinberg discussing his research on adolescents and their parents.

- Build your decision-making skills by trying your hand at the parenting and education "Scenarios."

Early Adulthood

*How many roads
must a man walk
down before you call
him a man?*
—BOB DYLAN
American Folk Singer, 20th Century

Early adulthood is a time for work and a time for love, sometimes leaving little time for anything else. For some of us, finding our place in adult society and committing to a more stable life take longer than we imagine. We still ask ourselves who we are and wonder if it isn't enough just to be. Our dreams continue and our thoughts are bold, but at some point we become more pragmatic. Sex and love are powerful passions in our lives—at time angels of light, at others fiends of torment. And we possibly will never know the love of our parents until we become parents ourselves. Section 7 contains two chapters: "Physical and Cognitive Development in Early Adulthood" (chapter 14) and "Socioemotional Development in Early Adulthood" (chapter 15).

Whatever you can do, or dream you can, begin it. Boldness has genius, power, and magic.

—JOHANN WOLFGANG VON GOETHE
German Playwright and Novelist, 19th Century

Physical and Cognitive Development in Early Adulthood

Learning Goals

1 *D*escribe the transition from adolescence to adulthood

2 *I*dentify the changes in physical development in young adults

3 *D*iscuss sexuality in young adults

4 *C*haracterize cognitive changes in early adulthood

5 *E*xplain the key dimensions of careers and work in early adulthood

Images of Life-Span Development
Florence Griffith Joyner

"When you have been second best for so long, you can either accept it or try to become the best. I made the decision to try to be the best"—Florence Griffith Joyner, Olympic gold medalist.

Florence Griffith Joyner, also known as "Flo-Jo," smashed Olympic and world records in the 100-meter and 200-meter dashes at 28 years of age. This was especially unusual because earlier sprint champions were in their early twenties. Through better weight training, eating habits, and remarkable self-discipline, Flo-Jo was able to accomplish her track goals at an age at which many thought such achievements were impossible.

In college, Flo-Jo had to juggle many aspects of her life to be successful. In addition to being a full-time college student, she also worked and commuted to school. Nonetheless, she not only became the NCAA champion in the 200-meter dash but she also managed to achieve high grades.

Flo-Jo grew up in poverty in the Watts area in Los Angeles. She never forgot her past and frequently gave back to the community. She often returned to speak to children and urged them to place academics ahead of athletics in their lives.

Florence Griffith Joyner unfortunately died an early death at the age of 38, apparently as the result of a seizure. A book she wrote prior to her death was later published (Griffith Joyner & Hanc, 1999). In it, she talked about the importance of finding a career that you like and making a deep commitment to be the best you can be in life and work.

In this chapter, we will explore many aspects of physical and cognitive development in early adulthood. These include some of the areas that were so important in Flo-Jo's life: seeking to reach peak physical performance, achieving, finding the right career match, and juggling roles. However, we will begin where we left off in the last major section of the book, "Adolescence," and address the transition from adolescent to adulthood.

1 THE TRANSITION FROM ADOLESCENCE TO ADULTHOOD

Becoming an Adult

The Transition from High School to College

As the Bob Dylan quotation at the opening of Section 7 says, "How many roads must a man walk down before you call him a man?" When does an adolescent become an adult? In chapter 12, we saw that it is not easy to tell when a girl or a boy enters adolescence ◀▥ p. 373. The task of determining when an individual becomes an adult is more difficult.

Becoming an Adult

In terms of age, recall from chapter 1 that we said the period of early adulthood is entered in the late teens or early twenties and lasts through the thirties ◀▥ p. 20. As many individuals make the transition from adolescence to adulthood, they face a complex and challenging world of work with highly specialized tasks. During this period, their income is often low and sporadic and they might change residences periodically. Marriage and a family are increasingly being delayed until the mid twenties or later. This period of extended economic and personal temporariness might last from two to eight years or even longer.

The age range from 18 to 25 recently has been labeled emerging adulthood (Arnett, 2000). During this time frame, individuals have left the dependency of childhood but have not yet entered the enduring responsibilities of adulthood. Experimentation and exploration characterize emerging adulthood. Many individuals at this point in their lives are still exploring which career path they want to follow, what they want their identity to be, and which lifestyle they want to adopt (such as single, cohabiting, or married).

One study examined emerging adults' perception of whether they were adults or not (Arnett, 2000). The majority of the 18- to 25-year-olds responded neither "yes" nor "no," but "in some respects yes, in some respects no" (see figure 14.1). In this study, it was not until the late twenties and early thirties that a clear majority said that they had reached adulthood. Thus, the emerging adults saw themselves as being in an in-between period, not adolescents, but not full-fledged adults, either.

The most widely recognized marker of entry into adulthood is the occasion when an individual first takes a more or less permanent, full-time job. This usually happens when individuals finish school, high school for some, college for others, postgraduate training for others. However, criteria for determining when an individual has left adolescence and entered adulthood are not clear-cut. Economic independence may be considered a criterion of adulthood. However, developing this independence is often a long, drawn-out process rather than an abrupt one. College graduates are increasingly returning to live with their parents as they attempt to get their feet on the ground economically. In one study, adolescents often cited taking responsibility for oneself and independent decision making as identifying the onset of adulthood (Scheer & Unger, 1994). And in another study, more than 70 percent of college students said that being an adult means accepting responsibility for the consequences of one's actions, deciding on one's own beliefs and values, and establishing a relationship with parents as an equal adult (Arnett, 1995).

The new freedoms and responsibilities of emerging adulthood represent major changes in individuals' lives. Although change characterizes the transition from adolescence to adulthood, keep in mind that considerable continuity still glues these periods together. For example, one recent longitudinal study found that religious views and behaviors were especially stable in emerging adults, and to a lesser degree, attitudes toward drugs were stable as well (Bachman & others, 2002).

What we have said about the determinants of adult status mainly characterize individuals in industrialized societies, especially Americans. Are the criteria for adulthood the same in developing countries as they are in the United States? In developing countries, marriage is more often a significant marker for entry into adulthood and this usually occurs much earlier than the adulthood markers in the United States (Arnett, 2000).

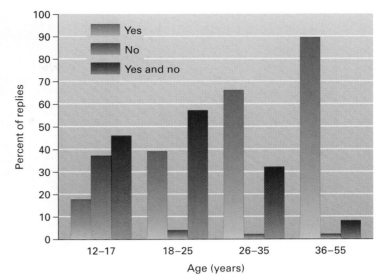

FIGURE 14.1 Self-Perceptions of Adult Status

In one study, individuals were asked, "Do you feel that you have reached adult status?" and were given a choice of answering "yes," "no," or "in some respects yes, in some respects no" (Arnett, 2000). As indicated in the graph, the majority of the emerging adults (18 to 25) responded "in some respects yes, in some respects no."

The Transition from High School to College

Just as the transition from elementary school to middle or junior high school involves change and possible stress, so does the transition from high school to college ◄||| p. 390. In many instances, there are parallel changes in the two transitions. Going from being a senior in high school to being a freshman in college replays the top-dog phenomenon of transferring from the oldest and most powerful group of students to the youngest and least powerful group of students that occurred earlier as adolescence began. For many of you, the transition from high school to college was not very long ago.

The transition from high school to college often involves positive as well as negative features. In college, students are likely to feel grown up, be able to spend more time with peers, have more opportunities to explore different lifestyles and values, and enjoy greater freedom from parental monitoring. However, college involves a larger, more impersonal school structure and an increased focus on achievement and its assessment. *What was your transition to college like?*

mhhe com/
santrockld9

Transition to College
The American College Freshman

The transition from high school to college involves movement to a larger, more impersonal school structure; interaction with peers from more diverse geographical and sometimes more diverse ethnic backgrounds; and increased focus on achievement and its assessment.

But, as with the transition from elementary to middle or junior high school, the transition from high school to college can involve positive features. Students are more likely to feel grown up, have more subjects from which to select, have more time to spend with peers, have more opportunities to explore different lifestyles and values, enjoy greater independence from parental monitoring, and be challenged intellectually by academic work (Santrock & Halonen, 2002).

Stress Stress is believed to be a major contributor to heart disease, cancer, lung problems, accidental injuries, cirrhosis of the liver, and suicide—six of the leading causes of death in the United States. Antianxiety drugs and ulcer medications are among the best-selling prescription drugs.

Today's college students experience more stress and are more depressed than in the past, according to a national study of more than 300,000 freshmen at more than 500 colleges and universities (Sax & others, 2001). In 2001, 28 percent (up from 16 percent in 1985) said they frequently "felt overwhelmed with what I have to do." And college freshmen in 2000 indicated that they felt more depressed than their counterparts from the 1980s had indicated. The pressure to succeed in college, get a great job, and make lots of money were pervasive concerns of these students.

In one study, the academic circumstances creating the most stress for students were tests and finals, grades and competition, professors and class environment, too many demands, papers and essay exams, career and future success, and studying (Murphy, 1996). The personal circumstances that caused the most stress for students were intimate relationships, finances, parental conflicts and expectations, and roommate conflicts.

Let's examine some ways to cope with stress, beginning with the negative ways:

- Repress it so you don't have to think about it.
- Take it out on other people when you feel angry or depressed.
- Keep your feelings to yourself.
- Tell yourself the problem will go away.
- Refuse to believe what is happening.
- Try to reduce the tension by drinking and eating more.

Fortunately, you can cope with stress in these positive ways:

- See stress as a challenge to be overcome rather than an overwhelming threat.
- Have good coping resources, such as friends, family, and a mentor. One recent study found that first-year students showed better adaptation to college when they had less family conflict (Feenstra & others, 2001).
- Develop an optimistic outlook and think positively. Thinking optimistically gives you the sense that you are controlling your environment rather than letting it control you. One recent study found that greater optimism, assessed at the beginning of the first semester of college, was linked with less stress and depression over the course of the semester (Brisette, Scheier, & Carver, 2002).
- Learn how to relax.

Happiness   What makes college students happy? One recent study of 222 undergraduates compared the upper 10 percent of college students who were very happy with average and very unhappy college students (Diener & Seligman, 2002). The very happy college students were highly social, more extraverted, and had stronger romantic and social relationships than the less happy college students (see figure 14.2). We will spend considerable time examining the social aspects of young adults in chapter 15.

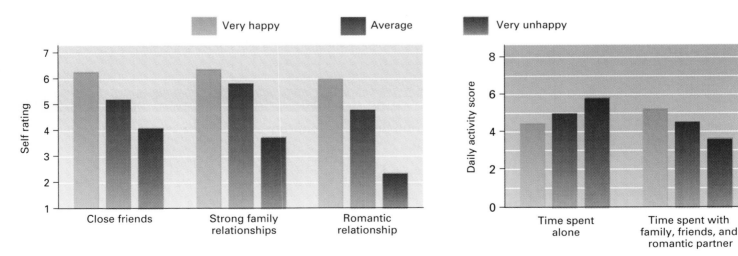

FIGURE 14.2 Characteristics of Very Happy College Students (Diener & Seligman, 2002)

Self-ratings were made on a scale of 1 to 7, with 1 being much below the average of college students on the campus studied (University of Illinois), and 7 being much above the average of college students on the campus. Daily activity scores reflect mean times with 1 representing no time, and 10 reflecting 8 hours per day.

Careers in Life-Span Development

Grace Leaf, College/Career Counselor

Grace Leaf is a counselor at Spokane Community College in Washington. She has a master's degree in educational leadership and is working toward a doctoral degree in educational leadership at Gonzaga University in Washington. Her job involves teaching orientation for international students, conducting individual and group advising, and doing individual and group career planning. Leaf tries to connect students with goals and values and help them design an educational program that fits their needs and visions.

Grace Leaf, counseling college students at Spokane Community College about careers.

Education The United States is becoming a more educated country. In 1998, 24 percent of the population over 25 years and older had completed four years or more of college, compared with only 17 percent in 1980 (U.S. Department of Education, 1999). Total college enrollment is expected to increase in the next decade as increasing numbers of high school graduates pursue higher education. In the last several decades, there has been a dramatic increase in the number of individuals who attend community colleges rather than four-year colleges, and the community college movement continues to expand.

What is college attendance like around the world? Canada has the largest percentage of 18- to 21-year-olds enrolled in college (41 percent), followed by Belgium (40 percent), France (36 percent), the United States (35 percent), Ireland (31 percent), and New Zealand (25 percent) (U.S. Department of Education, 1999). The greatest percentage increase in college attendance is taking place in Africa—128 percent from 1980 through 1996.

These figures do not include the many returning students who in the United States make up an increasing percentage of the college population. Returning students either did not go to college right out of high school or went to college, dropped out, and now have returned. More than one of every five full-time college students today is a returning student, and about two-thirds of part-time college students are (Sax & others, 2000). Many returning students have to balance their course work with commitments to a partner, children, job, and community responsibilities. Despite the many challenges that returning students face, they bring many strengths to campus, such as life experiences that can be applied to a wide range of issues and topics.

College counselors can be a good source of information about coping with stress and academic matters. To read about the work of college counselor Grace Leaf, see the Careers in Life-Span Development insert.

Review and Reflect

1 ### Describe the transition from adolescence to adulthood

REVIEW

- What are the criteria for becoming an adult?
- What is the transition from high school to college like?

REFLECT

- What do you think is the most important criterion for becoming an adult? Does it make sense to describe becoming an adult in terms of "emerging adulthood" over a period of years or is there a specific age at which someone becomes an adult? Explain.

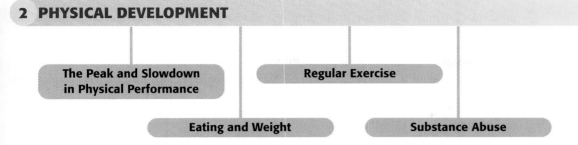

2 PHYSICAL DEVELOPMENT

- The Peak and Slowdown in Physical Performance
- Regular Exercise
- Eating and Weight
- Substance Abuse

For most individuals physical status not only reaches its peak in early adulthood, it also begins to decline during this period. Interest in health has increased among young adults, with special concerns about diet, weight, exercise, and addiction.

The Peak and Slowdown in Physical Performance

Most of us reach our peak physical performance under the age of 30, often between the ages of 19 and 26. This peak of physical performance occurs not only for the average young adult, but for outstanding athletes as well. Even though athletes as a group keep getting better than their predecessors—running faster, jumping higher, and lifting more weight—the age at which they reach their peak performance has remained virtually the same (Schultz & Curnow, 1988). However, as you saw in Images of Life-Span Development at the beginning of the chapter, some individuals such as Florence Griffith Joyner have been able to extend the "biological window" of peak performance to an older age in early adulthood.

Most swimmers and gymnasts reach their peak performance in their late teens. Golfers and marathon runners tend to peak in their late twenties. In other areas of athletics, peak performance is often in the early to mid twenties.

Not only do we reach our peak physical performance during early adulthood, but during this time we are also the healthiest. Few young adults have chronic health problems, and they have fewer colds and respiratory problems than when they were children. Most college students know what it takes to prevent illness and promote health. In one study, college students' ranking of health-protective activities—nutrition, sleep, exercise, watching one's weight, and so on—virtually matched that of licensed nurses (Turk, Rudy, & Salovey, 1984).

Although most college students know what it takes to prevent illness and promote health, they don't fare very well when it comes to applying this information to themselves. In one study, college students reported that they probably would never have a heart attack or drinking problem, but that other college students would (Weinstein, 1984). The college students also said no relation exists between their risk of heart attack and how much they exercise, smoke, or eat meat or high-cholesterol food such as eggs, even though they correctly recognized that factors such as family history influence risk. Many college students, it seems, have unrealistic, overly optimistic beliefs about their future health risks.

In early adulthood, few individuals stop to think about how their personal lifestyles will affect their health later in their adult lives. As young adults, many of us develop a pattern of not eating breakfast, not eating regular meals, and relying on snacks as our main food source during the day, eating excessively to the point where we exceed the normal weight for our age, smoking moderately or excessively, drinking moderately or excessively, failing to exercise, and getting by with only a few hours of sleep at night. These poor personal lifestyles were associated with poor health in one investigation of 7,000 individuals from the ages of 20 to 70 (Belloc & Breslow, 1972). In the Berkeley Longitudinal Study—in which individuals were evaluated over a period of 40 years—physical health at age 30 predicted life satisfaction at age 70, more so for men than women (Mussen, Honzik, & Eichorn, 1982).

After thirty, a body has a mind of its own.

—BETTE MIDLER
American Actress, 20th Century

There are some hidden dangers in the peaks of performance and health in early adulthood. Young adults can draw on physical resources for a great deal of pleasure, often bouncing back easily from physical stress and abuse. However, this can lead them to push their bodies too far. The negative effects of abusing one's body may not show up in the first part of early adulthood, but they probably will surface later in early adulthood or in middle adulthood (Csikszentmihalyi & Rathunde, 1998).

How are gender and ethnicity linked to health behavior and beliefs in young adults? One recent study found that male college students engaged in riskier health behaviors than female college students (Courtenay, McCreary, & Merighi, 2002). Among various ethnic groups in this study, Asian Americans reported the most risky health behaviors, especially in cigarette smoking. Latinos showed the greatest dietary health risks, which was most notable in their high fat intake.

Not only do we reach our peak in physical performance during early adulthood, but it is during this age period that we also begin to decline in physical performance. Muscle tone and strength usually begin to show signs of decline around the age of 30. Sagging chins and protruding abdomens may also begin to appear for the first time. The lessening of physical abilities is a common complaint among the just-turned-thirties. Says one 30-year-old, "I played tennis last night. My knees are sore and my lower back aches. Last month, it was my elbow that hurt. Several years ago it wasn't that way. I could play all day and not be sore the next morning." Sensory systems show little change in early adulthood, but the lens of the eye loses some of its elasticity and becomes less able to change shape and focus on near objects. Hearing peaks in adolescence, remains constant in the first part of early adulthood, and then begins to decline in the last part of early adulthood. And in the mid to late twenties, the body's fatty tissue increases.

The health profile of our nation's young adults can be improved by reducing the incidence of certain health-impairing lifestyles, such as overeating, and by engaging in health-improving lifestyles that include good eating habits, exercising regularly, and not abusing drugs.

Eating and Weight

In earlier chapters, we explored obesity in childhood (chapters 8 and 10) and examined the eating disorders of anorexia nervosa and bulimia nervosa in adolescence (chapter 12) ◀▥▥ pp. 239, 305, and 384. Now, we will turn our attention to obesity in the adult years and the extensive preoccupation that many adults have with dieting.

Obesity   Approximately one-third of the American population is overweight enough to be at increased risk for health problems such as hypertension, cardiovascular disease, and diabetes (Stunkard, 2000). Obesity often becomes more common with increased age, especially among women. *Body mass index*, (*BMI*) a measure of weight in relation to height, is used to determine whether an individual is obese or not (National Institutes of Health, 2000) (see figure 14.3).

Heredity   Until recently, the genetic component of obesity had been underestimated by scientists. Some individuals do inherit a tendency to be overweight. Researchers have documented that animals can be inbred to have a propensity for obesity (Blundell, 1984). Further, identical human twins have similar weights, even when they are reared apart. Estimates of the variance in body mass that can be explained by heredity range from 25 to 70 percent.

Weight (pounds)

	120	130	140	150	160	170	180	190	200	210	220	230	240	250
4'6"	29	31	34	36	39	41	43	46	48	51	53	56	58	60
4'8"	27	29	31	34	36	38	40	43	45	47	49	52	54	56
4'10"	25	27	29	31	34	36	38	40	42	44	46	48	50	52
5'0"	23	25	27	29	31	33	35	37	39	41	43	45	47	49
5'2"	22	24	26	27	29	31	33	35	37	38	40	42	44	46
5'4"	21	22	24	26	28	29	31	33	34	36	38	40	41	43
5'6"	19	21	23	24	26	27	29	31	32	34	36	37	39	40
5'8"	18	20	21	23	24	26	27	29	30	32	34	35	37	38
5'10"	17	19	20	22	23	24	26	27	29	30	32	33	35	36
6'0"	16	18	19	20	22	23	24	26	27	28	30	31	33	34
6'2"	15	17	18	19	21	22	23	24	26	27	28	30	31	32
6'4"	15	16	17	18	20	21	22	23	24	26	27	28	29	30
6'6"	14	15	16	17	19	20	21	22	23	24	25	27	28	29
6'8"	13	14	15	17	18	19	20	21	22	23	24	25	26	28

Height (vertical axis label)

▨ Underweight   ▨ Healthy weight   ▨ Overweight   ▨ Obese

FIGURE 14.3 Figuring Your Body Mass Index

Body mass index is a measure of weight in relation to height. Anyone with a BMI of 25 or more is considered overweight. People who have a body mass index of 30 or more (a BMI of 30 is roughly 30 pounds over a healthy weight) are considered obese. BMI has some limitations: It can overestimate body fat in people who are very muscular, and it can underestimate body fat in people who have lost muscle mass, such as the elderly.

Leptin (from the Greek word *leptos,* which means "thin") is a chemical substance that is involved in satiety (the condition of being full to satisfaction). Leptin, a protein that is released by fat cells, decreases food intake and increases energy expenditure (Obwerbauer & others, 2001). Leptin acts as an anti-obesity hormone (Misra & others, 2001). Initial research focused on the *ob mouse* (the label for this strain of mice), which has a low metabolism, overeats, and gets extremely fat. A particular gene called *ob* normally produces leptin. However, because of a genetic mutation, the fat cells of *ob* mice cannot produce leptin. When *ob* mice are given daily injections of leptin, their metabolic rate increases, they become more active, and they eat less. Consequently, their weight falls to normal. Figure 14.4 shows an untreated *ob* mouse and an *ob* mouse that has received injections of leptin. In humans, leptin concentrations have been linked with weight, percentage of body fat, weight loss in a single diet episode, and cumulative percentage of weight loss in all diet episodes (Benini & others, 2001). Today, scientists are interested in the possibility that leptin might help obese individuals lose weight (Wauters & others, 2001).

FIGURE 14.4 Leptin and Obesity

The *ob* mouse on the left is untreated; the one on the right has been given injections of leptin.

Set Point and Metabolism   The amount of stored fat in your body is an important factor in your *set point,* the weight maintained when no effort is made to gain or lose weight. Fat is stored in what are called adipose cells. When these cells are filled, you do not get hungry. When people gain weight—because of genetic predisposition, childhood eating patterns, or adult overeating—the number of their fat cells increases, and they might not be able to get rid of them. A normal-weight individual has 30 to 40 billion fat cells. An obese individual has 80 to 120 billion fat cells. Some scientists have proposed that these fat cells can shrink but might not go away.

Another factor in weight is **basal metabolism rate (BMR),** the minimal amount of energy an individual uses in a resting state. BMR varies with age and sex. Rates decline precipitously during adolescence and then more gradually in adulthood; they also are slightly higher for males than females (see figure 14.5). Many people gradually increase their weight over many years (Wing & Polley, 2001). To some degree the weight gain can be due to a declining basal metabolism rate.

Environmental Factors   The human gustatory system and taste preferences developed at a time when reliable food sources were scarce. Our earliest ancestors probably developed a preference for sweets, because ripe fruit, which is a concentrated source of sugar (and calories), was so accessible. Today many people still have a "sweet tooth," but unlike our ancestors' ripe fruit that contained sugar *plus* vitamins and minerals, the soft drinks and candy bars we snack on today often fill us with empty calories.

Strong evidence of the environment's influence on weight is the doubling of the rate of obesity in the United States since 1900. This dramatic increase in obesity likely is due to greater availability of food (especially food high in fat), energy-saving devices, and declining physical activity. Obesity is six times more prevalent among women with low incomes than among women with high incomes. Americans also are more obese than Europeans and people in many other areas of the world.

Ethnicity and Gender   A recent study found that African American and Latino women in their twenties and thirties become obese faster than their White counterparts, and Latino men become obese faster than White and African American men

mhhe com/
santrockld9

Why People Are Getting Fatter
Obesity
Heredity and Obesity

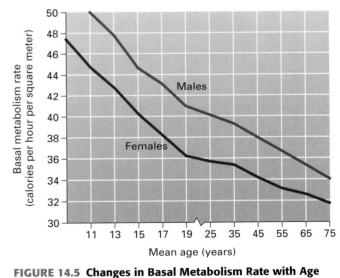

FIGURE 14.5 Changes in Basal Metabolism Rate with Age

BMR varies with age and sex. Rates are usually higher for males and decline proportionately with age for both sexes.

basal metabolism rate (BMR) The minimal amount of energy a person uses in a resting state.

Careers in Life-Span Development

Judith Rodin, University Professor, Health Psychology Researcher, and University President

Judith Rodin has conducted numerous research studies, especially in the area of eating behavior and women's health. She obtained her Ph.D. in psychology at the University of Pennsylvania and went on to teach and conduct research at Yale University. Her book *Body Traps* (Rodin, 1992) focuses on her belief that the American culture has unhealthy views of women's health, especially in its emphasis on extreme thinness as an ideal body build.

Judith Rodin returned to the University of Pennsylvania to become its president. In doing so, she became the first female to become president of an Ivy League university.

Judith Rodin (*center*) talking with college students at the University of Pennsylvania.

(McTigue, Garrett, & Popkin, 2002). Two possibilities might explain these findings (Brownell, 2002). There may be some biological vulnerability that makes some ethnic-gender groups more susceptible to obesity. Also, some individuals may be at risk for obesity because of their environment, as when their exposure to junk food and fast food is high and their opportunities to be active are minimal.

Dieting Ironically, while obesity is on the rise, dieting has become an obsession with many Americans. We will explore a number of factors in dieting, beginning with restrained eating.

Restrained Eaters Many people live their lives as one big long diet, interrupted by occasional hot fudge sundaes or chocolate chip cookies. They are **restrained eaters,** individuals who chronically restrict their food intake to control their weight. Restrained eaters are often on diets, are very conscious of what they eat, and tend to feel guilty after splurging on sweets. An interesting characteristic of restrained eaters is that when they stop dieting, they tend to binge eat—that is, eat large quantities of food in a short time.

The Use and Misuse of Diets The topic of dieting is of great interest to many diverse groups in the United States, including the public, health professionals, policy makers, the media, and the powerful diet and food industries. On one side are the societal norms that promote a very lean, aesthetic body. This ideal is supported by $30 billion a year in sales of diet books, programs, videos, foods, and pills. On the other side are health professionals and a growing minority of the press. Although they recognize the alarmingly high rate of obesity, they are frustrated by high relapse rates and the obsession with excessive thinness that can lead to chronic dieting and serious health risks (Brownell, 2000; Brownell & Rodin, 1994).

Although many Americans regularly embark on a diet, few are successful in keeping weight off long-term. Some critics argue that all diets fail (Wooley & Garner, 1991). However, studies show that some individuals do lose weight and maintain the loss (Brownell & Cohen, 1995). How often this occurs and whether some diet programs work better than others are still open questions.

What we do know about losing weight is that the most effective programs include an exercise component. Exercise not only burns up calories, but continues to elevate the person's metabolic rate for several hours *after* the exercise. Also, exercise lowers a person's set point for weight, which makes it easier to maintain a lower weight (Bennett & Gurin, 1982).

Dieting is a pervasive concern of many Americans, but the population is not uniform and many people who are on diets should not be. A 10 percent reduction in body weight might produce striking benefits for an older, obese, hypertensive man but be unhealthy for a female college student who is not overweight. The pressure to be thin, and thus diet, is greatest among young women, yet they do not have the highest risk of obesity.

Even when diets do produce weight loss, they can place the dieter at risk for other health problems. One main concern focuses on weight cycling (commonly called "yo-yo dieting"), in which the person is in a recurring cycle of dieting and weight gain (Wadden & others, 1996). Researchers have found a link between frequent changes in weight and chronic disease (Brownell & Rodin, 1994). Also, liquid diets and other very-low calorie strategies are related to gallbladder damage.

With these problems in mind, when overweight people diet and maintain their weight loss, they do become less depressed and reduce their risk for a number of health-impairing disorders (Christensen, 1996).

One individual who has conducted extensive research on eating behavior is Judith Rodin. To read about her work, see the Careers in Life-Span Development insert.

Regular Exercise

In 1961, President John F. Kennedy offered this message: "We are under-exercised as a nation. We look instead of play. We ride instead of walk. Our existence deprives us of the minimum of physical activity essential for healthy living." Without question, people are jogging, cycling, and aerobically exercising more today than in 1961, but far too many of us are still couch potatoes, spending most of our leisure time in front of the TV or a computer screen.

One of the main reasons that health experts want people to exercise is that it helps to prevent heart disease (Williams, 2001). Although exercise designed to strengthen muscles and bones or to improve flexibility is important to fitness, many health experts have stressed aerobic exercise. **Aerobic exercise** is sustained exercise—jogging, swimming, or cycling, for example—that stimulates heart and lung activity.

People in some occupations get more vigorous exercise than those in others (Howley, 2001). For example, longshoremen, who are on their feet all day and lift, push, and carry heavy cargo, have about half the risk of fatal heart attacks as co-workers like crane drivers and clerks, who have physically less demanding jobs. Elaborate studies of 17,000 male alumni of Harvard University found that those who exercised strenuously on a regular basis had a lower risk of heart disease and were more likely to still be alive in their middle adulthood years than their more sedentary counterparts (Lee, Hsieh, & Paffenbarger, 1995; Paffenbarger & others, 1986).

Some experts conclude that, regardless of other risk factors (smoking, high blood pressure, overweight, heredity), if you exercise enough to burn more than 2,000 calories a week, you can cut your risk of heart attack by an impressive two-thirds (Sherwood, Light, & Blumenthal, 1989). Burning up 2,000 calories a week through exercise requires a lot of effort, far more than most of us are willing to expend. To burn 300 calories a day, through exercise, you would have to do one of the following: swim or run for about 25 minutes, walk for 45 minutes at about 4 miles an hour, or participate in aerobic dancing for 30 minutes.

As a more realistic goal, health experts recommend that adults engage in 30 minutes or more of moderate-intensity physical activity on most, preferably all, days of the week. Most recommend that you should try to raise your heart rate to at least 60 percent of your maximum heart rate. However, only about one-fifth of adults are active at these recommended levels of physical activity. Examples of the physical activities that qualify as moderate or vigorous are listed in figure 14.6 on page 450.

Researchers have found that exercise benefits not only physical health, but mental health as well (King, 2000; Phillips, Kiernan, & King, 2001). In particular, exercise improves self-concept and reduces anxiety and depression (Moses & others, 1989).

Research on the benefits of exercise suggests that both moderate and intense activities produce important physical and psychological gains (Thayer & others, 1996). Some people enjoy rigorous, intense exercise. Others enjoy more moderate exercise routines. The enjoyment and pleasure we derive from exercise added to its aerobic benefits make exercise one of life's most important activities.

Here are some helpful strategies for building exercise into your life:

- *Reduce TV time.* Heavy TV viewing by college students is linked to poor health (Astin, 1983). Replace some of your TV time with exercise.

What role does exercise play in losing weight?

mhhe●com/
santrockld9

Aerobic Institute
Women and Exercise

aerobic exercise Sustained exercise (such as jogging, swimming, or cycling) that stimulates heart and lung activity.

Moderate	Vigorous
Walking, briskly (3 to 4 mph)	Walking, briskly uphill or with a load
Cycling, for pleasure or transportation (≤10 mph)	Cycling, fast or racing (>10 mph)
Swimming, moderate effort	Swimming, fast treading crawl
Conditioning exercise, general calisthenics	Conditioning exercise, stair ergometer or ski machine
Racket sports, table tennis	Racket sports, singles tennis or racketball
Golf, pulling cart or carrying clubs	Golf, practice at driving range
Canoeing, leisurely (2.0 to 3.9 mph)	Canoeing, rapidly (≥ 4 mph)
Home care, general cleaning	Moving furniture
Mowing lawn, with power mower	Mowing lawn, with hand mower
Home repair, painting	Home repair, fix-up projects

FIGURE 14.6 Moderate and Vigorous Physical Activities

- *Chart your progress.* Systematically recording your exercise workouts will help you to chart your progress. This strategy is especially helpful over the long term.
- *Get rid of excuses.* People make up all kinds of excuses for not exercising. A typical excuse is, "I don't have enough time." You likely do have enough time.
- *Imagine the alternative.* Ask yourself whether you are too busy to take care of your own health. What will your life be like if you lose your health?
- *Learn more about exercise.* The more you know about exercise, the more you are likely to start an exercise program and continue it.

Substance Abuse

In chapter 12, "Physical and Cognitive Development in Adolescence," we explored the nature of substance abuse in adolescence ◀║║ p. 381. Let's now examine the extent of substance abuse in college students and young adults.

Alcohol Heavy, binge drinking often increases in college, and it can take its toll on students (Bachman & others, 1996; Schulenberg, 1999; Schulenberg & Maggs, in press) (see figure 14.7). Chronic binge drinking is more common among college men than women and students living away from home, especially in fraternity houses (Schulenberg & others, 2000). In a national survey of drinking patterns on 140 campuses, almost half of the binge drinkers reported problems that included (Wechsler & others, 1994):

- missing classes,
- physical injuries,
- troubles with police, and
- having unprotected sex.

For example, binge-drinking college students were 11 times more likely to fall behind in school, 10 times more likely to drive after drinking, and twice as likely to have unprotected sex than college students who did not binge drink.

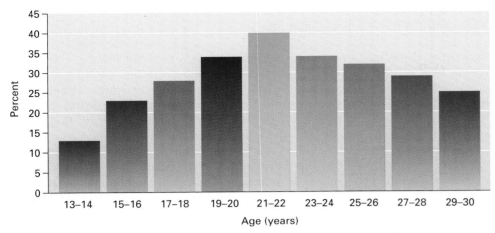

FIGURE 14.7 Binge Drinking in the Adolescence-Early Adulthood Transition

Note that the percentage of individuals engaging in binge drinking peaked at 21 to 22 years of age and then began to gradually decline through the remainder of the twenties. Binge drinking was defined as having five or more alcoholic drinks in a row in the past two weeks.

More than 40,000 full-time U.S. college students were asked about their drinking habits in 1993, 1997, 1999, and 2001 (Wechsler & others, 2002). Binge-drinking rates (men who drank five or more drinks in a row and women who drank four or more drinks at least once in the two weeks prior to the questionnaire) remained remarkably consistent—at about 44 percent—over the eight years. Further, almost 75 percent of underage students living in fraternities or sororities were binge drinkers and 70 percent of traditional-age college students who lived away from home were binge drinkers. The lowest rate of binge drinking—25 percent—occurred for students living at home with their parents.

A special concern is the increase in binge drinking by females during emerging adulthood. One study found a 125 percent increase in binge drinking at all-women colleges from 1993 through 2001 (Wechsler & others, 2002).

Fortunately, by the time individuals reach their mid twenties, many have reduced their use of alcohol and drugs. That is the conclusion reached by Jerald Bachman and his colleagues (1996, 2002) in a longitudinal analysis of more than 38,000 individuals. They were evaluated from the time they were high school seniors through their twenties. Here are some of the main findings in the study:

- College students drink more than youths who end their education after high school.
- Those who don't go to college smoke more.
- Singles use marijuana more than married individuals.
- Drinking is heaviest among singles and divorced individuals. Becoming engaged, married, or even remarried quickly brings down alcohol use. Thus, living arrangements and marital status are key factors in alcohol and drug use rates during the twenties.
- Individuals who considered religion to be very important in their lives and who frequently attended religious services are less likely to take drugs than their less religious counterparts.

Around the world, there are differences in alcohol use by religion and gender (Koenig, 2001; Melinder & Anderson, 2001). Catholics, Reform Jews, and liberal Protestants all consume alcohol at a fairly high level. Males drink alcohol more than females do.

Europeans, especially the French, drink alcohol at high rates. Estimates are that about 30 percent of French adults have impaired health related to alcohol

mhhe ●com/
santrockld9

CLearinghouse for Drug
Information
Alcoholism
Smoking/Tobacco Control
Smoking Cessation

consumption. Alcohol use is also high in Russia but its use in China is low. In some religions, such as the Mormon and Muslim religions, use of alcohol is forbidden.

Cigarette Smoking Converging evidence from a number of studies underscores the dangers of smoking or being around those who do (Millis, 1998; Pomerleaw, 2000). For example, smoking is linked to 30 percent of cancer deaths, 21 percent of heart disease deaths, and 82 percent of chronic pulmonary disease deaths. Second-hand smoke is implicated in as many as 9,000 lung cancer deaths a year. Children of smokers are at special risk for respiratory and middle-ear diseases.

Fewer people smoke today than in the past, and almost half of all living adults who ever smoked have quit. The prevalence of smoking in men has dropped from over 50 percent in 1965 to about 28 percent today (National Center for Health Statistics, 2000). However, more than 50 million Americans still smoke cigarettes today. And cigar smoking and tobacco chewing, with risks similar to those of cigarette smoking, have increased.

Most adult smokers would like to quit, but their addiction to nicotine often makes quitting a challenge. Nicotine, the active drug in cigarettes, is a stimulant that increases the smoker's energy and alertness, a pleasurable and reinforcing experience. Nicotine also stimulates neurotransmitters that have a calming or pain-reducing effect.

How can smokers quit? Five main methods are used to help smokers quit:

- *Using a substitute source of nicotine.* Nicotine gum, the nicotine patch, the nicotine inhaler, and nicotine spray work on the principle of supplying small amounts of nicotine to diminish the intensity of withdrawal. Recent research shows that the percentage of individuals who are still not smoking after five months ranges from 18 percent for the nicotine patch to 30 percent for the nicotine spray (Centers for Disease Control and Prevention, 2001).
- *Taking an antidepressant. Bupropion ST,* an antidepressant sold as Zyban, helps smokers control their cravings while they ease off nicotine. Recent research indicates that smokers using Zyban to quit have had a 30 percent average success rate for five months after they started taking the drug (Centers for Disease Control and Prevention, 2001).
- *Controlling stimuli associated with smoking.* This behavior modification technique sensitizes the smoker to social cues associated with smoking. For example, the smoker might associate a morning cup of coffee or a social drink with smoking. Stimulus control strategies help the smoker to avoid these cues or learn to substitute other behaviors for smoking.
- *Going "cold turkey."* Some people succeed by simply stopping smoking without making any major changes in their lifestyle. They decide they are going to quit and they do. Lighter smokers usually have more success with this approach than heavier smokers.

Studies indicate that when people do stop smoking their risk of cancer is reduced (Centers for Disease Control and Prevention, 2000). Five years after people stop smoking their health risk is noticeably lower than people who continue to smoke (U.S. Surgeon General's Report, 1990).

Addiction **Addiction** is a pattern of behavior characterized by an overwhelming involvement with using a drug and securing its supply. This can occur despite adverse consequences associated with the use of the drug. There is a strong tendency to relapse after quitting or withdrawal. Withdrawal symptoms consist of significant changes in physical functioning and behavior. Depending on the drug, these symptoms might include insomnia, tremors, nausea, vomiting, cramps, elevation of heart rate and blood pressure, convulsions, anxiety, and depression when a physically dependent person stops taking the drug. Experts on drug abuse use the term *addiction* to

addiction A pattern of behavior characterized by an overwhelming involvement with using a drug and securing its supply.

describe either a physical or psychological dependence on the drug or both (Pinger & others, 2001).

Controversy continues about whether addictions are diseases (Ray & Ksir, 2002). The **disease model of addiction** describes addictions as biologically based, lifelong diseases that involve a loss of control over behavior and require medical and/or spiritual treatment for recovery. In the disease model, addiction is either inherited or bred into a person early in life. Current or recent problems or relationships are not believed to be causes of the disease. Once involved in the disease, you can never completely rid yourself of it, according to this model. The disease model has been strongly promoted and supported by the medical profession and Alcoholics Anonymous (AA) (Humphreys, 2000).

In contrast to the disease model of addiction, which focuses on biological mechanisms, some psychologists believe that understanding addiction requires that it be placed in context as part of people's lives, their personalities, their relationships, their environments, and their perspectives. In this **life-process model of addiction,** addiction is not a disease but rather a habitual response and a source of gratification or security that can be understood best in the context of social relationships and experiences.

Each of these views of addiction—the disease model and the non-disease, life-process model—has its supporters.

About one-third of alcoholics recover whether they are in a treatment program or not. This figure was found in a long-term study of 700 individuals over 50 years and has consistently been found by other researchers as well (Vaillant, 1992). There is a "one-third rule" for alcoholism: by age 65, one-third are dead or in terrible shape, one-third are abstinent or drinking socially, and one-third are still trying to beat their addiction. A positive outcome and recovery from alcoholism are predicted by certain factors: (1) a strong negative experience related to drinking, such as a serious medical emergency or condition; (2) finding a substitute dependency to compete with alcohol abuse, such as meditation, exercise, or overeating (which of course has its own negative health consequences); (3) having new social supports (such as a concerned, helpful employer or a new marriage); and (4) joining an inspirational group, such as a religious organization or AA (Vaillant, 1992).

Review and Reflect

2 Identify the changes in physical development in young adults

REVIEW

- How does physical development peak and then slow down in early adulthood?
- What are some important things to know about eating and weight?
- What are the benefits of exercise?
- How extensive is substance abuse in young adults? What effects does it have on their lives?

REFLECT

- To discourage smoking, many governments now levy heavy taxes on cigarettes because of their negative health effects. Would you recommend that the U.S. government levy similar heavy taxes on fatty foods because of their negative health effects? Explain.

disease model of addiction The view that addictions are biologically based, lifelong diseases that involve a loss of control over behavior and require medical and/or spiritual treatment for recovery.

life-process model of addiction The view that addiction is not a disease but rather a habitual response and a source of gratification and security that can be understood only in the context of social relationships and experiences.

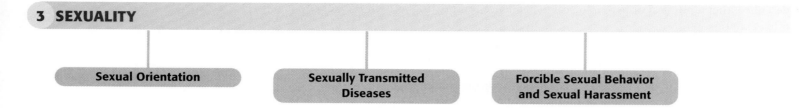

3 SEXUALITY

| Sexual Orientation | Sexually Transmitted Diseases | Forcible Sexual Behavior and Sexual Harassment |

We do not need sex for everyday survival the way we need food and water, but we do need it for the survival of the species. What is the nature of heterosexuality and homosexuality in the human species?

Sexual Orientation

Let's now explore sexual orientation and various aspects of heterosexual and homosexual attitudes and behaviors.

Heterosexual Attitudes and Behavior In a well-designed, comprehensive study of Americans' sexual patterns, Robert Michael and his colleagues (1994) interviewed more than 3,000 people from 18 to 59 years of age who were randomly selected, a sharp contrast from earlier samples that were based on unrepresentative groups of volunteers.

Here are some of the key findings from the 1994 Sex in America survey:

- Americans tend to fall into three categories: One-third have sex twice a week or more, one-third a few times a month, and one-third a few times a year or not at all.
- Married couples have sex the most and also are the most likely to have orgasms when they do. Figure 14.8 portrays the frequency of sex for married and noncohabiting individuals in the past year.
- Most Americans do not engage in kinky sexual acts. When asked about their favorite sexual acts, the vast majority (96 percent) said that vaginal sex was

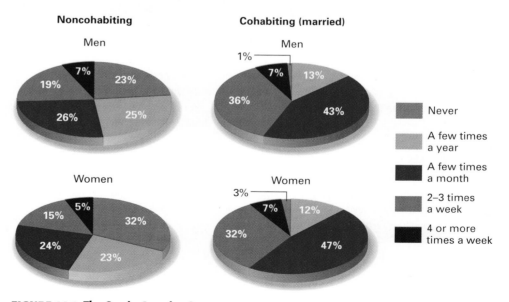

FIGURE 14.8 The Sex in America Survey

Percentages show noncohabiting and cohabiting (married) males' and females' responses to the question "How often have you had sex in the past year?"

"very" or "somewhat" appealing. Oral sex was in third place, after an activity that many have not labeled a sexual act—watching a partner undress.

- Adultery is clearly the exception rather than the rule. Nearly 75 percent of the married men and 85 percent of the married women indicated that they have never been unfaithful.
- Men think about sex far more than women do—54 percent of the men said they think about it every day or several times a day, whereas 67 percent of the women said they think about it only a few times a week or a few times a month.

In sum, one of the most powerful messages in the 1994 survey was that Americans' sexual lives are more conservative than previously believed. Although 17 percent of the men and 3 percent of the women said they have had sex with at least 21 partners, the overall impression from the survey was that sexual behavior is ruled by marriage and monogamy for most Americans.

Homosexual Attitudes and Behavior   Until the end of the nineteenth century, it was generally believed that people were either heterosexual or homosexual. Today, it is more accepted to view sexual orientation along a continuum from exclusive heterosexuality to exclusive homosexuality rather than as an either/or proposition (see figure 14.9). Some individuals are also *bisexual,* being sexually attracted to people of both sexes. In the Sex in America survey, 2.7 percent of the men and 1.3 percent of the women reported that they had had homosexual sex in the past year (Michael & others, 1994).

Why are some individuals homosexual and others heterosexual? Speculation about this question has been extensive (Herek, 2000). Homosexuals and heterosexuals have similar physiological responses during sexual arousal and seem to be aroused by the same types of tactile stimulation. Investigators find no differences between homosexuals and heterosexuals in a wide range of attitudes, behaviors, and adjustments (Bell, Weinberg, & Mammersmith, 1981). Homosexuality once was classified as a mental disorder, but both the American Psychiatric Association and the American Psychological Association discontinued this classification as a mental disorder in the 1970s.

Recently, researchers have explored the possible biological basis of homosexuality (D'Auqelli, 2000; Gladue, 1994). The results of hormone studies have been inconsistent. If male homosexuals are given male sex hormones (androgens), their sexual orientation doesn't change. Their sexual desire merely increases. A very early prenatal critical period might influence sexual orientation. In the second to fifth months after conception, exposure of the fetus to hormone levels characteristic of females might

mhhe com/
santrockld9

**Human Sexuality
American Sexual Behavior
Lesbian and Gay Issues**

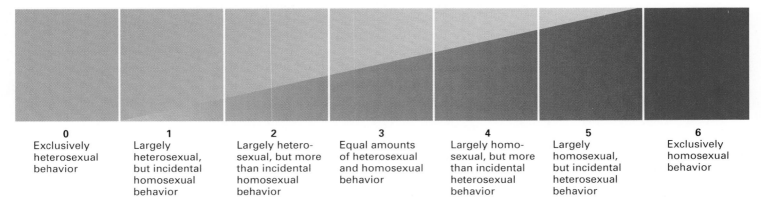

0	1	2	3	4	5	6
Exclusively heterosexual behavior	Largely heterosexual, but incidental homosexual behavior	Largely heterosexual, but more than incidental homosexual behavior	Equal amounts of heterosexual and homosexual behavior	Largely homosexual, but more than incidental heterosexual behavior	Largely homosexual, but incidental heterosexual behavior	Exclusively homosexual behavior

FIGURE 14.9 The Continuum of Sexual Orientation

The continuum ranges from exclusive heterosexuality, which Kinsey and associates (1948) rated as 0, to exclusive homosexuality (6). People who are about equally attracted to both sexes (ratings 2 to 4) are bisexual.

What likely determines an individual's sexual preference?

mhhe ● com/
santrockld9

Center for AIDS Prevention Studies

HIV/STD Education

Signs of HIV Infection in Females

sexually transmitted diseases (STDs)
Diseases that are contracted primarily through sex.

acquired immune deficiency syndrome (AIDS) A sexually transmitted disease caused by the HIV virus, which destroys the body's immune system.

cause the individual (male or female) to become attracted to males (Ellis & Ames, 1987). If this critical-period hypothesis turns out to be correct, it would explain why clinicians have found that sexual orientation is difficult, if not impossible, to modify.

With regard to anatomical structures, neuroscientist Simon LeVay (1991) found that an area of the hypothalamus that governs sexual behavior is twice as large (about the size of a grain of sand) in heterosexual males as in homosexual males. This area was found to be about the same size in homosexual males and heterosexual females. Critics of this research point out that many of the homosexuals in the study had AIDS and suggest that their brains could have been altered by the disease.

An individual's sexual orientation—homosexual, heterosexual, or bisexual—is most likely determined by a combination of genetic, hormonal, cognitive, and environmental factors (Baldwin & Baldwin, 1998). Most experts on homosexuality believe that no one factor alone causes homosexuality and that the relative weight of each factor can vary from one individual to the next. In effect, no one knows exactly why some individuals are homosexual. Scientists have a clearer picture of what does not cause homosexuality. For example, children raised by gay or lesbian parents or couples are no more likely to be homosexual than are children raised by heterosexual parents (Patterson, 2002). There also is no evidence that male homosexuality is caused by a dominant mother or a weak father, or that female homosexuality is caused by girls choosing male role models.

How can gays and lesbians adapt to a world in which they are a minority? According to psychologist Laura Brown (1989), gays and lesbians experience life as a minority in a dominant, majority culture. For lesbian women and gay men, developing a *bicultural identity* creates new ways of defining themselves. Brown believes that gays and lesbians adapt best when they don't define themselves in polarities, such as trying to live in an encapsulated gay or lesbian world completely divorced from the majority culture or completely accepting the dictates and bias of the majority culture. Balancing the demands of the two cultures—the minority gay/lesbian culture and the majority heterosexual culture—can often lead to more effective coping for homosexuals, says Brown.

Sexually Transmitted Diseases

Sexually transmitted diseases (STDs) are diseases that are primarily contracted through sex—intercourse as well as oral-genital and anal-genital sex. STDs affect about one of every six U.S. adults (National Center for Health Statistics, 2001). Among the main STDs are bacterial infections (such as gonorrhea, syphilis, and chlamydia), and STDs caused by viruses—genital herpes, genital warts, and AIDS. Figure 14.10 describes these sexually transmitted diseases.

No single STD has had a greater impact on sexual behavior, or created more public fear in the last several decades than AIDS (Kelly, 2002). **Acquired immune deficiency syndrome (AIDS)** is a sexually transmitted disease that is caused by the human immunodeficiency virus (HIV), which destroys the body's immune system. Following exposure to HIV, an individual's body is vulnerable to germs that a normal immune system could destroy.

As of June 2000, more than 26,000 cases of AIDS in 20- to 24-year-olds had been reported in the United States with about 80 percent of these being males and almost half intravenous (IV) drug users (Centers for Disease Control and Prevention, 2001). Because of education and the development of more effective drug treatments, deaths due to AIDS have begun to decline in the United States (National Center for Health Statistics, 2001). The greatest concern about AIDS is in sub-Saharan Africa, where it has reached epidemic proportions (World Health Organization, 2000).

Just asking a date about his or her sexual behavior does not guarantee protection from AIDS and other sexually transmitted diseases. For example, in one investigation, 655 college students were asked to answer questions about lying and sexual behavior (Cochran & Mays, 1990). Of the 422 respondents who said they were sexually active, 34 percent of the men and 10 percent of the women said they had lied so their part-

STD	Description/cause	Incidence	Treatment
Gonorrhea	Commonly called the "drip" or "clap." Caused by the bacterium *Neisseria gonorrhoeae*. Spread by contact between infected moist membranes (genital, oral-genital, or anal-genital) of two individuals. Characterized by discharge from penis or vagina and painful urination. Can lead to infertility.	500,000 cases annually in U.S.	Penicillin, other antibiotics
Syphilis	Caused by the bacterium *Treponema palladium*. Characterized by the appearance of a sore where syphilis entered the body. The sore can be on the external genitals, vagina, or anus. Later, a skin rash breaks out on palms of hands and bottom of feet. If not treated, can eventually lead to paralysis or even death.	100,000 cases annually in U.S.	Penicillin
Chlamydia	A common STD named for the bacterium *Chlamydia trachomatis*, an organism that spreads by sexual contact and infects the genital organs of both sexes. A special concern is that females with chlamydia may become infertile. It is recommended that adolescent and young adult females have an annual screening for this STD.	About 3 million people in U.S. annually; estimates are that 10 percent of adolescent girls have this STD.	Antibiotics
Genital herpes	Caused by a family of viruses with different strains. Involves an eruption of sores and blisters. Spread by sexual contact.	One of five U.S. adolescents and adults	No known cure but antiviral medications can shorten outbreaks
AIDS	Caused by a virus, the human immunodeficiency virus (HIV) that destroys the body's immune system. Semen and blood are the main vehicles of transmission. Common symptoms include fevers, night sweats, weight loss, chronic fatigue, and swollen lymph nodes.	4,000 13- to 19-year-olds in the U.S.; epidemic incidence in sub-Saharan adolescent girls	New treatments have slowed the progression from HIV to AIDS; no cure
Genital warts	Caused by the human papillomavirus, which does not always produce symptoms. Usually appear as small, hard painless bumps in the vaginal area, or around the anus. Very contagious. Certain high-risk types of this virus cause cervical cancer and other genital cancers. May recur despite treatment	About 5.5 million new cases annually; considered the most common STD in the U.S.	A topical drug, freezing, or surgery.

FIGURE 14.10 Sexually Transmitted Diseases

ner would have sex with them. Much higher percentages—47 percent of the men and 60 percent of the women—said they had been lied to by a potential sexual partner. When asked what aspects of their past they would be most likely to lie about, more than 40 percent of the men and women said they would understate the number of their sexual partners. Twenty percent of the men, but only 4 percent of the women, said they would lie about their results from an AIDS blood test.

What are some good strategies for protecting against AIDS and other sexually transmitted diseases? They include:

- *Knowing your and your partner's risk status.* Anyone who has had previous sexual activity with another person might have contracted an STD without being aware of it. Spend time getting to know a prospective partner before you have sex. Use this time to inform the other person of your STD status and inquire about your partner's. Remember that many people lie about their STD status.
- *Obtaining medical examinations.* Many experts recommend that couples who want to begin a sexual relationship should have a medical checkup to rule out STDs before they engage in sex. If cost is an issue, contact your campus health service or a public health clinic.
- *Having protected, not unprotected, sex.* When correctly used, latex condoms help to prevent many STDs from being transmitted. Condoms are most effective in preventing gonorrhea, syphilis, chlamydia, and AIDS. They are less effective against the spread of herpes.

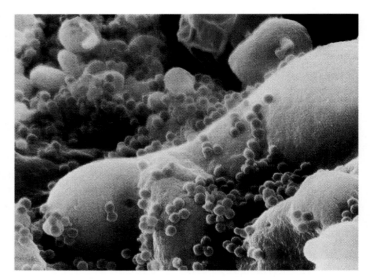

HIV attacking the body's immune system. Each blue sphere is an HIV virus.

What are some good strategies for protecting against AIDS and other sexually transmitted diseases? How effectively have you practiced these strategies?

- *Not having sex with multiple partners.* One of the best predictors of getting an STD is having sex with multiple partners. Having more than one sex partner elevates the likelihood that you will encounter an infected partner.

Forcible Sexual Behavior and Sexual Harassment

Too often, sexual behavior becomes forcible and is engaged in against another person's will. Also, concern about sexual harassment has increased in recent years.

Rape **Rape** is forcible sexual intercourse with a person who does not give consent. Legal definitions of rape differ from state to state. For example, in some states, husbands are not prohibited from forcing their wives to have intercourse, although this has been challenged in several states. Because of difficulties involved in reporting rape, the actual incidence is not easily determined. It appears that rape occurs most often in large cities, where it has been reported that 8 of every 10,000 women 12 years and older are raped each year. Nearly 200,000 rapes are reported each year in the United States.

An increasing concern is **date or acquaintance rape,** which is coercive sexual activity directed at someone with whom the individual is at least casually acquainted. Date rape is an increasing problem on college campuses (Rosen & Stith, 1995). As many as two-thirds of college males admit to fondling females against their will and one-half admit to forced sexual activity.

Why is rape so pervasive in the American culture? Among the causes given are that males are socialized to be sexually aggressive, to regard women as inferior beings, and to view their own pleasure as the most important objective. Researchers have found these common characteristics among rapists: aggression enhances the offender's sense of power or masculinity; rapists are angry at women generally; and they want to hurt and humiliate the victim (Browne & Williams, 1993).

Rape is a traumatic experience for the victim and those close to her (Bachar & Koss, 2002). The rape victim initially feels shock and numbness, and is often acutely disorganized. Some women show their distress through words and tears, others show more internalized suffering. As victims strive to get their lives back to normal, they may experience depression, fear, and anxiety for months or years. Sexual dysfunctions, such as reduced sexual desire and an inability to reach orgasm, occur in 50 percent of rape victims (Sprei & Courtois, 1988). Many rape victims make changes in their lifestyle—such as moving to a new apartment or refusing to go out at night. A woman's recovery depends on both her coping abilities and her psychological adjustment prior to the assault. Social support from parents, boyfriend or husband and others close to her are important factors in recovery, as is the availability of professional counseling, which sometimes is obtained through a rape crisis center (Allison & Wrightsman, 1993).

Although most victims of rape are women, male rape does occur. Men in prisons are especially vulnerable to rape, usually by heterosexual males who use rape as a means of establishing their dominance and power. Though it might seem impossible for a man to be raped by a woman, a man's erection is not completely under his voluntary control, and some cases of male rape by women have been reported (Sarrel & Masters, 1982). Although male victims account for fewer than 5 percent of all rapes, the trauma that males suffer is just as great as that experienced by females.

Sexual Harassment Women encounter sexual harassment in many different forms—from sexist remarks and covert physical contact (patting, brushing against

mhhe●com/
santrockld9

Sexual Assault

Sexual Harassment

rape Forcible sexual intercourse with a person who does not consent to it.

date or acquaintance rape Coercive sexual activity directed at someone with whom the perpetrator is at least casually acquainted.

their bodies) to blatant propositions and sexual assaults (Fitzgerald, 2000; Fitzgerald, Collinsworth, & Harned, 2002; Ogoski, 2001). Literally millions of women experience such sexual harassment each year in work and educational settings. Sexual harassment can result in serious psychological consequences for the victim. Sexual harassment is a manifestation of power and domination of one person over another. The elimination of such exploitation requires the development of work and academic environments that are compatible with the needs of women workers and students, providing them with equal opportunities to develop a career and obtain an education in a climate free of sexual harassment (Marks & Nelson, 1993). Sexual harassment of men by women does occur, but to a far less extent than the sexual harassment of women by men.

Review and Reflect

3 **Discuss sexuality in young adults**

REVIEW

- What is the nature of heterosexuality and homosexuality?
- What are sexually transmitted diseases? What are some important things to know about AIDS?
- What are the effects of forcible sexual behavior and sexual harassment?

REFLECT

- What can be done to reduce forcible sexual behavior and sexual harassment?

4 COGNITIVE DEVELOPMENT

Cognitive Stages   **Creativity**

To explore the nature of cognition in early adulthood, we will focus on issues related to cognitive stages and creative thinking.

Cognitive Stages

Are young adults more advanced in their thinking than adolescents? Let's explore what Piaget and others have said about this intriguing question.

Piaget's View   Piaget believed that an adolescent and an adult think qualitatively in the same way. That is, Piaget argued that formal operational thought (more logical, abstract, and idealistic than the concrete operational thinking of 7- to 11-year-olds) is entered in early adolescence at approximately 11 to 15 years of age ◀‖‖ p. 386. Piaget did believe that young adults are more *quantitatively* advanced in their thinking in the sense that they have more knowledge than adolescents. He also believed, as do information-processing psychologists, that adults especially increase their knowledge in a specific area, such as a physicist's understanding of physics or a financial analyst's knowledge about finance.

Some developmentalists believe it is not until adulthood that many individuals consolidate their formal operational thinking. That is, they may begin to plan and hypothesize about intellectual problems in adolescence, but they become more systematic and sophisticated at this as young adults. Nonetheless, many adults do not think in formal operational ways at all (Keating, 1980).

Realistic and Pragmatic Thinking   Other developmentalists believe that the idealism Piaget described as part of formal operational thinking decreases in early adulthood. This especially occurs as young adults move into the world of work and face the constraints of reality (Labouvie-Vief, 1986).

A related perspective on adult cognitive change was proposed by K. Warner Schaie and Sherry Willis (2000). They concluded that it is unlikely that adults go beyond the powerful methods of scientific thinking characteristic of the formal operational stage. However, Schaie argued that adults do progress beyond adolescents in their *use* of intellect. For example, he said that in early adulthood individuals often switch from acquiring knowledge to applying knowledge. This especially occurs as individuals pursue long-term career goals and attempt to achieve success in their work.

Reflective and Relativistic Thinking   William Perry (1970, 1999) also described some changes in cognition that take place in early adulthood. He said that adolescents often view the world in terms of polarities—right/wrong, we/they, good/bad. As youth move into adulthood, they gradually move away from this type of absolute thinking as they become aware of the diverse opinions and multiple perspectives of others. Thus, in Perry's view, the *absolute, dualistic thinking* (either/or) of adolescence gives way to the *reflective, relativistic thinking* of adulthood.

As we see next, some theorists have pieced together some of these different aspects of thinking and proposed a new qualitative stage of cognitive development.

Is There a Fifth, Postformal Stage?   Some theorists have pieced together cognitive changes in young adults and proposed a new stage of cognitive development. **Postformal thought** is qualitatively different from Piaget's formal operational thought. Postformal thought involves understanding that the correct answer to a problem requires reflective thinking and can vary from one situation to another, and that the search for truth is often an ongoing, never-ending process. Postformal thought also includes the belief that solutions to problems need to be realistic and that emotion and subjective factors can influence thinking (Kitchener & King, 1981; Kramer, Kahlbaugh, & Goldston, 1992). Researchers have found that young adults are more likely to engage in this postformal thinking than adolescents are (Commons & others, 1989).

As young adults engage in more reflective judgment when solving problems, they might think deeply about many aspects of politics, their career and work, relationships, and other areas of life (Labouvie-Vief & Diehl, 1999). They might understand that what might be the best solution to a problem at work (with a co-worker or boss) might not be the best solution at home (with a romantic partner). Many young adults also become more skeptical about there being a single truth and often are not willing to accept an answer as final. They also often recognize that thinking can't just be abstract but rather has to be realistic and pragmatic. And many young adults understand that emotions can play a role in thinking—for example, that one likely thinks more clearly in a calm, collected state than in an angry, highly aroused state.

How strong is the research evidence for a fifth, postformal stage of cognitive development? The fifth stage is controversial, and some critics argue that the research evidence has yet to be provided to document it as clearly a qualitatively more advanced stage than formal operational thought.

Creativity

In chapter 10, "Physical and Cognitive Development in Middle and Late Childhood," we studied creativity in children ◀▥ p. 324. The strategies for being creative in adulthood are essentially the same as in childhood. Here we focus on the issue of whether

postformal thought A form of thought that is qualitatively different from Piaget's formal operational thought. It involves understanding that the correct answer to a problem can require reflective thinking, that the correct answer can vary from one situation to another, and that the search for truth is often an ongoing, never-ending process. It also involves the belief that solutions to problems need to be realistic and that emotion and subjective factors can influence thinking.

U.S. Poet Laureate Mark Strand says that in his most creative moments he loses a sense of time and becomes absorbed in what he is doing. In this state, he feels he is dismantling meaning and remaking it. Strand comments that he can't stay in this absorbed frame of mind for an entire day. It comes and goes. His attention coils and uncoils. His focus sharpens and softens. When an idea clicks, he focuses intensely, transforming the idea into a vivid verbal image that communicates its essence to the reader.

Nina Holton, a leading contemporary sculptor, turns playful wild germs of ideas into stunning sculptures. She says that sculpture is a combination of wonderful, unique ideas and a lot of hard work. She comments that when she is introduced to people they often say, "It must be so exciting and wonderful being a sculptor." Holton loves her work, but says that most people see only its creative side, not the hard work.

Jonas Salk, who invented the polio vaccine, says that his best ideas come to him at night when he suddenly wakes up. After about five minutes of visualizing problems he had thought about the day before, he begins to see an unfolding, as if a poem, painting, story, or concept is about to take form. Salk also believes that many creative ideas are generated through conversations with others who have open, curious minds and positive attitudes. Salk's penchant for seeing emergent possibilities often brought him into conflict with people who had orthodox opinions.

creativity might decline at some point in adulthood and explore Mihaly Csikszentmihalyi's ideas about how to lead a more creative life.

Adult Developmental Changes   At the age of 30, Thomas Edison invented the phonograph, Hans Christian Anderson wrote his first volume of fairy tales, and Mozart composed *The Marriage of Figaro.* One early study of creativity found that individuals' most creative products were generated in their thirties and that 80 percent of the most important creative contributions were completed by age 50 (Lehman, 1960). More recently, researchers have found that creativity does peak in adulthood and then decline, but that the peak often occurs in the forties. However, qualifying any conclusion about age and creative accomplishments are (1) the magnitude of the decline in productivity, (2) contrasts across creative domains, and (3) individual differences in lifetime output (Simonton, 1996).

Even though a decline in creative contributions is often found in the fifties and later, the decline is not as great as commonly thought. An impressive array of creative accomplishments occur in late adulthood. Benjamin Franklin invented the bifocal lens when he was 78 years old; Goethe completed *Faust* when he was in his eighties. And one of the most remarkable examples of creative accomplishment in late adulthood can be found in the life of Henri Chevreul. After a distinguished career as a physicist, Chevreul switched fields in his nineties to become a pioneer in gerontological research. He published his last research paper just a year prior to his death at the age of 103!

Any consideration of decline in creativity with age requires consideration of the domain involved. In such fields as philosophy and history, older adults often show as much creativity as when they were in their thirties and forties. By contrast, in such fields as lyric poetry, abstract math, and theoretical physics, the peak of creativity is often reached in the twenties or thirties.

There also is extensive individual variation in the lifetime output of creative individuals. Typically, the most productive creators in any field are far more prolific than their least productive counterparts. The contrast is so extreme that the top 10 percent of creative producers frequently account for 50 percent of the creative output in a particular domain. For instance, only sixteen composers account for half of the music regularly performed in the classical repertoire.

Csikszentmihalyi's Ideas Mihaly Csikszentmihalyi (pronounced ME-high CHICK-sent-me-high-ee) (1995) interviewed 90 leading figures in art, business, government, education, and science to learn how creativity works. He discovered that creative people regularly experience a state he calls *flow,* a heightened state of pleasure we experience when we are engaged in mental and physical challenges that absorb us. Csikszentmihalyi (1997, 2000; Nakamura & Csikzsentmihalyi, 2002) believes everyone is capable of achieving flow. Based on his interviews with some of the most creative people in the world, the first step toward a more creative life is cultivating your curiosity and interest. How can you do this?

- *Try to be surprised by something every day.* Maybe it is something you see, hear, or read about. Become absorbed in a lecture or a book. Be open to what the world is telling you. Life is a stream of experiences. Swim widely and deeply in it, and your life will be richer.
- *Try to surprise at least one person every day.* In a lot of things you do, you have to be predictable and patterned. Do something different for a change. Ask a question you normally would not ask. Invite someone to go to a show or a museum you never have visited.
- *Write down each day what surprised you and how you surprised others.* Most creative people keep a diary, notes, or lab records to ensure that their experience is not fleeting or forgotten. Start with a specific task. Each evening record the most surprising event that occurred that day and your most surprising action. After a few days, reread your notes and reflect on your past experiences. After a few weeks, you might see a pattern of interest emerging in your notes, one that might suggest an area you can explore in greater depth.
- *When something sparks your interest, follow it.* Usually when something captures your attention, it is short-lived—an idea, a song, a flower. Too often we are too busy to explore the idea, song, or flower further. Or we think these areas are none of our business because we are not experts about them. Yet the world is our business. We can't know which part of it is best suited to our interests until we make a serious effort to learn as much about as many aspects of it as possible.
- *Wake up in the morning with a specific goal to look forward to.* Creative people wake up eager to start the day. Why? Not necessarily because they are cheerful, enthusiastic types but because they know that there is something meaningful to accomplish each day, and they can't wait to get started.
- *Take charge of your schedule.* Figure out which time of the day is your most creative time. Some of us are more creative late at night, others early in the morning. Carve out some time for yourself when your creative energy is at its best.
- *Spend time in settings that stimulate your creativity.* In Csikszentmihalyi's (1995) research, he gave people an electronic pager and beeped them randomly at different times of the day. When he asked them how they felt, they reported the highest levels of creativity when walking, driving, or swimming. I (your author) do my most creative thinking when I'm jogging. These activities are semiautomatic in that they take a certain amount of attention while leaving some time free to make connections among ideas. Another setting in which highly creative people report coming up with novel ideas is the sort of half-asleep, half-awake state we are in when we are deeply relaxed or barely awake.

To read further about Mihalyi Csikzentmihalyi's work, see the Careers in Life-Span Development insert. You will find out about the setting in which he gets his most creative ideas.

Careers in Life-Span Development

Mihaly Csikszentmihalyi, University Professor and Researcher

Mihaly Csikszentmihalyi, born in Hungary and a professor at the University of Chicago for many years, currently is a professor at Claremont Graduate School in California ◀||||| p. 30. Csikszentmihalyi has had a special interest in adolescents, initially conducting a number of research studies on what they do in their lives, the contexts in which they spend their time, and the people with whom they interact, and how they are feeling. He developed what is known as the experience sampling technique (the "beeper" technique) in which researchers give participants an electronic pager and contact them at random times, asking them a series of questions.

Csikszentmihalyi developed the concept of "flow"—the mental and emotional state people are in when they deeply enjoy what they are doing. Currently he is one of the main architects of changing psychology's focus from the negative to the positive, believing that for too long the field has studied the dark side of life and that it is high time psychologists started focusing more on the good aspects of people—things like optimistic thinking, being altruistic, having good relationships, and being creative.

He has conducted a study of highly creative people in different walks of life—business, the arts, science—to discover what they are thinking, feeling, and doing when they come up with their most creative insights (Csikszentmihalyi, 1995). One thing he found was that certain settings are more likely to stimulate creativity than others. *When and where do you get your most creative thoughts?*

Mihaly Csikszentmihalyi, in the setting where he gets his most creative ideas.

Review and Reflect

4 **Characterize cognitive changes in early adulthood**

REVIEW
- What changes in cognitive development in young adults have been proposed?
- Does creativity decline in adulthood? How can people lead more creative lives?

REFLECT
- What do you think are the most important cognitive changes that take place in young adults?

mhhe ●com/
santrockld9

Csikszentmihalyi

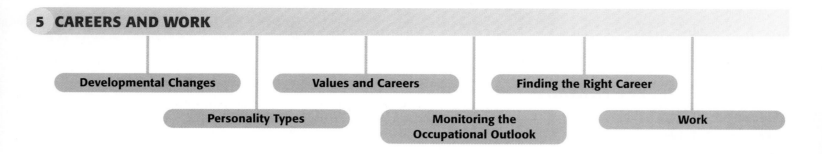

5 CAREERS AND WORK

Developmental Changes · Values and Careers · Finding the Right Career

Personality Types · Monitoring the Occupational Outlook · Work

At age 21, Thomas Smith graduated from college and accepted a job as a science teacher at a high school in Boston. At age 26, Mary Lou Hernandez graduated from medical school and took a job as an intern at a hospital in Los Angeles. At age 20, Barbara Breck finished her training at a vocational school and went to work as a computer programmer for an engineering firm in Chicago. Earning a living, choosing an occupation, establishing a career, and developing in a career—these are important themes of early adulthood.

Developmental Changes

Many children have idealistic fantasies about what they want to be when they grow up. For example, young children might want to be a superhero, a sports star, or a movie star. In the high school years, they often have begun to think about careers on a somewhat less idealistic basis. In their late teens and early twenties, their career decision making has usually turned more serious as they explore different career possibilities and zero in on the career they want to enter. In college, this often means choosing a major or specialization that is designed to lead to work in a particular field.

By their early and mid twenties, many individuals have completed their education or training and started to enter a full-time occupation. From the mid twenties through the remainder of early adulthood, individuals often seek to establish their emerging career in a particular field. They may work hard to move up the career ladder and improve their financial standing.

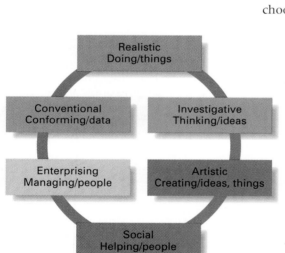

FIGURE 14.11 Holland's Model of Personality Types and Career Choices

Personality Types

Personality type theory is John Holland's (1987) view that it is important for individuals to select a career that matches up well with their personality type. Holland believes that when individuals find careers that fit their personality, they are more likely to enjoy the work and stay in the job longer than if they'd taken a job not suited to their personality. Holland proposed six basic career-related personality types: realistic, investigative, artistic, social, enterprising, and conventional (see figure 14.11):

- *Realistic.* They like the outdoors and working in manual activities. They often are less social, have difficulty in demanding situations, and prefer to work alone. This personality type matches up best with such jobs as laborer, farmer, truck driver, construction worker, engineer, and pilot.
- *Investigative.* They are interested in ideas more than people, are rather indifferent to social relationships, are troubled by emotional situations, and are often aloof and intelligent. This personality type matches up well with scientific, intellectually oriented professions.
- *Artistic.* They are creative and enjoy working with ideas and materials that allow them to express themselves in innovative ways. They value nonconformity,

personality type theory John Holland's view that it is important to match an individual's personality with a particular career.

freedom, and ambiguity. Sometimes they have difficulties in social relationships. Not many jobs match up with the artistic personality type. Consequently, some artistic individuals work in jobs that are their second or third choices and express their artistic interests through hobbies and leisure.

- *Social.* They like to work with people and tend to have a helping orientation. They like doing social things considerably more than engaging in intellectual tasks. This personality type matches up with jobs in teaching, social work, and counseling.
- *Enterprising.* They also are more oriented toward people than things or ideas. They may try to dominate others to reach their goals. They are often good at persuading others to do things. The enterprising type matches up with careers in sales, management, and politics.
- *Conventional.* They function best in well-structured situations and are skilled at working with details. They often like to work with numbers and perform clerical tasks rather than working with ideas or people. The conventional type matches up with such jobs as accountant, bank teller, secretary, or file clerk.

If all individuals (and careers) fell conveniently into Holland's personality types, career counselors would have an easy job. However, individuals are typically more varied and complex than Holland's theory suggests. Even Holland (1987) states that individuals rarely are pure types, and most persons are a combination of two or three types. Still, the basic idea of matching the abilities and attitudes of individuals to particular careers is an important contribution to the career development field. Holland's personality types are incorporated into the Strong-Campbell Interest Inventory, a widely used measure in career guidance.

Values and Careers

An important aspect of choosing a career is that it also match up with your values. When people know what they value most—what is important to them in life—they can refine their career choice more effectively. Some values are reflected in Holland's personality types, such as whether a person values working in a career that involves helping others or in a career in which creativity is valued. Among the values that some individuals think are important in choosing a career are working with people they like, working in a career with prestige, making a lot of money, being happy, not having to work long hours, being mentally challenged, having plenty of time for leisure pursuits, working in the right geographical location, and working where physical and mental health are important.

Monitoring the Occupational Outlook

It is a good idea for individuals to keep up with the occupational outlook for various fields. An excellent source is the *Occupational Outlook Handbook* (2002–2003), which is revised every two years.

Service-producing industries will account for most new jobs: Business, health, and professional services are projected to account for nearly 75 percent of job growth from 2000 to 2010. Employment in computer and data-processing services is projected to grow 86 percent in this time frame, ranking it as the fastest-growing industry. Indeed, the seven occupations with the fastest projected growth are all in the computer area (see figure 14.12). Employers today point out that no matter what their career aspirations, individuals will need computer skills to perform their job competently. The reality is that computer skills are not just nice to have—they are a must.

Jobs that require college degrees will be the fastest growing and highest paying. Jobs that require an associate degree from a community college

Holland's Personality Types

Steps to Successful Career Planning

Journal of Vocational Behavior Career Development Quarterly

Journal of Counseling Psychology

"Your son has made a career choice, Mildred. He's going to win the lottery and travel a lot."

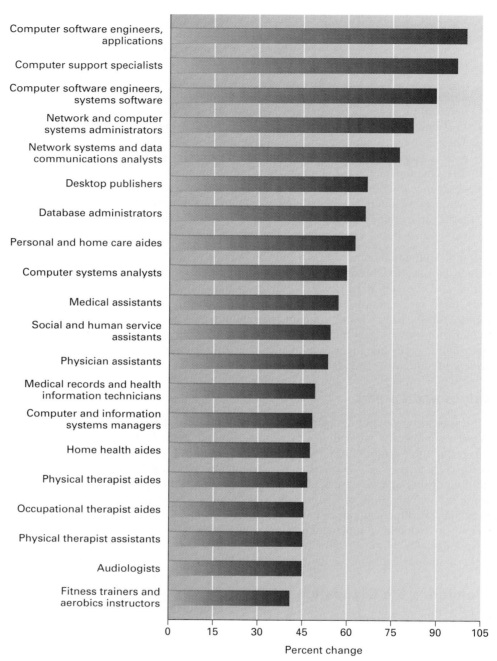

FIGURE 14.12 Percent Change in Employment in Occupations Projected to Grow the Fastest, 2000 to 2010.

are projected to increase more than 30 percent from 1998 to 2008, those that require a bachelor's degree or doctoral degree more than 25 percent, and those that require a master's degree more than 20 percent. All but a few of the highest-paying occupations require a college degree.

The labor force participation rates of women in nearly all age groups are projected to increase while that of men is anticipated to remain unchanged. The Asian American and Latino American labor forces are expected to increase faster than other

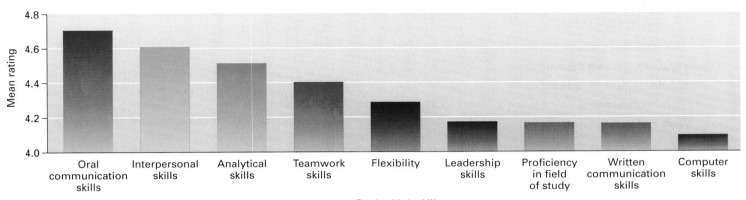

FIGURE 14.13 Desired Skills of an Ideal Job Candidate Rated by Employers

In a national survey of employers, desired characteristics of job applicants were rated on a scale of 1 = extremely unimportant to 5 = extremely important. Note how important communication skills were to the employers. Three of the four highest-rated skills were communication skills (oral, interpersonal, and teamwork).

ethnic groups, by 40 and 37 percent, respectively. It has been projected that by 2008, the Latino American labor force will be larger than the African American labor force.

Finding the Right Career

Take a few minutes and think about the career you want to pursue. What do you think the profile of an ideal job candidate in this career field would be?

To begin with, computer skills are increasingly important in most careers. In one national study, the communication skills of prospective job candidates were extremely important (Collins, 1996) (see figure 14.13). At the top of employers' wish lists of characteristics they desired in a future employee was oral communication skills.

To determine whether a candidate has the skills to succeed at the job, employers look for evidence in the candidate's accomplishments and experiences. In particular they look for

- leadership positions,
- involvement in campus organizations and extracurricular activities,
- relevant experiences in internships, part-time work, or co-ops, and
- good grades

The ideal job candidate presents a combination of these.

In choosing a career, it is a good idea to have several careers in mind rather than just one. Increasingly, individuals are having more than just one career in their adult working life.

Some good strategies for finding more information about a particular career are to see a career counselor, engage in personal networking (ask friends, family, and instructors if they know someone in a particular field who could be contacted for information), and scope out Internet networks and resources (extensive information about jobs and careers is available on the Internet).

Work

Work plays a powerful role in our lives. How much time do people spend in work? How can you get positive work experiences during college? What are some good strategies for nailing a job interview? What issues do dual-career couples face?

Occupational Outlook

Career and Job-Hunting Resources

What Color Is Your Parachute?

Job Interviewing

Work and Family Issues

Work defines individuals in fundamental ways (Osipow, 2000). Individuals identify with their work, and work shapes their lives in many ways. It is an important influence on their financial standing, housing, the way they spend their time, where they live, their friendships, and their health.

Most individuals spend about one-third of their adult lives at work. In one recent survey, 35 percent of Americans worked 40 hours a week, but 18 percent even worked 51 hours or more per week (Center for Survey Research at the University of Connecticut, 2000). Almost half of the individuals worked more than 40 hours a week. Only 10 percent worked less than 30 hours a week.

Work creates a structure and rhythm to life that is often missed when individuals do not work for an extended period of time. When unable to work, many individuals experience emotional distress and low self-esteem.

However, some aspects of work also create stress. Four main aspects of work settings are linked with employee stress and health problems (Moos, 1986): (1) high job demands such as having a heavy workload and time pressure; (2) inadequate opportunities to participate in decision making; (3) a high level of supervisor control; and (4) a lack of clarity about the criteria for competent performance.

Getting Positive Work Experiences During College Students can participate in cooperative education programs, internships, or part-time or summer work relevant to their field of study. This experience can be critical in helping students obtain the job they want when they graduate from college. Today's employers expect job candidates to have this type of experience. In a national survey of employers, almost 60 percent said their entry-level college hires had co-op or internship experience (Collins, 1996). Participating in these work experiences can be a key factor in whether you land the job you want when you graduate from college.

More than 1,000 colleges in the United States offer cooperative education (*co-op*) programs. A co-op is a paid apprenticeship in a career field that you are interested in pursuing. You may not be permitted to participate in a co-op program until your junior year.

The Job Interview How well you handle a job interview is a critical factor in obtaining a job. Here are some good strategies for how to get an interview and doing well in the job interview (Yate, 2002):

- *Resume.* This is important and you will need one. Resumes are used by employers to decide whether they want to interview you in the first place. Organize your resume, write it clearly, and don't use a lot of jargon.
- *Interview.* Don't wing an interview. Do your homework. Find out as much about your prospective employer as possible. What does the company/organization do? How successful is it? Employers are impressed by job candidates who have taken the time to learn about their organization. This is true whether you are interviewing for a part-time job at your college library or for a full-time job in a large corporation after you graduate from college.
- *Work experience.* Be prepared to give positive examples of your past work experience. Interviewers anticipate that your past work behavior is a good predictor of how well you do in this new job, so the examples you give from past jobs may seal your fate.
- *Interview questions.* Anticipate what questions you will be asked in the interview. Do some practice interviews. Some typical interview questions include: What is your greatest strength? What interests you the most about this job? Why should I hire you? Also be prepared for some zingers. For example, how would you respond to these questions: Tell me something you are not very proud of. Describe a situation in which your idea was criticized. These types of questions

"Uh-huh. Uh-huh. And for precisely how long were you a hunter-gatherer at I.B.M.?"

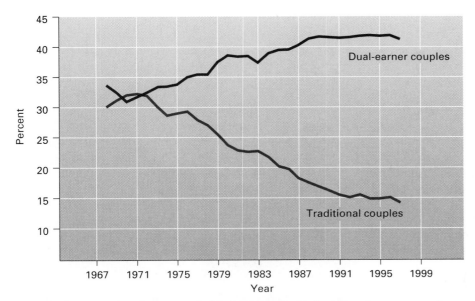

FIGURE 14.14 Changes in the Percentage of U.S. Traditional and Dual-Career Couples
Notice the dramatic increase in dual-earner couples in the last three decades. Traditional couples are those in which the husband is the sole breadwinner.

are used by interviewers to catch you off guard and determine how you handle a stressful situation.

- *Ask appropriate job-related questions yourself.* Review the job requirements with the interviewer.
- *Keep your cool.* Always leave in the same mannerly and polite way you entered.
- *Close of the interview.* As the interview closes, decide whether you want the job. If so, ask for it. If the job is not offered on the spot, ask when the two of you can talk again.
- *More.* That's not all. Immediately after the interview, type a follow-up letter. Keep it short, less than one page. Mail the letter within 24 hours after the interview. If you do not hear anything within five days, call the organization and ask about the status of the job.

Dual-Career Couples Although single-earner married families still make up a sizeable minority of families, the era of the stay-at-home-mom has given way to the era of the two-earner couple (Barnett, 2001) (see figure 14.14).

The increasing career commitment on the part of women has led to new work-related issues, such as the division of work and family responsibilities in dual-career couples (Barnett, 2001; Hyde & Barnett, 2001). Until recently, it had been assumed that men show less interest in home and family matters than women do.

However, recent research suggests that (Barnett, 2001; Barnett & others, 2001):

- *Men are increasing their responsibility for maintaining the home.* Men in dual-career families do about 45 percent of the housework. The decreasing gap between the time women and men spend in household and child-care tasks is mainly due to large increases in time spent by men.
- *Women are increasing their responsibility for breadwinning.* In terms of hourly earnings, a growing percentage of wives earn as much as or more than their husbands. This role reversal is present in about one-third of two-earner couples.
- *Men are showing greater interest in family and parenting.* The twenty first century is the first time that young men are reporting that family is at least as important to

Juggling Roles

In *Juggling: The Unexpected Advantages of Balancing Career and Home for Women and Their Families,* Faye Crosby (1991) described the advantages of multiple roles for women. She also discussed ways that the stress involved in juggling the roles can be reduced. Especially noteworthy when women "jugglers' are interviewed is the lack of free minutes they have. One woman in her thirties said she would just like to have a few more minutes in the day. When asked what she would do with the additional several hours, she said that she would relax after work before she started cooking dinner, or she would go to the gym and swim. She said that yesterday when she went to pick the kids up, she had a cake in the oven and worried that she would get stuck in traffic and it would burn up. Her final comment was that she would love not to have to be somewhere at a certain time. Jugglers identify the unrelenting pace of life as a persistent problem They speak of lacking time to relax, of pressured schedules, and of cramming weeks of work into the hours of the day.

Thus, not only do most jugglers derive a great deal of pleasure from life, they, like many other women in contemporary American society, feel stressed, stretched, and tired to the point of exhaustion. Virtually all women, especially jugglers, need competent support systems to help them cope with the multiple demands in their lives. A better national child-care policy and improved day care, as well as supportive others, can help to reduce the stress that many jugglers feel. Jugglers can build a network of adults who accept responsibility to help out, especially in times of emergency, no matter how minor.

The juggler is a real person who is striving to overcome obstacles in her path. As a society, we need to illuminate the features of our social structure that create unnecessary stress and unneeded heartache, and we need to work to change those features. We need to regard women's large-scale entry into the labor force as an unprecedented opportunity to build a better nation. As Crosby concludes, it is possible and desirable to regard the increasing number of women who are simultaneously spouse, parent, and career person as providing us all a chance to fashion social worlds that promote healthy communities, families, and individuals.

The character played by Diane Keaton (*above*), in the movie *Baby Boom,* lost her job when she couldn't find a way to juggle her career and family roles and still give her child adequate care and attention. Many U. S. corporations perceive flexible scheduling as an important management issue. Some individuals are turning down higher-paying jobs to take jobs with more flexibility. This is likely to be an increasing trend.

them as work (Barnett & others, 2001). Among men with more egalitarian attitudes, fatherhood is linked with a decrease of 9 hours per week at work, while among men with more traditional views, fatherhood is associated with an increase of almost 11 hours per week.

Thus, an important issue for many women and men is juggling career and family work (Milke & Peltola, 2000). To read further about this issue in women's lives, see the Sociocultural Worlds of Development box.

What are some changes in men's roles in home and family matters in the last 40 years?

Review and Reflect

5 **Explain the key dimensions of careers and work in early adulthood**

REVIEW

• What are some developmental changes in careers and work?
• How might personality types be linked to career choice?
• Why is it important to examine your values when thinking about a career?
• In which areas are there likely to be the greatest increase in jobs through 2010?
• What skills do employers want job applicants to have?
• How can people find the right career?
• What are some important things to know about work?

REFLECT

• What careers do you want to pursue? How much education will they take?

Reach Your Learning Goals

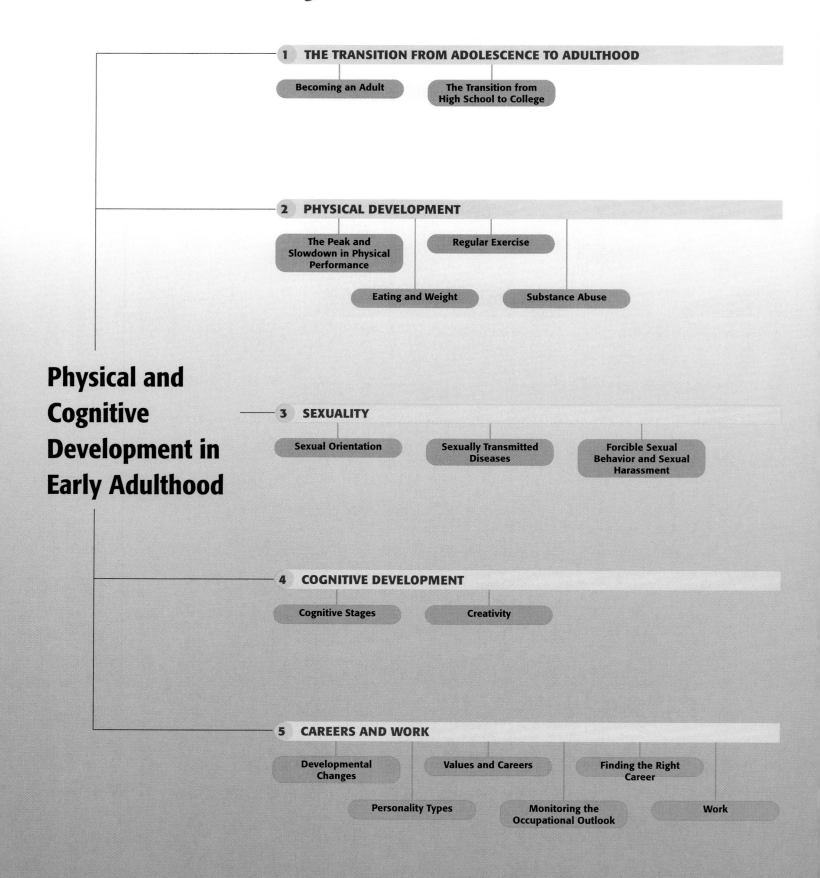

Physical and Cognitive Development in Early Adulthood

1 THE TRANSITION FROM ADOLESCENCE TO ADULTHOOD

- Becoming an Adult
- The Transition from High School to College

2 PHYSICAL DEVELOPMENT

- The Peak and Slowdown in Physical Performance
- Regular Exercise
- Eating and Weight
- Substance Abuse

3 SEXUALITY

- Sexual Orientation
- Sexually Transmitted Diseases
- Forcible Sexual Behavior and Sexual Harassment

4 COGNITIVE DEVELOPMENT

- Cognitive Stages
- Creativity

5 CAREERS AND WORK

- Developmental Changes
- Values and Careers
- Finding the Right Career
- Personality Types
- Monitoring the Occupational Outlook
- Work

Summary

1. Describe the transition from adolescence to adulthood

- During the transition to adulthood, there is often personal and economic temporariness. The transition is increasingly referred to as emerging adulthood, a time of experimentation and exploration. Two criteria for adult status are economic independence and independent decision making.
- There is both continuity and change in the transition to adulthood, and the transition can involve both positive and negative features. An increasing number of college students are returning students.

2. Identify the changes in physical development in young adults

- Peak physical status is often reached between 19 and 26 years of age. There is a hidden hazard in this time period—bad health habits are often formed then. Toward the latter part of early adulthood, a detectable slowdown in physical performance is apparent for most individuals.
- Obesity is a serious problem, with about one-third of Americans overweight enough to be at increased health risk. Heredity, set point, and basal metabolism are biological factors involved in obesity. Environmental factors and culture influence obesity. Ethnicity-gender factors are linked to obesity. Many divergent interests are involved in the topic of dieting. Restrained eating is an important dieting topic. Most diets don't work long-term. For those that do, exercise is usually an important component. Dieting can be harmful; however, when overweight people diet and maintain their weight loss, it can have positive effects.
- Both moderate and intense exercise produce important physical and psychological gains, such as lowered risk of heart disease and lowered anxiety.
- Although some reduction in alcohol use has occurred among college freshmen, binge drinking is still a major concern. By the mid twenties a reduction in drug use often takes place. A number of strategies, such as nicotine substitutes, have shown some success in getting smokers to quit but quitting is difficult because of the addictive properties of nicotine. Two strategies for intervening in addictions are the disease model and the life-process model, each of which has supporters.

3. Discuss sexuality in young adults

- Describing sexual practices in America always has been challenging. The 1994 Sex in America Survey was a major improvement over the earlier Kinsey survey. In the 1994 survey, Americans' sexual lives were portrayed as more conservative than in the earlier surveys. It generally is accepted to view sexual orientation along a continuum from exclusively heterosexual to exclusively homosexual. An individual's sexual preference likely is the result of a combination of genetic, hormonal, cognitive, and environmental factors.
- Also called STDs, sexually transmitted diseases are contracted primarily through sexual contact. Gonorrhea, syphilis, chlamydia, and genital herpes are among the most common STDs. The STD that has received the most attention in the last several decades is AIDS (acquired immune deficiency syndrome), which is caused by HIV, a virus that destroys the body's immune system. Some good strategies for protecting against AIDS and other STDs are to (1) know your and your partner's risk status; (2) obtain medical examinations; (3) have protected, not unprotected, sex; and (4) not have sex with multiple partners.
- Rape is forcible sexual intercourse with a person who does not give consent. Rape usually produces traumatic reactions in its victims. Sexual harassment occurs when one person uses his or her power over another individual in a sexual manner and can result in serious psychological consequences for the victim.

4. Characterize cognitive changes in early adulthood

- Formal operational thought, entered at age 11 to 15, is Piaget's final cognitive stage. Piaget did say that adults are quantitatively more knowledgeable than adolescents but that adults do not enter a new, qualitatively different stage. Some experts argue that the idealism of Piaget's formal operational stage declines in young adults, replaced by more realistic, pragmatic thinking. Perry said that adolescents often engage in dualistic, absolute thinking, while young adults are more likely to engage in reflective, relativistic thinking. Postformal thought is qualitatively different from Piaget's formal operational thought. It involves understanding that the correct answer might require reflective thinking and might vary from one situation to another, and that the search for truth is often never-ending. Also, the postformal stage includes the understanding that solutions to problems often need to be realistic and that emotion and subjective factors can be involved in thinking.
- Creativity peaks in adulthood, often in the forties, and then declines. However, (1) the magnitude of the decline is often slight; (2) the creativity-age link varies by domain; and (3) there is extensive individual variation in lifetime creative output. Based on interviews with leading experts in different domains, Csikszentmihalyi charted the way creative people go about living a creative life, such as waking up every morning with a mission and spending time in settings that stimulate their creativity.

5. Explain the key dimensions of careers and work in early adulthood

- Many young children have idealistic fantasies about a career. In the late teens and early twenties, their career thinking has usually turned more serious. By their early to mid twenties, many individuals have completed their education or training and started in a career. In the remainder of early adulthood, they seek to establish their emerging career and start moving up the career ladder.

- John Holland proposed that it is important for individuals to choose a career that is compatible with their personality type. He proposed six personality types from realistic to conventional.
- It is important to match up a career to your values. There are many different values, ranging from the importance of money to working in a preferred geographical location.
- Service-producing industries will account for the most jobs in American in the next decade. Employment in the computer industry is especially projected to grow rapidly. Jobs that require a college education will be the fastest growing and highest paying. Labor force participation of women will increase and so will that of Latinos and African Americans.
- In most careers today, oral communication skills and interpersonal skills are at the top of the list of what employers want in prospective employees.
- Personality types and values are important in finding the right career. It is a good idea to have several careers rather than just one. In terms of finding the right career, seeing a career counselor, engaging in personal networking, and scoping out Internet networks and resources are good strategies.
- Work defines people in fundamental ways and is a key aspect of their identity. Most individuals spend about one-third of their adult life at work. People often become stressed if they are unable to work but work also can produce stress, as when there is a heavy workload and time pressure. Getting positive work experiences during college might include cooperative education, internship, or part-time/summer work relevant to your field of study. The job interview can be critical in getting a job and a number of positive strategies can be followed. The increasing number of women who work in careers outside the home has led to new work-related issues. There has been a considerable increase in the time men spend in household work and child care.

Key Terms

basal metabolism rate (BMR) 447
restrained eaters 448
aerobic exercise 449
addiction 452

disease model of addiction 453
life-process model of addiction 453

sexually transmitted diseases (STDs) 456
acquired immune deficiency syndrome (AIDS) 456
rape 458

date or acquaintance rape 458
postformal thought 460
personality type theory 464

Key People

Robert Michael 454
Simon LeVay 456
Laura Brown 456

Jean Piaget 459
K. Warner Schaie and Sherry Willis 460

William Perry 460
Mihaly Csikszentmihalyi 462
John Holland 464

Faye Crosby 470

Taking It to the Net

1. Irina has always considered herself overweight, but not obese. She is 5 feet 4 inches tall and weighs 160 pounds. Calculate her body mass index (BMI) and use the guidelines to determine whether or not she is overweight or obese. What is your BMI?
2. Nanette is working part-time in her college human resources office. She has been asked to start gathering information for a

sexual harassment information booklet. What are the essential characteristics of sexual harassment and how should she communicate how the signs are identified?

Connect to www.mhhe.com/santrockld9 to research the answers and complete these exercises.

E-Learning Tools

To help you master the material in this chapter, you'll find a number of valuable study tools on the Student CD-ROM that accompanies this book. In addition, visit the Online Learning Center for *Life-Span Development,* ninth edition, where you'll find these valuable resources for chapter 14, "Physical and Cognitive Development in Early Adulthood."

- A number of self-assessments related to this chapter's content will challenge you to think about college life, your lifestyle, and career. These include:
  Exploring My College Experiences
  Comparing My Attitudes and Values with Those of Other College Students

  What Is My Health Style?
  Do I Abuse Drugs?
  How I Cope
  How Much Do I know About STDs?
  Matching My Personality Type to Careers
  My Career Goals
  How Do My Career Interests Link Up with Occupations that Are Expected to Have High Pay and the Largest Numerical Growth in Jobs from 1998 to 2008?
- Build your decision-making skills by trying your hand at the parenting and education "Scenarios."

C H A P T E R

15

Love is a canvas furnished by nature and embroidered by imagination.

—VOLTAIRE
French Essayist, 18th Century

Socioemotional Development in Early Adulthood

Chapter Outline		**Learning Goals**
CONTINUITY AND DISCONTINUITY FROM CHILDHOOD TO ADULTHOOD	**1**	**D**escribe continuity and discontinuity in temperament and attachment from childhood to adulthood
Temperament		
Attachment		
ATTRACTION, LOVE, AND CLOSE RELATIONSHIPS	**2**	**I**dentify some key aspects of attraction, love, and close relationships
Attraction		
The Faces of Love		
Loneliness		
MARRIAGE AND THE FAMILY	**3**	**D**iscuss marriage and the family
The Family Life Cycle		
Marriage		
Parental Roles		
THE DIVERSITY OF ADULT LIFESTYLES	**4**	**E**xplain the diversity of lifestyles
Single Adults		
Cohabiting Adults		
Divorced Adults		
Remarried Adults		
Gay and Lesbian Adults		
GENDER, RELATIONSHIPS, AND SELF-DEVELOPMENT	**5**	**C**haracterize the role of gender in relationships
Women's Development		
Men's Development		

Images of Life-Span Development
Edith, Phil, and Sherry—Searching for Love

Phil is a lovesick man. On two consecutive days he put expensive ads in New York City newspapers, urging, begging, pleading with a woman named Edith to forgive him and continue their relationship. The first ad read:

Edith

I was torn two ways. Too full of child to relinquish the lesser. Older now, a balance struck, that child forever behind me. Please forgive me, reconsider. Help make a new us; better now than before.

Phil

This ad was placed in the *New York Post* at a cost of $3,600. Another full-page ad appeared in the *New York Times* at a cost of $3,408. Phil's ads stirred up quite a bit of interest. Forty-two Ediths responded; Phil said he thought the whole process would be more private. As Phil would attest, relationships are very important to us. Some of us will go to almost any length and spend large sums of money to restore lost relationships.

Sherry is not searching for a particular man. She is at the point where she is, well, looking for Mr. Anybody. Sherry is actually more particular than she says, although she is frustrated by what she calls that "great man shortage" in this country. For every 100 men over 15 years of age who have never been married or are widowed or divorced, there are 123 women. For African Americans the ratio is 100 men for every 133 women.

William Novak (1983), author of *The Great American Man Shortage*, believes it is the quality of the gap that bothers most women. He says the quality problem stems from the fact that the combination of the feminist movement and women's tendency to seek therapy when their personal relationships do not work out has made women outgrow men emotionally. He points out that many women are saying to men, "You don't have to earn all the money anymore, and I don't want to have to do all the emotional work." Novak observes that the whole issue depresses many women because society has conditioned them to assume that their lack of a marriage partner is their fault. One 37-year-old woman told Novak, "I'm no longer waiting for a man on a white horse. Now I'd settle for the horse."

Love is of central importance in each of our lives, as it is in Phil's and Sherry's lives. Shortly, we will discuss the many faces of love, but first we will return to an issue we initially raised in chapter 1: continuity and discontinuity.

1 CONTINUITY AND DISCONTINUITY FROM CHILDHOOD TO ADULTHOOD

Temperament   **Attachment**

We no longer believe in the infant determinism of Freud's psychosexual theory, which argued that our personality as adults is virtually cast in stone by the time we are 5 years of age. But the first 20 years of life are not meaningless in predicting an adult's personality. And there is every reason to believe that later experiences in the early adult years are important in determining what the individual is like as an adult. In trying to understand the young adult's personality, it would be misleading to look only at the adult's life in present tense, ignoring the developmental unfolding of personality. So, too, would it be far off target to only search through a 30-year-old's first 5 to 10 years of life in trying to predict why he or she is having difficulty in a close relationship. The truth about adult personality development, then, lies somewhere between the infant determinism of Freud and a contextual approach that ignores the antecedents of the adult years altogether.

It is a common finding that the smaller the time intervals over which we measure personality characteristics, the more similar an individual will look from one measurement to the next. Thus, if we measure an individual's self-concept at the age of 20 and then again at the age of 30, we will probably find more stability than if we measured the individual's self-concept at the age of 10 and then again at the age of 30. Let's now explore some research findings that reflect these ideas about continuity and discontinuity.

Temperament

In chapter 7, we described *temperament* as an individual's behavioral style and characteristic emotional responses ◀▥ p. 210. How stable is temperament? Do young adults show the same behavioral style and characteristic emotional responses as when they were infants or young children?

Activity level is an important dimension of temperament. Is a child's activity level linked to her or his personality in early adulthood? In one longitudinal study, children who were highly active at age 4 were likely to be very outgoing at age 23, which reflects continuity (Franz, 1996). From adolescence into early adulthood, most individuals show fewer emotional mood swings, become more responsible, and engage in less risk-taking behavior, which reflects discontinuity (Caspi, 1998).

Is temperament in childhood linked with adjustment in adulthood? Here is what we know based on the few longitudinal studies that have been conducted on this topic (Caspi, 1998). Recall from chapter 7 the distinction between an easy and a difficult temperament ◀▥ p. 210. In one longitudinal study, children who had an easy temperament at 3 to 5 years of age were likely to be well-adjusted as young adults (Chess & Thomas, 1987). In contrast, many children who had a difficult temperament at 3 to 5 years of age were not well-adjusted as young adults. Also, other researchers have found that boys with a difficult temperament in childhood are less likely as adults to continue their formal education, whereas girls with a difficult temperament in childhood are more likely to experience marital conflict as adults (Wachs, 2000).

Inhibition is another temperament characteristic that has been studied extensively (Kagan, 2000; 2002). Researchers have found that individuals with an inhibited temperament in childhood are less likely as adults to be assertive or experience social support, and more likely to delay entering a stable job track (Wachs, 2000).

Yet another aspect of temperament involves emotionality and the ability to control one's emotions. In one longitudinal study, when 3-year-old children showed good control of their emotions and were resilient in the face of stress, they were likely to continue to handle emotions effectively as adults (Block, 1993). By contrast, when 3-year-olds had low emotional control and were not very resilient, they were likely to show problems in these areas as young adults.

In sum, these studies reveal some continuity between certain aspects of temperament in childhood and adjustment in early adulthood. However, keep in mind that these connections between childhood temperament and adult adjustment are based on only a small number of studies and more research is needed to verify these linkages. Indeed, Theodore Wachs (1994, 2000) proposed ways that linkages between temperament in childhood and personality in adulthood might vary depending on the intervening contexts in individuals' experience (see figure 15.1 on page 480).

Initial Temperament Trait: Inhibition

	Child A	Child B
	Intervening Context	
Caregivers	Caregivers (parents) who are sensitive and accepting, and let child set his or her own pace	Caregivers who use inappropriate "low level control" and attempt to force the child into new situations
Physical Environment	Presence of "stimulus shelters" or "defensible spaces" that the children can retreat to when there is too much stimulation	Child continually encounters noisy, chaotic environments that allow no escape from stimulation.
Peers	Peer groups with other inhibited children with common interests, so the child feels accepted	Peer groups consist of athletic extroverts, so the child feels rejected.
Schools	School is "undermanned" so inhibited children are more likely to be tolerated and feel they can make a contribution.	School is "overmanned" so inhibited children are less likely to be tolerated and more likely to feel undervalued.
	Personality Outcomes	
	As an adult, individual is closer to extroversion (outgoing, sociable) and is emotionally stable.	As an adult, individual is closer to introversion and has more emotional problems.

FIGURE 15.1 Temperament in Childhood, Personality in Adulthood, and Intervening Contexts

Varying experiences with caregivers, the physical environment, peers, and schools can modify links between temperament in childhood and personality in adulthood. The example given here is for inhibition.

Attachment

Attachment is another topic we highlighted in chapter 7, "Socioemotional Development in Infancy" ◀▥ p. 216. We also described attachment in chapter 13, "Sociomotional Development in Adolescence" ◀▥ p. 410. Let's examine attachment in young adults and the extent to which it is linked to attachment earlier in development.

The concepts of secure and insecure attachment continue to be used to describe attachment relationships in adulthood (Crowell & others, 2002; Main, 2000; Ryff & Singer, 2000; Shaver & Hazan, 1993). About 50 to 60 percent of adults in nonclinical samples are *securely attached*. These individuals provide realistic, coherent descriptions of their childhood and appear to understand how past experiences affect their current lives as adults. Approximately 25 to 30 percent of adults fall into the *insecure-dismissing* category of attachment. They don't want to discuss their relationships with their parents or do not seem invested in them. Their memories often focus on negative experiences such as being rejected or neglected by a parent. *Insecure-preoccupied* individuals make up about 15 percent of adults. In contrast to dismissing adults, preoccupied adults readily talk about their relationships but they tend to be incoherent and disorganized. They appear unable to move beyond their childhood issues with parents and often express anger toward them or ongoing efforts to please them.

Although relationships with romantic partners differ from those with parents in important ways (such as sexuality and reciprocal caregiving), romantic partners fulfill for adults some of the same needs as parents do for their children. Adults count on their romantic partners to be a secure base to which they can return and obtain comfort and security in stressful times.

Cindy Hazan and Phillip Shaver (1987; Shaver & Hazan, 1993) have examined the continuity between childhood attachment relationships and romantic relationships in a number of studies. They interview adults about their relationships with their parents as they were growing up and about their current romantic relationship. They find that the quality of childhood attachment relationships is linked with the quality of adult romantic relationships. For example, adults who report that they were securely attached to their parents are more likely to say that they have a secure attachment to their romantic partner than are adults who report having had an inse-cure attachment to their parents when they were growing up. In one longitudinal study, individuals who were securely attached to caregivers at 1 year of age also were likely to have secure attachments to parents and romantic partners 20 years later (Waters & others, 2000).

In sum, there appear to be some important continuities between attachment to parents as a child and attachment to parents and romantic partners as a young adult (Crowell & others, 2002; Fraley, 2002). Nonetheless, keep in mind that not all indi-viduals fit this pattern and that attachment styles are not cast in stone (Lewis, Feiring, & Rosenthal, 2000). For example, in the longitudinal study just described and in other studies, links between earlier and later attachments are lessened by stressful and dis-ruptive life experiences (such as the death of a parent or instability of caregiving) (Collins & Laursen, 2000). Also, some individuals revise their attachment styles as they experience relationships in their adult years (Baldwin & Fehr, 1995). For exam-ple, in one study, approximately 30 percent of young adults changed their attachment style over a four-year period (Kirkpatrick & Hazan, 1994).

mhhe ●com/
santrockld9
Adult Attachment
Relationships

Review and Reflect

1 **Describe continuity and discontinuity in temperament and attachment from childhood to adulthood**

REVIEW

- How stable is temperament from childhood to adulthood?
- How much does attachment change from childhood to adulthood?

REFLECT

- What was your temperament like as a child? What is it like now?

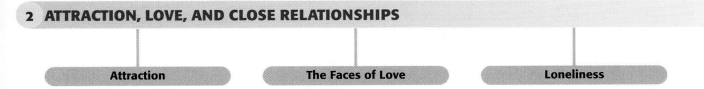

2 ATTRACTION, LOVE, AND CLOSE RELATIONSHIPS

Attraction   **The Faces of Love**   **Loneliness**

What attracts us to others and motivates us to spend more time with them? And an-other question needs to be asked, one that has intrigued philosophers, poets, and songwriters for centuries: What is love? Is it lustful and passionate? Or should we be more cautious in our pursuit of love, as a Czech proverb advises, "Do not choose your wife at a dance, but in the fields among the harvesters."

Of equal importance is why relationships dissolve. Many of us know all too well that an individual we thought was a marvelous human being with whom we wanted to spend the rest of our life may not turn out to be so marvelous after all. But often it is said that it is better to have loved and lost than never to have loved at all. Loneliness is a dark cloud over many individuals' lives, something few human beings want to feel. These are the themes of our exploration of close relationships: how they get started in the first place, the faces of love, intimacy, and loneliness.

Attraction

What attracts us to others and motivates us to spend more time with them? Does just being around someone increase the likelihood that a relationship will develop? Do birds of a feather flock together—that is, are we likely to associate with those who are similar to us? How important is physical attraction in a relationship?

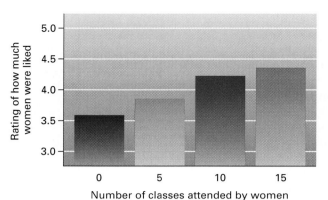

FIGURE 15.2 Exposure to Someone and the Extent To Which They Are Liked

The more frequently that students in a large college class saw women who had been planted there by researcher, the more they said they liked the women, even though they had not even interacted with them.

Familiarity and Similarity Physical proximity does not guarantee that we will develop a positive relationship with another person. Familiarity can breed contempt, but familiarity is a condition that is necessary for a close relationship to develop (Bornstein & D'Agostino, 1992). For the most part, friends and lovers have been around each other for a long time; they may have grown up together, gone to high school or college together, worked together, or gone to the same social events.

To test the importance of exposure and its effect on liking someone, researchers planted female students in a large college classroom (Moreland & Beach, 1992). The women did not interact with the professor or the other students. They just walked in and sat quietly in the first row where they were most likely to be seen. The females attended anywhere from 15 to 0 (the control group condition) classes. At the end of the term, the students were shown slides of the females and asked to rate the extent to which they liked them. As shown in figure 15.2, the more times they saw the women, the more they said they liked them.

Once we have been exposed to someone for a period of time, what is it that makes the relationship breed friendship and even love? Birds of a feather do indeed flock together. One of the most powerful lessons generated by the study of close relationships is that we like to associate with people who are similar to us (Berscheid, 2000). Our friends, as well as our lovers, are much more like us than unlike us (Berndt, 1996). We have similar attitudes, behavior, and characteristics, as well as clothes, intelligence, personality, other friends, values, lifestyle, physical attractiveness, and so on. In some limited cases and on some isolated characteristics, opposites may attract. An introvert may wish to be with an extravert, or someone with little money may wish to associate with someone who has a lot of money, for example. But overall we are attracted to individuals with similar rather than opposite characteristics. In one study, for example, the old adage "Misery loves company" was supported as depressed college students preferred to meet unhappy others while nondepressed college students preferred to meet happy others (Wenzlaff & Prohaska, 1989). The fact that individuals are attracted to each other on the basis of similar characteristics and attitudes is reflected in the questions that computer dating services ask their clients.

consensual validation An explanation of why individuals are attracted to people who are similar to them. Our own attitudes and behavior are supported and validated when someone else's attitudes and behavior are similar to our own.

Consensual validation provides an explanation of why people are attracted to others who are similar to them. Our own attitudes and behavior are supported when someone else's attitudes and behavior are similar to ours—their attitudes and behavior validate ours. People tend to shy away from the unknown. We might tend, instead, to prefer people whose attitudes and behavior we can predict. And similarity implies that we will enjoy doing things with the other person, which often requires a partner who likes the same things and has similar attitudes. In one study, self-verifying evaluations were especially important in marriage (Swann, De La Ronde, & Hixon, 1994).

Dilbert reprinted by permission of United Features Syndicate, Inc.

Physical Attraction   How important is *physical attraction* in a relationship? Many advertising agencies would have us believe it is the most important factor in establishing and maintaining a relationship. However, heterosexual men and women across many cultures differ on the importance they place on good looks when they seek an intimate partner. Women tend to rate as most important such traits as considerateness, honesty, dependability, kindness, and understanding; men prefer good looks, cooking skills, and frugality (Buss, 1999, 2000, 2001).

Some aspects of attractiveness vary across time in a particular culture. Consider the United States. In the 1950s, the soft, voluptuous Marilyn Monroe was the female ideal; today the ideal is the lean, athletic female.

The force of similarity also operates at a physical level. We usually seek out someone at our own level of attractiveness in both physical characteristics and social attributes. Most of us come away with a reasonably good chance of finding a "good match." Research indicates that this *matching hypothesis*—that although we might prefer a more attractive person in the abstract, in the real world we end up choosing someone who is close to our own level of attractiveness—holds up (Kalick & Hamilton, 1986).

Several additional points help to clarify the role of physical beauty and attraction in our close relationships. Much of the research has focused on initial or short-term encounters; researchers have not often evaluated attraction over the course of months and years (Murstein, Reif, & Syracuse-Siewert, 2002). As relationships endure, physical attraction probably assumes less importance. Rocky Dennis, as portrayed in the movie *Mask,* is a case in point. His peers and even his mother initially wanted to avoid Rocky, whose face was severely distorted, but over the course of his childhood and adolescent years, the avoidance turned into attraction and love as people got to know him. As Rocky's story demonstrates, familiarity can overcome even severe initial negative reactions to a person.

The Faces of Love

Once attraction initiates a relationship, other opportunities exist to deepen the relationship to love. *Love* refers to a vast and complex territory of human behavior. As you read about love, you will see that there are different types of love, such as friendship, romantic love, and affectionate love. Altruism, discussed in chapter 11, "Socioemotional Development in Middle and Late Childhood," also is classified as a type of love by some experts (Berscheid, 1988). To begin, though, we will focus on a very important theme in the lives of young adults—intimacy, which is especially important in friendship and affectionate love.

Intimacy   Let's explore Erik Erikson's view of intimacy, the role of intimacy in relationship maturity, and how people juggle the motivation for intimacy and the motivation for independence.

Erikson's Stage: Intimacy Versus Isolation   As we go through our adult lives, most of us are motivated to successfully juggle the development of identity and intimacy. Recall from our discussion in chapter 13 that Erik Erikson (1968) believes that identity versus identity confusion—pursuing who we are, what we are all about, and where we are going in life—is the most important issue to be negotiated in adolescence ◀▮▮▮ p. 405. Erikson thinks that intimacy should come after individuals are well on their way to establishing stable and successful identities. Intimacy is another life crisis in Erikson's scheme. If intimacy is not developed in early adulthood, the individual may be left with what Erikson calls "isolation." Intimacy versus isolation is Erikson's sixth developmental stage, which individuals experience in early adulthood ◀▮▮▮ p. 46. At this time, individuals face the task of forming intimate relationships with others. Erikson describes intimacy as finding oneself yet losing oneself in another person. If young adults form healthy friendships and an intimate relationship with another individual, intimacy will be achieved. If not, isolation will result.

*A*sk a toad what is beauty . . . he will answer that it is a female with two great round eyes coming out of her little head, a large flat mouth, a yellow belly and a brown back.

—Voltaire
French Essayist, 18th Century

Eric Stoltz as Rocky Dennis in the movie *Mask.* Rocky was unloved and unwanted as a young child because of his grotesque features. As his mother and peers got to know him, they became much more attracted to him. *What are some of the factors that influence our attraction to others?*

We are what we love.

—Erik Erikson
Danish-Born American Psychoanalyst and Author, 20th Century

mhhe ●com/
santrockld9

**Intimate Relationships
Ellen Berscheid's Research
Friendship**

---

romantic love Also called passionate love or eros, romantic love has strong sexual and infatuation components and often predominates in the early period of a love relationship.

An inability to develop meaningful relationships with others can harm an individual's personality. It may lead individuals to repudiate, ignore, or attack those who frustrate them. Such circumstances account for the shallow, almost pathetic attempts of youth to merge themselves with a leader. Many youth want to be apprentices or disciples of leaders and adults who will shelter them from the harm of the "out-group" world. If this fails, and Erikson believes that it must, sooner or later the individuals recoil into a self-search to discover where they went wrong. This introspection sometimes leads to painful depression and isolation. It may also contribute to a mistrust of others.

Intimacy and Independence The early adult years are a time when individuals usually develop an intimate relationship with another individual. An important aspect of this relationship is the commitment of the individuals to each other. At the same time, individuals show a strong interest in independence and freedom. Development in early adulthood often involves an intricate balance of intimacy and commitment on the one hand, and independence and freedom on the other.

Recall that intimacy is the aspect of development that follows identity in Erikson's eight stages of development. A related aspect of developing an identity in adolescence and early adulthood is independence. At the same time as individuals are trying to establish an identity, they face the difficulty of having to cope with increasing their independence from their parents, developing an intimate relationship with another individual, and increasing their friendship commitments. They also face the task of being able to think for themselves and do things without always relying on what others say or do.

The extent to which the young adult has begun to develop autonomy has important implications for early adulthood maturity. The young adult who has not sufficiently moved away from parental ties may have difficulty in both interpersonal relationships and a career. Consider the mother who overprotects her daughter, continues to support her financially, and does not want to let go of her. In early adulthood, the daughter may have difficulty developing mature intimate relationships and she may have career difficulties. When a promotion comes up that involves more responsibility and possibly more stress, she may turn it down. When things do not go well in her relationship with a young man, she may go crying to her mother.

The balance between intimacy and commitment, on the one hand, and independence and freedom, on the other, is delicate. Keep in mind that these important dimensions of adult development are not necessarily opposite ends of a continuum. Some individuals are able to experience a healthy independence and freedom along with an intimate relationship. These dimensions may also fluctuate with social and historical change. And keep in mind that intimacy and commitment, and independence and freedom, are not just concerns of early adulthood. They are important themes of development that are worked and reworked throughout the adult years. Next, we will explore another important aspect of adults' close relationships: romantic love.

Romantic Love **Romantic love** is also called passionate love, or eros. Poets, playwrights, and musicians through the ages have lauded the fiery passion of romantic love—and lamented the searing pain when it fails. Think for a moment about songs and books that hit the top of the charts. Chances are they are about love.

Romantic love has strong components of sexuality and infatuation, and it often predominates in the early part of a love relationship. Well-known love researcher Ellen Berscheid (1988) says that it is romantic love we mean when we say that we are "in love" with someone. It is romantic love she believes we need to understand if we are to learn what love is all about. Berscheid believes that sexual desire is the most important ingredient of romantic love.

In our culture, romantic love is the main reason we get married. In 1967, a famous study showed that most men maintained that they would not get married if they were not "in love." Women either were undecided or said that they would get married even if they did not love their prospective husband (Kephart, 1967). In the 1980s, both women and men tended to agree that they would not get married unless they were "in love." More than half of today's men and women say that not being "in love" is sufficient reason to dissolve a marriage (Berscheid, Snyder, & Omoto, 1989). Romantic love is especially important among college students. One study of unattached college men and women found that more than half identified a romantic partner, rather than a parent, sibling, or friend, as their closest relationship (Berscheid, Snyder, & Omoto, 1989).

Romantic love includes a complex intermingling of different emotions—fear, anger, sexual desire, joy, and jealousy, for example (Harris, 2002). Obviously, some of these emotions are a source of anguish (Daley & Hammen, 2002). One study found that romantic lovers were more likely than friends to be the cause of depression (Berscheid & Fei, 1977).

Affectionate Love   Love is more than just passion. **Affectionate love,** also called companionate love, is the type of love that occurs when someone desires to have the other person near and has a deep, caring affection for the person.

There is a growing belief that the early stages of love have more romantic ingredients, but as love matures, passion tends to give way to affection (Berscheid & Reis, 1998; Harvey & Weber, 2001). Phillip Shaver (1986) proposed a developmental model of love in which the initial phase of romantic love is fueled by a mixture of sexual attraction and gratification, a reduced sense of loneliness, uncertainty about the security of developing another attachment, and excitement from exploring the novelty of another human being. With time, he says, sexual attraction wanes, attachment anxieties either lessen or produce conflict and withdrawal, novelty is replaced with familiarity, and lovers either find themselves securely attached in a deeply caring relationship or distressed—feeling bored, disappointed, lonely, or hostile, for example. In the latter case, one or both partners may eventually seek a different close relationship.

Consummate Love   So far we have discussed two forms of love: romantic (or passionate) and affectionate (or companionate). Robert J. Sternberg (1988) described a third form of love, *consummate love*, which he said is the strongest, fullest type of love. Sternberg's triarchic theory of love can be thought of as a triangle with three main dimensions—passion, intimacy, and commitment. Passion, as described earlier, is physical and sexual attraction to another. Intimacy is emotional feelings of warmth, closeness, and sharing in a relationship. Commitment is our cognitive appraisal of the relationship and our intent to maintain the relationship even in the face of problems (Rusbult & others, 2001).

Sternberg's theory states that the ideal form of love involves all three dimensions (see figure 15.3). If passion is the only ingredient in a relationship (with intimacy and commitment low or absent), we are merely *infatuated*. An affair or a fling in which there is little intimacy and even less commitment would be an example. A relationship marked by intimacy and commitment but low or lacking in passion is called *affectionate love*, a pattern often found among couples who have been married for many years. If passion and commitment are present but intimacy is not, Sternberg calls the relationship *fatuous love*, as when one person worships another from a distance. But if couples share all three dimensions—passion, intimacy, and commitment—they will experience consummate love.

Friendship   Increasingly researchers are finding that friendship plays an important role in development throughout the human life span (Antonucci, 1990; Hartup, 1999) ◀ⅢⅢ p. 414. In the words of American historian Henry Adams, "One friend in life is much, two are many, and three hardly possible." **Friendship** is a form of close

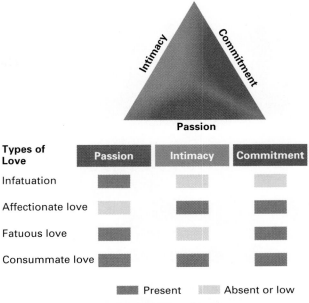

FIGURE 15.3 Sternberg's Triangle of Love

Sternberg identified three types of love: passion, intimacy, and commitment. Various combinations of these types of love result in these patterns of love: infatuation, affectionate love, fatuous love, and consummate love.

affectionate love   In this type of love (also called "companionate love"), an individual desires to have the other person near and has a deep, caring affection for the other person.

friendship   A form of close relationship that involves enjoyment, acceptance, trust, respect, mutual assistance, confiding, understanding, and spontaneity.

How is adult friendship different among female friends, male friends, and cross-sex friends?

relationship that involves enjoyment (we like to spend time with our friends), acceptance (we accept our friends without trying to change them), trust (we assume our friends will act in our best interest), respect (we think our friends make good judgments), mutual assistance (we help and support our friends and they us), confiding (we share experiences and confidential matters with a friend), understanding (we feel that a friend knows us well and understands what we like), and spontaneity (we feel free to be ourselves around a friend). In an inquiry of more than 40,000 individuals, many of these characteristics were given when people were asked what a best friend should be like (Parlee, 1979).

As we saw in chapter 11, friendship can serve many functions—such as companionship, intimacy/affection, support, and a source of self-esteem ◀||| p. 414. In some cases, friends can provide a better buffer from stress and be a better source of emotional support than family members. This might be because friends choose each other whereas family ties are obligatory. Individuals often select a friend in terms of such criteria as loyalty, trustworthiness, and support. Thus, it is not surprising that in times of stress individuals turn to their friends for emotional support (Fehr, 1996).

Zick Rubin (1970) argues that liking involves our sense that someone else is similar to us; it includes a positive evaluation of the individual. Loving, he believes, involves being close to someone; it includes dependency, a more selfless orientation toward the individual, and qualities of absorption and exclusiveness.

But friends and lovers are similar in some ways. In one study, friends and romantic partners shared the characteristics of acceptance, trust, respect, confiding, understanding, spontaneity, mutual assistance, and happiness (Davis, 1985). However, relationships with spouses or lovers were more likely to also involve fascination and exclusiveness.

As with children, adult friends usually come from the same age group. For many individuals, friendships formed in the twenties often continue through the twenties and into the thirties, although some new friends may be made in the thirties and some lost because of moving or other circumstances.

As in the childhood years, there are sex differences in adult friendship (Winstead & Griffin, 2002). Women have more close friends and their friendships are more intimate than men's. This intimacy involves more self-disclosure and exchange of emotional support. Adult male friendships are more competitive than those of females (Sharkey, 1993). For example, male friends disagree with each other more. Also, when adult female friends get together, they often talk, whereas adult male friends are more likely to engage in activities, especially outdoors. Of course, adult male friends talk, but it usually is a more distant, less intimate pattern of talk. Thus, the adult male pattern of friendship often involves keeping one's distance while sharing useful information.

When women talk with their friends, they expect to be able to openly express their feelings, reveal their weaknesses, and discuss their problems (Garner & Estep, 2002). They anticipate that their friends will listen at length to what they have to say and be sympathetic. In contrast, men are less likely to talk about their weaknesses with their friends, and they want practical solutions to their problems rather than sympathy (Tannen, 1990). Later in the chapter we will further explore these differences in the talk of women and men in relationships.

Keep in mind that these differences in same-sex adult friendship often are small (Sabini, 1995). For example, many men engage in self-disclosure and provide emotional support in their friendships.

But what about female-male friendship? Cross-sex friendships are more common among adults than among elementary school children, but not as common as same-sex friendships in adulthood (Fehr, 1996). Cross-sex friendships can provide both opportunities and problems. The opportunities involve learning more about common feelings and interests, and characteristics that both sexes have, as well as acquiring knowledge and understanding of beliefs and activities that historically have been reserved more for one sex than for the other. For example, in cross-sex friendships females might learn more about sports, cars, and the stock market. Males might learn more about relationships and to better appreciate art and classical music.

Problems can arise in cross-sex friendships because of the different expectations women and men have about the purpose of friendship. For example, a woman might expect a lot of sympathy from a male friend when she expresses an emotional problem to him but might instead receive back a directive solution rather than a shoulder to cry on (Tannen, 1990). Another problem that can plague an adult cross-sex friendship is unclear sexual boundaries (Swain, 1992). Men are more likely to try to turn a platonic friendship into a sexual relationship, and women often are offended by this. The ambiguity in sexual attraction can produce tension and confusion for both women and men in a cross-sex adult friendship.

Individuals who don't have friends are vulnerable to loneliness. Let's now explore what it is like to be lonely.

Loneliness

Recall that Erik Erikson (1968) believes that intimacy versus isolation is the key developmental issue for young adults to resolve. Social isolation can result in loneliness.

Each of us has times in our lives when we feel lonely, but for some people loneliness is a chronic condition. More than just an unwelcome social situation, chronic loneliness is linked with impaired physical and mental health (Cacioppo, 2002; McInnis & White, 2001). Chronic loneliness even can lead to an early death (Cuijpers, 2001).

Our society's emphasis on self-fulfillment and achievement, the importance we attach to commitment in relationships, and a decline in stable close relationships are among the reasons loneliness is common today (de Jong-Gierveld, 1987). Researchers have found that married individuals are less lonely than their nonmarried counterparts (never married, divorced, or widowed) in studies conducted in more than twenty countries (Perlman & Peplau, 1998).

How do you determine if you are lonely? Scales of loneliness ask you to respond to items like "I don't feel in tune with the people around me" and "I can find companionship when I want it." If you consistently respond that you never or rarely feel in tune with people around you and rarely or never can find companionship when you want it, you are likely to fall into the category of people who are described as moderately or intensely lonely (Russell, 1996).

mhhe●com/
santrockld9

Loneliness

Shyness

Loneliness and Life's Transitions   Loneliness is interwoven with how people pass through life transitions, such as a move to a different part of the country, a divorce, or the death of a close friend or family member. Another situation that often creates loneliness is the first year of college. When students leave the familiar world of their hometown and family to enter college, they especially can feel lonely. Many college freshmen feel anxious about meeting new people and developing a new social life can create considerable anxiety. As one student commented:

> My first year here at the university has been pretty lonely. I wasn't lonely at all in high school. I lived in a fairly small town—I knew everybody and everyone knew me. I was a member of several clubs and played on the basketball team. It's not that way at the university. It is a big place and I've felt like a stranger on so many occasions. I'm starting to get used to my life here and the last few months I've been making myself meet people and get to know them, but it has not been easy.

As this comment illustrates, freshmen rarely bring their popularity and social standing from high school into the college environment. There may be a dozen high school basketball stars, National Merit scholars, and former student council presidents in a single dormitory wing. Especially if students attend college away from home, they face the task of forming completely new social relationships.

One study found that two weeks after the school year began, 75 percent of 354 college freshmen felt lonely at least part of the time (Cutrona, 1982). More than

"What I'm trying to say, Mary, is that I want your site to be linked to my site."

© Mick Stevens from cartoonbank.com All Rights Reserved.

40 percent said their loneliness was moderate to severe. Students who were the most optimistic and had the highest self-esteem were more likely to overcome their loneliness by the end of their freshman year. Loneliness is not reserved for college freshmen, though. Upperclassmen are often lonely as well. In one recent study of more than 2,600 undergraduates, lonely individuals were less likely to actively cope with stress than individuals who were able to make friends (Cacioppo & others, 2000). Also in this study, lonely college students had higher levels of stress-related hormones and poorer sleep patterns than students who had positive relationships with others.

It is important to distinguish chronic loneliness from the desire of some people to have some time to themselves. Some individuals, especially those who are involved in intense careers that involve extensive interactions with people, value solitary time.

Loneliness and Technology   One of the factors that may be contributing to loneliness in contemporary society is technology. Although invention of the telephone more than a century ago seems to have decreased social isolation for many individuals and families, psychologists have found a link between TV viewing and loneliness. Correlation does not equal causation, but it does seem plausible that television can contribute to social disengagement.

Because most people isolate themselves at their computers when they use the Internet, the Internet also may increase disengagement. One study focused on 169 individuals during their first several years online (Kraut & others, 1998). In this study, greater use of the Internet was associated with declines in participants' communication with family members in the household and increases in depression and loneliness. At the same time, however, some people use the Internet to form potentially strong new ties (Bargh, McKenna, & Fitzsimons, in press; Clay, 2000). Especially for socially anxious and lonely individuals, the Internet may provide a safe way to begin contacts that eventually lead to face-to-face meetings and possibly even intimate relationships.

Strategies for Reducing Loneliness   If you are lonely, how can you become better connected with others? Here are some strategies:

- *Participate in activities that you can do with others.* Join organizations or volunteer your time for a cause you believe in. You likely will get to know others whose views are similar to yours. Going to just one social gathering can help you develop social contacts. When you go, introduce yourself to others and start a conversation. Another strategy is to sit next to new people in your classes or find someone to study with.
- *Be aware of the early warning signs of loneliness.* People often feel bored or alienated before loneliness becomes pervasive. Head off loneliness by becoming involved in new social activities.
- *Draw a diagram of your social network.* Determine whether the people in the diagram meet your social needs. If not, pencil in the people you would like to get to know.
- *Engage in positive behaviors when you meet new people.* You will improve your chances of developing enduring relationships if, when you meet new people, you are nice, considerate, honest, trustworthy, and cooperative. Have a positive attitude, be supportive of the other person, and make positive comments about him or her.
- *See a counselor or read a book on loneliness.* If you can't get rid of your loneliness on your own, you might want to contact the counseling services at your college. The counselor can talk with you about strategies for reducing your loneliness. You also might want to read a good book on loneliness. A good book is *Intimate Connections* by David Burns (1985).

Review and Reflect

2 **Identify some key aspects of attraction, love, and close relationships**

REVIEW

- What attracts someone to another person?
- What are some different types of love?
- What is the nature of loneliness and how does it affect people?

REFLECT

- If you were to give someone advice about love, what would it be?

3 MARRIAGE AND THE FAMILY

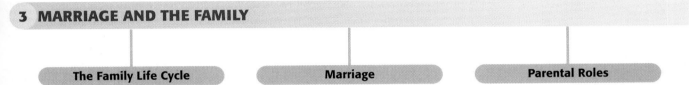

| The Family Life Cycle | Marriage | Parental Roles |

Should I get married? If I wait any longer, will it be too late? Will I get left out? Should I stay single or is it too lonely a life? If I get married, do I want to have children? How will it affect my marriage? These are questions that many young adults pose to themselves as they consider their lifestyle options. But before we explore these lifestyle options, let's examine the nature of the family life cycle.

The Family Life Cycle

As we go through life, we are at different points in the family life cycle. The six stages of the family life cycle are (Carter & McGoldrick, 1988) (see figure 15.4 on page 490):

- **Leaving home and becoming a single adult** is the first stage in the family life cycle, and it involves **launching,** the process in which youth move into adulthood and exit their family of origin. Adequate completion of launching requires that the young adult separate from the family of origin without cutting off ties completely or fleeing in a reactive way to find some form of substitute emotional refuge. The launching period is a time for the youth and young adult to formulate personal life goals, to develop an identity, and to become more independent before joining with another person to form a new family. This is a time for young people to sort out emotionally what they will take along from the family of origin, who they will leave behind, and what they will to develop into themselves.

  Complete cutoffs from parents rarely resolve emotional problems. The shift to adult-to-adult status between parents and children requires a mutually respectful and personal form of relating, in which young adults can appreciate parents as they are, needing neither to make them into what they are not nor to blame them for what they could not be. Neither do young adults need to comply with parental expectations and wishes at their own expense.

- The **new couple** is the second stage in the family life cycle, in which two individuals from separate families unite to form a new family system. This stage involves not only the development of a new marital system, but also a realignment with extended families and friends to include the spouse. Women's changing roles, the increasingly frequent marriage of partners from divergent cultural

leaving home and becoming a single adult The first stage in the family life cycle. It involves launching.

launching The process in which youth move into adulthood and exit their family of origin.

new couple Forming the new couple is the second stage in the family life cycle. Two individuals from separate families of origin unite to form a new family system.

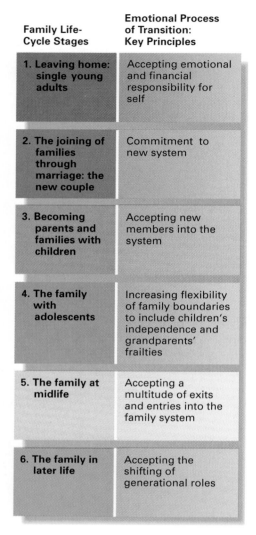

Family Life-Cycle Stages	Emotional Process of Transition: Key Principles
1. Leaving home: single young adults	Accepting emotional and financial responsibility for self
2. The joining of families through marriage: the new couple	Commitment to new system
3. Becoming parents and families with children	Accepting new members into the system
4. The family with adolescents	Increasing flexibility of family boundaries to include children's independence and grandparents' frailties
5. The family at midlife	Accepting a multitude of exits and entries into the family system
6. The family in later life	Accepting the shifting of generational roles

FIGURE 15.4 The Family Life Cycle

becoming parents and a family with children The third stage in the family life cycle. Adults who enter this stage move up a generation and become caregivers to the younger generation.

family with adolescents The fourth stage of the family life cycle, in which adolescent children push for autonomy and seek to develop their own identities.

family at midlife The fifth stage in the family life cycle, a time of launching children, linking generations, and adapting to midlife developmental changes.

family in later life The sixth and final stage in the family life cycle, involving retirement and, in many families, grandparenting.

backgrounds, and the increasing physical distances between family members are placing a much stronger burden on couples to define their relationships for themselves than was true in the past. Marriage is usually described as the union of two individuals, but in reality it is the union of two entire family systems and the development of a new, third system. Some experts on marriage and the family believe that marriage represents such a different phenomenon for women and men that we need to speak of "her" marriage and "his" marriage. In American society, women have anticipated marriage with greater enthusiasm and more positive expectations than men have.

- **Becoming parents and a family with children** is the third stage in the family life cycle. Entering this stage requires that adults now move up a generation and become caregivers to the younger generation. Moving through this lengthy stage successfully requires a commitment of time as a parent, understanding the roles of parents, and adapting to developmental changes in children. Problems that emerge when a couple first assumes the parental role are struggles with each other about taking responsibility, as well as refusal or inability to function as competent parents to children. We extensively discussed this stage of the family life cycle in chapters 7, 9, and 11 ◀▥ pp. 220, 276, and 349.
- The **family with adolescents** represents the fourth stage of the family life cycle. Adolescence is a period of development in which individuals push for autonomy and seek to develop their own identity. The development of mature autonomy and identity is a lengthy process, transpiring over at least 10 to 15 years. Compliant children become noncompliant adolescents. Parents tend to adopt one of two strategies to handle noncompliance. They either clamp down and put more pressure on the adolescent to conform to parental values, or they become more permissive and let the adolescent have extensive freedom. Neither is a wise overall strategy. A more flexible, adaptive approach is best. We discussed the family with adolescents in chapter 13 ◀▥ p. 410.
- The **family at midlife** is the fifth stage in the family life cycle. It is a time of launching children, playing an important role in linking generations, and adapting to midlife changes in development. Until about a generation ago, most families were involved in raising their children for much of their adult lives until old age. Because of the lower birth rate and longer life of most adults, parents now launch their children about 20 years before retirement, which frees many midlife parents to pursue other activities. We will discuss midlife families in greater detail in chapter 17.
- The **family in later life** is the sixth and final stage in the family life cycle. Retirement alters a couple's lifestyle, requiring adaptation. Grandparenting also chacacterizers many families in this stage. We will discuss the family in later life in chapter 20.

Figure 15.4 summarizes these stages of the family life cycle.

Some critics argue that the stage concept of the family life cycle is misleading. They argue that clearly defined stages often do not develop and the stages do not always occur in an orderly, sequential fashion (Elder, 1998). Further, they state that it is the variability associated with the stages which should be emphasized. For example, some women have children early (adolescence), or late (thirties, forties), some women have children outside of marriage, and some women have a career before parenthood or experience both simultaneously. Age and entry into these roles are increasingly independent. Further, many individuals have multiple families (such as children from a first marriage and children from a remarriage) and these may develop at different points in the life course.

Marriage

Our exploration of marriage focuses on some marital trends, expectations and myths about marriage, what makes marriages work, and the benefits of a good marriage.

Marital Trends   Until about 1930, stable marriage was widely accepted as a legitimate endpoint of adult development. In the last 60 years, however, we have seen
the emergence of personal fulfillment both inside and outside a marriage that com-
petes with marriages' stability as an adult developmental goal. The changing norm
of male-female equality in marriage has produced marital relationships that are
more fragile and intense than they were earlier in the twentieth century (Bradbury,
Fincham, & Beach, 2000). More adults are remaining single longer today, and the
average duration of a marriage in the United States is currently just over 9 years. In
1998, the U.S. average age for a first marriage climbed to 27 years for men and 25
years for women, higher than at any point in history (see figure 15.5). However, the
United States is still a marrying society. In 1998, 118 million individuals in the
United States were married, about 60 percent of the total population, which is a
drop of only about 5 percent since 1980. The divorce rate has begun to slow down,
although it still remains high—we will discuss divorced adults later in this chapter.
Even with adults remaining single for longer and divorce being a frequent occurrence, Americans still show a strong predilection for marriage—the proportion of
women who never marry remained at about 7 percent throughout the twentieth
century, for example.

In a recent national survey, young adults portrayed how they believe it is important for a marriage to be emotionally deep and communicative (Whitehead &
Popenoe, 2001):

- An overwhelming majority (94 percent) of never-married singles said that when
  you marry, you want your spouse to be your soul mate, first and foremost.
- A large majority of young adults indicated that it is unwise for a woman to rely
  on marriage for financial security.
- More than 80 percent of women said that it is more important for them to have
  a husband who can communicate his deepest feelings than to have a husband
  who makes a good living.
- A high percentage (86 percent) reported that marriage is hard work and a full-
  time job.

The sociocultural context is a powerful influence on marriage. The age at which
individuals marry, expectations about what the marriage will be like, and the developmental course of the marriage vary not only across historical time
within a given culture, but also across cultures. For example, a new marriage law took effect in China in 1981. The law sets a minimum age for
marriage—22 years for males, 20 years for females. Late marriage and
late childbirth are critical efforts in China's attempt to control population growth. More information about the nature of marriage in different cultures appears in the Sociocultural Worlds of Development box on
page 492.

Marital Expectations and Myths   Among the explanations of our nation's high divorce rate and high degree of dissatisfaction in many marriages is that we have such strong expectations of marriage. We expect our
spouse to simultaneously be a lover, a friend, a confidant, a counselor, a
career person, and a parent, for example. In one study, unhappily married
couples expressed unrealistic expectations about marriage (Epstein &
Eidelson, 1981).

Marriage therapists believe it is important to have realistic expectations about a marriage (Sharp & Ganong, 2000). Researchers have found
that unrealistic expectations are linked with lower levels of marital satisfaction (Larson & Holman, 1994). Similarly, individuals who have highly
romantic beliefs about marriage are likely to encounter disappointment as
they realize that sustaining their romantic ideal is not possible (Huston,
Neihuis, & Smith, 1997).

> *When two people are
> under the influence of the
> most violent, most insane,
> most delusive, and most
> transient of passions, they
> are required to swear that
> they will remain in that
> excited, abnormal, and
> exhausting condition
> continuously until death
> do them part.*
>
> —George Bernard Shaw
> *Irish Playwright, 20th Century*

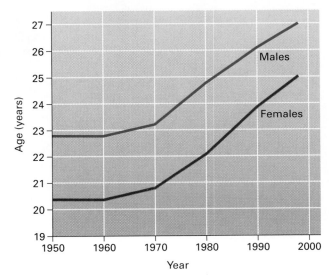

**FIGURE 15.5 Increase in Age at First Marriage in the
United States**

Shown here are average ages at first marriage in the United
States. Notice that since the 1960s, the age at which this important life event occurs has steadily increased.

Marriage Around the World

The traits that people look for in a marriage partner vary around the world. In one large-scale study of 9,474 adults from 37 cultures on six continents and five islands, people varied the most on how much they valued chastity—desiring a marital partner with no previous experience in sexual intercourse (Buss & others, 1990). Chastity was the most important factor in marital selection in China, India, Indonesia, Iran, Taiwan, and the Palestinian Arab culture. Adults from Ireland and Japan placed moderate importance on chastity. In contrast, adults in Sweden, Finland, Norway, the Netherlands, and Germany generally said that chastity was not important in selecting a marital partner.

In this study, domesticity was also valued in some cultures and not in others. Adults from the Zulu culture in South Africa, Estonia, and Colombia placed a high value on housekeeping skills in their marital preference. By contrast, adults in the United States, Canada, and all Western European countries except Spain said that housekeeping was not an important trait in their partner.

Religion plays an important role in marital preferences in many cultures. For example, Islam stresses the honor of the male and the purity of the female. It also emphasizes the woman's role in childbearing, child rearing, educating children, and instilling the Islamic faith in their children.

International comparisons of marriage also reveal that individuals in Scandinavian countries marry late, whereas their counterparts in Eastern Europe marry early (Blanchi & Spani, 1986). In Denmark, for example, almost 80 percent of the women and 90 percent of the men aged 20 to 24 have never been married. In Hungary less than 40 percent of the women and 70 percent of the men the same age have never been married. In Scandinavian countries, cohabitation is popular among young adults; however, most Scandinavians eventually marry. Only 5 percent of the women and 11 percent of the men in their early forties have never been married. Some countries such as Hungary encourage early marriage and childbearing to offset current and future population losses. Like Scandinavian countries, Japan has a high proportion of unmarried young people. However, rather than cohabitating as the Scandinavians do, unmarried Japanese young adults live at home longer with their parents before marrying.

Based on a review of many cross-cultural studies, these further conclusions were reached about love and marriage in the United States and Japan (Rothbaum & others, 2000). Traditionally, the Japanese family has had considerable influence on mate selection, and that influence continues to some degree today. In one-third to one-half of all marriages in Japan, initial contacts are still arranged by go-betweens. It also is common practice for parents to investigate the background of potential spouses for children.

In the United States, personal attraction dictates mate selection more than in Japan. Japanese Americans perceive that they have more choice and independence in selecting a mate than in Japan (Rothbaum & others, 2000).

Although romantic and passionate love are strong factors in many U.S. marriages, especially early in the marital relationship, in Japan, loyalty and commitment are more important (Dion & Dion, 1993; Yamagishi & Yamagishi, 1994). Divorce statistics bear out the emphasis on loyalty and commitment in Japan. The divorce rate in the United States is more than three times that of Japan (Kumagai, 1995). Conflict is not readily accepted in marital relations in Japan; rather, cohesion and cherishing the relationship are desired (Rothbaum & others, 2000).

(a)

(b)

(c)

(a) In Scandinavian countries, cohabitation is popular; only a small percentage of 20- to 24-year-olds are married. *(b)* Islam stresses male honor and female purity. *(c)* Loyalty and commitment are very important in Japanese marital relationships.

Underlying unrealistic expectations about marriage are numerous myths about marriage (Flanagan & others, 2001; Markman, 2000). A myth is a widely held belief unsupported by facts.

To study college students' beliefs in the myths of marriage, Jeffry Larson (1988) constructed a marriage quiz to measure college students' information about marriage and compared their responses with what is known about marriage in the research literature. The college students responded incorrectly to almost half of the items. Female students missed fewer items than male students, and students with a less romantic perception of marriage missed fewer items than more romantically inclined students.

What are some of the myths about marriage? They include these (Gottman & Silver, 1999):

- *Avoiding conflict will ruin your marriage.* Couples have different styles of conflict. Some avoid fights at all costs, some fight a lot, and some choose to "talk out" their differences and find solutions to problems without ever raising their voices. As long as the style works for both partners, no one style is necessarily better than the others. Couples can get into trouble if one partner wants to talk out a conflict while the other just wants to watch a favorite TV show that night.
- *Affairs are the main cause of divorce.* In most instances, it is the other way around. Marital problems send the couple on a downward trajectory, and one or both partners seek an intimate relationship outside of the marriage. In many instances, these affairs are not about sex but rather are about seeking to find friendship, support, understanding, respect, and caring.
- *Men are not biologically made for marriage.* This myth holds that men are philanderers by nature and thus ill suited for monogamy. This is sometimes called "the law of the jungle": the male of the species seeks to create as many offspring as possible and his allegiance to one mate restricts him from attaining this goal. Also involved is the view that the female's main task is to tend to her young, so she seeks a single mate who will provide for her and her children. However, as more women have sought employment outside the home, the rate at which women have extramarital affairs has increased dramatically; women's rate of extramarital affairs now slightly exceeds that of men.
- *Men and women are from different planets.* According to a best-selling book by John Gray (1992), men and women have serious relationship problems because he is from Mars and she is from Venus. Gender differences can contribute to marital problems, but they usually don't cause them. For example, the key factor in whether wives or husbands feel satisfied with the sex, romance, and passion in their marriage is the quality of the couple's friendship.

What Makes Marriages Work   John Gottman (1994; Gottman & Notarius, 2000; Gottman & Silver, 1999; Gottman & others, 1998) has been studying married couples' lives since the early 1970s. He uses extensive methods to study what makes marriages work. Gottman interviews couples about the history of their marriage, their philosophy about marriage, and how they view their parents' marriages. He videotapes them talking to each other about how their day went and evaluates what they say about the good and bad times of their marriages. Gottman also uses physiological measures to measure their heart rate, blood flow, blood pressure, and immune functioning moment by moment. He also checks back in with the couples every year to see how their marriage is faring. Gottman's research represents the most extensive assessment of marital relationships available. Currently he and his colleagues are following 700 couples in seven different studies.

John Gottman's Ideas

In his research, Gottman has found that seven main principles determine whether a marriage will work or not:

- *Establishing love maps.* Individuals in successful marriages have personal insights and detailed maps of each other's life and world. They aren't psychological strangers. In good marriages, partners are willing to share their feelings with each other. They use these "love maps" to express not only their understanding of each other but also their fondness and admiration.
- *Nurturing fondness and admiration.* In successful marriages, partners sing each other's praises. More than 90 percent of the time, when couples put a positive spin on their marriage's history, the marriage is likely to have a positive future.
- *Turning toward each other instead of away.* In good marriages, spouses are adept at turning toward each other regularly. They see each other as friends and this

What makes marriages work? What are the benefits of having a good marriage?

mhhe ● com/
santrockld9

Marriage Support
Journal of Family Psychology
Marriage and Family Therapy

friendship acts as a powerful shield against conflict. The friendship doesn't keep arguments from occurring, but it can prevent differences of opinion from overwhelming a relationship. In these good marriages, spouses respect each other and appreciate each other's point of view even though they might not agree with it.

- *Letting your partner influence you.* Bad marriages often involve one spouse who is unwilling to share power with the other. Although power-mongering is more common in husbands, some wives also show this problem. A willingness to share power and to respect the other person's view is a prerequisite to compromising.
- *Solving solvable conflicts.* Gottman has found two types of problems that occur in marriage: (1) perpetual and (2) solvable. Perpetual problems include spouses differing on whether to have children and one spouse wanting sex far more frequently than the other. Solvable problems include not helping each other reduce daily stresses and not being verbally affectionate. Unfortunately, more than two-thirds of marital problems fall into the perpetual category—those that won't go away. Fortunately, marital therapists have found that couples often don't have to solve their perpetual problems for the marriage to work. In his research, Gottman has found that resolving conflicts works best when couples start out solving the problem with a soft rather than a harsh approach, make an effort to make and receive repair attempts, regulate their emotions, compromise, and are tolerant of each other's faults. Conflict resolution is not about one person making changes, it is about negotiating and accommodating each other.

Work, stress, in-laws, money, sex, housework, a new baby: These are among the typical areas of marital conflict. Even in happy marriages, these areas are often hot buttons in a relationship. When there is conflict in these areas, it usually means that a husband and wife have different ideas about the tasks involved, their importance, or how they should be accomplished. If the conflict is perpetual, no amount of problem-solving expertise will fix it. The tension will decrease only when both partners feel comfortable living with the ongoing difference. However, when the issue is solvable, the challenge is to find the right strategy for dealing with it. Strategies include:

   a. Scheduling formal griping sessions about stressful issues
   b. Learning to talk about sex in a way that both partners feel comfortable with
   c. Creating lists of who does what to see how household labor is divided up

- *Overcoming gridlock.* One partner wants the other to attend church, the other is an atheist. One partner is a homebody, the other wants to go out and socialize a lot. Such problems often produce gridlock. Gottman believes the key to ending gridlock is not to solve the problem, but to move from gridlock to dialogue and be patient.
- *Creating shared meaning.* The more partners can speak candidly and respectfully with each other, the more likely it is that they will create shared meaning in their marriage. This also includes sharing goals with one's spouse and working together to achieve each other's goals.

The Benefits of a Good Marriage   Now that you know what makes a marriage work, are there any benefits to having a good marriage? There are. An unhappy marriage increases an individual's risk of getting sick by approximately one-third and can even shorten a person's life by an average of four years (Gove, Style, & Hughes, 1990). On the other hand, individuals who are happily married live longer, healthier lives than divorced individuals or those who are unhappily married (Cotten, 1999).

What are the reasons for these benefits of a happy marriage? People in happy marriages likely feel less physically and emotionally stressed, which puts less wear and tear on a person's body. Such wear and tear can lead to numerous physical ailments, such as high blood pressure and heart disease, as well as psychological problems such as anxiety, depression, and substance abuse.

Gender and Emotion in Marriage   Wives consistently disclose more to their partners than husbands do (Hendrick, 2002). And women tend to express more tenderness, fear, and sadness than their partners. A common complaint expressed by women in a marriage is that their husbands do not care about their emotional lives and do not express their own feelings and thoughts. Women often point out that they have to literally pull things out of their husbands and push them to open up. Men frequently respond either that they are open or that they do not understand what their wives want from them. It is not unusual for men to protest that no matter how much they talk it is not enough for their wives. Women also say they want more warmth as well as openness from their husbands. For example, women are more likely than men to give their partners a spontaneous kiss or hug when something positive happens. Overall, women are more expressive and affectionate than men in marriage, and this difference bothers many women (Fox & Murry, 2000; Streil, 2002).

Parental Roles

For many adults, parental roles are well planned and coordinated with other roles in life and developed with the individual's economic situation in mind. For others, the discovery that they are about to become parents is a startling surprise. In either event, the prospective parents may have mixed emotions and romantic illusions about having a child. Parenting consists of a number of interpersonal skills and emotional demands, yet there is little in the way of formal education for this task. Most parents learn parenting practices from their own parents—some they accept, some they discard. Husbands and wives may bring different viewpoints of parenting practices to the marriage. Unfortunately, when methods of parents are passed on from one generation to the next, both desirable and undesirable practices are perpetuated.

The needs and expectations of parents have stimulated many myths about parenting:

- The birth of a child will save a failing marriage.
- As a possession or extension of the parent, the child will think, feel, and behave like the parents did in their childhood.
- Children will take care of parents in old age.
- Parents can expect respect and get obedience from their children.

Unlike most approaches to helping couples, mine is based on knowing what makes marriages succeed rather than fail.

—**John Gottman**
Contemporary Psychologist,
University of Washington

Careers in Life-Span Development

Janis Keyser, Parent Educator

Janis Keyser is a parent educator and teaches in the Department of Early Childhood Education at Cabrillo College in California. In addition to teaching college classes and conducting parenting workshops, she also has co-authored a book with Laura Davis (1997), *Becoming the Parent You Want To Be, A Sourcebook of Strategies for the First Five Years.*

Keyser also writes as an expert on the iVillage website (http://www.parentsplace.com). And she also co-authors a nationally syndicated parenting column, "Growing Up, Growing Together." She is the mother of three, stepmother of five, grandmother of twelve, and great grandmother of six.

Janis Keyser (right), conducting a parenting workshop.

We never know the love of our parents until we have become parents.

—Henry Ward Beecher
American Clergyman, 19th Century

- Having a child means that the parents will always have someone who loves them and is their best friend.
- Having a child gives the parents a "second chance" to achieve what they should have achieved.
- If parents learn the right techniques, they can mold their children into what they want.
- It's the parents' fault when children fail.
- Mothers are naturally better parents than fathers.
- Parenting is an instinct and requires no training.

In earlier times, women considered being a mother a full-time occupation. Currently, there is a tendency to have fewer children, and, as birth control has become common practice, many individuals choose when they will have children and how many children they will raise. The number of one-child families is increasing, for example. Giving birth to fewer children and reduced demands of child care free a significant portion of a woman's life span for other endeavors. Three accompanying changes are that (1) as a result of the increase in working women, there is less maternal investment in the child's development; (2) men are apt to invest a greater amount of time in fathering; and (3) parental care in the home is often supplemented by institutional care (day care, for example) ◀ ▦ p. 222.

As more women show an increased interest in developing a career, they are not only marrying later, but also having children later (Grolnick & Gurland, 2001). What are some of the advantages of having children early or late? Some of the advantages of having children early are these: The parents are likely to have more physical energy (for example, they can cope better with such matters as getting up in the middle of the night with infants and waiting up until adolescents come home at night); the mother is likely to have fewer medical problems with pregnancy and childbirth; and the parents may be less likely to build up expectations for their children, as do many couples who have waited many years to have children. By contrast, there are also advantages to having children late: The parents will have had more time to consider their goals in life, such as what they want from their family and career roles; the parents will be more mature and will be able to benefit from their life experiences to engage in more competent parenting; and the parents will be better established in their careers and have more income for child-rearing expenses.

Parent educators seek to help individuals to become better parents. To read about the work of one parent educator, see the Careers in Life-Span Development insert.

A special concern that has recently surfaced involves many successful women feeling anxiety about being childless. A recent book, *Creating a Life: Professional Women and the Quest for Children* (Hewlett, 2002), described the results of interviews with 1,186 high-achieving career women (income in the top 10 percent of their age group) from 28 to 55 years of age. Among the findings were:

- Thirty-three percent were childless at age 40.
- Forty-two percent who worked in corporations were childless.
- Forty-nine percent of "ultraachievers" (earning more than $100,000 a year) were childless.

- Twenty-five percent of childless high achievers from 41 to 55 years of age would still like to have a child and 31 percent of "ultraachievers" would still like to have one.
- No high achiever from 41 to 55 years of age had a first child after age 39 and no "ultraachiever" had one after age 36.

Many of the study's childless women in their forties and fifties recommended that younger women spend more time envisioning what their life will be like when they become middle-aged and whether they want their life to include a child. They argue that many high-achieving women will ultimately be happier if they have a child in their twenties or thirties. Critics argue that the optimal age for motherhood depends on the individual and that many women become mothers after they are 35 years of age.

Review and Reflect

3 Discuss Marriage and the Family

REVIEW

- What are the six stages of the family life cycle?
- What characterizes marriage and marital relationships?
- What are some parental roles?

REFLECT

- Are there more pressures on marriage today than in the past? Explain.

4 THE DIVERSITY OF ADULT LIFESTYLES

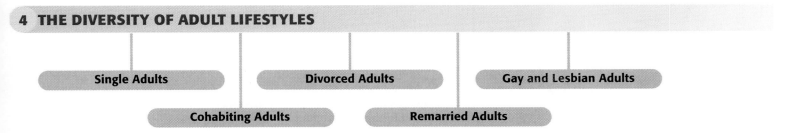

Single Adults   Divorced Adults   Gay and Lesbian Adults

Cohabiting Adults   Remarried Adults

Today's adult lifestyles are diverse. We have single-career families; dual-career families; single-parent families, including mother custody, father custody, and joint custody; the remarried or stepfamily; the kin family (made up of bilateral or intergenerationally linked members); and even the experimental family (individuals in multiadult households—communes—or cohabiting adults). And, of course, there are many single adults.

Single Adults

There is no rehearsal. One day you don't live alone, the next day you do. College ends. Your wife walks out. Your husband dies. Suddenly, you live in this increasingly modern condition, living alone. Maybe you like it, maybe you don't. Maybe you thrive on the solitude, maybe you ache as if in exile. Either way, chances are you are only half prepared, if at all, to be sole proprietor of your bed, your toaster, and your time. Most of us were raised in the din and clutter of family life, jockeying for a place in the bathroom in the morning, fighting over the last piece of cake, and obliged to compromise on the simplest of choices—the volume of the stereo, the channel on the

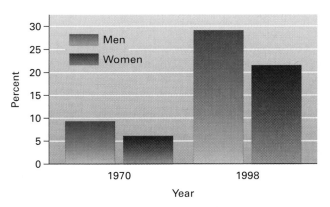

FIGURE 15.6 Percentage of Single Adults 30 to 34 Years of Age in 1970 and 1998

In less than three decades, the percentage of single adults 30 to 34 years of age more than tripled.

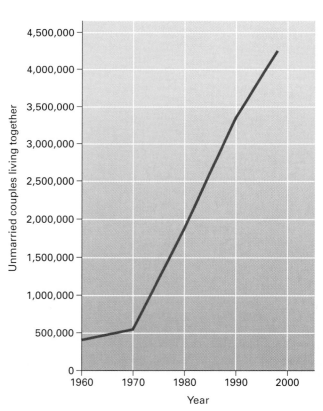

FIGURE 15.7 The Increase in Cohabitation in the United States

Since 1970, there has been a dramatic increase in the number of unmarried adults living together in the United States.

TV, for example. Few of us grew up thinking that home would be a way station in our life course.

There has been a dramatic rise in the percentage of single adults. In 1998, more than 46 million adult Americans (24 percent of the total American adults) who never had been married lived alone (U.S. Bureau of the Census, 2000). This is three times the percentage in 1970 (8 percent). As shown in figure 15.6, being single in the age period of the early thirties had shown a similar increase.

A history of myths and stereotypes is associated with being single, ranging from the "swinging single" to the "desperately lonely, suicidal single." Of course, most single adults are somewhere between these extremes.

What are some of the advantages of being single? They include time to make decisions about one's life course, time to develop personal resources to meet goals, freedom to make autonomous decisions and pursue one's own schedule and interests, opportunity to explore new places and try out new things, and availability of privacy.

Common problems of single adults focus on intimate relationships with other adults, confronting loneliness, and finding a niche in a society that is marriage oriented. Many single adults cite personal freedom as one of the major advantages of being a single adult. One woman who never married commented, "I enjoy knowing that I can satisfy my own whims without someone else's interferences. If I want to wash my hair at two o'clock in the morning, no one complains. I can eat when I'm hungry and watch my favorite television shows without contradictions from anyone. I enjoy these freedoms. I would feel very confined if I had to adjust to another person's schedule."

Some adults never marry. Initially, they are perceived as living glamorous, exciting lives. But once we reach the age of 30, there can be increasing pressure to settle down and get married. If a woman wants to bear children, she might feel a sense of urgency when she reaches 30. This is when many single adults make a conscious decision to marry or to remain single. As one 30-year-old male recently commented, "It's real. You are supposed to get married by 30—that is a standard. It is part of getting on with your life that you are supposed to do. You have career and who-am-I concerns in your twenties. In your thirties, you have to get on with it, keep on track, make headway, financially and familywise." But, to another 30-year-old, getting married is less important than buying a house and some property. A training manager for a computer company, Jane says, "I'm competent in making relationships and being committed, so I don't feel a big rush to get married. When it happens, it happens."

Cohabiting Adults

Cohabitation refers to living together in a sexual relationship without being married. Cohabitation has undergone considerable changes in recent years (Booth, Crouter, & Clements, 2001; Crooks & Bauer, 2002) (see figure 15.7). There has been a significant increase in both the number of adults who engage in this lifestyle and acceptance of what once was considered unconventional (Nock, 1995). In 1996, 6.75 percent of all couples in the United States were cohabiting. Twenty-five percent of individuals 19 to 24 years old and 42 percent of individuals 25 to 29 years old have cohabited at least once. These arrangements tend to be short-lived, with one-third lasting less than a year (Hyde & DeLamater, 2002). Less than 1 out of 10 lasts five years.

A number of couples view their cohabitation not as a precursor to marriage but rather as an ongoing lifestyle. These couples prefer the informality of living together to the more official aspects of marriage. They like being together because they want to, not because they are bound by a legal contract.

When unmarried adults cohabit, they can feel less pressure to live up to the expectations attached to being a "wife" or a "husband." Relationships in cohabitation tend to be more equal than in marriage (Wineberg, 1994). Also, there is less stigma attached to dissolving a cohabitation relationship than there is to divorce.

Although cohabitation offers some advantages, it also can produce some problems. Disapproval by parents and other family members can be severe, placing emotional strain on the cohabiting couple. Some cohabiting couples can have difficulty owning property jointly. Without a clear, written contract, legal rights on the dissolution of the relationship are less certain than in a divorce.

Some individuals believe that cohabitation improves their chances for choosing a partner with whom they will have a stable and happy marriage. Others believe just the opposite—that living together before marriage will have a more negative impact on future marriage. Which viewpoint is right?

Some researchers have found no differences in marital quality between individuals who earlier cohabited and those who did not (Newcomb & Bentler, 1980; Watson & DeMeo, 1987). Other researchers have found lower rates of marital satisfaction in couples who lived together before getting married (Booth & Johnson, 1988). For example, in one study of 13,000 individuals, married couples who cohabited prior to their marriage reported lower levels of happiness with and commitment to their marital relationship than their counterparts who had not previously cohabited (Nock, 1995). Also, in one study, living together prior to marriage was more likely to lead to divorce than when a couple did not live together prior to marriage (DeMaris & Rao, 1992). In a recent study, spouses who cohabited before marriage showed less support of their spouse than those who did not cohabit before marriage (Cohan & Kleinbaum, 2002). Further, in another recent study, after 10 years of marriage, 40 percent of couples who lived together first had divorced whereas 31 percent of those who had not cohabited first had divorced (Centers for Disease Control and Prevention, 2002).

In sum, researchers have not found that cohabitation leads to greater marital happiness and success. Rather, they have discovered either that it leads to no differences or evidence that cohabitation is not good for a marriage.

Divorced Adults

Divorce has become epidemic in our culture ◀▥ p. 283. The number of divorced adults rose from 4.3 million individuals (3 percent of the adult population) in 1970 to 19.4 million individuals (10 percent of the population) in 1998. The divorce rate was increasing annually by 10 percent, but has been declining since the 1980s. While divorce has increased for all socioeconomic groups, those in disadvantaged groups have a higher incidence of divorce. Youthful marriage, low educational level, and low income are associated with increases in divorce. So too is premarital pregnancy. One study revealed that half of the women who were pregnant before marriage failed to live with the husband for more than five years (Sauber & Corrigan, 1970).

If a divorce is going to occur, it usually takes place early in a marriage, peaking in the fifth to tenth years of marriage (National Center for Health Statistics, 2000) (see figure 15.8). Some partners in a troubled marriage might stay in it and try to work things out. If after several years these efforts don't improve the relationship, they might seek a divorce.

Many adults, even those who initiated the divorce, experience changes and challenges in their lives following marital dissolution (Amato, 2000; Hetherington, 2000). Both divorced women and

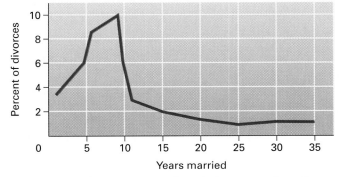

FIGURE 15.8 The Divorce Rate in Relation to Number of Years Married

Shown here is the percentage of divorces as a function of how long couples have been married. Notice that most divorces occur in the early years of marriage, peaking in the fifth to tenth years of marriage.

mhhe●com/
santrockld9

Psychological Aspects of Divorce
Divorced and Remarried Parents
Remarried Adults' Resources
Stepfamily Interventions

divorced men complain of loneliness, diminished self-esteem, anxiety about the unknowns in their lives, and difficulty in forming satisfactory new intimate relationships.

The stress of separation and divorce places both men and women at risk for psychological and physical difficulties (Hetherington & Stanley-Hagan, 2002; Kitzman & Gaylord, 2002). Separated and divorced women and men have higher rates of psychiatric disorders, admission to psychiatric hospitals, clinical depression, alcoholism, and psychosomatic problems, such as sleep disorders, than do married adults. There is increasing evidence that stressful events of many types—including marital separation—reduce the immune system's capabilities, rendering separated and divorced individuals vulnerable to disease and infection. In one study, the most recently separated women (one year or less) were more likely to show impaired immunological functioning than women whose separations had occurred several years earlier (one to six years) (Kiecolt-Glaser & Glaser, 1988). Also in this study, unhappily married individuals had immune systems that were not functioning as effectively as those of happily married individuals.

Custodial parents have concerns about child rearing and overload in their lives. Noncustodial parents register complaints about alienation from or lack of time with their children. Men show only modest declines in income following a divorce but women reveal a significant decline in income following a divorce, with estimates of the decline ranging from 20 to 35 percent. For divorced women, the financial decline means living in a less desirable neighborhood with fewer resources, less effective schools, and more deviant peer groups for their children. Nonetheless, the economic decline for women following a divorce has diminished as increasing numbers of women have a better education and job.

Psychologically, one of the most common characteristics of divorced adults is the difficulty they have in trusting someone else in a romantic relationship. Following a divorce, though, people's lives can take diverse turns. In E. Mavis Hetherington's research, men and women took six common pathways out of divorce (Hetherington and Kelly, 2002):

- *The enhancers.* Accounting for 20 percent of the divorced group, these females grew more competent, well-adjusted, and self-fufilled following their divorce. They were competent in multiple areas of life, showed a remarkable ability to bounce back from stressful circumstances, and create something meaningful out of the problems they encountered.
- *The good enoughs.* Consistently the largest group of divorced individuals, they were described as the average man and woman coping with divorce. They showed some strengths and some vulnerabilities and strengths, some success and some problems. When they encountered a problem, they tried to solve it. However, good enoughs planned less systematically and were less persistent than enhancers. Unlike enhancers, good enough women usually married men who educationally and economically looked like their first husbands, often moving into marriages that were not a great improvement over the first one.
- *The seekers.* This group was eager to find a new mate as soon as possible. At one year postdivorce, 40 percent of the men and 38 percent of women were classified as seekers. As individuals found new partners over time or became more secure or satisfied in their single life, the seeker category shrank and came to be predominated by men.
- *The libertines.* They often spent more time in singles bars and had more casual sex than their counterparts in the other divorce categories. However, by the end of the first year postdivorce, they often grew disillusioned with their sensation-seeking lifestyle and longed for a stable relationship.
- *The competent loners.* These individuals, which made up only about 10 percent of the divorced group, were well-adjusted, self-sufficient, and socially skilled. They had a successful career, an active social life, and a wide range of interests. However, unlike enhancers, competent loners had little interest in sharing their life with anyone else.

- *The defeated.* Some of these individuals had problems before their divorce, which worsened after the breakup when they found that the added stress of a failed marriage was more than they could handle. Others had problems because they had a spouse who had supported them, or in the case of a drinking problem, restricted them.

Hetherington recommends these strategies for divorced adults (Hetherington & Kelly, 2002):

- Look at divorce as an opportunity for personal growth and to build more fulfilling relationships.
- Think carefully about the decisions you make. The consequences of choices about work, lovers, and children may last a lifetime.
- Focus more on the future than the past. Set priorities and goals, and then work toward them.
- Capitalize on your strengths and the resources available to you.
- Don't expect to be successful and happy in everything you do. The road to a more satisfying life is likely to be bumpy and have many detours.
- Remember that you are never trapped by one pathway. Most of the divorced adults who were categorized as defeated immediately after divorce in Hetherington's research gradually moved on to a better life, but moving forward usually requires a great deal of effort.

Remarried Adults

In chapter 11, we discussed stepfamilies with a special emphasis on the effects of living in a stepfamily on children's development ◀|||| p. 350. Here we will continue our exploration of stepfamilies with a stronger focus on the relationships of remarried adults. On average, divorced adults remarry within four years after their divorce, with men doing this sooner than women.

Stepfamilies come in many sizes and forms. The custodial and noncustodial parents and stepparent all might have been married and divorced, in some cases more than once. These parents might have residential children from prior marriages and a large network of grandparents and other relatives. Regardless of their form and size, the newly reconstituted families face some unique tasks. The couple must define and strengthen their marriage and at the same time renegotiate the biological parent-child relationships and establish stepparent-stepchild and stepsibling relationships (Coleman, Ganong, & Fine, 2000; Hetherington & Stanley-Hagan, 2002).

The complex histories and multiple relationships make adjustment difficult in a stepfamily (Coleman, Ganong, & Weaver, 2001; Thomson & others, 2001). The difficulty of adjusting to life in a stepfamily is borne out by the data: only one-third of stepfamily couples stay remarried (Gerlach, 1998).

Why do remarried adults find it so difficult to stay remarried? For one thing, many remarry not for love but for financial reasons, for help in rearing children, and to reduce loneliness. They also might carry into the stepfamily negative relationship patterns that resulted in the failure of an earlier marriage. Remarried couples also experience more stress in rearing children than parents in never-divorced families (Ganong & Coleman, 1994).

Among the strategies that help remarried couples cope with the stress of living in a stepfamily are these (Visher & Visher, 1989):

- *Have realistic expectations.* Allow time for loving relationships to develop, and look at the complexity of the stepfamily as a challenge to overcome.
- *Develop new positive relationships within the family.* Create new traditions and ways of dealing with difficult circumstances that work. Allocation of time is especially important with all of the people involved. In this regard, the remarried couple needs to allot time alone for each other.

What are the research findings regarding the development and psychological well-being of children raised by gay and lesbian couples?

mhhe ● com/
santrockld9

Gay and Lesbian Relationships

Gay and Lesbian Adults

Researchers have found that gay and lesbian relationships are similar—in their satisfactions, loves, joys, and conflicts—to heterosexual relationships (Hyde & DeLamater, 2002; Peplau & Beals, 2002). For example, like heterosexual couples, gay and lesbian couples need to find a balance in their relationships that is acceptable to both partners in terms of romantic love, affection, how much autonomy is acceptable, and how equal the relationship will be. Lesbian couples especially place a high priority on equality in their relationships (Kurdek, 1995). In one study, gay and lesbian couples listed the areas of conflict in order of frequency: finances, driving style, affection and sex, being overly critical, and household tasks (Kurdek, 1995). The components of this list are likely to be familiar to heterosexual couples as well.

There are a number of misconceptions about homosexual couples. For example, many people think that one partner is masculine and the other feminine in a homosexual relationship. This appears to be true only in a small percentage of cases. Indeed, some researchers have found that gay and lesbian couples are more flexible in their gender roles than heterosexual individuals are (Marecek, Finn, & Cardell, 1988). Another misconception is that homosexual couples have a huge amount of sex. Again, this is true only of a small segment of the gay male population, and it is uncommon among lesbians. Yet another misconception about homosexual couples is that they don't get involved in long-term relationships. Researchers have found that homosexuals prefer long-term, committed relationships (Peplau & Beals, 2002). About half of committed gay male couples do have an open relationship that allows the possibility of sex (but not affectionate love) outside of the relationship. Lesbian couples usually do not have this open relationship.

One aspect of relationships in which heterosexual and homosexual couples differ involves the obstacles that make it difficult to end a relationship (Peplau & Beals, 2002). In this regard, the legal and social context of marriage creates barriers to breaking up that do not usually exist for same-sex partners (Peplau & Beals, 2002).

Increasingly, gay and lesbian couples are creating families that include children. This is controversial to many heterosexual individuals who view a gay or lesbian family as damaging to the development of a child. However, researchers have found that children growing up in gay or lesbian families are just as popular with their peers and there are no differences in the adjustment and mental health of children living in these families when they are compared with children in heterosexual families (Hyde & DeLamater, 2002). Also, the overwhelming majority of children growing up in a gay or lesbian family have a heterosexual orientation (Patterson, 1996, 2000).

Review and Reflect

4 **Explain the diversity of lifestyles**

REVIEW

- What characterizes single adults?
- What are the lives of cohabiting adults like?
- How does divorce affect adults?
- What are the lives of remarried parents like?
- What characterizes the lifestyles of gay and lesbian adults?

REFLECT

- Which type of lifestyle are you living today? What do you think are the advantages and disadvantages of this lifestyle for you? If you could have a different lifestyle, which one would it be? Why?

5 GENDER, RELATIONSHIPS, AND SELF-DEVELOPMENT

Women's Development   Men's Development

In chapters 9 and 11, we discussed a number of ideas about gender development in children ◀▥▥ pp. 272 and 334. Also, earlier in this chapter we explored gender in friendship, gender and family work, and the mother's and the father's roles. Here we will further examine gender by focusing on some issues involving gender, relationships, and self-development.

Do women and men hold different views of love? One recent study found that men conceptualize love in terms of passion while women think of love more in terms of friendship (Fehr & Broughton, 2001). However, both women and men view love in affectionate terms.

Women's Development

Jean Baker Miller (1986) has been an important voice in stimulating the examination of psychological issues from a female perspective. She believes that the study of women's psychological development opens up paths to a better understanding of all psychological development, male or female. She also concludes that when researchers examine what women have been doing in life, a large part of it is active participation in the development of others. In Miller's view, women often try to interact with others in ways that will foster the other person's development along many dimensions—emotionally, intellectually, and socially.

Most experts believe it is important for women to not only maintain their competency in relationships but to be self-motivated, too (Donelson, 1998). Miller believes that through increased self-determination, coupled with already developed relationship skills, many women will gain greater power in the American culture. And as Harriet Lerner (1989) concludes in her book *The Dance of Intimacy*, it is important for women to bring to their relationships nothing less than a strong, assertive, independent, and authentic self. She believes competent relationships are those in which the separate "I-ness" of both persons can be appreciated and enhanced while still staying emotionally connected to each other.

Deborah Tannen (1990) analyzed the talk of women and men. She reported that a common complaint that wives have about their husbands is, "He doesn't listen to me anymore." Another is, "He doesn't talk to me anymore." Lack of communication, while high on women's lists of reasons for divorce, is much less often mentioned by men.

Tannen distinguishes between rapport talk and report talk. *Rapport talk* is the language of conversation and a way of establishing connections and negotiating relationships. *Report talk* is public speaking, which men feel more comfortable doing. Men hold center stage through such verbal performances as storytelling, joking, or imparting information. Men learn to use talking as a way of getting and keeping attention. By contrast, women enjoy private speaking more, talk that involves discussing similarities and matching experiences. It is men's lack of interest in rapport talk that bothers many women.

Women's dissatisfaction with men's silence at home is captured in a typical cartoon setting of a breakfast table at which a husband and wife are sitting. He's reading the newspaper; she's glaring at the back of the newspaper. Another cartoon shows a husband opening a newspaper and asking his wife, "Is there anything you want to say to me before I

Gender and Communication
Women's Issues
Gender and Society

"You have no idea how nice it is to have someone to talk to."
Copyright © 1964 Don Orehek.

How might men be able to reconstruct their masculinity in positive ways?

*U*nderstanding the other's ways of talking is a giant leap across the communication gap between women and men, and a giant step toward opening lines of communication.

—Deborah Tannen
*Contemporary Sociologist,
Georgetown University*

The Men's Bibliography

**Psychological Study of
Men and Masculinity**

Male Issues

begin reading the newspaper?" The reader knows there isn't, but that as soon as he starts reading the paper, she will think of something. *To him, talk is for information.* So when his wife interrupts his reading, it must be to inform him of something he needs to know. So, since this is the case, she might as well tell him what she thinks he needs to know before he starts reading. *But for her, talk is for interaction.* She believes saying things is a way to show involvement; listening is a way to show caring and interest.

The problem, then, may not be an individual man, or even men's styles alone, but the difference between women's and men's styles. If so, both men and women can make adjustments. A woman can push herself to speak up without being invited, or begin to speak even at the slightest pause in talk. The adjustment should not be just one-sided. Men can learn that women who are not accustomed to speaking up in groups are not as free as they are to do so. By understanding this reluctance on the part of women, men can make them feel more comfortable by warmly encouraging and allowing them to speak rather than hogging public talk.

Men's Development

The male of the species—what is he really like? What are his concerns? According to Joseph Pleck's (1981, 1995) *role-strain* view, male roles are contradictory and inconsistent. Men not only experience stress when they violate men's roles, they also are harmed when they *do* act in accord with men's roles. Here are some of the areas where men's roles can cause considerable strain (Levant, 2002; Levant & Brooks, 1997):

- *Health.* Men live 8 to 10 years less than women do. They have higher rates of stress-related disorders, alcoholism, car accidents, and suicide. Men are more likely than women to be the victims of homicide. In sum, the male role is hazardous to men's health.
- *Male-female relationships.* Too often, the male's role involves images that men should be dominant, powerful, and aggressive and should control women. Also, the male role has involved looking at women in terms of their bodies rather than their minds and feelings. Earlier, we described Deborah Tannen's (1990) concept that men show too little interest in rapport talk and relationships. And

the male role has included the view that women should not be considered equal to men in work, earnings, and many other aspects of life. Too often these dimensions of the male role have produced men who have disparaged women, been violent toward women, and been unwilling to have equal relationships with women.

- *Male-male relationships.* Too many men have had too little interaction with their fathers, especially fathers who are positive role models. Nurturing and being sensitive to others have been considered aspects of the female role, and not the male role. And the male role emphasizes competition rather than cooperation. All of these aspects of the male role have left men with inadequate positive, emotional connections with other males.

To reconstruct their masculinity in more positive ways, Ron Levant (2002) believes, every man should (1) reexamine his beliefs about manhood, (2) separate out the valuable aspects of the male role, and (3) get rid of those parts of the masculine role that are destructive. All of this involves becoming more "emotionally intelligent"—that is, becoming more emotionally self-aware, managing emotions more effectively, reading emotions better (one's own emotions and others'), and being motivated to improve close relationships.

Review and Reflect

5 Characterize the role of gender in relationships

REVIEW

- What are some important aspects of the woman's role in relationships?
- What are some important aspects of the man's role in relationships?

REFLECT

- If you are female, what would you change about the way men function in relationships?
- If you are male, what would you change about the way women function in relationships?

Reach Your Learning Goals

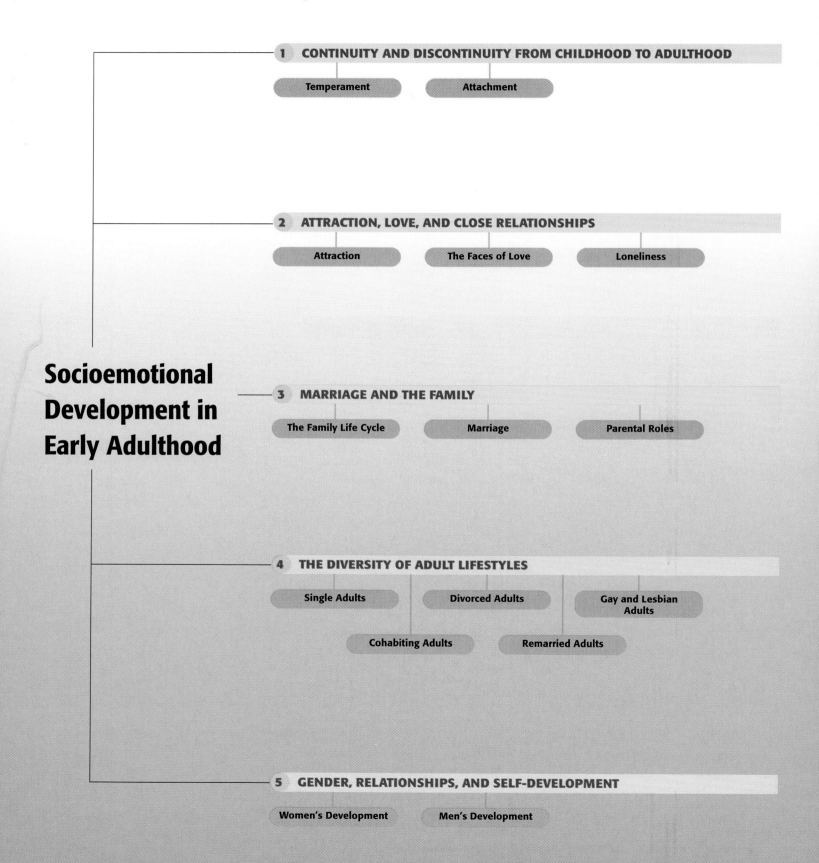

Socioemotional Development in Early Adulthood

1 CONTINUITY AND DISCONTINUITY FROM CHILDHOOD TO ADULTHOOD

Temperament   Attachment

2 ATTRACTION, LOVE, AND CLOSE RELATIONSHIPS

Attraction   The Faces of Love   Loneliness

3 MARRIAGE AND THE FAMILY

The Family Life Cycle   Marriage   Parental Roles

4 THE DIVERSITY OF ADULT LIFESTYLES

Single Adults   Divorced Adults   Gay and Lesbian Adults

Cohabiting Adults   Remarried Adults

5 GENDER, RELATIONSHIPS, AND SELF-DEVELOPMENT

Women's Development   Men's Development

Summary

1 Describe continuity and discontinuity in temperament and attachment from childhood to adulthood

- The first 20 years are important in predicting an adult's personality, but so, too, are continuing experiences in the adult years. Activity level in early childhood is linked with being an outgoing young adult. Young adults show fewer mood swings, are more responsible, and engage in less risk taking than adolescents. In some cases, temperament in childhood is linked with adjustment problems in early adulthood.
- Attachment styles in young adults are linked with their attachment history, although attachment styles can change in adulthood as adults experience relationships.

2 Identify some key aspects of attraction, love, and close relationships

- Familiarity precedes a close relationship. We like to associate with people who are similar to us. The principles of consensual validation and matching can explain this. Physical attraction is usually the most important in the early part of relationships, and criteria for physical attractiveness vary across cultures and historical time.
- Erikson theorized that intimacy versus isolation is the key developmental issue in early adulthood. There is a delicate balance between intimacy and commitment, on the one hand, and independence and freedom on the other. Romantic love, also called passionate love, is involved when we say we are "in love." It includes passion, sexuality, and a mixture of emotions, not all of which are positive. Affectionate love, also called companionate love, usually becomes more important as relationships mature. Shaver proposed a developmental model of love and Sternberg a triarchic model of love (passion, intimacy, and commitment). Friendship plays an important role in adult development, especially in terms of emotional support. Female, male, and female-male friendships often have different characteristics. For example, self-disclosure is more common in female friendships.
- Loneliness often emerges when people make life transitions, so it is not surprising that loneliness is common among college freshmen. Changes in loneliness are emerging as technology changes. A number of strategies were described to help lonely individuals become more socially connected.

3 Discuss marriage and the family

- There are six stages in the family life cycle: leaving home and becoming a single adult; the new couple; becoming parents and a family with children; the family with adolescents; the midlife family; and the family in later life.
- Even though adults are remaining single longer and the divorce rate is high, we still show a strong predilection for marriage. The age at which individuals marry, expectations about what the marriage will be like, and the developmental course of marriage may vary not only across historical time within a culture, but also across cultures. Unrealistic expectations and myths about marriage contribute to marital dissatisfaction and divorce. Among the marital myths are that avoiding conflict will ruin a marriage, men are not biologically made for marriage, and men and women are from different planets. Gottman has conducted extensive research on what makes marriages work. In his research these principles characterize good marriages: establishing love maps, nurturing fondness and admiration, turning toward each other instead of away, letting your partner influence you, solving solvable conflicts, overcoming gridlock, and creating shared meaning. The benefits of marriage include better physical and mental health and a longer life. Overall, women are more expressive and affectionate in marriage, and this difference bothers many women.
- For some, the parental role is well planned and coordinated. For others, there is surprise and sometimes chaos. There are many myths about parenting, among them the myth that the birth of a child will save a failing marriage. Families are becoming smaller, and many women are delaying childbirth until they have become well established in a career. There are some advantages to having children earlier in adulthood, and some advantages to having them later.

4 Explain the diversity of lifestyles

- Being single has become an increasingly prominent lifestyle. Myths and stereotypes about singles abound, ranging from "swinging single" to "desperately lonely, suicidal single." There are advantages and disadvantages to being single, autonomy being one of the advantages. Intimacy, loneliness, and finding a positive identity in a marriage-oriented society are concerns of single adults.
- Cohabitation is an increasing lifestyle for many adults. Cohabitation offers some advantages as well as problems. Cohabitation does not lead to greater marital happiness but rather to no differences or differences suggesting that cohabitation is not good for a marriage.
- Divorce has increased dramatically, although its rate of increase has begun to slow. Divorce is complex and emotional. In the first year following divorce, a disequilibrium in the divorced adult's behavior occurs, but by several years after the divorce, more stability has been achieved. The divorced displaced homemaker may encounter excessive stress. Men do not go through a divorce unscathed either.
- Stepfamilies are complex and adjustment is difficult. Only about one-third of remarried adults stay remarried.
- One of the most striking findings about gay and lesbian couples is how similar they are to heterosexual couples. There are a number of misconceptions about homosexual couples. Researchers have found that the children of gay and lesbian parents are as well adjusted as those of heterosexual couples. The overwhelming number of children in gay and lesbian families grow up to be heterosexual.

5 Characterize the role of gender in relationships

- Many experts believe that it is important for females to retain their competence and interest in relationships, but also to direct more effort into self-development. Tannen distinguishes between rapport talk, which many women prefer, and report talk, which many men prefer.

- Men have been successful at achieving but the male role involves considerable strain. It is possible to talk about the "male experience," but there is diversity among males, just as there is diversity among females.

Key Terms

Key People

Taking It to the Net

1. Yolanda, who is divorced with two young children, is contemplating a marriage proposal from her boyfriend Dana, also divorced with one young child. She is concerned about the potential issues that may arise from this union. What issues relating to stepfamilies and remarriage should Yolanda consider before making this decision about her future?
2. Kelly, at 29 years old, is surprised to hear about two close friends from college, both of whom are getting divorced after only a few years of marriage. One of these friends, April, tells her that "starter marriages" are happening more and more frequently. Is April correct about a growing trend of divorces before the age of 30, and if so, what might some of the factors behind this trend be?

Connect to www.mhhe.com/santrockld9 to research the answers and complete these exercises.

E-Learning Tools

To help you master the material in this chapter, you'll find a number of valuable study tools on the Student CD-ROM that accompanies this book. In addition, visit the Online Learning Center for *Life-Span Development*, ninth edition, where you'll find these valuable resources for chapter 15, "Socioemotional Development in Early Adulthood."

- A number of self-assessments will challenge you to examine your attitudes about relationships and finding a mate:
  Loneliness
  My Attachment Style
  Am I Ready for a Committed Relationship?
  Am I a Giver or a Taker in a Relationship?
  What is My Love Like?
  The Characteristics I Desire in a Potential Mate
  My Attitudes Toward Women
- Build your own decision-making skills by trying your hand at the parenting and education "Scenarios."

Middle Adulthood

Generations will depend on the ability of every procreating individual to face his children.
—ERIK ERIKSON
American Psychologist, 20th Century

In middle adulthood, what we have been forms what we will be. For some of us, middle age is such a foggy place, a time when we need to discover what we are running from and to and why. We compare our life with what we vowed to make it. In middle age, more time stretches before us, and some evaluations, however reluctant, have to be made. As the young-old polarity greets us with a special force, we need to join the daring youth with the discipline of age in a way that does justice to both. As middle-aged adults, we come to sense that the generations of living things pass in a short while and, like runners, hand on the torch of life. Section 8 consists of two chapters: "Physical and Cognitive Development in Middle Adulthood" (chapter 16) and "Socioemotional Development in Middle Adulthood" (chapter 17).

When more time stretches before one, some assessments, however, reluctantly and incompletely, begin to be made.

—JAMES BALDWIN
American Novelist, 20th Century

Physical and Cognitive Development in Middle Adulthood

Chapter Outline

Learning Goals

CHANGING MIDDLE AGE

1 *E*xplain how middle age is changing

PHYSICAL DEVELOPMENT

2 *D*iscuss physical changes in middle adulthood

Physical Changes

Health and Disease

Culture, Personality, Relationships, and Health

Mortality Rates

Sexuality

COGNITIVE DEVELOPMENT

3 *I*dentify cognitive changes in middle adulthood

Intelligence

Information Processing

CAREERS, WORK, AND LEISURE

4 *C*haracterize career development, work, and leisure in middle adulthood

Work in Midlife

Job Satisfaction

Career Challenges and Changes

Leisure

RELIGION AND MEANING IN LIFE

5 *E*xplain the roles of religion and meaning in life during middle adulthood

Religion and Adult Lives

Religion and Health

Meaning in Life

Images of Life-Span Development
Time Perspectives

Our perception of time depends on where we are in the life span. We are more concerned about time at some points in life than others (Schroots, 1996). Jim Croce's song "Time In A Bottle" reflects a time perspective that develops in the adult years:

> *If I could save time in a bottle*
> *The first thing that I'd like to do*
> *Is to save every day*
> *Till Eternity passes away*
> *Just to spend them with you…*
> *But there never seems to be enough time*
> *To do the things you want to do*
> *Once you find them*
> *I've looked around enough to know*
> *That you're the one I want to go*
> *Through time with*

—JIM CROCE, "Time in a Bottle"

Jim Croce's song connects time with love and the hope of going through time with someone we love. Love and intimacy are important themes of adult development. So is time. Middle-aged adults begin to look back to where they have been, reflecting on what they have done with the time they have had. They look toward the future more in terms of how much time remains to accomplish what they hope to do with their lives.

When young adults look forward in time to what their lives might be like as middle-aged adults, too often they anticipate that things will go downhill. However, like all periods of the human life span, for most individuals there usually are positive and negative features of middle age.

Interest in middle age is essentially a phenomenon of the late twentieth century and early twenty-first century. As you read in chapter 1, in 1900 the average life expectancy was 47 years of age ◀▥▥ p. 8. It only has been since a much larger percentage of people began living to older ages that it made any sense to label, describe, and investigate a period in the human life span called "middle adulthood."

1 CHANGING MIDDLE AGE

**Network on Successful
Midlife Development**

Exploring Middle Age

Each year, for $8, about 2.5 to 3 million Americans who have turned 50 become members of the American Association for Retired Persons (AARP). There is something incongruous about so many 50-year-olds joining a retirement group when hardly any of them are retired. Indeed, many of today's 50-year-olds are in better shape, more alert, and more productive than their 40-year-old counterparts from a generation or two earlier. As more people lead healthier lifestyles and medical discoveries help to stave off the aging process, the boundaries of middle age are being pushed upward. It looks like middle age is starting later and lasting longer for increasing numbers of active, healthy, and productive people. One recent study found that almost half of the individuals 65 to 69 years of age considered themselves middle-aged (National Council on Aging, 2000) and another study found a similar pattern: Half of the 60- to 75-year-olds viewed themselves as in middle age (Lachman, Maier, & Budner, 2000). Also, some individuals consider the upper boundary of midlife as the age at which they make the transition from work to retirement.

Sigmund Freud and Carl Jung studied midlife transitions around the turn of the twentieth century, but "midlife" came much earlier back then. As we just mentioned, in 1900 the average life expectancy was only 47 years of age; only 3 percent of the population lived past 65. Today, the average life expectancy is 77; 12 percent of the U.S. population is older than 65. As a much greater percentage of the population lives to an older age, the midpoint of life and what constitutes middle age or middle adulthood are getting harder to pin down (Staudinger & Bluck, 2001). In only one century, we have added 30 years to the average life expectancy. Statistically, the middle of life today is about 38 years of age—hardly any 38-year-olds, though, wish to be called "middle-aged"! What we think of as middle age comes later—anywhere from 40 to about 60 or 65 years of age. And as more people live longer, the 60 to 65 years upper boundary will likely be nudged upward. When the American Board of Family Practice asked a random sample of 1,200 Americans when middle age begins, 41 percent said it was when you worry about having enough money for health-care concerns, 42 percent said it was when your last child moves out, and 46 percent said it was when you don't recognize the names of music groups on the radio anymore (Beck, 1992).

Although middle adulthood has been a relatively neglected period of the human life span (except for pop psychology portrayals of the midlife crisis), this age period is beginning to be given more attention by life-span developmentalists (Lachman, 2001; Willis & Reid, 1999). One reason for the increased attention is that in the next several decades the largest cohorts in U.S. history will move through the middle-age years. From 1990 to 2015, the middle-aged U.S. population is projected to increase from 47 million to 80 million, a 72 percent increase. Because of the size of these baby-boom cohorts (recall from chapter 2 that a *cohort* is a group of people born in a particular year or time period), the median age of the U.S. population will increase from 33 years in 1990 to 42 years in 2050, reflecting the movement of "baby boomers" through middle age. The baby boomers are of interest to developmentalists not only because of their increased numbers but also because they are the best-educated and most affluent cohorts in history to pass through middle age.

Though the age boundaries are not set in stone, we will consider **middle adulthood** as the developmental period that begins at approximately 40 years of age and extends to about 60 years of age. However, as we just pointed out, for many increasingly healthy adults, middle age is starting later and lasting longer. Remember from our discussion in chapter 1 that we have not only a chronological age, but biological, psychological, and social ages.

For many people, middle adulthood is a time of declining physical skills and expanding responsibility; a period in which people become more conscious of the young-old polarity and the shrinking amount of time left in life; a point when individuals seek to transmit something meaningful to the next generation; and a time when people reach and maintain satisfaction in their careers.

But these characteristics don't describe everybody in middle age. As life-span expert Gilbert Brim (1992) commented, middle adulthood is full of changes, twists, and turns; the path is not fixed. People move in and out of states of success and failure.

A longitudinal study conducted by George Vaillant (2002) illustrates the variation in people's lives during middle adulthood and how this variation is linked to successful aging. Individuals were assessed at age 50 and then again at 75 to 80 years of age. As shown in figure 16.1, when individuals at 50 years of age were not heavy smokers, did not abuse alcohol, had a stable marriage, exercised, maintained a normal weight, and had good coping skills, they were more likely to be alive and happy at 75 to 80 years of age.

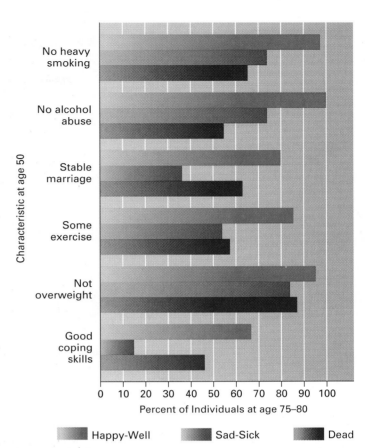

FIGURE 16.1 **Links Between Characteristics at Age 50 and Health and Happiness at Age 75 to 80**

In a longitudinal study, the characteristics shown above at age 50 were related to whether individuals were happy-well, sad-sick, or dead at age 75 to 80 (Vaillant, 2002).

*M*iddle age is a mix of new opportunities and expanding resources accompanied by declines in physical abilities.

—Lois Verbrugge
University of Michigan

middle adulthood The developmental period beginning at approximately 40 years of age and extending to about 60.

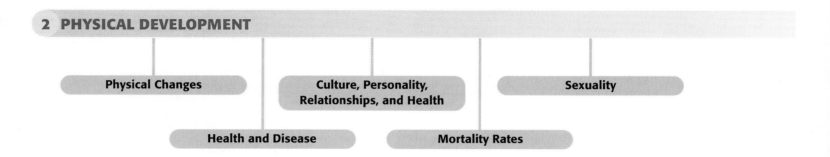

Review and Reflect

1 **Explain how middle age is changing**

REVIEW

• How is middle age today different than in past generations?

REFLECT

• How do you think you will experience (are experiencing or have experienced) middle age differently from your parents or grandparents?

2 PHYSICAL DEVELOPMENT

```
Physical Changes          Culture, Personality,          Sexuality
                          Relationships, and Health

        Health and Disease          Mortality Rates
```

I am 58 years old at the time I am writing this book. When I was a college student and my father was 56 years old, I thought he was really old. I could not conceive of myself ever being that old! But it happened, and now I've got a few gray hairs. I'm wearing reading glasses while I'm typing this sentence. I can't run as fast as I could, although I still run 10 to 15 miles every week to keep my body from falling apart. What physical changes accompany this change to middle adulthood?

Physical Changes

Unlike the rather dramatic physical changes that occur in early adolescence and the sometimes abrupt decline in old age, midlife physical changes are usually gradual (Merrill & Verbrugge, 1999) ◀▥ p. 372. Although everyone experiences some physical change due to aging in the middle adulthood years, the rates of this aging vary considerably from one individual to another. Genetic makeup and lifestyle factors play important roles in whether chronic disease will appear and when.

Visible Signs One of the most visible signs of physical changes in middle adulthood is physical appearance. The first outwardly noticeable signs of aging usually are apparent by the forties or fifties.

The skin begins to wrinkle and sag because of a loss of fat and collagen in underlying tissues. Small, localized areas of pigmentation in the skin produce aging spots, especially in areas that are exposed to sunlight, such as the hands and face. Hair becomes thinner and grayer due to a lower replacement rate and a decline in melanin production. Fingernails and toenails develop ridges and become thicker and more brittle.

Since a youthful appearance is stressed in our culture, many individuals whose hair is graying, whose skin is wrinkling, whose bodies are sagging, and whose teeth are yellowing strive to make

Famous actor Sean Connery as a young adult in his 20s (left) and as a middle-aged adult in his 50s (right). *What are some of the most outwardly noticeable signs of aging in the middle adulthood years?*

themselves look younger. Undergoing cosmetic surgery, dyeing hair, purchasing wigs, enrolling in weight reduction programs, participating in exercise regimens, and taking heavy doses of vitamins are common in middle age. One study found that middle-aged women focus more attention on facial attractiveness than do older or younger women (Nowak, 1977). In this same study, middle-aged women were more likely to perceive the signs of aging as having a negative effect on their physical appearance. In our culture, some aspects of aging in middle adulthood are taken as signs of attractiveness in men. Similar signs may be perceived as unattractive in women. Facial wrinkles and gray hair symbolize strength and maturity in men but may be perceived as unattractive in women.

Height and Weight Individuals lose height in middle age, and many gain weight. Adults lose about one-half inch of height per decade beginning in their forties (Memmler & others, 1995). On the average, body fat accounts for about 10 percent of body weight in adolescence; it makes up 20 percent or more in middle age.

Being overweight is a critical health problem in middle adulthood. For individuals who are 30 percent or more overweight, the probability of dying in middle adulthood increases by about 40 percent. Obesity increases the probability that an individual will suffer a number of other ailments, among them hypertension and digestive disorders.

In one recent large-scale study of middle-aged individuals, 7 of 10 said that they are overweight (Brim, 1999). Nearly half of the individuals over the age of 45 said they are less fit than they were five years ago.

Strength, Joints, and Bones As we saw in chapter 14, maximum physical strength often is attained in the twenties ◀▥ p. 445. Peak functioning of the body's joints also usually occurs in the twenties. Muscle strength decreases noticeably by the mid forties. A loss of strength especially occurs in the back and legs. It is estimated that about 10 to 15 percent of maximum strength is lost from age 35 to 60. The cushions for the movement of bones (such as tendons and ligaments) become less efficient in the middle adult years, a time when many individuals experience joint stiffness and more difficulty in movement.

Maximum bone density occurs by the mid to late thirties, from which point there is a progressive loss of bone. The rate of this bone loss begins slowly but accelerates in the fifties (Whitbourne, 2001). Women experience about twice the rate of bone loss as men. By the end of midlife, bones break more easily and heal more slowly.

Vision Accommodation of the eye—the ability to focus and maintain an image on the retina—experiences its sharpest decline between 40 and 59 years of age. In particular, middle-aged individuals begin to have difficulty viewing close objects, which means that many individuals have to wear glasses with bifocal lenses (Fozard & Gordon-Salant, 2001). The eye's blood supply also diminishes, although usually not until the fifties or sixties. The reduced blood supply may decrease the visual field's size and account for an increase in the eye's blind spot. Also, there is some evidence that the retina becomes less sensitive to low levels of illumination.

Hearing Hearing can also start to decline by the age of 40. Sensitivity to high pitches usually declines first. The ability to hear low-pitched sounds does not seem to decline much in middle adulthood, though. And men usually lose their sensitivity to high-pitched sounds sooner than women do. However, this sex difference might be due to men's greater exposure to noise in occupations such as mining, automobile work, and so on (Kline & Scialfa, 1996).

Researchers are identifying new possibilities for improving the vision and hearing of people as they age (Fozard & Gordon-Salant, 2001). One way this is being carried out is through better control of glare or background noise. Further, recent advances in hearing aids dramatically improve hearing for many individuals (Birren, 2002).

Women's Health in Middle Age
Men's Health in Middle Age

*M*iddle age is when your age starts to show around your middle.

—Bob Hope
American Comedian, 20th Century

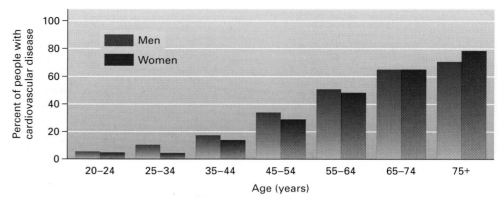

FIGURE 16.2 The Relation of Age and Gender to Cardiovascular Disease
Notice the sharp increase in cardiovascular disease in middle age.

Cardiovascular System   The cardiovascular system changes in middle adulthood. As indicated in figure 16.2, cardiovascular disease increases considerably in middle age (Hankinson & others, 2001). Fatty deposits and scar tissue slowly accumulate in the linings of blood vessels, gradually reducing blood flow to various organs, including the heart and brain. Fatty deposits can begin in adolescence. Thus, eating food high in fat content and being overweight in adolescence may have later life consequences (Birren, 2002).

Blood pressure, too, usually rises in the forties and fifties (Siegler & others, 1999). At menopause, a woman's blood pressure rises sharply and usually remains above that of a man through life's later years. Exercise, weight control, and a diet rich in fruits, vegetables, and whole grains can often help to stave off many cardiovascular problems in middle age.

Lungs   There is little change in lung capacity through most of middle adulthood. However, at about the age of 55, the proteins in lung tissue become less elastic. This change, combined with a gradual stiffening of the chest wall, decreases the lungs' capacity to shuttle oxygen from the air people breathe to the blood in their veins. As shown in figure 16.3, the lung capacity of individuals who are smokers drops precipitously in middle age, but if the individuals quit smoking their lung capacity improves, although not to the level of individuals who have never smoked (Williams, 1995).

Sleep   Some aspects of sleep become more problematic in middle age. The total number of hours slept usually remains the same as in early adulthood, but beginning in the forties, wakeful periods are more frequent and there is less of the deepest type of sleep (stage 4). The amount of time spent lying awake in bed at night begins to increase in middle age, and this can produce a feeling of being less rested in the morning (Katchadourian, 1987). Sleep problems in middle-aged and older adults are more common in individuals who use a higher number of prescription and nonprescription drugs, and who are depressed (Giron & others, 2002).

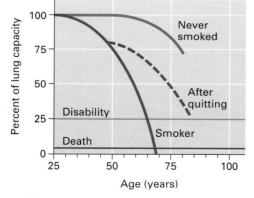

FIGURE 16.3 The Relation of Lung Capacity to Age and Cigarette Smoking

Lung capacity shows little change through middle age for individuals who have not smoked. However, smoking is linked with reduced lung capacity in middle-aged and older adults. When individuals stop smoking, their lung capacity becomes greater than those who continue to smoke, but not as great as the lung capacity individuals who have never smoked.

Health and Disease

In middle adulthood, the frequency of accidents declines and individuals are less susceptible to colds and allergies than in childhood, adolescence, or early adulthood. Indeed, many individuals live through middle adulthood without having a disease or persistent health problem. However, disease and persistent health problems become more common in middle adulthood for other individuals (Spiro, 2001). As indicated in figure 16.4, when individuals were asked to rate their health in early, middle, and late adulthood, they indicated that their health was not as good as in early adulthood

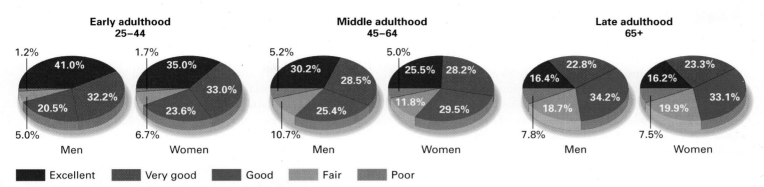

FIGURE 16.4 **Self-Rated Health at Different Points in Adulthood**

Individuals were asked "How would you rate your health?" on a scale from poor to excellent at different points in adulthood. Middle-aged adults rated their health as worse than young adults but better than older adults. The numbers represent the percentages of individuals in each group rating themselves at each of the points on the scale. Men rated their health better in midlife than women but this gender difference virtually disappeared in older adults.

but better than in late adulthood (National Center for Health Statistics, 1999). Note that men rated their health as somewhat better than women in midlife but in late adulthood the gender differences virtually disappeared.

Chronic disorders are characterized by a slow onset and a long duration. Chronic disorders are rare in early adulthood, increase in middle adulthood, and become common in late adulthood. Arthritis is the leading chronic disorder in middle age, followed by hypertension.

The most common chronic disorders in middle age vary for females and males. Men have a higher incidence of fatal chronic conditions (such as coronary heart disease, cancer and stroke); women have a higher incidence of nonfatal ones (such as arthritis, varicose veins, and bursitis).

Culture, Personality, Relationships, and Health

Emotional stability and personality are related to health in middle adulthood. In the Berkeley Longitudinal Study, as individuals aged from 34 to 50, those who were the most healthy were also the most calm, the most self-controlled, and the most responsible (Livson & Peskin, 1981). Let's now explore the role of culture in cardiovascular disease and two personality profiles that are associated with health and illness.

Culture and Cardiovascular Disease   Culture plays an important role in coronary disease. Cross-cultural psychologists believe that studies of migrant ethnic groups help shed light on the role culture plays in health. As ethnic groups migrate, the health practices dictated by their cultures change while their genetic predispositions to certain disorders remain constant (Ilola, 1990). The Ni-Hon-San Study (Nipon–Honolulu–San Francisco), part of the Honolulu Heart Study, is an ongoing study of approximately 12,000 Japanese men in Hiroshima and Nagasaki (Japan), Honolulu, and San Francisco. In the study, the Japanese men living in Japan have had the lowest rate of coronary heart disease, those living in Honolulu have had an intermediate rate, and those living in San Francisco have had the highest rate. Acculturation provides a valuable framework for understanding why the Japanese men's cholesterol level, glucose level, and weight all increased as they migrated and acculturated. As the Japanese men migrated farther away from Japan, their health practices, such as diet, changed. The Japanese men in California, for example, ate 40 percent more fat than the men in Japan.

Conversely, Japanese men in California have much lower rates of cerebrovascular disease (stroke) than Japanese men living in Japan. Businessmen in Japan tend to

chronic disorders Disorders that are characterized by slow onset and long duration. They are rare in early adulthood, they increase during middle adulthood, and they become common in late adulthood.

Health Promotion in African Americans, Latinos, Asian Americans, and Native Americans

There are differences within ethnic groups as well as among them. This is just as true of health among ethnic groups as it is of, say, family structure. The spectrum of living conditions and lifestyles within an ethnic group are influenced by social class, immigrant status, social and language skills, occupational opportunities, and such social resources as the availability of meaningful support networks—all of which can play a role in an ethnic minority member's health.

Prejudice and racial segregation are the historical underpinnings for the chronic stress of discrimination and poverty that adversely affects the health of many African Americans. Support systems, such as an extended family network, may be especially important resources to improve the health of African Americans and help them cope with stress (Boyd-Franklin, 1989).

Some of the same stressors mentioned for African Americans are associated with migration to the United States by Puerto Ricans, Mexicans, and Latin Americans. Language is often a barrier for unacculturated Latinos in doctor-patient communications. In addition, there is increasing evidence that diabetes occurs at an above-average rate in Latinos, making this disease a major health problem that parallels the above-average rate of high blood pressure among African Americans (Gardner & others, 1984).

Asian Americans are characterized by their broad diversity in national backgrounds and lifestyles. They range from highly acculturated Japanese Americans, who may be better educated than many White Americans and have excellent access to health care, to the many Indochinese refugees who have few economic resources and may be in poor health.

Cultural barriers to adequate health care include a lack of financial resources and poor language skills. In addition, members of ethnic minority groups are often unfamiliar with how the medical system operates, confused about the need to see numerous people, and uncertain about why they have to wait so long for service (Snowden & Cheung, 1990).

Other barriers may be specific to certain cultures, reflecting differing ideas regarding what causes disease and how it should be treated. For example, there are Chinese herbalists and folk healers in every Chinatown in the United States. Depending on their degree of acculturation to Western society, Chinese Americans may go to either a folk healer or a Western doctor first, but generally they will consult a folk healer for follow-up care. Chinese medicines are usually used for home care.

Native Americans view Western medicine as a source of crisis intervention, quick fixes for broken legs, or cures for other symptoms. They do not view Western medicine as a source for treating the causes of disease or for preventing disease. For example, they are unlikely to attend a seminar on preventing alcohol abuse. They also are reluctant to become involved in care that requires long-term hospitalization or surgery.

Health care professionals can increase their effectiveness with ethnic minority patients by improving their knowledge of patients' attitudes, beliefs, and folk practices regarding health and disease. Such information should be integrated into Western treatment rather than ignored at the risk of alienating patients.

---

consume vast quantities of alcohol and to chain-smoke, both of which are high-risk factors for stroke. As a result, stroke was the leading cause of death in Japan until it was surpassed by cancer in 1981. However, death rates from stroke for Japanese American men are at the same level as those of White American men. Researchers suspect that this level is related to a change in behavior. That is, Japanese American men consume less alcohol and smoke less than their counterparts in Japan. To read more about cultural factors in health, see the Sociocultural Worlds of Development box.

Type A/Type B Behavioral Patterns   In the late 1950s a secretary for two California cardiologists, Meyer Friedman and Ray Rosenman, observed that the chairs in their waiting rooms were tattered and worn, but only on the front edges. The cardiologists had noticed the impatience of their cardiac patients, who often arrived exactly on time for an appointment and were in a great hurry to leave. Subsequently they conducted a study of 3,000 healthy men between the ages of 35 and 59 over a period of eight years (Friedman & Rosenman, 1974). During the eight years, one group of men had twice as many heart attacks or other forms of heart disease as anyone else. And autopsies of the men who died revealed that this same group had coronary arteries that were more obstructed than those of other men. Friedman and Rosenman described the coronary disease group as characterized by **Type A behavior pattern,** a cluster of characteristics—being excessively competitive, hard-driven, impatient, and

Type A behavior pattern A cluster of characteristics—being excessively competitive, hard-driven, impatient, and hostile—thought to be related to the incidence of heart disease.

hostile—thought to be related to the incidence of heart disease. Rosenman and Friedman labeled the behavior of the other group, who were relaxed and easygoing, **Type B behavior pattern.**

However, further research on the link between Type A behavior and coronary disease indicates that the association is not as strong as Friedman and Rosenman believed (Suls & Swain, 1998; Williams, 1995, 2001). Researchers have examined the components of Type A behavior, such as hostility, competitiveness, a strong drive to accomplish goals, and impatience, to determine a more precise link with coronary risk. The Type A behavior component most consistently associated with coronary problems is hostility (Faber & Burns, 1996). People who are hostile outwardly or turn anger inward are more likely to develop heart disease than their less angry counterparts (Allan & Scheidt, 1996). Such people have been called "hot reactors" because of their intense physiological reactions to stress. Their hearts race, their breathing quickens, and their muscles tense up. Redford Williams (1995), a leading behavioral medicine researcher, believes that such people can develop the ability to control their anger and develop more trust in others, which he thinks can reduce their risk for heart disease.

The role of personality factors, including hostility, in health were examined in one longitudinal study of more than 1,500 men from 28 to 80 years of age with an average age of 47 at the initial assessment (Aldwin & others, 2001). Men who had high, increasing symptoms of poor health were characterized by hostility and anxiety, were overweight, and smoked. Those with few symptoms of poor health were emotionally stable, educated, thin, nonsmokers.

Hardiness   **Hardiness** is a personality style characterized by a sense of commitment (rather than alientation), control (rather than powerlessness), and a perception of problems as challenges (rather than threats). In the Chicago Stress Project, male business managers 32 to 65 years of age were studied over a five-year period. During the five years, most of the managers experienced stressful events, such as divorce, job transfers, the death of a close friend, inferior performance evaluations at work, and working at a job with an unpleasant boss. In one study, managers who developed an illness (ranging from the flu to a heart attack) were compared with those who did not (Kobasa, Maddi, & Kahn, 1982). The latter group was more likely to have a hardy personality. In another study, whether or not hardiness along with exercise and social support buffered stress and reduced illness in executives' lives was investigated (Kobasa & others, 1986). When all three factors were present in an executive's life the level of illness dropped dramatically (see figure 16.5 on page 522). This suggests the power of multiple buffers of stress, rather than a single buffer, in maintaining health (Maddi, 1998; Ouellette & DiPlacido, 2001).

Health and Social Relationships   In chapter 15, "Socioemotional Development in Early Adulthood," we saw that being in a happy marriage is linked with getting sick less, having less physical and emotional stress, and living longer than being in an unhappy marriage ◀‖‖ p. 500. These results hold for middle-aged as well as young adults.

Researchers also have revealed links between health in middle age and earlier pathways of relationships (Ryff & Singer, 2000). In one recent longitudinal study, individuals who were on a positive relationship pathway from childhood to middle age had significantly fewer biological problems (cardiovascular disease, physical decline) than their counterparts who were on a negative relationship pathway (Ryff & others, 2001). In another longitudinal study, adults who experienced more warmth and closeness with their parents during childhood had fewer diagnosed diseases (coronary artery disease, hypertension, ulcer, alcoholism) than those who did not experience warmth and closeness with their parents in childhood (Russek & Schwartz, 1997). These studies reflect continuity in development over many years in the human life span. Thus, health in middle age is related to the current quality of social relationships and to the pathways of those relationships earlier in development.

Type Z behavior
© 1987 The New Yorker Collection, Donald Reilly from cartoonbank.com. All Rights Reserved.

mhhe●com/
santrockld9

Behavioral Medicine

Controlling Anger and Developing Life Skills

All men should strive to learn before they die what they are running from, and to, and why.

—JAMES THURBER
American Novelist, 20th Century

Type B behavior pattern Being primarily calm and easygoing.

hardiness A personality style characterized by a sense of commitment (rather than alienation), control (rather than powerlessness), and a perception of problems as challenges (rather than threats).

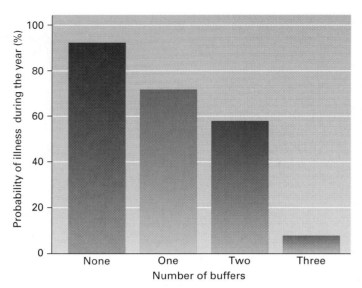

FIGURE 16.5 Illness in High-Stress Business Executives

In one study of high-stress business executives (all of whom were selected for this analysis because they were above the stress mean for the entire one year of the study), a low level of all three buffers (hardiness, exercise, and social support) involved a high probability of at least one serious illness in that year (Kobasa & others, 1986). High levels of one, two, and all three buffers decreased the likelihood of at least one serious illness occurring in the year of the study.

Cause of Death

1. Heart disease
2. Cancer
3. Cerebrovascular disease
4. Accidents
5. Pulmonary disease

FIGURE 16.6 Leading Causes of Death in Middle Adulthood

climacteric The midlife transition in which fertility declines.

menopause The complete cessation of a woman's menstruation, which usually occurs in the late forties or early fifties.

Mortality Rates

Infectious disease was the main cause of death until the middle of the twentieth century. As infectious disease rates declined and more individuals lived through middle age, chronic disorders increased.

Chronic diseases are now the main causes of death for individuals in middle adulthood (Merrill & Verbrugge, 1999). Heart disease is the leading cause of death in middle age, followed by cancer and cerebrovascular disease. In the first half of middle age, cancer claims more lives than heart disease; this is reversed in the second half.

Figure 16.6 shows the leading causes of death in middle age. Men have higher mortality rates than women for all of the leading causes of death.

Sexuality

What kind of changes characterize the sexuality of women and men as they go through middle age? **Climacteric** is a term that is used to describe the midlife transition in which fertility declines. Let's explore the substantial differences in the climacteric of women and men.

Menopause Most of us know something about menopause. But is what we know accurate? Stop for a moment and think about your knowledge of menopause. What is menopause? When does it occur? Can it be treated? Most of us share some assumptions about menopause—we might think that it is a disease, that it involves numerous complaints, that women who are undergoing menopause deeply regret losing their reproductive capacity, their sexuality, and their femininity, and that they become deeply depressed. Are these assumptions accurate?

Menopause is the time in middle age, usually in the late forties or early fifties, when a woman's menstrual periods completely cease. The average age at which women have their last period is 52. A small percentage of women—10 percent—go through menopause before 40. Just as puberty has been coming earlier in recent years, menopause has been coming later (Birren, 2002). Specific causes of the later incidence of menopause have not been documented, but improved nutrition and lower incidence of infectious diseases may be the reasons.

There is a dramatic decline in the production of estrogen by the ovaries. Estrogen decline produces some uncomfortable symptoms in some menopausal women—"hot flashes," nausea, fatigue, and rapid heartbeat, for example (Sommer, 2001). Some menopausal women report depression and irritability, but in some instances these feelings are related to other circumstances in the woman's life, such as becoming divorced, losing a job, caring for a sick parent, and so on (Gannon, 1998).

The comments of the following two women reveal the extensive variation menopause may bring. One woman commented, "I had hot flashes frequently for almost six months. I didn't get as embarrassed as some of my friends who also had hot flashes, but I found the 'heat wave' sensation uncomfortable." Another woman commented, "I am constantly amazed and delighted to discover new things about my body, something menstruation did not allow me to do. I have new responses, desires, sensations, freed and apart from the distraction of menses [periods]."

In a large-scale study of Americans in midlife, almost two-thirds of postmenopausal women said they felt relief that their periods had stopped (Brim, 1999). Only 1 percent said they felt "only regret" that they no longer had their period. Just over 50 percent of middle-aged women said they did not have hot flashes at all.

Why, then, do so many individuals have the idea that menopause is such a big deal? Why do we have so many erroneous assumptions—that menopausal women will lose their sexuality and femininity, that they will become deeply depressed, and that they will experience extensive physical pain? Much of the research on menopause is based on small, selective samples of women who go to physicians or therapists because they are having problems associated with menopause. These women are unrepresentative of the large population of women in the United States.

The problem of using a small, selective sample was reflected in popular author Gail Sheehy's (1991) book *The Silent Passage*. Sheehy writes about her own difficult experiences and reports the frustrations of a few women she chose to interview. Although Sheehy dramatically overstates the percentage of women who have serious problems with menopause, she does not overstate the stigma attached to menopause or the inadequate attention accorded it by the medical community (which is male-dominated).

Cross-cultural studies reveal wide variations in the menopause experience (Avis, 1999). For example, hot flashes are uncommon in Mayan women (Beyene, 1986). Asian women report fewer hot flashes than women in Western societies (Payer, 1991). It is difficult to determine the extent to which these cross-cultural variations in the menopause experience are due to genetic, dietary, reproductive, or cultural factors.

Our portrayal of menopause has been much more positive than its usual portrayals in the past. While menopause overall is not the negative experience for most women it was once thought to be, the loss of fertility is an important marker for women—it means that they have to make final decisions about having children. Women in their thirties who have never had children sometimes speak about being "up against the biological clock" because they cannot postpone questions about having children much longer.

Hormone replacement therapy (HRT) augments the declining levels of reproductive hormone production by the ovaries. HRT can consist of various forms of estrogen, and usually a progestin (Hlatky & others, 2002). The consensus at this time is that HRT reduces hot flashes, reduces sleep disturbances, helps to maintain the urogenital tract, and reduces bone loss (Sommer, 2001). HRT also reduces the risk of endometrial (the endometrium is the membrane that lines the uterus) cancer. However, in 2002, the National Institutes of Health stopped early a major clinical trial of the benefits and risks of combined estrogen and progestin in healthy menopausal women due to increased risks of breast cancer, coronary heart disease, and stroke. A separate study of estrogen alone in women who had a hysterectomy was allowed to continue unchanged because, at this point, the balance of risks and benefits for estrogen alone is uncertain.

The National Institutes of Health recommend that women with a uterus who are currently taking estrogen plus progestin should consult with their doctor to determine whether they should continue the hormone therapy. If they are taking the hormone treatment for short-term relief of symptoms, the benefits may outweigh the risks. However, the recent negative results for estrogen plus progestin suggest that long-term use of this type of hormone replacement therapy should be seriously reevaluated.

Hormonal Changes in Middle-Aged Men Do men go through anything like the menopause that women experience? That is, is there a male menopause? During middle adulthood, most men do not lose their capacity to father children, although there usually is a modest decline in their sexual hormone level and activity. Men experience hormonal changes in their fifties and sixties, but nothing like the dramatic drop in estrogen that women experience (Sommer, 2001). Testosterone production begins to decline about 1 percent a year during middle adulthood, and sperm count usually shows a slow decline, but men do not lose their fertility in middle age. What has been referred to as "male menopause," then, probably has less to do with hormonal change than with the psychological adjustment men must make when they are faced with declining physical energy and family and work pressures. Testosterone therapy has not been found to relieve such symptoms, suggesting that they are not induced by hormonal change.

Researchers have found that almost 50 percent of Canadian and American women have occasional hot flashes, but only 1 in 7 Japanese women do (Lock, 1998). *What factors might account for these variations?*

mhhe●com/
santrockld9

Menopause: Information and Resources

National Institute of Aging: Menopause

Medline: Menopause

Medline: Middle-Age Sexuality

Midlife Male Hormone Changes

In middle age, men's testosterone levels gradually drop, which can reduce their sexual drive. Their erections are less full and less frequent, and require more stimulation to achieve them. Researchers once attributed these changes to psychological factors, but increasingly they find that as many as 75 percent of the erectile dysfunctions in middle-aged men stem from physiological problems. Smoking, diabetes, hypertension, and elevated cholesterol levels are at fault in many erectile problems in middle-aged men (Crooks & Bauer, 2002).

Recently, the most attention in helping individuals with a sexual dysfunction has focused on Viagra, a drug designed to conquer impotence. Its success rate is in the range of 60 to 80 percent, and its prescription rate has outpaced such popular drugs as Prozac (antidepressant) and Rogaine (baldness remedy) in first-year comparisons (Padma-Nathan & Giuliano, 2001). Viagra also is being taken by some women to improve their sexual satisfaction. However, Viagra is not an aphrodisiac; it won't work in the absence of desire. The possible downside of Viagra involves headaches in 1 of 10 men, seeing blue (because the eyes contain an enzyme similar to the one on which Viagra works in the penis, about 3 percent of users develop temporary vision problems ranging from blurred vision to a blue or green halo effect), and blackouts (Viagra can trigger a sudden drop in blood pressure). Also, scientists do not know the long-term effects of taking the drug, although in short-term trials it appears to be a relatively safe drug.

Sexual Attitudes and Behavior   Although the ability of men and women to function sexually shows little biological decline in middle adulthood, sexual activity usually occurs on a less frequent basis than in early adulthood. Career interests, family matters, energy level, and routine may contribute to this decline. In the recent Sex in America survey, frequency of having sex was greatest for individuals aged 25 to 29 years old (47 percent had sex twice a week or more) and dropped off for individuals in their fifties (23 percent of 50- to 59-year-old males said they had sex twice a week or more, while only 14 percent of the females in this age group reported this frequency) (Michael & others, 1994). Figure 16.7 shows the age trends in frequency of sex from the Sex in America survey.

A spouse or live-in partner makes all the difference in whether sexual activity occurs, especially for women over 40 years of age. In one recent study conducted by the MacArthur Foundation, 95 percent of women in their forties with partners said that they have been sexually active in the last six months, compared with only 53 percent of those without partners (Brim, 1999). By their fifties, 88 percent of women living with a partner have been sexually active in the last six months, but only 37 per-

Age groups			Frequency of sex		
	Not at all	A few times per year	A few times per month	2–3 times a week	4 or more times a week
Men					
18–24	15	21	24	28	12
25–29	7	15	31	36	11
30–39	8	15	37	23	6
40–49	9	18	40	27	6
50–59	11	22	43	20	3
Women					
18–24	11	16	2	9	12
25–29	5	10	38	37	10
30–39	9	16	6	33	6
40–49	15	16	44	20	5
50–59	30	22	35	12	2

FIGURE 16.7 The Sex in America Survey: Frequency of Sex at Different Points in Adult Development

cent of those who are neither married nor living with someone say they have had sex in the last six months.

3 COGNITIVE DEVELOPMENT

| Intelligence | Information Processing |

We have seen that the decline in many physical characteristics in middle adulthood is not just imagined. Middle-aged adults might not see as well, run as fast, or be as healthy as in their twenties and thirties. But what about their cognitive skills? In chapter 14, "Physical and Cognitive Development in Early Adulthood," we saw that cognitive abilities are very strong in early adulthood ◀▥ p. 459. Do they decline as we enter and move through middle adulthood? To answer this question we will explore the possibility of cognitive changes in intelligence and information processing.

Intelligence

Our exploration of possible changes in intelligence in middle adulthood focuses on the concepts of fluid and crystallized intelligence, the Seattle Longitudinal Study, and cohort effects.

Fluid and Crystallized Intelligence   John Horn believes that some abilities begin to decline in middle age while others increase (Horn & Donaldson, 1980). Horn argues that **crystallized intelligence,** an individual's accumulated information and verbal skills, continues to increase in middle adulthood, while **fluid intelligence,** one's ability to reason abstractly, begins to decline in the middle adulthood years (see figure 16.8 on page 526).

Horn's data were collected in a cross-sectional manner. Remember from chapter 2, "The Science of Life-Span Development," that this involves assessing individuals of different ages at the same point in time ◀▥ p. 63. For example, a cross-sectional study might assess the intelligence of different groups of 40-, 50-, and 60-year-olds in a single evaluation, such as 1980. The average 40-year-old and the average 60-year-old were born in different eras, which produced different economic and educational opportunities. For example, as the 60-year-olds grew up they likely had fewer educational opportunities, which probably influenced their scores on intelligence tests.

crystallized intelligence Accumulated information and verbal skills, which increase with age, according to Horn.

fluid intelligence The ability to reason abstractly, which steadily declines from middle adulthood on, according to Horn.

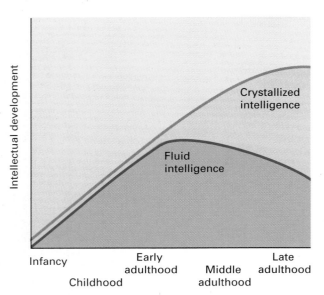

FIGURE 16.8 Fluid and Crystallized Intellectual Development Across the Life Span

According to Horn, crystallized intelligence (based on cumulative learning experiences) increases throughout the life span, but fluid intelligence (the ability to perceive and manipulate information) steadily declines from middle adulthood.

mhhe com/
santrockld9

K. Warner Schaie

Midlife Baby-Boomer Characteristics

Thus, if we find differences between 40- and 60-year-olds on intelligence tests when they are assessed cross-sectionally, these differences might be due to cohort effects related to educational differences rather than to age.

By contrast, remember from chapter 2 that in a longitudinal study, the same individuals are studied over a period of time ◀▥ p. 63. Thus, a longitudinal study of intelligence in middle adulthood might consist of giving the same intelligence test to the same individuals when they are 40, 50, and 60 years of age. As we see next, whether data on intelligence are collected cross-sectionally or longitudinally can make a difference in what is found about intellectual decline.

The Seattle Longitudinal Study K. Warner Schaie (1996) is conducting an extensive study of intellectual abilities in the adulthood years. Five hundred individuals initially were tested in 1956. New waves of participants are added periodically. The main focus in the Seattle Longitudinal Study has been on individual change and stability in intelligence. A psychometric, measurement-based approach, described in chapter 10, "Physical and Cognitive Development in Middle and Late Childhood," is used.

The main mental abilities tested were:

- *Vocabulary* (ability to understand ideas expressed in words)
- *Verbal memory* (ability to encode and recall meaningful language units, such as a list of words)
- *Number* (ability to perform simple mathematical computations such as addition, subtraction, and multiplication)
- *Spatial orientation* (ability to visualize and mentally rotate stimuli in two- and three-dimensional space)
- *Inductive reasoning* (ability to recognize and understand patterns and relationships in a problem and use this understanding to solve other instances of the problem)
- *Perceptual speed* (ability to quickly and accurately make simple discriminations in visual stimuli)

As shown in figure 16.9, the highest level of functioning for four of the six intellectual abilities occurred in the middle adulthood years (Willis & Schaie, 1999). For

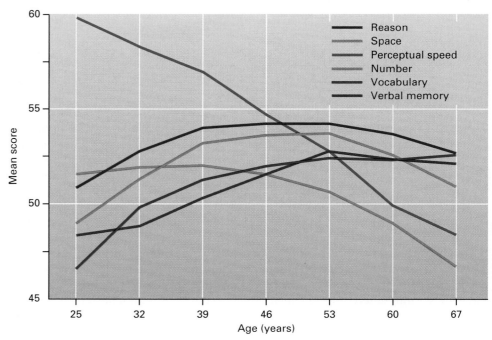

FIGURE 16.9 Longitudinal Changes in Six Intellectual Abilities from Age 25 to Age 67

both women and men, peak performance on vocabulary, verbal memory, inductive reasoning, and spatial orientation was attained in middle age. For only two of the six abilities—numerical ability and perceptual speed—were there declines in middle age. Perceptual speed showed the earliest decline, actually beginning in early adulthood.

When Schaie (1994) assessed intellectual abilities both cross-sectionally and longitudinally, he found decline more likely in the cross-sectional than in the longitudinal assessments. For example, as shown in figure 16.10, when assessed longitudinally, inductive reasoning increased until toward the end of middle adulthood, when it began to show a slight decline. By contrast, when assessed cross-sectionally, inductive reasoning showed a consistent decline in the middle adulthood years.

Interestingly, in terms of John Horn's ideas that were discussed earlier, middle age was a time of peak performance for both some aspects of crystallized intelligence (vocabulary) and fluid intelligence (spatial orientation and inductive reasoning) for the participants in the Seattle Longitudinal Study.

Thus, in Schaie's view, it is in middle adulthood, not early adulthood, that people reach a peak in their cognitive functioning for many intellectual skills.

Information Processing

Recall from our discussion of theories of development in chapter 2 and in a number of child development and adolescence chapters (8, 10, and 12), we also examined the information-processing approach to cognition ◀▥ pp. 50, 249, 314, and 389. Among the information-processing changes that take place in middle adulthood are those involved in speed of processing information, memory, expertise, and practical problem-solving skills.

Speed of Information Processing   As we saw in Schaie's (1994, 1996) Seattle Longitudinal Study, perceptual speed begins declining in early adulthood and continues to decline in middle adulthood. A common way to assess speed of information is through a reaction-time task, in which individuals simply press a button as soon as they see a light appear (Madden, 2001). Middle-aged adults are slower to push the button when the light appears than young adults are. However, keep in mind that the decline is not dramatic—under 1 second in most investigations. Also, for unknown reasons, the decline in reaction time is stronger for women than for men (Salthouse, 1994).

Memory   In Schaie's (1994, 1996) Seattle Longitudinal Study, verbal memory peaked in the fifties. However, in some other studies, verbal memory has shown a decline in middle age, especially when assessed in cross-sectional studies. For example, in several studies, when asked to remember lists of words, numbers, or meaningful prose, younger adults outperformed middle-aged adults (Salthouse, 1991; Salthouse & Skovronek, 1992). Although there still is some controversy about whether memory declines in the middle adulthood years, most experts conclude that it does decline (Salthouse, 2000). However, some experts argue that studies that have concluded there is a decline in memory during middle age often have compared young adults in their twenties with older middle-aged adults in their late fifties and even have included some individuals in their sixties (Schaie, 2000). In this latter view, memory decline in the early part of middle age either is nonexistent or minimal, not occurring until the latter part of middle age or late adulthood (Backman, Small, & Wahlin, 2001).

Aging and cognition expert Denise Park (2001) argues that starting in late middle age, more time is needed to learn new information. **Working memory** is closely linked to short-term memory but places more emphasis on memory as a place for mental work. Working memory is like a "workbench" where individuals can manipulate and assemble information when making decisions, solving problems, and comprehending written and spoken language (Baddeley, 2000). Linked to the slowdown in learning new information in late middle age, working memory capacity—the

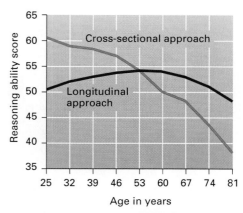

FIGURE 16.10 Cross-Sectional and Longitudinal Comparisons of Intellectual Change in Middle Adulthood

working memory Closely related to short-term memory but places more emphasis on mental work. Working memory is like a "workbench" where individuals can manipulate and assemble information when making decisions, solving problems, and comprehending written and spoken language.

Stephen J. Hawking is a world-renowned expert in physics. Hawking authored the best-selling book, *A Brief History of Time*. Hawking has a neurological disorder that prevents him from walking or talking. He communicates with the aid of a voice-equipped computer. *What distinguishes experts from novices?*

amount of information that can be immediately retrieved and used—becomes more limited (Leonards, Ibanez, & Giannakopoulous, 2002). Think of this situation as an overcrowded desk with many items in disarray. As a result of the overcrowding and disarray, long-term memory becomes less reliable, more time is needed to enter new information into long-term storage, and more time is required to retrieve the information. Thus, Park believes that much of the blame for declining memory in late middle age is a result of information overload that continues to build up as we go through the adult years.

Memory decline is more likely to occur when individuals don't use effective memory strategies, such as organization and imagery. By organizing lists of phone numbers into different categories or imagining the phone numbers as representing different objects around the house, many people can improve their memory in middle adulthood.

Expertise As we learned in chapter 10, *expertise* involves having an extensive, highly organized knowledge and understanding of a particular domain ◀‖‖ p. 315. Individuals can have expertise in areas as diverse as physics, art, or knowledge of wine. Developing expertise and becoming an "expert" in a field usually is the result of many years of experience, learning, and effort. Because it takes so long to attain, expertise often shows up more in the middle adulthood than in the early adulthood years (Clancy & Hoyer, 1994; Hoyer & Roodin, 2003).

Strategies that distinguish experts from novices include these:

- Experts are more likely to rely on their accumulated experience to solve problems.
- Experts often process information automatically and analyze it more efficiently when solving a problem in their domain than novices do.
- Experts have better strategies and shortcuts to solving problems in their domain than novices do.
- Experts are more creative and flexible in solving problems in their domain than novices are (Csikszentmihalyi, 1997).

Practical Problem Solving A final difference in the information processing of middle-aged and young adults involves solving practical problems. Nancy Denney (1986, 1990) assessed practical problem-solving abilities in adults by observing such circumstances as how they handled a landlord who would not fix their stove and what they did if a bank mistakenly did not deposit a check in their account. She found that the ability to solve such practical problems increased through the forties and fifties as individuals accumulated practical experience.

Review and Reflect

3 Identify cognitive changes in middle adulthood

REVIEW
- How does intelligence develop in middle adulthood?
- What changes take place in processing information during middle age?

REFLECT
- What do you think are the most important cohort effects that can influence the development of intelligence in middle age? How are these likely to change in the future?

4 CAREERS, WORK, AND LEISURE

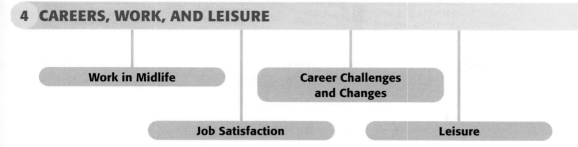

- Work in Midlife
- Career Challenges and Changes
- Job Satisfaction
- Leisure

What are some issues that workers face in midlife? Are middle-aged workers as satisfied with their jobs as young adult workers?

Work in Midlife

In the United States, approximately 80 percent of individuals 40 to 59 years of age are employed. In the 51 to 59 age group, slightly less than 25 percent do not work. More than half of this age group say that a health condition or an impairment limits the type of paid work that they do (Sterns & Huyck, 2001). Further, U.S. labor force participation is projected to grow to 37 percent for the 55 and older age group, a 6.5 percent increase over the participation rate for 1996 with the 55 to 64 age group to add 7.3 million workers (Schwerha & McMullin, 2002). The majority of these increases are expected to be in the service industry.

An important issue in midlife is whether individuals will continue to do the type of work that they want to do. Mental and physical capabilities will not be a major impediment for many middle-aged adults if they want to continue working.

For many people, midlife is a time of evaluation, assessment, and reflection in terms of the work they do and want to do in the future. Among the work issues that some people face in midlife are recognizing limitations in career progress, deciding whether to change jobs or careers, whether to rebalance family and work, and planning for retirement (Sterns & Huyck, 2001).

Job Satisfaction

Work satisfaction increases steadily throughout the work life— from age 20 to at least age 60, for both college-educated and non-college-educated adults (Rhodes, 1983) (see figure 16.11). This same pattern has been found for both women and men. Satisfaction probably increases because as we get older we get paid more, we are in higher positions, and we have more job security. There is also a greater commitment to the job as we get older. We take our jobs more seriously, have lower rates of avoidable absenteeism, and are more involved with our work in middle adulthood than in early adulthood. Younger adults are still experimenting with their work and still searching for the right occupation. They may be inclined to seek out what is wrong with their current job rather than focusing on what is right about it. For the most part, researchers have found the highest levels of physical and psychological well-being in people who are doing as much paid work as they would like to do (House, 1998; House & others, 1992).

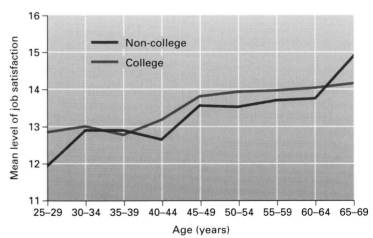

FIGURE 16.11 Age and Job Satisfaction

Job satisfaction increases with age, for both college- and non-college-educated adults. Among the reasons for increased satisfaction are more income, higher-status jobs, greater job security, and stronger job commitment.

Reprinted with special permission of North American Syndicate.

Is It Time to Change Jobs?
Women and Work in Midcareer

Career Challenges and Changes

The current middle-aged worker faces several important challenges in the twenty-first century (Avolio & Sosik, 1999). These include the globalization of work, rapid developments in information technologies, downsizing of organizations, and early retirement.

Globalization has replaced the traditional White male workforce with employees of different ethnic and national backgrounds. The proliferation of computer technology compels middle-aged adults to become increasingly computer literate to maintain their work competence (Csaja, 2001). To improve profits, many companies are restructuring and downsizing. One of the outcomes of this is to offer incentives to middle-aged employees to retire early—in their fifties, or in some cases even forties, rather than their sixties.

Some midlife career changes are self-motivated, others are the consequence of losing one's job (Moen, 1998; Moen & Wethington, 1999). Some individuals in middle age decide that they don't want to do the same work they have been doing for the rest of their lives (Hoyer & Roodin, 2003). One aspect of middle adulthood involves adjusting idealistic hopes to realistic possibilities in light of how much time individuals have before they retire and how fast they are reaching their occupational goals (Levinson, 1978, 1997). If individuals perceive that they are behind schedule, if their goals are unrealistic, they don't like the work they are doing, or their job has become too stressful, they could become motivated to change jobs.

Leisure

As adults, not only must we learn how to work well, but we also need to learn how to relax and enjoy leisure (Strain & others, 2002). With the kind of work ethic on which America is based, it is not surprising to find that many adults view leisure as boring and unnecessary. But even Aristotle recognized leisure's importance in life, stressing that we should not only work well but use leisure well. He described leisure as better because it was the end of work. How can we define leisure? **Leisure** refers to the pleasant times after work when individuals are free to pursue activities and interests of their own choosing—hobbies, sports, or reading, for example.

What is leisure in middle adulthood like? When Mark became 40 years old, he decided that he needed to develop some leisure activities and interests. He bought a personal computer and joined a computer club. Now Mark looks forward to coming home from work and "playing with his toy." At the age of 43, Barbara sent her last child off to college and told her husband that she was going to spend the next several years reading the many books she had bought but had never found time to read. Mark and Barbara chose different leisure activities, but their actions suggest that middle adulthood is a time when leisure activities assume added importance. For example, some developmentalists believe that middle adulthood is a time of questioning how time should be spent and of reassessing priorities (Gould, 1978).

leisure The pleasant times after work when individuals are free to pursue activities and interests of their own choosing.

Leisure can be an especially important aspect of middle adulthood because of the changes many individuals experience at this point in the adult life span (Mannell, 2000; McGuire, 2000). The changes include physical changes, relationship changes with spouse and children, and career changes. By middle adulthood, more money is available to many individuals, and there may be more free time and paid vacations. These midlife changes may produce expanded opportunities for leisure. For many individuals, middle adulthood is the first time in their lives when they have the opportunity to diversify their interests.

In one study, 12,338 men 35 to 57 years of age were assessed each year for five years regarding whether they took vacations or not (Gump & Matthews, 2000). Then, the researchers examined the medical and death records over nine years for men who lived for at least a year after the last vacation survey. Compared with those who never took vacations, men who went on annual vacations were 21 percent less likely to die over the nine years and 32 percent less likely to die of coronary heart disease. The qualities that lead men to pass on a vacation tend to promote heart disease, such as not trusting anyone to fill in while you are gone or fearing that you will get behind in your work and someone will replace you. These are behaviors that sometimes have been described as part of the Type A behavioral pattern.

Adults at midlife need to begin preparing psychologically for retirement. Constructive and fulfilling leisure activities in middle adulthood are an important part of this preparation (Kelly, 1996). If an adult develops leisure activities that can be continued into retirement, the transition from work to retirement can be less stressful.

Sigmund Freud once commented that the two things adults need to do well to adapt to society's demands are to work and to love. To his list we add "to play." In our fast-paced society, it is all too easy to get caught up in the frenzied, hectic pace of our achievement-oriented work world and ignore leisure and play. *Imagine your life as a middle-aged adult. What would be the ideal mix of work and leisure? What leisure activities do you want to enjoy as a middle-aged adult?*

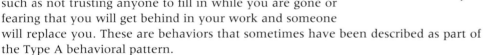

Review and Reflect

4 **Characterize career development, work, and leisure in middle adulthood**

REVIEW

- What are some issues that workers face in midlife?
- What is job satisfaction like in middle age?
- What career challenges and changes might people experience in middle adulthood?
- What characterizes leisure in middle age?

REFLECT

- What do you want your work life and leisure to be like in middle age? If you are middle aged, what is your work life and leisure like? If you are an older adult, what were they like in middle age?

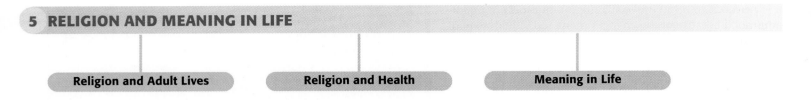

5   RELIGION AND MEANING IN LIFE

Religion and Adult Lives   **Religion and Health**   **Meaning in Life**

What role does religion play in our development as adults? Is meaning of life an important theme for many middle-aged adults?

Religion and Adult Lives

In the MacArthur Study of Midlife Development, more than 70 percent of the individuals said they are religious and consider spirituality a major part of their lives (Brim, 1999). However, that does not mean they are committed to a single religion or house of worship. About one-half said they attend religious services less than once a month or never. In another study, about three-fourths of Americans said that they pray (*Religion in America,* 1993).

In a recent longitudinal study of individuals from their early thirties through their late sixties/early seventies, a significant increase in spirituality occurred between late middle (mid fifties/early sixties) and late adulthood (Wink & Dillon, 2002) (see figure 16.12).

Religion also is an important aspect of people's lives around the world—98 percent of respondents in India, 88 percent in Italy, 72 percent in France, and 63 percent in Scandinavia say that they believe in God (Gallup, 1987).

Females have consistently shown a stronger interest in religion than males have (Bijur & others, 1993). Compared to men, they participate more in both organized and personal forms of religion, are more likely to believe in a higher power or presence, and are more likely to feel that religion is an important dimension of their lives. In the recent longitudinal study just described, the spirituality of women increased more than men in the second half of life (Wink & Dillon, 2002).

A series of recent studies have found that Americans are becoming less committed to particular religious denominations (such as Baptist or Catholic). They are more tolerant of other faiths and more focused on their own spiritual journeys (Paloutzian, 2000). This change may be partly generational, a consequence of postwar baby boomers' emphasis on experimentation and independent thinking that is reflected in a fluid religious orientation.

At the same time that many Americans show a strong interest in religion and believe in God, they also reveal a declining faith in mainstream religious institutions, in religious leaders, and in the spiritual and moral stature of the nation (*Religion in America,* 1993; Sollod, 2000).

In thinking about religion and adult development, it is important to consider the role of individual differences. Religion is a powerful influence in some adults' lives, whereas it plays little or no role in others' lives (Myers, 2000). Further, the influence of religion in people's lives may change as they develop. In John Clausen's (1993) longitudinal investigation, some individuals who had been strongly religious in their early adult years became less so in middle age; others became more religious in middle age.

Religion and Health

How might religion be related to physical health? to coping and happiness?

FIGURE 16.12   Level of Spirituality in Four Adult Age Periods

In a longitudinal study, the spirituality of individuals in four different adult age periods—early (30s), middle (40s), late middle (mid-50s/early 60s), and late (late 60s/early 70s) adulthood was assessed (Wink & Dillon, 2002). Based on responses to open-ended questions in interviews, the spirituality of the individuals was coded on a 5-point scale with 5 being the highest level of spirituality and 1 the lowest.

What roles do religion and spirituality play in the lives of middle-aged adults?

Religion and Physical Health   What might be some of the effects of religion on physical health? One example is cults or religious sects that encourage behaviors that are damaging to health. For example, some religious sects ignore sound medical advice or refuse pain-relieving medication. For individuals in the religious mainstream, there is generally either no link between religion and physical health or a positive effect. For example, in one review, five studies documented that religious commitment had a protective influence on blood pressure or hypertension rates (Levin & Vanderpool, 1989). Also, a number of studies have confirmed a positive association of religious participation and longevity (Gartner, Larson, & Allen, 1991; Hummer & others, 1999; Thoresen & Harris, 2002).

Why might religion promote physical health? There are several possible answers (Hill & Butter, 1995):

- *Lifestyle issues.* For example, religious individuals have lower drug use than their nonreligious counterparts (Gartner, Larson, & Allen, 1991).
- *Social networks.* The degree to which individuals are connected to others affects their health. Well-connected individuals have fewer health problems. Religious groups, meetings, and activities provide social connectedness for individuals (Collins & others, 1993).
- *Coping with stress.* Religion offers a source of comfort and support when individuals are confronted with stressful events (Pargament, 1990). Although research has not clearly demonstrated prayer's positive effect on physical health, some investigators argue that prayer might be associated with such positive health-related changes as a decrease in the perception of pain and reduced muscle tension (McCullough, 1995).

It also has been stressed that religious organizations might have a stronger influence on physical health by providing more health-related services. For example, they could sponsor community-based health education and health-testing programs.

Coping   What is the relation between religion and the ability to cope with stress? Some psychologists have categorized prayer and religious commitment as defensive coping strategies, arguing that they are less effective in helping individuals cope

mhhe com/
santrockld9

**Exploring the Psychology
of Religion**

Psychology of Religion Journals

**Mental Health, Religion,
and Culture**

Alice McNair, Pastoral Counselor

Alice McNair is a pastoral counselor in Mocksville, North Carolina. She has a doctorate in pastoral counseling from Northwestern University. Prior to her present position, McNair was director of the Pastoral Ministries Institute near Washington, D.C. She also is an ordained Baptist minister. She works with adolescents and adults, providing individual, marital, and family counseling.

than are life-skill, problem-solving strategies. However, recently researchers have found that some styles of religious coping are associated with high levels of personal initiative and competence, and that even when defensive religious strategies are initially adopted, they sometimes set the stage for the later appearance of more-active religious coping (Pargament & Park, 1995; Seifert, 2002; Tan, 2000). In one study, depression decreased during times of high stress when there was an increase in collaborative coping (in which people see themselves as active partners with God in solving problems) (Brickel & others, 1998). Also, in general, an intrinsic religious orientation tends to be associated with a sense of competence and control, freedom from worry and guilt, and an absence of illness, whereas an extrinsic orientation tends to be associated with the opposite characteristics (Ventis, 1995).

Instead of disintegrating during times of high stress, religious coping behaviors appear to function quite well in these periods (Bergin, 2000; Koenig, 1998). In one study, individuals were divided into those who were experiencing high stress and those with low stress (Manton, 1989). In the high-stress group, spiritual support was significantly related to personal adjustment (indicated by low depression and high self-esteem). No such links were found in the low-stress group. In a study of 850 medically ill patients admitted to an acute-care hospital, religious coping was related to low depression (Koenig & others, 1992). In John Clausen's (1993) analysis of individuals in the Berkeley Longitudinal Studies, the more-competent women and men in middle age were more likely than their less-competent counterparts to have a religious affiliation and involvement.

In sum, various dimensions of religiousness can help some individuals cope more effectively with their lives (Paloutzian, 2000; Thoresen & Harris, 2002). Religious beliefs can shape a person's psychological perception of pain or disability. Religious cognitions can play an important role in maintaining hope and stimulating motivation toward recovery. Because of its effectiveness in reducing distress, religious coping can help prevent denial of the problem and thus facilitate early recognition and more appropriate health-seeking behavior. Religion also can forestall the development of anxiety and depression disorders by promoting communal or social interaction. Houses of religious worship are a readily available, acceptable, and inexpensive source of support for many individuals, especially the elderly. The socialization provided by religious organizations can help prevent isolation and loneliness (Koenig & Larson, 1998).

Religious counselors often advise people about mental health and coping. To read about the work of one religious counselor, see the Careers in Life-Span Development insert.

Happiness Are people who have a meaningful faith happier than those who do not? Reviews of the happiness literature suggest that happy people do tend to have a meaningful religious faith (Diener, Lucas, & Oishi, 2002). Remember, though, that knowing that two factors correlate does not mean that one causes the other (just as in the case of religion and mental disorder co-occurring in a few individuals). A number of researchers have found that religiously active individuals report greater happiness than do those who are religiously inactive (Diener, Lucas, & Oishi, 2002). However, we don't know whether this connection means that faith enhances happiness or whether happiness induces faith.

Meaning in Life

Austrian psychiatrist Viktor Frankl's mother, father, brother, and wife died in the concentration camps and gas chambers in Auschwitz, Poland. Frankl survived the concentration camp and went on to write about meaning in life. In his book *Man's Search for Meaning*, Frankl (1984) emphasized each person's uniqueness and the finiteness of life. He believed that examining the finiteness of our existence and the certainty of death adds meaning to life. If life were not finite, said Frankl, we could spend our life doing just about whatever we please because time would continue forever.

Frankl said that the three most distinct human qualities are spirituality, freedom, and responsibility. Spirituality, in his view, does not have a religious underpinning. Rather, it refers to a human being's uniqueness—to spirit, philosophy, and mind. Frankl proposed that people need to ask themselves such questions as why they exist, what they want from life, and what the meaning of their life is.

It is in middle adulthood that individuals begin to be faced with death more often, especially the deaths of parents and other older relatives. Also faced with less time in their life, many individuals in middle age begin to ask and evaluate the questions that Frankl proposed.

Roy Baumeister (1991; Baumeister & Vohs, 2002) argues that the quest for a meaningful life can be understood in terms of four main needs for meaning that guide how people try to make sense of their lives:

- *Need for purpose.* Present events draw meaning from their connection with future events. Purposes can be divided into: 1) goals and 2) fulfillments. Life can be oriented toward a future anticipated state, such as living happily ever after or being in love.
- *Need for values.* This can lend a sense of goodness or positive characterization of life and justify certain courses of action. Values help people to determine whether certain acts are right or wrong. Frankl's (1984) view of meaning in life emphasized value as the main form of meaning that people need.
- *Need for a sense of efficacy.* This involves the belief that one can make a difference. A life with purposes and values but no efficacy might consist of a person knowing what is desirable but unable to do anything with that knowledge. With a sense of efficacy, people believe that they can control their environment, which has positive physical and mental health benefits (Bandura, 2001)
- *Need for self-worth.* Most individuals want to be good, worthy persons. Self-worth can be pursued individually, such as finding out that one is very good at doing something, or collectively, as when people find self-esteem from belonging to a group or category of people.

Review and Reflect

5 **Explain the roles of religion and meaning in life during middle adulthood**

REVIEW
- What are some characteristics of religion in middle-aged individuals?
- How is religion linked to physical and mental health?
- What roles does meaning in life play in middle adulthood?

REFLECT
- What are the most important aspects of meaning in life? Might the components of meaning in life vary depending on how old someone is? Explain.

Reach Your Learning Goals

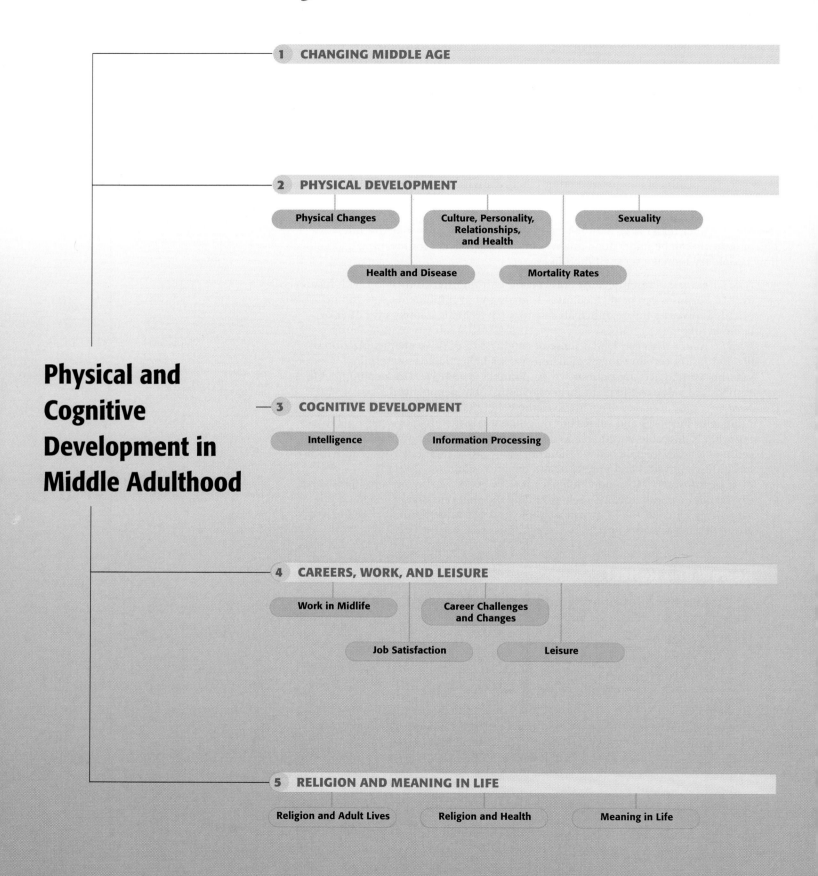

Physical and Cognitive Development in Middle Adulthood

1 CHANGING MIDDLE AGE

2 PHYSICAL DEVELOPMENT

- Physical Changes
- Culture, Personality, Relationships, and Health
- Sexuality
- Health and Disease
- Mortality Rates

3 COGNITIVE DEVELOPMENT

- Intelligence
- Information Processing

4 CAREERS, WORK, AND LEISURE

- Work in Midlife
- Career Challenges and Changes
- Job Satisfaction
- Leisure

5 RELIGION AND MEANING IN LIFE

- Religion and Adult Lives
- Religion and Health
- Meaning in Life

Summary

1 Explain how middle age is changing

- The age boundaries of middle age are not set in stone. As more people live to an older age, what we think of as middle age seems to be occurring later. Developmentalists are beginning to study middle age more probably because of the dramatic increase in the number of individuals entering this period of the life span. Middle age involves extensive individual variation. With this variation in mind, we will consider middle adulthood to be entered at about 40 and exited at approximately 60 years of age. Midlife changes are often gradual.

2 Discuss physical changes in middle adulthood

- Genetic and lifestyle factors play important roles in whether chronic diseases will appear and when.
- Among the physical changes are outwardly noticeable changes in physical appearance (wrinkles, aging spots); height (decrease) and weight (increase), strength, joints, and bones; vision; hearing; cardiovascular system; lungs; and sleep. In middle age, the frequency of accidents declines and individuals are less susceptible to colds and allergies.
- Chronic disorders rarely appear in early adulthood, increase in middle adulthood, and become more common in late adulthood. Arthritis is the leading chronic disorder in middle age, followed by hypertension. Men have more fatal chronic disorders, women more nonfatal ones in middle age.
- Culture plays an important role in coronary disease. The Type A behavior pattern has been proposed as having a link with heart disease, but it primarily is the hostility dimension of the pattern that is consistently associated with heart disease. Hardiness is a buffer of stress and is related to reduced illness. Health in middle age is linked to the current quality of social relationships and to developmental pathways of relationships.
- In middle age, the leading causes of death, in order, are heart disease, cancer, and cerebrovascular disease.
- *Climacteric* is the midlife transition in which fertility declines. Menopause is a marker that signals the end of childbearing capability, usually arriving in the late forties and early fifties. The vast majority of women do not have serious physical or psychological problems related to menopause. Hormone replacement therapy (HRT) augments the declining levels of reproductive hormone production by the ovaries. HRT consists of various forms of estrogen, and usually progestin. Although HRT reduces many short-term symptoms of menopause, its long-term use is no longer recommended by the National Institutes of Health because of its association with increases in breast cancer, coronary heart disease, and stroke. Men do not experience an inability to father children in middle age, although their testosterone levels decline. A male menopause, like the dramatic decline in estrogen in women, does not occur. Sexual behavior occurs less frequently in middle adulthood than in early adulthood.

Nonetheless, a majority of middle-aged adults show a moderate or strong interest in sex.

3 Identify cognitive changes in middle adulthood

- Horn argued that crystallized intelligence (accumulated information and verbal skills) continues to increase in middle adulthood whereas fluid intelligence (ability to reason abstractly) declines. Schaie found that, when assessed longitudinally, intellectual abilities are less likely to decline and are even more likely to improve than when assessed cross-sectionally in middle adulthood. The highest level of four intellectual abilities (vocabulary, verbal memory, inductive reasoning, and spatial ability) occurred in middle age.
- Speed of information processing, often assessed through reaction time, declines in middle adulthood. Although Schaie found that verbal memory increased in middle age, some researchers have found that memory declines in middle age. Working memory declines in late middle age. Memory is more likely to decline in middle age when individuals don't use effective strategies. Expertise involves having an extensive, highly organized knowledge and an understanding of a domain. Expertise often increases in the middle adulthood years. Practical problem solving often increases through the forties and fifties as individuals accumulate practical experience.

4 Characterize career development, work, and leisure in middle adulthood

- Midlife workers face a number of issues and for many people midlife is a time of reflection, assessment, and evaluation of their current work and what they plan to do in the future. One important issue is whether individuals will continue to do the type of work they want to do.
- Work satisfaction increases steadily throughout life—from age 20 to at least age 60—for both college-educated and non-college-educated adults.
- The current middle-aged worker faces such challenges as the globalization of work, rapid developments in information technologies, downsizing of organizations, and early retirement. Midlife job or career changes can be self-motivated or forced on individuals.
- We not only need to learn to work well, but we also need to learn to enjoy leisure. Midlife may be an especially important time for leisure because of the physical changes that occur and because of preparation for an active retirement.

5 Explain the roles of religion and meaning in life during middle adulthood

- Religion is an important dimension of many Americans' lives, as well as the lives of people around the world. Females show a stronger interest in religion than males do. It is important to consider individual differences in religious interest.

- In some cases, religion can be negatively linked to physical health, as when cults or religious sects restrict individuals from obtaining medical care. In mainstream religions, religion usually shows either a positive association or no association with physical health. Religion can play an important role in coping, for some individuals. Happy people tend to have a meaningful religious faith, but it is important to remember that the link is correlational, not causal.

- Frankl believes that examining the finiteness of our existence leads to exploration of meaning in life. Faced with death of older relatives and less time to live themselves, many middle-aged individuals increasingly examine life's meaning. Baumeister argues that a quest for a meaningful life involves four main needs: purpose, values, efficacy, and self-worth.

Key Terms

Key People

Taking It to the Net

1. In the past year 58-year-old Alan has experienced some lapses in memory. He sometimes forgets where he put his car keys, it may take him a few minutes to recall the name of someone he met on the golf course last week, and it takes him longer to balance his checkbook than it used to. Is Alan showing signs of dementia or normal age-related forgetfulness? What kinds of strategies can Alan use to maintain or even improve his memory?

2. Advances in health and hygiene mean that Americans tend to live longer. What do we need to know about how to cultivate physical health and productivity in America's aging population?

3. Harry can't decide whether to go to theological seminary to study for the ministry, or go to medical school. Recent polls indicate that his interests are not necessarily incompatible. What are people reporting about the role of religion in mental and physical health?

Connect to www.mhhe.com/santrockld9 to research the answers and complete these exercises.

E-Learning Tools

To help you master the material in this chapter, you'll find a number of valuable study tools on the Student CD-ROM that accompanies this book. In addition, visit the Online Learning Center for *Life-Span Development*, ninth edition, where you'll find these valuable resources for chapter 16, "Physical and Cognitive Development in Middle Adulthood."

- Ever thought about your religious or existential well-being? Complete the self-assessment, *My Spiritual Well-Being*, to see where you are on this scale. Then use the self-assessment, *What Is My Purpose in Life*, to explore this thought-provoking question.

- Build your decision-making skills by trying your hand at the parenting and education "Scenarios."

CHAPTER

17

The generations of living things pass in a short time, and like runners, hand on the torch of life.

—LUCRETIUS,
Roman Poet, 1st Century B.C.

Socioemotional Development in Middle Adulthood

Learning Goals

1 *D*escribe personality theories and development in middle adulthood

2 *D*iscuss stability and change in development during middle adulthood, including longitudinal studies

3 *I*dentify some important aspects of close relationships in middle adulthood

Images of Life-Span Development
Middle-Age Variations

Forty-five-year-old Sarah feels tired, depressed, and angry. She became pregnant when she was 17 and married Ben. They stayed together for three years, and then he left her for another woman. Sarah went to work as a salesclerk to help make ends meet. She remarried eight years later to Alan, who had two children of his own from a previous marriage. Sarah stopped working for several years, but then Alan started going out on her. She found out about it from a friend. Sarah stayed with Alan for another year. Finally he was gone so much that she could not take it anymore and decided to divorce him. Sarah went back to work again as a salesclerk; she has been in the same position for 16 years now. During those 16 years, she has dated a number of men, but the relationships never seemed to work out. Her son never finished high school and has drug problems. Her father just died last year, and Sarah is trying to help her mother financially, although she can barely pay her own bills. Sarah looks in the mirror and does not like what she sees. She sees her past as a shambles, and the future does not look rosy, either.

Forty-five-year-old Wanda feels energetic, happy, and satisfied. She graduated from college and worked for three years as a high school math teacher. She married Andy, who had just finished law school. One year later, they had their first child, Josh. Wanda stayed home with Josh for two years, then returned to her job as a math teacher. Even during her pregnancy, Wanda stayed active and exercised regularly, playing tennis almost every day. After her pregnancy, she kept up her exercise habits. Wanda and Andy had another child, Wendy. Now, as they move into their middle-age years, their children are both off to college, and Wanda and Andy are enjoying spending more time with each other. Last weekend they visited Josh at his college, and the weekend before they visited Wendy at her college. Wanda continued working as a high school math teacher until six years ago. She had developed computer skills as part of her job and taken some computer courses at a nearby college, doubling up during the summer months. She resigned her math teaching job and took a job with a computer company, where she has already worked her way into management. Wanda looks in the mirror and likes what she sees. She sees her past as enjoyable, although not without hills and valleys, and she looks to the future with zest and enthusiasm.

As with Sarah and Wanda, there are individual variations in the way people experience middle age. Let's now examine personality theories and development in middle age, including further ideas about individual variation.

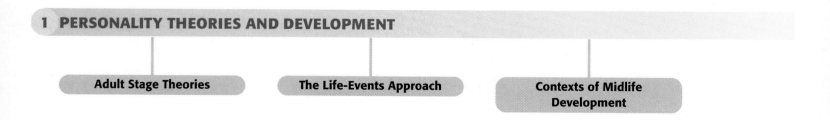

1 PERSONALITY THEORIES AND DEVELOPMENT

Adult Stage Theories **The Life-Events Approach** **Contexts of Midlife Development**

What is the best way to conceptualize middle age? Is it a stage or a crisis? How pervasive are midlife crises? How extensively is middle age influenced by life events? Is personality linked with the contexts, such as the point in history in which individuals go through midlife, their culture, and their gender?

Adult Stage Theories

Adult stage theories have been plentiful, and they have contributed to the view that midlife is a crisis in development. Two prominent adult stage theories are Erik Erikson's life-span view and Daniel Levinson's seasons of a man's life.

Erikson's Stage of Generativity Versus Stagnation Erikson (1968) believes that middle-aged adults face a significant issue in life—generativity versus stagnation, which is the name Erikson gave to the seventh stage in his life-span theory ◀▥ p. 46. Generativity encompasses adults' desire to leave a legacy of themselves to the next generation (Petersen, 2002). Through generativity, the adult achieves a kind of immortality by leaving one's legacy to the next generation. By contrast, stagnation (sometimes called "self-absorption") develops when individuals sense that they have done nothing for the next generation.

In George Vaillant's (2002) longitudinal studies of aging, one of which was described in chapter 16, in middle age, generativity (defined in this study as "taking care of the next generation") was more strongly related than intimacy to whether individuals would have an enduring and happy marriage at 75 to 80 years of age. One of the participants in Vaillant's studies said: "From twenty to thirty I learned how to get along with my wife. From thirty to forty I learned how to be a success at my job, and at forty to fifty I worried less about myself and more about the children" (p.114).

In a longitudinal study of Smith College women, generativity increased from the thirties through the fifties (Cole & Stewart, 1996; Roberts & Helson, 1997; Stewart, Ostrove, & Helson, 2001; Zucker, Ostrove, & Stewart, 2002) (see figure 17.1). Also in this study, another aspect of Erikson's theory—identity—was assessed in terms of "identity certainty" and this increased from the thirties through the fifties. Figure 17.2 describes the items that were used to assess generativity and identity certainty in the Smith College study.

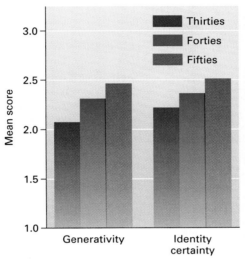

FIGURE 17.1 Changes in Generativity and Identity Certainty from the Thirties through the Fifties

Both generativity and identity certainty increased in Smith College women as they aged from their thirties through their fifties (Stewart, Ostrove, & Helson, 2001). The women rated themselves on a 3-point scale indicating the extent to which they thought the statements about generativity and identity creativity were descriptive of their lives.

Generativity

Feeling needed by people

Effort to ensure that young people get their chance to develop

Influence in my community or area of interest

A new level of productivity or effectiveness

Appreciation and awareness of older people

Having a wider perspective

Interest in things beyond my family

Identity certainty

A sense of being my own person

Excitement, turmoil, confusion about my impulses and potential (reversed)

Coming near the end of one road and not yet finding another (reversed)

Feeling my life is moving well

Searching for a sense of who I am (reversed)

Wishing I had a wider scope to my life (reversed)

Anxiety that I won't live up to opportunities (reversed)

Feeling secure and committed

FIGURE 17.2 Items Used to Assess Generativity and Identity Certainty

These items were used to assess generativity and identity certainty in the longitudinal study of Smith College women (Stewart, Ostrove, & Helson, 2001). In the assessment of identity certainty, five of the items involved reversed scoring (for example, if an individual scored high on the item "Searching for a sense of who I am," it was an indication of identity uncertainty rather identity certainty).

Middle-aged adults can develop generativity in a number of different ways (Kotre, 1984). Through biological generativity, adults conceive and give birth to an infant. Through parental generativity, adults provide nurturance and guidance to children. Through work generativity, adults develop skills that are passed down to others. And through cultural generativity, adults create, renovate, or conserve some aspect of culture that ultimately survives.

Through generativity, adults promote and guide the next generation by parenting, teaching, leading, and doing things that benefit the community (Pratt & others, 2001). Generative adults commit themselves to the continuation and improvement of society as a whole through their connection to the next generation. Generative adults develop a positive legacy of the self and then offer it as a gift to the next generation.

Does research support Erikson's theory that generativity is an important dimension of middle age? Yes, it does. In one study, Carol Ryff (1984) examined the views

Era of late adulthood: 60 to ?

Late adult transition: Age 60 to 65

Culminating life structure for middle adulthood: 55 to 60

Age 50 transition: 50 to 55

Entry life structure for middle adulthood: 45 to 50

Middle adult transition: Age 40 to 45

Culminating life structure for early adulthood: 33 to 40

Age 30 transition: 28 to 33

Entry life structure for early adulthood: 22 to 28

Early adult transition: Age 17 to 22

FIGURE 17.3 Levinson's Periods of Adult Development

of women and men at different ages across adulthood. The middle-aged adults especially were concerned about generativity and guiding younger adults. In another study, having a positive identity was linked with generativity in middle age (Vandewater, Ostrove, & Stewart, 1997). In another study, women developed generativity through different aspects of their lives (Peterson & Stewart, 1996). Generative women with careers found gratification through work; generative women who had not worked in a career experienced gratification through parenting.

In one modification of Erikson's theory, it was proposed that Erikson's three adult stages—involving intimacy (early adulthood), generativity (middle adulthood), and integrity (late adulthood)—are best viewed as developmental phases within identity. In this view, identity remains the central core of the self's development across all of the adult years (Whitbourne & Connolly, 1999).

Levinson's Seasons of a Man's Life In *The Seasons of a Man's Life* (1978), clinical psychologist Daniel Levinson reported the results of extensive interviews with forty middle-aged men. The interviews were conducted with hourly workers, business executives, academic biologists, and novelists. Levinson bolstered his conclusions with information from the biographies of famous men and the development of memorable characters in literature. Although Levinson's major interest focused on midlife change, he described a number of stages and transitions in the life span, ranging from 17 to 65 years of age, which are shown in figure 17.3.

Levinson emphasizes that developmental tasks must be mastered at each of these stages. In early adulthood, the two major tasks to be mastered are exploring the possibilities for adult living and developing a stable life structure. Levinson sees the twenties as a *novice phase* of adult development. At the end of one's teens, a transition from dependence to independence should occur. This transition is marked by the formation of a dream—an image of the kind of life the youth wants to have, especially in terms of a career and marriage. The novice phase is a time of reasonably free experimentation and of testing the dream in the real world.

From about the ages of 28 to 33, the man goes through a transition period in which he must face the more serious question of determining his goals. During the thirties, he usually focuses on family and career development. In the later years of this period, he enters a phase of *Becoming One's Own Man* (or BOOM, as Levinson calls it). By age 40, he has reached a stable location in his career, has outgrown his earlier, more tenuous attempts at learning to become an adult, and now must look forward to the kind of life he will lead as a middle-aged adult.

According to Levinson, the change to middle adulthood lasts about five years (ages 40 to 45) and requires the adult male to come to grips with four major conflicts that have existed in his life since adolescence: (1) being young versus being old, (2) being destructive versus being constructive, (3) being masculine versus being feminine, and (4) being attached to others versus being separated from them. Seventy to 80 percent of the men Levinson interviewed found the midlife transition tumultuous and psychologically painful, as many aspects of their lives came into question. According to Levinson, the success of the midlife transition rests on how effectively the individual reduces the polarities and accepts each of them as an integral part of his being.

Because Levinson interviewed middle-aged males, we can consider the data about middle adulthood more valid than the data about early adulthood. When individuals are asked to remember information about earlier parts of their lives, they may distort and forget things. The original Levinson data included no females, although Levinson (1987, 1996) reported that his stages, transitions, and the crisis of middle age hold for females as well as males. Levinson's work included no statistical analysis. However, the quality and quantity of the Levinson biographies are outstanding in the clinical tradition.

How Pervasive Are Midlife Crises? Levinson (1978) views midlife as a crisis, believing that the middle-aged adult is suspended between the past and the future, trying to cope with this gap that threatens life's continuity. George Vaillant (1977) concludes that just as adolescence is a time for detecting parental flaws and discovering the truth about childhood, the forties are a decade of reassessing and recording the truth about the adolescent and adulthood years. However, while Levinson sees midlife as a crisis, Vaillant believes that only a minority of adults experience a midlife crisis:

> Just as pop psychologists have reveled in the not-so-common high drama of adolescent turmoil, also the popular press, sensing good copy, had made all too much of the mid-life crisis. The term mid-life crisis brings to mind some variation of the renegade minister who leaves behind four children and the congregation that loved him in order to drive off in a magenta Porsche with a 25-year-old striptease artiste. As with adolescent turmoil, mid-life crises are much rarer in community samples. (pp. 222–223)

Vaillant's study—called the "Grant Study"—involved a follow-up of Harvard University men in their early thirties and in their late forties who initially had been interviewed as undergraduates. In Vaillant's words, "The high drama in Gail Sheehy's best-selling *Passages* was rarely observed in the lives of the Grant Study men" (p. 223).

The research studies listed here all document that midlife is not characterized by pervasive crises:

- One study assessed 3,032 Americans from 25 to 72 years of age (Brim, 1999). In this study, the individuals from 40 to 60 years of age were less nervous and worried than those under 40. The middle-aged adults reported a growing sense of control in their work and more financial security. The middle-aged adults also indicated a greater sense of environmental mastery—the ability to handle daily responsibilities—and autonomy than their younger counterparts.
- A longitudinal study of 2,247 individuals found few midlife crises (McCrae & Costa, 1990; Siegler & Costa, 1999). In this study, the emotional instability of individuals did not significantly increase through their middle-aged years (see figure 17.4).
- A study found that adults experienced a peak of personal control and power in middle age (Clark-Plaskie & Lachman, 1999).
- A study of individuals described as young (average age 19), middle-aged (average age 46), and older (average age 73) adults found that their ability to manage their environmental surroundings (environmental mastery) and self-determination (autonomy) increased in middle age (Keyes & Ryff, 1999) (see figure 17.5). Their investment in living (purpose in life) and desire for continued self-realization (personal growth) dropped slightly from early to middle adulthood but still remained high before declining in late adulthood.

Adult development experts are virtually unanimous in their belief that midlife crises have been exaggerated (Etaugh & Bridges, 2002; Reid & Willis, 1999). In sum:

- The stage theories place too much emphasis on crises in development, especially midlife crises.
- There often is considerable individual variation in the way people experience the stages, a topic that we will turn to next.

Individual Variations Stage theories especially focus on the universals of adult personality development. They try to pin down stages that all individuals go through

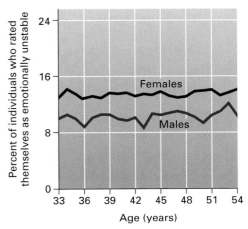

FIGURE 17.4 Emotional Instability and Age

In one longitudinal study, the emotional instability of individuals was assessed from age 33 to age 54 (Costa & McCrae, 1999; McCrae & Costa, 1990). No significant increase in emotional instability occurred during the middle-aged years.

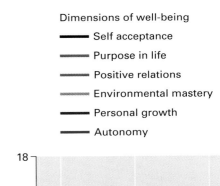

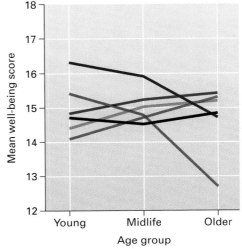

FIGURE 17.5 Age and Well-Being

In one study, six dimensions of well-being were assessed in three different age groups (young adults, middle-aged adults, and older adults) (Ryff & Keyes, 1998). An increase or little change in most of the dimensions of well-being occurred during middle adulthood.

in their adult lives. These theories do not adequately address individual variations in adult development. In one extensive study of a random sample of 500 men at midlife, it was concluded that there is extensive individual variation among men (Farrell & Rosenberg, 1981). In the individual variations view, middle-aged adults interpret, shape, alter, and give meaning to their lives.

The ability to set aside unproductive worries and preoccupations is believed to be an important factor in functioning under stress. In Vaillant's (1977, 2002) longitudinal study, pervasive personal preoccupations were maladaptive in both the work and the marriages of college students over a 30-year period after leaving college. Some individuals in this study had personal preoccupations, while others did not.

The Life-Events Approach

Age-related stages represent one major way to examine adult personality development. A second major way to conceptualize adult personality development is to focus on life events (Schwarzer & Schultz, 2003). In the early version of the life-events approach, life events were viewed as taxing circumstances for individuals, forcing them to change their personality (Holmes & Rahe, 1967). Such events as the death of a spouse, divorce, marriage, and so on were believed to involve varying degrees of stress, and therefore likely to influence the individual's development.

Today's life-events approach is more sophisticated (Cui & Vaillant, 1996; Hultsch & Plemons, 1979; McLeod, 1996). The **contemporary life-events approach** emphasizes on how life events influence the individual's development, but also mediating factors (physical health, family supports, for example), the individual's adaptation to the life event (appraisal of the threat, coping strategies, for example), the life-stage context, and the sociohistorical context (see figure 17.6). If individuals are in poor health and have little family support, life events are likely to be more stressful. One individual may perceive a life event as highly stressful, another individual may perceive the same event as a challenge. And a divorce may be more stressful after many years of marriage when adults are in their fifties than when they have only been married several years and are in their twenties (Chiriboga, 1982). Adults may be able to cope more effectively with divorce today than in the 1950s because divorce has become more commonplace and accepted in today's society.

Though the life-events approach is a valuable addition to understanding adult development, like other approaches to adult development, it has its drawbacks (Dohrenwend & Dohrenwend, 1978). One of the most significant drawbacks is that the life-events approach places too much emphasis on change. It does not adequately recognize the stability that, at least to some degree, characterizes adult development. Another drawback is that it may not be life's major events that are the primary sources of stress, but our daily experiences (Pillow, Zautra, & Sandler, 1996). Enduring a boring but tense job or marriage and living in poverty do not show up on scales of major life events. Yet the everyday pounding we take from these living conditions can add up to a highly stressful life and eventually illness. Some psychologists believe we can gain greater insight into the source of life's stresses by focusing more on daily hassles and daily uplifts (Lazarus & Folkman, 1984).

In one study of 210 Florida police officers, the day-to-day friction associated with an inefficient justice system and distorted press accounts of police work were more stressful than responding to a felony in progress or making an arrest (Spielberger & Grier, 1983). In another study, the most frequent daily hassles of college students were wasting time, concerns about meeting high standards, and being lonely (Kanner & others, 1981). Among the most frequent uplifts of the college students were entertainment, getting along well with friends, and completing a task. In this same study, the most frequent daily hassles of middle-aged adults were concerns about weight and the health of a family member, while their most frequent daily uplifts involved relating well with a spouse or lover, or a friend (see figure 17.7). And the middle-aged adults were more likely than the college students to report that their daily hassles

contemporary life-events approach Emphasizes that how a life event influences the individual's development depends not only on the life event, but also on mediating factors, the individual's adaptation to the life event, the life-stage context, and the sociohistorical context.

involved economic concerns (rising prices and taxes, for example). Critics of the daily-hassles approach argue that some of the same problems involved with life-events scales occur when daily hassles are assessed (Dohrenwend & Shrout, 1985). For example, knowing about an adult's daily hassles tells us nothing about physical changes, how the individual copes with hassles, and how the individual perceives hassles.

Contexts of Midlife Development

As people live through middle age, they do so in a number of contexts. Among those are historical contexts (cohort effects), gender, and culture.

Historical Contexts (Cohort Effects) Some developmentalists believe that changing historical times and different social expectations influence how different cohorts—remember that these are groups of individuals born in the same year or time period—move through the life span. Bernice Neugarten (1964) has been emphasizing the power of age-group or cohort since the 1960s. Our values, attitudes, expectations, and behaviors are influenced by the period in which we live. For example, individuals born during the difficult times of the Great Depression may have a different outlook on life than those born during the optimistic 1950s, says Neugarten.

Neugarten (1986) believes that the social environment of a particular age group can alter its **social clock**—the timetable according to which individuals are expected to accomplish life's tasks, such as getting married, having children, or establishing themselves in a career. Social clocks provide guides for our lives; individuals whose lives are not synchronized with these social clocks find life to be more stressful than those who are on schedule, says Neugarten. She argues that today there is much less agreement than in the past on the right age or sequence for the occurrence of major life events. For example, the age at which people get married, have children, become parents, go to school, and retire varies more than in previous decades.

One study found that, between the late 1950s and the late 1970s, there was a dramatic decline in adults' beliefs that there is a "right age" for major life events and

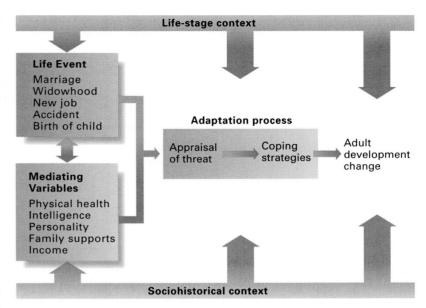

FIGURE 17.6 A Contemporary Life-Events Framework for Interpreting Adult Developmental Change

social clock The timetable according to which individuals are expected to accomplish life's tasks, such as getting married, having children, or establishing themselves in a career.

Daily Hassles	Percent of Times Checked		Daily Uplifts
Concerns about weight	52.4	76.3	Relating well with your spouse or lover
Health of family member	48.1	74.4	Relating well with friends
Rising prices of common goods	43.7	73.3	Completing a task
Home maintenance	42.8	72.7	Feeling healthy
Too many things to do	38.6	69.7	Getting enough sleep
Misplacing or losing things	38.1	68.4	Eating out
Yardwork or outside home maintenance	38.1	68.1	Meeting your responsibilities
Property, investment, or taxes	37.6	67.7	Visiting, phoning, or writing someone
Crime	37.1	66.7	Spending time with family
Physical appearance	35.9	65.5	Home (inside) pleasing to you

FIGURE 17.7 The Ten Most Frequent Daily Hassles and Uplifts of Middle-Aged Adults over a Nine-Month Period

achievements (Passuth, Maines, & Neugarten, 1984) (see figure 17.8). And in one study, Australian adults were asked the same questions about the best age for experiencing various life circumstances as Neugarten had asked American adults (Peterson, 1996). The Australian adults advocated later ages for marriage and grandparenthood, a younger age for leaving school, and a broader age range for retiring. In general, the Australians endorsed a wide age range for experiencing of life circumstances.

Trying to tease out universal truths and patterns about adult development from one birth cohort is complicated because the findings may not apply to another birth cohort. Most of the individuals studied by Levinson and Vaillant, for example, were born before and during the Great Depression. What was true for these individuals may not be true for today's 40-year-olds, born in the optimistic aftermath of World War II, or the post-baby-boom generation as they approach the midlife transition. The midlife men in Levinson's and Vaillant's studies might have been burned out at a premature age rather than reflect a normal developmental pattern of less stress (Rossi, 1989).

Gender Contexts   Critics say that the stage theories of adult development have a male bias (Deutsch, 1991). For example, the central focus of stage theories is on career choice and work achievement, which historically have dominated men's life choices and life chances more than women's. The stage theories do not adequately address women's concerns about relationships, interdependence, and caring (Gilligan, 1982). The adult stage theories have also placed little importance on childbearing and child rearing. Women's family roles are complex and often have a higher salience in their lives than in men's lives. The role demands that women experience in balancing career and family are usually not experienced as intensely by men.

One of the problems in making stage theory comparisons of males and females is the assumption of a normative sequence of development by the stage theories. That is,

Activity/event	Appropriate age range	Percent who agree (late '50s study)		Percent who agree (late '70s study)	
		Men	Women	Men	Women
Best age for a man to marry	20–25	80	90	42	42
Best age for a woman to marry	19–24	85	90	44	36
When most people should become grandparents	45–50	84	79	64	57
Best age for most people to finish school and go to work	20–22	86	82	36	38
When most men should be settled on a career	24–26	74	64	24	26
When most men hold their top jobs	45–50	71	58	38	31
When most people should be ready to retire	60–65	83	86	66	41
When a man has the most responsibilities	35–50	79	75	49	50
When a man accomplishes most	40–50	82	71	46	41
The prime of life for a man	35–50	86	80	59	66
When a woman has the most responsibilities	25–40	93	91	59	53
When a woman accomplishes most	30–45	94	92	57	48

FIGURE 17.8 Individuals' Conceptions of the Right Age for Major Life Events and Achievements: Late 1950s and Late 1970s

the stage theories assume that most people will encounter a given developmental stage at more or less the same time: graduation from high school and college, getting married, starting a family, becoming grandparents, and retiring, for example. However, our contemporary life challenges many of these "normative" experiences. Many women are returning to college to obtain an education and further their career a number of years after starting a family. Many other women are delaying marriage and childbearing until after they have successfully established a career. Yet other women continue in the tradition of women earlier in this century by getting married, having children, and not pursuing a career outside the home. As the roles of women have become more complex and varied, defining a normative sequence of development for them has become difficult, if not impossible.

Critics say the stage theories of adult development have a male bias by emphasizing career choice and achievement, and that they do not adequately address women's concerns about relationships, interdependence, and caring. The stage theories assume a normative sequence of development, but as women's roles have become more varied and complex, determining what is normative is difficult. *What kinds of changes have taken place in middle-aged women's lives in recent years?*

Many women who are now at midlife and beyond experienced a role shift in their late twenties, thirties, or beyond (Fodor & Franks, 1990). As they were engaging in traditional roles, the women's movement began and changed the lives of a substantial number of traditionally raised women and their families. Changes are still occurring for many midlife women. There is an increasing number of late-life divorces. And in an America obsessed with youth and beauty, there is a double standard of aging: Women must stay young, while men are allowed to age. In one study, most midlife women wanted to be at least 10 years younger (Rossi, 1989).

Basic changes in social attitudes regarding labor force participation, families, and gender roles have begun to broaden the opportunities available for women in middle adulthood as well as other life-span periods (Moen & Wethington, 1999). The effects of these changes are the most far-reaching for the baby-boom cohort now entering midlife. The employment patterns across the life span for women now in their middle adult years now more closely resemble those of males. (Contemporary Research Press, 1993).

Is midlife and beyond to be feared by women as a loss of youth and opportunity, a time of decline? Or is it a new prime of life, a time for renewal, for shedding preoccupations with a youthful appearance and body, and for seeking new challenges, valuing maturity, and enjoying change?

In one study, the early fifties were indeed a new prime of life for many women (Mitchell & Helson, 1990). In the sample of 700 women aged 26 to 80, women in their early fifties most often described their lives as "first-rate." Conditions that distinguished the lives of women in their early fifties from those of women in other age periods included more "empty nests," better health, higher income, and more concern for parents. Women in their early fifties showed confidence, involvement, security, and breadth of personality.

In sum, the view that midlife is a negative age period for women is stereotypical, as so many perceptions of age periods are (Aldwin & Levenson, 2001; Huyck, 1999). Midlife is a diversified, heterogeneous period for women, just as it is for men.

Cultural Contexts   We have already seen that midlife crises are less pervasive in the United States than is commonly believed (Chiriboga, 1989). How common are midlife crises in other cultures? There has been little cross-cultural research on middle adulthood, and adult stage theories, such as Levinson's, have not been tested in other cultures. In many cultures, though, especially nonindustrialized cultures, the concept of middle age is not very clear, or in some cases is absent. It is common in nonindustrialized societies to describe individuals as young or old, but not as middle-aged (Grambs, 1989). And some cultures have no words for "adolescent," "young adult," or "middle-aged adult."

Gusii dancers perform on habitat day in Nairobi, Kenya. Movement from one status to another in the Gusii culture is due primarily to life events, not age. The Gusii do not have a clearly labeled midlife transition.

Consider the Gusii culture, located south of the equator in the African country of Kenya. The Gusii divide the life course differently for females and males (LeVine, 1979):

Females	Males
1. Infant	1. Infant
2. Uncircumcised girl	2. Uncircumcised boy
3. Circumcised girl	3. Circumcised boy warrior
4. Married woman	4. Male elder
5. Female elder	

Thus, movement from one status to the next is due primarily to life events, not age, in the Gusii culture. While the Gusii do not have a clearly labeled midlife transition, some of the Gusii adults do reassess their lives around the age of 40. At this time, these Gusii adults examine their current status and the limited time they have remaining in their lives. Their physical strength is decreasing and they know they cannot farm their land forever, so they seek spiritual powers by becoming ritual practitioners or healers. As in the American culture, however, a midlife crisis in the Gusii culture is the exception rather than the rule.

What is middle age like for women in other cultures? It depends on the modernity of the culture and the culture's view of gender roles. Some anthropologists believe that middle age has more advantages in many nonindustrialized societies than in industrialized nations like the United States (Brown, 1985). As women reach middle age in many nonindustrialized societies, three changes take place that improve their status. First, they are often freed from cumbersome restrictions that were placed on them when they were younger. For example, in middle age they enjoy greater geographical mobility. Child care has ceased or can be delegated, and domestic chores are reduced. Commercial opportunities, visitation of relatives living at a distance, and religious opportunities provide an opportunity to venture forth from the village. A second major change brought on by middle age is a woman's right to exercise authority over specified younger kin. Middle-aged women can extract labor from younger family members. The work of the middle-aged woman tends to be administrative, delegating tasks and making assignments to younger women. The middle-aged woman also makes important decisions for certain members of the younger generation: what a grandchild is to be named, who is ready to be initiated, and who is eligible to marry whom. A third major change brought on by middle age in nonindustrialized societies is the eligibility of the woman for special statuses and the possibility that these provide recognition beyond the household. These statuses include the vocations of midwife, curer, holy woman, and matchmaker.

Review and Reflect

1 **Describe personality theories and development in middle adulthood**

REVIEW

- What are some adult stage theories of development?
- What is the life-events approach?
- How do contexts influence midlife development?

REFLECT

- Which approach makes more sense to you—adult stage or life events? Or do you think both approaches should be considered in understanding an adult's development? Explain your answer.

2 STABILITY AND CHANGE

| Longitudinal Studies | | Conclusions |

Recall from chapter 1 that an important issue in life-span development is the extent to which individuals show stability in their development versus the extent to which they change ◀▥ p. 24. A number of longitudinal studies have addressed the stability-change issue as they have assessed individuals at different points in their adult lives.

Longitudinal Studies

We will examine four longitudinal studies to help us understand the extent to which there is stability or change in adult development: Neugarten's Kansas City Study, Costa and McCrae's Baltimore Study, the Berkeley Longitudinal Studies, and Helson's Mills College Study.

Neugarten's Kansas City Study   One of the earliest longitudinal studies of adult personality development was conducted by Bernice Neugarten (1964). Known as the "Kansas City Study," it involved the investigation of individuals 40 to 80 years of age over a 10-year period. The adults were given personality tests, they filled out questionnaires, and they were interviewed.

Neugarten concluded that both stability and change characterized the adults as they aged. The characteristics that showed the most stability were styles of coping (such as avoiding problems or tackling them head-on), being satisfied with life, and being goal-directed. In terms of change, as individuals aged from 40 to 60 they became more passive and were more likely to be threatened by the environment.

Costa and McCrae's Baltimore Study   Another major study of adult personality development continues to be conducted by Paul Costa and Robert McCrae (1995, 1998). They focus on what are called the **big five factors of personality,** which consist of emotional stability (neuroticism), extraversion, openness to experience, agreeableness, and conscientiousness (see figure 17.9).

Using their five-factor personality test, Costa and McCrae (1995, 2000) studied approximately a thousand college-educated men and women aged 20 to 96, assessing the same individuals over a period of many years. Data collection began in the 1950s to the mid 1960s and is ongoing. Costa and McCrae concluded that considerable stability occurs in the five personality factors—emotional stability, extraversion, openness, agreeableness, and conscientiousness.

In one study, McCrae and his colleagues (1999) found consistent age trends in personality in a number of different cultures. In Germany, Croatia, Italy, Portugal, and

mhhe●com/
santrockld9

The Big Five
Paul Costa's Research

big five factors of personality Emotional stability (neuroticism), extraversion, openness to experience, agreeableness, and conscientiousness.

Emotional stability	Extraversion	Openness	Agreeableness	Conscientiousness
• Calm or anxious	• Sociable or retiring	• Imaginative or practical	• Softhearted or ruthless	• Organized or disorganized
• Secure or insecure	• Fun-loving or somber	• Interested in variety or routine	• Trusting or suspicious	• Careful or careless
• Self-satisfied or self-pitying	• Affectionate or reserved	• Independent or conforming	• Helpful or uncooperative	• Disciplined or impulsive

FIGURE 17.9 The Big Five Factors of Personality

Korea, older adults scored lower on extraversion and openness to experience than younger adults. In these countries, the older adults scored higher in agreeableness and conscientiousness than younger adults. Similar patterns of age changes also were found in a study of Chinese and American adults (Yang, McCrae, & Costa, 1998). Few cultural variations were found in these studies.

In another recent study, 285 adults from the United States (the Midwest) and 450 adults from China (Bejing) who were 20 to 87 years of age were given the California Psychological Inventory (CPI) (Labouvie-Vief & others, 2000). The CPI is a standardized personality test in which individuals respond to a large number of items that reflect a number of personality traits by saying whether the items are like them or not like them. Analysis of the results indicated that older adults were less extraverted and less flexible than their younger adult counterparts. The older adults were more likely to show self-control and engage in normative behavior than younger adults were. The age changes were more pronounced for the Chinese than for the American adults.

Berkeley Longitudinal Studies By far the longest-running longitudinal inquiry is the series of analyses called the Berkeley Longitudinal Studies. Initially, more than 500 children and their parents were studied in the late 1920s and early 1930s. The book *Present and Past in Middle Life* (Eichorn & others, 1981) profiles these individuals as they became middle-aged. The results from early adolescence through a portion of midlife did not support either extreme in the debate over whether personality is characterized by stability or change. Some characteristics were more stable than others, however. The most stable characteristics were the degree to which individuals were intellectually oriented, self-confident, and open to new experiences. The characteristics that changed the most included the extent to which the individuals were nurturant or hostile and whether they had good self-control or not.

John Clausen (1993), one of the researchers in the Berkeley Longitudinal Studies, believes that too much attention has been given to discontinuities for all members of the human species, as exemplified in the adult stage theories. Rather, he believes that some people experience recurrent crises and change a great deal over the life course, while others have more stable, continuous lives and change far less.

Helson's Mills College Study Another longitudinal investigation of adult personality development was conducted by Ravenna Helson and her colleagues (Helson, 1997, Helson, Mitchell, & Moane, 1984; Helson & Wink, 1992; Stewart, Osgrove, & Helson, 2001). They initially studied 132 women who were seniors at Mills College in California in the late 1950s and then studied them again when they were in their thirties, forties, and fifties. Helson and her colleagues distinguished three main groups among the Mills women: family-oriented, career-oriented (whether or not they also wanted families), and those who followed neither path (women without children who pursued only low-level work). Despite their different college profiles and their diverging life paths, the women in all three groups experienced some similar psychological changes over their adult years. However, the women in the third group changed less than those committed to career or family. Between the ages of 27 and the early forties, there was a shift toward less traditionally feminine attitudes, including greater dominance, greater interest in events outside the family, and more emotional stability. This may have been due to societal changes from the 1950s to the 1980s rather than to age changes.

During their early forties, many of the women shared the concerns that stage theorists such as Levinson found in men: concern for young and old, introspectiveness, interest in roots, and awareness of limitations and death. However, the researchers in the Mills College Study concluded that rather than being in a midlife crisis, what was being experienced was *midlife consciousness.* They also indicated that commitment to the tasks of early adulthood—whether to a career or family (or both)—helped women learn to control their impulses, develop interpersonal skills, become independent, and work hard to achieve goals. Women who did not commit themselves to one of these lifestyle patterns faced fewer challenges and did not develop as fully as the other women (Rosenfeld & Stark, 1987).

In the Mills study, some women moved toward becoming "pillars of society" in their early forties to early fifties. Menopause, caring for aging parents, and an empty nest were not associated with an increase in responsibility and self-control (Helson & Wink, 1992). The identity certainty and awareness of aging of the Mills college women increased from their thirties through their fifties (Stewart, Osgrove, & Helson, 2001).

Conclusions

What can be concluded about stability and change in personality development during the adult years? Avshalom Caspi and Brent Roberts (2001) recently concluded that the evidence does not support the conclusion that personality traits become completely fixed at a certain age in adulthood (Caspi & Roberts, 2001). However, they argue that change is typically not unlimited and in some cases the changes in personality are small. They also say that age is positively related to stability and that this link peaks in the fifties and sixties. That is, people show greater stability in their personality when they reach midlife than when they were younger adults. These findings support what is called a *cumulative personality model* of personality development, which states that with time and age people become more adept at interacting with their environment in ways that promote the stability of personality.

At age 55, actor Jack Nicholson said "I feel exactly the same as I've always felt: a slightly reined-in voracious beast." Nicholson felt his personality had not changed much. Some others might think they have changed more. *How much does personality change and how does it stay the same through adulthood?*

This does not mean that change is absent throughout midlife. Ample evidence shows that social contexts, new experiences, and sociohistorical changes can affect personality development. However, Caspi and Roberts (2001) concluded, as people get older, stability increasingly outweighs change.

Other researchers argue that stability in personality begins to set in at about 30 years of age (Costa & McCrae, 2000; McCrae, 2001). However, some researchers conclude that personality change can be extensive in the adult years (Lewis, 2001). And some people likely change more than others. In sum, there still is disagreement on how much stability and change characterize personality development in adulthood (Bertrand & Lachman, 2003).

Review and Reflect

2 **Discuss stability and change in development during middle adulthood, including longitudinal studies**

REVIEW

- Identify four longitudinal studies and explain their results.
- What conclusions can be reached about stability and change in development during middle adulthood?

REFLECT

- Why is it important to conduct longitudinal studies when investigating stability and change in development?

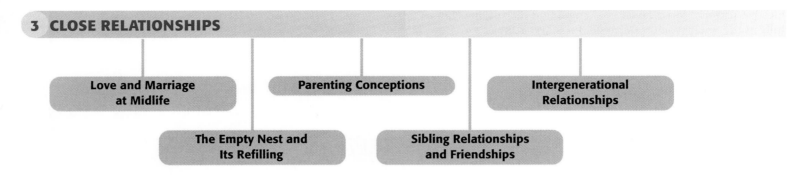

3 CLOSE RELATIONSHIPS

- Love and Marriage at Midlife
- The Empty Nest and Its Refilling
- Parenting Conceptions
- Sibling Relationships and Friendships
- Intergenerational Relationships

Attachment and love are important to our well-being throughout our lives. What are they like in middle age?

Love and Marriage at Midlife

Our exploration of love and marriage at midlife initially focuses on the increase in affectionate love that often takes place at midlife and the nature of marriage and divorce at this point in adulthood.

Affectionate Love   Remember from chapter 15 that two major forms of love are romantic love and affectionate love ◀▥ p. 484. The fires of romantic love are strong in early adulthood. Affectionate, or companionate, love increases during middle adulthood. That is, physical attraction, romance, and passion are more important in new relationships, especially in early adulthood. Security, loyalty, and mutual emotional interest become more important as relationships mature, especially in middle adulthood.

Marriage and Divorce   Even some marriages that were difficult and rocky during early adulthood turn out to be better adjusted during middle adulthood. Although the partners may have lived through a great deal of turmoil, they eventually discover a deep and solid foundation on which to anchor their relationship. In middle adulthood, the partners may have fewer financial worries, less housework and chores, and more time with each other. Partners who engage in mutual activities usually view their marriage as more positive at this time.

Most individuals in midlife who are married voice considerable satisfaction with being married. In one recent large-scale study of individuals in middle adulthood, 72 percent of those who were married said their marriage was either "excellent" or "very good" (Brim, 1999). Possibly by middle age, many of the worst marriages already have dissolved.

Are there any differences in the factors that predict whether couples will divorce in midlife compared to when they were younger adults? In chapter 15, "Socioemotional Development in Early Adulthood," we described John Gottman's extensive research on the factors that make a successful marriage ◀▥ p. 493. In a 14-year longitudinal study, Gottman and Robert Levenson (2000) recently found that couples who divorce in midlife tend to have a profile like the couple played by Annette Bening and Kevin Spacey in the movie *American Beauty:* cool and distant, with suppressed emotions. The midlife divorcing couples were alienated and avoidant. They were the kind of people you see in a restaurant who aren't talking with each other. It is a distant relationship with little or no laughter, love, or interest in each other. One of the divorcing midlife parents often feels like his or her life is "empty." The researchers found that when divorce occurs among younger adults (often in the first 7 years of a marriage) it is characterized by heated emotions that tend to burn out

Annette Bening and Kevin Spacey together in the movie, *American Beauty.* *How is their profile similar to what researchers have found in couples who divorce in midlife?*

the marriage early. The young divorcing couples frequently were volatile and expressive, full of disappointment that they let each other know about.

Divorce in middle adulthood may be more positive in some ways, more negative in others, than divorce in early adulthood. For mature individuals, the perils of divorce can be fewer and less intense than for younger individuals. They have more resources, and they can use this time as an opportunity to simplify their lives by disposing of possessions, such as a large home, which they no longer need. Their children are adults and may be able to cope with their parents' divorce more effectively. The partners may have attained a better understanding of themselves and may be searching for changes that could include the end to a poor marriage.

In contrast, the emotional and time commitment to marriage that has existed for so many years may not be lightly given up. Many midlife individuals perceive this as failing in the best years of their lives. The divorcer might see the situation as an escape from an untenable relationship, but the divorced partner usually sees it as betrayal, the ending of a relationship that had been built up over many years and that involved a great deal of commitment and trust.

The Empty Nest and Its Refilling

An important event in a family is the launching of a child into adult life, to a career or family independent of the family of origin ◀ꟼ p. 489. Parents face new adjustments as disequilibrium is created by a child's absence. In the **empty nest syndrome,** marital satisfaction decreases because parents derive considerable satisfaction from their children and the children's departure leaves parents with empty feelings.

Parents who live vicariously through their children might experience the empty nest syndrome, but most parents do not experience less marital satisfaction after their children have left home. Rather, for most parents marital satisfaction increases during the years after child rearing. With their children gone, marital partners have time to pursue career interests and more time for each other.

In today's uncertain economic climate, the refilling of the empty nest is becoming a common occurrence as adult children return to live at home after an unsuccessful career or a divorce. And some individuals don't leave home at all until their middle to late twenties because they cannot financially support themselves. The middle generation has always provided support for the younger generation, even after the nest is bare. Through loans and monetary gifts for education, and through emotional support, the middle generation has helped the younger generation. Adult children appreciate the financial and emotional support their parents provide them at a time when they often feel considerable stress about their career, work, and lifestyle. And parents feel good that they can provide this support.

However, as with most family living arrangements, there are both pluses and minuses when adult children return to live at home. Many parents have developed expectations that their adult children would be capable of supporting themselves. And adult children had expectations that they would be on their own as young adults. In one study, 42 percent of middle-aged parents said they had serious conflicts with their

Doonesbury   BY GARRY TRUDEAU

empty nest syndrome A decrease in marital satisfaction after children leave home, because parents derive considerable satisfaction from their children.

resident adult children (Clemens & Axelson, 1985). One of the most common complaints voiced by both adult children and their parents is a loss of privacy. The adult children complain that their parents restrict their independence, cramp their sex lives, reduce their rock music listening, and treat them as children rather than adults. Parents often complain that their quiet home has become noisy, that they stay up late worrying when their adult children will come home, that meals are difficult to plan because of conflicting schedules, that their relationship as a married couple has been invaded, and that they have to shoulder too much responsibility for their adult children. In sum, when adult children return home to live, a disequilibrium in family life is created, which requires considerable adaptation on the part of parents and their adult children. This living arrangement usually works best when there is adequate space, when parents treat their adult children more like adults than children, and when there is an atmosphere of trust and communication.

Parenting Conceptions

What is your relationship with your parents like? How do you perceive your parents? Do you think of them as emotional providers? financial supporters? Do you know how they became who they are? Has your perception of your parents changed as you have grown older? Several research studies recently have addressed how our relationships with and perception of our parents can change as we grow from adolescence through the adult years.

In a study of 73 women and men 50 to 60 years of age, many of the middle-aged parents said that as their children became adults they gained a new sense of appreciation for their commitment and influence as parents (Berquist, Greenberg, & Klaum, 1993). Other middle-aged parents expressed a sense of lost opportunity and said they wished they had better relationships with their adult children. When middle-aged parents mention disappointment regarding their adult children's development, they often say that they wish they had spent more time with them. Many men in the United States regret that they did not have a meaningful parenting experience.

In a longitudinal study that spans more than two decades, 30 college-educated women were interviewed about their identity development (Josselson, 1996). For all of the women, now in their forties, their relationship with their mother continues to be a part of their lives. The identity of the middle-aged women was frequently cast against the background of their mothers. In their early thirties, half of the women listed their mother as the person they felt closest to or second closest to among all the people in their lives. In their early forties, their mother often had been surpassed in importance by their spouse and sometimes their children on the list of "people you feel closest to," but their mother still frequently appeared in the second or third position.

In another study, individuals were interviewed at different points in adolescence and adult development, asking them about their perceptions of their parents (Labouvie-Vief & others, 1995). Younger individuals and those over the age of 60 primarily described their parents as providers of emotional and financial support. In contrast, during middle adulthood they were more likely to mention their parents' uniqueness and showed an awareness of the conditions that shaped their parents into the persons they were. These findings suggest that during middle adulthood we restructure our perceptions of our parents.

Sibling Relationships and Friendships

Sibling relationships also persist over the entire life span for most adults (Teti, 2001; White, 2001) ◄▥ p. 281. Eighty-five percent of today's adults have at least one living sibling. Sibling relationships in adulthood may be extremely close, apathetic, or highly rivalrous. The majority of sibling relationships in adulthood have been found to be close (Cicirelli, 1991). Those siblings who are psychologically close to each other in adulthood tended to be that way in childhood. It is rare for sibling closeness to develop for the first time in adulthood (Dunn, 1984).

Friendships continue to be important in middle adulthood just as they were in early adulthood (Antonucci, 1989). It takes time to develop intimate friendships, so friendships that have endured over the adult years are often deeper than those that have just been formed in middle adulthood.

Intergenerational Relationships

Intergenerational Connections

Intergenerational Programs and Projects

William Acquilino's Research

The Sandwich Generation

With each new generation, personality characteristics, attitudes, and values are replicated or changed. As older family members die, their biological, intellectual, emotional, and personal legacies are carried on in the next generation. Their children become the oldest generation and their grandchildren the second generation. As adult children become middle-aged they often develop more positive perceptions of their parents (Field, 1999). In one recent study, conflicts between mothers and daughters decreased across the life course in both the United States and Japan (Akiyama & Antonucci, 1999).

For the most part, family members maintain considerable contact across generations (Allen, Blieszener & Roberto, 2000; Bengtson, 2001). As we continue to stay connected with our parents and our children as we age, both similarity and dissimilarity across generations are found. For example, similarity between parents and an adult child is most noticeable in religion and politics, least in gender roles, lifestyle, and work orientation.

What are the most common conflicts that arise in relationships between parents and adult children? In one study, they included communication and interaction style (such as "He is always yelling" and "She is too critical"), habits and lifestyle choices (such as sexual activity, living arrangements), child-rearing practices and values (such as decisions about having children, being permissive or controlling), politics, religion, and ideology (such as lack of religious involvement) (Clarke & others, 1999). In this study, there were generational differences in perception of the main conflicts between parents and adult children. Parents most often listed habits and lifestyle choices; adult children cited communication and interaction style.

A consistent finding in intergenerational research is that parents and their young adult children differ in the way they describe their relationship. For example, in one study, middle-aged parents were especially likely to report that the relationship was closer (Acquilino, 1999). Another study found that parents continued to give more favorable evaluations of their relationships with adult children across 17 years in a longitudinal study (Giarrusso & Feng, 1999).

The relationship between parents and their adult children is related to the nature of their earlier relationship as these studies indicate:

- In a New Zealand study of the child-rearing antecedents of intergenerational relations, supportive family environments and parenting in childhood (assessed when the children were 3 to 15 years of age) were linked with more positive relationships (in terms of contact, closeness, conflict, and reciprocal assistance) between the children and their middle-aged parents when the children were 26 years (Belsky & others, 2001).
- In another study, individuals who felt trusted by their parents in adolescence reported greater closeness to their parents in early adulthood (Jacobs & Tanner, 1999). Also in this study, daughters who had experienced long-term lack of trust during adolescence were more alienated from their parents as young adults than sons who had similar experiences.
- In yet another study, the motivation of adult children to provide social support to their older parents was linked with

What is the nature of intergenerational relationships?

Intergenerational Relationships in Mexican American Families—The Effects of Immigration and Acculturation

In the last several decades, increasing numbers of Mexicans have immigrated to the United States, and their numbers are expected to increase. The pattern of immigration usually involves separation from the extended family. It may also involve separation of immediate family members, with the husband coming first and then later bringing his wife and children. Initially isolated, especially the wife, they experience considerable stress due to relocation and the absence of family and friends. Within several years, a social network is usually established in the ethnic neighborhood.

As soon as some stability in their lives is achieved, Mexican families may sponsor the immigration of extended family members, such as a maternal or paternal sister or mother who provides child care and enables the mother to go to work. In some cases the older generation remains behind and joins their grown children in old age. The accessibility of Mexico facilitates visits to and from the native village for vacations or at a time of crisis, such as when an adolescent runs away from home.

Three levels of acculturation often exist within a Mexican American family (Falicov & Karrer, 1980). The mother and the grandparents may be at the beginning level, the father at an intermediate level, and the children at an advanced level. The discrepancies between acculturation levels can give rise to conflicting expectations within the family. The immigrant parents' model of child rearing may be out of phase with the dominant culture's model, which may cause reverberations through the family's generations. For example, the mother and grandparents may be especially resistant to the demands for autonomy and dating made by adolescent daughters, and so may the father. And in recent years an increasing number of female youth leave their Mexican American homes to further their education, an event that is often stressful for families with strong ties to Mexican values.

As children leave home, parents begin to face their future as a middle-aged couple. This may be difficult for many Mexican American middle-aged couples because their value orientations have prepared them better for parenting than for relating as a married couple. Family therapists who work with Mexican Americans frequently report that a common pattern is psychological distance between the spouses and a type of emotional separation in midlife. The marital partners continue to live together and carry on their family duties but relate to each other only at a surface level. The younger generation of Mexican Americans may find it difficult to accept their parents' lifestyle, may question their marital arrangement, and may rebel against their value orientations. Despite the intergenerational stress that may be brought about by immigration and acculturation, the majority of Mexican American families maintain considerable contact across generations and continue to have a strong family orientation.

In case you're worried about what's going to become of the younger generation, it's going to grow up and start worrying about the younger generation.

—ROGER ALLEN
American Writer, 20th Century

earlier family experiences (Silverstein & others, 2002). Children who spent more time in shared activities with their parents and were given more financial support by them earlier in their lives provided more support to their parents when they became older.

Gender differences also characterize intergenerational relationships (Bengtson, 2001; Etaugh & Bridges, 2001). In one study, mothers and their daughters had much closer relationships during their adult years than mothers and sons, fathers and daughters, and fathers and sons (Rossi, 1989). Also in this study, married men were more involved with their wives' kin than with their own. And maternal grandmothers and maternal aunts were cited twice as often as their counterparts on the paternal side of the family as the most important or loved relative.

Middle-aged adults play an important role in intergenerational relationships (Williams & Nussbaum, 2001). They have been described as the "sandwich," "squeeze," or "overload" generation because of the responsibilities they have for their adolescent and young adult children on the one hand and their aging parents on the other (Etaugh & Bridges, 2001).

These simultaneous pressures from adolescents or young adult children and aging parents may contribute to stress in middle adulthood. Many middle-aged adults experience considerable stress when their parents become very ill and die. One survey found that when adults enter midlife 41 percent have both parents alive but that 77 percent leave midlife with no parents alive (Bumpass & Acquilino, 1994).

Recent analyses suggest that fewer middle-aged adults are "sandwiched" between multiple roles as caregiver to a parent and to their own children than often is reported in the media (Hoyer & Roodin, 2003). In one study, a large majority of middle-aged children did not have the responsibility of providing direct care for their parents (Rosenthal, Martin-Matthews, & Matthews, 1996). When this type of responsibility

Careers in Life-Span Development

Lillian Troll, Professor of Psychology and Life-Span Development and Researcher on Families and Aging Women

Lillian Troll has been a leading figure in the field of adult development and aging. She graduated from the University of Chicago with a joint major in psychology and premedicine. During World War II she dropped out of graduate school to work in Washington, where she helped develop the array of Army screening and achievement tests. After the war she became a suburban housewife and mother, following her husband's career moves from city to city. For a decade, the closest Troll came to a career in life-span development was founding a nursery school in New Jersey.

Many years later, after her divorce, Troll returned to the University of Chicago and, in 1967, completed a Ph.D. in life-span development. She then began teaching and conducting research on generations in the family and women's develop-

ment, first at Wayne State University in Detroit and then, as a 60-year-old grandmother, at Rutgers University Psychology Department ◀▥ p. 30. In 1986 she retired and moved to California, where she continued research at the University of California at San Francisco, by collaborating with Colleen Johnson on a longitudinal study of the "oldest old" (people over 85).

Lillian Troll (*left*) with participants in a study of aging women.

was required, it most often was assumed by daughters in their mid to late fifties who did not simultaneously have direct child-care or child-rearing responsibilities. In another study, the point at which some adult children have to take responsibility of caring for their parents usually coincided with the launch of their own adult children who were beginning their own careers and families (Soldo, 1996).

When adults immigrate to another country, intergenerational stress may also be increased. To read about the role of immigration and acculturation in intergenerational relationships among Mexican Americans, see the Sociocultural Worlds of Development box.

Lillian Troll has conducted research on intergenerational relations and women's development in midlife. To read about her work, see the Careers in Life-Span Development insert.

Review and Reflect

3 Identify some important aspects of close relationships in middle adulthood

REVIEW

- How can love and marriage at midlife be characterized?
- What is the empty nest? How has it been refilling?
- What are some parenting conceptions related to middle age?
- What are sibling relationships and friendships like in middle adulthood?
- What are relationships across generations like?

REFLECT

- Might there be distinctive phases of middle adulthood? Think about what you have read in this chapter and the previous one and describe what these subphases might be. Would they be linked to age? If so, how?

Reach Your Learning Goals

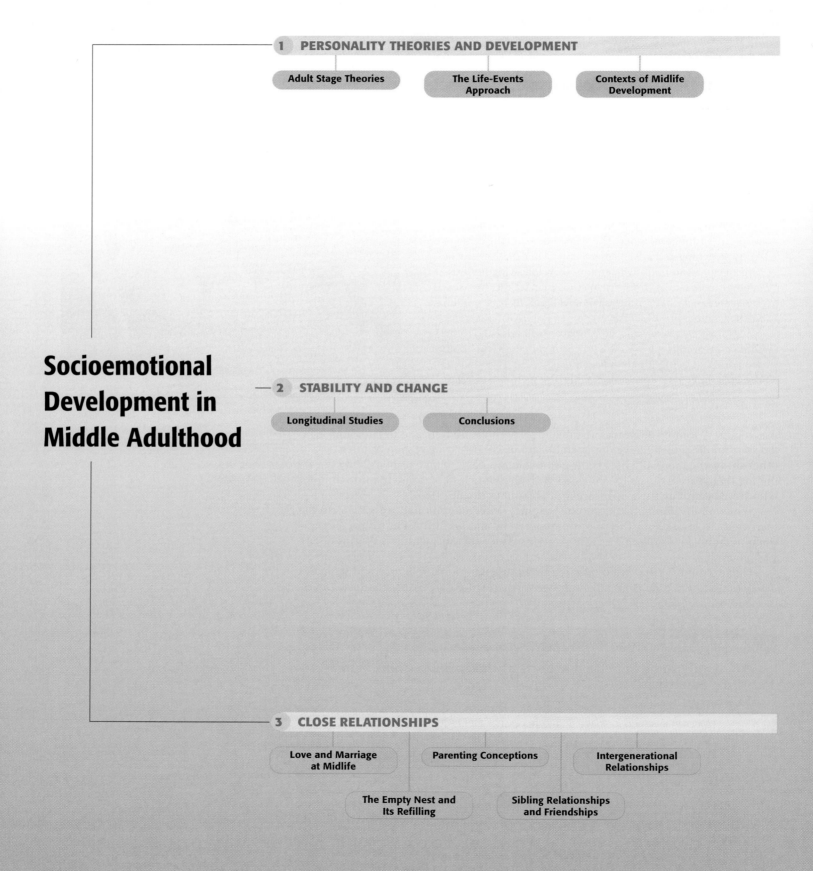

Socioemotional Development in Middle Adulthood

1 PERSONALITY THEORIES AND DEVELOPMENT

- Adult Stage Theories
- The Life-Events Approach
- Contexts of Midlife Development

2 STABILITY AND CHANGE

- Longitudinal Studies
- Conclusions

3 CLOSE RELATIONSHIPS

- Love and Marriage at Midlife
- The Empty Nest and Its Refilling
- Parenting Conceptions
- Sibling Relationships and Friendships
- Intergenerational Relationships

Summary

1 Describe personality theories and development in middle adulthood

- Erikson says that the seventh stage of the human life span, generativity versus stagnation, occurs in middle adulthood. Four types of generativity are biological, parental, work, and cultural. In Levinson's theory, developmental tasks should be mastered at different points in development and changes in middle age focus on four conflicts: being young versus being old, being destructive versus being constructive, being masculine versus being feminine, and being attached to others versus being separated from them. Levinson proposed that a majority of Americans, especially men, experience a midlife crisis. For the most part, though, midlife crises have been exaggerated. There is considerable individual variation in development during the middle adulthood years.

- In the early version of the life-events approach, life events produce taxing circumstances that create stress in people's lives. In the contemporary version of the life-events approach, how life events influence the individual's development depends not only on the life event, but also on mediating factors, adaptation to the event, the life-stage context, and the sociohistorical context.

- Neugarten believes that the social environment of a particular cohort can alter its social clock—the timetable according to which individuals are expected to accomplish life's tasks, such as getting married, having children, and establishing a career. Critics say that the adult stage theories are male biased because they place too much emphasis on achievement and careers. The stage theories do not adequately address women's concerns about relationships. Midlife is a heterogeneous period for women, as it is for men. For some women, midlife is the prime of their lives. In many nonindustrialized societies, a woman's status often improves in middle age. In many cultures, the concept of middle age is not clear. Most cultures distinguish between young adults and old adults.

2 Discuss stability and change in development during middle adulthood, including longitudinal studies

- In Neugarten's Kansas City Study, both stability and change were found. Styles of coping, life satisfaction, and being goal-directed were the most stable. Individuals became more passive and feared the environment more as they aged through middle adulthood. In Costa and McCrae's Baltimore Study, the big five personality factors—emotional stability, extraversion, openness to experience, agreeableness, and conscientiousness—showed considerable stability. In the Berkeley Longitudinal Studies, the extremes in the stability-change argument were not supported. The most stable

characteristics were intellectual orientation, self-confidence, and openness to new experiences. The characteristics that changed the most were nurturance, hostility, and self-control. In Helson's Mills College Study of women, there was a shift toward less traditional feminine characteristics from age 27 to the early forties, but this might have been due to societal changes. In their early forties, women experienced many of the concerns that Levinson described for men. However, rather than a midlife crisis, this is best called midlife consciousness.

- The issue of whether personality is stable or changes in adulthood continues to be debated. Some researchers believe that stability peaks in the fifties and sixties (Caspi & Roberts, 2001), others that it begins to stabilize at about 30 (Costa & McRae, 2000), and yet others argue for more change (Lewis, 2001). Some people change more than others.

3 Identify some important aspects of close relationships in middle adulthood

- Affectionate love increases in midlife, especially in marriages that have endured many years. A majority of middle-aged adults who are married say that their marriage is good or excellent. Researchers recently have found that couples who divorce in midlife are more likely to have a cool, distant, emotionally suppressed relationship, whereas divorcing young adults are more likely to have an emotionally volatile and expressive relationship. Divorce is a special concern.

- Rather than decreasing marital satisfaction as once thought, the empty nest increases it for most parents. An increasing number of young adults are returning home to live with their parents.

- In middle age, many individuals say they wish they had spent more time with their children, fathers wish they had been better parents, and many women maintain a close relationship with their mothers. During middle age, many individuals restructure their perceptions of parents and parenting.

- Sibling relationships continue throughout life. Some are close, others are distant. Friendships continue to be important in middle age.

- Continuing contact across generations in families usually occurs. Mothers and daughters have the closest relationships. The middle-aged generation has been called the "sandwich" or "squeezed" generation because it is caught between obligations to children and obligations to parents. The middle-aged generation plays an important role in linking generations.

Key Terms

Key People

Taking It to the Net

1. What did psychologist Daniel Goleman find about how Erik Erikson and his wife Joan dealt with his seventh developmental stage, generativity versus stagnation, in their own lives?
2. When 50-year-old Ron tells his teenage sons that he's enjoying midlife more than any other time in his life, they laugh and think their dad is joking. How does Ron's perspective match up with current research on men and midlife?

Connect to www.mhhe.com/santrockld9 to research the answers and complete these exercises.

E-Learning Tools

To help you master the material in this chapter, you'll find a number of valuable study tools on the Student CD-ROM that accompanies this book. In addition, visit the Online Learning Center for *Life-Span Development*, ninth edition, where you'll find these valuable resources for chapter 17, "Socioemotional Development in Middle Adulthood."

- Several self-assessments related to this chapter's topics will challenge you to apply concepts to your own life:

    How Generative Am I?
    Life Events and My Chance of Significant Illness in the Coming Year
    How Extraverted Am I?

- Build your decision-making skills by trying your hand at the parenting and education "Scenarios."

Late Adulthood

To be seventy years young is sometimes far more cheerful and hopeful than to be forty years old.
—OLIVER WENDELL HOLMES, SR.
American Physician, 19th Century

The rhythm and meaning of human development eventually wend their way to late adulthood, when each of us stands alone at the heart of the earth and suddenly it is evening. We shed the leaves of youth and are stripped by the winds of time down to the truth. We learn that life is lived forward but understood backward. We trace the connection between the end and the beginning of life and try to figure out what this whole show is about before it is out. Ultimately, we come to know that we are what survives of us. Section 9 contains three chapters: "Physical Development in Late Adulthood" (chapter 18), "Cognitive Development in Late Adulthood" (chapter 19), and "Socioemotional Development in Late Adulthood" (chapter 20).

CHAPTER 18

Each of us stands alone at the heart of the earth, pierced through by a ray of sunshine: And suddenly it is evening.

—SALVATORE QUASIMODO
Italian Poet, 20th Century

Physical Development in Late Adulthood

Chapter Outline

Learning Goals

1 *D*iscuss the biological aspects of longevity

2 *D*escribe how a person's brain and body change in late adulthood

3 *I*dentify health problems in older adults and how they can be treated

Images of Life-Span Development
Learning to Age Successfully

Jonathan Swift said, "No wise man ever wished to be younger." Without a doubt, a 70-year-old body does not work as well as it once did. It is also true that an individual's fear of aging is often greater than need be. As more individuals live to a ripe *and* active old age, our image of aging is changing. While on the average a 75-year-old's joints should be stiffening, people can practice not to be average. For example, a 75-year-old man might *choose* to train for and run a marathon; an 80-year-old woman whose capacity for work is undiminished might *choose* to make and sell children's toys.

Consider 85-year-old Sadie Halperin, who has been working out for 11 months at a rehabilitation center for the aged in Boston. She lifts weights and rides a stationary bike. She says that before she started working out, about everything she did—shopping, cooking, walking—was a major struggle. Sadie says she always felt wobbly and held on to a wall when she walked. Now she walks down the center of the hallways and reports that she feels wonderful. Initially she could lift only 15 pounds with both legs; now she lifts 30 pounds. At first she could bench-press only 20 pounds; now she bench-presses 50 pounds. Sadie's exercise routine has increased her muscle strength and helps her to battle osteoporosis by slowing the calcium loss from her bones, which can lead to deadly fractures (Ubell, 1992).

The story of Sadie Halperin's physical development and well-being raise some truly fascinating questions about life-span development, which we will explore in this chapter. They include: Why do we age, and what, if anything, can we do to slow down the process? How long can we live? What chance do you have of living to be 100? Do older adults have sex? Can certain eating habits and exercise help us live longer?

Eighty-five-year-old Sadie Halperin doubled her strength in exercise after just 11 months. Before developing an exercise routine, she felt wobbly and often had to hold on to a wall when she walked. Now she walks down the middle of hallways and says she feels wonderful.

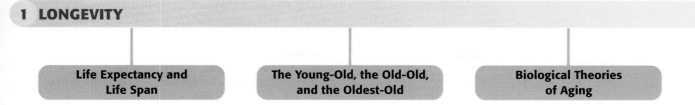

1 LONGEVITY

| Life Expectancy and Life Span | The Young-Old, the Old-Old, and the Oldest-Old | Biological Theories of Aging |

In his eighties, Linus Pauling argued that vitamin C slows the aging process. Aging researcher Roy Walford fasts two days a week because he believes undernutrition (not malnutrition) also slows the aging process. What do we really know about longevity?

Life Expectancy and Life Span

We are no longer a youthful society. Remember from chapter 1 that, as more individuals live to older ages, the proportion of individuals at different ages has become increasingly similar ◀▥ p. 8. Indeed, the concept of a period called "late adulthood" is a recent one—until the twentieth century most individuals died before they were 65.

Although a much greater percentage of persons live to an older age, the life span has remained virtually unchanged since the beginning of recorded history. **Life span** is the upper boundary of life, the maximum number of years an individual can live. The maximum life span of human beings is approximately 120 to 125 years of age. **Life expectancy** is the number of years that will probably be lived by the average person born in a particular year. Improvements in medicine, nutrition, exercise, and lifestyle have increased our life expectancy an average of 30 additional years since 1900.

The life expectancy of individuals born today in the United States is 77 years (80 for women, 74 for men). We will have more to say about the gender difference in life expectancy shortly. There is still a gap (7 years) between the life expectancy of Whites (77 years) and African Americans (70 years) in the United States, but the gap is narrowing. In 1970 the gap was 8 years (U.S. Bureau of the Census, 2000).

How does the United States fare in life expectancy compared to other countries around the world? Considerably better than some, a little worse than some others. For example, Okinawa has the highest life expectancy at birth today (81.2 years) while Afghanistan and Kenya have very low ones (47 years). Differences in life expectancies across countries are due to such factors as diet, health conditions, and medical care throughout the life span.

The figures just given are for life expectancy at birth. When individuals in the United States reach 65, how long can they expect to live? Today, they can expect to live an average of 18 more years (20 for females, 16 for males) (U.S. Bureau of the Census, 2000). To read about the factors that contribute to a long life span in Okinawa, see the Sociocultural Worlds of Development box on p. 572.

Centenarians   In 1980, there were only 15,000 centenarians in the United States. In the year 2000, there were 77,000, and it is projected that this number will increase to more than 1 million by 2050. Because of the increase in centenarians, they are now being studied more often. One view is that "the older you get, the sicker you get." However, researchers are finding that could be a myth. Recent research on 100-year-olds reveals that many of them have been quite healthy in their old age (Perls, 1999).

Clearly, genes play an important role in surviving to an extremely old age. But there are other influencing factors as well.

In the ongoing New England Centenarian Study, researchers so far have examined 169 individuals who are 100+ years of age (Perls, Lauerman, & Silver, 1999). The centenarians are a robust group. Among the characteristics of the 169 who made it to 100, only 3 have had cancer. A disproportionate number of them are women who have never been married.

mhhe●com/
santrockld9

Aging Links
Aging Research Center

life span The upper boundary of life, the maximum number of years an individual can live. The maximum life span of human beings is about 120 to 125 years of age.

life expectancy The number of years that will probably be lived by the average person born in a particular year.

To me old age is always fifteen years older than I am.

—BERNARD BARUCH
American Statesman, 20th Century

mhhe●com/
santrockld9

**New England Centenarian Study
Life Expectancy Calculator**

A misconception is that to live to be 100, an individual has to live a stress-free life. But in the New England study, a majority of the centenarians have had difficult lives, such as surviving the Holocaust and living in extreme poverty as an immigrant to the United States (Perls, Lauerman, & Silver, 1999). What has contributed to their survival is their ability to cope successfully with stress.

In one study, 1,200 centenarians were interviewed about many aspects of their lives (Segerberg, 1982). Through their eyes, life looks like this:

- Mary Butler said that finding something to laugh about every day is important. She believes a good laugh is better than a dose of medicine anytime.
- Elza Wynn concluded that he has been able to live so long because he made up his mind to live. He was thinking about dying when he was 77, but decided he would wait awhile.
- Anna Marie Robertson ("Grandma") Moses commented that she felt older at 16 than at any time since then. Even now that she's very old, she never thinks about being old.
- Billy Red Fox believes that being active and not worrying are important keys to living to be 100. At 95, he switched jobs to become a public relations representative. Even at 100, Billy travels 11 months of the year, making public appearances and talking to civic clubs.
- Duran Baez remarried at 50 and went on to have fifteen more children. At 100 years of age, he was asked, "Do you have any ambition you have not yet realized?" Duran replied, "No." He said that he had lived the kind of life he expected, raising a good family, never doing any harm to anybody, staying honest all his life, and finding out that people really do like him. Duran says, "That's enough for the time being."

What about you? What chance do you have of living to be 100? To find out, turn to figure 18.1. According to the items in figure 18.1, among the most important factors in longevity are heredity and family history, health (weight, diet, smoking, and exercise), education, personality, and lifestyle. To read further about living to a very old age, see the Sociocultural Worlds of Development box on page 572.

The rapid growth in the 85+ and 100+ age categories suggests that some potentially important change might lie ahead, such as these:

- Even if it is still an option, retiring at 65 might be too young for many of tomorrow's older adults.
- Increasing health and longer productivity of the elderly might offset some of the economic burden that planners have long assumed will exist for a graying America.
- Society's dismal view of old age might get a needed push toward a more positive image.

Sex Difference in Longevity Is there a sex difference in how long people live? Today, the life expectancy for females is 80 years of age, while for males it is 74. Beginning at age 25, females outnumber males; this gap widens during the remainder of the adult years. By the time adults are 75 years of age, more than 61 percent of the population is female; for those 85 and over, the figure is almost 70 percent female. Why? Social factors such as health attitudes, habits, lifestyles, and occupation are probably important. For example, men are more likely than women to die from the leading causes of death in the United States, such as cancer of the respiratory system, motor vehicle accidents, suicide, cirrhosis of the liver, emphysema, and coronary heart disease. These causes of death are associated with lifestyle. For example, the sex difference in deaths due to lung cancer and emphysema occurs because men are heavier smokers than women are.

However, if life expectancy is influenced extensively by the stress of work, the sex difference should be narrowing, because so many more women have entered the

This test gives you a rough guide for predicting your longevity. The basic life expectancy for males is age 73, and for females is 80. Write down your basic life expectancy. If you are in your fifties or sixties, you should add ten years to the basic figure because you have already proved yourself to be a durable individual. If you are over age sixty and active, you can even add another two years.

Life Expectancy

Decide how each item applies to you and add or subtract the appropriate number of years from you basic life expectancy.

1. Family history
___ Add five years if two or more of your grandparents lived to 80 or beyond.
___ Subtract four years if any parent, grandparent, sister, or brother died of a heart attack or stroke before 50.
___ Subtract two years if anyone died from these diseases before 60.
___ Subtract three years for each case of diabetes, thyroid disorder, breast cancer, cancer of the digestive system, asthma, or chronic bronchitis among parents or grandparents.

2. Marital status
___ If you are married, add four years.
___ If you are over twenty-five and not married, subtract one year for every unmarried decade.

3. Economic status
___ Add two years if your family income is over $60,000 per year.
___ Subtract three years if you have been poor for the greater part of your life.

4. Physique
___ Subtract one year for every ten pounds you are overweight.
___ For each inch your girth measurement exceeds your chest measurement deduct two years.
___ Add three years if you are over forty and not overweight.

5. Exercise
___ Add three years if you exercise regularly and moderately (jogging three times a week).
___ Add five years if you exercise regularly and vigorously (long-distance running three times a week).
___ Subtract three years if your job is sedentary.
___ Add three years if your job is active.

6. Alcohol
___ Add two years if you are a light drinker (one to three drinks a day).
___ Subtract five to ten years if you are a heavy drinker (more than four drinks per day).
___ Subtract one year if you are a teetotaler.

7. Smoking
___ Subtract eight years if you smoke two or more packs of cigarettes per day.
___ Subtract two years if you smoke one to two packs per day.
___ Subtract two years if you smoke less than one pack.
___ Subtract two years if your regularly smoke a pipe or cigars.

8. Disposition
___ Add two years if you are a reasoned, practical person.
___ Subtract two years if you are aggressive, intense, and competitive.
___ Add one to five years if you are basically happy and content with life.
___ Subtract one to five years if you are often unhappy, worried, and often feel guilty.

9. Education
___ Subtract two years if you have less than a high school education.
___ Add one year if you attended four years of school beyond high school.
___ Add three years if you attended five or more years beyond high school.

10. Environment
___ Add four years if you have lived most of your life in a rural environment.
___ Subtract two years if you have lived most of your life in an urban environment.

11. Sleep
___ Subtract five years if you sleep more than nine hours a day.

12. Temperature
___ Add two years if your home's thermostat is set at no more than 68° F.

13. Health care
___ Add three years if you have regular medical checkups and regular dental care.
___ Subtract two years if you are frequently ill.

___ **Your Life Expectancy Total**

FIGURE 18.1 Can You Live to Be 100?

labor force. Yet in the last 40 years, just the opposite has occurred. Apparently, self-esteem and work satisfaction outweigh the stress of work when the longevity of women is at issue.

The sex difference in longevity is also influenced by biological factors. In virtually all species, females outlive males. Women have more resistance to infections and degenerative diseases. For example, the female's estrogen production helps to protect her from arteriosclerosis (hardening of the arteries). And the additional X chromosome that women carry in comparison to men may be associated with the production of more antibodies to fight off disease.

The Young-Old, the Old-Old, and the Oldest-Old

Late adulthood, which begins in the sixties and extends to approximately 120 years of age, has the longest span of any period of human development—50 to 60 years. The

Living Longer in Okinawa

Individuals live longer on the Japanese island of Okinawa in the East China Sea than anywhere else in the world. In Okinawa, there are 34.7 centenarians for every 100,000 inhabitants, the highest ratio in the world. In comparison, the United States has about 10 centenarians for every 100,000 residents. The life expectancy in Okinawa is 81.2 years (86 for women, 78 for men), also highest in the world.

What is responsible for such longevity in Okinawa? Some possible explanations include (Willcox, Willcox, & Suzuki, 2002):

- *Diet.* Okinawans eat very healthy food, heavy on grains, fish, and vegetables, light on meat, eggs, and dairy products. The risk of dying of cancer is far lower among Okinawans than among Japanese and Americans (see figure 18.2). About 100,000 Okinawans moved to Brazil and quickly adopted the eating regimen of their new home, one heavy on red meat. The result: The life expectancy of the Brazilian Okinawans is now 17 years lower than Okinawa's 81 years!
- *Low-Stress Lifestyle.* The easygoing lifestyle in Okinawa more closely resembles that of a laid-back South Sea island than that of the high-stress world on the Japanese mainland.

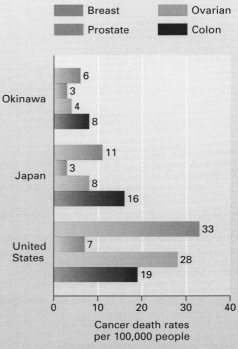

Toskiko Taira, 80, weaves cloth from the fibers of banana trees on a loom in Okinawa. She, like many Okinawans, believes that such sense of purpose helps people to live longer.

- *Caring Community.* Okinawans look out for each other and do not isolate or ignore their older adults. If older adults need help, they don't hesitate to ask a neighbor. Such support and caring is likely responsible for Okinawa having the lowest suicide rate among older women in East Asia, an area noted for its high suicide rate among older women.
- *Activity.* Many older adults in Okinawa are active, engaging in such activities as taking walks and working in their gardens. Many older Okinawans also continue working at their jobs.
- *Spirituality.* Many older adults in Okinawa find a sense of purpose in spiritual matters. Prayer is commonplace and believed to ease the mind of stress and problems.

Legend: Breast, Ovarian, Prostate, Colon

Okinawa: Breast 6, Prostate 3, Ovarian 4, Colon 8
Japan: Breast 11, Prostate 3, Ovarian 8, Colon 16
United States: Breast 33, Prostate 7, Ovarian 28, Colon 19

Cancer death rates per 100,000 people

FIGURE 18.2 Risks of Dying from Cancer in Okinawa, Japan, and the United States

The risk of dying from different forms of cancer is lower in Okinawa than in the United States and Japan (Willcox, Willcox, & Suzuki, 2002). Okinawans eat lots of tofu and soy products, which are rich in flavonoids (believed to lower the risk of breast and prostate cancer). They also consume large amounts of fish, especially tuna, mackerel, and salmon, which reduce the risk of breast cancer.

combination of the lengthy span with the dramatic increase in the number of adults living to older ages has led to increased interest in differentiating the late adulthood period. The most common demarcation is the young-old (65 to 74 years of age), old-old (75 to 84 years of age), and oldest-old (85 and older).

Many experts on aging, however, prefer to talk about such categories as the young-old, old-old, and oldest-old in terms of *function* rather than age. In chapter 1 we

One-hundred-year-old Iva Blake is among the oldest-old in America. Adapting to her changing circumstances, she still tends to her garden from a wheelchair. *What are some characteristics of the oldest-old?*

described age not only in terms of chronological age, but also in terms of biological age, psychological age, and social age ◀||||| p. 22. Thus, in terms of functional age—the person's actual ability to function—an 85-year-old might well be more biologically and psychologically fit than a 65-year-old (Neugarten & Neugarten, 1987). With this concept of functional age and its implication for individual differences in aging in mind, as you will see next, there still are some significant differences when the old age group segment still in their sixties is compared with the 85-and-older age group (Suzman & others, 1992).

The oldest-old are much more likely to be female. They also have a much higher susceptibility to disease and a far greater incidence of disability than do the young-old. Today's oldest-old are much more likely to be living in institutions, less likely to be married, and more likely to have low educational attainment. Their needs, capacities, and resources are often different from those of their young-old counterparts.

When thinking about the differentiation of late adulthood into subperiods, remember that every period or subperiod of development is heterogeneous. Even the oldest-old are a heterogeneous, diversified group (Roberts, Dunkle, & Haug, 1994). Many of the oldest-old function effectively, although others have outlived their social and financial supports and depend on society for their daily living. Almost one-fourth of the oldest-old are institutionalized and many report some limitation of activity or difficulties in performing personal-care activities. A significant number are cognitively impaired.

A substantial portion of the oldest-old function effectively. Society's preoccupation with the disability and mortality of the oldest-old has concealed the fact that the majority of older adults aged 80 and over continue to live in the community. More than one-third of older adults 80 and over who live in the community report that their health is excellent or good; 40 percent say they have no activity limitation (Suzman & others, 1992).

In one study of successful aging, physical performance (based on tests of balance, gait, lower-body strength and coordination, and manual dexterity) in 70- to 78-year-old women and men was related to participation in moderate and/or strenuous exercise activity and emotional support from social networks (Seeman & others, 1994). Shakespeare's image of the oldest-old in *As You Like It*—"mere oblivion, sans teeth, sans taste, sans everything"—clearly is not supported by the increasing research evidence that describes a more optimistic picture of a substantial portion of people in their eighties and older (Garfein & Herzog, 1995).

(a)

(b)

(*a*) Frenchwoman Jeanne Louise Calment, who recently died at the age of 122. Greater ages have been claimed, but scientists say the maximum human life span is about 120. (*b*) Heredity is an important component of how long we will live. For example, in figure 18.1, you were able to add five years to your life expectancy if two or more of your grandparents lived to 80 or beyond. And if you were born a female, you start out with a basic life expectancy that is seven years older than if you were born a male. The three sisters shown here are all in their eighties.

Biological Theories of Aging

A common belief is that aging characterizes changes which occur in the last part of the life span. While aging is most noticeable in middle and late adulthood, life-span developmentalists point out that biological aging actually begins at birth.

What are the biological explanations of aging? Intriguing explanations of why we age are provided by three biological theories: cellular clock theory, free-radical theory, and hormonal stress theory.

Cellular Clock Theory The **cellular clock theory** is Leonard Hayflick's (1977) view that cells can divide a maximum of about 75 to 80 times and that as we age the ability of cells to divide decreases. Hayflick found that cells extracted from older adults, in their fifties to seventies, divided fewer than 75 to 80 times. Based on the ways cells divide, Hayflick places the upper limit of the human life span at about 120 years. Thus, we rarely live to the end of our life-span potential.

In the last decade, scientists have added an extension to cellular clock theory (Warner & Hodes, 2000). Hayflick did not know why cells die. Recently, scientists have found that the answer might lie at the tip of chromosomes (Bodner & others, 1998; Martin & Buckwalter, 2001; Shay & Wright, 2000). *Telomeres* are DNA sequences that cap chromosomes. Each time a cell divides, the telomeres become shorter and shorter (see figure 18.3). After about 70 to 80 replications, the telomeres are dramatically reduced and the cell no longer can reproduce. Researchers also have found that injecting the enzyme *telomerase* into human cells grown in the laboratory can substantially extend the life of the cells beyond the approximately 75 to 80 normal cell divisions (Shay & Wright, 1999). In one study, age-related telomere erosion was linked with an impaired ability to recover from stress and an increased rate of cancer formation (Rudolph & others, 1999).

cellular clock theory Leonard Hayflick's theory that the maximum number of times that human cells can divide is about 75 to 80. As we age, our cells have less capability to divide.

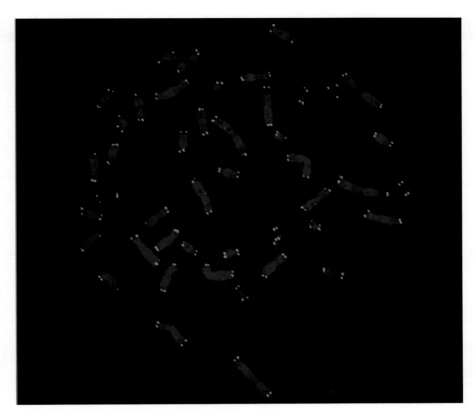

FIGURE 18.3 Telomeres and Aging
The photograph shows actual telomeres lighting up the tips of chromosomes.

Free-Radical Theory   A second microbiological theory of aging is the **free-radical theory,** which states that people age because inside their cells normal metabolism produces unstable oxygen molecules known as free radicals. These molecules ricochet around the cells, damaging DNA and other cellular structures. Like all organisms, cells generate waste when they metabolize energy. The problematic by-products of this process include these free-radical oxygen molecules. As the free radicals bounce around inside of cells, their damage can lead to a range of disorders, including cancer and arthritis (Hauck & Bartke, 2001; Knight, 2000).

Hormonal Stress Theory   The first two biological theories of aging—cellular clock and free-radical—focus on changes at the cellular level. A third biological theory of aging emphasizes changes at the hormonal level. **Hormonal stress theory** states that aging in the body's hormonal system can lower resilience to stress and increase the likelihood of disease (Finch & Seeman, 1999). The hypothalamic-pituitary-adrenal (HPA) axis is one of the body's main regulatory systems for responding to external stress and maintaining the body's internal equilibrium. Note that *hypothalamic* refers to the hypothalamus in the brain, *pituitary* to the body's master gland located near the hypothalamus, and *adrenal* to the two adrenal glands that sit just above the kidneys. Hormonal stress theory emphasizes that with aging, the hormones stimulated by stress that flow through the HPA system remain elevated longer than when individuals were younger. These prolonged, elevated levels of stress-related hormones are associated with increased risks for many diseases, including cardiovascular disease, cancer, diabetes, and hypertension.

Which of these three biological theories best explains aging? That question has not been answered yet. It might turn out that all of these biological processes are involved in aging.

What Causes Aging?

Telomeres Research

Research on Telomeres and Telomerase

Genetic Studies of Aging

free-radical theory A microbiological theory of aging that states that people age because inside their cells normal metabolism produces unstable oxygen molecules known as free radicals. These molecules ricochet around inside cells, damaging DNA and other cellular structures.

hormonal stress theory The theory that aging in the body's hormonal system can lower resilience to stress and increase the likelihood of disease.

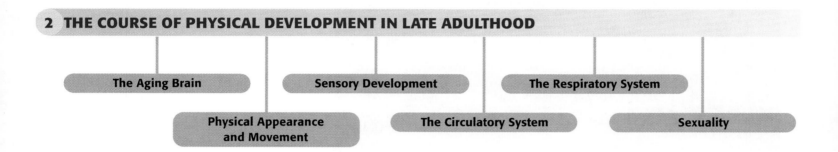

Review and Reflect

> **1** **Discuss the biological aspects of longevity**
>
> **REVIEW**
> * What is the difference between life span and life expectancy?
> * What is the difference between the young-old, old-old, and oldest-old?
> * What are three biological theories of aging?
>
> **REFLECT**
> * How long would you like to live? Why? Describe the oldest person you know? What is he or she like?

2 THE COURSE OF PHYSICAL DEVELOPMENT IN LATE ADULTHOOD

The Aging Brain

Physical Appearance and Movement

Sensory Development

The Circulatory System

The Respiratory System

Sexuality

Although there are inevitable age-associated increases in the risks of physical disability, the actual onset of such problems is not uniform. Acknowledgment of considerable variability in rates of decline in functioning has generated increased attention to factors involved in the successful maintenance of functional abilities with age (Birren, 1996; Whitbourne, 2000). One analysis involved the MacArthur Research Network on Successful Aging Study, a three-site longitudinal study of successful aging in women and men aged 70 to 79 years of age. In this study, physical performance (such as walking efficiency, maintaining balance, and repeatedly standing up and sitting down) did decline with age, but there was considerable individual variation (Seeman & others, 1994). The physical performance of older adults in poor health from low-income backgrounds was inferior to that of their higher-income, healthy counterparts. A majority of the older adults also maintained their physical performance over a three-year period in their seventies, and some even improved their performance in this time frame.

As we discuss the nature of physical development, we will chronicle age-related changes in physical decline, but we will also stress new developments in aging research that underscore how bodily powers decline slowly and that sometimes even lost function can be restored. In one survey, disabilities among older adults had declined almost 15 percent from 1982 to 1994 (Manton, Corder, Stallard, 1997). Exercise, fewer smokers, and improvements in medical care account for much of the decline in disability (Suzman, 1997).

The Aging Brain

What are some general findings about the aging brain? How much plasticity and adaptiveness does the aging brain retain?

General Slowdown in Central Nervous System Functioning   A general slowing of function characterizes the central nervous system, which begins in middle adulthood and increases in late adulthood (Birren, 2002). This slowdown can affect physical coordination and intellectual performance. After age 70, many adults no longer show a knee-jerk reflex and by age 90 most reflexes are virtually gone (Spence,

1989). The slowing of central nervous system functioning can impair the performance of older adults on intelligence tests, especially timed tests (Birren, Woods, & Williams, 1980).

Decreased Brain Lateralization

In chapter 5, "Physical Development in Infancy," we described how brain lateralization develops in childhood ◀▥ p. 153. Recall that lateralization is the specialization of function in one hemisphere of the brain or the other. Using neuroimaging techniques, researchers recently have found that brain activity in the prefrontal cortex is lateralized less in older adults than in younger adults when they are engaging in cognitive tasks (Cabeza, 2002; Dixit & others, 2000; Reuter-Lorenz, 2002). For example, figure 18.4 shows that when younger adults are given the task of recognizing words they have previously seen, they process the information primarily in the right hemisphere while older adults are more likely to use both hemispheres (Madden & others, 1999).

The decrease in lateralization in older adults might play a compensatory role in the aging brain. That is, using both hemispheres may improve the cognitive functioning of older adults. Researchers have found support for this view. For example, in one study, older adults who used both brain hemispheres were faster at completing a working memory task than their counterparts who primarily used only one hemisphere of their brain (Reuter-Lorenz & others, 2000). However, the decrease in lateralization may be a mere by-product of aging and reflect an age-related decline in the brain's ability to specialize functions. In this latter view, during childhood the brain becomes increasingly differentiated in terms of its functions; as adults become older, this process may become reversed. Support for the decrease in differentiation is found in the higher intercorrelations of performance on cognitive tasks in older adults than in younger adults (Baltes & Lindenberger, 1997).

Changes in Neurons

For decades it was believed that no new brain cells (neurons) are generated after the early childhood years. However, researchers recently discovered that adults continue to grow new brain cells throughout their lives (Gould & others, 1999; Nottebohm, 2002). Figure 18.5 shows that exercise and an enriched environment can generate new brain cells in adult mice.

Even in the late adulthood years, the brain has remarkable repair capability, losing only a portion of its ability to function (Anderton, 2002). The adaptive nature of the

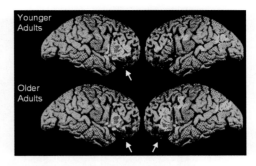

FIGURE 18.4 The Decrease in Brain Lateralization in Older Adults

Younger adults primarily used the right prefrontal region of the brain (top left photo) during a recall memory task, while older adults used both the left and right prefrontal regions (bottom two photos).

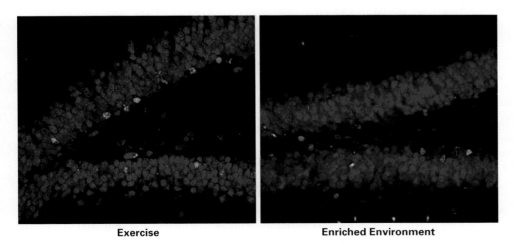

Exercise   Enriched Environment

FIGURE 18.5 Generating New Nerve Cells in Adult Mice

Researchers have found that exercise (running) and an enriched environment (a larger cage and many toys) can cause brain cells to divide and form new brain cells (Kempermann, van Praag, & Gage, 2000). Cells were labeled with a chemical marker that becomes integrated into the DNA of dividing cells (red). Four weeks later, they were also labeled to mark neurons (nerve cells). As shown here, both the running mice and the mice in an enriched environment had many cells that were still dividing (red) and others that had differentiated into new nerve cells (orange).

FIGURE 18.6 The Brains of the Mankato Nuns

Top: Sister Marcella Zachman (*left*) finally stopped teaching at age 97. Now, at 99, she helps ailing nuns exercise their brains by quizzing them on vocabulary or playing a card game called Skip-Bo, at which she deliberately loses. Sister Mary Esther Boor (*right*), also 99 years of age, is a former teacher who stays alert by doing puzzles and volunteering to work the front desk. *Below:* A technician holds the brain of a deceased Mankato nun. The nuns donate their brains for research that explores the effects of stimulation on brain growth.

brain in older adults was demonstrated in one study (Coleman, 1986). From the forties through the seventies, the growth of dendrites (the receiving part of the neuron or nerve cell) increased. But in very old people (in their nineties), dendritic growth no longer was taking place. Thus, dendritic growth might compensate for the possible loss of neurons through the seventies but not in the nineties. Lack of dendritic growth in older adults could be due to a lack of environmental stimulation.

Stanley Rapaport (1994), chief of the neurosciences laboratory at the National Institute on Aging, compared the brains of younger and older people engaged in the same tasks. The older brains literally rewired themselves to compensate for losses. If one neuron was not up to the job, neighboring neurons helped to pick up the slack. Rapaport concluded that as brains age, they can actually shift responsibilities for a given task from one region to another.

The Mankato Nuns An intriguing ongoing investigation of the brain involves nearly 700 nuns in a convent in Mankato, Minnesota (Danner, Snowdon, & Frieden, 2001; Griener, Snowden, & Griener, 1999; Kemper & others, 2001; Snowdon, 1995, 1997) (see figure 18.6). The nuns are the largest group of brain donors in the world. Examination of the nuns' donated brains, as well as others, has led neuroscientists to believe that the brain has a remarkable capacity to change and grow, even in old age. The Sisters of Notre Dame in Mankato lead an intellectually challenging life, and brain researchers recently have found that stimulating the brain with mental exercises can cause neurons to increase their dendritic branching.

Preventing and Treating Brain Diseases The capacity of the brain to change offers new possibilities for preventing and treating brain diseases:

- The onset of Alzheimer's disease symptoms might be delayed for years. The more educated people are, the less likely they are to develop Alzheimer's. This probably occurs because intellectual activity develops surplus brain tissue that compensates for tissue damaged by the disease.
- Older individuals might recover better from strokes. Even when areas of the brain are permanently damaged by stroke, new message routes can be created to get around the blockage or to resume the function of that area.

Physical Appearance and Movement

In chapter 16, "Physical and Cognitive Development in Middle Adulthood," we pointed out some changes in physical appearance that take place ◄▌▌ p. 516. In late adulthood, these changes become more pronounced. The changes are most noticeable in the form of facial wrinkles and age spots.

We also get shorter when we get older. From 30 to 50 years of age, men lose about 1/2 inch in height, then might lose another 3/4 inch from 50 to 70 years of age. The height loss for women could be as much as 2 inches from 25 to 75 years of age (Hoyer & Roodin, 2003). Note that there are large variations in the extent to which individuals become shorter in middle and late adulthood. The decrease in height is due to bone loss in the vertebrae.

Our weight usually drops after we reach 60 years of age. This likely occurs because we lose muscle, which also gives our bodies a more "sagging" look. Figure 18.7 shows the decline in percentage of muscle and bone from age 25 to age 75, and the corresponding increase in the percentage of fat. The good news is that exercise and appropriate weight lifting can help to reduce the decrease in muscle mass and improve the older person's body appearance. We will have more to say about this later in this chapter.

Older adults move slower than young adults and this difference occurs across a wide range of movement difficulty (see figure 18.8). General slowing of movement in older adults has been found in everyday tasks such as reaching and grasping, moving from one place to another, and continuous movement (Ketchman & Stelmach, 2001; Wishart & others, 2000).

Sensory Development

Sensory changes in late adulthood involve vision, hearing, taste, smell, touch, and pain.

Vision   In late adulthood, the decline in vision that began for most of us in early or middle adulthood becomes more pronounced (Kosnick & others, 1989). Night driving is especially difficult, to some extent because tolerance for glare diminishes. Dark adaptation is slower, meaning that older individuals take longer to recover their vision when going from well-lighted rooms to semidarkness. The area of the visual field becomes smaller, suggesting that a stimulus's intensity in the peripheral area of the visual field needs to be increased if the stimulus is to be seen. Events taking place away from the center of the visual field may not be detected.

This visual decline often can be traced to reduction in the quality or intensity of light reaching the retina. In extreme old age, these changes may cause severe difficulty in seeing. Large-print books and magnifiers may be needed in such cases.

In one study, sensory functioning in more than 500 adults 70 to 102 years of age was compared with competence in everyday activities (Marsiske, Klumb, & Baltes, 1997). Sensory acuity, especially in vision, was related to whether and how well elderly adults bathed and groomed themselves, completed household chores, engaged in intellectual activities, and watched TV.

One vision problem associated with aging is *cataracts,* which are cloudy, opaque areas in the lens of the eye that prevent light from passing through. This causes blurred vision. Surgery to remove cataracts is usually very successful and currently is the most common operation on individuals 65 years and older in the United States.

Another vision problem related to aging is *glaucoma,* a disease that involves a hardening of the eyeball because of fluid buildup in the eye. If untreated, glaucoma can destroy vision. It is a problem for 1 percent of individuals in their seventies and 10 percent of individuals in their nineties. Special eyedrops can be used to treat glaucoma.

Yet another vision problem that is linked with aging is *macular degeneration,* a disease involving deterioration of the retina. This affects 1 in 25 individuals from 66 to 74 years of age and 1 in 6 who are older. Macular degeneration is difficult to treat and is a leading cause of blindness in older adults. If the disease is detected early, it can be corrected with a laser.

Hearing   Although hearing impairment can begin in middle adulthood, it usually does not become much of an impediment until late adulthood (Fozard, 2000; Fozard & Gordon-Salant, 2001). Even then, some but not all hearing problems may be corrected by hearing aids. Only 19 percent of individuals from 45 to 54 years of age experience some type of hearing problem, but from 75 to 79 the figure has reached 75 percent (Harris, 1975). It has been estimated that 15 percent of the population over the age of 65 is legally deaf, usually due to the degeneration of the cochlea, the primary neural receptor for hearing in the inner ear (Olsho, Harkins, & Lenhardt, 1985).

Percentage of total weight

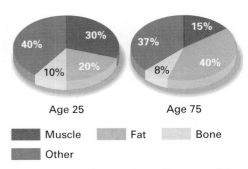

Age 25   Age 75

■ Muscle   ■ Fat   ■ Bone
■ Other

FIGURE 18.7 Changes in Body Composition of Bone, Muscle, and Fat from 25 to 75 Years of Age

Notice the decrease in bone and muscle and the increase in fat from 25 to 75 years of age.

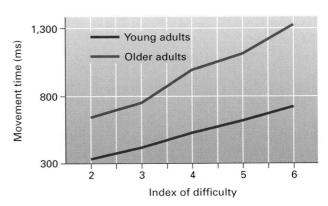

FIGURE 18.8 Movement and Aging

Older adults take longer to move than young adults and this occurs across a range of movement difficulty (Ketcham & Stelmach, 2001).

Perceptual System	Young-Old (65 to 74 years)	Old-Old (75 years and older)
Vision	There is a loss of acuity even with corrective lenses. Less transmission of light occurs through the retina (half as much as in young adults). Greater susceptibility to glare occurs. Color discrimination ability decreases.	There is a significant loss of visual acuity and color discrimination, and a decrease in the size of the perceived visual field. In late old age, people are at significant risk for visual dysfunction from cataracts and glaucoma.
Hearing	There is a significant loss of hearing at high frequencies and some loss at middle frequencies. These losses can be helped by a hearing aid. There is greater susceptibility to masking of what is heard by noise.	There is a significant loss at high and middle frequencies. A hearing aid is more likely to be needed than in young-old age.

FIGURE 18.9 Vision and Hearing Decline in the Young-Old and the Old-Old

Wearing two hearing aids that are balanced to correct each ear separately can sometimes help hearing-impaired adults.

Earlier we indicated that life-span developmentalists are increasingly making distinctions between the young-old (ages 65 to 74) and the old-old (75 to 84 years). This distinction is important in considering the degree of decline in various perceptual systems. As indicated in figure 18.9, the decline in the perceptual systems of vision and hearing is much greater in the old-old than in the young-old (Charness & Bosman, 1992).

Smell and Taste Most older adults lose some of their sense of smell or taste, or both (Schiffman, 1996). These decrements can reduce their enjoyment of food and their life satisfaction. One negative outcome for a decline in the sense of smell is less ability to detect smoke from a fire. Smell and taste losses often begin around 60 years of age. Compounds that stimulate the olfactory nerve have been added to foods to increase intake by elderly individuals. Also, there is less decline in smell and taste in healthy older adults than in their less healthy counterparts.

Many older adults often prefer highly seasoned foods (sweeter, spicier, saltier) to compensate for their diminished taste and smell (Hoyer & Roodin, 2003). This can lead to eating more low-nutrient, highly seasoned "junk food."

Touch Changes in touch are associated with aging (Gescheider, 1997). One study found that, with aging, individuals could detect touch less in the lower extremities (ankles, knees, and so on) than in the upper extremities (wrists, shoulders, and so on) (Corso, 1977). For most older adults, a decline in touch sensitivity is not problematic (Hoyer & Roodin, 2003).

Pain Older adults are less sensitive to pain and suffer from it less than younger adults (Harkins, Price, & Martinelli, 1986). Although decreased sensitivity to pain can help older adults cope with disease and injury, it can be harmful if it masks injury and illness that need to be treated.

The Circulatory System

Not long ago it was believed that cardiac output—the amount of blood the heart pumps—declines with age even in healthy adults. However, we now know that when heart disease is absent, the amount of blood pumped is the same regardless of an adult's age.

In the past, a 60-year-old with a blood pressure reading of 160/90 would have been told, "For your age, that is normal." Now medication, exercise, and/or a healthier diet might be prescribed to lower blood pressure. Most experts on aging recommend that consistent blood pressures at 160/90 and above should be treated to reduce the risk of heart attack, stroke, or kidney disease (Lakatta, 1992). A rise in blood pressure with age can be linked with illness, obesity, anxiety, stiffening of blood vessels, or lack of exercise. The longer any of these factors persist, the worse the individual's blood pressure gets (Rowe & Kahn, 1998).

The Respiratory System

Lung capacity drops 40 percent between the ages of 20 and 80, even without disease (Fozard, 1992). Lungs lose elasticity, the chest shrinks, and the diaphragm weakens. The good news, though, is that older adults can improve lung functioning with diaphragm-strengthening exercises. Severe impairments in lung functioning and death can result from smoking.

Sexuality

Aging does induce some changes in human sexual performance, more so in the male than in the female. Orgasm becomes less frequent in males, occurring in every second to third act of intercourse rather than every time. More direct stimulation usually is needed to produce an erection. From 65 to 80 years of age, approximately one out of four men have serious problems getting and/or keeping erections, and at over 80 years of age the percentage rises to one out of two men (Butler & Lewis, 2002).

In the absence of two circumstances—actual disease and the belief that old people are or should be asexual—sexuality can be lifelong. Even when actual intercourse is impaired by infirmity, other relationship needs persist, among them closeness, sensuality, and being valued as a man or a woman (Johnson, 1996).

Such a view, of course, is contrary to folklore, to the beliefs of many individuals in society, and even to many physicians and health-care personnel. Fortunately, many older adults have gone on having sex without talking about it, unabashed by the accepted and destructive social image of the dirty old man and the asexual, undesirable older woman.

In one study of older adults in their sixties, many were still having sex (Wiley & Bortz, 1996). The women rated kissing as one of the most satisfying sexual activities, while the men rated oral sex as the most satisfying. In another study of more than 1,200 older adults (mean age = 77), almost 30 percent had participated in sexual activity in the past month (Matthias & others, 1997). Two-thirds of the older adults were satisfied with their current level of sexual activity.

Various therapies for older adults who report sexual difficulties have been effective (Carbone & Seftel, 2002). In one study, sex education—which consisted largely of simply giving sexual information—led to increased sexual interest, knowledge, and activity in the elderly (White & Catania, 1981).

Review and Reflect

2 Describe how a person's brain and body change in late adulthood

REVIEW

- How much plasticity and adaptability does the aging brain have?
- What changes in physical appearance and movement characterize late adulthood?
- How do vision, hearing, smell and taste, touch, and sensitivity to pain change in older adults?
- How does the circulatory system change in older adults?
- How does the respiratory system change in older adults?
- What is the nature of sexuality in late adulthood?

REFLECT

- If you could interview the Mankato nuns, what questions would you want to ask them?

3 HEALTH

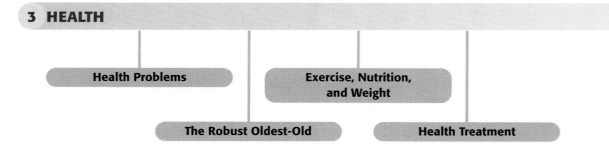

Health Problems

The Robust Oldest-Old

Exercise, Nutrition, and Weight

Health Treatment

How healthy are older adults? What types of health problems do they have? As we discuss the health of older adults, you will see that there are more healthy older adults than we used to envision.

Health Problems

As we age, the probability increases that we will have some disease or illness. For example, though many are still quite healthy overall, the majority of adults still alive at 80 years of age or older are likely to have some type of impairment.

In chapter 16, "Physical and Cognitive Development in Middle Adulthood," we defined *chronic disorders* as disorders with a slow onset and a long duration ◀▥ p. 519. Chronic diseases are rare in early adulthood, increase in middle adulthood, and become more common in late adulthood. As shown in figure 18.10, arthritis is the most common chronic disorder in late adulthood, followed by hypertension. Older women have a higher incidence of arthritis and hypertension, and are more likely to have visual problems, but are less likely to have hearing problems than older men are.

Although adults over the age of 65 often have a physical impairment, many of them can still carry on their everyday activities or work. Chronic conditions associated with the greatest limitation on work are heart conditions (52 percent), diabetes (34 percent), asthma (27 percent), and arthritis (27 percent).

Lifestyle, social, and psychological factors are linked with health in older adults (Siegler, Bosworth, & Poon, 2003). In the McArthur Studies of Successful Aging, engaging in physical activity had a protective effect on health in virtually every group of older adults assessed (Seeman & Chen, 2002). Also, emotional support was linked with better functioning in individuals with cardiovascular disease and self-efficacy was a protective factor for individuals with a history of cancer. Conflict in relationships was linked with greater decline in older adults with diabetes or hypertension. Low income is also strongly related to health problems in late adulthood. Approximately three times as many poor as nonpoor older adults report that their activities are limited by chronic disorders.

Causes of Death in Older Adults Nearly three-fourths of all older adults die of heart disease, cancer, or cerebrovascular disease (stroke). Chronic lung diseases, pneumonia and influenza, and diabetes round out the six leading causes of death among older adults. If cancer, the second leading cause of death in older adults, were completely eliminated, the average life expectancy would rise by only 1 to 2 years. However, if all cardiovascular and kidney diseases were eradicated, the average life expectancy of older adults would increase by approximately 10 years. This increase in longevity is already under way as the number of strokes among older adults has declined considerably in the last several decades. The decline in strokes is due to improved treatment of high blood pressure, a decrease in smoking, better diet, and an increase in exercise.

Ethnicity is linked with the death rates of older adults (Centers for Disease Control and Prevention, 2002). Among ethnic groups in the United States, African Americans have high death rates for stroke, heart disease, lung cancer, and female breast

> *How many of us older persons have really been prepared for the second half of life, for old age, and eternity?*
>
> —CARL JUNG
> *Swiss Psychoanalyst, 20th Century*

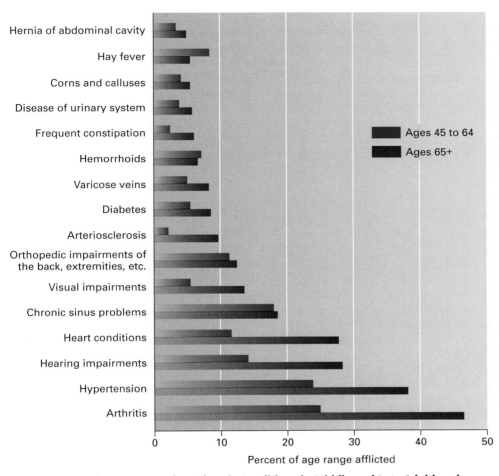

FIGURE 18.10 **The Most Prevalent Chronic Conditions in Middle and Late Adulthood**

cancer. Asian Americans and Latinos have low death rates for these diseases. In the last decade, death rates for most diseases in African Americans, Latinos, and Asian Americans have decreased. However, death rates for most diseases still remain high for African Americans (Centers for Disease Control and Prevention, 2002).

Arthritis   **Arthritis** is an inflammation of the joints accompanied by pain, stiffness, and movement problems. Arthritis is especially common in older adults. This disorder can affect hips, knees, ankles, fingers, and vertebrae. Individuals with arthritis often experience pain and stiffness, as well as problems in moving about and performing routine daily activities. There is no known cure for arthritis. However, the symptoms of arthritis can be reduced by drugs, such as aspirin, range-of-motion exercises for the afflicted joints, weight reduction, and, in extreme cases, replacement of the crippled joint with a prosthesis (Burke & others, 2003).

Osteoporosis   Normal aging involves some loss of bone tissue from the skeleton. However, in some instances loss of bone tissue can become severe. **Osteoporosis** is a chronic condition that involves an extensive loss of bone tissue. Osteoporosis is the main reason many older adults walk with a stoop. Women are especially vulnerable to osteoporosis, the leading cause of broken bones in women. Approximately 80 percent of the osteoporosis cases in the United States occur in females, 20 percent in males. Osteoporosis is more common in White, thin, and small-framed women. This aging disorder is related to deficiencies in calcium, vitamin D, estrogen depletion, and lack of exercise. To prevent osteoporosis, young and middle-aged women should eat foods

Arthritis
Osteoporosis

arthritis Inflammation of the joints that is accompanied by pain, stiffness, and movement problems; especially common in older adults.

osteoporosis A chronic condition that involves an extensive loss of bone tissue and is the main reason many older adults walk with a marked stoop. Women are especially vulnerable to osteoporosis.

rich in calcium, get more exercise, and avoid smoking. Calcium-rich foods include dairy products (low-fat milk and low-fat yogurt, for example) and certain vegetables (such as broccoli, turnip greens, and kale). Estrogen replacement therapy may also be recommended for middle-aged women at especially high risk for developing osteoporosis, except those with a family history of breast cancer. Alternate drugs such as Fosimax can be used to reduce the risk of osteoporosis. Older women should also get bone density checks.

A program of regular exercise might have the potential to prevent osteoporosis. In one study, women aged 50 to 70 lifted weights twice a week (Nelson & others, 1994). Their risk of osteoporosis and resulting broken bones was sharply reduced, while their balance and muscular strength improved.

Accidents Accidents are the seventh leading cause of death among older adults. Injuries resulting from a fall at home or during a traffic accident in which an older adult is a driver or an older pedestrian is hit by a vehicle are common. Each year, approximately 200,000 adults over the age of 65 (most of them women) fracture a hip in a fall. Half of these older adults die within 12 months, frequently from pneumonia. Because healing and recuperation are slower in older adults, an accident that is only a temporary setback for a younger person may result in long-term hospital or home care for an older adult. In one study, an exercise program reduced the risk of falls in elderly adults (Province & others, 1995). In another study, Tai Chi, a form of balance training, improved the coordination of older adults in challenging conditions (Wong & others, 2001).

The Robust Oldest-Old

Our image of the oldest-old (eighties and older) is predominantly of being disabled and frail. The implications of the projected rapid growth of the oldest-old population have often been pessimistic—an expensive burden of chronic disability in which the oldest-old often require the everyday help of other persons. However, as we discussed earlier in this chapter, the oldest-old are a heterogeneous group, and until recently this diversity has not been adequately recognized. Although almost one-fourth of the oldest-old are institutionalized, the majority live in the community and remain independent (Suzman & others, 1992).

Because so much attention has been given to chronic disabilities of the oldest-old, those who have aged successfully have gone virtually unnoticed and unstudied. An increased interest in successful aging is producing a more optimistic portrayal of the oldest-old than in the past (Perls, Lauerman, & Silver, 1999; Rowe & Kahn, 1998). Health service researchers are discovering that a relatively large portion of people in old age are low-cost users of medical services; a small percentage account for a large fraction of expenditures, and this usually occurs in the last year of life, a period that is expensive at any age. A surprisingly large portion of the oldest-old not only do not require personal assistance on a daily basis but also are physically robust, and some who are not initially robust recover their robustness. In a longitudinal study of a national sample of adults 80 years and older, 33 percent were classified as robust based on the following criteria: no difficulty in walking 1/4 mile, stooping, crouching, kneeling, lifting 10 pounds, or walking up 10 steps without resting (Suzman & others, 1992). About three-fourths of the robust older adults had no hospitalizations and had fewer than six doctor visits in the previous 12 months.

In this and other studies of very old adults, a sizable portion of individuals are free of disability, able to cope with their disabilities free of assistance, or able to recover their functioning over time (Freund & Riediger, 2003; Harris & others, 1989). Cataract surgery and a variety of rehabilitation strategies can improve the functioning of the oldest-old. Later in this chapter we will discuss how exercise programs can improve strength and mobility in older persons. For example, in one study, eight weeks of leg-strength training markedly improved the walking ability of nursing home residents who averaged 90 years of age (Fiatarone & others, 1990). One promising approach for preventing or intervening in osteoporosis is calcium supplementation.

In sum, earlier portraits of the oldest-old have been stereotypical. A substantial subgroup of the oldest-old are robust and active. And there is cause for optimism in the development of new regimens of prevention and intervention.

Exercise, Nutrition, and Weight

An important aspect of preventing health problems in older adults and improving their health is to encourage individuals to exercise more and to develop better nutritional habits.

Exercise   Although we may be in the evening of our lives in late adulthood, we are not meant to live out our remaining years passively. Everything we know about older adults suggests they are healthier and happier the more active they are. The possibility that regular exercise can lead to a healthier late adulthood and increase longevity has been raised. Let's examine several research studies on exercise and aging.

In one study, the cardiovascular fitness of 101 older men and women (average age = 67 years) was examined (Blumenthal & others, 1989). The older adults were randomly assigned to an aerobic exercise group, a yoga and flexibility control group, and a waiting list control group. The program lasted four months. Prior to and following the four-month program, the older adults underwent comprehensive physiological examinations. In the aerobic group, the older adults participated in three supervised exercise sessions per week for 16 weeks. Each session consisted of a 10-minute warm-up, 30 minutes of continuous exercise on a stationary bicycle, 15 minutes of brisk walking/jogging, and a 5-minute cool-down. In the yoga and flexibility control group, the older adults participated in 60 minutes of supervised yoga exercises at least twice a week for 16 weeks. Over the four-month period, the cardiovascular fitness—such as peak oxygen consumption, cholesterol level, and blood pressure—of the aerobic exercise group significantly improved. In contrast, the cardiovascular fitness of the yoga and waiting list groups did not improve.

In another study, exercise literally meant a difference in life or death for middle-aged and older adults (Blair, 1990). More than 10,000 men and women were divided into categories of low fitness, medium fitness, and high fitness (Blair & others, 1989). Then they were studied over a period of eight years. As shown in figure 18.11, sedentary participants (low fitness) were more than twice as likely to die during the eight-year time span of the study than those who were moderately fit and more than three times as likely to die as those who were highly fit. The positive effects of being physically fit occurred for both men and women in this study.

In yet another study, changes in level of physical activity and cigarette smoking were associated with risk of death during the middle and late adulthood years (Paffenbarger & others, 1993). Beginning moderately vigorous sports activity from the forties through the eighties was associated with a 23 percent lower risk of death, quitting cigarette smoking with a 41 percent lower death risk.

Gerontologists increasingly recommend strength training in addition to aerobic activity and stretching for older adults (Pennix & others, 2002; Rubenstein & others, 2000). The average person's lean body mass declines with age—about 6.6 pounds of lean muscle are lost each decade during the adult years. The rate of loss accelerates after age 45. Also, the average percentage ratio of muscle to fat for a 60- to 70-year-old woman is 44 percent fat. In a 20-year-old woman the ratio is 23 to 24 percent. Weight lifting can preserve and possibly increase muscle mass in older adults (Slade & others, 2002). In one study, it also reduced depression in the elderly (Singh, Clements, & Fiatarone, 1997).

Exercise is an excellent way to maintain health. Researchers continue to document its positive effects in older adults (Burke & others, 2001; Evans, 2000). Exercise helps people to live independent lives with dignity in late adulthood.

All we know about older adults indicates that they are healthier and happier the more active they are. Several decades ago, it was believed that older adults should be more passive and inactive to be well adjusted and satisfied with life. In today's world, we believe that while older adults may be in the evening of their life span, they are not meant to live out their remaining years passively.

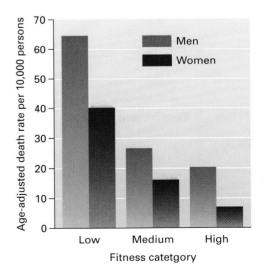

FIGURE 18.11 Physical Fitness and Mortality

In this study of middle-aged and older adults, being moderately fit or highly fit meant that individuals were less likely to die over a period of eight years than their low-fitness (sedentary) counterparts (Blair & others, 1989).

FIGURE 18.12 The Jogging Hog Experiment

Jogging hogs reveal the dramatic effects of exercise on health. In one investigation, a group of hogs was trained to run approximately 100 miles per week (Bloor & White, 1983). Then, the researchers narrowed the arteries that supplied blood to the hogs' hearts. The hearts of the jogging hogs developed extensive alternate pathways for blood supply, and 42 percent of the threatened heart tissue was salvaged compared to only 17 percent in a control group of nonjogging hogs.

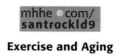

Exercise and Aging

At 80, 90, and even 100 years of age, exercise can help prevent elderly adults from falling down or even being institutionalized. Being physically fit means being able to do the things you want to do, whether you are young or old. More about researchers' investigations into exercise's positive benefits for health is shown in figure 18.12.

A recent review of research on exercise and aging reached these conclusions (Singh, 2002):

- *Exercise can minimize the physiological changes associated with aging and contribute to health and well-being.* Changes that can be modified by exercise include motor coordination, cardiovascular function, metabolism (cholesterol, for example), and attention span.
- *Exercise can optimize body composition as aging occurs.* Exercise can increase muscle mass and bone mass, as well as decrease bone fragility (Slade & others, 2002).
- *Exercise is related to prevention of common chronic diseases.* Exercise can reduce the risk of cardiovascular disease, type 2 diabetes, osteoporosis, stroke, and breast cancer (Miller & others, 2000).
- *Exercise is associated with improvement in the treatment of many diseases.* When exercise is used as part of the treatment, individuals with these diseases show improvement in symptoms: arthritis, pulmonary disease, congestive heart failure, coronary artery disease, hypertension, type 2 diabetes, and obesity (Jadelis & others, 2001; Wallace, Mills, & Browning, 1997).
- *Exercise is related to the prevention of disability and can be used effectively in the treatment of disability.* One study of more than 5,000 individuals found that physical activity was associated with slower progression of functional limitations and disability (Miller & others, 2000). Specifically, older adults who walked a mile at least once per week were less likely than their sedentary counterparts to progress to functional limitations over the six years of the study.
- *Exercise can be used as an adjunct to counteract the side effects of standard medical care and thus potentially improve overall disease and quality-of-life outcomes.* For example, depression is sometimes an unintended side effect of drugs used to treat hypertension and exercise may reduce the depression (Singh, 2002).
- *Exercise is linked to increased longevity.* Energy expenditure during exercise of at least 1,000 kcal/week reduces mortality by about 30 percent, while 2000 kcal/week reduces mortality by about 50 percent (Lee & Skerrett, 2001).

Nutrition and Weight Seventeenth-century English philosopher and essayist Francis Bacon was the first author to recommend scientific evaluation of diet and longevity. He advocated a frugal diet. Does a restricted intake of food increase longevity or could it possibly even extend the human life span?

Scientists have accumulated considerable evidence that food restriction in laboratory animals (in most cases rats) can increase the animals' life span (Goto & others, 2002; Hadley & others, 2001; Kirk, 2001; Mattson & others, 2002). Animals fed diets restricted in calories, although adequate in protein, vitamins, and minerals, live as much as 40 percent longer than animals given unlimited access to food. And chronic problems such as kidney disease appear at a later age. Diet restriction also delays biochemical alterations such as the age-related rise in cholesterol observed in both humans and animals.

Whether similar very low-calorie diets (in some instances the animals eat 40 percent less than normal) can stretch the human life span is not known (Roth & others, 2002). Most nutritional experts do not recommend very low-calorie diets for older adults; rather, they recommend a well-balanced, low-fat diet that includes the nutritional factors needed to maintain good health.

No one knows for certain how calorie restriction works to increase the life span of animals. Some scientists believe it might lower the level of free radicals or potentially toxic particles created by the breakdown of food. Others believe calorie restriction might trigger a state of emergency called "survival mode" in which the body eliminates all unnecessary functions to focus only on staying alive. Encouraged by the research on animals, the National Institutes of Health is planning calorie restriction studies on humans (Johannes, 2002). Calorie restriction of 30 percent in humans would translate into about 1,120 calories a day for the average woman and 1,540 for the average man.

Leaner men do live longer, healthier lives. In one study of 19,297 Harvard alumni, those weighing the least were less likely to die over the past three decades (Lee & others, 1993). The men were divided into five categories according to body mass index (a complex formula that takes into account weight and height). As body mass increased, so did risk of death. The most overweight men had a 67 percent higher risk of dying than the thinnest men. For example, the heaviest men (such as 181 pounds or more for a 5-foot-10-inch man) also had 2½ times the risk of death from cardiovascular disease. Currently, these researchers are studying the relation of body mass index to longevity in women and predict similar results to the study with men.

The Growing Controversy over Vitamins and Aging   For years, most experts on aging and health argued that a balanced diet was all that was needed for successful aging; vitamin supplements were not recommended. However, an increasing number of research studies raise questions about the practice of not recommending vitamin supplements for middle-aged and older adults. The new research suggests the possibility that some vitamin supplements—mainly a group called "antioxidants," which includes vitamin C, vitamin E, and beta-carotene—help to slow the aging process and improve the health of older adults.

The theory is that antioxidants counteract the cell damage caused by free radicals, which are produced both by the body's own metabolism and by environmental factors such as smoking, pollution, and bad chemicals in the diet. When free radicals cause damage (oxidation) in one cell, a chain reaction of damage follows. Antioxidants act much like a fire extinguisher, helping to neutralize free-radical activity. For example, people who took vitamin E supplements for two years significantly reduced their risk of heart disease—by up to 40 percent (Rimm & others, 1993). However, cancer and heart disease benefits of vitamin E and beta-carotene were not confirmed in a large-scale study of male smokers 50 years old and older in Finland (Alpha-Tocopherol, Beta-Carotene Cancer Prevention Study Group, 1994). Vitamin E users did have a significant reduction in prostate cancer in this study. One study found that centenarians had exceptionally high levels of vitamins A and E compared to healthy younger adults (Mecocci & others, 2000).

There is no evidence that antioxidants can increase the human life span, but some aging and health experts believe they can reduce a person's risk of becoming frail and sick in the later adult years. However, there are still a lot of blanks and uncertainties in what we know (Stern, 1993). That is, we don't know which vitamins should be taken, how large a dose should be taken, what the restraints are, and so on. Critics also argue that the key experimental studies documenting the effectiveness of the vitamins in slowing the aging process have not been conducted. The studies in this area thus far have been so-called population studies that are correlational rather than experimental in nature. Other factors—such as exercise, better health practices, and good nutritional habits—might be responsible for the positive findings about vitamins and aging rather than vitamins per se. Also, the free-radical theory is a theory and not a fact, and is only one of a number of theories about why we age.

With these uncertainties in mind, some aging experts still recommend vitamin supplements in the following range (Blumberg, 1993): 250 to 1,000 milligrams of vitamin C, 100 to 400 IU of vitamin E, and 15 to 30 milligrams of beta-carotene.

Possible links between vitamins and cognitive performance in older adults also have been the focus of increased research attention. A recent review of cross-sectional

Roy Walford's Views

Caloric Restriction and Aging Research

and longitudinal research studies concluded that taking B vitamins, especially folate, B_6, and B_{12}, is positively related to cognitive performance in older adults (Calvaresi & Bryan, 2001). This review also presented some evidence that supplementation with B vitamins can improve cognitive performance in older adults

Now that we have considered older adults' health problems and the roles of exercise and nutrition, let's turn our attention to the health treatment available to older adults.

Health Treatment

What is the quality of nursing homes and other extended-care facilities for older adults? What is the nature of the relationship between older adults and health-care providers?

Care Options   Only about 5 percent of adults 65 years of age and over reside in a nursing home at any point in time in our society. However, as older adults age, their probability of being in a nursing home or other extended-care facility increases. Twenty-three percent of adults 85 years of age and older live in nursing homes or other extended-care facilities.

Because of the inadequate quality of many nursing homes and the escalating costs of nursing home care, many gerontologists and geriatric specialists (*geriatrics* is the branch of medicine dealing with the health problems of the aged) believe alternatives to nursing homes need to be considered (Beith, 2002; Castle, 2001). These alternatives include home health care, day-care centers, and preventive medicine clinics (Fisk & Rogers, 2002). The alternatives are potentially less expensive than hospitals and nursing homes. They also are less likely to engender feelings of depersonalization and dependency that occur so often among residents of institutions (Greene & others, 1995).

Giving Options for Control and Teaching Coping Skills   An important factor related to health, and even survival, in a nursing home is the patient's feelings of control and self-determination. In a classic study, a group of older nursing home residents were encouraged to make more day-to-day choices and thus feel they had more responsibility for and control over their lives (Rodin & Langer, 1977). They began to decide such matters as what they ate, when their visitors could come, what movies they saw, and who could come to their rooms. A similar group in the same nursing home was told by the administrator how caring the nursing home was and how much the staff wanted to help, but these older nursing home residents were given no opportunities to take more control over their lives. Eighteen months later, the residents given responsibility and control were more alert and active, and said they were happier, than the residents who were only encouraged to feel that the staff would try to satisfy their needs. And the "responsible" or "self-control" group had significantly better improvement in their health than did the "dependent" group. Even more important was the finding that after 18 months only half as many nursing home residents in the "responsibility" group had died as in the "dependent" group (see figure 18.13). Perceived control over one's environment, then, may literally be a matter of life or death.

Ellen Langer (1989) argues that it is extremely important for aging individuals to understand that they can *choose* the way they think. She believes that most people do things out of habit. When people no longer know why they are doing something, these habits assume a mindless quality. Although there is nothing wrong with doing something out of habit, to change a habit people need to become mindful of why they are engaging in the habit. In her research, Langer (1989) has shown that one reason people act old (as by not making decisions or not carrying heavy things) is not that their bodies force them to act this way but rather that they have stored mental images of how old people act and then base their actions on these mental images. She demon-

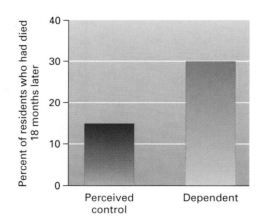

FIGURE 18.13 Perceived Control and Mortality

In the study by Rodin and Langer (1977), nursing home residents who were encouraged to feel more in control of their lives were more likely to be alive 18 months later than those who were treated to feel more dependent on the nursing home staff.

strated that when people were induced to think of themselves as younger, they showed many outward changes, such as a better posture and quicker gait. More basic changes also occurred, such as having a more positive outlook, better memory, and improved eyesight.

In another study, Richard Schulz (1976) gave nursing home residents different amounts of control over visits they received from local college students. Having control over the visits, or at least advance information about them, made the nursing home residents more active, happier, and healthier. This probably occurred because control makes life less stressful by making it more predictable. When the experiment ended, so did the visits by the college students. In a follow-up two years later, the nursing home residents who had been given control over scheduling of visits—and then had the visits, and the control, taken away—were doing worse psychologically than the others (Schulz & Hanusa, 1978). In sum, loss of control may even be worse than lack of control in some cases.

Ellen Langer (*left*) and Judith Rodin conducted a classic study of perceived control in nursing homes. *Was their study a correlational or an experimental study? How did they set up the study? What were the results?*

How can a psychological factor, such as the feeling of control, have such dramatic effects on health? Judith Rodin (1990) says that individuals who believe they have a high degree of control are more likely to feel that their actions can make a difference in their lives. Thus, they are more likely to take better care of themselves by eating healthier foods and exercising. In contrast, those who have reduced feelings of control are likely to feel that what they do will not make a difference. So they do not even bother to try to make a difference. Rodin also believes that the perception of control can have a direct effect on the body. For example, being in control reduces stress and its stress-related hormones. When stress-related hormones remain elevated, there is more wear and tear on the body. High blood pressure, heart disease, arthritis, and certain types of ulcers have all been linked with excessive stress.

Following up on this line of thinking, Rodin (1983) measured stress-related hormones in several groups of nursing home residents. Then, she taught the residents coping skills to help them deal better with day-to-day problems. They were taught how to say no when they did not want something, without worrying whether they would offend someone. They were given assertiveness training, and learned time management skills. After the training, the nursing home residents had greatly reduced levels of cortisol (a hormone closely related to stress that has been implicated in a number of diseases). The cortisol levels of the "assertive training" residents remained lower, even after 18 months. Further, these nursing home residents were healthier and had a reduced need for medication, compared to residents who had not been taught the coping skills. In sum, Rodin's research shows that simply giving nursing home residents options for control and teaching them coping skills can change their behavior and improve their health.

Trends in Health and Aging

Health and Aging: Cross-Cultural Comparisons

The Older Adult and Health-Care Providers   The attitudes of both the health-care provider and the older adult are important aspects of the older adult's health care (Greene & Adelman, 2001). Unfortunately, health-care providers too often share society's stereotypes and negative attitudes toward the elderly (Nussbaum, Pecchioni, & Crowell, 2001). In a health-care setting, these attitudes can take the form of avoidance, dislike, and begrudged tolerance rather than positive, hopeful treatment. Health-care personnel are more likely to be interested in treating younger persons who more often have acute problems with a higher prognosis for successful recovery. They often are less motivated to treat older persons, who are more likely to have chronic problems with a lower prognosis for successful recovery.

Careers in Life-Span Development

Deborah Radomski, Geriatric Nurse

Geriatric nurses seek to prevent or intervene in the chronic or acute health problems of older adults ◀|||| p. 35. They take courses in schools of nursing and obtain one or more degrees in nursing. Geriatric nurses take courses in biological sciences, nursing care, and mental health. They also experience supervised training in geriatric settings. They might work in hospitals, nursing homes, schools of nursing, or with geriatric medical specialists or psychiatrists in a medical clinic or in private practice.

Deborah Radomski is a geriatric nurse who works in a different context. She is a telemedic for Geriatric Associates of America, a Texas organization that provides health care to nursing homes. In a typical eight-hour day, she handles about 120 calls from nurses working with older adult patients.

Radomski obtained her undergraduate nursing degree from Lamar University and her master's degree in nursing from the University of Texas. She worked in various nursing positions at different hospitals before assuming her current telemedic job. Nursing homes especially use her services to inquire about such matters as dietary recommendations, exercise activities, illnesses, drugs, and medical emergencies. However, Radomski says there is only so much she can do over the phone. For example, if an older adult is in acute respiratory distress, she tells the caller to immediately take the person to the hospital.

Deborah Radomski (*right*) with one of her patients. Most of her work, though, now involves telemedicine.

Not only are physicians less responsive to older patients, but older patients often take a less active role in medical encounters with health-care personnel than do younger patients (Woodward & Wallston, 1987). Older adults should be encouraged to take a more active role in their own health care (Hummert & Nussbaum, 2001).

Geriatric nurses specialize in treating the health-care problems of older adults. To read about the work of one geriatric nurse, see the Careers in Life-Span Development insert.

How can health-care providers improve their attitudes toward older adults?

Review and Reflect

3 **Identify health problems in older adults and how they can be treated**

REVIEW

- What are some common health problems in older adults? What are the main causes of death in older adults?
- How can the robust oldest-old be described?
- How do exercise, nutrition, and weight influence development in late adulthood?
- What are some options and issues in the health treatment of older adults?

REFLECT

- What changes in your lifestyle now might help you age more successfully when you become an older adult?

Reach Your Learning Goals

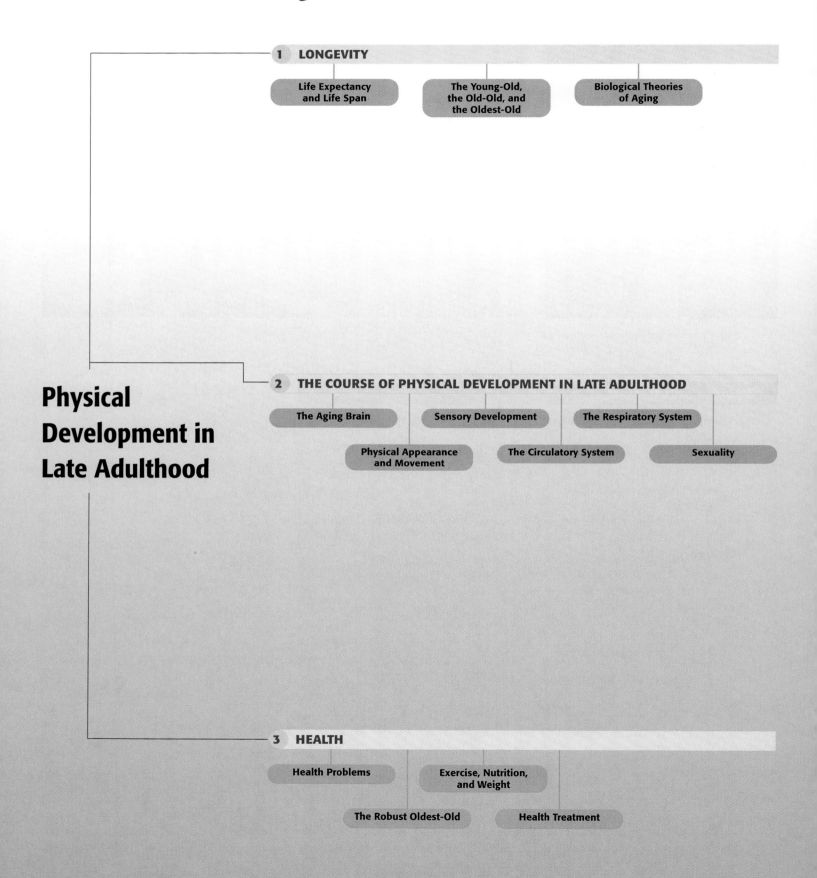

Physical Development in Late Adulthood

1   LONGEVITY

- Life Expectancy and Life Span
- The Young-Old, the Old-Old, and the Oldest-Old
- Biological Theories of Aging

2   THE COURSE OF PHYSICAL DEVELOPMENT IN LATE ADULTHOOD

- The Aging Brain
- Sensory Development
- The Respiratory System
- Physical Appearance and Movement
- The Circulatory System
- Sexuality

3   HEALTH

- Health Problems
- Exercise, Nutrition, and Weight
- The Robust Oldest-Old
- Health Treatment

Summary

1 Discuss the biological aspects of longevity

- Life expectancy refers to the number of years that will probably be lived by an average person born in a particular year. Life span is the maximum number of years an individual can live. Life expectancy has dramatically increased, life span has not. An increasing number of people are living to be 100 years or older. Many of these people are healthy for most of their older years and seem to cope with stress effectively. U.S. females live about six years longer on average than males do. The sex difference is likely due to biological and social factors.

- The young-old are 65 to 74 years of age, the old-old are 75 to 84 years of age, and the oldest-old are 85 years and older. The needs, capacities, and resources of the oldest-old are often different from their young-old counterparts. Significant numbers of the oldest-old function effectively and are in good health. A number of experts believe that when the terms *young-old, old-old,* and *oldest-old* are used, they should refer to functional age, not chronological age. Some 85-year-olds function far better than some 65-year-olds.

- Hayflick proposed the cellular clock theory, which states that cells can divide a maximum of about 75 to 80 times and that as we age, our cells become less capable of dividing. In the last decade, scientists have found that telomeres likely are involved in explaining why cells lose their capacity to divide. According to the free-radical theory, people age because unstable oxygen molecules called free radicals are produced in cells. According to the hormonal stress theory, aging in the body's hormonal system can lower resilience to stress and increase the likelihood of disease.

2 Describe how a person's brain and body change in late adulthood

- There is a general slowing of function in the central nervous system that begins in middle adulthood and increases in late adulthood. The brain becomes less lateralized in older adults. Researchers have recently found that older adults can generate new neurons. We lose some neurons as we age, but how many is debated. The aging brain retains considerable plasticity and adaptiveness. Growth of dendrites can take place in older adults. The brain has the capacity to virtually rewire itself to compensate for loss in older adults.

- The most obvious signs of aging are wrinkled skin and age spots on the skin. People get shorter as they age, and their weight often decreases after age 60 because of loss of muscle. The movement of older adults slows across a wide range of movement tasks.

- The visual system declines, but the vast majority of older adults can have their vision corrected so they can continue to work and function in the world. Hearing decline can begin in middle age but usually does not become much of an impediment until late adulthood. Hearing aids can diminish hearing problems for many older adults. Smell and taste can decline, although the decline is minimal in healthy older adults. Changes in touch sensitivity are associated with aging, although this does not present a problem for most older adults. Sensitivity to pain decreases in late adulthood.

- When heart disease is absent, the amount of blood pumped is the same regardless of an adult's age. High blood pressure no longer is just accepted but rather is treated with medication, exercise, and/or a healthy diet. Blood pressure can rise in older adults due to a number of factors, which can be modified.

- Lung capacity does drop, but older adults can improve lung functioning with diaphragm-strengthening exercises.

- Aging in late adulthood does include some changes in sexual performance, more for males than females. Nonetheless, there are no known age limits to sexual activity.

3 Identify health problems in older adults and how they can be treated

- As we age, our probability of disease or illness increases. Chronic disorders are rare in early adulthood, increase in middle adulthood, and become more common in late adulthood. The most common chronic disorder in late adulthood is arthritis. Nearly three-fourths of older adults die of heart disease, cancer, or stroke. Osteoporosis is the main reason many older adults walk with a stoop; women are especially vulnerable. Accidents are usually more debilitating to older than to younger adults.

- Early portraits of the oldest-old were too negative; there is cause for optimism in the development of new regimens and interventions.

- The physical benefits of exercise have clearly been demonstrated in older adults. Aerobic exercise and weight lifting are both recommended if the adults are physically capable of them. Food restriction in animals can increase the animals' life span, but whether this works with humans is not known. In humans, being overweight is associated with an increased mortality rate. Most nutritional experts recommend a well-balanced, low-fat diet for older adults, but do not recommend an extremely low-calorie diet. The vitamin and aging controversy focuses on whether vitamin supplements—especially the antioxidants vitamin C, vitamin E, and beta-carotene—can slow the aging process and improve older adults' health. Recent research has found a link between taking B vitamins and positive cognitive performance in older adults.

- Although only 5 percent of adults over 65 reside in nursing homes, 23 percent of adults 85 and over do. The quality of nursing homes varies enormously. Alternatives to nursing homes are being proposed. Simply giving nursing home residents options for control and teaching coping skills can change their behavior and improve their health. The attitudes of both the health-care provider and the older adult patient are important aspects of the older adult's health care. Too often health-care personnel share society's negative view of older adults.

Key Terms

Key People

Taking It to the Net

1. Do you think you will live to be 100? Investigate your chances of being a centenarian by reading the results from an ongoing Harvard University Medical School study.
2. Seventy-year-old Jack knows that regular exercise is important to maintain a healthy heart. But will exercise alone guarantee Jack a long and healthy life?
3. Patty's 85-year-old mother, who lives with her and her family, has begun eating less and less. She tells Patty, "Eating is no fun anymore. I can't taste anything." What can Patty do to make meals more appealing for her mother?

Connect to www.mhhe.com/santrockld9 to research the answers and complete these exercises.

E-Learning Tools

To help you master the material in this chapter, you'll find a number of valuable study tools on the Student CD-ROM that accompanies this book. In addition, visit the Online Learning Center for *Life-Span Development*, ninth edition, where you'll find these valuable resources for chapter 18, "Physical Development in Late Adulthood."

- Use the self-assessment, *My Beliefs About Aging*, to evaluate your perspectives on aging.
- Build your decision-making skills by trying your hand at the parenting and education "Scenarios."

CHAPTER

The night hath not yet come: We are not quite cut off from labor by the failing of light; some work remains for us to do and dare.

—HENRY WADSWORTH LONGFELLOW
American Poet, 19th Century

Cognitive Development in Late Adulthood

Chapter Outline

Chapter Outline		Learning Goals

COGNITIVE FUNCTIONING IN OLDER ADULTS   **1**

Multidimensionality and Multidirectionality

Education, Work, and Health

Use It or Lose It

Training Cognitive Skills

1 *D*escribe the cognitive functioning of older adults

WORK AND RETIREMENT   **2**

Work

Retirement in the United States and Other Countries

Adjustment to Retirement

2 *D*iscuss aging and adaptations to work and retirement

MENTAL HEALTH   **3**

Depression

Dementia, Alzheimer's Disease, and Other Afflictions

Fear of Victimization, Crime, and Elder Maltreatment

Meeting the Mental Health Needs of Older Adults

3 *C*haracterize mental health problems and their treatment in older adults

RELIGION   **4**

4 *E*xplain the role of religion in the lives of older adults

Images of Life-Span Development
Sister Mary

Sister Mary was born in 1892 in Philadelphia. She died in 1993 at 101 years of age. Mary was a remarkable woman who had high cognitive test scores even after she reached 100 years of age (Snowden, 1997). What is more remarkable is that she maintained this high level of cognitive competence despite having extensive neurofibrillary tangles and senile plaques, which are classic neurological characteristics of Alzheimer's disease.

Sister Mary taught full-time until she was 77 years old. Then for several years more she worked part-time as a math teacher and teacher's aide. She finally retired at 84, although she once commented that she never really retired: "I only retire at night."

Only 4 feet, 6 inches tall, and weighing only about 85 pounds, Sister Mary spent the last years of her life in the convent she had entered when she was a young girl. In her so-called retirement, she continued to give talks about various life and religious issues and to be active in the community. She was also an avid reader, often seen poring over newspapers and books with her magnifying glass.

Sister Mary was known for her great attitude. She had a wide smile and a warm, hearty laugh. When she asked her doctor if he was secretly giving her medicine to keep her alive and healthy, he replied that it was her wonderful attitude that was doing the trick.

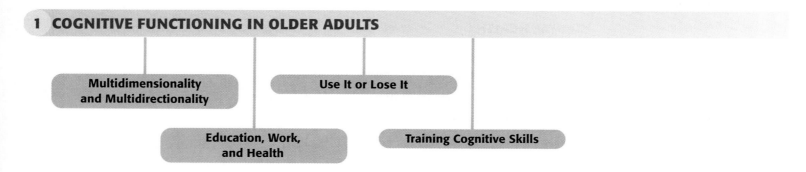

At the age of 70, John Rock invented the birth control pill. At age 76, Anna Mary Robertson Moses, better known as Grandma Moses, took up painting and became internationally famous, staging fifteen one-woman shows throughout Europe. At age 89, Arthur Rubinstein gave one of his best performances at New York's Carnegie Hall. When Pablo Casals was 95, a reporter asked him, "Mr. Casals, you are the greatest cellist who ever lived. Why do you still practice six hours a day?" Mr. Casals replied, "Because I feel like I am making progress" (Canfield & Hansen, 1995).

Multidimensionality and Multidirectionality

In thinking about the nature of cognitive change in adulthood, it is important to consider that cognition is a multidimensional concept (Dixon & Cohen, 2003). It is also important to consider that while some dimensions of cognition might decline as we age, others might remain stable or even improve.

Cognitive Mechanics and Cognitive Pragmatics Paul Baltes (1993, 2000) clarified the distinction between those aspects of the aging mind that show decline and

(*left*) Grandma Moses, known in her time as the "grand old lady of American art," took up painting at the age of 78 and continued to paint past her hundredth birthday. (*right*) Dr. Benjamin Spock, who become famous for his child-rearing advice, released his last book, *A Better World for Our Children*, in 1994 at the age of 89.

those that remain stable or even improve. He makes a distinction between "cognitive mechanics" and "cognitive pragmatics."

- **Cognitive mechanics** are the "hardware" of the mind and reflect the neurophysiological architecture of the brain developed through evolution. Cognitive mechanics consist of the speed and accuracy of the processes involved in sensory input, attention, visual and motor memory, discrimination, comparison, and categorization. Because of the strong influence of biology, heredity, and health on cognitive mechanics, their decline with aging is likely.
- **Cognitive pragmatics** are the culture-based "software programs" of the mind. Cognitive pragmatics include reading and writing skills, language comprehension, educational qualifications, professional skills, and also the type of knowledge about the self and life skills that help us to master or cope with life. Because of the strong influence of culture on cognitive pragmatics, their improvement into old age is possible. Thus, while cognitive mechanics may decline in old age, cognitive pragmatics may actually improve (see figure 19.1 on page 600).

Now that we have examined the distinction between cognitive mechanics and cognitive pragmatics, let's explore some of the more specific cognitive processes that reflect these two general domains. We begin with these aspects of cognitive mechanics: sensory/motor and speed of processing.

Sensory/Motor and Speed-of-Processing Dimensions

In the Berlin Study of Aging, the key factors that accounted for age differences in intelligence were visual and auditory acuity (Lindenberger & Baltes, 1994). Thus, sensory functioning was a strong late-life predictor of individual differences in intelligence. It is also now well accepted that the speed of processing information declines in late adulthood (Earles & Salthouse, 1995; Salthouse, 1996, 2000; Salthouse & Miles, 2002) (see figure 19.2 on page 600).

Although speed of processing information slows down in late adulthood, there is considerable individual variation in this ability. And it is not clear that this slowdown affects our lives in substantial ways. For example, in one experiment, the reaction

cognitive mechanics The "hardware" of the mind, reflecting the neurophysiological architecture of the brain as developed through evolution. Cognitive mechanics involve the speed and accuracy of the processes involving sensory input, visual and motor memory, discrimination, comparison, and categorization.

cognitive pragmatics The culture-based "software" of the mind. Cognitive pragmatics include reading and writing skills, language comprehension, educational qualifications, professional skills, and also the type of knowledge about the self and life skills that help us to master or cope with life.

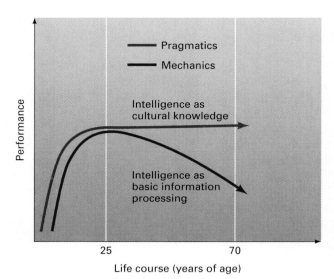

FIGURE 19.1 Theorized Age Changes in Cognitive Mechanics and Cognitive Pragmatics

Baltes argues that cognitive mechanics decline during aging, whereas cognitive pragmatics do not. Cognitive mechanics have a biological/genetic foundation; cognitive pragmatics have an experimental/cultural foundation.

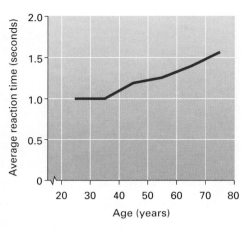

FIGURE 19.2 The Relation of Age to Reaction Time

In one study, the average reaction time began to slow in the forties and this decline accelerated in the sixties and seventies (Salthouse, 1994). The task used to assess reaction time required individuals to match numbers with symbols on a computer screen.

time and typing skills of typists of varying ages were studied (Salthouse, 1994). The older typists usually had slower reactions, but they actually typed just as fast as the younger typists. Possibly the older typists were faster when they were younger and had slowed down, but the results in another experimental condition suggested that something else was involved. When the number of characters that the typists could look ahead at was limited, the older typists slowed considerably; the younger typists were affected much less by this restriction. Thus, the older typists had learned to look farther ahead, allowing them to type as fast as their younger counterparts.

Attention   Three aspects of attention that have been investigated in older adults are selective attention, divided attention, and sustained attention:

- **Selective attention** is focusing on a specific aspect of experience that is relevant while ignoring others that are irrelevant. An example of selective attention is the ability to focus on one voice among many in a crowded room or a noisy restaurant. Another is making a decision about which stimuli to attend to when making a left turn at an intersection. Generally, older adults are less adept at selective attention than younger adults are (Rogers & Fisk, 2001). However, on simple tasks involving a search for a feature (such as determining whether a target item is present on a computer screen) and when individuals are given sufficient practice, age differences are minimal (Humphrey & Kramer, 1997).
- **Divided attention** involves concentrating on more than one activity at the same time. When the two competing tasks are reasonably easy, age differences among adults are minimal or nonexistent. However, the more difficult the competing tasks are, older adults divide attention less effectively than younger adults (Stein-Morrow & Soederberg Miller, 1999). In one study, the ability to engage in a conversation while simultaneously driving a simulator through highway traffic (in an experimental laboratory) was examined in 17 to 25-year-olds, 26 to 49-year-olds, and 50 to 80-year-olds (McKnight & McKnight, 1993). A nondistraction control condition also was included. Overall, the participants performed more poorly in the divided attention condition than in the nondistraction control condition. Also, the older adults (50 to 80 years old) performed worse in the

selective attention Focusing on a specific aspect of experience that is relevant while ignoring others that are irrelevant.

divided attention Concentrating on more than one activity at the same time.

divided attention condition than the younger two groups but not in the control condition. Thus, placing more demands on the attention of the older adults led them to perform more poorly on the driving task.

- **Sustained attention** is the state of readiness to detect and respond to small changes occurring at random times in the environment. Sometimes sustained attention is referred to as *vigilance*. Researchers have found that older adults perform as well as middle-aged and younger adults on measures of sustained attention (Berardi, Parasuraman, & Haxby, 2001).

Memory Let's examine a research study that addresses how we remember as we age. Non-Latino adults of various ages in the United States were studied to determine how much Spanish they remembered from classes they had taken in high school or college (Bahrick, 1984). The individuals chosen for the study had used Spanish very little since they initially learned it in high school or college. Not surprisingly, the young adults who had taken Spanish within the last 3 years remembered Spanish best. After that, the deterioration in memory was gradual (see figure 19.3). For example, older adults who had studied Spanish 50 years earlier remembered about 80 percent of what young adults did who had studied it in the last 3 years! The most important factor in the adults' memory of Spanish was not how long ago they studied it but how well they initially learned it—those who got an A in Spanish 50 years earlier remembered more Spanish than adults who got a C when taking Spanish only 1 year earlier.

Memory does change during aging, but not all memory changes with age in the same way (Balota, Dolan, & Duchek, 2000). The main dimensions of memory and aging that have been studied include episodic memory, semantic memory, cognitive resources (such as working memory and perceptual speed), memory beliefs, and noncognitive factors such as health, education, and socioeconomic factors (Smith, 1996).

Episodic Memory **Episodic memory** is the retention of information about the where and when of life's happenings (Tulving, 2000). For example, what was it like when your younger sister or brother was born, what happened to you on your first date, what were you doing when you heard that the Persian Gulf War had begun, and what did you eat for breakfast this morning?

Younger adults have better episodic memory than older adults (Piolino & others, 2002; Wingfield & Kahana, 2002). Older adults think that they can remember older events better than more recent events, typically reporting that they can remember what happened to them years ago but can't remember what they did yesterday. However, researchers consistently have found that, contrary to such self-reports, in older adults the older the memory, the less accurate it is. This has been documented in studies of memory for high school classmates, foreign language learned in school over the life span, names of grade school teachers, and autobiographical facts kept in diaries (Smith, 1996).

Semantic Memory **Semantic memory** is a person's knowledge about the world. It includes a person's fields of expertise (such as knowledge of chess, for a skilled chess player; general academic knowledge of the sort learned in school, such as knowledge of geometry; and "everyday knowledge" about the meanings of words, famous individuals, important places, and common things, such as who Nelson Mandela and Mahatma Gandhi are. Semantic memory appears to be independent of a an individual's personal identity with the past. For example, you can access a fact—such as "Lima is the capital of Peru"—and not have the foggiest idea of when and where you learned it.

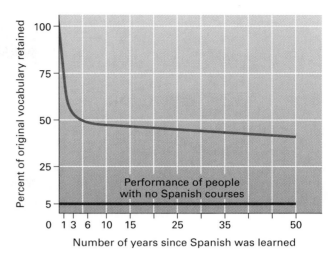

FIGURE 19.3 Memory for Spanish as a Function of Age Since Spanish Was Learned

An initial steep drop over about a three-year period in remembering the vocabulary learned in Spanish classes occurred. However, there was little dropoff in memory for Spanish vocabulary from 3 years after taking Spanish classes to 50 years after taking them. Even 50 years after taking Spanish classes, individuals still remembered almost 50 percent of the vocabulary.

sustained attention The state of readiness to detect and respond to small changes occurring at random times in the environment.

episodic memory The retention of information about the where and when of life's happenings.

semantic memory A person's knowledge about the world—including a person's fields of expertise, general academic knowledge of the sort learned in school, and "everyday knowledge."

Does semantic memory decline during aging? Older adults do often take longer to retrieve semantic information, but usually they can ultimately retrieve it. For the most part, episodic memory declines more in older adults than semantic memory (Parkin & Walter, 1992).

mhhe●com/
santrockld9

Cognitive Psychology Laboratory

Timothy Salthouse's Research

Fredda Blanchard-Field's Research

Cognitive Resources: Working Memory and Perceptual Speed   One view of memory suggests that a limited number of cognitive resources can be devoted to any cognitive task. Two important cognitive resource mechanisms are working memory and perceptual speed. Recall from chapter 16 that *working memory* is closely linked to short-term memory but places more emphasis on memory as a place for mental work ◀▥ p. 527. Working memory is like a mental "workbench" that allows individuals to manipulate and assemble information when making decisions, solving problems, and comprehending written and spoken language (Baddeley, 2000). Researchers have found declines in working memory during the late adulthood years (Leonards, Ibanez, & Giannakopoulos, 2002; Light, 2000; Oberauer & others, 2001; Park & others, 2002; Salthouse, 1994, 2000).

Perceptual speed is another cognitive resource that has been studied by researchers on aging. Perceptual speed is the ability to perform simple perceptual-motor tasks such as deciding whether pairs of two-digit or two-letter strings are the same or different or determining the time required to step on the brakes when the car directly ahead stops. Perceptual speed shows considerable decline in late adulthood, and it is strongly linked with decline in working memory (Salthouse, 2000).

Explicit and Implicit Memory   Researchers also have found that aging is linked with changes in explicit memory (O'Hanlon, Willcox, & Kemper, 2001). **Explicit memory** is memory of facts and experiences that individuals consciously know and can state. Explicit memory also is sometimes called *declarative memory.* Examples of explicit memory include being at a grocery store and remembering what you wanted to buy or recounting the events of a movie you have seen. **Implicit memory** is memory without conscious recollection; it involves skills and routine procedures that are automatically performed. Implicit memory is sometimes called *procedural memory.* Examples of implicit memory include unconsciously remembering how to drive a car, swing a golf club, or type on a computer keyboard.

Implicit memory is less likely to be adversely affected by aging than explicit memory (Schugens & others, 1997; Tulving, 2000). Thus, older adults are more likely to forget what items they wanted to buy at a grocery store (unless they wrote them down on a list and brought it with them) than they are to forget how to drive a car. Their perceptual speed might be slower in driving the car, but they remember how to do it.

Prospective Memory   **Prospective memory** involves remembering to do something in the future, such as remembering to take your medicine or remembering to do an errand. While some researchers have found a decline in prospective memory with age, a number of studies show that whether there is a decline is complex and depends on such factors as the nature of the task and what is being assessed (Cherry & LeCompte, 1999; Einstein & others, 2000; Kliegel, McDaniel, & Einstein, 2000; Vogels & others, 2002; West & Craik, 2001). For example, age-related deficits occur more often in time-based (such as remembering to call someone next Friday) than in event-based (remembering to tell your friend to read a particular book the next time you see her) prospective memory tasks.

Memory Beliefs   An increasing number of studies are finding that people's beliefs about memory play an important role in their actual memory (Cavanaugh, 2000). That is, what people tell themselves about their ability to remember matters. For example, some older adults might believe that their memory and other cognitive skills are inadequate and therefore avoid learning how to use a computer or shy away from

explicit memory Memory of facts and experiences that individuals consciously know and can state.

implicit memory Memory without conscious recollection; involves skills and routine procedures that are automatically performed.

prospective memory Involves remembering to do something in the future.

a training course in strategies for learning and retaining new information.

In one study, individuals with low anxiety about their memory skills and high self-efficacy regarding their use of memory in everyday contexts showed higher memory performance than their high-anxiety/low-self-efficacy counterparts (McDougall & others, 1999). Other researchers also are finding that positive or negative beliefs about one's memory skills are related to actual memory performance. Some critics, though, argue that memory beliefs do not have a significant impact on memory (Schaie, 2000).

Noncognitive Factors   Health, education, and socioeconomic status can influence an older adult's performance on memory tasks. Although such noncognitive factors as good health are associated with less memory decline in older adults, they do not eliminate memory decline.

One criticism of research on memory and aging is that it has relied primarily on laboratory tests of memory. The argument is that such tasks are contrived and do not represent the everyday cognitive tasks performed by older adults. If researchers used more everyday life memory tasks, would memory decline be found in older adults? A number of researchers have found that using more familiar tasks reduces age decrements in memory but does not eliminate them. Younger adults are better than older adults at remembering faces, routes through town, grocery items, and performed activities. In one study, young adults (20 to 40 years old) remembered news content in print, audio, and TV format better than old adults (60 to 80 years old) (Frieske & Park, 1999).

Older adults might not be as quick with their thoughts or behavior as younger people, but wisdom may be an entirely different matter. This older woman shares the wisdom of her experience with a classroom of children. *How is wisdom described by life-span developmentalists?*

Conclusions About Memory and Aging   Some, but not all, aspects of memory decline in older adults. The decline occurs primarily in episodic and working memory, not in semantic memory. A decline in perceptual speed is associated with memory decline. Successful aging does not mean eliminating memory decline, but reducing it and adapting to it. As we will see later in this chapter, older adults can use certain strategies to reduce memory decline.

Wisdom   Does wisdom, like good wine, improve with age? What is this thing we call "wisdom"? **Wisdom** is expert knowledge about the practical aspects of life that permits excellent judgment about important matters. This practical knowledge involves exceptional insight into human development and life matters, good judgment, and an understanding of how to cope with difficult life problems. Thus, wisdom, more than standard conceptions of intelligence, focuses on life's pragmatic concerns and human conditions (Baltes & Staudinger, 1998, 2000). This practical knowledge system can take many years to acquire, accumulating through intentional, planned experiences and accidental experiences. However, recent research has found no age differences in wisdom, with young adults showing as much wisdom as older adults (Baltes & Staudinger, 2000).

Wisdom involves solving practical problems. Fredda Blanchard-Fields (1996) reviewed the research on everyday problem solving in older adults. She concluded that, in contrast to research demonstrating a decline in older adults' ability to solve abstract problems, older adults' competency in problem solving is most evident in everyday types of situations.

Of course, not all older adults solve practical problems in competent ways. In one study, only 5 percent of adults' responses to life-planning problems were classified as wise, and the wise responses were equally distributed across the early, middle, and late adulthood years (Smith & Baltes, 1990).

wisdom   Expert knowledge about the practical aspects of life that permits excellent judgment about important matters.

It is always in season for the old to learn.

—Aeschylus
Greek Playwright, 5th Century B.C.

Education, Work, and Health

Education, work, and health are three important influences on the cognitive functioning of older adults. They are also three of the most important factors involved in understanding why cohort effects need to be taken into account in studying the cognitive functioning of older adults ◀‖‖‖ p. 65.

Education Successive generations in America's twentieth century have been better educated. Not only were today's older adults more likely to go to college when they were young adults than were their parents or grandparents, but more older adults are returning to college today to further their education than in past generations. Educational experiences are positively correlated with scores on intelligence tests and information-processing tasks, such as memory (Verhaeghen, Marcoen, & Goossens, 1995).

Older adults might seek more education for a number of reasons. They might want to better understand the nature of their aging. They might want to learn more about the social and technological changes that have produced dramatic changes in their lives. They might want to discover relevant knowledge and to learn relevant skills to cope with societal and job demands in later life. They might recognize that they need further education to remain competitive and stay in the workforce. Earlier, in the twentieth century, most individuals made career choices in adolescence and young adulthood and never wavered from those choices throughout their adult years. Today, that is not always the pattern. Technological changes have meant that some of the occupations of 15 years ago no longer exist. And some of today's occupations could not even be identified 15 years ago. Finally, older adults may seek more education to enhance their self-discovery and the leisure activities that will enable them to make a smoother adjustment to retirement.

Work Successive generations have also had work experiences that include a stronger emphasis on cognitively oriented labor. Our great-grandfathers and grandfathers were more likely to be manual laborers than were our fathers, who are more likely to be involved in cognitively oriented occupations. As the industrial society continues to be replaced by the information society, younger generations will have more experience in jobs that require considerable cognitive investment. The increased emphasis on information processing in jobs likely enhances an individual's intellectual abilities.

In one recent study, substantive complex work was linked with higher intellectual functioning in older adults (Schooler, Mulatu, & Oates, 1999). This research is consistent with findings in a wide range of disciplines, including animal-based neurobiology studies, which strongly suggest that exposure to complex environments increases intellectual functioning throughout the life course (Kempermann, Kuhn, & Gage, 1997).

Health Successive generations have also been healthier in late adulthood as better treatments for a variety of illnesses (such as hypertension) have been developed. Many of these illnesses have a negative impact on intellectual performance (Hultsch, Hammer, & Small, 1993). In one study, hypertension was related to decreased performance on the WAIS (Wechsler Adult Intelligence Scale) by individuals over the age of 60 (Wilkie & Eisdorpher, 1971). In one study, physical health and physical activity were positively related to cognitive performance in older adults (Anstey & Smith, 1999). The older the population, the more persons with health problems. Thus, some of the decline in intellectual performance found for older adults is likely due to health-related factors rather than to age per se (Comijs & others, 2002).

K. Warner Schaie (1994) concluded that some diseases are linked to cognitive dropoffs—these diseases include heart disease, diabetes, and high blood pressure.

Schaie does not believe the diseases directly cause mental decline. Rather, the lifestyles of the individuals with the diseases might be the culprits. For example, overeating, inactivity, and stress are related to both physical and mental decay (Christensen & others, 1996).

A number of research studies have found that exercise is linked to improved cognitive functioning (Kramer & others, 2002). Here are the results of two of these studies:

- In one study, community-dwelling women 65 years of age and older did not have cognitive impairment or physical limitations when they were initially assessed (Yaffe & others, 2001). Six to eight years later, the women with higher physical activity when they were initially assessed were less likely to experience cognitive decline.
- In one study, 124 individuals 60 to 75 years of age whose primary activity was sitting around the house were tested for their level of aerobic endurance and their level of cognitive functioning (Kramer & others, 1999). Cognitive functioning was assessed by tasks on working memory, planning, and scheduling. Half the group was randomly assigned to engage in yoga-type stretching activities and the other half was randomly assigned to start walking three times a week. After six months, the walkers averaged a mile in 16 minutes, a minute faster than at the beginning, and the stretchers had become more flexible. When their cognitive functioning was retested after six months, the walkers scored up to 25 percent higher on the cognitive tests than the stretchers did.

Other researchers have found that aerobic exercise is related to improved memory and reasoning (Clarkson-Smith & Hartley, 1989). Walking or any other aerobic exercise appears to get blood and oxygen pumping to the brain, which can help people think more clearly.

Related to the idea that health status is an important factor in the cognitive functioning of older adults is the **terminal drop hypothesis.** It states that death is preceded by a decrease in cognitive functioning over approximately a five-year period prior to death. Thus, distance from death in a subsequently deceased population should be correlated with performance on tests of cognitive functioning if they were administered during the critical five-year period (Riegel & Riegel, 1972). In investigations that compare older and younger adults, many more of the older adults than the younger adults are likely to be within five years of their death. The chronic diseases these older adults may have are likely to decrease their motivation, alertness, and energy to perform competently when they are given tests of cognitive functioning. Thus, the negative findings for older adults in some investigations that compare older adults with younger adults may be due in part to age from death rather than simply age from birth. One issue in considering terminal drop is in keeping with our emphasis on assessing a number of aspects of cognitive functioning rather than general intelligence alone. In one study, the terminal drop hypothesis was supported for tests of vocabulary, but not for numerical facility and perceptual speed (White & Cunningham, 1989).

Use It or Lose It

Changes in cognitive activity patterns might result in disuse and consequent atrophy of cognitive skills. This concept is captured in the adage "Use it or lose it." The mental activities that likely benefit the maintenance of cognitive skills in older adults are reading books, doing crossword puzzles, and going to lectures and concerts. The studies listed here support this idea:

- In an analysis of participants in the Victoria Longitudinal Study, when middle-aged and older adults participated in intellectually engaging activities it served to buffer them against cognitive decline (Hultsch & others, 1999). This also was

terminal drop hypothesis The hypothesis that death is preceded by a decrease in cognitive functioning over approximately a five-year period prior to death.

Careers in Life-Span Development

Sherry Willis, Researcher and Professor of Human Development

Sherry Willis obtained her Ph.D. from the University of Texas at Austin and has been a professor of human development at Pennsylvania State University since 1972 ◀▥ p. 30. She is one of the leading experts on cognitive development in adults. Willis has shown that older adults can be trained to improve their reasoning ability. She especially believes it is important for adults to use their cognitive abilities and believes that maintaining an active mental life is important.

Sherry Willis, Researcher and Professor of Human Development (*right*), assessing the cognitive skills of aging adults.

found in another longitudinal study over a 45-year time frame (Arbuckle & others, 1998).

- In a 4½-year longitudinal study of 801 Catholic priests 65 years and older, those who regularly read books, did crossword puzzle, or otherwise exercised their minds, were 47 percent less likely to develop Alzheimer's disease than the priests who rarely engaged in these activities (Wilson & others, 2002). Shortly, we will have much more to say about Alzheimer's disease.
- In a study of chess players from 20 to 80 years of age, their success in chess tournaments was more closely linked with the amount of time they engaged in deliberate practice than with their age (Charness, Krampe, & Mayr, 1996).

Training Cognitive Skills

If cognitive skills are atrophying in late adulthood, can they be retrained? There are essentially two main conclusions that can be derived from research: (1) There is plasticity, and training can improve the cognitive skills of many older adults; and (2) there is some loss in plasticity in late adulthood (Baltes, 1995).

As evidence of plasticity and the effectiveness of cognitive training, Sherry Willis and K. Warner Schaie (1986) studied approximately 400 adults, most of whom were older adults. Using individualized training, they improved the spatial orientation and reasoning skills of two-thirds of the adults. Nearly 40 percent of those whose abilities had declined returned to a level they had reached 14 years earlier.

Mnemonics can also be used to improve older adults' cognitive skills. **Mnemonics** are techniques that are designed to make memory more efficient. In the fifth century B.C., the Greek poet Simonides attended a banquet. After he left, the building collapsed, crushing the guests and maiming their bodies beyond recognition. Simonides was able to identify the bodies using a memory technique. He generated vivid images of each individual and pictured where they had sat at the banquet. The *method of loci,* Simonides' technique, was used in one study to improve the memory of older adults (Kliegl & Baltes, 1987). The method of loci involved practice with a map of forty Berlin landmarks. The older adults were also trained to use *chunking*—organizing items into meaningful or manageable units—to improve their memory of Berlin landmarks. Strategies for remembering telephone numbers, Social Security numbers, and license plate numbers are common examples of how chunking can help people remember large amounts of information in their everyday lives.

Using the method of loci and chunking, the elderly adults could recall more than 32 of the 40 Berlin landmarks. Later they were able to apply what they had learned in their method of loci and chunking training to recall long lists of digits. One 69-year-old woman correctly recalled 120 digits presented in intervals of eights. Such results suggest substantial memory capacity in healthy, mentally fit older adults. In another study, the method of loci was again effective in improving the memory of older adults (Kliegl, Smith, & Baltes, 1990). In yet another study, older adults benefited from

mnemonics Techniques designed to make memory more efficient.

mnemonic instruction, but not as much as younger adults (Verhaeghen & Marcoen, 1996).

In a seven-year-longitudinal study, Sherry Willis and Carolyn Nesselroade (1990) examined the effectiveness of cognitive training on the maintenance of fluid intelligence with advancing age (recall from chapter 16 that fluid intelligence involves the ability to reason abstractly). The older adults were taught strategies for identifying the rule or pattern required in problem solutions. Adults in their seventies and eighties performed at a higher level than they had in their late sixties following the cognitive training, which consisted of the trainer modeling the use of correct strategies in solving tasks, individual practice on training items, feedback about correct solutions of practice problems, and group discussion.

In one study, cognitive training helped remediate cognitive decline in older adults and enhanced the performance of individuals who were not showing decline (Saczynski, Willis, & Schaie, 1999). In this study, leisure activities and more time spent in communication were linked with positive cognitive training effects. In another study, instructing older adults to notice distinctions in pictures improved their memory of the pictures (Levy, Jennings, & Langer, 2001) (see figure 19.4).

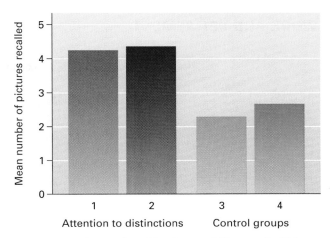

FIGURE 19.4 Improving Attention and Memory in Older Adults

In one study, older adult participants were randomly assigned to one of four attention interventions (Levy, Jennings, & Langer, 2001). In two of the groups, participants studying a set of pictures were told to notice either 3 (group 1) or 5 (group 2) distinctions. In two control groups, participants either were not given any directions related to attention (group 3) or just told to "pay attention." The older adults who viewed the pictures in terms of distinctions remembered more pictures than did the control groups.

Review and Reflect

1 Describe the cognitive functioning of older adults

REVIEW

- How is cognition multidimensional and multidirectional in older adults? What changes in cognitive processes take place in aging adults?
- How do education, work, and health affect cognition in aging adults?
- What is the concept of "use it or lose it"?
- To what extent can older adults' cognitive skills be trained?

REFLECT

- Can you think of older adults who have made significant contributions in late adulthood other than those we mentioned in the chapter? Spend some time reading about these individuals and evaluate how their intellectual interests contributed to their life satisfaction as older adults.

What percentage of older adults continue to work? How productive are they? Who adjusts best to retirement? What is the changing pattern of retirement in the United States and around the world? These are some of the questions we now examine.

Work

In the beginning of the twenty-first century, the percentage of men over the age of 65 who continue to work full-time is less than at the beginning of the twentieth century. The decline from 1900 to 2000 has been as much as 70 percent. An important change in older adults' work patterns is the increase in part-time work (Elder & Pavalko, 1993). The percentage of older adults who work part-time has steadily increased since the 1960s. Aging and work expert James House (1998) believes that many middle-aged workers would like to do less paid work while many older adults would like to do more.

Some individuals maintain their productivity throughout their lives. Some of these older workers work as many or more hours than younger workers. In the National Longitudinal Survey of Older Men, good health, a strong psychological commitment to work, and a distaste for retirement were the most important characteristics related to continued employment into old age (seventies and eighties) (Parnes & Sommers, 1994). The probability of employment also was positively correlated with educational attainment and being married to a working wife.

Especially important to think about is the large cohort of baby boomers—78 million people who will begin to reach traditional retirement age in 2010. Because this cohort is so large, we are likely to see increasing numbers of older adults continue to work (Yeats, Folts, & Knapp, 1999).

Cognitive ability is one of the best predictors of job performance in older adults. And older workers have lower rates of absenteeism, fewer accidents, and increased job satisfaction, compared with their younger counterparts (Warr, 1994). This means that the older worker can be of considerable value to a company, above and beyond the older worker's cognitive competence. Changes in federal law now allow individuals over the age of 65 to continue working. Also, remember from our discussion earlier in the chapter that substantively complex work is linked with a higher level of intellectual functioning (Schooler, Mulatu, & Oates, 1999). This likely is a reciprocal relation—that is, individuals with higher cognitive ability likely continue to work as older adults, and when they work in substantively complex jobs, this likely enhances their intellectual functioning (Schooler, 2001).

An increasing number of middle-aged and older adults are embarking on a second or a third career (Moen & Wethington, 1999. In some cases, this is an entirely different type of work or a continuation of previous work but at a reduced level. Many older adults also participate in unpaid work—as a volunteer or as an active participant in a voluntary association. These options afford older adults opportunities for productive activity, social interaction, and a positive identity.

Significant numbers of retirees only partially retire, moving to part-time employment by either reducing the number of hours they work on their career jobs or by taking on new (and frequently lower-paying) jobs (Han & Moen, 1998). Self-employed men are especially likely to continue paid employment, either on the same job or on a new job. Nearly one-third of the men who take on a part-time job do not do so until two years after their retirement (Burkhauser & Quinn, 1989).

In a recent survey, 80 percent of baby boomers said that they expect to work during the retirement years (Roper Starch Worldwide, 2000). The main reason they plan to work when they get older is to engage in part-time work for interest or enjoyment (35 percent), followed by income (23 percent), desire to start a business (17 percent), and the desire to try a different field of work (5 percent). In another recent survey, nearly 70 percent of current employees said that they expect to work for pay once they retire, mainly because they enjoy working and want to stay active and involved (Anthony Greenwald & Associates, 2000).

In summary, age affects many aspects of work (Cleveland & Shore, 1996). Nonetheless, many studies of work and aging— such as evaluation of hiring and performance—reveal inconsistent results. Important contextual factors, such as age composition of departments or applicant pools, occupations, and jobs, all affect decisions about older workers. It also is important to recognize that agist stereotypes of workers and of tasks can limit older workers' career opportunities and can encourage early retirement or other forms of downsizing that adversely affect older workers.

Retirement in the United States and Other Countries

A retirement option for older workers is a late-twentieth-century phenomenon in America (Atchley, 1996). Recall from our earlier discussion that a much higher percentage of older Americans worked full-time in the early 1900s than today. The Social Security system, which establishes benefits for older workers when they retire, was implemented in 1935. On the average, today's workers will spend 10 to 15 percent of their lives in retirement.

Ninety-two-year-old Russell "Bob" Harrell (*right*) puts in 12-hour days at Sieco Consulting Engineers in Columbus, Indiana. A highway and bridge engineer, he designs and plans roads. James Rice (age 48), a vice president of client services at Sieco, says that "Bob" wants to learn something new every day and that he has learned many life lessons from being around him. Harrell says he is not planning on retiring. *What are some variations in work and retirement in older adults?*

In 1967, the Age Discrimination Act made it a federal policy to prohibit the firing of employees because of their age before they reach the mandatory retirement age. In 1978, Congress extended the mandatory retirement age from 65 to 70 in business, industry, and the federal government. In 1986, Congress voted to ban mandatory retirement for all but a few occupations, such as police officer, firefighter, and airline pilot, where safety is an issue. Federal law now prohibits employers from firing older workers, who have seniority and higher salaries, just to save money. As mandatory retirement continues to lessen, older workers will face the decision of when to retire rather than be forced into retirement.

Although the United States has extended the retirement age upward, early retirement continues to be followed in large numbers. In many European countries, officials have experimented with various financial inducements designed to reduce or control unemployment by encouraging the retirement of older workers. Germany, Sweden, Great Britain, Italy, France, Czechoslovakia, Hungary, and Russia are among the nations that are moving toward earlier retirement. Nonetheless, currently in the Netherlands, there is an effort to recruit retired persons to reenter the workforce because of low unemployment in the country. More information about cultural variations in retirement appears in the Sociocultural Worlds of Development box on page 610.

Adjustment to Retirement

In thinking about adjustment to retirement, it is important to conceptualize retirement as a process rather than an event (Kim & Moen, 2001). Much of the research on

Work and Retirement in Japan, the United States, England, and France

Are a larger percentage of older adults in Japan in the labor force than in the United States and other industrialized countries? What are the attitudes of older Japanese adults toward work and retirement compared to their counterparts in other industrialized countries? To answer these questions, the Japanese Prime Minister's Office conducted national surveys of adults 60 years of age and older in four industrialized nations—Japan, the United States, England, and France. A much larger percentage of the men over 60 in Japan were in the labor force (57 percent) than in the United States (33 percent), England (13 percent), and France (8 percent).

When asked, "What do you think is the best age to retire?" a majority of the older men in England and France said 60 years of age. In sharp contrast, only 14 percent of the older men in Japan

and 16 percent of the older men in the United States chose such an early age to retire. Another question the older men in the four countries were asked was, "Where should an older person's income come from?" In Japan and the United States, the proportion of older men who favored saving while working was a least twice that advising reliance on Social Security. In contrast, older adult men in France and England favored reliance on Social Security.

The marked differences in the rate of employment among those over 60 in Japan and the United States, compared to England and France, are mainly due to attitudes and values about work, and about reliance on oneself (and on relatives, in the case of Japan) rather than on the government and its Social Security system.

**mhhe●com/
santrockld9**

AARP

Exploring Retirement

Baby Boomers and Retirement

Health and Retirement

retirement has been cross-sectional rather than longitudinal and has focused on men rather than women. One recent study found that men had higher morale when they had retired within the last two years compared to men who had been retired for longer periods of time (Kim & Moen, 2002). Let's examine some other factors that may be linked to well-being in retirement.

Older adults who adjust best to retirement are healthy, have adequate income, are active, are better educated, have an extended social network including both friends and family, and usually were satisfied with their lives before they retired (Gall, Evans, & Howard, 1997; Moen & Quick, 1998; Palmore & others, 1985). Older adults with inadequate income and poor health, and who must adjust to other stress that occurs at the same time as retirement, such as the death of a spouse, have the most difficult time adjusting to retirement (Stull & Hatch, 1984).

Flexibility is also a key factor in whether individuals adjust well to retirement. When people retire, they no longer have the structured environment they had when they were working, so they need to be flexible and discover and pursue their own interests (Eisdorfer, 1996). Cultivating interests and friends unrelated to work improves adaptation to retirement (Zarit & Knight, 1996).

Individuals who view retirement planning only in terms of finances don't adapt as well to retirement as those who have a more balanced retirement plan (Birren, 1996). It is important not only to plan financially for retirement, but to consider other areas of your life as well (Choi, 2001). What are you going to do with your leisure time? What are you going to do to stay active? What are you going to do socially? What are you going to do to keep your mind active?

Individuals who retire involuntarily are more unhealthy, depressed, and poorly adjusted than those who retire voluntarily (Swan, 1996). Options for control and self-determination are important aspects of older adults' mental health, the topic of our next section.

Review and Reflect

2 **Discuss aging and adaptations to work and retirement**

REVIEW

• What characterizes the work of older adults?

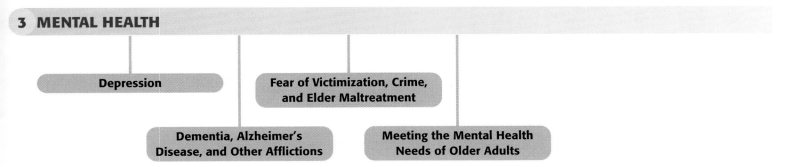

3 MENTAL HEALTH

Depression

Fear of Victimization, Crime, and Elder Maltreatment

Dementia, Alzheimer's Disease, and Other Afflictions

Meeting the Mental Health Needs of Older Adults

Although a substantial portion of the population can now look forward to a longer life, that life may unfortunately be hampered by a mental disorder in old age. This prospect is both troubling to the individual and costly to society. Mental disorders make individuals increasingly dependent on the help and care of others. The cost of mental health disorders in older adults is estimated at more than $40 billion per year in the United States. More important than the loss in dollars, though, is the loss of human potential and the suffering (Burns, Roth, & Christie, 1996). Although mental disorders in older adults are a major concern, older adults do not have a higher incidence of mental disorders than younger adults (Busse & Blazer, 1996).

Depression

Major depression is a mood disorder in which the individual is deeply unhappy, demoralized, self-derogatory, and bored. The person does not feel well, loses stamina easily, has a poor appetite, and is listless and unmotivated. Major depression has been called the "common cold" of mental disorders. Estimates of depression's frequency among older adults vary, although there is no evidence that depression is more common in older adults than in younger adults (Callahan & Wolinsky, 1995).

In the child, adolescent, and early adulthood years, females show greater depression than males (Nolen-Hoeksema & Ahrens, 2002) 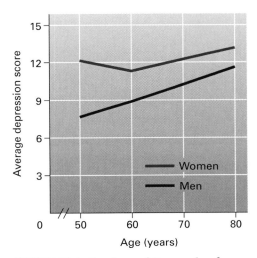 p. 428. Does this gender difference hold for middle-aged and older adults? One recent longitudinal study found greater depression in women than men at 50 and 60 years of age, but not at 80 years of age (Barefoot & others, 2001) (see figure 19.5). Men showed increases in depressive symptoms from 60 to 80 but women did not. In this cohort, men may have undergone more profound role shifts after 60 years of age because they were more likely than women to have retired from active involvement in the work world. Thus, the absence of a gender difference in depression in older adults may be cohort specific and may not hold as women who have entered to workforce in greater numbers are assessed in late adulthood.

Among the most common predictors of depression in older adults are earlier depressive symptoms, poor health, loss events such as death of a spouse, and low social support (Gatz, 1989; Nolen-Hoeksema & Ahrens, 2002). In one longitudinal study, widows showed elevated depressive symptoms up to two years following the death of

FIGURE 19.5 Gender and Depression from Age 50 to 80

One longitudinal study found higher depression scores in women than men at 50 and 60 but not at 80 (Barefoot & others, 2001). Men showed an increase in depressive symptoms from 50 to 80, but women did not.

major depression A mood disorder in which the individual is deeply unhappy, demoralized, self-derogatory, and bored. The person does not feel well, loses stamina easily, has poor appetite, and is listless and unmotivated. Major depression is so widespread that it has been called the "common cold" of mental disorders.

Former president Ronald Reagan was diagnosed with Alzheimer's disease at age 83.

**mhhe ●com/
santrockld9**

Dementia Web

Exploring Dementia

Dementia Research and Treatment

Dementia Caregivers

dementia A global term for any neurological disorder in which the primary symptoms involve a deterioration of mental functioning.

Alzheimer's disease A progressive, irreversible brain disorder characterized by a gradual deterioration of memory, reasoning, language, and eventually physical function.

a spouse (Turvey & others, 1999). In this longitudinal study, depression was likely to increase as older adults' health worsened (Fonda & Norgard, 1999). However, good social support and being socially integrated in the community helped to buffer the effects of declining health on depression in these individuals (Blazer, 2002).

One recent study of older adults (average age = 72.5 years) compared those with chronic mild depression and those who were not depressed (McGuire, Kiecolt-Glaser, & Glaser, 2002). The older adults who had chronic mild depression had worse immune system functioning, which resulted in less ability to fight off an infectious agent than their nondepressed counterparts.

Depression is a treatable condition, not only in young adults but in older adults as well (Alexopoulos & others, 2002; Haynie & others, 2001). Unfortunately, as many as 80 percent of older adults with depressive symptoms receive no treatment at all. Combinations of medications and psychotherapy produce significant improvement in almost four out of five elderly adults with depression (Koenig & Blazer, 1996).

Major depression can result not only in sadness, but also in suicidal tendencies. Nearly 25 percent of individuals who commit suicide in the United States are 65 years of age or older (Church, Siegel, & Fowler, 1988). The older adult most likely to commit suicide is a male who lives alone, has lost his spouse, and is experiencing failing health.

Dementia, Alzheimer's Disease, and Other Afflictions

Among the most debilitating of mental disorders in older adults are the dementias (Santacruz & Swagerty, 2001; Zarit & Downs, 1999). In recent years, extensive attention has been focused on the most common dementia, Alzheimer's disease. Other afflictions common in older adults are multi-infarct dementia and Parkinson's disease.

Dementia   **Dementia** is a global term for any neurological disorder in which the primary symptoms involve a deterioration of mental functioning. Individuals with dementia often lose the ability to care for themselves and can lose the ability to recognize familiar surroundings and people (including family members) (Laurin & others, 2001; Warner & Butler, 2002).

It is estimated that 20 percent of individuals over the age of 80 have dementia. More than seventy types or causes of dementia have been identified (Skoog, Blennow, & Marcusson, 1996).

The most common form of dementia is **Alzheimer's disease,** a progressive, irreversible disorder that is characterized by gradual deterioration of memory, reasoning, language, and eventually physical functioning (Mungas & others, 2002). More than 50 percent of dementias involve Alzheimer's disease. Approximately 10 to 20 percent of dementias stem from vascular disease (Epstein & Connor, 1999).

Alzheimer's Disease   Approximately 4 million adults in the United States have Alzheimer's disease. It has been predicted that Alzheimer's disease could triple in the next 50 years, as increasing numbers of people live to older ages. Because of the increasing prevalence of Alzheimer's disease, researchers have stepped up their efforts to discover the causes of the disease and find more effective ways to treat it (Bonde & Lange, 1998).

Because of differences in onset, Alzheimer's also is now described as *early-onset* (initially occurring in individuals younger than 65 years of age) or *late-onset* (which has its initial onset in individuals 65 years of age and older). Early-onset Alzheimer's disease is rare (about 10 percent of all cases) and generally affects people 30 to 60 years of age.

As Alzheimer's disease progresses, the brain deteriorates and shrinks. Figure 19.6 provides a comparison of the normally aging brain of a healthy individual and the brain of an individual with Alzheimer's disease.

Causes and Treatments   Alzheimer's disease is currently perceived as a puzzle with many pieces (Siegfried, 1995). For a number of years, scientists have tried to discover

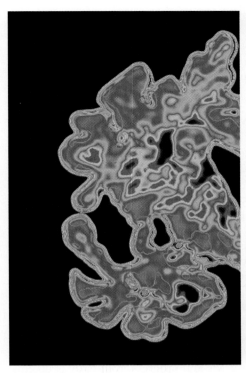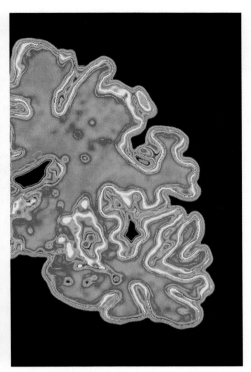

FIGURE 19.6 Two Brains: Normal Aging and Alzheimer's Disease

The brain image on the left is from a brain ravaged by Alzheimer's disease. The brain image on the right is from a brain of a normal aging individual. Notice the deterioration and shrinking in the Alzheimer's brain.

which piece of the puzzle is the cause of Alzheimer's disease. Today some scientists argue that the best strategy might be not to search for a single cause of Alzheimer's but to discover how to put all of the pieces together.

Alzheimer's disease was first diagnosed in 1906 by the German doctor Alois Alzheimer, but serious research on the disease did not begin until the 1950s, as Alzheimer's became more clearly distinguished from other types of dementia. In the 1970s, it was discovered that Alzheimer's involves a deficiency in the important brain messenger chemical acetylcholine, which plays an important role in memory (Hodges, 2000). Aricept is the main drug currently used to treat Alzheimer's, and it works by blocking chemicals that ordinarily cut acetylcholine apart (Camps & Munoz-Torrero, 2002).

Efforts to identify the cause of Alzheimer's have not yet been successful. What scientists now believe is that Alzheimer's disease is a complex unraveling of neural structure and function that likely involves many different molecular and cellular dimensions (Smith & others, 1995).

Alzheimer's disease might have a genetic basis in some individuals. ApoE4, an abnormal gene on chromosome 19, results in excess levels of a blood protein that carries cholesterol through the body. It has been estimated that the ApoE4 gene could play a role in as many as one-third of the cases of Alzheimer's disease. ApoE4 is associated with plaque formation in individuals with Alzheimer's disease (Holtzmann & others, 1999).

One of the main characteristics of Alzheimer's disease is the increasing number of *tangles* (tied bundles of protein that impair the functioning of neurons) and *plaques* (deposits that accumulate in the brain's blood vessels) (Galvan & others, 2002; Velez-Pardo, Lopera, & Del Rio, 2002). In the Images of Life-Span Development section at the

Memory loss is a common characteristic of Alzheimer's disease. Written reminders, like those shown here, can help individuals with Alzheimer's remember daily tasks.

Careers in Life-Span Development

Jan Weaver, Director of the Alzheimer's Association of Dallas

Dr. Jan Weaver joined the Alzheimer's Associations, Greater Dallas Chapter, as Director of Services and Education in 1999. Prior to that time, she served as associate director of education for the Texas Institute for Research and Education on Aging and director of the National Academy for Teaching and Learning About Aging at the University of North Texas. As a gerontologist, Dr. Weaver plans and develops services and educational programs that address patterns of human development related to aging. Among the services of the Alzheimer's Association that Weaver supervises are a resource center and helpline; a family assistance program, a care program, support groups, referral and information, educational conferences, and community seminars.

Dr. Weaver recognizes that people of all ages should have an informed and balanced view of older adults that helps them perceive aging as a process of growth and fulfillment rather than a process of decline and dependency. Her recent publications include editing a special issue of *Educational Gerontology*, published in 1999, that addresses the importance of aging education throughout the life span. Dr. Weaver earned her Ph.D. in sociology, with an emphasis in gerontology, from the University of North Texas in 1996.

Jan Weaver, giving a lecture on Alzheimer's disease.

beginning of this chapter, we described how Sister Mary was functioning quite well despite having tangles and plaques in her brain. The formation of tangles and plaques is a normal part of aging. However, in Alzheimer's disease these are much more pervasive.

Early Detection of Alzheimer's Disease Special brain scans, such as MRI (magnetic resonance imaging) can detect changes in the brain that are fairly typical of early - Alzheimer's disease even before symptoms develop (Li & others, 2002; Weatherford, 1999). In addition, certain spinal fluids give early signals of Alzheimer's disease. Recently a sophisticated urine test called the neural thread protein test has predicted the occurrence of Alzheimer's in some individuals two years before symptoms (such as memory loss) appeared. When positive, the urine test allows preventive measures to be initiated that delay the cognitive decline of Alzheimer's disease.

Progressive Decline There is a predictable, progressive decline in physical, cognitive, and social functioning when individuals have Alzheimer's disease (Morris & others, 2001). Most Alzheimer's patients, once diagnosed, live approximately eight years and progress from early problems of memory loss and declining intellectual function to later stages in which hospitalization in a near vegetative state ensues (Weatherford, 1999).

Caring for Individuals with Alzheimer's Disease A special concern is caring for Alzheimer's patients. Health-care professionals believe that the family can be an important support system for the Alzheimer's patient, but this support can have costs for the family, who can become emotionally and physically drained by the extensive care required for a person with Alzheimer's (Powers, Gallagher-Thompson, & Kraemer, 2002; Toseland & others, 2002; Yale, 1999). For example, depression has been reported in 50 percent of family caregivers for Alzheimer's patients (Redinbaugh, MacCallum, & Kiecolt-Glaser, 1995). Respite care has been developed to help people who have to meet the day-to-day needs of Alzheimer's patients. This type of care provides an important break away from the burden of providing chronic care.

There are many career opportunities for working with individuals who have Alzheimer's disease. To read about the work of a director of an Alzheimer's association, see the Careers in Life-Span Development insert.

Multi-Infarct Dementia **Multi-infarct dementia** involves a sporadic and progressive loss of intellectual functioning caused by repeated temporary obstruction of blood flow in cerebral arteries. The result is a series of mini-strokes. The term *infarct* refers to the temporary obstruction of blood vessels. It is estimated that 15 to 25 percent of dementias involve the vascular impairment of multi-infarct dementia.

Multi-infarct dementia is more common among men with a history of high blood pressure. The clinical picture of multi-infarct dementia is different than for Alzheimer's disease—many patients recover from multi-infarct dementia, whereas

multi-infarct dementia Sporadic and progressive loss of intellectual functioning caused by repeated temporary obstruction of blood flow in cerebral arteries.

Alzheimer's disease shows a progressive deterioration. The symptoms of multi-infarct dementia include confusion, slurring of speech, writing impairment, and numbness on one side of the face, arm, or leg (Hoyer & Roodin, 2003). However, after each occurrence, there usually is a rather quick recovery, although each succeeding occurrence is usually more damaging. Approximately 35 to 50 percent of individuals who have these transient attacks will have a major stroke within five years unless the underlying problems are treated. Especially recommended for these individuals are exercise, improved diet, and appropriate drugs, which can slow or stop the progression of the underlying vascular disease.

Parkinson's Disease   Another dementia is **Parkinson's disease,** a chronic, progressive disease characterized by muscle tremors, slowing of movement, and partial facial paralysis. Parkinson's disease is triggered by degeneration of dopamine-producing neurons in the brain (Kihara & others, 2002). Dopamine is a neurotransmitter that is necessary for normal brain functioning. Why these neurons degenerate is not known. The main treatment for Parkinson's disease involves the drug L-dopa, which is converted by the brain into dopamine. However, it is difficult to determine the correct level of dosage of this drug, and too much of it can produce schizophrenic symptoms.

Now that we have explored the nature of dementia, let's turn our attention to another problem that many elderly face: the fear of victimization and crime.

Muhammad Ali, one of the world's leading sports figures, has Parkinson's disease.

Fear of Victimization, Crime, and Elder Maltreatment

Some of the physical decline and limitations that characterize development in late adulthood contribute to a sense of vulnerability and fear among older adults (Gray & Acierno, 2002). For some older adults, the fear of crime may become a deterrent to travel, attendance at social events, and the pursuit of an active lifestyle. Almost one-fourth of older adults say they have a basic fear of being the victim of a crime. However, in reality, possibly because of the precautions they take, older adults are less likely than younger adults to be the victim of a crime. However, the crimes committed against older adults are likely to be serious offenses, such as armed robbery (Cohn & Harlow, 1993). Older adults are also victims of nonviolent crimes such as fraud, vandalism, purse snatching, and harassment. Estimates of the incidence of crimes against older adults may be low because older adults may not report crimes, fearing retribution from criminals or believing the criminal justice system cannot help them.

Elder maltreatment can be perpetrated by anyone, but it is primarily carried out by family members. As with child maltreatment, elder maltreatment can involve neglect or physical abuse. Older adults are most often abused by their spouses. A special concern is the burden older women carry in facing possible physical violence. In one study of 614 cases of abuse in Hillsborough County, Florida, 37 percent involved physical assault, most of the abused were women, they were most likely to be living with their spouse, and they were most likely to be over 60 years of age (VandeWeerd & Paveza, 1999). The perpetrators were most likely to be male spouses. Older women also were more likely than elderly men to suffer property damage and robbery, but in these cases the perpetrator was most likely to be a young male (18 to 29 years of age) who was not related to the victim.

Meeting the Mental Health Needs of Older Adults

Older adults receive disproportionately fewer mental health services (Sadavoy & others, 1996). One estimate is that only 2.7 percent of all clinical services provided by psychologists go to older adults, although individuals aged 65 and over make up more than 11 percent of the population. The proportion of community mental health services rendered to older adults has remained relatively stable—at or about 4 percent in the 1970s and 1980s (Lebowitz, 1987).

Psychotherapy can be expensive. Although reduced fees and sometimes no fee can be arranged in public hospitals for older adults from low-income backgrounds,

mhhe●com/
santrockld9

Multi-Infarct Dementia
National Parkinson Foundation
World Parkinson Disease Foundation
Resources for Parkinson's Disease
Stages in Parkinson's Disease

Parkinson's disease   A chronic, progressive disease characterized by muscle tremors, slowing of movement, and partial facial paralysis.

Margaret Gatz (*right*) has been a crusader for better mental health treatment of the elderly. She believes that mental health professionals need to be encouraged to include more older adults in their client lists and that we need to better educate the elderly about how they can benefit from therapy. *What are some common mechanisms of change that can be used to improve the mental health of older adults?*

many older adults who need psychotherapy do not get it (Knight & others, 1996). It has been said that psychotherapists like to work with young, attractive, verbal, intelligent, and successful clients (called YAVISes) rather than those who are quiet, ugly, old, institutionalized, and different (called QUOIDs). Psychotherapists have been accused of failing to see older adults because they perceive that older adults have a poor prognosis for therapy success, they do not feel they have adequate training to treat older adults, who may have special problems requiring special treatment, and they may have stereotypes that label older adults as low-status and unworthy recipients of treatment (Knight, Nordhus, & Satre, 2003; Knight & others, 1996).

There are many different types of mental health treatment available to older adults. Some common mechanisms of change that improve the mental health of older adults are (Gatz, 1989): (1) fostering a sense of control, self-efficacy, and hope; (2) establishing a relationship with a helper; (3) providing or elucidating a sense of meaning; and (4) promoting educative activities and the development of skills.

How can we better meet the mental health needs of older adults? First, psychologists must be encouraged to include more older adults in their client lists, and older adults must be convinced that they can benefit from therapy. Second, we must make mental health care affordable: Medicare currently pays lower percentages for mental health care than for physical health care, for example.

Review and Reflect

3 Characterize mental health problems and their treatment in older adults

REVIEW

• What is the nature of depression in older adults?
• What are dementia, Alzheimer's disease, and other afflictions like in older adults?
• How extensive is fear of victimization, crime, and maltreatment in older adults?
• How can the mental health needs of older adults be met?

REFLECT

• Older adults do not have more mental health problems than younger adults, although many people perceive that older adults have more mental problems. What might account for this misperception?

4 RELIGION

In chapter 16, we described religion and meaning in life with a special focus on middle age, including links between religion and health ◀▥ p. 532. Here we will continue our exploration of religion by describing its importance in the lives of many older adults.

In many societies around the world, the elderly are the spiritual leaders in their churches and communities. For example, in the Catholic church, more popes have been elected in their eighties than in any other 10-year period of the human life span.

The religious patterns of older adults have increasingly been studied (Levin, 1994). In one analysis, both older African Americans and older Whites attended religious services several times a month, said religion was important in their lives, read religious materials, listened to religious programming, and prayed frequently (Levin, Taylor, & Chatters, 1994). Also, in this analysis, older women had a stronger interest in religion than did older men.

When the significance of religion in people's lives has been assessed, individuals over 65 years of age are more likely than younger people to say that religious faith is the most significant influence in their lives, that they try to put religious faith into practice, and that they attend religious services (Gallup & Bezilla, 1992). In another survey, compared to younger adults, adults in old age were more likely to have a strong interest in spirituality and to pray (Gallup & Jones, 1989).

Is religion related to a sense of well-being and life satisfaction in old age? In one study of 836 older persons, it was. Religious practices—such as prayer and scripture reading—and religious feelings were associated with a sense of well-being, especially for women and individuals over 75 years of age (Koenig, Smiley, &

During late adulthood, many individuals increasingly engage in prayer. *How might this be linked with longevity?*

Gonzales, 1988). In one study, older adults' self-esteem was highest when they had a strong religious commitment and lowest when they had little religious commitment (Krause, 1995). In another study, a commitment to religion was linked with health and well-being in young, middle-aged, and older African American adults (Levin, Chatters, & Taylor, 1995). And in one study of low-income Latinos in San Diego, a strong religious orientation was associated with better health (Cupertino & Haan, 1999).

Religion can provide some important psychological needs in older adults, helping them face impending death, find and maintain a sense of meaningfulness and significance in life, and accept the inevitable losses of old age (Fry, 1999 Koenig & Larson, 1998). In one recent study, although church attendance decreased in older adults in their last year of life, their feelings of religiousness and the strength or comfort they received from religion were either stable or increased (Idler, Kasl, & Hays, 2001). Socially, the religious community can provide a number of functions for older adults, such as social activities, social support, and the opportunity to assume teaching and leadership roles. Older adults can become deacons, elders, or religion teachers, assuming leadership roles they might have been unable to take on before they retired (Cox & Hammonds, 1988).

Might praying or meditating actually be associated with longevity? In one recent study, they were (McCullough & others, 2000). Nearly 4,000 women and men 65 years and older, mostly Christians, were asked about their health and whether they prayed or meditated. Those who said they rarely or never prayed had about a 50 percent greater risk of dying during the six-year study compared with those who prayed or meditated at least once a month. In this study, the researchers controlled for many factors known to place people at risk for dying, such as smoking, drinking, and social isolation. It is possible that prayer and meditation lower the incidence of death in older adults because they reduce stress and dampen the body's production of stress hormones such as adrenaline. A decrease in stress hormones is linked with a number of health benefits, including a stronger immune system (McCullough & others, 2000).

mhhe com/
santrockld9

Spirituality and Health in Older Adults

Review and Reflect

4 **Explain the role of religion in the lives of older adults**

REVIEW
- What are some characteristics of religion in older adults?

REFLECT
- Do you think you will become more or less religious as an older adult? Explain.

Reach Your Learning Goals

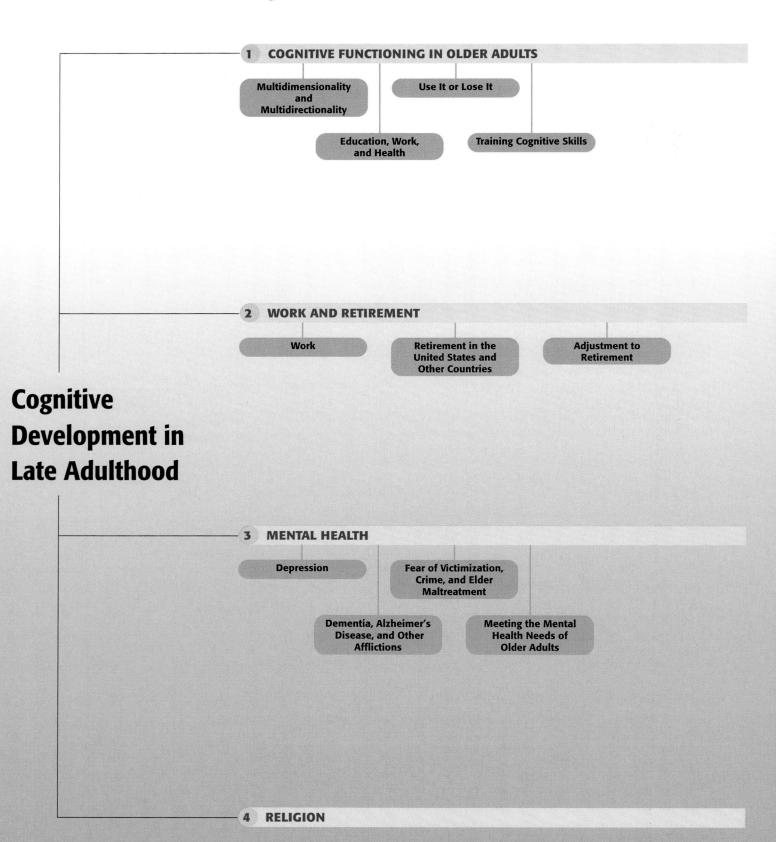

Cognitive Development in Late Adulthood

1 COGNITIVE FUNCTIONING IN OLDER ADULTS

- Multidimensionality and Multidirectionality
- Education, Work, and Health
- Use It or Lose It
- Training Cognitive Skills

2 WORK AND RETIREMENT

- Work
- Retirement in the United States and Other Countries
- Adjustment to Retirement

3 MENTAL HEALTH

- Depression
- Dementia, Alzheimer's Disease, and Other Afflictions
- Fear of Victimization, Crime, and Elder Maltreatment
- Meeting the Mental Health Needs of Older Adults

4 RELIGION

Summary

1 Describe the cognitive functioning of older adults

- Baltes emphasizes a distinction between cognitive mechanics (the neurophysiological architecture, including the brain) and cognitive pragmatics (the culture-based software of the mind). Cognitive mechanics are more likely to decline in older adults than are cognitive pragmatics. Researchers have found that sensory/motor and speed-of-processing dimensions decline in older adults. Some changes in attention take place in adulthood. In selective attention, older adults fare more poorly than younger adults in general but when tasks are simple and sufficient practice is given age differences are minimal. Likewise, for divided attention, on simple tasks, adult age differences are minimal but on difficult tasks older adults do worse than younger adults. Older adults perform as well as middle-aged and younger adults on measures of sustained attention. Younger adults have better episodic memory than older adults. Regarding semantic memory, older adults have more difficulty retrieving semantic information, but they usually can eventually retrieve it. Researchers have found declines in working memory and perceptual speed in older adults. Older adults are more likely to show declines in explicit than in implicit memory. Prospective memory involves remembering what to do in the future, and the relation of prospective memory to aging is complex. An increasing number of studies are finding that people's beliefs about memory play an important role in their memory performance. Noncognitive factors such as health, education, and socioeconomic status are linked with memory in older adults. Wisdom is expert knowledge about the practical aspects of life that permits excellent judgments about important matters. Although theorists propose that older adults have more wisdom, researchers usually find that younger adults show as much wisdom as older adults.
- Successive generations of Americans have been better educated. Education is positively correlated with scores on intelligence tests. Older adults may return to education for a number of reasons. Successive generations have had work experiences that include a stronger emphasis on cognitively oriented labor. The increased emphasis on information processing in jobs likely enhances an individual's intellectual abilities. Poor health is related to decreased performance on intelligence tests in older adults. Exercise is linked to higher cognitive functioning in older adults. The terminal drop hypothesis states that death is preceded by a decrease in cognitive functioning over a five-year period prior to death.
- Researchers are finding that older adults who engage in cognitive activities, especially challenging ones, have higher cognitive functioning that those who don't use their cognitive skills.
- There are two main conclusions that can be derived from research on training cognitive skills in older adults: (1) There is plasticity, and training can improve the cognitive skills of many older adults; and (2) there is some loss in plasticity in late adulthood.

2 Discuss aging and adaptations to work and retirement

- Today, the percentage of men over 65 who continue to work full-time is less than at the beginning of the twentieth century. An important change in older adults' work patterns is the increase in part-time work. Some individuals continue a life of strong work productivity throughout late adulthood.
- A retirement option for older workers is a late-twentieth-century phenomenon in the United States. The United States has extended the mandatory retirement age upward, and efforts have been made to reduce age discrimination in work-related circumstances. While the United States has moved toward increasing the age for retirement, many European countries are encouraging early retirement.
- Individuals who are healthy, have adequate income, are active, are better educated, have an extended social network of friends and family, and are satisfied with their lives before they retire adjust best to retirement.

3 Characterize mental health problems and their treatment in older adults

- Depression has been called the "common cold" of mental disorders. However, a majority of older adults with depressive symptoms never receive mental health treatment. Dementia is a global term for any neurological disorder in which the primary symptoms involve a deterioration of mental functioning. Alzheimer's disease is by far the most common dementia. This progressive, irreversible disorder is characterized by gradual deterioration of memory, reasoning, language, and eventually physical functioning. Special efforts are being made to discover the causes of Alzheimer's and effective treatments for it. Some experts believe Alzheimer's is a puzzle with many pieces.
- Special brain scans, analysis of spinal fluids, and a sophisticated urine test are being used to detect Alzheimer's before its symptoms appear. Alzheimer's disease involves a predictable, progressive decline. An important concern is caring for Alzheimer's patients and the burdens this places on caregivers. In addition to Alzheimer's disease, other types of dementia are multi-infarct dementia and Parkinson's disease.
- Some of the physical decline and limitations that characterize development in late adulthood contribute to a sense of vulnerability and fear among older adults. Almost one-fourth of older adults say they have a basic fear of being the victim of a crime. Older women are more likely than older men to be victimized or abused.
- A number of barriers to mental health treatment in older adults exist; older adults receive disproportionately less

mental health treatment. There are many different ways to treat the mental health problems of the elderly.

4 **Explain the role of religion in the lives of older adults**
- Many older adults are spiritual leaders in their church and community. Religious interest increases in old age and is related to a sense of well-being in the elderly.

Key Terms

cognitive mechanics 599
cognitive pragmatics 599
selective attention 600
divided attention 600
sustained attention 601

episodic memory 601
semantic memory 601
explicit memory 602
implicit memory 602
prospective memory 602

wisdom 603
terminal drop hypothesis 605
mnemonics 606
major depression 611
dementia 612

Alzheimer's disease 612
multi-infarct dementia 614
Parkinson's disease 615

Key People

Paul Baltes 598

Fredda Blanchard-Fields 603

K. Warner Schaie 604, 606

Sherry Willis 606, 607

Taking It to the Net

1. Jasper's 66-year-old father thinks he was passed over for a promotion because of his age. How can Jasper investigate whether his father has a legal claim based on age discrimination against his company? What rights do older workers have in their jobs?

2. Angela is interested in finding out more about how causes, nature, and treatment of depression change over the life span. Her Aunt Sadie has become very depressed as she has gotten older, and Angela worries her aunt might harm herself. What can Angela find out about the extent of depression in the elderly population and why it often goes undiagnosed, the causes, and the best treatment regimens?

3. Juan's grandfather has just been diagnosed with Alzheimer's disease. What do Juan and his family need to know about caring for his grandfather's physical needs? What legal and financial issues may need to be considered by Juan's family to help them better deal with this situation?

Connect to www.mhhe.com/santrockld9 to research the answers and complete these exercises.

E-Learning Tools

To help you master the material in this chapter, you'll find a number of valuable study tools on the Student CD-ROM that accompanies this book. In addition, visit the Online Learning Center for *Life-Span Development*, ninth edition, where you'll find these valuable resources for chapter 19, "Cognitive Development in Late Adulthood."

- Use the self-assessment, *My Perception of Older Workers*, to find out how your perspectives might differ from human resource professionals in the United States.
- Build your decision-making skills by trying your hand at the parenting and education "Scenarios."

I am the family face;
Flesh perishes, I live on,
Projecting trait and trace
Through time to times
anon,
And leaping from place
to place
Over oblivion.

—THOMAS HARDY
English Novelist and Poet,
19th Century

Socioemotional Development in Late Adulthood

Images of Life-Span Development
Bob Cousy

Bob Cousy was a star player on Boston Celtics teams that won numerous National Basketball Association championships. At age 68, he still sometimes plays 18 holes of golf in the morning and three sets of tennis in the afternoon. Says Cousy:

> I still thrive on competition, and when I feel those competitive juices flowing, I've got to find an outlet. Of course, at 68, it is not going to be playing basketball. Basketball's not a sport you grow old with. Sure, I can manage a few from the free-throw line, but being in shape for basketball is something you lose three months after you retire from the sport . . .
>
> Now I'm working in broadcasting. I'm a commentator for the Celtics' away games. I like it because I'm controlling my own destiny.

In addition to his work as a broadcaster for the Celtics, Cousy enjoys spending time with his wife, family, and close friends.

Bob Cousy's life as an older adult reflects some of the themes of socioemotional development in older adults that we will discuss in this chapter. These include the important role that being active plays in life satisfaction, adapting to changing skills, and the positive role of close relationships with friends and family in an emotionally fulfilling life.

Bob Cousy, as a Boston Celtics star when he was a young adult (*left*) and as an older adult (*right*). *What are some changes he has made in his life as an older adult?*

1 THEORIES OF SOCIOEMOTIONAL DEVELOPMENT

- Erikson's Theory
  - Disengagement Theory
- Activity Theory
  - Socioemotional Selectivity Theory
- Selective Optimization with Compensation Theory

We will explore five main theories of socioemotional development that focus on late adulthood: Erikson's theory, disengagement theory, activity theory, socioemotional selectivity theory, and selective optimization with compensation theory.

Erikson's Theory

We initially described Erik Erikson's (1968) eight stages of the human life span in chapter 2, and as we explored different periods of development in this book we examined the stages in more detail ◀▥ p. 46. Here we will discuss his final stage.

Integrity versus despair is Erikson's eighth and final stage of development, which individuals experience during late adulthood. This stage involves reflecting on the past and either piecing together a positive review or concluding that one's life has not been well spent. Through many different routes, the older adult may have developed a positive outlook in each of the preceding periods. If so, retrospective glances and reminiscences will reveal a picture of a life well spent, and the older adult will be satisfied (integrity). But if the older adult resolved one or more of the earlier stages in a negative way (being socially isolated in early adulthood or stagnated in middle adulthood, for example), retrospective glances about the total worth of his or her life might be negative (despair). Figure 20.1 on page 626 portrays how positive resolutions of Erikson's eight stages can culminate in wisdom and integrity for older adults.

Robert Peck's Reworking of Erikson's Final Stage Robert Peck (1968) reworked Erikson's final stage of development, integrity versus despair, by describing three developmental tasks, or issues, that men and women face when they become old:

- **Differentiation versus role preoccupation** involves redefining one's worth in terms of something other than work roles. Peck believes older adults need to pursue a set of valued activities so that time previously spent in an occupation and with children can be filled.
- **Body transcendence versus body preoccupation** involves coping with declining physical well-being. As older adults age, they may experience a chronic illness and considerable deterioration in their physical capabilities. For men and women whose identity has revolved around their physical well-being, the decrease in health and deterioration of physical capabilities may present a severe threat to their identity and feelings of life satisfaction. However, while most older adults experience illnesses, many enjoy life through human relationships that allow them to go beyond a preoccupation with their aging body.
- **Ego transcendence versus ego preoccupation** involves recognizing that while death is inevitable and likely not very far away, it is adaptive to be at ease with oneself by realizing one's contributions to the future through rearing of children or through vocations or hobbies.

Life Review Life review is prominent in Erikson's final stage of integrity versus despair. Life review involves looking back at one's life experiences, evaluating them,

integrity versus despair Erikson's eighth and final stage of development, which individuals experience in late adulthood. This involves reflecting on the past and either piecing together a positive review or concluding that one's life has not been well spent.

differentiation versus role preoccupation One of the three developmental tasks of aging described by Peck, in which older adults must redefine their worth in terms of something other than work roles.

body transcendence versus body preoccupation A developmental task of aging described by Peck, in which older adults must cope with declining physical well-being.

ego transcendence versus ego preoccupation A developmental task of aging described by Peck, in which older adults must come to feel at ease with themselves by recognizing that although death is inevitable and probably not too far away, they have contributed to the future through raising their children or through their vocations and ideas.

Conflict and Resolution	Culmination in Old Age
Old age Integrity vs. despair: wisdom	Existential identity; a sense of integrity strong enough to withstand physical disintegration.
Middle adulthood Generativity vs. stagnation: care	Caring for others, and empathy and concern.
Early adulthood Intimacy vs. isolation: love	Sense of complexity of relationships; value of tenderness and loving freely.
Adolescence Identity vs. confusion: fidelity	Sense of complexity of life; merger of sensory, logical, and aesthetic perception.
School age Industry vs. inferiority: competence	Humility; acceptance of the course of one's life and unfulfilled hopes.
Early childhood Initiative vs. guilt: purpose	Humor; empathy; resilience.
Toddlerhood Autonomy vs. shame: will	Acceptance of the cycle of life, from integration to disintegration.
Infancy Basic trust vs. mistrust: hope	Appreciation of interdependence and relatedness.

FIGURE 20.1 Erikson's View of How Positive Resolution of the Eight Stages of the Human Life Span Can Culminate in Wisdom and Integrity in Old Age

In Erikson's view, each stage of life is associated with a particular psychosocial conflict and a particular resolution. In this chart Erikson (1988) describes how the issue from each of the earlier stages can mature into the many facets of integrity and wisdom in old age. At left, Erikson is shown with his wife Joan, an artist.

interpreting them, and often reinterpreting them. Distinguished aging researcher Robert Butler (1975, 1996) believes the life review is set in motion by looking forward to death. Sometimes the life review proceeds quietly, at other times it is intense, requiring considerable work to achieve some sense of personality integration. The life review may be observed initially in stray and insignificant thoughts about oneself and one's life history. These thoughts may continue to emerge in brief intermittent spurts or become essentially continuous. One 76-year-old man commented, "My life is in the back of my mind. It can't be any other way. Thoughts of the past play on me. Sometimes I play with them, encouraging and savoring them; at other times I dismiss them."

Life reviews can include sociocultural dimensions, such as culture, ethnicity, and gender. Life reviews also can include interpersonal, relationship dimensions, including sharing and intimacy with family members or a friend. And life reviews can include personal dimensions, which might involve the creation and discovery of meaning and coherence. These personal dimensions might unfold in such a way that the pieces do or don't make sense to the older adult. In the final analysis, each person's life review is to some degree unique.

As the past marches in review, the older adult surveys it, observes it, and reflects on it (Cully, LaVoie, & Gfeller, 2001). Reconsideration of previous experiences and their meaning occurs, often with revision or expanded understanding taking place. This reorganization of the past may provide a more valid picture for the individual, providing new and significant meaning to one's life. It may also help prepare the individual for death, in the process reducing fear.

As the life review proceeds, the older adult may reveal to a spouse, children, or other close associates unknown characteristics and experiences that previously had been undisclosed. In return, they may reveal previously unknown or undisclosed truths. Hidden themes of great meaning to the individual may emerge, changing the nature of the older adult's sense of self. Successful aging, though, doesn't mean thinking about the past all of the time. In one study, older adults who were obsessed about the past were less well adjusted than older adults who integrated their past and present (Wong & Watt, 1991).

Disengagement Theory

Disengagement theory states that to cope effectively, older adults should gradually withdraw from society. This theory was proposed almost half a century ago (Cumming & Henry, 1961). In this view, older adults develop increasing self-preoccupation, decrease their emotional ties with others, and show less interest in society's affairs. By following these strategies of disengagement, it was believed, older adults would enjoy enhanced life satisfaction.

The theory generated a storm of protest and met with a quick death. We mention it because of its historical relevance. Although not formally proposed until 1961, it summarized the prevailing beliefs about older adults in the first half of the twentieth century.

Activity Theory

Activity theory states that the more active and involved older adults are, the more likely they are to be satisfied with their lives. Thus, activity theory is the exact opposite of disengagement theory. Researchers have found strong support for activity theory, beginning in the 1960s and continuing into the twenty-first century (Neugarten, Havighurst, & Tobin, 1968; Rook, 2000). These researchers have found that when older adults are active, energetic, and productive, they age more successfully and are happier than if they disengage from society.

Activity theory suggests that many individuals will achieve greater life satisfaction if they continue their middle-adulthood roles into late adulthood. If these roles are stripped from them (as in early retirement), it is important for them to find substitute roles that keep them active and involved.

Socioemotional Selectivity Theory

Socioemotional selectivity theory states that older adults become more selective about their social networks. Because they place a high value on emotional satisfaction, older adults spend more time with familiar individuals with whom they have had rewarding relationships. Developed by Laura Carstensen (1991, 1995, 1998), this theory argues that older adults deliberately withdraw from social contact with individuals peripheral to their lives while they maintain or increase contact with close friends and family members with whom they have had enjoyable relationships. This selective narrowing of social interaction maximizes positive emotional experiences and minimizes emotional risks as individuals become older.

Socioemotional selectivity theory challenges the stereotype that the majority of older adults are in emotional despair because of their social isolation. Rather, older adults consciously choose to decrease the total number of their social contacts in favor of spending increasing time in emotionally rewarding moments with friends and family. That is, they systematically hone their social networks so that available social partners satisfy their emotional needs.

Is there research evidence to support life-span differences in the composition of social networks? Longitudinal studies reveal far smaller social networks for older adults than for younger adults (Lee & Markides, 1990; Palmore, 1981). In one study of individuals 69 to 104 years of age, the oldest participants had fewer peripheral social contacts than the relatively younger participants but about the same number of close emotional relationships (Lang & Carstensen, 1994).

mhhe ● com/
santrockld9

**Activities Resources
for Older Adults**

disengagement theory The theory that to cope effectively, older adults should gradually withdraw from society.

activity theory The theory that the more active and involved older adults are, the more likely they are to be satisfied with their lives.

socioemotional selectivity theory The theory that older adults become more selective about their social networks. Because they place a high value on emotional satisfaction, older adults often spend more time with familiar individuals with whom they have had rewarding relationships.

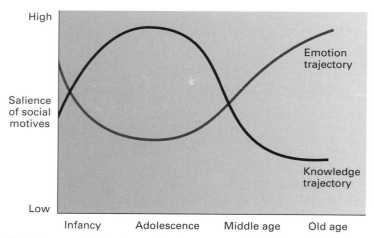

FIGURE 20.2 Idealized Model of Socioemotional Selectivity Through the Life Span

In Carstensen's theory of socioemotional selectivity, the motivation to reach knowledge-related and emotion-related goals changes across the life span.

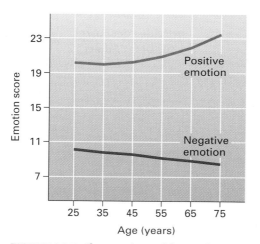

FIGURE 20.3 Changes in Positive and Negative Emotion Across the Adult Years

Positive and negative scores had a possible range of 6 to 30 with higher scores reflecting positive emotion and lower scores negative emotion. Positive emotion increased in the middle adulthood and late adulthood years while negative emotion declined.

selective optimization with compensation theory The theory that successful aging is related to three main factors: selection, optimization, and compensation.

Socioemotional selectivity theory also focuses on the types of goals that individuals are motivated to achieve (Carstensen, Isaacowitz, & Charles, 1999). It states that two important classes of goals are (1) knowledge-related and (2) emotional. This theory emphasizes that the trajectory of motivation for knowledge-related goals starts relatively high in the early years of life, peaking in adolescence and early adulthood and then declining in middle and late adulthood (see figure 20.2). The emotion trajectory is high during infancy and early childhood, declines from middle childhood through early adulthood, and increases in middle and late adulthood.

One of the main reasons given for these changing trajectories in knowledge-related and emotion-related goals involves the perception of time. As older adults perceive that they have less time left in their lives, they are motivated to spend more time seeking emotion-related goals rather than knowledge-related goals. Because striving for knowledge is so important from late adolescence to middle age, it is pursued relentlessly even at the cost of emotional satisfaction.

Researchers have found that across diverse samples (Norwegians, Catholic nuns, African Americans, Chinese Americans, and European Americans) older adults report better control of their emotions and fewer negative emotions than younger adults (Carstensen, Gottman, & Levensen, 1995; Lawton & others, 1992; Mroczek, 2001). Compared to younger adults, the feelings of older adults mellow. Emotional life is on a more even keel with fewer highs and lows. It may be that although older adults have less extreme joy, they have more contentment, especially when they are connected in positive ways with friends and family (Harlow & Cantor, 1996).

In one study using a very large U.S. sample, how emotion changes across the life span was examined (Mroczek & Kolarz, 1998). Older adults reported experiencing more positive emotion and less negative emotion than younger adults and the increase in positive emotion with age in adults increased at an accelerating rate (see figure 20.3). In sum, researchers have found that the emotional life of older adults is more positive than once believed (Carstensen, 1998; Mroczek, 2001; Ryan & La Guardia, 2000).

Laura Carstensen, who created socioemotional selectivity theory, is a leading theorist and researcher in the socioemotional aspects of aging. To read further about her work, see the Careers in Life-Span Development insert.

Selective Optimization with Compensation Theory

Selective optimization with compensation theory states that successful aging is linked with three main factors: selection, optimization, and compensation.

Selection is based on the concept that older adults have a reduced capacity and loss of functioning, which require a reduction in performance in most life domains. Optimization suggests that it is possible to maintain performance in some areas through continued practice and the use of new technologies. Compensation becomes relevant when life tasks require a level of capacity beyond the current level of the older adult's performance potential. Older adults especially need to compensate in circumstances with high mental or physical demands, such as when thinking about and memorizing new material very fast, reacting quickly when driving a car, or running fast. When older adults develop an illness, the need for compensation is obvious.

Selective optimization with compensation theory was proposed by Paul Baltes and his colleagues (Baltes & Baltes, 1990; Freund & Baltes, 2002; Krampe & Baltes, 2002; Marsiske & others, 1995). They describe the life of the late Arthur Rubinstein to illustrate their theory. When he was interviewed at 80 years of age, Rubinstein said that

Careers in Life-Span Development

Laura Carstensen, Psychology Professor and Director of Women's Studies Program

Laura Carstensen is a professor of psychology at Stanford University and also is director of the Institute for Gender and Women. She obtained her doctorate in clinical psychology from West Virginia University ◀▥ p. 32. Carstensen is a leading theorist and researcher in the socioemotional development of older adults. Her theory of socioemotional selectivity is gaining recognition as an important theory. She has conducted a number of research studies on adult development and aging, which have been supported by grants from the National Institute of Aging.

Laura Carstensen (*right*), in a caring relationship with an older woman.

three factors were responsible for his ability to maintain his status as an admired concert pianist into old age. First, he mastered the weakness of old age by reducing the scope of his performances and playing fewer pieces (which reflects *selection*). Second, he spent more time at practice than earlier in his life (which reflects *optimization*). Third, he used special strategies, such as slowing down before fast segments, thus creating the image of faster playing (which reflects *compensation*).

The process of selective optimization with compensation is likely to be effective whenever loss is prominent in a person's life. Loss is a common dimension of old age, although there are wide variations in the nature of the losses involved. Because of this individual variation, the specific form of selection, optimization, and compensation will likely vary depending on the person's life history, pattern of interests, values, health, skills, and resources.

In Baltes' view (1996, 2000; Krampe & Baltes, 2002), the selection of domains and life priorities is an important aspect of development. Life goals and priorities likely vary across the life course for most people. For many individuals, it is not just the sheer attainment of goals, but rather the attainment of *meaningful* goals, that makes life satisfying. In one study, younger adults were more likely to assess their well-being in terms of accomplishments and careers, whereas older adults were more likely to link well-being with good health and the ability to accept change. And as you read earlier in our discussion of socioemotional selectivity theory, emotion-related goals become increasingly important for older adults (Carstensen, 1998).

In one cross-sectional study, the personal life investments of 25- to 105-year-olds were assessed (Staudinger, 1996) (see figure 20.4 on page 630). From 25 to

FIGURE 20.4 Degree of Personal Life Investment at Different Points in Life

Shown here are the top four domains of personal life investment at different points in life. The highest degree of investment is listed at the top (for example, work was the highest personal investment from 25 to 34 years of age, family from 35 to 84, and health from 85 to 105).

34 years of age, participants said that they personally invested more time in work, friends, family, and independence, in that order. From 35 to 54 and 55 to 65 years of age, family became more important than friends to them in terms of their personal investment. Little changed in the rank ordering of persons 70 to 84 years old, but for participants 85 to 105 years old, health became the most important personal investment. Thinking about life showed up for the first time on the most important list for those who were 85 to 105 years old.

One point to note about the study just described is the demarcation of late adulthood into the subcategories of 70 to 84 and 85 to 105 years of age. This fits with our comments on several occasions that researchers increasingly do not study late adulthood as a homogeneous category.

Review and Reflect

1 Discuss five theories of socioemotional development and aging

REVIEW

- What is Erikson's theory of late adulthood?
- What is disengagement theory?
- What is activity theory?
- What is socioemotional selectivity theory and how does research support it?
- What is selective optimization with compensation theory?

REFLECT

- Which of the five theories best describes the lives of older adults you know? Explain.

2 THE SELF AND SOCIETY

The Self	Older Adults in Society

Do self-perceptions change in late adulthood? How are older adults perceived and treated by society?

The Self

Our exploration of the self focuses on changes in self-esteem, self-acceptance, and personal control. In chapter 13, we described how self-esteem drops in adolescence, especially for girls. How does self-esteem change in the adult years?

Self-Esteem   In the cross-sectional study of self-esteem described in chapter 13, a very large, diverse sample of 326,641 individuals from 9 to 90 were assessed (Robins & others, 2002). About two-thirds of the participants were from the United States. The individuals were asked to respond to the item, "I have high self-esteem," on the following 5-point scale:

1	2	3	4	5
Strongly Disagree				Strongly Agree

Self-esteem increased in the twenties, leveled off in the thirties and forties, rose considerably in the fifties and sixties, and then dropped significantly in the seventies and eighties (see figure 20.5). Through most of the adult years, the self-esteem of males was higher than the self-esteem of females. However, in the seventies and eighties, the self-esteem of males and females converged.

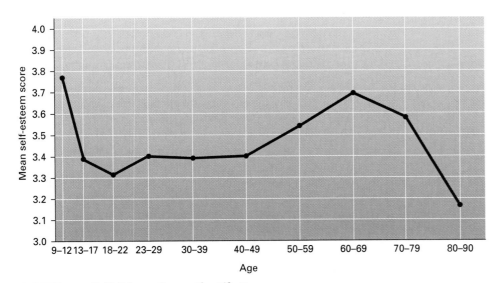

FIGURE 20.5 Self-Esteem Across the Life Span

One cross-sectional study found that self-esteem was high in childhood, dropped in adolescence, increased through early and middle adulthood, then dropped in the seventies and eighties (Robins & others, 2002). More than 300,000 individuals were asked the extent to which they have high self-esteem on a 5-point scale with 5 being "Strongly Agree" and 1 being "Strongly Disagree."

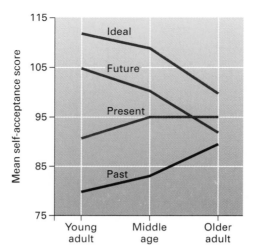

FIGURE 20.6 Changes in Self-Acceptance Across the Adult Years

Acceptance of ideal and future selves decreases with age, acceptance of past selves increases with age, and acceptance of present selves increases slightly in middle age and then leveled off.

Putting the results together with those discussed in chapter 13, self-esteem was high in childhood, declined in adolescence, increased throughout adulthood until the seventies, at which point it declined again. Males had higher self-esteem than females during most of the life span, although no differences were found in childhood or old age. The self-esteem of girls declined more than the self-esteem of boys in adolescence.

Why might self-esteem decline in older adults? Explanations include deteriorating physical health and negative societal attitudes toward older adults, although these factors were not examined in the large-scale study just described. Further research is needed to verify these developmental changes in self-esteem.

Self-Acceptance Another aspect of the self that changes across the adult years is self-acceptance. In one study, the self-acceptance of individuals at different points in adult development depended on whether they were describing their past, present, future, or ideal selves (Ryff, 1991). As shown in figure 20.6, young and middle-aged adults showed greater acceptance of their ideal and future selves than their present and past selves. However, in older adults there was little difference in acceptance of various selves because of decreased acceptance of ideal and future selves and increased acceptance of past selves.

Personal Control Developmentalists have shown a substantial increase in interest in the role of personal control in people's lives as they age (Heckhausen, 2001). *Personal control* involves the extent to which individuals believe that they are in control of what they do in life as opposed to being controlled by their environment.

The main way that personal control has been studied has been in terms of *locus of control.* An internal locus of control describes people who take responsibility for their behavior while an external locus of control refers to people who believe that other people, circumstances, or chance factors are responsible for their behavior. In one study, perceived control over one's development decreased through the adult years (Brandtstadter, 1999). However, perceived control depends on the domain being studied. For example, one study found lower perceived control over intelligence with increasing age (Soederberg, Miller, & Lachman, 1999) while another study revealed an increase in perceived control over marital support with age (Brandsttadter, 1999).

Jutta Heckhausen and her colleagues (Heckhausen, 1997, 2001; Heckhausen & Schultz, 1995; Heckhausen, Wrosch, & Fleeson, 2001) view control in terms of motivation and believe it is important to examine control-related strategies and the ability of people to control important outcomes in their lives. They distinguish between primary control striving and secondary control striving:

- *Primary control striving* refers to individuals' efforts to change the external world so that it meets their needs and desires. Primary control strategies are directed at attaining personal goals and overcoming obstacles. Persistence in striving for a goal ("When things don't go according to my plans, my motto is: 'Where there is a will, there's a way'") is an example of a primary control strategy.
- *Secondary control striving* targets individuals' inner worlds and their own motivation, emotion, and mental representation. Examples of secondary control striving are positive reappraisal ("I find I usually learn something from a difficult situation") and lowering aspirations ("When my expectations are not being met, I lower them").

In most instances, primary control is more adaptive than secondary control because in primary control individuals change their environment to meet their own needs and seek gains in their life. In secondary control, they often are trying to minimize losses or maintain their standing.

Primary and secondary control are believed to change through the life span. The ability to control outcomes is expected to increase substantially during the child, adolescent, and early adult years, level off in the middle adulthood years, and then decline in late adulthood (see figure 20.7). Secondary control increases in a similar manner to primary control through the early adult years, but unlike primary control, continues to increase through the middle adult and late adulthood years (see figure 20.7). Increasing physical and social challenges to primary control lead to increased use of secondary control strategies. Researchers have generally found that secondary control does increase in older adults (Grob, Little, & Wanner, 1999; Heckhausen & Schultz, 1995). One study focused on control strategies related to health or financial stress (Wrosch, Heckhausen, & Lachman, 2000). Primary control in the form of persistence in attaining a goal was positively related to perceived well-being in young adults. However, in middle and late adulthood, the secondary control strategy of positive reappraisal had a strong link with perceived well-being rather than persistence. The secondary control strategy of lowering aspirations was negative related to perceived well-being at all points in adulthood.

Older Adults in Society

Does society stereotype older adults? What are some social policy issues in an aging society? How do income and living arrangements affect older adults?

Stereotyping Older Adults   **Ageism** is prejudice against others because of their age, especially prejudice against older adults. Like sexism, it is one of society's uglier words. Many older adults face painful discrimination and might be too polite and timid to attack it (McMullin & Marshall, 2001; Perdue, 2000). Older adults might not be hired for new jobs or might be eased out of old ones because they are perceived as rigid or feebleminded, or because employing older adults is considered not cost-effective. They could be shunned socially, possibly because they are perceived as senile or boring. At other times, they might be perceived as children and described with adjectives such as "cute" and "adorable." The elderly might be edged out of their family life by children who see them as sick, ugly, and parasitic. In sum, older adults might be perceived as incapable of thinking clearly, learning new things, enjoying sex, contributing to the community, and holding responsible jobs—inhumane perceptions to be sure, but often painfully real.

In one study, young, middle-aged, and older adults had many of the same stereotypes of older adults (Hummert & others, 1994). Seven stereotypes of older adults were present in all age groups: *perfect grandmother, golden ager, John Wayne conservative, severely impaired, shrew/curmudgeon, despondent,* and *recluse*. Notice that this listing includes almost the same number of positive as negative stereotypes, with only one—*severely impaired*—being a traditional stereotype of old age.

The personal consequences of negative stereotyping about aging can be serious. A physician (60 years old himself) recently told an 80-year-old: "Well, of course, you are tired. You just need to slow down. Don't try to do so much. After all you are very old." Many older adults accept this type of advice even though it is rooted in age stereotyping rather than medical records. One recent study found that ageism was widespread with the most frequent type occurring when people showed disrespect for older adults followed by assumptions about ailments or frailty caused by age (Palmore, 2001).

The increased number of adults living to an older age has led to active efforts to improve society's image of the older adults, obtain better living conditions for older adults, and gain political clout. The American Association of Retired Persons (AARP), with more than 30 million members, is bigger than most countries. The Gray Panthers, with 80,000 members, pressures Congress on everything from health insurance to housing costs for older adults. These groups have developed a formidable gray lobbying effort in state and national politics.

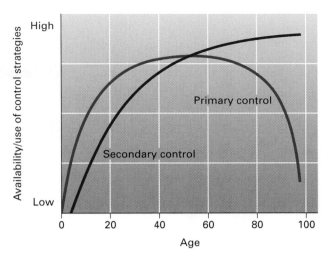

FIGURE 20.7 Theorized Changes in Primary and Secondary Control Strategies Across the Human Life Span

According to Heckhausen, primary control strategies increase in the child, adolescent, and early adult years, then level off in middle age, and finally decline in older adults. However, secondary control strategies continue to increase throughout the adult years.

ageism Prejudice against other people because of their age, especially prejudice against older adults.

The Gray Panthers are actively involved in pressuring Congress on everything from health insurance to housing costs. Along with the American Association for Retired Persons, they have developed a formidable gray lobbying effort in state and national politics. *What are some of the policy issues in an aging society?*

Policy Issues in an Aging Society The aging society and older persons' status in this society raise policy issues about the well-being of older adults. These include the status of the economy and the viability of the Social Security system, the provision of health care, supports for families who care for older adults, and generational inequity, each of which we consider in turn (Neugarten, 1988).

An important issue involving the economy and aging is the concern that our economy cannot bear the burden of so many older persons, who by reason of their age alone are usually consumers rather than producers. However, not all persons 65 and over are nonworkers and not all persons 18 to 64 are workers. And considerably more individuals in the 55 to 64 age group are in the workforce—three out of five men—than a decade ago. Thus, it is incorrect to simply describe older adults as consumers and younger adults as producers.

An aging society also brings with it various problems involving health care (Birren, 1993). Escalating health-care costs are currently causing considerable concern. One factor that contributes to the surge in health costs is the increasing number of older adults. Older adults have more illnesses than younger adults, despite the fact that many older adults report their health as good. Older adults see doctors more often, are hospitalized more often, and have longer hospital stays. Approximately one-third of the total health bill of the United States is for the care of adults 65 and over, who comprise only 12 percent of the population. The health-care needs of the elderly are reflected in Medicare, the program that provides health-care insurance to adults over 65 under the Social Security system. Of interest is the fact that the United States is the only industrialized nation that provides health insurance specifically for older adults rather than to the population at large, and the only industrialized nation currently without a national health-care system. Older adults themselves still pay about one-third of their total health-care costs. Thus, older adults as well as younger adults are adversely affected by rising medical costs.

A special concern is that while many of the health problems of older adults are chronic rather than acute, the medical system is still based on a "cure" rather than a "care" model. Chronic illness is long-term, often lifelong, and requires long-term, if not life-term, management. Chronic illness often follows a pattern of an acute period that may require hospitalization, followed by a longer period of remission, and then repetitions of this pattern. The patient's home, rather than the hospital, often becomes the center of managing the patient's chronic illness. In a home-based system, a new type of cooperative relationship between doctors, nurses, patients, family members, and other service providers needs to be developed. Health-care personnel need to be trained and be available to provide home services, sharing authority with the patient and perhaps yielding to it over the long term.

Eldercare is the physical and emotional caretaking of older members of the family, whether that care is day-to-day physical assistance or responsibility for arranging and overseeing such care. An important issue involving eldercare is how it can best be provided (Gonyea, 1994). With so many women in the labor market, who will replace them as caregivers? An added problem is that many caregivers are in their sixties, and many of them are ill themselves. They may find it especially stressful to be responsible for the care of relatives who are in their eighties or nineties.

In one study, two distinct systems of eldercare were found: individualistic and collectivistic (Pyke & Bengtson, 1996). Individualists approached parental caregiving

eldercare Physical and emotional caretaking for older members of the family, whether by giving day-to-day physical assistance or by being responsible for overseeing such care.

reluctantly and considered it a burden. They often reported that they did not have adequate time for it and they relied on formal supports. In contrast, in collectivistic families, parental caregiving was assumed by family members, who emphasized family ties.

Some gerontologists advocate that the government should provide financial support to families to help with home services or substitute for the loss of income if a worker reduces outside employment to care for an aging relative (England & others, 1991). Some large corporations are helping workers with parent-caring by providing flexible work schedules and creating more part-time or at-home jobs. Government supports have been slow to develop. One reason for their slow development is that some persons believe such government interventions will weaken the family's responsibility and thus have a negative effect on the well-being of older, as well as younger, adults.

Yet another policy issue involving aging is **generational inequity** (discussed initially in chapter 1): the view that our aging society is being unfair to its younger members because older adults pile up advantages by receiving an inequitably large allocation of resources. Some authors have argued that generational inequity produces intergenerational conflict and divisiveness in the society at large (Longman, 1987). The generational equity issue raises questions about whether the young should be required to pay for the old. One claim is that today's baby boomers, now in their forties and fifties, will receive lower Social Security payments than are presently being paid out, or none at all, when they reach retirement age if the economy takes a downturn.

The generational inequity issue sometimes also takes the form of whether the "advantaged" old population is using up resources that should go to disadvantaged children. The argument is that older adults are advantaged because they have publicly provided pensions, health care, food stamps, housing subsidies, tax breaks, and other benefits that younger age groups do not have. While the trend of greater services for the elderly has been occurring, the percentage of children living in poverty has been increasing.

Distinguished developmentalist Bernice Neugarten (1988) says it is undeniable that the large numbers of poor children are a disgrace to an affluent society like the United States. She stresses that the problem should not be viewed as one of generational equity, but rather as a major shortcoming of our broader economic and social policies. In conclusion, Neugarten envisions that we should be thinking about what a positive spirit of aging would mean to America, and to what extent this positive spirit could improve the range of options for people of all ages. Margaret Gatz (1992), an expert on aging, agrees.

Income   Older adults who are poor represent a special concern (Vartanian & McNamara, 2002). Recent census data suggest that although the overall number of older people living in poverty has declined since the 1960s, the percentage of older persons living in poverty has consistently remained in the 10 to 12 percent range since the early 1980s (U.S. Bureau of the Census, 2000). More than 25 percent of older women who live alone live in poverty. Also, the number of older single women just above the poverty line remains substantial. Poverty rates among ethnic minorities are two to three times higher than the rate for Whites. Combining sex and ethnicity, 60 percent of older African American women and 50 percent of older Latino women who live alone live in poverty. Also, the oldest-old are the age subgroup of the elderly most likely to be living in poverty.

Many older adults are understandably concerned about their income. The average income of retired Americans is only about half of what they earned when they were fully employed. Although retired individuals need less income for job-related and social activities, adults 65 and over spend a greater proportion of their income for food, utilities, and health care. They spend a smaller proportion for transportation, clothing, pension and life insurance, and entertainment than do adults under the age

generational inequity The view that our aging society is being unfair to its younger members because older adults pile up advantages by receiving inequitably large allocations of resources.

of 65. Social Security is the largest contributor to the income of older Americans (38 percent), followed by assets, earnings, and pensions.

The majority of older adults face a life of reduced income. Far too few middle-aged adults adequately plan for this (Vartanian & McNamara, 2002). For instance, middle-aged Americans who will retire in 20 to 25 years will need an income equal to 75 percent of their current annual expenditures (adjusted for inflation) to maintain their current middle-aged lifestyle.

Living Arrangements   One stereotype of older adults is that they are often residents in institutions—hospitals, mental hospitals, nursing homes, and so on. However, nearly 95 percent of older adults live in the community. Almost two-thirds of older adults live with family members—spouse, a child, a sibling, for example—while almost one-third live alone. The older people become, the greater are their odds for living alone. The majority of older adults living alone are widowed. As with younger adults, living alone as an older adult does not mean being lonely (Kasper, 1988). Older adults who can sustain themselves while living alone often have good health and few disabilities, and they may have regular social exchanges with relatives, friends, and neighbors.

For many years researchers who studied the living arrangements of older adults focused on special situations such as nursing homes, public housing, mobile-home parks, welfare hotels, or retirement communities. However, less than 10 percent of older adults live in these types of housing arrangements. Nonetheless, the quality of housing for the elderly is far from perfect. The vast majority of older adults prefer to live independently—either alone or with a spouse—rather than with a child, with a relative, or in an institution. However, too many of the elderly have inadequate housing. One recent study examined the relation between older adults' physical living environment and their self-rated health (Krause, 1996). Older adults who had the most dilapidated housing gave themselves worse health ratings than their counterparts who had better housing.

Only 5 percent of adults 65 years of age and older live in institutions, but the older adults become, the more likely they are to live in an institution. For example, 23 percent of adults 85 years and over live in institutions. The majority of the elderly adults in institutions are widows, many of whom cannot physically navigate their environment, are mentally impaired, or are incontinent (cannot control their excretory functions). Because the population is aging and because wives' life expectancies are increasing more rapidly than husbands', even greater numbers of widows are likely to be in institutions in the future.

Review and Reflect

2 Identify changes in the self and society in late adulthood

REVIEW

- How do self-esteem and self-acceptance change in late adulthood?
- How are older adults perceived and treated by society?

REFLECT

- What do you envision your life will be like as an older adult?

3 FAMILIES AND SOCIAL RELATIONSHIPS

- The Aging Couple
- Grandparenting
- Friendship
- Social Support and Social Integration

What are the relationships of aging couples like? What roles do grandparents play? What do friendships and social networks contribute to the lives of older adults?

The Aging Couple

The time from retirement until death is sometimes referred to as the "final stage in the marriage process." Retirement alters a couple's lifestyle, requiring adaptation. The greatest changes occur in the traditional family, in which the husband works and the wife is a homemaker. The husband may not know what to do with his time, and the wife may feel uneasy having him around the house all of the time. In traditional families, both partners may need to move toward more expressive roles. The husband must adjust from being the good provider to being a helper around the house; the wife must change from being only a good homemaker to being even more loving and understanding. Marital happiness as an older adult is also affected by each partner's ability to deal with personal conflicts, including aging, illness, and eventual death (Field, 1996).

Individuals who are married in late adulthood are usually happier than those who are single (Lee, 1978). Marital satisfaction is greater for women than for men, possibly because women place more emphasis on attaining satisfaction through marriage than men do. However, as more women develop careers, this sex difference may not continue.

Not all older adults are married. At least 8 percent of all individuals who reach the age of 65 have never been married. Contrary to the popular stereotype, older adults who have never been married seem to have the least difficulty coping with loneliness in old age. Many of them discovered long ago how to live autonomously and how to become self-reliant.

Few of us imagine older couples taking an interest in sex. We might think of them as being interested in a game of bridge or a conversation on the porch, but not much else. In fact, a number of older adults date. The increased health and longevity of older adults have resulted in a much larger pool of active older adults. And the increased divorce rate has added more older adults to this pool.

Regarding their sexuality, older adults may express their sexuality differently than younger adults, especially when engaging in sexual intercourse becomes difficult. Older adults especially enjoy touching and caressing as part of their sexual relationship. When older adults are healthy, they still may engage in sexual activities. However, companionship often becomes more important than sexual activity in older adults. Older couples emphasize intimacy over sexual prowess.

Grandparenting

Let's explore these aspects of grandparenting: How satisfying is it to be a grandparent? What roles do grandparents assume and what styles do they use when they interact with their grandchildren? What is the profile of grandparenting and how is it changing?

*G*row old with me!
The best is yet to be,
The last of life,
For which the first was made.

—**Robert Browning**
English Poet, 19th Century

mhhe.com/
santrockld9

Older Adults' Sexual Activity

mhhe ● com/
santrockld9

Today's Grandparent
Foundation of Grandparenting
The Grandparent Network
Adult Children and
Their Elderly Parents
Grandparent Visitation Rights

Satisfaction with Grandparenting   In one study, only a small minority (8 percent) of Australian grandparents said that they were more dissatisfied than satisfied with their grandparenting role (Peterson, 1999). A majority of grandparents say that grandparenting is easier than parenting. In one study, middle-aged grandparents (45 to 60 years of age) were more willing to give advice and to assume responsibility for watching and disciplining grandchildren than were older grandparents (60 years and older). Also, in another study, maternal grandparents interacted more with their grandchildren than paternal grandparents did (Bahr, 1989).

In one study, frequent contact with grandchildren predicted high levels of satisfaction in grandparenting for both grandmothers and grandfathers (Peterson, 1999). Also in this study, opportunities to observe their grandchildren's development and share in their activities were described as the best features of being a grandparent; lack of frequent contact with grandchildren was pointed to as the worst feature.

Grandparent Roles and Styles   What is the meaning of the grandparent role? Three prominent meanings are attached to being a grandparent (Neugarten & Weinstein, 1964). For some older adults, being a grandparent is a source of biological reward and continuity. In such cases, feelings of renewal (youth) or extensions of the self and family into the future emerge. For others, being a grandparent is a source of emotional self-fulfillment, generating feelings of companionship and satisfaction that may have been missing in earlier adult-child relationships. And for yet others, being a grandparent is not as important as it is for some individuals, and is experienced as a remote role.

The grandparent role may have different functions in different families, in different ethnic groups and cultures, and in different situations (Kivnick & Sinclair, 1996). For example, in one study of White, African American, and Mexican American grandparents and grandchildren, the Mexican American grandparents saw their grandchildren more frequently, provided more support for the grandchildren and their parents, and had more satisfying relationships with their grandchildren (Bengtson, 1985). And in a study of three generations of families in Chicago, grandmothers had closer relationships with their children and grandchildren and gave more personal advice than grandfathers did (Hagestad, 1985).

The diversity of grandparenting was also apparent in an early investigation of how grandparents interacted with their grandchildren (Neugarten & Weinstein, 1964). Three styles were dominant—formal, fun-seeking, and distant figures. In the formal style, the grandparent performed what was considered to be a proper and prescribed role. These grandparents showed a strong interest in their grandchildren, but left parenting to the parents and were careful not to give child-rearing advice. In the fun-seeking style, the grandparent was informal and playful. Grandchildren were a source of leisure activity; mutual satisfaction was emphasized. A substantial portion of grandparents were distant figures. In the distant-figure style, the grandparent was benevolent but interaction occurred on an infrequent basis. Grandparents who were over the age of 65 were more likely to display a formal style of interaction; those under 65 were more likely to display a fun-seeking style.

The Changing Profile of Grandparents   In 1997, the U.S. Bureau of the Census issued its first detailed portrait ever of many different living arrangements involving grandparents. Especially noticeable was the increasing number of grandchildren living with their grandparents (Fuller-Thompson & Minkler, 2001). In 1980, 2.3 million grandchildren lived with their grandparents, but in 2000 that figure had reached 5.6 million (U.S. Bureau of the Census, 2001). Forty-two percent of those grandparents are responsible for their grandchildren. Climbing divorce rates, adolescent pregnancies, and drug use are the main reason that grandparents are thrust back into the "parenting" role they thought they had shed.

Almost one-half of the grandchildren who move in with grandparents are raised by a single grandmother. These families are mainly African American (53 percent).

When both grandparents are raising grandchildren, the families are overwhelmingly White—63 percent when there are no parents around and 57 percent when the home has one or both of the parents.

Grandparents who take in grandchildren are in better health, are better educated, are more likely to be working outside the home, and are younger than grand-parents who move in with their children. Less than 20 percent of grandparents whose grandchildren move in with them are 65 years old or older. In one recent study of grandparents raising their grandchildren, younger grandparents, grandchildren with physical and psychological problems, and low family cohesion were associated with stress (Sands & Goldberg-Glen, 2000).

In chapter 17, "Socioemotional Development in Middle Adulthood," we discussed the "sandwich generation," the middle generation that may be financially and time squeezed because of having to be responsible for and care for both their children and their aging parents. In the 2000 U.S. Census report on grandparents, it was clear that not all middle-generation adults experience this generational squeeze. A majority of the grandparents who were living with their children contributed to the family in-come and provided child care while parents worked.

Partly because women live longer, there are more grandmothers than grand-fathers (2.9 million versus 1.7 million) who live with their children. About 70 percent of the grandparents who move in with their children are grandmothers. Only about 10 percent of the grandparents who move in with their children and grandchildren are in poverty. However, single grandmothers who move in with children who are raising children by themselves are much more likely to be in poverty (28 percent). Al-most half of the grandparents who move in with their children are immigrants.

As more individuals live to an old age and as more families live in varied family structures, we can expect the nature of the grandparent's role and social interaction with grandchildren to change (Smith & Drew, 2002). Because of the aging of our society, an increasing number of grandparents are also great-grandparents. At the

At the beginning of the twentieth century, the three-generation family was common, but now the four-generation family is common as well. Thus, an increasing number of grandparents are also great-grandparents. The four-generation family shown here is the Jordans—author John Santrock's mother-in-law, daughter, granddaughter, and wife.

*B*eing embedded in a
family is a positive aspect of
life for many older adults.

—LILLIAN TROLL

**Contemporary Developmental Psychologist,
University of California at San Francisco**

mhhe ● com/
santrockld9

Older Adults and Their Families

What role does social support play in the health of the elderly?

turn of the century, the three-generation family was common, but now the four-generation family is common. As divorce and remarriage have become more common, a special concern of grandparents is visitation privileges with their grandchildren. In the last 10 to 15 years, more states have passed laws giving grandparents the right to petition a court to legally obtain visitation privileges with their grandchildren. Now, even if a parent objects, grandparents may be permitted to spend time with their grandchildren. Whether such forced visitation rights for grandparents are in the child's best interest is still being debated.

Aging expert Lillian Troll (1994, 2000) has found in her research that older adults who are embedded in family relationships have much less distress than those who are family deprived. Next, we will consider these other aspects of social relationships in late adulthood: friendship, social support, and social integration.

Friendship

Aging expert Laura Carstensen (1997) concluded that people choose close friends over new friends as they grow older. And as long as they have several close people in their network, they seem content, says Carstensen.

In one recent study of 128 married older adults, women were more depressed than men if they did not have a best friend, but women who did have a friend reported lower levels of depression (Antonucci, Lansford, & Akiyama, 2001). Similarly, women who did not have a best friend were less satisfied with life than women who did have a best friend.

In one study of young-old and old-old adult friendships, there was more continuity than change in amount of contact with friends (Field, 1999). There were, however, more changes in older adult male than older adult female friendships. Older men declined in number of new friends, in their desire for close friendships, and in involvement beyond family activities, while older women did not change in these areas.

The mobility of our society increases the distance between older and younger adults. Friendships with unrelated adults may help to replace the warmth, companionship, and nurturance traditionally supplied by families. In sum, friends play an important role in the support systems of older adults (Jerrome & Wenger, 1999; Troll, 1999).

What happens when older adults' friends die? One study found that one way older adults dealt with this loss was to loosen up their requirements for what they considered a friend (Johnson & Troll, 1994). Once "friends" probably meant intimate companions to them. Now they include the woman passed in the hall or the deliverer of Meals on Wheels.

Social Support and Social Integration

In the *social convoy* model of social relations, individuals go through life embedded in a personal network of individuals from whom they give and receive social support (Antonucci & Akiyama, 2002; Antonucci, Lansford, & Akiyama, 2001; Antonucci, Vandewater, & Lansford, 2000). Social support can help individuals of all ages cope more effectively.

Social support can improve the physical and mental health of older adults (Pruchno & Rosenbaum, 2003). Social support is linked with a reduction in symptoms of disease and with the ability to meet one's own health-care needs (Cohen, Teresi, & Holmes, 1985). Social support also decreases the probability that an older adult will be institutionalized (Antonucci, 1990). Social support is associated with a lower incidence of depression in older adults (Joiner, 2000).

Social integration plays an important role in the lives of many older adults (Antonucci, Vandewater, & Lansford, 2000; Luszcz & Giles, 2002). Being lonely and socially isolated is a significant health risk factor in older adults (Rowe & Kahn, 1997). In one study, being part of a social network was related to longevity, especially for men (House, Landis, & Umberson, 1988). And in a longitudinal study, both women and men with more organizational memberships lived longer than their counterparts with low organizational participation (Tucker & others, 1999).

Remember from our earlier discussion of socioemotional selectivity theory that many older adults choose to have fewer peripheral social contacts and more emotionally positive contacts with friends and family. Thus, although the overall social activity of many older adults decreases, this does not mean that they are emotionally distraught about this. Rather, it could reflect their greater interest in spending more time in the small circle of their friends and families where they are less likely to experience negative emotional experiences.

Review and Reflect

3 Characterize the families and social relationships of aging adults

REVIEW

- How would you profile the aging couple?
- What is the nature of grandparenting?
- What is the friendship of older adults like?
- What roles do social support and social integration play in late adulthood?

REFLECT

- Baby boomers, now adults in midlife, were born in the aftermath of World War II during the high birthrate years from 1945 to 1960. The grandparents of baby boomers who still are alive are the oldest generation now living. How are the values of today's middle-aged baby boomers similar to or different from those of their grandparents, who were influenced by the Victorian era in which women were not supposed to work, drive a car, or enjoy sex? Compare the attitudes of these two generations in regard to gender roles, sexuality, and other aspects of life.

4 ETHNICITY, GENDER, AND CULTURE

Ethnicity	Gender	Culture

How is ethnicity linked to aging? Do gender roles change in late adulthood? What are the social aspects of aging in different cultures?

Ethnicity

Of special concern are ethnic minority older adults, especially African Americans and Latinos, who are overrepresented in poverty statistics (Hayward, Friedman, & Chen, 1996). Consider Harry, a 72-year-old African American who lives in a run-down hotel in Los Angeles. He suffers from arthritis and uses a walker. He has not been able to work for years, and government payments are barely enough to meet his needs.

Comparative information about African Americans, Latinos, and Whites indicates a possible double jeopardy for elderly ethnic minority individuals. They face problems related to *both* ageism and racism (Jackson, Chatters, & Taylor, 1993). Both the wealth and the health of ethnic minority older adults decrease more rapidly than for elderly

Whites (Edmonds, 1993). Older ethnic minority individuals are more likely to become ill but less likely to receive treatment. They are also more likely to have a history of less education, unemployment, worse housing conditions, and shorter life expectancies than their older White counterparts (Himes, Hogan, & Eggebeen, 1996). And many ethnic minority workers never enjoy the Social Security and Medicare benefits to which their earnings contribute, because they die before reaching the age of eligibility for benefits.

Despite the stress and discrimination older ethnic minority individuals face, many of these older adults have developed coping mechanisms that allow them to survive in the dominant White world (Markides & Rudkin, 1996). Extension of family networks helps elderly minority-group individuals cope with the bare essentials of living, and gives them a sense of being loved (Antonucci, Vandewater, & Lansford, 1998). Churches in African American and Latino communities provide avenues for meaningful social participation, feelings of power, and a sense of internal satisfaction. And residential concentrations of ethnic minority groups give their older members a sense of belonging. Thus, it always is important to consider individual variations in the lives of aging minorities (Whitfield & Baker-Thomas, 1999).

Gender

Do our gender roles change when we become older adults? Some developmentalists believe there is decreasing femininity in women and decreasing masculinity in men when they reach the late adulthood years (Gutmann, 1975). The evidence suggests that older men do become more feminine—nurturant, sensitive, and so on—but it appears that older women do not necessarily become more masculine—assertive, dominant, and so on (Turner, 1982). Keep in mind that cohort effects are especially important to consider in areas like gender roles. As sociohistorical changes take place and are assessed more frequently in life-span investigations, what were once perceived to be age effects may turn out to be cohort effects (Jacobs, 1994).

One study found that time spent in committed activities by older adults had shifted in opposite ways for women and men (Verbrugge, Gruber-Baldini, & Fozard, 1996). Between 1958 and 1992, older men decreased their time in paid work and spent more doing housework, home repairs, yardwork, shopping, and child care. By contrast, older women engaged in more paid work and decreased their time in housework.

A possible double jeopardy also faces many women—the burden of *both* ageism and sexism (Lopata, 1994). The poverty rate for older adult females is almost double that of older adult males. According to Congresswoman Mary Rose Oakar, the number one priority for midlife and older women should be economic security. She predicts that 25 percent of all women working today can expect to be poor in old age. Yet only recently has scientific and political interest in the aging woman developed. For many years, the aging woman was virtually invisible in aging research and in protests involving rights for older adults (Markson, 1995). An important research and political agenda for the twenty-first century is increased interest in the aging and the rights of older adult women.

Not only is it important to be concerned about older women's double jeopardy of ageism and sexism, but special attention also needs to be devoted to female ethnic minority older adults. They face what could be described as triple jeopardy—ageism, sexism, and racism (Burton, 1996; Markides, 1995). More information about being female, ethnic, and old appears in the Sociocultural Worlds of Development box.

Old Age Across Cultures and Time

Culture

What factors are associated with whether older adults are accorded a position of high status in a culture? Seven factors are most likely to predict high status for older adults in a culture (Sangree, 1989):

Being Female, Ethnic, and Old

Part of the unfortunate history of ethnic minority groups in the United States has been the negative stereotypes against members of their groups. Many have also been hampered by their immigrant origins in that they are not fluent or literate in English, may not be aware of the values and norms involved in American social interaction, and may have lifestyles that differ from those of mainstream America (Organista, 1994). Often included in these cultural differences is the role of women in the family and in society. Many, but not all, immigrant ethnic groups traditionally have relegated the woman's role to family maintenance. Many important decisions may be made by a woman's husband or parents, and she is often not expected to seek an independent career or enter the workforce except in the case of dire financial need.

Some ethnic minority groups may define an older woman's role as unimportant, especially if she is unable to contribute financially. However, in some ethnic minority groups, an older woman's social status improves. For example, older African American women can express their own needs and can be given status and power in the community. Despite their positive status in the African American family and the African American culture, African American women over the age of 70 are the poorest population group in the United States. Three of five older African American women live alone; most of them are widowed. The low incomes of older African American women translate into less than adequate access to health care. Substantially lower incomes for African American older women are related to the kinds of jobs they hold, which either are not covered by Social Security or, in the case of domestic service, are not reported even when reporting is legally required.

A portrayal of older African American women in cities reveals some of their survival strategies. They highly value the family as a system of mutual support and aid, adhere to the American work ethic, and view religion as a source of strength (Perry & Johnson, 1994). The use of religion as a way of coping with stress has a long history in the African American culture, with roots in the slave experience. The African American church came to fulfill needs and functions once met by religion-based tribal and community organizations that African Americans brought from Africa. In one study, the older African American women valued church organizations more than their male counterparts did, especially valuing the church's group activities (Taylor, 1982).

In sum, older African American women have faced considerable stress in their lives (Edmonds, 1993). In the face of this stress, they have shown remarkable adaptiveness, resilience, responsibility, and coping skills.

A special concern is the stress faced by older African American women, many of whom view religion as a source of strength to help them cope. *What are some other characteristics of being female, ethnic, and old?*

- Older persons have valuable knowledge.
- Older persons control key family/community resources.
- Older persons are permitted to engage in useful and valued functions as long as possible.
- There is role continuity throughout the life span.
- Age-related role changes involve greater responsibility, authority, and advisory capacity.
- The extended family is a common family arrangement in the culture, and the older person is integrated into the extended family.

Cultures vary in the prestige they give to older adults. In the Navajo culture, older adults are especially treated with respect because of their wisdom and extensive life experiences. *What are some other factors that are linked with respect for older adults in a culture?*

- In general, respect for older adults is greater in collectivistic cultures (such as China and Japan), than in individualistic cultures (such as the United States). However, some researchers are finding that this collectivistic/individualistic difference in respect for older adults is not as strong as it used to be and that in some cases older adults in individualistic cultures receive considerable respect (Antonucci, Vandewater, & Lansford, 2000).

Review and Reflect

4 **Summarize how ethnicity, gender, and culture are linked with aging**

REVIEW

- How does ethnicity modify the experience of aging?
- Do gender roles change in late adulthood? Explain.
- How is aging experienced in different cultures?

REFLECT

- What can America do to make being an older adult a more positive experience?

5 SUCCESSFUL AGING

For too long, older adults were perceived as always being in decline, and the positive dimensions of aging were ignored (Rowe & Kahn, 1997). Throughout our coverage of late adulthood, we have called attention to successful aging and how earlier stereotypes of aging are being overturned as researchers discover that being an older adult has many positive aspects  p. 633. We indicated that once developmentalists began focusing on the positive aspects of aging rather than primarily focusing on its negative aspects, they realized there are far more robust, healthy older adults than they

John Glenn's recent space mission is emblematic of our rethinking of older adults in terms of successful aging.

previously believed. In our discussion of aging, we have found that with a proper diet, an active lifestyle, mental stimulation and flexibility, positive coping skills, good social relationships and support, and the absence of disease, many of our abilities can be maintained, or in some cases even improved, as we get older. Improvements in medicine mean that increasing numbers of older adults with diseases can still lead active, constructive lives. Being active is especially important in successful aging (Freund & Riediger, 2003). Thus, older adults who get out and go to meetings, participate in church activities, go on trips, and exercise regularly are more satisfied with their lives than their counterparts who disengage from society and passively live out the last part of their lives (Mannell & Dupuis, 1996). In this chapter, we have seen that older adults who are emotionally selective, optimize their choices, and compensate effectively for any losses they might encounter increase their chances of aging successfully.

Successful aging also involves perceived control over the environment and a sense of self-efficacy (Bertrand & Lachman, 2003). In chapter 18, "Physical Development in Late Adulthood," we described how perceived control over the environment had a positive effect on nursing home residents' health and longevity ◀▥ p. 588. In recent years, the term *self-efficacy* has often been used to describe perceived control over the environment and the ability to produce positive outcomes (Bandura, 2000; Clarke-Plaskie & Lachman, 1999). Researchers have found that many older adults are quite effective in maintaining a sense of control and have a positive view of themselves (Brandstadter, Wentura, & Greve, 1993).

Review and Reflect

5 Explain how to age successfully

REVIEW

- What factors are linked with aging successfully?

REFLECT

- How might aging successfully in late adulthood be related to what people have done earlier in their lives?

Reach Your Learning Goals

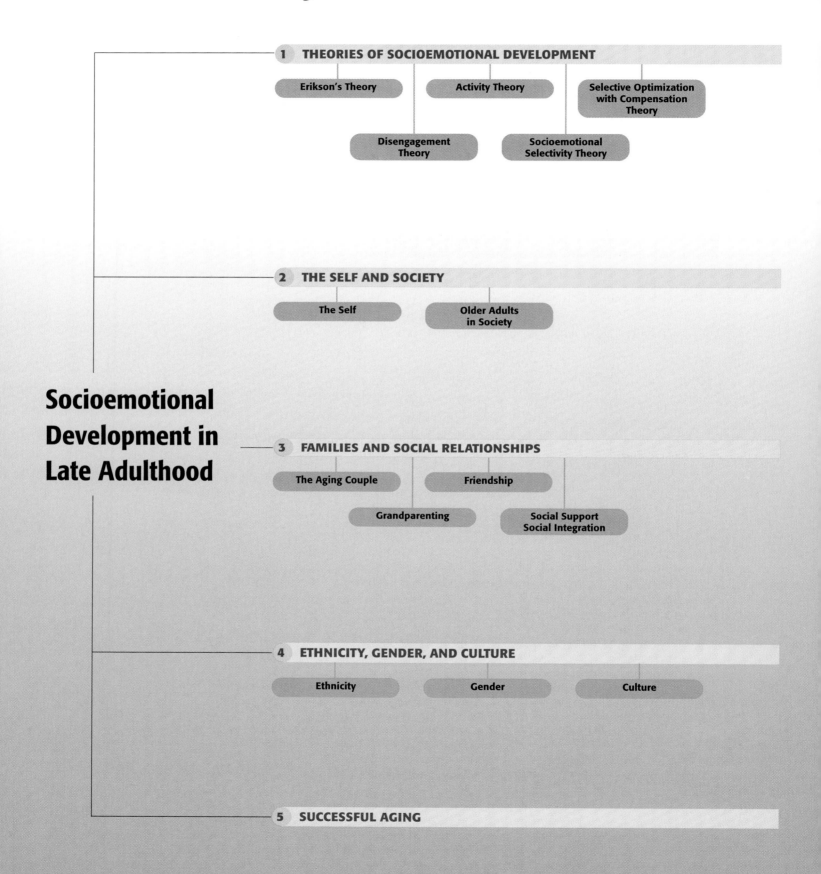

Socioemotional Development in Late Adulthood

1   THEORIES OF SOCIOEMOTIONAL DEVELOPMENT

- Erikson's Theory
- Activity Theory
- Selective Optimization with Compensation Theory
- Disengagement Theory
- Socioemotional Selectivity Theory

2   THE SELF AND SOCIETY

- The Self
- Older Adults in Society

3   FAMILIES AND SOCIAL RELATIONSHIPS

- The Aging Couple
- Friendship
- Grandparenting
- Social Support Social Integration

4   ETHNICITY, GENDER, AND CULTURE

- Ethnicity
- Gender
- Culture

5   SUCCESSFUL AGING

Summary

1 Discuss five theories of socioemotional development and aging

- Erikson's eighth and final stage of development, which individuals experience in late adulthood, involves reflecting on the past and either integrating it positively or concluding that one's life has not been well spent. Peck described three developmental tasks that older adults face: (1) differentiation versus role preoccupation, (2) body transcendence versus preoccupation, and (3) ego transcendence versus preoccupation. Life review is an important theme in Erikson's stage of integrity versus despair.
- Disengagment theory is no longer a viable view. It stated that to be satisfied with their lives older adults need to withdraw from society.
- Activity theory states that the more active and involved older adults are, the more likely they are to be satisfied with their lives. This theory has been strongly supported.
- Socioemotional selectivity theory states that older adults become more selective about their social networks. Because they place a high value on emotional satisfaction, they are motivated to spend more time with familiar individuals with whom they have had rewarding relationships. Knowledge-related and emotion-related goals change across the life span, with emotion-related goals being more important when individuals get older.
- Selective optimization with compensation theory states that successful aging is linked with three main factors: (1) selection, (2) optimization, and (3) compensation. These are especially likely to be relevant when loss occurs.

2 Identify changes in the self and society in late adulthood

- In one large-scale study, self-esteem increased through most of adulthood, but declined in the seventies and eighties. Further research is needed to verify these developmental changes in self-esteem. Changes in types of self-acceptance occur through the adult years as acceptance of ideal and future selves decreases with age and acceptance of past selves increases. There is increased interest in the relation of personal control to aging. The link between personal control and aging depends on the domain being studied. Heckhausen and her colleages distinguished beween primary control and secondary control with primary control more prominent in younger adults and secondary control more common in older adults.
- Ageism is prejudice against others because of their age. Too many negative stereotypes of older adults continue to exist. Social policy issues in an aging society include the status of the economy and the viability of the Social Security system, the provision of health care, eldercare, and generational inequity. Of special concern are older adults who are in poverty. Poverty rates are especially high among older women who live alone and ethnic minority older adults. Most older adults live in the community, not in institutions. Almost two-thirds of older adults live with family members.

3 Characterize the families and social relationships of aging adults

- Retirement alters a couple's lifestyle and requires adaptation. Married older adults are often happier than single older adults.
- Most grandparents are satisfied with their role. There are different grandparent roles and styles. The profile of grandparents is changing, due to such factors as divorce and remarriage.
- There is more continuity than change in friendship for older adults, although there is more change for males than for females.
- Social support is linked with improved physical and mental health in older adults. Older adults who participate in more organizations live longer than their counterparts who have low participation rates. Older adults often have fewer peripheral social ties but a strong motivation to spend time in relationships with close friends and family members that are rewarding.

4 Summarize how ethnicity, gender, and culture are linked with aging

- Aging minorities face special burdens, having to cope with the double burden of ageism and racism. Nonetheless, there is considerable variation in aging minorities.
- There is stronger evidence that men become more feminine (nurturant, sensitive) as older adults than there is that women become more masculine (assertive). Older women face a double jeopardy of ageism and sexism.
- Historically, respect for older adults in China and Japan was high, but today their status is more variable. Factors that predict high status for the elderly across cultures range from their valuable knowledge to integration into the extended family.

5 Explain how to age successfully

- Increasingly, the positive aspects of older adults are being studied. Factors that are linked with successful aging include an active lifestyle, positive coping skills, good social relationships and support, and self-efficacy.

Key Terms

integrity versus despair 625

differentiation versus role preoccupation 625

body transcendence versus body preoccupation 625

ego transcendence versus ego preoccupation 625

disengagement theory 627

activity theory 627

socioemotional selectivity theory 627

selective optimization with compensation theory 628

ageism 633

eldercare 634

generational inequity 635

Key People

Erik Erikson 625

Robert Peck 625

Robert Butler 626

Laura Carstensen 627

Paul Baltes 628

Jutta Heckhausen 632

Bernice Neugarten 635

Taking It to the Net

1. The viability of our Social Security program continues to be a hotly debated issue in our country, as evidenced in debates of the last presidential election. What are some of the reforms being suggested for this program, and how much Social Security might you receive?

2. Ted is the activities director at an adult retirement community. While talking to a friend who is a social worker, she suggested that Ted might want to develop a program in which the residents engage in the process of reminiscence and life-review. What benefits might the residents gain from such an activity?

3. Jessica, a 33-year-old single mother of three, has been diagnosed with breast cancer. Just as a precaution, Jessica has made arrangements for her parents to raise the children if something happens to her. What types of services and financial assistance would be available to Jessica's grandparents if they need to take on this responsibility?

Connect to www.mhhe.com/santrockld9 to research the answers and complete these exercises.

E-Learning Tools

To help you master the material in this chapter, you'll find a number of valuable study tools on the Student CD-ROM that accompanies this book. In addition, visit the Online Learning Center for *Life-Span Development*, ninth edition, where you'll find these valuable resources for chapter 20, "Socioemotional Development in Late Adulthood."

- Use the self-assessment, *How Satisfied Am I With My Life?*, to gain a better understanding of how you feel about your experiences and accomplishments in life.
- Build your decision-making skills by trying your hand at the parenting and education "Scenarios."

Endings

Years following years steal something every day; At last they steal us from ourselves away.
—ALEXANDER POPE
English Poet, 18th Century

Our life ultimately ends—when we approach life's grave sustained and soothed with unfaltering trust or rave at the close of day; when at last years steal us from ourselves; and when we are linked to our children's children's children by an invisible cable that runs from age to age. This final section contains one chapter: "Death and Grieving" (chapter 21).

*Sustained and soothed
by an unfaltering trust,
approach thy grave,
Like one who wraps the
Drapery of his couch
About him, and lies
down to pleasant
dreams.*

—William Cullen Bryant
American Poet, 19th Century

Death and Grieving

Learning Goals

*E*valuate issues in determining death and decisions regarding death

*D*escribe the roles of sociohistorical and cultural contexts in understanding death

*D*iscuss death and atttitudes about it at different points in development

*E*xplain the psychological aspects involved in facing one's own death and the contexts in which people die

*I*dentify ways to cope with the death of another person

Images of Life-Span Development
Princess Diana's Death

Princess Diana's sons William and Harry placed white flowers and a letter to their mother on her coffin. *In what ways do people mourn a death and grieve?*

Few deaths have captured the attention of the public as Princess Diana's did. Diana, Princess of Wales, died tragically in 1997 when the car she was traveling in crashed at high speed in Paris, France. Her body was subsequently returned to England and her funeral was held at Westminster Abbey. Following the funeral, which was televised around the world, the coffin was taken to the family's country estate for a private burial.

The elaborate, very formal funeral of Princess Diana is but one of many rituals of mourning. In this chapter you will read about many other types of mourning. Also, increasingly bodies are cremated rather than buried.

Death comes in many forms. For Princess Diana, only 37 years old and very healthy, it was very unexpected. For many people, it occurs in old age and can be expected after a long illness.

When an individual dies, those who have had a close relationship with the deceased typically engage in a grief process that can be brief or last for many years. In Princess Diana's case, her brother, Earl Spencer, gave a moving speech at the funeral in which he spoke of her kindness and how she would be missed. The grieving of her two sons—William and Harry, with whom she had very close, loving relationships—was especially important to their well-being. A noticeable form of grieving by William and Harry was their placement of white flowers on the coffin with a letter addressed to "Mummy."

After someone dies, individuals review the person's life and evaluate what they were like as a person and their contributions. Princess Diana was especially remembered for her charitable work and the positive image she brought to the British royal family. At her funeral, many individuals gave tributes to her, including Elton John, who wrote and sang in her memory a special version of his song "Candle in the Wind."

1 DEFINING DEATH AND LIFE/DEATH ISSUES

> **Issues in Determining Death**

> **Decisions Regarding Life, Death, and Health Care**

Is there one point in the process of dying that is *the* point at which death takes place, or is death a more gradual process? What are some decisions individuals can make about life, death, and health care?

Issues in Determining Death

Twenty-five years ago, determining if someone was dead was simpler than it is today. The end of certain biological functions, such as breathing and blood pressure, and the rigidity of the body (rigor mortis) were considered to be clear signs of death. In the past several decades, defining death has become more complex (Corr, Nabe, & Corr,

2003; Kyba, 2002). Consider the circumstance of Philadelphia Flyers hockey star Pelle Lindbergh, who slammed his Porsche into a cement wall on November 10, 1985. The newspaper headline the next day read, "Flyers' Goalie is Declared Brain Dead." In spite of the claim that he was "brain dead," the story reported that Lindbergh was listed in "critical condition" in the intensive care unit of a hospital.

Brain death is a neurological definition of death, which states that a person is brain dead when all electrical activity of the brain has ceased for a specified period of time. A flat EEG (electroencephalogram) recording for specified period of time is one criterion of brain death. The higher portions of the brain often die sooner than the lower portions. Because the brain's lower portions monitor heartbeat and respiration, individuals whose higher brain areas have died may continue breathing and have a heartbeat. The definition of brain death currently followed by most physicians includes the death of both the higher cortical functions and the lower brain stem functions.

Some medical experts argue that the criteria for death should include only higher cortical functioning. If the cortical death definition were adopted, then physicians could claim a person is dead who has no cortical functioning even though the lower brain stem is functioning. Supporters of the cortical death policy argue that the functions we associate with being human, such as intelligence and personality, are located in the higher cortical part of the brain. They believe that when these functions are lost, the "human being" is no longer alive.

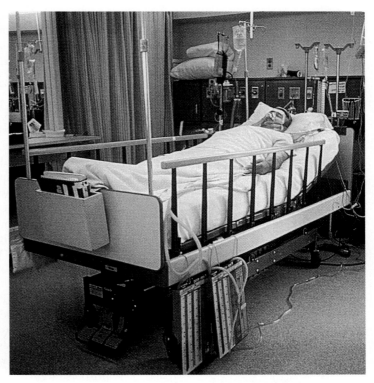

Advances in medical technology have complicated the definition of death. Controversy continues to swirl about what criteria should be used to determine when someone is dead. *What is this controversy about?*

Decisions Regarding Life, Death, and Health Care

In cases of catastrophic illness or emergency circumstances, patients might not be able to respond adequately to participate in decisions about their medical care, possibly even being comatose or irrational. To prepare for this type of situation, some individuals make choices earlier.

Natural Death Act and Advanced Directive   For many patients in a coma, it has not been clear what their wishes regarding termination of treatment might be if they still were conscious (Aiken, 2000). Recognizing that terminally ill patients might prefer to die rather than linger in a painful or vegetative state, the organization "Choice in Dying" created the Living Will. This document is designed to be filled in while the individual can still think clearly and expresses the person's desires regarding extraordinary medical procedures that might be used to sustain life when the medical situation becomes hopeless.

Physicians' concerns over malpractice suits and the efforts of people who support the Living Will concept have produced natural death legislation in many states. For example, California's Natural Death Act permits individuals who have been diagnosed by two physicians as terminally ill to sign an *advanced directive,* which states that life-sustaining procedures shall not be used to prolong their lives when death is imminent. An advanced directive must be signed while the individual still is able to think clearly. Laws in all fifty states now accept advanced directives as reflecting an individual's wishes.

Euthanasia   Euthanasia ("easy death") is the act of painlessly ending the lives of individuals who are suffering from an incurable disease or severe disability. Sometimes euthanasia is called "mercy killing." Distinctions are made between two types of euthanasia: passive and active.

brain death A neurological definition of death. A person is brain dead when all electrical activity of the brain has ceased for a specified period of time. A flat EEG recording is one criterion of brain death.

euthanasia The act of painlessly ending the lives of persons who are suffering from incurable diseases or severe disabilities; sometimes called "mercy killing."

Dr. Jack Kevorkian, who assisted a number of people in Michigan as they ended their lives through euthanasia. *Where do you stand on the use of active euthanasia?*

mhhe ●com/
santrockld9

Living Wills

Choice in Dying

Jack Kevorkian

Assisted Suicide

Exploring Euthanasia

Euthanasia Resources

passive euthanasia The withholding of available treatments, such as life-sustaining devices, allowing the person to die.

active euthanasia Death induced deliberately, as by injecting a lethal dose of a drug.

- **Passive euthanasia** occurs when a person is allowed to die by withholding available treatment, such as withdrawing a life-sustaining device. For example, this might involve turning off a respirator or a heart-lung machine.
- **Active euthanasia** occurs when death is deliberately induced, as when a lethal dose of a drug is injected.

Technological advances in life-support devices raise the issue of quality of life (Asch & Christakis, 1996; Jecker, 1996). Should individuals be kept alive in undignified and hopeless states? The trend is toward acceptance of passive euthanasia in the case of terminally ill patients. The inflammatory argument that once equated this practice with suicide rarely is heard today. However, experts do not yet entirely agree on the precise boundaries or the exact mechanisms by which treatment decisions should be implemented (Kelly & McLoughlin, 2002; Jennekens & Kater, 2002; Leeman, 2002). Can a comatose patient's life-support systems be disconnected when the patient has left no written instructions to that effect? Does the family of a comatose patient have the right to overrule the attending physician's decision to continue life-support systems? These are searching questions with no simple or universally agreed-upon answers. In one study of Canadian health-care workers, there was considerable variability in their decisions about whether to withdraw life support from critically ill patients (Cook & others, 1995).

The most widely publicized cases of active euthanasia involve the "assisted suicide" practiced by Jack Kevorkian, a Michigan physician (Roscoe & others, 2002). Kevorkian has assisted a number of terminally ill patients to end their lives. After a series of trials, Kevorkian was convicted of second-degree murder and given a long prison sentence.

Active euthanasia is a crime in most countries and in all states in the United States except one—Oregon. Active euthanasia is legal in the Netherlands and Uruguay (Sheldon, 2002). In 1994, the state of Oregon passed the Death with Dignity Act, which allows active euthanasia. Through 2001, ninety-one individuals were known to have died by active euthanasia in Oregon.

A survey of more than 900 physicians assessed their attitudes about active euthanasia (Walker, Gruman, & Blank, 1999). Most opposed active euthanasia, said that adequate pain control often eliminates the need for it, and commented that the primary role of the physician is to preserve life. They also reported that the potential for abuse in active euthanasia is substantial, and many believed that it is morally wrong.

Needed: Better Care for Dying Individuals   A report by a panel of experts concluded that death in America is often lonely, prolonged, and painful (Institute of Medicine, 1997). Dying individuals often get too little or too much care. Scientific advances sometimes have made dying harder by delaying the inevitable (Muth, 2000). Also, even though painkillers are available, too many people experience severe pain during the last days and months of life (Fine & Peterson, 2002). The panel of experts recommended that regulations be changed to make it easier for physicians to prescribe painkillers for dying patients who need them. The panel also pointed out that many health-care professionals have not been trained to provide adequate end-of-life care or understand how important it is.

End-of-life care should include respect for the goals, preferences, and choices of the patient and his or her family (Kirchoff, 2002; Wilson & Truman, 2002). Many patients who are nearing death want companionship (Finucane, 2002).

There are few fail-safe measures for avoiding pain at the end of life. Still, you can implement these suggestions (Cowley & Hager, 1995):

- Make a Living Will, and be sure there is someone who will draw your doctor's attention to it.
- Give someone the power of attorney and make sure this person knows your wishes regarding medical care.

- Give your doctors specific instructions—from "Do not resuscitate" (DNR) to "Do everything possible"—for specific circumstances.
- If you want to die at home, talk it over with your family and doctor.
- Check to see whether your insurance plan covers home care and hospice care.

Hospice is a humanized program committed to making the end of life as free from pain, anxiety, and depression as possible. Hospice's goals contrast with those of a hospital, which are to cure illness and prolong life. The hospice movement began toward the end of the 1960s in London, when a new kind of medical institution, St. Christopher's Hospice, opened. Little effort is made to prolong life at St. Christopher's—there are no heart-lung machines and there is no intensive care unit, for example. A primary goal is to bring pain under control and to help dying patients face death in a psychologically healthy way (Corr, Nabe, & Corr, 2003). The hospice also makes every effort to include the dying individual's family; it is believed that this strategy benefits not only the dying individual but family members as well, probably diminishing their guilt after the death (Mulholland, 2002).

The hospice movement has grown rapidly in the United States. Hospice advocates continue to underscore that it is possible to control pain for almost any dying individual and that it is possible to create an environment for the patient that is superior to that found in most hospitals (Hayslip, 1996).

Today more hospice programs are home-based, a blend of institutional and home care designed to humanize the end-of-life experience for the dying person. Whether the hospice program is carried out in the dying person's home, through a blend of home and institutional care, or in an institution often depends on medical needs and the availability of caregivers, including family and friends.

The widespread acceptance of hospices is evident in the more than 1,500 community groups that are involved nationally in establishing hospice programs. Hospices are more likely to serve people with terminal cancer than those with other life-threatening conditions (Kastenbaum, 2000).

Hospice care emphasizes **palliative care,** which involves reducing pain and suffering and helping individuals die with dignity. Health-care professionals work together to treat the dying person's symptoms, make the individual as comfortable as possible, show interest in the person and the person's family, and help them more effectively cope with death (Chochinov, 2002; Sheehan & Twaddle, 2002; Williams & Wheeler, 2001).

Hospice Net
Hospice Foundation of America
Better Care for the Dying

Review and Reflect

1 **Evaluate issues in determining death and decisions regarding death**

REVIEW

- What are some issues regarding the determination of death?
- What are some decisions to be made regarding life, death, and health care?

REFLECT

- Where do you stand on the issue of whether assisted suicide should be legal? Explain your answer.

hospice A humanized program committed to making the end of life as free from pain, anxiety, and depression as possible. The goals of hospice contrast with those of a hospital, which are to cure disease and prolong life.

palliative care Emphasized in hospice care; involves reducing pain and suffering and helping individuals die with dignity.

2 DEATH AND SOCIOHISTORICAL, CULTURAL CONTEXTS

Changing Historical Circumstances

Death in Different Cultures

When, where, and how people die have changed historically in the United States, and attitudes toward death vary across cultures.

Changing Historical Circumstances

We have already described one of the historical changes involving death—the increasing complexity of determining when someone is truly dead. Another historical change in death is in the age group it strikes most often. Two hundred years ago, almost one of every two children died before the age of 10, and one parent died before children grew up. Today, death occurs most often among older adults. Life expectancy has increased from 47 years for a person born in 1900 to 97 years for someone born today (U.S. Bureau of the Census, 2000). In 1900, most people died at home, cared for by their family. As our population has aged and become more mobile, more older adults die apart from their families. In the United States today, more than 80 percent of all deaths occur in institutions or hospitals. The care of a dying older person has shifted away from the family and minimized our exposure to death and its painful surroundings.

Death in Different Cultures

The ancient Greeks faced death as they faced life—openly and directly. To live a full life and die with glory was the prevailing goal of the Greeks. Individuals are more conscious of death in times of war, famine, and plague. Whereas Americans are conditioned from early in life to live as though they were immortal, in much of the world this fiction cannot be maintained. Death crowds the streets of Calcutta in daily overdisplay, as it does the scrubby villages of Africa's Sahel. Children live with the ultimate toll of malnutrition and disease, mothers lose as many babies as survive into adulthood, and it is rare that a family remains intact for many years. Even in peasant areas where life is better, and health and maturity may be reasonable expectations, the presence of dying people in the house, the large attendance at funerals, and the daily contact with aging adults prepare the young for death and provide them with guidelines on how to die. By contrast, in the United States it is not uncommon to reach adulthood without having seen someone die.

Most societies throughout history have had philosophical or religious beliefs about death, and most societies have a ritual that deals with death (Shepard, 2002) (see figure 21.1).

In most societies, death is not viewed as the end of existence—though the biological body has died, the spiritual body is believed to live on. This religious perspective is favored by most Americans as well. However, cultures differ in their perceptions of death and their reactions to it. In the Gond culture of India, death is believed to be caused by magic and demons. The members of the Gond culture react angrily to death. In the Tanala culture of Madagascar, death is believed to be caused by natural forces. The members of the Tanala culture show a much more peaceful reaction to death than their counterparts in the Gond culture. Other cultural variations in attitudes toward death include beliefs about reincarnation, which is an important aspect of the Hindu and Buddhist religions (Truitner & Truitner, 1993).

Perceptions of death vary and reflect diverse values and philosophies. Death may be seen as a punishment for one's sins, an act of atonement, or a judgment of a just

FIGURE 21.1 A Ritual Associated with Death
Family memorial day at the national cemetery in Seoul, Korea.

God. For some, death means loneliness; for others, death is a quest for happiness. For still others, death represents redemption, a relief from the trials and tribulations of the earthly world. Some embrace death and welcome it; others abhor and fear it. For those who welcome it, death may be seen as the fitting end to a fulfilled life. From this perspective, how we depart from earth is influenced by how we have lived.

In many ways, we in the United States are death avoiders and death deniers. This denial can take many forms:

- The tendency of the funeral industry to gloss over death and fashion lifelike qualities in the dead
- The adoption of euphemistic language for death—for example, *exiting, passing on, never say die,* and *good for life,* which implies forever
- The persistent search for a fountain of youth
- The rejection and isolation of the aged, who may remind us of death
- The adoption of the concept of a pleasant and rewarding afterlife, suggesting that we are immortal
- The medical community's emphasis on the prolongation of biological life rather than an emphasis on diminishing human suffering

mhhe.com/
santrockld9

Dying and Medicine in America
Culture and Death
Judaism and Death
Islam and Death
Hinduism and Death

Review and Reflect

2 **Describe the roles of sociohistorical and cultural contexts in understanding death**

REVIEW
- What are some changing sociohistorical circumstances regarding death?
- What are some variations in death across cultures?

REFLECT
- Why is the United States such a death-denying culture? How could this be changed?

3 A DEVELOPMENTAL PERSPECTIVE ON DEATH

Causes of Death and Expectations About Death

Attitudes Toward Death at Different Points in the Life Span

Do the causes of death vary across the human life span? Do we have different expectations about death as we develop through the life span? What are our attitudes toward death at different points in our development?

mhhe●com/
santrockld9

Causes of Death

Causes of Death and Expectations About Death

Although we often think of death as occurring in old age, death can occur at any point in the human life span. Death can occur during prenatal development through miscarriages or stillborn births. Death can also occur during the birth process or in the first few days after birth, which usually happens because of a birth defect or because infants have not developed adequately to sustain life outside the uterus. In chapter 5, "Physical Development in Infancy," we described *sudden infant death syndrome (SIDS),* in which infants stop breathing, usually during the night, and die without apparent cause. SIDS currently is the highest cause of infant death in the United States, with the risk highest at 4 to 6 weeks of age (American Academy of Pediatrics Task Force on Infant Sleep Position and SIDS, 2000).

In childhood, death occurs most often because of accidents or illness. Accidental death in childhood can be the consequence of such things as an automobile accident, drowning, poisoning, fire, or a fall from a high place. Major illnesses that cause death in children are heart disease, cancer, and birth defects, and it is not unusual for terminally ill children to distance themselves from their parents as they approach the final phase of their illness. The distancing may be due to the depression that many dying patients experience, or it may be a child's way of protecting parents from the overwhelming grief they will experience at the death. Most dying children know they have a terminal illness. Their developmental level, social support, and coping skills influence how well they cope with knowing they will die.

Compared to childhood, death in adolescence is more likely to occur because of motor vehicle accidents, suicide, and homicide. Many motor vehicle accidents that cause death in adolescence are alcohol-related.

Older adults are more likely to die from chronic diseases, such as heart disease and cancer, whereas younger adults are more likely to die from accidents. Older adults' diseases often incapacitate before they kill, which produces a course of dying that slowly leads to death. Of course, many young and middle-aged adults die of diseases, such as heart disease and cancer.

Younger adults who are dying often feel cheated more than do older adults who are dying (Kalish, 1987). Younger adults are more likely to feel they have not had the opportunity to do what they want to with their lives. Younger adults perceive they are losing what they might achieve; older adults perceive they are losing what they have.

Attitudes Toward Death at Different Points in the Life Span

The ages of children and adults influence the way they experience and think about death. A mature, adultlike conception of death includes an understanding that death is final and irreversible, that death represents the end of life, and that all living things die. Most researchers have found that, as children grow, they develop a more mature approach to death (Wass & Stillion, 1988).

Childhood Most researchers believe that infants do not have even a rudimentary concept of death. However, as infants develop an attachment to a caregiver, they can experience loss or separation and an accompanying anxiety. But young children do not perceive time the way adults do. Even brief separations may be experienced as total losses. For most infants, the reappearance of the caregiver provides a continuity of existence and a reduction of anxiety. We know very little about the infant's actual experiences with bereavement, although the loss of a parent, especially if the caregiver is not replaced, can negatively affect the infant's health.

Even children 3 to 5 years of age have little or no idea of what death really means. They may confuse death with sleep or ask in a puzzled way, "Why doesn't it move?" Preschool-aged children rarely get upset by the sight of a dead animal or by being told that a person has died. They believe that the dead can be brought back to life spontaneously by magic or by giving them food or medical treatment. Young children often believe that only people who want to die, or who are bad or careless, actually die. They also may blame themselves for the death of someone they know well, illogically reasoning that the event may have happened because they disobeyed the person who died.

Sometime in the middle and late childhood years more realistic perceptions of death develop. In one early investigation of children's perception of death, children 3 to 5 years of age denied that death exists, children 6 to 9 years of age believed that death exists but only happens to some people, and children 9 years of age and older recognized death's finality and universality (Nagy, 1948).

In a review of research on children's conception of death, it was concluded that children probably do not view death as universal and irreversible until about 9 years of age (Cuddy-Casey & Orvaschel, 1997). Most children under 7 do not see death as likely. Those who do, perceive it as reversible.

An expert on death and dying, Robert Kastenbaum (1997) takes a different view on developmental dimensions of death and dying. He believes that even very young children are acutely aware of and concerned about *separation* and *loss,* just as attachment theorist John Bowlby (1980) does. Kastenbaum also says that many children work hard at trying to understand death. Thus, instead of viewing young children as having illogical perceptions of death, Kastenbaum thinks a more accurate stance is to view them as having concerns about death and striving to understand it. To read further about Kastenbaum's work, see the Careers in Life-Span Development insert.

Most psychologists believe that honesty is the best strategy in discussing death with children. Treating the concept as unmentionable is thought to be an inappropriate strategy, yet most of us have grown up in a society in which death is rarely discussed. In one study, the attitudes of 30,000 young adults toward death were evaluated (Shneidman, 1973). More than 30 percent said they could not

Careers in Life-Span Development

Robert Kastenbaum, Geropsychologist

Robert Kastenbaum became interested in aging, death, and grieving in a culture—that of the United States—whose people felt uncomfortable talking about such matters. After obtaining his doctorate at the University of Southern California, he became one of the first geropsychologists (researchers who study the psychology of aging). After years of research, he became director of a hospital for the aged and introduced new programs for providing a more stimulating and supportive institutional environment. Kastenbaum helped to plan and evaluate the National Hospice Demonstration project, which confirmed the value of patient- and family-oriented care in the last phase of life. He was a cofounder of the National Caucus on Black Aging, established an interdisciplinary program in aging and human development at Arizona State University, and served for three decades as editor of the *International Journal of Aging and Human Development* and *Omega: Journal of Death and Dying.* His books include *Dorian Graying: Is Youth the Only Thing That Matters?*; *Defining Acts*; *Death as Drama*; *The Psychology of Death*; and *Death, Society, and Human Experience.*

Now retired from Arizona State University, Kastenbaum is devoting more time to writing theater pieces that deal with themes of aging and death. He wrote the words for the operas *Dorian* (premiered in New York City) and *Closing Time* (premiered in Tucson) and, most recently, the play *Tell Me About Tigers* (premiered in English and French versions in Montreal). A strong theme in both his research and his theater pieces has been how people face critical life-and-death situations and how this is affected by the values and relationships they have been developing throughout their lives.

Robert Kastenbaum, with a poster from one of the theater pieces he wrote.

mhhe ● com/
santrockld9

Discussing Death with Young Children

Grieving Children

Education About Death and Dying

**Association of Death
Education and Counseling**

recall any discussion of death during their childhood. An equal number said that, although death was discussed, the discussion took place in an uncomfortable atmosphere. Almost one of every two respondents said that the death of a grandparent was their first personal encounter with death.

In addition to honesty, what other strategies can be adopted in discussing death with children? The best response to the child's query about death might depend on the child's maturity level (Aiken, 2000). For example, the preschool child requires a less elaborate explanation than an older child. Death can be explained to preschool children in simple physical and biological terms. Actually, what young children need more than elaborate explanations of death is reassurance that they are loved and will not be abandoned. Regardless of children's age, adults should be sensitive and sympathetic, encouraging them to express their own feelings and ideas.

Adolescence   In adolescence, the prospect of death, like the prospect of aging, is regarded as a notion that is so remote that it does not have much relevance. The subject of death may be avoided, glossed over, kidded about, neutralized, and controlled by a cool, spectatorlike orientation. This perspective is typical of the adolescent's self-conscious thought; however, some adolescents do show a concern for death, both in trying to fathom its meaning and in confronting the prospect of their own demise (Baxter, Stuart, & Stewart, 1998).

Adolescents develop more abstract conceptions of death than children do. For example, adolescents describe death in terms of darkness, light, transition, or nothingness (Wenestam & Wass, 1987). They also develop religious and philosophical views about the nature of death and whether there is life after death.

You will also recall the concepts of adolescent egocentrism and personal fable from chapter 12, "Physical and Cognitive Development in Adolescence"—adolescents' preoccupation with themselves and their belief that they are invincible and unique. Thus, it is not unusual for adolescents to think that they are somehow immune to death and that death is something that happens to other people but not to them.

Adulthood   There is no evidence that a special orientation toward death develops in early adulthood. An increase in consciousness about death accompanies individuals' awareness that they are aging, which usually intensifies in middle adulthood. In our discussion of middle adulthood, we indicated that midlife is a time when adults begin to think more about how much time is left in their lives. Researchers have found that middle-aged adults actually fear death more than do young adults or older adults (Kalish & Reynolds, 1976). Older adults, though, think about death more and talk about it more in conversation with others than do middle-aged and young adults. They also have more direct experience with death as their friends and relatives become ill and die. Older adults are forced to examine the meanings of life and death more frequently than are younger adults.

In old age, one's own death may take on an appropriateness it lacked in earlier years. Some of the increased thinking and conversing about death, and an increased sense of integrity developed through a positive life review, may help older adults accept death. Older adults are less likely to have unfinished business than are younger adults. They usually do not have children who need to be guided to maturity, their spouses are more likely to be dead, and they are less likely to have work-related projects that require completion. Lacking such anticipations, death may be less emotionally painful to them. Even among older adults, however, attitudes toward death are sometimes as individualized as the people holding them. One 82-year-old woman declared that she had lived her life and was now ready to see it come to an end. Another 82-year-old woman declared that death would be a regrettable interruption of her participation in activities and relationships.

Review and Reflect

3 **Discuss death and attitudes about it at different points in development**

REVIEW

- What are some developmental changes in the causes of death and expectations for death?
- What are some attitudes about death at different points in development?

REFLECT

- What is your current attitude about death? Has it changed since you were an adolescent? If so, how?

4 FACING ONE'S OWN DEATH

- **Kübler-Ross' Stages of Dying**
- **Perceived Control and Denial**
- **The Contexts in Which People Die**

Knowledge of death's inevitability permits us to establish priorities and structure our time accordingly. As we age, these priorities and structurings change in recognition of diminishing future time. Values concerning the most important uses of time also change. For example, when asked how they would spend six remaining months of life, younger adults described such activities as traveling and accomplishing things they previously had not done; older adults described more inner-focused activities—contemplation and meditation, for example (Kalish & Reynolds, 1976).

Most dying individuals want an opportunity to make some decisions regarding their own life and death (Kastenbaum, 2000). Some individuals want to complete unfinished business; they want time to resolve problems and conflicts and to put their affairs in order. Might there be a sequence of stages we go through as we face death?

Kübler-Ross' Stages of Dying

Elisabeth Kübler-Ross (1969) divided the behavior and thinking of dying persons into five stages: denial and isolation, anger, bargaining, depression, and acceptance.

Denial and isolation is Kübler-Ross' first stage of dying, in which the person denies that death is really going to take place. The person may say, "No, it can't be me. It's not possible." This is a common reaction to terminal illness. However, denial is usually only a temporary defense and is eventually replaced with increased awareness when the person is confronted with such matters as financial considerations, unfinished business, and worry about surviving family members.

Anger is Kübler-Ross' second stage of dying, in which the dying person recognizes that denial can no longer be maintained. Denial often gives way to anger, resentment, rage, and envy. The dying person's question is, "Why me?" At this point, the person becomes increasingly difficult to care for as anger may become displaced and projected onto physicians, nurses, family members, and even God. The realization of loss is great, and those who symbolize life, energy, and competent functioning are especially salient targets of the dying person's resentment and jealousy.

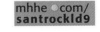

mhhe●com/
santrockld9

Kübler-Ross on Dying

denial and isolation Kübler-Ross' first stage of dying, in which the dying person denies that she or he is really going to die.

anger Kübler-Ross' second stage of dying, in which the dying person's denial gives way to anger, resentment, rage, and envy.

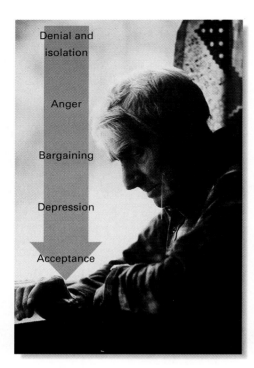

FIGURE 21.2 Kübler-Ross' Stages of Dying

According to Elisabeth Kübler-Ross, we go through five stages of dying: denial and isolation, anger, bargaining, depression, and acceptance. *Does everyone go through these stages, or go through them in the same order? Explain.*

bargaining Kübler-Ross' third stage of dying, in which the dying person develops the hope that death can somehow be postponed.

depression Kübler-Ross' fourth stage of dying, in which the dying person comes to accept the certainty of her or his death. A period of depression or preparatory grief may appear.

acceptance Kübler-Ross' fifth stage of dying, in which the dying person develops a sense of peace, an acceptance of her or his fate, and, in many cases, a desire to be left alone.

Bargaining is Kübler-Ross' third stage of dying, in which the person develops the hope that death can somehow be postponed or delayed. Some persons enter into a bargaining or negotiation—often with God—as they try to delay their death. Psychologically, the person is saying, "Yes, me, but . . ." In exchange for a few more days, weeks, or months of life, the person promises to lead a reformed life dedicated to God or to the service of others.

Depression is Kübler-Ross' fourth stage of dying, in which the dying person comes to accept the certainty of death. At this point, there is a period of depression or preparatory grief may appear. The dying person may become silent, refuse visitors, and spend much of the time crying or grieving. This behavior should be perceived as normal in this circumstance and is actually an effort to disconnect the self from all love objects. Attempts to cheer up the dying person at this stage should be discouraged, says Kübler-Ross, because the dying person has a need to contemplate impending death.

Acceptance is Kübler-Ross' fifth stage of dying, in which the person develops a sense of peace, an acceptance of one's fate, and in many cases, a desire to be left alone. In this stage, feelings and physical pain may be virtually absent. Kübler-Ross describes this fifth stage as the end of the dying struggle, the final resting stage before death. A summary of Kübler-Ross' dying stages is presented in figure 21.2.

What is the current evaluation of Kübler-Ross' approach? According to psychology death expert Robert Kastenbaum (1998, 2000) there are some problems with Kübler-Ross' approach:

- The existence of the five-stage sequence has not been demonstrated by either Kübler-Ross or independent research.
- The stage interpretation neglected the patients' total life situations, including relationship support, specific effects of illness, family obligations, and institutional climate in which they were interviewed.

Because of the criticisms of Kübler-Ross' stages of dying, some psychologists prefer to describe them not as stages but rather as potential reactions to dying. At any one moment, a number of emotions may wax and wane. Hope, disbelief, bewilderment, anger, and acceptance may come and go as individuals try to make sense of what is happening to them. However, we should not forget Kübler-Ross' pioneering efforts:

- Her contribution was important in calling attention to people who are attempting to cope with life-threatening illnesses.
- She did much to encourage giving needed attention to the quality of life for dying persons and their families.

In facing their own death, some individuals struggle until the end, desperately trying to hang on to their lives. Acceptance of death never comes for them. Some psychologists believe that the harder individuals fight to avoid the inevitable death they face and the more they deny it, the more difficulty they will have in dying peacefully and in a dignified way; other psychologists argue that not confronting death until the end may be adaptive for some individuals (Lifton, 1977).

Perceived Control and Denial

Perceived control and denial may work together as an adaptive strategy for some older adults who face death. When individuals are led to believe they can influence and control events—such as prolonging their lives—they may become more alert and cheerful. Remember from our discussion in chapter 18 that giving nursing home residents options for control improved their attitudes and increased their longevity (Rodin & Langer, 1977).

Denial also may be a fruitful way for some individuals to approach death. It is not unusual for dying individuals to deny death right up until the time they die. Life without hope represents learned helplessness in its most extreme form. Denial can protect us from the torturous feeling that we are going to die.

Denial can be adaptive or maladaptive. Denial can be used to avoid the destructive impact of shock by delaying the necessity of dealing with one's death. Denial can insulate the individual from having to cope with intense feelings of anger and hurt; however, if denial keeps us from having a life-saving operation, it clearly is maladaptive. Denial is neither good nor bad; its adaptive qualities need to be evaluated on an individual basis.

The Contexts in Which People Die

For dying individuals, the context in which they die is important. More than 50 percent of Americans die in hospitals, and nearly 20 percent die in nursing homes. For some people, their final days unfortunately are spent in isolation and fear (Clay, 1997).

Hospitals offer several important advantages to the dying individual—professional staff members are readily available, and the medical technology present may prolong life, for example, yet a hospital may not be the best place for many people to die. Most individuals say they would rather die at home (Kalish & Reynolds, 1976). Many feel, however, that they will be a burden at home, that there is limited space there, and that dying at home may alter prior relationships such as being cared for by one's children. Individuals who are facing death also worry about the competency and availability of emergency medical treatment if they remain at home. As we saw earlier in the chapter, an increasing number of people choose to die in the humane atmosphere of a hospice.

Review and Reflect

4 **Explain the psychological aspects involved in facing one's own death and the contexts in which people die**

REVIEW

- What are Kübler-Ross' five stages of dying? What conclusions can be reached about them?
- What roles do perceived control and denial play in facing one's own death?
- What are the contexts in which people die?

REFLECT

- How do you think you will psychologically handle facing your own death?

5 COPING WITH THE DEATH OF SOMEONE ELSE

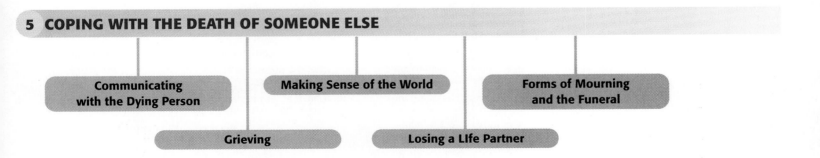

Communicating with the Dying Person   Making Sense of the World   Forms of Mourning and the Funeral

Grieving   Losing a Life Partner

Loss can come in many forms in our lives—divorce, a pet's death, loss of a job—but no loss is greater than that which comes through the death of someone we love and care for—a parent, sibling, spouse, relative, or friend. In the ratings of life's stresses that require the most adjustment, death of a spouse is given the highest number. How should we communicate with a dying individual? How do we cope with the death of someone we love?

Communicating with the Dying Person

Most psychologists believe that it is best for dying individuals to know that they are dying and that significant others know they are dying so they can interact and communicate with each other on the basis of this mutual knowledge. What are some of the advantages of this open awareness context for the dying individual? Four such advantages are: Dying individuals can close their lives in accord with their own ideas about proper dying; dying individuals may be able to complete some plans and projects, can make arrangements for survivors, and can participate in decisions about a funeral and burial; dying individuals have the opportunity to reminisce, to converse with others who have been important individuals in their life, and to end life conscious of what life has been like; and dying individuals have more understanding of what is happening within their bodies and what the medical staff is doing to them (Kalish, 1981).

In addition to an open communication system, what are some other suggestions for conversing with a dying individual? Some experts believe that conversation should not focus on mental pathology or preparation for death but should focus on strengths of the individual and preparation for the remainder of life. Since external accomplishments are not possible, communication should be directed more at internal growth. Keep in mind also that caring does not have to come from a mental health professional only; a concerned nurse, an attentive physician, a sensitive spouse, or an intimate friend can provide an important support system for a dying individual (De-Spelder & Strickland, 1996). Figure 21.3 presents some effective strategies for communicating with a dying person.

Grieving

Our exploration of grief focuses on dimensions of grieving, as well as cultural diversity in healthy grieving.

mhhe●com/ santrockld9

Exploring Death and Dying

Death, Dying, and Grieving

Death and Dying Resources

Death and Dying in America

1. Establish your presence, be at the same eye level; don't be afraid to touch the dying person—dying individuals are often starved for human touch.

2. Eliminate distraction—for example, ask if it is okay to turn off the TV. Realize that excessive small talk can be a distraction.

3. Dying individuals who are very frail often have little energy. If the dying person you are visiting is very frail, you may not want to visit for very long.

4. Don't insist that the dying person feel acceptance about death, if the dying person wants to deny the reality of the situation; on the other hand, don't insist on denial if the dying individual indicates acceptance.

5. Allow the dying person to express guilt or anger; encourage the expression of feelings.

6. Don't be afraid to ask the person what the prognosis (expected outcome) is for their illness. Discuss alternatives, unfinished business.

7. Sometimes dying individuals don't have access to certain others; ask the dying person if there is anyone he or she would like to see that you can contact.

8. Encourage the dying individual to reminisce, especially if you have memories in common.

9. Talk with the individual when she or he wishes to talk. If this is impossible, make an appointment and keep it.

10. Express your regard for the dying individual. Don't be afraid to express love, and don't be afraid to say good-bye.

FIGURE 21.3 Effective Strategies for Communicating with a Dying Person

Dimensions of Grieving **Grief** is the emotional numbness, disbelief, separation anxiety, despair, sadness, and loneliness that accompany the loss of someone we love. Grief is not a simple emotional state but rather a complex, evolving process with multiple dimensions (Bruce, 2002; Jacobs & others, 1987). In this view, pining for the lost person is one important dimension. Pining or yearning reflects an intermittent, recurrent wish or need to recover the lost person. Another important dimension of grief is separation anxiety, which not only includes pining and preoccupation with thoughts of the deceased person but also focuses on places and things associated with the deceased, as well as crying or sighing as a type of suppressed cry. Another dimension of grief is the typical immediate reaction to a loss discussed earlier—emotional blunting, numbness, disbelief, and outbursts of panic or extreme tearfulness. Yet another dimension of grief involves despair and sadness, which include a sense of hopelessness and defeat, depressive symptoms, apathy, loss of meaning for activities that used to involve the person who is gone, and growing desolation (Giddens & Giddens, 2000; Ringdal & others, 2001). This dimension does not represent a clear-cut stage but, rather, occurs repeatedly in one context or another shortly after a loss. Nonetheless, as time passes, pining and protest over the loss tend to diminish, although episodes of depression and apathy may remain or increase. The sense of separation anxiety and loss may continue to the end of one's life, but most of us emerge from grief's tears, turning our attention once again to productive tasks and regaining a more positive view of life (Powers & Wampold, 1994).

Researchers have found that the grieving process is more like a roller-coaster ride than an orderly progression of stages with clear-cut time frames (Lund, 1996). The ups and downs of grief often involve rapidly changing emotions, meeting the challenges of learning new skills, detecting personal weaknesses and limitations, creating new patterns of behavior, and forming new friendships and relationships (Holland, 2002). Fortunately, for most individuals the roller-coaster dimensions of grief become more manageable over time, with fewer abrupt highs and lows. But many grieving spouses still report that even though time has brought them some healing, they have never gotten over the loss. They have just learned to live with it.

Long-term grief is sometimes masked and can predispose individuals to become depressed and even suicidal (Davis, 2001; Kastenbaum, 1998, 2000). Good family communication can help reduce the incidence of depression and suicidal thoughts. For example, in one study, family members who communicated poorly with each other had more negative grief reactions six months later than those who communicated effectively with each other just after the loss of a family member (Schoka & Hayslip, 1999).

Grief counselors help individuals cope with their feelings of losing someone close to them (Mitchell & Catron, 2002; Worden, 2002). To read about the work of one grief counselor, see the Careers in Life-Span Development insert.

Cultural Diversity in Healthy Grieving Some orientations on grieving emphasize the importance of breaking bonds with the deceased and the return of survivors to autonomous lifestyles. People who persist in holding on to the deceased are believed to be in need of therapy. Recent conceptual and research analyses, however, have cast

Careers in Life-Span Development

Sara Wheeler, Certified College Grief Counselor

Sara Wheeler has a doctorate of science in nursing and is a certified grief counselor ◀▥▥ p. 35. She teaches in the College of Nursing at the University of Illinois, Urbana campus, and also conducts grief counseling. She is especially concerned with helping families cope with their losses and strategies that nurses can use to provide support, empathy, information, and guidance.

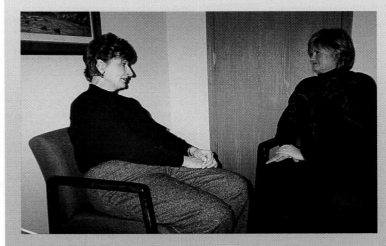

Sara Wheeler (*right*), conducting grief counseling.

It is sweet to mingle tears with tears; griefs, where they wound in solitude, wound more deeply.

—Seneca
Roman Poet, 1st Century

grief The emotional numbness, disbelief, separation anxiety, despair, sadness, and loneliness that accompany the loss of someone we love.

mhhe●com/
santrockld9

Grieving and the Loss of a Child
The Grieving Process
Grief Theories
Exploring Grief
Grief and Bereavement
Bereavement Resources

doubt on whether this uniform recommendation is always the best therapeutic advice (Reisman, 2001; Stroebe & others, 1992).

Analyses of non-Western cultures suggest that beliefs about continuing bonds with the deceased vary extensively. In contrast with Western beliefs, maintenance of ties with the deceased is accepted and sustained in the religious rituals of Japan. In the Hopi of Arizona, the deceased are forgotten as quickly as possible and life is carried on as usual. Their funeral ritual concludes with a breakoff between mortals and spirits. The diversity of grieving is nowhere more clear than in two Muslim societies—one in Egypt, the other in Bali. In Egypt, the bereaved are encouraged to dwell at length on their grief, surrounded by others who relate similarly tragic accounts and express their own sorrow. By contrast, in Bali, the bereaved are encouraged to laugh and be joyful rather than be sad.

In a longitudinal study of bereavement in the Netherlands, many people tended to maintain contact with the deceased, despite the contemporary emphasis on breaking such bonds (Stroebe & Stroebe, 1991). Many of the widowed persons were not planning a major break with their pasts, but rather were integrating the loss experience into their lifestyles and trying to carry on much as before the death of a loved one. Well over half "consulted" the deceased when having to make a decision. One widow said that she gained considerable comfort from knowing that this is exactly what her deceased husband would have wanted her to do. Similar findings have recently been reported regarding American widows (Shuchter & Zisook, 1993). A similar picture emerges in another recent study of parents of sons who died in two Israeli wars, 13 and 4 years earlier (Rubin, 1995). Even many years after the death of their son, the Israeli parents showed a strong involvement with and valuation of the son. They especially idealized the lost son in ways that were not present in the descriptions by a control group of parents of sons who had recently left home.

In summary, diverse groups of people grieve in a variety of ways. The diverse grieving patterns are culturally embedded practices (Witzum, Malkinson, & Rubin, 2001). Thus, there is no one right, ideal way to grieve. There are many different ways

How might grieving vary across individuals and cultures?

to feel about a deceased person and no set series of stages that the bereaved must pass through to become well adjusted. The stoic widower may need to cry out over his loss at times. The weeping widow may need to put her husband's wishes aside as she becomes the financial manager of her estate. What is needed is an understanding that healthy coping with the death of a loved one involves growth, flexibility, and appropriateness within a cultural context. This orientation is just beginning to appear in the fields of bereavement research and clinical practice.

Making Sense of the World

One beneficial aspect of grieving is that it stimulates many individuals to try to make sense of their world (Kalish, 1981, 1987). A common occurrence is to go over again and again all of the events that led up to the death. In the days and weeks after the death, the closest family members share experiences with each other, sometimes reminiscing over family experiences. In one recent study, women who became widowed in midlife were challenged by the crisis of their husband's death to examine meaningful directions for their lives (Danfroth & Glass, 2001).

Each individual may offer a piece of death's puzzle. "When I saw him last Saturday, he looked as though he were rallying," says one family member. "Do you think it might have had something to do with his sister's illness?" remarks another. "I doubt it, but I heard from an aide that he fell going to the bathroom that morning," comments yet another. "That explains the bruise on his elbow," says the first individual. "No wonder he told me that he was angry because he could not seem to do anything right," chimes in a fourth family member. So it goes in the attempt to understand why someone who was rallying on Saturday was dead on Wednesday.

When a death is caused by an accident or a disaster, the effort to make sense of it is pursued more vigorously. As added pieces of news come trickling in, they are integrated into the puzzle. The bereaved want to put the death into a perspective that they can understand—divine intervention, a curse from a neighboring tribe, a logical sequence of cause and effect, or whatever it may be.

Losing a Life Partner

Those left behind after the death of an intimate partner suffer profound grief and often endure financial loss, loneliness, increased physical illness, and psychological disorders, including depression (Hungerford, 2001; Stroebe & others, 1998). How they cope with the crisis varies considerably (Fry, 1999). Widows outnumber widowers by the ratio of 5 to 1, because women live longer than men, because women tend to marry men older than themselves, and because a widowed man is more likely to remarry. Widowed women are probably the poorest group in America, despite the myth of huge insurance settlements. One recent study found that most widows in the United States and Germany experienced a decline in living standards in the year following their husband's death, and many fell into poverty when they became widows (Hungerford, 2001).

Many widows are lonely. The poorer and less educated they are, the lonelier they tend to be. The bereaved are also at increased risk for many health problems, including death (Corr, Nable, & Corr, 2000; Fredman, Daly, & Lazur, 1995).

Optimal adjustment after a death depends on several factors (Leming & Dickinson, 2002). Women do better than men largely because, in our society, women are responsible for the emotional life of a couple, whereas men usually manage the finances and material goods (Fry, 2001). Thus, women have better networks of friends, closer relationships with relatives, and experience in taking care of themselves psychologically (Antonucci & others, 2001; Martin-Matthews, 1996). Older widows do better than younger widows, perhaps because the death of a partner is more expected for older women. For their part, widowers usually have more money than widows do, and they are much more likely to remarry (DiGiulio, 1989).

mhhe.com/santrockld9
Widows/Widowers
WidowNet

The Family and the Community in Mourning—
The Amish and Traditional Judaism

The family and the community have important roles in mourning in some cultures. Two of those cultures are the Amish and traditional Judaism (Worthington, 1989).

The Amish are a conservative Protestant sect with approximately 80,000 members in the United States, Ontario, and several small settlements in South and Central America. The Amish live in a family-oriented society in which family and community support are essential for survival. Today, they live at the same unhurried pace as that of their ancestors, using horses instead of cars and facing death with the same steadfast faith as their forebears. At the time of death, close neighbors assume the responsibility of notifying others of the death. The Amish community handles virtually all aspects of the funeral. Family members dress the body in white garments—the wearing of white clothes signifies the high ceremonial emphasis on death as a final rite of passage to a new and better life. The funeral service is held in a barn in warmer months and in a house during colder months. Calm acceptance of death, influenced by a deep religious faith, is an integral part of the Amish culture. Following the funeral, a high level of support is given to the bereaved family for at least a year. Visits to the family, special scrapbooks and handmade items for the family, new work projects started for the widow, and quilting days that combine fellowship and productivity are among the supports given to the bereaved family.

The family and community also have specific and important roles in mourning in traditional Judaism. The program of mourning is divided into graduated time periods, each with its appropriate practices. The observance of these practices is required of the spouse and the immediate blood relatives of the deceased. The first period is *aninut*, the period between death and burial. The next two periods make up *avelut*, or mourning proper. The first of these is *shivah*, a period of 7 days, which commences with the burial. This is followed by *sheloshim*, the 30-day period following the burial, including shivah. At the end of sheloshim, the mourning

process is considered over for all but one's parents. In this case, mourning continues for 11 months, although observances are minimal. The 7-day period of the shivah is especially important in mourning in traditional Judaism. The Jewish community provides considerable support during the mourning process. The mourners, sitting together as a group through an extended period, have an opportunity to project their feelings to the group as a whole. Visits from others during shivah may help the mourner deal with feelings of guilt. After shivah, the mourner is encouraged to resume normal social interaction. In short, it is customary for the mourners to walk together a short distance as a symbol of their return to society. In its entirety, the elaborate mourning system of traditional Judaism is designed to promote personal growth and to reintegrate the individual into the community.

An Amish funeral procession in Pennsylvania. The funeral service is held in the barn in the warmer months and in the house during the colder months. Following the funeral, a high level of support is given to the bereaved family for at least a year.

For either widows or widowers, social support helps them adjust to the death of a spouse (Boerner & Wortman, 1998; Kastenbaum, 1998). The Widow-to-Widow program, begun in the 1960s, provides support for newly widowed women. Its objective is to prevent the potentially negative effects of the loss. Volunteer widows reach out to other widows, introducing them to others who may have similar problems, leading group discussions, and organizing social activities. The program has been adopted by the American Association of Retired Persons and disseminated throughout the United States as the Widowed Person's Service. The model has since been adopted by numerous community organizations to provide support for those going through a difficult life transition that will confront the vast majority of us.

One recent study found that psychological and religious factors—such as personal meaning, optimism, the importance of religion, and access to religious support—were related to the psychological well-being of older adults following the loss of a spouse (Fry, 2001). Other studies have indicated that religiosity and coping skills are related to well-being following the loss of a spouse in late adulthood (Fry, 1999).

Forms of Mourning and the Funeral

In some cultures, a ceremonial meal is held; in others, a black armband is worn for one year following a death; and so on. Cultures vary in how they practice mourning (Adamolekun, 2001).

The funeral is an important aspect of mourning in many cultures. One consideration involves what to do with the body. Approximately 80 percent of corpses are disposed of by burial, the remaining 20 percent by cremation (Aiken, 2000; Cremation Association of America, 2000). Cremation is more popular in the Pacific region of the United States, less popular in the South. Cremation also is more popular in Canada than in the United States and most popular of all in Japan and many other Asian countries.

In one recent study, bereaved individuals who were personally religious derived more psychological benefits from a funeral, participated more actively in the rituals, and adjusted more positively to the loss (Hayslip, Edmondson, & Guarnaccia, 1999).

The funeral industry has been the source of controversy in recent years. Funeral directors and their supporters argue that the funeral provides a form of closure to the relationship with the deceased, especially when there is an open casket. Their dissenters, however, stress that funeral directors are just trying to make money; they further argue that the art of embalming is grotesque.

One way to avoid being exploited because bereavement has made us vulnerable to being talked into purchasing more expensive funeral arrangements is to purchase them in advance. However, most of us do not follow this procedure. In one survey, only 24 percent of individuals 60 and over had made any funeral arrangements (Kalish & Reynolds, 1976).

Some cultures have elaborate mourning systems. To learn about two cultures with extensive mourning systems, see the Sociocultural Worlds of Development box.

The art of living well and the art of dying well are one.
—EPICURUS
Greek Philosopher, 3rd Century B.C.

mhhe●com/
santrockld9

Buddhist Funeral Rites

Review and Reflect

5 **Identify ways to cope with the death of another person**

REVIEW

- What are some good strategies for communicating with a dying person?
- What is the nature of grieving?
- How is making sense of the world a beneficial outcome of grieving?
- What are some characteristics and outcomes of losing a life partner?
- What are some forms of mourning? What is the nature of the funeral?

REFLECT

- Is there a best or worst way to grieve? Explain.

Reach Your Learning Goals

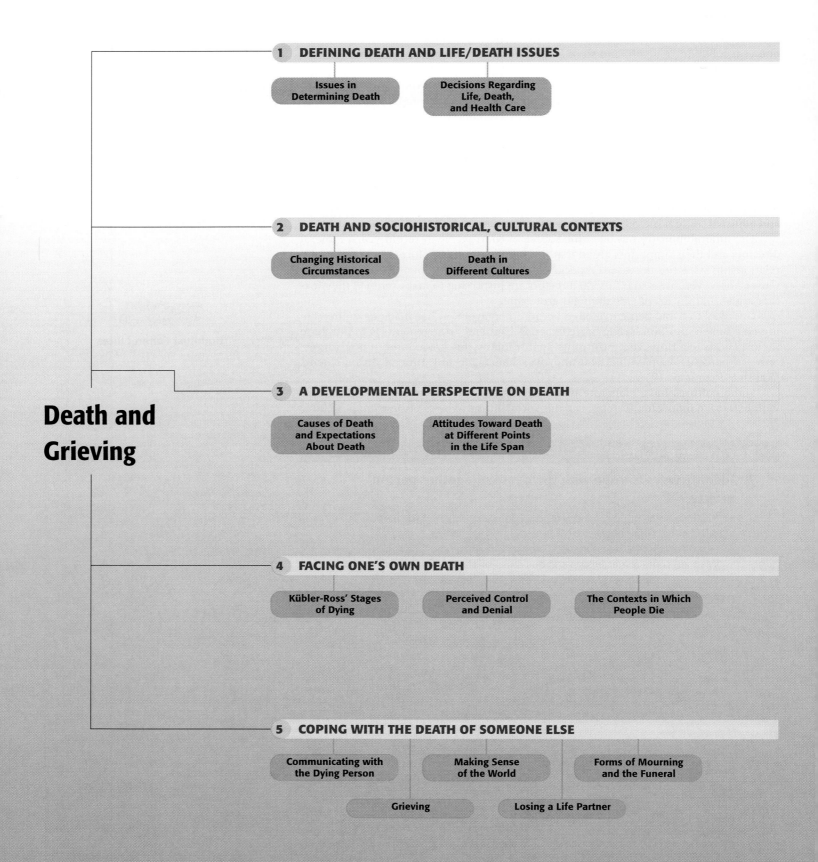

Death and Grieving

1 DEFINING DEATH AND LIFE/DEATH ISSUES

Issues in Determining Death

Decisions Regarding Life, Death, and Health Care

2 DEATH AND SOCIOHISTORICAL, CULTURAL CONTEXTS

Changing Historical Circumstances

Death in Different Cultures

3 A DEVELOPMENTAL PERSPECTIVE ON DEATH

Causes of Death and Expectations About Death

Attitudes Toward Death at Different Points in the Life Span

4 FACING ONE'S OWN DEATH

Kübler-Ross' Stages of Dying

Perceived Control and Denial

The Contexts in Which People Die

5 COPING WITH THE DEATH OF SOMEONE ELSE

Communicating with the Dying Person

Making Sense of the World

Forms of Mourning and the Funeral

Grieving

Losing a Life Partner

Summary

1 Evaluate issues in determining death and decisions regarding death

- Twenty-five years ago, determining if someone was dead was simpler than it is today. Brain death is a neurological definition of death, which states that a person is brain dead when all electrical activity of the brain has ceased for a specified period of time. Medical experts debate whether this should mean the higher and lower brain functions or just the higher cortical functions.
- The Natural Death Act and advanced directive are increasingly used. Euthanasia is the act of painlessly ending the life of a person who is suffering from an incurable disease or disability. Distinctions are made between active and passive euthanasia. The need for more humanized care for the dying person includes the development of hospice programs. Hospice care has a palliative care emphasis.

2 Describe the roles of sociohistorical and cultural contexts in understanding death

- When, where, and why people die have changed historically. Today, death occurs most often among older adults. More than 80 percent of all deaths in the United States now occur in a hospital or an institution. Our exposure to death in the family has been minimized.
- Most societies throughout history have had philosophical or religious beliefs about death, and most societies have rituals that deal with death. Most cultures do not view death as the end of existence—spiritual life is thought to continue. The United States has been described as a death-denying and death-avoiding culture.

3 Discuss death and attitudes about it at different points in development

- Although death is more likely to occur in late adulthood, death can come at any point in development. The deaths of some persons, especially children and younger adults, are often perceived to be more tragic than those of others, such as very old adults, who have had an opportunity to live a long life. In children and younger adults, death is more likely to occur because of accidents but in older adults is more likely to occur because of chronic diseases.
- Infants do not have a concept of death. Preschool children also have little concept of death, often showing little or no upset at the sight of a dead animal or person. Preschool children sometimes blame themselves for a person's death. In the elementary school years, children develop a more realistic orientation toward death. Most psychologists believe honesty is the best strategy for helping children cope with death. Death may be glossed over in adolescence. Adolescents have more abstract, philosophical views of death than children do. There is no evidence that a special orientation toward death emerges in early adulthood. Middle adulthood is a time when adults show a heightened consciousness about death and death anxiety. Older adults often show less death anxiety than middle-aged adults, but older adults experience and converse about death more. Attitudes about death may vary considerably among adults of any age.

4 Explain the psychological aspects involved in facing one's own death and the contexts in which people die

- Kübler-Ross proposed five stages: denial and isolation, anger, bargaining, depression, and acceptance. Not all individuals go through the same sequence. Some individuals may struggle to the end.
- Perceived control and denial may work together as an adaptive orientation for the dying individual. Denial can be adaptive or maladaptive, depending on the circumstance.
- Most deaths in the United States occur in hospitals; this has advantages and disadvantages. Most individuals say they would rather die at home, but they worry that they will be a burden and they worry about the lack of medical care.

5 Identify ways to cope with the death of another person

- Most psychologists recommend an open communication system; this system should not dwell on pathology or preparation for death but should emphasize the dying person's strengths.
- Grief is the emotional numbness, disbelief, separation, anxiety, despair, sadness, and loneliness that accompany the loss of someone we love. Grief is multidimensional and in some cases may last for years. There are cultural variations in grieving.
- The grieving process may stimulate individuals to strive to make sense out of their world; each individual may contribute a piece to death's puzzle.
- Usually the most difficult loss is the death of a spouse. The bereaved are at risk for many health problems. Social support benefits widows and widowers.
- Forms of mourning vary across cultures. An important aspect of mourning in many cultures is the funeral. In recent years, the funeral industry has been the focus of controversy.

Key Terms

Key People

Taking It to the Net

1. Herman's mother has Parkinson's disease. He wants her to make some difficult end-of-life decisions while she still can. He and his mother discuss the options of a health-care power of attorney, a Living Will, and/or a DNR. What are the different purposes of these documents and what is the family's involvement in these decisions?

2. Letitia, a recent widow, is interested in starting a program for widowed women in her community. In order to start the process to request funding, she is exploring her options in foundation grants. As part of this process, she will need to investigate the available data on the nature and extent of widowhood in the United States today, including the age, sex, and socioeconomic status of widowed people. What type of information is available to her and her group?

3. Ellen has taken care of her mother throughout her long, lingering illness that has just been diagnosed as terminal. Ellen does not think she alone can provide the type of care necessary to take care of her mother in her final weeks. Her neighbor suggested she contact the local hospice. What does a hospice offer to families in this situation and how is it different from a nursing home?

Connect to www.mhhe.com/santrockld9 to research the answers and complete these exercises.

E-Learning Tools

To help you master the material in this chapter, you'll find a number of valuable study tools on the Student CD-ROM that accompanies this book. In addition, visit the Online Learning Center for *Life-Span Development*, ninth edition, where you'll find these valuable resources for chapter 21, "Death and Grieving."

- Use the self-assessment, *How Much Anxiety Do You Have About Death*, to explore your own feelings about the end of life.
- Build your decision-making skills by trying your hand at the parenting and education "Scenarios."

The Journey of Life

We have come to the end of this book. I leave you with the following montage of thoughts and images that convey the power, complexity, and beauty of human development.

Life-Span Development has been about life's rhythm and meaning, about turning mystery into understanding, and about weaving together a portrait of who we were, are, and will be. From the first cries of a newborn baby to the final prayers of an elderly adult, we arrive, laugh, grow, play, seek, work, question, hope, mate, quarrel, sing, achieve, and care.

NOTE: The descriptions in the Epilogue are based on quotations presented throughout the text.

The rhythm and meaning of human development involve beginnings, when questions of whence and whither, when and how, are asked. How from so simple a beginning do endless forms develop and grow and mature? What was this organism, what is it now, and what will it become? Birth's fragile moment arrives, when the newborn is on a threshold between two worlds.

As newborns, we were not empty-headed organisms. We cried, kicked, coughed, sucked, saw, heard, and tasted. We slept a lot, and occasionally we smiled, although the meaning of our first smiles was not entirely clear. We crawled and then we walked, a journey of a thousand miles beginning with a single step. With each forward step we left some ghost of ourselves behind. Sometimes we conformed, sometimes others conformed to us. Our development was a continuous creation of more complex forms, and our helpless kind demanded the meeting eyes of love. We split the universe into two halves: "me" and "not me." And we juggled the need to curb our own will with becoming what we could will freely.

*I*n early childhood, our greatest untold poem was being only 4 years old. We skipped, played, and ran all the day long, never in our lives so busy, busy becoming something we had not quite grasped yet. Who knew our thoughts, which we worked up into small mythologies all our own. While our thoughts and feelings took wings, the blossoms of our heart no wind could touch. Our small world widened as we discovered new refuges and new people. When we said "I," we meant something totally unique, not to be confused with any other.

I n middle and late childhood, we were on a different plane, belonging to a generation and a feeling properly our own. It is the wisdom of human development that at no other time are we more ready to learn than at the end of early childhood's period of expansive imagination. Our thirst was to know and to understand. Our parents continued to cradle our lives, but our growth was also being shaped by successive choirs of friends. We did not think much about the future or the past, but enjoyed the present.

In no order of things was adolescence the simple time of life for us. We clothed ourselves with rainbows and went "brave as the zodiac," flashing from one end of the world to the other. We tried on one face after another, searching for a face of our own. We wanted our parents to understand us and hoped they would give us the privilege of understanding them. We wanted to fly but found that first we had to learn to stand and walk and climb and dance. In our most pimply and awkward moments we became acquainted with sex. We played furiously at adult games but were confined to a society of our own peers. Our generation was the fragile cable by which the best and the worst of our parents' generation was transmitted to the present. In the end, there were but two lasting bequests our parents could leave us—one being roots, the other wings.

Early adulthood is a time for work and a time for love, sometimes leaving little time for anything else. For some of us, finding our place in adult society and committing to a more stable life take longer than we imagine. We still ask ourselves who we are and wonder if it isn't enough just to be. Our dreams continue and our thoughts are bold, but at some point we become more pragmatic. Sex and love are powerful passions in our lives—at times angels of light, at others fiends of torment. And we possibly will never know the love of our parents until we become parents ourselves.

In middle adulthood, what we have been forms what we will be. For some of us, middle age is such a foggy place, a time when we need to discover what we are running from and to and why. We compare our life with what we vowed to make it. In middle age, more time stretches before us and some evaluations have to be made, however reluctantly. As the young/old polarity greets us with a special force, we need to join the daring of youth with the discipline of age in a way that does justice to both. As middle-aged adults, we come to sense that the generations of living things pass in a short while and, like runners, hand on the torch of life.

*T*he rhythm and meaning of human development eventually wend their way to late adulthood, when each of us stands alone at the heart of the earth and "suddenly it is evening." We shed the leaves of youth and are stripped by the winds of time down to the truth. We learn that life is lived forward but understood backward. We trace the connection between the end and the beginning of life and try to figure out what this whole show is about before it is over. Ultimately, we come to know that we are what survives of us.

O ur life ultimately ends—when we approach life's grave sustained and soothed with unfaltering trust or rave at the close of day; when, at last, years steal us from ourselves; and when we are linked to our children's children's children by an invisible cable that runs from age to age.

I hope that this book has been not only a window to the life span of *Homo sapiens* but also a window to your own personal journey in life.

Glossary

A

acceptance Kübler-Ross' fifth stage of dying, in which the dying person develops a sense of peace, an acceptance of her or his fate, and, in many cases, a desire to be left alone. 664

accommodation Occurs when individuals adjust to new information. 48

acquired immune deficiency syndrome (AIDS) A sexually transmitted disease caused by the HIV virus, which destroys the body's immune system. 456

active (niche-picking) genotype environment correlations Correlations that exist when children seek out environments they find compatible and stimulating. 102

active euthanasia Death induced deliberately, as by injecting a lethal dose of a drug. 656

activity theory The theory that the more active and involved older adults are, the more likely they are to be satisfied with their lives. 627

addiction A pattern of behavior characterized by an overwhelming involvement with using a drug and securing its supply. 452

adolescent egocentrism The heightened self-consciousness of adolescents. 388

adoption study A study in which investigators seek to discover whether, in behavior and psychological characteristics, adopted children are more like their adoptive parents, who provided a home environment, or more like their biological parents, who contributed their heredity. Another form of the adoption study is to compare adoptive and biological siblings. 88

aerobic exercise Sustained exercise (such as jogging, swimming, or cycling) that stimulates heart and lung activity. 449

affectionate love In this type of love (also called "companionate love"), an individual desires to have the other person near and has a deep, caring affection for the other person. 485

affordances Opportunities for interaction offered by objects that are necessary to perform functional activities. 169

ageism Prejudice against other people because of their age, especially prejudice against older adults. 633

altruism Unselfish interest in helping another person. 344

Alzheimer's disease A progressive, irreversible brain disorder characterized by a gradual deterioration of memory, reasoning, language, and eventually physical function. 612

amnion The life-support system that is a bag or envelope that contains a clear fluid in which the developing embryo floats. 114

androgyny The presence of positive masculine and feminine characteristics in the same individual. 347

anger cry A cry similar to the basic cry, with more excess air forced through the vocal chords. 207

anger Kübler-Ross' second stage of dying, in which the dying person's denial gives way to anger, resentment, rage, and envy. 663

animism The belief that inanimate objects have "lifelike" qualities and are capable of action. 243

anorexia nervosa An eating disorder that involves the relentless pursuit of thinness through starvation. 384

Apgar Scale A widely used method to assess the health of newborns at one and five minutes after birth. The Apgar Scale evaluates infants' heart rate, respiratory effort, muscle tone, body color, and reflex irritability. 134

arthritis Inflammation of the joints that is accompanied by pain, stiffness, and movement problems; especially common in older adults. 583

assimilation (Piaget) Occurs when individuals incorporate new information into their existing knowledge. 48

assimilation (cultural) The absorption of ethnic minority groups into the dominant group, which often involves the loss of some

or virtually all of the behavior and values of the ethnic minority group. 424

associative play Play that involves social interaction with little or no organization. 289

attachment A close emotional bond between an infant and a caregiver. 215

attention deficit hyperactivity disorder (ADHD) A disability in which children consistently show one or more of the following characteristics: (1) inattention, (2) hyperactivity, and (3) impulsivity. 308

authoritarian parenting A restrictive punitive style in which parents exhort the child to follow their directions and to respect work and effort. The authoritarian parent places firm limits and controls on the child and allows little verbal exchange. Authoritarian parenting is associated with children's social incompetence. 277

authoritative parenting A parenting style in which parents encourage their children to be independent but still place limits and controls on their actions. Extensive verbal give-and-take is allowed, and parents are warm and nurturant toward the child. Authoritative parenting is associated with children's social competence. 277

autonomous morality The second stage of moral development, in Piaget's theory, displayed by older children (about 10 years of age and older). The child becomes aware that rules and laws are created by people and that, in judging an action, one should consider the actor's intentions as well as the consequences. 271

B

bargaining Kübler-Ross' third stage of dying, in which the dying person develops the hope that death can somehow be postponed. 664

basal metabolism rate (BMR) The minimal amount of energy a person uses in a resting state. 239, 447

basic cry A rhythmic pattern usually consisting of a cry, a briefer silence, a shorter inspiratory whistle that is higher pitched than the main cry, and then a brief rest before the next cry. 207

basic-skills-and-phonetics approach The idea that reading instruction should teach both phonemic awareness and phonics. 326

Bayley Scales of Infant Development Scale developed by Nancy Bayley, which are widely used in the assessment of infant development. The current version has three components: a mental scale, a motor scale, and an infant behavior profile. 191

becoming parents and a family with children The third stage in the family life cycle. Adults who enter this stage move up a generation and become caregivers to the younger generation. 490

behavior genetics The study of the degree and nature of behavior's basis in heredity. 88

big five factors of personality Emotional stability (neuroticism), extraversion, openness to experience, agreeableness, and conscientiousness. 551

biological age A person's age in terms of biological health. 22

biological processes Changes in an individual's physical nature. 18

blastocyst The inner layer of cells that develops during the germinal period. These cells later develop into the embryo. 113

body transcendence Versus body preoccupation a developmental task of aging described by Peck, in which older adults must cope with declining physical well-being. 625

bonding The formation of a close connection, especially a physical bond between parents and their newborn in the period shortly after birth. 137

brain death A neurological definition of death. A person is brain dead when all electrical activity of the brain has ceased for a specified period of time. A flat EEG recording is one criterion of brain death. 655

brainstorming A technique in which individuals are encouraged to come up with creative ideas in a group, play off each other's ideas, and say practically whatever comes to mind. 325

Brazelton Neonatal Behavioral Assessment Scale A test given several days after birth to assess newborns' neurological development, reflexes, and reactions to people. 134

breech position The baby's position in the uterus that causes the buttocks to be the first part to emerge from the vagina. 135

bulimia nervosa An eating disorder in which the individual consistently follows a binge-and-purge pattern. 385

canalization The process by which characteristics take a narrow path, or developmental course. Apparently, preservative forces help to protect a person from environmental extremes. 87

care perspective The moral perspective of Carol Gilligan, that views people in terms of their connectedness with others and emphasizes interpersonal communication, relationships with others, and concern for others. 343

case study An in-depth look at a single individual. 61

cellular clock theory Leonard Hayflick's theory that the maximum number of times that human cells can divide is about 75 to 80. As we age, our cells have less capability to divide. 574

centration The focusing of attention on one characteristic to the exclusion of all others. 244

cephalocaudal pattern The sequence in which the greatest growth occurs at the top-of-the-head with physical growth in size, weight, and feature differentiation gradually working from top to bottom. 149

child-centered kindergarten Education that involves the whole child by considering both the child's physical, cognitive, and social development and the child's needs, interests, and learning styles. 256

chromosomes Threadlike structures that come in 23 pairs, one member of each pair coming from each parent. Chromosomes are made up of the genetic substance DNA. 83

chronic disorders Disorders that are characterized by slow onset and long duration. They are rare in early adulthood, they increase during middle adulthood, and they become common in late adulthood. 519

chronological age The number of years that have elapsed since a person's birth; what is usually meant by "age." 22

climacteric The midlife transition in which fertility declines. 522

clique A small group that ranges from 2 to about 12 individuals, averaging about 5 to 6 individuals, and can form because adolescents engage in similar activities. 415

cognitive developmental theory of gender The theory that children's gender typing occurs after they have developed a concept of gender. Once they consistently conceive of themselves as male or female, children often organize their world on the basis of gender. 275

cognitive mechanics The "hardware" of the mind, reflecting the neurophysiological architecture of the brain as developed through evolution. Cognitive mechanics involve speed and accuracy of the processes involving sensory input, visual and motor memory, discrimination, comparison, and categorization. 599

cognitive pragmatics The culture-based "software" of the mind. Cognitive pragmatics include reading and writing skills, language comprehension, educational qualifications, professional skills, and also the type of knowledge about the self and life skills that help us to master or cope with life. 599

cognitive processes Changes in an individual's thought, intelligence, and language. 18

cohort effects Effects due to a person's time of birth or generation but not to actual age. 65

commitment Marcia's term for the part of identity development in which adolescents show a personal investment in what they are going to do. 406

connectedness According to Cooper and her colleagues, connectedness consists of two dimensions: mutuality (sensitivity to and respect for others' views) and permeability (openness to others' views). 407

consensual validation An explanation of why individuals are attracted to people who are similar to them. Our own attitudes and behavior are supported and validated when someone else's attitudes and behavior are similar to our own. 482

conservation In Piaget's theory, awareness that altering an object's or a substance's appearance does not change its basic properties. 244

constructive play Play that combines sensorimotor/practice repetitive activity with symbolic representation of ideas. Constructive play occurs when children engage in self-regulated creation or construction of a product or a problem solution. 290

contemporary life-events approach Emphasizes that how a life event influences the individual's development depends not only on the life event, but also on mediating factors, the individual's adaptation to the life event, the life-stage context, and the socio-historical context. 546

context The settings, influenced by historical, economic, social, and cultural factors, in which development occurs. 13

continuity-discontinuity issue The issue regarding whether development involves gradual, cumulative change (continuity) or distinct stages (discontinuity). 23

control processes Cognitive processes that do not occur automatically but require work and effort. These processes are under the learner's conscious control and can be used to improve memory. They are also appropriately called strategies. 315

controversial children Children who are frequently nominated both as someone's best friend and as being disliked. 353

conventional reasoning The second, or intermediate, level in Kohlberg's theory of moral development. Internalization is intermediate. Individuals abide by certain standards (internal), but they are the standards of others (external), such as parents or the laws of society. 341

convergent thinking Thinking that produces one correct answer and is characteristic of the kind of thinking tested by standardized intelligence tests. 324

cooperative play Play that involves social interaction in a group with a sense of group identity and organized activity. 289

coordination of secondary circular reactions Piaget's fourth sensorimotor substage, which develops between 8 and 12 months of age. In this substage, several significant changes take place involving the coordination of schemes and intentionality. 184

correlational research The goal is to describe the strength of the relationship between two or more events or characteristics. 61

creativity The ability to think in novel and unusual ways and to come up with unique solutions to problems. 324

crisis Marcia's term for a period of identity development during which the adolescent is choosing from among meaningful alternatives. 406

critical thinking Thinking reflectively and productively, as well as evaluating the evidence. 315

cross-cultural studies Comparisons of one culture with one or more other cultures. These provide information about the degree to which development is similar, or universal, across cultures, and to the degree to which it is culture-specific. 14

cross-sectional approach A research strategy in which individuals of different ages are compared at one time. 63

crowd A larger group structure than a clique, a crowd is usually formed based on reputation and members may or may not spend much time together. 415

crystallized intelligence Accumulated information and verbal skills, which increase with age, according to Horn. 525

cultural-familial retardation Retardation that is characterized by no evidence of organic brain damage, but the individual's IQ is between 50 and 70. 323

culture The behavior patterns, beliefs, and all other products of a group that are passed on from generation to generation. 13

culture-fair tests Tests of intelligence that are designed to be free of cultural bias. 321

date or acquaintance rape Coercive sexual activity directed at someone with whom the perpetrator is at least casually acquainted. 458

dating scripts The cognitive models that adolescents and adults use to guide and evaluate dating interactions. 417

deferred imitation Imitation that occurs after a time delay of hours or days. 190

dementia A global term for any neurological disorder in which the primary symptoms involve a deterioration of mental functioning. 612

denial and isolation Kübler-Ross' first stage of dying, in which the dying person denies that she or he is really going to die. 663

depression Kübler-Ross' fourth stage of dying, in which the dying person comes to accept the certainty of her or his death. A period of depression or preparatory grief may appear. 664

descriptive research Has the purpose of observing and recording behavior. 58

development The pattern of change that begins at conception and continues through the life cycle. 7

developmental quotient (DQ) An overall developmental score that combines subscores in motor, language, adaptive, and personal-social domains in the Gesell assessment of infants. 191

developmentally appropriate practice Education that focuses on the typical developmental patterns of children (age-appropriateness) and the uniqueness of each child (individual-appropriateness). 256

differentiation versus role preoccupation One of the three developmental tasks of aging described by Peck, in which older adults must redefine their worth in terms of something other than work roles. 625

difficult child A child who tends to react negatively and cry frequently, who engages in irregular daily routines, and who is slow to accept new experiences. 210

disease model of addiction The view that addictions are biologically based, lifelong diseases that involve a loss of control over behavior and require medical and/or spiritual treatment for recovery. 453

disengagement theory The theory that to cope effectively, older adults should gradually withdraw from society. 627

dishabituation An infant's renewed interest in a stimulus. 189

divergent thinking Thinking that produces many answers to the same question and is characteristic of creativity. 324

divided attention Concentrating on more than one activity at the same time. 600

DNA A complex molecule that contains genetic information. 83

doula A caregiver who provides continuous physical, emotional, and educational support to the mother before, during, and after childbirth. 129

Down syndrome A form of mental retardation, caused by the presence of an extra (47th) chromosome. 90

dynamic systems theory The new perspective on motor development in infancy that seeks to explain how motor behaviors are assembled for perceiving and acting. 167

dyslexia A category of learning disabilities involving a severe impairment in the ability to read and spell. 307

easy child A child who is generally in a positive mood, who quickly establishes regular routines in infancy, and who adapts easily to new experiences. 210

eclectic theoretical orientation An orientation that does not follow any one theoretical approach, but rather selects from each theory whatever is considered the best in it. 56

ecological theory Bronfenbrenner's environmental systems theory that focuses on five environmental systems: microsystem, mesosystem, exosystem, macrosystem, and chronosystem. 54

ecological view The view that perception functions to bring organisms in contact with the environment and to increase adaptation. 169

ego transcendence versus ego Preoccupation a developmental task of aging described by Peck, in which older adults must come to feel at ease with themselves by recognizing that although death is inevitable and probably not too far away, they have contributed to the future through raising their children or through their vocations and ideas. 625

egocentrism The inability to distinguish between one's own perspective and someone else's (salient feature of the first substage of preoperational thought). 242

eldercare Physical and emotional caretaking for older members of the family, whether by giving day-to-day physical assistance or by being responsible for overseeing such care. 634

embryonic period The period of prenatal development that occurs two to eight weeks after conception. During the embryonic period, the rate of cell differentiation intensifies, support systems for the cells form, and organs appear. 113

emotion Feeling, or affect, that can involve physiological arousal (a fast heartbeat, for example), conscious experience (thinking about being in love with someone, for example), and behavioral expression (a smile or grimace, for example). 206

emotional intelligence A form of social intelligence that involves the ability to monitor one's own and others' feelings and emotions, to discriminate among them, and to use this information to guide one's thinking and action. 339

emotional regulation Effectively managing arousal to adapt and reach a goal. 209

empty nest syndrome A decrease in marital satisfaction after children leave home, because parents derive considerable satisfaction from their children. 555

episodic memory The retention of information about the where and when of life's happenings. 601

Erikson's theory Includes eight stages of human development. Each stage consists of a unique developmental task that confronts individuals with a crisis that must be faced. 46

ethnic gloss Using an ethnic label such as African American or Latino in a superficial way that portrays an ethnic group as being more homogeneous than it really is. 70

ethnic identity An enduring, basic aspect of the self that includes a sense of membership in an ethnic group and the attitudes and feelings related to that membership. 408

ethnicity A characteristic based on cultural heritage, nationality characteristics, race, religion, and language. 14

ethology Stresses that behavior is strongly influenced by biology, is tied to evolution, and is characterized by critical or sensitive periods. 53

euthanasia The act of painlessly ending the lives of persons who are suffering from incurable diseases or severe disabilities; sometimes called "mercy killing." 655

evocative genotype-environment correlations Correlations that exist when the child's genotype elicits certain types of physical and social environments. 102

evolutionary psychology A contemporary approach that emphasizes the importance of adaptation, reproduction, and survival of the fittest in explaining behavior. 81

experiment A carefully regulated procedure in which one or more of the factors believed to influence the behavior being studied are manipulated while all other factors are held constant. 62

explicit memory Memory of facts and experiences that individuals consciously know and can state. 602

family at midlife The fifth stage in the family life cycle, a time of launching children, linking generations, and adapting to midlife developmental changes. 490

family in later life The sixth and final stage in the family life cycle, involving retirement and, in many families, grandparenting. 490

family with adolescents The fourth stage of the family life cycle, in which adolescent children push for autonomy and seek to develop their own identities. 490

fetal alcohol syndrome (FAS) A cluster of abnormalities that appears in the offspring of mothers who drink alcohol heavily during pregnancy. 119

fetal period The prenatal period of development that begins two months after conception and lasts for seven months, on the average. 115

fine motor skills Motor skills that involve more finely tuned movements, such as finger dexterity. 163

first habits and primary circular reactions Piaget's second sensorimotor substage, which develops between 1 and 4 months of age. In this substage, infants' reflexes evolve into adaptive schemes that are more refined and coordinated. 184

fluid intelligence The ability to reason abstractly, which steadily declines from middle adulthood on, according to Horn. 525

fragile X syndrome A disorder involving an abnormality in the X chromosome, which becomes constricted and, often, breaks. 91

free-radical theory A microbiological theory of aging that states that people age because inside their cells normal metabolism produces unstable oxygen molecules known as free radicals. These molecules ricochet around inside cells, damaging DNA and other cellular structures. 757

friendship A form of close relationship that involves enjoyment, acceptance, trust, respect, mutual assistance, confiding, understanding, and spontaneity. 485

games Activities engaged in for pleasure that include rules and often competition with one or more individuals. 290

gender The social and psychological dimension of being male or female. 14, 272

gender identity The sense of being male or female, which most children acquire by the time they are 3 years old. 272

gender role A set of expectations that prescribes how females or males should think, act, and feel. 272

gender schema Individual's attention and behavior are guided by an internal motivation to conform to gender-based sociocultural standards and stereotypes. 275

gender stereotypes Broad categories that reflect our impressions and beliefs about females and males. 345

generation inequity An aging society's being unfair to its younger members because older adults pile up advantages by receiving inequitably large allocations of resources. 17

generational inequity The view that our aging society is being unfair to its younger members because older adults pile up advantages by receiving inequitably large allocations of resources. 635

genes Units of hereditary information composed of DNA. Genes carry information that enables cells to reproduce themselves and manufacture the proteins that maintain life. 83

genotype A person's genetic heritage; the actual genetic material. 86

germinal period The period of prenatal development that takes place in the first two weeks after conception. It includes the creation of the zygote, continued cell division, and the attachment of the zygote to the uterine wall. 113

gifted Having above-average intelligence (an IQ of 130 or higher) and/or superior talent for something. 323

gonads The sex glands, the testes in males and the ovaries in females. 374

grasping reflex A neonatal reflex that occurs when something touches the infant's palms. The infant responds by grasping tightly. 162

grief The emotional numbness, disbelief, separation anxiety, despair, sadness, and loneliness that accompany the loss of someone we love. 667

gross motor skills Motor skills that involve large muscle activities, such as walking. 163

habituation Repeated presentation of the same stimulus, which causes reduced attention to the stimulus. 189

hardiness A personality style characterized by a sense of commitment (rather than alienation), control (rather than powerlessness), and a perception of problems as challenges (rather than threats). 521

heritability A concept that refers to the fraction of variance in IQ in a population that is attributed to genetics. 100

heteronomous morality The first stage of moral development, in Piaget's theory, occurring from approximately 4 to 7 years of age. Justice and rules are conceived of as unchangeable properties of the world, removed from the control of people. 271

hormonal stress theory The theory that aging in the body's hormonal system can

lower resilience to stress and increase the likelihood of disease. 575

hormones Powerful chemical substances secreted by the endocrine glands and carried through the body by the bloodstream. 373

hospice A humanized program committed to making the end of life as free from pain, anxiety, and depression as possible. The goals of hospice contrast with those of a hospital, which are to cure disease and prolong life. 657

hypothalamus A structure in the higher portion of the brain that monitors eating, drinking, and sex. 373

hypotheses Specific assumptions and predictions that can be tested to determine their accuracy. 43

hypothetical-deductive reasoning Piaget's formal operational concept that adolescents have the cognitive ability to develop hypotheses, or best guesses, about ways to solve problems, such as an algebraic equation. 287

identity achievement Marcia's term for adolescents who have undergone a crisis and have made a commitment. 406

identity diffusion Marcia's term for adolescents who have not yet experienced a crisis (explored meaningful alternatives) or made any commitments. 406

identity foreclosure Marcia's term for adolescents who have made a commitment but have not experienced a crisis. 406

identity moratorium Marcia's term for adolescents who are in the midst of a crisis, but their commitments are either absent or vaguely defined. 406

imaginary audience Adolescents' belief that others are as interested in them as they themselves are; attention-getting behavior motivated by a desire to be noticed, visible, and "on stage." 388

imminent justice The concept that, if a rule is broken, punishment will be meted out immediately. 271

implicit memory Memory without conscious recollection; involves skills and routine procedures that are automatically performed. 602

inclusion Educating a child with special education needs full-time in the regular classroom. 309

individual differences The stable, consistent ways that people are different from each other. 317

individuality According to Cooper and her colleagues, individuality consists of two dimensions: self-assertion (the ability to have and communicate a point of view) and separateness (the use of communication patterns to express how one is different from others). 407

individualized education plan (IEP) A written statement that spells out a program tailored to a child with a disability. The plan should be (1) related to the child's learning capacity, (2) specially constructed to meet the child's individual needs and not merely a copy of what is offered to other children, and (3) designed to provide educational benefits. 309

indulgent parenting A style of parenting in which parents are highly involved with their children but place few demands or controls on them. Indulgent parenting is associated with children's social incompetence, especially a lack of self-control. 277

infant-directed speech Speech often used by parents (in which case it sometimes is called "parentese") and other adults when they talk to babies. It has a higher than normal pitch and involves the use of simple words and sentences. 198

infinite generativity An individual's ability to generate an infinite number of meaningful sentences using a finite set of words and rules, which makes language a highly creative enterprise. 194

information-processing theory Emphasizes that individuals manipulate information, monitor it, and strategize about it. Central to this theory are the processes of memory and thinking. 50

innate goodness view The idea, presented by Swiss-born philosopher Jean-Jacques Rousseau, that children are inherently good. 8

insecure avoidant babies Babies that show insecurity by avoiding the caregiver. 217

insecure disorganized babies Babies that show insecurity by being disorganized and disoriented. 217

insecure resistant babies Babies that often cling to the caregiver, then resist her by fighting against the closeness, perhaps by kicking or pushing away. 217

integrity versus despair Erikson's eighth and final stage of development, which individuals experience in late adulthood. This involves reflecting on the past and either piecing together a positive review or concluding that one's life has not been well spent. 625

intelligence Problem-solving skills and the ability to learn from and adapt to the experiences of everyday life. 317

intelligence quotient (IQ) A person's mental age divided by chronological age, multiplied by 100. 317

intermodal perception The ability to relate and integrate information about two or more sensory modalities, such as vision and hearing. 174

internalization The developmental change from behavior that is externally controlled to behavior that is controlled by internal standards and principles. 341

internalization of schemes Piaget's sixth and final sensorimotor substage, which develops between 18 and 24 months of age. In this substage, the infant's mental functioning shifts from a purely sensorimotor plane to a symbolic plane, and the infant develops the ability to use primitive symbols. 185

intimacy in friendships Self-disclosure and the sharing of private thoughts. 352

intuitive thought substage Piaget's second substage of preoperational thought, in which children begin to use primitive reasoning and want to know the answers to all sorts of questions (between 4 and 7 years of age). 244

justice perspective A moral perspective that focuses on the rights of the individual; individuals independently make moral decisions. 343

juvenile delinquent An adolescent who breaks the law or engages in behavior that is considered illegal. 424

Klinefelter syndrome A disorder in which males have an extra X chromosome, making them XXY instead of XY. 91

kwashiorkor A condition caused by a deficiency in protein in which the child's abdomen and feet become swollen with water. 159

laboratory A controlled setting in which many of the complex factors of the "real world" are removed. 59

language A form of communication based on a system of symbols. In humans language is characterized by infinite generativity and rule systems. 194

language acquisition device (LAD) A biological endowment, hypothesized by Chomsky, that enables the child to detect certain language categories, such as phonology, syntax, and semantics. 197

lateralization Specialization of function in one hemisphere of the cerebral cortex or the other. 153

launching The process in which youths move into adulthood and exit their family of origin. 489

learning disability A disability that involves (1) having normal intelligence or above; (2) having difficulties in at least one academic area and usually several; and (3) having no other problem or disorder, such as mental retardation, that can be determined as causing the difficulty. 307

least restrictive environment (LRE) The concept that a child with a disability must be educated in a setting that is as similar as possible to the one in which children who do not have a disability are educated. 309

leaving home and becoming a single adult The first stage in the family life cycle. It involves launching. 489

leisure The pleasant times after work when individuals are free to pursue activities and interests of their own choosing. 530

life expectancy The number of years that will probably be lived by the average person born in a particular year. 569

life span The upper boundary of life, the maximum number of years an individual can live. The maximum life span of human beings is about 120 to 125 years of age. 559

life-history records Records of information about a lifetime chronology of events and activities that often involve a combination of data records on education, work, family, and residence. 61

life-process model of addiction The view that addiction is not a disease but rather a habitual response and a source of gratification and security that can be understood only in the context of social relationships and experiences. 453

life-span perspective The view that development is lifelong, multidimensional, multidirectional, plastic, multidisciplinary, involves growth, maintenance and regulation, and is contextual. 9

longitudinal approach A research strategy in which the same individuals are studied over a period of time, usually several years or more. 63

long-term memory A relatively permanent type of memory that holds huge amounts of information for a long period of time. 314

low-birthweight infant An infant that weighs less than 5½ pounds at birth. 131

major depression A mood disorder in which the individual is deeply unhappy, demoralized, self-derogatory, and bored. The person does not feel well, loses stamina easily, has poor appetite, and is listless and unmotivated. Major depression is so widespread that it has been called the "common cold" of mental disorders. 611

marasmus A wasting away of body tissues in the infant's first year, caused by severe protein-calorie deficiency. 159

meiosis The process by which cells in the reproductive organs divide into gametes (sperm in males, eggs in females), which have half of the genetic material of the parent cell. 84

memory A central feature of cognitive development, pertaining to all situations in which an individual retains information over time. 190

menarche A girl's first menstruation. 373

menopause The complete cessation of a woman's menstruation, which usually occurs in the late forties or early fifties. 522

mental age (MA) Binet's measure of an individual's level of mental development, compared with that of others. 317

mental retardation A condition of limited mental ability in which an individual has a low IQ, usually below 70 on a traditional test of intelligence, and has difficulty adapting to everyday life. 323

metacognition Cognition about cognition, or knowing about knowing. 316

middle adulthood The developmental period beginning at approximately 40 years of age and extending to about 60. 515

mitosis The process of cell division by which each chromosome in a cell's nucleus duplicates itself. 84

mnemonics Techniques designed to make memory more efficient. 606

Montessori approach An educational philosophy in which children are given considerable freedom and spontaneity in choosing activities and are allowed to move from one activity to another as they desire. 256

moral development Development that involves thoughts, feelings, and actions regarding rules and conventions about what people should do in their interactions with other people. 270

Moro reflex A neonatal startle response that occurs in reaction to a sudden, intense noise or movement. When startled, the newborn arches its back, throws its head back, and flings out its arms and legs. Then the newborn rapidly closes its arms and legs to the center of the body. 162

multi-infarct dementia Sporadic and progressive loss of intellectual functioning caused by repeated temporary obstruction of blood flow in cerebral arteries. 614

myelination The process in which the nerve cells are covered and insulated with a layer of fat cells, which increases the speed at which information travels through the nervous system. 236

natural childbirth Developed in 1914 by Dick-Read, this method attempts to reduce the mother's pain by decreasing her fear through education about childbirth and relaxation techniques during delivery. 130

naturalistic observation Observing behavior in real-world settings. 59

nature-nurture issue Nature refers to an organism's biological inheritance, nurture to environmental influences. The "nature" proponents claim biological inheritance is the most important influence on development; the "nurture" proponents claim that environmental experiences are the most important. 23

neglected children Children who are infrequently nominated as a best friend but are not disliked by their peers. 353

neglectful parenting A style of parenting in which the parent is very uninvolved in the child's life; it is associated with children's social incompetence, especially a lack of self-control. 277

neo-Piagetians Developmentalists who have elaborated on Piaget's theory, believing that more emphasis should be given to

information processing, strategies, and precise cognitive steps. 314

neuron Nerve cell that handles information processing at the cellular level. 150

new couple forming The new couple is the second stage in the family life cycle. Two individuals from separate families of origin unite to form a new family system. 489

nonshared environmental experiences The child's own unique experiences, both within the family and outside the family, that are not shared by another sibling. Thus, experiences occurring within the family can be part of the "nonshared environment." 103

normal distribution A symmetrical distribution with most cases falling in the middle of the possible range of scores and a few scores appearing toward the extremes of the range. 317

object permanence The Piagetian term for one of an infant's most important accomplishments: understanding that objects and events continue to exist, even when they cannot directly be seen, heard, or touched. 185

onlooker play Play in which the child watches other children play. 289

operations In Piaget's theory, internalized sets of actions that allow children to do mentally what they formerly did physically. 242

organic retardation Mental retardation that involves some physical damage and is caused by a genetic disorder or brain damage. 323

organogenesis Organ formation that takes place during the first two months of prenatal development. 114

original sin view Advocated during the Middle Ages, the belief that children were born into the world as evil beings and were basically bad. 7

osteoporosis A chronic condition that involves an extensive loss of bone tissue and is the main reason many older adults walk with a marked stoop. Women are especially vulnerable to osteoporosis. 583

pain cry A sudden appearance of loud crying without preliminary moaning and a long initial cry followed by an extended period of breath holding. 207

palliative care Emphasized in hospice care; involves reducing pain and suffering and helping individuals die with dignity. 657

parallel play Play in which the child plays separately from others, but with toys like those the others are using or in a manner that mimics their play. 289

Parkinson's disease A chronic, progressive disease characterized by muscle tremors, slowing of movement, and partial facial paralysis. Muhammed Ali, one of the world's leading sports figures, has Parkinson's disease. 615

passive euthanasia The withholding of available treatments, such as life-sustaining devices, allowing the person to die. 656

passive genotype-environment correlations Correlations that occur because biological parents provide an environment that matches their own genetic tendencies and their children inherit genetic tendencies from their parents. 102

perception The interpretation of what is sensed. 168

personal fable The part of adolescent egocentrism that involves an adolescent's sense of uniqueness and invincibility. 388

personality type theory John Holland's view that it is important to match an individual's personality with a particular career. 464

phenotype The way an individual's genotype is expressed in observed and measurable characteristics. 86

phenylketonuria (PKU) A genetic disorder in which an individual cannot properly metabolize a substance needed for production of proteins in the body. PKU is now easily detected but, if left untreated, results in mental retardation and hyperactivity. 92

phonology A language's sound system. 195

Piaget's theory States that children actively construct their understanding of the world and go through four stages of cognitive development. 47

pituitary gland An important endocrine gland that controls growth and regulates other glands. 373

placenta A life-support system that consists of a disk-shaped group of tissues in which small blood vessels from the mother and offspring intertwine. 113

pluralism The coexistence of distinct ethnic and cultural groups in the same society. Individuals with a pluralistic stance usually advocate that cultural differences be maintained and appreciated. 424

popular children Children who are frequently nominated as a best friend and are rarely disliked by their peers. 424

postformal thought A form of thought, proposed as a fifth stage, that is qualitatively different from Piaget's formal operational thought. It involves understanding that the correct answer to a problem can require reflective thinking, that the correct answer can vary from one situation to another, and that the search for truth is often an ongoing, never-ending process. It also involves the belief that solutions to problems need to be realistic and that emotion and subjective factors can influence thinking. 460

postpartum period The period after childbirth when the mother adjusts, both physically and psychologically, to the process of childbirth. This period lasts for about six weeks or until her body has completed its adjustment and returned to a near prepregnant state. 135

practice play Play that involves repetition of behavior when new skills are being learned or when physical or mental mastery and coordination of skills are required for games or sports. Sensorimotor play, which often involves practice play, is primarily confined to infancy, while practice play can be engaged in throughout life. 290

preconventional reasoning The lowest level in Kohlberg's theory of moral development. The individual shows no internalization of moral values-moral reasoning is controlled by external rewards and punishment. 341

prepared childbirth Developed by French obstetrician Ferdinand Lamaze, this childbirth strategy is similar to natural childbirth but includes a special breathing technique to control pushing in the final stages of labor and a more detailed anatomy and physiology course. 130

pretense/symbolic play Play in which the child transforms the physical environment into a symbol. 290

preterm infants Those born three weeks or more before the pregnancy has reached its full term. 131

primary circular reaction A scheme based on the infant's attempt to reproduce an interesting or a pleasurable event that initially occurred by chance. 184

Project Head Start A government-funded program that is designed to provide children from low-income families the opportunity to acquire the skills and experiences important for school success. 60, 258

prospective memory Involves remembering to do something in the future. 602

proximodistal pattern The sequence in which growth starts at the center of the body and moves toward the extremities. 149

psychoanalytic theory Describes development as primarily unconscious and heavily colored by emotion. Behavior is merely a surface characteristic and the symbolic workings of the mind have to be analyzed to understand behavior. Early experiences with parents are emphasized. 44

psychoanalytic theory of gender A theory deriving from Freud's view that the preschool child develops a sexual attraction to the opposite-sex parent, by approximately 5 or 6 years of age renounces this attraction because of anxious feelings, and subsequently identifies with the same-sex parent, unconsciously adopting the same-sex parent's characteristics. 273

psychological age An individual's adaptive capacities compared to those of other individuals of the same chronological age. 22

puberty A period of rapid skeletal and sexual maturation that occurs mainly in early adolescence. 372

R

rape Forcible sexual intercourse with a person who does not consent to it. 458

reaction range The range of possible phenotypes for each genotype, suggesting the importance of an environment's restrictiveness or richness. 87

reciprocal socialization Socialization that is bidirectional; children socialize parents, just as parents socialize children. 221

reflexive smile A smile that does not occur in response to external stimuli. It happens during the month after birth, usually during irregular patterns of sleep, not when the infant is in an alert state. 208

rejected children Children who are infrequently nominated as a best friend and are actively disliked by their peers. 353

reproduction The process that, in humans, begins when a female gamete (ovum) is fertilized by a male gamete (sperm). 84

restrained eaters Individuals who chronically restrict their food intake to control their weight. Restrained eaters are often on diets, are very conscious of what they eat, and tend to feel guilty after splurging on sweets. 448

rite of passage A ceremony or ritual that marks an individual's transition from one status to another. Most rites of passage focus on the transition to adult status. 420

romantic love Also called passionate love, or eros, romantic love has strong sexual and infatuation components and often predominates in the early period of a love relationship. 484

rooting reflex A newborn's built-in reaction that occurs when the infant's cheek is stroked or the side of the mouth is touched. In response, the infant turns its head toward the side that was touched, in an apparent effort to find something to suck. 161

S

scaffolding In cognitive development, Vygotsky used this term to describe the changing support over the course of a teaching session, with the more-skilled person adjusting guidance to fit the child's current performance level. In parenting, the concept of scaffolding refers to parental behavior that supports children's efforts, as in turn-taking. 221, 246

scheme In Piaget's theory, a cognitive structure that helps individuals organize and understand their experiences. 183

secondary circular reactions Piaget's third sensorimotor substage, which develops between 4 and 8 months of age. In this substage, the infant becomes more object-oriented, or focused on the world, moving beyond preoccupation with the self in sensorimotor interactions. 184

secure attachment The infant uses a caregiver as a secure base from which to explore the environment. Ainsworth believes that secure attachment in the first year of life provides an important foundation for psychological development later in life. 217

selective attention Focusing on a specific aspect of experience that is relevant while ignoring others that are irrelevant. 600

selective optimization with compensation theory The theory that successful aging is related to three main factors: selection, optimization, and compensation. 628

self-concept Domain-specific evaluations of the self. 337

self-esteem The global evaluative dimension of the self. Self-esteem is also referred to as self-worth or self-image. 337

self-understanding The child's cognitive representation of self, the substance and content of the child's self-conceptions. 269

semantic memory A person's knowledge about the world-including a person's fields of expertise, general academic knowledge of the sort learned in school, and "everyday knowledge." 601

sensation The product of the interaction between information and the sensory receptors-the eyes, ears, tongue, nostrils, and skin. 168

sensorimotor play Behavior engaged in by infants to derive pleasure from exercising their existing sensorimotor schemas. 289

separation protest An infant's distress over being separated from his or her caregiver. 209

sequential approach A combined cross-sectional, longitudinal design. 64

seriation The concrete operation that involves ordering stimuli along a quantitative dimension (such as length). 312

service learning A form of education that promotes social responsibility and service to the community. 396

sexually transmitted diseases (STDs) Diseases that are contracted primarily through sex. 379, 456

shared environmental experiences Children's common environmental experiences that are shared with their siblings, such as their parents' personalities and intellectual orientation, the family's social class, and the neighborhood in which they live. 103

short-term memory The memory component in which individuals retain information for up to 30 seconds, assuming there is no rehearsal. 251

sickle-cell anemia A genetic disorder that affects the red blood cells and occurs most often in people of African descent. 92

simple reflexes Piaget's first sensorimotor substage, which corresponds to the first month after birth. In this substage, the basic means of coordinating sensation and action is through reflexive behaviors, such as rooting and sucking, which the infant has at birth. 184

slow-to-warm-up child A child who has a low activity level, is somewhat negative , and displays a low intensity mood. 210

small for date infants Also called small for gestational age infants, these infants' birthweights are below normal when the length of pregnancy is considered. Small for date infants may be preterm or full term. 131

social age Social roles and expectations related to a person's age. 22

social clock The timetable according to which individuals are expected to accomplish life's tasks, such as getting married, having children, or establishing themselves in a career. 547

social cognitive theory The view of psychologists who emphasize behavior, environment, and cognition as the key factors in development. 52

social cognitive theory of gender A theory that emphasizes that children's gender development occurs through the observation and imitation of gender behavior and through the rewards and punishments children experience for gender-appropriate and -inappropriate behavior. 273

social constructivist approach An approach that emphasizes the social contexts of learning and that knowledge is mutually built and constructed. Vygotsky's theory reflects this approach. 247

social play Play that involves social interactions with peers. 290

social policy A national government's course of action designed to promote the welfare of its citizens. 15

social referencing "Reading" emotional cues in others to help determine how to act in a particular situation. 209

social smile A smile in response to an external stimulus, which, early in development, typically is in response to a face. 208

socioemotional processes Changes in an individual's relationships with other people, emotions, and personality. 18

socioemotional selectivity theory The theory that older adults become more selective about their social networks. Because they place a high value on emotional satisfaction, older adults often spend more time with familiar individuals with whom they have had rewarding relationships. 627

solitary play Play in which the child plays alone and independently of others. 288

stability-change issue The issue of whether development is best described as involving stability or as involving change. This issue involves the degree to which we become older renditions of our early experience or instead develop into someone different from who we were at an earlier point in development. 24

standardized test A test with uniform procedures for administration and scoring. Many standardized tests allow a person's performance to be compared with the performance of other individuals. 60

Strange Situation An observational measure of infant attachment that requires the infant to move through a series of introductions, separations, and reunions with the caregiver and an adult stranger in a prescribed order. 217

stranger anxiety An infant's fear and wariness of strangers; it tends to appear in the second half of the first year of life. 209

sucking reflex A newborn's built-in reaction of automatically sucking an object placed in its mouth. The sucking reflex enables the infant to get nourishment before it has associated a nipple with food. 161

sudden infant death syndrome (SIDS) A condition that occurs when an infant stops breathing, usually during the night, and suddenly dies without an apparent cause. 157

sustained attention The state of readiness to detect and respond to small changes occurring at random times in the environment. 601

symbolic function substage Piaget's first substage of preoperational thought, in which the child gains the ability to mentally represent an object that is not present (between 2 and 4 years of age). 242

tabula rasa view The idea, proposed by John Locke, that children are like a "blank tablet." 7

telegraphic speech The use of short and precise words to communicate; young children's two- and three-word utterances characteristically are telegraphic. 196

temperament An individual's behavioral style and characteristic way of emotional response. 210

teratogen From the Greek word tera, meaning "monster." Any agent that causes a birth defect. The field of study that investigates the causes of birth defects is called teratology. 117

terminal drop hypothesis The hypothesis that death is preceded by a decrease in cognitive functioning over approximately a five-year period prior to death. 605

tertiary circular reactions, novelty, and curiosity Piaget's fifth sensorimotor substage, which develops between 12 and 18 months of age. In this substage, infants become intrigued by the variety of properties that objects possess and by the multiplicity of things they can make happen to objects. 185

theory of mind Refers to the awareness of one's own mental processes and the mental processes of others. 252

theory An interrelated, coherent set of ideas that helps to explain events and make predictions. 43

top-dog phenomenon The circumstance of moving from the top position in elementary school to the lowest position in middle or junior high school. 391

transitivity The ability to logically combine relations to understand certain conclusions. 312

triarchic theory of intelligence Sternberg's theory that intelligence consists of analytical intelligence, creative intelligence, and practical intelligence. 319

trophoblast The outer layer of cells that develops in the germinal period. These cells provide nutrition and support for the embryo. 113

Turner syndrome A disorder in females in which either an X chromosome is missing, making the person XO instead of XX, or the second X chromosome is partially deleted. 91

twin study A study in which the behavioral similarity of identical twins is compared with the behavioral similarity of fraternal twins. 88

Type A behavior pattern A cluster of characteristics-being excessively competitive, hard-driven, impatient, and hostile-thought to be related to the incidence of heart disease. 520

Type B behavior pattern Being primarily calm and easygoing. 521

umbilical cord A life-support system containing two arteries and one vein that connects the baby to the placenta. 114

unoccupied play Play in which the child is not engaging in play as it is commonly understood and might stand in one spot, or perform random movements that do not seem to have a goal. 288

Vygotksky's theory A sociocultural cognitive theory that emphasizes how culture and social interaction guide cognitive development. 50

whole-language approach An approach to reading instruction based on the idea that instruction should parallel children's natural language learning. Reading materials should be whole and meaningful. 326

wisdom Expert knowledge about the practical aspects of life that permits excellent judgment about important matters. 603

working memory Closely related to short-term memory but places more emphasis on mental work. Working memory is like a "workbench" where individuals can manipulate and assemble information when making decisions, solving problems, and comprehending written and spoken language. 527

XYY syndrome A disorder in which males have an extra Y chromosome. 91

zone of proximal development (ZPD) Vygotsky's term for tasks too difficult for children to master alone but that can be mastered with assistance. 246

zygote A single cell formed through fertilization. 84

References

A

Abbassi, V. (1998). Growth and normal puberty. *Pediatrics (Suppl.), 102 (2)* 507–511.

Abel, E. L., Kruger, M., & Burd, L. (2002). Effects of maternal and paternal age on Caucasian and Native American preterm births and birth weights. *American Journal of Perinatology, 19,* 49–54.

Aboud, F., & Skerry, S. (1983). Self and ethnic concepts in relation to ethnic constancy. *Canadian Journal of Behavioral Science, 15,* 3–34.

Acquilino, W. (1999). Two views of one relationship: Comparing parents' and young adult children's reports of the quality of intergenerational relations. *Journal of Marriage and the Family, 61,* 858–870.

Acredolo, L. P., & Hake, J. L. (1982). Infant perception. In B. B. Wolman (Ed.). *Handbook of developmental psychology.* Englewood Cliffs, NJ: Prentice Hall.

Adamolekun, K. (2001). Survivors' motives for extravagant funerals among the Yorubas of western Nigeria. *Death Studies, 25,* 609–619.

Adams, R. J. (1989). Newborns' discrimination among mid- and long-wavelength stimuli. *Journal of Experimental Child Psychology, 47,* 130–141.

Adams, R., & Laursen, B. (2001). The organization and dynamics of adolescent conflict with parents and friends. *Journal of Marriage and the Family, 63,* 97–110.

Addis, A., Magrini, N., & Mastroiacovo, P. (2001). Drug use during pregnancy. *Lancet, 357,* 800.

Adler, T. (1991, January). Seeing double? Controversial twins study is widely reported, debated. *APA Monitor, 22,* 1, 8.

Adolph, K. E. (1997). Cognitive-motor learning in infant locomotion. *Monographs of the Society for Research in Child Development.*

Ahluwalia, I. B., Tessaro, I., Grumer-Strawn, L. M., MacGowan, C., & Benton-Davis, S. (2000). Georgia's breast-feeding promotion program for low-income women. *Pediatrics, 105,* E-85–E-87.

Ahn, N. (1994). Teenage childbearing and high school completion: Accounting for individual heterogeneity. *Family Planning Perspectives, 26,* 17–21.

Aiken, L. (2000). *Dying, death, and bereavement* (4th ed.). Mahwah. NJ: Erlbaum.

Ainsworth, M. D. S. (1979). Infant-mother attachment. *American Psychologist, 34,* 932–937.

Aisner, D. R., Wright, W. E., & Shay, J. W. (2001). Telomerase regulation: Not just flipping the switch. *Current Opinion in Genetics and Development, 12,* 80–85.

Akiyama, H., & Antonucci, T. C. (1999, November). *Mother-daughter dynamics over the life course.* Paper presented at the meeting of the Gerontological Association of America, San Francisco.

Alan Guttmacher Institute. (1998). *Teen sex and pregnancy.* New York: Author.

Alan Guttmacher Institute. (1999). *Facts in brief: Teen sex and pregnancy.* New York: Author.

Alan Guttmacher Institute. (2000, February 24). *United States and the Russian Federation lead the developed world in teenage pregnancy rates.* New York: Author.

Aldwin, C. M., & Levenson, M. R. (2001). Stress, coping, and health at midlife: A developmental perspective. In M. E. Lachman (Ed.), *Handbook of midlife development.* New York: John Wiley.

Aldwin, C. M., Spiro, A., Levenson, M. R., & Cupertino, A. P. (2001). Longitudinal findings from the Normative Aging Study: III. Personality, individual health trajectories, and mortality. *Psychology and Aging, 16,* 450–465.

Alexander, A., Anderson, H., Heilman, P. C. & others. (1991). Phonological awareness training and remediation of analytic decoding deficits in a group of severe dyslexics. *Annals of Dyslexia, 41,* 193–206.

Alexander, J. M., McIntire, D. D., & Leveno, K. J. (2001). Prolonged pregnancy: Induction of labor and cesarean births. *Obstetrics and Gynecology, 97,* 911–915.

Alexopoulos, G., Buckwalter, K., Olin, J., Martinez, R., Wainscott, C., & Krishnan, K. (2002). Comorbidity of late life depression: an opportunity for research on mechanisms and treatment. *Biological Psychiatry, 52,* 543.

Allan, R., & Scheidt, S. (Eds.). (1996). *Heart and mind.* Washington, DC: American Psychological Association.

Allen, J. P., & Hauser, S. T. (1994, February). *Adolescent-family interactions as predictors of qualities of parental, peer, and romantic relationships at age 25.* Paper presented at the meeting of the Society for Research on Adolescence, San Diego.

Allen, J. P., & Kuperminc, G. P. (1995, March). *Adolescent attachment, social competence, and problematic behavior.* Paper presented at the meeting of the Society for Research in Child Development, Indianapolis.

Allen, J. P., March, P., McFarland, C., McElhaney, K. B., Land, D. J., Jodl, K., & Peck, S. (2002). Attachment and autonomy as predictors of the development of social skills and delinquency during midadolescence. *Journal of Consulting and Clinical Psychology, 70,* 56–66.

Allen, K. R., Blieszener, R., & Roberto, K. A. (2000). Families in middle and later years: A review and critique of research in the 1990s. *Journal of Marriage and the Family, 62,* 911–926.

Allen, M., Brown, P., & Finlay, B. (1992). *Helping children by strengthening families.* Washington, DC: Children's Defense Fund.

Allison, J. A., & Wrightsman, L. S. (1993). *Rape: The misunderstood crime.* Newbury Park, CA: Sage.

Alpha-Tocopherol, Beta-Carotene Cancer Prevention Study Group. (1994). The effect of Vitamin E and beta-carotene on the incidence of lung cancer and other cancers in non-smokers. *New England Journal of Medicine, 330,* 1029–1035.

Amabile, T. M. (1993). Commentary. In D. Goleman, P. Kaufman, & M. Ray. *The Creative Spirit.* New York: Plume.

Amabile, T. M., & Hennesey, B. A. (1992). The motivation for creativity in children. In A. K. Boggiano & T. S. Pittman (Eds.), *Achievement and motivation.* New York: Cambridge.

Amato, P. R. (2000). The consequences of divorce for adults and children. *Journal of Marriage and the Family, 62,* 1269–1287.

Amato, P. R., & Booth, A. (1996). A prospective study of divorce and parent-child relationships. *Journal of Marriage and the Family, 58,* 356–365.

Amato, P. R., & Keith, B. (1991). Parental divorce and the well-being of children: A meta-analysis. *Psychological Bulletin, 110,* 26–46.

American Academy of Pediatrics. (2000). Suicide and suicide attempts in adolescence. *Pediatrics, 105,* 871–874.

American Academy of Pediatrics. (2001). *Toilet training.* Available on the World Wide Web at: http://www.aap.org/family./toil.htm.

American Academy of Pediatrics (AAP) Committee on Drugs. (1994). The transfer of drugs and other chemicals into human milk. *Pediatrics, 93,* 137–150.

American Academy of Pediatrics (AAP) Work Group on Breastfeeding. (1997). Breastfeeding and the use of human milk. *Pediatrics, 100,* 1035–1039.

American Academy of Pediatrics Task Force in Infant Positioning and SIDS. (2000). Changing concepts of sudden infant death syndrome. *Pediatrics, 105,* 650–656.

American Association for Protecting Children. (1986). *Highlights of official child neglect and abuse reporting: 1984.* Denver: American Humane Association.

Amsterdam, B. K. (1968). *Mirror behavior in children under two years of age.* Unpublished doctoral dissertation, University of North Carolina, Chapel Hill.

Anderson, C. A., & Bushman, B. J. (2002). Human aggression. *Annual Review of Psychology* (Vol. 53). Palo Alto, CA: Annual Reviews.

Anderson, D. R., Huston, A. C., Schmitt, K., Linebarger, D. L., & Wright, J. C. (2001). Early childhood viewing and adolescent behavior: The recontact study. *Monographs of the Society for Research in Child Development, 66,* (1, Serial No. 264).

Anderson, D. R., Lorch, E. P., Field, D. E., Collins, P. A., & Nathan, J. G. (1985, April). *Television viewing at home: Age trends in visual attention and time with TV.* Paper presented at the biennial meeting of the Society for Research in Child Development, Toronto.

Anderson, E., Greene, S. M., Hetherington, E. M., & Clingempeel, W. G. (1999). The dynamics of parental remarriage. In E. M. Hetherington (Ed.), *Coping with divorce, single parenting, and remarriage.* Mahwah, NJ: Erlbaum.

Anderton, B. H. (2002). Aging of the brain. *Mechanisms of Aging and Development, 123,* 811–817.

Anstey, K. J., & Smith, G. A. (1999). Interrelationships among biological markers of aging, health, activity, acculturation, and cognitive performance in late adulthood. *Psychology and Aging, 14,* 605–618.

Anthony Greenwald & Associates. (2000). *Current views toward retirement: A poll.* New York: Author.

Antonucci, T. C. (1989). Understanding adult social relationships. In K. Kreppner & R. M. Lerner (Eds.), *Family systems and life-span development.* Hillsdale, NJ: Erlbaum.

Antonucci, T. C. (1990). Social supports and relationships. In R. H. Binstock & L. K. George (Eds.), *Handbook of aging and the social sciences.* San Diego: Academic Press.

Antonucci, T. C., & Akiyama, H. (2002). Aging and close relationships over the life span. *International Society for the Study of Behavioural Development Newsletter* (1, Serial No. 41), 2–5.

Antonucci, T. C., Lansford, J. E., & Akiyama, H. (2001). The impact of positive and negative aspects of marital relationships and friendships on the well-being of older adults. In J. P. Reinhardt (Ed.), *Negative and positive support.* Mahwah, NJ: Erlbaum.

Antonucci, T. C., Lansford, J. E., Schaabeg, L., Smith, J., Baltes, M., Akiyama, H., Takahashi, K., & Fuhrer, R. (2001). Widowhood and illness: A comparison of social network characteristics in France, Germany, Japan, and the United States. *Psychology and Aging, 16,* 655–665.

Antonucci, T. C., Vandewater, E. A., & Lansford, J. E. (1998). Extended family relationships. In H. S. Friedman (Ed.), *Encyclopedia of mental health* (Vol. 2). San Diego: Academic Press.

Antonucci, T. C., Vandewater, E. A., & Lansford, J. E. (2000). Adulthood and aging: Social processes and development. In A. Kazdin (Ed.), *Encyclopedia of psychology.* Washington, DC, & New York: American Psychological Association and Oxford University Press.

Arbuckle, T. Y., Maag, U., Pushkar, D., & Chalkelsen, J. S. (1998). Individual differences in trajectory of intellectual development over 45 years of adulthood. *Psychology and Aging, 13,* 663–675.

Archer, S. L. (Ed.). (1994). *Intervention for adolescent identity development.* Newbury Park, CA: Sage.

Archibald, A. B., Graeber, J. A., & Brooks-Gunn, J. (1999). Associations among parent-adolescent relationships, pubertal growth, dieting, and body image in young adolescent girls: A short-term longitudinal study. *Journal of Research on Adolescence, 9,* 395–415.

Archibald, A. B., Graber, J.A., & Brooks-Gunn, J. (2003). Pubertal processes and physical growth in adolescence. In G. Adams & M. Berzonsky (Eds.), *Blackwell handbook of adolescence.* Malden, MA: Blackwell.

Archibald, S. L., Fennema-Notetine, C., Gamst, A., Riley, E. P., Mattson, S. N., & Jernigan, T. L. (2001). Brain dysmorphology in individuals with severe prenatal alcohol exposure. *Developmental Medicine and Child Neurology, 43,* 148–154.

Arendt, R., Angelopouos, J., Salvator, A., & Singer, L. (1999). Motor development of cocaine-exposed children at age two years. *Pediatrics, 103,* 86–92.

Arnett, J. J. (1995, March). *Are college students adults?* Paper presented at the meeting of the Society for Research in Child Development, Indianapolis.

Arnett, J. J. (2000). Emerging adulthood. *American Psychologist, 55,* 469–480.

Aronson, E. (1986, August). *Teaching students things they think they already know about: The case of prejudice and desegregation.* Paper presented at the meeting of the American Psychological Association, Washington, DC.

Arshad, S. H. (2001). Food allergen avoidance in primary prevention of food allergy. *Allergy, 56,* 113–116.

Asch, D. A., & Christakis, N. A. (1996). Why do physicians prefer to withdraw some forms of life support over others? Intrinsic attributes of life-sustaining treatments are associated with physicians' preferences. *Medical Care, 34,* 103–111.

Astin, A. W. (1993). *What matters in college.* San Francisco: Jossey-Bass.

Atchley, R. C. (1976). *The sociology of retirement.* Cambridge, MA: Schenkman.

Attie, I., & Brooks-Gunn, J. (1989). Development of eating problems in adolescent girls: A longitudinal study. *Developmental Psychology, 25,* 70–79.

Avis, N. E. (1999). Women's health at midlife. In S. L. Willis & J. D. Reid (Eds.), *Life in the middle: Psychological and social development in middle age.* San Diego: Academic Press.

Avolio, B. J., & Sosik, J. J. (1999). A life-span framework for assessing the impact of work on white-collar workers. In S. L. Willis & J. D. Reid (Eds.), *Life in the middle: Psychological and social development in middle age.* San Diego: Academic Press.

Azar, S. T. (2002). Parenting and child maltreatment. In M. H. Bornstein (Ed.), *Handbook of parenting* (2nd ed., Vol. 4). Mahwah, NJ: Erlbaum.

B

Bachar, K. J., & Koss, M. P. (2002). Rape. In J. Worell (Ed.), *Encyclopedia of women and gender.* San Diego: Academic Press.

Bachman, J. G., Johnston, L. D., O'Malley, P., & Schulenberg, J. (1996). Transitions in drug use during late adolescence and young adulthood. In J. A. Graber, J. Brooks-Gunn, & A. C. Petersen (Eds.), *Transitions through adolescence.* Mahwah, NJ: Erlbaum.

Bachman, J. G., O'Malley, P. M., Schulenberg, J., Johnston, L. D., Bryant, A. L., & Merline, A. C. (2002). *The decline of substance abuse in young adulthood.* Mahwah, NJ: Erlbaum.

Backman, L., Small, B. J., & Wahlin, A. (2001). Aging and memory: Cognitive and behavioral processes. In J. E. Birren & K. W. Schaie (Eds.), *Handbook of the psychology of aging* (5th ed.). San Diego: Academic Press.

Baddeley, A. (2000). Short-term and working memory. In E. Tulving & F. I. M. Craik (Eds.), *The Oxford handbook of memory.* New York: Oxford University Press.

Baer, J. S., Barr, H. M., Bookstein, F. L., Sampson, P. D., & Streissguth, A. P. (1998). Prenatal alcohol exposure and family history of alcoholism in the etiology of adolescent alcohol problems. *Journal of Studies on Alcohol, 59,* 533–543.

Bagwell, C. L., Newcomb, A. F., & Bukowski, W. M. (1994, February). *Early adolescent friendship as a predictor of adult adjustment: A twelve-year follow-up investigation.* Paper presented at the biennial meeting of the Society for Research on Adolescence, San Diego.

Bahr, S. J. (1989). Prologue: A developmental overview of the aging family. In S. J. Bahr & E. T. Peterson (Eds.), *Aging and the family.* Lexington, MA: Lexington Books.

Bahrick, H. P. (1984). Semantic memory content in permastore: Fifty years of memory for Spanish learned in school. *Journal of Experimental Psychology: General, 113,* 1–35.

Bailey, B., Forget, S., & Koren, G. (2002). Pregnancy outcome of women who failed appointments at a teratogen information service clinic. *Reproductive Toxicology, 16,* 77–80.

Baillargeon, R. (1986). Representing the existence and the location of hidden objects: Object permanence in 6- and 8-month-old infants. *Cognition, 23,* 21–41.

Baillargeon, R. (1995). The object concept revisited: New directions in the investigation of infants' physical knowledge. In C. E. Granrud (Ed.), *Visual perception and cognition in infancy.* Hillsdale, NJ: Erlbaum.

Bakeman, R., & Brown, J. V. (1980). Early interaction: Consequences for social and mental development at three years. *Child Development, 51,* 437–447.

Bakker, E., Van Gool, J. D., Van Sprundel, M., Van Der Auwera, C., & Wyndaele, J. J. (2002). Results of a questionnaire evaluating the effects of different methods of toilet training on achieving bladder control. *British Journal of Urology International, 90,* 456–461.

Baldwin, J. D., & Baldwin, J. I. (1998). Sexual behavior. In H. S. Friedman (Ed.), *Encyclopedia of mental health* (Vol. 3). San Diego: Academic Press.

Baldwin, M., & Fehr, B. (1995). On the instability of attachment ratings. *Personal Relationships, 2,* 247–261.

Baldwin, S., & Hoffman, J. P. (2002). The dynamics of self-esteem: A growth curve analysis. *Journal of Youth and Adolescence, 31,* 101–113.

Balota, D. A., Dolan, P. O., & Duchek, J. M. (2000). Memory changes in healthy older adults. In E. Tulving & F. I. M. Craik (Eds.), *The Oxford handbook of memory.* New York: Oxford University Press.

Baltes, P. B. (1987). Theoretical propositions of life-span developmental psychology: On the dynamics between growth and decline. *Developmental Psychology, 23,* 611–626.

Baltes, P. B. (1993). The aging mind: Potentials and limits. *Gerontologist, 33,* 580–594.

Baltes, P. B. (1995, September). Unpublished review of J. W. Santrock's *Life-span development,* 6th ed. (New York: McGraw-Hill).

Baltes, P. B. (1996, August). *On the incomplete architecture of human ontogenesis.* Invited award address presented at the meeting of the American Psychological Association, Toronto.

Baltes, P. B. (2000). Life-span developmental theory. In A. Kazdin (Ed.), *Encyclopedia of psychology.* Washington, DC, & New York: American Psychological Association and Oxford University Press.

Baltes, P. B., & Baltes, M. M. (1990). Psychological perspectives on successful aging: The model of selective optimization with compensation. In P. B. Baltes & M. M. Baltes (Eds.), *Successful aging: Perspectives from the behavioral sciences.* New York: Cambridge University Press.

Baltes, P. B., & Lindenberger, U. (1997). Emergence of a powerful connection between sensory and cognitive functions across the adult life span: A new window to the study of cognitive aging? *Psychology and Aging, 12,* 12–21.

Baltes, P. B., Reese, H. W., & Lipsitt, L. P. (1980). Life-span developmental psychology. *Annual Review of Psychology, 31,* 65–110.

Baltes, P. B., & Staudinger, U. M. (1998). Wisdom. In H. S. Friedman (Ed.), *Encyclopedia of mental health* (Vol. 3). San Diego: Academic Press.

Baltes, P. B., & Staudinger, U. M. (2000). Wisdom. *American Psychologist, 55,* 122–136.

Baltes, P. B., Staudinger, U. M., & Lindenberger, U. (1999). Lifespan psychology: Theory and application to intellectual functioning. *Annual Review of Psychology, 50,* 471–507.

Bandstra, E. S., Morrow, C. E., Anthony, J. C., Haynes, V. L., Johnson, A. L., Xue, L., & Audrey, Y. (2000, May). *Effects of prenatal cocaine exposure on attentional processing in children through five years of age.* Paper presented at the joint meetings of the Pediatric Academic Societies and the American Academy of Pediatrics, Boston.

Bandura, A. (1965). Influence of models' reinforcement of contingencies on the acquisition of imitative responses. *Journal of Personality and Social Psychology, 1,* 589–595.

Bandura, A. (1977). *Social learning theory.* Englewood Cliffs, NJ: Prentice-Hall.

Bandura, A. (1986). *Social foundations of thought and action: A social cognitive theory.* Englewood Cliffs, NJ: Prentice Hall.

Bandura, A. (1998, August). *Swimming against the mainstream: Accentuating the positive aspects of humanity.* Paper presented at the meeting of the American Psychological Association, San Francisco.

Bandura, A. (2000). Self-efficacy. In A. Kazdin (Ed.), *Encyclopedia of psychology.* Washington, DC, & New York: American Psychological Association and Oxford University Press.

Bandura, A. (2000). Social cognitive theory. In A. Kazdin (Ed.), *Encyclopedia of psychology.* Washington, DC, & New York: American Psychological Association and Oxford University Press.

Bandura, A. (2001). Social cognitive theory. *Annual Review of Psychology* (Vol. 52). Palo Alto, CA: Annual Reviews.

Bandura, A. (2002). Selective moral disengagement in the exercise of moral agency. *Journal of Moral Education, 31,* 101–119.

Bandura, A. (2002). Social cognitive theory. *Annual Review of Psychology,* Vol. 52. Palo Alto, CA: Annual Reviews.

Banks, E. C. (1993, March). *Moral education curriculum in a multicultural context: The Malaysian primary curriculum.* Paper presented at the biennial meeting of the Society for Research in Child Development, New Orleans.

Banks, J. A. (1995). Multicultural education: Its effects on students' racial and gender role attitudes. In J. A. Banks & C. A. M. Banks (Eds.), *Handbook of research on multicultural education.* New York: Macmillan.

Banks, J. A. (1997). Approaches to multicultural education reform. In J. A. Banks & C. A. M. Banks (Eds.), *Multicultural education.* Boston: Allyn & Bacon.

Banks, M. S., & Salapatek, P. (1983). Infant visual perception. In P. H. Mussen (Ed.), *Handbook of child psychology* (4th ed., Vol. 2). New York: Wiley.

Barefoot, J. C., Mortensen, E. L., Helms, J., Avlund, K., & Schroll, M. (2001). A longitudinal study of gender differences in depressive symptoms from age 50 to 80. *Psychology and Aging, 16,* 342–345.

Bargh, J. A., McKenna, K. Y. A., & Fitzsimons, G. (in press). Can you see the real me? Self-presentation and social perception on the Internet. *Journal of Social Issues.*

Barnes, D. L. (2002). What midwives need to know about postpartum depression. *Midwifery Today, 61,* 18–19.

Barnett, D., Ganiban, J., & Cicchetti, D. (1999). Maltreatment, negative expressivity, and the development of type D attachments from 12 to 24 months of age. In J. I. Vondra & D. Barnett (Eds.), *Monograph of the Society for Research in Child Development, 64* (3, Serial No. 258), 97–118.

Barnett, R. C. (2002). Work-family balance. In J. Worell (Ed.), *Encyclopedia of women and gender.* San Diego: Academic Press.

Barnett, R. C., Gareis, K. C., James, J. B., & Steele, J. (2001, August). *Planning ahead: College seniors' concerns about work-family conflict.* Paper presented at the meeting of the American Psychological Association, San Francisco.

Barnett, S. B., & Maulik, D. (2001). Guidelines and recommendations for safe use of Doppler ultrasound in perinatal applications. *Journal of Maternal and Fetal Medicine, 10,* 75–84.

Barr, H. M., & Streissguth, A. P. (2001). Identifying maternal self-reported alcohol use associated with fetal alcohol disorders. Alcoholism: *Clinical and Experimental Research, 25,* 283–287.

Barrett, D. E., Radke-Yarrow, M., & Klein, R. E. (1982). Chronic malnutrition and child behavior. Effects of calorie supplementation on social and emotional functioning at school age. *Developmental Psychology, 18,* 541–556.

Bates, A. S., Fitzgerald, J. F., Dittus, R. S., & Wollinsky, F. D. (1994). Risk factors for underimmunization in poor urban infants. *Journal of the American Medical Association, 272,* 1105–1109.

Bates, J. E. (2001). Adjustment style in childhood as a product of parenting and temperament. In T. D. Wachs & G. A. Kohnstamm (Eds.), *Temperament in context.* Mahwah, NJ: Erlbaum.

Baudry, M. (2003). Synapses and synaptic transmission and integration. In V. S. Ramachandran (Ed.), *Encyclopedia of the human brain.* San Francisco: Academic Press.

Bauer, P. J., Wenner, J. A., Dropik, P. L., & Wewerka, S. S. (2000). Parameters of remembering and forgetting in the transition from infancy to early childhood. *Monographs of the Society for Research in Child Development, 65* (4, Serial No. 263).

Baum, A. S. (2000). Genetic disorders. In A. Kazdin (Ed.), *Encyclopedia of psychology.* Washington, DC, & New York: American

Psychological Association and Oxford University Press.

Baum, A., Revenson, T. A., & Singer, J. E. (Eds.) (2001). *Handbook of health psychology.* Mahwah, NJ: Erlbaum.

Baumeister, R. F. (1991). *Meaning of life.* New York: Guilford.

Baumeister, R. F. (1993). *Self-esteem: The puzzle of low self-regard.* New York: Plenum Press.

Baumeister, R. F., & Vohs, K. D. (2002). The pursuit of meaningfulness in life. In C. R. Snyder & S. J. Lopez (Eds.), *Handbook of positive psychology.* New York: Oxford University Press.

Baumrind, D. (1971). Current patterns of parental authority. *Developmental Psychology Monographs, 4* (1, Pt. 2).

Baumrind, D. (1991). Effective parenting during the early adolescent transition. In P. A. Cowan & E. M. Hetherington (Eds.), *Advances in family research* (Vol. 2). Hillsdale, NJ: Erlbaum.

Baumrind, D. (1999, November). Unpublished review of J. W. Santrock's *Child development,* 9th ed. (New York: McGraw-Hill).

Baumrind, D., Larzelere, R. E., & Cowan, P. A. (2002). Ordinary physical punishment: Is it harmful? Comment on Gershoff. *Psychological Bulletin, 128,* 590–595.

Bauserman, R. (2002). Child adjustment in joint-custody versus sole-custody arrangements: A meta-analytic review. *Journal of Family Psychology, 16,* 91–102.

Baxter, G. W., Stuart, W. J., & Stewart, W. J. (1998). *Death and the adolescent.* Toronto: University of Toronto Press.

Bayley, N. (1969). *Manual for the Bayley Scales of Infant Development.* New York: Psychological Corporation.

Bayley, N. (1970). Development of mental abilities. In P. H. Mussen (Ed.), *Manual of child psychology* (3rd ed., Vol. 1). New York: Wiley.

Beagles-Roos, J., & Gat, I. (1983). Specific impact of radio and television on children's story comprehension. *Journal of Educational Psychology, 75,* 128–137.

Beal, C. R. (1994). *Boys and girls: The development of gender roles.* Boston: McGraw-Hill.

Bechtold, A. G., Busnell, E. W., & Salapatek, P. (1979, April). *Infants' visual localization of visual and auditory targets.* Paper presented at the meeting of the Society for Research in Child Development, San Francisco.

Beck, M. (1992, December 7). Middle Age. *Newsweek*, pp. 50–56.

Bednar, R. L., Wells, M. G., & Peterson, S. R. (1995). *Self-esteem* (2nd ed.). Washington, DC: American Psychological Association.

Begley, S. (1997). How to build a baby's brain. *Newsweek Special Issue*. Spring/Summer, 28–32.

Behrman, R. E., Kliegman, R., & Jenson, H. B. (Eds.) (2000). *Nelson's textbook of pediatrics* (16th ed.). London: Harcourt International.

Beith, B. H. (2002). Needs and requirements in health care for the older adults: Challenges and opportunities for the new millennium. In W. A. Rogers & A. D. Fisk (Eds.), *Human factors interventions for the health care of older adults*. Mahwah, NJ: Erlbaum.

Bell, A. P., Weinberg, M. S., & Mamersmith, S. K. (1981). *Sexual preference*. New York: Simon & Schuster.

Bell, M. A., & Fox, N. A. (1992). The relations between frontal brain electrical activity and cognitive development during infancy. *Child Development, 63,* 1142–1163.

Bell, S. M., & Ainsworth, M. D. S. (1972). Infant crying and maternal responsiveness. *Child Development, 43,* 1171–1190.

Belle, D. (1999). *The after school lives of children*. Mahwah, NJ: Erlbaum.

Bellinger, D., Leviton, A., Waternaux, C., Needleman, H., & Rabinowitz, M. (1987). Longitudinal analysis of prenatal and postnatal lead exposure and early cognitive development. *New England Journal of Medicine, 316,* 1037–1043.

Belloc, N. B., & Breslow, L. (1972). Relationships of physical health status and health practices. *Preventive Medicine, 1,* 409–421.

Belsky, J. (1981). Early human experience: A family perspective. *Developmental Psychology, 17,* 3–23.

Belsky, J., & Eggebeen, D. (1991). Early and extensive maternal employment/child care and 4–6-year-olds socioemotional development: Children of the National Longitudinal Survey of Youth. *Journal of Marriage and the Family, 53,* 1083–1099.

Belsky, J., Jaffe, S., Hsieh, K., & Silva, P. (2001). Child-rearing antecedents of intergenerational relations in young adulthood: A prospective study. *Developmental Psychology, 37,* 801–813.

Belson, W. (1978). *Television violence and the adolescent boy*. London: Saxon House.

Bem, S. L. (1977). On the utility of alternative procedures for assessing psychological androgyny. *Journal of Consulting and Clinical Psychology, 45,* 196–205.

Bengtson, V. L. (1985). Diversity and symbolism in grandparental roles. In V. L. Bengtson & J. Robertson (Eds.), *Grandparenthood*. Newbury Park, CA: Sage.

Bengtson, V. L. (2001). Beyond the nuclear family: The increasing importance of multigenerational bonds. *Journal of Marriage and the Family, 63,* 1–16.

Bennett, W. I., & Gurin, J. (1982). *The dieter's dilemma: Eating less and weighing more*. New York: Basic Books.

Benini, A. L., Camilloni, M. A., Scordato, C., Lezzi, G., Savia, G., Oriani, G., Bertoli, S., Balzola, F., Liuzzi, A., & Petroni, M. L. (2001). Contribution of weight cycling to serum leptin in human obesity. *International Journal of Obesity and Related Metabolic Disorders, 25,* 721–726.

Benson, P. (1993). *The troubled journey*. Minneapolis: Search Institute.

Berardi, A., Parasuraman, R., & Haxby, J. V. (2001). Overall vigilance and sustained attention decrements in healthy aging. *Experimental Aging Research, 27,* 19–39.

Bergin, A. E. (2000). Religious values and mental health. In A. Kazdin (Ed.), *Encyclopedia of psychology*. Washington, DC, & New York: American Psychological Association and Oxford University Press.

Bergin, D. (1988). Stages of play development. In D. Bergin (Ed.), *Play as a medium for learning and development*. Portsmouth, NH: Heinemann.

Berko Gleason, J. (2000). Language: An overview. In A. Kazdin (Ed.), *Encyclopedia of psychology*. Washington, DC, & New York: American Psychological Association and Oxford University Press.

Berko Gleason, J. (2001). *The development of language* (5th ed.). Boston: Allyn & Bacon.

Berko Gleason, J. (2002). Unpublished review of J. W. Santrock's *Life-span development*, 9th ed. (New York: McGraw-Hill).

Berko, J. (1958). The child's learning of English morphology. *Word, 14,* 150–177.

Berlin, L., & Cassidy, J. (2000). Understanding parenting. Contributions of attachment theory and research. In J. D. Osofsky & H. E. Fitzgerald (Eds.), *WAIMH handbook of infant mental health* (Vol. 3). New York: Wiley.

Berlyne, D. E. (1960). *Conflict, arousal, and curiosity*. New York: McGraw-Hill.

Berndt, T. J. (1996). Transitions in friendship and friends' influence. In J. A. Graber, J. Brooks-Gunn, & A. C. Petersen (Eds.), *Transitions through adolescence*. Mahwah, NJ: Erlbaum.

Berndt, T. J. (1999). Friends' influence on children's adjustment. In W. A. Collins & B. Laursen (Eds.), *Relationships as developmental contexts*. Mahwah, NJ: Erlbaum.

Berndt, T. J. (2002). Friendship quality and social development. *Current Directions in Psychological Science, 11,* 7–10.

Berndt, T. J., & Perry, T. B. (1990). Distinctive features and effects of early adolescent friendships. In R. Montemayor (Ed.), *Advances in adolescent research*. Greenwich, CT: JAI Press.

Bernier, M. O., Plu-Bureau, G., Bossard, N., Ayzac, L., Thalabard, J. C. (2000). Breastfeeding and risk of breast cancer: A metaanalysis of published studies. *Human Reproduction Update, 6(4),* 374–386.

Berquist, W. H., Greenberg, E. M., & Klaum, G. A. (1993). *In our fifties*. San Francisco: Jossey-Bass.

Berscheid, E. (1988). Some comments on love's anatomy: Or, whatever happened to old-fashioned lust? In R. J. Sternberg (Ed.), *Anatomy of love*. New Haven, CT: Yale University Press.

Berscheid, E. (2000). Attraction. In A. Kazdin (Ed.), *Encyclopedia of psychology*. Washington, DC, & New York: American Psychological Association and Oxford University Press.

Berscheid, E., & Fei, J. (1977). Sexual jealousy and romantic love. In G. Clinton & G. Smith (Eds.), *Sexual jealousy*. Englewood Cliffs, NJ: Prentice Hall.

Berscheid, E., & Reis, H. T. (1998). Attraction and close-relationships. In D. T. Gilbert, S. T. Fiske, & G. Lindzey (Eds.), *Handbook of social psychology* (4th ed., Vol. 2). New York: McGraw-Hill.

Berscheid, E., Snyder, M., & Omato, A. M. (1989). Issues in studying close relationships. In C. Hendrick (Ed.), *Close relationships*. Newbury Park, CA: Sage.

Bertrand, R. M., & Lachman, M. E. (2003). Personality development in adulthood and old age. In I. B. Weiner (Ed.), *Handbook of psychology, Vol. VI*. New York: Wiley.

Best, D. (2002). Cross-cultural gender roles. In J. Worell (Ed.), *Encyclopedia of women and gender*. San Diego: Academic Press.

Best, J. W., & Kahn, J. V. (2003). *Research in education* (9th ed.). Boston: Allyn & Bacon.

Beyene, Y. (1986). Cultural significance and physiological manifestations of menopause: A biocultural analysis. *Culture, Medicine and Psychiatry, 10,* 47–71.

Bianchi, S. M., & Spani, D. (1986). *American women in transition*. New York: Russell Sage Foundation.

Bijur, P. E., Wallston, K. A., Smith, C. A., Lifrak, S., & Friedman, S. B. (1993, August). *Gender differences in turning to religion for coping*. Paper presented at the meeting of the American Psychological Association, Toronto.

Billman, J. (2003). *Observation and participation in early childhood settings: A practicum guide* (2nd ed.). Boston: Allyn & Bacon.

Billy, J. O. G., Rodgers, J. L., & Udry, J. R. (1984). Adolescent sexual behavior and friendship choice. *Social Forces, 62,* 653–678.

Bingham, C. R., & Crockett, L. J. (1996). Longitudinal adjustment patterns of boys and girls experiencing early, middle, and late sexual intercourse. *Developmental Psychology, 32,* 647–658.

Birren, J. E. (1993). Fifteen commandments for responsible old age. In R. N. Butler & K. Kiikuni (Eds.), *Who is responsible for my old age?* New York: Springer.

Birren, J. E. (Ed.). (1996). *Encyclopedia of gerontology.* San Diego: Academic Press.

Birren, J. E. (2002). Unpublished review of J. W. Santrock's *Life-span development,* 9th ed. (New York: McGraw-Hill).

Birren, J. E., & Schaie, K. W. (Eds.). (2001). *Handbook of the psychology of aging* (5th ed.). San Diego: Academic Press.

Birren, J. E., Woods, A. M., & Williams, M. V. (1980). Behavioral slowing with age: Causes, organization, & consequences. In L. W. Poon (Ed.), *Aging in the 1980s: Psychological issues.* Washington, DC: American Psychological Association.

Bissada, A., & Briere, J. (2002). Child abuse: Physical and sexual. In J. Worell (Ed.), *Encyclopedia of women and gender.* San Diego: Academic Press.

Bjorklund, D. F., & Bering, J. M. (2001, April). *Evolutionary developmental psychology.* Paper presented at the meeting of the Society for Research in Child Development, Minneapolis.

Bjorklund, D. F., & Rosenbaum, K. (2000). Middle childhood: Cognitive development. In A. Kazdin (Ed.), *Encyclopedia of psychology.* Washington, DC, & New York: American Psychological Association and Oxford University Press.

Blachman, B. A., Ball, E., Black, R., & Tangel, D. (1994). Kindergarten teachers develop phoneme awareness in low-income inner-city classrooms: Does it make a difference? In B. A. Blachman (Ed.), *Reading and writing.* Mahwah, NJ: Erlbaum.

Black, J. E. (2001, April). *Complex and interactive effects of enriched experiences on brain development.* Paper presented at the meeting of the Society for Research in Child Development, Minneapolis.

Blair, C., & Ramey, C. (1996). Early intervention with low birth weight infants: The path to second generation research. In M. J. Guralnick (Ed.). *The effectiveness of early intervention.* Baltimore: Paul H. Brookes.

Blair, S. N. (1990, January). *Personal communication.* Aerobics Institute, Dallas.

Blair, S. N., Kohl, H. W., Paffenbarger, R. S., Clark, D. G., Cooper, K. H., & Gibbons, L. W. (1989). Physical fitness and all-cause mortality: A prospective study of healthy men and women. *Journal of the American Medical Association, 262,* 2395–2401.

Blanchard-Fields, F. (1996). Decision making and everyday problem solving. In J. E. Birren (Ed.), *Encyclopedia of gerontology* (Vol. 1). San Diego: Academic Press.

Blazer, D. (2002). *Depression in late life* (3rd ed.). New York: Springer.

Block, J. (1993). Studying personality the long way. In D. Funder, R. D. Parke, C. Tomlinson-Keasey, & K. Widaman (Ed.), *Studying lives through time.* Washington, DC: American Psychological Association.

Block, J. H., & Block, J. (1980). The role of ego-control and ego-resiliency in the organization of behavior. In W. A. Collins (Ed.), *Minnesota symposium on child psychology* (Vol. 13). Minneapolis: University of Minnesota Press.

Block, N. (2002). How heritability misleads about race. In J. M. Fish (Ed.), *Race and intelligence.* Mahwah, NJ: Erlbaum.

Bloom, L. (1993). *The transition from infancy to language: Acquiring the power of expression.* Cambridge, England: Cambridge University Press.

Bloom, L. (1998). Language acquisition in developmental context. In W. Damon (Ed.), *Handbook of child psychology* (5th ed., Vol. 5). New York: Wiley.

Bloom, L., Lifter, K., & Broughton, J. (1985). The convergence of early cognition and language in the second year of life: Problems in conceptualization and measurement. In M. Barrett (Ed.), *Single word speech.* London: Wiley.

Bloor, C., & White, F. (1983). *Unpublished manuscript.* University of California at San Diego, LaJolla, CA.

Blum, L. M. (2000). *At the breast: Ideologies of breastfeeding and motherhood in the contemporary United States.* Boston: Beacon Press.

Blumberg, J. (1993, June 2). Commentary in "Lowly vitamin supplements pack a big health punch." *USA Today,* p. 3D.

Blumenfeld, P. C., Pintrich, P. R., Wessles, K., & Meece, J. (1981, April). *Age and sex differences in the impact of classroom experiences on self-perceptions.* Paper presented at the biennial meeting of the Society of Research in Child Development, Boston.

Blumenthal, J. A., Emery, C. F., Madden, D. J., George, L. K., Coleman, R. E., Riddle, M. W., McKee, D. C., Reasoner, J., & Williams, R. S. (1989). Cardiovascular and behavioral effects of aerobic exercise training in healthy older men and women. *Journal of Gerontology: Medical Sciences, 44,* M147–157.

Blumenthal, J., Jeffries, N. O., Castellanos, F. X., Liu, H., Zidjdenbos, A., Paus, T., Evans, A. C., Rapoport, J. L., & Giedd, J. N. (1999). Brain development during childhood and adolescence: A longitudinal MRI study. *Nature Neuroscience, 10,* 861–863.

Blundell, J. E. (1984). Systems and interactions: An approach to the pharmacology of feeding. In A. J. Stunkdard & E. Stellar (Eds.), *Eating and its disorders.* New York: Raven Press.

Bodnar, A. G., Ouellette, M., Frolkis, M., Holt, S. E., Chiu, C.-P., Morin, G. B., Harley, C. B., Shay, J. W., & Wright, W. E. (1998). Extension of lifespan by introduction of telomerase in normal human cells. *Science, 279,* 349–352.

Boerner, K., & Wortman, C. B. (1998). Grief and loss. In H. S. Freeman (Ed.), *Encyclopedia of mental health* (Vol. 2). San Diego: Academic Press.

Bogenschneider, K. (2002). *Family policy matters.* Mahwah, NJ: Erlbaum.

Bohlin, G., & Hagekull, B. (1993). Stranger wariness and sociability in the early years. *Infant Behavior and Development, 16,* 53–67.

Bolen, J. C., Bland, S. D., & Sacks, J. J. (1999, April). *Injury prevention behaviors: Children's use of occupant restraints and bicycle helmets.* Paper presented at the meeting of the Society for Research in Child Development, Albuquerque.

Bolger, K. E., & Patterson, C. J. (2001). Developmental pathways from child maltreatment to peer rejection. *Child Development, 72,* 549–568.

Bonde, M. W., & Lange, K. L. (1998). Alzheimer's disease. In H. S. Friedman (Ed.), *Encyclopedia of mental health* (Vol. 1). San Diego: Academic Press.

Bonk, C. J., & Cunningham, D. J. (1999). Searching for learner-centered, constructivist, and sociocultural components of collaborative educational learning tools. In C. J. Bonk & K. S. King (Eds.), *Electronic collaborators.* Mahwah, NJ: Erlbaum.

Bonvillian, J. D., Orlansky, M. D., & Novack, L. L. (1983). Developmental milestones: Sign language and motor development. *Child Development, 54,* 1435–1445.

Bookstein, F. L., Streissguth, A. P., Sampson, P. D., Connor, P. D., & Barr, H. M. (2002). Corpus callosum shape and neuropsychological deficits in adult males with heavy fetal alcohol exposure. *Neuroimage, 15,* 233–251.

Booth, A., & Crouter, A. C. (Eds.) (1999). *Does it take a village?* Mahwah, NJ: Erlbaum.

Booth, A., Crouter, A. C., & Clements, M. (Eds.). (2001). *Couples in conflict.* Mahwah, NJ: Erlbaum.

Booth, A., & Johnson, D. (1988). Premarital cohabitation and marital success. *Journal of Family Issues, 9,* 255–272.

Bornstein, M. H. (2000). Unpublished review of J. W. Santrock's *Life-span development,* 8th ed. (New York: McGraw-Hill).

Bornstein, M. H. (Ed.) (2002). *Handbook of parenting,* 2nd ed. New York: Wiley.

Bornstein, M. H., & Arterberry, M. E. (1999). Perceptual development. In M. H. Bornstein & M. E. Lamb (Eds.), *Developmental psychology: An advanced textbook* (4th ed.). Mahwah, NJ: Erlbaum.

Bornstein, M. H., & Bradley, R. H. (Eds.). (2003). *Socioeconomic status, parenting, and child development.* Mahwah, NJ: Erlbaum.

Bornstein, M. H., & Sigman, M. D. (1986). Continuity in mental development from infancy. *Child Development, 57,* 251–274.

Bornstein, R. F., & D'Agostino, P. R. (1992). Stimulus recognition and the mere exposure effect. *Journal of Personality and Social Psychology, 63,* 545–552.

Borowsky, I. W., Ireland, M., & Resnick, M. D. (2001). Adolescent suicide attempts: Risks and protectors. *Pediatrics, 107,* 485–493.

Bosma, H. A., & Kunnen, E. S. (Eds.). (2001). *Identity and emotion.* New York: Cambridge University Press.

Botwinick, J. (1978). *Aging and behavior* (2nd ed.). New York: Springer.

Bouchard, T. J. (1995, August). *Henuibility of intelligence.* Paper presented at the meeting of the American Psychological Association, New York, NY.

Bouchard, T. J., Lykken, D. T., McGue, M., Segal, N. L., & Tellegen, A. (1990). Source of human psychological differences. The Minnesota Study of Twins Reared Apart. *Science, 250,* 223–228.

Bouchey, H. A., & Furman, W. (2003). Dating and romantic relationships in adolescence. In G. Adams & M. Berzonsky (Eds.), *Blackwell handbook of adolescence.* Malden, MA: Blackwell.

Bower, B. (1985). The left hand of math and verbal talent. *Science News, 127,* 263.

Bower, B. (1999, March 20). Minds on the move. Science News, 1–5.

Bowlby, J. (1969). *Attachment and loss* (Vol. 1). London: Hogarth Press.

Bowlby, J. (1980). *Attachment and loss: Vol. 3. Loss, sadness, and depression.* New York: Basic Books.

Bowlby, J. (1989). *Secure and insecure attachment.* New York: Basic Books.

Boyd-Franklin, N. (1989). *Black families in therapy. A multisystems approach.* New York: Guilford Press.

Boyer, K., & Diamond, A. (1992). Development of memory for temporal order in infants and young children. In A. Diamond (Ed.), *Development and neural bases of higher cognitive function.* New York: New York Academy of Sciences.

Brabeck, M. (2000). Kohlberg, Lawrence. In A. Kazdin (Ed.), *Encyclopedia of psychology.* Washington, DC, & New York: American Psychological Association and Oxford University Press.

Bracken, M. B., Eskenazi, B., Sachse, K., McSharry, J., Hellenbrand, K., & Leo-Summers, L. (1990). Association of cocaine use with sperm concentration, motility, and morphology. *Fertility and Sterility, 53,* 315–322.

Bradbury, F. D., Fincham, F. D., & Beach, S. R. H. (2000). Research on the nature and determinants of marital satisfaction: A decade in review. *Journal of Marriage and the Family, 62,* 964–980.

Bradley, R. H., & Corwyn, R. F. (2002). Socioeconomic status and child development. *Annual Review of Psychology* (Vol. 53). Palo Alto, CA: Annual Reviews.

Bradley, R. H., Corwyn, R. F., McAdoo, H. P., & Coll, C. G. (2001). The home environments of children in the United States. Part I: Variations by age, ethnicity, and poverty status. *Child Development, 72,* 1844–1867.

Bramswig, J. H. (2001). Long-term results of growth hormone therapy in Turner syndrome. *Endocrinology, 15,* 5–13.

Brandstädter, J. (1999). Sources of resilience in the aging self. In T. M. Hess & F. Blanchard-Fields (Eds.), *Social cognition and aging* (pp. 123–141). San Diego: Academic Press.

Brandstadter, J., Wentura, D., & Greve, W. (1993). Adaptive resources of the aging self: Outlines of an emergent perspective. *Journal of Behavioral Development, 16,* 323–349.

Brannon, L. (2002). *Gender: psychological perspectives.* Boston: Allyn & Bacon.

Brazelton, T. B. (1956). Sucking in infancy. *Pediatrics, 17,* 400–404.

Brazelton, T. B. (1998, September 7). Commentary. *Dallas Morning News,* p. C2.

Brazelton, T. B., Nugent, J. K., & Lester, B. M. (1987). Neonatal behavioral assessment scale. In J. D. Osofsky (Ed.), *Handbook of infant development* (2nd ed.). New York: Wiley.

Bredekamp, S. (1987). *Developmentally appropriate practice in early childhood programs serving children from birth through age 8.* Washington, DC: National Association for the Education of Young Children.

Bremner, G. (2002). Cognitive development: Knowledge of the physical world. In A. Fogel & G. Bremner (Eds.), *Blackwell handbook of infant development.* London: Blackwell.

Brenner, R. A., Trumble, A. C., Smith, G. S., Kessler, E. P., & Overpeck, M. D. (2001). Where children drown, 1995. *Pediatrics, 108,* 85–89.

Brent, R. L., & Fawcett, L. B. (2000, May). *Environmental causes of human birth defects: What have we learned about the mechanism, nature, and etiology of congenital malformations in the past 50 years?* Paper presented at the joint meetings of the Pediatric Academic Societies and the American Academy of Pediatrics, Boston.

Bretherton, I., Stolberg, U., & Kreye, M. (1981). Engaging strangers in proximal interaction: Infants' social initiative. *Developmental Psychology, 17,* 746–755.

Brickel, C. O., Ciarrocchi, J. W., Sheers, N. J., Estadt, B. K., Powell, D. A., & Pargament, K. I. (1998). Perceived stress, religious coping styles, and depressive affect. *Journal of Psychology and Christianity, 17,* 33–42.

Brim, G. (1992, December 7). Commentary, *Newsweek,* p. 52.

Brim, O. (1999). *The MacArthur Foundation study of midlife development.* Vero Beach, FL: MacArthur Foundation.

Brisette, I., Scheier, M. F., & Carver, C. S. (2002). The role of optimism in social network development, coping, and psychological adjustment during a life transition. *Journal of Personality and Social Psychology, 82,* 102–111.

Brody, G. H., & Ge, X. (2001). Linking parenting processes and self-regulation to psychological functioning and alcohol use during early adolescence. *Journal of Family Psychology, 15,* 82–94.

Brody, J. E. (1994, April 6). The value of breast milk. *New York Times,* p. C11.

Brody, N. (2000). Intelligence. In A. Kazdin (Ed.), *Encyclopedia of psychology.* Washington, DC, & New York: American Psychological Association and Oxford University Press.

Brodzinsky, D. M., Lang, R., & Smith, D. W. (1995). Parenting adopted children. In M. H. Bornstein (Ed.), *Handbook of parenting* (Vol. 3). Hillsdale, NJ: Erlbaum.

Brodzinsky, D. M., Schechter, D. E., Braff, A. M., & Singer, L. M. (1984). Psychological and academic adjustment in adopted children. *Journal of Consulting and Clinical Psychology, 52,* 582–590.

Bronfenbrenner, U. (1986). Ecology of the family as a context for human development: Research perspectives. *Developmental Psychology, 22,* 723–742.

Bronfenbrenner, U. (2000). Ecological theory. In A. Kazdin (Ed.), *Encyclopedia of psychology.* Washington, DC, & New York: American Psychological Association and Oxford University Press.

Bronfenbrenner, U., & Morris, P. (1998). The ecology of developmental processes. In W. Damon (Ed.), *Handbook of child psychology* (5th ed., Vol. 1). New York: Wiley.

Brook, J. S., Brook, D. W., Gordon, A. S., Whiteman, M., & Cohen, P. (1990). The psychological etiology of adolescent drug use: A family interactional approach. *Genetic, Social, and General Psychology Monographs, 116,* 110–267.

Brook, J. S., Whiteman, M., Balka, E. B., Win, P. T., & Gursen, M. D. (1998). Drug use among Puerto Ricans: Ethnic identity as a protective factor. *Hispanic Journal of Behavioral Sciences, 20,* 241–254.

Brooks, J. B. (1999). *The process of parenting* (5th ed.). Mountain View, CA: Mayfield.

Brooks, J. G., & Brooks, M. G. (1993). *The case for constructivist classrooms.* Alexandria, VA: Association for Supervision and Curriculum.

Brooks, J. G., & Brooks, M. G. (2001). *The case for constructivist classrooms.* Upper Saddle River, NJ: Prentice Hall.

Brooks-Gunn, J., & Graber, J. (1999). *What's sex got to do with it? The development of health and sexual identities during adolescence.* Unpublished manuscript, Columbia University, New York City.

Brooks-Gunn, J., Han, W. J., & Waldfogel, J. (2002). Maternal employment and child cognitive outcomes in the first three years of life: The NICHD Study of Early Child Care. *Child Development, 73,* 1052–1072.

Brooks-Gunn, J., Klebanov, P. K., & Duncan, G. J. (1996). Ethnic differences in children's intelligence test scores: Role of economic deprivation, home environment, and maternal characteristics. *Child Development, 67,* 396–408.

Brooks-Gunn, J., & Paikoff, R. (1993). "Sex is a gamble, kissing is a game": Adolescent sexuality, contraception, and sexuality. In S. P. Millstein, A. C. Petersen, & E. O. Nightingale (Eds.), *Promoting the health behavior of adolescents.* New York: Oxford University Press.

Brooks-Gunn, J., & Paikoff, R. (1997). Sexuality and developmental transitions during adolescence. In J. Schulenberg, J. Maggs, & K. Hurrelmann (Eds.), *Health risks and developmental transitions during adolescence.* New York: Cambridge University Press.

Brooks-Gunn, J., & Warren, M. P. (1989). The psychological significance of secondary sexual characteristics in 9- to 11-year-old girls. *Child Development, 59,* 161–169.

Brouwers, E. P. M., van Baar, A. L., & Pop, V. J. M. (2001). Maternal anxiety during pregnancy and subsequent infant development. *Infant Behavior and Development, 24,* 95–106.

Brown, B. B. (1999). "You're going with whom?!": Peer group influences on adolescent romantic relationships. In W. Furman, B. B. Brown, & C. Feiring (Eds.), *The development of romantic relationships in adolescence.* Cambridge: Cambridge University Press.

Brown, B. B. (2003). Crowds, cliques, and friendships. In G. Adams & M. Berzonsky (Eds.), *Blackwell handbook of adolescence.* Malden, MA: Blackwell.

Brown, B. B., & Lohr, M. J. (1987). Peer-group affiliation and adolescent self-esteem: An integration of ego-identity and symbolic-interaction theories. *Journal of Personality and Social Psychology, 52,* 47–55.

Brown, J. D., Steele, J. R., & Walsh-Childers, K. (Eds.). (2002). *Sexual teens, sexual media.* Mahwah, NJ: Erlbaum.

Brown, J. K. (1985). Introduction. In J. K. Brown & V. Kerns (Eds.), *In her prime: A new view of middle-aged women.* South Hadley, MA: Bergin & Garvey.

Brown, L. S. (1989). New voices, new visions: Toward a lesbian/gay paradigm for psychology. *Psychology of Women Quarterly, 13,* 445–458.

Brown, R. (1973). *A first language: The early stages.* Cambridge, MA: Harvard University Press.

Brown, R. (1986). *Social Psychology* (2nd ed.). New York: Free Press.

Browne, A., & Williams, K. R. (1993). Gender, intimacy, and lethal violence: Trends from 1976 through 1987. *Gender and Society, 7,* 78–98.

Brownell, K. D. (2002, June 18). Commentary. *USA Today,* p. 8D.

Brownell, K. D., & Cohen, L. R. (1995). Adherence to dietary regimens. *Behavioral Medicine, 20,* 226–242.

Brownell, K. D., & Rodin, J. (1994). The dieting maelstrom: Is it possible to lose weight? *American Psychologist, 9,* 781–791.

Bruce, C. A. (2002). The grief process for patient, family, and physician. *Journal of the American Osteopathic Association, 102,* (9, Supplement 3), S28–S32.

Bruce, J. M., Olen, K., & Jensen, S. J. (1999, April). *The role of emotion and regulation in social competence.* Paper presented at the meeting of the Society for Research in Child Development, Albuquerque.

Bruck, M., & Ceci, S. (1999). The suggestibility of young children's memory. *Annual Review of Psychology* (Vol. 50). Palo Alto, CA: Annual Reviews.

Bruer, J. T. (1999). *The myth of the first three years.* New York: Free Press.

Bryant, J., & Bryant, J. A. (Eds.) (2001). *Television and the American family.* Mahwah, NJ: Erlbaum.

Buchanan, C. M. (2001, August). *Understanding the variability in children's adjustment after divorce.* Paper presented at the meeting of the American Psychological Association, San Francisco.

Buhrmester, D. (1998). Need fulfillment, interpersonal competence, and the developmental contexts of early adolescent friendship. In W. M. Bukowski & A. F. Newcomb (Eds.), *The company they keep: Friendship in childhood and adolescence.* New York: Cambridge University Press.

Buhrmester, D. (2001, April). *Romantic development: Does age at which romantic involvement start matter?* Paper presented at the meeting of the Society for Research in Child Development, Minneapolis.

Buhrmester, D., & Carbery, J. (1992, March). *Daily patterns of self-disclosure and adolescent adjustment.* Paper presented at the biennial meeting of the Society for Research on Adolescence, Washington, DC.

Buhrmester, D., & Furman, W. (1987). The development of companionship and intimacy. *Child Development, 58,* 1101–1113.

Bulterys, M. (2001). Preventing vertical HIV transmissions in the year 2000. *Placenta, 22,* S5–S12.

Bumpass, L., & Aquilino, W. (1994). *A social map of midlife: Family and work over the middle life course.* Center for Demography & Ecology, University of Wisconsin, Madison, WI.

Bumpus, M. F., Crouter, A. C., & McHale, S. M. (2001). Parental autonomy granting during adolescence: Exploring gender differences in context. *Developmental Psychology, 37,* 161–173.

Burchinal, M. R. (2001, April). *Using the Phase 1 data set of the NICHD Study of Early Child Care.* Paper presented at the meeting of the Society for Research in Child Development, Minneapolis.

Burchinal, M. R., Roberts, J. E., Nabors, L. A., & Bryant, D. M. (1996). Quality of center child care and infant cognitive and language development. *Child Development, 67,* 606–620.

Burke, G. L., Arnold, A. M., Bild, D., Cushman, M., Fried, O., Newman, A., & Robbins, C. (2001). Factors associated with healthy aging. *Journal of the American Geriatric Society, 49,* 254–262.

Burke, H. M., Zautra, A. J., Davis, M. C., Schultz, A. S., & Reich, J. W. (2003). Arthritis and musculoskeletal conditions. In I. B. Weiner (Ed.), *Handbook of psychology,* Vol. IX. New York: Wiley.

Burkhauser, R. V., & Quinn, J. F. (1989). American patterns of work and retirement. In W. Schmall (Ed.), *Redefining the process of retirement.* Berlin: Springer.

Burns, A., Roth, M., & Christie, S. (1996). The natural history of mental disorder in old age. *International Journal of Geriatric Psychiatry, 11,* 7–14.

Burns, D. (1985). *Intimate connections.* New York: William Morrow.

Burton, L. M., & Allison, K. W. (1995). Social context and adolescence: Alternative perspectives on developmental pathways for African-American teens. In L. J. Crockett & A. C. Crouter (Eds.), *Pathways through adolescence.* Hillsdale, NJ: Erlbaum.

Burton, L. M. (1996). The timing of childbearing, family structure, and the role of responsibilities of aging Black women. In E. M. Hetherington & E. A. Blechman (Eds.), *Stress, coping, and resilience in children and families.* Hillsdale, NJ: Erlbaum.

Burts, D. C., Hart, C. H., Charlesworth, R., Hernandez, S., Kirk, L., & Mosley, J. (1989, March). *A comparison of the frequences of stress behaviors observed in kindergarten children in classrooms with developmentally appropriate and developmentally inappropriate instructional practices.* Paper presented at the meeting of the American Educational Research Association, San Francisco.

Bush, P. G., Mayhew, T. M., Abramovich, D. R., Aggett, P. J., Burke, M. D., & Page, K. R. (2001). Maternal cigarette smoking and oxygen diffusion across the placenta. *Placenta, 21,* 824–833.

Bushman, B. J., & Huesmann, L. R. (2001). Effects of televised violence on aggression. In D. Singer & J. Singer (Eds.), *Handbook of children and the media.* Thousand Oaks, CA: Sage.

Buss, D. M. (1995). Psychological sex differences: Origins through sexual selection. *American Psychologist, 50,* 164–168.

Buss, D. M. (1999). *Evolutionary psychology: The new science of the mind.* Boston: Allyn & Bacon.

Buss, D. M. (2000). Evolutionary psychology. In A. Kazdin (Ed.), *Encyclopedia of psychology.* Washington, DC, & New York: American Psychological Association and Oxford University Press.

Buss, D. M. (2001). Human nature and culture: an evolutionary psychology perspective. *Journal of Personality, 69,* 955–978.

Buss, D. M., & others. (1990). International preferences in selecting mates: A study of 37 cultures. *Journal of Cross-Cultural Psychology, 21,* 5–47.

Busse, E. W., & Blazer, D. G. (1996). *The American Psychiatric Press textbook of geriatric psychiatry* (2nd ed.). Washington, DC: American Psychiatric Press.

Butler, R. N. (1975). *Why survive? Being old in America.* New York: Harper & Row.

Butler, R. N. (1996). Global aging: Challenges and opportunities of the next century. *Ageing International, 21,* 12–32.

Butler, R. N., & Lewis, M. (2002). *The new love and sex after 60.* New York: Ballentine.

Butz, A. M., Pulsifer, M., Marano, N., Belcher, H., Lears, M. K., & Royall, R. (2001). Effectiveness of a home intervention for perceived child behavioral problems and parenting stress in children with in utero drug exposure. *Archives of Pediatric and Adolescent Medicine, 155,* 1029–1037.

Buzwell, S., & Rosenthal, D. (1996). Constructing a sexual self: Adolescents' sexual self-perceptions and sexual risk-taking. *Journal of Research on Adolescence, 6,* 489–513.

Bybee, J. (Ed.). (1999). *Guilt and children.* San Diego: Academic Press.

Byrnes, J. P. (1997). *The nature and development of decision making.* Mahwah, NJ: Erlbaum.

Byrnes, J. P. (2001). *Minds, brains, and learning.* New York: Guilford Press.

Byrnes, J. P. (2003). Cognitive development during adolescence. In G. Adams & M. Berzonsky (Eds.), *Blackwell handbook of adolescence.* Malden, MA: Blackwell.

C

Cabeza, R. (2002). Hemispheric asymmetry reduction in older adults: The HAROLD model. *Psychology and Aging, 17,* 85–100.

Cacioppo, J. T. (2002). Emotion and health. In R. J. Davidson, K. R. Sherer, & H. H. Goldsmith (Eds.), *Handbook of affective sciences.* New York: Oxford University Press.

Cacioppo, J. T., Ernst, J. M., Burleson, M. H., McClintock, M. K., Malarkey, W. B., Hawkley, L. C., Kowalewski, R. B., Paulsen, A., Hobson, J. A., Hugdahl, K., Spiegel, D., Berntson, G. G. (2000). Lonely traits and concomitant physiological processes: The MacArthur Social Neuroscience Studies. *International Journal of Psychophysiology, 35,* 143–154.

Calabrese, R. L., & Schumer, H. (1986). The effects of service activities on adolescent alienation. *Adolescence, 21,* 675–687.

Call, K., Riedel, A., Hein, K., McLoyd, V., Kipke, M., & Petersen, A. (2003). Adolescent health and well-being in the 21st century: A global perspective. In R. Larson, B. Brown, & J. Mortimer (Eds.), *Adolescents' preparation for the future: Perils and promises.* Malden, MA: Blackwell.

Callahan, C. M., & Wolinsky, F. D. (1995). Hospitalization for major depression among older Americans. *Journal of Gerontology: Medical Sciences, 50A,* M196–M202.

Callan, J. E. (2002). Gender development: Psychoanalytic perspectives. In J. Worrel (Ed.), *Encyclopedia of women and gender.* San Diego: Academic Press.

Callender, E. S., Rickard, L., Rinksy-Eng, J. (2001). Knowledge and use of folic acid supplementation: A study of

Colorado women whose pregnancies were affected by a fetal neural tube defect. *Clinical Investigations in Medicine, 24,* 124–128.

Calvaresi, E., & Bryan, J. (2001). B vitamins, cognition, and aging: A review. *Journal of Gerontology: Psychological Sciences, 56B,* 327–339.

Camaioni, L. (2002). Early language. In U. Goswami (Ed.), *Blackwell handbook of childhood cognitive development.* Malden, MA: Blackwell.

Cameron, J., Cowan, L., Holmes, B., Hurst, P., & McLean, M. (Eds.). (1983). *International handbook of educational systems.* New York: Wiley.

Cameron, J. R., Hansen, R., & Rosen, D. (1989). Preventing behavioral problems in infancy through temperament assessment and parental support programs. In W. B. Carey & S. C. McDevitt (Eds.), *Clinical and education applications of temperament research.* Amsterdam: Swets & Zeitlinger.

Campbell, L., Campbell, B., & Dickinson, D. (1999). *Teaching and learning through multiple intelligences* (2nd ed.). Boston: Allyn & Bacon.

Campa, B. E., Connor-Smith, J. K., Saltzman, H., Thomsen, A. H., & Wadsworth, M. E. (2001). Coping with stress during childhood and adolescence: Problems, progress, and potential in theory and research. *Psychological Bulletin, 127,* 87–127.

Campos, J. J. (2001, April). *Emotion in emotional development: Problems and prospects.* Paper presented at the meeting of the Society for Research in Child Development, Minneapolis.

Campos, J. J., Langer, A., & Krowitz, A. (1970). Cardiac responses on the visual cliff in prelocomotor human infants. *Science, 170,* 196–197.

Camps, P., & Munoz-Torrero, D. (2003). Cholinergic drugs in pharmacotherapy of Alzheimer's disease. *Mini-Review of Medicinal Chemistry, 2,* 11–25.

Canfield, J., & Hansen, M. V. (1995). *A second helping of chicken soup for the soul.* Deerfield Beach, FL: Health Communications.

Canfield, R. L., & Haith, M. M. (1991). Young infants' visual expectations for symmetric and asymmetric stimulus sequences. *Developmental Psychology, 27,* 198–208.

Caporael, L. R. (2001). Evolutionary psychology. *Annual Review of Psychology* (Vol. 52). Palo Alto, CA: Annual Reviews.

Carbone, D. J., & Seftel, A. D. (2002). Erectile dysfunctions: Diagnosis and treatment in older men. *Geriatrics, 57(9),* 18–24.

Carbonne, B., Tsatsaris, V., & Goffinet, F. (2001). The new tocolytics. *Gynecology, Obstetrics, and Fertility, 29,* 316–319.

Carnegie Corporation. (1989). *Turning points: Preparing youth for the 21st century.* New York: Author.

Carnegie Council on Adolescent Development. (1995). *Great transitions.* New York: Author.

Carstensen, L. L. (1991). Selectivity theory: Social activity in life-span context. *Annual Review of Gerontology and Geriatrics, 11,* 195–217.

Carstensen, L. L. (1995). Evidence for a life-span theory of socioemotional selectivity. *Current Directions in Psychological Science, 4,* 151–156.

Carstensen, L. L. (1997, August). *Psychology and the aging revolution.* Symposium presented at the meeting of the American Psychological Association, Chicago.

Carstensen, L. L. (1998). A life-span approach to social motivation. In J. Heckhausen & C. Dweck (Eds.), *Motivation and self-regulation across the life span.* New York: Cambridge University Press.

Carstensen, L. L., Gottman, J. M., & Levenson, R. W. (1995). Emotional behavior in long-term marriage. *Psychology and Aging, 10,* 140–149.

Carstensen, L. L., Isaacowitz, D. M., & Charles, S. T. (1999). Taking time seriously: A theory of socioemotional selectivity. *American Psychologist, 54,* 165–181.

Carter, B., & McGoldrick, M. (1989). Overview: The changing family life cycle—A framework for family therapy. In B. Carter & M. McGoldrick (Eds.), *The changing family life cycle* (2nd ed.). Boston: Allyn & Bacon.

Carter-Saltzman, L. (1980). Biological and sociocultural effects on handedness: Comparison between biological and adoptive families. *Science, 209,* 1263–1265.

Carver, K., Joyner, K., & Udry, J. R. (in press). National estimates of romantic relationships. In P. Florsheim (Ed.), *Adolescent romantic relations and sexual behavior: Theory, research, and practical implications.* Mahwah, NJ: Erlbaum.

Carver, L. J., & Bauer, P. J. (1999). When the event is more than the sum of its parts: Nine-month-olds' long-term ordered recall. *Memory, 7,* 147–174.

Carver, L. J., & Bauer, P. J. (2001). The dawning of a past: The emergence of long-term explicit memory in infancy. *Journal of Experimental Psychology: General, 130,* (4), 726–745.

Carver, L. J., Bauer, P. J., & Nelson, C. A. (2000). Associations between infant brain activity and recall memory. *Developmental Science, 3,* 234–246.

Case, R. (1999). Conceptual development in the child and the field: A personal view of the Piagetian legacy. In E. K. Skolnick, K. Nelson, S. A. Gelman, & P. H. Miller (Eds.), *Conceptual development.* Mahwah, NJ: Erlbaum.

Case, R., Kurland, D. M., & Goldberg, J. (1982). Operational efficiency and the growth of short-term memory span. *Journal of Experimental Child Psychology, 33,* 386–404.

Case, R., & Mueller, M. P. (2001). Differentiation, integration, and covariance mapping as fundamental processes in cognitive and neurological growth. In J. L. McClelland & R. S. Siegler (Eds.), *Mechanisms of cognitive development.* Mahwah, NJ: Erlbaum.

Casey, B. J. (2002). Neuroscience: Windows into the human brain. *Science, 296,* 1408–1409.

Casey, B. J., Durston, S., & Fossella, J. A. (2001). Evidence for a mechanistic model of cognitive control. *Clinical Neuroscience Research, 1,* 267–282.

Casey, B. M., McIntire, D. D., Leveno, K. J. (2001). The continuing value of the Apgar score on the assessment of newborn infants. *New England Journal of Medicine, 344,* 467–471.

Caspi, A. (1998). Personality development across the life course. In W. Damon (Ed.), *Handbook of child psychology* (Vol. 3). New York: Wiley.

Caspi, A., & Roberts, B. W. (2001). Personality development across the life course: The argument for change and continuity. *Psychological Inquiry, 12,* 49–66.

Cassidy, J., & Berlin, L. J. (1994). The insecure/ambivalent pattern of attachment: Theory and research. *Child Development, 65,* 971–991.

Cassidy, J., & Shaver, P. R. (Eds.) (1999). *Handbook of attachment: Theory, research, and clinical applications.* New York: Guilford.

Castle, N. G. (2001). Innovation in nursing homes. *The Gerontologist, 41* (No. 2), 161–172.

Cauce, A. M., Domenech-Rodriquez, M., Paradise, M., Cochran, B. N., Shea, J. M., Srebnik, D., & Baydar, N. (2002). Cultural and contextual influences in mental health help seeking: A focus on ethnic minority youth. *Journal of Consulting and Clinical Psychology, 70,* 44–55.

Cauffman, B. E. (1994, February). *The effects of puberty, dating, and sexual involvement on* *dieting and disordered eating in young adolescent girls.* Paper presented at the meeting of the Society for Research on Adolescence, San Diego.

Caulfield, R. A. (2001). *Infants and toddlers.* Upper Saddle River, NJ: Prentice Hall.

Cavanaugh, J. (2000, January). Commentary. *American Psychologist, 31,* p. 25.

Ceballo, R. E. (1999, April). *The psychological impact of children's perceptions of neighborhood danger and collective efficacy.* Paper presented at the meeting of the Society for Research in Child Development, Albuquerque.

Ceci, S. J. (2000). Bronfenbrenner, Urie. In A. Kazdin (Ed.), *Encyclopedia of psychology.* Washington, DC, & New York: American Psychological Association and Oxford University Press.

Ceci, S. J., & Gilstrap, L. L. (2000). Determinants of intelligence: Schooling and intelligence. In A. Kazdin (Ed.), *Encyclopedia of psychology.* Washington, DC, & New York: American Psychological Association and Oxford University Press.

Center for Survey Research at the University of Connecticut. (2000). *Hours on the job.* Storrs: University of Connecticut, Center for Survey Research.

Centers for Disease Control and Prevention. (2000). *HIV/AIDS surveillance report.* Atlanta: Author.

Centers for Disease Control and Prevention. (2001). *Sexually transmitted diseases.* Atlanta: Author.

Centers for Disease Control and Prevention. (2001). *Strategies for stopping smoking.* Atlanta, GA: Author.

Centers for Disease Control and Prevention. (2002). *Cohabitation, marriage, divorce, and remarriage in the United States.* Atlanta: Author.

Centers for Disease Control and Prevention. (2002). Trends in racial and ethnic-specific rates for health status indicators: United States, 1990–1998. *Healthy People 2000: Statistical Notes, 23,* 1–16.

Chan, A., Keane, R. J., & Robinson, J. S. (2001). The contribution of maternal smoking to preterm birth, small for gestational age, and low birth weight among Aboriginal and non-Aboriginal births in South Australia. *Medical Journal of Australia, 174,* 389–393.

Charness, N., & Bosman, E. A. (1992). Human factors and aging. In F. I. M. Craik & T. A. Salthouse (Eds.), *The handbook of aging and cognition.* Hillsdale, NJ: Erlbaum.

Charness, N., Krampe, R. T., & Mayr, U. (1996). The role of practice and coaching in entrepreneurial skill domains: An international comparison of life-span chess skill acquisition. In K. A. Ericsson (Ed.), *The road to excellence: The acquisition of expert performance in the arts, sciences, sports, and games.* Mahwah, NJ: Erlbaum.

Chase-Lansdale, P. L., Coley, R. L., & Grining, C. P. L. (2001, April). *Low-income families and child care.* Paper presented at the meeting of the Society for Research in Child Development, Minneapolis.

Chauhuri, J. H., & Williams, P. H. (1999, April). *The contribution of infant temperament and parent emotional availability to toddler attachment.* Paper presented at the meeting of the Society for Research in Child Development, Albuquerque.

Chavkin, W. (2001). Cocaine and pregnancy—time to look at the evidence. *Journal of the American Medical Association, 285,* 1626–1628.

Chen, C., & Stevenson, H. W. (1989). Homework: A cross-cultural comparison. *Child Development, 60,* 551–561.

Chen, X., Hastings, P. D., Rubin, K. H., Chen, H., Cen, G., & Stewart, S. L. (1998). Childrearing attitudes and behavioral inhibition in Chinese and Canadian toddlers: A cross-cultural study. *Developmental Psychology, 34,* 677–686.

Chen, Z., & Siegler, R. S. (2000). Across the great divide: Bridging the gap between understanding of toddlers' and older children's thinking. *Monograph of the Society for Research in Child Development, 65* (2).

Chen, Z., & Siegler, R. S. (2000). Intellectual development in childhood. In R. J. Sternberg (Ed.), *Handbook of intelligence.* New York: Cambridge University Press.

Cheng, T. L., Fields, C. B., Brenner, R. A., Wright, J. L., Lomax, T., & Schedit, P. C. (2000). Sports injuries: An important cause of morbidity in urban youth. *Pediatrics, 105,* E32–33.

Cherlin, A. J., & Furstenberg, F. F. (1994). Stepfamilies in the United States: A reconsideration. In J. Blake & J. Hagen (Eds.), *Annual review of sociology.* Palo Alto, CA: Annual Reviews.

Cherry, K. E., & LeCompte, D. L. (1999). Age and individual differences influence prospective memory. *Psychology and Aging, 14,* 60–76.

Chess, S., & Thomas, A. (1977). Temperamental individuality from childhood to

adolescence. *Journal of Child Psychiatry, 16,* 218–226.

Chess, S., & Thomas, A. (1987). *Origins and evolution of behavior disorders.* Cambridge, MA: Harvard University Press.

Chi, M. T. (1978). Knowledge structures and memory development. In R. S. Siegler (Ed.), *Children's thinking: What develops?* Hillsdale, NJ: Erlbaum.

Children's Defense Fund. (2002). *State of America's children.* Washington, DC: Author.

Child Trends. (2001). *Trends among Hispanic children, youth, and families.* Washington, DC: Author.

Chilsom, J. (2001). Evolution of the management and prevention of childhood lead poisoning. *Environmental Research, 86,* 111–121.

Chiriboga, D. A. (1982). Adaptation to marital separation in later and earlier life. *Journal of Gerontology, 37,* 109–114.

Chiriboga, D. A. (1989). Mental health at the midpoint: Crisis, challenge, or relief? In S. Hunter & M. Sundel (Eds.), *Midlife myths.* Newbury Park, CA: Sage.

Chisholm, K. (1998). A three-year follow-up of attachment and indiscriminate friendliness in children adopted from Romanian orphanages. *Child Development, 69,* 1092–1106.

Chochinov, H. M. (2002). Dignity-conserving care—a new model for palliative care: Helping the patient feel valued. *Journal of the American Medical Association, 287,* 2253–2260.

Choi, N. G. (2001). Relationship between life satisfaction and postretirement employment among older women. *International Journal of Aging and Human Development, 52,* 45–70.

Chomsky, N. (1957). *Syntactic structures.* The Hague: Mouton.

Christensen, H., Korten, A., Jorm, A. F., Henderson, A. S., Scott, R., & MacKinnon, A. J. (1996). Activity levels and cognitive functioning in an elderly community sample. *Age and Aging, 25,* 72–80.

Christensen, L. (1996). *Diet-behavior relationships.* Washington, DC: American Psychological Association.

Christian, K., Bachnan, H. J., & Morrison, F. J. (2001). Schooling and cognitive development. In R. J. Sternberg & E. L. Grigorenko (Eds.), *Environmental effects on cognitive development.* Mahwah, NJ: Erlbaum.

Chun, K. M., & Akutsu, P. D. (2003). Acculturation among ethnic minority families. In K. M. Chun, P. B. Organista, & G. Marin (Eds.), *Acculturation*. Washington, DC: American Psychological Association.

Church, D. K., Siegel, M. A., & Fowler, C. D. (1988). *Growing old in America*. Wylie, TX: Information Aids.

Cicchetti, D. (2001). How a child builds a brain. In W. W. Hartup & R. A. Weinberg (Eds.), *Child psychology in retrospect and prospect*. Mahwah, NJ: Erlbaum.

Cicchetti, D. (2001, April). *The emergence, evolution, and future of developmental psychopathology*. Paper presented at the meeting of the Society for Research in Child Development, Minneapolis.

Cicchetti, D., Ganiban, J., & Barnet:, D. (1991). Contributions from the study of high risk populations to understanding the development of emotion regulation. In J. Garber & K. Dodge (Eds.), *The development of emotion regulation and dysregulation*. New York: Cambridge University Press.

Cicchetti, D., & Toth, S. L. (1998). Perspectives on research and practice in developmental psychology. In W. Damon (Ed.), *Handbook of child psychology* (Vol. 4). New York: Wiley.

Cicirelli, V. G. (1991). Sibling relationships in adulthood. *Marriage and Family Review, 16,* 291–310.

Clancy, S. M., & Hoyer, W. J. (1994). Age and skill in visual search. *Developmental Psychology, 30,* 545–552.

Clark, E. (2000). Language acquisition. In A. Kazdin (Ed.), *Encyclopedia of psychology*. Washington, DC, & New York: American Psychological Association and Oxford University Press.

Clark, S. D., Zabin, L. S., & Hardy, J. B. (1984). Sex, contraception, and parenthood: Experience and attitudes among urban black young men. *Family Planning Perspectives, 16,* 77–82.

Clarke, E. J., Preston, M., Raksin, J., & Bengtson, V. L. (1999). Types of conflicts and tensions between older adults and adult children. *Gerontologist, 39,* 261–270.

Clarkson-Smith, L., & Hartley, A. A. (1989). Relationships between physical exercise and cognitive abilities in older adults. *Psychology and Aging, 4,* 183–189.

Clausen, J. A. (1993). *American lives*. New York: Free Press.

Clay, R. A. (1997, April). Helping dying patients let go of life in peace. *APA Monitor,* p. 42.

Clay, R. A. (2000, April). Linking up online: Is the Internet enhancing interpersonal connections or leading to greater social isolation? *Monitor on Psychology, 31,* 20–23.

Clemens, A. W., & Axelson, L. J. (1985). The not-so-empty nest: The return of the fledgling adult. *Family Relations, 34,* 259–264.

Cleveland, J. N., & Shore, L. M. (1996). Work and employment. In J. E. Birren (Ed.), *Encyclopedia of aging* (Vol. 2). San Diego: Academic Press.

Clifford, B. R., Gunter, B., & McAleer, J. L. (1995). *Television and children*. Hillsdale, NJ: Erlbaum.

Clifton, R. K., Morrongiello, B. A., Kulig, J. W., & Dowd, J. M. (1981). Developmental changes in auditory localization in infancy. In R. N. Aslin, J. R. Alberts, & M. R. Petersen (Eds.), *Development of perception* (Vol. 1). Orlando, FL: Academic Press.

Clifton, R. K., Muir, D. W., Ashmead, D. H., & Clarkson, M. G. (1993). Is visually guided reaching in early infancy a myth? *Child Development, 64,* 1099–1110.

Cnattingius, S., Bergstrom, R., Lipworth, L., & Kramer, M. S. (1998). Prepregnancy weight and the risk of adverse pregnancy outcomes. *New England Journal of Medicine, 338,* 147–152.

Cnattingius, S., Signorello, L. B., Anneren, G., Classon, B., Ekbom, A., Ljunger, E., Blot, W. J., McLaughlin, J. K., Petersson, G., Rane, A., & Granath, F. (2000). Caffeine intake and the risk of first-trimester spontaneous abortion. *New England Journal of Medicine, 343,* 1839–1845.

Cochran, S. D., & Mays, V. M. (1990). Sex, lies, and HIV. *New England Journal of Medicine, 322*(11), 774–775.

Cohan, C. L., & Kleinbaum, S. (2002). Toward a greater understanding of the cohabitation effect: Premarital cohabitation and marital communication. *Journal of Marriage and Family, 64,* 180–192.

Cohen, C. I., Teresi, J., & Holmes, D. (1985). Social networks, stress, adaptation, and health. *Research on Aging, 7,* 409–431.

Cohen, G. J. (2000). *American Academy of Pediatrics guide to your child's sleep: Birth through adolescence*. New York: Villard Books.

Cohen, L. B., & Cashon, C. H. (2003). Infant perception and cognition. In I. B. Weiner (Ed.), *Handbook of psychology* (Vol. VI). New York: Wiley.

Cohn, E., & Harlow, K. (1993, October). *Elders as victims: Randomized studies in two states*. Paper presented at the meeting of the

Gerontological Association of America, New Orleans.

Coie, J. (1999, November). Unpublished review of J. W. Santrock's *Child development,* 9th ed. (New York: McGraw-Hill).

Colby, A., Kohlberg, L., Gibbs, J., & Lieberman, M. (1983). A longitudinal study of moral judgment. *Monographs of the Society for Research in Child Development* (Serial No. 201).

Cole, E. R., & Stewart, A. J. (1996). Black and White women's political activism: Personality development, political identity and social responsibility. *Journal of Personality and Social Psychology, 71,* 130–140.

Coleman, M., Ganong, L., & Fine, M. (2000). Reinvestigating remarriage: Another decade of progress. *Journal of Marriage and the Family, 62,* 1288–1307.

Coleman, M., Ganong, L., & Weaver, S. E. (2001). Relationship maintenance and enhancement in remarried families. In J. H. Harvey & A. Wenzel (Eds.), *Close romantic relationships*. Mahwah, NJ: Erlbaum.

Coleman, P. D. (1986, August). *Regulation of dendritic extent: Human aging brain and Alzheimer's disease*. Paper presented at the meeting of the American Psychological Association, Washington, DC.

Coles, R. (1970). *Erik H. Erikson: The growth of his work*. Boston: Little, Brown.

Coley, R. (2001). *Differences in the gender gap: Comparisons across/racial/ethnic groups in the United States*. Princeton, NJ: Educational Testing Service.

Coll, C. T. G., Meyer, E. C., & Brillion, L. (1995). Ethnic and minority parenting. In M. H. Bornstein (Ed.), *Children and parenting* (Vol. 2). Hillsdale, NJ: Erlbaum.

Coll, C. T. G., & Pachter, L. M. (2002). Ethnic and minority parenting. In M. H. Bornstein (Ed.), *Handbook of parenting* (2nd ed., Vol. 4). Mahwah, NJ: Erlbaum.

College Board. (1996, August 22). *News from the College Board*. New York: The College Entrance Examination Board.

Collins, M. (1996, Winter). The job outlook for '96 grads. *Journal of Career Planning, 51*–54.

Collins, N. L., Dunke-Schetter, C., Lobel, M., & Scrimshaw, S. C. M. (1993). Social support and pregnancy: Psychological correlates of birth outcomes and postpartum depression. *Journal of Personality and Social Psychology, 65,* 1243–1258.

Collins, W. A. (2002, April). *More than a myth: The developmental significance of romantic*

relationships during adolescence. Presidential address delivered at the Meeting of the Society for Research on Adolescence, New Orleans.

Collins, W. A., & Laursen, B. (2000). Adolescent relationships: The art of fugue. In C. Hendrick & S. S. Hendrick (Eds.), *Close relationships: A sourcebook.* Thousand Oaks, CA: Sage.

Collins, W. A., Maccoby, E. E., Steinberg, L., Hetherington, E. M., & Bornstein, M. H. (2000). Contemporary research on parenting: The case for nature and nurture. *American Psychologist, 55,* 218–232.

Collins, W. A., Maccoby, E. E., Steinberg, L., Hetherington, E. M., & Bornstein, M. H. (2001). Toward nature WITH nurture. *American Psychologist, 56,* 171–173.

Collins, W. A., Madsen, S. D., & Susman-Stillman, A. (2002). Parenting during middle childhood. In M. Bornstein (Ed.), *Handbook of parenting* (2nd ed.). Mahwah, NJ: Erlbaum.

Comas-Díaz, L. (2001). Hispanics, Latinos, or Americanos: The evolution of identity. *Cultural Diversity and Ethnic Minority Psychology, 7,* 115–120.

Comer, J. P. (1988). Educating poor minority children. *Scientific American, 259,* 42–48.

Comer, J. P., Haynes, N. M., Joyner, E. T., & Ben-Avie, M. (1996). *Rallying the whole village: The Comer process for reforming urban education.* New York: Teachers College Press.

Comijs, H., Deeg, D., Dik, M., Twisk, J., & Jonker, C. (2002). *Memory complaints.* Unpublished manuscript, Department of Psychiatry, Vrije University, Amsterdam, The Netherlands.

Committee on Drugs. (2000). Use of psychoactive medication during pregnancy and possible effects on the fetus and newborn. *Pediatrics, 105,* 880–887.

Committee on Fetus and Newborn. (2000). Prevention and management of pain and stress in the newborn. *Pediatrics, 105,* 454–461.

Committee on Pediatric AIDS. (2000). Identification and care of HIV-exposed and HIV-infected infants, children, and adolescents. *Pediatrics, 106,* 149–153.

Committee on Sports Medicine and Fitness. (2000). Injuries in youth soccer: A subject review. *Pediatrics, 105,* 659–661.

Committee on Substance Abuse. (2000). Fetal alcohol syndrome and alcohol-related neurodevelopmental disorders. *Pediatrics, 106,* 258–261.

Commoner, B. (2002). Unraveling the DNA myth: The spurious foundation of genetic engineering. *Harper's Magazine, 304,* 39–47.

Commons, M. L., Sinnott, J. D., Richards, F. A., & Armon, C. (1989). *Adult development: Vol. 1. Comparisons and applications of developmental models.* New York: Praeger.

Compas, B. E., & Grant, K. E. (1993, March). *Stress and adolescent depressive symptoms: Underlying mechanisms and processes.* Paper presented at the biennial meeting of the Society for Research in Child Development, New Orleans.

Comstock, G., & Scharrar, E. (1999). *Television.* San Diego: Academic Press.

Condry, K. F., Smith, W. C., & Spelke, E. S. (2001). Development of perceptual organization. In F. Lacerda, C. von Hofsten, & M. Heimann (Eds.), *Emerging cognitive abilities in infancy.* Mahwah, NJ: Erlbaum.

Conger, R. D., & Ge, X. (1999). Conflict and cohesion in parent-adolescent relations: Changes in emotional expression. In M. J. Cox & J. Brooks-Gunn (Eds.), *Conflict and cohesion in families.* Mahwah, NJ: Erlbaum.

Conger, R., & Reuter, M. (1996). Siblings, parents, and peers: A longitudinal study of social influences in adolescent risk for alcohol use and abuse. In G. H. Brody (Ed.), *Sibling relationships: Their causes and consequences.* Norwood, NJ: Ablex.

Contemporary Research Press. (1993). *American working women: A statistical handbook.* Dallas: Author.

Cook, D. J., Guyatt, G. H., Jaeschke, R., Reeve, J., Spanier, A., King, D., Molloy, D., Willan, A., & Streiner, D. (1995). Determinants in Canadian health care workers of the decision to withdraw life support from the critically ill. *Journal of the American Medical Association, 273,* 703–708.

Cooper, C. R., & Grotevant, H. D. (1989, April). *Individuality and connectedness in the family and adolescent's self and relational competence.* Paper presented at the meeting of the Society for Research in Child Development, Kansas City.

Cooper, C. R., Grotevant, H. D., Moore, M. S., & Condon, S. M. (1982, August). *Family support and conflict: Both foster adolescent identity and role taking.* Paper presented at the meeting of the American Psychological Association, Washington, DC.

Corr, C. A., Nabe, C. M., & Corr, D. M. (2000). *Death and dying: Life and living* (3rd ed.), Belmont, CA: Wadsworth.

Corr, C. A., Nabe, C. M., & Corr, D. M. (2003). *Death and dying, life and living* (4th ed.), Belmont, CA: Wadsworth.

Corsini, R. J. (1999). *The dictionary of psychology.* Philadelphia: Brunner/Mazel.

Corso, J. F. (1977). Auditory perception and communication. In J. E. Birren & K. W. Schaie (Eds.), *Handbook of the psychology of aging* (2nd ed.). New York: Van Nostrand Reinhold.

Cosey, E. J., & Bechtel, G. A. (2001). Family support and prenatal care among unmarried African American teenage primiparas. *Journal of Community Health and Nursing, 18,* 107–114.

Cosmides, L., Tooby, J., Cronin, H., & Curry, O. (Eds.). (2003). *What is evolutionary psychology? Explaining the new science of the mind.* New Haven, CT: Yale University Press.

Costa, P. T., & McCrae, R. R. (1995). Solid ground on the wetlands of personality: A reply to Black. *Psychological Bulletin, 117,* 216–220.

Costa, P. T., & McCrae, R. R. (1998). Personality assessment. In H. S. Friedman (Ed.), *Encyclopedia of mental health* (Vol. 3). San Diego: Academic Press.

Costa, P. T., & McCrae, R. R. (1999). Contemporary personality psychology: Implications for geriatric neuropsychiatry. In C. E. Coffey and J. L. Cummings (Eds.), *Textbook of geriatric neuropsychiatry* (2nd ed.). Washington, DC: American Psychiatric Press.

Costa, P. T., & McCrae, R. R. (2000). Contemporary personality psychology. In C. E. Coffey and J. L. Cummings (Eds.), *Textbook of geriatric neuropsychiatry.* Washington, DC: American Psychiatric Press.

Cotten, S. R. (1999). Marital status and mental health revisited: Examining the importance of risk factors and resources. *Family Relations, 48,* 225–233.

Council of Economic Advisors. (2000). *Teens and their parents in the 21st century: An examination of trends in teen behavior and the role of parent involvement.* Washington, DC: Author.

Courtenay, W. H., McCreary, D. R., & Merighi, J. R. (2002). Gender and ethnic differences in health beliefs and behaviors. *Journal of Health Psychology, 7,* 291–231.

Cowan, C. P., & Cowan, P. A. (2000). *When partners become parents.* Mahwah, NJ: Erlbaum.

Cowan, C. P., Cowan, P. A., Heming, G., & Boxer, C. (1995). *Preventive interventions with parents of preschoolers on the children's* *adaptation to kindergarten.* Paper presented at the meeting of the Society for Research in Child Development, New Orleans.

Cowan, P. A., & Cowan, C. P. (2002). What an intervention design reveals about how parents affect their children's academic behavior and behavior problems. In J. G. Borkowski, S. L. Ramey, & M. Bristol-Power (Eds.), *Parenting and the child's world.* Mahwah, NJ: Erlbaum.

Cowley, G. (1998, April 6). Why children turn violent. *Newsweek*, pp. 24–25.

Cowley, G., & Hager, M. (1995, December 4). Terminal care: Too painful, too prolonged. *Newsweek*, pp. 74–75.

Cox, H., & Hammonds, A. (1998). Religiosity, aging, and life satisfaction. *Journal of Religion and Aging, 5,* 1–21.

Crawford, M., & Unger, R. (2000). *Women and gender* (3rd ed.). New York: McGraw-Hill.

Cremation Association of America. (2000). *Fact sheet.* Milwaukee, WI: Author.

Crick, N. R., Grotpeter, J. K., & Bigbee, M. A. (2002). Relationally and physically aggressive children's intent attributions and feelings of distress for relational and instrumental peer provocations. *Child Development, 73,* 1134–1142.

Crick, N. R., Nelson, D. A., Morales, J. R., Cullerton-Sen, C., Casas, J. F., Hickman, S. (2001). Relational victimization in childhood and adolescence: I hurt you through the grapevine. In J. Juvonen & S. Graham (Eds.), *Peer harassment in school: The plight of the vulnerable and victimized.* New York: Guilford Press.

Crockenberg, S. B. (1986). Are temperamental differences in babies associated with predictable differences in caregiving? In J. V. Lerner & R. M. Lerner (Eds.), *Temperament and social interaction during infancy and childhood.* San Francisco: Jossey-Bass.

Crockett, L. J., Raffaelli, M., & Moilanen, K. (2003). Adolescent sexuality: Behavior and meaning. In G. Adams & M. Berzonsky (Eds.), *Blackwell handbook of adolescence.* Malden, MA: Blackwell.

Crooks, R., & Baur, K. (2002). *Our sexuality* (8th ed.). Belmont, CA: Wadsworth.

Crosby, F. J. (1991). *Juggling.* New York: Free Press.

Crowell, J. A., Treboux, D., Gao, Y., Fyffe, C., Pan, H., & Waters, E. (2002). Assessing secure base behavior in adulthood: development of a measure, links to adult attachment representations, and relations to couples' communication and reports of

relationships. *Developmental Psychology, 38,* 679–693.

Crowley, K., Callahan, M. A., Tenenbaum, H. R., & Allen, E. (2001). Parents explain more to boys than to girls during shared scientific thinking. *Psychological Science, 12,* 258–261.

Croyle, R. T. (2000). Genetic counseling. In A. Kazdin (Ed.), *Encyclopedia of psychology.* Washington, DC, & New York: American Psychological Association and Oxford University Press.

Csaja, S. J. (2001). Technological change and the older worker. In J. E. Birren & K. W. Schaie (Eds.), *Handbook of the psychology of aging* (5th ed.). San Diego: Academic Press..

Csikszentmihalyi, M. (1995). *Creativity.* New York: HarperCollins.

Csikszentmihalyi, M. (1997). *Finding flow.* New York: Basic Books.

Csikszentmihalyi, M. (2000). Creativity: An overview. In A. Kazdin (Ed.), *Encyclopedia of psychology.* Washington, DC, & New York: American Psychological Association and Oxford University Press.

Csikszentmihalyi, M., & Rathunde, K. (1998). The development of the person: An experiential perspective on the ontogenesis of psychological complexity. In W. Damon (Ed.), *Handbook of child psychology* (5th ed., Vol. 1). New York: Wiley.

Cuddy-Casey, M., & Orvaschel, H. (1997). Children's understanding of death in relation to child suicidality and homicidality. *Death Studies, 17,* 33–45.

Cui, X., & Vaillant, G. E. (1996). Antecedents and consequences of negative life events in adulthood: A longitudinal study. *American Journal of Psychiatry, 153,* 123–126.

Cuijpers, P. (2001). Mortality and depressive symptoms in inhabitants of residential homes. *International Journal of Geriatric Psychiatry, 16,* 131–138.

Cullen, K. (2001). *Context and eating behavior in children.* Unpublished research, Children's Nutrition Research Center, Baylor School of Medicine, Houston.

Cully, J. A., LaVoie, D., & Gfeller, J. D. (2001). Reminiscence, personality, and psychological functioning in older adults. *The Gerontologist, 41 (No. 1),* 89–95.

Cumming, E., & Henry, W. (1961). *Growing old.* New York: Basic Books.

Cummings, E. M. (1987). Coping with background anger in early childhood. *Child Development, 58,* 976–984.

Cummings, M. (2003). Human heredity (6th ed.). Belmont, CA: Wadsworth.

Cupertino, A. P., & Haan, M. N. (1999, November). *Religiosity and health among elderly Latinos.* Paper presented at the meeting of the Gerontological Society of America, San Francisco.

Curran, K., DuCette, J., Eisenstein, J., & Hyman, I. A. (2001, August). *Statistical analysis of the cross-cultural data: The third year.* Paper presented at the meeting of the American Psychological Association, San Francisco.

Cushner, K. H. (1999). *Human diversity in action.* New York: McGraw-Hill.

Cushner, K. H. (2003). *Human diversity in action* (2nd ed.). New York: McGraw-Hill.

Cushner, K. H., & Brislin, R. W. (1995). *Intercultural interactions* (2nd ed.). Newbury Park, CA: Sage.

Cushner, K. H., McClelland, A., & Safford, P. (1996). *Human diversity and education.* (2nd ed.). New York: McGraw-Hill.

Cutrona, C. E. (1982). Transition to college: Loneliness and the process of social adjustment. In L. A. Peplau & D. Perlman (Eds.), *Loneliness.* New York: Wiley.

D

Daley, S. E., & Hammen, C. (2002). Depressive symptoms and close relationships during the transition to adulthood: Perspectives from dysphoric women, their best friends, and their romantic partners. *Journal of Consulting and Clinical Psychology, 70,* 129–141.

Damon, W. (1988). *The moral child.* New York: Free Press.

Damon, W., & Hart, D. (1988). *Self-understanding in childhood and adolescence.* New York: Cambridge University Press.

Damon, W., & Hart, D. (1992). Self-understanding and its role in social and moral development. In M. H. Bornstein & M. E. Lamb (Eds.), *Developmental psychology: An advanced textbook* (3rd ed.). Hillsdale, NJ: Erlbaum.

Danforth, M. M., & Glass, J. C. (2001). Listen to my words, give meaning to my sorrow: A study in cognitive constructs in middle-aged bereaved widows. *Death Studies, 25,* 513–548.

Danner, D., Snowdon, D., & Friesen, W. (2001). Positive emotions in early life and longevity: Findings from the Nun Study.

Journal of Personality and Social Psychology, 80 (5): 813–814.

Darwin, C. (1859). *On the origin of species.* London: John Murray.

Dattilio, F. M. (Ed.). (2001). Case studies in couple and family therapy. New York: Guilford.

D'Augelli, A. (2000). Sexual orientation. In A. Kazdin (Ed.), *Encyclopedia of psychology,* Washington, DC, & New York: American Psychological Association and Oxford University Press.

Davidson, J. (2000). Giftedness. In A. Kazdin (Ed.), *Encyclopedia of psychology.* Washington, DC, & New York: American Psychological Association and Oxford University Press.

Davies, K. (2001). *Cracking the genome.* New York: Free Press.

Davis, G. F. (2001). Loss and duration of grief. *Journal of the American Medical Association, 285,* 1152–1153.

Davis, K. E. (1985, February). Near and dear: Friendship and love compared. *Psychology Today,* pp. 22–29.

Davis, L., & Keyser, J. (1997). *Becoming the parent you want to be: A sourcebook of strategies for the first five years.* New York: Broadway Books.

Davison, G. C., & Neale, J. M. (2001). *Abnormal psychology* (8th ed.). New York: Wiley.

Davison, K. K., & Birth, L. L. (2001). Weight status, parent reaction, and self-concept in five-year-old girls. *Pediatrics, 107,* 46–53.

Davisson, M. T., Gardiner, K., & Costa, A. C. (2001). Report of the ninth international workshop on the molecular biology of human chromosome 21 and Down syndrome. *Cytogenetic Cell Genetics, 92,* 1–22.

Daws, D. (2000). *Through the night.* San Francisco: Free Association Books.

DeCasper, A. J., & Spence, M. J. (1986). Prenatal maternal speech influences newborn's perception of speech sounds. *Infant Behavior and Development, 9,* 133–150.

deHaan, M., & Nelson, C. A. (1999). Brain activity differentiates face and object processing in 6-month-old infants. *Developmental Psychology, 35,* 1113–1121.

de Jong-Gierveld, J. (1987). Developing and testing a model of loneliness. *Journal of Personality and Social Psychology, 53,* 119–128.

DeLamater, J., & MacCorquodale, P. (1979). *Premarital sexuality.* Madison: University of Wisconsin Press.

DeLoache, J. (2001). The symbol-mindedness of young children. In W. W. Hartup & R. A. Weinberg (Eds.), *Child psychology in retrospect and prospect.* Mahwah, NJ: Erlbaum.

DeMarie, D., Abshier, D. W., & Ferron, J. (2001, April). *Longitudinal study of predictors of memory improvement over the elementary school years: Capacity, strategies, and metamemory revisited.* Paper presented at the meeting of the Society for Research in Child Development, Minneapolis.

DeMaris, A., & Rao, K. (1992). Premarital cohabitation and subsequent marital stability in the United States: A reassessment. *Journal of Marriage and the Family, 54,* 178–190.

Demetriou, A. (2001, April). *Towards a comprehensive theory of intellectual development.* Paper presented at the meeting of the Society for Research in Child Development, Minneapolis.

Dempster, F. N. (1981). Memory span: Sources of individual and developmental differences. *Psychological Bulletin, 80,* 63–100.

Denham, S. A. (1998). *Emotional development in young children.* New York: Guilford.

Denmark, F. L., Russo, N. F., Frieze, I. H., & Eschuzur, J. (1988). Guidelines for avoiding sexism in psychological research: A report of the ad hoc committee on nonsexist research. *American Psychologist, 43,* 582–585.

Denney, N. W. (1986, August). *Practical problem solving.* Paper presented at the meeting of the American Psychological Association, Washington, DC.

Denney, N. W. (1990). Adult age differences in traditional and practical problem solving. *Advances in Psychology, 72,* 329–349.

Denny, C. B. (2001). Stimulant effects in attention deficit hyperactivity disorder. *Journal of Clinical Child Psychology, 30,* 98–109.

Derman-Sparks, L. (1989). *Anti-bias curriculum.* Washington, DC: National Association for the Education of Young Children.

DeSpelder, L. A., & Strickland, A. L. (1996). *The last dance: Encountering death and dying* (4th ed.). Mountain View, CA: Mayfield.

Dettmer, P., Dyck, N., & Thurston, L. (2002). *Consultation, collaboration, and teamwork for students with special needs* (4th ed.). Boston: Allyn & Bacon.

Deutsch, F. M. (1991). Women's lives: The story not told by theories of development. *Contemporary Psychology, 36,* 237–238.

Dewey, J. (1933). *How we think.* Lexington, MA: D.C. Heath.

de Wolff, M. S., & van Ijzendoorn, M. H. (1997). Sensitivity and attachment: A meta-analysis on parental antecedents of infant attachment. *Child Development, 68,* 571–591.

Diamond, A. (2001). A model system for studying the role of dopamine in the pre-frontal cortex during early development in humans: Early and continuously treated phenylketonuria. In C. Nelson & M. Luciana (Eds.), *Handbook of developmental cognitive neuroscience.* Cambridge, MA: MIT Press.

Diener, E., Lucas, R. E., & Oishi, S. (2002). Emotion-focused approaches and subjective well-being: The science of happiness and life-satisfaction. In C. R. Snyder & S. J. Lopez (Eds.), *Handbook of positive psychology.* New York: Oxford University Press.

Diener, E., Lucas, R. E., & Oishi, S. (2002). Subjective well-being: The science of happiness and satisfaction. In C. R. Snyder & S. J. Lopez (Eds.), *Handbook of positive psychology.* New York: Oxford University Press.

Diener, E., & Seligman, M. E. P. (2002). Very happy people. *Psychological Science, 13,* 81–84.

Dieter, J. N., Field, T., Hernandez-Reif, M., Jones, N. A., Lecanuet, J. P., Salman, F. A., & Redzepi, M. (2001). Maternal depression and increased fetal activity. *Journal of Obstetrics and Gynecology, 21,* 468–473.

DiGiulio, R. C. (1989). *Beyond widowhood.* New York: Free Press.

Dion, K. K., & Dion, K. L. (1993). Individualistic and collectivistic perspectives on gender and the cultural context of love and intimacy. *Journal of Social Issues, 49,* 53–69.

Dishion, T. (2001, April). *Understanding and preventing adolescent drug use.* Paper presented at the meeting of the Society for Research in Child Development, Minneapolis.

Dixit, N. K., Gerton, B. K., Dohn, P., Meyer-Lindenberg, A., & Berman, K. F. (2000, June). *Age-related changes in rCBF activation during an N-Back working memory paradigm occur prior to age 50.* Paper presented at the Human Brain Mapping meeting, San Antonio, TX.

Dixon, R., & Cohen, A. (2003). Cognitive development in adulthood. In I. B. Weiner (Ed.), *Handbook of psychology,* Vol. VI. New York: Wiley.

Dobzhansky, T. G. (1977). *Evolution.* New York: W. H. Freeman.

Dodge, K. A. (1983). Behavioral antecedents of peer social status. *Child Development, 54,* 1386–1399.

Dodge, K. A. (2000). Developmental psychology. In M. H. Ebert, P. T. Loosen, & B. Nurcombe (Eds.). *Current diagnosis and treatment in psychiatry.* East Norwalk, CT: Appleton & Lange.

Dodge, K. A. (2001). The science of youth violence prevention: Progressing from developmental psychopathology to efficacy to effectiveness in public policy. *American Journal of Preventive Medicine, 20,* 63–70.

Dohrenwend, B. S., & Dohrenwend, B. P. (1978). Some issues in research on stressful life events. *Journal of Nervous and Mental Disease, 166,* 7–15.

Dohrenwend, B. S., & Shrout, P. E. (1985). "Hassles" in the conceptualization and measurement of life stress variables. *American Psychologist, 40,* 780–785.

Donelson, F. E. (1998). *Women's experiences.* Mountain View, CA: Mayfield.

Donnerstein, E. (2002). Media violence. In J. Worell (Ed.), Encyclopedia of gender and women. San Diego: Academic Press.

Donovan, P. (1993). *Testing positive: Sexually transmitted disease and the public health response.* New York: Alan Guttmacher Institute.

Dorn, L. D., & Lucas, F. L. (1995, March). *Do hormone-behavior relations vary depending upon the endocrine and psychological status of the adolescent?* Paper presented at the meeting of the Society for Research in Child Development, Indianapolis.

Dornbusch, S., & Kaufman, J. (2001). The social structure of the U.S. high school. In T. Urdan & F. Pajares (Eds.), *Adolescence and education.* Greenwich, CT: IAP.

Dorr, A., Rabin, B. E., & Irlen, S. (2002). Parents, children, and the media. In M. H. Bornstein (Ed.), *Handbook of parenting* (2nd ed., Vol. 5). Mahwah, NJ: Erlbaum.

Dowda, M., Ainsworth, B. E., Addy, C. L., Saunders, R., & Riner, W. (2001). Environmental influences, physical activity, and weight status in 8- to 16-year-olds. *Archives of Pediatric and Adolescent Medicine, 155,* 711–717.

Downey, G., & Bonica, C. A. (1997, April). *Characteristics of early adolescent dating relationships.* Paper presented at the meeting of the Society for Research in Child Development, Washington, DC.

Drew, C., & Hardman, M. L. (2000). *Mental retardation* (7th ed.). Columbus, OH: Merrill.

Dryfoos, J. G. (1990). *Adolescents at risk: Prevalence and prevention.* New York: Oxford University Press.

Dunkel-Schetter, C. (1998). Maternal stress and preterm delivery. *Prenatal and Neonatal Medicine, 3,* 39–42.

Dunkel-Schetter, C. (1999, August). *Is maternal stress a risk factor for adverse birth outcomes?* Paper presented at the meeting of the American Psychological Association, Boston.

Dunkel-Schetter, C., Gurung, R. A. R., Lobel, M., & Wadhwa, P. D. (2001). Stress processes in pregnancy and birth. In A. Baum, T. A. Revenson, & J. E. Singer (Eds.), *Handbook of health psychology.* Mahwah, NJ: Erlbaum.

Dunn, J. (1984). Sibling studies and the developmental impact of critical incidents. In P. B. Baltes & O. G. Brim (Eds.), *Life-span development and behavior* (Vol. 6). Orlando, FL: Academic Press.

Dunn, J., Davies, L. C., O'Connor, T. G., & Sturgess, W. (2001). Family lives and friendships: The perspectives of children in step-, single-parent, and nonstep families. *Journal of Family Psychology, 15,* 272–287.

Dunnewold, A., & Sanford, D. G. (1994). *Postpartum survival guide.* Oakland: New Harbinger.

Durrant, J. E. (2002). Trends in youth crime and well-being since the abolition of corporal punishment in Sweden. *Youth and Society, 3,* 437–455.

Durrant, R., & Ellis, B. (2003). Evolutionary psychology. In I.B. Weiner (Ed.), *Handbook of psychology* (Vol. III). New York: Wiley.

Dusek, J. B., & McIntyre, J. G. (2003). Self-concept and self-esteem development. In G. Adams & M. Berzonsky (Eds.), *Blackwell handbook of adolescence.* Malden, MA: Blackwell.

Eagle, M. (2000). Psychoanalytic theory: History of the field. In A. Kazdin (Ed.), *Encyclopedia of psychology.* Washington, DC, & New York: American Psychological Association and Oxford University Press.

Eagly, A. H. (2001). Social role theory of sex differences and similarities. In J. Worell (Ed.), *Encyclopedia of women and gender.* San Diego: Academic Press.

Eagly, A. H., & Crowley, M. (1986). Gender and helping behavior: A meta-analytic review of the social psychological literature. *Psychological Bulletin, 100,* 283–308.

Eagly, A. H., & Steffen, V. J. (1986). Gender and aggressive behavior: A meta-analytic review of the social psychological literature. *Psychological Bulletin, 100,* 309–330.

Earles, J. L., & Salthouse, T. A. (1995). Interrelations of age, health, and speed. *Journal of Gerontology: Psychological Sciences, 50B,* 33–41.

Eccles, J. (2000). Adolescence: Social patterns, achievements, and problems. In A. Kazdin (Ed.), *Encyclopedia of psychology.* Washington, DC, & New York: American Psychological Association and Oxford University Press.

Eccles, J. (2000). Gender socialization. In A. Kazdin (Ed.), *Encyclopedia of psychology.* Washington, DC, & New York: American Psychological Association and Oxford University Press.

Eccles, J. (2001, April). *Gender and ethnicity as developmental contexts.* Paper presented at the meeting of the Society for Research in Child Development, Minneapolis.

Eccles, J. (2003). Education: Junior and high school. In G. Adams & M. Berzonsky (Eds.), *Blackwell handbook of adolescence.* Malden, MA: Blackwell.

Eccles, J., Wigfield, A., & Byrnes, J. (2003). Cognitive development in adolescence. In I. B. Weiner (Ed.), *Handbook of psychology* (Vol. VI). New York: Wiley.

Edelman, M. W. (1997, April). *Children, families and social policy.* Paper presented at the meeting of the Society for Research in Child Development, Washington, DC.

Edmonds, M. M. (1993). Physical health. In J. S. Jackson, L. M. Chatters, & R. J. Taylor (Eds.), *Aging in Black America.* Newbury Park, CA: Sage.

Educational Testing Service. (1992, February). *Cross-national comparison of 9–13 year olds' science and math achievement.* Princeton, NJ: Author.

Egeland, B., Jacobvitz, D., & Sroufe, L. A. (1988). Breaking the cycle of abuse. *New Directions for Child Development, 11,* 77–92.

Eggebeen, D. J., & Knoester, C. (2001). Does fatherhood matter for men? *Journal of Marriage and the Family, 63,* 381–393.

Ehrlich, R., Jordaan, E., Du Toit, D., Potter, P., Volmink, J., Zwarenstein, M., & Weinberg, E. (2001). Household smoking and bronchial hyperresponsiveness in children with asthma. *Journal of Asthma, 38,* 239–251.

Eichorn, D. H., Clausen, J. A., Haan, N., Honzik, M. P., & Mussen, P. H. (Eds.). (1981). *Present and past in middle life.* New York: Academic Press.

Eiferman, R. R. (1971). Social play in childhood. In R. Herron & B. Sutton-Smith (Eds.), *Child's play.* New York: Wiley.

Eiger, M. S., & Olds, S. W. (1999). *The complete book of breastfeeding* (3rd ed.). New York: Bantam.

Einstein, G. O., McDaniel, M. A., Manzi, M., Cochran, B., & Baker, M. (2000). Prospective memory and aging: Forgetting intentions over short delays. *Psychology and Aging, 15,* 671–683.

Eisdorfer, C. (1996, December). Interview. *APA Monitor,* 35.

Eisenberg, N. (Ed.). (1982). *The development of prosocial behavior.* New York: Wiley.

Eisenberg, N. (2001). Emotion-regulated regulation and its relation to quality of social functioning. In W. W. Hartup & R. A. Weinberg (Eds.), *Child psychology in retrospect and prospect.* Mahwah, NJ: Erlbaum.

Eisenberg, N., Fabes, R. A., Guthrie, I. K., & Reiser, M. (2002). The role of emotionality and regulation in children's social competence and adjustment. In L. Pulkkinen & A. Caspi (Eds.), *Paths to successful development.* New York: Cambridge University Press.

Eisenberg, N., Martin, C. L., & Fabes, R. A. (1996). Gender development and gender effects. In D. C. Berliner & R. C. Calfee (Eds.), *Handbook of educational psychology.* New York: Macmillan.

Ekwo, E. E., & Moawad, A. (2000). Maternal age and preterm births in a black population. *Pediatric Perinatal Epidemiology, 2,* 145–151.

Elder, G. H. (1998). The life course and human development. In W. Damon (Ed.), *Handbook of child development* (5th ed.). New York: Wiley.

Elder, G. H., & Pavalko, E. K. (1993). Work careers in men's later years: Transitions, trajectories, and historical change. *Journal of Gerontology, 48,* S180–S191.

Elias, M. (1998, June 23). For 50 years pediatrics has taken giant steps. *USA Today,* pp. 1, 2D.

Elicker, J. (1996). A knitting tale: Reflections on scaffolding. *Childhood Education, 72,* 29–32.

Elkind, D. (1970, April 5). Erik Erikson's eight ages of man. *New York Times Magazine.*

Elkind, D. (1976). *Child development and education: A Piagetian perspective.* New York: Oxford University Press.

Elkind, D. (1988, January). Educating the very young: A call for clear thinking. *NEA Today,* pp. 22–27.

Ellis, L., & Ames, M. A. (1987). Neurohormonal functioning and sexual orientation. *Psychological Bulletin, 101,* 233–258.

Elmes, D. G., Kantowitz, B. H., & Roedinger, H. L. (2003). *Research methods in psychology* (7th ed.). Belmont, CA: Wadsworth.

Emde, R. N., Gaensbauer, T. G., & Harmon, R. J. (1976). Emotional expression in infancy: A biobehavioral study. *Psychological Issues: Monograph Series, 10* (37).

Emery, R. E., Laumann-Billings, L., Waldron, M. C., Sbarra, D. A., & Dillon, P. (2001). Child custody mediation and litigation: Custody, contact, and coparenting 12 years after initial dispute resolution. *Journal of Consulting and Clinical Psychology, 69,* 323–332.

England, L. J., Kendrick, J. S., Gargiullo, P. M., Zhniser, S. C., & Hannon, W. H. (2001). Measures of maternal tobacco exposure and infant birth weight at term. *American Journal of Epidemiology, 153,* 954–960.

England, S. E., Linsk, N. L., Simon-Rusinowitz, L., & Keigher, S. M. (1991). Paying kin for care: Agency barriers to formalizing informal care. *Journal of Aging and Social Policy, 2,* 63–86.

Ennett, S., & Bauman, K. (1996). Adolescent social networks: School, demographic, and longitudinal considerations. *Journal of Adolescent Research, 11,* 194–215.

Enoch, M. A., & Goldman, D. (2002). Problem drinking and alcoholism: Diagnosis and treatment. *American Family Physician, 65,* 441–448.

Enright, R. D., Lapsley, D. K., Dricas, A. S., & Fehr, L. A. (1980). Parental influence on the development of adolescent autonomy and identity. *Journal of Youth and Adolescence, 9,* 529–546.

Epstein, D. K., & Connor, J. R. (1999, Fall). Dementia in the elderly: An overview. *Generations,* pp. 9–16.

Epstein, J. A., Botvin, G. J., & Diaz, T. (1998). Linguistic acculturation and gender effects on smoking among Hispanic youth. *Preventive Medicine, 27,* 538–589.

Epstein, N., & Eidelson, R. J. (1981). Unrealistic beliefs of clinical couples: Their relationship to expectations, goals, and satisfaction. *American Journal of Family Therapy, 9,* 13–21.

Erikson, E. H. (1950). *Childhood and society.* New York: W. W. Norton.

Erikson, E. H. (1968). *Identity: Youth and crisis.* New York: W. W. Norton.

Erikson, E. H. (1969). *Ghandi's truth.* New York: Norton.

Eskenazi, B., Stapleton, A. L., Kharrazi, M., & Chee, W. Y. (1999). Associations between maternal decaffeinated and caffeinated coffee consumption and fetal growth and gestational duration. *Epidemiology, 10,* 242–249.

Etaugh, C. A., & Bridges, J. S. (2001). Midlife transitions. In J. Worell (ed.), *Encyclopedia of women and gender.* San Diego: Academic Press.

Etaugh, C., & Bridges, J. S. (2001). *Psychology of women: A life-span perspective.* Boston: Allyn & Bacon.

Etzel, R. (1988, October). *Children of smokers.* Paper presented at the American Academy of Pediatrics meeting, New Orleans.

Evans, W. (2000). Exercise strategies should be designed to increase muscle power. *Journal of Gerontology: Medical Sciences, 55A,* M309–M310.

F

Faber, D., & Burns, J. W. (1996). Anger management style, degree of expressed anger, and gender influence on cardiovascular recovery from interpersonal harassment. *Journal of Behavioral Medicine, 19,* 55–72.

Fagan, J. F. (1992). Intelligence: A theoretical viewpoint. *Current Directions in Psychological Science, 1,* 82–86.

Fagot, B. I., Leinbach, M. D., & O'Boyle, C. (1992). Gender labeling, gender stereotyping, and parenting behaviors. *Developmental Psychology, 28,* 225–230.

Fagot, B. I., Rodgers, C. S., & Leinbach, M. D. (2000). Theories of gender socialization. In T. Eckes & H. M. Trautner (Eds.), *The developmental social psychology of gender.* Mahwah, NJ: Erlbaum.

Falbo, T., & Poston, D. L. (1993). The academic, personality, and physical outcomes of only children in China. *Child Development, 64,* 18–35.

Falicov, C., & Karrer, B. (1980). Cultural variations in the family life cycle: The Mexican American family. In E. Carter & M. McGoldrick (Eds.), *The family life cycle: A framework for family therapy.* New York: Gardner Press.

Famy, C., Streissguth, A. P., & Unis, A. S. (1998). Mental illness in adults with fetal alcohol syndrome or fetal alcohol effects. *American Journal of Psychiatry, 155,* 552–554.

Fang, J., Madhaven, S., & Alderman, M. H. (1999). Low birth weight: Race and maternal nativity—Impact of community income. *Pediatrics, 103,* e5.

Fantz, R. L. (1963). Pattern vision in newborn infants. *Science, 140,* 296–297.

Faraone, S. V., & Doyle, A. E. (2001). The nature and heritability of attention deficit hyperactivity disorder. *Child and Adolescent Psychiatric Clinics of North America, 10,* 299–316.

Farrell, M. P., & Rosenberg, S. D. (1981). *Men at mid-life.* Boston: Auburn House.

Feenstra, J. S., Banyard, V. L., Rines, E. N., & Hopkins, K. R. (2001). First-year students' adaptation to college: The role of family variables and individual coping. *Journal of College Student Development, 42,* 106–111.

Fehr, B. (1996). *Friendship processes.* Thousand Oaks, CA: Sage.

Fehr, B., & Broughton, R. (2001). Gender and personality differences in conceptions of love: An interpersonal theory analysis. *Personal Relationships, 8,* 115–136.

Feinberg, M., & Hetherington, E. M. (2001). Differential parenting as a within-family variable. *Journal of Family Psychology, 15,* 22–37.

Feiring, C. (1996). Concepts of romance in 15-year-old adolescents. *Journal of Research on Adolescence, 6,* 181–200.

Feldman, H. D. (2001, April). *Contemporary developmental theories and the concept of talent.* Paper presented at the meeting of the Society for Research in Child Development, Minneapolis.

Feldman, R., Greenbaum, C. W., & Yirmiya, N. (1999). Mother-infant affect synchrony as an antecedent of the emergence of self-control. *Developmental Psychology, 35,* 223–231.

Feldman, S. S. (1999). Unpublished review of J. W. Santrock's *Adolescence,* 8th ed. (New York: McGraw-Hill).

Feldman, S. S., & Elliott, G. R. (1990). Progress and promise of research on normal adolescent development. In S. S. Feldman & G. Elliott (Eds.), *At the threshold: The developing adolescent.* Cambridge, MA: Harvard University Press.

Feldman, S. S., Turner, R., & Aruajo, K. (1999). Interpersonal context as an influence on sexual timetables of youths: Gender and ethnic effects. *Journal of Research on Adolescence, 9,* 25–52.

Feldman, S. S., & Weinberger, D. A. (1994). Self-restraint as a mediator of family influences on boys' delinquent behavior: A longitudinal study. *Child Development, 65,* 195–211.

Ferguson, D. M., Harwood, L. J., & Shannon, F. T. (1987). Breastfeeding and subsequent social adjustment in 6- to 8- year-old children. *Journal of Child Psychology and Psychiatry, 28,* 378–386.

Ferguson, D. M., Horwood. L. J., & Beautrais, A. L. (1999). Is sexual orientation related to mental health problems and suicidality in young people? *Archives of General Psychiatry, 56,* 876–880.

Fernald, A. (2001). Two hundred years of research on the early development of language comprehension. In W. W. Hartup & R. A. Weinberg (Eds.), *Child psychology in retrospect and prospect.* Mahwah, NJ: Erlbaum.

Fernandez, O., Sabharwal, M., Smiley, T., Pastuszak, A., Koren, G., & Einarson, T. (1998). Moderate to heavy caffeine consumption during pregnancy and relationship to spontaneous abortion and abnormal fetal growth: A meta-analysis. *Reproductive Toxicology, 12,* 435–444.

Ferrer-Wreder, L., Lorene, C. C., Kurtines, W., Briones, E., Bussell, J., Berman, S., & Arrufat, O. (2002). Promoting identity development in marginalized youth. *Journal of Adolescent Research, 17,* 168–187.

Fiatarone, M. A., Marks, E. C., Meredith, C. N., Lipsitz, L. A., & Evans, W. J. (1990). High intensity strength training in nonagenarians: Effects on skeletal muscle. *Journal of the American Medical Association, 263,* 3029–3034.

Field, A. E., Cambargo, C. A., Taylor, C. B., Berkey, C. S., Roberts S. B., & Colditz, G. A. (2001). Peer, parent, and media influences on the development of weight concerns and frequent dieting among preadolescent and adolescent girls and boys. *Pediatrics, 107,* 54–60.

Field, D. (1996). Review of relationships in old age by Hansson & Carpenter. *Contemporary Psychology, 41,* 44–45.

Field, D. (1999). A cross-cultural perspective on continuity and change in social relations in old age: Introduction to a special issue. *International Journal of Aging and Human Development, 48,* 257–262.

Field, T. (1990). *Infancy.* Cambridge, MA: Harvard University Press.

Field, T. (1992, September). Stroking babies helps growth, reduces stress. *Brown University Child and Adolescent Behavior Letter,* pp. 1, 6.

Field, T. (2000). Child abuse. In A. Kazdin (Ed.), *Encyclopedia of psychology.* Washington, DC, & New York: American Psychological Association and Oxford University Press.

Field, T. (2001). Massage therapy facilitates weight gain in preterm infants. *Current Directions in Psychological Science, 10,* 51–55.

Field, T. M. (1998). Massage therapy effects. *American Psychologist, 53,* 1270–1281.

Field, T. M., Grizzle, N., Scafidi, F., & Schanberg, S. (1996). Massage and relaxation therapies' effects on depressed adolescent mothers. *Adolescence, 31,* 903–911.

Field, T. M., Hernandez-Reif, M., Taylor, S., Quintino, O., & Burman, I. (1997). Labor pain is reduced by massage therapy. *Journal of Psychosomatic Obstetrics and Gynecology, 18,* 286–291.

Field, T., Schanberg, S. M., Scafidi, F., Bauer, C. R., Vega-Lahr, N., Garcia, R., Nystrom, J., & Kuhn, C. (1986). Tactile/kinesthetic stimulation effects on preterm neonates. *Pediatrics, 77,* 654–658.

Fields, R. (1998). *Drugs in perspective* (3rd ed.). New York: McGraw-Hill.

Fifer, B., & Grose-Fifer, J. (2001). Prenatal development and risk. In A. Fogel & G. Bremner (Eds.), *Blackwell handbook of infant development.* London: Blackwell.

Finch, C. E., & Seeman, T. E. (1999). Stress theories of aging. In V. L. Bengtson, & K. W. Schaie (Eds.). *Handbook of theories of aging.* New York: Springer.

Fine, P. G., & Peterson, D. (2002). Caring what dying patients care about caring. *Journal of Pain Symptom Management, 23,* 267–268.

Finucane, T. E. (2002). Care of patients nearing death: Another view. *Journal of the American Geriatric Society, 50,* 551–553.

Fischer, K. W., & Bidell, T. R. (1998). Dynamic development of psychological structures in action and thought. In W. Damon (Ed.), *Handbook of child psychology* (Vol. 1). New York: Wiley.

Fischer, K. W., & Rose, S. P. (1995, Fall). Concurrent cycles in the dynamic development of brain and behavior. *SRCD Newsletter,* pp. 3–4, 15–16.

Fisk, A. D., & Rogers, W. A. (2002). Health care of older adults: The promise of human factors research. In W. A. Rogers & A. D. Fisk (Eds.), *Human factors interventions for the health care of older adults.* Mahwah, NJ: Erlbaum.

Fitzgerald, H., Mann, T., Cabrera, N., & Wong, M. M. (2003). Diversity in caregiving contexts. In I.B. Weiner (Ed.), *Handbook of psychology* (Vol. VI.). New York: Wiley.

Fitzgerald, L. (2000). Sexual harassment. In A. Kazdin (Ed.), *Encyclopedia of psychology.* Washington, DC, & New York: American Psychological Association and Oxford University Press.

Fitzgerald, L., Collinsworth, L. L., & Harned, M. S. (2002). Sexual harassment. In J. Worell (Ed.), *Encyclopedia of women and gender.* San Diego: Academic Press.

Flanagan, C. (2002, April). *Inclusion and reciprocity: Developmental sources of social trust and civic hope.* Paper presented at the meeting of the Society for Research on Adolescence, New Orleans.

Flanagan, C., & Faison, N. (2001). Youth civic development: Implications of research for social policy and programs. *Social Policy Report, XV* (No. 1), 1–14.

Flanagan, C., Gill, S., & Gallay, L. (1998, November). *Intergroup understanding, social justice, and the "social contract" in diverse communities of youth: Foundations for civic understanding.* Project report prepared for the workshop on research to improve intergroup relations among youth, Forum on Adolescence, Board on Children, Youth, and Families, National Research Council, Washington, DC.

Flanagan, K. M., Clements, M. L., Whitton, S. W., Portney, M. J., Randall, D. W., & Markman, H. J. (2001). Retrospect and prospect in the psychological study of marital and couple relationships. In J. P. McHale & W. S. Grolnick (Eds.), *Retrospect and prospect in the psychological study of families.* Mahwah, NJ: Erlbaum.

Flannery, D. J., Hussey, D., Biebelhausen, L., & Wester, K. (2003). Crime, delinquency, and youth gangs. In G. Adams & M. Berzonsky (Eds.), *Blackwell handbook of adolescence.* Malden, MA: Blackwell.

Flavell, J. H. (1999). Cognitive development: Children's knowledge about the mind. *Annual Review of Psychology* (Vol. 50). Palo Alto, CA: Annual Reviews.

Flavell, J. H., Friedrichs, A., & Hoyt, J. (1970). Developmental changes in memorization processes. *Cognitive Psychology, 1,* 324–340.

Flavell, J. H., Miller, P. H., & Miller, S. (2002). *Cognitive development* (4th ed.). Upper Saddle River, NJ: Prentice Hall.

Flick, L., White, D. K., Vemulapalli, C., Stulac, B. B., & Kemp, J. S. (2001). Sleep position and the use of soft bedding during bed sharing among African American infants at increased risk for sudden infant death syndrome. *Journal of Pediatrics, 138,* 338–343.

Flohr, J. W., Atkins, D. H., Bower, T. G. R., & Aldridge, M. A. (2001, April). *Infant music preferences.* Paper presented at the meeting of the Society for Research in Child Development, Minneapolis.

Flynn, J. R. (1999). Searching for justice: The discovery of IQ gains over time. *American Psychologist, 54,* 5–20.

Fodor, I., G., & Franks, V. (1990). Women in midlife and beyond. The new prime of life? *Psychology of Women Quarterly, 14,* 445–449.

Foege, W. (2000). *The power of immunization. The progress of nations.* New York: UNICEF.

Fogel, A. (2001). *Infancy* (4th ed.). Belmont, CA: Wadsworth.

Fonda, S. J., & Norgard, T. M. (1999, November). *Patterns and correlates of change in depressive symptoms among community-dwelling elderly.* Paper presented at the meeting of the Gerontological Society of America, San Francisco.

Ford, K., Sohn, W., & Lepkowski, J. (2001). Characteristics of adolescents' sexual partners and their association with use of condoms and other contraceptive methods. *Family Planning Perspectives, 33,* 100–105, 132.

Forrest, J. D., & Singh, S. (1990). The sexual and reproductive behavior of American women, 1982–1988. *Family Planning Perspectives, 22,* 206–214.

Fox, B., & Hull, M. (2002). *Phonics for the teacher of reading* (8th ed.). Upper Saddle River, NJ: Merrill.

Fox, G. L., & Murry, V. M. (2000). Gender and families: Feminist perspectives and family research. *Journal of Marriage and the Family, 62,* 1160–1172.

Fozard, J. L. (1992, December 6). Commentary in "We can age successfully." *Parade Magazine,* pp. 14–15.

Fozard, J. L. (2000). Sensory and cognitive changes with age. In K. W. Schaie & M. Pietrucha (Eds.), *Mobility and transportation in the elderly.* New York: Springer.

Fozard, J. L., & Gordon-Salant, S. (2001). Changes in vision and hearing with aging. In J. E. Birren & K. W. Schaie (Eds.), *Handbook of the psychology of aging* (5th ed.). San Diego: Academic Press.

Fraga, C. G., Motchnik, P. A., Shigenaga, M. K., Helbock, H. J., Jacob, R. A., & Ames, B. N. (1991). Ascorbic acid protects against endogenous oxidative DNA damage in human sperm. *Proceedings of the National Academy of Sciences of the United States, 88,* 11003–11006.

Fraiberg, S. (1959). *The magic years.* New York: Scribner's.

Fraley, R. C. (2002). Attachment stability from infancy to adulthood: Meta-analysis and dynamic modeling of developmental mechanisms. *Personality and Social Psychology Review, 6,* 123–151.

Frank, D. A., Augustyn, M., Knight, W. G., Pell, T., & Zuckerman, B. (2001). Growth, development, and behavior in early childhood following prenatal cocaine exposure: a systematic review. *Journal of the American Medical Association, 285,* 1613–1625.

Franke, T. M. (2000, Winter). The role of attachment as a protective factor in adolescent violent behavior. *Adolescent & Family Health, 1,* 29–39.

Frankl, V. (1984). *Man's search for meaning.* New York: Basic Books.

Franz, C. E. (1996). The implications of preschool tempo and motoric activity level for personality decades later. Reported in A. Caspi, Personality development across the life course, in W. Damon (Ed.), *Handbook of child psychology,* Vol. 3 (New York: Wiley), p. 337.

Frederikse, M., Lu, A., Aylward, E., Barta, P., Sharma, T., & Pearlson, G. (2000). Sex differences in inferior lobule volume in schizophrenia. *American Journal of Psychiatry, 157,* 422–427.

Fredman, L., Daly, M. P., & Lazur, A. M. (1995). Burden among White and Black caregivers to elderly adults. *Journal of Gerontology, 50B,* S110–S118.

Fredrickson, D. D. (1993). Breastfeeding research priorities, opportunities, and study criteria: What we learned from the smoking trial. *Journal of Human Lactation, 3,* 147–150.

Freedman, J. L. (1984). Effects of television violence on aggressiveness. *Psychological Bulletin, 96,* 227–246.

French, S. A., Story, M., & Jeffery, R. W. (2001). Environmental influences on eating and physical activity. *Annual Review of Public Health, 22,* 309–335.

Freud, A., & Dann, S. (1951). Instinctual anxiety during puberty. In A. Freud (Ed.), *The ego and its mechanisms of defense.* New York: International Universities Press.

Freud, S. (1917). *A general introduction to psychoanalysis.* New York: Washington Square Press.

Freund, A. M., & Baltes, P. B. (2002). Life-management strategies of selection, optimization, and compensation: Measurement by self-report and construct validity. *Journal of Personality and Social Psychology, 82,* 642–662.

Freund, A. M., & Riediger, M. (2003). Successful aging. In I. B. Weiner (Ed.), *Handbook of psychology,* Vol. VI. New York: Wiley.

Fried, P. A., & Smith, A. M. (2001). A literature review of the consequences of prenatal marijuana exposure. An emerging theme of a deficiency in executive function. *Neurotoxicology and Teratology, 23,* 1–11.

Fried, P. A., & Watkinson, B. (1990). 36- and 48-month neurobehavioral follow-up of children prenatally exposed to marijuana, cigarettes, and alcohol. *Developmental and Behavioral Pediatrics, 11,* 49–58.

Friedman, M., & Rosenman, R. (1974). *Type A behavior and your heart.* New York: Knopf.

Frieske, D. A., & Park, D. C. (1999). Memory for news in young and old adults. *Psychology and aging, 14,* 90–98.

Fry, P. S. (1999, November). *Significance of religiosity and spirituality to psychological well being of older adults.* Paper presented at the meeting of the Gerontological Society of America, San Francisco.

Fry, P. S. (1999, November). *Widows' regrets of action and inaction in coping with spousal loss: A follow-up.* Paper presented at the meeting of the Gerontological Society of America, San Francisco.

Fry, P. S. (2001). The unique contribution of key existential factors to the prediction of psychological well-being of older adults following spousal loss. *The Gerontologist, 41,* 69–81.

Fuligni, A. J., & Yoshikawa, H. (2003). Socioeconomic resources, poverty, and child development among immigrant families. In M. H. Bornstein & R. H. Bradley (Eds.), *Socioeconomic status, parenting, and child development.* Mahwah, NJ: Erlbaum.

Fuller-Thomson, E., & Minkler, M. (2001). American grandparents providing extensive care to their grandchildren: Prevalence and profile. *The Gerontologist, 41* (No. 2), 201–209.

Furman, W., & Buhrmester, D. (1992). Age and sex differences in perceptions of networks of personal relationships. *Child Development, 63,* 103–115.

Furman, W., & Wehner, E. A. (1999). Adolescent romantic relationships: A developmental perspective. In S. Shulman & W. A. Collins (Eds.), *New directions for child development: Adolescent romantic relationships.* San Francisco: Jossey-Bass.

Furth, H. G., & Wachs, H. (1975). *Thinking goes to school.* New York: Oxford University Press.

G

Gadpaille, W. J. (1996). *Adolescent suicide.* Washington, DC: American Psychological Association.

Galambos, N. L., & Maggs, J. L. (1989, April). *The after-school ecology of young adolescents and self-reported behavior.* Paper presented at the biennial meeting of the Society for Research in Child Development, Kansas City.

Gall, M. D., Borg, W. R., & Gall, J. P. (2003). *Educational research* (7th ed.). Boston: Allyn & Bacon.

Gall, T. L., Evans, D. R., & Howard, J. (1997). The retirement adjustment process: Changes in well-being of male retirees across time. *Journal of Gerontology, 52B,* 110–117.

Gallup, G. H. (1987). *The Gallup poll: Public opinion 1986.* Wilmington, DE: Scholarly Resources.

Gallup, G. H., & Bezilla, R. (1992). *The religious life of young Americans.* Princeton, NJ: Gallup Institute.

Gallup, G. H., & Jones, S. (1989). *One hundred questions and answers: Religion in America.* Princeton, NJ: Gallup Institute.

Galotti, K. M., Kozberg, S. F. (1996). Adolescents' experience of a life-framing decision. *Journal of Youth and Adolescence, 25,* 3–16.

Galotti, K. M., Kozberg, S. F., & Farmer, M. C. (1990, March). *Gender and developmental differences in adolescents' conceptions of moral reasoning.* Paper presented at the meeting of the Society for Research in Adolescence, Atlanta.

Galvin, M., David, J. P., Delacourte, A., Luna, J., & Mena, R. (2002). Sequence of neurofibrillary changes in aging and Alzheimer's disease: A confocal study with phospho-tau antibody AD2. *Journal of Alzheimer's Disease, 4,* 417–425.

Gannon, L. (1998). Menopause. In H. S. Friedman (Ed.), *Encyclopedia of mental health* (Vol. 2). San Diego: Academic Press.

Ganong, L. H., & Coleman, M. (1994). *Remarried family relationships.* Thousand Oaks, CA: Sage.

Gao, Y., Elliott, M. E., & Waters, E. (1999, April). *Maternal attachment representations and support for three-year-olds' secure base behavior.* Paper presented at the meeting of the Society for Research in Child Development, Albuquerque.

Garbarino, J. (1999). *Lost boys: Why our sons turn violent and how we can save them.* New York: Free Press.

Garbarino, J. (2001). Violent children. *Archives of Pediatrics & Adolescent Medicine, 155,* 1–2.

Garbarino, J., Dubrow, N., Kostelny, K., & Pardo, C. (1992). *Children in danger.* San Francisco: Jossey-Bass.

Gard, J. W., Alexander, J. M., Bawdon, R. E., & Albrecht, J. T. (2002). Oxytocin preparation stability in several common intravenous solutions. *American Journal of Obstetrics and Gynecology, 186,* 496–498.

Gardner, H. (1983). *Frames of mind.* New York: Basic Books.

Gardner, H. (1993). *Multiple intelligences.* New York: Basic Books.

Gardner, H. (2002). The pursuit of excellence through education. In M. Ferrari (Ed.), *Learning from extraordinary minds.* Mahwah, NJ: Erlbaum.

Gardner, L. I., Stern, M. P., Haffner, S. M., Gaskill, S. P., Hazuda, H. P., Relethford, J. H., & Eifter, C. W. (1984). Prevalence of diabetes in Mexican Americans: Relationships to percent of gene pool derived from Native American sources. *Diabetes, 33,* 86–92.

Garfein, A. J., & Herzog, A. R. (1995). Robust aging among the young-old, old-old, and oldest-old. *Journal of Gerontology, 50B,* S77–S87.

Garmezy, N. (1985). Stress-resistant children: The search for protective factors. In J. E. Stevenson (Ed.), Recent research in developmental psychopathology. *Journal of Child Psychology and Psychiatry Book Supplement, 4,* 213–233.

Garmezy, N. (1993). Children in poverty: Resilience despite risk. *Psychiatry, 56,* 127–136.

Garner, D. M., & Desai, J. J. (2001). Eating disorders in children and adolescents. In J. N. Hughes, A. M. La Greca, & J. C. Conoley (Eds.), *Handbook of psychological services for children and adolescents.* New York: Oxford University Press.

Garner, P. W., & Estep, K. M. (2002). Empathy and emotional expressivity. In J. Worell (Ed.), *Encyclopedia of women and gender.* San Diego: Academic Press.

Gartner, J., Larson, D. B., & Allen, G. D. (1991). Religious commitment and mental health: A review of the empirical literature. *Journal of Psychology and Theology, 19,* 6–25.

Gatz, M. (1989). Clinical psychology and aging. In M. Storandt & G. R. VandenBos (Eds.), *The adult years: Continuity and change.* Washington, DC: American Psychological Association.

Gatz, M. (1992). The mental health system and older adults. *American Psychologist, 47,* 741–751.

Gelman, R. (1969). Conservation acquisition: A problem of learning to attend to relevant attributes. *Journal of Experimental Child Psychology, 7,* 67–87.

Gelman, R., & Brenneman, K. (1994). Domain specificity and cultural variation are not inconsistent. In L. A. Hirschfeld & S. Gelman (Eds.), *Mapping the mind: Domain specificity in cognition and culture.* New York: Cambridge University Press.

Gelman, R., & Williams, E. M. (1998). Enabling constraints for cognitive development and learning. In W. Damon (Ed.), *Handbook of child psychology* (5th ed., Vol. 4). New York: Wiley.

Gelman, S. A., & Opfer, J. E. (2002). Development of the animate-inanimate distinction. In U. Goswami (Ed.), *Blackwell handbook of childhood cognitive development.* Malden, MA: Blackwell.

Geltman, P. L., Brown, M. J., & Cochran, J. (2001). Lead poisoning among refugee children settled in Massachusetts, 1995 to 1999. *Pediatrics, 108,* 158–162.

Gerlach, P. (1998). *Stepfamily in formation.* Chicago: Stepfamily Association of Illinois.

Gershoff, E. T. (2002). Corporal punishment by parents and associated child behaviors and experiences: A meta-analysis and theoretical review. *Psychological Bulletin, 128,* 539–579.

Gescheider, G. A. (1997). *Psychophysics: The fundamentals.* Mahwah, NJ: Erlbaum.

Geschwind, N., & Behan, P. O. (1984). Laterality, hormones, and immunity. In N. Geschwind & A. M. Galaburda (Eds.), *Cerebral dominance: The biological foundations.* Cambridge, MA: Harvard University Press.

Gesell, A. L. (1934). *An atlas of infant behavior.* New Haven, CT: Yale University Press.

Gesell, A. L. (1934). *Infancy and human growth.* New York: Macmillan.

Gewirtz, J. (1977). Maternal responding and the conditioning of infant crying: Directions of influence within the attachment-acquisition process. In B. C. Etzel, J. M. LeBlanc, & D. M. Baer (Eds.), *New developments in behavioral research.* Hillsdale, NJ: Erlbaum.

Giarrusso, R., & Feng, D. (1999, November). *The influence of life transitions on the intergenerational stake phenomenon.* Paper presented at the meeting of the Gerontological Association of America, San Francisco.

Gibbons, J. L. (2000). Gender development in cross-cultural perspective. In T. Eckes & H. M. Trautner (Eds.), *The developmental social psychology of gender.* Mahwah, NJ: Erlbaum.

Gibbs, J. C. (1993, March). *Inductive discipline's contribution to moral motivation.* Paper presented at the biennial meeting of the Society for Research in Child Development, New Orleans.

Gibson, E. J. (1969). *Principles of perceptual learning and development.* New York: Appleton-Century-Crofts.

Gibson, E. J. (1989). Exploratory behavior in the development of perceiving, acting, and the acquiring of knowledge. *Annual Review of Psychology, 39.* Palo Alto, CA: Annual Reviews.

Gibson, E. J. (2001). *Perceiving the affordances.* Mahwah, NJ: Erlbaum.

Gibson, E. J., Riccio, G., Schmuckler, M. A., Stoffregen, T. A., Rosenberg, D., & Taormina, J. (1987). Detection of the traversability of surfaces by crawling and walking infants. *Journal of Experimental Psychology: Human Perception and Performance, 13,* 533–544.

Gibson, E. J., & Walk, R. D. (1960). The "visual cliff." *Scientific American, 202,* 64–71.

Gibson, J. H., Harries, M., Mitchell, A., Godfrey, R., Lunt, M., & Reeve, J. (2000). Determinants of bone density and prevalence of osteopenia among female runners in their second to seventh decades of age. *Bone, 26,* 591–598.

Gibson, J. J. (1966). *The senses considered as perceptual systems.* Boston: Houghton Mifflin.

Gibson, J. J. (1979). *The ecological approach to visual perception.* Boston: Houghton Mifflin.

Giddens, S., & Giddens, O. (2000). *Coping with grieving and loss.* New York: Rosen.

Gielchinsky, Y., Rojansky, N., Fasoliotis, S. J., & Ezra, Y. (2002). Placenta accreta—summary of 10 years: A survey of 310 cases. *Placenta, 23,* 210–214.

Gilligan, C. (1982). *In a different voice.* Cambridge, MA: Harvard University Press.

Gilligan, C. (1990). Teaching Shakespeare's sister. In C. Gilligan, N. Lyons, & T. Hammer (Eds.), *Making connections: The relational worlds of adolescent girls at Emme Willard School.* Cambridge, MA: Harvard University Press.

Gilligan, C. (1992, May). *Joining the resistance: Girls' development in adolescence.* Paper presented at the symposium on development and vulnerability in close relationships, Montreal.

Gilligan, C. (1996). The centrality of relationships in psychological development: A puzzle, some evidence, and a theory: In G. G. Noam & K. W. Fischer (Eds.), *Development and vulnerability in close relationships.* Hillsdale, NJ: Erlbaum.

Gilligan, C. (1998). *Minding women: Reshaping the education realm.* Cambridge, MA: Harvard University Press.

Gilligan, C., & Attanucci, J. (1988). Two moral orientations. In C. Gilligan, J. V. Ward, J. M. Taylor, & B. Bardige (Eds.), *Mapping the moral domain.* Cambridge, MA: Harvard University Press.

Giron, M. S. T., Forsell, Y., Bernsten, C., Thorslund, M., Winblad, B., & Fastborn, J. (2002). Sleep problems in a very old population: Drug use and clinical correlates. *Journal of Gerontology: Medical Sciences, 57A,* M236–M240.

Gladue, B. A. (1994). The biopsychology of sexual orientation. *Current Directions in Psychological Science, 3,* 150–154.

Glei, D. A. (1999). Measuring contraceptive use patterns among teenage and adult women. *Family Planning Perspectives, 31,* 73–80.

Goelman, H., Andersen, C. J., Anderson, J., Gouzouasis, P., Kendrick, M., Kindler, A., Porath, M., & Young-Koh, J. (2003). Early childhood education. In I. B. Weiner (Ed.), *Handbook of psychology,* Vol. VII. New York: Wiley.

Gojdamaschko, N. (1999). Vygotsky. In M. A. Runco & S. Pritzker (Eds.), *Encyclopedia of creativity.* San Diego: Academic Press.

Goldfield, E. C., & Wolff, P. H. (2002). Motor development in infancy. In A. Slater & M. Lewis (Eds.), *Infant development.* New York: Oxford University Press.

Goldin-Meadow, S. (1979). The development of language-like communication without a language model. *Science, 197,* 401–403.

Goldsmith, H. H. (1988, August). *Does early temperament predict late development?* Paper presented at the meeting of the American Psychological Association, Atlanta.

Goldsmith, H. H., & Gottesman, I. I. (1981). Origins of variation in behavioral style: A longitudinal study of temperament in young twins. *Child Development, 52,* 91–103.

Goldstein, J. M., Seidman, L. J., Horton, N. J., Makris, N., Kennedy, D. N., Caviness, V. S., Faraone, S. V., & Tsuang, M. T. (2001). Normal sexual dimorphism of the adult human brain assessed by in vivo magnetic resonance imaging. *Cerebral Cortex, 11,* 490–497.

Goldstein-Ferber, S. (1997, April). *Massage in preterm infants.* Paper presented at the Child Development Conference, Bar-Ilan, Israel.

Goldwater, P. N. (2001). SIDS: More facts and controversies. *Medical Journal of Australia, 174,* 302–304.

Goleman, D. (1995). *Emotional intelligence.* New York: Basic Books.

Goleman, D., Kaufman, P., & Ray, M. (1993). *The creative spirit.* New York: Plume.

Golombok, S., MacCallum, F., & Goodman, E. (2001). The "test-tube" generation: Parent-child relationships and the psychological well-being of in vitro fertilization children at adolescence. *Child Development, 72,* 599–608.

Gonyea, J. G. (1994). Introduction to the issue on work and eldercare. *Research on Aging, 16,* 3–6.

Gonzales, N. A., Knight, G. P., Morgan Lopez, A., Saenz, D., & Sirolli, A. (in press). Acculturation and the mental health of Latino youths: An integration and critique of the literature. In J. M. Contreras, K. A. Kerns, & A. M. Neal-Barnett (Eds.), *Latino children and families in the United States.* Westport, CT: Greenwood.

Gonzalez-del Angel, A. A., Vidal, S., Saldan, Y., del Castillo, V., Angel, M., Macias, M., Luna, P., & Orozco, L. (2000). Molecular diagnosis of the fragile X and FRAXE syndromes in patients with mental retardation of unknown cause in Mexico. *Annals of Genetics, 43,* 29–34.

Goodman, R. A., Mercy, J. A., Loya, F., Rosenberg, M. L., Smith, J. C., Allen, N. H., Vargas, L., & Kolts, R. (1986). Alcohol use and interpersonal violence: Alcohol detected in homicide victims. *American Journal of Public Health, 76,* 144–149.

Goodstadt, L., & Ponting, C. P. (2001). Sequence variation and disease in the wake of the draft human genome. *Human Molecular Genetics, 20,* 2209–2214.

Goto, S., Takashasi, R., Araki, S., & Nakamoto, H. (2002). Dietary restriction initiated in late adulthood can reverse age-related alterations of protein and protein metabolism. *Annals of the New York Academy of Science, 959,* 50–60.

Gottfried, A. E., Gottfried, A. W., & Bathurst K. (2002). Maternal and dual-earner employment status and parenting. In M. H. Bornstein (Ed.), *Handbook of parenting* (2nd ed., Vol. 2). Mahwah, NJ: Erlbaum.

Gottlieb, G. (1998). Normally occurring environmental and behavioral influences on gene activity: From central dogma to probabilistic epigenesis. *Psychological Review, 105,* 792–802.

Gottlieb, G. (2000). Nature and nurture theories. In A. Kazdin (Ed.), *Encyclopedia of psychology.* Washington, DC, & New York: American Psychological Association and Oxford University Press.

Gottlieb, G. (2002). Origin of species: The potential significance of early experience for evolution. In W. W. Hartup & R. A. Weinberg (Eds.), *Child psychology in retrospect and prospect.* Mahwah, NJ: Erlbaum.

Gottlieb, G., Wahlsten, D., & Lickliter, R. (1998). The significance of biology for human development: A developmental psychobiological systems view. In W. Damon (Ed.), *Handbook of child psychology* (5th ed., Vol. 1). New York: Wiley.

Gottlieb, G. L. (2001). Influence of strategy on muscle activity during impact movements. *Journal of Motor Behavior, 33,* 235–242.

Gottman, J. M. (1994). *Why marriages succeed or fail.* New York: Simon & Schuster.

Gottman, J. M., Coan, J., Carrere, S., & Swanson, C. (1998). Predicting marital happiness and stability from newlywed interactions. *Journal of Marriage and the Family, 60,* 5–22.

Gottman, J. M., & Levenson, R. W. (2000). The timing of divorce: Predicting when a couple will divorce over a 14-year period. *Journal of Marriage and the Family, 62,* 737–745.

Gottman, J. M., & Notarius, C. I. (2000). Decade review: Observing marital interaction. *Journal of Marriage and the Family, 62,* 927–947.

Gottman, J. M., & Parker, J. G. (Eds.). (1987). *Conversations of friends.* New York: Cambridge University Press.

Gottman, J. M., Ryan, K. D., Carrere, S., & Erley, A. M. (2002). Toward a scientifically based marital therapy. In H. A. Liddle & D. A. Santisteban (Eds.), *Family psychology.* Washington, DC: American Psychological Association.

Gottman, J. M., & Silver, N. (1999). *The seven principles for making marriages work.* New York: Crown.

Gould, E., Reeves, A. J., Graziano, M. S., & Gross, C. G. (1999). Neurogenesis in the neocortex of adult primates, *Science, 286* (1), 548–552.

Gould, M. (2001, December 5). *Science for all: Just growing pains? The mental health of our children.* Washington, DC: National Institute of Mental Health.

Gould, R. L. (1978). *Transformations: Growth and change in adult life.* New York: Simon & Schuster.

Gould, S. J. (1981). *The mismeasure of man.* New York: W. W. Norton.

Gounin-Decarie, T. (1996). Revisiting Piaget, or the vulnerability of Piaget's infancy theory in the nineties. In G. G. Noam & K. W. Fischer (Eds.), *Development and vulnerability in close relationships.* Hillsdale, NJ: Erlbaum.

Gove, W. R., Style, C. B., & Hughes, M. (1990). The effect of marriage on the well-being of adults: A theoretical analysis. *Journal of Health and Social Behavior, 24,* 122–131.

Graber, J. A., & Brooks-Gunn, J. (2001). *Co-occurring eating and depressive problems: An 8-year study of adolescent girls.* Unpublished manuscript, Center for Children and Families, Columbia University.

Graber, J. A., & Brooks-Gunn, J. (2002). Adolescent girls' sexual development. In G. M. Wingood & R. J. DiClemente (Eds.), *Handbook of sexual and reproductive health.* New York: Plenum.

Graham, K. M. (2001, April). *Child survival: A right, not a need.* Paper presented at the meeting of the Society for Research in Child Development, Minneapolis.

Grambs, J. D. (1989). *Women over forty* (rev. ed.), New York: Springer.

Grant, J. P. (1993). *The state of the world's children.* New York: UNICEF and Oxford University Press.

Grant, J. P. (1997). *State of the world's children.* New York: UNICEF and Oxford University Press.

Grantham-McGregor, S., Ani, C., & Fernald, L. (2001). The role of nutrition in cognitive development. In R. J. Sternberg & E. L. Grigorenko (Eds.), *Environmental effects on cognitive abilities.* Mahwah, NJ: Erlbaum.

Gray, J. (1992). *Men are from Mars, women are from Venus.* New York: HarperCollins.

Gray, M. J., & Acierno, R. (2002). Symptom presentation of older adult crime victims: description of a clinical sample. *Journal of Anxiety Disorders, 16,* 299–309.

Green, L. A., Fryer, G. E., Yawn, B. P., Lanier, D., & Dovey, S. M. (2001). The ecology of medical care revisited. *New England Journal of Medicine, 344,* 2021–2025.

Greenberger, E., & Steinberg, L. (1986). *When teenagers work: The psychological social costs of adolescent employment.* New York: Basic Books.

Greene, M. G., & Adelman, R. D. (2001). Building the physician-older patient relationship. In M. L. Hummert & J. F. Nussbaum (Eds.), *Aging, communication, and health.* Mahwah, NJ: Erlbaum.

Greene, V. L., Lovely, M. E., Miller, M. D., & Ondrich, J. I. (1995). Reducing nursing home use through community long-term care: An optimization analysis. Journal of *Gerontology: Social Sciences, 50B,* S259–S268.

Greenhill, L. L., Findlings, R. L., Swanson, J. M., & the MPH MR ADHD Study Group. (2002). A double-blind, placebo-controlled study of modified-release methylphenidate in children with attention-deficit/hyperactivity disorder. *Pediatrics, 109,* e39.

Greeno, J. G., Collins, A. M., & Resnick, L. (1996). Cognition and learning. In D. C. Berliner & R. C. Chafee (Eds.), *Handbook of educational psychology.* New York: Macmillian.

Greenough, W. T. (1997, April 21). Commentary in article, "Politics of biology." *U. S. News & World Report,* p. 79.

Greenough, W. T. (1999, April). *Experience, brain development, and links to mental retardation.* Paper presented at the meeting of the Society for Research in Child Development, Albuquerque.

Greenough, W. T. (2001, April). *Nature and nurture in the brain development process.* Paper presented at the meeting of the Society for Research in Child Development, Minneapolis.

Greenough, W. T., Klintsova, A. Y., Irvan, S. A., Galvez, R., Bates, K. E., & Weiler, I. J. (2001). Synaptic regulation of protein synthesis and the fragile X protein. *Proceedings of the National Academy of Science USA, 98,* 7101–7106.

Greven, P. (1991). *Spare the child: The religious roots of punishment and the psychological impact of physical abuse.* New York: Knopf.

Griener, P. A., Snowdon, D. A., & Griener, L. H. (1999). Self-rated function, self-rated health, and postmortem evidence of brain infarcts: Finding from the Nun study. *Journal of Gerontology: Social Sciences, 54B,* S219–S222.

Griffith-Joyner, F., & Hanc, J. (1999). *Running for dummies.* Foster City, CA: IDG Books.

Grigorenko, E. (2000). Heritability and intelligence. In R. J. Sternberg (Ed.), *Handbook of intelligence.* New York: Cambridge University Press.

Grigorenko, E. L. (2001). Developmental dyslexia: An update on genes, brains, and environments. *Journal of Child Psychology and Psychiatry, 42,* 91–125.

Grigorenko, E. L. (2001). The invisible danger: The impact of ionizing radiation on cognitive development and functioning. In R. J. Sternberg & E. L. Grigorenko (Eds.), *Environmental effects on cognitive abilities.* Mahwah, NJ: Erlbaum.

Grob, A., Little, T. D., & Wanner, B. (1999). Control judgements across the lifespan. *International Journal of Behavioral Decisions, 23,* 833–854.

Grolnick, W. S., Bridges, L. J., & Connell, J. P. (1996). Emotion regulation in two-year-olds: Strategies and emotional expression in four contexts. *Child Development, 67,* 928–941.

Grolnick, W. S., & Gurland, S. T. (2001). Mothering: Retrospect and prospect. In J. P. McHale & W. S. Grolnick (Eds.), *Retrospect and prospect in the psychological study of families.* Mahwah, NJ: Erlbaum.

Gross, R. T. (1984). Patterns of maturation: Their effects on behavior and development. In M. D. Levine & P. Satz (Eds.), *Middle childhood: Development and dysfunction.* Baltimore: University Park Press.

Grossmann, K., Grossmann, K. E., Spangler, G., Suess, G., & Unzner, L. (1985). Maternal sensitivity and newborns' orientation responses as related to quality of attachment in Northern Germany. In I. Bretherton & E. Waters (Eds.), Growing points of attachment theory and research. *Monographs of the Society for Research in Child Development, 50* (1–2, Serial No. 209).

Grotevant, H. D., & McRoy, R. G. (1990). Adopted adolescents in residential treatment: The role of the family. In D. M. Brodzinsky & M. D. Schechter (Eds.), *The psychology of adoption.* New York: Oxford University Press.

Grusec, J., Davidov, M., & Lundell, L. (2002). Prosocial and helping behavior. In P. K. Smith & C. H. Hart (Eds.), *Blackwell handbook of childhood social development.* Malden, MA: Blackwell.

Guilford, J. P. (1967). *The structure of intellect.* New York: McGraw-Hill.

Gump, B., & Matthews, K. (2000 March). *Annual vacations, health, and death.* Paper presented at the meeting of American Psychosomatic Society, Savannah, GA.

Gunnar, M. R., Malone, S., & Fisch, R. O. (1987). The psychobiology of stress and coping in the human neonate: Studies of the adrenocortical activity in response to stress in the first week of life. In T. Field, P. McCabe, & N. Scheiderman (Eds.). *Stress and coping.* Hillsdale, NJ: Erlbaum.

Gur, R. C., Mozley, L. H., Mozley, P. D., Resnick, S. M., Karp, J. S., Alavi, A., Arnold, S. E., & Gur, R. E. (1995). Sex differences in regional cerebral glucose metabolism during a resting state. *Science, 267,* 528–531.

Gurwitch, R. H., Silovksy, J. F., Schultz, S., Kees, M., & Burlingame, S. (2001). *Reactions and guidelines for children following trauma/disaster.* Norman, OK: Department of Pediatrics, University of Oklahoma Health Sciences Center.

Gutmann, D. L. (1975). Parenthood: A key to the comparative study of the life cycle. In N. Datan & L. Ginsberg (Eds.), *Life-span developmental psychology: Normative life crises.* New York: Academic Press.

Gyamfi, P., Brooks-Gunn, J., & Jackson, A. P. (2001). Associations between employment and financial and parental stress in low-income single Black mothers. In M. C. Lennon (Ed.), *Welfare, work, and well-being.* New York: Haworth Press.

H

Hack, M., Flannery, D. J., Schlucter, M., Cartar, L., Borawski, E., & Klein, N. (2002). Outcomes in young adulthood for very-low-birth-weight infants. *New England Journal of Medicine, 346,* 149–157.

Hadley, E. C., Dutta, C., Finkelstein, J., Harris, T., Lane, M., Roth, G., Sherman, S., & Starke-Reed, P. (2001). Human implications of caloric restriction's effects on aging in laboratory animals. *Journal of Gerontology, 56A (Suppl.),* 5–7.

Hagestad, G. O. (1985). Continuity and connectedness. In V. L. Bengston (Ed.), *Grandparenthood.* Beverly Hills, CA: Sage.

Hahn, C. S., & DiPietro, J. A. (2001). In vitro fertilization and the family: Quality of parenting, family functioning, and child psychosocial adjustment. *Developmental Psychology, 37,* 37–48.

Hahn, D. B., & Payne, W. A. (2003). *Focus on health* (6th ed.). New York: McGraw-Hill.

Hahn, W. K. (1987). Cerebral lateralization of function: From infancy through childhood. *Psychological Bulletin, 101,* 376–392.

Haith, M. M. (1991, April). *Setting a path for the 90s: Some goals and challenges in infant-sensory and perceptual development.* Paper presented at the Society for Research in Child Development, Seattle.

Haith, M. M., & Benson, J. B. (1998). Infant cognition. In W. Damon (Ed.), *Handbook of child psychology* (5th ed., Vol. 2). New York: Wiley.

Haith, M. M., Hazen, C., & Goodman, G. S. (1988). Expectation and anticipation of dynamic visual events by 3.5 month old babies. *Child Development, 59*, 467–479.

Hakuta, K. (2000). Bilingualism. In A. Kazdin (ed.), *Encyclopedia of psychology.* Washington, DC, & New York: American Psychological Association and Oxford University Press.

Hall, G. S. (1904). *Adolescence* (Vols. 1 & 2). Englewood Cliffs, NJ: Prentice Hall.

Hall, R. T. (2000). Prevention of premature birth: Do pediatricians have a role? *Pediatrics, 105*, 1137–1140.

Hallahan, D. P., & Kaufman, J. M. (2003). *Exceptional learners* (9th ed.). Boston: Allyn & Bacon.

Halonen, J., & Santrock, J. W. (1999). *Psychology: Contexts and applications.* New York: McGraw-Hill.

Halpern, D. (2002). Sex difference research: Cognitive abilities. In J. Worell (Ed.), *Handbook of women and gender.* San Diego: Academic Press.

Halpern, I. F., & Brand, K. L. (1999, April). *The role of temperament in children's emotion reactions and coping responses to stress.* Paper presented at the meeting of the Society for Research in Child Development, Albuquerque.

Hamburg, D. A. (1997). Meeting the essential requirements for healthy adolescent development in a transforming world. In R. Takanishi & D. Hamburg (Eds.), *Preparing adolescents for the 21st century.* New York: Cambridge University Press.

Hammen, C. (2003). Mood disorders. In I. B. Weiner (Ed.), *Handbook of psychology* (Vol. VIII). New York: Wiley. P.15

Han, S. K., & Moen, P. (1998). *Clocking out: Multiplex time use in retirement.* Bronfenbrenner Life Course Center Working Paper Series No. 98-03m. Ithaca, NY: Cornell University.

Hand, I. L., Noble, L., McVeigh, T. J., Kim, M., & Yoon, J. J. (2001). The effects of intrauterine cocaine exposure on the respiratory status of the very low birthweight infant. *Journal of Perinatology, 6*, 372–375.

Hankinson, S. E., Colditz, G. A., Manson, J. E., & Speizer, F. E. (2001). *Healthy women, healthy lives.* Dallas: American Heart Association.

Harkins, S. W., Price, D. D., & Martinelli, M. (1986). Effects of age on pain perception. *Journal of Gerontology, 41*, 58–63.

Harkness, S., & Super, C. M. (1995). Culture and parenting. In M. H. Bornstein (Ed.), *Handbook of parenting* (Vol. 3). Hillsdale, NJ: Erlbaum.

Harkness, S., & Super, C. M. (2002). Culture and parenting. In M. H. Bornstein (Ed.), *Handbook of parenting* (2nd ed., Vol. 2). Mahwah, NJ: Erlbaum.

Harlow, H. F. (1958). The nature of love. *American Psychologist, 13*, 673–685.

Harlow, R. E., & Cantor, N. (1996). Still participating after all these years: A study of life task participation in later life. *Journal of Personality and Social Psychology, 71*, 1235–1249.

Harris, C. R. (2002). Sexual and romantic jealousy in heterosexual and homosexual adults. *Psychological Science, 13*, 7–12.

Harris, G., Thomas, A., & Booth, D. A. (1990). Development of salt taste in infancy. *Developmental Psychology, 26*, 534–538.

Harris, J. R. (1998). *The nurture assumption: Why children turn out the way they do: Parents matter less than you think and peers matter more.* New York: Free Press.

Harris, L. (1975). *The myth and reality of aging in America.* Washington, DC: National Council on Aging.

Harris, L. (1987, September 3). The latchkey child phenomena. *Dallas Morning News,* pp. 1A, 10A.

Harris, L. (1997). *A national poll of children and exercise.* Washington, DC: Lou Harris & Associates.

Harris, T., Koyar, M. G., Suzman, R., Kleinman, J. C., & Feldman, J. J. (1989). Longitudinal study of physical ability in the oldest old. *American Journal of Public Health, 79*, 698–702.

Hart, B., & Risley, T. R. (1995). *Meaningful differences.* Baltimore, MD: Paul Brookes.

Hart, C. H., Burts, D. C., Durland, M. A., Charlesworth, R., DeWolf, M., & Fleege, P. O. (1998). Stress behaviors and activity type participation of preschoolers in more and less developmentally appropriate classrooms: SES and sex differences. *Journal Research in Childhood Education, 12*, 176–196.

Hart, C. H., Charlesworth, R., Burts, D. C., & DeWolf, M. (1993, March). *The relationship of attendance in developmentally appropriate or inappropriate kindergarten classrooms to first-grade behavior.* Paper presented at the biennial meeting of the Society for Research in Child Development, New Orleans.

Harter, S. (1990). Self and identity development. In S. S. Feldman & G. R. Elliott (Eds.), *At the threshold: The developing adolescent.* Cambridge, MA: Harvard University Press.

Harter, S. (1998). The development of self-representations. In W. Damon (Ed.), *Handbook of child psychology* (5th ed., Vol. 3). New York: Wiley.

Harter, S. (1999). *The construction of the self.* New York: Guilford.

Harter, S. (2002). Review of Santrock, *Child Development,* 10th ed. New York: McGraw-Hill.

Harter, S., & Marold, D. B. (1992). Psychosocial risk factors contributing to adolescent suicide ideation. In G. Noam & S. Borst (Eds.), *Child and adolescent suicide.* San Francisco: Jossey-Bass.

Harter, S., & Whitesell, N. (2001, April). *What we have learned from Columbine: The impact of self-esteem on suicidal and violent ideation among adolescents.* Paper presented at the meeting of the Society for Research in Child Development, Minneapolis.

Hartshorne, H., & May, M. S. (1928–1930). *Moral studies in the nature of character: Studies in the nature of character.* New York: Macmillan.

Hartup, W. W. (1983). The peer system. In P. H. Mussen (Ed.), *Handbook of child psychology* (4th ed., Vol. 4). New York: Wiley.

Hartup, W. W. (1996). The company they keep: Friendships and their development significance. *Child Development, 67*, 1–13.

Hartup, W. W. (1999, April). *Peer relations and the growth of the individual child.* Paper presented at the meeting of the Society for Research in Child Development, Albuquerque.

Hartup, W. W. (2000). Middle childhood: Socialization and social context. In A. Kazdin (Ed.), *Encyclopedia of psychology.* Washington, DC, & New York: American Psychological Association and Oxford University Press.

Hartup, W. W. (2001, April). *Relationships and the development of social competence: Friends and enemies.* Paper presented at the meeting of the Society for Research in Child Development, Minneapolis.

Hartup, W. W., & Abecassis, M. (2002). Friends and enemies. In P. K. Smith & C. H. Hart (Eds.), *Blackwell handbook of childhood social development.* Malden, MA: Blackwell.

Hartup, W. W., & Laursen, B. (1999). Relationships as developmental contexts: Retrospective themes and contemporary issues. In W. Andrew Collins & B. Laursen (Eds.), *Relationships as developmental contexts.* Mahwah, NJ: Erlbaum.

Harvey, J. H., & Weber, A. L. (2001). *Odyssey of the heart* (2nd ed.). Mahwah, NJ: Erlbaum.

Haselager, G. J. T., Cilessen, A. H. N., Van Lieshout, C. F. M., Riksen-Walraen, J. M. A., & Hartup, W. W. (2002). Heterogeneity among peer-rejected boys across middle childhood: Developmental pathways of social behavior. *Developmental Psychology, 38,* 446–456.

Hauck, S. J., & Bartke, A. (2001). Free radical defenses in the liver and kidney of human growth hormone transgenic mice. *Journal of Gerontology, 56A (No. 4),* B153–B162.

Hawkins, J. A., & Berndt, T. J. (1985, April). *Adjustment following the transition to junior high school.* Paper presented at the biennial meeting of the Society for Research in Child Development, Toronto.

Hayflick, L. (1977). The cellular basis for biological aging. In C. E. Finch & L. Hayflick (Eds.), *Handbook of the biology of aging.* New York: Van Nostrand.

Haynie, D. A., Berg, S., Johansson, B., Gatz, M., & Zarit, S. H. (2001). Symptoms of depression in the oldest old: A longitudinal study. *Journal of Gerontology, 56B (No. 2),* P111–P118.

Hayslip, B. (1996). Hospice. In J. E. Birren (Ed.), *Encyclopedia of gerontology* (Vol. 1). San Diego: Academic Press.

Hayslip, B., Edmondson, R., & Guarnaccia, C. (1999, November). *Religiousness, perceptions of funerals, and bereavement adjustment in adulthood.* Paper presented at the meeting of the Gerontological Society of America, San Francisco.

Hayward, M. D., Friedman, S., & Chen, H. (1996). Race inequities in men's retirement. *Journal of Gerontology, 51A,* S1–S10.

Hazan, C., & Shaver, P. R. (1987). Romantic love conceptualized as an attachment process. *Journal of Personality and Social Psychology, 52,* 522–524.

Health Management Resources. (2001). *Child health and fitness.* Boston: Author.

Heath, S. B., & McLaughlin, M. W. (Eds.). (1993). *Identity and inner-city youth.* New York: Teacher College Press.

Heckhausen, J. (1997). Developmental regulation across adulthood: Primary and secondary control of age-related challenges. *Developmental Psychology, 33,* 176–187.

Heckhausen, J. (2001). Adaptation and resilience in midlife. In M. E. Lachman (Ed.), *Handbook of midlife development.* New York: John Wiley.

Heckhausen, J., & Schultz, R. (1995). A life-span theory of control. *Psychological Review, 102,* 284–304.

Heckhausen, J., Wrosch, C., & Fleeson, W. (2001). Developmental regulation before and after a developmental decline: The sample case of "biological clock" for childbearing. *Psychology and Aging, 16,* 400–413.

Heinicke, C. M. (2002). The transition to parenting. In M. H. Bornstein (Ed.), *Handbook of parenting* (2nd ed.). Mahwah, NJ: Erlbaum.

Hellige, J. B. (2003). Laterality. In V. S. Ramachandran (Ed.), *Encyclopedia of the human brain.* San Francisco: Academic Press.

Helson, R. (1997, August). *Personality change: When is it adult development?* Paper presented at the meeting of the American Psychological Association, Chicago.

Helson, R., Mitchell, V., & Moane, G. (1984). Personality change in women from college to midlife. *Journal of Personality and Social Psychology, 53,* 176–186.

Helson, R., & Wink, P. (1992). Personality change in women from the early 40s to early 50s. *Psychology and Aging, 7,* 46–55.

Helwig, C., & Turiel, E. (2002). Moral reasoning and social development. In P. K. Smith & C. H. Hart (Eds.), *Blackwell handbook of childhood social development.* Malden, MA: Blackwell.

Hendrick, S. (2002). Intimacy and love. In J. Worell (Ed.), *Encyclopedia of women and gender.* San Diego: Academic Press.

Hendry, J. (1995). *Understanding Japanese society.* London: Routledge.

Hendry, J. (1999). *Social anthropology.* New York: Macmillan.

Henry, D. B., Tolan, P. H., & Gorman-Smith, D. (2001). Longitudinal family and peer group effects on violence and nonviolent delinquency. *Journal of Clinical Child Psychology, 30,* 172–186.

Hepper, P. G., Shahidullah, S., & White, R. (1990). Origins of fetal handedness. *Nature, 347,* 431.

Herek, G. (2000). Homosexuality. In A. Kazdin (Ed.), *Encyclopedia of psychology.* Washington, DC, & New York: American Psychological Association and Oxford University Press.

Herrill, R., Goldberg, J., True, W. R., Ramakrishnan, V., Lyons, M., Eisen, S., & Tsuang, M. T. (1999). Sexual orientation and suicidality: A co-twin control study in adult men. *Archives of General Psychiatry, 56,* 867–874.

Herrnstein, R. J., & Murray, C. (1994). *The bell curve: Intelligence and class structure in modern life.* New York: Free Press.

Hetherington, E. M. (1989). Coping with family transitions: Winners, losers, and survivors. *Child Development, 60,* 1–14.

Hetherington, E. M. (1993). An overview of the Virginia Longitudinal Study of Divorce and Remarriage with a focus on early adolescence. *Journal of Family Psychology, 7,* 39–56.

Hetherington, E. M. (1999). Social capital and the development of youth from non-divorced, divorced, and remarried families. In W. A. Collins & B. Laursen (Eds.), *Relationships as developmental contexts.* Mahwah, NJ: Erlbaum.

Hetherington, E. M. (2000). Divorce. In A. Kazdin (ed.), *Encyclopedia of psychology.* Washington, DC, & New York: American Psychological Association and Oxford University Press.

Hetherington, E. M., Bridges, M., & Insabella, G. M. (1998). What matters? What does not? Five perspectives on the association between marital transitions and children's adjustment. *American Psychologist, 53,* 167–184.

Hetherington, E. M., & Kelly, J. (2002). *For better or for worse: Divorce reconsidered.* New York: Norton.

Hetherington, E. M., Reiss, D., & Plomin, R. (Eds.). (1994). *Separate social worlds of siblings: The impact of nonshared environment on development.* Hillsdale, NJ: Erlbaum.

Hetherington, E. M., & Stanley-Hagan, M. (2002). Parenting in divorced and remarried families. In M. H. Bornstein (Ed.), *Handbook of parenting* (2nd ed., Vol. 3). Mahwah, NJ: Erlbaum.

Heuwinkel, M. K. (1996). New ways of learning 5 new ways of teaching. *Childhood Education, 72,* 27–31.

Hewlett, S. A. (2002). *Creating a life: Professional women and the quest for children.* New York: Talk Miramax Books.

Hill, C. R., & Stafford, F. P. (1980). Parental care of children: Time diary estimate of quantity, predictability, and variety. *Journal of Human Resources, 15,* 219–239.

Hill, J. O., & Trowbridge, F. L. (1998). Childhood obesity: Future directions and research priorities. *Pediatrics, 101,* 570–574.

Hill, J., Waldfogel, J., Brooks-Gunn, J., & Han, W. (2001, November). *Towards a better estimate of causal links in child policy: The case of maternal employment and child outcomes.* Paper presented at the Association for Public Policy Analysis and Management Fall Research Conference, Washington, DC.

Hill, P. C., & Butter, E. M. (1995). The role of religion in promoting physical health. *Journal of Psychology and Christianity, 14,* 141–155.

Hill, R. D., Thorn, B. L., Bowling, J., Morrison, A. (Eds.). (2002). *Geriatric residential care.* Mahwah, NJ: Erlbaum.

Himes, C. L., Hogan, D. P., & Eggebeen, D. J. (1996). Living arrangements of minority elders. *Journal of Gerontology. 51A,* S42–S48.

Hirsch, B. J., & Rapkin, B. D. (1987). The transition to junior high school: A longitudinal study of self-esteem, psychological symptomatology, school life, and social support. *Child Development, 58,* 1235–1243.

Hirsch-Pasek, K., Hyson, M., Rescorla, L., & Cone, J. (1989, April). *Hurrying children: How does it affect their academic, social, creative, and emotional development?* Paper presented at the Society for Research in Child Development meeting, Kansas City.

Hitch, G. J., Towse, J. N., & Hutton, U. (2001). What limits children's working memory span? Theoretical accounts and applications for scholastic development. *Journal of Experimental Psychology: General, 130,* 184–198.

Hlatky, M. A., Boothroyd, D., Vittinghoff, E., Shaprt, P., & Whooley, M. A. (2002). Quality-of-life and depressive symptoms in postmenopausal women after receiving hormone replacement therapy. *Journal of the American Medical Association, 287,* 591–597.

Hobel, C. J., Dunkel-Schetter, C., Roesch, S. C., Castro, L. C., & Arora, C. P. (1999). Maternal plasma corticotrophin-releasing hormone associated with stress at 20 weeks' gestation in pregnancies ending in preterm delivery. *American Journal of Obstetrics and Gynecology, 180,* S257–S263.

Hodges, J. R. (2000). Memory in the dementias. In E. Tulving & F. I. M. Craik (Ed.), *The Oxford handbook of memory.* New York: Oxford University Press.

Hoff, E. (2003). Language development in childhood. In I. B. Weiner (Ed.), *Handbook of psychology* (Vol. VI). New York: Wiley.

Hoff, E., Laursen, B., & Tardiff, T. (2002). Socioeconomic status and parenting. In M. H. Bornstein (Ed.), *Handbook of parenting* (2nd ed., Vol. 2). Mahwah, NJ: Erlbaum.

Hoff-Ginsberg, E., & Lerner, S. (1999, April). *The nature of vocabulary differences related to socioeconomic status at two and four years.* Paper presented at the meeting of the Society for Research in Child Development, Albuquerque.

Hoffman, L. W. (1989). Effects of maternal employment in two-parent families. *American Psychologist, 44,* 283–293.

Hoffman, L. W., & Youngblade, L. M. (1999). *Mothers at work: Effects on children's well-being.* New York: Cambridge.

Hoffman, M. L. (1970). Moral development. In P. H. Mussen (Ed.), *Manual of child psychology* (3rd ed., Vol. 2). New York: Wiley.

Hoffman, M. L. (2002). *Empathy and moral development.* New York: Cambridge University Press.

Hoffman, S., Foster, E., & Furstenberg, F. (1993). Reevaluating the costs of teenage childbearing. *Demography, 30,* 1–13.

Hogan, D. M., & Tudge, J. (1999). Implications of Vygotsky's theory for peer learning. In A. M. O'Donnell & A. King (Eds.), *Cognitive perspectives on peer learning.* Mahwah, NJ: Erlbaum.

Holding, S. (2002). Current state of screening for Down syndrome. *Annals of Clinical Biochemistry, 39,* 1–11.

Holland, J. C. (2002). Management of grief and loss: medicine's obligation and challenge. *Journal of the American Medical Women's Association, 57,* 95–96.

Holland, J. L. (1987). Current status of Holland's theory of careers: Another perspective. *Career Development Quarterly, 36,* 24–30.

Hollier, L. M., Harstad, T. W., Sanchez, P. J., Twickler, D. M., & Wendel, G. D. (2001). Fetal syphilis: Clinical and laboratory characteristics. *Obstetrics and Gynecology, 97,* 947–953.

Holmbeck, G. N. (1996). A model of family relational transformations during the transition to adolescence: Parent-adolescent conflict and adaptation. In J. A. Graber, J. Brooks-Gunn, & A. C. Petersen (Eds.), *Transitions through adolescence.* Hillsdale, NJ: Erlbaum.

Holmes, T. H., & Rahe, R. H. (1967). The social readjustment rating scale. *Journal of Psychosomatic Research, 11,* 213–218.

Holtzen, D. W. (2000). Handedness and professional tennis. *International Journal of Neuroscience, 105,* 101–119.

Holtzmann, D. M., Bales, K. R., Wu, S., Bhat, P., Parsadanian, M., Fagan, A. M., Chang, L. K., Sun, Y., & Pauyl, S. M. (1999). Expression of human apolipoprotein E reduces amyloid-beat deposition in a mouse model of Alzheimer's disease. *Journal of Clinical Investigation, 103,* R15–R21.

Honein, M. A., Paulozzi, L. J., Mathews, T. J., Erickson, J. D., & Wong, L. Y. (2001). Impact of folic acid fortification of the U.S. food supply on the occurrence of tube defects. *Journal of the American Medical Association, 285,* 2981–2986.

Hopkins, B. (1991). Facilitating early motor development: An intracultural study of West Indian mothers and their infants living in Britain. In J. K. Nugent, B. M. Lester, & T. B. Brazelton (Eds.), *The cultural context of infancy: Vol. 2. Multicultural and interdisciplinary approaches to parent-infant relations.* Norwood, NJ: Ablex.

Hopkins, B., & Westra, T. (1988). Maternal handling and motor development: An intracultural study. *Genetic Psychology Monographs, 14,* 377–420.

Hopkins, B., & Westra, T. (1990). Motor development, maternal expectations, and the role of handling. *Infant Behavior and Development, 13,* 117–122.

Hopkins, J. R. (2000). Erikson, E. H. (2000). In A. Kazdin (Ed.), *Encyclopedia of psychology.* Washington, DC, & New York: American Psychological Association and Oxford University Press.

Hoppu, U., Kalliomaki, M., Laiho, K., & Isolauri, E. (2001). Breast milk—immunomodulatory signals against allergenic diseases, *Allergy, 56,* 23–26.

Horn, J. L., & Donaldson, G. (1980). Cognitive development II: Adulthood development of human abilities. In O. G. Brim & J. Kagan (Eds.), *Constancy and change in human development.* Cambridge, MA: Harvard University Press.

Horney, K. (1967). *Feminine psychology.* New York: W. W. Norton.

Hotchner, T. (1997). *Pregnancy and childbirth.* New York: Avon.

House, J. S. (1998). Commentary: Age, work, and well-being. In K. W. Schaie & C. Schooler (Eds.), *The impact of work on older adults.* New York: Springer.

House, J. S., Kessler, R. C., Herzog, R. C., Mero, R. P., Kinney, A. M., & Breslow, M. J. (1992). Social stratification, age, and health. In K. W. Schaie, D. Blazer, & J. S. House (Eds.), *Aging, health behaviors, and health outcomes.* Mahwah, NJ: Erlbaum.

House, J. S., Landis, K. R., & Umberson, D. (1988). Social relationships and health. *Science, 241,* 540–545.

Howard, R. W. (2001). Searching the real world for signs of rising population intelligence. *Personality & Individual Differences, 30,* 1039–1058.

Howe, M. L. (1997). Children's memory for traumatic experiences. *Learning and Individual Differences, 9,* 153–174. (p. 349)

Howell, E. M. (2001). The impact of Medicaid expansions for pregnant women: A synthesis of the evidence. *Medical Care Research Review, 58,* 3–30.

Howes, C. (1988, April). *Can the age of entry and the quality of infant child care predict behaviors in kindergarten?* Paper presented at the International Conference on Infant Studies, Washington, DC.

Howley, E. T. (2001). Type of activity: Resistance, aerobic and leisure versus occupational physical activity. *Medical Science and Sports Exercise, 33 (Suppl.),* S364–369.

Hoyer, W. J. & Roodin, P. A. (2003). *Adult development and aging* (5th ed.). New York: McGraw-Hill.

Hoyer, W. J., Rybash, J. M., & Roodin, P. A. (1999). *Adult development and aging* (4th ed.). New York: McGraw-Hill.

Hoyle, R. H., & Judd, C. M. (2002). *Research methods in social psychology* (7th ed.). Belmont, CA: Wadsworth.

Huesmann, L. R. (1986). Psychological processes promoting the relation between exposure to media violence and aggressive behavior by the viewer. *Journal of Social Issues, 42,* 125–139.

Hultsch, D. F., Hammer, M., & Small, B. J. (1993). Age differences in cognitive performance in later life: Relationships to self-reported health and activity life style. *Journal of Gerontology, 48,* P1–P11.

Hultsch, D. F., Hertzog, C., Small, B. J., & Dixon, R. A. (1999). Use it or lose it: Engaged lifestyle as a buffer of cognitive decline in aging? *Psychology and Aging, 14,* 245–263.

Hultsch, D. F., & Plemons, J. K. (1979). Life events and life-span development. In P. B. Baltes & O. G. Brim (Eds.), *Life-span development and behavior.* New York: Academic Press.

Hummer, R. A., Rogers, R. G., Nam, C. B., & Ellison, C. G. (1999). Religious involvement and U.S. adult mortality. *Demography, 36,* 272–285.

Hummert, M. L., Garstka, T. A., Shaner, J. L., & Strahm, S. (1994). Stereotypes of the elderly held by young, middle-aged, and elderly adults. *Journal of Gerontology, 49,* P240–P249.

Hummert, M. L., & Nussbaum, J. F. (Eds.). (2001). *Aging, communication, and health.* Mahwah, NJ: Erlbaum.

Humpheys, K. (2000). Alcoholics Anonymous. In A. Kazdin (Ed.), *Encyclopedia of psychology.* Washington, DC, & New York: American Psychological Association and Oxford University Press.

Humphrey, D. G., & Kramer, A. F. (1997). Age differences in visual search for feature, conjunction, and triple-conjunction targets. *Psychology and Aging, 12,* 704–717.

Hungerford, T. L. (2001). The economic consequences of widowhood on elderly women in the United States and Germany. *The Gerontologist, 41 (No. 1),* 103–110.

Hunsley, M., & Thoman, E. B. (2002). The sleep of co-sleeping infants when they are not co-sleeping: Evidence that co-sleeping is stressful. *Developmental Psychobiology, 40,* 14–22.

Huston, A. (1999, August). *Employment interventions for parents in poverty: How do children fare?* Paper presented at the meeting of the Society for Research in Child Development, Albuquerque.

Huston, A. C. (1983). Sex-typing. In P. H. Mussen (Ed.). *Handbook of child psychology* (4th ed., Vol. 4). New York: Wiley.

Huston, A. C., McLoyd, V. C., & Coll, C. G. (1994). Children and poverty: issues in contemporary research. *Child Development, 65,* 275–282.

Huston, T. L., Neihuis, S., & Smith, S. (1997, November). *Divergent experiential and behavioral pathways leading to marital distress and divorce.* Paper presented at the meeting of the National Council on Family Relations, Washington, DC.

Huttenlocher, J., Haight, W., Bruk, A., Seltzer, M., & Lyons, T. (1991). Early vocabulary growth: Relation to language input and gender. *Developmental Psychology, 27,* 236–248.

Huttenlocher, P. R., & Dabholkar, A. S. (1997). Regional differences in synaptogenesis in human cerebral cortex. *Journal of Comparative Neurology, 37 (2),* 167–178.

Huyck, M. H. (1999). Gender roles and gender identity in midlife. In S. L. Willis & J. D. Reid (Eds.), *Life in the middle.* San Diego: Academic Press.

Huyck, M. H., & Hoyer, W. J. (1982). *Adult development and aging.* Belmont, CA: Wadsworth.

Hyde, J. S. (1993). Meta-analysis and the psychology of women. In F. L. Denmark & M. A. Paludi (Eds.), *Handbook on the psychology of women.* Westport, CT: Greenwood.

Hyde, J. S., & Barnett, R. C. (2001). Women, men, work and family: A new theoretical view. *The American Psychologist, 56* (10).

Hyde, J. S., & DeLamater, J. D. (2003). *Understanding human sexuality* (8th ed.). New York: McGraw-Hill.

Hyde, J. S., & Mezulis, A. H. (2001). Gender differences in research: Issues and critique. In J. Worell (Ed.), *Encyclopedia of women and gender.* San Diego: Academic Press.

Hyde, J. S., & Plant, E. A. (1995). Magnitude of psychological gender differences: Another side of the story. *American Psychologist, 50,* 159–161.

Hyman, I. E., & Loftus, E. F. (2001). False childhood memories and eye-witness errors. In M. L. Eisen, J. A. Quas, & G. S. Goodman, (Eds.) *Memory and suggestibility in the forensic interview.* Mahwah, NJ: Erlbaum.

Hymel, S., McDougall, P., & Renshaw, P. (2002). Peer acceptance/rejection. In P. K. Smith & C. H. Hart (Eds.), *Blackwell handbook of childhood social development.* Malden, MA: Blackwell.

I

Iannucci, L. (2000). *Birth defects.* New York: Enslow.

Idler, E. L., Stanislav, V. K., & Hays, J. C. (2001). Patterns of religious practice and belief in the last year of life. *Journal of Gerontology: Social Sciences, 56B,* S326–S334.

Ilola, L. M. (1990). Culture and health. In R. W. Brislin (Ed.), *Applied cross-cultural psychology.* Newbury Park, CA: Sage.

Inglehart, R. (1990). *Culture shift in advanced industrial society.* Princeton, NJ: Princeton University Press.

Inoff-Germain, G., Arnold, G. S., Nottelmann, E. D., Susman, E. J., Cutler, G. B., & Chrousos, G. P. (1988). Relations between hormone levels and observational measures of aggressive behavior of young adolescents in family interactions. *Developmental Psychology, 24,* 124–139.

Institute of Medicine. (1997, June). *Approaching death: Improving care at the end of life.* Washington, DC: National Academy of Sciences.

Intons-Peterson, M. (1996). Memory aids. In D. Hermann, C. McEvoy, C. Hertzog, P. Hertel, & M. Johnson (Eds.), *Basic and applied memory research* (Vol. 2). Hillsdale, NJ: Erlbaum.

Izard, C. (2000). Affect. In A. Kazdin (Ed.), *Encyclopedia of psychology.* Washington, DC, & New York: American Psychological Association and Oxford University Press.

J

Jaakkola, J. J., Nafstad, P., & Magnus, P. (2001). Environmental tobacco smoke, parental atopy, and childhood asthma. *Environmental Health Perspectives, 109,* 579–582.

Jackson, J. S., Chatters, L. M., & Taylor, R. J. (Eds.). (1993). *Aging in Black America.* Newbury Park, CA: Sage.

Jacob, N., Van Gestel, S., Derom, C., Theiry, E., Vernon, P., Derom, R., & Vlietinck, R. (2001). Heritability estimates of intelligence in twins: Effect of chorion type. *Behavior Genetics, 31,* 209–217.

Jacobs, J. E., & Klaczynski, P. A. (2002). The development of judgment and decision making during childhood and adolescence. *Current Directions in Psychological Science, 11,* 145–149.

Jacobs, J. E., & Potenza, M. (1990, March). *The use of decision-making strategies in late adolescence.* Paper presented at the meeting of the Society for Research in Adolescence, Atlanta.

Jacobs, J. E., & Tanner, J. L. (1999, August). *Stability and change in perceptions of parent-child relationships.* Paper presented at the meeting of the Gerontological Association of America, San Francisco.

Jacobs, R. H. (1994). His and her aging: Differences, difficulties, dilemmas, delights. *Journal of Geriatric Psychiatry, 27,* 113–128.

Jacobs, S. C., Dosten, T. R., Kasl, S. V., Ostfield, A. M., Berkman, L., & Charpentier, M. P. H. (1987). Attachment theory and multiple dimensions of grief. *Omega, 18,* 41–52.

Jacobson, J. L., Jacobson, S. W., Fein, G. G., Schwartz, P. M., & Dowler, J. (1984). Prenatal exposure to an environmental toxin: A test of the multiple-effects model. *Developmental Psychology, 20,* 523–532.

Jacobson, J. L., Jacobson, S. W., Padgett, R. J., Brumitt, G. A., & Billings, R. L. (1992). Effects of prenatal PCB exposure on cognitive processing efficiency and sustained attention. *Developmental Psychology, 28,* 297–306.

Jadelis, K., Miller, M., Ettinger, W., & Messier, S. (2001). Strength, balance, and the modifying effects of obesity and knee pain: Results from the Observational Arthritis Study in Seniors (OASIS). *Journal of the American Geriatric Society, 49,* 884–891.

Jaffee, S. R. (2002). Pathways to adversity in young adulthood among early childbearers. *Journal of Family Psychology, 16,* 38–49.

James, W. (1890/1950). *The principles of psychology.* New York: Dover.

Jecker, N. S. (1996). Ethics and euthanasia. In J. E. Birren (Ed.), *Encyclopedia of gerontology* (Vol. 1). San Diego: Academic Press.

Jeffery, H. E., Megevand, A., Page, H., & Page, M. (2000). Why the prone position is a risk factor in sudden infant death syndrome. *Pediatrics, 104,* 263–269.

Jenkins, A. M., Albee, G. W., Paster, V. S., Sue, S., Baker, D., Comaz-Diaz, L., Puente, A., Suinn, R. M., Caldwell-Colbert, A. T., Williams, V. J., & Root, M. P. P. (2003). Ethnic minorities. In I. B. Weiner (Ed.), *Handbook of psychology* (Vol. I). New York: Wiley.

Jenkins, J. M., & Astington, J. W. (1996). Cognitive factors and family structure associated with theory of mind development in young children. *Developmental Psychology, 32,* 70–78.

Jennekens, F. G., & Kater, L. (2002). Physician-assisted death. *New England Journal of Medicine, 347,* 1043.

Jensen, A. R. (1969). How much can we boost IQ and scholastic achievement? *Harvard Educational Review, 39,* 1–123.

Jerrome, D., & Wenger, G. C. (1999). Stability and change in late-life friendships. *Aging and Society, 19,* 661–676.

Jessor, R., Turbin, M. S., & Costa, F. (1998). Protective factors in adolescent health behavior. *Journal of Personality and Social Psychology, 75,* 788–800.

Jeynes, W. H. (2002). The relationship between the consumption of various drugs by adolescents and their academic achievement. *American Journal of Alcohol Abuse, 28,* 15–32.

Ji, B. T., Shu, X. O., Linet, M. S., Zheng, W., Wacholde, S., Gao, Y. T., Ying, D. M., & Jin, F. (1997). Paternal cigarette smoking and the risk of childhood cancer among offspring of nonsmoking mothers. *Journal of the National Cancer Institute, 89,* 238–244.

Jiao, S., Ji, G., & Jing, Q. (1996). Cognitive development of Chinese urban only children and children with siblings. *Child Development, 67,* 387–395.

Jinon, S. (1996). The effect of infant massage on growth of the preterm infant. In C. Yarbes-Almirante & M. De Luma (Eds.), *Increasing safe and successful pregnancy.* Amsterdam: Elsevier.

Jirtle, R. L., Sander, M., & Barrett, J. C. (2000). Genomic imprinting and environmental disease susceptibility. *Environmental Health Perspectives, 108,* 271–278.

Johannes, L. (2002, June 3). The surprising rise of a radical diet: "Calorie restriction." *The Wall Street Journal,* pp. A1, A10.

Johnson, B. K. (1996). Older adults and sexuality. A multidimensional perspective. *Journal of Gerontological Nursing, 22,* 6–15.

Johnson, C. (1990, May). The new woman's ethics report. *New Woman,* p. 6.

Johnson, C. L., & Troll, L. E. (1994). Constraints and facilitators to friendships in late late life. *Gerontologist, 34,* 79–87.

Johnson, J., Dupuis, V., Musial, D., Hall, G., & Gollnick, D. (2002). *Introduction to the foundations of American Education* (12th ed.). Boston: Allyn & Bacon.

Johnson, M. H. (1999). Developmental neuroscience. In M. H. Bornstein & M. E. Lamb (Eds.), *Developmental psychology: An advanced textbook* (4th ed.). Mahwah, NJ: Erlbaum.

Johnson, M. H. (2000). Infancy: Biological processes. In A. Kazdin (Ed.), *Encyclopedia of psychology.* Washington, DC, & New York: American Psychological Association and Oxford University Press.

Johnson, M. H. (2001). Functional brain development during infancy. In A. Fogel & G. Bremner (Eds.), *Blackwell handbook of infant development.* London: Blackwell.

Johnson, M. K., Beebe, T., Mortimer, J. T., & Snyder, M. (1998). Volunteerism in adolescence: A process perspective. *Journal of Research on Adolescence, 8,* 309–332.

John-Steiner, V., & Mahn, H. (2003). Sociocultural contexts for teaching and learning. In I. B. Weiner (Ed.), *Handbook of psychology* (Vol. VII). New York: Wiley.

Johnston, C., & Leung, D. W. (2001). Effects of medication, behavioral, and combined treatments on parents' and children's attributions for the behavior of children with attention-deficit hyperactivity disorder, *Journal of Consulting and Clinical Psychology, 69,* 67–76.

Johnston, L. D., O'Malley, P. M., & Bachman, J. G. (1992, January 25). *Most forms of drug use decline among American high school and college students.* News release, Institute of Social Research, University of Michigan, Ann Arbor.

Johnston, L. D., O'Malley, P. M., & Bachman, J. G. (2001, December). *Monitoring the future, 2001.* Ann Arbor, MI: Institute for Social Research, University of Michigan.

Joiner, T. E. (2000). Depression: Current developments and controversies. In S. H. Qualls & N. Abeles (Eds.), *Psychology and the aging revolution.* Washington, DC: American Psychological Association.

Jones, G., Riley, M., & Dwyer, T. (2000). Breastfeeding early in life and bone mass in prepubertal children: A longitudinal study. *Osteoporosis International, 11,* 146–152.

Jones, L. (1984). White-black achievement differences: The narrowing gap. *American Psychologist, 39,* 1207–1213.

Jones, M. C. (1965). Psychological correlates of somatic development. *Child Development, 36,* 899–911.

Josselson, R. (1996). *On becoming the same age as one's mother.* Paper presented at the meeting of the American Psychological Association, Toronto.

Jusczyk, P. W. (2002). Language development: from speech perception to first words. In A. Slater & M. Lewis (Eds.), *Infant development.* New York: Oxford University Press.

Jusczyk, P. W., & Hohne, E. A. (1997). Infants' memory for spoken words. *Science, 277,* 1984–1986.

K

Kagan, J. (1984). *The nature of the child.* New York: Basic Books.

Kagan, J. (1987). Perspectives on infancy. In J. D. Osofsky (Ed.), *Handbook on infant development* (2nd ed.). New York: Wiley.

Kagan, J. (1992). Yesterday's promises, tomorrow's promises. *Developmental Psychology, 28,* 990–997.

Kagan, J. (1997). Temperament and the reaction to unfamiliarity. *Child Development, 68,* 139–143.

Kagan, J. (1998). The biology of the child. In W. Damon (Ed.), *Handbook of child psychology* (5th ed., Vol. 3). New York: Wiley.

Kagan, J. (1998). *The power of parents.* Available on the world wide web at: http://psychplace.com.

Kagan, J. (2000). Temperament. In A. Kazdin (Ed.), *Encyclopedia of psychology.* Washington, DC, & New York: American Psychological Association and Oxford University Press.

Kagan, J. (2002). Behavioral inhibition as a temperamental category. In R. J. Davidson, K. R. Scherer, & H. H. Goldsmith (Eds.), *Handbook of affective sciences.* New York: Oxford University Press.

Kagan, J. J., Kearsley, R. B., & Zelazo, P. R. (1978). *Infancy: Its place in human development.* Cambridge, MA: Harvard University Press.

Kagan, J., & Snidman, N. (1991). Infant predictors of inhibited and uninhibited behavioral profiles. *Psychological Science, 2,* 40–44.

Kahn, A., Swaguchi, T., Sawaguchi, A., Groswasser, J., Franco, P., Scaillet, S., Kelmanson, I., & Dan, B. (2002). Sudden infant deaths: from epidemiology to physiology. *Forensic Science International, 130,* Supplement: 8.

Kalick, S. M., & Hamilton, T. E. (1986). The matching hypothesis reexamined. *Journal of Personality and Social Psychology, 51,* 673–682.

Kalish, R. A. (1981). *Death, grief, and caring relationships.* Monterey, CA: Brooks/Cole.

Kalish, R. A. (1987). Death. In G. L. Maddox (Ed.), *Encyclopedia of aging.* New York: Springer.

Kalish, R. A., & Reynolds, D. K. (1976). *An overview of death and ethnicity.* Farmingdale, NY: Baywood.

Kaltiala-Heino, R., Rimpela, M, Rantanen, P., & Laippala, P. (2001). Adolescent depression. *Journal of Affective Disorders, 64,* 155–166.

Kamerman, S. B. (1989). Child care, women, work, and the family: An international overview of child-care services and related policies. In J. S. Lande, S. Scarr, & N. Gunzenhauser (Eds.), *Caring for children: Challenge to America.* Hillsdale, NJ: Erlbaum.

Kamerman, S. B. (2000a). Parental leave policies. *Social Policy Report of the Society for Research in Child Development, XIV* (No. 2), 1–15.

Kamerman, S. B. (2000b). From maternity to paternity child leave policies. *Journal of the Medical Women's Association, 55,* 98–99.

Kamii, C. (1985). *Young children reinvent arithmetic: Implications of Piaget's theory.* New York: Teachers College Press.

Kamii, C. (1989). *Young children continue to reinvent arithmetic.* New York: Teachers College Press.

Kanner, A. D., Coyne, J. C., Schaefer, C., & Lazarus, R. S. (1981). Comparison of two modes of stress measurement: Daily hassles and uplifts versus major life events. *Journal of Behavioral Medicine, 4,* 1–39.

Kantrowitz, B. (1991, Summer). The good, the bad, and the difference. *Newsweek,* pp. 48–50.

Kaplow, J. B., Curran, P. J., Dodge, K. A., & the Conduct Problems Prevention Research Group. (2002). Child, parent, and peer predictors of early-onset substance use: A multisite longitudinal study. *Journal of Abnormal Child Psychology, 30,* 199–216.

Karns, J. T. (2001). Health, nutrition, and safety. In A. Fogel & G. Bremner (Eds.), *Blackwell handbook of infant development.* London: Blackwell.

Kasper, J. D. (1988). *Aging alone: Profiles and projections.* Report of the Commonwealth Fund Commission: Elderly People Living Alone. Baltimore: Commonwealth Fund Commission.

Kastenbaum, R. J. (1997). Unpublished review of J. W. Santrock's *Life-span development,* 7th ed. (New York: McGraw-Hill).

Kastenbaum, R. J. (1998). *Death, society, and human experience* (6th ed.). Upper Saddle River, NJ: Prentice Hall.

Kastenbaum, R. J. (2000). *The psychology of death* (3rd ed.). New York: Springer.

Katchadoourian, H. (1987). *Fifty: Midlife in perspective.* New York: W. H. Freeman.

Katz, L., & Chard, S. (1989). *Engaging the minds of young children: The project approach.* Norwood, NJ: Ablex.

Kaufman, P. (2001). Dropping out of school: Detours in the life course. In T. Urdan & F. Pajares (Eds.), *Adolescence and education.* Greenwich, CT: IAP.

Kaugers, A. S., Russ, S. W., & Singer, L. T. (2000, May). *Self-regulation among cocaine-exposed four-year-old children.* Paper presented at the joint meetings of the Pediatric Academic Societies and the American Academy of Pediatrics, Boston.

Kausler, D. H. (1994). *Learning and memory in normal aging.* San Diego: Academic Press.

Keating, D. P. (1990). Adolescent thinking. In S. S. Feldman & G. R. Elliott (Eds.), *At the threshold: The developing adolescent.* Cambridge, MA: Harvard University Press.

Keller, A., Ford, L., & Meacham, J. (1978). Dimensions of self-concept in preschool children. *Developmental Psychology, 14,* 483–489.

Kelly, B. D., & McLoughlin, D. M. (2002). Euthanasia, assisted suicide, and psychiatry: A Pandora's box. *British Journal of Psychiatry, 181,* 278–279.

Kelly, J. A. (2002). Safer sex behaviors. In J. Worell (Ed.), *Encyclopedia of women and gender.* San Diego: Academic Press.

Kelly, J. B. (2001). Legal and educational interventions for families in residence and contact disputes. *Australian Journal of Family Law, 15,* 92–113.

Kelly, J. R. (1996). Leisure. In J. E. Birren (Ed.), *Encyclopedia of gerontology* (Vol. 2). San Diego: Academic Press.

Kemper, S., Greiner, L. H., Marquis, J. G., Prenovost, K., Mitzner, T. L. (2001). Language decline across the life span: Findings from the Nun Study. *Psychology and Aging, 16* (2): 227–239.

Kempermann, G., Kuhn, H. G., & Gage, F. H. (1997). More hippocampal neurons in adult mice living in an enriched environment. *Nature, 386,* 493–495.

Kempermann, G., van Praag, H., & Gage, F. H. (2000). Activity-dependent regulation of neuronal plasticity and self repair. *Progress in Brain Research, 127,* 35–48.

Kennell, J. H., & McGrath, S. K. (1999). Commentary: Practical and humanistic lessons from the third world for perinatal caregivers everywhere. *Birth, 26,* 9–10.

Kephart, W. M. (1967). Some correlates of romantic love. *Journal of Marriage and the Family, 29,* 470–474.

Kerr, M. (2001). Culture as a context for temperament. In T. D. Wachs & G. A. Kohnstamm (Eds.), *Temperament in context.* Mahwah, NJ: Erlbaum.

Kessen, W., Haith, M. M., & Salapatek, P. (1970). Human infancy. In P. H. Mussen (Ed.), *Manual of child psychology* (3rd ed., Vol. 1). New York: Wiley.

Ketchum, C. J., & Stelmach, G. E. (2001). Age-related declines in motor control. In J. Birren & K. W. Schaie (Eds.), *Handbook of the psychology of aging* (5th ed.). San Diego: Academic Press.

Keyes, C. L. M., & Ryff, C. D. (1998). Generativity in adult lives: Social structure contours and quality of life consequences. In D. P. McAdams & E. de St. Aubin (Eds.), *Generativity and adult development: How and why we care for the next generation.* Washington, DC: American Psychological Association.

Keyes, C., & Ryff, C. (1999). Psychological well-being in midlife. In S. L. Willis & J. D. Reid (Eds.), *Life in the middle.* San Diego: Academic Press.

Kiecolt-Glaser, J. K., & Glaser, R. (1988). Behavioral influences on immune function. In T. Field, P. McCabe, & N. Schneiderman (Eds.), *Stress and coping across development.* Hillsdale, NJ: Erlbaum.

Kiess, W., Galler, A., Reich, A., Muller, G., Kapellen, T., Deutscher, J., Raile, K., &

Kratzch, J. (2001). Clinical aspects of obesity in childhood and adolescence. *Obesity Reviews, 2,* 29–36.

Kihara, T., Shimohama, S., Sawada, H., Honda, K., Nakamizo, T., Kanki, R., Yamashita, H., & Akaike, A. (2002). Protective effect of dopamine D2 agonists in cortical neurons via the phosphatidylinositol 3 kinase cascade. *Journal of Neuroscience Research, 70(3),* 274–282.

Kilbride, H. W., Thorstad, K. K., & Daily, D. K. (2000, May). *Preschool outcome for extremely low birth weight infants compared to their full term siblings.* Paper presented at the joint meeting of the Pediatric Academic Societies and American Academy of Pediatrics, Boston.

Kim, J. E., & Moen, P. (2001). Is retirement good or bad for subjective well-being? *Current Directions in Psychological Science, 3,* 83–87.

Kim, J. E., & Moen, P. (2002). Retirement transitions, gender, and psychological well-being: A life-course, ecological model. *Journal of Gerontology: Psychological Sciences, 57B,* P212–P222.

Kimura, D. (2000). *Sex and cognition.* Cambridge, MA: MIT Press.

King, A. (2000). Exercise and physical activity. In A. Kazdin (Ed.), *Encyclopedia of psychology.* Washington, DC, & New York: American Psychological Association and Oxford University Press.

King, N. (1982). School uses of materials traditionally associated with children's play. *Theory and Research in Social Education, 10,* 17–27.

Kinsey, A. C., Pomeroy, W. B., & Martin, E. E. (1948). *Sexual behavior in the human male.* Philadelphia: W. B. Saunders.

Kirchhoff, K. T. (2002). Promoting a peaceful death in the ICU. *Critical Care Nursing Clinics of North America, 14,* 201–206.

Kirk, K. L. (2001). Dietary restriction and aging. *Journal of Gerontology, 56A* (No. 2), B123–B129.

Kirk, R. E. (2003). Experimental design. In I. B. Weiner (Ed.), *Handbook of psychology* (Vol. II). New York: Wiley.

Kirkpatrick, L. A., & Hazan, C. (1994). Attachment styles and close relationships: A four-year prospective study. *Personal Relationships, 1,* 123–142.

Kisilevsky, B. S. (1995). The influence stimulus and subject variables on human fetal responses to sound and vibration. In J-P Lecaunet, W. P. Fifer, M. A. Krasnegor, & W. P. Smotherman (Eds.), *Fetal development.* Hillsdale, NJ: Erlbaum.

Kitchener, K. S., & King, P. M. (1981). Reflective judgment: Concepts of justification and their relationship to age and education. *Journal of Applied Developmental Psychology, 2,* 89–111.

Kite, M. (2002). Gender stereotypes. In J. Worell (Ed.), *Encyclopedia of women and gender.* San Diego: Academic Press.

Kitzman, K. M., & Gaylord, N. K. (2002). Divorce and child custody. In J. Worell (Ed.), *Encyclopedia of women and gender.* San Diego: Academic Press.

Kivnick, H. Q., & Sinclair, H. M. (1996). Grandparenthood. In J. E. Birren (Ed.), *Encyclopedia of gerontology* (Vol. 1). San Diego: Academic Press.

Klaczynski, P. A., & Narasimham, G. (1998). Development of scientific reasoning biases: Cognitive versus ego-protective explanations. *Developmental Psychology, 34,* 175–187.

Klaus, M. H., Kennell, J. H., & Klaus, P. H. (1993). *Mothering the mother.* Reading, MA: Addison-Wesley.

Klaus, M., & Kennell, H. H. (1976). *Maternal-infant bonding.* St. Louis: Mosby.

Klesges, L. M., Johnson, K. C., Ward, K. D., & Barnard, M. (2001). Smoking cessation in pregnant women. Obstetrics and Gynecological Clinics of North America, 28, 269–282.

Kliegl, M., McDaniel, M. A., & Einstein, G. O. (2000). Plan formation, retention, and execution in prospective memory: A new approach and age-related effects. *Memory and Cognition, 28,* 1041–1049.

Kliegl, R., & Baltes, P. B. (1987). Theory-guided analysis of mechanisms of development and aging through testing-the-limits and research on expertise. In C. Schooler & K. W. Schaie (Eds.), *Cognitive functioning and social structure over the life course.* Norwood, NJ: Ablex.

Kliegl, R., Smith, J., & Baltes, P. B. (1990). On the locus and process of magnification of age differences during mnemonic training. *Developmental Psychology, 26,* 894–904.

Kline, D. W., & Scialfa, C. T. (1996). Visual and auditory aging. In J. E. Birren & K. W. Schaie (Eds.), *Handbook of the psychology of aging* (4th ed.). San Diego: Academic Press.

Kling, K. C., Hyde, J. S., Showers, C. J., & Buswell, B. N. (1999). Gender differences in self-esteem: A meta-analysis. *Psychological Bulletin, 125,* 470–500.

Klitzing, K. V., Simoni, H., & Burgin, D. (1999, April). *Mother, father, and infant: The triad from pre-natal representations to post-natal interactions.* Paper presented at the meeting of the Society for Research in Child Development, Albuquerque.

Klug, W. S., & Cummings, M. R. (2003). *Genetics: A molecular perspective.* Upper Saddle River, NJ: Prentice Hall.

Knecht, S., Drager, B., Deppe, M., Bobe, L., Lohmann, H., Floel, A., Ringelstein, E. B., & Henningsen, H. (2000). Handedness and hemispheric language dominance in healthy humans. *Brain, 135,* 2512–2518.

Knight, B. G., Nordus, I. H., & Satre, D. D. (2003). Psychotherapy with older adults. In I. B. Weiner (Ed.), *Handbook of psychology,* Vol. VIII. New York: Wiley.

Knight, B. G., Teri, L., Wohlford, P., & Santos, J. (Eds.). (1996). *Mental health services for older adults.* Washington, DC: American Psychological Association.

Kobak, R. (1999). The emotional dynamics of disruptions in attachment relationships: Implications for theory, research, and clinical intervention. In J. Cassidy & P. Shaver (Eds.), *Handbook of attachment.* New York: Guilford.

Kobasa, S. C., Maddi, S. R., & Kahn, S. (1982). Hardiness and health: A prospective study. *Journal of Personality and Social Psychology, 42,* 168–177.

Kobasa, S. C., Maddi, S. R., Puccetti, M. C., & Zola, M. (1986). Relative effectiveness of hardiness, exercise, and social support as resources against illness. *Journal of Psychosomatic Research, 29,* 525–533.

Kochanska, G. (1999, April). *Applying a temperament model to the study of social development.* Paper presented at the meeting of the Society for Research in Child Development, Albuquerque.

Koenig, H. G. (Ed.). (1998). *Handbook of religion and mental health.* San Diego: Academic Press.

Koenig, H. G. (2001). Religion and medicine II: Religion, mental health, and related behaviors. *International Journal of Psychiatry, 31,* 97–109.

Koenig, H. G., & Blazer, D. G. (1996). Depression. In J. E. Birren (Ed.), *Encyclopedia of gerontology* (Vol. 1). San Diego: Academic Press.

Koenig, H. G., Cohen, H. J., Blazer, D. G., Pieper, C., Meador, K. G., Shelp, F., Goldi, V., & DiPasquale, R. (1992). Religious coping and depression in elderly hospitalized medically ill men. *American Journal of Psychiatry, 149,* 1693–1700.

Koenig, H. G., Larson, D. B. (1998). Religion and mental health. In H. S. Friedman (Ed.), *Encyclopedia of mental health* (Vol. 3). San Diego: Academic Press.

Koenig, H. G., Smiley, M., & Gonzales, J. A. T. (1988). *Religion, health, and aging.* New York: Greenwood Press.

Kohlberg, L. (1958). *The development on modes of moral thinking and choice in the years 10 to 16.* Unpublished doctoral dissertation, University of Chicago.

Kohlberg, L. (1966). A cognitive-developmental analysis of children's sex-role concepts and attitudes. In E. E. Maccoby (Ed.), *The development of sex differences.* Palo Alto, CA: Stanford University Press.

Kohlberg, L. (1969). Stage and sequence: The cognitive-developmental approach to socialization. In D. A. Goslin (Ed.), *Handbook of socialization theory and research.* Chicago: Rand McNally.

Kohlberg, L. (1976). Moral stages and moralization: The cognitive-developmental approach. In T. Lickona (Ed.), *Moral development and behavior.* New York: Holt, Rinehart & Winston.

Kohlberg, L. (1986). A current statement of some theoretical issues. In S. Modgil & C. Modgil (Eds.), *Lawrence Kohlberg.* Philadelphia: Falmer.

Kopp, C. B., & Neufeld, S. J. (2002). Emotional development during infancy. In R. J. Davidson, K. R. Scherer, & H. H. Goldsmith (Eds.), *Handbook of affective sciences.* New York: Oxford University Press.

Koriat, A., Goldsmith, M., Pansky, A. (2000). Toward a psychology of memory accuracy. *Annual Review of Psychology* (Vol. 51). Palo Alto, CA: Annual Reviews.

Kosnik, W., Winslow, L., Kline, D., Rasinski, K., & Sekuler, R. (1989). Visual changes in daily life through adulthood. *Journal of Gerontology: Psychological Sciences, 43,* P63–P70.

Koss-Chioino, J. D., & Vargas, L. (1999). *Working with Latino Youth.* San Francisco: Jossey-Bass.

Kotler, J. A., Wright, J. C., & Huston, A. C. (2001). Television use in families with children. In J. Bryant & J. A. Bryant (Eds.), *Television and the American Family.* Mahwah, NJ: Erlbaum.

Kotlowitz, A. (1991). *There are no children here.* New York: Anchor Books.

Kotovsky, L., & Baillargeon, R. (1994). Calibration-based reasoning about collision events in 11-month-old infants. *Cognition, 51,* 107–129.

Kotre, J. (1984). *Outliving the self: Generativity and the interpretation of lives.* Baltimore: Johns Hopkins University Press.

Kottak, C. P. (2002). *Cultural anthropology* (9th ed.). New York: McGraw-Hill.

Kozol, J. (1991). *Savage inequalities.* New York: Crown.

Kozulin, A. (2000). Vygotsky. In A. Kazdin (Ed.). *Encyclopedia of psychology.* Washington, DC, & New York: American Psychological Association and Oxford University Press.

Kramer, A. F., Hahn, S., Cohen, N. J., Banich, M. T., McAuley, E., Harrison, C., Chason, J., Vakil, E., Bardell, L., Boileau, R., & Colcombe, A. (1999, July). Ageing, fitness, and neurocognitive function. *Nature, 400,* 418–419.

Kramer, A. F., Hahn, S., McAuley, E., Cohen, N. J., Banich, M. T., Harrison, C., Chason, J., Boileau, R. A., Bardell, L., Colcombe, A., & Vakil, E. (2002). Exercise, aging and cognition: Healthy body, healthy mind? In A. D. Fisk & W. Rogers (Eds.), *Human factors interventions for the health care of older adults.* Mahwah, NJ: Erlbaum.

Kramer, D. A., Kahlbaugh, P. E., & Goldston, R. B. (1992). A measure of paradigm beliefs about the social world. *Journal of Gerontology, 47,* 180–189.

Kramer, M. S., & others. (2001). Promotion of breastfeeding intervention trial. *Journal of the American Medical Association, 285* (No. 4), 413–420.

Krampe, R. T., & Baltes, P. B. (2002). Intelligence as adaptive resource development and resource allocation: A new look through the lens of SOC and expertise. In R. J. Sternberg & E. L. Grigorenko (Eds.), *Perspectives on the psychology of abilities, competencies, and expertise.* New York: Cambridge University Press.

Krause, N. (1995). Religiosity and self-esteem among older adults. *Journal of Gerontology: Psychological Sciences, 50B,* P236–P246.

Krause, N. (1996). Neighborhood deterioration and self-rated health in later life. *Psychology and Aging, 11,* 342–352.

Kraut, R., Patterson, M., Lundmark, V., Kiesler, S., Mukopadhyay, T., & Scherlis, W. (1998). Internet paradox. *American Psychologist, 53,* 1017–1031.

Kreppner, K. (2001). Retrospect and prospect in the study of families as systems. In J. P. McHale & W. S. Grolnick (Eds.), *Retrospect and prospect in the psychological study of families.* Mahwah, NJ: Erlbaum.

Kreutzer, M., Leonard, C., & Flavell, J. H. (1975). An interview study of children's knowledge about memory. *Monographs of the Society for Research in Child Development.* 40 (1, Serial No. 159).

Krimer, L. S., Goldman-Rakic, P. S. (2001). Prefrontal microcircuits. *Journal of Neuroscience, 21,* 3788–3796.

Kroger, J. (2003). Identity development during adolescence. In G. Adams & M. Berzonsky (Eds.), *Blackwell handbook of adolescence.* Malden, MA: Blackwell.

Kübler-Ross, E. (1969). *On death and dying.* New York: Macmillan.

Kuebli, J. (1994, March). Young children's understanding of everyday emotions. *Young Children,* pp. 36–48.

Kuhl, P. K. (1993). Infant speech perception: A window on psycholinguistic development. *International Journal of Psycholinguistics, 9,* 33–56.

Kuhl, P. K. (2000). A new view of language acquisition. *Proceedings of the National Academy of Science, 97* (22), 11850–11857.

Kuhn, D. (1999). A developmental model of critical thinking. *Educational Researcher, 28,* 16–25.

Kuhn, D. (2000). Adolescent thought processes. In A. Kazdin (Ed.), *Encyclopedia of psychology.* Washington, DC, & New York: American Psychological Association and Oxford University Press.

Kumagai, F. (1995). Families in Japan: Beliefs and realities. *Journal of Comparative and Family Studies, 18,* 135–163.

Kumari, A. S. (2001). Pregnancy outcome in women with morbid obesity. International *Journal of Gynecology and Obstetrics, 73,* 101–107.

Kupersmidt, J. B., & Coie, J. D. (1990). Preadolescent peer status, aggression, and school adjustment as predictors of externalizing problems in adolescence. *Child Development, 61,* 1350–1363.

Kupersmidt, J. B., & Patterson, C. (1993, March). *Developmental patterns of peer relations and aggression in the prediction of externalizing behavior problems.* Paper presented at the biennial meeting of the Society for Research in Child Development, New Orleans.

Kurdek, L. A. (1995). Developmental changes in relationship quality in gay and lesbian cohabiting couples. *Developmental Psychology, 31,* 86–94.

Kwak, H. K., Kim, M., Cho, B. H., & Ham, Y. M. (1999, April). *The relationship between children's temperament, maternal control strategies, and children's compliance.* Paper presented at the meeting of the Society

for Research in Child Development, Albuquerque.

Kyba, F. C. (2002). Legal and ethical issues in end-of-life care. *Critical Care Nursing Clinics of North America, 14,* 141–155.

L

La Greca, A. M., Silverman, W. K., Vernberg, E. M., & Roberts, M. C. (Eds.). (2002). *Helping children cope with disasters and terrorism.* Washington, DC: American Psychological Association.

Labouvie-Vief, G. (1986, August). *Modes of knowing and life-span cognition.* Paper presented at the meeting of the American Psychological Association, Washington, DC.

Labouvie-Vief, G., & Diehl, M. (1999). Self and personality development. In J. C. Kavanaugh & S. K. Whitbourne (Eds.), *Gerontology: An interdisciplinary perspective.* New York: Oxford University Press.

Labouvie-Vief, G., Diehl, M., Chiodo, L. M., & Coyle, N. (1995). Representations of self and parents across the life span. *Adult Development, 7,* 207–222.

Labouvie-Vief, G., Diehl, M., Tarnowksi, A., & Shen, J. (2000). Age differences in personality: Findings from the United States and China. *Journal of Gerontology: Psychological Sciences, 55B,* P4–P17.

Lachman, M. E. (Ed.). (2001). *Handbook of midlife development.* New York: John Wiley.

Lachman, M. E., Maier, H., & Budner, R. (2000). *A portrait of midlife.* Unpublished manuscript, Brandeis University, Waltham, MA.

Lackmann, G. M., Salzberger, U., Tollner, U., Chen, M., Carmella, S. G., & Hecht, S. S. (1999). Metabolites of a tobacco-specific carcinogen in urine from newborns. *Journal of the National Cancer Institute, 91,* 459–465.

Ladd, G. W. (1999). Peer relationships and social competence during early and middle childhood. *Annual Review of Psychology* (Vol. 50). Palo Alto, CA: Annual Reviews.

Ladd, G. W., Buhs, E., & Troop, W. (2002). School adjustment and social skills training. In P. K. Smith & C. H. Hart (Eds.), *Blackwell handbook of childhood social development.* Malden, MA: Blackwell.

Laible, D. J., Carlo, G., & Raffaeli, M. (2000). The differential relations of parent and peer attachment to adolescent adjustment. *Journal of Youth and Adolescence, 29,* 45–53.

Lakatta, E. S. (1992, December 6). Commentary in "We can age successfully." *Parade Magazine,* p. 15.

Lamb, M. E. (1986). *The father's role: Applied perspectives.* New York: Wiley.

Lamb, M. E. (1994). Infant care practices and the application of knowledge. In C. B. Fisher & R. M. Lerner (Eds.), *Applied developmental psychology.* New York: McGraw-Hill.

Lamb, M. E. (2000). The history of research on father involvement: An overview. *Marriage and Family Review, 29,* 23–42.

Lamb, M. E., Frodi, A. M., Hwant, C. P., Frodi, M., & Steinberg, J. (1982). Mother- and father-infant interaction involving play and holding in traditional and nontraditional Swedish families. *Developmental Psychology, 18,* 215–221.

Lang, F. R., & Carstensen, L. L. (1994). Close emotional relationships in late life: Further support for proactive aging in the social domain. *Psychology and Aging, 9,* 315–324.

Langer, E. (1989). *Mindfulness.* Reading, MA: Addison-Wesley.

Langston, W. (2002). *Research methods manual for psychology.* Belmont, CA: Wadsworth.

Larsen, R. J., & Buss, D. M. (2002). *Personality psychology: Domains of knowledge about human nature.* New York: McGraw-Hill.

Larson, J. (1988). The marriage quiz: College students' beliefs in selected areas of marriage. *Family Relations, 37,* 3–11.

Larson, J. H., & Holman, T. B. (1994). Premarital predictors of marital quality and stability. *Family Relations, 43,* 228–237.

Larson, R. W. (1999, September). Unpublished review of J. W. Santrock's *Adolescence,* 8th ed. (New York: McGraw-Hill).

Larson, R. W., Brown, B., & Mortimer, J. (2003). *Adolescents' preparation for the future: Perils and promises.* Malden, MA: Blackwell.

Larson, R. W., Clore, G. L., & Wood, G. A. (1999). The emotions of romantic relationships. In W. Furman, B. B. Brown, & C. Feiring (Eds.), *The development of romantic relationships in adolescence.* New York: Cambridge University Press.

Larson, R., & Richards, M. (1994). *Divergent realities: The emotional lives of mothers, fathers, and adolescents.* New York: Basic Books.

Laurin, D., Verreault, R., Lindsay J., MacPherson, K., & Rockwood, K. (2001). Physical activity and risk of cognitive impairment and dementia in elderly persons. *Archives of Neurology, 58,* 498–504.

Lawton, M. P., Kleban, M. H., Rajagopal, D., & Dean, J. (1992). The dimensions of affective experience in three age groups. *Psychology and Aging, 7,* 171–184.

Lazarus, R. S., & Folkman, S. (1984). *Stress, appraisal, and coping.* New York: Springer.

Le Vay, S. (1994). The sexual brain. Cambridge, MA: MIT Press.

Leadbeater, B. J. R., & Way, N. (2001). *Growing up fast.* Mahwah, NJ: Erlbaum.

Lebowitz, B. D. (1987). Mental health services. In G. L. Maddox (Ed.), *The encyclopedia of aging.* New York: Springer.

Lee, D. J., & Markides, K. S. (1990). Activity and mortality among aged persons over an eight-year period. *Journals of Gerontology: Social Sciences, 45,* S39–S42.

Lee, G. R. (1978). Marriage and morale in late life. *Journal of Marriage and the Family, 40,* 131–139.

Lee, I. M., Hsieh, C., & Paffenbarger, O. (1995). Exercise intensity and longevity in men. *Journal of the American Medical Association, 273,* 1179–1184.

Lee, I. M., Manson, J. E., Hennekens, C. H., & Paffenbarger, R. S. (1993). Body-weight and mortality: A 27-year-follow-up. *Journal of the American Medical Association, 270,* 2823–2828.

Lee, I. M., & Skerrett, P. J. (2001). Physical activity and all-cause mortality: What is the dose-response relation? *Medical Science and Sports Exercise, 33* (6 Suppl.), S459–S471.

Leeman, C. P. (2002). Physician-assisted death. *New England Journal of Medicine, 347,* 1041–1042.

Lehman, H. C. (1960). The age decrement in outstanding scientific creativity. *American Psychologist, 15,* 128–134.

Leifer, A. D. (1973). *Television and the development of social behavior.* Paper presented at the meeting of the International Society for the Study of Behavioral Development, Ann Arbor, MI.

Leming, M. R., & Dickinson, G. E. (2002). *Understanding death, dying, and bereavement* (5th ed.). Belmont, CA: Wadsworth.

Lenders, C. M., McElrath, T. F., & Scholl, T. O. (2000). Nutrition in pregnancy. *Current Opinions in Pediatrics, 12,* 291–296.

Lenoir, C. P., Mallet, E., & Calenda, E. (2000). Siblings of sudden infant death syndrome and near miss in about 30 families: Is there a genetic link? *Medical Hypotheses, 54,* 408–411.

Leonards, U., Ibanez, V., & Giannakopoulos, P. (2002). The role of stimulus type in age-related changes of visual working memory. *Experimental Brain Research, 146,* 172–183.

Leong, F. T. L. (2000). Cultural pluralism. In A. Kazdin (Ed.), *Encyclopedia of psychology.* Washington, DC, & New York: American Psychological Association and Oxford University Press.

Lerner, H. G. (19989). *The dance of intimacy.* New York: Harper & Row.

Lerner, J. V. (2000). Parent-child relationship: Childhood. In A. Kazdin (Ed.), *Encyclopedia of psychology.* Washington, DC, & New York: American Psychological Association and Oxford University Press.

Lerner, R. M. (2002). *Concepts and theories of human development* (3rd ed.). Mahwah, NJ: Erlbaum.

Lester, B. (2000). Unpublished review of J. W. Santrock's *Life-span development* (8th ed.) (New York: McGraw-Hill).

Levant, R. F. (2002). Men and masculinity. In J. Worell (Ed.), *Encyclopedia of women and gender.* San Diego: Academic Press.

Levant, R. F., & Brooks, G. R. (1997). *Men and sex: New psychological perspectives.* New York: Wiley.

LeVay, S. (1991). A difference in the hypothalamic structure between heterosexual and homosexual men. *Science, 253,* 1034–1037.

Levelt, W. J. M. (1989). Speaking: From intention to articulation. Cambridge, MA: MIT Press.

Leventhal, A. (1994, February). *Peer conformity during adolescence: An integration of developmental, situational, and individual characteristics.* Paper presented at the meeting of the Society for Research on Adolescence, San Diego.

Levin, J. S. (1994). *Religion in aging and health.* Thousand Oaks, CA: Sage.

Levin, J. S., Chatters, L. M., & Taylor, R. J. (1995). Religious effects on health status and life satisfaction among Black Americans. *Journal of Gerontology: Social Sciences, 50B,* S154–S163.

Levin, J. S., Taylor, R. J., & Chatters, L. M. (1994). Race and gender differences in religiosity among older adults: Findings from four national surveys. *Journal of Gerontology, 49,* S137–S145.

Levin, J. S., & Vanderpool, H. Y. (1989). Is religion therapeutically significant for hypertension? *Social Science and Medicine, 29,* 69–78.

LeVine, S. (1979). *Mothers and wives: Gusii women of East Africa.* Chicago: University of Chicago Press.

Levinson, D. J. (1978). *The seasons of a man's life.* New York: Knopf.

Levinson, D. J. (1987, August). *The seasons of a woman's life.* Paper presented at the meeting of the American Psychological Association, New York.

Levinson, D. J. (1996). *Seasons of a woman's life.* New York: Alfred Knopf.

Levy, B. R., Jennings, P., & Langer, E. J. (2001). Improving attention in old age. *Journal of Adult Development, 8,* 189–192.

Levy, T. M. (Ed.). (1999). *Handbook of attachment interventions.* San Diego: Academic Press.

Lewis, C., & Carpendale, J. (2002). Social cognition. In P. K. Smith & C. H. Hart (Eds.), *Blackwell handbook of childhood social development.* Malden, MA: Blackwell.

Lewis, M. (1993). Self-conscious emotions: Embarrassment, pride, shame, and guilt. In M.. Lewis & J. Haviland (Eds.), *The handbook of emotions.* New York: Guilford Press.

Lewis, M. (1995). Embarrassment: The emotion of self-exposure and evaluation. In J. Tangney & K. Fischer (Eds.), *Self-conscious emotions: The psychology of shame, guilt, embarrassment and pride.* New York: Guilford Press.

Lewis, M. (1997). *Altering fate: Why the past does not predict the future.* New York: Guilford Press.

Lewis, M. (2001). Issues in the study of personality development. *Psychological Inquiry, 12,* 67–83.

Lewis, M. (2003). Early emotional development. In A. Slater & M. Lewis (Eds.), *Introduction to infant development.* New York: Oxford University Press.

Lewis, M., & Brooks-Gunn, J. (1979). *Social cognition and the acquisition of the self.* New York: Plenum.

Lewis, M., Feiring, C., & Rosenthal, S. (2000). Attachment over time. *Child Development, 71,* 707–720.

Lewis, M., & Ramsay, D. S. (1999). Effect of maternal soothing and infant stress response. *Child Development, 70,* 11–20.

Lewis, R. (2003). *Human genetics* (5th ed.). New York: McGraw-Hill.

Li, S. J., Li, Z., Wu, G., Zhang, M. J., Franczak, M., & Antuono, P. G. (2002). Alzheimer disease: evaluation of functional MR imaging index as a marker. *Radiology, 225,* 253–259.

**Lifshitz, F., Pugliese, M. T., Moses, N., &
Weyman-Daum, M.** (1987). Parental health
beliefs as a cause of nonorganic failure to
thrive. *Pediatrics, 80,* 175–182.

Lifton, R. J. (1977). The sense of immortal-
ity: On death and the continuity of life. In
H. Feifel (Ed.), *New meanings of death.* New
York: McGraw-Hill.

Light, L. L. (2000). Memory changes in
adulthood. In S. H. Qualls & N. Abeles (Eds.),
Psychology and the aging revolution. Washington,
DC: American Psychological Association.

**Lightwood, J. M., Phibbs, C. S., &
Glantz, S. A.** (1999). Short-term health
and economic benefits of smoking cessation.
Pediatrics, 104, 1312–1320.

Limber, S. P. (1997). Preventing violence
among school children. *Family Futures, 1,*
27–28.

Lindbohm, M. (1991). Effects of paternal
occupational exposure in spontaneous abor-
tions. *American Journal of Public Health, 121,*
1029–1033.

Lindenberger, U., & Baltes, P. B. (1994).
Sensory functioning and intelligence in old
age: A strong connection. *Psychology and
Aging, 9,* 339–355.

Lippa, R. A. (2002). *Gender, nature, and nurture.* Mahwah, NJ: Erlbaum.

Liprie, M. L. (1993). Adolescents' contributions to family decision making. In B. H.
Settles, R. S. Hanks, & M. B. Sussman (Eds.),
*American families and the future: Analyses of
possible destinies.* New York: Haworth Press.

Lipsitz, J. (1983, October). *Making it the hard
way: Adolescents in the 1980s.* Testimony presented at the Crisis Intervention Task Force,
House Select Committee on Children, Youth,
and Families, Washington, DC.

Lipsitz, J. (1984). *Successful schools for young
adolescents.* New Brunswick, NJ: Transaction.

**Livesley, W. J., Jang, K. L., & Vernon,
P. A.** (2003). Genetic basis of personality
structure. In I. B. Weiner (Ed.), *Handbook of
psychology* (Vol. V). New York: Wiley.

Livesly, W., & Bromley, D. (1973). *Person
perception in childhood and adolescence.* New
York: Wiley.

Livson, N., & Peskin, H. (1981). Psycho-
logical health at age 40. Prediction from
adolescent personality. In D. M. Eichorn,
J. Clausen, N. Haan, M. Honzik, & P. Mussen
(Eds.), *Present and past in middle life.* New York:
Academic Press.

Lock, A. (2002). Preverbal communication.
In U. Goswami (Ed.), *Blackwell handbook of
childhood cognitive development.* Malden, MA:
Blackwell.

Lock, M. (1998). Menopause: Lessons from
anthropology. *Psychosomatic Medicine, 60,*
410–419.

Lockman, J. J. (2000). A perception-action
perspective on tool use development. *Child
Development, 71,* 137–144.

Loebel, M., & Yali, A. M. (1999, August).
*Effects of positive expectancies on adjustment to
pregnancy.* Paper presented at the meeting of
the American Psychological Association,
Boston.

**Loeber, R., DeLamatre, M., Keenan, K., &
Zhang, Q.** (1998). A prospective replication
of developmental pathways in disruptive
and delinquent behavior. In R. Cairns,
L. Bergman, & J. Kagan (Eds.), *Methods and
models for studying the individual.* Thousand
Oaks, CA: Sage.

Loeber, R., & Farrington, D. P. (Eds.).
(2001). *Child delinquents: Development, intervention and service needs.* Thousand Oaks, CA: Sage.

**London, M. L., Ladewig, P. W., Olds, S. B.,
& Ladewig, P. W.** (2000). *Maternal newborn
nursing care* (4th ed.). Boston: Addison-Wesley.

Long, T., & Long, L. (1983). *Latchkey children.* New York: Penguin.

Longman, P. (1987). *Born to pay: The new
politics of aging in America.* Boston: Houghton-
Mifflin.

Lopata, H. Z. (1994). *Circles and settings:
Role changes of American women.* Albany State
University of New York Press.

Lorenz, K. Z. (1965). *Evolution and the modification of behavior.* Chicago: University of
Chicago Press.

Lott, B. L., & Maluso, D. (2001). Gender
development: Social learning. In J. Worrel
(Ed.), *Encyclopedia of women and gender.* San
Diego: Academic Press.

**Lowe, X., Eskenazi, B., Nelson, D. O.,
Kidd, S., Alme, A., & Wyrobek, A. J.**
(2001). Frequency of XY sperm increases
with age in fathers of boys with Klinefelter
syndrome. *American Journal of Human Genetics,
69,* 1046–1054.

Luciana, M., Sullivan, J., & Nelson, C. A.
(2001). Associations between phenylalanine-
to-tyrosine ratios and performance on tests of
neuropsychological function in adolescents
treated early and continuously for phenylketonuria. *Child Development, 72,* 1637–1652.

Lund, D. A. (1996). Bereavement and loss.
In J. E. Birren (Ed.), *Encyclopedia of gerontology*
(Vol. 1). San Diego: Academic Press.

Luria, A., & Herzog, E. (1985, April).
Gender segregation across and within settings.
Paper presented at the biennial meeting of

the Society for Research in Child Development, Toronto.

Luszcz, M., & Giles, L. (2002). Benefits of
close social relationships for health and
longevity of older adults. *International Society
for the Study of Behavioural Development
Newsletter* (1, Serial No. 41), 15–16.

Lynch, E. W., & Hanson, M. J. (1993).
*Developing cross-cultural competence: A guide for
working with young children and their families.*
Baltimore: Paul H. Brookes.

Lyon, G. R. (1996). Learning disabilities.
Future of Children, 6 (1), 54–76.

Lyon, G. R., & Moats, L. C. (1997). Critical
conceptual and methodological considerations in reading intervention research. *Journal of Learning Disabilities, 30,* 578–588.

Lyon, T. D., & Flavell, J. H. (1993). Young
children's understanding of forgetting over
time. *Child Development, 64,* 789–800.

**Lyytinen, P., Rasku-Puttonen, H.,
Poikkeus, A., Laakso, M., & Ahonen, T.**
(1994). Mother-child teaching strategies and
learning disabilities. *Journal of Learning Disabilities, 27,* 186–192.

M

Maas, J. B. (1998). *Power sleep.* New York:
Villard Books.

Maccoby, E. E. (1984). Middle childhood in
the context of the family. In *Development
during middle childhood.* Washington, DC:
National Academy Press.

Maccoby, E. E. (1987, November). Interview with Elizabeth Hall: All in the family.
Psychology Today, pp. 54–60.

Maccoby, E. E. (1992). The role of parents
in the socialization of children: An historical
overview. *Developmental Psychology, 28,*
1006–1018.

Maccoby, E. E. (1993, March). *Trends and issues in the study of gender role development.* Paper
presented at the biennial meeting of the Society for Research in Child Development, New
Orleans.

Maccoby, E. E. (1998). *The two sexes:
Growing up apart, coming together.* Cambridge, MA: Harvard University Press.

Maccoby, E. E. (1999). The uniqueness of
the parent-child relationship. In W. A.
Collins, & B. Laursen (Eds.), *Relationships as
developmental contexts.* Mahwah, NJ: Erlbaum.

Maccoby, E. E. (2001, April). *Influencing policy through research.* Paper presented at the
meeting of the Society for Research in Child
Development, Minneapolis.

Maccoby, E. E. (2002). Gender and group process: A developmental perspective. *Current Directions in Psychological Science, 11,* 54–57.

Maccoby, E. E. (2002). Parenting effects. In J. G. Borkowski, S. L. Ramey, & M. Bristol-Power (Eds.), *Parenting and the child's world.* Mahwah, NJ: Erlbaum.

Maccoby, E. E., & Jacklin, C. N. (1974). *The psychology of sex differences.* Palo Alto, CA: Stanford University Press.

Maccoby, E. E., & Mnookin, R. H. (1992). *Dividing the child: Social and legal dilemmas of custody.* Cambridge, MA: Harvard University Press.

MacDorman, M. F., & Singh, G. K. (1998). Midwifery care, social and medical factors, and birth outcomes in the USA. *Journal of Epidemiology and Community Health, 52,* 310–317.

MacFarlane, J. A. (1975). Olfaction in the development of social preferences in the human neonate. In *Parent-infant interaction. Ciba Foundation Symposium No. 33.* Amsterdam: Elsevier.

MacLean, W. E. (2000). Down syndrome. In A. Kazdin (Ed.), *Encyclopedia of psychology.* Washington, DC, & New York: American Psychological Association and Oxford University Press.

Madden, D. J. (2001). Speed and timing of behavioral processes. In J. E. Birren & K. W. Schaie (Eds.), *Handbook of the psychology of aging* (5th ed.). San Diego: Academic Press.

Madden, D. J., Gottlob, L. R., Denny, L. L., Turkington, T. G., Provenzale, J. M., Hawk, T. C., et al. (1999). Aging and recognition memory: Changes in regional cerebral blood flow associated with components of reaction time distributions. *Journal of Cognitive Neuroscience, 11,* 511–520.

Maddi, S. (1998). Hardiness. In H. S. Friedman (Ed.), *Encyclopedia of mental health* (Vol. 3). San Diego: Academic Press.

Mader, S. S. (2002). *Human biology* (7th ed.). New York: McGraw-Hill.

Maggs, J. L., Schulenberg, J., & Hurrelmann, K. (1997). Developmental transitions in adolescence: Health promotion implications. In J. Schulenberg, J. L. Maggs, & K. Hurrelmann (Eds.), *Health risks and developmental transitions during adolescence.* New York: Cambridge University Press.

Magnuson, K. A., & Duncan, G. J. (2002). Parents in poverty. In M. H. Bornstein (Ed.), *Handbook of parenting* (2nd ed., Vol. 4). Mahwah, NJ: Erlbaum.

Mahler, M. (1979). *Separation-individuation* (Vol. 2). London: Jason Aronson.

Main, M. (2000). Attachment theory. In A. Kazdin (Ed.), *Encyclopedia of psychology.* Washington, DC, & New York: American Psychological Association and Oxford University Press.

Maizels, M., Rosenbaum, D., & Keating, B. (1999). *Getting to dry: How to help your child overcome bedwetting.* Cambridge, MA: Harvard Common Press.

Major, B., Barr, L., Zubek, J., & Babey, S. H. (1999). Gender and self-esteem: A meta-analysis. In W. Swann & J. Langlois (Eds.), *Sexism and stereotypes in modern society: The gender science of Janet Taylor Spence.* Washington, DC: Psychological Association.

Makrides, M., Neumann, M., Simmer, K., Pater, J., & Gibson, R. (1995). Are long-chain polyunsaturated fatty acids essential nutrients in infancy? *Lancet, 345,* 1463–1468.

Malinosky-Rummell, R., & Hansen, D. J. (1993). Long-term consequences of childhood physical abuse. *Psychological Bulletin, 114,* 68–79.

Malinowski, B. (1927). *Sex and repression in savage society.* New York: Humanities Press.

Mandler, J. M. & McDonough, L. (1995). Long-term recall in infancy. *Journal of Experimental Child Psychology, 59,* 457–474.

Mandler, J. M. (1990). A new perspective on cognitive development. *American Scientist, 78,* 236–243.

Mandler, J. M. (1998). Representation. In W. Damon (Ed.), *Handbook of child psychology* (5th ed., Vol. 2). New York: Wiley.

Mandler, J. M. (2000). Unpublished review of J. W. Santrock's *Life-Span Development,* 8th ed. (New York: McGraw-Hill).

Mannell, R. C. (2000). Older adults, leisure, and wellness. *Journal of Leisurability, 26,* 3–10.

Mannell, R. C., & Dupuis, S. (1996). Life satisfaction. In J. E. Birren (Ed.), *Encyclopedia of gerontology* (Vol. 2). San Diego: Academic Press.

Mannessier, L., Alie-Daram, S., Roubinet, F., & Brossard, Y. (2000). Prevention of fetal hemolytic disease: It is time to take action. Transfusions in *Clinical Biology, 7,* 527–532.

Mannino, D. M., Moorman, J. E., Kingsley, B., Rose, D., & Repace, J. (2001). Health effects related to environmental tobacco smoke exposure in the United States. *Archives of Pediatric and Adolescent Medicine, 155,* 36–41.

Manton, K. G., Corder, L., & Stallard, E. (1997, March 18). Chronic disability in elderly United States populations, 1982–1994. *Proceedings of the National Academy of Sciences, 94,* 2593–2598.

Manton, K. I. (1989). The stress-buffering role of spiritual support: Cross-sectional and prospective investigations. *Journal for the Scientific Study of Religion, 28,* 310–323.

Maracek, J., Kimmel, E. B., Crawford, M. E., & Hare-Muston, R. (2003). Psychology of women and gender. In I. B. Weiner (Ed.), *Handbook of psychology* (Vol. I). New York: Wiley.

Marcia, J. E. (1980). Ego identity development. In J. Adelson (Ed.), *Handbook of adolescent psychology.* New York: Wiley.

Marcia, J. E. (1994). The empirical study of ego identity. In H. A. Bosma, T. L. G. Graafsma, H. D. Grotevant, & D. J. De Levita (Eds.), *Identity and development.* Newbury Park, CA: Sage.

Marcus, D. L., Mulrine, A., & Wong, K. (1999, September 13). How kids learn. *U.S. News & World Report,* pp. 44–50.

Marecek, J., Finn, S. E., & Cardell, M. (1988). Gender roles in the relationships of lesbians and gay men. In J. P. De Cecco (Ed.), *Gay relationships.* New York: Harrington Park Press.

Markides, K. S. (1995). Aging and ethnicity. *Gerontologist, 35,* 276–277.

Markides, K. S., & Rudkin, L. (1996). Race and ethnic diversity. In J. E. Birren (Ed.), *Encyclopedia of gerontology* (Vol. 2). San Diego: Academic Press.

Markman, H. J. (2000). Marriage. In A. Kazdin (Ed.), *Encyclopedia of psychology.* Washington, DC, & New York: American Psychological Association and Oxford University Press.

Markowitz, M. (2000). Lead poisoning. *Pediatrics in Review, 21,* 327–335.

Marks, M. A., & Nelson, E. S. (1993). Sexual harassment on campus: Effects of professor gender on perception of sexually harassing behaviors. *Sex Roles, 28,* 207–218.

Markson, E. W. (1995). Older women: The silent majority? *Gerontologist, 35,* 278–281.

Marsiske, M., Klumb, P. L., & Baltes, M. M. (1997). Everyday activity patterns and sensory functioning in old age. *Psychology and Aging, 12,* 444–457.

Marsiske, M., Lang, F. R., Baltes, M. M., & Baltes, P. B. (1995). Selective optimization with compensation: Life-span perspectives on successful human development. In R. A. Dixon & L. Bäckman (Eds.), *Compensating for psychological deficits and declines: Managing losses and promoting gains* (pp. 35–79). Hillsdale, NJ: Erlbaum.

Martin, C. L., & Dinella, L. (2002). Gender development: Gender schema theory. In J. Worrel (Ed.), *Encyclopedia of women and gender.* San Diego: Academic Press.

Martin, E. W., Martin, R., & Terman, D. L. (1996). The legislative and litigation history of special education. *Future of Children, 6* (1), 25–53.

Martin, J. A., & Buckwalter, J. A. (2001). Biomarkers of aging. *Journal of Gerontology, 56A* (No. 4), B172–B179.

Martinez-Pasarell, O., Nogues, C., Bosch, M., Egozcue, J., & Templado, C. (1999). Analysis of sex chromosome aneupolidy in sperm from fathers of Turner syndrome patients. *Human Genetics, 104,* 345–349.

Martin-Matthews, A. (1996). Widowhood and widowerhood. In J. E. Birren (Ed.), *Encyclopedia of gerontology* (Vol. 2). San Diego: Academic Press.

Masten, A. S. (1999). Resilience comes of age: Reflections on the past and outlook for the next generation of research. In M. D. Glantz, J. Johnson, & L. Huffman (Eds.), *Resilience and development.* New York: Plenum Press.

Matheny, A. P., & Phillips, K. (2001). Temperament and context: Correlates of home environment with temperament continuity and change. In T. D. Wachs & G. A. Kohnstamm (Eds.), *Temperament in context.* Mahwah, NJ: Erlbaum.

Matsumoto, D. (Ed.). (2001). *The handbook of culture and psychology.* New York: Oxford University Press.

Matthias, R. F., Lubben, J. E., Atchison, K. A., & Schweitzer, S. O. (1997). Sexual activity and satisfaction among very old adults: Results from a community-dwelling Medicare population survey. *Gerontologist, 37,* 6–14.

Mattson, M. P., Duan, W., Chan, S. L., Cheng, A., Haughey, N., Gary, D. S., Guo, Z., Lee, J., & Furukawa, K. (2002). Neuroprotective and neurorestorative signal transduction mechanisms in brain aging: modification by genes, diet, and behavior. *Neurobiology of Aging, 23,* 707.

Matusov, E., Bell, N., & Rogoff, B. (2001). *Schooling as cultural process: Working together and guidance by children from schools differing in collaborative practices.* Unpublished manuscript, University of Delaware.

Maughan, A., & Cicchetti, D. (2002). Impact of child maltreatment and interadult violence on children's emotion regulation difficulties and socioemotional adjustment. *Child Development, 73,* 1525–1542.

Maurer, D. (2001, April). *Variations in plasticity in visual development.* Paper presented at the meeting of the Society for Research in Child Development, Minneapolis.

Maurer, D., & Salapatek, P. (1976). Developmental changes in the scanning of faces by young infants. *Child Development, 47,* 523–527.

Mauro, V. P., Wood, I. C., Krushel, L., Crossin, K. L., & Edelman, G. M. (1994). Cell adhesion alters gene transcription in chicken embryo brain cells and mouse embryonal carcinoma cells. *Proceedings of the National Academy of Sciences USA, 91,* 2868–2872.

Maxson, S. (2003). Behavioral genetics. In I. B. Weiner (Ed.), *Handbook of psychology* (Vol. III). New York: Wiley.

Mayer, R. E. (2003). Memory and information processes. In I. B. Weiner (Ed.), *Handbook of psychology* (Vol. VII). New York: Wiley.

McAdoo, H. P. (Ed.). (1999). *Family ethnicity* (2nd ed.). Newbury Park, CA: Sage.

McAdoo, H. P. (2002). African-American parenting. In M. H. Bornstein (Ed.), *Handbook of parenting* (2nd ed., Vol. 4). Mahwah, NJ: Erlbaum.

McCall, R. B., & Carriger, M. S. (1993). A meta-analysis of infant habituation and recognition memory performance as predictors of later IQ. *Child Development, 64,* 57–79.

McCarty, M. E., & Ashmead, D. H. (1999). Visual control of reaching and grasping in infants. *Developmental Psychology, 35,* 620–631.

McCombs, B. L. (2003). Research to policy for guiding educational reform. In I. B. Weiner (Ed.), *Handbook of psychology* (Vol. VII). New York: Wiley.

McCormick, C. B. (2003). Metacognition and learning. In I. B. Weiner (Ed.), *Handbook of psychology,* Vol. VII. New York: Wiley.

McCormick, M. C. (2001). Prenatal care—necessary, but not sufficient. *Health Services Research, 36,* 399–403.

McCrae, R. R. (2001). Traits through time. *Psychological Inquiry, 12,* 85–87.

McCrae, R. R., & Costa, P. T. (1990). *Personality in adulthood.* New York: Guilford.

McCrae, R. R., Costa, P. T., Lima, M. P., Simoes, A., Ostendorf, F., et al. (1999). Age differences in personality across the adult lifespan: Parallels in five cultures. *Developmental Psychology, 35,* 466–477.

McCullough, M. E. (1995). Prayer and health: Conceptual issues, research review, and research agenda. *Journal of Psychology and Theology, 23,* 15–29.

McCullough, M. E., Hoyt, W. T., Larson, D. B., Koenig, H. G., & Thoresen, C. (2000). Religious involvement and mortality: A meta-analytic review. *Health psychology, 19,* 211–222.

McDougall, G. J., Strauss, M. E., Holston, E. C., & Martin, M. (1999, November). *Memory self-efficacy and memory-anxiety as predictors of memory performance in at-risk elderly.* Paper presented at the meeting of the Gerontological Society of America, San Francisco.

McGrath, S., Kennell, J., Suresh, M., Moise, K., & Hinkley, C. (1999, May). *Doula support vs. epidural analgesia: Impact on cesarean rates.* Paper presented at the meeting of the Society for Pediatric Research, San Francisco.

McGue, M., Bouchard, Jr. T. J., Iacono, W. G., & Lykken, D. T. (1993). Behavioral genetics of cognitive ability: A life-span perspective. In R. Plomin & G. R. McClearn (Eds.), *Nature, nurture, and psychology.* Washington, DC: American Psychological Association.

McGuire, F. (2000). What do we know? Not much. The state of leisure and aging research. *Journal of Leisurability, 26,* 97–100.

McGuire, L., Kiecolt-Glaser, & Glaser, R. (2002). Depressive symptoms and lymphocyte proliferation in older adults. *Journal of Abnormal Psychology, 111,* 192–197.

McGuire, S. (2001). Are behavioral genetic and socialization research compatible? *American Psychologist, 56,* 171.

McHale, J. P., Lauretti, A. F., & Kuersten-Hogan, R. (1999, April). *Linking family-level patterns to father-child, mother-child, and marital relationship qualities.* Paper presented at the meeting of the Society for Research in Child Development, Albuquerque.

McHale, J. P., Luretti, A., Talbot, J., & Pouquette, C. (2001). Retrospect and prospect in the psychological study of marital and couple relationships. In J. P. McHale & W. S. Grolnick (Eds.), *Retrospect and prospect in the psychological study of families.* Mahwah, NJ: Erlbaum.

McHale, J., Johnson, D., & Sinclair, R. (1999). Family dynamics, preschoolers' family representations, and preschool peer relationships. *Early Education and Development, 10,* 373–401.

McHale, J., Khazan, I., Erera, P., Rotman, T., DeCourcey, W., & McConnell, M. (2002). Coparenting in diverse family systems. In M. H. Bornstein (Ed.), *Handbook of parenting* (2nd ed., Vol. 3). Mahwah, NJ: Erlbaum.

McInnis, G. J., & White, J. H. (2001). A phenomenological exploration of loneliness in the older adult. *Archives of Psychiatric Nursing, 15,* 128–139.

McKenna, J. J., Mosko, S. S., & Richard, C. A. (1997). Bedsharing promotes breast-feeding. *Pediatrics, 100,* 214–219.

McKnight, A. J., & McKnight, A. S. (1993). The effect of cellular phone use upon driver attention. *Accident Analysis and Prevention, 25,* 259–265.

McLeod, J. D. (1996). Life events. In J. E. Birren (Ed.,) *Encyclopedia of gerontology* (Vol. 1). San Diego: Academic Press.

McLoyd, V. C. (1998). Children in poverty: Development, public policy, and practice. In W. Damon (Ed.), *Handbook of child psychology* (5th ed., Vol. 4). New York: Wiley.

McLoyd, V. C. (1999). Cultural influences in a multicultural society: Conceptual and methodological issues. In A. S. Masten (Ed.), *Cultural processes in child development.* Mahwah, NJ: Erlbaum.

McLoyd, V. C. (2000). Poverty. In A. Kazdin (Ed.), *Encyclopedia of psychology.* Washington, DC, & New York: American Psychological Association and Oxford University Press.

McLoyd, V. C., & Smith, J. (2002). Physical discipline and behavior problems in African American, European American, and Hispanic children: Emotional support as a moderator. *Journal of Marriage and Family, 64,* 40–53.

McMillan, J. H., & Wergin, J. F. (2002). *Understanding and Evaluating educational research* (2nd ed.). Upper Saddle River, NJ: Prentice Hall.

McMullin, J. A., & Marshall, V. W. (2001). Ageism, age relations, and garment industry work in Montreal. *The Gerontologist, 41* (No. 1), 111–119.

McNamara, F., & Sullivan, C. E. (2000). Obstructive sleep apnea in infants. *Journal of Pediatrics, 136,* 318–323.

McNamara, F., Lijowska, A. S., & Thach, B. T. (2002). Spontaneous arousal activity in infants during NREM and REM sleep. *Journal of Physiology, 538,* 263–269.

McTigue, K. M., Garrett, J. M., & Popkin, B. M. (2002). The natural history of the development of obesity in a cohort of young U.S. adults between 1981 and 1998. *Annals of Internal Medicine, 136,* 857–864.

McVeigh, C. A., Baafi, M., & Williamson, M. (2002). Functional status after fatherhood: An Australian study. *Journal of Obstetrics, Gynecology, and Neonatal Nursing, 31,* 165–171.

McVey, G. L., Pepler, D., Davis, D., Flett, G. L., & Abdolell, M. (2002). Risk and protective factors associated with disordered eating during early adolescence. *Journal of Early Adolescence, 22,* 75–95.

Mecocci, P., Olidori, M. C., Troiano, L., Cherubin, A., Cecchetti, R., Pini, G., Straatman, M., Monti, D., Stahl, W., Sies, W., Franceschi, C., & Senin, U. (2000). Plasma antioxidants and longevity: A study on healthy centenarians. *Free Radical Biology and Medicine, 28,* 1243–1248.

Mehler, J., Jusczyk, P. W., Lambertz, G., Halsted, N., Bertoncini, J., & Amiel-Tison, C. (1988). A precursor of language acquisition in young infants. *Cognition, 29,* 132–178.

Melby, J. N., & Vargas, D. (1996, March). *Predicting patterns of adolescent tobacco use.* Paper presented at the meeting of the Society for Research on Adolescence, Boston.

Melinder, K. A., & Andersson, R. (2001). The impact of structural factors on the injury rate in different European countries. *European Journal of Public Health, 11,* 301–308.

Meltzoff, A. N. (1988). Infant imitation and memory: Nine-month-old infants in immediate and deferred tests. *Child Development, 59,* 217–225.

Meltzoff, A. N. (2000). Learning and cognitive development. In A. Kazdin (Ed.), *Encyclopedia of psychology.* Washington, DC, & New York: American Psychological Association and Oxford University Press.

Meltzoff, A. N., & Gopnik, A. (1997). *Words, thoughts, and theories.* Cambridge, MA: MIT Press.

Meltzoff, A. N., & Moore, M. K. (1999). A new foundation for cognitive development: The birth of the representational infant. In E. K. Skolnick, K. Nelson, S. A. Gelman, & P. H. Miller (Eds.), *Conceptual development.* Mahwah, NJ: Erlbaum.

Memmler, R. L., Cohen, B. J., Wood, D. L., & Schweglr, J. (1995). *The human body in health and disease* (8th ed.). Philadelphia: Lippincott Williams & Wilkins.

Menyuk, P., Liebergott, J., & Schultz, M. (1995). *Early language development in full-term and premature infants.* Hillsdale, NJ: Erlbaum.

Meredith, N. V. (1978). Research between 1960 and 1970 on the standing height of young children in different parts of the world. In H. W. Reece & L. P. Lipsitt (Eds.),. *Advances in child development and behavior* (Vol. 12). New York: Academic Press.

Merrick, J., Aspler, S., & Schwartz, G. (2001). Should adults with phenylketonuria have diet treatment? *Mental Retardation, 39,* 215–217.

Merrill, S. S., & Verbrugge, L. M. (1999). Health and disease in midlife. In S. L. Willis & J. D. Reid (Eds.), *Life in the middle: Psychological and social development in middle age.* San Diego: Academic Press.

Michael, R. T., Gagnon, J. H., Laumann, E. O., & Kolata, G. (1994). *Sex in America.* Boston: Little, Brown.

Michel, G. L. (1981). Right-handedness: A consequence of infant supine head-orientation preference? *Science, 212,* 685–687.

Michel, R. S. (2000). Toilet training. *Pediatric Review, 20,* 240–245.

Milke, M. A., & Peltola, P. (2000). Playing all the roles: Gender and the work-family balancing act. *Journal of Marriage and the Family, 61,* 476–490.

Miller, B. C., Bayley, B. K., Christensen, M., Leavitt, S. C., & Coyl, D. D. (2003). Adolescent pregnancy and childbearing. In G. Adams & M. Berzonksy (Eds.), *Blackwell handbook of adolescence.* Malden, MA: Blackwell.

Miller, B. C., Fan, X., Christensen, M., Grotevant, H. D., & von Dulmen, M. (2000). Comparisons of adopted and non-adopted adolescents in a large, nationally representative sample. *Child Development, 71,* 1458–1473.

Miller, J. B. (1986). *Toward a new psychology of women* (2nd ed.). Boston: Beacon Press.

Miller, J. G. (1995, March). *Culture, context, and personal agency: The cultural grounding of self and morality.* Paper presented at the meeting of the Society for Research in Child Development, Indianapolis.

Miller, M., Rejeski, W., Reboussin, B., Ten Have, T., & Ettinger, W. (2000). Physical activity, functional limitations, and disability in older adults. *Journal of the American Geriatric Society, 48,* 1264–1272.

Miller, P. H. (2001). *Theories of developmental psychology* (4th ed.). New York: Worth.

Miller, P. H., & Seier, W. L. (1994). Strategy utilization deficiencies in children: When, where, and why. In H. W. Reese (Ed.), *Advances in child development and behavior* (Vol. 24). New York: Academic Press.

Miller-Jones, D. (1989). Culture and testing. *American Psychologist, 44,* 360–366.

Millis, R. M. (1998). Smoking. In H. S. Friedman (Ed.), *Encyclopedia of mental health* (Vol. 3). San Diego: Academic Press.

Minuchin, P. (2001). Looking toward the horizon: Present and future in the study of family systems. In J. P. McHale & W. S. Grolnick (Eds.), *Retrospect and prospect in the psychological study of families.* Mahwah, NJ: Erlbaum.

Minuchin, P. O., & Shapiro, E. K. (1983). The school as a context for social development. In P. H. Mussen (Ed.), *Handbook of child psychology* (4th ed., Vol. 4). New York: Wiley.

Mischel, W. (1973). Toward a cognitive social learning reconceptualization of personality. *Psychological Review, 80,* 252–283.

Mischel, W. (1995, August). *Cognitive-affective theory of person-environment psychology.* Paper presented at the meeting of the American Psychological Association, New York City.

Mishell, D. (2000). *2000 Yearbook of obstetrics.* St. Louis: Mosby.

Misra, A., Arora, N., Mondal, S., Pandey, R. M., Jailkhani, B., Peshin, S., Chaudhary, D., Saluja, T., Singh, P., Chandra, S., Luithra, K., & Vikram, N. K. (2001). Relation between plasma leptin and anthropometric and metabolic covarites in lean and obese diabetic and hyperlipdaemic Asian Northern Indian subjects. *Diabetes, Nutrition, and Metabolism, 14,* 18–26.

Mitchell, E. A., Stewart, A. W., Crampton, P., & Salmond, C. (2000). Deprivation and sudden infant death syndrome. *Social Science and Medicine, 51,* 147–150.

Mitchell, M., & Catron, G. (2002). Teaching grief and bereavement: Involving support groups in educating student midwives. *The Practicing Midwife, 5,* 26–27.

Mitchell, V., & Helson, R. (1990). Women's prime of life: Is it the 50s? *Psychology of Women Quarterly, 14,* 451–470.

Mizes, J. S., & Miller, K. J. (2000). Eating disorders. In M. Herson & R. T. Ammerman (Eds.), *Advanced abnormal child psychology* (2nd ed.). Mahwah, NJ: Erlbaum.

Modell, J., & Elder, G. H. (2002). Child development in history: So what's new. In W. W. Hartup & R. A. Weinberg (Eds.), *Child psychology in retrospect and prospect.* Mahwah, NJ: Erlbaum.

Moely, B. E., Santulli, K. A., & Obach, M. S. (1995). Strategy instruction, metacognition, and motivation in the elementary school classroom. In F. E. Weinert & W. Schneider (Eds.), *Memory performance and competencies.* Mahwah, NJ: Erlbaum.

Moen, P. (1998). Recasting careers: Changing reference groups, risks, and realities. *Generations, 22,* 40–45.

Moen, P., & Quick, H. E. (1998). Retirement. In H. S. Friedman (Ed.), *Encyclopedia of mental health* (Vol. 3). San Diego: Academic Press.

Moen, P., & Wethington, E. (1999). Midlife development in a life course context. In S. L. Willis & J. D. Reid (Eds.), *Life in the middle: Psychological and social development in middle age.* San Diego: Academic Press.

Mohan, R. M., Golding, S., & Paterson, D. J. (2001). Intermittent hypoxia improves atrial tolerance to subsequent anoxia and reduces stress protein expression. *Acta Physiology Scandinavia, 172,* 89–95.

Monk, C., Fifer, W. P., Sloan, R. P., & Myers, M. M. (2000, May). *Individual differences in fetal cardiac reactivity are associated with maternal anxiety and infant birth weight.* Paper presented at the joint meetings of the Pediatric Academic Societies and the American Academy of Pediatrics, Boston.

Montemayor, R. (1982). The relationship between parent-adolescent conflict and the amount of time adolescents spend with parents, peers, and alone. *Child Development, 53,* 1512–1519.

Moody, R. (2001). Adoption: Women must be helped to consider all options. *British Medical Journal, 323,* 867.

Moore, C., & Lemmon, K. (2001). *The self in time.* Mahwah, NJ: Erlbaum.

Moore, D. (2001). *The dependent gene.* New York: W. H. Freeman.

Moos, R. H. (1986). Work as a human context. In M. S. Pallack & R. Perloff (Eds.), *Psychology and work: Productivity, change, and employment.* Washington, DC: American Psychological Association.

Moreland, R. L., & Beach, R. (1992). Exposure effects in the classroom: The development of affinity among students. *Journal of Experimental Social Psychology, 28,* 255–276.

Morelli, G. A., Rogoff, B., Oppenheim, D., & Goldsmith, D. (1992). Cultural variation in infants' sleeping arrangements: Questions of independence. *Developmental Psychology, 28,* 604–613.

Morris, J. C., Storandt, M., Miller, J. P., McKeel, D., Price, J., Rubin, E. H., & Berg, L. (2001). Mild cognitive impairment represents early-stage Alzheimer's disease. *Archives of Neurology, 58,* 397–405.

Morrongiello, B. A., Fenwick, K. D., & Chance, G. (1990). Sound localization acuity in very young infants: An observer-based testing procedure. *Developmental Psychology, 26,* 75–84.

Morrow, L. (1988, August 8). Through the eyes of children. *Time,* pp. 32–33.

Moses, J., Steptoe, A., Mathews, A., & Edwards, S. (1989). The effects of exercise training on mental well-being in a normal population: A controlled trial. *Journal of Psychosomatic Research, 33,* 47–61.

Moshman, D. (1999). *Adolescent psychological development: Rationality, morality, and identity.* Mahwah, NJ: Erlbaum.

Mounts, N. S. (2002). Parental management of adolescent peer relationships in context: The role of parenting style. *Journal of Family Psychology, 16,* 58–69.

Mozingo, J. N., Davis, M. W., Droppleman, P. G., & Merideth, A. (2000). "It wasn't working" women's experiences with short-term breast feeding. *American Maternal Journal of Nursing, 25,* 120–126.

Mroczek, D. K., & Kolarz, C. M. (1998). The effect of age on positive and negative affect: A developmental perspective on happiness. *Journal of Personality and Social Psychology, 75,* 1333–1349.

Mroczek, D. K. (2001). Age and emotion in adulthood. *Current Directions in Psychological Science, 10,* 87–90.

Mueller, N., & Silverman, N. (1989). Peer relations in maltreated children. In D. Cicchetti & V. Carlson (Eds.), *Child maltreatment.* New York: Cambridge University Press.

Mulholland, H. (2002). Hospice care: A few home truths. *Nursing Times, 98 (40),* 11.

Mullis, I. V. S. (1999, April). *Using TIMSS to gain new perspectives about different school organizations and policies.* Paper presented at the meeting of the American Educational Research Association, Montreal.

Mumme, D. L., Fernald, A., & Herrera, C. (1996). Infant's responses to facial & emotional signals in a social referencing paradigm. *Child Development, 67,* 3219–3237.

Mungas, D., Reed, B. R., Jagust, W. J., DeCarli, C., Mack, W. J., Kramer, J. H., Weiner, M. W., Schuff, N., & Chui, H. C. (2002). Volumetric MRI predicts rate of cognitive decline related to AD and cerebrovascular disease. *Neurology, 59,* 867–873.

Murnane, R. J., & Levy, F. (1996). *Teaching the new basic skills.* New York: Free Press.

Murphy, M. C. (1996). Stressors on the college campus: A comparison of 1985 and 1993. *Journal of College Student Development, 37,* 20–28.

Murray, J. P. (2000). Media effects. In A. Kazdin (Ed.), *Encyclopedia of psychology.* Washington, DC, & New York: American Psychological Association and Oxford University Press.

Murstein, B. I., Reif, J. A., & Syarcuse-Siewert, G. (2002). Comparison of the function of exchange in couples of similar and differing physical attractiveness. *Psychological Reports, 91,* 299–314.

Mussen, P. H., Honzik, M., & Eichorn, D. (1982). Early adult antecedents of life satisfaction at age 70. *Journal of Gerontology, 37,* 316–322.

Muth, A. S. (Ed.). (2000). *Death and dying sourcebook: Basic consumer health information for the layperson about end-of-life care and related ethical issues.* Detroit: Omnigraphics.

Myers, D. G. (2000). *The American paradox.* New Haven, CT: Yale University Press.

Myers, D. L. (1999). *Excluding violent youths from juvenile court: The effectiveness of legislative waiver.* Doctoral dissertation, University of Maryland, College Park.

Nader, K. (2001). Treatment methods for childhood trauma. In J. P. Wilson, M. J. Friedman, & J. Lindy (Eds.), *Treating psychological trauma and PTSD.* New York: Guilford Press.

Naglieri, J. (2000). Stanford-Binet Intelligence Scale. In A. Kazdin (Ed.), *Encyclopedia of psychology.* Washington, DC, & New York: American Psychological Association and Oxford University Press.

Nagy, M. (1948). The child's theories concerning death. *Journal of Genetic Psychology, 73,* 3–27.

Nahas, G. G. (1984). *Marijuana in science and medicine.* New York: Raven Press.

Nakamura, J., & Csikszentmihalyi, M. (2002). The concept of flow. In C. R. Snyder & S. J. Lopez (Eds.), *Handbook of positive psychology.* New York: Oxford University Press.

Nansel, T. R., Overpeck, M., Pilla, R., Ruan, W., Simons-Morton, B., & Scheidt, P. (2001). Bullying behaviors among U.S. youth. *Journal of the American Medical Association, 285,* 2094–2100.

Narang, A., & Jain, N. (2001). Haemolytic disease of newborn. *Indian Journal of Pediatrics, 68,* 167–172.

Nash, J. M. (1997, February 3). Fertile minds. *Time,* pp. 50–54.

National and Community Service Coalition. (1995). *Youth volunteerism.* Washington, DC: Author.

National Assessment of Educational Progress. (1998). *National report: 1998.*

Washington, DC: National Center for Education Statistics.

National Assessment of Educational Progress. (2001). *National report: 2000.* Washington, DC: National Center for Education Statistics.

National Association for the Education of Young Children. (1986). Position statement on developmentally appropriate practice in programs for 4- and 5-year-olds. *Young Children 41,* 20–29.

National Center for Children Exposed to Violence. (2001). *Statistics.* New Haven, CT: Author.

National Center for Education Statistics. (2001). *Dropout rates in the United States: 2000.* Washington, DC: U.S. Department of Education.

National Center for Health Statistics. (1999). Current estimates from the National Health Interview Survey, 1996. *Vital and Health Statistics, Series 10* (No. 200). Atlanta: Centers for Disease Control and Prevention.

National Center for Health Statistics. (2000). *Health United States, 2000, with adolescent health chartbook.* Bethesda, MD: U.S. Department of Health and Human Services.

National Center for Health Statistics. (2000). *Health United States, 1999.* Atlanta: Centers for Disease Control and Prevention.

National Center for Health Statistics. (2001). *Causes of death.* Hyattsville, MD: Department of Health and Human Services.

National Center for Health Statistics. (2001). *Health United States, 2001.* Atlanta: Centers for Disease Control and Prevention.

National Center for Health Statistics. (2002). *New CDC report tracks trends in cesarean births and VCACs during the 1990s.* Atlanta: Centers for Disease Control and Prevention.

National Center on Addiction and Substance Abuse. (2001). *2000 teen survey.* New York: Author.

National Commission on the High School Year. (2001). *Youth at the crossroads: Facing high school and beyond.* Washington, DC: The Education Trust.

National Council on Aging. (2000, March). *Myths and realities survey results.* Washington, DC: Author.

National Institutes of Health. (2002). *Body mass index table.* Bethesda, MD: Author.

National Research Council. (1999). *How people learn.* Washington, DC: National Academy Press.

National Vital Statistics Reports. (2001). Deaths and death rates for the 10 leading causes of death in specified age groups. *National Vital Statistics Reports, 48* (No. 11), Table 8.

National Vital Statistics Reports. (2001). *Deaths: Preliminary data for 1999* (Vol. 49, No. 3). 1–25.

Natsopoulos, D., Kiosseoglou, G., Xeroxmeritou, A., & Alevriadou, A. (1998). Do the hands talk on the mind's behalf? Differences in language between left- and right-handed children. *Brain and Language, 64,* 182–214.

Navarrete, C., Martinez, I., & Salamanca, F. (1994). Paternal line of transmission in chorea of Huntington with very early onset. *Genetic Counseling, 5,* 175–178.

Neisser, U., Boodoo, G., Bouchard, T. J., Boykin, A. W., Brody, N., Ceci, S. J., Halpern, D. F., Loehlin, J. C., Perloff, R. J., Sternberg, R., & Urbina, S. (1996). Intelligence: Knowns and unknowns. *American Psychologist, 51,* 77–101.

Nelson, C. (1999). Research description. *Institute of Child Development biennial report.* Minneapolis: Institute of Child Development.

Nelson, K. (1999). Levels and modes of representation: Issues for the theory of conceptual change and development. In E. K. Skolnick, K. Nelson, S. A. Gelman, & P. H. Miller (Eds.), *Conceptual development.* Mahwah, NJ: Erlbaum.

Nelson, M. E., Fiatarone, M. A., Moranti, C. M., Trice, I., Greenberg, R. A., & Evans, W. J. (1994). Effects of high-intensity strength training on multiple risk factors for osteoporotic fractures: A randomized controlled trial. *Journal of the American Medical Association, 272,* 1909–1914.

Nelson-LeGall, S., & Kelly, K. (2001, April). *Gender and ethnicity in the schoolroom.* Paper presented at the meeting of the Society for Research in Child Development, Minneapolis.

Neugarten, B. L. (1964). *Personality in middle and late life.* New York: Atherton.

Neugarten, B. L. (1986). The aging society. In A. Pifer & L. Bronte (Eds.), *Our aging society: Paradox and promise.* New York: W. W. Norton.

Neugarten, B. L. (1988, August). *Policy issues for an aging society.* Paper presented at the meeting of the American Psychological Association, Atlanta.

Neugarten, B. L., Havighurst, R. J., & Tobin, S. S. (1968). Personality and patterns of aging. In B. L. Neugarten (Ed.), *Middle age and aging.* Chicago: University of Chicago Press.

Neugarten, B., & Neugarten, D. (1987, May). The changing meaning of age. *Psychology Today,* 44–51.

Neugarten, B. L., & Weinstein, K. K. (1964). The changing American grandparent. *Journal of Marriage and the Family, 26,* 199–204.

Newcomb, M. D., & Bentler, P. M. (1988). Substance use and abuse among children and teenagers. *American Psychologist, 44,* 242–248.

Newcomb, M., & Bentler, P. (1980). Assessment of personality and demographic aspects of cohabitation and marital success. *Journal of Personality Development, 4,* 11–24.

Newell, K., Scully, D. M., McDonald, P. V., & Baillargeon, R. (1989). Task constraints and infant grip configurations. *Developmental Psychobiology, 22,* 817–832.

NHANES. (2001, March). *National Health and Nutrition Examination Surveys.* Washington, DC: U.S. Department of Health and Human Services.

NICHD Early Child Care Research Network. (2000). Factors associated with fathers' caregiving activities and sensitivity with young children. *Developmental Psychology, 14,* 200–219.

Nichols, F. H., & Humenick, S. S. (2000). *Childbirth education* (2nd ed.). London: Harcourt International.

Nock, S. (1995). A comparison of marriages and cohabiting relationships. *Journal of Family Issues, 16,* 53–76.

Nolen-Hoeksema, S. (1990). *Sex differences in depression.* Stanford, CA: Stanford University Press.

Nolen-Hoeksema, S. (2001). *Abnormal psychology* (2nd ed.). New York: McGraw-Hill.

Nolen-Hoeksema, S., & Ahrens, C. (2002). Age differences and similarities in correlates of depressive symptoms. *Psychology and Aging, 17,* 116–124.

Nottebohm, F. (2002). Neuronal replacement in the adult brain. *Brain Research Bulletin, 57,* 737–750.

Nottelmann, E. D., Susman, E. J., Blue, J. H., Inoff-Germain, G., Dorn, L. D., Loriaux, D. L., Cutler, G. B., & Chrousos, G. P. (1987). Gonadal and adrenal hormone correlates of adjustment in early adolescence. In R. M. Lerner & T. T. Foch (Eds.), *Biological-psychological interactions in early adolescence.* Hillsdale, NJ: Erlbaum.

Novak, W. (1983). *The great American man shortage.* New York: Rawson.

Nowak, C. A. (1977). Does youthfulness equal attractiveness? In L. E. Troll, J. Israel, & K. Israel (Eds.), *Looking ahead: A woman's guide to the problems and joys of growing older.* Englewood Cliffs, NJ: Prentice Hall.

Nugent, K., & Brazelton, T. B. (2000). Preventive infant mental health: Uses of the Brazelton scale. In J. D. Osofsky & H. E. Fitzgerald (Eds.), *WAIMH Handbook of infant mental health* (Vol. 2). New York: Wiley.

Nussbaum, J. F., Pecchioni, L., & Crowell, T. (2001). The older patient-health care provider relationship in a managed care environment. In M. L. Hummert & J. F. Nussbaum (Eds.), *Aging, communication, and health.* Mahwah, NJ: Erlbaum.

O'Hanlon, L., Wilcox, K. A., & Kemper, S. (2001). Age differences in implicit and explicit associative memory: Exploring elaborative processing effects. *Experimental Aging Research, 27,* 341–359.

Oberauer, K., Demmrich, A., Mayr, U., & Kliegl, R. (2001). Dissociating retention and access in working memory. *Memory and cognition, 29,* 18–33.

Oberbauer, A. M., Rundstadler, J. A., Murray, A. D., & Havel, P. J. (2001). Obesity and elevated plasma leptin concentration in oMT1A-o growth hormone transgenic mice. *Obesity Research, 9,* 51–58.

Occupational Outlook Handbook. (2002–2003). Washington, DC: U.S. Department of Labor, Bureau of Labor Statistics.

Oehninger, S. (2001). Strategies for the infertile man. *Seminars in Reproductive Medicine, 19,* 231–238.

Offer, D., Ostrov, E., Howard, K. I., & Atkinson, R. (1988). *The teenage world: Adolescents' self image in ten countries.* New York: Plenum.

Ogbu, J. U. (1989, April). *Academic socialization of Black children: An innoculation against future failure?* Paper presented at the meeting of the Society for Research in Child Development, Kansas City.

Ogbu, J. U. (2002). Cultural amplifiers of intelligence. In J. M. Fish (Ed.), *Race and intelligence.* Mahwah, NJ: Erlbaum.

Ogbu, J. U., & Stern, P. (2001). Caste status and intellectual ability. In R. J. Sternberg & E. L. Grigorenko (Eds.), *Environmental effects on cognitive abilities.* Mahwah, NJ: Erlbaum.

Okagaki, L. (2000). Determinants of intelligence: Socialization of intelligence. In A. Kazdin (Ed.), *Encyclopedia of psychology.* Washington, DC, & New York: American Psychological Association and Oxford University Press.

Olivardia, R., Pope, H. G., Mangweth, B., & Hudson, J. I. (1995). Eating disorders in college men. *American Journal of Psychiatry, 152,* 1279–1284.

Olsho, L. W., Harkins, S. W., & Lenhardt, M. L. (1985). Aging and the auditory system. In J. E. Birren & K. W. Schaie (Eds.), *Handbook of the psychology of aging* (2nd ed.). New York: Van Nostrand Reinhold.

Olson, H. C. (2000). Fetal alcohol syndrome. In A. Krazdin (Ed.), *Encyclopedia of psychology.* Washington, DC, & New York: American Psychological Association and Oxford Unversity Press.

Olszewski-Kubilius, P. (2003). Gifted education programs and procedures. In I. B. Weiner (Ed.), *Handbook of psychology* (Vol. VII). New York: Wiley.

Olweus, D. (1980). Bullying among schoolboys. In R. Barnen (Ed.), *Children and violence.* Stockholm: Adaemic Litteratur.

Orbanic, S. (2001). Understanding bulimia. *American Journal of Nursing, 101,* 35–41.

Organista, K. C. (1994). Overdue overview of elderly Latino mental health. *Contemporary Psychology, 39,* 61–62.

Oshio, S., Johnson, P., & Fullerton, J. (2002). The 1999–2000 task analysis of American nurse-midwifery/midwifery practice. *Journal of Midwifery and Women's Health, 47,* 35–41.

Osipow, S. (2000). Work. In A. Kazdin (Ed.), *Encyclopedia of psychology.* Washington, DC, & New York: American Psychological Association and Oxford University Press.

Ostrea, E. M., Whitehall, J. S., & Laken, M. A. (2000, May). *Prevalence of fetal exposure to environmental toxins: An international study.* Paper presented at the joint meetings of the Pediatric Academic Societies and the American Academy of Pediatrics, Boston.

Ouellette, S. C., & DiPlacido, J. (2001). Personality's role in the protection and enhancement of health. In A. Baum, T. A. Revenson, & J. E. Singer (Eds.), *Handbook of health psychology.* Mahwah, NJ: Erlbaum.

Overton, W. F. (2003). Development across the life span. In I. B. Weiner (Ed.), *Handbook of psychology* (Vol. VI). New York: Wiley.

Overton, W. F., & Byrnes, J. P. (1991). Cognitive development. In R. M. Lerner, A. C. Petersen, and J. Brooks-Gunn (Eds.), *Encyclopedia of adolescence* (Vol. 1). New York: Garland.

Owen, M. (2001, April). *Family measures in the Phase 1 data set of the NICHD Study of Early Child Care.* Paper presented at the meeting of the Society for Research in Child Development, Minneapolis.

P

Padma-Nathan, H., & Giuliano, F. (2001). Oral drug therapy for erectile dysfunction. *Urology Clinics of North America, 28,* 321–334.

Paffenbarger, O., Hyde, R. T., Wing, A. L., & Hsieh, C. (1986). Physical activity, all-cause mortality, and longevity of college alumni. *New England Journal of Medicine, 324,* 605–612.

Paffenbarger, R. S., Hyde, R. T., Wing, A. L., Lee, I., Jung, D. L., & Kampter, J. B. (1993). The association of changes in physical-activity level and other life-style characteristics with mortality among men. *New England Journal of Medicine, 328,* 538–545.

Paikoff, R. L., Buchanan, C. M., & Brooks-Gunn, J. (1991). Hormone-behavior links at puberty, methodological links in the study of. In R. M. Lerner, A. C. Petersen, & J. Brooks-Gunn (Eds.), *Encyclopedia of adolescence.* New York: Garland.

Palmore, E. (1981). *Social patterns in normal aging: Findings from the Duke Longitudinal Study.* Durham, NC: Duke University Press.

Palmore, E. (2001). The ageism survey: First findings. *The Gerontologist, 41,* 572–575.

Palmore, E. B., Burchett, B. M., Fillenbaum, C. G., George, L. K., & Wallman, L. M. (1985). *Retirement: Causes and consequences.* New York: Springer.

Paloutzian, R. (2000). *Invitation to the psychology of religion* (3rd ed.). Boston: Allyn & Bacon.

Paludi, M. A. (2002). *Psychology of women* (2nd ed.). Upper Saddle River, NJ: Prentice Hall.

Panchaud, C., Singh, S., Feivelson, D., & Darroch, J. E. (2000). Sexually transmitted diseases among adolescents in developed countries. *Family Planning Perspectives, 32,* 24–32.

Pargament, K. I. (1990). God help me: Toward a theoretical framework of coping for the psychology of religion. In M. L. Lynn & D. O. Moberg (Eds.), *Research in the social scientific study of religion* (Vol. 2). Greenwich, CT: JAI Press.

Pargament, K. I., & Park, C. L. (1995). Merely a defense? Examining psychologists' stereotype of religion. *Journal of Social Issues.*

Park, D. (2001). Commentary in Restak, R. *The secret life of the brain.* Washington, DC: Joseph Henry Press.

Park, D. C., Lautenschalger, G., Hedden, T., Davidson, N. S., Smith, A. D., & Smith, P. K. (2002). Models of visuospatial and verbal memory across the adult life span. *Psychology and Aging, 17,* 299–320.

Parke, R. D. (1995). Fathers and families. In M. H. Bornstein (Ed.), *Children and parenting* (Vol. 3). Hillsdale, NJ: Erlbaum.

Parke, R. D. (2000). Father involvement: A developmental psychology perspective. *Marriage and Family Review, 29,* 43–58.

Parke, R. D. (2001). Parenting in the new millennium. In J. P. McHale & W. S. Grolnick (Eds.), *Retrospect and prospect in the psychological study of families.* Mahwah, NJ: Erlbaum.

Parke, R. D. (2002). Fathering. In M. H. Bornstein (Ed.), *Handbook of parenting* (2nd ed.). Mahwah, NJ: Erlbaum.

Parke, R. D., & Buriel, R. (1998). Socialization in the family: Ethnic and ecological perspectives. In W. Damon (Ed.), *Handbook of child psychology* (5th ed., Vol. 3). New York: Wiley.

Parkin, A. J., & Walter, B. M. (1992). Recollective experience, normal aging, and frontal dysfunction. *Psychology and Aging, 7,* 290–298.

Parlee, M. B. (1979, April). The friendship bond: PT's survey report on friendship in America. *Psychology Today,* pp. 43–54, 113.

Parnes, H. S., & Sommers, D. G. (1994). Shunning retirement: Work experiences of men in their seventies and early eighties. *Journal of Gerontology, 49,* S117–S124.

Parten, M. (1932). Social play among preschool children. *Journal of Abnormal and Social Psychology, 27,* 243–269.

Pascali-Bonaro, D. (2002). Pregnant and widowed on September 11: The birth community reaches out. *Birth, 29,* 62–64.

Pasch, L. A. (2001). Confronting fertility problems. In A. Baum, T. A. Revenson, & J. E. Singer (Eds.), *Handbook of health psychology.* Mahwah, NJ: Erlbaum.

Passuth, P. M., Maines, D. R., & Neugarten, B. L. (1984). *Age norms and age constraints twenty years later.* Paper presented at the annual meeting of the Midwest Sociological Society, Chicago.

Patterson, C. J. (1995). Sexual orientation and human development: An overview. *Developmental Psychology, 31,* 3–11.

Patterson, C. J. (2000). Family relationships of lesbians and gay men. *Journal of Marriage and the Family, 62,* 1052–1069.

Patterson, C. J. (2002). Lesbian and gay parenthood. In M. H. Bornstein (Ed.), *Handbook of parenting* (2nd ed.). Mahwah, NJ: Erlbaum.

Patterson, G. R., DeBaryshe, B. D., & Ramsey, E. (1989). A developmental perspective on antisocial behavior. *American Psychologist, 44,* 329–355.

Pavlov, I. P. (1927). In G. V. Anrep (Trans.), *Conditioned reflexes.* London: Oxford University Press.

Payer, L. (1991). The menopause in various cultures. In H. Burger & M. Boulet (Eds.), *A portrait of the menopause.* Park Ridge, NJ: Parthenon.

Pearlin, L. I. (1994). The study of the oldest-old: Some promises and puzzles. *International Journal of Aging and Human Development, 38,* 91–98.

Peck, R. C. (1968). Psychological developments in the second half of life. In B. L. Neugarten (Ed.), *Middle age and aging.* Chicago: University of Chicago Press.

Pellegrini, A. D. (2002). Bullying, victimization, and sexual harassment during the transition to middle school. *Educational Psychologist, 37,* 151-164.

Pennington, B. F., & Lefly, D. L. (2001). Early reading development in children at family risk for dyslexia. *Child Development, 72,* 816–833.

Penninx, B. W., Rejeski, W. J., Pandya, J., Miller, M. E., Di Bari, M., Applegate, W. B., & Pahor, M. (2002). Exercise and depressive symptoms: A comparison of aerobic and resistance exercise effects on emotional and physical function in older persons with high and low depressive symptomatology. *Journal of Gerontology: Psychological and Social Sciences, 57,* P124–P132.

Peplau, L. A., & Beals, K. P. (2001). Lesbians, gays, and bisexuals in relationships. In J. Worell (Ed.), *Encyclopedia of women and gender.* San Diego: Academic Press.

Perdue, C. W. (2000). Ageism. In A. Kazdin (Ed.), *Encyclopedia of psychology.* Washington, DC, & New York: American Psychological Association and Oxford University Press.

Perez-Febles, A. M. (1992). *Acculturation and interactional styles of Latina mothers and their infants.* Unpublished honors thesis, Brown University, Providence, RI.

Perkins, D. F., & Borden, L. M. (2003). Positive behaviors, problem behaviors, and resiliency in adolescence. In I. B. Weiner (Ed.), *Handbook of psychology* (Vol. VI). New York: Wiley.

Perlman, D., & Peplau, L. A. (1998). Loneliness. In H. S. Friedman (Ed.), *Encyclopedia of mental health* (Vol. 2). San Diego: Academic Press.

Perls, T. (1999, November). *An Internet-based life expectancy calculator.* Paper presented at the meeting of the Gerontological Association of America, San Francisco.

Perls, T., Lauerman, J. F., & Silver, M. H. (1999). *Living to 100.* New York: Basic Books.

Perry, C. M., & Johnson, C. L. (1994). Families and support networks among African American oldest-old. International *Journal of Aging on Human Development, 38,* 41–50.

Perry, W. G. (1970). *Forms of intellectual and ethical development in the college years.* New York: Holt, Rinehart & Winston.

Perry, W. G. (1999). *Forms of ethical and intellectual development in the college years: A scheme.* San Francisco: Jossey Bass.

Perse, E. M. (2001). *Media effects and society.* Mahwah, NJ: Erlbaum.

Peskin, E. G., & Rein, G. M. (2002). A guest editorial: What is the correct cesarian rate and how do we get there? *Obstetrics and Gynecological Survey, 57,* 189–190.

Peskin, H. (1967). Pubertal onset and ego functioning. *Journal of Abnormal Psychology, 72,* 1–15.

Petersen, A. C. (1979, January). Can puberty come any faster? *Psychology Today,* pp. 45–56.

Petersen, A. C. (1993). Creating adolescents: The role of context and process in developmental trajectories. *Journal of Research on Adolescence, 3,* 1–18.

Peterson, B. E. (2002). Longitudinal analysis of midlife generativity, intergenerational roles, and caregiving. *Psychology and Aging, 17,* 161–168.

Peterson, B. E., & Stewart, A. J. (1996). Antecedents and contexts of generativit motivation at midlife. *Psychology and Aging, 11,* 21–33.

Peterson, C. C. (1996). The ticking of the social clock: Adults' beliefs about the timing of transition events. *International Journal of Aging and Human Development, 42,* 189–203.

Peterson, C. C. (1999). Grandfathers' and grandmothers' satisfaction with the grandparenting role: Seeking new answers to old questions. *International Journal of Aging and Human Development, 49,* 61–78.

Peterson, K. S. (1997, September 3). In high school, dating is a world into itself. *USA Today,* pp. 1–2D.

Peth-Pierce, R. (1998). *The NICHD Study of Early Child Care.* Washington, DC: National Institute of Child Health and Human Development.

Petitto, L., & Marentette, P. (1991). Babbling in the manual mode: Evidence for the ontogeny of language. *Science, 251,* 1493–1496.

Phillips, D. A., Friedman, S. L., Huston, A. C., & Weinraub, M. (1999, April). *The roles of work and poverty in the lives of families with young children.* Paper presented at the meeting of the Society for Research in Child Development, Albuquerque.

Phillips, D. A., Voran, K., Kisker, E., Howes, C., & Whitebook, M. (1994). Child care for children in poverty: Opportunity or inequity? *Child Development, 65,* 472–492.

Phillips, W. T., Kiernan, R. M., & King, A. C. (2001). The effects of physical activity on physical and psychological health. In A. Baum, T. A. Revenson, & J. E. Singer (Eds.), *Handbook of health psychology.* Mahwah, NJ: Erlbaum.

Phinney, J. S. (1989). Stages of ethnic identity development in minority group adolescents. *Journal of Early Adolescence, 9,* 34–49.

Phinney, J. S. (1996). When we talk about American ethnic groups, what do we mean? *American Psychologist, 51,* 918–927.

Phinney, J. S. (2000). Ethnic identity. In A. Kazdin (Ed.), *Encyclopedia of psychology.* Washington, DC, & New York: American Psychological Association and Oxford University Press.

Phinney, J. S. (2003). Ethnic identity and acculturation. In K. M. Chun, P. B. Organista, & G. Marin (Eds.), *Acculturation.* Washington, DC: American Psychological Association.

Phinney, J. S., & Alipura, L. L. (1990). Ethnic identity in college students from four ethnic groups. *Journal of Adolescence, 13,* 171–183.

Phinney, J. S., & Devich-Navarro, M. (1997). Variations in bicultural identification among African American and Mexican American adolescents. *Journal of Research on Adolescence, 7,* 3–32.

Phinney, J. S., Ferguson, D. L., & Tate, J. D. (1997). Intergroup attitudes among ethnic minority adolescents: A causal model. *Child Development, 68,* 955–969.

Phinney, J. S., Ong, A., & Madden, T. (2000). Cultural values and intergenerational discrepancies in immigrant and non-immigrant families. *Child Development, 71,* 528–539.

Piaget, J. (1932). *The moral judgment of the child.* New York: Harcourt Brace Jovanovich.

Piaget, J. (1952). *The origins of intelligence in children.* New York: International Universities Press.

Piaget, J. (1952a). Jean Piaget. In C. A. Murchison (Ed.). *A history of psychology in autobiography* (Vol. 4). Worcester, MA: Clark University Press.

Piaget, J. (1954). *The construction of reality in the child.* New York: Basic Books.

Piaget, J. (1962). *Play, dreams, and imitation.* New York. W. W. Norton.

Piaget, J., & Inhelder, B. (1969). *The child's conception of space* (F. J. Langdon & J. L. Lunzer, Trans.). New York: W. W. Norton.

Pick, H. L. (1997). Review of J. W. Santrock's *Child development,* 8th ed. (New York: McGraw-Hill).

Pierce, K. M., Hamm, J. V., & Vandell, D. L. (1997, April). *Experiences in after-school programs and children's adjustment at school and at home.* Paper presented at the meeting of the Society for Research in Child Development, Washington, DC.

Pillow, D. R., Zautra, A. J., & Sandler, I. (1996). Major life events and minor stressors: Identifying mediational links in the stress process. *Journal of Personality and Social Psychology, 70,* 381–394.

Pinger, R. R., Payne, W. A., Hahn, D. B., & Hahn, E. J. (2001). *Drugs* (4th ed.). New York: McGraw-Hill.

Pinker, S. (1994). *The language instinct.* New York: HarperCollins.

Piolino, P., Desgranges, B., Benali, K., & Eustache, F. (2002). Episodic and semantic remote autobiographical memory in aging. *Memory, 10,* 239–357.

Pittenger, D. (2003). *Behavioral research design and analysis.* New York: McGraw-Hill.

Pittman, K., & Diversi, M. (2003). Social policy for the 21st century. In R. Larson, B. Brown, & J. Mortimer (Eds.), *Adolescents' preparation for the future: Perils and promises.* Malden, MA: Blackwell.

Plackslin, S. (2000). *Mothering the new mother: Women's feelings and needs after childbirth—A support and resource guide.* New York: Newmarket Press.

Pleck, J. H. (1995). The gender-role strain paradigm. In R. F. Levant & W. S. Pollack (Eds.), *A new psychology of men.* New York: Basic Books.

Plomin, R. (1993, March). *Human behavioral genetics and development: An overview and update.* Paper presented at the biennial meeting of the Society for Research in Child Development, New Orleans.

Plomin, R., Asbury, K., & Dunn, J. (2001). Why are children in the same family so different? Nonshared environment a decade later. *Canadian Journal of Psychiatry, 46,* 225–233.

Plomin, R., DeFries, J. C., McClearn, G. E., & McGuffin, P. (2001). *Behavioral genetics* (4th ed.). New York: Worth.

Plomin, R., Reiss, D., Hetherington, E. M., & Howe, G. W. (1994). Nature and nurture: Contributions to measures of the family environment. *Developmental Psychology, 30,* 32–43.

Polivy, J., & Herman, C. P. (2002). Causes of eating disorders. *Annual Review of Psychology* (Vol. 53). Palo Alto, CA: Annual Reviews.

Polivy, J., Herman, C. P., Mills, J., & Brock, H. (2003). Eating disorders in adolescence. In G. Adams & M. Berzonsky (Eds.), *Blackwell handbook of adolescence.* Malden, MA: Blackwell.

Pollack, H. A. (2001). Sudden infant death syndrome, maternal smoking during pregnancy, and the cost-effectiveness of smoking cessation intervention. *American Journal of Public Health, 91,* 432–436.

Pollack, H. A., & Frohna, J. G. (2001). A competing risk model of sudden death syndrome incidence in two U.S. birth cohorts. *Journal of Pediatrics, 138,* 661–667.

Pollitt, E. P., Gorman, K. S., Engle, P. L., Martorell, R., & Rivera, J. (1993). Early supplementary feeding and cognition. *Monographs of the Society for Research in Child Development, 58* (7, Serial No. 235).

Pomerleau, O. (2000). Smoking. In A. Kazdin (Ed.), *Encyclopedia of psychology.* Washington, DC, & New York: American Psychological Association and Oxford University Press.

Ponterotto, J. G., Casas, J. M., Suzuki, L. A., & Alexander, C. M. (Eds.). (2001). *Handbook of multicultural counseling.* Thousand Oaks, CA: Sage.

Posner, J. K., & Vandell, D. L. (1994). Low-income children's after-school care: Are there benefits of after-school programs? *Child Development, 65,* 440–456.

Potter, S. M., Zelazo, P. R., Stack, D. M., & Papageorgiou, A. N. (2000). Adverse effects of fetal cocaine exposure on neonatal auditory information processing. *Pediatrics, 105,* e40–e41.

Potvin, L., Champagne, F., & Laberge-Nadeau, C. (1988). Mandatory driver training and road safety: The Quebec experience. *American Journal of Public Health, 78,* 1206–1212.

Powers, D. V., Gallagher-Thompson, D., & Kraemer, H. C. (2002). Coping and depression in Alzheimer's caregivers: Longitudinal evidence of stability. *Journal of Gerontology: Psychological Science, 57B,* P205–P211.

Powers, L. E., & Wampold, B. E. (1994). Cognitive-behavioral factors in adjustment to adult bereavement. *Death Studies, 18,* 1–24.

Pratt, M. W., Danso, H. A., Arnold, M. L., Norris, J. E., & Filyer, R. (2001). Adult generativity and the socialization of adolescents. *Journal of Personality, 69,* 89–120.

Pressley, M. (2000). What should comprehension instruction be the instruction of? In M. Kamil (Ed.), *Handbook of reading research.* Mahwah, NJ: Erlbaum.

Pressley, M. (2003). Literacy and literacy instruction. In I. B. Weiner (Ed.), *Handbook of psychology* (Vol. VII). New York: Wiley.

Pressley, M., Wharton-MacDonald, R., Allington, R., Block, C. C., Morrow, L., Tracey, D., Baker, K., Brooks, G., Cronin, J., Neson, E., & Woo, D. (2001). A study of effective first grade literacy instruction. *Scientific Studies of Reading, 15,* 35–58.

Province, M. A., Hadley, E. C., Hornbrook, M. C., Lipitz, L. A., Miller, J. P., Mulrow, C. D., Ory, M. G., Sattin, R. W., Tinetti, M. E., & Wolf, S. L. (1995). The effects of exercise on falls in elderly patients. *Journal of the American Medical Association, 273,* 1341–1347.

Pruchno, R., & Rosenbaum, J. (2003). Social relationships in adulthood and old age. In I. B. Weiner (Ed.), *Handbook of psychology, Vol. VI.* New York: Wiley.

Pruett, M. K., & Jackson, T. D. (2001). Perspectives on the divorce process. *Journal of the American Academy of Psychiatry and Law, 29,* 18–28.

Putnam, S. P., Sanson, A. V., & Rothbart, M. K. (2002). Child temperament and parenting. In M. H. Bornstein (Ed.), *Handbook of parenting* (2nd ed.). Mahwah, NJ: Erlbaum.

Pyke, K. D., & Bengtson, V. L. (1996). Caring more or less: Individualistic and collectivist systems of family eldercare. *Journal of Marriage and the Family, 58,* 379–392.

Qutub, M., Klapper, P., Vallely, P., & Cleator, G. (2001). Genital herpes in pregnancy: Is screening cost effective? *International Journal of STD and AIDS, 12,* 14–16.

Rabin, B. E., & Dorr, A. (1995, March). *Children's understanding of emotional events on family television series.* Paper presented at the meeting of the Society for Research in Child Development, Indianapolis.

Raffaelli, M., & Ontai, L. (in press). "She's sixteen years old and there's boys calling over to the house": An exploratory study of sexual socialization in Latino families. *Culture, Health, and Sexuality.*

Ramey, C. T., & Campbell, F. A. (1984). Preventive education for high-risk children: Cognitive consequences of the Carolina Abecedarian Project. *American Journal of Mental Deficiency, 88,* 515–523.

Ramey, C. T., Campbell, F. A., & Blair, C. (2001). Enhancing the life course for high-risk children: Results from the Abecedarian project. In J. Crane (Ed.), *Social programs that work.* New York: Sage.

Ramey, C. T., Campbell, F. A., Burchinal, M., Skinner, M. L., Gardner, D. M., & Ramey, S. L. (2000). Persistent effects of early intervention on high-risk children and their mothers. *Applied Developmental Science, 4,* 2–14.

Ramey, C. T., Ramey, S. L., & Lanzi, R. G. (2001). Intelligence and experience. In R. J. Sternberg & E. I. Grigorenko (Eds.), *Environment effects on cognitive development.* Mahwah, NJ: Erlbaum.

Ramey, C. T., & Ramey, S. L. (1998). Early prevention and early experience. *American Psychologist, 53,* 109–120.

Ramey, S. L., & Ramey, C. T. (2000). Early childhood experiences and developmental competence. In S. Danziger & J. Waldfogel (Eds.), *Securing the future: Investing in children from birth to college.* New York: Russell Sage Foundation.

Ramphal, C. (1962). *A study of three current problems in education.* Unpublished doctoral dissertation, University of Natal, India.

Ransjo-Arvidson, A. B., Matthiesen, A. S., Nissen, L. G., Widstrom, A. M., & Uvnas-Moberg, K. (2001). Maternal analgesia during labor disturbs newborn behavior: Effects on breastfeeding, temperature, and crying. *Birth, 28,* 5–12.

Rapaport, S. (1994, November 28). Interview. *U.S. News & World Report,* p. 94.

Rapport, M. D., Chung, K. M., Shore, G., & Issacs, P. (2001). A conceptual model of child psychopathology: Implications for understanding a deficit hyperactivity disorder and treatment effectiveness. *Journal of Clinical Child Psychology, 30,* 48–58.

Raudenbush, S. (2001). Longitudinal data analysis. *Annual Review of Psychology* (Vol. 52). Palo Alto, CA: Annual Reviews.

Raven, P. H., Johnson, G. B., Singer, S., & Loso, J. (2002). *Biology* (6th ed.). New York: McGraw-Hill.

Ray, O. S., & Ksir, C. (2002). *Drugs, society, and human behavior* (9th ed.). New York: McGraw-Hill.

Redinbaugh, E. M., MacCallum, J., & Kiecolt-Glaser, J. K. (1995). Recurrent syndromal depression in caregivers. *Psychology and Aging, 10,* 358–368.

Reid, J. D., & Willis, S. L. (1999). Middle age: New thoughts, new directions. In S. L. Willis & J. D. Reid (Eds.), *Life in the middle.* San Diego: Academic Press.

Reid, P. T., & Zalk, S. R. (2001). Academic environments: Gender and ethnicity in U.S. higher education. In J. Worell (Ed.), *Encyclopedia of women and gender.* San Diego: Academic Press.

Reifman, A. (2001). Models of parenting and adolescent drinking. *American Psychologist, 56,* 170–171.

Reis, D., Neiderhiser, J. M., Hetherington, E. M., & Plomin, R. (2000). *The relationship code.* Cambridge, MA: Harvard University Press.

Reisman, A. S. (2001). Death of a spouse: Basic assumptions and continuation of bonds. *Death Studies, 25,* 445–460.

Relier, J. P. (2001). Influence of maternal stress on fetal behavior and brain development. *Biology of the Neonate, 79,* 168–171.

Religion in America. (1993). Princeton, NJ: Princeton Religious Research Center.

Remafedi, G., Resnick, M., Blum, R., & Harris, L. (1992). Demography of sexual orientation in adolescents. *Pediatrics, 89* (4), 714–721.

Rest, J. (1999). *Postconventional moral thinking.* Mahwah, NJ: Erlbaum.

Reuter-Lorenz, P. (2002). New visions of the aging mind and brain. *Trends in Cognitive Science, 6,* 394.

Reuter-Lorenz, P. A., Jonides, J., Smith, E. S., Hartley, A., Miller, A., Marshuetz, C., et al. (2000). Age differences in the frontal lateralization of verbal and spatial working memory revealed by PET. *Journal of Cognitive Neuroscience, 12,* 174–187.

Reynolds, A. J. (1999, April). *Pathways to long-term effects in the Chicago Child-Parent Center Program.* Paper presented at the meeting of the Society for Research in Child Development, Albuquerque.

Rhodes, J. E., Grossman, J. B., & Resch, N. L. (2000). Agents of change: Pathways through which mentoring relationships influence adolescents' academic adjustment. *Child Development, 71,* 1662–1671.

Rhodes, S. R. (1983). Age-related differences in work attitudes and behavior: A review and conceptual analysis. *Psychological Bulletin, 93,* 329–367.

Rice, J. (2002). Family roles and patterns: Contemporary trends. In J. Worrel (Ed.), *Encyclopedia of women and gender.* San Diego: Academic Press.

Rickards, A. L., Kelly, E. A., Doyle, L. W., & Callahan, C. (2001). Cognition, academic progress, behavior, and self-concept at 14 years of very low birthweight children. *Journal of Developmental and Behavioral Pediatrics, 22,* 11–18.

Ridgeway, D., Waters, E., & Kuczaj, S. A. (1985). Acquisition of emotion-descriptive language: Receptive and productive vocabulary norms for ages 18 months to 6 years. *Developmental Psychology, 21,* 901–908.

Riegel, K. F., & Riegel, R. M. (1972). Development, drop, and death. *Developmental Psychology, 6,* 306–319.

Rigby, K. (2002). Bullying in childhood. In P. K. Smith & C. H. Hart (Eds.), *Blackwell handbook of childhood social development.* Malden, MA: Blackwell.

Rimberg, H. M., & Lewis, R. J. (1994). Older adolescents and AIDS: Correlates of self-reported safer sex practices. *Journal of Research on Adolescence, 4,* 453–464.

Rimm, E. B., Stampfer, M. J., Ascherio, A., Giovannucci, E., Colditz, G. A., & Willett, W. C. (1993). Vitamin E consumption and the risk of coronary heart disease in men. *New England Journal of Medicine, 328,* 1450–1456.

Ringdal, G. I., Jordhoy, M. S., Ringdal, K., & Kaasa, S. (2001). The first year of grief and bereavement in close family members to individuals who have died of cancer. *Palliative Medicine, 15,* 91–105.

Roberts, B. L., Dunkle, R., & Haug, M. (1994). Physical, psychological, and social resources as moderators of stress to mental health of the very old. *Journal of Gerontology, 49,* S35–S43.

Roberts, B. W., & Helson, R. (1997). Changes in culture, changes in personality: The influence of individualism in a longitudinal study of women. *Journal of Personality and Social Psychology, 72,* 641–651.

Robins, R. W., Trzesniewski, K. H., Tracey, J. L., Potter, J., & Gosling, S. D. (2002). Age differences in self-esteem from age 9 to 90. *Psychology and Aging, 17,* 423–434

Robinson, D. P., & Greene, J. W. (1988). The adolescent alcohol and drug problem: A practical approach. *Pediatric Nursing, 14,* 305–310.

Rochat, P. (2002). Origins of self concept. In G. Bremner & A. Fogel (Eds.), *The Blackwell handbook of infant development.* Malden, MA: Blackwell.

Rode, S. S., Chang, P., Fisch, R. O., & Sroufe, L. A. (1981). Attachment patterns of infants separated at birth. *Developmental Psychology, 17,* 188–191.

Rodin, J. (1983). Behavioral medicine: Beneficial effects of self-control training in aging. *International Review of Applied Psychology, 32,* 153–181.

Rodin, J. (1992). *Body traps.* New York: William Morrow.

Rodin, J., & Langer, E. J. (1977). Long-term effects of a control-relevant intervention with the institutionalized aged. *Journal of Personality and Social Psychology, 35,* 397–402.

Rogers, A. (1987). *Questions of gender differences: Ego development and moral voice in adolescence.* Unpublished manuscript, Department of Education, Harvard University.

Rogers, W. A., & Fisk, A. D. (2001). Attention in cognitive aging research. In J. E. Birren & K. W. Schaie (Eds.), *Handbook of the psychology of aging* (5th ed.). San Diego: Academic Press.

Rogoff, B. (1998). Cognition as a collaborative process. In W. Damon (Ed.), *Handbook of child psychology* (5th ed., Vol. 2). New York: Wiley.

Rogoff, B., Turkanis, C. G., & Bartlett, L. (Eds.) (2001). *Learning together.* New York: Oxford University Press.

Rohner, R. P., & Rohner, E. C. (1981). Parental acceptance-rejection and parental control: Cross-cultural codes. *Ethnology, 20,* 245–260.

Rook, K. S. (2000). The evolution of social relationships in later adulthood. In S. H. Qualls & N. Abeles (Eds.), *Psychology and the aging revolution.* Washington, DC: American Psychological Association.

Roopnarine, J. L., & Johnson, J. E. (2000). *Approaches to early childhood education.* Columbus, OH: Merrill.

Roosa, M. W., Dumka, L. E., Gonzales, N. A., & Knight, G. P. (2002). Cultural/ethnic issues and the prevention scientist in the 21st century. *Prevention & Treatment, 5,* 1–13.

Roper Starch Worldwide. (2000). *Attitudes toward retirement: A poll.* New York: Author.

Roscoe, L. A., Malphurs, J. E., Dragovic, L. J., & Cohen, D. (2002). A comparison of characteristics of Kevorkian euthanasia cases and physician-assisted suicides in Oregon. *The Gerontologist, 41,* 439–446.

Rose, A. A., Feldman, J. F., McCarton, C. M., & Wolfson, J. (1988). Information processing in seven-month-old infants as a function of risk status. *Child Development, 59,* 489–603.

Rose, L. C., & Gallup, A. M. (2000). The 32nd annual Phi Delta Kappa/Gallup Poll of the public's attitudes toward the public schools. *Phi Delta Kappan, 82* (No. 10), 41–58.

Rose, S., & Frieze, I. R. (1993). Young singles' contemporary dating scripts. *Sex Roles, 28,* 499–509.

Rosen, K. H., & Stith, S. M. (1995). Women terminating abusive dating relationships: A qualitative study. *Journal of Personal and Social Relationships, 12,* 155–160.

Rosenblith, J. F. (1992). *In the beginning* (2nd ed.). Newbury Park, CA: Sage.

Rosenfeld, A., & Stark, E. (1987, May). The prime of our lives. *Psychology Today.* pp. 62–72.

Rosenstein, D., & Oster, H. (1988). Differential facial responses to four basic tastes in newborns. *Child Development, 59,* 1555–1568.

Rosenthal, C. J., Martin-Matthews, A., & Matthews, S. H. (1996). Caught in the middle? Occupancy in multiple roles and help to parents in a national probability sample of Canadian adults. *Journal of Gerontology: Psychological Sciences and Social Sciences, 51B,* S274–S283.

Rosenzweig, M. R. (1969). Effects of heredity and environment on brain chemistry, brain anatomy, and learning ability in the rat. In M. Monosevitz, G. Lindzey, & D. D. Thiessen (Eds.), *Behavioral genetics.* New York: Appleton-Century-Crofts.

Rosenzweig, M. R. (2000). Ethology. In A. Kazdin (Ed.), *Encyclopedia of psychology.* Washington, DC, & New York: American Psychological Association and Oxford University Press.

Rosnow, R. L. (1995). Teaching research ethics through role-playing and discussion. In M. E. Ware & D. E. Johnson (Eds.), *Demonstrations and activities in teaching psychology* (Vol. 1). Mahwah, NJ: Erlbaum.

Rossi, A. S. (1989). A life-course approach to gender, aging, and intergenerational relations. In K. W. Schaie & C. Schooler (Eds.), *Social structure and aging.* Hillsdale, NJ: Erlbaum.

Roth, G. S., Lane, M. A., Ingram, D. K., Mattison, J. A., Elahi, D., Tobin, J. D., Muller, D., & Metter, E. J. (2002). Biomarkers of caloric restriction may predict longevity in humans. *Science, 297,* 811.

Roth, J., & Brooks-Gunn, J. (2000). What do adolescents need for healthy development? Implications for youth policy. *Social Policy Report, 14* (1), 3–19.

Rothbart, M. K., & Bates, J. E. (1998). Temperament. In W. Damon (Ed.), *Handbook of child psychology* (5th ed., Vol. 3). New York: Wiley.

Rothbart, M. K, & Putnam, S. P. (2002). Temperament and socialization. In L. Pulkkinen & A. Caspi (Eds.), *Paths to successful development.* New York: Cambridge University Press.

Rothbart, M. L. K. (1971). Birth order and mother-child interaction, *Dissertation Abstracts, 27,* 45–57.

Rothbaum, F., Poll, M., Azuma, H., Miyake, K., & Weisz, J. (2000). The development of close relationships in Japan and the United States: Paths of symbiotic harmony and generative tension. *Child Development, 71,* 1121–1142.

Rovee-Collier, C. (1987). Learning and memory in children. In J. D. Osofsky (Ed.), *Handbook of infant development* (2nd ed.). New York: Wiley.

Rovee-Collier, C. (2001). Infant learning and memory. In A. Fogel & G. Bremner (Eds.), *Blackwell handbook of infant development.* London: Blackwell.

Rovee-Collier, C., & Barr, R. (2002). Infant learning and memory. In G. Bremner &

A. Fogel (Eds.), *Blackwell handbook of infant development.* Malden, MA: Blackwell.

Rovira, M. T., Antorn, M. T., Paya, A., Castellanos, E., Mur, A., & Carreras, R. (2001). Human immunodeficiency virus infection in pregnant women, transmission, and zidovudine therapy. *European Journal of Obstetrics, Gynecology, and Reproductive Biology, 97,* 46–49.

Rowe, D. C. (2001). The nurture assumption persists. *American Psychologist, 56,* 168–169.

Rowe, J. W., & Kahn, R. L. (1997). *Successful aging.* New York: Pantheon Books.

Rowe, J. W., & Kahn, R. L. (1998). *Successful aging.* New York: Pantheon Books.

Rowe, S. M., & Wertsch, J. V. (2002). Vygotsky's model of cognitive development. In U. Goswami (Ed.), *Blackwell handbook of childhood cognitive development.* Malden, MA: Blackwell.

Rubenstein, L. Z., Josephson, K. R., Trueblood, P. R., Loy, S., Harker, J. O., Pietruszka, F. M., & Robbins, A. S. (2000). Effects of group exercise program on strength, mobility, and falls among fall-prone elderly men. *Journal of Gerontology: Medical Sciences, 55A,* M317–M321.

Rubin, D. H., Krasilnikoff, P. A., Leventhal, J. M., Weile, B., & Berget, A. (1986, August 23). Effect of passive smoking on birthweight. *The Lancet,* 415–417.

Rubin, K. (2000). Middle childhood: Social and emotional development. In A. Kazdin (Ed.), *Encyclopedia of psychology.* Washington, DC, & New York: American Psychological Association and Oxford University Press.

Rubin, K. H., Maioni, T. L., & Hornung, M. (1976). Free play behaviors in middle and lower social class preschoolers: Parten and Piaget revisited. *Child Development, 47,* 414–419.

Rubin, S. (1995). On life after the death of a son in war: Theory and research with the two-track model of bereavement. *Psychology: Israel Journal, 5* (1), 70–84.

Rubin, Z. (1970). Measurement of romantic love. *Journal of Personality and Social Psychology, 16,* 265–273.

Rubin, Z., & Mitchell, C. (1976). Couples research as couples counseling. *American Psychologist, 31,* 17–25.

Ruble, D. (2000). Gender constancy. In A. Kazdin (Ed.), *Encyclopedia of psychology.* Washington, DC., and New York: American Psychological Association and Oxford University Press.

Rudolph, K. L., Chang, S., Lee, H., Gottlieb, G. J., Greider, C., & DePinho, R. A. (1999). Longevity, stress response, and cancer in aging telomerase-deficient mice. *Cell, 96,* 701–712.

Rumberger, R. W. (1995). Dropping out of middle school: A multilevel analysis of students and schools. *American Educational Research Journal, 3,* 583–625.

Runco, M. (2000). Research on the processes of creativity. In A. Kazdin (Ed.), *Encyclopedia of psychology.* Washington, DC, & New York: American Psychological Association and Oxford University Press.

Rusbult, C. E., Olsen, N., Davis, J. L., & Hannon, P. A. (2001). Commitment and relationship maintenance mechanisms. In J. H. Harvey & A. Wenzel (Eds.), *Close romantic relationships.* Mahwah, NJ: Erlbaum.

Russek, L. G., & Schwartz, G. E. (1997). Feelings of parental caring predict health status in midlife: A 35-year follow-up of the Harvard Mastery Study of Stress. *Journal of Behavioral Medicine, 30,* 1–13.

Russell, D. W. (1996). UCLA Loneliness Scale (Version 3): Reliability, validity and factor structure. *Journal of Personality, Assessment, 66,* 20–43.

Russell, S. T., & Joyner, K. (2001). Adolescent and suicide risk: evidence from a national study. *American Journal of Public Health, 91,* 1276–1281.

Rutter, M. (2002). Nature, nurture, and development: From evangelism through science toward policy and practice. *Child Development, 73,* 1–21.

Ryan, A. S. (1997). The resurgence of breastfeeding in the United States. *Pediatrics, 99,* E-12.

Ryan, R. M., & La Guardia, J. G. (2000). What is being optimized?: Self-determination theory and basic psychological needs. In S. H. Qualls & N. Abeles (Eds.), *Psychology and the aging revolution.* Washington, DC: American Psychological Association.

Ryff, C. D. (1984). Personality development from the inside: The subjective experience of change in adulthood and aging. In P. B. Baltes & O. G. Brim (Eds.), *Life-span development and behavior.* New York: Academic Press.

Ryff, C. D. (1991). Possible selves in adulthood and old age: A tale of shifting horizons. *Psychology and Aging, 6,* 286–295.

Ryff, C. D., & Keyes, C. L. M. (1995). The Structure of Psychological Well-Being Revisited. *Journal of Personality and Social Psychology, 69,* 719–727.

Ryff, C. D., & Singer, B. (2000). Interpersonal flourishing: A positive health agenda for the new millennium. *Personality and Social Psychology Review, 4,* 30–44.

Ryff, C. D., Singer, B., Wing, E. H., & Love, G. D. (2001). Elective affinities and uninvited agonies: Mapping emotion with significant others onto health. In C. D. Ryff & B. Singer (Eds.), *Emotion, social relationships, and health.* New York: Oxford University Press.

S

Saarni, C. (1999). *The development of emotional competence.* New York: Guilford.

Sabini, J. (1995). *Social psychology* (2nd ed.). New York: Norton.

Saczynski, J. S., Willis, S. L., & Schaie, K. W. (1999, November). *Cognitive training effects in normal, non-demented elderly: Associated variables and maintenance of training gains.* Paper presented at the meeting of the Gerontological Society of America, San Francisco.

Sadavoy, J., Lazarus, L. W., Jarvik, L. E., & Grossberg, G. T. (Eds.). (1996). *Comprehensive review of geriatric psychiatry* (2nd ed.). Washington, DC: American Psychiatric Press.

Sadker, M. P., & Sadker, D. M. (2003). *Teachers, schools, and society* (6th ed.). New York: McGraw-Hill.

Sagan, C. (1977). *The dragons of Eden.* New York: Random House.

Salkind, N. J. (2003). *Exploring research* (5th ed.). Upper Saddle River, NJ: Prentice Hall.

Salovy, P., & Mayer, J. D. (1990). Emotional intelligence. Imagination, *Cognition, and Personality, 9,* 185–211.

Salthouse, T. A. (1991). *Theoretical perspectives on cognitive aging.* Mahwah, NJ: Erlbaum.

Salthouse, T. A. (1994). The aging of working memory. *Neuropsychology, 8,* 535–543.

Salthouse, T. A. (1994). The nature of influence of speed on adult age differences in cognition. *Developmental Psychology, 30,* 240–259.

Salthouse, T. A. (1996). General and specific speed mediation of adult age differences in memory. *Journal of Gerontology, 51A,* P30–P42.

Salthouse, T. A. (2000). Adulthood and aging: Cognitive processes and development. In A. Kazdin (ed.), *Encyclopedia of psychology.* Washington, DC, & New York: American Psychological Association and Oxford University Press.

Salthouse, T. A., & Miles, J. D. (2002). Aging and time-sharing aspects of executive control. *Memory and Cogniton, 30,* 572–582

Salthouse, T. A., & Skovronek, E. (1992). Within-context assessment of working memory. *Journal of Gerontology, 47,* P110–P117.

Samaniego, R. Y., & Gonzales, N. A. (1999). Multiple mediators of the effects of acculturation status on delinquency for Mexican American adolescents. *American Journal of Community Psychology, 27,* 189–210.

Samour, P. Q., Helm, K. K., & Lang, C. E. (Eds.). (2000). *Handbook of pediatric nutrition* (2nd ed.). Aspen, CO: Aspen.

Samuels, M., & Samuels, N. (1996). *New well pregnancy book.* New York: Fireside.

Sands, R. G., & Goldberg-Glen, R. S. (2000). Factors associated with stress among grandparents raising their grandchildren. *Family Relations, 49,* 97–105.

Sangree, W. H. (1989). Age and power: Life-course trajectories and age structuring of power relations in East and West Africa. In D. I. Kertzer & K. W. Schaie (Eds.), *Age structuring in comparative perspective.* Hillsdale, NJ: Erlbaum.

Sanson, A., & Rothbart, M. K. (1995). Child temperament and parenting. In M. H. Bornstein (Ed.), *Handbook of parenting* (Vol. 4). Hillsdale, NJ: Erlbaum.

Santacruz, K. S., & Swagerty, D. (2001). Early diagnosis of dementia. *American Family Physician, 63,* 703–13.

Santiseban, D. A., & Mitrani, V. B. (2003). The influence of acculturation processes on the family. In K. M. Chun, P. B. Organista, & G. Marin (Eds.), *Acculturation.* Washington, DC: American Psychological Association.

Santrock, J. W. (2001). *Educational Psychology.* New York: McGraw-Hill.

Santrock, J. W., & Halonen, J. A. (2002). *Your guide to college success* (2nd ed.). Belmont, CA: Wadsworth.

Santrock, J. W., Sitterle, K. A., & Warshak, R. A. (1988). Parent-child relationships in stepfather families. In P. Bronstein & C. P. Cowan (Eds.), *Fatherhood today: Men's changing roles in the family.* New York: Wiley.

Santrock, J. W., & Warshak, R. A. (1979). Father custody and social development in boys and girls. *Journal of Social Issues, 35,* 112–125.

Saraswathi, T. S., & Mistry, J. (2003). The cultural context of child development. In I. B. Weiner (Ed.), *Handbook of psychology* (Vol. VI). New York: Wiley.

Sarigiani, P. A., & Petersen, A. C. (2000). Adolescence: Puberty and biological maturation. In A. Kazdin (Ed.), *Encyclopedia of psychology*. Washington, DC, & New York: American Psychological Association and Oxford University Press.

Sarrel, P., & Masters, W. (1982). Sexual molestation of men by women. *Archives of Human Sexuality, 11*, 117–131.

Sauber, M., & Corrigan, E. M. (1970). *The six year experience of unwed mothers as parents*. New York: Community Council of Greater New York.

Savin-Williams, R. C. (2001). *Mom, dad, I'm gay*. Washington, DC: American Psychological Association.

Sax, L. J., Astin, A. W., Korn, W. S., & Mahoney, K. M. (2000). *The American freshman: National norms for fall 2000*. Los Angeles: UCLA, Higher Education Research Institute.

Sax, L. J., Lindholm, J. A., Astin, A. W., Korn, W. S., & Mahoney, K. M. (2001). *The American freshman: National norms for fall 2001*. Los Angeles: Higher Education Research Institute, UCLA.

Scafidi, F., & Field, T. M. (1996). Massage therapy improves behavior in neonates born to HIV-positive mothers. *Journal of Pediatric Psychology, 21*, 889–897.

Scarr, S. (1984, May). Interview. *Psychology Today*. pp. 59–63.

Scarr, S. (1993). Biological and cultural diversity: The legacy of Darwin for development. *Child Development, 64*, 1333–1353.

Scarr, S. (2000). Day care. In A. Kazdin (Ed.), *Encyclopedia of Psychology*. Washington, DC, & New York: American Psychological Association and Oxford University Press.

Scarr, S., & Weinberg, R. A. (1980). Calling all camps! The war is over. *American Sociological Review, 45*, 859–865.

Scarr, S., & Weinberg, R. A. (1983). The Minnesota adoption studies: Genetic differences and malleability. *Child Development, 54*, 253–259.

Schachter, S. C., & Ransil, B. J. (1996). Handedness distributions in nine professional groups. *Perceptual and Motor Skills, 82*, 51–63.

Schaffer, H. R. (1996). *Social development*. Cambridge, MA: Blackwell.

Schaie, K. W. (1993). The Seattle longitudinal studies of adult intelligence. *Current Directions in Psychological Science, 2*, 171–175.

Schaie, K. W. (1994). The life course of adult intellectual abilities. *American Psychologist, 49*, 304–313.

Schaie, K. W. (1996). *Intellectual development in adulthood: The Seattle Longitudinal Study*. New York: Cambridge University Press.

Schaie, K. W. (2000). Unpublished review of J. W. Santrock's *Life-span development*, 8th ed. (New York: McGraw-Hill).

Schaie, K. W., & Willis, S. L. (2000). A stage theory model of adult development revisited. In R. Rubinstein, M. Moss, & M. Kleban (Eds.), *The many dimensions of aging: Essays in honor of M. Powell Lawton*. New York: Springer.

Schaie, K. W., & Willis, S. L. (2001). *Adult development and aging* (5th ed.). Upper Saddle River, NJ: Prentice Hall.

Schalagar, B. L., Brown, T. T., Lugar, H. M., Visscher, K. M., Miezin, F. M., & Petersen, S. E. (2002). Functional neuroanatomical differences between adults and school-age children in processing single words. *Science, 296*, 1476–1479.

Scheer, S. D., & Unger, D. G. (1994, February). *Adolescents becoming adults: Attributes for adulthood*. Paper presented at the meeting of the Society for Research on Adolescence, San Diego.

Schiffman, S. S. (1996). Smell and taste. In J. E. Birren (Ed.), *Encyclopedia of gerontology*. San Diego: Academic Press.

Schlegel, M. (2000). All work and play. *Monitor on Psychology, 31* (11), 50–51.

Schneider, B. H., Atkinson, L., & Tardif, C. (2001). Child-parent attachment and children's peer relations: A quantitative review. *Developmental Psychology, 37*, 86–100.

Schneider, W. (2002). Memory development in children. In U. Goswami (Ed.), *Blackwell handbook of childhood cognitive development*. Malden, MA: Oxford University Press.

Schneider, W., & Pressley, M. (1997). *Memory development from 2 to 20* (2nd ed.). Mahwah, NJ: Erlbaum.

Schnorr, T. M., & others. (1991). Video-display terminals and the risk of spontaneous abortion. *New England Journal of Medicine, 324*, 727–733.

Schoendorf, K. C., & Kiely, J. L. (1992). Relationship of sudden infant death syndrome to maternal smoking during and after pregnancy. *Pediatrics, 90*, 905–908.

Schoka, E., & Hayslip, B. (1999, November). *Grief and the family system: The roles of communication, affect, and cohesion*. Paper presented at the meeting of the Gerontological Society of America, San Francisco.

Schooler, C. (2001). The intellectual effects of the demands of the work environment. In R. J. Sternberg & E. L. Grigorenko (Eds.), *Environmental effects on cognitive abilities*. Mahwah, NJ: Erlbaum.

Schooler, C., Mulatu, S., & Oates, G. (1999). The continuing effects of substantively complex work on the intellectual functioning of older workers. *Psychology and Aging, 14*, 483–506.

Schrag, S. G., & Dixon, R. L. (1985). Occupational exposure associated with male reproductive dysfunction. *Annual Review of Pharmacology and Toxicology, 25*, 467–592.

Schroots, J. J. F. (1996). Time: Concepts and perceptions. In J. E. Birren (Ed.), *Encyclopedia of gerontology* (Vol. 2). San Diego: Academic Press.

Schrum, L., & Berenfeld, B. (1997). *Teaching and learning in the information age: A guide to telecommunications*. Boston: Allyn & Bacon.

Schuchter, S., & Zisook, S. (1993). The course of normal grief. In M. Stroebe, W. Stroebe, & R. O. Hanson (Eds.), *Handbook of bereavement*. New York: Cambridge University Press.

Schugens, M. M., Daum, I., Spindler, M., & Birbaumer, N. (1997). Differential effects of aging on explicit and implicit memory. *Aging, Neuropsychology, and Cognition, 4*, 33–44.

Schulenberg, J. (1999, June). *Binge drinking trajectories before, during, and after college: More reasons to worry from a developmental perspective*. Invited paper presented at the meeting of the American Psychological Society, Denver.

Schulenberg, J., & Maggs, J. L. (in press). A developmental perspective on alcohol use and heavy drinking during adolescence and the transition to early adulthood. *NIAAA Monographs*.

Schulenberg, J., O'Malley, P. M., Bachman, J. G., & Johnson, L. D. (2000). "Spread your wings and fly": The course of health and well-being during the transition to young adulthood. In L. Crockett & R. Silbereisen (Eds.), *Negotiating adolescence in times of social change*. New York: Cambridge University Press.

Schultz, R. (1976). Effects of control and predictability on the physical and psychological well-being of the institutionalized aged. *Journal of Personality and Social Psychology, 33*, 563–573.

Schultz, R., & Curnow, C. (1988). Peak performance and age among super athletes: Track and field, swimming, baseball, tennis, and golf. *Journal of Gerontology, 43*, P113–P120.

Schultz, R., & Hanusa, B. H. (1978). Long-term effects of control and predictability-enhancing interventions: Findings and ethical issues. *Journal of Personality and Social Psychology, 11*, 1194–1201.

Schum, T. R., Kolb, T. M., McAuliffe, T. L., Simms, M. D., Underhill, R. L., & Lewis, M. (2002). Sequential acquisition of toilet-training skills: A descriptive study of gender and age differences in normal children. *Pediatrics, 109,* E-48.

Schum, T. R., McAuliffe, T. L., Simms, M. D., Walter, J. A., Lewis, M., & Pupp, R. (2001). Factors associated with toilet training in the 1990s. *Ambulatory Pediatrics, 1,* 79–86.

Schwartz, D., & Mayaux, M. J. (1982). Female fecundity as a function of age: Results of artificial insemination in nulliparous women with azoospermic husbands. *New England Journal of Medicine, 306,* 304–406.

Schwarzer, R., & Schultz, U. (2003). Stressful life events. In I. B. Weiner (Ed.), *Handbook of psychology,* Vol. IX. New York: Wiley.

Schweitzer, J. B., Cummins, T. K., & Kant, C. A. (2001). Attention deficit hyperactivity disorder. *Medical Clinics of North America, 85,* 757–777.

Schwerha, D. J., & McMullin, D. L. (2002). Prioritizing ergonomic research in aging for the 21st century American workforce. *Experimental Aging Research, 28,* 99–110.

Schwitzer, A. M., Rodriquez, L. E., Thomas, C., & Salami, L. (2001). The eating disorders NOS profile among college women. *Journal of American College Health, 49,* 157–166.

Scott-Jones, D. (1995, March). *Incorporating ethnicity and socioeconomic status in research with children.* Paper presented at the meeting of the Society for Research in Child Development, Indianapolis.

Sears, R. R., & Feldman, S. S. (Eds.). (1973). *The seven ages of man.* Los Altos, CA: Kaufmann.

Seeman, T. E., Charpentier, P. A., Berkman, L. F., Tinetti, M. E., Guralnik, J. M., Albert, M., Blazer, D., & Rowe, J. W. (1994). Predicting changes in physical performance in a high-functioning elderly cohort: MacArthur Studies of Successful Aging. *Journal of Gerontology, 49,* M97–M108.

Seeman, T. E., & Chen, X. (2002). Risk and protective factors for physical functioning in older adults with and without chronic conditions: MacArthur Studies of Successful Aging. *Journal of Gerontology: Social Sciences, 57B,* S135–S144.

Segerberg, O. (1982). *Living to be 100: 1200 who did and how they did it.* New York: Scribner's.

Seidman, E. (2000). School transitions. In A. Kazdin (Ed.), *Encyclopedia of psychology.* Washington, DC, & New York: American Psychological Association and Oxford University Press.

Seifert, L. S. (2002). Toward a psychology of religion, spirituality, meaning-search, and aging: Past research and practical application. *Journal of Adult Development, 9,* 61–78.

Semba, R. D., & Neville, M. C. (1999). Breast-feeding, mastitis, and HIV transmission: Nutritional implications. *Nutrition Review, 57,* 146–153.

Seroczynski, A. D., Jacquez, F. M., & Cole, D. (2003). Depression and suicide during adolescence. In G. Adams & M. Berzonsky (Eds.), *Blackwell handbook of adolescence.* Malden, MA: Blackwell.

Serpell, R. (2000). Determinants of intelligence: Culture and intelligence. In A. Kazdin (Ed.), *Encyclopedia of psychology.* Washington, DC, & New York: American Psychological Association and Oxford University Press.

Sharkey, W. (1993). Who embarrasses whom? Relational and sex differences in the use of intentional embarrassment. In P. J. Kalbfleisch (Ed.), *Interpersonal communication.* Mahwah, NJ: Erlbaum.

Sharma, A. R., McGue, M. K., & Benson, P. L. (1996). The emotional and behavioral adjustment of adopted adolescents. Part I: Age at adoption. *Children and Youth Services Review, 18,* 101–114.

Sharma, A. R., McGue, M. K., & Benson, P. L. (1998). The psychological adjustment of United States adopted adolescents and their nonadopted siblings. *Child Development, 69,* 791–802.

Sharp, E. A., & Ganong, L. H. (2000). Awareness about expectations: Are unrealistic beliefs changed by integrative teaching. *Family Relations, 49,* 71–76.

Shaughnessy, J. J., Zechmeister, E. B., & Zechmeister, J. S. (2003). *Research methods in psychology* (6th ed.). New York: McGraw-Hill.

Shaver, P. (1986, August). *Being lonely, falling in love: Perspectives from attachment theory.* Paper presented at the meeting of the American Psychological Association, Washington, DC.

Shaver, P. R., & Hazan, C. (1993). Adult romantic attachment: Theory and evidence. In W. H. Jones & D. Perlman (Eds.), *Advances in personal relationships.* London: Jessica Kingsley.

Shaw, G. M. (2001). Adverse human reproductive outcomes and electromagnetic fields. *Bioelectromagnetics, 5,* (Suppl.), S5–S18.

Shay, J. W., & Wright, W. E. (1999). Telomeres and telomerase in the regulation of cellular aging. In V. A. Bohr, B. F. Clark, & T. Stevenser (Eds.), *Molecular biology of aging.* Copenhagen, Denmark: Munksgaard.

Shay, J. W., & Wright, W. E. (2000). The use of telomerized cells for tissue engineering. *Nature Biotechnology, 18,* 22–23.

Sheehan, M. K., & Twaddle, M. (2002). *Caring, 10 (10),* 10–11.

Sheehy, G. (1991). *The silent passage.* New York: Random House.

Sheldon, T. (2002). World Medical Association isolates Netherlands on euthanasia. *British Medical Journal, 325,* 675.

Shepard, G. H. (2002). Three days for weeping: dreams, emotions, and death in Peruvian Amazon. *Medical Anthropology Quarterly, 16,* 200–209.

Sherwood, A., Light, K. C., & Blumenthal, J. A. (1989). Effects of aerobic exercise training on hemodynamic responses during psychosocial stress in normotensive and borderline hypertensive Type A men: A preliminary report. *Psychosomatic Medicine, 51,* 123–136.

Shields, S. A. (1991). Gender in the psychology of emotion: A selective research review. In K. T. Strongman (Ed.), *International review of studies on emotion.* (Vol.) New York: Wiley.

Shields, S. A., & Eyssell, K. M. (2001). History of the study of gender psychology. In J. Worell (Ed.), *Encyclopedia of women and gender.* San Diego: Academic Press.

Shiono, P. H., & Behrman, R. E. (1995, spring). Low birth weight: Analysis and recommendations. *Future of Children, 5* (1), 4–18.

Shiraev, E., & Levy, D. (2001). *Introduction to cross-cultural psychology.* Boston: Allyn & Bacon.

Shneidman, E. S. (1973). *Deaths of man.* New York: Quadrangle/New York Times.

Shonk, S. M., & Cicchetti, D. (2001). Maltreatment, competency deficits, and risk for academic and behavioral maladjustment, *Developmental Psychology, 37,* 3–17.

Siegel, L. S. (1989, April). *Perceptual-motor, cognitive, and language skills as predictors of cognitive abilities at school age.* Paper presented at the biennial meeting of the Society for Research in Children, Kansas City.

Siegel, L. S. (2003). Learning disabilities. In I. B. Weiner (Ed.), *Handbook of psychology* (Vol. VII). New York: Wiley.

Siegfried, T. (1995, April 8). Seeing big picture will be key to solving Alzheimer's puzzle. *Dallas Morning News,* p. 7D.

Siegler, I. C., Bosworth, H. B., & Poon, L. W. (2003). Disease, health, and aging. In I. B. Weiner (Ed.), *Handbook of psychology* (Vol. VI). New York: Wiley.

Siegler, I. C., & Costa, P. T. (1999, August). *Personality change and continuity in midlife: UNC Alumni Heart Study.* Paper presented at the meeting of the American Psychological Association, Boston.

Siegler, I. C., Kaplan, B. H., Von Dras, D. D, & Mark, D. B. (1999). Cardiovascular health: A challenge for midlife. In S. L. Willis & J. D. Reid (Eds.), *Life in the Middle: Psychological and social development in middle age.* San Diego: Academic Press.

Siegler, R. S. (1998). *Children's thinking* (3rd ed.). Upper Saddle River, NJ: Prentice Hall.

Siegler, R. S. (2001). Children's discoveries and brain-damaged patients' rediscoveries. In J. L. McClelland & R. J. Siegler (Eds.), *Mechanisms of cognitive development.* Mahwah, NJ: Erlbaum.

Signore, C. (2001). Rubella. *Primary Care Update in Obstetrics and Gynecology, 8,* 133–137.

Silfverdal, S. A., Bodin, L., Ulanova, M., Hahn-Zoric, M., Hanson, L. A., & Olcen, P. (2002). Long term enhancement of the IgG2 antibody response to Haemophilus influenzae type b by breast-feeding. *Pediatric Infectuous Disease Journal, 21,* 816–822.

Silverstein, L. B. (2001). Father and families. In J. P. McHale & W. S. Grolnick (Eds.), *Retrospect and prospect in the psychological study of families.* Mahwah, NJ: Erlbaum.

Silverstein, M., Conroy, S. J., Wang, H., Giarrusso, R., & Bengston, V. L. (2002). Reciprocity in parent-child relation over the adult life course. *Journal of Gerontology: Psychological Sciences and Social Sciences, 57B,* S3–S13.

Simmons, R. G., & Blyth, D. A. (1987). *Moving into adolescence.* Hawthorne, NY: Aldine.

Simons, J., Finlay, B., & Yang, A. (1991). *The adolescent and young adult fact book.* Washington, DC: Children's Defense Fund.

Simons-Morton, B., Haynie, D. L., Crump, A. D., Eitel, P., & Saylor, K. E. (2001). Peer and parent influences on smoking and drinking among early adolescents. *Health Education & Behavior, 28,* 95–107.

Simonton, D. K. (1996). Creativity. In J. E. Birren (Ed.), *Encyclopedia of aging.* San Diego: Academic Press.

Singer, D. G. (1993). Creativity of children in a changing world. In G. L. Berry & J. K. Asamen (Eds.), *Children and television: Images in a changing sociocultural world.* Newbury Park, CA: Sage.

Singer, L. T., Arendt, R., Fagan, J., Minnes, S., Salvator, A., Bolek, T., & Becker, M. (1999). Neonatal visual information processing in cocaine-exposed and non-exposed infants. *Infant Behavior and Development, 22,* 1–15.

Singh, M. A. F. (2002). Exercise comes of age: Rationale and recommendations for a geriatric exercise prescription. *Journal of Gerontology: Medical Sciences, 57A,* M262–M282.

Singh, N. A., Clements, K. M., & Fiatarone, M. A. (1997). A randomized controlled trial of progressive resistance training in depressed elders. *Journal of Gerontology, 52A,* M27–M35.

Singh, S., Wulf, D., Samara, R., & Cuca, Y. P. (2000). Gender differences in the timing of first intercourse: Data from 14 countries. *International Family Planning Perspectives, 26,* 21–28, 43.

Skinner, B. F. (1938). *The behavior of organisms: An experimental analysis.* New York: Appelton-Century-Crofts.

Skinner, B. F. (1957). *Verbal behavior.* New York: Appelton-Century-Crofts.

Skoog, I., Blennow, K., & Marcusson, J. (1996). Dementia. In J. E. Birren (Ed.), *Encyclopedia of gerontology* (Vol. 1). San Diego: Academic Press.

Slater, A. (2001). Visual perception. In A. Fogel & G. Bremner (Eds.), *Blackwell handbook of infant development.* London: Blackwell.

Slater, A., Field, T., & Hernandez-Reif, M. (2002). The development of the senses. In A. Slater & M. Lewis (Eds.), *Infant development.* New York: Oxford University Press.

Slater, A., Morison, V., & Somers, M. (1988). Orientation discrimination and cortical function in the human newborn. *Perception, 17,* 597–602.

Slobin, D. (1972, July) Children and language: They learn the same way all around the world. *Psychology Today,* pp. 71–76.

Slomkowski, C., Rende, R., Conger, K. J., Simons, R. L., & Conger, R. D. (2001). Sisters, brothers, and delinquency: Social influence during early and middle adolescence. *Child Development, 72,* 271–283.

Small, S. A. (1990). *Preventive programs that support families with adolescents.* Washington, DC: Carnegie Council on Adolescent Development.

Smith, A. D. (1996). Memory. In J. E. Birren (Ed.), *Encyclopedia of gerontology* (Vol. 2). San Diego: Academic Press.

Smith, J., & Baltes, P. B. (1990). Wisdom-related knowledge: Age-cohort differences in responses to life-planning problems. *Developmental Psychology, 26,* 494–505.

Smith, L., & Hattersley, J. (2000). *The smart guide to preventing SIDS.* New York: Smart.

Smith, L. M., Chang, L., Yonekura, M. L., Gilbride, K., Kuo, J., Poland, R. E., Walot, I., & Ernst, T. (2001). Brain proton magnetic resonance spectroscopy and imaging in children exposed to cocaine in utero. *Pediatrics, 107,* 227.

Smith, M. A., Sayre, L. M., Monnier, V. M., & Perry, G. (1995). Radical aging in Alzheimer's disease. *Trends in Neuroscience, 18,* 172–176.

Smith, P. K., & Drew, L. M. (2002). Grandparenthood. In M. H. Bornstein (Ed.), *Handbook of parenting* (2nd ed.). Mahwah, NJ: Erlbaum.

Smith, P. K., & others. (2002). Definitions of bullying: A comparison of terms used, and age and gender differences, in a fourteen-country international comparison. *Child Development, 73,* 1119–1133.

Smolak, L., & Striegel-Moore, R. (2002). Body image concerns. In J. Worell (Ed.), *Encyclopedia of women and gender.* San Diego: Academic Press.

Snarey, J. (1987, June). A question of morality. *Psychology Today,* pp. 6–8.

Snowden, D. A. (1995). *An epidemiological study of aging in a select population and its relationship to Alzheimer's disease.* Unpublished manuscript, Sanders Brown Center on Aging, Lexington, KY.

Snowden, D. A. (1997). Aging and Alzheimer's disease: Lessons from the nun study. *Gerontologist, 37,* 150–156.

Snowden, L. R., & Cheung, F. K. (1990). Use of inpatient mental health services by members of ethnic minority groups. *American Psychologist, 45,* 347–355.

Snyder, H. N., & Sickmund, M. (1999, October). *Juvenile offenders and victims: 1999 national report.* Washington, DC: National Center for Juvenile Justice.

Soederberg Miller, L. M., & Lachman, M. (1999, August). *Stress reactivity and cognitive performance in adulthood.* Paper presented at the annual meeting of the American Psychological Association, Boston.

Sokal, L., & Seifert, K. (2001, April). *Gender schematic development within the family context.* Paper presented at the meeting of the Society for Research in Child Development, Minneapolis.

Soldo, B. J. (1996). Cross-pressures on middle-aged adults: A broader view. *Journal of*

Gerontology: Psychological Sciences and Social Sciences, 51B, S271–S273.

Sollod, R. N. (2000). Religious and spiritual practices. In A. Kazdin (Ed.), *Encyclopedia of psychology.* Washington, DC, & New York: American Psychological Association and Oxford University Press.

Sommer, B. (2001). Menopause. In J. Worell (Ed.), *Encyclopedia of women and gender.* San Diego: Academic Press.

Soong, W. T., Chao, K. Y., Jang, C. S., & Wang, J. D. (1999). Long-term effect of increased lead absorption on intelligence of children. *Archives of Environmental Health, 54,* 297–301.

Sorokin, P. (2002). New agents and future directions in biotherapy. *Clinical Journal of Oncological Nursing, 6,* 19–24.

Sowter, B., Doyle, L. W., Morley, C. J., Altmann, A., & Halliday, J. (1999). Is sudden infant death syndrome still more common in very low birth weight infants in the 1990s? *Medical Journal of Australia, 171,* 411–413.

Spear, H. J., & Kulbok, P. A. (2001). Adolescent health behaviors and related factors: A review. *Public Health Nursing, 18,* 82–93.

Spearman, C. E. (1927). *The abilities of man.* New York: Macmillan.

Spelke, E. S. (1979). Perceiving bimodally specified events in infancy. *Developmental Psychology, 5,* 626–636.

Spelke, E. S. (1988). The origins of physical knowledge. In L. Weiskrantz (Ed.), *Thought Without Language.* New York: Oxford University Press.

Spelke, E. S. (1991). Physical knowledge in infancy: Reflections on Piaget's theory. In S. Carey & R. Gelman (Eds.), *The epigenesis of mind: Essays on biology and cognition.* Hillsdale, NJ: Erlbaum.

Spelke, E. S., & Newport, E. L. (1998). Nativism, empiricism, and the development of knowledge. In W. Damon (Ed.), *Handbook of child psychology* (5th ed., Vol. 2). New York: Wiley.

Spelke, E. S., & Owsley, C. J. (1979). Intermodal exploration and knowledge in infancy. *Infant Behavior and Development, 2,* 13–28.

Spence, A. P. (1989). *Biology of human aging.* Englewood Cliffs, NJ: Prentice Hall.

Spence, J. T., & Buckner, C. E. (2000). Instrumental and expressive traits, trait stereotypes, and sexist attitudes: What do they signify? *Psychology of Women Quarterly, 24,* 44–62.

Spence, J. T., & Helmreich, R. (1978). *Masculinity and femininity: Their psychological dimensions.* Austin: University of Texas Press.

Spence, M. J., & DeCasper, A. J. (1987). Prenatal experience with low-frequency maternal voice sounds influences neonatal perception of maternal voice samples. *Infant Behavior and Development, 10,* 133–142.

Spencer, M. B. (1990). Commentary in Spencer, M. B., & Dornbusch, S. Challenges in studying ethnic minority youth. In S. S. Feldman & G. R. Elliott (Eds.), *At the threshold: The developing adolescent.* Cambridge, MA: Harvard University Press.

Spencer, M. B. (1999). Social and cultural influences on school adjustment: The application of an identity-focused cultural ecological perspective. *Educational Psychologist, 34,* 43–57.

Spencer, M. B., & Dornbusch, S. M. (1990). Challenges in studying minority youth. In S. S. Feldman & G. R. Elliott (Eds.), *At the threshold: The developing adolescent.* Cambridge, MA: Harvard University Press.

Spencer, M. B., Noll, E., Stoltzfuz, J., & Harpalani, V. (2001). Identity and school adjustment: Revisiting the "acting white" assumption. *Educational Psychologist, 36,* 21–30.

Spielberger, C. D., & Grier, K. (1983). Unpublished manuscript, University of South Florida, Tampa.

Spiro, A. (2001). Health in midlife: Toward a lifespan view. In M. E. Lachman (Ed.), *Handbook of midlife development.* New York: John Wiley.

Sprei, J. E., & Courtois, C. A. (1988). The treatment of women's sexual dysfunctions arising from sexual assault. In R. A. Brown & J. R. Fields (Eds.), *Treatment of sexual problems in individual and couples therapy.* Great Neck, NY: PMA.

Spring, J. (1998). *The intersection of cultures.* New York: McGraw-Hill.

Springer, S. P., & Deutsch, G. (1985). *Left brain, right brain.* San Francisco: Freeman.

Sroufe, L. A. (2000, Spring). The inside scoop on child development: Interview. *Cutting through the hype.* Minneapolis: College of Education and Human Development, University of Minnesota.

Sroufe, L. A. (2001). From infant attachment to adolescent autonomy: Longitudinal data on the role of parents in development. In J. Borkowski, S. Ramey, & M. Bristol-Power (Eds.), *Parenting and your child's world.* Mahwah, NJ: Erlbaum.

Sroufe, L. A., Egeland, B., & Carlson, E. A. (1999). One social world: The integrated development of parent-child and peer relationships. In W. A. Collins & B. Laursen (Eds.), *Minnesota symposium on child psychology,* vol. 31. Mahwah, NJ: Erlbaum.

Sroufe, L. A., & Waters, E. (1976). The ontogenesis of smiling and laughter: A perspective on the organization of development in infancy. *Psychological Review, 83,* 173–198.

Sroufe, L. A., Waters, E., & Matas, L. (1974). Contextual determinants of infant affectional response. In M. Lewis & L. Rosenblum (Eds.), *Origins of fear.* New York: Wiley.

St. Pierre, R., Layzer, J., & Barnes, H. (1996). *Regenerating two-generation programs.* Cambridge, MA: Abt Associates.

Stanhope, L., & Corter, C. (1993, March). *The mother's role in the transition to siblinghood.* Paper presented at the biennial meeting of the Society for Research in Child Development, New Orleans.

Stattin, H., & Magnusson, D. (1990). *Pubertal maturation in female development: Paths through life* (Vol. 2). Hillsdale, NJ: Erlbaum.

Staudinger, U. M. (1996). Psychologische Produktivitat und Selbstenfaltung im Alter. In M. M. Baltes & L. Montada (Eds.), *Produktives Leben im Alter.* Frankfurt: Campus.

Staudinger, U. M., & Bluck, S. (2001). A view on midlife development from life-span theory. In M. E. Lachman (Ed.), *Handbook of midlife development.* New York: John Wiley.

Steinberg, L. D. (1986). Latchkey children and susceptibility to peer pressure: An ecological analysis. *Developmental Psychology, 22,* 433–439.

Steinberg, L. D., & Caufman, E. (2001). Adolescents as adults in court. *Social Policy Report, SRC D, XV* (No. 4), 1–13.

Steinberg, L. D., & Silk, J. S. (2002). Parenting adolescents. In M. Bornstein (Ed.), *Handbook of parenting* (2nd ed., Vol. 1). Mahwah, NJ: Erlbaum.

Steiner, J. E. (1979). Human facial expressions in response to taste and smell stimulation. In H. Reese & L. Lipsitt (Eds.), *Advances in child development and behavior* (Vol. 13). New York: Academic Press.

Stein-Morrow, E. A. L. & Soederberg Miller, L. M. (1999). Basic cognitive processes. In J. C. Cavanaugh & S. K. Whitbourne (eds.), *Gerontology: An interdisciplinary perspective.* New York: Oxford University Press.

Stern, D. N., Beebe, B., Jaffe, J., & Bennett, S. L. (1977). The infant's stimulus world during social interaction: A study of caregiver behaviors with particular reference to repetition and timing. In H. R. Schaffer (Ed.), *Studies in mother-infant interaction.* London: Academic Press.

Stern, J. S. (1993, June 2). Commentary in "Lowly vitamin supplements pack a big health punch." *USA Today,* p. 3D.

Sternberg, R. J. (1986). *Intelligence applied.* San Diego: Harcourt Brace Jovanovich.

Sternberg, R. J. (1988). *The triangle of love.* New York: Basic Books.

Sternberg, R. J. (1999). Intelligence. In M. A. Runco & S. Pritzker (Eds.), *Encyclopedia of creativity.* San Diego: Academic Press.

Sternberg, R. J. (2002). Individual differences in cognitive development. In U. Goswami (Ed.), *Blackwell handbook of childhood cognitive development.* Malden, MA: Blackwell.

Sternberg, R. J. (2003). Contemporary theories of intelligence. In I. B. Weiner (Ed.), *Handbook of psychology* (Vol. VII). New York: Wiley.

Sternberg, R. J., & Grigorenko, E. L. (Eds.). (2001). *Environmental effects on cognitive abilities.* Mahwah, NJ: Erlbaum.

Sterns, H. L., & Huyck, H. (2001). The role of work in midlife. In M. E. Lachman (Ed.), *Handbook of midlife development.* New York: John Wiley.

Steur, F. B., Applefield, J. M., & Smith, R. (1971). Televised aggression and interpersonal aggression of preschool children. *Journal of Experimental Child Psychology, 11,* 442–447.

Stevenson, H. G. (1995, March). *Missing data: On the forgotten substance of race, ethnicity, and socioeconomic classifications.* Paper presented at the meeting of the Society for Research in Child Development, Indianapolis.

Stevenson, H. W. (1995). Mathematics achievement of American students: First in the world by 2000? In C. A. Nelson (Ed.), *Basic and applied perspectives in learning, cognition, and development.* Minneapolis: University of Minnesota Press.

Stevenson, H. W. (2000). Middle childhood: Education and schooling. In A. Kazdin (Ed.), *Encyclopedia of psychology.* Washington, DC, & New York: American Psychological Association and Oxford University Press.

Stevenson, H. W., & Hofer, B. K. (1999). Education policy in the United States and abroad: What we can learn from each other.

In G. J. Cizek (Ed.), *Handbook of educational policy.* San Diego: Academic Press.

Stevenson, H. W., Lee, S., & Stigler, J. W. (1986). Mathematics achievement of Chinese, Japanese, and American children. *Science, 231,* 693–699.

Stewart, A. J., Ostrove, J. M., & Helson, R. (2001). Middle aging in women: Patterns of personality change from the 30s to the 50s. *Journal of Adult Development, 8,* 23–37.

Stice, E., Presnell, K., & Spangler, D. (2002). Risk factors for binge eating onset in adolescent girls: A 2-year prospective investigation. *Health Psychology, 21,* 131–138.

Stouthamer-Loeber, M., Loeber, R., Wei, E., Farrington, D. P., & Wikstrom, P. H. (2002). Risk and promotive effects in the explanation of persistent serious delinquency in boys. *Journal of Consulting and Clinical Psychology, 70,* 111–123.

Strain, L. A., Grabusie, C. C., Searle, M. S., & Dunn, N. J. (2002). Continuing and ceasing leisure activities in later life: A longitudinal study. *The Gerontologist, 42,* 217–223.

Strass, P. (2002). Postpartum depression support. *Canadian Nurse, 98,* 25–28.

Straus, M. A. (2001). *Beating the devil out of them* (2nd ed.). New Brunswick, NJ: Transaction Publishers.

Straus, M. A. (2003). *The primordial violence: Corporal punishment by parents, cognitive development, and crime.* Walnut Creek, CA: Alta Mira Press.

Straus, M. A., Sugarman, D. B., & Giles-Sims, J. (1997). Spanking by parents and subsequent antisocial behavior of children. *Archives of Pediatric and Adolescent Medicine, 151,* 761–767.

Strauss, R. S. (2001). Environmental tobacco smoke and serum vitamin C levels in children. *Pediatrics, 107,* 540–542.

Streil, J. (2002). Marriage: Still "his" and "hers"? In J. Worell (Ed.), *Encyclopedia of women and gender.* San Diego: Academic Press.

Streissguth, A. P., Martin, D. C., Sandman, B. M., Kirchner, G. L., & Darby, B. L. (1984). Intrauterine alcohol and nicotine exposure: Attention and reaction time in four-year-old children. *Developmental Psychology, 20,* 533–543.

Striegel-Moore, R. H., Silberstein, L. R., & Rodin, J. (1993). The social self in bulimia nervosa: Public self-consciousness, social anxiety, and perceived fraudulence. *Journal of Abnormal Psychology, 102,* 297–303.

Stroebe, M., Gergen, M. H., Gergen, K. J., & Stroebe, W. (1992). Broken hearts or broken bonds: Love and death in historical perspective. *American Psychologist, 47,* 1205–1212.

Stroebe, M., & Stroebe, W. (1991). Does "grief work" work? *Journal of Consulting and Clinical Psychology, 59,* 57–65.

Stroebe, M., Stroebe, W., Schut, H., & van den Bout, J. (1998). Bereavement. In H. S. Friedman (Ed.), *Encyclopedia of mental health* (Vol. 1). San Diego: Academic Press.

Stull, D. E., & Hatch, L. R. (1984). Unraveling the effects of multiple life changes. *Research on Aging, 6,* 560–571.

Stunkard, A. (2000). Obesity. In A. Kazdin (Ed.), *Encyclopedia of psychology.* Washington, DC, & New York: American Psychological Association and Oxford University Press.

Sue, S. (1990, August). *Ethnicity and culture in psychological research and practice.* Paper presented at the meeting of the American Psychological Association, Boston.

Sullivan, H. S. (1953). *The interpersonal theory of psychiatry.* New York: W. W. Norton.

Sullivan, K., & Sullivan, A. (1980). Adolescent-parent separation. *Developmental Psychology, 16,* 93–99.

Sullivan, L. (1991, May 25). U.S. secretary urges TV to restrict "irresponsible sex and reckless violence." *Boston Globe,* p. A1.

Suls, J., & Swain, A. (1998). Type A-Type B personalities. In H. S. Friedman (Ed.), *Encyclopedia of mental health* (Vol. 3). San Diego: Academic Press.

Suomi, S. J., Harlow, H. F., & Domek, C. J. (1970). Effect of repetitive infant-infant separations of young monkeys. *Journal of Abnormal Psychology, 76,* 161–172.

Super, C., & Harkness, S. (1997). The cultural structuring of child development. In J. W. Berry, Y. H. Poortinga, & J. Pandey (Eds.), *Handbook of cross-cultural psychology: Vol. 2. Theory and method.* Boston: Allyn & Bacon.

Susman, E. J., Dorn, L. D., & Schiefelbein, V. L. (2003). Puberty, sexuality, and health. In I. B. Weiner (Ed.), *Handbook of psychology* (Vol. VI). New York: Wiley.

Susman, E. J., Murowchick, E., Worrall, B. K., & Murray, D. A. (1995, March). *Emotionality, adrenal hormones, and context interactions during puberty and pregnancy.* Paper presented at the meeting of the Society for Research in Child Development, Indianapolis.

Sutton-Smith, B. (2000). Play. In A. Kazdin (Ed.), *Encyclopedia of psychology.* Washington,

DC, & New York: American Psychological Association and Oxford University Press.

Suzman, R. (1997, March 18). Commentary, *USA Today*, p. 1A.

Suzman, R. M., Harris, T., Hadley, E. C., Kovar, M. G., & Weindruch, R. (1992). The robust oldest old: Optimistic perspectives for increasing healthy life expectancy. In R. M. Suzman, D. P. Willis, & K. G. Manton (Eds.), *The oldest old*. New York: Oxford University Press.

Swaab, D. F., Chung, W. C., Kruijver, F. P., Hofman, M. A., & Ishunina, T. A. (2001). Structural and functional sex differences in the human hypothalamus. *Hormones and Behavior, 40,* 93–98.

Swain, S. O. (1992). Men's friendships with women. In P. M. Nardi (Ed.), *Gender in intimate relationships*. Belmont, CA: Wadsworth.

Swan, G. E. (1996). Interview. *APA Monitor,* p. 35.

Swann, W. B., De La Ronde, C., & Hixon, J. G. (1994). Authenticity and positive strivings in marriage and courtship. Journal of *Personality and Social Psychology, 66,* 857–869.

Swanson, J. M., & others. (2001). Clinical relevance of the primary findings of MTA: Success rates based on severity of ADHD and ODD symptoms at the end of treatment. *Journal of the American Academy of Child and Adolescent Psychiatry, 40,* 168–179.

T

Taddio, A., Katz, J., Ilersich, A. L., & Koren, G. (1997). Effect of neonatal circumcision on pain response during subsequent routine vaccination. *Lancet, 349,* 599–603.

Takahashi, K. (1990). Are the key assumptions of the "Strange Situation" procedure universal? A view from Japanese research. *Human Development, 33,* 23–30.

Tamis-Lemonda, C. S., Bornstein, M. H., & Baumwell, L. (2001). Maternal responsiveness and children's achievement of language milestones. *Child Development, 72,* 748–767.

Tan, S. Y. (2000). Religion and psychotherapy: An overview. In A. Kazdin (Ed.), *Encyclopedia of psychology*. Washington, DC, & New York: American Psychological Association and Oxford University Press.

Tannen, D. (1990). *You just don't understand: Women and men in conversation*. New York: Ballantine.

Taylor, H. G., Klein, N., & Hack, M. (1994). Academic functioning in <750 gm birthweight children who have normal cognitive abilities: Evidence for specific learning disabilities. *Pediatric Research 35,* 289A.

Taylor, S. P. (1982). Mental health and successful coping among Black women. In R. C. Manuel (Ed.), *Minority aging*. Westport, CT: Greenwood Press.

Tenenbaum, H. R., Callahan, M., Alba-Speyer, C., & Sandoval, L. (2002). Parent-child science conversations in Mexican descent families: Educational background, activity, and past experience as moderators. *Hispanic Journal of Behavioral Sciences, 24,* 225–248.

Tercyak, K. P., Johnson, S. B., Roberts, S. E., & Cruz, A. Z. (2001). Psychological response to prenatal genetic counseling and amniocentesis. *Patient Educational Counseling, 43,* 73–84.

Terman, D. L., Larner, M. B., Stevenson, C. S., & Behrman, R. E. (1996). Special education for students with disabilities: Analysis and recommendations. *The Future of Children 6* (1), 4–24.

Terman, L. (1925). *Genetic studies of genius: Vol. 1. Mental and physical traits of a thousand gifted children*. Standford, CA: Stanford University Press.

Tesser, A. (2000). Self-esteem. In A. Kazdin (Ed.). *Encyclopedia of psychology*. Washington, DC, & New York: American Psychological Association and Oxford University Press.

Teti, D. M. (2001). Retrospect and prospect in the study of sibling relationships. In J. P. McHale & W. S. Grolnick (Eds.), *Retrospect and prospect in the psychological study of families*. Mahwah, NJ: Erlbaum.

Teti, D. M., Sakin, J., Kucera, E., Caballeros, M., & Corns, K. M. (1993, March). *Transitions to siblinghood and security of firstborn attachment: Psychosocial and psychiatric correlates of changes over time*. Paper presented at the biennial meeting of the Society for Research in Child Development, New Orleans.

Tetreault, M. K. T. (1997). Classrooms for diversity: Rethinking curriculum and pedagogy. In J. A. Banks & C. A. Banks (Eds.), *Multicultural education* (3rd ed.). Boston: Allyn & Bacon.

Tharp, R. G. (1994). Intergroup differences among Native Americans in socialization and child cognition: An ethogenetic analysis. In P. M. Greenfield & R. Cocking (Eds.), *Cross-cultural roots of minority child development*. Mahwah, NJ: Erlbaum.

Tharp, R. G., & Gallimore, R. (1988). *Rousing minds to life: Teaching, learning, and schooling in social context*. New York: Cambridge University Press.

Thayer, J. F., Rossy, I., Sollers, J., Friedman, B. H., & Allen, M. T. (1996, March). *Relationships among heart period variability and cardiodynamic measures vary as a function of fitness*. Paper presented at the meeting of the American Psychosomatic Society, Williamsburg, VA.

The Conduct Problems Prevention Research Group. (2002). Evaluation of the first 3 years of the Fast Track prevention trial with children at high risk for adolescent conduct problems. *Journal of Abnormal Child Psychology, 30,* 19–35.

Thelen, E. (1995). Motor development: A new synthesis. *American Psychologist, 50,* 79–95.

Thelen, E. (2000). Perception and motor development. In A. Kazdin (Ed.), *Encyclopedia of psychology*. Washington, DC, & New York: American Psychological Association and Oxford University Press.

Thelen, E. (2001). Dynamic mechanisms of change in early perceptual-motor development. In J. L. McClelland & R. S. Siegler (Eds.), *Mechanisms of cognitive development*. Mahwah, NJ: Erlbaum.

Thomas, A., & Chess, S. (1991). Temperament in adolescence and its functional significance. In R. M. Lerner, A. C. Petersen, & J. Brooks-Gunn (Eds.), *Encyclopedia of adolescence* (Vol. 2). New York: Garland.

Thomas, K. (1998, November 4). Teen cyberdating is a new wrinkle for parents, too. *USA Today,* p. 9D.

Thompson, P. M., Giedd, J. N., Woods, R. P., MacDonald, D., Evans, A. C., & Toga, A. W. (2000). Growth patterns in the developing brain detected by using continuum mechanical tensor maps. *Nature, 404,* 190–193.

Thompson, R. A. (1994). Emotion regulation: A theme in search of a definition. Monographs of the Society for Research in *Child Development, 59* (Serial No. 240), 2–3.

Thompson, R. A. (1999). The individual child: Temperament, emotion, self, and personality. In M. H. Bornstein & M. E. Lamb (Eds.), *Developmental psychology: An advanced textbook* (4th ed.). Mahwah, NJ: Erlbaum.

Thompson, R. A. (2000). Early experience and socialization. In A. Kazdin (Ed.), *Encyclopedia of psychology*. Washington, DC, & New York: American Psychological Association and Oxford University Press.

Thompson, R. A., & Nelson, C. A. (2001). Developmental science and the media. *American Psychologist, 56,* 5–15.

Thomson, E., Mosley, J., Hanson, T. L., McLanahan, S. S. (2001). Remarriage, cohabitation, and changes in mothering behavior. *Journal of Marriage and the Family, 63,* 370–380.

Thoresen, C. E., & Harris, A. H. S. (2002). Spirituality and health: What's the evidence and what's needed? *Annals of Behavioral Medicine, 24,* 3–13.

Thorton, A., & Camburn, D. (1989). Religious participation and sexual behavior and attitudes. *Journal of Marriage and the Family, 49,* 117–128.

Thurstone, L. L. (1938). *Primary mental abilities.* Chicago: University of Chicago Press.

Timins, J. K. (2001). Radiation during pregnancy. *New Jersey Medicine, 98,* 29–33.

Tobin, J. J., Wu, D. Y. H., & Davidson, D. H. (1989). *Preschool in three cultures.* New Haven, CT: Yale University Press.

Tolan, P. H. (2001). Emerging themes and challenges in understanding youth violence. *Journal of Clinical Child Psychology, 30,* 233–239.

Torff, B. (2000). Multiple intelligences. In A. Kazdin (Ed.), *Encyclopedia of psychology.* Washington, DC, & New York: American Psychological Association and Oxford University Press.

Toseland, R. W., McCallion, P., Gerber, T., & Banks, S. (2002). Predictors of health and human services use by persons with dementia and their family caregivers. *Social Science and Medicine, 55,* 1255–1266.

Toth, S. L., Manley, J. T., & Cicchetti, D. (1992). Child maltreatment and vulnerability to depression. *Development and Psychopathology, 4,* 97–112.

Tough, S. C., Newburn-Cook, C., Johnston, D. W., Svenson, L. W., Rose, S., & Belik, J. (2002). Delayed childbearing and its impact on population rate changes in lower birth weight, multiple birth, and preterm delivery. *Pediatrics, 109,* 399–403.

Trappe, R., Laccone, F., Cobilanschi, J., Meins, M., Huppke, P., Hanefeld, F., & Engel, W. (2001). MECP2 mutations in sporadic cases of Rett syndrome are almost exclusively of paternal origin. *American Journal of Human Genetics, 68,* 1093–1101.

Trasler, J. (2000). Paternal exposures: Altered sex ratios. *Teratology, 62,* 6–7.

Trasler, J. M., & Doerksen, T. (2000, May). *Teratogen update: Paternal exposure-reproductive risks.* Paper presented at the joint meeting of the Pediatric Academic Societies and American Academy of Pediatrics, Boston.

Travis, C. B. (2001). Gender development: Evolutionary perspectives. In J. Worrel (Ed.), *Encyclopedia of women and gender.* San Diego: Academic Press.

Treffers, P. E., Eskes, M., Kleiverda, G., & van Alten, D. (1990). Home births and minimal medical interventions. *Journal of the American Medical Association, 246,* 2207–2208.

Trehub, S. E., Schneider, B. A., Thorpe, L. A., & Judge, P. (1991). Observational measures of auditory sensitivity in early infancy. *Developmental Psychology, 27,* 40–49.

Triandis, H. C. (2001). Individualism and collectivism. In D. Matsumoto (Ed.), *The handbook of culture and personality.* New York: Oxford University Press.

Trimble, J. E. (1988, August). *The enculturation of contemporary psychology.* Paper presented at the meeting of the American Psychological Association, New Orleans.

Troiano, R. P., & Flegal, K. M. (1998). Overweight children and adolescents: Description, epidemiology, and demographics. *Pediatrics, 101,* 497–504.

Troist, A., Moles, A., Panepuccia, L., Lo Russo, D., Palla, G., & Scucchi, S. (2002). Serum cholesterol levels and mood symptoms in the postpartum period. *Psychiatry Research, 109,* 213–219.

Troll, L. E. (1994). Family-embedded versus family-deprived oldest-old: A study of contrasts. *International Journal of Aging and Human Development, 38,* 51–64.

Troll, L. E. (1999). Questions for future studies: Social relationships in old age. *International Journal of Aging and Human Development, 48,* 347–351.

Troll, L. E. (2000). Transmission and transmutation. In J. E. Birren & J. J. F. Schroots (Eds.), *A history of geropsychology in autobiography.* Washington, DC: American Psychological Association.

Truitner, K., & Truitner, N. (1993). Death and dying in Buddhism. In D. P. Irish & K. F. Lundquist (Eds.), *Ethnic variations in dying, death, and grief: Diversity in universality.* Washington, DC: Taylor & Francis.

Tubman, J. G., & Windle, M. (1995). Continuity of difficult temperament in adolescence: Relations with depression, life events, family support, and substance abuse. *Journal of Youth and Adolescence, 24,* 133–152.

Tucker, J. S., Schwartz, J. E., Clark, K. M., & Friedman, H. S. (1999). Age-related changes in the associations of social network ties with mortality risk. *Psychology and Aging, 14,* 564–571.

Tulving, E. (2000). Concepts of memory. In E. Tulving & F. I. M. Craik (Eds.), *The Oxford handbook of memory.* New York: Oxford University Press.

Turecki, S., & Tonner, L. (1989). *The difficult child.* New York: Bantam.

Turk, D. C., Rudy, T. E., & Salovey, P. (1984). Health protection: Attitudes and behaviors of LPN's teachers, and college students. *Health Psychology, 3,* 189–210.

Turner, B. F. (1982). Sex-related differences in aging. In B. B. Wolman (Ed.), *Handbook of developmental psychology.* Englewood Cliffs, NJ: Prentice Hall.

Turvey, C. L., Carney, C., Arndt, S., & Wallace, R. B. (1999, November). *Conjugal loss and syndromal depression in a sample of elders ages 70 years and older.* Paper presented at the meeting of the Gerontological Society of America, San Francisco.

U

U.S. Bureau of the Census. (2000). *Census 2000 data.* Washington, DC: Author.

U.S. Bureau of the Census. (2000). *Death Statistics.* Washington, DC: Author.

U.S. Bureau of the Census. (2000). *Statistical abstracts of the United States.* Washington, DC: U.S. Government Printing Office.

U.S. Bureau of the Census. (2001). *Census data: 2000.* Washington, DC: Author.

U.S. Department of Education. (1996). *Number and disabilities of children and youth served under IDEA.* Washington, DC: Office of Special Education Programs, Data Analysis System.

U.S. Department of Education. (1999). *Digest of education statistics.* Washington. DC: Author.

U.S. Department of Education. (2000). *To assure a free and appropriate public education of all children with disabilities.* Washington, DC: U.S. Office of Education.

U.S. Department of Energy (2001). *The human genome project.* Washington, DC: Author.

U.S. Department of Health and Human Services. (2001). *Youth violence.* Rockville, MD: Author.

U.S. General Accounting Office. (1987, September). *Prenatal care: Medicaid recipients and uninsured women obtain insufficient care.* A report to the Congress of the United States, HRD-97-137. Washington, DC: GAO.

U.S. Surgeon General's Report. (1990). *The health benefits of smoking cessation.* Bethesda, MD: U.S. Department of Health and Human Services.

Ubell, C. (1992, December 6). We can age successfully *Parade,* pp. 14–15.

Underwood, M. (2002). Sticks and stones and social exclusion: Aggression among boys and girls. In P. K. Smith & C. H. Hart (Eds.), *Blackwell handbook of childhood social development.* Malden, MA: Blackwell.

UNICEF. (2001). *UNICEF statistics: Low birthweight.* Geneva: Author.

UNICEF. (2002). *The state of the world's children 2002: Leadership.* Geneva: UNICEF.

United Nations. (2001). *Education for development.* New York: Author.

United Nations. (2002). *Improving the quality of life of girls.* New York: Author.

Vaillant, G. E. (1977). *Adaptation to life.* Boston: Little, Brown.

Vaillant, G. E. (1992). Is there a natural history of addiction? In C. P. O'Brien & J. H. Jaffe (Eds.), *Addictive states.* Cambridge, MA: Harvard University Press.

Vaillant, G. E. (2002). *Aging well.* Boston: Little, Brown.

Valencia, R. R., & Suzuki, L. A. (2001). *Intelligence testing and minority students.* Thousand Oaks, CA: Sage.

Valsiner, J. (2000). *Culture and human development.* Thousand Oaks, CA: Sage.

Van Beveren, T. T. (2002). *Prenatal development and the newborn.* Unpublished manuscript, University of Texas at Dallas, Richardson.

van den Boom, D. C. (1989). Neonatal irritability and the development of attachment. In G. A. Kohnstamm, J. E. Bates, & M. K. Rothbart (Eds.), *Temperament in childhood.* New York: Wiley.

Van Hoorn, J., Nourot, P. M., Scales, B., & Alward, K. R. (1999). *Play at the center of the curriculum.* Columbus, OH: Merrill.

van Ijzendoorn, M. H., & Kroonenberg, P. M. (1988). Cross-cultural patterns of attachment: A meta-analysis of the Strange Situation. *Child Development, 59,* 147–156.

Vandell, D. L., & Wilson, K. S. (1988). Infants' interactions with mother, sibling, and peer: Contrasts and relations between interaction systems. *Child Development, 48,* 176–186.

Vandewater, E. A., Ostrove, J. M., & Stewart, A. J. (1997). Predicting women's well-being in mid-life: The importance of personality development and social role involvements. *Journal of Personality and Social Development, 72,* 1147–1160.

VandeWeerd, C., & Paveza, G. (1999, November). *Physical violence in old age: A look at the burden of women.* Paper presented at the meeting of the Gerontological Society of America, San Francisco.

Varoqueaux, F. (2003). Synaptogenesis. In V. S. Ramachandran (Ed.), *Encyclopedia of the human brain.* San Diego: Academic Press.

Vartanian, T. P., & McNamara, J. M. (2002). Older women in poverty: The impact of midlife factors. Journal of Marriage and *Family, 64,* 532–548.

Velez-Pardo, C., Lopera, F., Del Rio, J. M. (2002). DNA damage does not correlate with amyloid-beat-plagques and neurofibrillary tangles in familial Alzheimer's disease Presenilin-1 mutation. *Journal of Alzheimer's Disease, 2,* 47–57.

Ventis, W. L. (1995). The relationships between religion and mental health. *Journal of Social Issues, 51,* 33–48.

Ventura, S. J., Martin, J. A., Curtin, S. C., & Mathews, T. J. (1997, June 10). *Report of final natality statistics, 1995.* Washington, DC: National Center for Health Statistics.

Verbrugge, L. M., Gruber-Baldini, A. L., & Fozard, J. L. (1996). Age differences and age changes in activities: Baltimore Longitudinal Study of Aging. *Journal of Gerontology: Social Sciences, 51B,* S30–S41.

Verhaeghen, P., & Marcoen, A. (1996). On the mechanisms of plasticity in young and older adults after instruction in the method of loci: Evidence for an amplification model. *Psychology and Aging, 11,* 164–178.

Verhaeghen, P., Marcoen, A., & Goossens, L. (1995). Facts and fiction about memory aging: A quantitative integration of research findings. *Journal of Gerontology, 48,* P157–P171.

Verklan, M. T. (2002). Physiological variability during transition to extrauterine life. *Critical Care Nursing Quarterly, 24,* 41–56.

Vidal, F. (2000). Piaget's theory. In A. Kazdin (Ed.), *Encyclopedia of psychology.* Washington, DC, & New York: American Psychological Association and Oxford University Press.

Visher, E., & Visher, J. (1989). Parenting coalitions after remarriage: Dynamics and therapeutic guidelines. *Family Relations, 38,* 65–70.

Vogels, W. W., Dekker, M. R., Brouwer, W. H., & de Jong, R. (2002). Age-related changes in event-related prospective memory performance: a comparison of four prospective memory tasks. *Brain and Cognition, 49,* 341-362.

Vurpillot, E. (1968). The development of scanning strategies and their relation to visual differentiation. *Journal of Experimental Child Psychology, 6,* 632–650.

Vygotsky, L. S. (1962). *Thought and language.* Cambridge, MA: MIT Press.

Wachs, T. D. (1994). Fit, context and the transition between temperament and personality. In C. Halverson, G. Kohnstamm, & R. Martin (Eds.), *The developing structure of personality from infancy to adulthood.* Hillsdale, NJ: Erlbaum.

Wachs, T. D. (2000). *Necessary but not sufficient.* Washington, DC: American Psychological Association.

Wachs, T. D., & Bates, J. E. (2002). Temperament. In G. Bremner & A. Fogel (Eds.), *The Blackwell handbook of infant development.* Malden, MA: Blackwell.

Wachs, T. D., & Kohnstamm, G. A. (Eds.). (2001). *Temperament in context.* Mahwah, NJ: Erlbaum.

Wadden, T. A., Foser, G. D., Stunkard, A. J., & Conill, A. M. (1996). Effects of weight cycling on the resting energy expenditure and body composition of obese women. *Eating Disorders, 19,* 5–12.

Waddington, C. H. (1957). The strategy of the genes. London: Allen & Son.

Wahlsten, D. (2000). Behavioral genetics. In A. Kazdin (Ed.), *Encyclopedia of psychology.* Washington, DC, & New York: American Psychological Association and Oxford University Press.

Wakschlag, L. S., Chase-Lansdale, P. L., & Brooks-Gunn, J. (1996, March). *Not just "ghosts in the nursery": Contemporaneous intergenerational relationships and parenting in* *young African American families.* Paper presented at the meeting of the Society for Research on Adolescence, Boston.

Walden, T. (1991). Infant social referencing. In J. Garber & K. Dodge (Eds.), *The development of emotional regulation and dysregulation.* New York: Cambridge University Press.

Walker, C., Gruman, C., & Blank, K. (1999, November). *Physician-assisted suicide: Looking beyond the numbers.* Paper presented at the meeting of the Gerontological Society of America, San Francisco.

Walker, H. (1998, May 31). Youth violence: Society's problem. *Eugene Register Guard,* p. 1C.

Walker, L. (2001). Battering in adult relationships. In J. Worell (Ed.), *Encyclopedia of women and gender.* San Diego: Academic Press.

Walker, L. J. (1991). Sex differences in moral development. In W. M. Kurtines & J. Gewirtz (Eds.), *Moral behavior and development* (Vol. 2). Hillsdale, NJ: Erlbaum.

Wallace, M., Mills, B., & Browning, C. (1997). Effects of cross-training on markers of insulin resistance/hyperinsulinemia. *Medical Science and Sports Exercise, 29,* 1170–1175.

Walsh, L. A. (2000, Spring). The inside scoop on child development: Interview. *Cutting through the hype.* Minneapolis: College of Education & Human Development, University of Minnesota.

Wang, X., Zuckerman, B., Kaufman, G., Pearson, C., Wang, G., Chen, C., Wise, P., Bauchner, H., & Xu, X. (2000, May). *Maternal cigarette smoking, genetic susceptibility, and birthweight.* Paper presented at the joint meeting of the Pediatric Academic Societies and the American Academy of Pediatrics, Boston.

Ward, B. M., Lambert, S. B., & Lester, R. A. (2001). Rubella vaccination in prenatal and postnatal women: Why not use MM? *Medical Journal of Australia, 174,* 311–312.

Wardle, J., Gutherie, C., Sanderson, S., Birch, L., & Plomin, R. (2001). Food and activity preferences in children of lean and obese parents. *International Journal of Obesity and Related Metabolic Disorders, 25,* 971–977.

Warner, H. R., & Hodes, R. J. (2000, Spring). Telomere length, telomerase, and aging: Hype, hope, and reality. *Generations, 24,* 48–53.

Warner, J., & Butler, R. (2002). Dementia. *Clinical Evidence, 7,* 846–866.

Warr, P. (1994). Age and employment. In M. Dunnette, L. Hough, & H. Triandis (Eds.), *Handbook of industrial and organizational psychology* (Vol. 4). Palo Alto, CA: Consulting Psychologists Press.

Warrick, P. (1992, March 1). The fantastic voyage of Tanner Roberts. *Los Angeles Times,* pp. El. 12,13.

Warshak, R. A. (2001). Personal communication, Department of Psychology, University of Texas at Dallas, Richardson.

Wass, H., & Stillion, J. M. (1988). Death in the lives of children and adolescents. In H. Wass, F. M. Berardo, & R. A. Neimeyer (Eds.), *Dying: Facing the facts* (2nd ed.). Washington, DC: Hemisphere.

Watemberg, N., Silver, S., Harel, S., & Lerman-Sagie, T. (2002). Significance of microcephaly among children with developmental disabilities. *Journal of Child Neurology, 17,* 117–122.

Waterman, A. S. (1992). Identity as an aspect of optimal psychological functioning. In G. R. Adams, T. P. Gullotta, & R. Montemayor (Eds.), *Adolescent identity formation.* Newbury Park, CA: Sage.

Waterman, A. S. (1997). An overview of service-learning and the role of research and evaluation in service-learning programs. In A. S. Waterman (Ed.), *Service learning.* Mahwah, NJ: Erlbaum.

Waters, E. (2001, April). *Perspectives on continuity and discontinuity in relationships.* Paper presented at the meeting of the Society for Research in Child Development, Minneapolis.

Waters, E., Merrick, S., Albersheim, L., Treboux, D., & Crowell, J. (2000). Attachment theory from infancy to adulthood: A 20-year-longitudinal study of relations between infant Strange Situation classification and attachment representations in adulthood. *Child Development, 71,* 684–689.

Watson, J. B. (1928). *Psychological care of infant and child.* New York: W. W. Norton.

Watson, J. B., & Rayner, R. (1920). Conditioned emotional reactions. *Journal of Experimental Psychology, 3,* 1–14.

Watson, R., & DeMeo, P. (1987). Premarital cohabitation vs. traditional courtship and subsequent marital adjustment: A replication and follow-up. *Family Relations, 36,* 193–197.

Wauters, M., Mertens, I., Chagnon, M., Rankinen, T., Considine, R. V., Chagnon, Y. C., Van Gaal, L. F., & Bouchard, C. (2001). Polymorphisms in the leptin receptor gene, body composition, and fat distribution in overweight and obese women. *International Journal of Obesity and Related Metabolic Disorders, 25,* 714–720.

Weatherford, W. (1999, October 31). Alzheimer's disease—What's new? *Dallas Morning News,* p. 4P.

Wechsler, H., Davenport, A., Sowdall, G., Moetykens, B., & Castillo, S. (1994). Health and behavioral consequences of binge drinking in college. *Journal of the American Medical Association, 272,* 1672–1677.

Wechsler, H., Lee, J. E., Kuo, M., & Lee, H. (2000). College binge drinking in the 1990s—A continuing health problem: Results from the Harvard University School of Public Health 1999 College Alcohol Study. *Journal of American College Health, 48,* 199–210.

Wechsler, H., Lee, J. E., Kuo, M., Seibring, M., Nelson, T. F., & Lee, H. (2002). Trends in college binge drinking during a period of increased prevention efforts: Findings from 4 Harvard School of Public Health college alcohol study surveys: 1993–2001. *Journal of American College Health, 50,* 203–217.

Weeks, A. D., & Mirembe, F. M. (2002). The retained placenta—new insights into an old problem. *European Journal of Obstetrics, Gynecology, and Reproductive Biology, 102,* 109–110.

Weikart, D. P. (1993). *Long-term positive effects in the Perry Preschool Head Start program.* Unpublished data, High Scope Foundation, Ypsilanti, MI.

Weincke, J. K., Thurston, S. W., Kelsey, K. T., Varkonyi, A., Wain, J. C., Mark, E. J., & Christiani, D. C. (1999). Early age at smoking initiation and tobacco carcinogen DNA damage in the lung. *Journal of the National Cancer Institute, 91,* 614–619.

Weinraub, M., Horuath, D. L., & Gringlas, M. B. (2002). Single parenthood. In M. H. Bornstein (Ed.), *Handbook of parenting* (2nd ed., Vol. 3). Mahwah, NJ: Erlbaum.

Weinstein, N. D. (1984). Reducing unrealistic optimism about illness susceptibility. *Health Psychology, 3,* 431–457.

Weiss, R. E. (2001). *Pregnancy and birth: Rh factor in pregnancy.* Available on the Internet at: http://www.about.com.

Weizmann, F. (2000). Bowlby, John. In A. Kazdin (Ed.), *Encyclopedia of psychology.* Washington, DC, & New York: American Psychological Association and Oxford University Press.

Wellman, H. M. (1997, April). *Ten years of theory of mind: Telling the story backwards.* Paper presented at the meeting of the Society for Research in Child Development, Washington, DC.

Wellman, H. M. (2000). Early Childhood. In A. Kazdin (Ed.), *Encyclopedia of psychology.*

Washington, DC, & New York: American Psychological Association and Oxford University Press.

Wellman, H. M. (2002). Understanding the psychological world: Developing a theory of mind. In U. Goswami (Ed.), *Blackwell handbook of childhood cognitive development.* Malden, MA: Blackwell.

Wellman, H. M., Cross, D., & Watson, J. (2001). Meta-analysis of theory-of-mind development: The truth about false belief. *Child Development, 72,* 655–684.

Wenestam, C. G., & Wass, H. (1987). Swedish and U.S. Children's thinking about death: A qualitative study and cross-cultural comparison. *Death Studies, 11,* 99–121.

Wentworth, R. A. L. (1999). *Montessori for the millennium.* Mahwah, NJ: Erlbaum.

Wentzel, K. R., & Asher, S. R. (1995). The academic lives of neglected, rejected, popular, and controversial children. *Child Development, 66,* 754–763.

Wenzlaff, R. M., & Prohaska, M. L. (1989). When misery loves company: Depression, attributions, and responses to others' moods. *Journal of Experimental Social Psychology, 25,* 220–223.

Werker, J. F., & LaLonde, C. E. (1988). Cross-language speech perception: Initial capabilities and developmental change. *Developmental Psychology, 24,* 672–683.

Werner, E. E. (1989). High risk children in young adulthood: A longitudinal study from birth to 32 years. *American Journal of Orthopsychiatry, 59,* 72–81.

Wertlieb, D. (2003). Applied developmental science. In I. B. Weiner (Ed.), *Handbook of psychology* (Vol. VI). New York: Wiley.

West, R., & Craik, F. I. M. (2001). Influences on the efficiency of prospective memory in younger and older adults. *Psychology and Aging, 16,* 682–696.

Whalen, C. K. (2001). ADHD treatment in the 21st century: Pushing the envelope *Journal of Clinical Child Psychology, 30,* 136–140.

Whiffen, V. (2001). Depression. In J. Worell (Ed.), *Encyclopedia of women and gender.* San Diego: Academic Press.

Whitbourne, S. K. (2000). Adult development and aging: Biological processes and physical development. In A. Kazdin (Ed.), *Encyclopedia of psychology.* Washington, DC, & New York: American Psychological Association and Oxford University Press.

Whitbourne, S. K. (2001). The physical aging process in midlife: Interactions with psychological and sociocultural factors. In M. E. Lachman (Ed.), *Handbook of midlife development.* New York: John Wiley.

Whitbourne, S. K., & Connolly, L. A. (1999). The developing self in midlife. In S. L. Willis & J. D. Reid (Eds.), *Life in the middle.* San Diego: Academic Press.

White, B., Castle, P., & Held, R. (1964). Observations on the development of visually directed reaching. *Child Development, 35,* 349–364.

White, C. B., & Catania, J. (1981). Psychoeducational intervention for sexuality with the aged, family members of the aged, and people who work with the aged. *International Journal of Aging and Human Development.*

White, C. W., & Coleman, M. (2000). *Early childhood education.* Columbus, OH: Merrill.

White, J. W. (2002). Aggression and gender. In J. Worell (Ed.), *Encyclopedia of gender and women.* San Diego: Academic Press.

White, L. (2001). Sibling relationships over the life course. *Journal of Marriage and the Family, 63,* 555–568.

White, N., & Cunningham, W. R. (1989). Is terminal drop pervasive or specific? *Journal of Gerontology: Psychological Sciences, 43,* P141–144.

Whitehead, B. D., & Popence, D. (2001). Unpublished manuscript: *The state of our unions: The social health of marriage in America.* Piscataway, NJ: Rutgers, The State University of New Jersey.

Whitfield, K. E., & Baker-Thomas, T. (1999). Individual differences in aging minorities. *International Journal of Aging and Human Development, 48,* 73–79.

Whiting, B. B. (1989, April). *Culture and interpersonal behavior.* Paper presented at the biennial meeting of the Society for Research in Child Development, Kansas City.

Whiting, B. B., & Edwards, C. P. (1988). *Children of different worlds.* Cambridge, MA: Harvard University Press.

Whitley, B. E. (2002). *Principles of research in behavioral science* (2nd ed.). New York: McGraw-Hill.

Whitman, T. L., Borkowski, J. G., Keogh, D. A., & Weed, K. (2001). *Interwoven lives.* Mahwah, NJ: Erlbaum.

Wickelgren, I. (1999). Nurture helps to mold able minds. *Science, 283,* 1832–1834.

Wiesner, M., & Ittel, A. (2002). Relations of pubertal timing and depressing symptoms to substance use in early adolescence. *Journal of Early Adolescence, 22,* 5–23.

Wiley, D., & Bortz, W. M. (1996). Sexuality and aging—usual and successful. *Journal of Gerontology, 51A,* M142–M146.

Wilkie, F., & Eisdorfer, C. (1971). Intelligence and blood pressure in the aged. *Science, 172,* 959–962.

Willcox, B. J., Willcox, M. D., & Suzuki, M. (2002). *The Okinawa Program.* New York: Crown.

Williams, A., & Nussbaum, J. F. (2001). *Intergenerational communication across the life span.* Mahwah, NJ: Erlbaum.

Williams, C. R. (1986). *The impact of television: A natural experiment in three communities.* New York: Academic Press.

Williams, J. E., & Best, D. L. (1982). *Measuring sex stereotypes: A thirty-nation study.* Newbury Park, CA: Sage.

Williams, J. E., & Best, D. L. (1989). *Sex and psyche: Self-concept viewed cross-culturally.* Newbury Park, CA: Sage.

Williams, M. A., & Wheeler, M. S. (2001). Palliative care: What is it? *Home Healthcare Nurse, 19,* 550–556.

Williams, M. E. (Ed.). (1995). *The American Geriatric Society's complete guide to aging.* Nevada City, CA: Harmony Books.

Williams, R. B. (1995). Coronary prone behaviors, hostility, and cardiovascular health. In K. Orth-Gomer & N. Schneiderman (Eds.), *Behavioral medicine approaches to cardiovascular disease prevention.* Mahwah, NJ: Erlbaum.

Williams, R. B. (2001). Hostility (among other psychosocial risk factors). In A. Baum, T. A. Revenson, & J. E. Singer (Eds.), *Handbook of health psychology.* Mahwah, NJ: Erlbaum.

Willis, S. L., & Nesselroade, C. S. (1990). Long-term effects of fluid ability training in old age. *Developmental Psychology, 26,* 905–910.

Willis, S. L., & Reid, S. L. (1999). *Life in the middle: Psychological and social development in middle age.* San Diego: Academic Press.

Willis, S. L., & Schaie, K. W. (1986). Training the elderly on the ability factors of spatial orientation and inductive reasoning. *Psychology and Aging, 1,* 239–247.

Willis, S. L., & Schaie, K. W. (1994). Assessing everyday competence in the elderly. In C. Fisher & R. Lerner (Eds.), *Applied developmental psychology.* Hillsdale, NJ: Erlbaum.

Willis, S. L., & Schaie, K. W. (1999). Intellectual functioning in midlife. In S. L. Willis & J. D. Reid (Eds.), *Life in the middle:*

Psychological and social development in middle age. San Diego: Academic Press.

Wilson, B. (2001, April). *The role of television in children's emotional development and socialization.* Paper presented at the meeting of the Society for Research in Child Development, Minneapolis.

Wilson, D. M., & Truman, C. D. (2002). Addressing myths about end-of-life care: Research into the use of acute care hospitals over the last five years of life. *Journal of Palliative Care, 18,* 29–38.

Wilson, J. F. (2003). *Biological foundations of human behavior.* Belmont, CA: Wadsworth.

Wilson, M. N., & Hall, F. D. (2000). Cultural diversity. In A. Kazdin (Ed.), *Encyclopedia of psychology.* Washington, DC, & New York: American Psychological Association and Oxford University Press.

Wilson, R. S., Mendes de Leon, C. F., Barnes, L. L., Schneider, J. A., Bienias, J., Evans, D. A., & Bennett, D. A. (2002). Participation in cognitively stimulating activities and risk of incident Alzheimer disease. *Journal of the American Medical Association, 287,* 742–748.

Wilson-Shockley, S. (1995). *Gender differences in adolescent depression: The contribution of negative affect.* M.S. Thesis, University of Illinois at Urbana-Champaign.

Windle, M., & Windle, R. C. (2003). Alcohol and other substance use and abuse. In G. Adams & M. Berzonsky (Eds.), *Blackwell handbook of adolescence.* Malden, MA: Blackwell.

Windle, W. F. (1940). *Physiology of the human fetus.* Philadelphia: W. B. Saunders.

Wineberg, H. (1994). Marital reconciliation in the United States: Which couples are successful? *Journal of Marriage and the Family, 56,* 80–88.

Wing, R. R., & Polley, B. A. (2001). Obesity. In A. Baum, T. A. Revenson, & J. E. Singer (Eds.), *Handbook of health psychology.* Mahwah, NJ: Erlbaum.

Wingfield, A., & Kahana, M. J. (2002). The dynamics of memory retrieval in older adulthood. *Canadian Journal of Experimental Psychology, 56(3),* 187-199.

Wink, P., & Dillon, M. (2002). Spiritual development across the adult life course: Findings from a longitudinal study. *Journal of Adult Development, 9,* 79–94.

Winner, E. (1986, August). Where pelicans kiss seals. *Psychology Today,* pp. 24–35.

Winner, E. (1996). *Gifted children: Myths and realities.* New York: Basic Books.

Winsler, A., Diaz, R. M., & Montero, I. (1997). The role of private speech in the transition from collaborative to independent task performance in young children. *Early Childhood Research Quarterly, 12,* 59–79.

Winstead, B., & Griffin, J. L. (2002). Friendship styles. In J. Worell (Ed.), *Encyclopedia of women and gender.* San Diego: Academic Press.

Wintre, M. G., & Vallance, D. D. (1994). A developmental sequence in the comprehension of emotions: Intensity, multiple emotions, and valence. *Developmental Psychology, 30,* 509–514.

Wishart, L. R., Lee, T. D., Murdoch, J. E., & Hodges, N. J. (2000). Effects of aging on automatic and effortful processes in bimanual coordination. *Journal of Gerontology, 53B (2),* P85–P94.

Witherington, D. W., Campos, J. J., & Hertenstein, M. (2002). Principles of emotion and its development in infancy. In G. Bremner & A. Fogel (Eds.), *The Blackwell handbook of infant development.* Malden, MA: Blackwell.

Witkin, H. A., Mednick, S. A., Schulsinger, R., Bakkestrom, E., Christiansen, K. O., Goodenbough, D. R., Hirchhorn, K., Lunsteen, C., Owen, D. R., Philip, J., Ruben, D. B., & Stocking, M. (1976). Criminality in XYY and XXY men. *Science, 193,* 547–555.

Witztum, E., Malkinson, R., & Rubin, S. S. (2001). Death, bereavement, and traumatic loss in Israel: A historical and cultural analysis. *International Journal of Psychiatry, 38,* 157–170.

Wong, A. M., Lin, Y. C., Chou, S. W., Tang, F. T., & Wong, P. Y. (2001). Coordination exercise and postural stability in elderly people: Effect of Tai Chi Chuan. *Archives of Physical Medicine & Rehabilitation, 82,* 608–612.

Wong, D. L., Hockenberry-Eaton, M., Wilson, D., Winkelsein, M. L., & Schwartz, P. (2001). *Wong's essentials of pediatric nursing* (6th ed.). St. Louis: Mosby.

Wong, D. L., Perry, S. E., & Hockenberry, M. (2001). *Maternal child nursing care* (2nd ed.). St. Louis: Mosby.

Wong, P. T. P., & Watt, L. M. (1991). What types of reminiscence are associated with successful aging? *Psychology and Aging, 6,* 272–279.

Woodrich, D. L. (1994). *Attention-deficit hyperactivity disorder: What every parent should know.* Baltimore: Paul H. Brookes.

Woodward, N. J., & Wallston, B. S. (1987). Age and health-care beliefs: Self-efficacy as a mediator of low desire for control. *Psychology and Aging, 2,* 3–8.

Wooley, S. C., & Garner, D. M. (1991). Obesity treatment: The high cost of false hope. *Journal of the American Dietetic Association, 91,* 1248–1251.

Worden, J. W. (2002). *Grief counseling and grief therapy* (3rd ed.). New York: Springer.

Worell, J. (Ed.). (2001). *Encyclopedia of women and gender.* San Diego: Academic Press.

World Health Organization. (2000, February 2). *Adolescent health behavior in 28 countries.* Geneva: Author.

Worobey, J., & Belsky, J. (1982). Employing the Brazelton scale to influence mothering: An experimental comparison of three strategies. *Developmental Psychology, 18,* 736–743.

Worthington, E. L. (1989). Religious faith across the life span: Implications for counseling and research. *Counseling Psychologist, 17,* 555–612.

Wright, M. R. (1989). Body image satisfaction in adolescent girls and boys. *Journal of Youth and Adolescence, 18,* 71–84.

Wrosch, C., Heckhausen, J., & Lachman, M. E. (2000). Primary and secondary control strategies for managing health and financial stress across adulthood. *Psychology and Aging, 15,* 387–399.

Y

Yaffe, K., Barnes, D., Nevitt, M., Lui, L., & Covinsky, K. (2001). A prospective study of physical activity and cognitive decline in elderly women. *Archives of Internal Medicine, 161,* 1703–1708.

Yale, R. (1999, Fall). Support groups and other services for individuals with early-stage Alzheimer's disease. *Generations,* pp. 57–62.

Yamagishi, T., & Yamagishi, M. (1994). Trust and commitment in the United States and Japan. *Motivation and Emotion, 18,* 129–166.

Yang, J., McCrae, R. R., & Costa, P. T. (1998). Adult age differences in personality traits in the United States and the People's Republic of China. *Journal of Gerontology: Psychological Sciences, 53B,* P375–P383.

Yates, M. (1995, March). *Political socialization as a function of volunteerism.* Paper presented at the meeting of the Society for Research in Child Development, Indianapolis.

Yates, M. (2002). *Knock 'em dead.* Boston: Adams Media.

Yeats, D. E., Folts, W. E., & Knapp, J. (1999). Older workers' adaptation to a changing workplace: Employment issues for the 21st century. *Educational Gerontology, 25,* 331–347.

Yin, Y., Buhrmester, D., & Hibbard, D. (1996, March). *Are there developmental changes in the influence of relationships with parents and friends on adjustment during early adolescence?* Paper presented at the meeting of the Society for Research on Adolescence, Boston.

Young, D. (2001). The nature and management of pain: What is the evidence? *Birth, 28,* 149–151.

Young, K. T. (1990). American conceptions of infant development from 1955 to 1984: What the experts are telling parents. *Child Development, 61,* 17–28.

Young, S. K., & Shahinfar, A. (1995, March). *The contributions of maternal sensitivity and child temperament to attachment status at 14 months.* Paper presented at the meeting of the Society for Research in Child Development, Indianapolis.

Youniss, J., Silbereisen, R., Christmas-Best, V., Bales, S., Diversi, M., & McLaughlin, M. (2003). Civic and community engagement of adolescents in the 21st century. In R. Larson, B. Brown, & J. Mortimer (Eds.), *Adolescents' preparation for the future: Perils and promises.* Malden, MA: Blackwell.

Yu, V. Y. (2000). Developmental outcome of extremely preterm infants. *American Journal of Perinatology, 17,* 57–61.

Zajonc, R. B. (2001). The family dynamics of intellectual development. *American Psychologist, 56,* 523–524.

Zarit, S. H., & Downs, M. G. (1999, Fall). State of the art for practice in dementia: Introduction. *Generations,* pp. 6–8.

Zarit, S. H., & Knight, B. G. (Eds.). (1996). *A guide to psychotherapy and aging.* Washington, DC: American Psychological Association.

Zeskind, P. S., Gingras, J. L., Campbell, K. D., & Donnelly, K. (1999, April). *Prenatal cocaine exposure disrupts fetal autonomic regulation.* Paper presented at the meeting of the Society for Research in Child Development, Albuquerque.

Zeskind, P. S., Klein, L., & Marshall, T. R. (1992). Adults' perceptions of experimental modifications of durations and expiratory sounds in infant crying. *Developmental Psychology, 28,* 1153–1162.

Zigler, E. F., & Hall, N. W. (2000). Child development and social policy. New York: McGraw-Hill.

Zigler, E. F., & Styfco, S. J. (1994). Head Start: Criticisms in a constructive context. *American Psychologist, 49,* 127–132.

Zimmer-Gemback, M. J., & Collins, W. A. (2003). Autonomy development during adolescence. In G. Adams & M. Berzonsky (Eds.), *Blackwell handbook of adolescence.* Malden, MA: Blackwell.

Zimmerman, R. S., Khoury, E., Vega, W. A., Gil, A. G., & Warheit, G. J. (1995). Teacher and student perceptions of behavior problems among a sample of African American, Hispanic, and non-Hispanic White students. *American Journal of Community Psychology, 23,* 181–197.

Zoppi, M. A., Ibba, R. M., Putzolu, M., Floris, M., & Monni, K. G. (2001). Nuchal translucency and the acceptance of invasive prenatal chromosomal diagnosis in women aged 35 and older. *Obstetrics and Gynecology, 97,* 916–920.

Zucker, A. N., Ostrove, J. M., & Stewart, A. J. (2002). College educated women's personality development in adulthood: Perceptions and age differences. *Psychology and Aging, 17,* 236–244.

Zuk, C. V., & Zuk, G. H. (2002). Origins of dreaming. *American Journal of Psychiatry, 159,* 495–496.

Zukow-Goldring, P. (2002). Sibling caregiving. In M. H. Bornstein (Ed.), *Handbook of parenting* (Vol. 3). Mahwah, NJ: Erlbaum.

Credits

Chapter 1

Fig. 1.4 "Home Environments of Infants by Ethnicity and Poverty Status," Bradley, et al., 2001, The Home Environments of Children in the United States, Part I, *Child Development*, 72, 1844–1867. Adapted by permission of the Society for Research in Child Development. **Fig. 1.7** From Inglehart, Robert; *Culture Shift in Advanced Industrial Society*. Copyright © 1990 by Princeton University Press. Reprinted by permission of Princeton University Press.

Chapter 3

Fig. 3.1 Baltes, P.B., Staudinger, U.M., & Lindenberger, U., 1999, "Lifespan Psychology," *Annual Review of Psychology*, 50, p. 474, Figure 1. Reprinted with permission, from the *Annual Review of Psychology*, Volume 50. Copyright © 1999 by Annual Reviews, www.annualreview.org. **Fig. 3.2** From John Santrock, *Psychology*, 7th Edition. Copyright © 2003 The McGraw-Hill Companies. Reproduced with permission of The McGraw-Hill Companies. **Fig. 3.4** From Santrock, *Children*, 5/e. Copyright © 1997 The McGraw-Hill Companies. Reproduced with permission of The McGraw-Hill Companies. **Fig. 3.6** From NOVA at www.pbs.org/wgbh/nova/genome/survey.html. Copyright © 2002 WGBH/Boston. **Fig. 3.12** From John Santrock, *Children*, 5th Edition. Copyright © 1997 The McGraw-Hill Companies. Reproduced with permission of The McGraw-Hill Companies. **Fig. 3.13** Reproduced from "Enhancing the Life Course for High-Risk Children: Results from the Abecedarian Project," by Craig T. Ramey, Frances A. Campbell, and Clancy Blair. In Jonathan Crane (Ed.), *Social Programs that Work*. Copyright © 1998 Russell Sage Foundation, 112 East 64th Street, New York, NY 10021. Reprinted with permission. **Fig. 3.14** From "The Increase in IQ Scores from 1932 to 1997," by Dr. Ulric Neisser. Reprinted by permission. **Fig. 3.15** John Santrock, *Children*, 7th Edition. Copyright © 2003 The McGraw-Hill Companies. Reproduced with permission of The McGraw-Hill Companies.

Chapter 4

Fig. 4.3 From John Santrock, *Children*, 5th Edition. Copyright © 1997 The McGraw-Hill Companies. Reproduced with permission of The McGraw-Hill Companies. **Fig. 4.4** Reprinted from *Pregnancy, Childbirth and the Newborn: The Complete Guide*, with permission of its publisher, Meadowbrook Press. Copyright © 1984 by the Childbirth Association of Seattle. **Fig. 4.6** From John Santrock, *Children*, 7th Edition. Copyright © 2003 The McGraw-Hill Companies. Reproduced with permission of The McGraw-Hill Companies. **Fig. 4.9** From Virginia A. Apgar, 1975, "A Proposal for a New Method of Evaluation of a Newborn Infant," in *Anesthesia and Analgesia*, Vol. 32, pp. 260–267. Reprinted by permission.

Chapter 5

Fig. 5.2 From John Santrock, *Child Development*, 9th Edition. Copyright © 2001 The McGraw-Hill Companies. Reproduced with permission of The McGraw-Hill Companies. **Fig. 5.3** Reprinted by permission of the publisher from *The Postnatal Development of the Human Cerebral Cortex*, Vol. 1-VIII, by Jesse LeRoy Conel. Cambridge, MA: Harvard University Press, Copyright © 1939, 1975 by the President and Fellows of Harvard College. **Fig. 5.4** From John Santrock, *Topical Life-Span Development*. Copyright © 2002 The McGraw-Hill Companies. Reproduced with permission of The McGraw-Hill Companies. **Fig. 5.9** Reprinted with permission from H.P. Roffward, J.M. Muzio and W.C. Dement, 1966, "Ontogenetic Development of Human Dream Sleep Cycle," *Science*, Vol. 152, pp. 604–609. **Fig. 5.10** From John Santrock, *Children*, 5th Edition. Copyright © 1997 The McGraw-Hill Companies. Reproduced with permission of The McGraw-Hill Companies. **Fig. 5.11** From John Santrock, *Child Development*, 9th Edition. Copyright © 2001 The McGraw-Hill Companies. Reproduced with permission of The McGraw-Hill Companies. **Fig. 5.15** From John Santrock, *Child Development*, 9th Edition. Copyright © 2001 The McGraw-Hill Companies. Reproduced with permission of The McGraw-Hill Companies.

Chapter 6

Fig. 6.3 From John Santrock, *Children*, 7th Edition. Copyright © 2003 The McGraw-Hill Companies. Reproduced with permission of The McGraw-Hill Companies. **Fig. 6.5** From Slater, A., Morison, V. & Somers, M., 1988, "Orientation Discrimination and Cortical Functions in the Human Newborn," *Perception*, Vol. 17, pp. 597–602, Fig. 1 and Table 1. Reprinted by permission of Pion, London. **Figs. 6.8, 6.9, 6.10** From John Santrock, *Children*, 7th Edition. Copyright © 2003 The McGraw-Hill Companies. Reproduced with permission of The McGraw-Hill Companies.

Chapter 7

Fig. 7.1 Reprinted by permission of the publisher from *Infancy: Its Place in Human Development* by Jerome Kagan, R.B. Kearsley and P.R. Zelazo, p. 107. Cambridge, MA: Harvard University Press, Copyright © 1978 by the President and Fellows of Harvard College. **Fig. 7.2** From John Santrock, *Life-Span Development*, 4th Edition. Copyright © 1999 The McGraw-Hill Companies. Reproduced with permission of The McGraw-Hill Companies. **Fig. 7.4** Adapted from M.D.S. Ainsworth & S.M. Bell, 1971, "Attachment, Exploration, and Separation: Illustrated by the Behavior of One-Year-Olds in a Strange Situation," *Child Development*, Vol. 41, (1), pp. 49–67. Reprinted by permission of Society for Research in Child Development. **Fig. 7.5** From van Ijzendoorn & Kroonenberg, 1988, "Cross Cultural Patterns of Attachment," *Child Development*, 59, 147–156. Adapted by permission of the Society for Research in Child Development. **Fig. 7.6** From Jay Belsky, "Early Human Experiences: A Family Perspective," in *Developmental Psychology*, Vol. 17, pp. 3–23. Copyright © 1981 by the American Psychological Association. Reprinted with permission. **Fig. 7.7** From John Santrock, *Children*, 5th Edition. Copyright © 1997 The McGraw-Hill Companies. Reproduced with permission of The McGraw-Hill Companies.

Chapter 8

Fig. 8.1 Reprinted from *Human Biology and Ecology*, by Albert Damon, with the permission of W.W. Norton & Company, Inc. Copyright © 1977 by W.W. Norton & Company, Inc. **Fig. 8.2** From John Santrock, *Children*, 7th Edition. Copyright © 2003 The McGraw-Hill Companies. Reproduced with permission of The McGraw-Hill Companies. **Fig. 8.3** From G.J. Schirmer (Ed.) *Performance Objectives for Preschool Children*, Adapt Press, Sioux Falls, SD, 1974. **Fig. 8.4** From G.J. Schirmer (Ed.) *Performance Objectives for Preschool Children*, Adapt Press, Sioux Falls, SD, 1974. **Fig. 8.5** From John Santrock, *Children*, 7th Edition. Copyright © 2003 The

McGraw-Hill Companies. Reproduced with permission of The McGraw-Hill Companies. **Fig. 8.6** From John Santrock, *Psychology*, 7/e. Copyright © 2003 The McGraw-Hill Companies. Reproduced with permission of The McGraw-Hill Companies. **Fig. 8.7** "The Symbolic Drawings of Young Children," reprinted courtesy of D. Wolf and J. Nove. **Fig. 8.12** From Santrock, *Children*, 7th Edition. Copyright © 2003 The McGraw-Hill Companies. Reproduced with permission of The McGraw-Hill Companies. **Fig. 8.13** After Dempster (1981) "Memory Span." *Psychological Bulletin*, 80, 63–100. **Fig. 8.15** After Wellman, Cross & Watson (2001). "Meta-Analysis of Theory of Mind Development: The Truth About False Belief." *Child Development*, 72, 655–684. **Fig. 8.16** From Jean Berko, 1958, "The Child's Learning of English Morphology," in *Word*, Vol. 14, p. 154. **Fig. 8.17** From *Young Children*, Vol. 41, pp. 23–27, September 1986. Reprinted with permission from the National Association for the Education of Young Children. **Fig. 8.18** After Tobin, Wu & Davidson (1989). *Preschool in Three Cultures*. New Haven, CT: Yale University Press.

Chapter 9

Fig. 9.1 From Santrock, *Children*, 7/e. Copyright © 2003 The McGraw-Hill Companies. Reproduced with permission of The McGraw-Hill Companies. **Fig. 9.5** From Curran, K., DuCette, J., Eisenstein, J. & Hyman, I.A., August 2001, "Statistical Analysis of the Cross-Cultural Data: The Third Year," Paper presented at the meeting of the American Psychological Association, San Francisco, CA. Reprinted by permission. **Fig. 9.9** From Anderson, et al., 2001, Early Childhood Viewing and Adolescent Behavior, *Monographs of the Society for Research in Child Development*, Vol. 66 (1), Serial No. 264. Adapted by permission of the Society for Research in Child Development.

Chapter 10

Fig. 10.1 After data presented by Health Management Resources 2001. *Child Health and Times*. Boston: Health Management Resources. **Fig. 10.2** From John Santrock, *Children*, 6th Edition. Copyright © 2000 The McGraw-Hill Companies. Reproduced with permission of The McGraw-Hill Companies. **Fig. 10.3** Tables II-II and II-III. "To Assure the Free and Appropriate Public Education of All Children With Disabilities," Washington, DC: U.S. Department of Education, 2000. **Fig. 10.5** From Chi, M.T.H. "Knowledge Structures and Memory Development," in R.S. Siegler (Ed.) *Children's Thinking: What Develops?* Copyright © 1978 Lawrence Erlbaum Associates. Reprinted by permission. **Fig. 10.8** "Sample Item from the Raven Progressive Matrices Test," from *Raven's Standard Progressive Matrices*, Item A5. Reprinted by permission of J.C. Raven Ltd. **Fig. 10.10** NAEP, 2000. Reading Achievement: 2000, Washington, DC: National Center for Educational Statistics. **Fig. 10.11** After Johnson & Newport, 1991. Critical Period Effects of

Universal Properties of Language. The Status of subjacency in the Acquisition of Second Language. *Cognition*, 39, 251–258.

Chapter 11

Fig. 11.2 From Colby, et al., 1983, "A Longitudinal Study of Moral Judgment," *Monographs of the Society for Research in Child Development*, Serial No. 201. Reprinted with permission of the Society for Research In Child Development. **Fig. 11.5** From Nansel, et al., 2001, "Bullying Behaviors Among U.S. Youth," *Journal of the American Medical Association*, Vol. 285, pp. 2094–2100. **Fig. 11.6** Reprinted with permission from Stevenson, Lee & Stigler, 1986, Figure 6, "Mathematics Achievement of Chinese, Japanese and American Children," *Science*, Vol. 231, pp. 693–699. Copyright " 1986 American Association for the Advancement of Science.

Chapter 12

Figs. 12.1, 12.2, 12.5 From John Santrock, *Adolescence*, 8th Edition. Copyright © 2001 The McGraw-Hill Companies. Reproduced with permission of The McGraw-Hill Companies. **Figs. 12.3, 12.4, 12.8** From John Santrock, *Children*, 7th Edition. Copyright © 2003 The McGraw-Hill Companies. Reproduced with permission of The McGraw-Hill Companies. **Fig. 12.6** Johnson, L.D., O'Malley, P.M., & Bachman, J.G., 2001, "The Monitoring of the Future: National Results on Adolescent Drug Use," Washington, DC: National Institute on Drug Abuse.

Chapter 13

Fig. 13.5 From "Romantic Development: Does Age at Which Romantic Involvement Starts Matter?" by Duane Buhrmester, April 2001, paper presented at the meeting of the Society for Research in Child Development, Minneapolis, MN. Reprinted with permission from the author.

Chapter 14

Page 437 Bob Dylan, "Blowin' in the Wind." Copyright © 1962 by Warner Brothers Music. Copyright renewed in 1990 by Special Rider Music. All rights reserved. International copyright secured. Reprinted by permission. **Fig. 14.1** From J. Arnett, "Emerging Adulthood," in *American Psychologist*, Vol. 55, pp. 469–480, Fig. 2. Copyright ©2000 by the American Psychological Association. Reprinted with permission. **Fig. 14.2** From Diener & Seligman, 2002, "Very Happy People," *Psychological Science*, Vol. 13, pp. 81–84. Reprinted with permission from Blackwell Publishers. **Fig. 14.3** From National Institutes of Health. **Fig. 14.5** From L.L. Langley, *Physiology of Man*. Copyright © 1972 Van Nostrand Reinhold. Reprinted by permission of L.L. Langley. **Fig. 14.6** From Pate, et al., *Journal of the American Medical Association*, 273, 404.

Copyright © 1995 American Medical Association. Reprinted by permission. **Fig. 14.7** From Bachman, J.G., et al., "Transitions in Drug Use During Late Adolescence and Young Adulthood," in J.A. Graber, J.Brooks-Gunn & A.C. Petersen (Eds.) *Transitions Through Adolescence*. Copyright © 1986 Lawrence Erlbaum Associates. Reprinted by permission. **Fig. 14.8** From *Sex in America*, by Robert Michael, et al. Copyright © 1994 by CSG Enterprises, Inc., Edward O. Laumann, Robert Michael, and Gina Kolata. By permission of Little, Brown and Company. **Fig. 14.10** From John Santrock, *Children*, 7th Edition. Copyright © 2003 The McGraw-Hill Companies. Reproduced with permission of The McGraw-Hill Companies. **Fig. 14.11** Reproduced by special permission of the publisher, Psychological Assessment Resources from *Making Vocational Choices: A Theory of Vocational Choices and Work Environments*. Copyright © 1973, 1985, 1992 by Psychological Assessment Resources, Inc. All rights reserved. **Fig. 14.12** From *Occupational Outlook Handbook*, 2002–2003, Ch. 8, U.S. Department of Labor. **Fig. 14.14** Figure from "Work-Family Balance," by R. Barnett, in *Encyclopedia of Woman and Gender: Sex Similarities and Differences and the Impact of Society on Gender*, 2 Volume Set, Judith Worell (Ed.). Copyright © 2001 Elsevier Science (USA). Reproduced by permission of the publisher.

Chapter 15

Fig. 15.1 From Wachs, T.D. "Fit, Context, and the Transition Between Temperament and Personality," in C. Halverson, G. Kohnstamm & R. Martin (Eds.) *The Developing Structure of Personality from Infancy to Adulthood*. Copyright © 1994 Lawrence Erlbaum Associates. Reprinted by permission. **Fig. 15.2** Figure from "Exposure Effects in the Classroom" by Moreland and Beach in *Journal of Experimental Social Psychology*, Volume 28, 255–276. Copyright © 1992 Elsevier Science (USA). Reproduced with special permission from the publisher. **Fig. 15.4** Reproduced by special permission of the publisher, Psychological Assessment Resources, Inc. from *The Changing Family Life Cycle*, 2/e. Copyright © 1989 by Psychological Assessment Resources, Inc. All rights reserved. **Figs. 15.5, 15.6, 15.7** U.S. Bureau of the Census, 2000. **Figure 15.8** National Center for Health Statistics, 2000.

Chapter 16

Page 514 From Jim Croce, "Time in a Bottle." Copyright © 1972, 1985 Denjac Music Co. Reprinted with permission. **Fig. 16.2** Adapted from *Newsweek*, Health for Life, special section, Fall/Winter 2001. Copyright © 2001 Newsweek, Inc. All rights reserved. Reprinted by permission. **Fig. 16.3** Adapted from *Newsweek*, Health for Life, special section, Fall/Winter 2001. Copyright © 2001 Newsweek, Inc. All rights reserved. Reprinted by permission. **Fig. 16.4** National Center for Health Statistics, 1999. **Fig. 16.6**

National Center for Health Statistics, 1998. **Fig. 16.7** From *Sex in America* by Robert Michael, et al. Copyright © 1995 by CSG Enterprises, Inc. Edward O. Laumann, Robert Michael, and Gina Kolata. Reprinted with permission from Little, Brown & Company. **Fig. 16.11** From *Men in Their Forties: The Transition to Middle Age,* by Lois M. Tamir, 1982. Used by permission of Springer Publishing Company, New York 10012.

Chapter 17

Figs. 17.1, 17.2 From Stewart, Osgrove & Helson, 2002, "Middle Aging in Women: Patterns of Personality Change from the 30s to the 50s," Fig. 3, *Journal of Adult Development,* Vol. 8, pp. 23–37. Reprinted with permission from Kluwer Academic Publishers. **Fig. 17.5** After Keyes and Ryff, (1999), "Psychological Well-Being in Mid-Life," in S.L. Willis and J.D. Reid (Eds.), *Life in the Middle,* San Diego: Academic Press. **Fig. 17.7** From A.D. Kenner, et al. in *Journal of Behavioral Medicine,* Vol. 4, 1981. Reprinted by permission of Plenum Publishers. **Fig. 17.8** From D.F. Hultsch and J.K. Plemons, "Life Events and Life Span Development," in *Life Span Development and Behavior,* Vol., 2, by P.B. Baltes and O.G. Brun (Eds.) Copyright © 1979 Academic Press. Reprinted by permission.

Chapter 18

Fig. 18.1 From *The Psychology of Death, Dying and Bereavement* by Richard Schulz. Copyright © 1978 The McGraw-Hill Companies. Reproduced with permission of The McGraw-Hill Companies. **Fig. 18.2** From *The Okinawa Program* by Bradley J. Willcox, D. Craig Willcox and Makoto Suzuki. Copyright © 2001 by Bradley J. Willcox, D. Craig Willcox and Makoto Suzuki. Used by permission of Clarkson Potter Publishers, a division of Random House, Inc. **Fig. 18.7** Adapted from *Newsweek,* Health for Life, special section, Fall/Winter 2000. Copyright © 2000 Newsweek, Inc. All rights reserved. Reprinted by permission. **Fig. 18.10** Data from Advocate from the U.S. Senate Special Committee on Aging, "Aging in America," p. 50, U.S. Government Printing Office, Washington, DC, 1983.

Chapter 20

Fig. 20.1 From "Erikson's View . . . Conflict and Resolution: Culmination in Old Age." Copyright © 1988 by *The New York Times.* Reprinted by permission. **Fig. 20.2** From L. Carstensen, et al., "The Social Context of Emotion" in the *Annual Review of Geriatrics and Gerontology* by Schaie/Lawton, 1997, Vol. 17, p. 331. Used by permission of Springer Publishing Company, New York 10012. **Fig. 20.3** From D. Mroczek and C.M. Kolarz, "The Effect of Age in Positive and Negative Affect" in *Journal of Personality and Social Psychology,* Vol. 75, pp. 1333–1349. Copyright © 1998 by the American Psychological Association. Adapted with permission. **Fig. 20.5**

From Robins, et al., "Age Differences in Self-Esteem from 9 to 90," in *Psychology and Aging,* in-press. Copyright © 2002 by the American Psychological Association. Adapted with permission. **Fig. 20.7** From R. Schulz and J. Heckhausen, "A Life Span Model of Successful Aging" in *American Psychologist,* Vol. 51, pp. 702–714. Copyright © 1996 by the American Psychological Association. Reprinted with permission.

PHOTO CREDITS

Section Openers

1: © David Young-Wolff/Photo Edit; **2:** © Petit Format/Nestle/Photo Researchers, Inc.; **3:** Northern Telecom & J. Walther Thompson Advertising; **4:** © Tom Prettyman/Photo Edit; **5:** © Tom Rosenthal/SuperStock; **6:** © Butch Martin/The Image Bank/Getty Images; **7:** © Ariel Skelley/CORBIS; **8:** © Barros & Barros/The Image Bank/Getty Images; **9:** © Adamsmith/SuperStock; **10:** © Dennis Stock/Magnum Photos

Chapter 1

Opener: © Charles Gupton/Stone/Getty Images; **p. 6 (top):** © Seana O'Sullivan/CORBIS/Sygma; **p. 6 (bottom):** © AP/Wide World Photos; p. 10: Courtesy K. Warner Schaie; **p. 12:** Courtesy of Luis Vargas; **p. 13:** © National Associate for the Education of Young Children, Robert Maust/Photo Agora; **p. 14:** © Nancy Agostini; **p. 15:** © James Pozarik/Liaison Agency/Getty Images News Service; **p. 16:** Courtesy of Marian Wright Edelman, The Children's Defense Fund, photograph by Rick Reinhard; **p. 17:** © Dennis Brack Ltd./Black Star/Stock Photo; **1.6 (left to right):** Courtesy of Landrum Shettles; John Santrock; © Joe Sohm/The Image Works; © CORBIS website; © James L. Shaffer; © Vol. 155/CORBIS; © CORBIS website; © CORBIS website; **p. 25:** © Joel Gordon 1995

Chapter 2

Opener: © Michael Krasowitz/FPG/Getty Images; **p. 44:** © Bettmann/CORBIS; **p. 47:** © Bettmann/CORBIS; **p. 48:** © CORBIS; **p. 49:** © Yves de Braine/Black Star/Stock Photo; **p. 50:** A.R. Lauria/Dr. Michael Cole, Laboratory of Human Cognition, University of California, San Diego; **p. 51:** © Bettmann/CORBIS; **p. 52:** Courtesy of Stanford University News Service; **p. 53:** Photo by Nina Leen/Life Magazine. © Time, Inc.; **p. 56 (top):** Courtesy of Urie Bronfenbrenner; **p. 56 (Freud):** © Bettmann Archives; (Pavlov): © The Bettmann Archive; (Piaget): © Yves de Braine/Black Star/Stock Photo; (Vygotsky): A.R. Lauria/Dr. Michael Cole, Laboratory of Human Cognition, University of California, San Diego; (Skinner): Courtesy of Jane Reed,

Howard University News Office; **(Erikson):** © UPI/Bettmann Newsphotos; **(Bandura):** Courtesy of Stanford University News Service; **(Bronenbrenner):** Courtesy of Urie Bronfenbrenner; **p. 61:** © Paul Popper Ltd., 2002; **p. 58:** © Richard T. Nowitz/Photo Researchers, Inc.; **2.12a:** © Photo Researchers, Inc.; **2.12b:** © AP/Wide World Photos; **2.12c:** © AP/Wide World Photos; **2.12d:** © Bettmann/CORBIS; **2.12e:** © Sukie Hill Photographer; **2.12f:** © Lawrence Migdale/Photo Researchers, Inc.; **p. 69 (left):** © AFP/CORBIS; **p. 69 (right):** © Stuart McClymont/Stone/Getty Images; **p. 70:** Courtesy of Pam Trotman Reid

Chapter 3

Opener: © Hua China Tourism Press, Shao/The Image Bank/Getty Images; **p. 80:** © Enrico Ferorelli Enterprises; **3.3:** © Sundstrom/Liaison Agency/Getty Images News Service; **3.5ab:** © Custom Medical Stock Photo; **p. 90:** © Joel Gordon 1989; **p. 92:** Courtesy of Holly Ishmael; **p. 93:** © Andrew Eccles/Outline Press; **p. 94:** © Jacques Pavlousky/Sygma/CORBIS; **p. 95:** © Ambassador/CORBIS/SYGMA; **p. 104:** © Joel Gordon 1999

Chapter 4

Opener: Photo Lennart Nilsson/Albert Bonniers Forlag AB, *A Child is Born,* Dell Publishing Company; **p. 115:** © David Young-Wolff/Photo Edit; **4.3 (all):** Photo Lennart Nilsson/Albert Bonniers Forlag AB., *A Child is Born,* Dell Publishing Company; **4.5:** Courtesy of Ann Streissguth; **p. 120:** © John Chiasson/Liaison Agency/Getty Images News Service; **p. 121:** © R.I.A./Liaison Agency/Getty Images News Service; **p. 123:** © Betty Press/Woodfin Camp & Associates; **p. 124 (top):** © Alon Reininger/Contract Press Images; **p. 124 (bottom):** © Charles Gupton/Stock Boston; **p. 125:** Courtesy of Rachel Thompson; **p. 126:** © Viviane Moos; **p. 128:** © SIU/Peter Arnold, Inc.; **p. 129:** © Nancy DeVore/Anthro-Photo; **p. 130:** Courtesy of Linda Pugh; **p. 131:** © Charles Gupton/Stock Boston; **p. 133:** Courtesy of Dr. Tiffany Field; **4.9:** © Stephen Marks, Inc./The Image Bank/Getty Images; **p. 136:** © Michael Newman/Photo Edit; **p. 138:** © Tony Schanuel

Chapter 5

Opener: © Kate Connell/Stone/Getty Images; **5.2:** Photo Lennart Nilsson/Albert Bonniers Forlag; **5.5:** © 1999 Kenneth Jarecke/Contact Press Images; **5.6:** © A. Glauberman/Photo Researchers, Inc.; **5.7ab:** Courtesy of Dr. Harry T. Chugani, Children's Hospital of Michigan; **5.8a:** © David Grugin Productions, Inc. Reprinted by permission.; **5.8b:** Image courtesy of Dana Boatman, Ph.D., Department of Neurology, John Hopkins University, reprinted with permission from *The Secret Life of the Brain,* Joseph Henry Press; **p. 158 (top):** © Bruce

McAllister/Image Works; **p. 158 (bottom):** © Bob Dammrich/The Image Works; **p. 159:** Courtesy of The Hawaii Family Support Center, Healthy Start Program; **p. 160:** Courtesy of T. Berry Brazelton; **p. 165 (top):** © Michael Greenlar/The Image Works; **p. 165 (bottom):** © Frank Baily Studios; **5.12:** © Judith Canty/Stock Boston; **p. 167:** Courtesy of Esther Thelen; **5.13 (all):** Courtesy of Dr. Charles Nelson; **5.14b:** © David Linton; **5.16:** © Enrico Ferorelli Enterprises; **5.17:** © Joe McNally/Sygma/CORBIS; **5.18a:** © Michael Siluk; **5.18b:** © Dr. Melanie Spence, University of Texas; **5.19:** © Jean Guichard/Sygma/CORBIS; **5.20a-c:** From D. Rosenstein and H. Oster "Differential Facial Responses to Four Basic Tastes in Newborns," *Child Development*, Vol. 59, 1988. © Society for Research in Child Development, Inc.

Chapter 6

Opener: © Sally and Richard Greenhill; **6.2 (left & right):** © Doug Goodman/Photo Researchers; **6.4:** Courtesy of Dr. Carolyn Rovee-Collier; **6.6:** © Enrico Ferorelli Enterprises; **p. 193:** Courtesy of John Santrock; **6.7 (left & right):** Courtesy of Dr. Patricia K. Kuhl, Center for Mind, Brain & Learning, University of Washington; **p. 196:** © ABPL Image Library/Animals Animals/Earth Scenes; **p. 197:** © Tim Davis/CORBIS

Chapter 7

Opener: © Jamie Marcial/SuperStock; **p. 206:** © Andy Sacks/Stone/Getty Images; **p. 208:** © Andy Cox/Stone/Getty Images; **p. 211:** © Michael Tcherevkoff/The Image Bank/Getty Images; **p. 212:** © Judith Oddie/Photo Edit; **7.2 (right):** © Myrleen Ferguson Cate/Photo Edit; **7.3 (left):** © Martin Rogers/Stock Boston; **7.4 (left):** © Daniel Grogan; **p. 219:** © David Young-Wolff/Photo Edit; **p. 221:** © Comstock, Inc.; **p. 224:** Courtesy of Rashmi Nakre, The Hattie Daniels Day Care Center

Chapter 8

Opener: © Jeffry W. Myers/Stock Boston; **p. 235:** © Bob Daemmrich/The Image Works; **p. 238:** © Eyewire Vol. EP078 /Getty Images; **p. 241:** Courtesy of Barbara Deloian; **8.8:** © Paul Fusco/Magnum Photos; **p. 247:** © James Wertsch/Washington University; **8.10:** © Elizabeth Crews/The Image Works; **8.11 (left):** A. R. Lauria/Dr. Michael Cole, Laboratory of Human Cognition, University of California, San Diego; **(right):** © Bettmann/CORBIS; **p. 249:** © Bob Daemmrich/The Image Works; **p. 252:** © 1999 James Kamp; **p. 253:** © Nita Winter; **p. 255:** © Roseanne Olson/Stone/Getty Images; **8.17:** © David Young-Wolff/Photo Edit; **p. 259:** © Robert Wallis/SIPA Press, Newsweek, April 17, 1989; **p. 260:** Courtesy of Yolanda Garcia

Chapter 9

Opener: © Hermine Dreyfuss/Photo Researchers; **p. 274:** © Suzanne Sasz/Photo Researchers, Inc.; **9.4:** © Peter Correz/StoneGetty Images; **p. 281:** Courtesy of Darla Botkin; **p. 282:** © Christopher Arnesen/Stone/Getty Images; **p. 284:** © 1999 Joel Gordon; **p. 285:** © Karen Kasmauski/Woodfin Camp; **p. 286:** © Spencer Grant/Photo Edit; **p. 289:** © Richard Hutchings/Photo Edit

Chapter 10

Opener: © Eyewire Vol. EP049/Getty Images; **p. 302:** © P. West/San Jose Mercury News/Sygma/CORBIS; **p. 304:** © Joe McNally/Time, Inc.; **p. 305:** Courtesy of Sharon McLeod; **p. 308:** © David Young-Wolff/Photo Edit; **p. 309:** © Will McIntyre/Photo Researchers, Inc.; **p. 313:** © Archives Jean Piaget, Universite De Geneve, Switzerland; **p. 314:** © Bernheim/Woodfin Camp; **p. 316:** Courtesy of Laura Martin; **p. 320:** © Joe McNally; **10.9:** © Jill Cannefax/EKM-Nepenthe; **p. 324:** Courtesy of Sterling C. Jones, Jr.; **p. 327:** © Richard Howard; **p. 328:** Courtesy of Salvador Tamayo

Chapter 11

Opener: © Vol. 100/PhotoDisc/Getty; **p. 340:** © Reutuers/NewMedia Inc./CORBIS; **p. 344:** © Keith Carter Photography; **p. 348:** © Catherine Gehm; **p. 350:** © Michael Newman/Photo Edit; **p. 353:** © PhotoDisc/Getty Images website; **p. 356:** © Lonnie Harp; **p. 358:** © Mike Yamashita/Woodfin Camp; **p. 359:** © John S. Abbott; **p. 360:** © Eiji Miyazawa/Black Star/Stock Photo

Chapter 12

Opener: © Cindy Charles/Photo Edit; **p. 371:** © M. Regine/The Image Bank/Getty Images; **p. 378:** © Lawrence Migdale/Stock Boston; **p. 380:** Courtesy of Lynn Blankinship; **12.7a:** © Mark Richards/Photo Edit; **12.7b:** Courtesy of National Institute of Drug Abuse; **p. 385:** © Tony Freeman/Photo Edit; **p. 388:** © Stewart Cohen/Stone/Getty Images; **p. 389:** © Susan Lapides 2002; **p. 392:** © Mark Antman/The Image Works; **p. 394:** Courtesy of Armando Ronquillo; **p. 395:** © H. Yamaguchi/Gamma Liaison/Getty Images News Service; **p. 396:** © Tony Freeman/Photo Edit; **p. 397:** Courtesy of Constance Flanagan, Professor of Youth Civic Development, Pennsylvania State University

Chapter 13

Opener: © Mary Kate Denny/Photo Edit; **p. 409:** © Bob Daemmrich/The Image Works; **13.3:** © Spencer Grant/Photo Edit; **p. 415:** © Tony Freeman/Photo Edit; **p. 416:** © Michael

Siluk/The Image Works; **p. 418:** © Tessa Codrington/Stone/Getty Images; **p. 420:** © Daniel Laine; **p. 422:** Courtesy of Carola Suarez-Orozco, photo by Kris Snibble/Harvard News Office; **p. 423:** Courtesy of El Puente Academy; **p. 426:** © Charlie Neuman/SDUT/Zuma; **p. 427:** Courtesy of Rodney Hammond; **p. 428:** © Jim Smith/Photo Researchers; **p. 431:** Courtesy of Peter Benson, Director, Search Institute

Chapter 14

Opener: © PictureQuest; **p. 440:** © Bettmann/CORBIS; **p. 442:** © PhotoDisc/Getty Images website; **p. 444:** Courtesy of Grace Leaf; **14.4:** © 1995 Amgen, Inc.; **p. 448:** Courtesy of Judith Rodin; **p. 449:** © Lori Adamski Peek/Stone/Getty Images; **p. 456:** © 1996 Rob Lewine/The Stock Market; **p. 457:** © Boehringer Ingelheim International GmbH, Photo Lennart Nilsson/Albert Bonniers Forlag AB; **p. 458:** © Barry O'Rourke/The Stock Market; **p. 461 (left):** AP/Wide World Photos; **p. 461 (middle):** Courtesy Nina Holton; **p. 461 (right):** Courtesy of Jim Cox/The Salk Institute; **p. 463:** Courtesy Mihaly Csikszentmihalyi; **p. 470:** © Shooting Star; **p. 471:** © Tom & Dee Ann McCarthy/CORBIS/Stock Market

Chapter 15

Opener: © Helen Norman/CORBIS; **p. 483:** Universal (Courtesy of The Picture Desk); **p. 486 (top):** © David Young-Wolff/Photo Edit; **p. 486 (middle):** © Tony Freeman/Photo Edit; **p. 486 (bottom):** © James McLoughlin/Stone/Getty Images; **p. 492 (left):** © Explorer/J.P. Nacivet/Photo Researchers; **p. 492 (middle):** © Dean Press Images/Image Works; **p. 492 (right):** © David Hanover/Stone/Getty Images; **p. 494:** © Ronald Mackechnie/Stone/Getty Images; **p. 496:** Courtesy of Janis Keyser; **p. 502:** © S. Gazin/The Image Works; **p. 504:** © Eye-Wire Vol. EP036/Getty Images

Chapter 16

Opener: © Zephyr Pictures/Index Stock; **p. 516 (left):** © Bettmann/CORBIS; **p. 516 (right):** © Matthew Mendelsohn/CORBIS; **p. 523:** © 1998 Tom & Dee McCarthy/The Stock Market; **16.7:** © Vol. 155/CORBIS; **p. 528:** © Reuters Newmedia Inc/CORBIS; **p. 531:** © Chris Cheadle/Stone/Getty Images; **p. 533:** © Tony Freeman/Photo Edit

Chapter 17

Opener: © Rob Lewine/The Stock Market; **17.3 (top):** © CORBIS website; **17.3 (middle):** © Eyewire/Getty website; **17.3 (bottom):** © Vol. 67/PhotoDisc; **17.8 (top):** © Bettmann/CORBIS; **17.8 (bottom):** © EyeWire/Getty Images website; **p. 549:** © Rhoda Sidney/Photo Edit; **p. 550:** © Betty Press/Woodfin Camp & Associates; **p. 553:** © Bettmann/CORBIS; **p. 554:** © Everett Collection; **p. 557:** © William Hubbell/Woodfin Camp & Associates; **p. 559:** Courtesy of Lillian Troll

Chapter 18

Opener: © A. Ramey/Photo Edit; **p. 568:** © John Goodman; **p. 572:** © USA Today, Paul Wiseman, photographer. Reprinted with permission.; **p. 573:** © Jim Richardson/Westlight/ CORBIS; **p. 574a:** © Pascal Parrot/Sygma; **p. 574b:** © Thomas Del Brase; **18.3:** Courtesy of Dr. Jerry Shay, PhD., UT Southwestern Medical Center; **18.4:** From R. Cabeza, et al., "Age-related; differences in neural activity during memory encoding and retrieval: A positron emission tomography study" in *Journal of Neuroscience,* 17, 391–400, 1997.; **18.5:** Courtesy of Dr. Fred Gage; **18.6 (top & bottom):** © James Balog; **18.10:** © George Gardner/The Image Works; **p. 585:** © Bob Daemmrich/Stock Boston; **18.12:** Courtesy of Colin M. Bloor; **p. 589:** Courtesy of Ellen Langer; **p. 590:** Courtesy of Debra Radomski; **p. 591 (left):** © Julian Hirshowitz/CORBIS; **p. 591 (right):** © Jose Luis Pelaez, Inc./CORBIS

Chapter 19

Opener: © Cleo Photography/Photo Edit; **p. 599 (left):** © Cornell Capa/Magnum Photos;

p. 599 (right): © Kirkland/Sygma; **p. 603:** © Elizabeth Crews; **p. 606:** Courtesy of Dr. Sherry Willis; **p. 609:** © Greg Sailor; **p. 612:** © Bettmann/CORBIS; **19.6 (left & right):** © Alfred Pasieka/Science Photo Library/Photo Researchers, Inc.; **p. 613:** © Ira Wyman/Sygma; **p. 614:** Courtesy of Jan W. Weaver; **p. 615:** © AP/Wide World Photos; **p. 616:** Courtesy of Donna Polisar; **p. 617:** © Bryan Peterson/The Stock Market

Chapter 20

Opener: © Chuck Savage/The Stock Market/ CORBIS; **p. 624 (left):** © AP/Wide World Photos; **p. 624 (right):** Photo by Steve Lipofsky BasketballPhoto.com; **20.1:** © Sarah Putman/ Picture Cube/Index Stock; **p. 629:** Courtesy of Laura Carstensen; **20.4 (left to right):** © Eye-wire/Getty Images website; © PhotoDisc/Getty Images website; © Corbis website; © PhotoDisc website; © Vol. 34/CORBIS; **p. 634:** Photo by Mariou Ruiz/Time Magazine/Time, Inc.; **p. 639:** John Santrock; **p. 640:** © Frank Conaway/Index Stock; **p. 643:** © G. Wayne Floyd/Unicorn Stock Photos; **p. 644:** © Suzi Moore-McGregor/ Woodfin Camp & Associates; **p. 645:** © NASA/ Liaison Agency/Getty Images News Service

Chapter 21

Opener: © Stan Honda/AP Wide World Photos; **p. 654:** © AP/Wide World Photos; **p. 655:** © Herb Snitzer/Stock Boston; **p. 656:** © Detroit

News/Gamma Liaison/Getty Images News Service; **21.1:** © Patrick Ward/Stock Boston; **p. 661:** Courtesy of Robert Kastenbaum; **21.2:** © Eastcott Momatinck/The Image Works; **p. 667:** Courtesy of Sara Wheeler; **p. 668:** © Phyllis Picarci/International Stock; **p. 670:** © Hermine Dreyfuss/Photo Researchers

Epilogue

2: Photo Lennart Nilsson/Albert Bonniers Forlag AB, *A Child is Born,* Dell Publishing Company; **3:** © Kate Connell/Stone/Getty Images; **4:** © Barbara Feigles/Stock Boston; **5:** © Vol. EP049 Eyewire/Getty Images; **6:** © Chuck Savage/ Corbis Stock Market; **7:** © PhotoDisc/Getty website; **8:** © LWA-JDC/CORBIS/Stock Market; **9:** © Dick Durrance/Woodfin Camp; **10:** © Dennis Stock/Magnum Photos

Name Index

D

H

O

P

Q

R

Subject Index

Q